ENVIRONMENTAL LAW AND POLICY IN INDIA

ENVIRONMENTAL LAW
AND
POLICY IN INDIA

Cases, Materials and Statutes

Second Edition

SHYAM DIVAN
ARMIN ROSENCRANZ

OXFORD

UNIVERSITY PRESS

OXFORD
UNIVERSITY PRESS

YMCA Library Building, Jai Singh Road, New Delhi 110 001

Oxford University Press is a department of the University of Oxford. It furthers the
University's objective of excellence in research, scholarship, and education
by publishing worldwide in

Oxford   New York

Auckland   Bangkok   Buenos Aires   Cape Town   Chennai
Dar es Salaam   Delhi   Hong Kong   Istanbul   Karachi   Kolkata
Kuala Lumpur   Madrid   Melbourne   Mexico City   Mumbai   Nairobi
Sao Paulo   Shanghai   Singapore   Taipei   Tokyo   Toronto

and an associated company in Berlin

Oxford is a registered trade mark of Oxford University Press
in the UK and in certain other countries

Published in India
By Oxford University Press, New Delhi

© Shyam Divan and Armin Rosencranz 2001

The moral rights of the author have been asserted
Database right Oxford University Press (maker)
First published by Oxford University Press 2001
Oxford India Paperbacks 2002
Second Impression 2002

ISBN   019   5661737

Typeset in Times
By Eleven Arts, Keshav Puram, Delhi 110 035
Printed at Roopak Printers, Delhi-110 032
Published by Manzar Khan, Oxford University Press
YMCA Library Building, Jai Singh Road, New Delhi 110 001

TO MADHAVI AND ROBBIE

PREFACE

Early in 1983, I received a letter from Professor P. Leelakrishnan inviting me to an international weekend seminar on air and water pollution at the University of Cochin. I replied that 13,000 miles was a long way to go to take part in a seminar; but if he wanted me for a semester, I would certainly consider it. One thing led to another and I was granted a Fulbright award to teach environmental law at the University of Cochin, followed by a month of lectures at the University of Poona. My course in environmental law was one of the first such courses to be taught in India. Before I left India in 1984, the Ford Foundation asked me to submit a proposal for a book on Indian environmental law. Eventually I was awarded a grant from Ford, India to organize such a book. For several years I worked with R. Sudarshan, the extraordinarily able assistant director of Ford, India during the 1980s.

I decided at the onset that my book would be modelled on the law books used in American law schools: it would contain cases, articles and statutes, as well as notes and questions to guide law students. My second decision was to find an Indian co-author on whom I could rely to secure and interpret current cases dealing with the whole range of environmental issues.

I was very fortunate to find, through mutual colleagues, a recent L.L.M. graduate of Boalt Hall (the law school at the University of California, Berkeley)— Shyam Divan. The first edition of *Environmental Law and Policy in India* came out in 1991, and went through two supplementary printings. It seemed to fill a need within the community of law students, law teachers, practising lawyers and judges, as well as environmental activists.

After four years had passed, and after accepting another Fulbright professorship to teach the National Law School of India's first environmental law course in 1992, Shyam and I entered into discussions with Ford program officers Jeff Campbell and Maja Daruwala. This led to a new grant to prepare a thoroughly revised and updated second edition. We all agreed that the second edition would pay special attention to equity issues, and to the environmental problems of the urban and rural poor. This edition has been in preparation for five years.

Many have contributed unstintingly of their time and energy to produce this book. Major research has been conducted by Bharath Jairaj, a graduate of my India Visiting Environmental Law Fellows Program, who practises environmental law in Chennai. The book has benefitted from the insights shared by my colleagues and friends: Gautam Patel, Kerban Anklesaria and Rajeev Dhavan. Medha Patkar and

Pervin Jehangir graciously gave their time to comment on a draft of the Narmada section. Vivek Divan compiled the statutes in the appendix. The manuscript preparation has been in the highly competent hands of Farzana Shaikh and Dipali Pawaskar.

   While all these people, and most of all our supportive families, deserve our praise and thanks, the two co-authors are alone responsible for the book's failings.

Stanford, California   ARMIN ROSENCRANZ
January 2001

ACKNOWLEDGEMENTS

The authors acknowledge the following publishers and authors for permissions to reprint excerpts from books and periodicals cited.

The Centre for Science and Environment (CSE) for Agarwal, 'Politics of Environment II' in *The State of India's Environment 1984–85: The Second Citizens' Report*, 1986; *Floods, Flood Plains and Environmental Myths: The Third Citizens' Report*, 1991; *State of India's Environment: The Citizens' Fifth Report*, 1999; Sharma, 'When a River Weeps', *Down to Earth*, 15 November 1997; and *Slow Murder: The Deadly Story of Vehicular Pollution in India*, 1996.

Oxford University Press (OUP) for World Commission on Environment and Development, *Our Common Future*, 1987; Gadgil and Guha, *This Fissured Land: An Ecological History of India*, 1993; Guha, *The Unquiet Woods: Ecological Change and Peasant Resistance in the Himalayas*, 1991; and Singh, *Common Property and Common Poverty: India's Forests, Forest Dwellers and the Law*, 1986.

The Sameeksha Trust for reproductions from the *Economic and Political Weekly* (EPW) from Divan, 'Cleaning the Ganga', EPW, 1 July 1995; Chopra, 'Forest and Other Sectors: Critical Role of Government Policy', EPW, 24 June 1995; and Kibel and Rosencranz, 'A Blanket Spread too Thin: Compensation for Bhopal's Victims', EPW, 2 July 1994.

The United Nations Development Programme for Rosencranz, Pandian and Campbell, *Economic Approaches for a Green India*, 1999; The Hindu for Kalpana Sharma, 'The Farakka Fallout', *The Hindu*, New Delhi, 29–30 April 1997; Island Press for Gretchen C. Daily, *Nature's Services*, 1997; University of Pennsylvania Press for Rosencranz, Divan and Scott, 'Legal and Political Repercussions in India' in *Learning from Disaster: Risk Management after Bhopal*, edited by Sheila Jasanoff, 1994; and the School of Legal Studies, Cochin University for M.K. Prasad, 'Silent Valley Case: An Ecological Assessment', 8 *Cochin University Law Review*, 128, 1984.

Darryl D'Monte and the CSE for *Temples or Tombs? Industry versus Environment: Three Controversies*, 1985; D'Monte and the India International Centre for 'Storm over Silent Valley', 9 *IIC Quarterly*, 288, 1982; Romila Thapar and OUP for *Asoka and the Decline of the Mauryas*, second edition, 1973; V.K. Gupta, *Kautilyan Jurisprudence*, 1987; P.M. Bakshi, 'Corporate Executives and the Pollution Law', 2 *Company Law Journal*, 61, 1986, Lori Udall for Udall and

Kleiner, 'Human Rights Violations Associated with the World Bank Finance Sarovar Dam Project in Western India', *Third International Narmada Symposium*, Tokyo, 29 August 1992; and O.P. Dwivedi for *India's Environmental Policies, Programmes and Stewardship*, 1997.

SUMMARY OF CONTENTS

TABLE OF CONTENTS

TABLE OF CASES

1

INTRODUCTION

A. ENVIRONMENTAL REGULATION IN THE 1990s: AN OVERVIEW

India employs a range of regulatory instruments to preserve and protect its natural resources. As a system for doing so, the law works badly, when it works at all. The legislature is quick to enact laws regulating most aspects of industrial and development activity, but chary to sanction enforcement budgets or require effective implementation. Across the country, government agencies wield vast power to regulate industry, mines and other polluters but are reluctant to use their power to discipline violators. The judiciary, a spectator to environmental despoliation for more than two decades, has recently assumed a pro-active role of public educator,[1] policy maker,[2] super-administrator,[3] and more generally, *amicus* environment. The flurry of legislation, lax enforcement and assertive judicial oversight have combined to create a unique implementation dichotomy: one limb represented by the hamstrung formal regulatory machinery comprised of the pollution control boards, forest bureaucracies and state agencies; the other, consisting of a non-formal, *ad hoc* citizen and court driven implementation mechanism. As we shall see throughout this book, the development of environmental law in the 1990s is largely the story of India's judiciary responding to the complaints of its citizens against environmental degradation and administrative sloth.

When environmental laws were first enacted in the 1970s, there was little to

---

[1] e.g., *M.C. Mehta v Union of India* AIR 1992 SC 382 (court directions to broadcast and telecast ecology programmes on the electronic media and include environmental study in school and college curricula).

[2] e.g., *S. Jagannath v Union of India* AIR 1997 SC 811 (directions prohibiting non-traditional acquaculture along the coast); *M.C.Mehta v Union of India* AIR 1996 (2) SCALE 92 (court directions for the introduction of unleaded petrol vehicles).

[3] e.g., *T.N. Godavarman Thirumulkpad v Union of India* AIR 1997 SC 1228 (judicial supervision over the implementation of national forest laws); *M.C. Mehta v Union of India* 1992 (Supp.2) SCC 633 (directions in the *Ganga Pollution Case* to riparian industries, tanneries and distilleries regarding abatement of pollution).

distinguish the field of environmental law from the general body of law. For instance, when Parliament enacted the Water Act of 1974, it adhered to the pattern of numerous other Indian statutes and created yet another agency-administered licensing system—this time to control effluent discharges into water. A breach of the Act invited judge-imposed penalties. The body of case law, too, was unremarkable. Most of the pre-1980 'environmental cases' were either actions in tort or standard agency prosecutions under an environmental statute. Moreover, during this early period the environment enjoyed no special protection from the judiciary.

All this was transformed, in part, by the spate of fresh legislation passed after the Bhopal gas leak disaster of December, 1984. The new laws and rules are impressive in their range: They cover hitherto unregulated fields, such as noise, vehicular emissions, hazardous waste, hazardous micro-organisms, the transportation of toxic chemicals, coastal development and environment impact assessment. The state of Maharashtra has introduced urban heritage regulations and an industry location policy designed to protect river basins. Stringent penalties introduced into the older pollution control laws, specifically, the Water and Air Acts, have raised the cost of non-compliance.

Equally significant, we find in these laws a governmental effort to supplement the old licensing regime with an array of new regulatory techniques. *Public hearings* under the Environment Impact Assessment Regulations of 1994 provide a forum to non-governmental organisations to voice their concerns to project proponents. *Citizens' initiative* provisions, together with a statutory 'right to information', now enable an aggrieved citizen to directly prosecute a polluter after examining government records and data. The *technology-forcing deadlines,* issued under the central Motor Vehicles Rules of 1989, compel the manufacturers of petrol and diesel vehicles to upgrade their technologies (perhaps even re-tool their plants) to meet the prescribed emission standards by a particular date. Mandatory *workers' participation* in plant safety and stringent *penalties on high level management* for the breach of factory safety regulations, are expected to reduce industrial accidents.

Another feature of the new regime is the vesting of enormous administrative power in the enforcement agencies. For example, a pollution control board may direct a polluter to shut down an offending factory or order the withdrawal of its power supply. Previously, the board had to approach a magistrate to enjoin the polluter. This shift away from judicial to administrative enforcement of environmental laws was intended to improve compliance. Earlier, few agencies had the financial and legal resources to speedily launch prosecutions and battle the cases through multiple appeals. With the change in the enforcement strategy, however, the burden of initiating a court action now rests on an aggrieved polluter, who must challenge the agency's order in court. Consequently, from a lawyer's standpoint, the agency merely has the task of defending its administrative order.

The new legislation has spawned new enforcement agencies and strengthened the older ones. Some of these agencies perform specialised tasks. Consider the authorities constituted under the Environment Impact Assessment (EIA) Regulations of 1994. The Union Ministry of Environment and Forests is responsible for evaluating

EIA reports submitted by project proponents. Generally, for large projects the review is carried out in consultation with a committee of experts. Responding to a suggestion by the Supreme Court,[4] the Union Government has established a National Coastal Management Authority and corresponding state level agencies. Further, the past decade has seen a growth in the budget and staff of the Central and state pollution control boards, charged with implementing the Water and Air Acts. Consequently, there is a some improvement in the enforcement of these laws in at least some of the states and union territories.

Despite these initiatives, the quality of the urban and rural environment continues to decline. The root cause of this problem is the slack performance of the enforcement agencies. Several factors inhibit agency functioning, not least among them being a lack of budgetary support. The Bihar pollution control board (BPCB), which administers pollution laws in the second most populous state of the union, is continuously starved of funds. For several years the state government withheld funding, restricting BPCB expenditure to less than a third of its modest requisition.[5] Depriving the enforcement agencies of funds has meant inadequate technical staff and supporting infrastructure for monitoring and control. Ten years after Parliament enacted the Water Act in 1974, the BPCB did not have a single laboratory or analyst to test effluent samples.[6] Political interference[7] and a lack of will to confront entrenched industrial and commercial interests, also contribute to poor administration. Besides, it is widely perceived that the effectiveness of some agencies is curtailed by institutional graft.[8] This laxity and indifference has invited judicial strictures from the High Courts[9] and the Supreme Court.[10]

Recently, the Supreme Court lamented:

> If the mere enactment of laws relating to the protection of environment was to ensure a clean and pollution free environment, then India would, perhaps, be the least polluted country in the world. But, this is not so. There are stated to be over 200 Central and State statutes which have at least some concern with environmental protection, either directly or indirectly. The plethora of such enactments has, unfortunately, not resulted in preventing environmental degradation which, on the contrary, has increased over the years.[11]

---

[4] *Indian Council for Enviro-Legal Action v Union of India* 1996 (5) SCC 281, 303.

[5] B. Desai, *Water Pollution in India* 146 (1990).

[6] *Id.* at 131.

[7] *Haryana Pollution Board Disbanded*, TIMES OF INDIA, Delhi, 13 May 1992. The board was dissolved shortly after it served a prosecution notice on the Chief Minister's son-in-law.

[8] The Punjab pollution control board was superseded in 1996 after the state government received complaints regarding maladministration and harassment. An enquiry revealed that some of the board decisions were 'highly suspect.' *G.S. Oberoi v State of Punjab* AIR 1998 P & H 67.

[9] *Bayer (India) Ltd. v State of Maharashtra* 1994 (4) BOM.C.REP. 309, 330; *Pravinbhai Patel v State of Gujarat* 1995 (2) GUJ.L.R. 1210, 1234; *V. Lakshmipathy v State of Karnataka* AIR 1992 KAR 57, 70; *Suo Motu v Vatva Industries Association* AIR 2000 GUJ 33, 35.

[10] *M.C. Mehta v Union of India* 1998 (3) SCALE 602 and 1998 (4) SCALE 326.

[11] *Supra* note 4, at 293.

Although courts are ill-equipped to take over enforcement functions, the dismal performance of government agencies has compelled the higher judiciary to secure compliance through public interest litigations. Leading by example, the Supreme Court has persuaded the High Courts of several states to set apart a greater share of judicial resources to environmental cases.[12] In numerous cases discussed in this book, you will find the Supreme Court stepping into the shoes of the administrator, marshalling resources, issuing directions to close down factories, requiring the implementation of environmental norms, cutting through bureaucratic gridlock and so on. As a result of this drive, hundreds of factories have installed effluent treatment plants and there is a heightened environmental awareness among administrators, the subordinate judiciary, police and municipal officials, all of whom are involved in implementing the court's orders. More generally, the Supreme Court has succeeded in building up a sustained pressure on polluters, where the pollution control boards had failed.

This new pattern of judge-driven implementation is supported by a broad political consensus. When it comes to challenging influential industries, labour-intensive enterprises and municipalities, bureaucrats are glad to let the judiciary bell the cat. Thus far, few politically sensitive development projects have been delayed or stalled due to environment-related judicial intervention and the major political parties appear reconciled to the expanded environmental jurisdiction. The public and media have generally applauded and indeed, often triggered judicial initiatives. One of the most encouraging trends during the past decade is the growing numbers of concerned individuals, citizen groups and non-governmental organisations exerting pressure on state agencies through the courts.

Although the expanded judicial role appears secure for the present, this trend is unlikely to continue beyond the near term. Court dockets are full and judges are conscious that systemic changes in a country as vast as India are unlikely to be brought about by judicial intervention alone. If judicial activism is to have a lasting impact, a political will in the form of substantial budgetary allocations for environment and increased community pressure on enforcement agencies, are imperative. Court-administered implementation can at best supplement, not replace, the formal agency-dependent enforcement mechanism.

B. THE NATURE OF ECOSYSTEMS

UNITED STATES COUNCIL ON ENVIRONMENTAL QUALITY, ENVIRONMENTAL QUALITY: FIRST ANNUAL REPORT, 6 (1970)

Ecology is the science of the intricate web of relationships between living organisms and their living and nonliving surroundings. These interdependent living and nonliving

---

[12] For example, the High Courts at Bombay, Calcutta, Madras and the Gujarat High Courts have a designated 'green bench'.

parts make up *ecosystems.* Forests, lakes, and estuaries are examples. Larger ecosystems or combinations of ecosystems, which occur in similar climates and share a similar character and arrangement of vegetation, are *biomes.* The Arctic tundra, prairie grasslands, and the desert are examples. The earth, its surrounding envelope of life-giving water and air, and all its living things comprise the *biosphere.* Finally, man's total *environmental system* includes not only the biosphere but also his interactions with his natural and manmade surroundings.

Changes in ecosystems occur continuously. Myriad interactions take place at every moment of the day as plants and animals respond to variations in their surroundings and to each other. Evolution has produced for each species, including man, a genetic composition that limits how far that species can go in adjusting to sudden changes in its surroundings. But within these limits the several thousand species in an ecosystem, or for that matter, the millions in the biosphere, continuously adjust to outside stimuli. Since interactions are so numerous, they form long chains of reactions. Thus small changes in one part of an ecosystem are likely to be felt and compensated for eventually throughout the system.

Dramatic examples of change can be seen where man has altered the course of nature. It is vividly evident in his well-intentioned but poorly thought out tampering with river and lake ecosystems. The Aswan Dam was primarily built to generate electric power. It produced power, but it also reduced the fish population in the Mediterranean, increased the numbers of disease-bearing aquatic snails, and markedly lowered the fertility of the Nile Valley.

* * *

The stability of a particular ecosystem depends on its diversity. The more interdependencies in an ecosystem, the greater the chances that it will be able to compensate for changes imposed upon it. A complex tropical forest with a rich mosaic of interdependencies possesses much more stability than the limited plant and animal life found on the Arctic tundra, where instability triggers frequent, violent fluctuations in some animal populations, such as lemmings and foxes. The least stable systems are the single crops—called monocultures—created by man. A cornfield or lawn has little natural stability. If they are not constantly and carefully cultivated, they will not remain cornfields or lawns but will soon be overgrown with a wide variety of hardier plants constituting a more stable ecosystem.

The chemical elements that make up living systems also depend on complex, diverse sources to prevent cyclic shortages or oversupply. The oxygen cycle, which is crucial to survival, depends upon a vast variety of green plants, notably plankton in the ocean. Similar diversity is essential for the continued functioning of the cycle by which atmospheric nitrogen is made available to allow life to exist. This cycle depends on a wide variety of organisms, including soil bacteria and fungi, which are often destroyed by persistent pesticides in the soil.

NOTES AND QUESTIONS

1. In considering how a legal system might respond to protect the environment against degradation, the gaps and uncertainties in our knowledge about environmental disruption must be stressed. For example, a substance may be known to cause cancer when its fibres or particles are inhaled by workers over several years. But what if the same substance is inhaled by a worker over a short period? Should the legal system compensate the worker, even though epidemiological and toxicological data may not exist or may be confusing and uncertain with regard to short-term exposures?

Uncertainty also exacerbates the difficulties of those who prescribe standards for the discharge of pollutants. Most scientists believe that it is not possible to identify health effect 'thresholds' for pollutants. (A threshold is the concentration at which sensitive individuals suffer adverse health effects.) Almost any non-zero concentration of a pollutant will adversely affect some sensitive individuals. And scientists are seldom unanimous on where to draw the line. Thus, decision-makers must simply pick a particular emission or discharge standard, amidst a cloud of ambiguous evidence. This makes standard-setting for pollutants seem unsystematic and random.

This 'number game' in standard setting is exemplified by the national minimum standard in respect of a parameter for industrial effluent, namely, sodium. In view of the high incidence of sodium in the natural water in some regions, the effluent parameter published in this regard was deleted from the statute before it was brought into force.[13]

2. Environmental problems are complex, not only in their causes and effects, but also in how they relate to each other. Eliminating pollution from one medium often transfers it to another. For example, when we protect the air and human health by not burning toxic chemical wastes, our alternative is usually to bury the wastes, thereby risking eventual contamination of the soil and groundwater. Frequently, it is these complexities and interdependencies that make environmental problems so obstinate.

3. The uncertainty in our understanding of environmental issues is brought out in the debate about the causes of floods in the river basins of the Ganga and Brahmaputra. During the 1980s, a number of reports[14] strengthened the perception that the floods in the sub-Himalayan plains were caused primarily by poor land use practices and deforestation by the villagers dwelling in the Himalayan foothills. This notion was challenged in the report excerpted below:

---

[13] The national minimum standard in respect of sodium, notified on 19 May 1993 with effect from 1 January 1994 *vide* the Environment (Protection) Second Amendment Rules of 1993 was deleted by a further amendment on 31 December 1993.

[14] e.g., Myers, *Environmental Repurcussions of Deforestation in the Himalayas*, 2 JR. OF WORLD FOREST RES. MNGM. 63 (1986); World Resources Institute, *Tropical Forests: A Call for Action* (1985).

CENTRE FOR SCIENCE AND ENVIRONMENT; FLOODS, FLOOD PLAINS AND ENVIRONMENTAL MYTHS: THE THIRD CITIZENS' REPORT, 147 (1991)

The Indus, Ganga and Brahmaputra valleys have always been flood prone. Even when the Himalayan mountains were uninhabited and the forest cover intact, major floods visited these valleys and disrupted human civilisation. Ancient Indian literature is full of references to devastating floods. People who built cities like Varanasi, Prayag and Patliputra were faced with a dilemma. They wanted to be close to the major rivers, which were the arteries of communication and commerce, they were also afraid of the floods these would bring. They, therefore, carefully chose the site of their cities along more stable rivers and on relatively flood proof bluffs. As a result, some of these cities have lasted for thousands of years whereas major cities could never emerge in other areas where rivers were flashy and volatile.

The Himalayan mountains, being the youngest in the world, lashed by intense rainstorms and highly seismic, give rise to extremely flashy rivers which come down laden with enormous quantities of silt. This is inherent to the ecology of the Himalayan ranges, and floods, therefore, are inherent to the ecology of the flood plains of the Indus, Ganga and Brahmaputra valleys. Deforestation over the last few centuries has definitely exacerbated the flashiness of the Himalayan rivers and their silt load but they are naturally so flashy and silt laden that the increase over the natural condition does not seem to be particularly high.

There is a tremendous paucity of scientific data but based on available knowledge and people's perception, two tentative conclusions can be reached. Firstly, the afforestation of the Himalayan mountains can reduce the problem of floods in the submontane plains only to a minor extent. Environmentalists should not enter into a game of one-upmanship with water engineers. There is no evidence to believe that ecological solutions like afforestation will control floods any more than engineering solutions like dams and embankments have been able to. People in the plains will have to deal with floods whether the Himalayan ranges are covered with forests. It is interesting to note that in the Assam valley it is the northern tributaries of the Brahmaputra which come down from the relatively forested slopes of Bhutan and Arunachal Pradesh that create more flood and silt problems than the southern tributaries which come down from the deforested slopes of Nagaland, Cachar hills and Meghalaya where shifting cultivation is practiced on a more extensive scale.

Secondly, ecological changes that have taken place in the lowlands themselves, because of technological interventions to control floods and encroach upon the flood plains, has exacerbated the problem far more than the ecological changes in the mountainous uplands. The natural drainage system in the plains has been willfully destroyed. Massive rivers have been embanked; drainage channels have been blocked off; and natural depressions and wetlands have been steadily encroached upon and reclaimed for agriculture. All this has not only increased the flood problem as a physical phenomenon but also, the societal susceptibility to floods.

By claiming that the destruction of the uplands is the cause of the growing agony in the low lands, environmentalists are providing arguments for a very dirty

kind of politics, which pits the relatively powerful people of the plains against the
less powerful people of the hills. Every time there is a flood in north Bihar, the chief
minister of Bihar gets an opportunity to blame Nepal. Every time there is a flood in
Assam, the local leaders blame the upland tribal communities and their shifting
cultivation practices in Arunachal Pradesh, Nagaland, Meghalaya, Manipur and
Mizoram. And, every time there is a flood in Bangladesh, the president of Bangladesh
can indulge in rhetorical politics against India. Whereas the truth is that every time
there is a flood in these respective areas, these leaders should be seriously looking
for changes they can make in the management of the flood plains themselves.
Something they just do not wish to tackle.

C. POPULATION GROWTH AND ECONOMIC INCENTIVES: TWO CAUSES OF ENVIRONMENTAL DISRUPTION

The World Commission on Environment and Development headed by Gro Harlem
Brundtland, Prime Minister of Norway, was set up as an independent body by the
United Nations in 1983. Its task was to fashion a global agenda for change, which
would ensure that human progress would be sustained through development without
bankrupting the resources of future generations. The following excerpt from the
influential report of the Brundtland Commission, clearly poses the nexus between
population control and sustainable development. The second reading in this section
is a brief excerpt from a report of the United Kingdom's Royal Commission on
Environmental Pollution. The Royal Commission describes the manner in which
economic incentives as well as legal and institutional arrangements contribute to
the pollution problem.

WORLD COMMISSION ON ENVIRONMENT AND DEVELOPMENT; OUR COMMON FUTURE, 95 (1987)

In 1985, some 80 million people were added to a world population of 4.8 billion.
Each year the number of human beings increases, but the amount of natural resources
with which to sustain this population, to improve the quality of human lives, and to
eliminate mass poverty remains finite. On the other hand, expanding knowledge
increases the productivity of resources.

Present rates of population growth cannot continue. They already compromise
many governments' abilities to provide education, health care, and food security for
people, much less their abilities to raise living standards. This gap between numbers
and resources is all the more compelling because so much of the population growth
is concentrated in low-income countries, ecologically disadvantaged regions, and
poor households.

Yet the population issue is not solely about numbers. And poverty and resource
degradation can exist on thinly populated lands, such as the drylands and the tropical
forests. People are the ultimate resource. Improvements in education, health, and
nutrition allow them to better use the resource they command, to stretch them further.

In addition, threats to the sustainable use of resources come as much from inequalities in people's access to resources and from the ways in which they use them as from the sheer numbers of people. Thus, concern over the 'population problem' also calls forth concern for human progress and human equality.

Nor are population growth rates the challenge solely of those nations with high rates of increase. An additional person in an industrial country consumes far more and places far greater pressure on natural resources than an additional person in the Third World. Consumption patterns and preferences are as important as numbers of consumers in the conservation of resources.

Thus many governments must work on several fronts—to limit population growth; to control the impact of such growth on resources and, with increasing knowledge, enlarge their range and improve their productivity; to realize human potential so that people can better husband and use resources; and to provide people with forms of social security other than large numbers of children. The means of accomplishing these goals will vary from country to country, but all should keep in mind that sustainable economic growth and equitable access to resources are two of the more certain routes towards lower fertility rates.

Giving people the means to choose the size of their families is not just a method of keeping population in balance with resources; it is a way of assuring—especially for women—the basic human right of self-determination. The extent to which facilities for exercising such choices are made available is itself a measure of a nation's development. In the same way, enhancing human potential not only promotes development but helps to ensure the right of all to a full and dignified life.

ROYAL COMMISSION ON ENVIRONMENTAL POLLUTION; FIRST REPORT, 4 (1971)

WHY THERE IS A POPULATION PROBLEM

The problem we face is how to strike a balance between the benefits of a rising standard of living, and its costs in terms of deterioration of the physical environment and the quality of life. In the past the danger of polluting air, water and land was not fully recognised, but now there is no doubt that it is a matter of great concern.

* * *

It may well be asked why it is that there should be a growing conflict between economic and technological advance on the one hand, and the quality of the environment on the other. There are two main reasons. One is rooted in a basic law of nature: it is impossible to add to the material resources with which the world is endowed and impracticable to dispose of waste materials outside the world and its envelope of air. Industry transforms natural resources and in doing so depletes some of them and spoils others—for example, our water resources—as a result of the undesirable accumulation of waste products. The second reason for the growing conflict is largely economic. Little can be done about the first reason, for even the most powerful legislatures cannot change the laws of nature; but many things can be done about the second. Governments can protect the environment through legal and institutional arrangements.

The economic reason why society may not strike the right balance between economic output and the quality of the environment is that the costs of many kinds of pollution are borne not by the polluters, but by somebody else. As a result these 'external' costs will not, in general, be taken fully into account by firms, individuals or other bodies who cause pollution. The other side of the coin is that those who spend money on reducing pollution may not always be the people who gain from the resulting improvement in the environment. This applies both to 'tangible' pollution, such as the poisoning of fish in polluted waters, and to 'intangible' pollution, such as unpleasant smells or ugly landscapes.

This characteristic of pollution has three main consequences:

(a) Output of goods and services which give rise to pollution tends to be pushed beyond the socially optimum point. Also, expenditure to reduce pollution will often be inadequate. It is true not only for private firms or individuals: it is true also for public authorities. For example, it is hardly surprising that a large proportion of the many sewage works in this country are inadequate, since it may well be that the benefits from better installations—in the form of cleaner effluent and hence cleaner rivers—would be enjoyed only by communities living further downstream. In such cases all the benefits are external to the sewage authority, which therefore has little inducement to improve its plant.

(b) There is generally not enough incentive to reduce the amount of pollution per unit of output of the goods and services responsible, so that not enough resources and effort are devoted to this objective. For example, if it becomes cheaper to distribute milk in plastic containers instead of glass bottles, this will be done whether or not the production and disposal of plastic containers impose higher pollution costs per unit of milk consumed than does the use of glass bottles. It is true, of course, that technological innovation in some industries has reduced the amounts of pollution per unit of output; for example, the switch from coal to other resources of fuel over the last two decades has greatly reduced the amount of certain kinds of airborne pollution per unit of industrial output. But this benefit to the environment has been fortuitous; we cannot rely on technological innovation automatically to reduce environmental pollution.

(c) Insofar as pollution costs are not borne by those who cause pollution or by the purchasers of their products, but by people who happen to be victims of the pollution, some of the total welfare resulting from the economic activity of the community is being redistributed away from the victims of pollution in favour of other groups in the community. Manufacturers whose production gives rise to pollution make greater profits than they would if they were obliged to bear the full social costs of their production, and purchasers of their goods buy them at a lower price than they would if the price had to cover the full social costs involved. Therefore both manufacturers and purchasers gain at the expense of other members of the community who may suffer in one way or another from the pollution.

POLLUTION ABATEMENT VERSUS OTHER CLAIMS ON RESOURCES

None of this implies—as is often believed to be the case—that all forms of pollution must cease. All production involves some costs, whether they are borne by the polluter or are external costs borne by others; but this is not a reason for stopping all production: £10 of external costs are no more costly to society than £10 of the normal costs of the labour or capital that are used by firms in the ordinary course of business. The fact that some pollution costs are not borne by those who make or purchase a product merely reflects the particular institutional arrangements of society. Consider, for example, the costs of purifying polluted water: these costs would be no less if sewage authorities and the users of rivers were united in some common body (as they are not at present) so that the costs were incurred by the same body which was responsible for the pollution. Similarly, the fact that airline operators do not have to pay to soundproof the homes of people who live near airports, is merely the result of particular legal and institutional arrangements and does not mean that the costs to society of the necessary soundproofing are any greater. Alternative legal or institutional arrangements could, in principle, be made to ensure that the costs of pollution caused by noise did enter into the calculations of the polluters like any other production costs. These costs would then play their full part in determining how far society should go in reducing pollution, and would no doubt lead to less pollution, other things being equal. But the costs to society of any given reduction in pollution would not necessarily be affected.

Thus, the problem which has often to be faced is, not how to stop pollution altogether, but how far it should be reduced. One implication of [the preceding analysis] is that some productive activities have been pushed too far, not that they should cease altogether. To abolish all such activities, and hence deprive society entirely of their benefits in order to eliminate one particular form of social cost, would be a clear case of throwing the baby away with the bath water. Another implication ... is that inadequate attention and resources are likely to be devoted to reducing pollution per unit of output, not that there is no limit to the amount of resources which should be devoted to this end. The more we spend on abating pollution the less we have available for other desirable expenditures.

The social benefits of cleaner air and water, less noise and a more pleasant landscape, have to be put into perspective with other claims on resources, such as housing, health and education, or private consumption and investment. Nobody would suggest that the allocation of resources amongst these uses should be based on an 'all-or-nothing' approach. For example, it would hardly be suggested that health has some absolute priority over all other social needs. Ideally we might all like to have pure water and complete freedom from noise and dirty air; but in practice we might tolerate some shortcomings in the environment in the interests of having, say, better schools, or better health or cultural facilities than we now enjoy. So long as resources are limited, choices have to be made between alternative ways of using them. There is no social merit in making exaggerated claims for one particular form of expenditure to the detriment of others which, to many people, may be more important.

NOTES AND QUESTIONS

1. At current growth rates, world population will increase from 6 billion to 8.4 billion in 30 years and perhaps to 15 billion at the end of the 21st century. The great bulk of the increase will come in poorer nations, whose resources are already under great pressure. Productive arable land, water, energy sources and biological diversity are all declining—based on data on worldwide ground water depletion, deforestation and soil erosion. Already 1.1 billion people are malnourished and as many as 2 billion people live in poverty. Is the answer to the world's environmental problems then conservation and sustainable development? Or is the real answer population control? Is the population issue a ploy by the developed world to deflect attention away from the resource-intensive lifestyles in the North? What about similar lifestyles practiced by the elite in the South?

2. There are other factors—political and technological—that contribute to environmental degradation. A democratic polity is usually more responsive to environmental problems than an authoritarian regime. But a democratic system has its shortcomings: Governments frequently adopt short-term, populist measures unmindful of their long-term impacts. Incremental decision-making that most closely approximates the status quo is usual for a government that must win a not-too-distant election. Consequently, short-term stability is prime, while long-term stability and welfare are at a discount. In such a system it is difficult to persuade a government to take unpopular measures that would benefit future generations and strengthen the long-term stability of society.

3. How can the legal system respond to favour ecologically benign technologies over more harmful ones? What incentives and disincentives would you propose to ensure that industries adopt appropriate technologies?

D. COMMON PROPERTY AND ECOSYSTEM SERVICES

Those persons who are most deeply affected by environmental deterioration in India, are the poor. They are the first victims of poor sanitation, bad air, contaminated water and scarce wood for fuel and fodder. India's poor are the ones who suffer most from the deterioration and loss of the nation's precious 'commons': water, air, soil and forest. For millions of Indians their only wealth is common property resources; and this is threatened by environmental degradation. The noted environmentalist, Anil Agarwal, develops this theme in the essay excerpted below. The second reading in this section is a persuasive tract by the late academic, Chhatrapati Singh. Singh argues that the appropriation of common property resources by the state is the root cause of poverty and the destruction of our natural resources.

AGARWAL; POLITICS OF ENVIRONMENT—II, IN CENTRE FOR SCIENCE AND ENVIRONMENT; THE STATE OF INDIA'S ENVIRONMENT 1984–85: THE SECOND CITIZENS' REPORT, 362 (1986)

The post-independence political debate in India has centered on two major issues: equity and growth. The environmental concern has added a third dimension: sustainability. India's biggest challenge today is to identify and implement a development process that will lead to greater equity, growth and sustainability.

The environment is not just pretty trees and tigers, threatened plants and ecosystems. It is literally the entity on which we all subsist, and on which the entire agricultural and industrial development depends. Development can take place at the cost of the environment only until a point. Beyond that point it will be like the foolish man who was trying to cut the very branch on which he was sitting. Development without concern for the environment can only be short-term development. In the long term, it can only be anti-development and can go on only at the cost of enormous human suffering, increased poverty and oppression. India may be rapidly approaching that point.

* * *

Let us look at a few cases of how the destruction of nature has affected the lives of people in India. One very dramatic area where government policies have consistently increased conflict is forests. The entire tribal population, and millions of other forest dwelling people, depend on the forests for their very existence. Destruction of forests has meant the social, cultural and economic destruction of the tribal populations in particular. Beginning with the British and continuing with free India, the government has decided to control the forest resource itself, leaving little or no control in the hands of the forest dwellers. Government control over forests has definitely meant a reallocation of forest resources away from the needs of local communities and into the hands of urban and industrial India. The end result is both increased social conflict and increased destruction or transformation of the ecological resource itself.

Yet another major component of the country's physical environment is grazing lands. The destruction of the grazing lands has meant enormous hardships for poor people, especially for the nomadic groups in the country. Few people know that India has nearly 200 castes engaged in pastoral nomadism, which add up to nearly 6 per cent of India's population. India is unique in the world in terms of the diversity of animals associated with pastoral nomadism. There are shepherds of camels in Rajasthan and in Gujarat, of donkeys in Maharashtra, of yaks in Ladakh, of pigs in Andhra Pradesh, and even of ducks in south India. Sheep, goats and cattle are of course the main nomadic animals.

A number of factors, including land reforms and development programmes, which have promoted expansion of agriculture to marginal lands, have steadily led to an erosion of grazing lands. The Rajasthan Canal is a fine example of a government programme that has transformed extensive grazing lands into agricultural lands. No effort was made by the government to ensure that the nomads who used these grazing lands earlier would benefit from the canal on a priority basis. In almost every village, the panchayat lands traditionally used as gaucher lands, have been encroached upon by powerful interest groups and privatised. Nomadic groups have been increasingly impoverished over the last 30 years and an ever-increasing number is being forced to give up their traditional occupation to become landless labourers or urban migrants.

* * *

What we see in India is growing conflict over the use of natural resources and, in particular, over biomass between the two sectors of the country's economy; the cash economy (or the modern sector) on one hand and the non-monetized, biomass-based subsistence economy (the traditional sector) on the other.

* * *

As even those forms of biomass that are used by the poor become commercialised, the access of the poor to those biomass sources gets automatically reduced because of limited purchasing power. The trend towards commercialization of firewood has been so rapid in the last 15 years that it is now rare to find poor households using much firewood, especially in the shape of logs. Firewood is no longer a fuel of the poor but of the relatively rich. The poor now subsist on qualitatively inferior sources of biomass fuels: crop wastes, weeds, twigs, cowdung and whatever organic kachra (waste) that they can find. In fact, if one goes to a village, one will see that even the firewood, crop wastes and cow dung are fuels used according to the family's economic status—crop wastes usually being at the lowest end of the pecking order.

Unfortunately, several scientific agencies, thinking that 'crop wastes' are actually wastes, have begun to undertake research on commercial utilisation of crop wastes. Technologies like fuel briquetting plants and small scale paper mills based on crop residues are being heavily promoted by the government. This raises prices of fuel and fodder and directly hits poor landless peasants, who now have to rely heavily on the mercy of landed farmers to allow them to take these wastes away, which they will do only as long as they are non-commercial entities to them.

* * *

If we are to construct a concept like Gross Nature Product, we would find that for the poor it is this indicator which is many times more important than the conventional Gross National Product. In fact, we can even say that those who do not get much from the conventional GNP—the poor—are the ones who are most critically dependent on the Gross Nature Product. The Gross National Product cannot be allowed to destroy or transform the Gross Nature Product.

Just as the economists get very worried about the structure of the Gross National Product, it is equally important, if they have the poor in mind, that they get worried about the structure of the Gross Nature Product. It is not just the quantity of biomass that is important for meeting basic household needs but also its diversity: sources of biomass within any village ecosystem must be diverse enough to meet the diverse household needs of fuel, fodder, building materials and herbs, and of raw materials for artisans.

The diversity in nature has also acted as insurance during periods of emergency by reducing societal vulnerability. During periods of drought and resulting crop failures, which are recurring phenomena in many parts of India, fruits from trees, and roots, leaves and wild animals in the forests, used to become an important, alternative source of nutrition.

* * *

The answer to India's immediate problem of poverty lies in increasing the biomass available in nature and increasing it in a manner that access to it is ensured on an equitable basis. But giving a relevant 'green cover' to the country—the real Green Revolution—would probably require the most holistic thinking that planners, economists and scientists have ever known. The conflicts and complementarities in the existing land use patterns have to be extremely well understood. Otherwise land-use patterns will remain as chaotic as today.

* * *

Immediately, at least, the country must recognize that a clear biomass policy is desperately needed, which recognises the competing uses for biomass in society, especially between biomass-based industry and poor households and sets clear priorities on the use of biomass in a situation of scarcity. The needs of the poor must be specified as a priority use of biomass in the existing situation of environmental degradation. A beginning definitely needs to be made with the proposed Forest Policy and with rural energy planning in general.

If India fails to recreate nature on a massive scale in a manner that generates employment and equity, not only its villages but also its cities will become unlivable. Many people prefer to call the urban migrants economic refugees from the countryside. But to my mind many of them are really ecological refugees, displaced by dams, by mines, by deforestation, by destruction of grazing lands, by floods, by droughts, by urban expansion, and what not. We have today the world's fourth largest urban population. Before the end of the century we will be the largest. Managing this huge urban population will call for extraordinary political and managerial sagacity and altogether new approaches, something we cannot learn from the rest of the world. But one thing is definite, if the process of urbanization continues to create the same demands on our rural environment, it will only accelerate the destruction of the rural environment and in turn make the urban environment impossible to manage. India cannot survive without a low-energy, low-resource input urbanisation. ... Only a holistic approach to our problems and dedicated political will to solve them will work.

SINGH; COMMON PROPERTY AND COMMON POVERTY: INDIA'S FORESTS, FOREST DWELLERS AND THE LAW, 1 (1986)

It is common knowledge that India is facing an environmental crisis. But what precisely is the crisis? Experts tell us it means the denudation of forests and the increase in waste land and pollution; so they and the state order the planting of trees, the cleaning up of rivers and the creation of new administrative infrastructures to achieve these ends. But do these measures really address themselves to the true crisis? Who has paused to reflect on the basic causes that have led to such massive deforestation and pollution? If the causes still persist, to what end is all this afforestation and purification directed? Will not new forests be hacked away again, and will not clean rivers be polluted sooner or later again? Deforestation and the increase in waste land and pollution are *effects*; the real need is to identify the *causes*.

* * *

The natural world is meant to be shared by all, whereas we have divided up its resources in terms of 'property' on the basis of needs, customs and laws, as well as by mere fiat and force. Property can be classified into two generic types: private and common. Within private property, only an individual and his family have legal rights to the benefits arising from its resources and capital. Within common property, access and utility are not limited to an individual and his family but are shared commonly by many people. Common property can be further classified as being of two distinct types; that which is the product of organized human labour, and that which is the product of nature's labour. In the former type feature public transport, entertainment places, service offices, hospitals, etc. These things are now generally called 'public property'. In the latter class fall natural forests, ponds, lakes, rivers and streams, ores, mineral fuels, sand, mud, limestone, and other types of stones and salts. All such common property yields natural resources. The term 'natural resources' is often mistakenly applied to minerals and oils only, but fish, wood, birds, mud, wild grass, salts and various other objects are as much natural resources as minerals. In terms of their consumption such resources are as economically significant as minerals and oils.

Now, if one looks at land records, agrarian records, records of the Forest Department (from around 1865 onwards), as well as literary sources, it is evident that till the end of the last century and in all historical periods before that at least 80 percent of India's natural resources were common property, with only about 20 percent being privately utilized. Given the uncertainty of records, even a ratio of 90:10 for common versus private property would not be an unlikely estimate. Records on common property are of course difficult to find, but their extent and type can be deducted from the knowledge of the overall geography of India and records of private holdings.

This extensive common property has provided the resource base for a non-cash, non-market economy. A whole range of necessary resources has been freely available to the people. Thus, commonly available wood, shrubs and cowdung has been utilized for cooking and heating; mud, bamboo and palm leaves for housing; wild grass and shrubs as animal fodder; and a variety of fruits and vegetables as food. There has been, thus, only a minimal cost for the basic energy, food and housing resources. The only costs involved have been personal labour and transportation. Even today most rural Indians depend upon common property resources for their energy and housing needs, and in some ways also for their food requirements. The dependency of free common property resources is the greatest in tribal areas, somewhat less in rural areas, and least in urban areas. The inhabitants of rural and tribal areas, however, form the majority of the Indian population.

Around 1865 and thereafter the British began the process of the privatization of common property resources. They did this by creating numerous permanent settlements on common property lands, declaring many 'reserved forests', 'protected forests' and 'revenue land'. After Independence Indians not only accepted these classifications but also attempted to enforce them with greater zeal.

* * *

The consequences of the legalised and *de facto* privatization of common property resources have been to turn the non-economy into a market economy, in other words the charging of a price for most primary resources which were free earlier. Indian rural people now pay a much higher price for their energy requirements than urban people. Wood and shrubs are sold to them at a higher price than to industries. Since wood has a much lower calorific value than gas, rural people end up spending a far greater amount of money in cooking an equivalent amount of food than urban gas users. Similarly, rural and tribal people end up spending a great deal of money on housing, the raw materials for which, till recent times, were free for them. The situation with food resources is similar.

The basic reason for rural and tribal poverty, therefore, is nothing but the privatization of common property resources in a non equitable manner. After Independence the government has put forwarded numerous plans for the removal of poverty. But all such economic plans have concerned themselves only with *private* property in land. The government has attempted to increase the purchasing power of the poor through land reforms, and by providing agrarian inputs, loans, etc. But none of the Five Year Plans, 20 Point Programs, and various other 'development' plans, takes into account the natural common resources which were available as free wealth. By rapidly increasing the prices of common resources the government, the industrialists and the urban rich are taking away from rural and tribal people much more than they are giving them through aids, loans and land reforms. The proof is in the fact that rural poverty and disparity in wealth have increased in actual monetary terms, not merely in terms of the number of poor people.

_____

In the next reading, Gretchen Daily introduces the new but important notion of ecosystem services, stressing the need for policy-makers to develop institutional frameworks to protect and sustain the earth's life-support systems.

DAILY; WHAT ARE ECOSYSTEM SERVICES?
IN NATURE'S SERVICES, 3 (1997)

Ecosystem services are the conditions and processes through which natural ecosystems, and the species that make them up, sustain and fulfil human life. They maintain biodiversity and the production of *ecosystem goods*, such as seafood, forage, timber, biomass fuels, natural fibre, and many pharmaceuticals, industrial products, and their precursors. The harvest and trade of these goods represent an important and familiar part of the human economy. In addition to the production of goods, ecosystem services are the actual life-support functions, such as cleansing, recycling, and renewal, and they confer many intangible aesthetic and cultural benefits as well.

One way to appreciate the nature and value of ecosystem services (originally suggested by John Holdren) is to imagine trying to set up a happy, day-to-day life on the moon. Assume for the sake of argument that the moon miraculously already had some of the basic conditions for supporting human life, such as an atmosphere and climate similar to those on earth. After inviting your best friends and packing your prized possessions, a BBQ grill, and some do-it-yourself books, the big question would be, which of earth's millions of species do you need to take with you?

Tackling the problem systematically, you could first choose from among all the species exploited directly for food, drink, spice, fibre and timber, pharmaceuticals, industrial products (such as waxes, lac, rubber and oils), and so on. Even being selective, this list could amount to hundreds of even several thousand species. The space ship would be filling up before you'd even begun adding the species crucial to *supporting* those at the top of your list. Which are these unsung heroes? No one knows which—nor even approximately how many—species are required to sustain human life. This means that rather than listing species directly, you would have to list instead the life-support functions required by your lunar colony; then you could guess at the types and numbers of species required to perform each. At a bare minimum, the spaceship would have to carry species capable of supplying a whole suite of ecosystem services that earthlings take for granted. These services include:

- purification of air and water
- mitigation of floods and droughts
- detoxification and decomposition of wastes
- generation and renewal of soil and fertility

- pollination of crops and natural vegetation
- control of the vast majority of potential agricultural pests
- dispersal of seeds and translocation of nutrients
- maintenance of biodiversity, from which humanity has derived key elements of its agricultural, medicinal, and industrial enterprise
- protection from the sun's harmful ultraviolet rays
- partial stabilization of climate
- moderation of temperature extremes and the force of winds and waves
- support of diverse human cultures
- providing of aesthetic beauty and intellectual stimulation that lift the human spirit.

Armed with this preliminary list of services, you could begin to determine which types and numbers of species are required to perform each. This is no simple task! Let's take the soil fertility case as an example. Soil organisms play important and often unique roles in the circulation of matter in every ecosystem on earth; they are crucial to the chemical conversion and physical transfer of essential nutrients to higher plants, and all larger organisms, including humans, depend on them. The abundance of soil organisms is absolutely staggering; under a square yard of pasture in Denmark, for instance, the soil was found to be inhabited by roughly 50,000 small earthworms and their relatives, 50,000 insects and mites, and nearly 12 million roundworms. And that is not all. A single gram (a pinch) of soil has yielded an estimated 30,000 protozoa, 50,000 algae, 400,000 fungi, and billions of individual bacteria. Which to bring to the moon? Most of these species have never been subjected to even cursory inspection. Yet the sobering fact of the matter is, as Ed Wilson put it: they don't need us, but we need them.

Ecosystem services are generated by a complex of natural cycles, driven by solar energy, that constitute the workings of the biosphere—the thin layer near earth's surface that contains all known life. The cycles operate on very different scales. Biogeochemical cycles, such as the movement of the element carbon through the living and physical environment, are truly global and reach from the top of the atmosphere to deep into soils and ocean-bottom sediments. Life cycles of bacteria, in contrast, may be completed in an area much smaller than the period at the end of this sentence. The cycles also operate at very different rates. The biogeochemical cycling of carbon, for instance, occurs at orders of magnitude faster than that of phosphorus, just as the life cycles of microorganisms may be orders of magnitude faster than those of trees.

All of these cycles are ancient, the product of billions of years of evolution, and have existed in forms very similar to those seen today for at least hundreds of millions of years. They are absolutely pervasive, but unnoticed by most human being going about their daily lives. Who, for example, gives a thought to the part of the carbon cycle that connects him or her to the plants in the garden outside, to plankton in the Indian Ocean, or to Julius Caesar? Noticed or not, human beings depend utterly on the continuation of natural cycles for their very existence. If the life cycles of predators that naturally control most potential pests of crops were interrupted, it is unlikely that pesticides could satisfactorily take their place. If the life cycle of pollinators of plants of economic importance ceased, society would face serious social and economic consequences. If the carbon cycle were badly disrupted, rapid climatic change could threaten the existence of civilization. In general, human beings lack both the knowledge and the ability to substitute for the functions performed by these and other cycles.

For millennia, humanity has drawn benefits from these cycles without causing global disruption. Yet, today, human influence can be discerned in the most remote reaches of the biosphere: deep below earth's surface in ancient aquifers, far out to sea on tiny tropical islands, and up in the cold, thin air high above Antarctica. Virtually no place remains untouched—chemically, physically, or biologically—by the curious and determined hand of humanity. Although much more by accident than by design, humanity now controls conditions over the entire biosphere.

Interestingly, the nature and value of Earth's life-support systems have been illuminated primarily through their disruption and loss. Thus, for instance, deforestation has revealed the critical role of forests in the hydrological cycle—in particular, in mitigating flood, drought, and the forces of wind and rain that cause erosion. Release of toxic substances, whether accidental or deliberate, has revealed the nature and value of physical and chemical processes, governed in part by a diversity of microorganisms, that disperse and break down hazardous materials. Thinning of the stratospheric ozone layer sharpened awareness of the value of its service in screening out harmful ultraviolet radiation.

A cognizance of ecosystem services, expressed in terms of their loss, dates back at least to Plato and probably much earlier:

What now remains of the formerly rich land is like the skeleton of a sick man with all the fat and soft earth wasted away and only the bare framework remaining. Formerly, many of the mountains were arable. The plains that were full of rich soil are now marshes. Hills that were once covered with forests and produced abundant pasture now produce only food for bees. Once the land was enriched by yearly rains, which were not lost, as they are now, by flowing from the bare land into the sea. The soil was deep, it absorbed and kept the water ... and the water that soaked into the hills fed springs and running streams everywhere. Now the abandoned shrines at spots where formerly there were springs attest that our description of the land is true.

Ecosystem services have also gained recognition and appreciation through efforts to substitute technology for them. The overuse of pesticides, for example, leading to the decimation of natural pest enemies and concomitant promotion of formerly benign species to pest status, has made apparent agriculture's dependence upon natural pest control services. The technical problems and cost of hydroponic systems—often prohibitive even for growing high-priced, speciality produce—underscore human dependence upon ecosystem services supplied by soil. Society is likely to value more highly the services listed above, and to discover (or rediscover) an array of services not listed, as human impacts on the environment intensify and the costs and limits of technological substitution become more apparent.

E. COURTS AND THE ENVIRONMENT

Throughout this book we will see how the courts, especially the High Courts and the Supreme Court of India, have seized opportunities presented by cases to protect the environment. Judicial action must be seen, however, as only one of many tools to bring about environmental improvement. In many situations, lobbying, public education and political action by mobilizing people, are far more effective mechanisms than the bringing of a lawsuit.

Before we examine individual cases, there are some features of the judicial process that should be recognized. First, judges are non-specialists, relatively insulated from the political process. This has its advantages. Generalist judges have a broader vision of national policies and interests than the parochial stand of specialist government agencies charged with establishing large, environmentally disruptive, industrial and developmental projects. Moreover, since judges are not involved in electoral politics, they may be more willing than the other wings of government to take unpopular decisions that are beneficial in the long run.

A second feature of the judicial process is that it frequently compels the defendant project authority to increase environment-related spending. For example, if the location of a project is challenged in court by an environmental group, the promoters frequently spend more funds on environmental impact appraisal and pollution abatement, than they otherwise might.

Third, it should be remembered that the courts can only respond to the cases that come before them. They can rarely effect systemic or society-wide changes in environmental conditions. Finally, unlike administrative decision-making, the judicial process is highly structured. Accordingly, policy implications of a case are sometimes ignored. This possibility often persuades judges to defer to the supposed expertise of governmental agencies.

However, since the late 1980s, the Supreme Court and a few High Courts have embarked on complex administrative exercises. One example is the *Ganga Pollution Case*,[15] a massive judicial effort to help clean the river Ganga. Here, the litigation-affected parties were several hundred, posing an immense management problem for the court. The sprawling dimensions of the *Ganga Case* prompted the court during Justice Kuldip Singh's tenure to evolve new procedures. Unlike conventional litigations, affected polluters were dissuaded from filing documents in the court's registry. All affidavits were tendered before the respective pollution control boards. In this manner, the court reduced its administrative burden. Moreover, to tailor its directions to each situation, the court issued orders piecemeal. What at the end of the day read like one comprehensive court order, was in fact a series of directions—dictated one paragraph at a time—and punctuated by brief arguments on each issue. It was this procedure that enabled the court to respond with specificity to each situation.

---

[15] *M.C. Mehta v Union of India* AIR 1988 SC 1037 and 1115.

Throughout this period of judicial activism, the Bar has made important contributions to the development of environmental jurisprudence. The leading environmental lawyer, M.C. Mehta has through his petitions and interim applications set the national agenda in the fields of water and air pollution, vehicular emission control, preservation of the coast, and the translocation of heavy industry away from urban areas. His example has inspired dozens of other advocates in the High Courts to pursue polluting industry and negligent enforcement agencies. Among them, the late Ajit Padiwal of Gujarat tenaciously battled factories around Ahmedabad that had blighted agricultural fields by discharging untreated effluents. In a large number of such public interest litigations, the legal assistance is rendered *pro bono* or at a nominal fee.

Moreover, the role of the Bar has extended beyond pleading the case in court. In many of the cases reviewed in this book you will find lawyers serving as fact finding commissioners or serving on committees charged with implementing court orders. Recently, the Supreme Court has appointed senior advocates as *amicus curiae*, to assist the court in tackling complex environmental and policy issues. With the advent of special environment tribunals and fora, the role of the Bar will grow in the coming years with a strong likelihood of a new specialization developing among its members.

2

ENVIRONMENTAL POLICY IN INDIA

This chapter explores environmental policy in India and its impact on regulation. The opening readings are from ancient Indian law. The most detailed and perceptive of these are the provisions found in Kautilya's *Arthashastra* written between 321 and 300 BC.[1] Kautilya was the prime minister of the Magadha Empire during the reign of Chandragupta Maurya. The *Arthashastra* is divided into 14 books that discuss a wide range of subjects, including administration, law, industry, commerce and foreign policy. Although the principal provisions dealing with the environment are in Book Two, some *shloka*s (stanzas) are found elsewhere in the work. The readings from the *Arthashastra* in this chapter collect these scattered *shloka*s and present them in an organized form.

The core material in this chapter are on forest policy and legislation from the colonial period to the present. They serve as a window to the varying nature and increasingly intense demands on India's natural resources and the government's policy response.

Several factors that have influenced Indian forestry have affected policy governing other natural resources as well. Short-sighted commercial and industrial policies that have rapidly reduced the forest cover since independence, have also contributed to erosion and the decline of India's wildlife. Moreover, the bureaucratic structure of India's forest law, which excludes citizens (forest dwellers) from participating in the decision-making process, is characteristic of most other environmental legislation. The following critique of forestry, therefore, illuminates a much wider field of governmental policy and practice than just forests: More generally, it provides an insight into the politics of resource conservation in India.

The final set of readings track the Indian Government's environmental policy since the 1970s, and stress the shift in the government's attitude from 'environment versus development' to 'environment *and* development'.

[1] V. Gupta, *Kautilyan Jurisprudence* 1 (1987).

A. READINGS FROM ANCIENT INDIAN LAW

GUPTA; KAUTILYAN JURISPRUDENCE, 155 (1987)

LAW CONCERNING FORESTS

State to maintain forests: The ruler shall not only protect produce-forests, elephant-forests but also set up new ones. Forests shall be grown, one for each forest produce and factories for goods made from forest produce shall be erected, and foresters working in the produce-forests shall be settled there.

Selling of trees: For cutting the tender sprouts of trees in city parks that bear flowers on fruits or yield shade the fine shall be six *pana*s, for cutting small branches twelve *pana*s; for cutting stout branches twenty four *pana*s, for destroying trunks the fine shall be the first amercement; for uprooting the tree the middlemost amercement. In the case of plants which bear flowers or fruits, or provide shade, half of the above fines shall be levied, also in case of trees in places of pilgrimage, forests of hermits or cremation grounds. In the case of trees at the boundaries, or that are worshipped or in sanctuaries, double the above fines shall be levied.

Damaging forests: The superintendent of forest produce shall cause forest produce to be brought in by guards in the produce-forests. He shall establish factories for forest produce. He shall fix adequate fines and compensations to be levied on those who cause any damage to productive forests except in calamities.

Forest produce: The ruler shall exploit timber forests and elephant forests. He shall establish factories for goods made from them.

Spies in the guise of traders shall ascertain the quantity and price of the royal merchandise obtained from forests.

Forest reserves for wild animals: On the borders of the country or in any other suitable locality, animal forests shall be established where all animals are welcomed as guests and given full protection.

Protection of wild life: The superintendent of slaughter-house shall punish, with the highest amercement, a person for entrapping, killing or injuring deer, bison, birds or fish which are declared to be under state protection or who are kept in reserved parks; the middle amercement on householders for these offences in reserved park enclosures. For entrapping, killing or injuring fish and birds whose killing is forbidden, he shall impose a fine of twenty-six *pana*s and three quarters, for entrapping deer and beasts, double that. One-sixth of live animals and birds shall be let off in forests under state's protection. Sea-fishes having the form of an elephant, horse, man, bull, or donkey, cranes or fishes from lakes, rivers, tanks or canals and birds for sports or auspicious birds, heron, lapwing, osprey, swan, ruddy goose, pheasant, *bhrngaraja, chakora, mattakokila,* peacock, parrot and *madanasarika* and also other birds and deers, shall be protected from all dangers of injury; for transgression of this rule, the fine shall be the first amercement.

Animals from reserved parks or protected ones, if found grazing in a field, after intimating the forest officers, shall be driven out without being hurt or killed. Stray cattle shall be driven out by the use of ropes or whips. For causing injury to them in other ways, the fine for physical injury shall be imposed. Those animals that attack or whose offence is clear shall be restrained through all possible ways. Wild animals, beasts, deer belonging to sanctuaries shall, when harmful, be killed or bound in places outside the reserved forests.

Fee for hunting: Of those whose killing is permitted and who are not protected in enclosures, the superintendent of slaughter-house shall receive one-sixth share of fishes and birds, one-tenth share of deer and beasts, in addition to a duty.

THAPAR; ASOKA AND THE DECLINE OF THE MAURYAS, 264 (2nd ED. 1973)

5TH PILLAR EDICT

Thus speaks the Beloved of the Gods, the king Piyadassi: When I had been consecrated for twenty-six years I forbade the killing of the following species of animals, namely: parrots, *maina*s, red-headed ducks [?], *cakravaka*-geese, swans *nandi-mukha*s [birds encountered in rice fields?], pigeons, bats, ants, tortoises, boneless fish, *vedaveyaka*s, *puputa*s of the Ganges [fish?], skate, porcupines, squirrels, deer, lizards, domesticated animals, rhinoceroses, white pigeons, domestic pigeons, and all quadrupeds which are of no utility and are not eaten. She goats, ewes, and sows which are with young or are giving suck are not to be killed, neither are their young up to the age of six months. Capons must not be made. Chaff which contains living things must not be set on fire. Forests must not be burned in order to kill living things or without any good reason. An animal must not be fed with another animal.

On the first full moon days of the three four-monthly seasons, and for three days when the full moon falls on the star Tisya, and the fourteenth and fifteenth of the bright fortnight, and the first of the dark, and regularly on fast days, fish are not to be caught or sold. And on these same days in the elephant-park and fisheries, other classes of animals likewise must not be killed. On the eighth, fourteenth, and fifteenth days of fortnight, on the days of the star Tisya and Punarvasu, on the three first full moons of the four monthly seasons, and on festival days, bulls, goats, rams, boars, and other animals which it is customary to castrate are not to be castrated. On the days of the stars Tisya and Punarvasu, on the first full moon days of the four-monthly seasons, and on the fortnights following them, cattle and horses are not to be branded.

In the period [from my consecration] to [the anniversary on which] I had been consecrated twenty-six years, twenty five releases of prisoners have been made.

B. READINGS ON FOREST POLICY AND LEGISLATION

GADGIL & GUHA; THIS FISSURED LAND: AN ECOLOGICAL HISTORY OF INDIA, 118 (1993)

By around 1860, Britain had emerged as the world leader in deforestation, devastating its own woods and the forests of Ireland, South Africa and north-eastern United

States to draw timber for shipbuilding, iron-smelting and farming. Upon occasion, the destruction of forests was used by the British to symbolize political victory. Thus in the early nineteenth century, and following its defeat of the Marathas, the East India Company razed to the ground teak plantations in Ratnagiri nurtured and grown by the legendary Maratha admiral Kanhoji Angre * * * Their early treatment of the Indian forests also reinforces the claim that 'the destructive energy of the British race all over the world' was rapidly converting forests into deserts. Until the later decades of the nineteenth century, the Raj carried out a 'fierce onslaught' on the subcontinent's forests. With oak forests vanishing in England, a permanent supply of durable timber was required for the Royal Navy as 'the safety of the empire depended on its wooden walls'. In a period of fierce competition between the colonial powers, Indian teak, the most durable of shipbuilding timbers, saved England during the war with Napoleon and the later maritime expansion. To tap the likely sources of supply, search parties were sent to the teak forests of India's west coast. Ships were built in dockyards in Surat and on the Malabar coast, as well as from teak imported into England * * * The revenue orientation of colonial land policy also worked towards the denudation of forests. As their removal added to the class of land assessed for revenue, forests were considered 'an obstruction to agriculture and consequently a bar to the prosperity of the Empire'. The dominant thrust of agrarian policy was to extend cultivation and 'the watchword of the time was to destroy the forests with this end in view'.

This process greatly intensified in the early years of the building of the railway network after about 1853. While great chunks of forest were destroyed to meet the demand for railway sleepers, no supervision was exercised over the felling operations; a large number of trees was felled and lay rotting on the ground. The sub-Himalayan forests of Garhwal and Kumaon, for example, were all 'felled in even to desolation', and 'thousands of trees were felled which were never removed, nor was their removal possible'.

* * *

The imperial forest department was formed in 1864, with the help of experts from Germany, the country which was at that time the leading European nation in forest management. The first inspector-general of forests, Dietrich Brandis, had been a botanist at Bonn University before his assignment in India. The awesome task of checking the deforestation of past decades required, first and foremost, forging legal mechanisms to assert and safeguard state control over forests. It was in this dual sense that the railways constituted the crucial watershed with respect to forest management in India—the need was felt to start an appropriate department, and for its effective functioning legislation was required to curtail the previously untouched access enjoyed by rural communities. This was an especially difficult task as, in many cases, the proprietary right of the state in forests had been 'deliberately alienated' in favour of peasant and tribal communities. Before its late recognition of the strategic importance of forests, the policy of the colonial state had been to recognize forests and waste land as the property of the village communities within whose boundaries these fell.

The first attempt at asserting state monopoly was through the Indian Forest Act of 1865. This was replaced thirteen years later by a far more comprehensive piece of legislation. Yet the latter act (to serve in time as a model for forest legislation in other British colonies) was passed only after a prolonged and bitter debate within the colonial bureaucracy. This controversy ... has a particular resonance for us today: the protagonists of the earlier debate put forth arguments strikingly similar to those advanced by participants in the contemporary debate about the environment in India.

Hurriedly drafted, the 1865 act was passed to facilitate the acquisition of those forest areas that were earmarked for railway supplies. It merely sought to establish the claims of the state to the forests it immediately required, subject to the proviso that existing rights not be abridged. Almost immediately, the search commenced for a more stringent and inclusive piece of legislation. A preliminary draft, prepared by Brandis in 1869, was circulated among the various presidencies. A conference of forest officers, convened in 1874, then went into the defects of the 1865 act and the details of a new one.

* * *

Adducing no evidence, Baden-Powell [a senior civil servant] claimed that 'the right of the state to dispose of or retain for public use the waste and forest area, is among the most ancient and undisputed of features in oriental Sovereignty'. 'In India', an official primer on forest law likewise affirmed, 'the government is by ancient law ... the general owner of all unoccupied and waste lands'. Whatever the historical evidence for this claim (scanty, at best), its purpose was clear: to pave the way for the formal assertion of ownership over forests and waste by the colonial state. The 'right' of oriental governments in the forest, insisted Baden-Powell, 'passed on to, and was accepted by, the British government'. Others were more blunt. 'The right of conquest', thundered one forest official, 'is the strongest of all rights—it is a right against which there is no appeal.'

Counterposed to this claim of an age-old right was the total denial of the legitimacy of any state intervention in the forest. The Madras government, which emerged as the most articulate official spokesman for village interests, rejected Baden-Powell's tendentious distinction between legally proven 'rights' and 'privileges' exercised without written sanction. 'All instances of the use of the forest by the people' it argued, 'should be taken as presumptive evidence of property therein'. Both 'private grantees and village and tribal communities', an early nationalist organization likewise pointed out, 'have cherished and maintained these rights [in the forest] with the same tenacity with which private property in land is maintained elsewhere'.

* * *

The 1878 act was a comprehensive piece of legislation which, by one stroke of the executive pen, attempted to obliterate centuries of customary use by rural populations all over India. It provided for three classes of forests. 'Reserved forests' consisted of compact and valuable areas, well connected to towns, which would lend themselves to sustained exploitation. In reserved forests a legal separation of rights was aimed for, it being thought advisable to safeguard total state control by a permanent settlement that either extinguished private rights, transferred them elsewhere, or in exceptional cases allowed their limited exercise. In the second category, the so-called 'protected forests' (also controlled by the state), rights were recorded but not settled. However, control was firmly maintained by outlining detailed provisions for the reservation of particular tree species as and when they became commercially valuable, and for closing the forest whenever required to grazing and fuelwood collection. Given increased commercial demand and their relatively precarious position from the government's point of view, protected areas were gradually converted into reserved forests where the state could exercise fuller control * * * The act also provided for the constitution of a third class of forests—village forests—although the option was not exercised by the government over the most part of the subcontinent. Finally, the new legislation greatly enlarged the punitive sanctions available to the forest administration, closely regulating the extraction and transit of forest produce and prescribing a detailed set of penalties for transgressions of the act.

* * *

The continuity between the forest policies of colonial and independent India is exemplified by the national forest policy of 1952. Upholding the 'fundamental concepts' of its predecessor—the forest policy of 1894—it reinforces the right of the state to exclusive control over forest protection, production, and management. With the integration of the princely states into the Indian union, the forest department in fact considerably enlarged its domain in the early years of independence. While inheriting the institutional framework of colonial forestry, however, the new government put it to slightly different uses. The one major difference in the post-1947 situation has been the rapid expansion of forest-based industry. [T]he demands of the commercial-industrial sector have replaced strategic imperial needs as the cornerstone of forest policy and management.

In the next tract, Ramachandra Guha presents a powerful defence of peasant values.

GUHA; THE UNQUIET WOODS: ECOLOGICAL CHANGE AND PEASANT RESISTANCE IN THE HIMALAYA, 191 (1991)

Reflecting on the century of social protest culminating in the Chipko Andolan, what is especially striking from the perspective of the sociology of peasant protest is the persistence of conflicts over forest rights in India. The forest conflicts in Europe ... were representative of a particular historical epoch, when the rise of capitalism undermined the basis of subsistence agriculture. Bitter as these struggles were, they greatly diminished in scope and intensity with the maturing of the Industrial

Revolution and the absorption of surplus workers in the cities or through emigration to the colonies. Simultaneously, the intensification of agriculture at home and the widening of the food production base through colonization greatly reduced the dependence of farming and stock-rearing on the forest. Subjected to commercial exploitation under sustained-yield silviculture, the forest has itself been transformed into an industrial enterprise run on capitalist lines. Of course, the forest continues to be an arena of conflict in Europe, as the labour force engaged in timber harvesting seeks to improve its wages and working conditions. The battle *for* the forest, however, between commercial forestry and the rural community, has, with the victory of industrial capitalism, been transformed into a battle *in* the forest. Although commercial forestry in India has created its own tensions between contractors and labourers, these conflicts pale into insignificance when compared with the continuing struggle between peasants and the state over control and use of the forest. The battle for the forest remains a very visible part of the social and ecological landscape.

* * *

In much of the Third World the 'wave of progress' has not yet rolled over the peasantry. In the incompleteness of this transition some scholars see a glimmer of hope. Concluding his fine study of Adivasi movements in western India David Hardiman writes: 'As yet, full fledged capitalism represents in these region only a possibility, not an achievement. The adivasis' values have deeper roots with a resilience which provides us with at least some source of hope'.

* * *

From an ecological perspective, therefore, peasant movements like Chipko are not merely a defence of the little community and its values, but also an affirmation of a way of life more harmoniously adjusted with natural processes. At one level they are defensive, seeking to escape the tentacle of the commercial economy and the centralizing state; at yet another level they are assertive, actively challenging the ruling-class vision of a homogenizing urban-industrial culture. It is this fusion of what I have termed the 'private' (peasant movement) and 'public' (ecological movement) profiles that has lent to Chipko a distinctive quality and strength. Far from being the dying wail of a class about to drop down the trapdoor of history, the call of Chipko represents one of the most innovative responses to the ecological and cultural crisis of modern society. It is a message we may neglect only at our own peril.

NOTES AND QUESTIONS

1. In 1988 the Union Government announced a new National Forest Policy. The policy endeavours to strike a balance between conservation, the commercial exploitation of forest resources and rights of local communities. Is a policy document, unsupported by legislation, likely to transform prevailing conditions? Is any forest reform possible without the repeal of the Forest Act of 1927 and its colonial framework?

2. In the wake of the pro-business economic liberalization policies of government since 1991, is the voice of Chipko a cry in the wilderness? Or are grassroot movements such as Chipko the only check against ecological degradation by the industrial juggernaut?

C. EARLY ENVIRONMENTAL LEGISLATION

A survey of early environmental legislation indicates the nature and levels of governmental awareness to environmental issues. Apart from forest laws, nineteenth century legislation also partially regulated two other aspects of India's environment: water pollution and wildlife.[2] These laws, however, had a narrow purpose and limited territorial reach.

The Shore Nuisance (Bombay and Kolaba) Act of 1853, one of the earliest laws concerning water pollution, authorised the collector of land revenue in Bombay to order the removal of any nuisance below the high-water mark in Bombay harbour. In 1857, an attempt was made to regulate the pollution produced by the Oriental Gas Company by imposing fines on the company and giving a right of compensation to anyone whose water was 'fouled' by the company's discharges.[3]

The Indian Penal Code, enacted in 1860, imposed a fine on a person who voluntarily 'fouls the water of any public spring or reservoir'. In addition, the Code penalized negligent acts with poisonous substances that endangered life or caused injury and proscribed public nuisances. The Indian Easements Act of 1882 protected riparian owners against 'unreasonable' pollution by upstream users. The Indian Fisheries Act passed in 1897, penalised the killing of fish by poisoning water and by using explosives. Legislative provisions regulating the discharge of oil into port waters[4] and prohibiting the poisoning of water in forests[5] were also enacted prior to independence.

Two early post-independence laws touched on water pollution. Section 12 of the Factories Act of 1948 required all factories to make 'effective arrangements' for waste disposal and empowered state governments to frame rules implementing this directive. Second, river boards, established under the River Boards Act of 1956 for the regulation and development of inter-state rivers and river valleys, were empowered to prevent water pollution. In both these laws, prevention of water pollution was only incidental to the principal objective of the enactment.

The earliest laws aimed at controlling air pollution were the Bengal Smoke

---

[2] See generally, Mathur, *A Federal Legislative History of Control of Water Pollution in India* in LEGAL CONTROL OF ENVIROMENTAL POLLUTION 86–94 (S. Agarwal ed. 1980); Ramakrishna, *The Emergence of Environmental Laws in the Developing Countries: A Case Study of India* 12 ECOLOGY L.Q. 907 (1985); and Kothari, Pande, Singh & Variava, *Management of National Parks and Sanctuaries in India: A Status Report* 106–7 (1989).

[3] Sections 15–17, Oriental Gas Company Act of 1857.

[4] Section 21, Indian Ports Act of 1908.

[5] Section 26, Indian Forest Act of 1927.

Nuisance Act of 1905 and the Bombay Smoke Nuisance Act of 1912.

In the field of wildlife protection, early legislation was limited to specific areas and particular species. In 1873, Madras enacted the first wildlife statute for the protection of wild elephants. The law introduced a general prohibition on the destruction of wild elephants and imposed a penalty on those who violated the embargo. The first effort by the Central Government came six years later with the passing of the Elephants' Preservation Act of 1879. In 1887, the Centre enacted the Wild Birds Protection Act prohibiting the possession or sale of wild birds recently killed or taken, during notified breeding seasons.[6]

In 1912, the Central Government enacted a broader Wild Birds and Animals Protection Act. Extending to most of British India, this law specified closed hunting seasons and regulated the hunting of designated species through licences. Indeed, all the statutes related primarily to the regulation of hunting and did not regulate trade in wildlife and wildlife products—both major factors in the decline of Indian wildlife. As a consequence, wildlife depredation continued and many species became extinct.

The first comprehensive law for the protection of wildlife and its habitat was perhaps the Hailey National Park Act of 1936 which established the Hailey (now Corbett) National Park in the State of Uttar Pradesh.

This review suggests that early legislative efforts were piecemeal and inadequate. Not until the 1970s did the Central Government begin enacting comprehensive environmental laws. The next set of readings trace the transformation in government policy, from environmental indifference to environmental concern, that guided India into an era of comprehensive environmental regulation.

D. READINGS ON INDIA'S ENVIRONMENTAL POLICY IN THE 1970s

In the summer of 1972, Stockholm staged the first UN Conference held specifically to consider global environmental conditions. Heads of state and high government officials from 113 countries participated in the deliberations which culminated in the adoption of a Declaration and an Action Plan. Prime Minister Indira Gandhi, was amongst the leaders of the Third World who addressed the conference.

GANDHI; ADDRESS OF PRIME MINISTER INDIRA GANDHI AT THE UNITED NATIONS CONFERENCE ON THE HUMAN ENVIRONMENT, Stockholm, 14 June 1972

On the one hand the rich look askance at our continuing poverty—on the other, they warn us against their own methods. We do not wish to impoverish the environment

---

[6] e.g., Rules published in the *Bombay Government Gazette*, 20 July 1911, page 1219 notifying the breeding season for the Talegaon Dabhade Municipality.

any further and yet we cannot for a moment forget the grim poverty of large numbers of people. Are not poverty and need the greatest polluters? For instance, unless we are in a position to provide employment and purchasing power for the daily necessities of the tribal people and those who live in or around our jungles, we cannot prevent them from combing the forest for food and livelihood; from poaching and from despoiling the vegetation. When they themselves feel deprived, how can we urge the preservation of animals? How can we speak to those who live in villages and in slums about keeping the oceans, the rivers and the air clean when their own lives are contaminated at the source? The environment cannot be improved in conditions of poverty. Nor can poverty be eradicated without the use of science and technology.

* * *

There are grave misgivings that the discussion on ecology may be designed to distract attention from the problems of war and poverty. We have to prove to the disinherited majority of the world that ecology and conservation will not work against their interest but will bring an improvement in their lives. To withhold technology from them would deprive them of vast resources of energy and knowledge. This is no longer feasible nor will it be acceptable.

The environmental problems of developing countries are not the side effects of excessive industrialization but reflect the inadequacy of development. The rich countries may look upon development as the cause of environmental destruction, but to us it is one of the primary means of improving the environment for living, of providing food, water, sanitation and shelter, of making the desert green and the mountains habitable.

* * *

The ecological crises should not add to the burdens of the weaker nations by introducing new considerations in the political and trade policies of rich nations. It would be ironic if the fight against pollution were to be converted into another business, out of which a few companies, corporations, or nations would make profit at the cost of the many.

* * *

It has been my experience that people who are at cross purposes with nature are cynical about mankind and ill-at-ease with themselves. Modern man must re-establish an unbroken link with nature and with life. He must again learn to invoke the energy of growing things and to recognize as did the ancients in India centuries ago, that one can take from the Earth and the atmosphere only so much as one puts back to them. In their hymn to Earth, the sages of the Atharva Veda chanted: I quote,
'What of thee I dig out, let that quickly grow over, Let me not hit
thy vitals, or thy heart.'

So can man himself be vital and of good heart and conscious of his responsibility.

* * *

DWIVEDI; INDIA'S ENVIRONMENTAL POLICIES, PROGRAMMES AND STEWARDSHIP, 54 (1997)

The year 1972 marks a watershed in the history of environmental management in
India. Prior to 1972 environmental concerns such as sewage disposal, sanitation, and
public health were dealt with by different federal ministries, and each pursued these
objectives in the absence of a proper coordination system at the federal or the intergovernmental level. When the twenty-fourth UN General Assembly decided to convene a conference on the human environment in 1972, and requested a report from
each member country on the state of the environment, a Committee on the Human
Environment under the chairmanship of Pitambar Pant, member of the Planning
Commission, was set up to prepare India's report. By May 1971 three reports had
been prepared: 'Some Aspects of Environmental Degradation and its Control in India', 'Some Aspects of Problems of Human Settlement in India' and 'Some Aspects
of Rational Management of Natural Resources'. With the help of these reports, the
impact of the population explosion on the natural environment and the existing state
of environmental problems were examined. By early 1972 it had been realized (as
observed in the Fourth Five Year Plan earlier) that unless a national body was established to bring about greater coherence and coordination in environmental policies
and programmes and to integrate environmental concerns in the plans for economic
development, an important lacuna would remain in India's planning process. Consequently on 12 April 1972 a National Committee on Environmental Planning and
Coordination (NCEPC) was established. ...

As a result of the reports' stress on the need to establish greater coordination
and integration in environmental policies and programmes, in February 1972 a
National Committee on Environmental Planning and Coordination (NCEPC) was
established in the Department of Science and Technology.

The NCEPC was an apex advisory body in all matters relating to environmental
protection and improvement. At its inception the Committee consisted of fourteen
members drawn from various disciplines concerned with environmental management.
Most of the non-official members were specialists. The committee was to plan and
coordinate, but the responsibility for execution remained with the various ministries
and government agencies. ...

Over time the composition of the NCEPC changed significantly (committee
members were appointed for a two-year term). While the membership of NCEPC
increased from 14 in 1972 to 24 in 1977 to 35 in 1979, the number of non-officials
decreased. The committee also became unwieldy, and decision making more complex.
Greater bureaucratization occurred with the addition of more secretaries. The first
committee enjoyed some political clout, but this gradually waned. Consequently the

cooperation of other departments also decreased, exacerbated by the fact that different departments had started to view the committee as an intruder.

* * *

The Fifth Five Year Plan (1974–79) stressed that the NCEPC should be involved in all major industrial decisions, so that environmental goals would be taken fully into account. The Plan also emphasized that the pursuit of development goals would not be less likely to cause a reduction in the quality of life if a link and balance between development planning and environmental management was maintained. In this context the Minimum Needs Programme (concerning rural and elementary education, rural health and sanitation, nutrition, drinking water, provision of housing sites and slum improvement) received a fairly high priority, and was expected to minimize environmental pollution and degradation in rural areas and reduce poverty levels.

In this Sixth Five Year Plan (1980–85), an entire chapter on 'Environment and Development' was included that emphasized sound environmental and ecological principles in land use, agriculture, forestry, marine exploitation, mineral extraction, fisheries, energy production and human settlements. It provided environmental guidelines to be used by administrators and resource managers when formulating and implementing programmes, and lay down an institutional structure for environmental management by the central and state governments. Although the document was alarmist in approach, it provided a good starting from which to address the degraded environmental conditions in India. ...

The basic approach taken by the Seventh Plan (1985–90) was to emphasize sustainable development in harmony with the environment, as the federal government had recognized the negative effects that development programmes were having on the environment, and the pressure on project planners and managers to pursue their developmental activities singlemindedly and thus lose sight of environmental and ecological imperatives. ... The Plan called for the government and voluntary agencies to work together to create environmental awareness, because improving the quality of the environment required the involvement of the entire public: 'This is a philosophy which must permeate the entire effort in the field of environment'. However even today this basic philosophy has still not taken hold because the earlier emphasis on industrialization, agri-business and power-generation projects, with little concern for environmental protection, has not relinquished its grip on decision makers.

By the late 1980s it had dawned on the leaders of India that poverty and under-development, as opposed to development activities, had led to many of the country's environmental problems, and that such problems could not longer be sidestepped. That is why the Seventh Plan recognized that 'the nation's planning for economic growth and social well-being in each sector must always take note of the need to protect environmental resources, and where possible, must work to secure improvement in environmental quality.'

The Eight Five Year Plan (1992–97), because of the uncertain political situation in India, came out in 1992 rather than 1990. It gave an important place to the environment by moving it to the fourth category of subjects examined in the text. The Plan stated:

> Systematic efforts have been made since the Sixth Plan period to integrate environmental considerations and imperatives in the planning process in all the key socio-economic sectors. As a result of sustained endeavour, planning in all major sectors like industry, science and technology, agriculture, energy and education includes environmental consideration.

The Planning Commission set up an expert committee to formulate long-term sectoral (including environment and forest) policies. It also noted that many environmental problems were continuing to cause serious concern, for example the loss of topsoil and vegetative cover, the degradation of forests, continuing pollution by toxic substances, careless industrial and agricultural practices, and unplanned urban growth. It acknowledged that environmental degradation was seriously threatening the economic and social progress of the country, and that 'Our future generations may discover that life support systems have been damaged beyond repair.'

E. POLICY SINCE THE MID-1980s

The continuing decline in the quality of the environment, together with the tragedy at Bhopal in which a leak from a pesticide factory killed more than 2,500 people and injured several thousand others, has spurred the Central Government and a few state governments to adopt stronger environmental policies, to enact fresh legislation and to create, reorganize and expand administrative agencies.

In December, 1988 the Union Ministry of Environment and Forests constituted a committee to recommend a framework and an action plan for the conservation of resources. The committee, which was comprised of eminent scientists, journalists, environmentalists and senior bureaucrats, prepared a draft policy statement for a national conservation strategy and invited comments and suggestions on the draft from hundreds of respondents across the country. After assimilating the responses received from governmental and non-governmental organizations, the committee submitted a report to the Union Government in April 1990.[7] Based on the recommendations of the committee, the Government of India adopted a National Conservation Strategy and Policy Statement on Environment and Development in June, 1992 (NCS).[8] The preamble to the NCS adopts the policy of 'sustainable development' and declares the government's commitment to re-orient policies and action 'in unison with the environmental perspective'.[9] The NCS proceeds to recognize the enormous dimensions

---

[7] Ministry of Environment and Forests, Government of India, *Report of the Core Committee for Recommending a National Strategy for Conservation and Sustainable Development* (April, 1990).

[8] Ministry of Environment and Forests, Government of India, *National Conservation Strategy and Policy Statement on Environment and Development* (June, 1992).

[9] *Id.* at paras 1.1 and 1.4.

of the environmental problems facing India and declares strategies for action in various spheres such as agriculture, forestry, industrial development, mining and tourism. Special sections in the NCS deal with the rehabilitation of persons ousted by large development projects; the role of non-governmental organizations; and the special relationship between women and the environment.

In February 1992 the Union Government published its policy for the abatement of pollution.[10] This statement declares the objective of the government to integrate environmental considerations into decision-making at all levels. To achieve this goal, the statement adopts fundamental guiding principles, namely, (i) prevention of pollution *at source*; (ii) the adoption of the *best available technology*; (iii) the *polluter pays* principle; and (iv) *public participation* in decision making.[11] Expanding on the public partnership theme, the statement declares:

> The public must be aware in order to be able to make informed choices. A high government priority will be to educate citizens about environmental risks, the economic and health dangers of resource degradation and the real cost of natural resources. Information about the environment will be published periodically. Affected citizens and non-governmental organisations play a role in environmental monitoring and therefore allowing them to supplement the regulatory system and recognising their expertise where such exists and their commitment and vigilance, will also be cost effective. Access to information to enable public monitoring of environmental concerns, will be provided for.
>
> Public interest litigation has successfully demonstrated that responsible non-governmental organisations and public spirited individuals can bring about significant pressure on polluting units for adopting abatement measures. This commitment and expertise will be encouraged and their practical work supported.[12]

There has been considerable activity in some states, too. In early 1997 Maharashtra announced a policy to restore the quality of its river waters and achieve ambient water quality standards. The policy classifies river stretches into zones and designates permissible industrial use within each zone.[13] A few months later Haryana announced a comprehensive conservation policy to improve pollution control.[14]

---

[10] Ministry of Environment and Forests, Government of India, *Policy Statement for Abatement of Pollution* (26 February 1992).

[11] *Id.* at para 3.3.

[12] *Id.* at para 11.1.

[13] Maharashtra Pollution Control Board, *Classification of River Waters and Guidelines for Location of Industrial Activity* (1997).

[14] *Action Plan for Clean Environment*, THE HINDU, New Delhi, 29 April 1997.

The policy statements, in themselves, are not enforceable in a court of law. However, these statements represent a broad political consensus and amplify the duties of government under the directive principles of state policy contained in Part IV of the Constitution. In the hands of a creative judge the policy documents referred to above may serve as an aid for interpreting environmental statutes or for spelling out the obligations of government agencies under environmental laws. For example, in *State of Himachal Pradesh v Ganesh Wood Products* [15] the Supreme Court relied upon the National Forest Policy and the State Forest Policy of Himachal Pradesh to invalidate a decision taken by the state industrial project authority. The authority approved the establishment of units which manufactured 'katha' from the scarce khair tree without considering factors such as the availability of khair trees and the adverse impact on the forests in the state. The court held that the policy of economic liberalization has to be understood in the light of the National Forest Policy and forest laws enacted by the government. The court cautioned government departments against ignoring the forest policies and warned that disregard of these policies would imperil government decisions.

In many instances, judges are reluctant to adopt a pro-active approach by compelling government departments to take measures to improve the quality of the environment. In this situation, a clear statement of policy may persuade the judge to prefer an environment friendly interpretation over a more conservative approach. The policy statements may also weigh with a court at the interlocutory stage when assessing the balance of convenience and the potential harm to the public interest. At the end of the day, unless the government policy is backed by adequate budgetary allocations, changes to the statutory regime and a bureaucratic will, the government's intentions are apt to remain on paper.

F. LIBERALIZATION AND ECONOMIC APPROACHES

Since 1991 India has adopted new economic policies to spur development. In an effort to integrate the Indian economy with global trade, the government has reduced industrial regulation, lowered international trade and investment barriers and encouraged export-oriented enterprise. Some commentators fear that liberalization will exacerbate environmental problems and increase inequities.[16] We close this chapter with a more positive assessment of economic tools and a call to rein in pollution through a system of economic incentives.

---

[15] AIR 1996 SC 149.

[16] R. Sudarshan, *Liberalisation and the Environment*, THE HINDU, New Delhi, 19 April 1996 and A. Kothari, *Environment and New Economic Policies*, ECONOMIC & POLITICAL WEEKLY, 29 April 1995 p. 924.

ROSENCRANZ, PANDIAN AND CAMPBELL; ECONOMIC APPROACHES FOR A GREEN INDIA, 1 (1999)

Despite the progress made under India's environmental command and control regulations, India's environment is degrading rapidly. A recent World Bank study estimates that environmental damage in India amounts to US $ 9.7 billion per year, or 4.5 percent of India's Gross Domestic Product. The 1995 Economic Survey of the Government of India indicates that 90 percent of water in 241 larger cities is polluted; moreover, 54 percent of the urban and 97 per cent of the rural population have no sanitation facilities. Together vehicles, factories and power plants discharge 3,000 tons of pollutants into New Delhi's air each day. Allocations to prevent and control pollution have been cut by 35.5 per cent over the last five years—a time when the government's economic liberalization policies are likely to increase the pollution problem.

The quality of life for many citizens, particularly those residing in urban areas, is at an unacceptable level. In fact, the most challenging environmental problems facing India stem from the rapid growth of large, polluting industries in urban areas. For years, industrial development came without either planning or environmental controls.

* * *

In sum, the command and control regulatory approach towards environment protection in India has failed to do the job. Penalties are too trivial to deter polluters; bribes often subvert regulatory intent; and the government agencies rarely use their power to shut down offending industries because of the economic dislocation that would result. Market driven solutions to environmental problems, as a complement to existing laws and rules, could result in a better use of scarce societal resources and better environmental protection as industry itself decides how to use its resources to abate pollution.

* * *

By market-based incentives, we are referring to policies and strategies that use incentives and disincentives to achieve a level of environmental protection beyond what the unregulated marketplace would otherwise provide. This definition accepts the basic premise, initially put forward by British economist Arthur Pigou, that government regulation in the environmental sector is necessary because the benefits of environmental protection, and the costs of environmental degradation are not inherently reflected in the price of goods and services.

Market-based incentives follow the 'polluter pays principle'. As the costs of creating pollution rise due to the play of market forces, the rational polluter has an economic incentive to reduce the pollution. The benefit of market-driven reform is that the polluters will reduce their emission levels where the imposition of controls is least costly.

Environmental markets create incentives to develop innovative and affordable pollution control technology. The polluter will develop the technology or modify the production process to emit less pollutants and correspondingly retain more money. By contrast, command and control laws encourage polluters to evade or thwart the regulations or else bribe their way out of complying with them because it is cheaper to do so. Moreover, industry is placed in a reactive rather than proactive role in regard to the development of pollution control technology.

In an era of governmental fiscal austerity towards the environment, permits, taxes and charges can be earmarked for their most efficient use. Since those approaches encourage the regulated community to move beyond the *status quo* in environmental protection technology, the funds raised can be doubly effective. Economists recognize that certain taxes discourage social 'goods' such as taxes on labour that discourage work effort, or taxes on savings that reduce the amount available for investment. Environmental taxes do not result in such tax distortions, but rather discourage 'bads' such as pollution. Taken a step further, environmental taxes can yield a 'double dividend' if the revenue from them is used to reduce and mitigate the effect of the aforementioned tax distortions.

* * *

However, economic approaches face numerous obstacles, especially in India. First and foremost, the command and control bureaucracy, ineffective though it may be, has been in place for over 20 years. The Pollution Control Boards, like any entrenched bureaucracy, will be jealous of their mission, and will be likely to see market-based approaches as unwelcome competition unless they have full charge over the administration and implementation of the new schemes. (Since the PCBs have been subcompetent in administering and implementing existing programs, it would be politically unsound to give them new responsibilities without a major overhaul, including professionalization and increased funding, of the Boards themselves).

Any new program will increase regulatory uncertainty and will on that ground alone meet resistance from polluters. A market-based program may raise the highly political questions of how much pollution to allow in an air or water basin, or how to allocate pollution permits. Such a program may alarm people living near industrial complexes, who may feel that pollution permits will inevitably increase local pollution levels.

NOTES AND QUESTIONS

1. What kind of economic incentives are best suited for India: taxes, charges, or tradeable pollution permits? What might industry prefer?

2. In the West, market-driven approaches have yielded mixed results. While US power companies have conserved energy (and reduced pollution) by offering rebates and subsidies to consumers who install efficient technologies, in other sectors, rich industries have bought marketable emission permits to avoid tighter pollution control.

3

CONSTITUTIONAL AND LEGISLATIVE PROVISIONS

Indian environmental statutes chiefly employ a system of licensing and criminal sanctions to preserve natural resources and regulate their use. Civil compensation recovered through private citizens' suits plays a peripheral role in the overall regulatory strategy. Pollution charges, fees or other economic approaches to discourage pollution are largely untried.

Until recently, the implementation of environmental laws was the exclusive province of specially constituted state agencies which issued permits and prosecuted violators in the ordinary criminal courts. Since 1986, enforcement techniques have been strengthened. These laws now permit *private* prosecutions and more significantly, empower state agencies to shut down polluting industries or stop their supply of water and power. This last enforcement method, in theory, promises quick results because it combines in a single state agency the old divided enforcement scheme of government prosecutions that required both administrative and judicial action to discipline violators. As we shall see from a number of public interest litigations discussed in this book, the performance of most enforcement agencies—whether it be the pollution control boards, forest bureaucracies or local town planning authorities—has been dismal. Few bureaucrats have effectively exercised their authority unless compelled to do so by judicial oversight. The judicial role in securing enforcement through public interest litigation lies outside the formal *statutory* framework and has been assumed by the higher judiciary in discharge of its *constitutional* obligations.

In this chapter we digest the primary regulatory statutes and examine in some detail the Environment (Protection) Act of 1986. India's international obligations under important multilateral treaties and conventions complement the municipal law and are dealt with in a separate chapter at the end of this book. Quite a few international law norms have been assimilated into domestic law by judgments of the apex court. But first, to put the whole regulatory framework in perspective, we examine the constitutional provisions that relate to the environment.

A. CONSTITUTIONAL PROVISIONS AND THE ENVIRONMENT

I. FUNDAMENTAL NORMS

The Indian Constitution is amongst the few in the world that contains specific provisions on environmental protection. The directive principles of state policy and the fundamental duties chapters explicitly enunciate the national commitment to protect and improve the environment. Judicial interpretation has strengthened this constitutional mandate.

In a case where the Supreme Court intervened to protect the forest wealth and wildlife from the ravages of mining in and around Sariska sanctuary in the Alwar district of Rajasthan, the court viewed its own constitutional role thus:

> This litigation concerns environment. A great American Judge emphasizing the imperative issue of environment said that he placed Government above big business, individual liberty above Government and environment above all. The issues and concerns in this case far transcend the trivialities and inhibitions of an adversarial litigation. All the parties must be forthcoming in a concerted effort to find a satisfying solution to the problem which, in more ways than one, is typical of the Indian predicament. We are, therefore, entitled to expect that the State Government and the mining-entrepreneurs in their own enlightened self interest will discard the adversarial litigative stance. *The issues of environment must and shall receive the highest attention from this Court.*[1]

This approach has led the Supreme Court to derive, adopt and apply a range of principles to guide the development of environmental jurisprudence. Notable amongst the *fundamental norms* recognized by the court are:

(1) Every person enjoys the right to a wholesome environment, which is a facet of the right to life guaranteed under Article 21 of the Constitution of India.[2]

(2) Enforcement agencies are under an obligation to strictly enforce environmental laws.[3]

(3) Government agencies may not plead non-availability of funds, inadequacy of staff or other insufficiencies to justify the non-performance of their obligations under environmental laws.[4]

---

[1] Emphasis supplied. *Tarun Bharat Sangh, Alwar v Union of India (Sariska Case)* Writ Petition (Civil) No. 509 of 1991, Supreme Court, 14 May 1992 (M.N. Venkatachaliah and B.P. Jeevan Reddy, JJ.).

[2] *Subhash Kumar v State of Bihar* AIR 1991 SC 420, 424; *M.C. Mehta v Union of India (Delhi Stone Crushing Case)* 1992 (3) SCC 256, 257; and *Virender Gaur v State of Haryana* 1995 (2) SCC 577, 581. See A. Rosencranz and S. Rustomjee, *Citizens' Right to a Healthful Environment*, 25 ENVIR. POL. & LAW 324 (1995).

[3] *Indian Council for Enviro-Legal Action v Union of India (CRZ Notification Case)* 1996 (5) SCC 281, 294, 301.

[4] *Dr. B.L. Wadehra v Union of India (Delhi Garbage Case)* AIR 1996 SC 2969, 2976.

(4) The 'polluter pays' principle which is a part of the basic environmental law of the land requires that a polluter bear the remedial or clean up costs as well as the amounts payable to compensate the victims of pollution.[5]

(5) The 'precautionary principle' requires government authorities to anticipate, prevent and attack the causes of environmental pollution. This principle also imposes the onus of proof on the developer or industrialist to show that his or her action is environmentally benign.[6]

(6) Government development agencies charged with decision making ought to give due regard to ecological factors including (a) the environmental policy of the Central and state government; (b) the sustainable development and utilization of natural resources; and (c) the obligation of the present generation to preserve natural resources and pass on to future generations an environment as intact as the one we inherited from the previous generation.[7]

(7) Stringent action ought to be taken against contumacious defaulters and persons who carry on industrial or development activity for profit without regard to environmental laws.[8]

(8) The power conferred under an environmental statute may be exercised only to advance environmental protection and not for a purpose that would defeat the object of the law.[9]

(9) The state is the trustee of all natural resources which are by nature meant for public use and enjoyment. The public at large is the beneficiary of the sea-shore, running waters, air, forests and ecologically fragile lands. These resources cannot be converted into private ownership.[10]

II. DIVISION OF LEGISLATIVE AUTHORITY

Under India's federal system, governmental power is shared between the Union or 'Central' Government and the 26 state governments. Part XI of the Constitution

[5] *Indian Council for Enviro-Legal Action v Union of India (Bichhri Case)* AIR 1996 SC 1446, 1466; *Vellore Citizens' Welfare Forum v Union of India,* AIR 1996 SC 2715, 2721; and *S. Jagannath v Union of India (Shrimp Culture Case)* AIR 1997 SC 811, 846, 850.

[6] *Vellore Citizens' Welfare Forum v Union of India* AIR 1996 SC 2715, 2721; *S. Jagannath v Union of India (Shrimp Culture Case)* AIR 1997 SC 811, 846; and *A.P. Pollution Control Board v Prof. M.V. Nayadu* AIR 1999 SC 812, 819.

[7] *State of Himachal Pradesh v Ganesh Wood Products* AIR 1996 SC 149, 159, 163.

[8] *Indian Council for Enviro-Legal Action v Union of India (Bichhri Case)* AIR 1996 SC 1446, 1468; *Pratibha Co-operative Housing Society Ltd. v State of Maharashtra* AIR 1991 SC 1453, 1456; *Pleasant Stay Hotel v Palani Hills Conservation Council* 1995 (6) SCC 127, 139; and *M.I. Builders v Radhey Shyam Sahu* AIR 1999 SC 2468, 2505.

[9] *Bangalore Medical Trust v B.S. Muddappa* AIR 1991 SC 1902, 1911, 1924; *Virender Gaur v State of Haryana* 1995 (2) SCC 577, 583; and *Indian Council for Enviro-Legal Action v Union of India (CRZ Notification Case)* 1996 (5) SCC 281, 299, 302.

[10] *M.C. Mehta v Kamal Nath (Span Motels Case)* 1997 (1) SCC 388; and *M.I Builders v Radhey Shyam Sahu* AIR 1999 SC 2468, 2498.

governs the legislative and administrative relations between the Union and the states.

Parliament has the power to legislate for the whole country, while the State Legislatures are empowered to make laws for their respective states. Article 246 of the Constitution divides the subject areas of legislation between the Union and the states. The Union List (List I) in the Seventh Schedule to the Constitution contains 97 subjects over which Parliament has exclusive powers to legislate. These include defence, foreign affairs, atomic energy, interstate transportation, shipping, major ports, regulation of air traffic, regulation and development of oilfields, mines and mineral development and interstate rivers. The State Legislatures have exclusive power to legislate with respect to 66 subjects in the State List (List II), such as public health and sanitation, agriculture, water supplies, irrigation and drainage and fisheries.

Under the Concurrent List (List III), both Parliament and the State Legislatures have overlapping and shared jurisdiction over 52 subject areas including forests, the protection of wildlife, mines and mineral development not covered in the Union List, population control and family planning, minor ports and factories.

Parliament has residual power to legislate on subjects not covered by the three Lists.[11] When a central law conflicts with a state law on a concurrent subject, the former prevails. A state law passed subsequent to the central law will prevail, however, if it has received Presidential Assent under Article 254.

Parliament is also empowered to legislate in the 'national interest' on matters enumerated in the State List.[12] In addition, Parliament may enact laws on state subjects, for states whose legislatures have consented to central legislations. Thus, the Water (Prevention and Control of Pollution) Act of 1974 was enacted by Parliament pursuant to consent resolutions passed by 12 State Legislatures.

From an environmental standpoint, the allocation of legislative authority is an important one: Some environmental problems such as sanitation and waste disposal, are best tackled at the local level. Others, like water pollution and wildlife protection, are better regulated by uniform national laws.

The Constituent Assembly that framed India's Constitution did not specifically consider the question of whether Parliament or the State Legislatures should regulate environmental matters. Instead, the distribution of environmental subjects within the three Lists was influenced by the Government of India Act of 1935 and by the conflict between those who wished to create a strong Centre and others who preferred to secure more powers for the states.[13] Understandably, there was a tussle for control over natural resources such as forests and fisheries which were important economic subjects. In July, 1949 the Drafting Committee of the Constituent Assembly convened a meeting of the Premiers of the Indian states and provinces and the

---

[11] Article 248.
[12] Article 249.
[13] See generally, H. Seervai, *Constitutional Law of India: A Critical Commentary* 164–71 (Vol. I, 1991); and S. Rao, *The Framing of India's Constitution: Select Documents* 315 (Vol. IV, 1968).

representatives of central ministers to discuss the division of legislative powers.[14]

At this meeting, proposals from the Ministry of Agriculture that 'Forests' and 'Fisheries' be transferred from the State List to the Concurrent List were strongly opposed by the provincial representatives.[15] The ministry argued that the forests affect the agricultural development and prosperity of the country as a whole, and no province or state should, even inadvertently, follow a policy that could be detrimental to the rest of the country. 'For instance, floods which cause considerable havoc in the plains may be the result of indiscriminate felling in the catchment areas under the control and jurisdiction of an entirely different Province.'[16] But the arguments failed, the proposals were rejected and the topic 'Forests' was classified as a state subject.[17]

Another proposal, jointly sponsored by the Ministries of Health and Home Affairs, aimed at removing 'Public Health and Sanitation' from the State List and placing it with 'Vital Statistics including registration of births and deaths' in the Concurrent List. It was argued that central legislation would be necessary to prevent the spread of diseases from one province to another. Unconvinced, the Premiers of the United Provinces, Assam, Bombay and Bihar, successfully resisted the move. Only the second part, placing 'Vital Statistics' in the Concurrent List, was accepted at the meeting.[18]

Elsewhere in these deliberations, the Ministry of Health successfully proposed an expansion of Parliament's power to regulate interstate rivers so that pollution of rivers by industrial wastes and sewage could be controlled. The ministry proposed that the draft Entry 74 in the Union List be widened to read: 'The development of *inter-State rivers and* inter-State waterways for purposes of flood control, irrigation, navigation and hydroelectric power *and for other purposes, where such development under the control of the Union is declared by Parliament by law to be expedient in the public interest.*'[19] This instance of environmental sensitivity was exceptional. The larger question of a decentralized versus a centralized federal structure prevailed over the issue of whether the central or State Legislatures were better situated to regulate environmental matters.

III. THE FORTY-SECOND AMENDMENT ACT

Environmental protection and improvement were explicitly incorporated into the Constitution by the Constitution (Forty-Second Amendment) Act of 1976. Article

[14] S. Rao, *id.*

[15] *Id.* at 635.

[16] S. Rao, *The Framing of India's Constitution: A Study* 633 (Vol. V, 1968).

[17] The Constitution (Forty–Second Amendment) Act of 1976 moved 'Forests' to the Concurrent List.

[18] S. Rao, *supra* note 13, at 634–5.

[19] Proposal emphasized. As finally adopted, Item 56 of the Union List (corresponding to draft Entry 74) reads: 'Regulation and development of inter–State rivers and river valleys to the extent to which such regulation and development under the control of the Union is declared by Parliament by law to be expedient in the public interest.'

48A was added to the directive principles of state policy. It declares: 'The State shall endeavour to protect and improve the environment and to safeguard the forests and wild life of the country.' Article 51A(g) in a new chapter entitled 'Fundamental Duties', imposes a similar responsibility on every citizen 'to protect and improve the natural environment including forests, lakes, rivers and wild life, and to have compassion for living creatures. ...' Although the language in the two articles differs, the differences appear to relate to form rather than to substance. Together, the provisions highlight the national consensus on the importance of environmental protection and improvement and lay the foundation for a jurisprudence of environmental protection.[20]

There was considerable debate in Parliament over the wording of draft Article 48A. In the Lok Sabha several amendments were moved. One of them required the state to 'conserve and develop the water, soil and other natural resources', while another proposed to ensure that the state's efforts to protect and improve the environment would not harm tribal forest dwellers. None of these amendments were accepted by the government, which took the position that the broad terms of a directive principle need not contain details.[21]

Welcoming the provision, members in the Rajya Sabha[22] proposed that the Article should also mention 'mineral wealth' and require the government to 'undertake adequate and effective measures to check environmental pollution.' Both amendments were rejected by the government as the existing wording was considered wide enough to cover the amendments' underlying concerns.[23]

IV. THE DIRECTIVE PRINCIPLES OF STATE POLICY

The directive principles are policy prescriptions that guide the government. Some of them are in the nature of economic rights that India could not guarantee when the Constitution was enacted, but that were expected to be realised in succeeding years. Although unenforceable by a court, the directive principles are increasingly being cited by judges as complementary to the fundamental rights.[24] In several environmental cases the courts have been guided by the language of Article 48A.[25]

---

[20] M.C. Mehta v State of Orissa AIR 1992 ORI 225, 227.

[21] The Lok Sabha is the House of the People (Lower House of Parliament). Lok Sabha Debates, Eighteenth Session, Fifth Series, Vol. LXV, No. 5, Oct. 29, 1976, columns 94–116. The Constitution (Forty–Fourth Amendment) Bill of 1976 after passage became the Constitution (Forty–Second Amendment) Act of 1976.

[22] House of the States (Upper House of Parliament).

[23] Parliamentary Debate: Rajya Sabha: Official Report, Vol. XCVIII, No. 5, Nov. 9, 1976, columns 158–71.

[24] e.g., Som Prakash Rekhi v Union of India AIR 1981 SC 212, 221–2.

[25] Virender Gaur v State of Haryana 1995 (2) SCC 571, 580; Indian Council for Enviro–Legal Action v Union of India (Bichhri Case) AIR 1996 SC 1446, 1459; M.C. Mehta v Union of India AIR 1988 SC 1037, 1038; Rural Litigation and Entitlement Kendra, Dehradun v State of Uttar Pradesh AIR 1988 SC 2187, 2199; and Kinkeri Devi v State of Himachal Pradesh AIR 1988 HP 4, 8.

Indeed, the Supreme Court has held:

> Whenever a problem of ecology is brought before the Court, the Court is bound to bear in mind Art. 48A of the Constitution ... and Art. 51 A(g). ... When the Court is called upon to give effect to the Directive Principle and the fundamental duty, the Court is not to shrug its shoulders and say that priorities are a matter of policy and so it is a matter for the policy-making authority. The least that the Court may do is to examine whether appropriate considerations are borne in mind and irrelevancies excluded. In appropriate cases, the Court may go further, but how much further will depend on the circumstances of the case. The Court may always give necessary directions. However the Court will not attempt to nicely balance relevant considerations. When the question involves the nice balancing of relevant considerations the Court may feel justified in resigning itself to acceptance of the decision of the concerned authority.[26]

Similarly, the Andhra Pradesh High Court has interpreted Article 48A as imposing 'an obligation' on the government, including courts, to protect the environment.[27]

India's rich cultural heritage is at times endangered by large development projects and short-sighted locational decisions. For example, emissions by industry which were permitted to come up in and around Agra threaten the Taj Mahal, a monument protected under the Ancient Monuments and Archeological Sites and Remains Act of 1958 and a World Heritage Site recognized by the 1972 UNESCO Convention for the Protection of the World Cultural and Natural Heritage.[28] In such situations, a court may be guided by the directive principle in Article 49, which casts a duty on the state 'to protect every monument or place or object of artistic or historic interest declared by or under law made by Parliament to be of national importance, from spoliation, disfigurement, destruction, removal, disposal or export, as the case may be.' Moreover, in view of the range of international treaties on different aspects of environmental protection (covered in chapter fifteen), the state's obligation to 'foster respect for international law and treaty obligations' in Article 51(c), read in conjunction with the specific treaty provisions, may also serve to strengthen the hands of a pro-conservation judge.

V. ARTICLE 253 AND ENVIRONMENTAL LEGISLATION

The Forty-Second Amendment also expanded the list of concurrent powers in the Constitution. The amendment introduced a new entry, 'Population Control and Family Planning,' while 'Forests' and 'Protection of Wild Animals and Birds' were moved from the State List to the Concurrent List.

---

[26] *Sachidanand Pandey v State of West Bengal* AIR 1987 SC 1109, 1114–15.

[27] *T. Damodar Rao v The Special Officer, Municipal Corporation of Hyderabad* AIR 1987 AP 171, 181.

[28] *Reprinted in* 11 I.L.M. 1358 (1972).

Article 253 of the Constitution empowers Parliament to make laws implementing India's international obligations as well as any decision made at an international conference, association or other body. Article 253 states: 'Notwithstanding anything in the foregoing provisions of this Chapter, Parliament has power to make any law for the whole or any part of the territory of India for implementing any treaty, agreement or convention with any other country or countries or any decision made at any international conference, association or other body.' Entry 13 of the Union List covers: 'Participation in international conferences, associations and other bodies and implementing of decisions made thereat.' In view of the broad range of issues addressed by international conventions, conferences, treaties and agreements, Article 253 read with Entry 13 apparently gives Parliament the power to enact laws on virtually any entry contained in the State List.

Parliament has used its power under Article 253 read with Entry 13 of the Union List to enact the Air (Prevention and Control of Pollution) Act of 1981 and the Environment (Protection) Act of 1986.[29] The preambles to both laws state that these Acts were passed to implement the decisions reached at the United Nations Conference on the Human Environment held at Stockholm in 1972. At the conference, members of the United Nations agreed to work to preserve the world's natural resources, and called on each country to carry out this goal.

The broad language of Article 253 suggests that in the wake of the Stockholm Conference in 1972, Parliament has the power to legislate on all matters linked to the preservation of natural resources.[30] Parliament's use of Article 253 to enact the Air Act and Environment Act confirms this view. The subjects 'Forests' and 'Preservation of Wild Animals and Birds' relate to natural resources. It appears, therefore, that the expansion of concurrent powers by the Forty-Second Amendment in 1976 only made explicit, powers that Parliament already possessed under Article 253.

VI. FEDERALISM: SOME ISSUES

On occasion, the division of power under India's federal structure has led to tensions between the Centre and the states in matters concerning regional development and the preservation of natural resources. The areas of stress include coastal development and the commercial exploitation of mineral resources around federally protected areas. In some instances, such as development in the Dahanu Taluka

[29] S. *Jagannath v Union of India (Shrimp Culture Case)* AIR 1997 SC 811, 844, 846.

[30] In 1980 the Tiwari Committee recommended that a new entry on 'Environmental Protection' be introduced in the Concurrent List to enable the Central Government to legislate on environmental subjects. The Committee's recommendation was based on a note from the Indian Academy of Environmental Law which observed that there was no direct entry in the Seventh Schedule enabling Parliament to enact comprehensive environmental laws. The note, however, did not consider Parliament's power under Article 253. Department of Science and Technology, Government of India, *Report of the Committee for Recommending Legislative Measures and Administrative Machinery for Ensuring Environmental Protection* para 3.15 (1980).

of Maharashtra, the state government has turned openly hostile to the imposition of central regulations.

Town planning, building regulations and local zoning are state subjects.[31] Consequently, provisions for development along the coast and foreshore are found in several municipal statutes and the land codes of the coastal states. These local laws, however, proved inadequate to protect the coastal ecology, prompting the Central Government to impose stringent national coastal development norms in 1991. The norms severely restrict the nature of development in a 500 m. wide strip along the entire Indian coast, adding up to more than 3000 sq.km. of land. Understandably, several state governments are irate at the sweeping assumption of power by the Centre,[32] particularly since the coastal norms are *delegated* legislation issued by the executive under the Environment (Protection) Rules of 1986 which, in turn, were framed under the Environment (Protection) Act of 1986 (EPA).

In the *Shrimp Culture Case*,[33] the Supreme Court upheld the power of the Union Government to frame coastal regulations in view of Parliament's competence under Article 253 read with Entry 13, List I of the Seventh Schedule to the Constitution, to enact the EPA for implementing the decisions taken at the 1972 Stockholm Conference.[34] The court went further and recognized that the coastal regulations 'shall have overriding effect and shall prevail over the law made by the legislatures of the states.'[35]

Another contentious issue relates to the quarrying of mineral deposits in areas close to forest lands and wildlife reserves. Central statutes designed to protect forests and prevent the destruction of wildlife habitat are viewed by some states as a needless fetter on industrial activity and mining. Several state governments, notably Rajasthan[36] and Gujarat[37] are anxious to encourage the commercial exploitation of minerals and have worked hard to neutralize federal protection in these areas.

The picturesque Dahanu Taluka, one of the richest horticultural districts in India, has strained Centre-state relations. In June 1991 the Union Ministry of

[31] These topics fall under the heads 'Land' and 'Local government' which are items 18 and 5 of List II (State List) in the Seventh Schedule to the Constitution.

[32] *Coastal Zone Rules to be Amended Soon*, ECONOMIC TIMES, New Delhi, 13 November 1996. Maharashtra expressed strong reservations on the incursion by the Centre in its counter affidavit dated 10 August 1994 filed before the Supreme Court in *Bittu Sehgal v Union of India*, Writ Petition (Civil) No. 231 of 1994.

[33] *S. Jagannath v Union of India* AIR 1997 SC 811, 846.

[34] United Nations Conference on the Human Environment.

[35] *Supra* note 33.

[36] *Shekhawat Irritated by Centre's Move to Amend Forest Act*, INDIAN EXPRESS, Bombay, 1 February 1995; and *Tarun Bharat Sangh, Alwar v Union of India (Sariska Case)* 1993 Supp (3) SCC 115, 128.

[37] See *Consumer Education and Research Society v Union of India (Narayan Sarovar Case–I)* Special Civil Application No. 1313 of 1993, Gujarat High Court, 22–4 March 1995 (B.N. Kirpal, C.J. and H.L. Gokhale, J.).

Environment and Forests notified a scheme of restrictions under the EPA limiting industrial activity in this ecologically sensitive area. Maharashtra has decried the Central scheme[38] claiming that it stifles legitimate development activity in a part of its territory and has lobbied hard for lifting the restrictions.

The division of authority between the Centre and the states has also prompted some central agencies to resist compliance with state town planning regulations. In Maharashtra for instance, until the 1981 decision of the Bombay High Court in the *Sassoon Harbour Case,*[39] (implicitly settling the issue against the central agencies), several central authorities resisted regulation under the local town planning laws.

B. ENVIRONMENTAL PROTECTION AND FUNDAMENTAL RIGHTS

I. THE RIGHT TO A WHOLESOME ENVIRONMENT

Encouraged by an atmosphere of freedom and articulation in the aftermath of the Emergency,[40] the Supreme Court entered one of its most creative periods. Specifically, the court fortified and expanded the fundamental rights enshrined in Part III of the Constitution. In the process, the boundaries of the fundamental right to life and personal liberty guaranteed in Article 21 were expanded to include environmental protection.[41]

The Supreme Court strengthened Article 21 in two ways. First, it required laws affecting personal liberty to also pass the tests of Article 14 and Article 19 of the Constitution,[42] thereby ensuring that the procedure depriving a person of his or her personal liberty be reasonable, fair and just.[43] Second, the court recognized several unarticulated liberties that were implied by Article 21. It is by this second method that the Supreme Court interpreted the right to life and personal liberty to include the right to a wholesome environment.

The first indication of the right to a wholesome environment may be traced to

---

[38] Affidavit of the state government, *supra* note 32.

[39] *Shyam Chainani v The Board of Trustees of the Port of Bombay* Appeal No. 151 of 1980 in Misc. Pet. No. 58 of 1980, Bombay High Court, 30 April 1981.

[40] On 25 June 1975 a Proclamation of Emergency was issued on the ground of 'internal disturbance' threatening the security of India. A widespread denial of civil and political rights followed. The proclamation was revoked in March, 1977 shortly after the Indira Gandhi government was swept out of power in a national election.

[41] Article 21 states: 'No person shall be deprived of his life or personal liberty except according to procedure established by law.'

[42] *Maneka Gandhi v Union of India* AIR 1978 SC 597, 623–4. Article 14 enshrines the right to equality before law and protects a person against arbitrary or unreasonable state action. Article 19 enumerates certain fundamental rights, such as the right to freedom of speech and expression and the right to form associations or unions.

[43] *Francis Coralie Mullin v The Administrator, Union Territory of Delhi* AIR 1981 SC 746, 749–50.

the *Dehradun Quarrying Case*.[44] In July, 1983, representatives of the Rural Litigation and Entitlement Kendra, Dehradun wrote to the Supreme Court alleging that illegal limestone mining in the Mussoorie–Dehradun region was devastating the fragile ecosystems in the area. On 14 July, the court directed its registry to treat the letter as a writ petition under Article 32 of the Constitution, with notice to the government of Uttar Pradesh and the collector of Dehradun. Over the years the litigation grew increasingly complex. By the time the court issued its final judgment in August, 1988, it had heard lengthy arguments from the Central and state governments, government agencies and mine lessees; appointed several expert committees; and passed at least five comprehensive, interim orders. None of these orders, however, articulate the fundamental right to a healthful environment.

Eight years after entertaining the *Dehradun Quarrying Case*, the Supreme Court revealed the basis of its jurisdiction to entertain environmental cases. In *Subhash Kumar v State of Bihar*[45] the court held that the right to life includes the right to enjoy unpolluted air and water. If anything endangers or impairs the quality of life in derogation of law, a citizen has a right to move the Supreme Court under Article 32 of the Constitution. Expanding upon this theme in a town planning case, *Virender Gaur v State of Haryana*,[46] the court observed:

> Article 21 protects the right to life as a fundamental right. Enjoyment of life ... including [the right to live] with human dignity encompasses within its ambit, the protection and preservation of environment, ecological balance free from pollution of air and water, sanitation, without which life cannot be enjoyed. Any contra acts or actions would cause environmental pollution. Environmental, ecological, air, water pollution, etc. should be regarded as amounting to violation of Article 21. Therefore, hygienic environment is an integral facet of right to healthy life and it would be impossible to live with human dignity without a human and healthy environment. ... [T] here is a constitutional imperative on the State Government and the municipalities, not only to ensure and safeguard proper environment but also an imperative duty to take adequate measures to promote, protect and improve both the man-made and the natural environment.[47]

In addition, several High Courts have explicitly recognized an environmental dimension to Article 21. For example, while considering a writ petition to enjoin

---

[44] *Rural Litigation and Entitlement Kendra, Dehradun v State of Uttar Pradesh* AIR 1988 SC 2187.
[45] AIR 1991 SC 420, 424. Also see *M.C. Mehta v Union of India (Delhi Stone Crushing Case)* 1992 (3) SCC 256, 257; and *Chameli Singh v State of Uttar Pradesh* AIR 1996 SC 1051, 1053. When deriving the right to shelter under Article 21 the Supreme Court held that this right would include 'the right to *decent environment* and a reasonable accomodation to live in.' *Shantistar Builders v Narayan K. Totame* AIR 1990 SC 630.
[46] 1995 (2) SCC 577.
[47] *Id.* at 580–1.

the Life Insurance Corporation and the Income-tax Department from building residential houses in a recreational zone, the Andhra Pradesh High Court held:

> [I]t would be reasonable to hold that the enjoyment of life and its attainment and fulfillment guaranteed by Article 21 of the Constitution embraces the protection and preservation of nature's gifts without [which] life cannot be enjoyed. There can be no reason why practice of violent extinguishment of life alone should be regarded as violative of Article 21 of the Constitution. The slow poisoning by the polluted atmosphere caused by environmental pollution and spoilation should also be regarded as amounting to violation of Article 21 of the Constitution. ...
>
> It, therefore, becomes the legitimate duty of Courts as the enforcing organs of Constitutional objectives to forbid all action of the State and the citizen from upsetting the environmental balance. In this case the very purpose of preparing and publishing the development plan is to maintain such an environmental balance. The object of reserving certain area as a recreational zone would be utterly defeated if private owners of the land in that area are permitted to build residential houses. It must, therefore, be held that the attempt of the Life Insurance Corporation of India and the Income-tax Department to build houses in this area is contrary to law and also contrary to Article 21 of the Constitution.[48]

Judges of the High Courts of Rajasthan,[49] Kerala,[50] Himachal Pradesh,[51] Karnataka[52] and Madhya Pradesh[53] too, have observed that environmental degradation violates the fundamental right to life.

II. THE RIGHT TO LIVELIHOOD

Another aspect of the right to life—the right to livelihood—can potentially check government actions with an environmental impact that threaten to dislocate poor people and disrupt their lifestyles. Conservative estimates place the figure of India's project displaced people over the past four decades at 16 million[54] no more than a quarter of whom were satisfactorily rehabilitated. The Morse Report to the World Bank which reviewed the Sardar Sarovar project on the Narmada notes that the

---

[48] *T. Damodar Rao v The Special Officer, Municipal Corporation of Hyderabad* AIR 1987 AP 171, 181.
[49] *L.K. Koolwal v State of Rajasthan* AIR 1988 RAJ 2, 4; and *Arvind Textiles v State of Rajasthan* AIR 1994 RAJ 195, 197.
[50] *Madhavi v Tilakan* 1988 (2) KER.L.T. 730, 731; *Attakoya Thangal v Union of India* 1990 (1) KER.L.T. 580, 583; and *Law Society of India v Fertilizers and Chemicals Travancore Ltd.* AIR 1994 KER 308, 370.
[51] *Kinkri Devi v State of Himachal Pradesh* AIR 1988 HP 4, 9.
[52] *V. Lakshmipathy v State of Karnataka* AIR 1994 KAR 57, 67.
[53] *K.C. Malhotra v State of Madhya Pradesh* AIR 1994 MP 48, 52; and *Hamid Khan v State of Madhya Pradesh* AIR 1997 MP 191, 193.
[54] World Bank, *Resettlement and Development* 2/11 (1994).

'record of resettlement and rehabilitation in India ... has been unsatisfactory in virtually every project with a large resettlement component.'[55]

The Supreme Court recognized the right to livelihood in the case of *Olga Tellis v Bombay Municipal Corporation*.[56] The petitioners, a journalist and two pavement dwellers, challenged a government scheme to deport pavement dwellers from Bombay to their places of origin. The main plank of the petitioners' argument was that the right to life includes the right to livelihood, and since the pavement dwellers would be deprived of their livelihood if they were evicted from their slum and pavement dwellings, their eviction would be tantamount to deprivation of their life, and was hence unconstitutional. Accepting the petitioners' argument, the court held:

> Deprive a person of his right to livelihood and you shall have deprived him of his life. ... The State may not by affirmative action, be compellable to provide adequate means of livelihood or work to the citizens. But, any person, who is deprived of his right to livelihood except according to just and fair procedure established by law, can challenge the deprivation as offending the right to life conferred by Art. 21.[57]

The court directed the municipal corporation to provide alternative sites or accommodation to the slum and pavement dwellers within a reasonable distance of their original sites; to earnestly pursue a proposed housing scheme for the poor; and to provide basic amenities to slum dwellers.[58]

Thereafter, in *Banawasi Seva Ashram v State of Uttar Pradesh*,[59] the Supreme Court detailed safeguards to protect tribal forest dwellers who were being ousted from their forest land by the National Thermal Power Corporation Limited (NTPC) for the Rihand Super Thermal Power Project. The court permitted the acquisition of the land only after the NTPC agreed to provide certain court-approved facilities to the ousted forest dwellers.[60] In other Article 32 petitions, the court has passed interim orders requiring state agencies to resettle and rehabilitate tribals who were being displaced by dams.[61]

---

[55] *Sardar Sarovar: Report of the Independent Review* 351 (1992). The report was prepared by Bradford Morse, former UNDP Director and was commissioned by the World Bank.

[56] AIR 1986 SC 180.

[57] *Id.* at 194.

[58] *Id.* at 204.

[59] AIR 1987 SC 374. In the course of its order the court observed that the tribals 'for generations had been using the jungles around for collecting the requirements for their livelihood—fruits, vegetables, fodder, flowers, timber, animals by way of sport and fuelwood.' Although not explicitly referred to in the order, Article 21 and the right to livelihood were impliedly relied on by the court. (Subsequent orders in the same case are reported at 1987 (1) SCALE 1149, 1992 (1) SCC 117, AIR 1992 SC 920 and 1993 (2) SCC 612).

[60] AIR 1987 SC 374, 378.

[61] *Karanjan Jalasay Y.A.S.A.S. Samiti v State of Gujarat* AIR 1987 SC 532 and *Gramin Sewa Sanstha v State of Uttar Pradesh* 1986 (Supp) SCC 578. Neither order explicitly refers to Article 21 or the right to livelihood.

Can the right to livelihood be asserted to prevent environmentally disruptive projects that threaten to uproot villagers and consequently, deprive them of their livelihood? Consider a case where the government sanctions the construction of a large dam without an adequate environmental impact analysis[62] and without public scrutiny. Is the government acting reasonably? Does the procedure leading to the government decision—a decision which will jeopardize the livelihood of thousands of villagers—meet the *Olga Tellis* standard of being a just and fair procedure established by law?

III. THE RIGHT TO EQUALITY

Apart from Article 21, the right to equality guaranteed in Article 14 of the Constitution may also be infringed by government decisions that have an impact on the environment.[63] Article 14, among other things, strikes at arbitrariness 'because an action that is arbitrary must necessarily involve a negation of equality.'[64]

Thus, urban environmental groups frequently resort to Article 14 to quash 'arbitrary' municipal permissions for construction that are contrary to development regulations. Besides, Article 14 may also be invoked to challenge government sanctions for mining and other activities with high environmental impact, where the permissions are 'arbitrarily' granted without an adequate consideration of environmental impacts.[65] In *State of Himachal Pradesh v Ganesh Wood Products*,[66] the Supreme Court held that a decision making authority must give due weight and regard to ecological factors such as the environmental policy of government and the sustainable use of natural resources. A government decision that fails to take into account relevant considerations affecting the environment is invalid.[67]

Is it possible to derive *a right to intergenerational equity* from Articles 21 and 14? The central tenet of the theory of intergenerational equity is the right of each generation of human beings to benefit from the cultural and natural inheritance from past generations as well as the *obligation* to preserve such heritage for future generations. Intergenerational equity requires conserving the diversity and quality of biological resources, and of renewable resources such as forests, water and soils.[68]

[62] Environmental Impact Analysis (EIA) is an exercise to evaluate the probable changes in the various socio–economic and bio–physical characteristics in the environment which may result from a proposed project. EIA is undertaken to reduce to a minimum the possibility of an action causing unanticipated changes in the environment. It assists decision–makers in considering the environmental costs and benefits of the proposed project. Where the benefits sufficiently exceed the costs of the project, the project may be environmentally justified.

[63] Article 14 states: 'The State shall not deny to any person equality before the law or the equal protection of the laws within the territory of India.'

[64] *Ajay Hasia v Khalid Mujib Shervardi* AIR 1981 SC 487, 499.

[65] See generally, *Kinkri Devi.v State of Himachal Pradesh* AIR 1988 HP 4, 9.

[66] AIR 1996 SC 149, 159, 163.

[67] *Id.*; and *Pleasant Stay Hotel v Palani Hills Conservation Council* 1995 (6) SCC 127, 136, 139, 140.

[68] See note on *Goa Guidelines on Intergenerational Equity* in 27 I.L.M. 1108 (1988) and the chapter on International Environmental Law.

Can this 'right' be invoked to preserve archaeological monuments or genetic resources threatened with destruction by state action or inaction?

In *Ganesh Wood Products Case* the Supreme Court recognized the obligation of the present generation to preserve natural resources for the next and future generations.[69] Likewise, in the *CRZ Notification Case*,[70] the Supreme Court observed that environmental statutes were enacted to ensure a good quality of life for unborn generations since it is they who must bear the brunt of ecological degradation.

IV. FREEDOM TO TRADE VIS-A-VIS ENVIRONMENTAL PROTECTION

As environmental regulation grows more stringent and its enforcement becomes more vigorous, industrial challenge to agency action is likely to increase. Courts will then need to balance environmental interests with the fundamental right to carry on any occupation, trade or business guaranteed in Article 19(1)(g).[71] For example, effluent discharge standards prescribed by the pollution control boards may be challenged under Article 19 for being excessive (too stringent to comply with, despite using the best available technology) or otherwise unreasonable. Likewise, unreasonable government decisions relating to the siting or translocation of industry may also be assailed under Article 19(1)(g).

Such future clashes between industry and enforcement agencies are presaged in the case of *Abhilash Textile v Rajkot Municipal Corporation,* excerpted below. Here, the Gujarat High Court was required to balance the right to carry on business against the danger to public health from the discharge of 'dirty water' onto public roads and drains. While the court adopts a commendable pro-environment stance, is the judgment well-reasoned?

ABHILASH TEXTILE v RAJKOT MUNICIPAL CORPORATION
AIR 1988 GUJ 57

ORDER:

Is there any right to carry on business or trade in unregulated manner and cause nuisance to the public and also become a health hazard to the society at large? If no, can the petitioners claim any right to be heard before they are asked to discontinue or prevent the nuisance? This, in substance, is the question which needs to be examined in this group of petitions.

In these four petitions in all 165 petitioners who are conducting the business of dyeing and printing works at different places in the city of Rajkot challenge the

---

[69] *Supra* note 66.

[70] *Indian Council for Enviro–Legal Action v Union of India, (CRZ Notification Case)* 1996 (5) SCC 281, 293.

[71] Article 19(1)(g) states: 'All citizens shall have the right ... to practise any profession, or to carry on any occupation, trade or business.'

notice issued by the respondent-Municipal Commissioner which is produced at Annexure-A to the petitions.

* * *

In this notice it is stated that at the place mentioned therein the petitioners are discharging dirty water from the factory on public road/public drainage without purifying the same, thereby causing damage to the public health. Moreover, it is stated that on 11 November 1986 when the place was visited by the Commissioner himself it was found that by discharging dirty water nuisance was being created. Hence each petitioner has been called upon to prevent the discharge of dirty water without the same being purified, within seven days from the date of receipt of the notice and they are also directed to inform the Commissioner regarding compliance. It is further stated that if there is failure to comply with the notice, under the powers conferred upon the Municipal Commissioner, he shall have to take steps to close the factory with a view to prevent the illegal discharge of dirty water.

The petitioners contended that they are carrying on the business for last about 20 to 25 years and the industry is providing employment to twenty to thirty thousand families; the proposed action as stated in the notice will have harsh consequences and the petitioners may have to close down their business. Having regard to the very harsh consequences it is submitted that before issuing the notice the respondent-Municipal Commissioner ought to have afforded an opportunity of being heard to the petitioners. Reliance is placed on the decision of the Supreme Court in the case of *Maneka Gandhi v Union of India* AIR 1978 SC 597. The learned counsel for the petitioners relied upon the following observations of the Supreme Court occurring in para 32 of the judgment:

It is well established that even where there is no specific provision in a statute or rules made thereunder for showing cause against action proposed to be taken against an individual, *which affects the rights of that individual,* the duty to give reasonable opportunity to be heard will be implied from the nature of the function to be performed by the authority which has the power to take punitive or damaging action.

The learned counsel for the petitioners submitted that the proposed action will have civil consequences inasmuch as the closing down of the factories will adversely affect the petitioners; they will have to close down their business and their right to carry on the business will be adversely affected. Similarly, very harsh consequences will follow and therefore, the notice Annexure-A which has been issued without affording an opportunity of being heard should be held to be illegal and void. [The court then set out the provisions of the Municipal Act defining a nuisance; providing for the licensing of trades that might cause a nuisance; and empowering the Municipal Commissioner to restrain nuisance-causing activities.]

In the background of the aforesaid statutory provisions can it be said that the petitioners have a right to carry on the business so as to cause nuisance and be a health hazard to the public at large? Article 19(1)(g) of the Constitution confers right upon every citizen to practice any profession or to carry on any occupation, trade or business. But this fundamental right is subject to reasonable restrictions which may be placed in the interest of the general public as provided for in sub-clause (6) of Article 19 itself. No one has a right to carry on business so as to cause nuisance to the society. One cannot carry on the business in the manner by which the business activity becomes a health hazard to the entire society. The fundamental right to carry on trade or business is subject to reasonable restrictions and regulations that may be placed in the interest of the general public.

It may also be noted that by discharge of effluent water on public road and/or in the public drainage system the entire environment of the locality gets polluted. The provisions regarding fundamental duties of the citizens contained in Article 51A(g) of the Constitution enjoins upon all the citizens to protect and improve the natural environment * * * By the impugned notice the respondent-Municipal Commissioner has simply reminded the petitioners of their fundamental duty. The petitioners cannot assert their right, much less fundamental right, to carry on business without any regard to the fundamental duty. In a complex society, in which we live today, no one can claim absolute freedom without incurring any obligation whatsoever for the general well being. The Article 51-A regarding fundamental duties of citizens has been inserted in the Constitution by Forty Second Amendment and it has come into force with effect from 3 January 1977. Even in absence of the provisions with regard to fundamental duty as enshrined in Article 51-A of the Constitution, the Supreme Court has held that such restrictions placed on the fundamental right to carry on trade or business are in the interest of the general public and constitutionally valid and no citizen can claim absolute right to carry on business without complying with the restrictions placed in this behalf.

* * *

The contention that the petitioners are carrying on business for last about 20 to 30 years has also no merit. If the petitioners wish to carry on the business they may have to incur expenditure and they must provide for purification-plant before discharging the effluent water on public road or in the public drainage system. This is the minimum requirement for carrying on the business which they must comply with. If they have to incur expenditure for the purification-plant the same must be considered as part of the cost of the business. The petitioners cannot be allowed to reap profit at the cost of the public health. This is the mandate of the law. This is what the Commissioner has proposed to do by serving the impugned notice upon the petitioners.

The only ground urged before me is that the notice has been issued without affording an opportunity of being heard and therefore it is violative of the principles of natural justice. As shown hereinabove the petitioners have not been able to show that they have any right, much less a fundamental right, to carry on their business without complying with the requirement of the law. Hence there is no substance in this contention. No other contention is raised.

* * *

In the facts and circumstances of the case it is hoped that before taking any coercive steps the respondent-Municipal Commissioner will give some more time to the petitioners to mend their ways and prevent the nuisance. This observation is made with a view to see that several workmen employed by the numerous factories may not be tendered unemployed on account of the fact that the petitioners are carrying on their business in unregulated manner. Subject to the aforesaid observations, the petitions are rejected. Notice discharged. Ad interim relief granted earlier stands vacated in each petition.

QUESTIONS

In holding that the petitioners have no fundamental right to carry on business without complying with municipal laws, the court appears to pre-judge the very issue the petitioners were seeking to agitate before the municipal commissioner. Instead, should not the court have *upheld* the principle requiring a personal hearing and then declined to intervene under Article 226 on the ground that the petitioners had no case on the merits?

In the *Sushila Saw Mill Case*, excerpted below, the Supreme Court was asked to invalidate section 4 of the Orissa Saw Mills and Saw Pits (Control) Act of 1991 which prohibited saw mills from operating in a forest or within a buffer of 10 kilometres from a forest. The law was enacted to preserve the state's forests and stop illegal felling of trees. When the 1991 Act came into force, Sushila mill which had been running for a decade in the Keonjhar district of Orissa, found that it fell within the prohibited zone. The mill challenged the ban in the Orissa High Court, contending that the complete bar violated its fundamental right under Article 19(1)(g). The High Court was not impressed and dismissed the writ petition. The mill carried the matter to the Supreme Court in a special leave petition under Article 136 of the Constitution.

SUSHILA SAW MILL v STATE OF ORISSA
AIR 1995 SC 2484

ORDER: * * *

The right to carry on trade or business envisaged under Article 19(1)(g) is subject to statutory regulation. When the statute prescribes total prohibition to continue to operate even the existing saw mills situated within the prohibited area, the right to carry on trade or business is subject to the provisions of the Act. Proviso to Section 4(1) puts a total embargo on the right to carry on trade or business in saw milling operation or sawing operation within the prohibited area. It is settled law that in the public interest restriction under Article 19(1)(g) may in certain rare cases include total prohibition.

This Court in *Narendra Kumar v Union of India* AIR 1960 SC 430, held that it is reasonable to think that makers of the Constitution considered the word 'restriction' to be sufficiently wide to save laws inconsistent with Article 19(1), or taking away the rights conferred by the Article, provided this inconsistency or taking away was reasonable in the interest of the different matters mentioned in the clause. There can be no doubt, therefore, that they intended the word 'restriction' to include cases of prohibition also in certain rare cases. The contention that a law prohibiting the exercise of a fundamental right is in no case saved cannot, therefore, be accepted. It is seen that the reserved forest is being denuded or depleted by illicit felling. Thereby denudation of the reserved forest was noticed by the legislature. The preservation of the forest is a matter of great public interest and one of the rare cases that demanded the total ban by the legislature. The Act came to be enacted to impose a total ban in prohibited area for the period during which the ban is in operation, to carry on saw mills business or sawing operation within the prohibited area. It is, therefore, clear that the statute intends to impose a total ban which is found to be in 'public interest'. The individual interest, therefore, must yield place to the public interest. Accordingly, it is neither arbitrary nor unreasonable. ... It is true that by geographical contiguity, Keonjhar District appears to have been situated within the prohibited area but that in the legislative mandate that the entire area covered within the prohibited zone is treated as a class as against the other area. Therefore, when the limits of that district are within prohibited zone of the reserved or protected or forest area etc. or within 10 kms it is a legislative scheme to give effect to the legislative object in the public interest to preserve forest wealth and environment and to put an end to illicit felling of forest growth. Therefore, it is a class legislation; it is not discriminatory and does not offend Article 14 or Article 301 of the Constitution. It is a valid law. The special leave petition is accordingly dismissed.

NOTES AND QUESTIONS

1. Would the outcome of the case have been different if not one, but several saw mills employing hundreds of workers were involved?

2. The court was extremely deferential to the legislature in upholding the ban. Is this because India's forests are in a devastated condition? Or more generally, would all prohibitions in aid of environmental protection meet the court's standard, i.e., 'a matter of great public interest and one of the rare cases that demand a total ban by the legislature'?

C. DIGEST OF ENVIRONMENTAL LEGISLATION

Although there are over two hundred central and state statutes that have some bearing on environmental protection,[72] in most cases the environmental concern is incidental

---

[72] Department of Science and Technology, Government of India, *Report of the (Tiwari) Committee for Recommending Legislative Measures and Administrative Machinery for Ensuring Environmental Protection* para 3.1 (1980).

to the law's principal object. For example, the Indian Fisheries Act of 1897 prohibited the destruction of fish by the use of explosives or by poisoning the water. Such scattered and piecemeal 'environmental' provisions held the field until the 1970s.[73]

In that decade, the evolution of national environmental policies resulted in Parliament enacting comprehensive laws in the fields of wildlife protection and water pollution. In the early 1980s, nationwide forest conservation and air pollution laws were passed. The Bhopal tragedy in December, 1984 caused a surge in environmental legislation: An umbrella Environment (Protection) Act (EPA) was passed in 1986, followed by amendments tightening the laws relating to air and water pollution and to hazardous activities. The 1990s witnessed fresh legislation dealing with insurance cover for hazardous industries, new laws setting up an environmental tribunal and appellate authority, amendments to the wildlife regime and a spate of central regulations under the EPA. To provide an overview of environmental regulation in India this section digests the principal national environmental statutes.

INTERPRETATION OF ENVIRONMENTAL STATUTES

Frequently, judges must choose between two possible interpretations of an environmental statute, one that advances environmental protection, and the other favouring some other interest such as industry, jobs or the need for energy. In this situation a judge may be persuaded to a pro-environment construction on the basis of rules for the interpretation of statutes. A strong statement by the Supreme Court favouring a pro-environment interpretation was in the *Sariska Case*,[74] where the court held:

> This litigation concerns environment. A great American Judge emphasising the imperative issue of environment said that he placed Government above big business, individual liberty above Government and environment above all. ... The issues of environment must and shall receive the highest attention from this Court.

Environment statutes are regarded as 'beneficient' legislation, enacted to advance the directive principle of state policy contained in Article 48A of the Constitution. Being beneficient legislation, it is the duty of the court to adopt an interpretation favouring ecological preservation.

Another related rule requires courts to adopt a 'purposive' interpretation, or an approach that advances the purpose which the legislature had in mind when enacting the law. For example, in *V. Shankar Reddy v State of Andhra Pradesh*,[75] a division

---

[73] At the state level, however, there are a few isolated instances of pre–1970 comprehensive environmental laws. e.g., the Orissa River Pollution Prevention Act of 1953 and the Maharashtra Prevention of Water Pollution Act of 1969.

[74] *Tarun Bharat Sangh, Alwar v Union of India* Writ Petition (Civil) No.509 of 1991, Supreme Court, 14 May 1992 (M.N. Venkatachaliah and B.P. Jeevan Reddy, JJ.).

[75] 1992 (2) ANDH.L.T. 514, 529.

bench of the Andhra Pradesh High Court upheld the invalidation of a government order permitting a forest to be cleared, since the order was against the purpose of the legislation, which was forest conservation. Occasionally, powers delegated to enforcement agencies under environmental laws are exercised for a purpose that undermines the object of the law. This is impermissible. In the *Bangalore Medical Trust Case*,[76] for instance, the Supreme Court held that discretion vested in an authority must be exercised for the purpose of attaining the objects of the law. A plot reserved for a public park could not be allotted arbitrarily to a private hospital by altering the town planning scheme. The alteration did not improve the scheme and, therefore, was contrary to the *purpose* for which the power to alter the scheme was conferred.

THE AIR (PREVENTION AND CONTROL OF POLLUTION) ACT OF 1981

To implement the decisions taken at the United Nations Conference on the Human Environment held at Stockholm in June, 1972 Parliament enacted the nationwide Air Act under Article 253 of the Constitution. The Act's statement of objects and reasons contains the government's explanation of the contents and the scope of the law, and its concern for the 'detrimental effect [of air-pollution] on the health of the people as also on animal life, vegetation and property.'

The Air Act's framework is similar to the one created by its predecessor, the Water Act of 1974. To enable an integrated approach to environmental problems, the Air Act expanded the authority of the central and state boards established under the Water Act, to include air pollution control. States not having water pollution boards were required to set up air pollution boards.

Under the Air Act, all industries operating within designated air pollution control areas must obtain a 'consent' (permit) from the state boards. The states are required to prescribe emission standards for industry and automobiles after consulting the Central board and noting its ambient air quality standards.

Prior to its amendment in 1987, the Air Act was enforced through mild court-administered penalties on violators. The 1987 amendment strengthened the enforcement machinery and introduced stiffer penalties. Now, the boards may close down a defaulting industrial plant or may stop its supply of electricity or water. A board may also apply to a court to restrain emissions that exceed prescribed standards. Notably, the 1987 amendment introduced a citizens' initiative provision into the Air Act and extended the Act to include noise pollution.

The Rules issued under the Air Act focus on procedural matters.

THE WATER (PREVENTION AND CONTROL OF POLLUTION) ACT OF 1974

The Water Act of 1974 was the culmination of over a decade of discussion and deliberation between the Centre and the states. The history and the preamble of the

---

[76] *Bangalore Medical Trust v B.S. Muddappa* AIR 1991 SC 1902, 1911, 1924.

Water Act suggest that only state governments can enact water pollution legislation. The Act, therefore, was passed by Parliament pursuant to enabling resolutions by twelve states, under Article 252(1) of the Constitution. Article 252 empowers Parliament to enact laws on state subjects for two or more states, where the State Legislatures have consented to such legislation.

The Act vests regulatory authority in state boards and empowers these boards to establish and enforce effluent standards for factories discharging pollutants into bodies of water. A Central board performs the same functions for union territories and coordinates activities among the states.

The boards control sewage and industrial effluent discharges by approving, rejecting or conditioning applications for consent to discharge. The state boards also minimize water pollution by advising state governments on appropriate sites for new industry.

Prior to its amendment in 1988, enforcement under the Water Act was achieved through criminal prosecutions initiated by the boards, and through applications to magistrates for injunctions to restrain polluters. The 1988 amendment strengthened the Act's implementation provisions. Now, a board may close a defaulting industrial plant or withdraw its supply of power or water by an administrative order; the penalties are more stringent; and a citizens' initiative provision bolsters the enforcement machinery. In Gujarat the amendments introduced in 1988 have not been adopted by a resolution of the legislature under Article 252. As a result, the 1988 amendments do not apply to that state.[77]

THE WATER (PREVENTION AND CONTROL OF POLLUTION) CESS ACT OF 1977

The Water Cess Act was passed to help meet the expenses of the Central and state water boards. The Act creates economic incentives for pollution control through a differential tax structure (with higher rates applicable to defaulting units) and requires local authorities and certain designated industries to pay a cess (tax) for water consumption. These revenues are used to implement the Water Act. The Central Government, after deducting the expenses of collection, pays the Central board and the states such sums as it deems necessary to enforce the provisions of the Water Act. To encourage capital investment in pollution control, the Act gives a polluter a 25 per cent rebate of the applicable cess upon installing effluent treatment equipment and meeting the applicable norms.

THE WILD LIFE (PROTECTION) ACT OF 1972

In 1972, Parliament enacted the Wild Life Act pursuant to the enabling resolutions of 11 states under Article 252(1) of the Constitution. The Wild Life Act provides for state wildlife advisory boards, regulations for hunting wild animals and birds, establishment of sanctuaries and national parks, regulations for trade in wild animals,

---

[77] *Pravinbhai J. Patel v State of Gujarat* 1995 (2) GUJ.L.R. 1210, 1216.

animal products and trophies, and judicially imposed penalties for violating the Act. Harming endangered species listed in Schedule I of the Act is prohibited throughout India. Hunting other species, like those requiring special protection (Schedule II), big game (Schedule III), and small game (Schedule IV) is regulated through licensing. A few species classified as vermin (Schedule V) may be hunted without restrictions. The Act is administered by wildlife wardens and their staff.

An amendment to the Act in 1982, introduced provisions permitting the capture and transportation of wild animals for the scientific management of animal populations. Comprehensive amendments to the parent Act in 1991 resulted in the insertion of special chapters dealing with the protection of specified plants and the regulation of zoos. The new provisions also recognized the needs of tribals and forest dwellers and introduced changes to advance their welfare.

THE PUBLIC LIABILITY INSURANCE ACT OF 1991

This law (PLIA) was enacted to provide immediate relief to the victims of an accident involving a hazardous substance. To achieve this object, the Act imposes 'no-fault' liability upon the owner of the hazardous substance and requires the owner to compensate the victims irrespective of any neglect or default on her part. The PLIA stipulates the maximum compensation for injury or death at Rs. 25,000 and limits compensation in respect of damage to private property to Rs. 6000. The right of a victim to claim additional relief under any other law is expressly reserved.

The Act obligates every owner to take out an insurance policy covering potential liability from an accident. An 'accident' is defined to cover a sudden unintended occurrence while 'handling' any hazardous substance resulting in continuous, intermittent or repeated exposure leading to death or injury to any person, or damage to property or the environment. Accidents by reason of war or radio-activity are excluded from the scope of the Act. The expression 'handling' is defined widely to include manufacture, trade, and transport of hazardous substances.

Along with the insurance premium, every owner must make a contribution to an Environmental Relief Fund established by the Central Government. The fund is designed to provide relief to the victims of an accident. The principal administrative authority under the PLIA is the collector, who is required to verify the occurrence of an industrial accident, give publicity to the event, invite applications for compensation and award relief.

The Act was amended in 1992 to introduce provisions relating to the relief fund. Rules framed in 1991 lay down the procedure for inviting and processing compensation applications and also cap the potential liability of an insurer at Rs. 450 million.

THE NATIONAL ENVIRONMENT TRIBUNAL ACT OF 1995

This Act (NETA) builds on the foundation laid in the PLIA and substantially alters the law of torts relating to toxic substances in India. NETA extends the principle of 'no-fault' liability, which first received statutory recognition under the PLIA, *beyond* the statutory compensation limits prescribed under the 1991 Act. NETA applies in cases where death or injury to any person or damage to any property is caused by an accident during the handling of any hazardous substance. Both Acts adopt the same definition for the expressions 'accident' and 'handling'.

NETA empowers the Centre to establish a national tribunal at New Delhi with power to entertain applications for compensation, hold an inquiry into each such claim and make an award determining the compensation to be paid. The tribunal is empowered to make interim awards after granting an opportunity to the affected party and may determine its own procedure for processing the compensation claims, consistent with the principles of natural justice.

Section 19 of NETA imposes a bar on all civil courts from entertaining 'any application or action' for any claim or compensation which may be entertained or dealt with by the tribunal. An award under the Act may be challenged before the Supreme Court or impugned in a petition to the High Court under Articles 226 and 227.[78]

THE NATIONAL ENVIRONMENT APPELLATE AUTHORITY ACT OF 1997

This statute requires the Central Government to constitute a national environment appellate authority for hearing appeals against orders granting environmental clearance in areas where restrictions are imposed on setting up any industry or carrying on any operation or process. Being cognate to the Environment (Protection) Act of 1986, this statute is discussed in the next section.

THE MINES AND MINERALS (REGULATION AND DEVELOPMENT) ACT OF 1957

As the short title suggests, the thrust of this law is to promote the prospecting of minerals and the development of mines. Recognizing the devastating environmental impact of mining activity in several regions across the country, Parliament amended the Act in 1986 to introduce provisions which would require greater environmental sensitivity whilst conducting mining operations.

Section 4A permits government to terminate a prospecting licence or mining lease in order to preserve the natural environment or prevent pollution or harm to public health, monuments, buildings and other structures. Sections 13 and 15 empower the Centre and the states to frame rules to restore vegetation destroyed by mining operations in any area.

THE INDIAN FOREST ACT OF 1927

Although it embodies the colonial policies of the pre-independence era, the Forest Act of 1927 remains in force. This Act consolidates, with minor changes, the provisions of the Indian Forest Act of 1878 and its amending Acts.

---

[78] *L. Chandra Kumar v Union of India* AIR 1997 SC 1125, 1154.

The 1927 Act deals with four categories of forests, namely, reserved forests, village forests, protected forests, and non-government (private) forests. A state may declare forest lands or waste lands as reserved forests, and may sell the produce from these forests. Any unauthorized felling of trees, quarrying, grazing and hunting in reserved forests is punishable with a fine or imprisonment, or both. Reserved forests assigned to a village community are called village forests. The state governments are empowered to designate protected forests and may prohibit the felling of trees, quarrying and the removal of forest produce from these forests. The preservation of protected forests is enforced through rules, licences and criminal prosecutions.

The Forest Act is administered by forest officers who are authorized to compel the attendance of witnesses and the production of documents, to issue search warrants and to take evidence in an inquiry into forest offences. Such evidence is admissible in a magistrate's court.

THE FOREST (CONSERVATION) ACT OF 1980

Alarmed at India's rapid deforestation and the resulting environmental degradation, the Central Government enacted the Forest (Conservation) Act in 1980. As amended in 1988, the Act requires the approval of the Central Government before a state 'dereserves' a reserved forest, uses forest land for non-forest purposes, assigns forest land to a private person or corporation, or clears forest land for the purpose of reforestation. An Advisory Committee constituted under the Act advises the Centre on these approvals.

THE INSECTICIDES ACT OF 1968

The Insecticides Act was designed to implement the recommendations of the Kerala and Madras Food-Poisoning Cases Inquiry Commission, which inquired into several deaths from insecticide-contaminated food in April and May, 1958. The Act established a Central Insecticides Board to advise the Centre and the states on technical aspects of the Act. A committee of this Board registers insecticides after examining their formulas and verifying claims regarding their safety and efficacy.

The manufacture and distribution of insecticides is regulated through licensing. A violation of the Act's registration and licensing provisions can lead to prosecution and penalties. The Central and state governments are vested with emergency powers to prohibit the sale, distribution and use of dangerous insecticides.

The following observations in the Tiwari Committee Report of September, 1980 are still current:

This Act, which regulates all aspects of the use of pesticides, has not encouraged strongly enough the move away from the use of organo-chlorine pesticides which are in disfavour all over the world for their proven detrimental effects on the various living natural resources of the environment. The use of biological and integrated pest control in India has hardly caught on in any significant measure. The implementation of the provisions of this Act for monitoring pesticide residues in the environment is totally inadequate. It is hence not surprising that increasing levels of pesticide residues are being recorded in foodstuffs, animal tissues and even human fat. Meanwhile, resistance of pests such as the malarial mosquito to chemical pesticides is on the rise.

The Insecticides Rules of 1971 prescribe the procedures for licensing, packaging, labelling and transporting insecticides. They also provide for workers' safety during the manufacture and handling of insecticides through protective clothing, respiratory devices and medical facilities.

THE ATOMIC ENERGY ACT OF 1962

The regulation of nuclear energy and radioactive substances in India is governed by the Atomic Energy Act of 1962, and the Radiation Protection Rules of 1971. Under the Act, the Central Government is required to prevent radiation hazards, guarantee public safety and the safety of workers handling radioactive substances, and ensure the disposal of radioactive wastes. Nuclear research, the manufacture and transport of radioactive substances, and the production and supply of atomic energy and nuclear-generated electricity also fall within the Centre's authority.

The Centre's apparently unfettered power to withhold from the public what it deems to be 'restricted information,' shrouds India's nuclear activities in secrecy. The government may classify as 'restricted information' any unpublished information regarding the location, quality, quantity, processing, acquisition and disposal of radioactive substances; the theory, design, construction and operation of nuclear reactors and of industrial plants that produce radioactive substances; and any information relating to nuclear research.

THE FACTORIES ACT OF 1948

Passed shortly after the Bhopal tragedy and the Supreme Court's judgment in the *Shriram Gas Leak Case,*[79] the 1987 amendment to the Factories Act introduced special provisions on hazardous industrial activities.

The 1987 amendment empowers the states to appoint site appraisal committees to advise on the initial location of factories using hazardous processes. The occupier of every hazardous unit must disclose to her workers, the Factory Inspector and the local authority all particulars regarding health hazards at the factory, and the preventive measures taken. These preventive measures must be publicized among the workers and nearby residents. Every occupier must also draw up an emergency disaster control plan, which must be approved by the Chief Inspector.

The occupier is required to maintain workers' medical records and must

---

[79] *M.C. Mehta v Union of India* AIR 1987 SC 965.

employ operations and maintenance personnel who are experienced in handling hazardous substances. The permissible limits of exposure to toxic substances are prescribed in the Second Schedule to the Act. Safety committees consisting of workers and managers are required periodically to review the factory's safety measures.

The Factories Act after its 1987 amendment, defines 'occupier' as a very senior level manager. Such person is held responsible for compliance with the Act's new provisions relating to hazardous processes. Non-compliance exposes the occupier to stiff penalties.

D. THE ENVIRONMENT (PROTECTION) ACT OF 1986

In the wake of the Bhopal tragedy, the Government of India enacted the Environment (Protection) Act of 1986 (EPA) under Article 253 of the Constitution. The purpose of the Act is to implement the decisions of the United Nations Conference on the Human Environment of 1972, in so far as they relate to the protection and improvement of the human environment and the prevention of hazards to human beings, other living creatures, plants and property. The EPA is an 'umbrella' legislation designed to provide a framework for Central Government coordination of the activities of various central and state authorities established under previous laws, such as the Water Act and Air Act. It is also an 'enabling' law, which articulates the essential legislative policy on environmental protection and delegates wide powers to the executive to *enable* bureaucrats to frame necessary rules and regulations. Since the time it entered the statute book, the Act has served to back a vast body of subordinate environmental legislation in India.

I. THE SCOPE OF THE ACT

The scope of the EPA is broad, with 'environment' defined to include water, air and land and the inter-relationships which exist among water, air and land, and human beings and other living creatures, plants, micro-organisms and property. [80] 'Environmental pollution' is the presence of any environmental pollutant, defined as any solid, liquid, or gaseous substance present in such concentration as may be, or may tend to be, injurious to the environment.[81] 'Hazardous substances' include any substance or preparation which may cause harm to human beings, other living creatures, plants, micro-organisms, property or the environment.[82]

Section 3(1), of the Act empowers the Centre 'to take all such measures as it deems necessary or expedient for the purpose of protecting and improving the quality of the environment and preventing, controlling and abating environmental pollution.'

[80] Section 2(a).
[81] Section 2(b) and (c).
[82] Section 2(e).

Specifically, the Central Government is authorized to set new national standards for the quality of the environment (ambient standards) as well as standards for controlling emissions and effluent discharges; to regulate industrial locations; to prescribe procedures for managing hazardous substances; to establish safeguards for preventing accidents; and to collect and disseminate information regarding environmental pollution.

Section 23 of the Act empowers the Centre to delegate its powers and functions to any officer, state government or other authority. Section 24 of the EPA ensures that the provisions of this Act and subordinate rules or orders *override* any other law. A broad rule-making power is conferred on the Central Government under sections 6 and 25.

NOTES

1. The primary legislative responses to the Bhopal gas leak tragedy of December, 1984 were the Bhopal Act of 1985 [83] and the EPA. Consequently, the EPA bears the stamp of the legislature's immediate concern to strengthen the regulatory framework for hazardous industry and pollution control: One out of the four chapters in the Act (chapter 3) is devoted to environmental pollution; section 6 empowers the Centre to frame rules for pollution control;[84] and almost all the specific subjects of legislative concern enumerated in section 3 deal with industrial pollution.[85]

This legislative focus soon translated into a range of central rules and regulations laying down pollution norms and regulating toxic substances. Since the early 1990s, however, the breath of government action under the EPA has extended to the protection of ecologically sensitive areas such as the coast and the introduction of economic incentives through a product labelling scheme called 'Ecomark'.

2. The potentially broad sweep of the EPA is suggested by the range of issues mentioned in the Statement of Object and Reasons accompanying the Bill: 'The decline of environmental quality has been evidenced by increasing pollution, loss of vegetal cover and biological diversity, excessive concentrations of harmful chemicals in the ambient atmosphere and in food chains, growing risks of environmental accidents and threats to life support systems.'[86]

3. In the *Shrimp Culture Case*,[87] the question arose whether provisions in state

[83] The Bhopal Gas Leak Disaster (Processing of Claims) Act was passed to ensure that claims arising out of the disaster would be dealt with speedily, effectively and equitably. The Union Government was authorised to sue on behalf of Indian claimants in foreign forums.

[84] This provision is in addition to the general rule–making power under section 25.

[85] This provision enables the Central Government to take all necessary measures to protect and improve the environment.

[86] Referred to by the Supreme Court in *S. Jagannath v Union of India (Shrimp Culture Case)* AIR 1997 SC 811, 844.

[87] *Id.* at 846.

laws regulating coastal prawn farms were valid, despite a conflict with the EPA regulations. The Supreme Court clarified that the coastal regulations notified under the EPA would prevail over state legislation. This judgment bolsters section 24 of the EPA which declares the overriding effect of the Act and subordinate rules in relation to any other central or state law.

II. DELEGATED LEGISLATION

The mass of subordinate legislation framed under the EPA by the Department of Environment, Forests and Wildlife of the Central Ministry of Environment and Forests falls under four broad categories: pollution control; hazardous substance regulation; environment impact assessment; and the protection of the coast and other ecologically fragile areas. Most of these regulations are analysed in greater detail under the related chapters later in the book. Here, we summarize the broad features of the rules.

Pollution Control

Section 7 of the EPA prohibits the discharge or emission of environmental pollutants in excess of the prescribed standards. To implement this mandate, the government has framed the Environment (Protection) Rules of 1986 (EPR). The standards are set out in the schedules appended to the EPR. Broadly, there are three types of standards: *source* standards which require the polluter to restrict at source the emission and discharge of environmental pollutants; *product* standards, which fix the pollution norms for new manufactured products such as cars; and *ambient* standards to set maximum pollutants loads in the air, and to guide regulators on the environmental quality that ought to be maintained for healthy living.

Schedule I lays down industry-specific standards for effluent discharge and emissions in respect of 89 designated industries. Every industrial unit must comply with the norms within one year of their publication[88] or such shorter period that may be ordered by the pollution control board.[89] In respect of any specific industry the Central Government may extend the lead time for compliance beyond one year.[90] In cases where the standards were prescribed prior to 16 January 1991 the industry was required to achieve compliance by the year end.[91]

In cases where the polluter is not covered by Schedule I, the unit must comply with the general standards for discharge of environmental pollutants prescribed in Schedule VI.[92] The general standards are also referred to as the 'minimum national standards' since they represent the parameters which every industry, at the very least, must meet until specific standards under Schedule I are notified. The pollution

[88] Rule 3(3).
[89] Rule 3(4).
[90] *Id.*
[91] Rule 3(5).
[92] Rule 3(3A).

control boards are empowered to specify stricter standards than those published in respect of any industry, operation or process, where necessary.[93]

Regarding product standards, new motor vehicles must meet emission[94] and noise limits.[95] Consumer durables such as air conditioners, refrigerators and air coolers and some types of construction equipment manufactured after 31 December 1993 are required to meet prescribed noise levels.[96]

In addition to the source and product norms, Schedules III and VII prescribe national ambient air quality standards in respect of noise and other air pollutants. The levels of ambient air quality have been fixed after providing an adequate margin of safety to protect public health, vegetation and property.

Supplementing the EPR are the Noise Pollution (Regulation and Control) Rules which were enforced on 14 February 2000. These Rules prescribe ambient air quality standards in respect of noise for industrial, commercial and residential areas as well as designated 'silence zones'. The Rules impose restrictions on the use of loud speakers and public address systems and cast a duty on district magistrates and police commissioners to ensure that noise levels do not exceed the norms.

Hazardous Substance Regulation

The Hazardous Wastes (Management and Handling) Rules, issued under the Act in July, 1989 have introduced a permit system to regulate the handling and disposal of hazardous wastes. These Rules fix responsibility for the proper handling, storage and disposal of such wastes on the person generating the wastes.

The Manufacture, Storage and Import of Hazardous Chemicals Rules of November, 1989 spell out the responsibilities of those handling hazardous substances (other than hazardous wastes). Under these Rules, a hazardous industry is required to identify major accident hazards, take adequate preventive measures and submit a safety report to the designated authority. An importer of hazardous chemicals must furnish complete product safety information to the competent authority and must transport the imported chemicals in accordance with the Central Motor Vehicle Rules of 1989.

In August, 1996 the Central Government framed the Chemical Accidents (Emergency, Planning, Preparedness and Response) Rules. These Rules require the Centre to constitute a Central Crisis Group (CCG)[97] for the management of chemical accidents and to set up a quick response mechanism termed as the Crisis Alert System.[98] The CCG is the apex body for dealing with major chemical accidents and providing expert guidance to contain the damage caused by such accidents.

---

[93] Rule 3(2), (3A).
[94] Schedule IV.
[95] Schedule VI.
[96] *Id.*
[97] Rule 3.
[98] Rule 4.

The Rules also contemplate the setting up of crisis groups at the state, district or local levels to assist the administration in prevention and control measures.

Rules to regulate the manufacture, use, import, export and storage of hazardous micro-organisms and genetically engineered cells were issued under the Environment Act in December, 1989. Under these Rules a Genetic Engineering Approval Committee has been establised in the Ministry of Environment and Forests to licence experiments in, and field trials of, genetically engineered organisms.

In July 1998, the Central Government issued the Bio-Medical Waste (Management and Handling) Rules, to regulate hospitals, clinics, veterinary institutions and other persons generating bio-medical wastes. The Rules introduce a licensing and reporting system requiring institutions to segregate, and dispose of designated categories of bio-medical waste in the prescribed manner.

Environment Impact Assessment

The first attempt at a comprehensive statutory environment impact assessment (EIA) programme began on 27 January 1994 when the Union Ministry of Environment and Forests issued a notification dealing with mandatory EIA. The notification mandates a public hearing and requires the project proponent to submit an EIA report, an environment management plan, details of the public hearing and a project report to the impact assessment agency for clearance, with further review by a committee of experts in certain cases. The impact assessment agency is the ministry itself. The EIA Regulations apply to 29 designated projects/industries which are enumerated in Schedule I to the notification.

In April 1997, the ministry took a first step towards de-centralizing the EIA regulatory machinery by shifting the responsibility for environmental site clearance in respect of thermal power projects to the states. This notification describes the categories of thermal power plants falling within state government purview[99] and largely replicates the procedure under the principal notification of 1991.[100]

Coastal Regulations and Protection
of Specified Areas

In addition to the EIA requirements, specific prohibitions and regulations operate in designated ecologically sensitive areas. The widest in reach and scope are the Coastal Zone Regulations issued in February, 1991. These regulations strictly control development activity including tourism within a strip of 500 meters from the sea shore, along the entire coast of India. While some activities such as setting up of new industry and the expansion of existing factories are completely prohibited, other types of commercial activity are restricted. Building activity is regulated depending upon the level of urbanization and the ecological sensitivity of the coastal region.

[99] Schedule I.
[100] Schedule II.

In response to specific environmental threats, industrial activity has also been curbed by central notifications in some ecologically sensitive regions like the horticultural belt in the Dahanu region in Maharashtra,[101] the Himalayan foothills around Doon valley,[102] the coastal Murud-Janjira area in the Raigad district of Maharashtra,[103] the congested Antop Hill locality in Bombay[104] and parts of the Aravalli Range in Rajasthan and Haryana.[105] Most of these notifications were issued in response to specific environmental threats to each region.

The Ecomark Scheme

In 1991, the Department of Environment, Forests and Wildlife announced a scheme for labelling environment friendly products. The objects of the scheme are to encourage manufacturers to introduce environment friendly products, reward genuine initiatives to reduce adverse environmental impacts and assist consumers in making an informed, responsible choice while purchasing goods. The label known as 'Ecomark' may be used by the manufacturers of the consumer goods who meet the environment criteria notified by the Central Government for the purpose of the scheme. Though qualification criteria have long been published for a number of goods such as soaps, detergents, paper and paints the scheme has yet to gain acceptance. Not a single product carries the Ecomark.

In a more recent initiative to alter consumption patterns, the Centre framed the Recycled Plastic Manufacture and Usage Rules of 1999. The Rules prohibit vendors of foodstuffs from packing their wares in bags or containers made from recycled plastics. If foodstuffs are to be sold in plastic bags, the carry bag must be made of virgin plastic. Moreover, the Rules provide that all carry bags must have a minimum thickness of 20 microns. The Rules adopt a novel enforcement strategy by requiring the Plastics Industry Association to implement self-regulatory measures.

NOTES AND QUESTIONS

1. Many of the regulations notified under the EPA are characterized by shoddy drafting. Consider the restraint imposed under regulation 6(2) of the 1991 Coastal Regulations:

[101] Notification dated 20 June 1991. The orchards of Dahanu were threatened by the possibility of rapid industrialization after a large thermal power plant came up in the area.
[102] Notification dated 1 February 1989. Doon valley was harmed by extensive limestone quarrying.
[103] Notification dated 6 January 1989. A coastal strip of about 30 km. was threatened by several giant industrial projects. This notification encouraged environmentalists to press for national coastal norms which took final shape in February, 1991.
[104] Notification dated 9 February 1990. The residents of Antop Hill lived under a continuous threat from vast quantities of hazardous chemicals stored in the neighbourhood.
[105] Notification dated 7 May 1992. Limestone quarrying threatened the Project Tiger reserve in the Alwar district of Rajasthan.

Buildings shall be permitted neither on the seaward side of the existing road ... nor on seaward side of existing authorised structures.

Numerous key expressions in the EPR ('land for irrigation' standards, 'inland surface water' standards), the Coastal Regulations ('reconstruction', 'authorized structure') and other rules are not defined, adding to the uncertainty.

Printing errors in the official gazette abound. For example, the EPR had two schedules that were numbered 'II'; Schedule VI to these Rules incorrectly refers to rule 3A instead of *sub-rule 3(3A)*; and there are misprints in Schedule VI to the EIA Regulations for thermal power stations as well. Inexplicably, the EPR prescribes noise standards for automobiles, domestic appliances and construction equipment at *two* places: items 46 and 47 at Schedule I and Part E of Schedule VI.

2. The slipshod drafting may, at times, have a serious regulatory impact and confuse administrators. For example, a reading of rule 3 of the EPR suggests that the provisions in Schedule VI *do not* apply in cases where industry-specific standards are set out in Schedule I. Rule 3(3A) appears to restrict the application of Schedule VI to 'industrial operations or processes *other than* those industries, operations or processes for which standards have been specified in Schedule I.' However, a reading of Schedule VI suggests otherwise. Industry-specific waste water generation standards mentioned in Part B of Schedule VI relate to several industries that are covered by Schedule I such as caustic soda, tanneries, integrated iron and steel plants and sugar units. Likewise, the industry-specific load based standards for waste water set out in Part C of Schedule VI cover industries such as oil refineries which are already covered by Schedule I. Though it is difficult to reconcile the language of rule 3(3A) to the contents of Schedule VI, it appears that only Parts A and D of Schedule VI, containing general effluent and emission standards, do not apply where the industry is covered by Schedule I. Parts B, C and E of Schedule VI as well as the annexures to Schedule VI seem to apply to *all* polluting industries whether or not covered by Schedule I of the EPR.

3. The statutory annexures to Schedule VI lay down important guidelines for the state pollution control boards. While enforcing the standards, the boards should ensure use of the *best available technology*; *recycling* of waste water and *reuse* of other materials; and the implementation of clean technologies by industry in order to increase *fuel efficiency*. While permitting discharge of effluents and emissions the assimilative capacity of the receiving bodies should also be kept in view so that the intended use of the receiving water body is not affected.

4. Section 7 of the EPA prohibits a person carrying on any industry, operation or process from discharging or emitting pollutants in excess of the prescribed standards. Although there is no express provision in the Act requiring the pollution control boards to enforce these standards, this scheme is implicit in the EPR. Sections 17(g) of the Water Act and Air Act empower the state boards to lay down standards for effluent discharge and emission and many state boards have notified norms under these two Acts. At times the pollution control board norms vary from

the EPA standards. Which standards apply—those issued under the EPA or the standards published by the state boards? Assuming the EPA standards prevail, should not Parliament repeal sections 17(g) and should not the boards reduce the confusion by annulling their own standards? At least one leading pollution case affecting several hundred units was decided by the Gujarat High Court without regard to the EPA standards and on the basis of the state board norms.[106]

5. Sub-rules 5(2) and (3) of the EPR contain a salutary safeguard requiring the Central Government to follow a pre-publication procedure before imposing any restrictions on industrial activity. The department must invite objections from members of the public to the proposed regulations, consider the objections and then publish the final regulations. This practice introduces transparency and citizen participation in the law making process. The EIA Regulations, the Coastal Regulations and the notifications issued to protect specified areas, were all framed after following the pre-publication procedure. On 16 March 1994 new sub-rule 5(4) was introduced, permitting the Centre to dispense with the pre-publication requirement in the 'public interest'. Since then, this clause has provided the department with a convenient handle to dispense with the pre-publication and comment procedure.

On 4 May 1994 a few weeks after sub-rule 5(4) was inserted, the department diluted the EIA Regulations by changing the mandatory public hearing requirement into a discretionary procedure and permitting preparatory activities such as the felling of trees and land acquisition to proceed even before site clearance was obtained. Was the department justified in hurrying through the amendment without following the pre-publication procedure? The amending notification makes a general reference to 'public interest' but gives no specific reason. Was the government trying to avoid public outcry against the dilution? Should the government take recourse to the 'public interest' clause to weaken environmental regulations? The department now routinely dispenses with the pre-publication procedure.[107]

III. SECTIONS 3 AND 5 OF THE EPA

Section 3(1) confers very wide powers on the Central Government 'to take all such measures as it deems necessary or expedient for the purpose of protecting and improving the quality of the environment and preventing, controlling and abating environmental pollution.' Sub-section (2) illustrates the types of measures that the Centre may adopt under sub-section (1). Amongst those is the power to restrict areas in which industries may be set up, which enabled the Coastal Regulations, the EIA Regulations and the notifications to protect special areas like the Doon valley and Dahanu. Commenting on the genesis of the Coastal Regulations in the *CRZ*

---

[106] *Pravinbhai J. Patel v State of Gujarat* 1995 (2) GUJ.L.R. 1210.

[107] e.g., notification dated 31 January 1997 amending the Coastal Regulations and notification dated 10 April 1997 amending the EIA Regulations.

Notification Case,[108] the Supreme Court observed that the principal notification of 1991 was issued under section 3(1) and 3(2)(v) of the EPA 'presumably after a lot of study [was] undertaken by the government. Normally, such notifications are issued after a detailed study and examination of all relevant issues.'

Section 3(3) permits the Central Government to constitute one or more authorities to implement the Act. Under section 5 of the Act, such an authority may issue binding directions in writing to any person, officer or authority. Section 5 clarifies that the power to issue directions includes the power to close, prohibit or regulate any industry, operation or process as well as the power to stop supply of energy, water or other service.

In the *Bichhri Case,*[109] chemical industries in an industrial complex in Bichhri, Rajasthan devastated the environment by discharging untreated toxic chemicals and sludge. All the regulatory agencies including the Central Government failed to perform their tasks. While considering whether a court in its writ jurisdiction was empowered to direct remedial measures and recover the clean up costs from the polluter, the Supreme Court examined the scope of sections 3 and 5 of the EPA:

> Section 5 clothes the Central Government (or its delegates) with the power to issue directions for achieving the objects of the Act. Read with the wide definition of 'environment' in Section 2(a), Sections 3 and 5 clothe the Central Government with all such powers as are 'necessary or expedient for the purpose of protecting and improving the quality of the environment'. The Central Government is empowered to take all measures and issue all such directions as are called for the above purpose. In the present case, the said powers will include giving directions for the removal of sludge, for undertaking remedial measures and also the power to impose the cost of remedial measures on the offending industry and utilise the amount so recovered for carrying out remedial measures. This Court can certainly give directions to the Central Government/its delegates to take all such measures, if in a given case this Court finds that such directions are warranted.[110]

Environmentalists, non-governmental organizations and academics have long commended the idea of an autonomous agency along the lines of the US Environment Protection Agency, to oversee the enforcement of the EPA. Although the Central Government may create a specialist agency under section 3(3), thus far, the Centre has chosen to leave implementation of the EPA to the Union Ministry of Environment and Forests. The executive's reluctance, however, hasn't deterred the Supreme Court from directing the Centre to set up an authority under section 3(3) of the EPA when the court considered it necessary.

[108] *Indian Council for Enviro–Legal Action v Union of India* 1996 (5) SCC 281, 296.
[109] *Indian Council for Enviro–Legal Action v Union of India* AIR 1996 SC 1446.
[110] *Id.* at 1464.

In *Vellore Citizens' Welfare Forum v Union of India*,[111] the court was dealing with the extensive damage caused by untreated effluent discharged by tanneries in Tamil Nadu. Turning to section 3(3) of the EPA, the court observed:

> The main purpose of the Act is to create an authority or authorities under section 3(3) of the Act with adequate powers to control pollution and protect the environment. It is a pity that till date no authority has been constituted by the Central Government. The work which is required to be done by the authority in terms of section 3(3) read with other provisions of the Act is being done by this court and other courts in the country. It is high time that the Central Government realises its responsibility and statutory duty to protect the degrading environment in the country.[112]

The Supreme Court directed the Centre to constitute an authority under section 3(3) with all necessary powers to deal with the situation created by the tanneries and other polluting industries in the state. A retired High Court judge was placed at the head of the new authority, which was to have persons with expertise in pollution control and environment protection as members. The authority was requested to identify the persons who had suffered because of the pollution, name the polluters liable to compensate the victims, assess the compensation to be paid and the costs of the remedial measures. The authority was asked to periodically review compliance by the tanneries and to direct relocation of any industry where necessary.

In the *Bayer Case*[113] the Supreme Court acknowledged its lack of expertise to resolve the complex issues arising from a demand to relocate hazardous industries away from urban areas. Bayer had petitioned the Bombay High Court to restrain the city of Thane from allowing residential buildings to come up within a kilometre of its factory. Bayer asked for the safety zone since it used hazardous chemicals at its plant and was anxious to minimize the impact of an industrial accident. The High Court accepted the company's plea and restrained development.[114] Against this judgment, some of the affected builders appealed to the Supreme Court, where the case took a dramatic turn. One of the arguments that seemed to find favour with the apex court was that Bayer shift out, not the proposed buildings. After several hearings, the court directed the Union Government to constitute a special authority under section 3(3) of the EPA to resolve the relocation issues raised in the case.

In the *CRZ Notification Case*[115] the Supreme Court noted the poor enforcement of environmental laws and recognized the administrative burden on the pollution control boards which prevented them from effectively implementing the Coastal Regulations. The court requested the Union Government to consider setting up State Coastal

[111] AIR 1996 SC 2715.
[112] *Id.* at 2724.
[113] *F.B. Taraporawala v Bayer India Ltd.* AIR 1997 SC 1846.
[114] *Bayer (India) Ltd. v State of Maharashtra* 1994 (4) BOM.C.REP.309.
[115] *Indian Council for Enviro–Legal Action v Union of India* 1996 (5) SCC 281.

Management Authorities in each state or zone and also a National Coastal Management Authority under section 3(3) of the EPA to assume the responsibility of enforcing these Regulations. The coastal authorities were established in November, 1998.

The ambit of section 5 of the EPA was explained by the Gujarat High Court in two cases concerning pollution of the Kharicut canal. *Pravinbhai J. Patel v State of Gujarat*,[116] was a mammoth public interest litigation spanning several months and covering more than one thousand industrial units in Ahmedabad. After a prolonged hearing and several interim orders, a division bench of the court issued a range of final directions requiring the closure of polluting units, setting deadlines for compliance and levying a compensatory charge on polluters for the benefit of the affected villagers. The court acknowledged that normally it was for the state government (as a delegate of the Centre) to issue appropriate closure directions under section 5 and that it was no part of a court's duty to do so. 'Where, however, there is a complete abdication of authority by the government and the court comes to the conclusion, like in the present case, that the government has failed to discharge its statutory duty, and which failure has resulted in the violation of the fundamental rights of the petitioners and lacs of other people guaranteed under Article 21 of the Constitution, then the court is left with no option but to issue appropriate direction to the government to pass the necessary orders under section 5 of the Environment Act.'[117] The court observed that under the EPA the government was the custodian of a clean environment and that its power under section 5 was coupled with a duty to exercise the power whenever the need arose.[118]

We carry an excerpt from an earlier case, where Justice Abhichandani of the Gujarat High Court placed environmental values above the rules of natural justice. Do you agree with his approach?

NARULA DYEING & PRINTING WORKS v UNION OF INDIA
AIR 1995 GUJ 185

In this group of matters, the petitioners—industrial units, have challenged the action of the State Government taken under S.5 of the Environmental (Protection) Act, 1986 (hereinafter referred to as 'the said Act'), giving directions to them to stop production activities and take necessary steps to units to conform to the standard specified by the Gujarat Pollution Control Board and not to restart the production activities without the permission of State Government and Forest and Environment Department. The directions were issued by the Forest and Environment Department of the Government to these three industrial units under the impugned orders dt. 19th October, 1994.

The petitioners in Special Civil Application No.12136/94 is a partnership firm carrying on business in textile processing and having its units in the G.I.D.C. Estate

---

[116] 1995 (2) GUJ.L.R. 1210.
[117] *Id.* at 1253.
[118] *Id.* at 1235.

zone at Handa, Ahmedabad. The said petitioner had applied for consent of the Gujarat Pollution Control Board (hereinafter referred to as the State Board) under S.25(2) of the Water (Prevention and Control of Pollution) Act, 1974 (hereinafter referred to as 'the Water Act'). A consent letter was issued in its favour on 26th Nov. 1981 by the State Board as per Annexure 'B' to the petition. According to this petitioner, it had constructed 'water treatment plant' which was functional. It is contended that, however, the drainage provided by the G.I.D.C. was not of sufficient capacity and due to overflow, the water discharged by other factories entered the premises of the factory of this petitioner. This petitioner had filed a suit being Civil Suit No.5391/93 in the City Civil Court at Ahmedabad on receiving a notice from the G.I.D.C. that action would be taken for disconnecting the water supply. The said suit is pending. According to the petitioner, samples were taken by the State Board for analysis of the effluent and a report dt.13th Oct. 1993 of the State Board showed PH factor at 6.06 which was within the tolerance limits. It is contended that no notice was issued to the petitioner before making the impugned order dt. 19th Oct. 1994. It is also contended that the action was taken on the basis of letter dt. 10th Oct, 1994 of the State Board, a copy of which was not supplied to the petitioner.

* * *

In all these cases, directions have been issued under S.5 of the Act in view of the fact that the discharge of trade effluents and polluted waste water entered the Kharicut Canal and polluted the underground strata resulting in damage to the crops and to the fertile lands in Kheda District. It is recorded in the impugned orders that the State Government had received many complaints regarding damage to the crop and the land due to such discharge of effluent. In case of all these petitioners, it was stated in the orders issued on them that they were not operating any effluent treatment plant and were discharging their effluents without treatment.

It was contended by the learned counsel appearing for the petitioners in these three matters that the impugned action of giving directions under S.5 of the Act has been taken without giving any opportunity of being heard to these petitioners. It was contended that the State Government could not have dispensed with the hearing before issuing the impugned order. It was also contended that the PH factor was within the tolerance limit.

On behalf of the State Government and other respondents, it was contended that these units were not having an operative effluent treatment plant and that they had not abided by the terms of the consent letters given by the State Board under S.25 (2) of the Water Act. The petitioners had not fulfilled the conditions of the consent letters. In the affidavits-in-reply filed on behalf of the respondents, it is stated that these petitioners were discharging polluted waste water without treatment and this resulted in an extensive damage to the crops and fertile lands in Hatar Taluka of Kheda District. Taking into account the extensive damage which was resulting due to the discharge of untreated effluents by these petitioners and other similar indus-trial units, closure orders were issued under S.5 of the said Act against as many as thirteen units which admittedly were discharging untreated effluents in the Kharicut Canal. It has been stated that having taken into consideration the various aspects of the matter and after satisfying itself about the urgency, the impugned action was taken by the authority by dispensing with the issuance of notice of hearing as provided under R.4(5) of the Rules framed under the said Act. After considering several representations received by the Department as well as by the Hon'ble the Chief Minister from agriculturists, framers and other citizens, the impugned action was taken against these industrial units.

In case of the petitioner in Special Civil Application No.12136/94, it has been stated that though consent was granted by the State Board with condition to provide effluent treatment plant within six months, it was found that the industry was discharging effluent not conforming to the standards and, therefore, three complaints were filed under the provisions of the Water Act on 4–1–1988, 19–1–1988 and 10–11–1989. It is also stated that inspection of the said industry was also carried on, on 27–5–1990, 23–5–1991, 14–5–1992 and 19–7–1993 and it was found that the industry was not operating effluent treatment plant and was discharging effluents not conforming to the standards. Based on the inspection reports on 3–9–1993 the Board requested G.I.D.C. to disconnect the water supply of this industry. Again on 22–1–1993 and 18–1–1994 this industry was required to upgrade effluent treatment plant and to submit a time bound programme in respect thereof. On 29–7–1994, the state board carried out inspection of this industry and found that the effluent treatment plant was not being operated.

* * *

In Special Civil Application No.12136/94, the analysis report dt. 31st July, 1993 showed excess of total suspended solids which was 295 as against the prescribed 100. It also showed excess over tolerance limits in case of Bio-chemical Oxygen demand which was 206 as against the prescribed 150 in the schedule item and 30 in the consent letter of the Board, the Chemical Oxygen demand was 520 which was in excess of the tolerance limit of 250 prescribed in the consent order of the Board. Similarly, the analysis report dt. 13th October, 1993 showed suspended solids at 526 as against 100, dissolved solids at 3823 against the tolerance limit of 2500 and the bio-chemical oxygen demand 1622 as against 30 prescribed in the consent order. The analysis report dt. 29th July, 1994 also showed excess of suspended solids which was 204 and excess of biochemical oxygen demand which was 196. The chemical oxygen demand was 5.15 as against the prescribed tolerance limit of 250 in the consent letter of the State Board.

* * *

The requirement of giving opportunity to file objections against the proposed directions which can be issued under S.5 of the Act can be dispensed with only when the Central Government is of the opinion that in view of the likelihood of a grave injury to the environment, it is not expedient to provide such opportunity. As noted above, the powers of the Central Government have been delegated to the State by Notification dt. 10–2–1988. The State Government in its deliberation on 3rd and 4th Oct., 1994 took into account the gravity of the situation and it was decided to issue directions as are contained in the impugned orders dt. 19th Oct., 1994 directing closure of these units. It was decided to take action without giving any show cause notice under R.4(5) of the said Rules, in view of the grave and serious pollution caused to the irrigation canal because of discharge of effluent by thirteen industries which had caused severe damage to the crops and fertile land and environment at large. The material on record clearly shows that the State Government was of the opinion that grave injury was being caused by discharge of such effluent into the irrigation canal resulting in severe damage to crops and fertile lands. The Biochemical oxygen demand tests applied to these petitioners showed that the tolerance limits were exceeded. The Biochemical oxygen demand test is widely used to determine the pollutional strength of domestic and industrial wastes in terms of oxygen that they will require if discharged into natural water courses in which aerobic conditions exist. The test is one of the most important in stream-pollution-control activities. Similarly, chemical oxygen demand test is widely used for measuring pollutional strength of domestic and industrial wastes. This test allows measurement of waste in terms of the total quantity of oxygen required for oxidation to carbon-dioxide and water. The trade effluents which contained various characteristics in excess of tolerance limits would undoubtedly ruin the fertility on the soil on which they come to be released. The release of such trade effluents in Kharicut canal which is meant for irrigation of lands obviously would result in damage to the crops and the fields to which the polluted water was being carried. When applied to a plant—soil system, oils and grease constituent of industrial wastes can affect seed germination of crop growth and yield. ... There were several complaints received by the Hon'ble the Chief Minister and the concerned Department regarding the pollution caused due to release of untreated effluents in river Khari. This naturally called for immediate action, and the record shows that urgent action was overdue. Therefore, if the State Government became suddenly aware of its duties and took action for preventing further damage to the crops and the agricultural lands, it cannot be said that there was justification for such action because it was not taken earlier. The gravity of the situation was in the extent of damage which was resulting due to discharge of such effluents. The Government was fully empowered to dispense with the opportunity being given for filing objections against the proposed directions in such cases of grave injury to the environment. The provisions of R.4(5) are intended to safeguard the environment from any grave injury to it and in the present case it has been amply borne out that the release of the effluents by the petitioners units was resulting in pollution of the irrigation canal causing vast damage to the crops and the agricultural fields. This fact has been recorded in writing in the impugned orders dt. 19th October, 1994. The petitioners did not operate effluent treatment plant and could not be allowed to release untreated effluents resulting in damage to the fertile lands of Kheda District. The State Government was, therefore, fully justified in proceeding under R.4(5) of the said Rule while exercising its delegated powers for issuing directions under S.5 of the Act as in the impugned orders. These petitions are therefore without any substance and are rejected.

* * *

NOTES AND QUESTIONS

1. Since 1988, the Gujarat pollution control board (GPCB) knew that Narula Dyeing was flouting effluent norms, but took no action. Was this due to the board's declared preference for 'persuasion' over coercive action?[119] Who was more persuasive—Narula or the GPCB? Why?

2. Having allowed Narula Dyeing to operate for all these years in breach of the norms, was the state justified in bypassing the prior notice procedure?

3. Justice Abhichandani's judgment in *Narula Dyeing* was affirmed by a Division Bench of the Gujarat High Court in *Pravinbhai J. Patel v State of Gujarat.*[120]

4. In *Narula Dyeing*, the industries argued that the power under section 5 of the EPA could be exercised by the Central Government alone and not the state. Even otherwise, the impugned directions suffered from the vice of excessive delegation since there were no guidelines to control administrative discretion. The High Court rejected these grounds since section 23 of the EPA empowered the Centre to delegate its functions and by a notification dated 10 February 1988 the Centre had conferred its power under section 5 on Gujarat.[121] The court also found sufficient guidance for the exercise of power under section 5 in section 3 of the EPA and the nature of functions required to be discharged by the Central Government under the Act.[122]

5. A division bench of the Orissa High Court refused to aid a soap factory which was asked to stop operations until it cleaned up its act and met the prescribed effluent standards. One of the grounds urged by the petitioner was that the section 5 direction was passed without giving a reasonable opportunity to be heard, since no personal hearing was granted. Reviewing the provisions of rule 4 of the Environment (Protection) Rules which lay down the procedure for directions issued under section 5, the High Court found that the requirement for granting an opportunity to be heard did not include a personal hearing and that it was sufficient if an opportunity for filing written objections was granted.[123]

6. Occassionally, a court may find that the government has over-stepped its jurisdiction in ordering closure and may frame a less stringent compliance programme for the defaulting unit.[124]

---

[119] Gujarat Pollution Control Board, *Guidelines on Environmental Pollution Control* 1.6 (1988).

[120] 1995 (2) GUJ.L.R.1210, 1244.

[121] The Central Government delegated its power under section 5 to all the state governments (except Arunachal Pradesh and Nagaland) under six notifications issued between 1988 and 1991. The notification in respect of Arunachal Pradesh and Nagaland was issued on 15 July 1998.

[122] In *Indian Council for Enviro–Legal Action v Union of India (CRZ Notification Case)* 1996 (5) SCC 281, 302, the Supreme Court held that directions under section 5 'have necessarily to be in accordance with the provisions of law and to give protection to environment.'

[123] *Mahabir Soap and Gudakhu Factory v Union of India* AIR 1995 ORI 218, 223.

[124] *Rajiv Singh v State of Bihar* AIR 1992 PAT 86.

IV. Violations and Penalties Under the Act

The EPA was the first environmental statute to give the Central Government authority to issue direct written orders, including orders to close, prohibit, or regulate any industry, operation or process or to stop or regulate the supply of electricity, water or any other service.[125] Other powers granted to the Central Government to ensure compliance with the Act include the power of entry for examination, testing of equipment and other purposes[126] and the power to take samples of air, water, soil or any other substance from any place for analysis.[127]

The Act explicitly prohibits discharges of environmental pollutants in excess of prescribed regulatory standards.[128] There is also a specific prohibition against handling hazardous substances except in compliance with regulatory procedures and standards.[129] Persons responsible for discharges of pollutants in excess of prescribed standards must prevent or mitigate the pollution and must report the discharge to governmental authorities.[130]

The Act provides for fairly severe penalties. Any person who fails to comply with or contravenes any of the provisions of the Act, or the rules, orders, or directions issued under the Act shall be punished, for each failure or contravention, with a prison term of up to five years or a fine of up to Rs. 100,000 or both. The Act imposes an additional fine of up to Rs. 5,000 for every day of continuing violation.[131] If a failure or contravention occurs for more than one year after the date of conviction an offender may be punished with a prison term which may extend to seven years.[132]

Corporate officials directly in charge of a company's business are liable for offences under the Act, unless the official can establish that the offence was committed without his or her knowledge or that he or she exercised all due diligence to prevent the commission of the offence.[133] In addition, if an offence is committed with the consent or connivance of, or is attributable to any neglect on the part of any director, manager, secretary or other officer, that person shall also be liable for the offence.[134] Similar provisions extend liability to the heads of departments of government and other department officers.[135]

Section 24 provides that if any act or omission constitutes an offence punishable under the EPA as well as any other law, the offender shall be liable to be punished under the *other* law and not under the EPA.

---

[125] Section 5. Later, similar provisions were introduced in the Air Act and the Water Act.
[126] Section 10.
[127] Section 11.
[128] Section 7.
[129] Section 8.
[130] Section 9(1).
[131] Section 15(1).
[132] Section 15(2).
[133] Section 16(1).
[134] Section 16(2).
[135] Section 17.

NOTES AND QUESTIONS

1. Section 24 of the Act is a curious and controversial provision. Generally, more recent legislation which conflicts with previous legislation supersedes the previous legislation. Standards established under the Environment (Protection) Act are also the subject of other statutes, such as the Water Act and Air Act. Until the amendment of the Air Act in 1987 and the Water Act in 1988, both these laws prescribed less stringent penalties than did the EPA. This situation led one commentator to describe the Environment (Protection) Act as a cobra that is seemingly fierce but has no venom in its fangs.[136]

2. Consider another serious problem with section 24. Suppose the Water Act allows discharge of a higher concentration of a particular pollutant than the concentration permissible under the EPA. If a factory discharges waste water containing the pollutant at a level higher than allowed under the EPA but within the allowable limits of the Water Act, does the Water Act penalty provision apply? Are there other problems with having two statutes—with different standards and penalty provisions—regulating release of the same pollutants?

3. Will this legislative scheme lead to more, or less, effective enforcement of environmental laws? One of the basic purposes of law is to promote uniformity and predictability in the application of rules and regulations. Does a scheme of deferring to earlier overlapping statutes promote this purpose?

4. Section 5 gives the Centre broad powers to enforce the Act, including the power to order the closure of any industry. Do workers whose employers are ordered by the government to close or curtail operations have a constitutional right to be heard by a court concerning the government's action? Should the government weigh the costs to these workers in lost jobs against the benefits to society before ordering closure of a polluting operation?

V. ENFORCEMENT OF THE ACT

One of the recurring themes in the Supreme Court judgments of the 1990s is the poor implementation of environmental laws. In the *CRZ Notification Case*, excerpted below, the court said that tolerating the infringement of an enacted law was worse than not enacting it at all. In this case, the petitioners challenged the 1994 amendment to the main notification of February 1991, introducing national Coastal Regulations. The petitioners argued that the amendments were invalid since they relaxed the provisions of the parent notification and would lead to ecological degradation. Allowing the petition, the court struck down the amendments which were likely to cause environmental harm. We excerpt portions of this judgment where the court surveyed environmental law enforcement.

---

[136] D'Monte, *Environment Law Has No Teeth*, 1 Encology No. 4, 24–25 (Sept. 1986).

INDIAN COUNCIL FOR ENVIRO-LEGAL ACTION v UNION OF INDIA
1996 (5) SCC 281

ORDER: * * *

If the mere enactment of the laws relating to the protection of environment was to ensure a clean and pollution free environment, then India would, perhaps, be the least polluted country in the world. But, this is not so. There are stated to be over 200 Central and state statutes which have at least some concern with environment protection, either directly or indirectly. The plethora of such enactments has, unfortunately, not resulted in preventing environmental degradation which on the contrary, has increased over the years.

                              * * *

It is with a view to protect and preserve the environment and save it for the future generations and to ensure good quality of life that the Parliament enacted the anti-pollution laws, namely, the Water Act, Air Act and the Environment (Protection) Act, 1986. These Acts and Rules framed and Notification issued thereunder contain provisions which prohibit and/or regulate certain activities with a view to protect and preserve the environment. When a law is enacted containing some provisions which prohibits certain types of activities, then, it is of utmost importance that such legal provisions are effectively enforced. If a law is enacted but is not being voluntarily obeyed, then it has to be enforced. Otherwise, infringement of law, which is actively or passively condoned for personal gain, will be encouraged which will in turn lead to a lawless society. Violation of anti-pollution laws not only adversely affects the existing quality of life but the non-enforcement of the legal provisions often results in ecological imbalance and degradation of environment, the adverse affect of which will have to be borne by the future generations.

The present case also shows that having issued the main Notification, no follow-up action was taken either by the coastal States and Union Territories or by the Central Government. The provisions of the main Notification appear to have been ignored and, possibly, violated with impunity. The coastal States and Union Territory Administrations were required to prepare Management Plans within a period of one year from the date of the Notification but this was not done. The Central Government was to approve the plans which were to be prepared but it did not appear to have reminded any of the coastal States or the Union Territory Administrations that the plans had not been received by it. Clause 4 of the main Notification required the Central Government and the State Governments as well as Union Territory Administrations to monitor and enforce the provisions of the main Notification, but no effective steps appear to have been taken and this is what led to the filing of the present Writ Petition.

There is no challenge to the validity of main Notification. Counsel for all the parties are agreed that the main Notification is valid and has to be enforced. Instances have been given by the petitioner as well as some of the intervenors where in different States, infringement of the main Notification is taking place but no action has been taken by the authorities concerned. The courts are ill-equipped and it is not their function to see day to day enforcement of law. This is an executive function which it is bound to discharge. A public interest litigation like the present, would not have been necessary if the authorities, as well as the people concerned, had voluntarily obeyed and/or complied with the main Notification or if the authorities who were entrusted with the responsibility, had enforced the main Notification. It is only the failure of enforcement of this Notification which has led to the filing of the present petition. The effort of this court while dealing with public interest litigation relating to environmental issues, is to see that the executive authorities take steps for implementation and enforcement of law. As such the court has to pass orders and give directions for the protection of the fundamental rights of the people. Passing of appropriate orders requiring the implementation of the law cannot be regarded as the Court having usurped the functions of the Legislature or the Executive. The orders are passed and directions are issued by the Court in discharge of its judicial functions, namely, to see that if there is a complaint by a petitioner regarding the infringement of any Constitutional or other legal right, as a result of any wrong action or inaction on the part of the State, then such wrong should not be permitted to continue.

NOTES AND QUESTIONS

1. Generally, most enforcement agencies have failed to discharge their obligations under environmental laws. What are the reasons for poor implementation?

2. Are the courts capable of transforming the enforcement culture? Does judicial intervention through public interest litigations strengthen the enforcement machinery or is it likely to further enfeeble administrators who may await court orders before taking action?

3. The EPA contains significant innovations for its enforcement, not contained in any other pollution abatement legislation at the time of the Act's adoption. For example, section 19 provides that *any person,* in addition to authorized government officials, may file a complaint with a court alleging an offence under the Act. This citizens' initiative provision requires that the person give notice of not less than 60 days of the alleged offence and the intent to file a complaint with the government official authorized to make such complaints.

The citizens' initiative provision appears to give the public significant powers to enforce the EPA. One commentator, however, has characterized the provision as an 'eye wash'. He notes that only government officials are given the power under the Act to collect samples needed as evidence of a violation of the Act. In addition, during the sixty days' notice period required for the government to decide whether to proceed against the alleged violator, the offending industry has time to clean up traces of the offence and prepare itself for the collection of samples.[137] What if the

---

[137] Agarwal, *Significance & Perspective Impact of India's Environment (Protection) Act, 1986,* 1 Encology No. 7, 28–29 (1986).

government decides to file a complaint against the alleged polluter but then does not diligently pursue prosecution? Should a citizen be allowed to file a separate action or intervene in the ongoing prosecution?

As a matter of practice, the citizens' initiative provision is seldom used. There are no significant reported decisions in cases arising from a citizen's complaint under section 19 of the EPA. Most environmental groups and concerned citizens prefer to obtain redress through the public interest litigation channel developed by the High Courts and the Supreme Court under their constitutional jurisdiction.

4. The Act allows, but does not require, the Central Government to obtain reports, returns, statistics, accounts, and other information in relation to its functions under the Act from any person, officer, state government or other authority. [138] Rule 14 of the Environment (Protection) Rules requires every polluter to file an annual environment statement containing the prescribed particulars. Could the citizens' initiative provision become an effective enforcement tool if industries were required to make mandatory public reports concerning their pollutant discharges? Severe penalties could be imposed for false reporting and the government could undertake random sampling to ensure that industries are complying with the reporting requirements. Mandatory reports submitted by industry under the Clean Water Act in the United States have been used by citizens' groups as evidence in suits filed against polluters.

5. In *Rural Litigation & Entitlement Kendra v State of Uttar Pradesh,*[139] the Supreme Court considered whether to order the closure of limestone mining operations that were affecting the water quality and degrading forest land in the Doon Valley. The defendant mining companies argued that because the issue of location of industries was one of the powers given to the Central Government under the EPA, the courts no longer have jurisdiction to consider the issue. The court summarily rejected this argument, noting that the Act does not purport to oust jurisdiction and that indeed the Act perhaps could not constitutionally oust the Supreme Court's jurisdiction.

VI. THE NATIONAL ENVIRONMENT APPELLATE AUTHORITY ACT OF 1997

This Act (NEAA) requires the Union Government to establish a body known as the National Environment Appellate Authority to hear appeals against orders granting environmental clearance in designated areas where industrial activity is proscribed or restricted by regulations framed under the EPA. The Appellate Authority is chaired by a retired judge of the Supreme Court or a Chief Justice of a High Court and has its head office at Delhi.

Restrictions on industrial activity may be imposed by the Centre under section 3(1) and 3(2)(v) of the EPA, and as we have seen this power has been exercised by the Union Government to regulate industrial activity along the coast as well as in

[138] Section 20.
[139] AIR 1988 SC 2187.

ecologically sensitive regions like the Doon valley, Dahanu and Murud-Janjira in Maharashtra and parts of the Aravalli Range. Likewise, the Environment Impact Assessment Regulations of January, 1994 were introduced in exercise of the Centre's power under these provisions.

Section 11 of the NEAA requires an appeal to be filed within 30 days of the impugned order granting conditional or unconditional environmental clearance or where the delay is explained, within 90 days. The appellate jurisdiction is restricted to cases where environmental clearance is granted and does not extend to cases where clearance is refused. The categories of 'aggrieved persons' who are conferred a right of appeal are enumerated in section 11(2). They include a person likely to be affected by the environmental clearance and an association of persons 'likely to be affected by such order and functioning in the field of environment'. The Appellate Authority is required to dispose of the appeal within 90 days of its filing. Section 15 of the NEAA bars a civil court or other authority from entertaining any appeal in matters falling within the jurisdiction of the Appellate Authority.

NOTES AND QUESTIONS

1. Does the phrase 'any association of persons ... likely to be affected by such order and functioning in the field of environment' appearing in section 11(2) entitle *all* non-governmental organizations having a genuine concern for the environment to file an appeal, or is the expression restricted to local organizations alone? Should a court liberally interpret the standing requirement? Or was the intent of Parliament to restrict the standing criteria to local groups?

2. Is the 30 day appeal period fair? Remember, there is no requirement under most of the regulatory notifications which mandate for the environmental clearance orders to be published. How is a citizen to learn about an environmental clearance which is granted? What type of publicity requirement would ensure fairness? How are local citizens to learn about the material and record which were considered by the clearing authority when there is no provision for making such records available to the public?

3. Does section 15 exclude the writ jurisdiction of the High Courts and the Supreme Court conferred under the Constitution?

4. In *A.P. Pollution Control Board v Prof. M.V. Nayudu*,[140] the Supreme Court held that in addition to its statutory jurisdiction, the Appellate Authority also had an advisory role to play in complicated environmental matters that were referred to it by the Supreme Court or the High Courts.

[140] AIR 1999 SC 812.

4

JUDICIAL REMEDIES AND PROCEDURES

Generally, modern environmental law provides for a system of regulation by statute. Administrative agencies created under environmental statutes are required to implement legislative mandates. Frequently, for lack of staff, money or will, these agencies fail to implement the laws under which they operate, and ecological degradation continues unabated. In this event, the citizen has a choice of three civil remedies to obtain redress: (1) a common law tort action against the polluter; (2) a writ petition to compel the agency to enforce the law and to recover clean up or remedial costs from the violator; or (3) in the event of damage from a hazardous industry accident, an application for compensation under the Public Liability Insurance Act of 1991 or the National Environment Tribunal Act of 1995. Among the civil remedies, the writ jurisdiction is the most popular; the action in tort but rarely used; and the statutory remedies, largely untried. Supplementing the redressal machinery is the National Environment Appellate Authority Act of 1997 which creates an appellate forum to test the validity of environmental clearances for industrial projects granted under the EPA.[1] In addition, if the pollution amounts to a 'public nuisance', a remedy under the Criminal Procedure Code of 1973 is also available. Finally, a citizen may make a criminal complaint under section 19 of the EPA or the corresponding provisions under the Water Act and the Air Act to trigger the prosecution of polluters.

In this chapter we examine these judicial remedies. To help contrast private nuisance cases with public nuisance cases, the opening section on torts is followed by the section on public nuisance. Next, we examine the writ procedure, and the citizens' initiative provisions. The second half of this chapter contains three sections on more general topics: Public interest litigations, class actions and freedom of information and the right to know. Taken together, these seven sections comprise the environmental lawyer's procedural armoury.

---

[1] Environment (Protection) Act of 1986.

A. TORT LAW

Actions brought under tort law are among the oldest of the legal remedies to abate pollution. Most pollution cases in tort law fall under the categories of nuisance, negligence and strict liability. To these traditional categories, the Supreme Court has added a new class based on the principle of 'absolute' liability. This norm was developed by the court in the post-Bhopal period in response to the spread of hazardous industries and was later adopted by the legislature.[2]

The rules of tort law were introduced into India under British rule. Initially, disputes arising within the Presidency towns of Calcutta, Madras and Bombay were subjected to common law rules.[3] Later, Indian courts outside the Presidency towns were required by Acts of British Parliament and Indian laws to reconcile disputes according to justice, equity and good conscience where there was no applicable statute.[4] Consequently, in suits for damages for torts (civil wrongs), courts followed the English common law in so far as it was consonant with these principles. By the eighteenth century, Indian courts had evolved a blend of tort law adapted to Indian conditions.[5] Common law based tort rules continue to operate under Article 372 of the Indian Constitution which ensured the continuance of existing laws.

In *Vellore Citizens' Welfare Forum v Union of India*,[6] the Supreme Court traced the source of the constitutional and statutory provisions that protect the environment to the 'inalienable common law right' of every person to a clean environment. Quoting from Blackstone's Commentaries on the English law of nuisance published in 1876, the court held that since the Indian legal system was founded on English common law, the right to a pollution-free environment was a part of the basic jurisprudence of the land.[7]

I. DAMAGES AND INJUNCTION

A plaintiff in a tort action may sue for damages or an injunction, or both.

Damages

Damages are the pecuniary compensation payable for the commission of a tort. Damages may be either 'substantial' or 'exemplary'. Substantial damages are awarded to compensate the plaintiff for the wrong suffered. The purpose of such damages is

---

[2] Both the Public Liability Insurance Act of 1991 and the National Environment Tribunal Act of 1995 adopt this norm.

[3] 'Common Law' refers to the customary law of England derived from judicial decisions, in contrast with legislative enactments.

[4] S. Desai & K. Desai, *Ramaswamy Iyer's The Law of Torts* 21 (8th ed. 1987).

[5] M. Setalvad, *The Common Law of India* 53 (1960).

[6] AIR 1996 SC 2715.

[7] *Id.* at 2722. For a general review of tort law principles see *Jay Laxmi Salt Works (P).Ltd. v State of Gujarat* 1994 (4) SCC 1.

restitution, i.e. to restore the plaintiff to the position he or she would have been in if the tort had not been committed. Such damages, therefore, correspond to a fair and reasonable compensation for the injury.

Exemplary damages are intended to punish the defendant for the outrageous nature of his or her conduct, as for instance, when he or she persists in causing a nuisance after being convicted and being fined for it.[8] The object of the court in such cases is to deter the wrongdoer. The deterrence objective has recently prompted the Supreme Court to add a fresh category to the type of cases where exemplary damages may be awarded, viz., when harm results from an enterprise's hazardous or inherently dangerous activity. In the *Shriram Gas Leak Case*,[9] oleum gas escaped from a unit of the Shriram Foods and Fertilizer Industries and injured a few Delhi citizens. The court observed that in such cases, compensation 'must be correlated to the magnitude and capacity of the enterprise because such compensation must have a deterrent effect. The larger and more prosperous the enterprise, the greater must be the amount of compensation payable by it. ...'[10]

Damages awarded in tort actions in India are notoriously low, and pose no deterrent to the polluter. Lengthy delays in the adjudication of cases combined with chronic inflation dilute the value of any damages that a successful plaintiff may receive. Consequently, although in theory damages are the principal relief in a tort action, in practice injunctive reliefs are more effective in abating pollution. Accordingly, litigation strategies must shift away from the conventional common law emphasis on damages. Lawyers in India intent on abating pollution may seek a temporary injunction against the polluter followed by a perpetual injunction on decree. Damages should be viewed as a bonus.

Injunction

An injunction is a judicial process where a person who has infringed, or is about to infringe the rights of another, is restrained from pursuing such acts. An injunction may take either a negative or a positive form. It may require a party to refrain from doing a particular thing or to do a particular thing. Injunctions are granted at the discretion of the court.

Injunctions are of two kinds, temporary and perpetual. The purpose of a temporary injunction is to maintain the state of things at a given date until trial on the merits. It is regulated by sections 94 and 95 as well as Order 39 of the Code of Civil Procedure of 1908. It may be granted on an interlocutory application[11] at any stage of a suit. It remains in force until the disposal of the suit or until further orders of the court.

[8] *J.C. Galstaun v Dunia Lal Seal* (1905) 9 CWN 612, 617.
[9] *M.C. Mehta v Union of India* AIR 1987 SC 1086.
[10] *Id.* at 1099.
[11] An application made between the commencement and end of a suit.

Rule 1 of Order 39 provides that temporary injunctions may be granted where it is proved:

> '(a) that any property in dispute in a suit is in danger of being wasted, damaged or alienated by any party to the suit, or wrongfully sold in execution, of a decree, or
> (b) that the defendant threatens, or intends, to remove or dispose of his property with a view to defrauding his creditors, or
> (c) that the defendant threatens to dispossess the plaintiff or otherwise cause injury to the plaintiff in relation to any property in dispute in the suit. ...'

The Supreme Court has held that courts also have an inherent power to issue a temporary injunction in circumstances that are not covered by the provisions of Order 39 when the court is satisfied that the interests of justice so require.[12]

The grant or refusal of a temporary injunction is governed by three well established principles: (1) the existence of a *prima facie* case (a showing on the facts that the plaintiff is very likely to succeed in the suit); (2) the likelihood of irreparable injury (an injury that cannot be adequately compensated for in damages) if the injunction is refused; and (3) that the balance of convenience requires the issue of the injunction (a showing that the inconvenience to the plaintiff if the temporary injunction is withheld exceeds the inconvenience to the defendant if he or she is restrained).

Perpetual injunctions are regulated by sections 37 to 42 of the Specific Relief Act of 1963. A perpetual injunction permanently restrains the defendant from doing the act complained of. It is granted at a court's discretion after judging the merits of the suit. A perpetual injunction is intended to protect the plaintiff indefinitely (so that he or she need not resort to successive actions in respect of every infringement), assuming that the circumstances of the case remain essentially unchanged.

A court may permanently restrain the defendant where damages do not provide adequate relief or where the injunction would prevent a multiplicity of proceedings. Thus, where hazardous dust from a brick grinding machine polluted the air of a neighbouring medical practitioner's consulting room, the polluter was permanently restrained from operating the machine.[13] A court may grant an injunction even though the anticipated damage may not be very serious, as long as the damage is continuous or frequent. The 'balance of convenience' test also applies to the award of a permanent injunction: The court must be satisfied that the damage that the defendant would suffer by the grant of the injunction is outweighed by the damage the plaintiff would suffer if the injunction was refused. Finally, the court will consider the injunction's impact on third parties, for example,

[12] *Manohar Lal Chopra v Rai Baja Seth Hiralal* AIR 1962 SC 527, 532.
[13] *Ram Baj Singh v Babulal* AIR 1982 ALL 285.

when the granting of an injunction would throw a large number of people out of work.

II. NUISANCE, NEGLIGENCE, STRICT LIABILITY AND ABSOLUTE LIABILITY

Nuisance

Modern environmental law has its roots in the common law relating to nuisance. A nuisance is an unlawful interference with the plaintiff's use or enjoyment of land. A plaintiff must, therefore, prove some injury to his enjoyment of property and his own interest in that property. An occupier of the property can sue for nuisance.

Ordinarily, a nuisance means anything that annoys, hurts or offends; but for an interference to be an *actionable nuisance,* the conduct of the defendant must be unreasonable. Further, a nuisance must not be momentary, but must continue for some time: A single, short inconvenience is not actionable. A nuisance would include offensive smells, noise, air pollution, and water pollution.

There are two kinds of nuisance—public and private. A public nuisance injures, annoys or interferes with the quality of life of a class of persons who come within its neighborhood. It is an unreasonable interference with a general right of the public. It is both a tort and a crime.

The remedies for a public nuisance are: (1) a criminal prosecution for the offence of causing a public nuisance;[14] (2) a criminal proceeding before a magistrate for removing a public nuisance;[15] (3) a civil action by the Advocate General or by two or more members of the public with permission of the court, for a declaration, an injunction, or both.[16]

A private nuisance is a substantial and unreasonable interference with the use and enjoyment of land. Reasonableness of the defendant's conduct is the central question in nuisance cases. To determine 'reasonableness', courts will be guided by the ordinary standard of comfort prevailing in the neighbourhood. Minor discomforts that are common in crowded cities will not be viewed as a nuisance by the courts.

An action for private nuisance may seek injunctive relief as well as damages. In cases of a continuing cause of action, such as pollution of a stream by factory wastes or smoke emissions from a chimney, the proper course is to sue for an injunction. Repeated actions for damages may be brought to recover the loss sustained up to the date of the court's decree; but future losses, which are contingent on the continuance of the wrong, are not usually awarded. Damages offer poor relief since the plaintiff would be compelled to bring successive actions. Ordinarily, therefore, courts grant the plaintiff an injunction where a nuisance exists or is threatened, unless he or she is guilty of improper conduct or delay.

---

[14] Section 268 of the Indian Penal Code of 1860.

[15] Sections 133–144 of the Code of Criminal Procedure of 1973.

[16] Section 91 of the Code of Civil Procedure of 1908. In the absence of special damage this is the only available civil remedy. A private action can be maintained against a public nuisance where the plaintiff has suffered particular damage beyond that suffered by all the other persons affected by the nuisance.

A two decade journey through four tiers of courts culminated in the dismissal of an action to restrain a baking oven from being operated in a residential locality in *Kuldip Singh v Subhash Chandra Jain*.[17] The plaintiff, Subhash Chandra Jain, feared that the baking oven and 12 foot chimney built by his neighbour would cause a nuisance when the bakery commenced. The trial court restrained the defendant since operation of the oven 'would result in emitting smell and generating heat and smoke which taken together would amount to nuisance.' The Supreme Court drew a distinction between an existing nuisance and a future nuisance: 'In case of a future nuisance, a mere possibility of injury will not provide the plaintiff with a cause of action unless the threat be so certain or imminent that an injury actionable in law will arise unless prevented by an injunction. The Court may not require proof of absolute certainty or a proof beyond reasonable doubt before it may interfere; but a strong case of probability that the apprehended mischief will in fact arise must be shown by the plaintiff.' In a remarkable conclusion, the apex court found that the plaintiff's apprehension about a smoking oven next door causing a nuisance was not justified by the pleadings or the evidence and dismissed the suit.

In *B. Venkatappa v B. Lovis*,[18] the Andhra Pradesh High Court upheld the lower court's mandatory injunction directing the defendant to close the holes in a chimney facing the plaintiff's property. The court ensured enforcement of its order by authorizing the plaintiff to seal the holes at the defendant's cost, if the defendant failed to do so. The High Court stated that the smoke and fumes that materially interfered with ordinary comfort were enough to constitute an actionable nuisance and that actual injury to health need not be proved. The court also observed that the existence of other sources of discomfort in the neighbourhood were no defence, provided that the source complained of materially added to the discomfort. The court rejected the defence that the plaintiff 'came to the nuisance': 'The fact that the nuisance existed long before the complainant occupied his premises, does not relieve the offender unless he can show that as against the complainant he has acquired a right to commit nuisance complained of.'[19]

The 1905 judgment of the Calcutta High Court in *J. C. Galstaun v Dunia Lal Seal*, excerpted below, may be the earliest reported pollution control case in India. Apart from its historical significance, the case is important because it shows how the common law regulatory system can check polluters in a pre-industrialized society. But would this system, unaided by statute, be sufficient today? While reading the judgment, notice: (a) the polluter's defences (rejected by this court at the beginning of the last century, but still raised today); and (b) the award of Rs. 1000 in damages— a very large amount at that time.

---

[17] 2000 (2) SCALE 582.

[18] AIR 1986 AP 239.

[19] The 'right to commit nuisance complained of', refers to a prescriptive right to emit smoke acquired under section 15 of the Indian Easements Act of 1882, or a right acquired by the authority of a statute. A right to cause a *public nuisance*, however, cannot be obtained by prescription.

J.C. GALSTAUN v DUNIA LAL SEAL
(1905) 9 CWN 612

PARGITER, J.:

This appeal arises out of a suit for a perpetual injunction to abate a nuisance and for damages on account of the same.

The Plaintiff has a garden-house in the Manicktollah Municipality in the suburbs of Calcutta and the Defendant has a shellac factory situated 200 or 300 yards to the north-west of it. The Defendant discharges the refuse-liquid of his manufactory into a Municipal drain that passes along the north of the Plaintiff's garden, and the Plaintiff alleges, first, that the liquid is foul-smelling and noxious to the health of the neighbourhood and specially to himself, and, secondly, that it has damaged him in health, comfort and the market value of his garden property. The Plaintiff has, therefore, asked for a perpetual injunction against the Defendant to restrain him from discharging the liquid refuse into the Municipal drain and for five thousand rupees as damages.

The Defendant admitted that the refuse-liquid from his shellac factory was discharged into the Municipal drain, but he denied that it was noxious or that it had injuriously affected the Plaintiff's property. He said he had been conducting the manufactory in a lawful and reasonable manner from the year 1896 and that it did not constitute a nuisance. He alleged that his factory had been licensed by the Municipality and that he had not caused the Plaintiff any damage and that the Plaintiff had no cause of action against him.

The Subordinate Judge decreed the suit, granted a perpetual injunction and awarded the Plaintiff a thousand rupees as damages. The Defendant has now appealed and has maintained the same pleas here as he did in the first court.

The first point is to ascertain the truth about the refuse-liquid and its character. [The court reviewed the evidence.]

Our conclusion on all the evidence adduced is that when the Defendant's factory was in full working, the refuse-liquid when first discharged into the Municipal drain was offensive, that is contained animal and vegetable matter, that decomposition cannot but have begun soon after it was discharged, that the liquid was subject to evaporation in the drain during the dry months which constituted the working season, that it became thick and sluggish in a very short time, and that the organic matter accumulated in the drain and gave off a stench which was highly offensive and noxious. That is, we find, that the refuse-liquid constituted a legal nuisance when discharged, and created a serious nuisance in its passage through the Municipal drain.

The Defendant made some attempt to prove that the stench arose not from his refuse but from the insanitary condition of the Plaintiff's garden. [This contention was rejected by the court.]

The Defendant has ... contended that the refuse-liquid is not noxious when it leaves the factory; that the refuse may become noxious if it stagnates; that the stagnation is really due to the faulty nature of the Municipal drain, which cannot carry the liquid off speedily and efficiently because of the partial block at the culvert; that if the Municipality would put the drain into good condition, there would be no nuisance; and that he cannot, therefore, be responsible for those injurious consequences.

Comparing these contentions with the findings which we have already expressed, it is clear that the essential question at issue in this suit is this: Whether the Defendant is at liberty to discharge into this Municipal drain such a refuse-liquid as we have described. We are of opinion that he can claim no such right.

In the first place, the Municipality did not admit that the Defendant had any such right, for it prosecuted him twice for allowing the refuse-liquid to flow into the drain, first, in the year 1897, and again, not long afterwards. The Defendant, it appears, gave a promise that he would not allow the liquid to flow into the drain and the prosecution (apparently the first one) was withdrawn. For a few months, he turned the liquid into a pit which he dug, but afterwards he reverted to the old practice of discharging it into the drain. In the second prosecution, he was convicted and fined. The Municipality tried to prevent the discharge of the liquid into the drain first by blocking the mouth of the drain, and afterwards by putting up an iron plate with masonry, but both these preventions were broken and removed. From these facts it appears that the Municipality tried to enforce the Municipal law against the Defendant but succeeded only partially and ultimately gave up the contest.

* * *

[The Defendant] cannot shift the responsibility on to the Municipality by contending that, if the Municipality would improve the drain so as to carry off all the refuse quickly, there would be no nuisance. This contention rests on a serious misconception of the rights and duties created under the Municipal law. No private person can claim a right to foul an ordinary drain by discharging into it what it was not intended to carry off, and then throw on the Municipality an obligation to alter the drain in order to remedy the nuisance that he has produced; nor can he say that other persons must meanwhile put up with such nuisance.

The Defendant's action consists of two parts; first, he has discharged the refuse—liquid into the drain; and, secondly, he has done so knowing that it cannot be efficiently carried away, but must stagnate, decompose and give off an offensive and intolerable stench.

The first part of his action constitutes a legal nuisance which the Plaintiff is entitled to restrain. Carrying on an offensive trade so as to interfere with another's health and comfort or his occupation of property has been constantly held in England to be a legal nuisance against which the courts will give relief.

* * *

The second part of the Defendant's action also constitutes a legal nuisance. Defendant is responsible for the consequences that arise necessarily out of his action. The case of *Ogston v Aberdeen District Tramways Company* [LR (1897) AP.CAS. 111 (1896)] has some points in resemblance with the present case. There a Tramway Company after heavy falls of snow used to clear the snow off its track and to heap it upon the side of the streets; then it scattered salt to make the snow melt in the grooves of its track in order to facilitate its own traffic, with the result that the fluid mixture of salt and snow permeated the heaps of snow and, forming a freezing compound, caused annoyance and injury to the other traffic in the streets. The Town Council did not take any immediate steps to remove the briny slush which was left upon the streets. It was held that the Tramway Company had committed a nuisance which was not sanctioned by either the general or the special Tramways Acts, and that the default of the Town Council did not affect the primary liability of the Tramway Company.

In that case, the Company put forward much the same propositions as have been put forward in this case. They contended that they were within their statutory rights, or that their action, if not expressly licensed by the statutes, was sanctioned by implication for the necessary purposes of the Tramway. But these pleas were disallowed. The statutes did not sanction what the Company did nor did they give the Company any right to create a nuisance. We have already pointed out that the Defendant's plea in the present case that he was entitled to discharge his refuse into the drain cannot prevail.

* * *

For these reasons, we think that the Plaintiff is entitled to restrain the Defendant from discharging the refuse-liquid of his factory into the Municipal drain. From the history of this case it appears that the Defendant has successfully resisted Municipal control, that he has enlarged his factory and that he has been discharging a greater volume of refuse-liquid into the drain. It is plain that if no injunction is issued, there will be nothing to prevent him from aggravating the present nuisance by further enlarging his factory and discharging still more refuse into the drain. An injunction for the permanent stoppage of the nuisance is the only effectual remedy, and we have abundance of authority for issuing an injunction in the cases decided in England.

With regard to the question of the damage caused to the Plaintiff, objections have been urged against the opinion formed by the Subordinate Judge. Persistence in a proved nuisance has been held in England to be a just cause for giving exemplary damages, (see Pollock's Law of Torts, 6th edition, Chap. X, 407). The Defendant has certainly persisted in spite of Municipal warning. This, therefore, is not a case in which the damages awarded should be nominal. There can be no doubt that material injury has been caused to the Plaintiff and the damages should be substantial; and, while holding this view, we think that the Subordinate Judge's estimate is reasonable and not excessive. For these reasons, we affirm the decree of the court below and dismiss this appeal with costs.

QUESTIONS

Despite the plaintiffs' success in *Galstaun's Case,* if a similar situation arose today, is a common law action advisable? What other options may the victim consider? What changes since 1905 might influence the choice of the remedy?

In *Ram Baj Singh's Case,* excerpted below, the plaintiff successfully restrained the defendant from using a brick grinding machine that generated dust and polluted the air. Note in this case: (a) the court's recognition of a private right of action arising from a public nuisance; (b) the liberal test employed by the court to determine the existence of a nuisance; (c) the issue of an injunction apparently without examining the balance of convenience; and (d) the evidentiary problems faced by the plaintiff.

RAM BAJ SINGH v BABULAL
AIR 1982 ALL 285

JUDGMENT:

The plaintiff-appellant has been denied the relief sought by him on the ground that [a] brick grinding machine of the defendant did not cause any substantial injury or special damage to the plaintiff. Learned Counsel appearing for the plaintiff has argued before me that the two courts below have not correctly appreciated the meaning of the expressions 'substantial injury' and 'special damage', as used in law.

The plaintiff-appellant commenced the action giving rise to this second appeal for permanent injunction to restrain the defendant-respondent from running his brick-grinding machine.

It is not in controversy between the parties that the plaintiff is a Medical Practitioner. He has built a consulting chamber before the brick-grinding machine was erected by the defendant-respondent. There is a controversy between parties as to whether the consulting chamber was established by the plaintiff in the year 1962 or in the year 1965. * * * It is also not disputed that the brick-grinding machine is electrically propelled and that it is situated at a distance of about 40 feet from the consulting chamber of the plaintiff-appellant in a north-eastern direction. There is a road which intervenes between the consulting chamber of the plaintiff-appellant and the brick-grinding machine.

The grievance of the plaintiff-appellant was that the brick-grinding machine was generating dust which polluted the atmosphere and entered the consulting chamber of the plaintiff-appellant and caused physical inconvenience to him and his patients who came to his chamber. It was further stated that the said machine had been set up by the defendant-respondent without any permission or licence from the Municipal Board.

The defendant-respondent contested the suit. He did not deny that the machine was erected by him in April, 1965. He contended that no dust emanated during the process of grinding bricks and there was no question of any pollution being caused in the atmosphere. He further stated that the bricks were moistened before being subjected to grinding process and no dust resulted therefrom. He further stated that his machine did not produce any noise and according to him, the erection and working of the machine did not cause any nuisance—whether public or private. He concluded by saying that the suit had been filed against him only on account of enmity and the same was not legally sustainable. The trial court came to the conclusion that the brick grinding machine had been erected by the defendant-respondent in the year

1965 without obtaining any licence from the appropriate authority. It further held that the dust did emanate and pollute the atmosphere and that such dust was injurious to health. It also came to the conclusion that the dust produced by the machine entered the consulting chamber of the plaintiff-appellant depending on the direction of the wind. It further found that the defence taken up by the defendant-respondent was false and the evidence produced by him could not be relied upon. It, however, dismissed the suit of the plaintiff-appellant on the finding that the dust resulting from the machine did not cause any substantial injury either to the plaintiff or to his patients. The trial court also went into the question as to whether the machine belonging to the defendant-respondent caused any actionable nuisance to the plaintiff-appellant and decided that [issue] against him.

* * *

[A] person is ordinarily entitled to do any thing on his own property, provided that doing of such a thing is lawful. His conduct, however, becomes a private nuisance when the consequence of his acts no longer remain confined to his own property but spill over in a substantial manner to the property belonging to another person. However, anything done by a person on his property, repercussions of which are felt on the neighbour's land, may not always be a nuisance. The consequences of anything done by the owner of a land on his own land which are also felt over the neighbouring land may be of such a trivial nature that no reasonable person would object to the same. No precise or universal formula has been devised to determine the distinction between a trivial consequence of an act or a consequence which can be termed to be of substantial magnitude. The test which has always been found to be useful in distinguishing the two sets of cases is the test of ascertaining the reaction of a reasonable person according to the ordinary usage of mankind living in a particular society in respect of the thing complained of.

After a land had been built upon, the owner of the building cannot expect to have air of the same quality which existed before the building was erected. The freshness of the air is necessarily diminished by the erection of the building. If the whole locality in which the building is situated is built upon, the quality of freshness of air will be diminished further and the same may become tainted to a certain extent. But when something is done by the owner of a neighbouring land upon his own land which is not comfortable or is wholly uncomfortable with physical comfort and human existence, the person aggrieved gets a right to sue. The act of the neighbour of which he will complain will be an actionable nuisance. At this stage, a note of caution may be sounded. In order to judge whether the air has been polluted to an extent that it has ceased to be comfortable with human comfort and existence, the standard to be employed again is the standard of a sober and reasonable mind. Concepts of elegant and dainty living will be wholly out of place. Further in judging the question of this comfort of danger to human existence on account of the act complained of, the location of a property is also a relevant circumstance. A person living in an industrial locality cannot claim to have as much fresh air as a person living in a non-industrial area.

* * *

[A]ccording to the findings of the two [lower] courts ... the consulting chamber of the plaintiff-appellant started functioning before the machine was set up by the defendant-respondent.

The two [lower] courts ... have been largely influenced by the fact that the plaintiff-appellant did not examine any of his patients to prove that any actual damage was caused to them on account of the dust emanating from the machine of the defendant-respondent. They have also referred to the statement of the plaintiff-appellant and have held that the plaintiff admitted that the damage caused to his patients was recorded in his register and the same had not been produced. From this omission on the part of the plaintiff, they have drawn an adverse inference against him and have come to the conclusion that the plaintiff-appellant has failed to establish that any special damage or any substantial injury was caused to him.

The expression 'special damage' is used in law to indicate a damage caused to a party in contra-distinction to damage caused to the public at large. The damage caused to the public at large on account of a nuisance is referred in law as a public nuisance. [The court referred to the public nuisance provisions in the Indian Penal Code and the Code of Criminal Procedure.] However, there may be cases where a single act may amount to a public nuisance and also give rise to a cause of action to an individual to sue on the basis of private nuisance. For instance, if night soil is heaped by the side of a public highway, it may be a nuisance to the general public and the persons who pass along the said highway. At the same time it may be a private nuisance to a person who lives in a house which adjoins the place where night soil is collected. All that the law requires is that when an act amounts to public nuisance, an individual can sue in his own right only if he is able to prove special damage to himself i.e., damage which is personal to him as opposed to the damage or inconvenience caused to the public at large or to a section of the public.

The expression 'special damage' was found by the text book writers to be somewhat inaccurate and confusing. In later editions of the text books such as Salmond on Torts, the expression which has been used is 'particular damage'. It actually follows from the findings recorded by the two courts below that the plaintiff had succeeded in establishing damage which was particular to himself. It has been held by the court of appeal that dust emanated from the crushing of bricks was a public hazard and was bound to cause injury to the health of the persons. It has further held that dust from bricks entered in sufficient quantity into the consulting chamber of the plaintiff-appellant so that a thin red coating was visible on the clothes of the persons sitting there. In view of these findings it is difficult to comprehend how it could be said that the plaintiff had failed to prove that special damage was not being caused to him on account of the offending brick grinding machine.

Coming to the question of substantial injury, I have already indicated above that every injury is considered to be substantial which a reasonable person considers to be so. In assessing the nature of substantial injury, the test to be applied is again the appraisement made of the injury by a reasonable person belonging to the society. The expression does not take into account the susceptibilities of hypersensitive person or persons attuned to a dainty mode of living. No other meaning can be assigned or has been assigned to the expression 'substantial injury.' In view of the fact found by the two courts below concurrently, it was impossible to hold that no substantial injury was being caused to the plaintiff-appellant. Causing of actual damage by the act complained of as a nuisance is besides the point. If actual damage or actual injury were to be the criterion a person will have to wait before the injury becomes palpable or demonstrable before instituting a suit for its abatement. My opinion, in this point is fortified by the views of the text book writers and the decided cases. Any act would amount to a private nuisance which can reasonably be said to cause injury, discomfort or annoyance to a person.

For reasons stated above, this appeal must succeed.

NOTES AND QUESTIONS

1. On the basis of the evidence adduced, the High Court concluded that the plaintiff's consulting rooms started functioning *before* the brick grinding machine was set up by the defendant. The court, therefore, was not required to resolve the issue of the plaintiff having come to the nuisance. If the brick grinding machine had been functioning before the plaintiff started his consultancy, would the case have had a different outcome? In this situation, might the court have preferred the softer relief of damages?

2. While judges in India routinely deal with cases involving a breach of a statute, tort cases involving subjective standards of 'reasonableness' are rare occurrences. In this situation, judges often seek a *statutory basis* to support their view of 'reasonableness'. The brick grinding machine was being operated without an appropriate government licence. Did this factor weigh with the court while deciding that the machine was being used unreasonably? Would the court have been more circumspect in restraining the defendant if the machine had been properly licensed by the municipal authorities?

3. The court dispenses with the balance of convenience test before granting the mandatory injunction. Similarly, the injunction's impact on third parties is apparently not considered. What are some of the factors that the court could have considered before reaching its decision?

4. The court employs a liberal test for nuisance, holding that air pollution amounts to a nuisance where it causes injury, discomfort or annoyance to a 'reasonable person'. Significantly, the court rejects a health-based standard that would require the plaintiff to prove actual injury: 'Causing of actual damage by the act complained of as a nuisance is besides the point. If actual damage or actual injury were to be the criterion, a person will have to wait before the injury becomes palpable or demonstrable before instituting a suit... .'

Apart from the problem of latent health effects, such a standard would also immeasurably increase the evidentiary burden on the plaintiff: Medical evidence would need to be adduced and the causal link between the pollutant and the injury would have to be established. In contrast, the 'reasonable person' standard may easily be met by adducing non-technical evidence.

But does the common law standard of 'reasonableness' provide a satisfactory basis for regulating pollution? Should not pollution regulation be designed to protect the most vulnerable segments of the population and not merely the 'average' or 'reasonable person'?

5. For a discussion on the nuisance test for excessive noise, see *Radhey Shiam v Gur Prasad Serma*.[20]

6. Since 1989 the Environment (Protection) Rules prescribe ambient noise levels for industrial, commercial and residential areas as well as silence zones. In 1996, the Centre notified National Ambient Air Quality Standards (NAAQS) for several pollutants such as sulphur dioxide, suspended particulate matter, respirable particulate matter, carbon monoxide, etc. The NAAQS standards allow an adequate margin of safety to protect public health, vegetation and property [21] and may guide a civil court in assessing the reasonableness of a smoke nuisance or excessive noise.

7. Does the 'polluter pays' principle, recently adopted by the Supreme Court,[22] strengthen nuisance law? As explained by the Supreme Court, this principle not only requires the polluter to compensate the victims of the pollution but also requires her to foot the bill for remedial costs to restore the damaged ecology.

Negligence

A common law action for negligence may be brought to prevent environmental pollution. In an action for negligence, the plaintiff must show that (1) the defendant was under a duty to take reasonable care to avoid the damage complained of; (2) there was a breach of this duty; and (3) the breach of duty caused the damage. The degree of care required in a particular case depends on the surrounding circumstances and varies according to the risk involved and the magnitude of the prospective injury.

An act of negligence may also constitute a nuisance if it unlawfully interferes with the enjoyment of another's right in land. Similarly, it may also amount to a breach of the rule of strict liability in *Rylands v Fletcher*,[23] if the negligent act allows the escape of anything dangerous which the defendant has brought on the land.

The causal connection between the negligent act and the plaintiff's injury is often the most problematic link in pollution cases. Where the pollutant is highly toxic and its effect is immediate, as with the methyl isocyanate that leaked from the Union Carbide plant in Bhopal, the connection is relatively straightforward. The causal link is more tenuous when the effect of the injury remains latent over long periods of time

[20] AIR 1978 ALL 86.
[21] Note 1, Schedule VII, Environment (Protection) Rules of 1986.
[22] *Indian Council for Enviro-Legal Action v Union of India (The Bichhri Case)* AIR 1996 SC 1446; and *Vellore Citizens' Welfare Forum v Union of India* AIR 1996 SC 2715.
[23] (1868) LR 3 HL 330.

and can eventually be attributed to factors other than the pollutant, or to polluters other than the defendant.[24]

The *Mukesh Textile Mills Case,* excerpted below, is one of the few reported pollution cases in which a judgment was rendered for damages. Note (a) the defences raised by the mill; (b) the witnesses examined by the parties to establish their respective contentions; (c) the discussion on the mitigation of damages; and (d) the manner in which the court quantified damages.

MUKESH TEXTILE MILLS (P) LTD. v H.R. SUBRAMANYA SASTRY
AIR 1987 KANT 87

VENKATACHALIAH, J.:

Appellant-Mukesh Textile Mills (P) Ltd., the defendant in the court below, has a sugar factory in Harige Village, Shimoga District. Adjacent to the sugar factory, on the north, the respondents-plaintiffs own several extents of land irrigated by a distributory channel of the Barda Reservoir canal. The water channel runs West to East, in between the premises of the sugar factory on the south and respondents' lands on the north.

Appellant stores molasses, a by-product in the manufacture of sugar, in three tanks in the factory premises. Two of them are steel tanks and the third, a mud one with earthen embankment, is close to the respondents' land separated only by the said water-channel. At the material point of time, some 8000 tonnes of molasses were stored in the earthen tank.

It would appear that the northern-embankment of this earthen tank had become dilapidated having been dug into by rodents and as a result, on the night of 16th of April 1970, the northern embankment collapsed and a large quantity of molasses in the tank overflowed and emptied themselves into the water channel, inundated and spread over respondents' land. The inundation of water, fully laden with the molasses, damaged the standing paddy and sugarcane crop raised by the respondents.

Respondents brought the present suit O.S. 26 of 1972 on the file of the Civil Judge, Shimoga, for damages of Rs. 35,000/- contending that extensive cultivation of paddy and sugarcane had been damaged.

Originally, the defence was one of denial that the molasses had so inundated respondents' land; but later the appellant sought, and was granted, leave to include by amendment the following defence:

> That in any event as the breach of the tank wherein the molasses was stored was due to the burrowing activity of the rodents in the said tank precincts, this was an Act of God and the defendant is in no way liable to answer the suit claim even granting that the plaintiff has suffered damages by reason of his crops being destroyed. The defendant could not have seen this burrowing by rodents.

---

[24] In numerous American suits brought against asbestos manufacturers by asbestos workers suffering from lung cancer, several courts reduced the damage award on the theory that a plaintiff's habit of smoking cigarettes had contributed, or could have contributed, to his condition. Some courts dismissed the suit entirely when the plaintiff had been a cigarette smoker.

On these pleadings, the court below framed the necessary and relevant issues. On the plaintiffs side—P.W.1—a Revenue Inspector; P.W.2 a Photographer, P.W.3—the Shanbogue and P.W.4—the Patel of Harige Village were examined. The first plaintiff tendered evidence as P.W.5.

On the side of the appellant-defendant, D.W.1—the Chief Chemist of the Factory; P.W.2 and P.W.3—the Cane Superintendent and the Manager, respectively of the factory, were examined. A number of documents were marked on either side.

On an appreciation of the evidence available on record, the court below held that as a result of a breach of the retaining wall of the mud tank molasses overflowed contaminated the water channel resulting in the inundation of respondents' land by molasses laden water and that the breach of the wall of the tank and the consequent damage suffered by respondents were attributable to actionable negligence on the part of the appellant. In regard to the quantum of damages the court below held that the claim as put forward by the respondents was somewhat exaggerated and that the loss of crops was only in respect of 14 acres of paddy and 3 acres of sugarcane Rs. 10,500/- and 4,200/- respectively, in all, Rs. 14,700/- was awarded as damages.

* * *

On the contentions urged at the hearing, the following points fall for determination in this appeal:

(a) Whether the breach of the molasses-tank and the inundation of crops by molasses laden water was the direct consequence of appellant's omission to keep the said tank in a state of good repair?

(b) Even if the breach was attributable to appellant's neglect, whether the damage to the crop was too remote and the result of an independent cause?

(c) Whether, at all events, the respondents ought to have mitigated the damages and their omission in this behalf disentitles them to relief and,

(d) Whether the damages of Rs.14,700/- awarded are supportable on the evidence on record?

Re: Point (a): [The appellant-defendant did not press the plea that the damage arose due to an 'Act of God.']

The liability of the appellant rests at least on two principles. One is that the appellant, who had stored large quantities of molasses in a mud tank had the duty to take reasonable care in the matter of maintenance, in a state of good repair, of the embankments of the tank. The duty, no doubt, is not simply to act carefully but not to cause injury carelessly. The doctrine of legal causation, in reference both to the creation of liability and to measurement of damages is much discussed. So is the place of 'causation' and 'foreseeability' in the tort of 'negligence'.

But in this case it was virtually admitted that the rodents had burrowed holes into the earthen embankment of the tank rendering its walls weak. Both from the foreseeability test and of initial causation it must be held that the appellant is liable. Appellant could reasonably have foreseen that damage was likely to be caused if there was a breach of the tank. There was clearly a duty-situation and appellant had omitted to do what a reasonable man, in those circumstances, would have done or would not have omitted to do. The damage that was likely to occur to the neighbouring land by a breach of a tank in which were stored 8000 tonnes of molasses was reasonably foreseeable, engendering a duty-situation. No defence was forthcoming that the tank had been inspected periodically and all reasonable steps taken to keep it in a state of good repair.

The second ground of liability is this: Appellant by storing a large quantity of molasses on the land had put the land to a non-natural use and if a person collects on his premises things which are intrinsically dangerous, or might become dangerous, if they escape, he has a liability, if things so stored escape and cause damage. This is the rule in *Rylands v Fletcher* (1868) LR 3 HL 330 in which Blackburn, J. enunciated the rule thus:

> We think that the true rule of the law is that the person who for his own purposes brings on his lands and collects and keeps there anything likely to do mischief if it escapes, must keep it at his peril, and if he does not do so, is prima facie answerable for all the damages which is the natural consequence of its escape.

On either of the two principles, a duty-situation emerges and the appellant must be held liable for the consequence of the escape of the fluid from its tank. * * *

Looked at from any side, the present one is a clear case of a duty-situation and also one of omission to discharge it on the part of the appellant. Point (a) is held against the appellant.

Re: Point (b): [Counsel for the appellant-defendant suggests] a defence of a 'novus actus interveniens.' If damage results from the intervention of acts of an independent third-party, it may be very difficult to discover the causal-connection between such damage and the original wrongful act.

In this case, the plea of 'novus actus' has absolutely no foundation. The chain of events set into motion by the negligence of the appellant, in improper maintenance of the tank which resulted in the breach of the tank and the damage caused to the crops, constitutes a direct and uninterrupted chain of events. It all happened in the night. The molasses contaminated the water in the channel and through it, the crops. The appeal to the principle of 'novus actus' appears to be somewhat misplaced. Point (b) is answered accordingly.

Re: Point (c): The contention of the [Counsel for the appellant] pushed to its logical conclusions, is that though the respondents' land was infested with molasses, the respondents' remedy was simple enough—if fresh water had been allowed to further irrigate and inundate the lands, the contamination would have been washed out. Learned Counsel submitted that as the respondents had not shown that they had so taken the requisite care to mitigate the damages they are not entitled to any damages. This plea was not taken in the court below. There is no material to show that such a process would have been really effective and practicable. [Since the appellant had failed to discharge the onus of proof, the court held that the plea of mitigation fails.]

Re: Point (d): We have examined the evidence on record on this point. The court below held that there was paddy crop on 14 acres and sugarcane crop on 3 acres.

The court below estimated the probable yield at 15 pallas of paddy per acre. Valuing paddy at Rs. 50/- per palla, the court below estimated the loss of paddy crop at Rs. 10,500/-. The yield from 3 acres of sugarcane was estimated at 60 tonnes valued at Rs. 70/- per ton. That brought in a further sum of Rs. 4200/-. D.W. 2 himself admitted the existence of the paddy and sugarcane crop. There is other material also to support this finding apart from the evidence of the 1st plaintiff. (P.W.5)

However, there is some force in what [appellant's counsel] said about the gross value of the crops having been taken while the crops had not been ready for harvest and required some more expenditure for their maintenance for sometime more before harvest and that the expenses for its upkeep and maintenance of the crops and expenses of harvest having to be deducted. We think that it is appropriate to deduct some amount from the damages awarded towards such expenditure, which was reasonably expected to be incurred. Accordingly, we deduct a sum of Rs. 2,500/- on this score. The damages awarded would, therefore, have to be scaled down to Rs. 12,200/- from Rs. 14,700/- This is our finding on Point (d).

In the result, this appeal is allowed in part, only in relation to the quantum of damages. In modification of the judgment and decree under appeal, the suit is decreed in a sum of Rs.12,200/- on which respondent-plaintiff shall be entitled to interest at 6% from the date of suit till the date of realization. The respondents shall be entitled to their costs in the suit proportionate to their success. The appellant shall, however, bear and pay its own costs in the court below. Both the parties are left to bear and pay their own costs in the appeal. Ordered accordingly.

Appeal partly allowed.

NOTES AND QUESTIONS

1. In a suit for damages, a plaintiff may sue for every prospective loss that would naturally result from the defendant's conduct. Thus, if the molasses had harmed future cultivation, the plaintiff could have obtained prospective damages as well. In such a situation, the plaintiff's evidentiary burden would have been considerable. He or she would have had to adduce expert evidence to establish the type and extent of damage to the soil. Who might possess such expertise? Where can such expertise be obtained?

2. Damages for past as well as prospective loss resulting from the same cause must be recovered in a single suit as more than one suit will not lie on the same cause of action.[25] Assume that some future damage caused by the molasses remained latent for several years before being discovered. Is it fair that the suit for damages for the loss of the standing crops should preclude a suit for latent injuries discovered in the future? Should the principle of *res judicata* apply to such cases?

3. After 14 years of litigation, the High Court ordered damages of Rs. 12,200

[25] This is governed by the principle of *res judicata* enunciated in section 11 of the Code of Civil Procedure of 1908.

with interest at 6 per cent per year from the date of the suit. The High Court reduced the subordinate court's award by Rs. 2,500. Was this necessary? Does compensation afford fair relief when it ignores the high litigation costs of bringing a suit and battling it through multiple appeals? Shouldn't a court be conscious of the fall in the value of the currency? Is the award of interest at 6 per cent per year at all realistic?

4. In an appeal filed by the Rajkot Municipal Corporation contesting a decree for damages awarded to the widow and children of a pedestrian killed by a falling tree, the Supreme Court held:

> The conditions in India have not developed to such an extent that a corporation can keep constant vigil by testing the healthy condition of the trees in the public places, roadsides, highways frequented by passers-by. There is no duty to maintain regular supervision thereof. ... Consequently, there would be no common law right to file a suit for tort of negligence.[26]

Apparently, 'conditions in India' developed quite swiftly. Two years later, without reference to *Rajkot*, the Supreme Court upheld a decree against the Delhi Municipal Corporation where a scooterist was killed by a falling tree. The court agreed with the finding of the trial court that the municipal corporation had been negligent in discharging its duty of care to road users.[27]

Strict Liability

The rule in *Rylands v Fletcher*[28] holds a person *strictly liable* when he brings or accumulates on his land something likely to cause harm if it escapes, and damage arises as a natural consequence of its escape. But 'strict' liability is subject to a number of exceptions that considerably reduce the scope of its operation. Exceptions that have been recognized are: (1) an act of God (natural disasters such as an earthquake or flood); (2) the act of a third party (e.g., sabotage); (3) the plaintiff's own fault; (4) the plaintiff's consent; (5) the natural use of land by the defendant (i.e., strict liability applies to a non-natural user of land); and (6) statutory authority.

Absolute Liability

With the expansion of chemical-based industries in India, increasing number of enterprises store and use hazardous substances. These activities are not banned because they have great social utility (e.g., the manufacture of fertilisers and pesticides). Traditionally, the doctrine of strict liability was considered adequate to regulate such hazardous enterprises. The doctrine allows for the growth of hazardous industries, while ensuring that such enterprises will bear the burden of the damage they cause

---

[26] *Rajkot Municipal Corporation v Manjulaben Jayantilal Nakum* 1997 (9) SCC 552, 601.

[27] *Municipal Corporation of Delhi v Sushila Devi* AIR 1999 SC 1929, 1933.

[28] *Supra* note 23. For a discussion on 'strict liability' and the *Rylands'* rule see *Jay Laxmi Salt Works (P) Ltd. v State of Gujarat* 1994 (4) SCC 1.

when a hazardous substance escapes. Shortly after the Bhopal gas leak tragedy of 1984, the traditional doctrine was replaced by the rule of 'absolute' liability, a standard *stricter* than strict liability. Absolute liability was first articulated by the Supreme Court and has since been adopted by Parliament.

The genesis of absolute liability was the *Shriram Gas Leak Case*[29] which was decided by the Supreme Court in December 1986. The case originated in a writ petition filed in the Supreme Court by the environmentalist and lawyer, M.C. Mehta as a public interest litigation. The petition sought to close and relocate Shriram's caustic chlorine and sulphuric acid plants which were located in a thickly populated part of Delhi. Shortly after Mehta filed this petition, on 4 December 1985 oleum leaked from Shriram's sulphuric acid plant causing widespread panic in the surrounding community.

Chief Justice Bhagwati, who presided over the Supreme Court bench, was concerned for the safety of Delhi's citizens. Moreover, the Chief Justice saw in the oleum leak a way of influencing the pending and far more important *Bhopal Gas Leak Case*. In the first reported order in *Shriram*, the Chief Justice observed that the principles and norms for determining the liability of large enterprises engaged in the manufacture and sale of hazardous products were 'questions of the greatest importance particularly since, following upon the leakage of MIC gas from the Union Carbide Plant in Bhopal, lawyers, judges and jurists are considerably exercised as to what controls, whether by way of relocation or by way of installation of adequate safety devices, need to be imposed upon [hazardous industries], what is the extent of liability of such corporations and what remedies can be devised for enforcing such liability with a view to securing payment of damages to the person affected by such leakage of liquid or gas.'[30]

Union Carbide hinted at a 'sabotage theory' to shield itself from the claims of the Bhopal victims. It was suggested that a disgruntled employee working in the pesticide factory owned by Carbide's Indian subsidiary may have triggered the escape of the gas. Such a theory afforded a defense under the rule of strict liability laid down in *Rylands v Fletcher*.[31] But any faith Union Carbide may have reposed in the sabotage theory was soon shaken by Chief Justice Bhagwati's rejection of the *Rylands'* rule in situations involving hazardous industries. In his last judgment before retirement, Chief Justice Bhagwati spoke for the court:

> We are of the view that an enterprise which is engaged in a hazardous or inherently dangerous industry which poses a potential threat to the health and safety of the persons working in the factory and residing in the surrounding areas owes an absolute and non-delegable duty to the community to ensure that no harm results to anyone on account of hazardous or inherently dangerous

[29] *M.C. Mehta v Union of India* AIR 1987 SC 1086.
[30] *M.C. Mehta v Union of India* AIR 1987 SC 965.
[31] *Supra* note 23.

nature of the activity which it has undertaken. ... We would therefore hold that where an enterprise is engaged in a hazardous or inherently dangerous activity and harm results to anyone on account of an accident in the operation of such hazardous or inherently dangerous activity resulting, for example, in the escape of toxic gas the enterprise is strictly and absolutely liable to compensate all those who are affected by the accident and *such liability is not subject to any of the exceptions* which operate vis-a-vis the tortious principle of strict liability under the rule in *Rylands v Fletcher*.[32]

The absolute liability theory laid down by the Supreme Court in *Shriram* was first applied by the Madhya Pradesh High Court to support its award of interim compensation to the Bhopal victims.[33] In light of *Shriram,* Justice Seth of the High Court described the liability of the enterprise to be 'unquestionable.'

However, soon thereafter the wisdom of the theory was questioned by Chief Justice Ranganath Misra who presided over the proceedings before the Supreme Court for a review of the *Bhopal Case* settlement.[34] Chief Justice Misra in his concurring judgment observed that the issue before the *Shriram* court was whether the delinquent company came within the ambit of 'state' under Article 12 of the Constitution so as to be subject to the discipline of Article 21 and to proceedings under Article 32 of the Constitution. Thus, according to the Chief Justice, what was said about the departure from the *Rylands v Fletcher* rule 'was essentially obiter'.[35]

Justice Venkatachaliah (speaking for Justices K.N. Singh, N.D. Ojha and himself) in the main judgment in the *Bhopal Review* also cast doubt on the absolute liability standard. He implicitly rejected the Madhya Pradesh High Court view that after the no-exception standard of *Shriram*, Carbide's liability was 'unquestionable'. The Supreme Court held that Carbide was entitled to its day in court when its defenses, legal and factual, would have to be tested. In Justice Venkatachaliah's words:

At the same time, it is necessary to remind ourselves that in bestowing a second thought whether the settlement is just, fair and adequate, we should *not* proceed on the premises that the liability of the UCC has been firmly established. It is *yet to be decided* if the matter goes to trial. Indeed, UCC has seriously contested the basis of its alleged liability. ... Every effort should be made to protect the victims from the prospects of a protracted, exhausting and uncertain litigation. While we do not intend to comment on the merits of the claims and of the defenses, factual and legal, arising in the suit, it is fair to

---

[32] Emphasis supplied. *Supra* note 29, at 1099.

[33] *Union Carbide Corporation v Union of India* Civil Revision No. 26 of 1988, 4 April 1988. This judgment was never implemented in view of the final settlement between the parties.

[34] *Union Carbide Corporation v Union of India (Bhopal Review)* AIR 1992 SC 248.

[35] *Id.* at 261. *Obiter dictum* are words of a judgment unnecessary for the decision of the case.

recognise that the suit involves complex questions as to the basis of UCC's liability and assessment of the quantum of compensation in a mass tort action.[36]

In recognizing Carbide's right to raise and urge defenses the court stepped back from the 'without exception' absolute liability principle declared in *Shriram*.

Meanwhile in January, 1991 Parliament enacted the Public Liability Insurance Act, giving statutory recognition to 'no-fault' liability in small measure. The victims of a hazardous industrial accident were now entitled to compensation at prescribed levels, without proof of negligence. The maximum compensation under the Act on a 'no-fault' basis however, is *limited* to Rs. 25,000; although the right of a victim to claim larger damages is expressly reserved. To safeguard the interest of victims, the law requires all hazardous enterprises to obtain sufficient insurance cover.

The application of absolute liability was extended *without limitation* by the National Environment Tribunal Act of 1995 to all cases where death or injury to a person (other than a workman) or damage to any property or the environment result from an accident involving a hazardous substance. The 'owner', who is defined to mean a person who owns or has control over the handling of any hazardous substance at the time of the accident, is liable to compensate the victims on a 'no-fault' basis. Applications for compensation may be made to the tribunal established under the Act. The heads under which compensation may be claimed are set out in the schedule to the Act and in addition to the omnibus entry 'any other claim arising out of or connected with any activity of handling hazardous substances', they include death; injury; medical expenses; damage to private property; expenses incurred by government authorities in providing relief and rehabilitation; loss or harm to animals, crops, trees and orchards; and loss of business or of employment. Although the law was enacted in June, 1995, it was not in force, at the time of writing this chapter.

In the *Bichhri Case* excerpted below, a Supreme Court bench of two Judges grappled with the seemingly divergent views expressed by the five-judge constitution benches in the *Shriram* and *Bhopal Review* cases. While the judges may not be faulted for preferring the *Shriram* dictum, are there any errors that weaken the force of the reasoning?

INDIAN COUNCIL FOR ENVIRO-LEGAL ACTION v UNION OF INDIA
AIR 1996 SC 1446

B.P. JEEVAN REDDY, J.:   * * *

Bichhri is a small village in Udaipur District of Rajasthan. To its north is a major industrial establishment, Hindustan Zinc Limited, a public sector concern. That did not affect Bichhri. Its woes began somewhere in 1987 when the fourth respondent

---

[36] Emphasis supplied. *Id.* at 306.

herein, Hindustan Agro Chemicals Limited started producing certain chemicals like Oleum (said to be concentrated form of sulphuric acid) and Single Super Phosphate. The real calamity occurred when a sister concern, Silver Chemicals (Respondent 5), commenced production of 'H' acid in a plant located within the same complex. 'H' acid was meant for export exclusively. Its manufacture gives rise to enormous quantities of highly toxic effluents—in particular, iron-based and gypsum-based sludge—which if not properly treated, pose grave threat to Mother Earth. It poisons the earth, the water and everything that comes in contact with it. Jyoti Chemicals (Respondent 8) is another unit established to produce 'H' acid besides some other chemicals. Respondents 6 and 7 were established to produce fertilizers and a few other products.

All the units/factories of Respondents 4 to 8 are situated in the same complex and are controlled by the same group of individuals. All the units are what may be called 'chemical industries'. The complex is located within the limits of Bichhri village.

Because of the pernicious wastes emerging from the production of 'H' acid, its manufacture is stated to have been banned in the western countries. But the need of 'H' acid continues in the West. That need is catered to by the industries like the Silver Chemicals and Jyoti Chemicals in this part of the world. (A few other units producing 'H' acid have been established in Gujarat, as would be evident from the decision of the Gujarat High Court in *Pravinbhai Jashbhai Patel v State of Gujarat*, a decision rendered by one of us, B.N. Kirpal, J. as the Chief Justice of that court.) Silver Chemicals is stated to have produced 375 MT of 'H' acid. The quantity of 'H' acid produced by Jyoti Chemicals is not known. It says that it produced only 20 MT as trial production, and no more. Whatever quantity these two units may have produced, it has given birth to about 2400–2500 MT of highly toxic sludge (iron-based sludge and gypsum-based sludge) besides other pollutants. Since the toxic untreated waste waters were allowed to flow out freely and because the untreated toxic sludge was thrown in the open in and around the complex, the toxic substances have percolated deep into the bowels of the earth polluting the aquifers and subterranean supply of water. The water in the wells and streams has turned dark and dirty rendering it unfit for human consumption. It has become unfit for cattle to drink and for irrigating land. The soil has become polluted rendering it unfit for cultivation, the mainstay of the villagers. The resulting misery to the villagers needs no emphasis. It spread disease, death and disaster in the village and the surrounding areas. This sudden degradation of earth and water had an echo in Parliament too. An Hon'ble Minister said, action was being taken, but nothing meaningful was done on the spot. The villagers then rose in virtual revolt leading to the imposition of Section 144 CrPC by the District Magistrate in the area and the closure of the Silver Chemicals in January 1989. It is averred by the respondents that both the units, Silver Chemicals and Jyoti Chemicals have stopped manufacturing 'H' acid since January 1989 and are closed. We may assume it to be so. Yet the consequences of their action remain—the sludge, the long-lasting damage to earth, to underground water, to human beings, to cattle and the village economy. It is with these consequences that we are to contend with in this writ petition.

The present social action litigation was initiated in August 1989 complaining precisely of the above situation and requesting for appropriate remedial action. To the writ petition, the petitioner enclosed a number of photographs illustrating the enormous damage done to water, cattle, plants and to the area in general. A good amount of technical data and other material was also produced supporting the averments in the writ petition.

[The judgment considers the pleadings, interim orders passed by the court and the submission of the parties before turning to the applicable tort law principle.]

[W]e are of the opinion that any principle evolved in this behalf should be simple, practical and suited to the conditions obtaining in this country. We are convinced that the law stated by this court in *Oleum Gas Leak Case* (*M.C. Mehta v Union of India* AIR 1986 SC 1086) is by far the more appropriate one—apart from the fact that it is binding upon us. (We have disagreed with the view that the law stated in the said decision is *obiter*). According to this rule, once the activity carried on is hazardous or inherently dangerous, the person carrying on such activity is liable to make good the loss caused to any other person by his activity *irrespective* of the fact whether he took reasonable care while carrying on his activity. The rule is premised upon the very nature of the activity carried on. In the words of the Constitution Bench, such an activity:

... can be tolerated only on condition that the enterprise engaged in such hazardous or inherently dangerous activity indemnifies all those who suffer on account of the carrying on of such hazardous or inherently dangerous activity regardless of whether it is carried on carefully or not.

The Constitution Bench has also assigned the reason for stating the law in the said terms. It is that the enterprise (carrying on the hazardous or inherently dangerous activity) alone has the resource to discover and guard against hazards or dangers— and not the person affected *and* the practical difficulty (on the part of the affected person) in establishing the absence of reasonable care or that the damage to him was foreseeable by the enterprise.

Once the law in *Oleum Gas Leak case* is held to be the law applicable, it follows, in the light of our findings recorded here in before, that Respondents 4 to 8 are absolutely liable to compensate for the harm caused by them to the villagers in the affected area, to the soil and to the underground water and hence, they are bound to take all necessary measures to remove the sludge and other pollutants lying in the affected area ... and also to defray the cost of the remedial measures required to restore the soil and the underground water sources. Sections 3 and 4 of Environment (Protection) Act confers upon the Central Government the power to give directions of the above nature and to the above effect. Levy of costs required for carrying out remedial measures is implicit in Sections 3 and 4 which are couched in very wide and expansive language. Appropriate directions can be given by this court to the Central Government to invoke and exercise those powers with such modulations as are called for in the facts and circumstances of this case.

* * *

NOTES AND QUESTIONS

1. Although the Public Liability Insurance Act of 1991 and the National Environment Tribunal Act of 1995 ('NETA') were on the statute book when the *Bichhri Case* was decided, the court makes no reference to these laws. Is the judgment *per incuriam*? Do these provisions strengthen the Supreme Court's reasoning or do they militate against the opinion?

2. NETA was not in force on the date of judgment in *Bichhri*. Possibly, in the assessment of the Central Government which was responsible for bringing the law into force, the time was not ripe for introducing the new standard. Should this have persuaded the court to reject the absolute liability standard?

3. Confronted by the strong language of Chief Justice Misra in the *Bhopal Review Case* where he finds the *Shriram* 'absolute liability' standard to be in the nature of a passing observation and therefore not binding, the *Bichhri* court disagrees with the Misra opinion and notes 'the majority judgment delivered by M.N. Venkatachaliah, J. ... has not expressed any opinion on the issue.'

4. Do the vacillations on the question of absolute liability—*Shriram, Bhopal Review, Bichhri*—suggest a preference for expediency over principle? Bear in mind the broad objective of the court in each case.

5. In its operative order, the court relegated the Bichhri villagers to the remedy of individual suits for compensation. Should not the court, in exercise of its expansive jurisdiction under Article 21, have awarded compensation in the writ proceedings? What are the pitfalls in adopting a summary procedure?

6. In a part of the judgment not excerpted above, the Supreme Court surveyed developments to the *Rylands* rule. In England, the rule continues to afford an independent head for claiming damages whereas in Australia the rule is absorbed in the tort of negligence.

7. In the *Vellore Case*,[37] the Supreme Court bench presided over by Justice Kuldip Singh referred to the absolute liability principle in the context of pollution caused by the discharge of untreated effluent by industries in Tamil Nadu. This case did not involve an industrial accident nor did it concern the escape or discharge of a toxic substance—which constitute the class of cases to which 'absolute liability' is applied. The *Vellore* court, however, rolled together the 'polluter pays principle' (applicable to *non-toxic* pollution cases) with the absolute liability standard (applicable to *toxic* torts). 'The "Polluter Pays Principle" as interpreted by this court [in *Bichhri*] means that the absolute liability for harm to the environment extends not only to compensate the victims of pollution but also the cost of restoring the environmental degradation.'[38] Is the extension of 'absolute liability' to non-toxic pollution cases justified? On what principle?

---

[37] *Vellore Citizens Welfare Form v Union of India* AIR 1996 SC 2715.
[38] *Id.* at 2721. Also see *M.C. Mehta v Union of India (Taj Trapezium)* AIR 1997 SC 734.

B. PUBLIC NUISANCE

A public nuisance may be broadly defined as an unreasonable interference with a general right of the public. Because a public nuisance interferes with a public right, it is not tied to interference with the enjoyment and use of property; and remedies against a public nuisance are, therefore, available to every citizen.

Section 268 of the Indian Penal Code of 1860 defines the offence of a public nuisance:

A person is guilty of a public nuisance who does any act or is guilty of an illegal omission which causes any common injury, danger or annoyance to the public or to the people in general who dwell or occupy property in the vicinity, or which must necessarily cause injury, obstruction, danger or annoyance to persons who may have occasion to use any public right.

The section also provides that '[a] common nuisance is not excused on the ground that it causes some convenience or advantage.'

Persons who conduct 'offensive' trades and thereby pollute the air, or cause loud and continuous noises that affect the health and comfort of those dwelling in the neighbourhood are liable to prosecution for causing a public nuisance. The penalty for this offence is merely Rs.200, which makes it pointless for a citizen to initiate a prosecution under section 268 by a complaint to a magistrate.[39]

A much better course would be to utilize the remedies provided in sections 133 to 144 of the Code of Criminal Procedure of 1973. Section 133 provides an independent, speedy and summary remedy against public nuisance.[40] The section empowers a magistrate to pass a 'conditional order' for the removal of a public nuisance within a fixed period of time.[41] The magistrate may act on information received from a police report or any other source including a complaint made by a citizen.[42] Although the magistrate's power to issue a conditional order under section 133 appears discretionary, the Supreme Court has interpreted the language to be

---

[39] A complaint may be made under section 190 of the Code of Criminal Procedure of 1973.

[40] A magistrate has no jurisdiction under section 133 to entertain private disputes between neighbours. For example, a flour mill that only disturbed a neighbouring family but no other residents in the locality, constituted a private nuisance actionable in tort and not a public nuisance. *Dhareppa Ballapa Gondai v Sub-Divisional Magistrate* 1984 (2) KAR.L.J. 444, 449–450.

[41] The order is 'conditional' because it is only a preliminary order. The order may be made absolute (final) only after giving the opposing party sufficient opportunity to be heard. The Kerala High Court has held that an order closing a polluting factory is illegal where no conditional order was first issued. *Vallikadar Assainar v P.K. Moideenkutty* 1999 CRI. L.J. 4228.

[42] For example, in *K. Ramachandra Mayya v District Magistrate* 1985 (2) KAR.L.J. 289, the High Court approved of the magistrate's order shutting down a stone quarry, where the magistrate acted on complaints from neighbouring residents that the blasting of rocks at the quarry caused damage from flying stone chips.

mandatory.[43] Once a magistrate has before him evidence of a public nuisance, he must order removal of the nuisance, within a fixed time.[44]

The person directed to remove the nuisance (the opposite party) must either comply with the order or show cause against it. Where he or she opposes the order, the court must initiate an inquiry and call on the parties to adduce evidence. Moreover, to assist the inquiry, the magistrate may direct a local investigation to ascertain facts or summon expert witnesses. If measures are necessary to prevent imminent danger or serious injury to the public, the court may issue an injunction pending an inquiry. When a person fails to appear and show cause, or when the court is satisfied on the evidence adduced that the initial order was proper, the order is made final. Otherwise it is vacated.

Failure to comply with a final order within the specified time attracts the penalty provided by section 188 of the Indian Penal Code for disobedience of an order of a public servant. Further, the court may carry out the order and recover costs from the defaulter. A magistrate is also empowered to prohibit repetition or continuance of a public nuisance.

A magistrate, however, may not pass a final order that exceeds the conditional order in scope. For instance, in *Gobind Singh v Shanti Sarup*[45] the conditional order required a baker to demolish within 10 days an oven and chimney that emitted smoke 'injurious to the health and physical comfort of the people living or working in the proximity.' In the final order, the magistrate went beyond the conditional order and completely prohibited the baker from carrying on his trade. The Supreme Court found the final order far too broad and narrowed its scope to require the baker to demolish the offending oven and chimney within a month. The baker, however, was allowed to practice his trade.

Are the powers of a magistrate to deal with pollution under section 133 curtailed by the Air (Prevention and Control of Pollution) Act of 1981 or the Water (Prevention and Control of Pollution) Act of 1974? In *Nagarjuna Paper Mills Ltd. v Sub-Divisional Magistrate and Divisional Officer, Sangareddy,*[46] the Andhra Pradesh High Court considered a petition from a magistrate's conditional order shutting down a paper mill that had failed to take adequate pollution control measures. The mill challenged the order, claiming that the state pollution control board had exclusive power to regulate air and water pollution. Rejecting this argument, the High Court upheld the magistrate's power to regulate pollution by restraining a public nuisance. This view was also adopted by a division bench of the Kerala High Court in *Krishna Panicker v Appukuttan Nair,*[47] overruling a contrary opinion expressed in *Tata Tea Ltd. v State of Kerala.*[48]

---

[43] *Municipal Council, Ratlam v Vardhichand* AIR 1980 SC 1622.

[44] In urgent cases, a magistrate may direct the *immediate* removal of a nuisance. *Supra* note 42 at 295. Also see section 145 of the Code of Criminal Procedure of 1973.

[45] AIR 1979 SC 143.

[46] 1987 CRI.L.J.2071.

[47] 1993 (1) KER. L.T. 771.

[48] 1984 KER. L.T. 645.

In *Municipal Council, Ratlam v Vardhichand,* excerpted below, the Supreme Court for the first time treated an environmental problem differently from an ordinary tort or public nuisance. Environmental pollution in *Ratlam* affected a large community of poor people and arose from a combination of diffuse causes: private polluters, slack and under-financed enforcement agencies, and haphazard town planning. In view of these peculiarities, the court tailored the existing public nuisance remedy to provide relief.

The judgment explicitly recognizes the impact of a deteriorating urban environment on the poor, and links the provision of basic public health facilities to both human rights and the directive principles in the Constitution. The court commends an activist judiciary to compel municipalities to provide proper sanitation and drainage, thereby enabling the poor to live with dignity.

Although the language of Justice Krishna Iyer is flowery in parts, the judgment is notable for the principles it enunciates. Notice the court's interpretation of the nature of a magistrate's power under section 133; the court's response to the municipality's plea of budgetary constraints; and the relief granted by the court.

MUNICIPAL COUNCIL, RATLAM v VARDHICHAND
AIR 1980 SC 1622

KRISHNA IYER, J.:

The key question we have to answer is whether by affirmative action a court can compel a statutory body to carry out its duty to the community by constructing sanitation facilities at great cost and on a time-bound basis. At issue is the coming of age of that branch of public law bearing on community actions and the court's power to force public bodies under public duties to implement specific plans in response to public grievances.

[The court described conditions of filth and stench resulting from the absence of public sanitation facilities or drains.]

The Sub-Divisional Magistrate, Ratlam, was moved to take action under S. 133 Cr. P.C. to abate the nuisance by ordering the municipality to construct drain pipes with flow of water to wash the filth and stop the stench. The Magistrate found the facts proved, made the direction sought and scared by the prospect of prosecution under Section 188 I.P.C. for violation of the order under S. 133 Cr. P.C., the municipality rushed from court to court till, at last, years after, it reached this court as the last refuge of lost causes. Had the municipal council and its executive officers spent half this litigative zeal on cleaning up the street and constructing the drains by rousing the people's sramdan resources and laying out the city's limited financial resources, the people's needs might have been largely met long ago.

The Magistrate, whose activist application of S. 133, Cr. P.C. for the larger purpose of making the Ratlam municipal body do its duty and abate the nuisance by affirmative action, has our appreciation. [The court reproduced lengthy extracts from the Magistrate's order describing the extremely unhygenic and insanitary conditions in a locality of Ratlam and the unsuccessful efforts of tormented residents to activate the municipality.]

The Magistrate held in the end:

Thus after perusing the evidence I come to this conclusion and after perusing the applications submitted by the persons residing on the New Road area from time to time to draw the attention of the non-applicants to remove the nuisance, the non-applicants have taken no steps whatsoever to remove all these public nuisances.

He issued the following order which was wrongly found unjustified by the Sessions court, but rightly upheld by the High Court:

Therefore, for the health and convenience of the people residing in that particular area all the nuisance must be removed and for that the following order is hereby passed:

(1)The Town Improvement Trust with the help of Municipal Council must prepare a permanent plan to make the proper flow in the said Nallah which is flowing in between Shastri Colony and New Road. Both the non-applicants must prepare the plan within six months and they must take proper action to give it a concrete form.

(2) According to para 13 a few places are described which are either having the same drains and the other area is having no drain and due to this the water stinks there; so the Municipal Council and the Town Improvement Trust must construct the proper drainage system and within their own premises where there is no drain it must be constructed immediately and all this work should be completed within six months.

(3) The Municipal Council should construct drains from the jail to the bridge behind the southern side of the houses so that the water flowing from the septic tanks and the other water flowing outside the residential houses may be channelised and it may stop stinking and it should have a proper flow so that the water may go easily towards the main Nallah. All these drains should be constructed completely within six months by the Municipal Council.

(4) The places where the pits are in existence the same should be covered with mud so that the water may not accumulate in those pits and it may not breed mosquitoes. The Municipal Council must complete this work within two months.

A notice under Section 141 of the Criminal Procedure Code (Old Code) may be issued to the non-applicants Nos. 1 and 2 so that all the works may be carried out within the stipulated period. Case is hereby finalised.

* * *

We proceed on the footing, as we indicated even when leave to appeal was sought, that the malignant facts of municipal callousness to public health and sanitation, held proved by the Magistrate, are true. What are the legal pleas to absolve the municipality from the court's directive under S. 133, Cr. P.C.? [The court set out section 133.]

So the guns of Section 133 go into action wherever there is public nuisance. The public power of the magistrate under the Code is a public duty to the members of the public who are victims of the nuisance, and so he shall exercise it when the jurisdictional facts are present as here. * * * Discretion becomes a duty when the beneficiary brings home the circumstances for its benign exercise.

If the order is defied or ignored, Section 188 I.P.C. come into penal play:

188. Whoever, knowing that, by an order promulgated by a public servant lawfully empowered to promulgate such order, he is directed to abstain from a certain act, or to take certain order with certain property in his possession or under his management, disobeys such direction and if such disobedience causes or tends to cause danger to human life, health or safety, or causes or tends to cause a riot or affray, shall be punished with imprisonment of either description for a term which may extend to six months, or with fine which may extend to one thousand rupees, or with both.

There is no difficulty in locating who has the obligation to abate the public nuisance caused by the absence of primary sanitary facilities. [The court set out section 123 of the M.P. Municipalities Act of 1961.]

The statutory setting being thus plain, the municipality cannot extricate itself from its responsibility. Its plea is not that the facts are wrong but that the law is not right because the municipal funds being insufficient it cannot carry out the duties under S. 123 of the Act. This 'alibi' made us issue notice to the State which is now represented by counsel ... before us. The plea of the municipality that notwithstanding the public nuisance financial inability validly exonerates it from statutory liability has no juridical basis. The Criminal Procedure Code operates against statutory bodies and others regardless of the cash in their coffers, even as human rights under Part III of the Constitution have to be respected by the State regardless of budgetary provision. Likewise, S. 123 of the Act has no saving clause when the municipal council is penniless. Otherwise a profligate statutory body or pachydermic governmental agency may legally defy duties under the law by urging in self-defence a self-created bankruptcy or perverted expenditure budget. That cannot be.

Section 133, Cr. P.C. is categoric, although reads discretionary. Judicial discretion when facts for its exercise are present, has a mandatory import. Therefore, when the Sub-Divisional Magistrate, Ratlam, has, before him, information and evidence, which disclose the existence of a public nuisance and on the materials placed, he considers that such unlawful obstruction or nuisance should be removed from any public place which may be lawfully used by the public, he shall act. Thus, his judicial power shall, passing through the procedural barrel, fire upon the obstruction or nuisance, triggered by the jurisdictional facts. The Magistrate's responsibility under S. 133 Cr. P.C. is to order removal of such nuisance with a time to be fixed in the order. This is a public duty implicit in the public power to be exercised on behalf of the public and pursuant to a public proceeding. Failure to comply with the direction will be visited with a punishment contemplated by S. 188, I.P.C. Therefore, the Municipal Commissioner or other executive authority bound by the order under S. 133, Cr. P.C. shall obey the direction because disobedience, if it causes obstruction or annoyance or injury to any persons lawfully pursuing their employment, shall be punished with simple imprisonment or fine as prescribed in the Section. The offence is aggravated if the disobedience tends to cause danger to human health or safety. The imperative tone of S. 133, Cr. P.C. read with the punitive temper of S. 188 I.P.C. makes the prohibitory act a mandatory duty.

* * *

We agree with the High Court in rejecting the plea that the time specified in the order is unworkable. The learned judges have rightly said:

It is unfortunate that such contentions are raised in 1979 when these proceedings have been pending since 1972. If in seven years' time the Municipal Council intended to remedy such a small matter there would have been no difficulty at all. Apart from it, so far as the directions are concerned, the learned Magistrate, it appears, was reasonable. So far as direction No. I is concerned, the learned Magistrate only expected the Municipal Council and the Town Improvement Trust to evolve a plan and to start planning about it within six months: the learned Magistrate has rightly not fixed the time limit within which that plan will be completed. Nothing more reasonable could be said about direction No. I.

A strange plea was put forward by the Municipal Council before the High Court which was justly repelled, viz., that the owners of houses had gone to that locality on their own choice with eyes open and, therefore, could not complain if human excreta was flowing, dirt was stinking, mosquitoes were multiplying and health was held hostage. A public body constituted for the principal statutory duty of ensuring sanitation and health cannot outrage the court by such an ugly plea. Luckily, no such contention was advanced before us. The request for further time for implementation of the magistrate's order was turned down by the High Court since no specific time-limit was accepted by the municipality for the fulfilment of the directions. A doleful statement about the financial difficulties of the municipality and the assurance that construction of drains would be taken up as soon as possible had no meaning. The High Court observed:

Such assurances, it appears, are of no avail as unfortunately these proceedings for petty little things like clearing of dirty water, closing the pits and repairing of drains have taken more than seven years and if these seven years are not sufficient to do the needful, one could understand that by granting some more time it could not be done.

The High Court was also right in rejecting the Additional Sessions Judge's recommendation to quash the Magistrate's order on the impression that Section 133, Cr. P.C. did not provide for enforcement of civic rights. Wherever there is a public nuisance, the presence of S. 133, Cr. P.C. must be felt and any contrary opinion is contrary to the law. In short, we have no hesitation in upholding the High Court's view of the law and affirmation of the Magistrate's order.

* * *

Three proposals have been put forward before us in regard to the estimated cost of the scheme as directed by the Magistrate. The Magistrate had not adverted to the actual cost of the scheme nor the reasonable time that would be taken to execute it. As stated earlier, it is necessary to ascertain how far the scheme is feasible and how heavy the cost is likely to be. The court must go further to frame a scheme and then fix time-limits and even oversee the actual execution of the scheme in compliance with the court's order.

* * *

In our view, what is important is to see that the worst aspects of the insanitary conditions are eliminated, not that a showy scheme beyond the means of the municipality must be undertaken and half done. From that angle we approve scheme 'C' which costs only around Rs.6 lakhs. We fix a time limit of one year for completing execution of the work according to that scheme. We further direct that the work shall begin within two months from today and the Magistrate shall inspect the progress of the work every three months broadly to be satisfied that the order is being implemented bona fide. Breaches will be visited with the penalty of S. 188, I.P.C.

We make the further supplementary directions which we specifically enjoin upon the municipal authority and the State Government to carry out.

1. We direct the Ratlam Municipal Council (RI) to take immediate action, within its statutory powers, to stop the effluents from the Alcohol Plant flowing into the street. The State Government also shall take action to stop the pollution. The Sub-Divisional Magistrate will also use his power under S. 133, I.P.C., to abate the nuisance so caused. Industries cannot make profit at the expense of public health. Why has the Magistrate not pursued this aspect?

2. The Municipal Council shall, within six months from today, construct a sufficient number of public latrines for use by men and women separately, provide water supply and scavenging service morning and evening so as to ensure sanitation. The health officer of the Municipality will furnish a report, at the end of the six-monthly term, that the work has been completed. We need hardly say that the local people will be trained in using and keeping these toilets in clean condition. Conscious co-operation of the consumers is too important to be neglected by representative bodies.

3. The State Government will give special instructions to the Malaria Eradication Wing to stop mosquito breeding in Ward 12. The Sub-Divisional Magistrate will issue directions to the officer concerned to file a report before him to the effect that the work has been done in reasonable time.

4. The municipality will not merely construct the drains but also fill up cesspools and other pits of filth and use its sanitary staff to keep the place free from

accumulations of filth. After all, what it lays out on prophylactic sanitation is a gain on its hospital budget.

5. We have no hesitation in holding that if these directions are not complied with the Sub-Divisional Magistrate will prosecute the officers responsible. Indeed, this court will also consider action to punish for contempt in case of report by the Sub-Divisional Magistrate of willful breach by any officer.

We are sure that the State Government will make available by way of loans or grants sufficient financial aid to the Ratlam Municipality to enable it to fulfil its obligations under this order. The State will realize that Art. 47 makes it a paramount principle of governance that steps are taken for the improvement of public health as amongst its primary duties. The municipality will also slim its budget on low priority items and elitist projects to use the savings on sanitation and public health. It is not our intention that the ward which has woken up to its rights alone need be afforded these elementary facilities. We expect all the wards to be benefited without litigation. The pressure of the judicial process, expensive and dilatory, is neither necessary nor desirable if responsible bodies are responsive to duties.

* * *

We dismiss this petition subject to the earlier mentioned modifications.

Petition dismissed.

NOTES AND QUESTIONS

1. The *Ratlam* judgment illustrates how an activist court can transform seemingly dull legislation into a powerful mandate to protect the environment. The judgment builds on two key interpretations. First, the court held that budgetary constraints did not absolve a municipality from performing its statutory obligation to provide sanitation facilities. Second, the court interpreted section 133 to impose a *mandatory* duty on a magistrate to remove a public nuisance *whenever* one exists. Reading these obligations together, the court supported the magistrate's order to compel the municipality to implement a sanitation scheme within a definite time frame.

Despite its vast potential, the *Ratlam* judgment remains under-used. Citizens' petitions to stir indolent municipalities into action are still rare. In another respect, however, the lead provided by *Ratlam* has been widely followed: Judicial activism now characterises the outcome of most environmental litigation.

2. In its judgment, the court condemned as an 'outrage' the municipality's plea that the affected persons came to the nuisance. Does the court's dictum also preclude a *private* respondent from raising this plea in a public nuisance case?

3. To ensure the implementations of its directions, the Supreme Court relied on a number of methods: Judicial oversight, deadlines, the threat of prosecution under section 188 of the Indian Penal Code, and the threat to use its power to punish

for contempt (the disobedience of a court order). But a critical weakness remained. Where were the funds to finance the sanitation scheme to come from? The judgment merely expressed the hope that the state government would assist the municipality, and required the municipality to slim its budget on 'low priority items and elitist projects'. What could the court have done if the state government had declined to grant any financial aid? Could the court have ordered an appropriation of funds?

4. The primary duty of a municipality to provide sanitation may also be enforced through a writ petition. Compare the *Ratlam* judgment with the Rajasthan High Court's order in *Rampal's Case,* which is excerpted later in this chapter.

In *P. C. Cherian v State of Kerala,* excerpted below, the Kerala High Court considered whether carbon particles ('carbon black') emitted from two rubber factories amounted to an actionable public nuisance under section 133. Note the court's willingness to take judicial notice of the health effects of air pollution and the court's exercise in balancing the community interest against the interest of the workers keeping their jobs.

P.C. CHERIAN v STATE OF KERALA
1981 KER.L.T. 113

JANAKI AMMA, J.:   * * *

Although the petitioners denied that their factories were responsible for the deposit of carbon black in the neighbourhood, there are documents produced which clearly make out a case of pollution at their instance. Ext. A3 in M.C. No. 4 of 1978 is a letter written by the Production Manager of the Padinjarekkara Factory to the Parish priest, of the Veroor Catholic Church. In that letter the manager undertook to do all that was possible for the prevention of carbon black flying and invited from the priest suggestions other than those involving stoppage of work. Ext. A4 is the proceedings of a conference convened by the concerned Ministers which was attended by the representatives of the two factories meant for the stoppage of pollution due to black carbon. There is also evidence that the petitioners undertook to defray the expenses incurred by the St. Joseph's Church for removal of the carbon deposits on the walls of the Church. In the face of the above evidence the findings in the two cases that carbon black was emanating from the factories of the petitioners contaminating the atmosphere and was causing deposits of carbon in the neighbourhood do not call for interference. That the devices stated to have been adopted by the two factories to prevent black carbon from escaping in the atmosphere are grossly inadequate is also established beyond doubt.

The further question is whether there is weight in the contention that carbon has no toxic effect on human body and dissemination of carbon is not a public nuisance. It is sheer commonsense that if the atmosphere gets contaminated with carbon particles, visible or invisible, there is every risk that they would get themselves deposited on the bodies, and get into the respiratory organs of the people residing in the neighbourhood. The evidence is that the particles get deposited on the wearing apparel of the people and the walls of buildings, not to mention the other umpteen articles which may get affected by the deposit. This is therefore an outstanding instance of air pollution which has become a menace to people in the industrial cities. The term air pollution according to the definition adopted by the W. H. O., is limited to the situations in which the outdoor ambient atmosphere contains materials in concentrations which are harmful to man and his environment. 'Air pollution has been shown to increase the incidences of emphysema, bronchitis, pneumonia and asthma. It is suspected of being an ancillary cause of lung cancer and arteriosclerosis. Air pollution obscures vision, damages buildings, destroys crops and alters weather' (See Environmental Legislation by Williams and Hurley page 34). The Supreme Court remarked in *Ratlam Municipality v Vardhichand* (AIR 1980 SC 1622):

> Public nuisance, because of pollutants being discharged by big factories to the detriment of the poorer sections, is a challenge to the social justice component of the rule of law.

To hold that the deposit of carbon black in the instant cases is a public nuisance it need not necessarily be a hazard to the health of the people. The word public nuisance is not defined in the Code; but S. 2(y) of the Code states that words and expressions not defined therein but defined in the Indian Penal Code have meanings respectively assigned to them in that Code. [Section] 268 of the Indian Penal Code defines public nuisance as follows:

> Public nuisance: A person is guilty of a public nuisance, who does any act or is guilty of an illegal omission which causes any common injury, danger or annoyance to the public or to the people in general who dwell or occupy property in the vicinity, or which must necessarily cause injury, obstruction, danger or annoyance to persons who may have occasion to use any public right.

Thus, under the definition any act which causes annoyance to the public is a public nuisance. There is no scope for doubt that carbon black on the clothes of the residents which make them soiled, and their deposit on food articles would cause annoyance to their owners. The manner in which the work in the factories of the petitioners was being conducted amounted to a public nuisance and was also injurious to the health and physical comfort of the community.

An argument was advanced at the time of hearing that there is no evidence as to which of the two factories involved was responsible for the emanation of carbon and the court only proceeded on the footing that it was the carbon black from the two factories together that was causing nuisance. This does not appear to be correct. The court has entered separate findings in the two cases that the working of the concerned factory, viz., the service mixing in large quantities of carbon for supplying major tyre factories is injurious to the physical comfort of the community.

The argument based on the decision in *Ram Autar v State of UP* (AIR 1962 SC 1794), that the stoppage of work of the factories would deprive the workers there of their means of livelihood has no application in the cases before us because the danger that the general public has to face by the service mixing of carbon without adequate equipments to prevent dissemination of carbon outweighs the advantage in the form of jobs for a few persons and that too under threat of hazards to their own health.

We have no hesitation in holding that the magistrate was justified in invoking his powers under S. 133 of the Code, in initiating action against the petitioners and in directing them to stop the service mixing of carbon in their factories. We, however, make it clear that it is open to the petitioners to restart the work of service mixing of carbon after introducing gadgets or equipments which would prevent dissemination of carbon black into the atmosphere. In order to avoid further trouble and a repetition of similar action against them they may choose the equipments in consultation with qualified experts in the field of environmental hygiene and to the satisfaction of the authorities concerned.

The Criminal Revision Petitions are dismissed with the above directions.

NOTES AND QUESTIONS

1. The court weighed the danger to the general public from the continued 'service mixing of carbon' against the loss of jobs for a few workers, and found that the former outweighs the latter. Is such balancing permissible under section 133? Does the Supreme Court's interpretation in *Ratlam* (that section 133 imposes a *mandatory* duty on the magistrate to abate a public nuisance), preclude such a balancing exercise?

2. Although the court held that it was not necessary to establish toxicity before restraining a public nuisance (mere annoyance to the public was enough), it went on to observe that carbon black was, indeed, injurious to the public health. The court's conclusion on the toxicity of carbon black was supported, not by scientific proof, but by 'sheer common sense'. The court reasoned: (a) that carbon particles cause air pollution; (b) that air pollution has been shown to increase the incidences of emphysema, bronchitis, pneumonia and asthma and is suspected of being an ancillary cause of lung cancer and arteriosclerosis; and (c) therefore, carbon particles are hazardous to health. The court's reasoning appears flawed, as it does not follow from (a) and (b) that *every* air pollutant harms health. Was judicial notice of the possible health effects of suspended carbon particles justifiable in this case?

C. THE WRIT JURISDICTION

I. SOURCE OF THE WRIT JURISDICTION

Articles 32 and 226 of the Constitution of India empower the Supreme Court and the High Courts, respectively, to issue directions or orders or writs, including writs of *habeas corpus, mandamus, prohibition, quo warranto* and *certiorari*. Writs of mandamus, certiorari and prohibition are generally resorted to in environmental matters.

The relative speed, simplicity and cheapness of the writ remedy have made it immensely popular with litigants. Ordinarily, the delay between the filing of a writ petition and the granting of a writ is far less than the time required to obtain a decree in a suit;[49] and in writs there are fewer intervening proceedings between filing and judgment. The filing fee for a writ is nominal compared with the high *ad valorem* court fees[50] that must be paid in an ordinary civil suit. In addition, the expense of presenting oral evidence is eliminated as facts are set forth in the affidavits of the parties. Further, approaching the highest courts directly for a writ reduces the likelihood of prolonged litigation in subsequent appeals.

The power to issue writs has been borrowed in India from England, where the prerogative writs have been issued for centuries. Prior to the Constitution's adoption, the three High Courts at Calcutta, Madras and Bombay, had the power to issue these writs under the Charter Act of 1861.[51] Other High Courts did not possess this power. The Constituent Assembly, which created India's Constitution, saw these writs as an effective means of enforcing fundamental rights, and consequently conferred on the Supreme Court and all the High Courts the power to issue these writs.[52]

The Supreme Court has interpreted Article 21, which guarantees the fundamental right to life and personal liberty, to include the right to a wholesome environment.[53] Accordingly, a litigant may assert his or her right to a healthful environment against the state, by a writ petition to either the Supreme Court or a High Court.

II. WRITS OF MANDAMUS, PROHIBITION AND CERTIORARI

The writ powers of the Supreme Court and the High Courts under Articles 32 and 226 are not confined to the prerogative writs derived from English law but extend to 'directions or orders or *writs in the nature of* habeas corpus, mandamus, prohibition, quo warranto and certiorari.' The term 'writs in the nature of' widens the court's discretion in granting relief by releasing Indian courts from the procedural technicalities that govern the issue of these writs under English Law.[54] A court may issue an order in the nature of these writs in all appropriate cases so long as it observes the broad and fundamental principles that govern such writs in English law.[55] The court may also

---

[49] For example, in the Bombay High Court the delay in a writ petition is 6 years compared to over 15 years for a suit.

[50] Fees related to the value of the suit.

[51] The Indian High Courts Act of 1861 is popularly called the Charter Act. For a discussion on the source of the writ jurisdiction, see the judgment of Madon, J. in *Prabodh Verma v State of Uttar Pradesh* AIR 1985 SC 167, 182.

[52] H. Seervai, *Constitutional Law of India: A Critical Commentary* 1450 (Vol 2, 1993).

[53] *Subhash Kumar v State of Bihar* AIR 1991 SC 420; and *Virendra Gaur v State of Haryana* AIR 1995 SC 577.

[54] M. Jain & S. Jain, *Principles of Administrative Law* 513 (1986).

[55] *T. C. Basappa v T. Nagappa* AIR 1954 SC 440, 443.

issue directions and orders to vindicate the petitioner's rights. The court may grant declaratory relief,[56] issue an injunction or quash the impugned action without recourse to a specific writ. Indeed, a notable feature of the writ process is the court's flexibility in choosing an appropriate relief.

A court can issue a writ of mandamus to command action by a public authority when an authority is vested with power and wrongfully refuses to exercise it. A mandamus can also be issued to undo what has been done in contravention of a statute. This writ can issue against an administrative, quasi-judicial or judicial authority.[57]

An applicant seeking a mandamus must show that the duty sought to be enforced is a duty of a public nature (i.e., a duty created under the Constitution, a statute or some rule of common law) and that the duty is mandatory and not discretionary in nature. Normally a mandamus does not lie against a private individual, but it might be issued where it is proved that the individual was colluding with a public authority.[58] Before a mandamus is issued, the court must be satisfied that the petitioner had demanded justice and that the concerned authority had refused the demand.[59]

For instance, a mandamus would lie against a municipality that fails to construct sewers and drains, clean streets and clear garbage. Likewise, a state pollution control board may be compelled to take action against an industry discharging pollutants beyond the permissible level.

Rampal's Case, excerpted below, illustrates the use of the writ process in securing government action to improve the urban environment. It also shows the simplicity of the writ procedure compared with the more cumbersome prosecution of a suit to enforce common law rights.

RAMPAL v STATE OF RAJASTHAN
AIR 1981 RAJ 121

ORDER:

The petitioners are residents of Mundara Mohalla, situated in the town of Mandal in Bhilwara District. Their case is that in Mundara Mohalla, there is a blind lane and a common Chowk in the centre, which is surrounded by the houses of the petitioners and others. The petitioners' grievance is that water of domestic use, including dirty water from the houses of the Mohalla, as also rain water has collected in the chowk and because there is no drain for the discharge of the accumulated water, there is growth of moss and insects and there is possibility of spread of epidemics. The petitioners have relied upon a letter written in this connection by the Medical and Health Officer, Government Hospital, Bhilwara, on 18 June 1979, to the Executive Officer of the Municipal Board, Mandal inviting his attention to the fact that stagnant water, which

---

[56] *Kavalappara Kottarathil Kochuni v State of Madras* AIR 1959 SC 725, 732–733.
[57] M. Jain & S. Jain, *supra* note 54, at 520.
[58] *Sohan Lal v Union of India* AIR 1957 SC 529, 532.
[59] *Saraswati Industrial Syndicate Ltd. v Union of India* AIR 1975 SC 460, 468.

has collected in the common chowk of the Mundara Mohalla, has become the breeding place of mosquitoes and insects and may cause the spread of diseases. The Medical and Health Officer in his aforesaid letter expressed the view that immediate steps should be taken for making a permanent arrangement for the disposal of such water as has collected in the chowk and which has caused a nuisance, for the residents of the area. As the Municipal Board has not cared to take any action in the matter, the petitioners have filed a writ of Mandamus praying for a direction to the Municipal Board for removal and discharge of filthy and dirty water and the construction of proper drainage or sewers for the discharge of such water.

Section 98 of the Rajasthan Municipalities Act, 1959 ... falls under Chapter VI which deals with the primary and secondary functions of the Municipal Boards. Amongst the primary duties enumerated in Section 98 of the Act, it has been provided that the Municipal board should make reasonable provisions for cleaning public streets, places and sewers and all spaces not being private property and removing noxious vegetation and removing filth, rubbish or other noxious and offensive matter and constructing drains, sewers, drainage works etc. [The court set out the relevant provisions of Section 98.]

For the proper performance of duties imposed upon the Municipal Boards under Section 98 of the Act, all sewers, drains, privies, water closets, house-gullies and cesspools within the municipality have been placed under the survey and control of the Municipal Boards by the provisions of Section 174 of the Act and under Section 175 of the Act the Boards have been authorized to construct covered sewers and drains and make other constructions in order to carry out any drainage scheme. The boards are also authorised to control the drainage system in respect of private houses under Section 176 and the owners of houses and empty buildings and land within the municipality are enjoined to connect their sewers and drains with the municipal drains. Thus, under S. 174 to 187, extensive powers have been given to the Municipal Boards for the purpose of maintaining cleanliness within the municipal area by repairing the existing drains, directing the construction of new drains and controlling the drainage system. The Municipal Boards are thus primarily responsible for maintaining sanitation and for taking proper steps for creating and maintaining healthy conditions within the municipal area.

The Municipal Board, Mandal has not filed any reply and it has not been contended by its learned counsel that it is not the duty of the Municipal board to remove or discharge the accumulated water and construct proper drainage system for the discharge of water accumulated in the chowk in Mundara Mohalla.

The only question, therefore, which arises for consideration in this writ petition is as to whether this court should issue a Mandamus to the Municipal Board to construct the sewers and drains for the discharge of domestic including dirty water, as well as rain water. In *Municipal Corporation v Advance Builders (P.) Ltd.* (AIR 1972 SC 793), it was held by their Lordships of the Supreme Court that since development and planning is primarily for the benefit of the public, the local body was under an obligation to perform its duty in accordance with the provisions of the Act. In the present case also, the statute imposes a duty upon the Municipal Boards and they are under a statutory obligation to perform such duties enumerated in Section 98 of the Act in accordance with the provisions in Chapter IX of the Act relating to drainage. It may be pointed out that the Municipal Board has no discretion in the matter and it cannot refuse to discharge the obligations, duties and functions, which have been imposed upon it and are enumerated in Section 98 as primary functions. When the statute imposes a duty, the performance and non-performance of which is not a matter of discretion, then this court has a power to issue a mandamus directing the local body to do what the statute requires to be done. The Municipal Board is under a statutory obligation to construct sewers and drains for the discharge of water, both domestic as well as rain, which is likely to cause public nuisance, if allowed to accumulate for a long time. There can be no doubt that if the water and the filth is allowed to accumulate for a long time the place would become the breeding ground for mosquitoes, insects and is liable to become cause for spread of diseases. In these circumstances, it would be proper and reasonable in the present case if the Municipal Board is directed to perform its statutory duties in this respect.

The writ petition is, accordingly, allowed and the Municipal Board, Mandal is directed to remove the water and filth collected in the chowk in Mundara Mohalla, Mandal by the construction of proper sewers and drains, so as to remove the cause of possible nuisance in the locality, within a period of three months. As the Municipal Board has not opposed the writ petition, the parties are left to bear their own costs.

Petition allowed.

NOTES AND QUESTIONS

1. Had the municipality pleaded an inability to construct the drain because of a lack of finances, should the court have refused relief?

2. Apart from a writ petition, what other legal remedies could Rampal have pursued to secure the same relief?

3. In *E. Sampath Kumar v Government of Tamil Nadu*,[60] the Madras High Court held that a neighbour troubled by the excessive noise pollution and vibrations caused by electrical motors, diesel engines and generators used by a hotel, could maintain a writ petition. The High Court rejected the hoteliers' plea that the proper remedy would be a civil suit. The court issued several directions to abate the nuisance and directed the authorities to periodically inspect the hotel.

The writs of certiorari and prohibition are designed to restrain public authorities from acting in excess of their authority. Certiorari is an order to an inferior court or quasi-judicial body to transmit the record of pending proceedings to the superior court for its review. Prohibition prevents a lower court or tribunal from assuming a

[60] 1998 AIHC 4498.

jurisdiction which it does not possess. The expansion of the concept of natural justice and the emergence of the 'fairness' requirement even in administrative functions, has blurred the distinction between quasi-judicial and administrative functions.[61] Certiorari and prohibition are now regarded as general remedies against an improper exercise of power by administrative as well as quasi-judicial authorities.[62]

The writs of certiorari and prohibition are issued where an authority (1) acts in excess of jurisdiction; (2) acts in violation of the rules of natural justice; (3) acts under a law which is unconstitutional; (4) commits an error apparent on the face of the record; and (5) reaches factual findings that are not supported by the evidence.[63] The fundamental distinction between certiorari and prohibition is that they are issued at different stages of the proceedings. Prohibition is issued when the matter is pending before an authority. The writ prohibits the concerned authority from proceeding any further with the matter. Certiorari is issued only after the concerned authority has decided the question before it.

For example, a writ of certiorari will lie against a municipal authority that considers a builder's application and permits construction contrary to development rules such as a height restriction, or that disregards zoning requirements and wrongly sanctions an office building in an area reserved for a garden. Certiorari would also lie against a state pollution control board that considers the application of an industry and wrongly permits it to discharge effluents beyond prescribed levels.

III. LIMITATIONS ON THE WRIT JURISDICTION

Although Articles 32 and 226 give the courts wide latitude to grant relief, the courts have imposed restraints on their own writ power. These pertain to the petitioner's standing to institute proceedings *(locus standi),* the exhaustion of alternative remedies, the principle of *res judicata,* and the time within which a writ may be sought (laches).

Neither Article 32 nor Article 226 describe who may seek redress from the courts. The rules of locus standi in relation to writs are judicial policies. Traditionally, locus standi was restrictive: Only an 'aggrieved person' could petition the courts for a writ of certiorari, prohibition or mandamus. Until the early 1980s, only the person directly affected by the administrative action in question could challenge it.[64] According to this view, a person could assert a public right or interest only by showing that he or she had suffered an injury not suffered by others. During the 1980s, the Supreme Court recognized that where a public wrong or public injury is caused by the state, any member of the public acting in good faith can maintain an action for redress.[65] In particular, any member of the public may approach the court on behalf of a person or

---

[61] *A.K. Kraipak v Union of India* AIR 1970 SC 150, 154.

[62] M. Jain & S. Jain, *supra* note 54, at 525.

[63] *Id.*

[64] *Calcutta Gas Company (Prop.) Ltd. v State of West Bengal* AIR 1962 SC 1044, 1047.

[65] *People's Union for Democratic Rights v Union of India* AIR 1982 SC 1473, 1483.

persons who have suffered a legal wrong and are unable themselves to petition the court by reason of poverty, disability, or their socially or economically disadvantaged position.[66] More than any other factor, the liberalization of the doctrine of standing in writ petitions has been responsible for the rapid growth in public interest litigation in India, and has provided easy access to the higher courts.

When a fundamental right, including the right to a wholesome environment, has been violated, relief through Articles 32 and 226 is fully appropriate. Where no fundamental right is involved, a High Court will decline to exercise its jurisdiction if an equally effective remedy is available and has not been used. The writ is an extraordinary remedy, and courts are reluctant to encourage petitioners who circumvent prescribed statutory procedure for correcting administrative action.[67] This rule of exhaustion of remedies can be waived by a court in a suitable case where, for instance, the impugned action violates the principles of natural justice, or where a government authority has exceeded its jurisdiction. The issue of an alternative remedy, however, is unlikely to arise in environmental writs, since existing environmental laws do not create alternative fora for dispute resolution or the redress of public grievances.[68] With the rapid increase in the complexity of environmental laws, the need for expertise in resolving environmental disputes may result in the establishment of special tribunals.[69] A beginning in this regard was made with the enactment of the National Environment Tribunal Act in 1995 and the National Environment Appellate Authority Act in 1997. Both these tribunals have a very limited jurisdiction confined to the adjudication of claims arising from hazardous industrial accidents (NETA) and disputes relating to project siting (NEAAA).[70] The National and State Coastal Management Authorities constituted in November 1998 may reduce the coastal ecology cases filed before the high courts. The authorities are empowered to investigate into violations of Coastal Zone Regulations and issue remedial directions.

A petitioner must pursue her remedy within a reasonable time of the cause of action arising, and a writ petition may be rejected on the ground of inordinate delay. This doctrine of *laches* has even been applied to petitions asserting a breach of a fundamental right, although the courts may be more indulgent when a fundamental right is involved and where the impugned action is manifestly erroneous or

---

[66] *Id.*

[67] e.g., the High Courts are reluctant to entertain disputes arising under the Income Tax Act of 1961, as the statute creates a hierarchy of authorities from which a person may obtain redress.

[68] By 'environmental writs' we mean petitions to abate pollution or prevent environmental degradation. Note that Section 28 of the Water Act and Section 31 of the Air Act provide the alternative remedy of administrative appeals to polluters who are dissatisfied with pollution control board decisions. Thus, a polluter's petition challenging a board decision may be resisted on the ground that an alternative remedy is available.

[69] The Supreme Court has suggested the establishment of environmental courts on a regional basis in *M.C. Mehta v Union of India* AIR 1987 SC 965 and *Indian Council for Enviro-Legal Action v Union of India* AIR 1996 SC 1446.

[70] At the time of writing NETA was not in force.

unauthorized. Where no prejudice is caused to the other party from the petitioner's lack of diligence, the courts generally measure the delay by referring to the statutory limitation for the filing of similar suits prescribed by the Limitation Act of 1963.

The doctrine of *laches* is often relaxed in environmental actions brought in the public interest. The court is usually indulgent, being aware of the financial constraints and obstacles that environmentalists face in obtaining authentic information and documentation.

The principle of *res judicata* has been applied to writ proceedings by judicial interpretation. Once a writ petition is rejected on its merits by the Supreme Court or a High Court, a subsequent writ petition cannot be moved in the same court on the same cause of action. Normally, *res judicata* also precludes a petition to the Supreme Court alleging the violation of a fundamental right, once the same petition has been dismissed on its merits by a High Court.[71]

IV. ARTICLES 32 AND 226

The Supreme Court's jurisdiction under Article 32 is more limited than the jurisdiction of the High Courts under Article 226. Article 32 guarantees the right to seek the Supreme Court's enforcement of fundamental rights. Moreover, Article 32 is itself a fundamental right and, therefore, cannot be abridged by legislation. An indispensable condition for invoking the Supreme Court's jurisdiction under Article 32 is the violation of a fundamental right conferred in Part III of the Constitution. Thus, an illegal government action that does not infringe a fundamental right cannot be challenged in writ proceedings under Article 32. In contrast, the writ jurisdiction of the High Courts under Article 226 may be invoked not only for the enforcement of a fundamental right but for 'any other purpose' as well. Ordinary legal rights may also be asserted through a writ petition in the High Court. For instance, although the freedom of trade, commerce and intercourse embodied in Article 301 is not a fundamental right and, therefore, cannot be enforced in a petition under Article 32,[72] such a right may be enforced in a High Court under Article 226. Invoking the High Court writ jurisdiction is the most popular method to obtain judicial review of administrative action. Article 226 cannot be curtailed by legislation, since it is a constitutional provision.

Thus, the Supreme Court and the High Courts have concurrent jurisdictions for the enforcements of fundamental rights. A person complaining of an infringement of fundamental rights may seek redress in either forum. As noted earlier, if the High Court is approached first, and the petition for relief is dismissed on its merits, the principle of *res judicata* will preclude a further petition to the Supreme Court under Article 32. The petitioner may, however, appeal to the Supreme Court under Article 133 or obtain special leave to appeal under Article 136.

Financial and tactical considerations influence the choice between the Supreme

---

[71] *Daryao v State of UP* AIR 1961 SC 1457, 1465, 1466.
[72] *Ram Chandra Palai v State of Orissa* AIR 1956 SC 298, 305.

Court and a High Court for an environmental writ petition. Typically, litigating in the Supreme Court is more expensive because of higher lawyers' fees and travel costs. Nevertheless, a petition challenging a programme or project which affects more than one state, such as a dam over a long river, should be moved in the Supreme Court. Ordinarily, High Court judges are reluctant to pass orders which might disrupt planning and investment outside their jurisdiction.[73] Supreme Court judges are more likely to examine the issue from a national perspective and pass orders affecting several states. Similarly, the Supreme Court is more likely to intervene in a project involving large investments, or connected with important government policy, such as the location of a nuclear power station. High Court judges tend to be more deferential to the legislature and the executive in such matters.

The crowding of the Supreme Court docket by a spate of environmental public interest litigations prompted the court to issue a notice to bar associations across the country, seeking their response on how to check the tide of petitions filed under Article 32.[74] In the *CRZ Notification Case*[75] the Supreme Court offered a partial solution to the problem: Since the High Courts were better placed to understand local conditions and the impact of environmental law violations, they ought to tackle issues which arise or pertain to the geographical areas within their respective states. Generally, the Supreme Court continues to entertain fresh public interest litigations under Article 32 where the issue involved has national implications or requires central monitoring such as the protection of forests[76] and the formulation of national guidelines for the proper collection and management of municipal solid waste (garbage). [77]

Finally, the nature of court orders in public interest litigation depends on the personality of the judge. The decision whether to petition under Article 32 or 226 is sometimes made after comparing the inclinations of the judges of the Supreme Court and the High Court who are likely to consider the petition.

V. JUDICIAL REVIEW AND SPECIAL CONSIDERATIONS

The scope of judicial review in environmental cases was explained by the Supreme Court in the *Calcutta Taj Hotel Case*,[78] where a group of citizens challenged the location of a hotel on the ground that the construction would interfere with the flight path of migratory birds. After referring to the constitutional provisions relating to environment, the court outlined the scope of judicial review thus:

---

[73] Normally, a writ issued by a High Court cannot run beyond its territorial jurisdiction. Nevertheless, a writ issued in one state can indirectly affect neighbouring states. For example, an injunction restraining development plans on a river in one state, could affect development activities in other states through which the river flows.

[74] *Howrah Ganatantrik Nagarik Samity v State of West Bengal* 1995 (5) SCALE 224.

[75] *Indian Council for Enviro-Legal Action v Union of India* 1996 (5) SCC 281, 301.

[76] *T.N. Godavarman Thirumulkpad v Union of India* AIR 1997 SC 1228.

[77] *Almitra Patel v Union of India* AIR 1998 SC 993.

[78] *Sachidanand Pandey v State of West Bengal* AIR 1987 SC 1109, 1115.

The least that the court may do is to examine whether appropriate considerations are borne in mind and irrelevancies excluded. In appropriate cases the court may go further but how much further must depend on the circumstances of the case. The court may always give necessary directions. However, the court will not attempt to nicely balance relevant considerations. When the question involved the nice balancing of relevant considerations, the court may feel justified in resigning itself to acceptance of the decision of the concerned authorities.

Likewise, in a challenge directed against the location of a thermal power station in the horticulture-rich Dahanu region on the coast of Maharashtra, the Supreme Court declined to interfere after holding that the court's role was restricted to examining whether the government had taken into account all relevant aspects and was not influenced by extraneous material in reaching its final decision.[79]

The broad language of Articles 32 and 226 has enabled the courts to fashion relief and pass orders consistent with their own assessment of the public interest and principles of equity. In a petition under Article 226, the High Court has jurisdiction over issues of both fact and law; but ordinarily such a petition is based on facts established by affidavit. A High Court's reluctance to receive evidence in an Article 226 proceeding is a rule of practice and not of jurisdiction.

In environmental disputes that involve complicated questions of fact to be resolved after recording evidence, a suit is the appropriate remedy, rather than a writ petition. For example, if pollution injures health, a suit for damages is appropriate since medical evidence and evidence to establish causation would have to be adduced.[80]

The Supreme Court may not refuse to entertain a petition under Article 32 merely because it involves disputed questions of fact.[81] A writ court wishing to inquire into a disputed question of fact has the inherent power to appoint a commission to adduce evidence on its behalf. In several public interest litigations, the Supreme Court and the High Courts have appointed fact-finding commissions to investigate the petition's allegations. For example, in *L.K. Koolwal v State of Rajasthan*[82] a citizen of Jaipur petitioned the Rajasthan High Court for a mandamus, directing the Jaipur Municipal Council to clean certain areas of the city. The court appointed a Commissioner to inspect the areas, and to report on the nature and extent of the problem. On the basis of the Commissioner's report, the court issued directions to clean the designated areas.

---

[79] *Dahanu Taluka Environment Protection Group v Bombay Suburban Electricity Supply Company Ltd.* 1991 (2) SCC 539, 541. Also see *Tehri Bandh Virodhi Sangarsh Samiti v State of Uttar Pradesh* 1992 Supp (1) SCC 44; and *Dr. Shivrao Shantaram Wagle v Union of India* AIR 1988 SC 952.

[80] A writ is also inappropriate in such a case because damages are not normally awarded under Articles 32 and 226.

[81] *Supra* note 56, at 734.

[82] AIR 1988 RAJ 2.

There is a large backlog of cases in most High Courts. In a writ petition in the Bombay High Court, at least six years will elapse between filing and judgment. Expedited petitions in this court take over two years to be heard. In the Delhi High Court the delay is eight to ten years. In environmental cases, such delays defeat the purpose of the writ petition unless appropriate interim orders are obtained at the admission stage. The interim order is usually an injunction against, or a direction to, an authority. Long delays in obtaining judgment highlight the importance of effective argument at the admission stage, where the crucial interim orders are issued.

A recent innovation in public interest litigations that has helped overcome judicial delays is the notion of a continuing mandamus. This technique involves securing compliance through periodic 'interim' directions. Here, the court does not formally admit the petition, but prods the recalcitrant agency to perform its duty within a time frame. The case is posted every few months to monitor the agency's performance and for further 'interim' directions.

D. STATUTORY REMEDIES

In addition to the common law and constitutional remedies discussed above, Parliament has provided special channels of redress in certain types of environmental cases. The Public Liability Insurance Act of 1991 (PLIA) and the National Environment Tribunal Act of 1995 (NETA) provide a summary remedy to the victims of a hazardous industrial accident. Both laws adopt a 'no-fault' liability standard, all but abolishing the defenses available to the owner of the hazardous facility, and create a speedy claims-disposal machinery. Under the PLIA, claims upto Rs. 25,000 may be filed before the district collector, with the jurisdiction for awarding larger amounts vesting in the national tribunal constituted under the ETA.

The National Environment Appellate Authority Act of 1997 creates an appellate forum where affected citizens may assail the environmental approval granted for siting a development project. The appellate authority examines the validity of decisions taken by the environment impact assessment (EIA) authority under the EIA regulations of 1994. This law, in tandem with the public hearing requirements under the EIA regulations, introduces a measure of transparency in the EIA procedure. It also provides a speedy dispute resolution mechanism to enable the project proponent to assess where he or she stands on environmental issues.

Until the enactment of the Environment (Protection) Act of 1986, the power to prosecute under Indian environmental laws belonged exclusively to the government. Citizens had no direct statutory remedy against a polluter who, for example, discharged an effluent beyond the permissible limit. Section 19 of the Environment Act brought about a change. Under this section, a citizen may prosecute an offender by a complaint to a magistrate. Prior to complaining, however, he or she must give the government 60 days notice of his or her intention to complain. This notice is intended to alert the government to the offence so that it may itself take appropriate remedial action.

Similar provisions allowing citizen participation in the enforcement of pollution laws are now found in section 43 of the Air Act as amended in 1987 and in section 49 of the Water Act as amended in 1988. Significantly, both of these amended sections also require pollution control boards to disclose relevant internal reports to a citizen seeking to prosecute a polluter. The ease of the writ procedure and the willingness of judges to adjudicate complex environmental issues on the basis of affidavit-evidence in public interest litigation has led to the neglect of the private prosecution machinery. Private prosecutions entail adherence to strict rules of evidence. Besides, those seeking to launch a private prosecution are discouraged by the sampling requirements under the pollution control laws which confer the power to draw the effluent samples exclusively on government officials. Pollution control board officials from Tamil Nadu, Karnataka and Maharashtra confirm that until January, 1999 there were no successful private prosecutions in their states.[83]

E. PUBLIC INTEREST LITIGATION

Since the 1980s, public interest litigation (PIL) has altered both the litigation landscape and the role of the higher judiciary in India. Instead of being asked to resolve private disputes, Supreme Court and High Court judges were asked to deal with public grievances over flagrant human rights violations by the state or to vindicate the public policies embodied in statutes or constitutional provisions. This new type of judicial business is collectively called 'public interest litigation.'[84] Most environmental actions in India fall within this class.

In a conventional dispute involving, for example, a breach of contract, litigation is a mode of dispute resolution between private parties. Such litigation has several characteristics: First, it is bipolar and adversarial. Second, the case has a retrospective orientation: The court must decide questions of fact and law pertaining to past events. Third, right and remedy are closely inter-related. Fourth, the lawsuit is bounded in time and effect. Judicial involvement ends with the determination of the disputed issues, and the impact is limited to the parties before the court. Fifth, the whole process is driven and controlled by the actions of the parties. The judge is a neutral umpire.

In a public interest case, the subject matter of litigation is typically a grievance against the violation of basic human rights of the poor and helpless or about the content or conduct of government policy. The petitioner seeks to champion a public cause for the benefit of all society. Again, the focus dictates the principal features of the litigation. First, since the litigation is not strictly adversarial, the scope of the controversy is flexible. Parties and official agencies may be joined (and even substituted) as the litigation unfolds; and new and unexpected issues may emerge to

---

[83] Presentations by the respective boards at a seminar 'Reforming Indian Environmental Laws', Nat. Law School of Ind. Univ. Bangalore, 30, 31 January 1999.

[84] The label 'social action litigation' is preferred by some jurists.

dominate the case. Second, the orientation of the case is prospective. The petitioner seeks to prevent an egregious state of affairs or an illegitimate policy from continuing into the future. Third, because the relief sought is corrective rather than compensatory, it does not derive logically from the right asserted. Instead, it is fashioned for the special purpose of the case, sometimes by a quasi-negotiating process between the court and the responsible agencies. Fourth, it is difficult to delimit the duration and effect of this new kind of litigation. Prospective judicial relief implies continuing judicial involvement. The parties often return to the court for fresh directions and orders. Finally, because the relief is sometimes directed against government policies, it may have impacts that extend far beyond the parties in the case. In view of these features, judges must play a large role in organizing and shaping the litigation and in supervizing the implementation of relief. This activist role of the PIL judge contrasts with the passive umpireship traditionally associated with judicial functions.[85]

I. EXPANDED STANDING AND THE EMERGENCE OF PIL IN INDIA

Public interest litigation in India was initiated and fostered by a few judges of the Supreme Court.[86] The method they used to redress public grievances was, to relax the traditional rules governing standing (*locus standi*). Standing is required to have a court hear one's case. Since a court will not hear a party unless he or she has a sufficient stake in the controversy, judicial perception of who has sufficient interest (i.e., 'the person aggrieved') is critical. The Supreme Court has lowered the standing barriers by widening the concept of 'the person aggrieved'.

Traditionally, only a person whose *own right* was in jeopardy was entitled to seek a remedy.[87] When extended to public actions, this meant that a person asserting a public right or interest had to show that he or she had suffered some special injury over and above what members of the public had generally suffered. Thus, diffuse public injuries such as air pollution affecting a large community were difficult to redress.

---

[85] See generally, Chayes, *The Role of the Judge in Public Law Litigation*, 89 Harvard Law Review 1281 (1976); Chayes, *Foreword: Public Law Litigation and the Burger Court*, 96 Harvard Law Review 4 (1982); and *Sheela Barse v Union of India* AIR 1988 SC 2211.

[86] The most notable contributions were made by Justice Krishna Iyer and Justice Bhagwati. From an international perspective, the evolution of 'public interest law' is an American contribution. Many trace its beginnings to the landmark desegregation decisions of the 1950s when the US Supreme Court required schools in southern American states to end racial segregation. See *Brown v Board of Education (Brown II)* 349 U.S. 294, 299 (1955). In the 1960s, major PIL centres in the US handled issues relating to civil rights and the problems of the poor. By the mid-1970s, long before its inception in India, PIL embraced such diverse issues as consumer protection, environmental protection, land use, occupational health and safety, health care, media access and employment benefits. During the 1980s, PIL declined in the United States. See generally, Chayes, *Id.*; and Cunningham, *Public Interest Litigation in Indian Supreme Court: A Study in the Light of American Experience,* 29 J.I.L.I. 494 (1987).

[87] There are several narrow but notable exceptions to this traditional rule. For example, any person can move a writ of *habeas corpus* for the production of a detained person; and a minor may sue through his or her parent or guardian.

Even under the traditional standing doctrine, a narrow exception has been available to citizens bringing environmental actions against local authorities. A rate payer,[88] for example, may compel municipal authorities to perform their public duties although the rate payer has suffered no individualized harm. Thus, a rate payer's right to challenge an illegal sanction to convert a building into a cinema was upheld by the Supreme Court in *K. Ramdas Shenoy v The Chief Officers, Town Municipal Council, Udipi.*[89]

The traditional view of standing also effectively prevented the grievances of India's poor from being heard by a court. Frequently, the poor and underprivileged are unwilling to assert their rights because of poverty, ignorance or fear of social or economic reprisals from dominant sections of the community. These disabilities could be reduced if, as in the case of a minor or a detained person, the law allowed a concerned citizen to sue on behalf of the underprivileged. The classical theory of *locus standi,* however, precludes such representation, and thereby keeps the grievances of the poor from reaching the courts.

Standing for the Poor and Oppressed: 'Representative Standing'

In the 1970s, two forces combined to erode the doctrinal limitations of standing. The first of these arose at the start of the decade with the spreading concern for social justice and the emergence of the legal aid movement. Justices Krishna Iyer and Bhagwati of the Supreme Court, who delivered the early judgments liberalizing standing, were also deeply involved in fostering legal service institutions for the weak and the poor.[90] Significantly, both judges served extra-judicially on the national Committee on Juridicare, which, in its final report in August, 1977, expressly recommended the broadening of the rule of *locus standi* as a means of encouraging PIL.[91] The report envisioned PIL as a channel, by which the poor and oppressed could gain access to the courts and to judge-fashioned remedies.

Donning their judicial robes, these judges then proceeded to implement the recommendation of their own report.[92] In cases involving the underprivileged, the Supreme Court began to override the procedural obstacles and technicalities that

---

[88] Someone who pays rate, cess or assessment on the value of his or her property. Rates are paid to the municipality and are applied to local public purposes.

[89] AIR 1974 SC 2177.

[90] Government of Gujarat, *Report of the Legal Aid Committee* (1971) (Chairperson: P.N. Bhagwati, then the Chief Justice of the Gujarat High Court); Government of India, Ministry of Law, Justice and Company Affairs, *Report of the Expert Committee on Legal Aid: Processual Justice to the People* (1973) (Chairperson: Justice V.R. Krishna Iyer).

[91] Government of India, Ministry of Law, Justice and Company Affairs, *Report on National Juridicare: Equal Justice-Social Justice,* 61 (1977) (The Committee on Juridicare was composed of Justice Bhagwati [Chairperson] and Justice Krishna Iyer [Member]).

[92] At least one Supreme Court judgment, delivered before the Juridicare Report, similarly urged an expansion of standing. 'Test litigations, *pro bono publico* and like broadened forms of legal proceedings are in keeping with the current accent on justice to the common man and a necessary disincentive to those who wish to bypass the real issues on the merits by suspect reliance on peripheral, procedural

had until then obstructed redress. Rather than reject a petition for lack of standing, the court chose to expand standing so that it could decide the substantive issues affecting the rights of the underprivileged.

This modification of the traditional rule of standing which permits the poor and oppressed to be represented by volunteers may be described as '*representative standing*'.[93] Representative standing cases in the Supreme Court have helped secure the release of bonded labourers,[94] obtain pension for retired government employees,[95] and improve the living conditions of inmates at a protective home for women.[96] In *Hussainara Khatoon v Home Secretary, State of Bihar*[97] the court implicitly recognized the standing of a public spirited lawyer to move a petition on behalf of 18 prisoners awaiting trials for very long periods in jails in the State of Bihar. The petition led to the discovery of over 80,000 prisoners,[98] some of whom had been languishing in prisons for periods longer than they would have served, if convicted.[99] Likewise, in *People's Union for Democratic Rights v Union of India*[100] the court allowed a group of social activists to petition on behalf of exploited government construction workers, who were being paid less than the statutory minimum wage. The court observed:

> Here the workmen whose rights are said to have been violated and to whom a life of basic human dignity has been denied are poor, ignorant, illiterate humans who, by reason of their poverty and social and economic disability, are unable to approach the courts for judicial redress and hence the petitioners have, under the liberalised rule of standing, *locus standi* to maintain the present writ petition espousing the cause of the workmen.[101]

Standing in Cases of Executive Inaction or Abuse: 'Citizen Standing'

This second modification of the classical standing doctrine, where a concerned citizen (or voluntary organization) may sue, not as a representative of others but in his or her

---

shortcomings. ... Public interest is promoted by a spacious construction of *locus standi* in our socio-economic circumstances. ...' (Per Krishna Iyer, J. in *Mumbai Kamgar Sabha v Abdulbhai Faizullabhai* AIR 1976 SC 1455, 1458).

[93] The term is Cunningham's. *Supra* note 86 at 498.

[94] *Bandhua Mukti Morcha v Union of India (Bonded Labourers Case)* AIR 1984 SC 802. (The petitioners were an organization dedicated to liberate bonded labourers).

[95] *D.S. Nakara v Union of India (Pensioners Case)* AIR 1983 SC 130. (The principal petitioners, 'Common Cause' were a voluntary organization).

[96] *Dr. Upendra Baxi v State of Uttar Pradesh* (1983) 2 SCC 308. (The petitioner was a law professor).

[97] AIR 1979 SC 1360 and *Hussainara (II)* at 1369. There are two reported orders in the same case.

[98] Cunningham, *supra* note 86 at 499.

[99] Although essentially a *habeas corpus* case, it is widely recognized as the earliest example of PIL in the Supreme Court. Though the case title carries the name of several prisoners, the petitioner was the advocate, Kapila Hingorani.

[100] AIR 1982 SC 1473.

[101] *Id.* at 1483.

own right as a member of the citizenry to whom a public duty is owed, may be termed 'citizen standing'.[102] The force that impelled this liberalization of standing stemmed from the need to check the abuse of executive authority in a modern welfare state. Enormous regulatory and fiscal authority is vested in the administrative agencies of the Indian Government. On occasion, these agencies misuse their power and funds. If a public authority acting illegally causes a specific legal injury to a person or a specific group of persons, a private action for redress would lie under the traditional doctrine of standing. At times, however, the injury arising may be diffuse, e.g., where government policy threatens to undermine judicial independence, or where official inaction threatens to harm the environment. In such cases, the restrictive traditional doctrine precludes relief and renders the executive action immune from judicial scrutiny.

Under increasing pressure to curb instances of official lawlessness with diffuse impacts, the Supreme Court expanded standing to enable a citizen to challenge such government actions in the public interest, though the citizen had not suffered any individualized harm. An early suggestion of this trend is evinced in *Fertilizer Corporation Kamgar Union v Union of India,*[103] where a trade union challenged the sale of old machinery and a plant belonging to a state-owned corporation on the ground that the sale was arbitrary and violated the workers' right to occupation under Article 19(1)(g) of the Constitution. The court rejected the petition because it found no merit in either claim.

However, on the issue of the trade union's standing, Chief Justice Chandrachud (delivering an opinion for Fazal Ali and Koshal, JJ. and himself) observed:

> If public property is dissipated, it would require a strong argument to convince the court that representative segments of the public or at least a segment of the public which is directly interested and affected would have no right to complain of the infraction of public duties and obligations. ... We are not too sure if we would have refused relief to the workers if we had found that the sale was unjust, unfair or mala fide.[104]

Concurring, Justice Krishna Iyer (speaking for Bhagwati, J. and himself) developed the theme even further:

> The argument is, who are you to ask about the wrong committed or illegal act of the Corporation if you have suffered no personal injury to property, body, mind or reputation? ... Law as I conceive it, is a social audit and this audit function can be put into action only when someone with real public interest ignites the jurisdiction. We cannot be scared by the fear that all and sundry will be litigation-happy and waste their time and money and the time of the court

---

[102] Once again, the phrase is Cunningham's. *Supra* note 86 at 500.
[103] AIR 1981 SC 344.
[104] *Id.* at 350.

through false and frivolous cases. ... Public interest litigation is part of the process of participate justice and 'standing' in civil litigation of that pattern must have liberal reception at the judicial doorsteps. ... If a citizen is no more than a wayfarer or officious intervener without any interest or concern beyond what belongs to any one of the 660 million people of this country, the door of the court will not be ajar for him. But [if] he belongs to an organization which has special interest in the subject matter, if he has some concern deeper than that of a busybody, he cannot be told off at the gates, although whether the issue raised by him is justiciable may still remain to be considered. I, therefore, take the view that the present petition would clearly have been permissible under Article 226.[105]

It was a small step from here for Justice Bhagwati to hold, in *S.P. Gupta v Union of India*,[106] that even where no specific legal injury had been suffered, any concerned citizen may sue to check the damage to the public interest and uphold the rule of law. Subsequent Supreme Court judgments have interpreted Justice Bhagwati's opinion as laying down the ratio on the issue of standing.[107] Though *S.P. Gupta* was overruled in the *SCARA Case*[108] on the main issue relating to the primacy of the judiciary in the appointment of High Court and Supreme Court judges, the *S.P. Gupta* judgment continues to be relied upon on other issues,[109] which were not before the *SCARA* bench.

Citizen standing has also enabled individuals to check the abuse of public office by high government functionaries;[110] to challenge government policies[111] and to test the legality of a fiscal policy that favoured tax dodgers.[112]

The early environmental cases decided by the Supreme Court, which have resulted in the closure of limestone quarries in the Dehradun region,[113] the installation of safeguards at a chlorine plant in Delhi[114] and the closure of polluting tanneries on the Ganges,[115] fall within this category of citizen standing cases.

---

[105] *Id.* at 354–6.

[106] (*Judges' Transfer Case*), AIR 1982 SC 149, 194.

[107] *People's Union for Democratic Rights v Union of India* AIR 1982 SC 1473.

[108] *Supreme Court Advocates-on-Record Association v Union of India* AIR 1994 SC 268.

[109] e.g. *C. Ravichandran Iyer v Justice A.M. Bhattacharjee* 1995(5) SCC 457.

[110] *P.B. Samant v State of Maharashtra, (Cement Case)* 1982 (1) BOM. C.REP. 367. (The Bombay High Court judgment led to the resignation of Chief Minister Antulay of Maharashtra). *Raju v State of Karnataka, (Arrak Liquor Bottling Case)* 1986 (1) KARN. L.REP. 164. (The Karnataka High Court judgment led to the resignation of Chief Minister Hegde of Karnataka). *Shiv Sagar Tiwari v Union of India* 1996 (6) SCC 558 and 1996 (6) SCC 599. (Out of turn allotment of government accommodation by the urban development minister).

[111] *Supra* note 106.

[112] *R.K. Garg v Union of India (Bearer Bonds Case)* AIR 1981 SC 2138.

[113] *Rural Litigation and Entitlement Kendra v State of Uttar Pradesh (Dehradun Quarrying Case)* AIR 1985 SC 652.

[114] *M.C. Mehta v Union of India (Shriram Gas Leak Case)* AIR 1987 SC 965.

[115] *M.C. Mehta v Union of India (Ganga Pollution [Tanneries] Case)* AIR 1988 SC 1037.

In the *Ganga Pollution (Municipalities) Case*,[116] the Supreme Court upheld the standing of a Delhi resident to sue the government agencies whose prolonged neglect had resulted in severe pollution of the river. Justice Venkataramiah's opinion in this case supports the notion of citizen standing:

> [The petitioner] is a person interested in protecting the lives of people who make use of the water flowing in the river Ganga and his right to maintain the petition cannot be disputed. The nuisance caused by the pollution of the river Ganga is a public nuisance, which is widespread in range and indiscriminate in its effect and it would not be unreasonable to expect any particular person to take proceedings to stop it as distinct from the community at large. The petition has been entertained as a Public Interest Litigation. On the facts and in the circumstances of the case we are of the view that the petitioner is entitled to move this court in order to enforce the statutory provisions which impose duties on the municipal authorities and the Boards constituted under the Water Act.[117]

II. LOCUS STANDI TODAY: SCOPE AND RESTRICTIONS

In 1981, a seven judge bench of the Supreme Court delivered a definitive judgment on standing in the *Judges' Transfer Case*.[118] Although every judge delivered a separate opinion, there was general agreement with Justice Bhagwati's view on the issue of *locus standi*. Justice Bhagwati upheld the standing of practicing lawyers to challenge a government policy to transfer High Court judges, thereby undermining judicial independence. His judgment comprehensively describes the enlarged scope of what we have termed 'representative standing' (A), and 'citizen standing' (B):

> (A) It may therefore now be taken as well established that where a legal wrong or a legal injury is caused to a person or to determinate class of persons by reason of violation of any constitutional or legal right or any burden is imposed in contravention of any constitutional or legal provision or without authority of law or any such legal wrong or legal injury or legal burden is threatened and such person or determinate class of persons is by reason of poverty, helplessness or disability or socially or economically disadvantaged position, unable to approach the court for relief, any member of the public can maintain an application for an appropriate direction, order or writ in the High Court under Art. 226 and in case of any fundamental right of such person or determinate class of persons, in this court under Art. 32 seeking judicial redress for the legal wrong or injury caused to such person or determinate class of persons. ... But we must hasten to make it clear that the individual who moves the court for

---

[116] *M.C. Mehta v Union of India* AIR 1988 SC 1115.

[117] *Id.* at 1126.

[118] *Supra* note 106. See text accompanying *supra* notes 107-9.

judicial redress in cases of this kind must be acting bona fide with view to vindicating the cause of justice and if he is acting for personal gain or private profit or out of political motivation or other oblique consideration, the court should not allow itself to be activised at the instance of such person and must reject his application at the threshold, whether it be in the form of a letter addressed to the court or even in the form of a regular writ petition filed in court.[119]

(B) If public duties are to be enforced and social collective 'diffused' rights and interests are to be protected, we have to utilize the initiative and zeal of public-minded persons and organizations by allowing them to move the court and act for a general or group interest, even though they may not be directly injured in their own rights. It is litigation—litigation undertaken for the purpose of redressing public injury, enforcing public duty, protecting social, collective, 'diffused' rights and interests or vindicating public interest, and any citizen who is acting bona fide and who has sufficient interest has to be accorded standing. What is sufficient interest to give standing to a member of the public would have to be determined by the court in each individual ease. It is not possible for the court to lay down any hard and fast rule or any strait-jacket formula for the purpose of defining or delimiting 'sufficient interest' It has necessarily to be left to the discretion of the court.[120]

Unfortunately, as a rule of practice, neither the litigants nor the courts make the distinction between representative and citizen standing. Indeed, some later Supreme Court judgments have failed to appreciate this distinction and have muddled the separate rationales into a confused (and seemingly narrower) single doctrine.[121]

In *Subash Kumar*[122] the Supreme Court reprimanded the petitioner for abusing the process of the court. Subash Kumar, an influential businessman, wanted to carry away slurry from the Tata Iron & Steel Company's ponds. Kumar tried various means to pressure the company into giving him business. When the company refused, he filed a public interest litigation under Article 32, claiming that the slurry discharged from the coal washeries was polluting the Bokaro river and was a serious health risk to the neighbouring community. He asked the court to prohibit TISCO's discharges. His interim application, however, revealed the real purpose: Kumar sought the court's permission to carry away the slurry flowing into the river. The Supreme Court saw through Kumar's game, found no merit in the allegations of

---

[119] *Supra* note 106 at 189.
[120] *Id.* at 192.
[121] e.g., *Forward Construction Company v Prabhat Mandal* AIR 1986 SC 391, 393; *Sachidanand Pandey v State of West Bengal (Calcutta Taj Hotel Case)* AIR 1987 SC 1109, 1134; and *Ramsharan Autyanuprasi v Union of India* AIR 1989 SC 549, 553. The expanded standing doctrine as formulated in all three judgments appears to ignore the 'citizen standing' dimension.
[122] *Subash Kumar v State of Bihar* AIR 1991 SC 420.

pollution and held that the petitioner was out to harass the company and make a profit to boot. The court dismissed the petition with costs, holding:

> Personal interest cannot be enforced through the process of this court under Art. 32 of the Constitution in the garb of a public interest litigation. Public interest litigation contemplates legal proceedings for vindication or enforcement of fundamental rights of a group of persons or community which are not able to enforce their fundamental rights on account of their incapacity, poverty or ignorance of law. A person invoking the jurisdiction of this court under Art.32 must approach this court for the vindication of the fundamental rights of affected persons and not for the purpose of vindication of his personal grudge or enmity. It is [the] duty of this court to discourage such petition and to ensure that the course of justice is not obstructed or polluted by unscrupulous litigants by invoking the extraordinary jurisdiction of this court for personal matters under the garb of the public interest litigation.[123]

Likewise, in *Chhetriya Pardushan Mukti Sangharsh Samiti v State of UP*,[124] the Supreme Court rejected a petition which was motivated by an ancient grudge and enmity. Declaring, 'We must protect society from so-called protectors', the court held that in view of the long history of animosity and the *prima facie* compliance with pollution statutes, there was no justification for judicial intervention. During the hearing, the industry furnished materials to show that the petitioner had a record of blackmailing people and that criminal charges were pending against him in this regard.

The Madhya Pradesh High Court disapproved the tactic employed to stall an industrial project in *Jayant Vitamins Ltd. v Rampur Distillery and Chemical Company Ltd.*[125] Jayant Vitamins claimed that the respondents' solvent extraction factory, when operating, would pollute the atmosphere and harm the bulk drugs manufactured at Jayant's plant. Moreover, the new plant was hazardous and the location was against the siting guidelines for industries. After perusing the record, the court discovered the hidden agenda of the petitioners. Jayant Vitamins needed the adjacent plot to expand its own unit and the petition was but a tactic to pressurize Rampur Distillery to sell the land. Dismissing the petition, the court held 'the bogey of pollution should not be allowed to be raised for ulterior selfish motives by disgruntled litigants to hamper or stop the process of industrialization.'[126]

III. THE RELAXATION OF PROCEDURES

The procedural requirements of litigation that ensure fairness and uniformity at the trial of conventional, adversarial lawsuits, may not be necessary in PIL cases. Judges

---

[123] *Id.* at 424.
[124] AIR 1990 SC 2060.
[125] 1992(3) COMP.L.JR.1.
[126] *Id.* at 13.

like to view PIL as a collaborative effort between the court, the citizen and the public official, where procedural safeguards have a diminished utility and may be relaxed to enable relief: '[I]t has to be remembered that every technicality in the procedural law is not available as a defence when a matter of grave public importance is for consideration before the court.'[127]

For instance, the Supreme Court and the High Courts frequently treat letters written to individual judges or the court as writ petitions.[128] These letters usually contain a bare outline of the grievance, the unsuccessful steps taken by the writer to secure relief from official agencies, and a request to the court to set matters right. A case in point is the *Dehradun Quarrying Case*,[129] where the Supreme Court directed a letter from the Rural Litigation and Entitlement Kendra, Dehradun, to be treated as a writ petition under Article 32 of the Constitution. The letter alleged that illegal limestone quarrying was devastating the fragile environment in the Himalayan foothills around Mussoorie. Satisfied that the matter merited inquiry, the Supreme Court first issued notices to the State of Uttar Pradesh and the collector of Dehradun to appear before the court. Then, as a clearer picture of the facts, regulatory structures and policies emerged, other affected parties—the Union Government, concerned government agencies and the mine owners— were also impleaded. By August 1988, when the Supreme Court delivered its final order, five years after it had received the letter, the litigation had grown into one of the most complex environmental cases handled by an Indian court.

In another case, a journalist complained to the Supreme Court that the national coastline was being sullied by unplanned development that violated a Central Government directive. The Supreme Court registered the letter as a writ petition, requested the court's legal aid committee to appoint a lawyer for the petitioner and issued notice to the Union Government and the governments of all the coastal states.[130]

Occasionally, the courts have relaxed procedural rules in other respects as well. In the *Shriram Gas Leak Case*,[131] the Supreme Court allowed an unconnected cause of action to be urged, without requiring amendments to the petition. The original petition sought the closure of Shriram's hazardous industrial plant and its relocation away from Delhi's populated localities. While the petition was pending, oleum gas escaped from the plant and harmed some persons, who filed applications for compensation in

---

[127] *Rural Litigation and Entitlement Kendra, Dehra Dun v State of Uttar Pradesh (Dehradun Quarrying Case)* AIR 1988 SC 2187, 2195.

[128] While letters written to *individual* judges have in the past been treated as writ petitions, the practice has been deprecated. The proper course is to address letters to the court. (See the separate opinions of Pathak, J. and Sen, J. in *Bandhua Mukti Morcha v Union of India* AIR 1984 SC 802, 848. But see the Bhagwati, J. opinion in *M.C. Mehta v Union of India (Shriram Gas Leak Case)* AIR 1987 SC 1086, 1090).

[129] *Supra* note 127.

[130] *Mahesh R. Desai v Union of India* Writ Petition No. 989 of 1988.

[131] *Supra* note 128.

the original 'closure and relocation' writ petition. Shriram urged the court not to decide the issue arising from the compensation claim, since no such claim had been made in the original petition, nor had the petitioner amended the petition to incorporate a compensation plea. The court overruled this objection, stating that a 'hypertechnical approach' that defeated the ends of justice was inappropriate in PIL cases.

IV. THE NEW CHALLENGES: FACTS, EXPERTISE AND SUPERVISION

As PIL cases began crowding the court docket—frequently in the form of letters or skimpy petitions based on newspaper reports—the judges hearing these cases were pressed to evolve new procedures and techniques to facilitate this new type of litigation. Broadly speaking, judicial innovation was required to: (1) secure detailed facts, since the petitioners' information was usually sketchy; (2) receive expert testimony in cases involving complex social or scientific issues; and (3) ensure the continuous supervision of prospective judicial orders.

To construct a complete framework of the facts, a judge often requires the concerned public officials to furnish detailed, comprehensive affidavits. Sometimes, as where a swift, impartial assessment of the facts is needed and the official machinery is unreliable, slow or biased, an affidavit may be unhelpful. In such cases, the courts appoint special commissions to gather facts and data. The power to appoint commissions is an inherent power of the Supreme Court under Article 32 of the Constitution and of the High Courts under Article 226.[132]

Since the commissioner is almost always a responsible person, the report of the commission is treated as *prima facie* evidence of the facts and data gathered. Once the report is received by the court, copies of it are supplied to the parties, who may choose to dispute the contents of the report in an affidavit. The court then considers the report in light of the affidavits, and proceeds to decide the issues.

In a petition for directions to the municipal authority of Jaipur to solve the city's acute sanitation problems, the Rajasthan High Court appointed a commissioner to report on the insanitary conditions in various parts of the city.[133] This commissioner apparently discharged his task to the court's satisfaction.

In another environmental petition, however, the Bombay High Court's experience with a commissioner was less sanguine.[134] The petition challenged the development permission for a beach resort on the Goa coast. Since work at the beach site had commenced, the court appointed a commissioner to inspect and report on the extent of the construction. In his report, the commissioner went beyond his fact-finding task of describing the development on the beach and commented on the legality of the structures. The High Court criticized the commissioner for exceeding his brief, and rejected the subjective portions of the report.

---

132 *Supra* note 94, at 816, 817, 845, and 849.
133 *L.K. Koolwal v State of Rajasthan* AIR 1988 RAJ 2.
134 *Sergio Carvalho v State of Goa* 1989 (1) GOA LAW TIMES 276, 302.

In pollution cases, the Supreme Court frequently relies on the National Environment Engineering Research Institute, Nagpur (NEERI) to visit the affected locality and submit its field report.[135] Several techniques have evolved to manage the litigation process in complex cases involving scores of parties. For example, the court may dissuade industry from filing pleadings in the court registry and instead require the polluter to file affidavits before the pollution control board;[136] appoint an *amicus curiae*[137] to peruse, analyse and collate the material filed by various respondents;[138] and appoint commissions to inspect the situation in the field.[139]

Yet another technique used by courts to ease the environmental petitioner's evidentiary burden, is the resort to a judicial notice of the 'facts'. For example, in a petition seeking to reduce pollution of the river Ganga, the Supreme Court dispensed with the need for hard scientific proof on the health effects of the pollution, the damage it caused to riparian property, and the manner in which it harmed the livelihood of those living downstream. In view of certain books and writings brought to the court's notice, the judges simply *assumed* that such injuries either had occurred or were likely to occur, and proceeded to issue remedial directions.[140]

Likewise, in *Anthony Lawrence Quadors v Municipal Corporation of Greater Bombay,*[141] the Bombay High Court took judicial notice of the poor state of the city's roads after the on-set of the monsoon. Here, the secretary of a taxi drivers union and a newspaper editor petitioned the court to compel the municipal authorities to maintain the roads in good condition. Ultimately, the petition was withdrawn after the Municipal Corporation agreed to implement the recommendations of a court-appointed committee of experts.

More recently, under the Supreme Court's formulation of the 'precautionary principle', the onus of proof is on the developer or industrialist to show that his or her action is environmentally benign. This principle was applied in *Vellore Citizens' Welfare Forum v Union of India*[142] and the *Taj Trapezium Case.*[143]

Frequently, independent scientific expertise is essential to inform judicial decision-making in environmental cases.[144] Judges in such cases usually appoint a

---

[135] e.g. *M.C. Mehta v Union of India (Calcutta Tanneries)* 1997(2) SCC 411.
[136] *Anil Kumar Karanwal v State of UP* 1996 (3) SCALE 61.
[137] A friend of the court.
[138] *T.N. Godavarman Thirumulkpad v Union of India* 1997 (3) SCC 312. This was the first major environmental case in which the Supreme Court used the services of an *amicus curae*. The role of the *amicus curae* extends to making submissions on the law.
[139] *Pravinbhai Jashbhai Patel v State of Gujarat* Spl. Civ. Appl. No.770 of 1995, Gujarat High Court, 10 May 1996.
[140] *Supra* note 115; also see *supra* note 116.
[141] Writ Petition No. 1129 of 1981, Bombay High Court, orders dated 4 October 1983 and 11 April 1985.
[142] AIR 1996 SC 2715.
[143] *M.C. Mehta v Union of India* AIR 1997 SC 734.
[144] *Supra* note 114, at 981.

committee of experts to probe scientific questions and advise the court on a course of action. Like special commissions, the expert committees are appointed under the inherent powers of the Supreme Court and the High Courts under Articles 32 and 226 of the Constitution. Since eminent scientists drawn from leading institutions compose these committees, the court treats their opinion with great deference.

Faced with the allegation that imported Irish butter targeted for distribution in Bombay was contaminated by the nuclear fallout from the Chernobyl disaster, the Supreme Court appointed an expert committee to determine whether the imported milk and dairy products were safe for human consumption. When the committee reported that the milk products were safe, the court released the butter for distribution.[145]

In the *Shriram Gas Leak Case,* the Supreme Court solicited the help of several expert committees. For instance, the Nilay Choudhary Committee was requested to advise the court on whether Shriram's hazardous chemical plant, which was located in Delhi, should be allowed to recommence operations in view of the danger to the neighbourhood. The committee was also asked to suggest measures to reduce the environmental threat that the plan posed.[146]

In the *Dehradun Quarrying Case,*[147] the Supreme Court enlisted an expert committee to evaluate the environmental impact of limestone quarrying operations in the Mussoorie-Dehradun region. Significantly, the court used the committee mechanism for another purpose as well, viz., to *supervise* the implementation of judicial orders. A 'monitoring committee' was formed to oversee the running of three limestone mines that had been allowed to continue operations, and to monitor reforestation measures in the region. A 'rehabilitation committee' was also set up to rehabilitate the mine owners whose mines had been closed by the court without payment of compensation. The rehabilitation committee was to ensure that the displaced mine owners were given alternative mining sites in other parts of the country.

V. DIRECTIONS AND RELIEF

Since the principal relief in PIL is prospective and affirmative rather than compensatory, the tight linkage between right and remedy that characterizes traditional litigation is attenuated in these cases. Remedial orders are fashioned *ad hoc* to accommodate a range of interests and do not always flow from a narrow determination of rights and liabilities. Moreover, since there is wide discretion, the temperament of the judge, his or her compassion for the grievance and the nature of the grievance itself, invariably influence the outcome of a case. As a result, it is frequently impossible to identify a single clear cut solution in PIL cases.

---

[145] *Shivarao Shantaram Wagle v Union of India (Irish Butter Case)* AIR 1988 SC 952.
[146] *Supra* note 114, at 969.
[147] *Supra* note 127.

Rights and Remedies

This disconnection between right and remedy is seen early in Indian PIL. The Supreme Court found injunctive reliefs, which are traditionally used to protect the interests of the parties until a final decision is reached on their rights, to be inadequate and unsuited for redressing public grievances. For example, the urgency in human rights cases affecting large numbers of poor people, or the intricacies in cases where fact-finding commissions or expert committees had to be constituted, demanded immediate, comprehensive, interim orders even *before* a decision on the rights. Characterizing these orders as 'remedies without rights', Cunningham describes their use by the Supreme Court in two leading cases:

> In the first public interest case, *Hussainara,* litigated before the Indian Supreme Court, the court issued four interim orders within the first four months following the filing of the writ petition. These orders set norms for releasing undertrial prisoners on personal bonds, ended the practice of 'protective custody' for crime victims and witnesses, ordered release of all prisoners in the State of Bihar who had been awaiting trial for a longer period than the maximum sentence for which they could be convicted, directed that free legal aid be given to all indigent accused, held that a speedy trial was a constitutional right, imposed an affirmative duty on magistrates to inform undertrial prisoners of their right to bail and legal aid, and ordered the release of all undertrials in Bihar for whom investigations had been pending for more than six months without an extension being granted by the magistrate. After this initial surge of activity, *Hussainara* has remained pending before the court for the last seven years without further decisions or final judgment.
>
> *Hussainara* thus set a pattern which the Supreme Court has followed in many public interest cases: immediate and comprehensive interim relief prompted by urgent need expressed in the writ petition with a long deferral of final decision as to factual issues and legal liabilities. ... Most recently in the *Shriram Fertilizer Gas Leak* case the court ordered the plant to be closed, set up a victim compensation scheme, and then ordered the plant reopening subject to extensive directions, all within ten weeks of the gas leak, without first deciding whether it had jurisdiction under article 32 to order relief against a private corporation.[148]

Relief in most of the PIL cases in the Supreme Court is obtained through interim orders. The new judicial emphasis on the effective implementation of environmental laws has prompted judges to monitor compliance through periodic reports filed in court by the government agency. Generally, short interim directions in the nature of a 'continuing mandamus' are passed at frequent intervals. Non-

[148] Cunningham, *supra* note 86, at 511.

compliance with court orders is met with judicial strictures, action in contempt of court or fines.

Judicial Activism

A second characteristic of many PIL cases is the court's ingress into fields traditionally reserved for the executive. Finding the executive response to be absent or deficient, the Supreme Court has used its interim directions to influence the quality of administration, 'making it more responsive than before to the constitutional ethic and law'.[149] Occasionally, the court has even created its own crude administrative machinery to remove a public hardship.

Prof. Baxi describes this gradual judicial takeover of 'the direction of administration in a particular arena from the executive' as 'creeping jurisdiction'.[150] A good illustration of the Supreme Court's 'creeping jurisdiction' is the *Dehradun Quarrying Case* where 'the Supreme Court considered, balanced and resolved competing policies—including the need for development, environmental conservation, preserving jobs, and protecting substantial business investments—in deciding to close a number of limestone quarries in the Mussoorie Hills and to allow others to continue operating under detailed conditions. In rendering this judgment the court reviewed the highly technical reports of various geological experts and gave varying weight to the expert opinions.'[151]

The article excerpted below describes the methodology adopted in the *Ganga Pollution Case* and points to the gains as well as the pitfalls in environmental law enforcement through the courts. Note the result-oriented approach of the court and the procedures adopted to secure strict enforcement of the pollution laws.

DIVAN; CLEANING THE GANGA, Economic and
Political Weekly, 1 July 1995, p. 1557

> Short of putting on their gum boots and wading into the murky waters of the Ganga to clean up the mess, a bench of the Supreme Court has been doing a whole lot and more to restore the health of the river. Justice Kuldip Singh over the past two years has cajoled, prodded and driven recalcitrant industries and public authorities in the Ganga basin to comply with pollution norms.
>
> Even in conventional litigation, Singh brings to his court an informal style rooted in common sense. A public interest litigation to clean up the Ganga has caught the judge's fancy. Each Friday finds the judge in his elements, anxious to improve the environment. A huge shoal of advocates, administrators, company executives, and public officials attentively follow the court proceedings as a range of snappy

[149] U. Baxi, *Taking Suffering Seriously: Social Action Litigation in the Supreme Court of India*, 29 The Review (International Commission of Jurists) 37, 42 (December 1982).

[150] *Id.*

[151] Cunningham, *supra* note 86, at 516-517.

judicial directions are issued week upon week. At present the Kuldip Singh court is tackling hundreds of large polluting industries in Uttar Pradesh, Bihar, and West Bengal; a slew of small municipalities that discharge untreated sewage into the river; half a dozen municipal corporations in the three states; the Eastern railways; giant thermal power plants; numerous small units such as tanneries and almost everyone else despoiling the river. The litigation-affected parties are several hundred. How does the court manage the show?

The traditional view of litigation frowns upon judges who embark on such massive administrative exercises. Judges are required to retain their objectivity; impartiality and aloofness. They ought not soil their judicial robes by entering the administrative area and taking decisions which are within the province of specialist enforcement agencies. This is old hat for the *Ganga* court. A new wisdom guides its approach. Dismayed at the persistent flouting of Parliament's mandate to clean the rivers, by polluters and pollution control boards alike, the court is unwilling to sit idly by.

The rigor of formal court procedures and statutory requirements are diluted in favour of a summary, result-oriented process. The main thrust is to substitute the ineffective administrative directives issued by the pollution control boards (PCBs) under the Water Act and the Environment (Protection) Act, with judicial orders, the disobedience of which invites contempt of court action and penalties. In view of the finality of the apex court's orders, there are few options for the polluters but to comply.

The court's first task is to identify the erring polluters. For this it looks to M.C. Mehta, the well known environmentalist and advocate, who petitioned the court in 1985 to clean up the river.

Once the polluters are identified, the court orders each firm to meet the effluent standards within a period of three months, or else face closure. Justice Singh hopes that the shadow of closure will stir hard headed businessmen to treat their factory effluents. To emphasize the urgency, the orders threatening closure are issued *exparte*, that is, without hearing the company. The court directs the PCBs to immediately serve notice on the unwary polluters, setting out the Supreme Court's deadline. Compliance must be reported to the board. At the end of the period, each board files a status report together with recommendations for future action. The willing are granted extensions to clean up their act. But for the obstinate, it's closure.

Where the discharge levels are achieved, the board is asked to inspect the working of the ETP and report to the court. Given the dismal record of the PCBs, it is no surprise that even this elementary task is at times entrusted by the court to the National Environmental Engineering Institute (NEERI), Nagpur.

The sprawling dimensions of the *Ganga* case have pressed the court to evolve new procedures. Unlike usual litigations, affected polluters are dissuaded from filing documents in the court's registry. All affidavits must be tendered before the respective boards. In this manner, the court hopes to reduce its administrative burden. Moreover, to tailor its directions to each situation, the *Ganga* court issues orders piecemeal. What at the end of the day reads like the comprehensive court order, is in fact a series of directions—dictated one paragraph at a time—and punctuated by brief arguments on each issue. It is this procedure that enables the court to respond with specificity to each situation.

Does the *Ganga* court then, get straight 'A's? At first blush, yes. Hundreds of factories have installed ETPs. Small scale units are busy complying with minimum standards for effluent discharge. The municipalities are creeping towards compliance. Bihar's thermal power stations at Bokaro and Patratu have ordered equipment to abate pollution. Even the Eastern Railways, after much foot-dragging, has agreed to treat the waste water gushing out from Howrah station.

More generally, the Supreme Court has succeeded in building up a sustained pressure on industry and municipalities, where the PCBs have failed. Throughout the Ganga basin there is heightened environmental awareness among administrators, the subordinate judiciary, police and municipal officials, all of whom are involved in implementing the Supreme Court's orders.

Impressive as all this may seem, unless the PCBs are overhauled quickly the gains will soon dissipate. There are limits to what a gung ho court can do in the face of an indifferent bureaucracy. The boards in the Ganga states appear resigned to doing no work except for a knee-jerk response to judicial orders. Besides, the word on the street is that the Supreme Court's orders are misused by dishonest board officials to line their own pockets. Unless a bribe is paid, an unfavourable report is made to the court.

There are other pitfalls. The massive administrative tasks assumed by the court, will sooner or later expose judges to criticism previously directed at administrators. Arbitrariness in passing closure orders without attention to special factors or hearing the affected party, are but a few of the concerns voiced by lawyers. None of this lends to the prestige of the court. Indeed, if a subordinate judge dares to assume the expansive administrative role of the *Ganga* court, he would probably be admonished for exceeding his jurisdiction.

If the Supreme Court's activism is to have a lasting impact, a new political will in the form of budgetary allocations at the municipal level and greater community pressure on board officials is necessary. Left to themselves, the PCBs will revert to a culture of slipshod enforcement.

NOTE

Two cases that illustrate the PIL process in solving environmental problems are *Janaki Nathubhai Chhara v Sardarnagar Municipality* [152] and *Citizens Action Committee v Civil Surgeon, Mayo (General) Hospital.* [153] These cases exhibit collaboration among litigants and the bench; the flexible character of the pleadings; the negotiations through which the courts ensure relief; and the activist role of the PIL judge.

Justice Pathak in his concurring opinion in the *Bonded Labourers Case,* excerpted below, cautions against the dangers of excessive judicial activism in PIL.

[152] AIR 1986 GUJ 49.
[153] AIR 1986 BOM 136.

In this case, the Supreme Court treated a letter from an organization dedicated to liberate bonded labourers as a writ petition, and appointed a commissioner to verify allegations that several stone quarry workers in the State of Haryana were forced to work under 'inhuman and intolerable' conditions, contrary to various social welfare laws. The court passed detailed directions for the release and rehabilitation of the bonded labourers.

BANDHUA MUKTI MORCHA v UNION OF INDIA
AIR 1984 SC 802

PATHAK, J: * * *

Where the court embarks upon affirmative action in the attempt to remedy a constitutional imbalance within the social order, few critics will find fault with it so long as it confines itself to the scope of its legitimate authority. But there is always the possibility, in public interest litigation, of succumbing to the temptation of crossing into territory which properly pertains to the Legislature or to the executive Government. For in most cases the jurisdiction of the court is invoked when a default occurs in executive administration, and sometimes where a void in community life remains unfilled by legislative action. The resulting public grievance finds expression through social action groups, which consider the court an appropriate forum for removing the deficiencies. Indeed, the citizen seems to find it more convenient to apply to the court for the vindication of constitutional rights than appeal to the executive or legislative organs of the State.

In the process of correcting executive error or removing legislative omission the Court can so easily find itself involved in policy making of a quality and a degree characteristic of political authority, and indeed run the risk of being mistaken for one. An excessively political role identifiable with political governance betrays the court into functions alien to its fundamental character, and tends to destroy the delicate balance envisaged in our constitutional system between its three basic institutions. The Judge, conceived in the true classical mould, is an impartial arbiter, beyond and above political bias and prejudice, functioning silently in accordance with the Constitution and his judicial conscience. Thus does he maintain the legitimacy of the institution he serves and honour the trust which his office has reposed in him.

The affirmative schemes framed in public interest litigation by the court sometimes require detailed administration under constant judicial supervision over protracted periods. The lives of large sections of the people, some of whom have had no voice in the decision, are shaped and ordered by mandatory court action extending into the future. In that context, it is as well to remember that public approval and public consent assume material importance in its successful implementation. In contrast with policy making by legislation, where a large body of legislators debate on a proposed legislative enactment, no such visual impact can be perceived when judicial decrees are forged and fashioned by a few judicial personages in the confines of a court. The mystique of the robe, at the stage of decision-making, is associated traditionally with cloistered secrecy and confidentiality and the end-result commonly issues as a final definitive act of the court. It is a serious question whether in every case the same awesome respect and reverence will endure during different stages of affirmative action seeking to regulate the lives of large numbers of people, some of whom never participated in the judicial process.

* * *

An activist court, spearheading the movement for the development and extension of the citizen's constitutional rights, for the protection of individual liberty and for the strengthening of the socio-economic fabric in compliance with declared constitutional objectives, will need to move with a degree of judicial circumspection. In the centre of a social order changing with dynamic pace, the court needs to balance the authority of the past with the urges of the future.

* * *

There is great merit in the court proceeding to decide an issue on the basis of strict legal principle and avoiding carefully the influence of purely emotional appeal. For that alone gives the decision of the court a direction which is certain, and unfaltering, and that especial permanence in legal jurisprudence which makes it a base for the next step forward in the further progress of the law. Indeed, both certainty of substance and certainty of direction are indispensable requirements in the development of the law, and invest it with the credibility which commands public confidence in its legitimacy.

This warning is of especial significance in these times, during a phase of judicial history when a few social action groups tend to show evidence of presuming that in every case the court must bend and mould its decision to popular notions of which way a case should be decided.

* * *

NOTES AND QUESTIONS

1. In 1991 M.C. Mehta, advocate and environmentalist, petitioned the Supreme Court to direct the exhibition and broadcast of environmental messages and information by the media.[154] Mehta also sought the introduction of 'environment' as a compulsory subject in schools and colleges. The Supreme Court issued detailed directions regarding the compulsory screening of slides and documentaries in cinema halls and the broadcast of programmes on radio and television. The University Grants

---

[154] *M.C. Mehta v Union of India* AIR 1992 SC 382.

Commission was told to prescribe courses on the environment in the university syllabi; and the state governments and education boards were directed to take immediate steps to include environment in the school curricula.

Was the Supreme Court's order justified? Is it the business of justices to decide educational priorities from the middle school upward to the graduate level? Ought they decide what movie and television viewers should watch? How was Article 21 violated justifying the exercise of jurisdiction under Article 32? The court's foray is difficult to support on jurisprudential grounds. The court has little expertise in matters of eduction and the media. Moreover, as known to movie and television viewers and school or under-graduate students, the Supreme Court's directions are seldom obeyed. Does this erode the prestige of the Supreme Court?

2. The court's approach in the *M.C. Mehta Media Case* is hard to reconcile with Justice Mukharji's plea in *State of Himachal Pradesh v Umed Ram Sharma*,[155] for judicial restraint in public interest cases. The petition arose from a demand by the villagers in Simla district for a road to their village. While upholding the High Court judgment directing the state government to construct the road as soon as possible, the Supreme Court cautioned:

> The State Government has assured this court that they would carry out this direction. The court must know its limitations in these fields. The court should bring about an urgency in executing lethargy if any, in a particular case but it must remember the warning of Benjamin N. Cardozo in *'The Nature of Judicial Process'* at page 141 of the book:
>
> The judge, even when he is free, is still not wholly free. He is not to innovate at pleasure. He is not a knight-errant roaming at will in pursuit of his own ideal of beauty or of goodness. He is to draw his inspiration from consecrated principles. He is not to yield to spasmodic sentiment, to vague and unregulated benevolence. He is to exercise a discretion informed by tradition, methodized by analogy, disciplined by system, and subordinated to 'the primordial necessity of order in the social life.' Wide enough in all conscience is the field of discretion that remains.

In a similar vein in *Asif Hameed v State of Jammu and Kashmir*,[156] the court held: 'The Constitution does not permit the court to direct or advise the executive in matters of policy or to sermonize qua any matter which under the constitution lies within the sphere of legislature or executive.'

3. For another opinion urging judicial restraint in PIL 'so that this salutary type of litigation does not lose its credibility', see Justice Khalid's observations in *Sachidanand Pandey v State of West Bengal*.[157] Here, the construction of the Calcutta

---

[155] AIR 1986 SC 847.
[156] AIR 1989 SC 1899.
[157] *Supra* note 121.

Taj Hotel was delayed for six years while administrative agencies and courts considered whether a proposed six-storey hotel would impede the flight pattern of migratory birds.

4. In the 1990s the Supreme Court set the national environmental agenda on a range of ecological issues. It did so through judicial orders in public interest litigations (PILs) filed by citizens, non-governmental organizations and environmental groups. Dismayed at the poor enforcement record of government agencies, the apex court set apart large amounts of judicial time and resources to address public grievances. As noted earlier, the court evolved a new procedure in the nature of a 'continuing mandamus', where a series of interim directions are issued to officials and their performance monitored through periodic compliance reports. During this period the emphasis shifted to implementation of natural resource laws. It was hoped that vigorous judicial scrutiny in select cases would have a salutary effect on the work culture and performance of the environmental bureacracy.[158]

F. CLASS ACTIONS

In a class action one or more members of a numerous class, having 'the same interest', may sue or defend on behalf of themselves and all the other members of the class. It is a procedural device designed to promote efficiency and fairness in the handling of large numbers of similar claims. A 'representative' or 'class' suit is recognized under Order I Rule 8 of the Code of Civil Procedure of 1908.

Class suits are an exception to the general rule of compulsory joinder of all interested parties. They are allowed on the premise that members of the class who are made parties will protect their *own interests,* and in protecting them, the interest *of the absent members* of the class will also be protected.

Why have class suits? One purpose is to provide an economical and convenient forum for disposing of similar lawsuits. Also, class suits are justified on the grounds of fairness: All members of the class are treated equally, and, if they are successful as plaintiffs, they share in the recovery.

Sometimes a suit between individuals may affect the interests of numerous non-parties. For example, the judgment in a petition by a few members of a trade challenging a zoning policy that prohibits the trade in whole sections of a city, would affect absent members of that trade as well. All traders who might be affected are given notice of the suit and are allowed to be joined as parties.

Additionally, separate suits could result in the establishment of inconsistent obligations for persons opposing the class. For example, where a number of victims of air pollution file separate suits to enjoin the polluter (in the same or different

---

[158] The lead provided by the Supreme Court, was followed by a number of High Courts, notably Kerala, Gujarat, Bombay, Madras and Calcutta which also adopted similar strategies to improve enforcement.

courts) the separate orders in the different proceedings might create conflicting obligations for the polluter. In Suit A, all emissions may be prohibited; in Suit B, emission reduction in a phased manner may be ordered; and in Suit C, the court may refuse to enjoin the polluter. A class action would prevent such conflicts.

Finally, class suits may spread the cost of litigation among numerous litigants and make the suit affordable when it otherwise would not be. For example, consumer class suits to recover damages for defective products might enable numerous small claims to be jointly adjudicated.

I. ORDER 1 RULE 8

Rule 8 of Order 1 of the Code of Civil Procedure of 1908, as it stands after the Code's 1976 amendment, prescribes the following conditions for a representative action: (1) that the class be numerous; (2) that members of the class have 'the same interest' in the suit; (3) that the court permit a few persons to sue or be sued on behalf of the entire class; and (4) that the court issue notice of the suit to all persons having the same interest.

The rule also permits any member of the class to join the class action if he or she so wishes and provides that no class action may be compromised or settled until the court issues notice to all the members of the class. Further, where a person sues or defends a class suit without due diligence, the court is empowered to substitute another member of the class in his or her place. Most important, a decree passed in a representative suit binds all members of the class.

The Same Interest

The existence and configuration of a class under rule 8 of Order 1 are determined by whether the persons claiming to constitute a class have 'the same interest' in the suit. Since rule 8 is a rule of procedure, the term 'the same interest' must receive a liberal construction; it ought not to be loaded down by arbitrary and technical restrictions. Liberally construed, the term requires a *community of interest* among the members of the class in the questions of law and fact involved.

This construction is fortified by the explanation to the rule, introduced by the 1976 amendment, which states: 'For the purpose of determining whether the persons who sue or are sued or defend, have the same interest in one suit, it is not necessary to establish that such persons have the same cause of action as the persons on whose behalf, or for whose benefit, they sue or are sued, or defend the suit, as the case may be.' Taking 'cause of action' to mean the bundle of facts which together with the applicable law gives the plaintiff a right of relief against the defendant, the explanation clearly suggests that there need not be an *identity* of facts, claim or interests amongst the members. Common general interest between class members is sufficient. Indeed, the rule seems to call for an accommodation of the inevitable diversities of situation so long as there is a unity of interest among the members of the class, and the representatives have an interest in the controversy common with those represented.

The judgment of the full bench of the Madras High Court in *Kodika Goundar v Velandi Goundar,* delivered before the 1976 amendment, correctly describes the ambit of Order 1, rule 8:

> In deciding therefore whether leave has to be granted or in considering whether a suit already instituted under O.1, R.8 is maintainable the principal consideration that should weigh with a court is whether it is satisfied that there is sufficient community of interest as between the plaintiffs or defendants as the case may be to justify the adoption of the procedure provided under O.1, R.8. ... The nature of a claim whether it is a suit for a declaration of a right, or an injunction or an action for money on contract or on tort—is not very material in considering whether a suit would be filed under the simplified procedure of O.1, R.8.[159]

Significantly, the court also held that a class action for damages was permissible.[160]

II. CLASS ACTIONS AND THE ENVIRONMENT

Although an examination of class suits in India shows that the class action device has been rarely, if ever, used in any personal injury tort case, there is no reason why it cannot be shaped into an instrument for the vindication of group interests in environmental torts. In fact, in most environmental cases, it is hard to conceive of individual relief apart from class relief. A class action would measurably assist in securing redress.

The most obvious use of class action is in mass disasters of the sort that occurred in Bhopal. In the wake of the Bhopal tragedy, the Indian Government filed a class action suit on behalf of all the victims, in accordance with the terms of the Bhopal Gas Leak Disaster (Processing of Claims) Act of 1985.

More generally, a class action may be used in all torts that have an impact on a large number of people. Where effluents discharged by an industry into a river kills fish and imperils the livelihood of several villagers downstream, the effect of pollution on any individual fisherman might be too small to justify a conventional lawsuit seeking compensation. In the aggregate, however, the impact on all the affected fishermen may be substantial enough to seek redress in a class action suit. On a practical level, while an individual fisherman might not be able to bear the cost of litigation, the group as a whole may find it easier to finance a single class action suit.

Reversing the class alignment, the defendant class action by an individual plaintiff is an effective way to enjoin a large number of polluters, as the *Ganga Pollution (Tanneries) Case* shows:

---

[159] AIR 1955 MAD 281, 286.

[160] But see *dicta* in *H.A.J. Gidney v Anglo Indian and Domiciled European Association*, AIR 1930 RANG 177, 181.

When this petition came up for preliminary hearing, the court directed the issue of notice under Order I of Rule 8 of the Code of Civil Procedure treating this case as a representative action by publishing the gist of the petition in the newspapers in circulation in northern India and calling upon all the industrialists and the municipal councils having jurisdiction over the areas through which the river Ganga flows to appear before court and to show cause as to why directions should not be issued to them as prayed by the petitioner asking them not to allow the trade effluents and the sewage into the river Ganga without appropriately treating them before discharging them into the river. Pursuant to the said notice a large number of industrialists and local bodies have entered appearance before the court. Some of them have filed counter-affidavits explaining the steps taken by them for treating the trade effluents before discharging them into the river.[161]

III. CLASS SUITS AND PIL WRITS

At present most environmental actions in India are brought under Articles 32 and 226 of the Constitution. As we have seen, the writ procedure is preferred over the conventional suit because it is speedy, relatively inexpensive and offers direct access to the highest courts of the land. Nevertheless, class action suits also have advantages. For instance, courts as a rule do not grant monetary compensation in writ proceedings. Generally, monetary recoveries from tortfeasors in environmental cases can only be obtained through a suit.

A second advantage class action suits offer is that detailed evidence may be adduced during the trial. Thus far, the environmental violations that have reached the courts have been so gross that judges were able to decide most issues on the basis of affidavits. With the increasing use of toxic chemicals in Indian agriculture and industry, there is a strong likelihood of more subtle, more difficult-to-prove environmental disputes reaching the courts. These disputes will probably be litigated in a more sophisticated and combative fashion than present day PIL. Technical experts may be required to submit to cross-examination. Causality between the pollutant and the harm may have to be rigorously established. The class action procedure appears more suited than the writ procedure to accommodate such complexities. Moreover, where there are large number of victims or where the victims are poor or disadvantaged, the delay endemic in the disposal of suits might not pose a problem. In such cases, directions for an expedited hearing of the class suit could be obtained from the court where the class action is filed or from a superior court.

This is not to suggest that the class suit as a procedural device is without problems. Radical individuality amongst a few members can threaten the integrity of a class; dissent within a class concerning liability or relief can

---

[161] *M.C. Mehta v Union of India* AIR 1988 SC 1037, 1038.

complicate litigation and objections by a few members may jeopardize settlements.

In the United States, the *Agent Orange* litigation[162] exemplifies the large class action lawsuit. In this case, thousands of Vietnam veterans collectively sued the manufacturers of a toxic chemical used as a defoliant in the Vietnam war. They claimed that the chemical, commonly named Agent Orange—a form of dioxin—caused them to suffer long-term chronic physical injury and also emotional injury. The litigation was complicated by the fact that there was no incontrovertible evidence that Agent Orange actually caused any of the claimed disability.

In this case, litigants formed factions, and fought among themselves. This factionalism did not, however, derail the judge-administered settlement: The judge was strong and decisive, and refused to let that happen. (The judge seemed convinced that the litigants would lose in a trial because of their large evidentiary burden.) The settlement award totalled US$ 250 million. This amount was to be distributed in two ways, namely cash awards to those who appear to have suffered the most severe injuries; and the delivery of rehabilitative services and health care to all other present and future claimants.

Another U.S. class action suit involved the Dalkon Shield,[163] an intrauterine contraceptive device that caused incidents of sterility and birth defects. This case was resolved successfully: Money was awarded promptly, with relatively small administrative or transactional costs.

As we have seen, a pragmatic spirit animates the amended Order 1, rule 8. It is now up to lawyers in India to use this rule to its full potential in environmental cases.

G. FREEDOM OF INFORMATION AND THE RIGHT TO KNOW

Public access to government information enables citizens to exercise their political choice meaningfully. Secrecy erodes the legitimacy of elected governments. A regime that conceals its actions and policies cannot be judged by the electorate and cannot be held accountable for its misdeeds. Moreover, governments in modern welfare states exercise vast powers that affect economic interests and impinge on a citizen's liberty. These powers are susceptible to misuse for private gain. The right to be informed of public acts helps check the abuse of executive power. Data that forms the basis of decision-making may at times be taken out of context, and bureaucrats may deliberately suppress certain viewpoints to favour others. Openness in government corrects these tendencies and raises the quality of decision-making. The right to know also strengthens participatory democracy. A peoples' right to influence government, other than through periodic elections, is widely recognized. Armed with information on government programmes, citizens may influence decision-making through representations, lobbying and public debate.

---

[162] *In Re: Agent Orange Product Liability Litigation*, 818 F. 2d. 145-280 (2nd Circuit, 1987).
[163] *In Re: A.H. Robins Co., Inc.*, 58 U.S.L.W. 2006 (4th Circuit, 1989).

The right to know is especially critical in environmental matters. For example, government decisions to site dams may displace thousands of people and deprive them of their lifestyles and livelihood. A responsible government, therefore, ought to widely publicize its river development plans and ought to be receptive to public feedback. But in the case of the Mansi-Wakal project intended to meet Udaipur's potable water requirements, none of the people who were to be displaced by the inundation were given basic information. Officials refused to part with the project report until villagers and activists held protest demonstrations.[164] Don't these citizens have a *right* to this information? Isn't the government under a *duty* to inform them? And isn't this obligation even greater in a society where large segments of the population are illiterate or unaware of their legal rights?

Information on the proposed location of nuclear power stations and hazardous industries directly affect the lives and health of neighbouring communities. As the Bhopal Gas Leak disaster grimly illustrates, pervasive ignorance to the dangers of methyl isocyanate contributed to the cause and the magnitude of the tragedy. Surely the government is obliged to fully disclose the proposed location of hazardous facilities and to consult local communities before reaching a decision. As the *Brundtland Report* [165] argues:

> Some large projects ... require participation of a different basis. Public inquiries and hearings on the development and environment impacts can help greatly in drawing attention to different points of view. Free access to relevant information and the availability of alternative sources of technical expertise can provide an informed basis for public discussion. When the environmental impact of a proposed project is particularly high, public scrutiny of the case should be mandatory and, wherever feasible, the decision should be subject to prior public approval, perhaps by referendum.[166]

Access to government records helps litigants construct the necessary fact base for legal actions. For example, information secured from municipal records has enabled urban environmental groups to expose the complicity between agencies and private builders.

I. JASANOFF; THE BHOPAL DISASTER AND THE RIGHT TO KNOW, 27 Social Science and Medicine 1113 (1988)

> The tragedy in Bhopal can be seen not merely as a failure of technology, but as a failure of knowledge. The accident might not have happened at all—in any case, its impact could have been greatly lessened—if the right people had obtained the right

---

[164] Centre for Science and Environment, *The State of India's Environment: The Citizens' Fifth Report* 149 (1999).

[165] World Commission on Environment and Development, *Our Common Future* (1987).

[166] *Id.* at 63-64.

information at a time when they were capable of appreciating it and taking appropriate preventive action. Reconstructions of the events in Bhopal show that there were striking gaps both in the information available about MIC and in the process of communicating this information within and outside the Union Carbide organization. A central challenge for future [right-to-know (RTK)] policies is to bridge the information gaps and the communication gaps that are likely to arise in the course of technology transfer.

In designing new RTK laws for transferred technologies, an important concern should be the production of more systematic, accurate and comprehensive characterizations of risk. Identifying the toxicological properties of individual chemicals, such as MIC, is a necessary, but by no means sufficient, step towards creating an adequate information base about hazardous industries. Probabilistic risk assessment and environmental impact analysis should both be made prerequisites to the siting of dangerous facilities. In carrying out such evaluations for transferred technologies, both private and public sector decision-makers should be sensitive to differing local circumstances in importing countries, including cultural and behavioural patterns in the workforce and the community. One lasting lesson of Bhopal is that the remote headquarters of multinational corporations are not necessarily the best places for performing such wide-ranging analyses. In order to take all relevant factors into account, and to give them due weight, much closer collaboration is required among parent companies, their foreign subsidiaries, and citizens and public authorities in technology-importing countries.

To improve the flow of information about hazardous technologies, the circles of those with a right to know and those with a duty to disclose should both be wider than under existing laws. Community right-to-know provisions have received a considerable boost in the United States after Bhopal. It is to be hoped that governments of developing countries will recognize the need for similar guarantees for their citizens. Public interest groups with demonstrated capabilities for risk management should be drawn as far as possible into the network of information sharing, reinforcing the lines of communications between industry, government and the general public.

At the same time, new policy initiatives are required in both technology-exporting and technology-importing countries in order to strengthen the disclosure obligations of hazardous industries, as well as their duty to act preventively when there is evidence of risk. Exporting countries, for example, could require that foreign governments be notified not only before the sale of banned or regulated products, but also before the construction of hazardous facilities. Importing countries, for their part, have to build a technical and administrative infrastructure capable of processing hazard information, drawing, where appropriate, on experts located outside government. Multinational corporations should take pains to distribute responsibility for health and safety in reasonable ways across their organizational structure and to ensure that managers understand clearly how this responsibility is allocated. Finally, an effective, internationally enforceable system of sanctions and penalties is needed to hold corporations accountable if they fall short of meeting their duties of disclosure and prevention.

Claims concerning trade secrecy present a high threshold barrier against any attempt to broaden the right to know. However, numerous statutes in the industrialized countries support the principle that health and safety considerations can override claims of confidentiality and compel at least a limited disclosure of hazard information. Such a principle should be applied to cross-national transfers of technology, although attempts to internationalize the health and environmental data developed by multinational corporations can be expected to encounter stiff opposition.

Bhopal finally raises questions about the limits of the right to know as a strategy for controlling risk. From the standpoint of many who were ultimately caught up in the disaster—workers, ordinary citizens, political officials—knowledge would have been most beneficial at the time Union Carbide made its basic decision about what manufacturing process should be employed in Bhopal. Wider consultation at this stage might have led to a different appraisal of risks and benefits of alternative technologies and resulted in the construction of a plant more suited to Indian conditions. Yet the choice of technology has traditionally been regarded as a corporate prerogative failing outside the scope of RTK laws. The fact that this choice led to catastrophe in Bhopal has been blamed on the absence of a technological culture in India. One could, however, with more justice blame Bhopal on a blinkered corporate culture that makes technology transfer decisions without even a rudimentary understanding of their social implications. To broaden this partial vision, the importers, consumers and potential victims of technology have to arm themselves with knowledge so that they can judge the appropriateness of different technological options. Ultimately, the right to know can only have meaning if it is supplemented by a right to participate in choosing and operating the imported technology. The tragedy of Bhopal will indeed be compounded if this lesson gets lost in an overly narrow, legalistic debate about the pros and cons of transnational information sharing.

II. EXECUTIVE MISUSE OF THE OFFICIAL SECRETS ACT

Non-disclosure of information is the norm in India; openness is the exception.[167] There is no national enactment in India imposing a duty on the government to supply information to an individual seeking it.[168] Instead, government actions are thickly veiled by the archaic Official Secrets Act of 1923. This draconian law was enacted by the British to guard against activities considered detrimental to the security of the Raj. Hardly altered in the five decades since independence, the law retains its colonial menace. The Act proscribes the disclosure of any 'secret' official information, without defining the word 'secret'. Thus, subject to judicial review, the Act grants government a *carte blanche* to withhold almost any information it chooses to.

[167] M. Jain & S. Jain, *Principles of Administrative Law* 890–900 (1986).
[168] In May, 1997, Tamil Nadu became the first state to introduce a right to information law. Although 23 'exceptions' or excluded classes of information make up most of the body of the Act, the Citizen, Consumer & Civil Action Group, Madras, has generally found government departments to be responsive to requisitions for information. Interview with Bharath Jairaj, CAG; 22 April 1999. Conducted by S. Divan. Several common law countries have such laws. e.g., U.S.A.'s Freedom of Information Act of 1966, Australia's Freedom of Information Act of 1982 and New Zealand's Official Information Act of 1982.

III. JUDICIAL RECOGNITION OF THE RIGHT TO KNOW

Under pressure to allow greater citizen access to official information, the judiciary is gradually shaping the broad contours of the right to know. Supreme Court judges have derived the right to know from two distinct constitutional sources—the fundamental right to freedom of speech and expression guaranteed in Article 19(l)(a) and the fundamental right to life and personal liberty enshrined in Article 21.

Justice Mathew in *State of Uttar Pradesh v Raj Narain*[169] was the first to recognise the citizen's right to know:

> In a government of responsibility like ours, where all the agents of the public must be responsible for their conduct, there can be but few secrets. The people of this country have a right to know every public act, everything that is done in a public way, by their public functionaries. They are entitled to know the particulars of every public transaction in all its bearing. The right to know, which is derived from the concept of freedom of speech, though not absolute, is a factor which should make one wary, when secrecy is claimed for transactions which can, at any rate, have no repercussion on public security, see *New York Times Co. v United States* (1971) 403 U.S.713. To cover with veil of secrecy, the common routine business, is not in the interest of the public. Such secrecy can seldom be legitimately desired. It is generally desired for the purpose of parties and politics or personal self-interest or bureaucratic routine. The responsibilities of officials to explain and to justify their acts is the chief safeguard against oppression and corruption.

Justice Bhagwati, too, in *S.P. Gupta v Union of India (Judges' Transfer Case)*,[170] recognized the right to know to be implicit in the right to free speech and expression. In *Dinesh Trivedi v Union of India*,[171] the Supreme Court once again acknowledged the vital importance of open government in a participative democracy.

Justice Mukharji in *Reliance Petrochemicals Ltd. v Proprietors of Indian Express Newspapers Bombay Pvt. Ltd.*[172] recognized the right to know as emanating from the right to life: 'We must remember that the people at large have a right to know in order to be able to take part in a participatory development in the industrial life and democracy. Right to know is a basic right [to] which citizens of a free country aspire [in the broadening horizon of the right to life] under Article 21 of our Constitution. That right has reached new dimensions and urgency. The right puts greater responsibility upon those who take upon the responsibility to inform.' The strong link between Article 21 and the right to know is evident in

[169] AIR 1975 SC 865, 884.
[170] AIR 1982 SC 149, 234. Justice Bhagwati's opinion is quoted in the Bombay High Court judgment in *Bombay Environmental Action Group v Pune Cantonment Board*, excerpted later in this section.
[171] 1997 (4) SCC 306, 314.
[172] AIR 1989 SC 190, 202.

environmental matters where secret government decisions may affect health, life and livelihood.

IV. JUDICIAL DEVELOPMENTS

The following judgment of the Bombay High Court and order of the Supreme Court significantly strengthen a citizen's access to official environmental information.

The Bombay High Court in its unreported judgment excerpted below, considered whether a recognized environmental group has a right to examine municipal permissions granted to private builders. The environmental group believed that construction on five plots within the cantonment was illegal and, therefore, it sought inspection of the relevant municipal documents. The cantonment board, however, refused to grant inspection, forcing the group to petition the court.

BOMBAY ENVIRONMENTAL ACTION GROUP v
PUNE CANTONMENT BOARD
Bombay High Court
A.S. Writ Petition No. 2733 of 1986
7 October 1986

DHARMADHIKARI, J.:

The petitioners wanted that they should be granted either inspection or copies of applications made for building permissions, plans accompanying such applications and all official proceedings relating to such permissions, including renewals thereof. Since this request of the petitioners was not granted, the petitioners have filed the present Writ Petition for a declaration that it was incumbent upon the Cantonment Board to disclose to the petitioners and other citizens and/or grant to the petitioners or other citizens inspection of all these documents and materials and they have, therefore, prayed for a necessary Writ and/or directions.

[Counsel] appearing for the petitioners, contended before us that under Art. 19(1)(a) of the Constitution of India, a citizen has a right to get such information. Even under the relevant provisions of the Act, a public body like the respondent Cantonment Board cannot refuse to give inspection of these public documents. This is more so when the petitioners, which is an Action Group, want to help the Cantonment Board in maintaining the environmental balance within its territorial jurisdiction and the documents asked for cannot be termed as secret or confidential.

* * *

In support of his contentions, [Counsel] has mainly relied upon the observations of the Supreme Court in *S.P. Gupta and others v President of India and others* A.I.R. 1982 S.C. 149, and particularly upon the following observations:

This is the new democratic culture of an open society towards which every liberal democracy is moving and our country should be no exception. The concept of an open government is the direct emanation from the right to know which seems to be implicit in the right of free speech and expression guaranteed under Article 19(1)(a). Therefore, disclosures of information in regard to the functioning of Government must be the rule and secrecy an exception justified only where the strictest requirement of public interest so demands. The approach of the court must be to attenuate the area of secrecy as much as possible consistently with the requirement of public interest, bearing in mind all the time that disclosure also serves an important aspect of public interest.

* * *

However, it was contended by ... the learned Counsel appearing for the respondents, that these observations of the Supreme Court cannot be read torn from their context and should be restricted to the provisions of Art.74 and Sections 123 and 162 of the Evidence Act viz., to the cases where a privilege is claimed and it cannot be held that they lay down a general rule. In the present case, the Cantonment Board is not claiming any privilege qua any document and, therefore, the said decision is not relevant for deciding the controversy raised in this Writ Petition. We find it difficult to accept this contention ... The Supreme Court in *S. P. Gupta's Case* has in terms construed the scope of Art. 19(1)(a) of the Constitution. If Art. 19(1)(à) takes in its import the disclosure of information in regard to the functioning of the Government and the right to know about it, which is implicit in the right of free speech and expression guaranteed under Art. 19(1)(a) of the Constitution of India, then the right of inspection as claimed by the petitioners in this Writ Petition must flow from the said fundamental right.

* * *

The apprehension expressed by [Counsel for the respondents] that if such right is given to a citizen, then the working of the Cantonment Board will not only be affected but will come to a standstill is also without any substance. To say the least, in this Writ Petition we are not dealing with the right of each and every citizen generally. We would like to confine ourselves to the rights of recognized social action groups whose activities deserve to be appreciated.

* * *

Real democracy cannot be worked by men sitting at the top. It has to be worked from below by the people of every village and town. That sovereignty resides in and flows from the people. So said the Father of the Nation in whose name we swear. Therefore, 'Who will watch the watchman' is the vexed question before our democracy.

* * *

NOTES

1. The judgment is of seminal importance because it transforms the right to know from judicial rhetoric into a substantive, enforceable right. The court finds the right to inspection to flow from the fundamental right to free speech and expression. More significantly, it recognizes the right to know to be a distinct, self-contained right, *independent* from the governments' claim to privilege under the Indian Evidence Act of 1872.[173] This is notable because the observations on the right to know by both Justice Mathew in *Raj Narains' Case*[174] as well as Justice Bhagwati in the *Judges' Transfer Case*[175] were made while considering government claims to privilege. A timid court could easily have accepted the respondents' contentions and restricted its application of the 'right to know' principle to cases where privilege is claimed.

2. Equally significant, the court upholds the petitioners' right to know *without* requiring any proof of government irregularity. It appears, therefore, that the right to know may be asserted even where no illegalities are alleged. Indeed, the only requirements for a recognized environmental action group asserting this right are that the group must act *'bona fide'*[176] and for a 'genuine purpose'. Finally, the judgment is important because by granting relief under Article 226, the High Court opens the speedy, inexpensive writ remedy to recognized social action groups seeking access to official environmental information.

In a different case between the same parties—*Bombay Environmental Action Group v Pune Cantonment Board*—the petitioners sought the Supreme Courts' special leave to appeal under Article 136 of the Constitution after the Bombay High Court had rejected their petition under Article 226. The petition challenged the construction of 'Sterling Centre', a building in the Pune cantonment area.

BOMBAY ENVIRONMENTAL ACTION GROUP v
PUNE CANTONMENT BOARD
Supreme Court of India
SLP (Civil) No. 11291 of 1986
13 October 1986

ORDER: * * *

Special leave petition is rejected on the facts and circumstances of the present case. We may make it clear that it is not in every case where construction has started or rights of

---

[173] Section 123 read with section 162 of the Indian Evidence Act enables the government to refrain from disclosing the contents of documents ('privileged documents') whose disclosure would injure the public interest.

[174] *Supra* note 169.

[175] *Supra* note 170.

[176] In good faith—honestly, openly and sincerely.

third parties have intervened that the courts will necessarily refuse to exercise their discretion to grant relief under Article 226. Every case must depend on its special facts and circumstances and there may be cases where the ends of justice may demand that the High Court should intervene and grant relief despite the rights of third parties having come into existence where the petitioner may not be guilty of laches or of undue delay. We would direct the Pune Cantonment Board to take care while giving sanction for construction to ensure that none of the Bye-laws is violated. We would particularly draw the attention of the Pune Cantonment Board to Bye-Law 10 of which observance must be strictly secured in the future. We would also direct that any person residing within the area of a local authority or any social action group or interest group or pressure group shall be entitled to take inspection of any sanction granted or plan approved by such local authority in construction of buildings along with the related papers and documents if such individual or social action group or interest group or pressure group wishes to take such inspection, except of course in cases where in the interests of security such inspection cannot be permitted.

NOTES AND QUESTIONS

1. While the Bombay High Court judgment[177] restricted access to municipal urban development documents to 'recognized social action groups', the Supreme Court's order extends this right to all persons residing within the area as well as to any social action group, interest group or pressure group. A second respect in which the Supreme Court's order appears broader is that it carves a very limited 'interests of security' exception to the right to know. The High Court judgment, apparently, conferred a wider discretion on the municipal officer as it allowed them to withhold municipal records whenever a request for inspection was 'not made for a genuine purpose'.

2. What is the precedential value of the Supreme Court order? Article 141 of the Constitution states: 'The law declared by the Supreme Court shall be binding on all courts within the territory of India.' But this does not mean that every sentence uttered by a judge of the Supreme Court is binding. In *Union of India v All India Services Pensioners Association*[178] the Supreme Court stated: 'The special leave petitions were not dismissed without reasons. This court had given reasons for dismissing the special leave petitions. When such reasons are given, the decision becomes one which attracts Article 141 of the Constitution. ...' Is the *Bombay Environmental Action Group* order a 'reasoned order' within the meaning of Article 141?

V. ENVIRONMENTAL LAWS AND ACCESS TO OFFICIAL INFORMATION

Both the Air Act and the Water Act as amended in 1987 and 1988 respectively, oblige pollution control boards to disclose relevant internal reports to a citizen seeking

---

[177] A.S. Writ Petition No. 2733 of 1986, reproduced earlier.
[178] AIR 1988 SC 501.

to prosecute a polluter. These disclosure provisions are unique among Indian laws. They ought to bolster citizen actions, and may also help to discipline polluters who are able to forestall prosecutions because they have the ear of board officials.

Provisos to section 43 of the Air Act and section 49 of the Water Act, however, allow a board to withhold any report if it considers that disclosure would be against 'the public interest'. This qualification to the right of information seems unnecessary. It is difficult to envision a situation where the disclosure of reports on pollution could harm the public.

Since citizens' prosecutions are still rare, the extent of a board's obligation to disclose information has yet to be judicially construed. Nonetheless, it seems clear that a mandamus will issue against a board when it unreasonably delays in disclosing documents that it would ordinarily use to prosecute a polluter.

The Environmental Impact Assessment Regulations of 1994 as amended in 1997, confer a right on members of the public to access the 'executive summary' of a proposal prepared by the project proponent. In theory, this access is meant to enable citizens to participate at a public hearing. In practical terms, the limited access prevents concerned citizens from effectively questioning the project. Unless citizens are permitted access to *all* relevant environmental studies and reports (and not just an executive summary authored by the project proponent), the public hearings will remain a formality.

5

WATER POLLUTION CONTROL

The Indian legal system provides four major sources of law for addressing water pollution problems: (1) a comprehensive scheme of administrative regulation through the permit system of the Water (Prevention and Control of Pollution) Act of 1974; (2) provisions of the Environment (Protection) Act of 1986 relating to water quality; (3) public nuisance actions against polluters, including municipalities charged with controlling water pollution; and (4) the common law right of riparian owners to unpolluted water. In addition, the Union Government's Department of Environment, Forests and Wildlife has developed an action plan for the prevention of pollution of the Ganga and a National River Conservation Plan which is scheduled to be completed in March 2005. The Supreme Court of India and the High Courts have added to the force of these laws by hearing public interest writ petitions that seek implementation of measures to prevent water pollution.

We open this chapter with a reading from the *Span Motels Case*, where the Supreme Court lays down a frame of reference to guide natural resource managers. In borrowing the public trust doctrine from American case law, the court supplies a common property vision of water resources and a wellspring for future environmental jurisprudence.

In 1995, Span Motels built a resort on the bank of the Beas river between Kullu and Manali in Himachal Pradesh. Kamal Nath, formerly the Union Minister of Environment and Forests, had links to the hotelier, who had encroached a swathe of forest land. The encroachment was 'validated' in 1993–94, during Nath's tenure as minister. During the 1995 monsoons, the river engulfed part of the land and threatened the resort. In an effort to protect its property, both before and after the 1995 floods, Span Motels carried out substantial work (dredging, construction of concrete barriers, wire crates, etc.) to deflect the flow of the river. Justice Kuldip Singh of the Supreme Court was only a couple of weeks from retirement when he delivered the following judgment on 13 December 1996.

M.C. MEHTA v KAMAL NATH
1997 (1) SCC 388

KULDIP SINGH, J: * * *

The forest lands which have been given on lease to the Motel by the State Government are situated at the bank of River Beas. Beas is a young and dynamic river. It runs through Kullu Valley between the mountain ranges of the Dhauladhar in the right bank and the Chandrakheni in the left. The river is fast-flowing, carrying large boulders, at the times of flood. When water velocity is not sufficient to carry the boulders, those are deposited in the channel often blocking the flow of water. Under such circumstances the river stream changes its course, remaining within the valley but swinging from one bank to the other. The right bank of the River Beas where the Motel is located mostly comes under forest, the left bank consists of plateaus, having steep bank facing the river, where fruit orchards and cereal cultivation are predominant. The area being ecologically fragile and full and scenic beauty should not have been permitted to be converted into private ownership and for commercial gains.

The notion that the public has a right to expect certain lands and natural areas to retain their natural characteristic is finding its way into the law of the land.

* * *

The ancient Roman Empire developed a legal theory known as the 'Doctrine of the Public Trust.' It was founded on the ideas that certain common properties such as rivers, seashore, forests and the air were held by Government in trusteeship for the free and unimpeded use of the general public. Our contemporary concern about 'the environment' bear a very close conceptual relationship to this legal doctrine. Under the Roman law these resources were either owned by no one (*res nullious*) or by every one in common (*res communious*). Under the English common law, however, the Sovereign could own these resources but the ownership was limited in nature, the Crown could not grant these properties to private owners if the effect was to interfere with the public interests in navigation or fishing. Resources that were suitable for these uses were deemed to be held in trust by the Crown for the benefit of the public. Joseph L. Sax, Professor of Law, University of Michigan—proponent of the Modern Public Trust Doctrine has given the historical background of the Public Trust Doctrine as under:

> The source of modern public trust law is found in a concept that received much attention in Roman and English Law—the nature of property rights in rivers, the sea, and the seashore. That history has been given considerable attention in the legal literature and need not be repeated in detail here. But two points should be emphasized. First, certain interests, such as navigation and fishing, were sought to be preserved for the benefit of the public; accordingly, property used for those purposes was distinguished from general public property which the sovereign could routinely grant to private owners. Second, while it was understood that in certain common properties—such as the seashore, highways, and running water—'perpetual use was dedicated to

the public', it has never been clear whether the public had an enforceable right to prevent infringement of those interests. Although the State apparently did protect public uses, no evidence is available that the public rights could be legally asserted against a recalcitrant government.

The public trust doctrine primarily rests on the principle that certain resources like air, sea, waters and the forests have such a great importance to the people as a whole that it would be wholly unjustified to make them a subject of private ownership. The said resources being a gift of nature, they should be made freely available to everyone irrespective of the status in life. The doctrine enjoins upon the Government to protect the resources for the enjoyment of the general public rather than to permit their use for private ownership or commercial purposes. According to Professor Sax the Public Trust Doctrine imposes the following restrictions on governmental authority:

Three types of restrictions on governmental authority are often thought to be imposed by the public trust: first, the property subject to the trust must not only be used for a public purpose, but it must be held available for use by the general public; second, the property may not be sold, even for a fair cash equivalent; and third the property must be maintained for particular types of uses.

[The court reviewed a number of U.S. Court decisions, particularly the judgment of the Supreme Court of California in the *Mono Lake Case* (*National Audubon Society v Superior Court of Alpine County*, 33 Cal 3d 419). In *Mono Lake*, the environmentalists filed a suit against the city of Los Angeles which was drawing water from streams that fed Mono Lake, a large saline lake rich in brine shrimps and bird life. As a result of the diversion, the lake level was falling, marring the scenic beauty and imperiling the birds. Upholding the plaintiff's claim that the public trust doctrine could be used to supercede Los Angeles' water diversion, the California Supreme Court held:

Thus, the public trust is more than an affirmation of State power to use public property for public purposes. It is an affirmation of the duty of the State to protect the people's common heritage of streams, lakes, marshlands and tidelands, surrendering that right of protection only in rare cases when the abandonment of that right is consistent with the purposes of the trust. The State has an affirmative duty to take the public trust into account in the planning and allocation of water resources, and to protect public trust use whenever feasible. Just as the history of this State shows that appropriation may be necessary for efficient use of water despite unavoidable harm to public trust values, it demonstrates that an appropriative water rights system administered without consideration of the public trust may cause unnecessary and unjustified harm to trust interest.]

It is no doubt correct that the public trust doctrine under the English common law extended only to certain traditional uses such as navigation, commerce and fishing. But the American Courts in recent cases have expanded the concept of the public trust doctrine. The observations of the Supreme Court of California in *Mono Lake Case* clearly show the judicial concern in protecting all ecologically important lands, for example fresh water, wetlands or riparian forests. The observations of the Court in *Mono Lake Case* to the effect that the protection of ecological values is among the purposes of public trust, may give rise to an argument that the ecology and the environment protection is relevant factor to determine which lands, waters or airs are protected by the public trust doctrine.

* * *

Our legal system—based on English common law—includes the public trust doctrine as part of its jurisprudence. The State is the trustee of all natural resources which are by nature meant for public use and enjoyment. Public at large is the beneficiary of the seashore, running waters, airs, forests and ecologically fragile lands. The State as a trustee is under a legal duty to protect the natural resources. These resources meant for public use cannot be converted into private ownership.

We are fully aware that the issues presented in this case illustrate the classic struggle between those members of the public who could preserve our rivers, forests, parks and open lands in their pristine purity and those charged with administrative responsibilities who, under the pressure of the changing needs of an increasingly complex society, find it necessary to encroach to some extent upon open lands heretofore considered inviolate to change. The resolution of this conflict in any given case is for the legislature and not the courts. If there is a law made by Parliament or the State Legislatures the courts can serve as an instrument of determining legislative intent in the exercise of its powers of judicial review under the Constitution. But in the absence of any legislation, the executive acting under the doctrine of public trust cannot abdicate the natural resources and convert them into private ownership, or for commercial use. The aesthetic use and the pristine glory of the natural resources, the environment and the ecosystem of our country cannot be permitted to be eroded for private, commercial or any other use unless the courts finds it necessary, in good faith, for the public good and in public interest to encroach upon the said resources.

Coming to the facts of the present case, large area of the bank of River Beas which is part of protected forest has been given on a lease purely for commercial purposes to the Motels. We have no hesitation in holding that the Himachal Pradesh Government committed patent breach of public trust by leasing the ecologically fragile land to the Motel management. Both the lease transactions are in patent breach of the trust held by the State Government. The second lease granted in the year 1994 was virtually of the land which is a part of the riverbed.

* * *

We therefore direct and order as under:

1. The public trust doctrine, as discussed by us in this judgment is a part of the law of the land.

2. The prior approval granted by the Government of India, Ministry of Environment and Forest by the letter dated 24–11–1993 and the lease deed dated

11–4–1994 in favour of the Motel are quashed. The lease granted to the Motel by the said lease deed in respect of 27 bighas and 12 biswas of area, is cancelled and set aside. The Himachal Pradesh Government shall take over the area and restore it to its original-natural conditions.

    3. The Motel shall pay compensation by way of cost for the restitution of the environment and ecology of the area. The pollution caused by various constructions made by the Motel in the riverbed and the banks of River Beas has to be removed and reversed. We direct NEERI through its Director to inspect the area, if necessary, and give an assessment of the cost which is likely to be incurred for reversing the damage caused by the Motel to the environment and ecology of the area. NEERI may take into consideration the report by the Board in this respect.

    4. The Motel through its management shall show cause why pollution fine in addition be not imposed on the Motel.

* * *

NOTES AND QUESTIONS

    1. The public trust doctrine has vast potential and may serve as a touchstone to test executive action with a significant environmental impact. For example, it may extend to common property cases where officials permit development along the seashore or the non-recreational use of playgrounds. It may also apply to un-regulated areas such as the exploitation of ground water.

    2. In the United States, the public trust doctrine as an environment protection theory developed over several years. The Indian Supreme Court, untroubled by the absence of any Indian precedent in this field, simply imported the doctrine and declared that it was a part of the law of the land. What are the implications of this approach on the rule of law; especially the tenets of predictability and certainty?

    3. It was in December, 1996 that the public trust doctrine was articulated for the first time in India in this case. When the doctrine was articulated in *Mono Lake*, it was used in that very case. Legal doctrines always apply to the case at hand, as well as prospectively.

    4. At the end of the day, Span Motels was trying to save its buildings from being washed away. Is that objectionable? Was the judicial response on over-reaction? Or was the court seeking to emphasize ecological values by making an example of a powerful government functionary?

    5. Does the public trust doctrine apply only to the allocation of pristine natural resources or does it extend to pollution cases as well? Are not river polluters 'allocating' to themselves clean water at the cost of downstream users? What are

the implications of this doctrine on pollution control boards charged with issuing consents or permits to water and air polluters?

6. In addition to the orders excerpted above, the court issued a direction to the Himachal Pradesh pollution control board to prevent all hotels, institutions and factories from discharging untreated waste water into the Beas. Is it a good judicial practice to issue general directions which travel beyond the scope of the petition? Are they justified because they strengthen the hands of the board officials?

7. In *M.I. Builders v Radhey Shyam Sahu,*[1] the Supreme Court held that allowing an underground shopping complex to come up below a public park violated the public trust doctrine. The court directed the demolition of the structures and restoration of the park.

A. WATER POLLUTION: SCOPE OF THE PROBLEM

The following readings provide descriptions of the nature and scope of the water pollution problem in India. The excerpt from the Citizens' Report is an overview of the problem. The excerpt from Anju Sharma's study of the Yamuna focuses on the effects of Delhi's untreated discharges into the river.

CENTRE FOR SCIENCE AND ENVIRONMENT; STATE OF INDIA'S ENVIRONMENT: THE CITIZENS' FIFTH REPORT, 59 (1999)

Polluting a river is dangerous because a river is the primary source of drinking water for towns and cities downstream of the point of pollution. Broadly, the causes of water pollution can be ascribed to:

Urbanization: Many of the towns and cities that came up on the banks of a river did not give a thought to the problem of urban sewage. Most of the sewage was conveniently allowed to flow into the rivers. The 25 large towns and cities on the Ganga, for instance, generate 1,340 million litres per day (mld) sewage. Prior to the Ganga Action Plan over 95 percent of this entered the river without being treated. Add to this the rapid increase in industrial pollution at these urban centres. Effluents from industries, many a time containing toxics and heavy metals, drain into the rivers. Ironically, the water of the same dirty river is the source of drinking water for another town downstream.

Municipal water treatment facilities in India, at present, do not remove traces of heavy metals. Given the fact that heavily polluted rivers are the major sources of municipal water for most towns and cities along their courses, it is believed that every consumer has been, over the years, exposed to unknown quantities of pollutants in the water they have consumed. To add to this, Indian towns and cities have grown in an unplanned manner over the years due to huge population increase in these

[1] AIR 1999 SC 2468.

settlements. The direct result on the rivers, which receive untreated sewage, is that the concentrated sewage flow has increased.

Industrial pollution: Most Indian rivers and freshwater streams are polluted by industrial wastes or effluents. All these industrial wastes are toxic to life forms that consume this water. This could harm the liver, kidneys, reproductive system, respiratory system or the nervous system. Water treatment facilities in India do not remove traces of heavy metals from water. (Technologically, the present treatment facilities are incapable of treating micropollutants like heavy metals and pesticides. Upgrading to improve treatment facilities, which are expensive, will be able to treat these pollutants.) Hence, traces of heavy metals in water enter the body of the consumer.

Withdrawal of water: Heavy abstraction of freshwater for irrigation and other purposes leaves almost no water in rivers. The only water that flows in the rivers thereafter is that from sewers, drains and seepage of groundwater. The Yamuna, for example, has almost no water at Tajewala in Haryana, where the Eastern Yamuna Canal and the Western Yamuna Canal abstract all the water for irrigation. Similarly, the upper and the lower Ganga canals have left the Ganga downstream dry.

Agricultural runoff and improper agricultural practices: Traces of fertilizers and pesticides are washed into the nearest waterbodies at the onset of the monsoons or whenever there are heavy showers. As the point of entry of such agricultural inputs is diffused throughout the river basin, they are termed non-point sources of pollution. Consumers are also affected by agricultural contaminants such as fertilizers and pesticides that run off from fields into rivers.

'An uneducated farmer tends not to go by the recommended dosage (of pesticides), nor does he bother about worker protection,' says A K Dikshit, senior scientist with the Indian Agricultural Research Institute, New Delhi. 'The recommendations are made on the basis of careful scientific research. But, in the Indian context, the farmer generally uses his own interpretations, often using excess fertilizers and pesticides,' adds Dikshit. When pesticides and fertilizers are used more than the recommended doses, they remain in the soil. While some of this may become inert over a period of time, traces end up in the closest waterbody. This could be in the form or irrigation or monsoon runoff. As Indian rivers are the primary source of drinking water in most municipalities, their pollution means that the municipal drinking water is contaminated with pesticides and fertilizer residues.

* * *

Religious and social practices: Carcasses of cattle and other animals disposed of in the so-called 'holy' rivers add to the pollution load. In keeping with ancient rituals, the dead are still cremated on river banks. Spiralling wood prices also have resulted in partially burnt bodies often being flung into rivers. The tradition of throwing unburnt bodies of holy men, infants and those who succumb to contagious diseases, into rivers, has given the issue of pollution in Indian rivers an unhealthy social dimension. Mass bathing in a river during religious festivals is another environmentally harmful practice. Studies have indicated that the biochemical oxygen demand goes up drastically when tens of thousands of people simultaneously take a 'holy dip'. Religious practices also demand that offerings from a *puja* be immersed in a river. It is now common to see people immersing offerings in plastic bags, further adding to the pollution load of a river.

Indian rivers showcase the price paid for mindless development; a classic example of pay-off between rapid population and economic growth and environmental degradation.

SHARMA; WHEN A RIVER WEEPS ..., DOWN TO EARTH, 15 April 1996, p. 27

Delhi discharges more than 2,000 millions litres per day (mld) of waste water into the Yamuna. Of this, only 300 mld is contributed by the industrial sector. The bulk of the pollutants come from untreated sewage, dumped into the river because the city administration lacks sufficient sewage treatment facilities. 'The administration has facilities to treat only 1,270 mld,' admits J C Kala, joint secretary, Union ministry of environment and forests (MEF).

Even the existing treatment facilities are underutilized. A report published by the Delhi pollution control committee (1993) revealed that a mere 31.8 mld of sewage is treated sufficiently for disposal into the river. The existing sewage plants are capital- and power-intensive. Sewage goes untreated into the river during machinery and power break-downs; in other cases, badly situated sewage treatment plants (STPs) get flooded during the rains.

As a result, though Delhi covers only two percent of the length and basin area of the river, it contributes 71 percent of the waste water discharged into the river everyday! And since most of the Yamuna waters that flow into the city are used up to cater to Delhi's extravagant requirements, what remains of the river after Delhi has finished with it, is undiluted sewage. 'Even an optimum flow of water is not maintained,' points out Sureshwar Sinha, founding member of Pani Morcha, an organisation committed to improving the quantity and quality of Delhi's water supply.

The situation is worse during summer. The average annual flow in Yamuna is estimated to be about 100 billion kilolitres, of which 80 percent is during the three monsoon months. With very little water flowing through it through the other months, the assimilation capacity of the river is considerably reduced—sewage is neither diluted nor dispersed.

* * *

Asphyxiation of Yamuna begins the moment it enters Delhi at Wazirabad in the north. About 1,800 mld of untreated sewage finds its way through 18 notorious *nullahs* (drains) and ends up in the river at various points along its 22 km stretch through Delhi.

Industrial waste from Delhi's 20 large, 25 medium and about 93,000 small-scale industrial units also flows into the river through these drains. By the time it leaves south Delhi at Okhla and for 490 km thereafter (until it is joined by the river Chambal), the Yamuna is a dead river. The water which the Central Pollution Control Board (CPCB) categorizes as fit for drinking at Wazirabad is deemed unfit for even bathing at Okhla. The dissolved oxygen (DO) and biological oxygen demand (BOD) levels at Wazirabad and Okhla differ dramatically; while DO level at Wazirabad was 12.5 mg/l in 1987, it decreased to 4.5 mg/l at Okhla. The BOD levels, meanwhile, were at a low of about 4 mg/l at Wazirabad in the same year, and shot up to 70 mg/l in Okhla.

In 1991, Phase II of the Ganga Action Plan (GAP) was launched for cleaning up tributaries like Yamuna, Gomti and Damodar; Rs. 340 crores was pledged for the Yamuna in 1993, 50 percent of which was to be borne by state governments. The Yamuna Action Plan (YAP) covered six towns of Haryana, 11 towns of Uttar Pradesh and Delhi. 'YAP aims at intercepting, diverting and treating municipal waste water,' says Kala.

Among other schemes, the project included the construction of community toilets, electric and improved wood-based crematoria, afforestation and development of *ghats* within a period of five years. But two years later, much of this is yet to begin. Though 12 more STPs are needed to deal with the sewage in Delhi, the YAP's contribution will only be two STPs, effectively taking care of only 20 mld of sewage. The rest are to be set up by the Delhi administration. But little has been done despite an outlay of Rs. 282 crores for sewage disposal in the city's Eighth Five Year Plan.

A 2 March 1995 directive from the Supreme Court to the MEF—to sanction the STPs within one week—following a public interest petition filed by lawyer M C Mehta in 1985 and then again in 1994, may hurry things up. The STPs have been sanctioned, and Kala expects them to be ready in a year's time.

Another public interest petition was filed by Sinha in 1993 demanding a stay order on YAP until it was reviewed on the basis of successes and failures of the GAP. 'Several reports on GAP have branded its failure,' says Sinha. 'There is no reason to expect that the Yamuna plan, modeled on GAP, would succeed. What is likely is that huge amounts of public funds and precious time are going to be wasted.'

To support his allegations, Sinha quotes from several reports. A study conducted by the National Environmental Engineering Research Institute, Nagpur, in 1991, when a major part of GAP had been completed, showed no improvement in the amount of fecal coliform in Ganga waters. Another report by S.K. Mishra and S.N. Upadhyay from the Institute of Technology, Benaras Hindu University, showed that the installation of sewage pumps near the bathing *ghats* in Varanasi had made little difference to the pollution levels. Under YAP, a similar plan to install sewage pumps near the *ghats* in Mathura awaits implementation.

Sinha complains that YAP accepts a low flow of water during lean season as normal. The Yamuna's low flow leaves no scope for the river to clean itself. 'The minimum flow requirement for any river should be at least 285 cu m /sec,' says CPCB's R C Trivedi. 'But the flow in Delhi goes down to 5 cu m/ sec during summer. Aquatic life, needing a minimum flow of 10 cu m/sec, dies. So, even if we could somehow divert pollution from the river, it would not help unless the flow is maintained.'

Strangely enough, reducing industrial waste is not on YAP's agenda. 'Industrial pollution will be left to better implementation of pollution control laws,' says Kala. But T. Venugopal CPCB's pollution assessment department head, admits that preventing industrial pollution from entering the river is a difficult job. Besides, he adds, the overall impact of pollution reduction through these laws is never felt because new industries are always coming up.

NOTES

After waiting five years for the pollution control authorities in Delhi and Haryana to end pollution of the Yamuna, the Supreme Court turned up the heat in 1999. On 27 August 1999 the court observed:

> The overwhelming majority of people of this State and those who depend upon the quality of the river water cannot be allowed to be held at ransom by a small percentage of persons polluting the river aided and abetted, in a way, by government inaction.[2]

The court prohibited the discharge of industrial effluents into the river, required monitoring stations to be established on each of the drains leading to the river, and required the administration to take effective measures against industry.

B. THE WATER ACT

The Water (Prevention and Control of Pollution) Act of 1974 is a complex statute which has been in effect for over two decades. Many features of the Act have been challenged in the courts. In this section we discuss the framework of the Water Act and analyse major issues including the scope of judicial relief authorized by the Act, constitutional challenges to the Act, liability of corporate officers, and funding of the administration of the Act.

I. FRAMEWORK OF THE WATER ACT

The Water Act of 1974 represented one of India's first attempts to deal comprehensively with an environmental issue. Parliament adopted minor amendments to the Act in 1978 and revised the Act in 1988 to more closely conform to the provisions of the Environment (Protection) Act of 1986.

Water is a subject in the State List under the Constitution.[3] Consequently, the Water Act, a central law, was enacted under Article 252(1) of the Constitution, which empowers the Union Government to legislate in a field reserved for the states, where two or more State Legislatures consent to a central law. All the states have approved implementation of the Water Act as enacted in 1974.[4]

The Water Act establishes a Central and state pollution control boards. The Central board may advise the Central Government on water pollution issues, coordinate the activities of state pollution control boards, sponsor investigation

---

[2] *News Item 'Hindustan Times' A.Q.F.M. Yamuna v Central Pollution Control Board* 1999 (5) SCALE 418, 419. Subsequent orders are reported at 2000 (1) SCALE 134; 2000 (1) SCALE 657; and 2000 (3) SCALE 122.

[3] Entry 17, List II, Seventh Schedule.

[4] However, the 1988 amendment has yet to be adopted by all the states.

and research relating to water pollution, and develop a comprehensive plan for the control and prevention of water pollution.[5] The Central board also performs the functions of a state board for the union territories. In conflicts between a state board and the Central board, the Central board prevails. Since 1982, the Central board has been attached to the Union Government's Department of Environment, Forests, and Wildlife.

The Water Act is comprehensive in its coverage, applying to streams, inland waters, subterranean waters, and sea or tidal waters. Standards for the discharge of effluent or the quality of the receiving waters are not specified in the Act itself. Instead, the Act enables state boards to prescribe these standards.[6]

The Act provides for a permit system or 'consent' procedure to prevent and control water pollution. The Act generally prohibits disposal of polluting matter in streams, wells and sewers or on land in excess of the standards established by the state boards.[7] A person must obtain consent from the state board before taking steps to establish any industry, operation or process, any treatment and disposal system or any extension or addition to such a system which might result in the discharge of sewage or trade effluent into a stream, well or sewer or onto land.[8] The state board may condition its consent by orders that specify the location, construction and use of the outlet as well as the nature and composition of new discharges. The state board must maintain and make public a register containing the particulars of the consent orders. The Act empowers a state board, upon thirty days notice to a polluter, to execute any work required under a consent order which has not been executed. The board may recover the expenses for such work from the polluters.

Other functions of the state boards specified by the Water Act include: (1) planning a comprehensive programme for prevention, control, and abatement of water pollution in the state; (2) encouraging, conducting, and participating in investigations and research of water pollution problems; (3) inspecting facilities for sewage and trade effluent treatment; and (4) developing economical and reliable methods of treatment of sewage and trade effluents.[9] The Act gives the state boards the power of entry and inspection to carry out their functions.[10] Moreover, a state board may take certain emergency measures if it determines that an accident or other unforeseen event has polluted a stream or well. These measures include removing the pollutants, mitigating the damage, and issuing orders to the polluter prohibiting effluent discharges.

The 1988 amendment introduced a new section 33A which empowers state

---

[5] Section 16.
[6] Section 17(g). The Environment (Protection) Act of 1986 gives the Central Government similar authority to establish water quality and effluent standards throughout India.
[7] Section 24.
[8] Section 25. Section 26 requires that persons releasing water pollutants prior to the adoption of the Water Act must also meet the consent requirements of section 25.
[9] Section 17.
[10] Section 23.

boards to issue directions to any person, officer or authority, including orders to close, prohibit or regulate any industry, operation or process and to stop or regulate the supply of water, electricity or any other service. Prior to the adoption of section 33A, a state board could issue direct orders to polluters under section 32 of the Act. A state board, however, could only exercise this power if the pollution arose from 'any accident or other unforeseen act or event'. Moreover, a state board's authority to issue orders under section 32 was limited to orders directed to the polluter, not to government officials or other parties. The state boards can also apply to courts for injunctions to prevent water pollution under section 33 of the Act. Under section 41, the penalty for failure to comply with a court order under section 33 or a direction from the board under section 33A is punishable by fines and imprisonment.

The amendments also increased the power of the Central board relative to the state boards. Under section 18 of the Act, the Central Government may determine that a state board has failed to comply with Central board directions and that because of this failure an emergency has arisen. The Central Government may then direct the Central board to perform the functions of the state board.

The 1988 amendments modified section 49 to allow citizens to bring actions under the Water Act. Now a state board must make relevant reports available to complaining citizens, unless the board determines that the disclosures would harm 'public interest'. Previously, the Act allowed courts to recognize only those actions brought by a board, or with a previous written sanction of a board.

NOTES AND QUESTIONS

1. The power to issue direct orders given to pollution control boards under section 33A may result in a decrease of section 33 actions against polluters. Note, however, that the courts are still involved in enforcing section 33A orders since the state boards have no direct power to exact fines, order imprisonment or otherwise compel compliance with their directions other than penalty actions filed with the courts under the Act.

Faced with an obstinate industry that refused to obey its closure order under section 33A, the state board in *Executive Apparel Processors v Taluka Executive Magistrate*,[11] directed the deputy commissioner to seize the unit and secure compliance. The commissioner's office moved the respondent-magistrate, who ordered closure. In revision, the Karnataka High Court quashed the magistrate's order holding that the board had no power to get its closure orders executed through the deputy commissioner but could initiate penalty proceedings under section 41.

2. Gujarat has not passed a resolution under Article 252(1) of the Constitution, making the amendment of 1988 applicable to the state. The result is that neither section

[11] 1997 (4) KAR.L.J. 181.

33A nor some of the important amendments made in the parent Act have been extended to Gujarat.[12] The High Court has urged the state government to quickly remove the lacuna.[13]

3. Under section 33A, the directions of the state boards are subject to any directions issued by the Central Government. As a matter of policy, should the Central Government be allowed to countermand a section 33A direction from a state board? Which authority is better situated to evaluate local water pollution problems—the Central Government or state boards? Which authority is better insulated from pressure by industry and local governments?

The harsh consequences that flow from a section 33A order persuaded the Madhya Pradesh High Court to insist upon strict compliance with the principles of natural justice. A pollution control board may not issue a closure order on extraneous considerations that travel beyond the grounds stated in the show cause notice.[14]

4. Highlighting the poor implementation of the Water Act, Kerban Anklesaria describes the law as a set of 'rules without regulation'.[15] Her critique of the Act begins at the composition of the state water boards which are packed with state government nominees and representatives of government companies.[16] There is hardly an independent voice on the board representing the affected citizen or environmentalist. According to Anklesaria the penalties are too low to deter defaulters. She would like to see them raised. She would also spur citizen prosecutions under section 49 by offering compensatory costs to concerned citizens who successfully prosecute a violator.

5. The facts in *Travancore Cochin Chemicals Ltd. v Kerala Pollution Control Board*,[17] illustrate foot-dragging by government officials in enforcing the Act. In 1975, the board gave the company consent to discharge effluents into the Periyar river until 31 January 1976. The board subsequently determined that the company was not complying with the conditions of the consent. The board was particularly concerned that the company might be discharging highly toxic mercury. Despite this concern, the board repeatedly extended consent to discharge effluents based on the company's assurances that it would install a plant to treat the effluents. The board also asked the state government to deal with the problem.

Finally, in 1984, after eight years of alleged illegal polluting by the company, the board filed an action under section 33, requesting an order to restrain the company from polluting the river. In 1983, however, because of a change in the rules

[12] *Pravinbhai J. Patel v State of Gujarat* 1995 (2) GUJ.L.R.1210, 1216.

[13] *Suo Motu v Bhavna Textile Pvt. Ltd.* 1997 (2) GUJ.L.HER. 760.

[14] *Mandu Distilleries Pvt. Ltd. v Madhya Pradesh Pradushan Niwaran Mandal* AIR 1995 MP 57, 63.

[15] K. Anklesaria, *A Judicial Regime of Environment Protection: The Case of the Indian Water Act* (unpublished manuscript; 1998).

[16] Section 4.

[17] Crim. Misc. Pet. No. 556/84, Kerala High Court, 12 April 1985, *reprinted in* Central Board for the Prevention and Control of Water Pollution ('CBPCWP'), *Judicial Interpretation of Water Pollution Control Laws*, 135 (1985).

implementing the Act, the company had submitted to the board a new application for consent to discharge. The board had not acted on that application. The company challenged the board's action in the Kerala High Court on the basis of section 25(7) of the Water Act, which provides that a state board must act on an application for consent to discharge within four months of the date of the application. If the board does not act on the application, its consent is deemed to have been given unconditionally at the end of the four month period.

The court ruled in favour of the company, finding that the 1983 application superseded the previously given conditional consent and that the company had an unconditional right to discharge into the river. The court added that the board must issue orders under section 27(2) of the Act to negate the implied unconditional consent before the court could entertain a section 33 petition.

In addition to chastising the board for its lack of diligence in prosecuting the company, the court also criticized both the state and Central boards for issuing conflicting orders to the company. The state board ordered the company to install a treatment plant at the same time that the Central board advised the company to wait two months for testing of new technology before installing a plant.

6. Section 25 of the Water Act obliges municipal bodies to obtain the consent of the state board before discharging sewage from new outlets. Section 26 requires municipal bodies to secure consent in respect of the sewers which were existing at the time when the Act was brought into force. Despite these provisions having long been in the statute book, most local bodies have neglected their obligation, prompting the Supreme Court to direct the Central board and the state boards to ensure compliance by municipalities.[18]

7. The citizens' initiative provision requires that courts take cognizance of an alleged violation of the Water Act upon the complaint of any person who has given 60 days notice to the appropriate state board or official. Under sections 20 and 21, however, only officials of the boards are empowered to obtain information and take samples from polluting enterprises. The citizens' initiative provision requires the boards to release relevant information, but does not require them to undertake investigations of alleged water pollution.

Does a complainant under the Water Act have any other means of compelling a board to investigate alleged water pollution, for example a writ of mandamus? Can the citizen complainant request a discovery order from the court to compel the alleged polluter to reveal information and provide samples?

Consider also the discretion of a board to withhold reports whose release it deems to be against the public interest. No definition of the 'public interest' is provided in the Water Act. Under what circumstances would it be in the public interest for a board to withhold information relevant to a citizens' prosecution?

---

[18] *Almitra Patel v Union of India* 1997 (6) SCALE 12 (SP). The failure of the Cuttack Municipality to apply for consent was noted by the Orissa High Court in *M.C. Mehta v State of Orissa* AIR 1992 ORI 225.

8. Section 21 of the Act provides detailed procedures for sampling effluents. The analysis of a sample is not admissible into evidence in any legal proceeding under the Act, unless the sample is taken in accordance with that section. In *Delhi Bottling Co. Pvt. Ltd. v Central Board for the Prevention and Control of Pollution*,[19] the Central board took a sample of trade effluent from a bottling company's discharge stream. The board analysed the sample and determined that the trade effluent did not conform to the requirements of the consent order granted to the company. The board sued under section 33 and the magistrate's court issued an injunction requiring the company to establish a treatment plant. The company challenged the injunction claiming that a representative of the company, present at the sampling, had requested that a sample be analysed by the Delhi administration laboratory as provided under section 21(e) of the Act. This analysis was not carried out.

Based on the pleadings, the court ruled in favour of the company, holding that samples not taken in strict compliance with section 21 are inadmissible as evidence and, therefore, the board had not proved that the company was violating its consent orders. Given the clear language of the statute and the court's determination of the facts, the ruling was correct. Note, however, that the company did not challenge the results of the analysis itself, the integrity of the sampling method, or the method of analysis. In addition, the requirement that polluters be given notice before a board may take a sample gives the polluters the opportunity to temporarily reduce or cease releasing pollutants during the period the sample is taken.

In *Delhi Bottling* the court set aside the magistrate's order. The board must now commence a new action against the company to obtain judicial relief, resulting in a long delay. Consider whether the court could have issued an alternative order. For example, could the court have ordered the magistrate to retain jurisdiction of the case until samples could be taken in compliance with the Water Act? Could the court require that such samples be taken while the company was carrying on normal operations at the plant?

The Gujarat High Court also shares the view that the provisions of section 21 relating to sampling are mandatory and must be substantially complied with by the prosecuting board. However, where the polluter does not make a request for part of the sample drawn after due notice, the magistrate ought to frame the charge and she would not be justified in discharging the accused.[20]

9. Ordinarily, judges are reluctant to exercise their discretionary jurisdiction in favour of polluters, particularly where the industry fails to invest in effluent treatment facilities.[21] In a rare departure, the Patna High Court indulged Shiv Shankar Chemical Industries Pvt. Ltd., an ethyl alchohol manufacturer located close to

[19] AIR 1986 DEL 152.

[20] *Dahyabhai K. Solanki v Kashiram Textiles Mills Pvt. Ltd.* 1994 (2) GUJ.L.R.1166.

[21] e.g. *Narula Dyeing & Printing Works v Union of India* AIR 1995 GUJ 185, 191 and *Pravinbhai J. Patel v State of Gujarat, supra* note 12.

Rajpura village near Bhagalpur.[22] In breach of its consent, Shiv Shankar failed to establish an effluent treatment plant (ETP). When the consent lapsed, the board refused to extend it, compelling the company to shut down its distillery. The distillery challenged the refusal under Article 226 before the High Court, where its case was heard along with a public interest litigation complaining against the harmful discharges from the factory.

On a balance of the rival contentions, the High Court permitted Shiv Shankar to re-start its production on the condition that it adopted various interim measures until the ETP became operational. In effect, the High Court directed the board to extend its consent on the terms imposed on the polluter in the judgment.

The Patna High Court was apparently persuaded by the recommendations of a court-appointed expert committee. Though the committee found the distillery's effluent 'highly polluting', it noted that the waters in the wells of village Rajpura were clean and did not show any evidence of pollution. To safeguard the villagers, the court directed the company to bear the medical expenses of any person suffering due to the effluent.

10. *Narula Dyeing and Printing Works v Union of India*,[23] is a strong pro-environment judgment where Justice Abhichandani of the Gujarat High Court repelled the challenge to closure orders issued by the state government under section 5 of the Environment (Protection) Act of 1986. Narula Dyeing was releasing untreated effluents into the Kharicut Canal for over a decade, though its 12 year old consent required the firm to set up a treatment plant within 6 months. Stressing the importance of the conditions in the consent relating to the nature, composition, temperature, volume, rate of discharge, etc. of the industrial effluent, the court held:

> [A] mere consent order issued by the State Board under Section 25(2) did not entitle the applicants to discharge trade effluents and it was incumbent upon the applicants to comply with the conditions mentioned in the consent order, as also to put up the effluent treatment plants within the time prescribed in the consent order. Failure of complying with the requirement of putting up effluent treatment plant resulted in lapse of the consent. Therefore, mere fact that consent orders were obtained by the Petitioners cannot insulate them against the requirement of putting up the effluent treatment plants and complying with the standards of tolerance limits prescribed.[24]

One of the conditions in the consent letter was that the consent would lapse unless the treatment plants were set up within 6 months.

11. The Water Act regulates water pollution through a system of 'command and control.' Effluent discharge standards are established and persons whose discharges

---

[22] *Rajiv Singh v State of Bihar* AIR 1992 PAT 86.
[23] *Supra* note 21.
[24] *Id.* at 189.

exceed the standards are subject to fines and imprisonment. Other means of regulation are possible. For example, the government could establish an upper limit of allowable pollutant release based on public health standards and charge fees based on the amount of the pollutant released within those limits. Under this system, polluters would have an economic incentive to reduce pollution if the fees are higher than the costs of reducing pollution. Would a fee system be any less burdensome to administer than a command and control system? How should the government use revenues obtained through a fee system?

12. Parliament has enacted a positive economic incentive for controlling water pollution. The Water (Prevention and Control of Pollution) Cess Act of 1977 levies a cess on water consumed by certain industries and local authorities. A rebate of 25 per cent of the cess is given for the installation of a water treatment plant and compliance with section 25 of the Water Act and standards set under the Environment (Protection) Act of 1986.

13. Difficulties faced by Surana Oils and Derivatives (India) Ltd. (SODL) in establishing a factory to manufacture castor oil derivatives illustrate the uncertainties in an environmental case. Since the factory was located close to Himayat Sagar Lake which supplied water to Hyderabad, the Andhra Pradesh pollution control board rejected SODL's application for consent. SODL challenged the refusal before the appellate authority and adduced evidence to show that it had adopted the latest eco-friendly technology with all safeguards. The appellate authority reviewed the material and on being satisfied that the factory 'is not a polluting industry', asked the board to grant consent. The decision of the appellate authority was challenged in public interest litigations filed before the High Court. The High Court declined to interfere since the matter was highly technical and it was inappropriate for a court exercising its writ jurisdiction to sit in appeal over the order of the appellate authority. The Supreme Court used the opportunity presented by the special leave petition filed by the board and an environmental group, to explain the precautionary principle and the special principle of burden of proof in environmental cases. The apex court remitted the matter to the National Environment Appellate Authority for an expert opinion on whether SODL should be allowed to operate at the controversial site.[25]

II. Scope of Judicial Relief Under the Water Act

Judicial opinion concerning the scope of section 33 of the Water Act is divided. In the following excerpt from the *Pondicherry Papers Ltd. Case,* note the doctrines invoked by the Madras High Court in its ruling that courts have broad powers to fashion orders under section 33.

[25] *A.P. Pollution Control Board v Prof. M.V. Nayudu* AIR 1999 SC 812. The High Court judgment is reported at *Society for Preservation of Environment and Quality of Life v Industries Department* 1998 (3) ANDH.L.T.516.

PONDICHERRY PAPERS LTD. v CENTRAL BOARD FOR PREVENTION AND CONTROL OF WATER POLLUTION
Madras High Court
Cri.M.P.No. 4662 and 4663 of 1978
March 21, 1980[26]

[The Central board, acting as a state board for Pondicherry, applied to a magistrate's court under Section 33 of the Water Act seeking an injunction restraining a paper company from discharging effluent until the company constructed a water treatment plant as required by the conditions of the board's consent orders. The magistrate issued an injunction. The company filed a motion to quash the injunction on the grounds that a magistrate does not have the authority under Section 33 to order compliance with a consent order.]

ORDER: * * *

The next question is what are the powers of the Magistrate when such an application is made. Sub-section (3) deals with these powers. The Court may make an order restraining the petitioner from polluting the water in any stream or well and in doing so, it may in that order direct the petitioner to desist from taking such action as is likely to cause pollution, or, as the case may be, remove from such stream or well such matter, or it can authorize the Board [to do so] under sub-section 3(ii). As has been held in *Sub-Divisional Officer, Faizabad v Shambhoo Narian Singh* (AIR 1970 SC 140) it is well recognised that where an Act confers a jurisdiction it impliedly also grants the power of doing all such acts or employing such means as are essentially necessary to its execution, but before implying the existence of such a power, the Court must be satisfied that the existence of that power is absolutely essential for the discharge of the power conferred and not merely that it is convenient to have such a power.

* * *

In *Dr. Indiremani Dyarelai Gupta v Nathu* (1963(l) SCR 721) it has been held [that] to judge whether legally a power could be vested in a statutory body, the proper rule of interpretation is that unless the nature of the power was such as to be inconsistent with the purpose for which the body was created, or unless the particular power was contra indicated by any specific provision of the Act, any power which furthers the provision of the Act, could be legally conferred.

* * *

The Water (Prevention and Control of Pollution) Act is a social welfare legislation, enacted for the purpose of prevention of pollution of water and for maintaining or restoring wholesomeness of water. Therefore, the Act has to be strictly enforced and

---

[26] We have corrected apparent grammatical errors in the judgment and have added punctuation to enhance readability. *Reprinted in* CBPCWP, *supra* note 17 at 73.

every effort should be made to carry out the true intent of the legislation. On these principles, the Magistrate has to act when an application is filed under Section 33 and it would be for him to determine according to the circumstances of the case what order he should pass in order to give effect to the provisions of the Act and to remove the pollution or prevent it.

The Madras High Court clearly found that based on the doctrines of implied powers and strict enforcement of public welfare legislation, courts have broad powers to fashion injunctive relief under section 33 of the Water Act. The Allahabad High Court implicitly adopts this view.[27] Compare this approach with that of the Delhi High Court in the following excerpt. The Central board has issued consent orders to a bottling company on the condition that the company build a water treatment plant. The company failed to build the plant and was polluting a nearby river with its effluent. The board obtained an injunction under section 33 restraining the company from polluting and ordering the company to build the treatment plant. The company challenged the injunction in the Delhi High Court.

DELHI BOTTLING CO. PVT. LTD. v CENTRAL BOARD FOR THE PREVENTION AND CONTROL OF WATER POLLUTION
AIR 1986 DEL 152

ORDER: * * *

The learned Magistrate also took note of the fact that the petitioners had not erected any treatment plant as per Cl.5 of the consent order. [Petitioner's counsel] submitted that there was no absolute obligation on the part of the petitioners to erect a separate treatment plant so long as they were not discharging the effluents contrary to the parameters as provided in the consent order. Be that as it may, the true interpretation of the impugned order is that restraint order has been passed against the petitioners restraining them from discharging their effluents in the stream which do not conform to the quality as per the standards prescribed by the Board in its consent order and thereby causing pollution of the stream. We cannot read between the order that a direction has been given to erect a treatment plant. Such a direction is also perhaps not envisaged by the provisions of S.33(1) of the Act. [Section] 33(1) only provides for the passing of a restraint order by the court against the Company for ensuring stoppage of apprehended pollution of water in the stream in which trade effluents of the Company are discharged. I, therefore, need not go into the question as to whether the petitioners' non-erection of a treatment plant was such an act on which the impugned order was justified. The restraint order is also not based on that

---

27 *Sir Shadi Lal Enterprises Ltd. v Chief Judicial Magistrate, Saharanpur* 1990 CRI. L.J. 522.

footing. For the non-erection of the treatment plant the Board has the power to launch prosecution against the defaulting Company under the provisions of S.41 of the Act.

* * *

NOTES AND QUESTIONS

1. In *Delhi Bottling*, the Delhi High Court considered section 33(1) but ignored section 33(2) which empowers a court to 'make such an order as it may deem fit' upon receiving a section 33 application from a board. The court did not consider the doctrines of implied powers and public welfare that the Pondicherry Papers court found so compelling. The reluctance of courts to exercise broad injunctive powers under section 33 may be one reason for granting state boards the authority to issue directions under section 33A. Note the broad power granted to the boards under section 33A of the Act.

2. The Madras High Court found that the scope of injunctive relief under section 33 is limited only by the intent of the Water Act and provisions of the Act that 'contra indicate' certain relief. Following the approach of the Madras High Court, could a court in response to a section 33 application order a company to take measures to prevent water pollution that are not required by a board's consent orders? Should the courts and public authorities issuing orders or directions under the Water Act consider the financial ability of polluters to comply?

3. The power of a magistrate to direct industry to 'desist' from causing pollution, is the subject of a long and painstaking analysis by the Gujarat High Court.[28] In July and August 1984, the magistrate, Surat, issued interim orders restraining several accused industrial units from discharging effluent outside their factories until the criminal cases were finally heard. In revision, the sessions judge modified these orders since in his view, the injunction operated to ban manufacture and was therefore beyond the magistrate's jurisdiction. Restoring the orders of the magistrate, the High Court held that the desist orders did not necessarily imply closure since the industries could opt to continue discharges *after* establishing effluent treatment facilities. If the industries chose not to spend on abatement, they would have to close: Parliament had armed magistrates with this coercive power after balancing the community interest against the interest of individual units.

The eight year passage of this case through three tiers of courts, prompted

---

[28] *Gujarat Water Pollution Control Board v Kohinoor Dyeing and Printing Works* 1993 (2) GUJ. L.R. 1368.

Justice Vaidya to inquire into the pendency of pollution prosecutions in the state. On 1 April 1993 over 1100 cases were pending across the districts of Gujarat. Describing the role of the pollution control board and the courts as 'trustees' for the public in matters of environmental degradation, the High Court framed guidelines for the expeditious disposal of pollution-related prosecutions. Two years later, the guidelines appear to have had little effect and the backlog of prosecutions remained just as high.[29]

III. CONSTITUTIONAL CHALLENGES TO SECTION 33 RESTRAINING ORDERS

A tactic of polluters to avoid restraining orders under Section 33 is a motion to quash the order on the grounds that the Water Act violates the fundamental right to carry on a trade or business guaranteed by Article 19(1)(g) of the Constitution of India.

The Rajasthan High Court balanced the interests protected by the Water Act against the competing interests protected by Article 19(1)(g) in the following case. A lower court had issued a restraining order against textile companies that were discharging effluents after the expiration of consent orders from the state and Central boards. The companies filed writ petitions in the Rajasthan High Court challenging the validity of the restraining order.

AGGRAWAL TEXTILE INDUSTRIES v STATE OF RAJASTHAN
Rajasthan High Court
S.B.C. Writ Petition No. 1375/80
March 2, 1981[30]

ORDER:

[Petitioners' counsel] has vehemently argued that the problem of prevention of water pollution is a problem of vast magnitude and that it would be beyond the means of an individual to prevent or control the pollution resulting from an industry set up by him and that the prohibition contained in Section 24 of the Act would result in complete closure of the business of the petitioners and that it would thus result in imposing unreasonable restrictions to carry on their trade and business. I am unable to accept the aforesaid contention. ... It is true that the prevention and control of pollution of water may involve expenditure beyond the means of a particular individual carrying on any particular industry and it may require co-operation amongst various units and ... the local authorities to effectively prevent and control such pollution. The Act also envisages that one of the functions of the State Board is to plan a comprehensive programme for the prevention, control or abatement of pollution of streams and wells in the State and to secure the execution thereof and to evolve economical and reliable methods of treatment of sewage and trade effluent, having regard to the peculiar conditions of soils, climate and water resources of different regions. But, this does not mean that an

[29] As on 31 March 1995, the pending prosecutions under the Water Act and Air Act were 1330 and 162, respectively. Gujarat Pollution Control Board, *Annual Report: 1994–95*. Research conducted by Bharath Jairaj.

[30] *Reprinted in* CBPCWP, *supra* note 17 at 32.

individual, while exercising his right to carry on his trade or business, is free to pollute the source of supply of water to other citizens, and thereby cause harm to the interest of the general public. It cannot be disputed that pollution of water is a very serious hazard for the health of the general public, and the provisions of the Act which seek to provide for the prevention and control of water pollution and maintaining or restoring the wholesomeness of water are enacted in the interest of the general public.

* * *

The question which next arises for consideration is, whether the aforesaid restriction that has been placed by Section 24 of the Act is an unreasonable restriction. ... [S]ub-section (2) of Section 24 enables a person to cause or permit a trade effluent to enter into a stream provided the consent of the State Government is obtained. Sections 25 and 26 of the Act make provisions for the grant of consent by the State Board for discharging any sewage or trade effluent into a stream or well. Section 28 provides for an appeal against an order made by the State Board under Sections 25 and 26, and a further right of revision is conferred under Section 29 of the Act. This shows that the Act contains adequate provisions for grant of consent by the State Board as well as provisions for appeal and revision against the orders passed by the State Board so as to enable a person to carry on his trade or business after obtaining the consent of the State Board. It is, therefore, not possible to hold that Section 24(l) imposes unreasonable restrictions on the right of the petitioners to carry on their trade or business.

* * *

NOTES AND QUESTIONS

1. Since the decision in *Aggrawal Textile Industries,* the Supreme Court has explicitly recognized the right to a wholesome environment as being an aspect of the fundamental right to life guaranteed by Article 21 of the Constitution.[31] How will this development affect challenges to section 33 injunctions based on the fundamental right to carry on a trade or business guaranteed by the Article (19)(1)(g)? Would it be more difficult for a court to find that a restriction on effluent discharge was unreasonable? What balance should the courts strike between these rights?

2. Another major challenge to section 33 restraining orders is the contention that *ex parte* restraining orders issued against polluters violate principles of natural justice embodied in the Constitution.[32] A pre-decisional hearing must be granted to

---

[31] *Subhash Kumar v State of Bihar* AIR 1991 SC 420.

[32] *Ex parte* orders are issued before the alleged polluter has an opportunity to be heard by the Court.

the polluter before a court issues a section 33 restraining order.[33] This rule of fairplay may be relaxed, however, in the case of an emergency, such as where the effluent discharged poses an imminent threat to public health.

3. The Gujarat High Court has suggested a number of measures to ensure that pollution related cases are disposed of expeditiously.[34] Board officials should take effective steps for the service of the summons upon the accused; prepare cases thoroughly; resist adjournments; seek exemplary costs to deter the accused from adopting dilatory tactics; and vigorously pursue appeals in the superior court. The High Court also directed the subordinate judiciary not to adjourn cases; to record the plea of the accused without delay; to ensure that all necessary witnesses are examined at the earliest; and to adopt a pro-active approach so that the objects of the Water Act are attained.

IV. CRIMINAL LIABILITY

The Water Act establishes criminal penalties of fines and imprisonment for noncompliance with section 33 orders, section 20 directions concerning information, section 32 emergency orders and section 33A directions issued by a state board.[35] Polluters violating the Act are also subject to criminal penalties.[36] The 1988 amendments to the Water Act increased the penalties for these offences, bringing them into line with the 1987 amendments to the Air Act.

Section 47 of the Water Act extends liability for violations committed by companies to certain corporate employees and officials. The Act also extends liability for violations to heads of government departments when a department has committed a violation, unless the department head can prove that the offence was committed without his knowledge or that he exercised all due diligence to prevent the commission of the offence.[37]

The following commentary discusses the liability of corporate officials and employees under the Water Act.

BAKSHI; CORPORATE EXECUTIVES AND
THE POLLUTION LAW, (1986) 2 Comp. L.J. 61

> Section 47 of the Water Pollution Act contains the usual provision to the effect that where an offence under the Act has been committed by a company, every person, who, at the time of the commission of the offence, 'was in charge of, and was responsible to the company for the conduct of the business of the company, as well as the company, shall be deemed to be guilty of the offence and shall be liable to be proceeded against and punished accordingly.' Under the proviso to this section, such company official is exempt

---

[33] *Megh Shyam Sharma v State of Uttar Pradesh* 1985 ALL.L.J.1195.
[34] *Supra* note 28, at 1392, 1393.
[35] Section 41.
[36] Sections 43 and 44.
[37] Section 48.

from punishment, if he proves that the offence had been committed without his knowledge, or that he had exercised all due diligence to prevent the commission of such offence. ... Company officials may well like to bear in mind that statutory provisions making company officials liable are contained in almost every Central Act that is enacted in recent times. In a way, such provisions impose a fictional liability on the company officer.

The provision usually runs in two sub-sections. The first sub-section provides—as does section 47 of the Water Pollution Act (referred to above)—that every person who is in charge of and responsible to the company for the conduct of the affairs of the company 'is liable' for the offence (in addition to the company), unless he can prove that the offence had been committed without his knowledge or that he had exercised all due diligence to prevent its commission. The second sub-section usually provides that where an offence (under the relevant Act) has been committed by a company, and it is proved that the offence is due to the connivance of or attributable to any neglect on the part of any director, manager, secretary or other officer of the company, then such director, manager, secretary or other officer shall also be deemed to be guilty of the offence and shall be liable to be proceeded against and punished accordingly. This sub-section, it may be noted, is not confined to a person 'in charge' of the company and responsible for its affairs. It applies to every officer of the company, however small he may be. But his connivance or neglect has to be proved. In this sense, its scope is narrow. But in another respect, the scope is wide, inasmuch as it does not require actual participation or mental support of the officer. In the context of pollution law and offences under such laws, such a provision in the Act would mean that if a company's production manager or technical director has been remiss in ensuring that the pollution regulations have been strictly complied with, then he would become punishable for the relevant offence under the Act. He may be miles away from the scene of the offence and may not have sanctioned its commission. He might even have been unaware of it. And yet, he would become criminally liable. Wilfully permitting the offence is not necessary in the Water Pollution Act, though such was the shape of the provision in some earlier Central Acts imposing criminal liability on corporate officials.

NOTES AND QUESTIONS

1. Not surprisingly, given the threat of imprisonment and fines, the liability of individual corporate officials has been the subject of extensive litigation. Challenges to actions against corporate officials generally are in the form of motions to quash the action, brought under section 482 of the Code of Criminal Procedure which recognizes the inherent powers of a High Court to prevent an abuse of the judicial process or to secure the ends of justice.

Many courts have refused to grant these motions when they are based on technical defects in pleadings.[38] In *Uttar Pradesh Pollution Control Board v Modi Distillery,*[39] the Supreme Court reversed an order quashing a prosecution under

[38] e.g. *Medwin Hospitals v State of AP* 1999 (2) ANDH. L.T. 471.
[39] AIR 1988 SC 1128.

section 44 of the Water Act. The state board initiated the prosecution under section 47 against a company and its corporate officials. The board's complaint erroneously designated corporate officials as officials of Modi Distillery, instead of Modi Industries Limited. The corporate officials sought to quash the prosecution on the grounds that under section 47 corporate officials could not be prosecuted if the company was not also prosecuted.

The Supreme Court was particularly hostile to the claims of the corporate officials because, in this case, the officials had failed to respond to the board's request for information concerning the corporation. The Supreme Court also found that the technical flaw in the complaint could be easily removed by having the matter remitted to the chief judicial magistrate with a direction to call upon the state board to make the formal amendment in the averments of the complaint by simply substituting the proper name of the company. The court's attitude is clearly expressed in the following statement from the opinion:

> It would be a travesty of justice if the big business house of Messrs Modi Industries Limited is allowed to defeat the prosecution launched and avoid facing the trial on a technical flaw which is not incurable for their alleged deliberate and wilful breach of the provisions contained in Sections 25(1) and 26. ...

Twelve years after *Modi Distillery* the farce continues. In *UP Pollution Control Board v Mohan Meakins Ltd.* 2000 (2) SCALE 532, the Supreme Court revived a prosecution launched in 1983 against the company and its directors, that had been erroneously quashed by the sessions court. The case had languished in the lower courts for sixteen years. 'Those who discharge noxious polluting effluents into streams may be unconcerned about the enormity of the injury which it inflicts on the public health at large, the irreparable impairment it causes on the acquatic organisms, the deleteriousness it imposes on the life and health of animals. So the courts should not deal with the prosecution for offences under the Act in a casual or routine manner.' Who are to blame for the abject delays? Who gains—and who pays?

2. In *K.K. Nandi v Amitabha Bannerjee*,[40] the Calcutta High Court rejected a motion to quash a prosecution against the manager of a beer company. The manager argued that the complaint was defective because it did not enumerate how he was responsible for the operations of the plant and how he had violated sections 25 and 26 of the Act. The court rejected the argument and ruled that a person designated as manager of a company is *prima facie* liable under section 47 of the Act. Whether or not the person designated 'manager' was in fact in overall charge of the affairs of the factory and whether or not he had any knowledge of the violations of the Act were held to be questions of fact which could be considered at the trial.

3. The Patna High Court, in *Mahmud Ali v State of Bihar*,[41] allowed the state to

[40] 1983 CRI.L.J. 1479.
[41] AIR 1986 PAT 133.

implead the managing director of a company charged with violating the Water Act, when it was shown at the trial that he was responsible for the violation. The managing director was not named in the complaint. The court relied on section 319 of the Criminal Procedure Code which allows the court to take cognizance of persons not included in the original complaint if the evidence at the trial points to their culpability.

4. In *J.S. Huja v State*,[42] the Allahabad High Court considered an application to quash a complaint filed by the Uttar Pradesh pollution control board. Since the company was discharging its effluent without obtaining consent, the board prosecuted the secretary and the directors of the company, alleging that they were responsible for the conduct of the day to day business of the company and were guilty of the omission. The applicants pleaded that they had retired and in any event, could not be prosecuted since they were not 'responsible to the company for the conduct of the business'. The High Court rejected the application holding that disputed questions of fact cannot be looked into under section 482. The complaint must be examined as filed and since there was a clear allegation that the applicants were responsible for the conduct of the work of the company when the offence was committed, there was no reason to quash the complaint.

5. In *Z. Kotasek v State of Bihar*,[43] the Patna High Court considered an application to quash an order passed by a magistrate taking cognisance of a complaint filed by the Bihar pollution control board against the Bata Shoe Company and its manager. The company was located on the banks of the Ganga and discharged a vast quantity of untreated effluent into the river. Despite several requests urging the company to secure the statutory consent and install appropriate treatment facilities, the company failed to comply with the board's requisitions. The applicants' case was that the board had not sanctioned the complaint; the manager was not liable; the complaint was 'premature' since recent analysis reports were not considered by the board; and that the state board had no jurisdiction since the Ganga was an inter-state river. The High Court rejected each of these submissions on the facts and held that the board had jurisdiction to regulate polluters discharging effluents at a point within the state.

The Gujarat High Court has upheld the chairman's right to accord sanction to prosecute a polluter, where the state board delegates this function to the chairman.[44] Moreover, the non-production of the sanction at the time of filing the complaint would not thwart the prosecution. Under beneficent legislation such as pollution control laws, procedural infirmities do not hamper the case. The High Court directed the trial court to accord priority to the case and dispose of it within three months.[45]

6. Trans Asia Carpets Ltd. tried to use its precarious financial position to advantage. In December 1990 it became 'sick' and applied to the Board for Industrial and Financial Reconstruction to frame a rehabilitation scheme to revive the unit.

---

[42] 1990 ALL L.J.41; 1989 CRI. L.J. 1334.

[43] 1984 CRI. L.J. 683.

[44] *Gujarat Pollution Control Board v Indian Chemicals Manufacturer* 1990(2) GUJ. L.R.1306.

[45] *Industrial Chemical Works v Dahyabhai K. Solanki* 1993(2) GUJ. L.R. 1318.

Meanwhile, the company released its untreated trade effluent into a drain which led to the river Karve. When the state board prosecuted the unit for discharging its trade effluent into a stream without obtaining the consent of the board, the company filed an application to the Allahabad High Court to quash the proceedings, claiming immunity from prosecution in terms of section 22 of the Sick Industrial Companies (Special Provisions) Act of 1985. Section 22 bars coercive proceedings against the property of the company and prevents the prosecution of civil suits filed for the recovery of dues. The High Court held that the protection to sick companies did not extend to prosecutions under the Water Act. All issues relating to the extent of pollution and whether the discharge was made into a 'stream' would be decided by the magistrate in the course of the trial.[46]

7. One of the few reported decisions in a case where the board successfully prosecuted the polluter is the Punjab and Haryana High Court judgment in *Haryana State Board v Jai Bharat Woollen Finishing Works*.[47] Jai Bharat discharged untreated effluent into an open drain in Panipat city without obtaining the consent of the board. A number of notices issued by the board were ignored by the firm and eventually on the basis of a test sample, the board prosecuted the firm, one of its partners and its manager. The trial court acquitted the accused on the ground that the discharge was onto vacant land and did not constitute an offence. Partly allowing the board's appeal, the High Court held that the discharge of a trade effluent, without consent of the board did constitute an offence. It made no difference whether the trade effluent was discharged into a municipal drain or flowed directly onto land. However, the court held that in the absence of proof that the concerned partner was in charge of or was responsible to the firm for the conduct of business, it would not be possible to convict the partner. On this interpretation, the court upheld the acquittal of a sleeping partner who did not participate in the business of the firm, while imposing a nominal fine of Rs. 3,000 on the firm and Rs. 2,500 on its manager.

8. Most state pollution control boards have enjoyed little success in bringing to book violators under pollution control laws. Does the fault lie with the boards, the laws, the courts or some other factor? What systemic changes might improve the success rate?

The provisions of section 40 of the Air Act are similar to section 47 of the Water Act. Contrast the reasoning of the Madhya Pradesh High Court and the Punjab and Haryana High Court in the following cases.

---

[46] *Trans Asia Carpets Ltd. v State of UP* 1992 ALL. L.J.357; 1992 CRI. L.J.673.
[47] 1993 FOR.L.T.101.

N.A. PALKHIVALA v M.P. PRADUSHAN NIWARAN MANDAL
1990 CRI. L.J. 1856

GULAB C. GUPTA, J: * * *

The petitioner No.1 is the Chairman of M/s Associated Cement Company Limited, a public limited company engaged in manufacture of cement at various places including at Jamul Cement Works, Durg. The petitioner No. 2 is the Deputy Chairman of the said company. The non-applicant-complainant claims to be the Board constituted under Section 4 of the Air (Prevention and Control of Pollution) Act, 1981 (hereinafter referred to as the Act) and filed a complaint against the petitioners and their company alleging offence punishable under Sections 37 and 39 read with Section 40 of the Act. It was alleged that the industry run by petitioners is covered by the schedule of the Act and uses lime as a raw-material. It was also alleged that the Industry obtained consent of the complainant under Section 21 of the Act on 27–9–84 for the period from 1–9–84 to 31–8–85 on condition that they will strengthen air pollution control devices and will install such equipments in all polluting sections. The non-applicant, therefore alleged that progress of E.S.P. installation was to be submitted to the complainant-Board regularly and their installation completed within six months. The non-applicant further alleged that the industry failed to comply with the condition of the consent letter resulting in danger to public and plant life. The non-applicant Board had rejected the application for renewal of consent for the period after 1–5–85 but in spite of it, the industry was being run in violation of the provisions of Act. It was, therefore, submitted that the industry was contravening the provision under Section 21 and was liable to be punished under Section 37 and 39 of the Act. It appears that the learned Magistrate took cognisance of the offence disclosed in the said complaint and issued process to the petitioners for their appearance. The petitioners have entered appearance and sought exemption from personal appearance from the learned Magistrate which has been granted.

There appears to be no dispute that the consent alleged to have been granted by the non-applicant-Board on 27–9–1984 was granted to the General Manager of Jamul Cement Works who has also been prosecuted alongwith the petitioners. The present application is not on his behalf and, therefore even if this application is allowed, the criminal case would proceed against the said General Manager. The petitioners submit that simply because they are Chairman and Dy.Chairman of the Board of Directors of the Company, it cannot be assumed that they have knowledge of the working of the cement plant at Jamul or the violation of the conditions of the consent letter issued by the non-applicant-Board in favour of the General Manager. They, therefore, submit that they are not directly incharge of the conduct of the business of the company and hence not within the purview of Section 40 of the Act. They, therefore, submit that they are not liable to be prosecuted. The learned Counsel for the non-applicant, however, submits that duties and responsibilities attached to the offices held by the petitioners are sufficient to make them liable under Section 40(1) of the Act and it will be their burden to prove that the offence was committed without their knowledge.

[The court examined the provisions of the complaint; noted that there was no mention about the duties and responsibilities of the petitioners; and referred to the provisions of the Companies Act of 1956 relating to directors.]

The complaint as noticed earlier, alleges criminal offence by the company and makes the petitioners responsible for the same in view of the Section 40 of the Act. Section 40 of the Act reads as under:

40. *Offences by Companies:* (1) Where an offence under this Act has been committed by a company, every person who at the time of the offence was committed, was directly in-charge of, and responsible to the company for the conduct of the business of the company, as well as the company, shall be deemed to be guilty of the offence and shall be liable to be proceeded against and punished accordingly.

Provided that nothing contained in this sub-section shall render any such person liable to any punishment provided in this Act, if he proves that the offence was committed without his knowledge or that he exercised all due diligence to prevent the commission of such offence.

A bare reading of this provision shows that every person who at the time the offences was committed, was directly incharge of and responsible to the company for the conduct of the business of the company, would also be liable to be punished for the said offence. The words 'directly in-charge of' are significant in this regard and exclude persons who are indirectly responsible for the business of the company. Under the circumstances it was the obligation of the non-applicant to allege by making specific averments in the complaint that the petitioners by virtue of the offices held by them, remain directly in-charge of and responsible to the Company for the conduct of the business of the company.

* * *

The facts of the instant case, however, point to [the] contrary. The contravention, in the instant case involves non-compliance of condition of permission granted to the General Manager and there is nothing on record to point that the said violation was even remotely connected with any policy matter. Indeed, if the inference is to be drawn, it will have to be drawn against the non-applicant. Every company running a factory will be presumed to be doing so because it was willing to abide by all statutory obligations. It will, therefore, be difficult to put the blame on the Chairman and Dy. Chairman for any such non-compliance. This Court is, therefore, unable to give the benefit of *S.K. Bhargava's case* [M.Cr. No. 3172/1989 decided on 6.12.1989 (MP)] to the non-applicant. The decisions in *K.K. Nandi v Amitabh Banerjee* [1983 Cr.L.J. 1479] and *Dr. Z. Kotasek v State of Bihar* [1984 Cr.L.J. 683] were also cited to justify prosecutions of the petitioners. Both these cases deal with the liability of the Manager of the company and say nothing about the Chairman and Dy. Chairman. The Manager of the company would be liable even on the basis of decision in *Delhi Municipality's* case [AIR 1983 SC 67]. The duties and responsibilities of the Manager have no resemblance to the duties and responsibilities of the Chairman and Dy. Chairman and hence these decisions would also not help the non-applicant. It is, therefore, possible to hold that the Chairman and Dy. Chairman of the Company by virtue of office held by them cannot be prosecuted for offences committed by the company as they are not the persons directly in-charge of, and responsible to the company for the conduct of its business as required under Section 40 of the Act. It was, therefore, the obligation of the non-applicant-complainant to specifically allege facts from which it could be reasonably inferred that the Chairman and Dy.Chairman of the company were directly in-charge of, and responsible for the conduct of the business of the company.

Application of these legal principles to the present factual situation would lead to one and only result *i.e.* the prosecution of the petitioners for the alleged violation of the provisions of Act is not in accordance with law. Must this prosecution be, therefore, quashed in exercise of powers under Section 482 of the Criminal Procedure Code?

[After reviewing the authorities, the High Court quashed the proceedings in respect of the two petitioners and permitted the case to proceed against the other accused persons in accordance with law].

HARYANA POLLUTION CONTROL BOARD
v BHARAT CARPETS LIMITED
1993 FOR.L.T. 97

AMARJEET CHAUDHARY, J.:

[The Haryana board challenged the order of the magistrate, Faridabad dismissing the board's complaint since nobody on behalf of the board appeared when the case was called out. As a result, four accused who were officers of the first respondent were acquitted. The acquitted persons included S.N.C. Bakshi and D.P. Gupta who were described by the counsel for the respondent as 'small functionaries of the company.' It was claimed that both of them were not involved in the day-to-day business of the company. Bakshi was the chief security officer and Gupta's designation was production officer. Reviewing the evidence on record and the provisions of section 47 of the Water Act, the court held:]

Thus the evidence on record and proviso to Section 47 of the Act leave no manner of doubt that none of the respondents i.e., S.N.C. Bakshi and D.P.Gupta can be said to have committed any offence as they were not responsible for conduct of the day-to-day business of the company and as such cannot be proceeded against.

Section 47 of the Act is *pari materia* to Section 23–C of the Foreign Exchange Regulation Act, 1947 and Section 34 of the Drugs and Cosmetics Act, 1940. In *State of Karnataka v Pratap Chand* AIR 1981 SC 872 it was held that a partnership firm charged for the offences under Section 18 (a)(ii) and (c) of the Drugs and Cosmetics Act, the partner of the firm who was in overall control of the day-to-day business of the firm would alone be liable to be convicted and the partner who was not in such control would not be proceeded with merely because he had the right to participate in the business of the firm under the terms of the partnership deed. In *G.L. Gupta v D.N. Mehta* AIR 1971 SC 28 it was observed as follows:

What then does the expression 'a person in charge and responsible for the conduct of the affairs of a company' mean? It will be noticed that the word 'company' includes a firm or other association and the same test must apply to a director in charge and a partner of a firm in charge of business. It seems to us that in the context a person 'in charge' must mean that the person should be in overall control of the day-to-day business of the company or firm. This inference follows from the working of Section 23-C(2). It mentions director, who may be a party to the policy being followed by a company and yet not be in charge of the business of the company. Further it mentions Manager, who usually is in charge of the business but not in overall charge. Similarly, the other officers may be in charge of only some part of business.

Keeping in view that above observation, and from the evidence in the present case it can be concluded that the Managing Director and Chairman of the Company who were in overall control of the day-to-day business of the company, could have been held to be liable and not S.N.C. Bakshi and D.P. Gupta as they were neither in charge of the company nor were acquainted with the day-to-day business of the company.

Considering all the pros and cons of the matter, we have come to the conclusion that this appeal fails and the same is hereby dismissed.

Appeal Dismissed.

QUESTIONS

1. Go for the company chairman, advises the Punjab and Haryana High Court. Don't prosecute the chairman, says Madhya Pradesh. What is a board to do? Can you reconcile the judgments?

2. Which strategy is superior for securing compliance: prosecuting the local factory management or the senior-most company official? Was the Madhya Pradesh High Court justified in interfering at a pre-trial stage? Might the eminence of the petitioner have influenced the outcome of the case?

V. THE WATER CESS ACT

Parliament adopted the Water Cess (Prevention and Control of Pollution) Act of 1977 to provide funds for the Central and state pollution control boards. The Act empowers the Central Government to impose a cess on water consumed by industries listed in Schedule I of the Act. Specified industries and local authorities are subject to the cess if they use water for purposes listed in Schedule II of the Act, which includes: (1) industrial cooling, spraying in mine pits, or 'boiler feed'; (2) domestic purposes; (3) processing which results in water pollution by biodegradable water pollutants; or (4) processing which results in water pollution by water pollutants which are not easily biodegradable or are toxic. A rebate of twenty-five per cent of the cess is given to complying industries and authorities.

Many companies challenged imposition of the cess, claiming that they were not within the specified industries. Consider the Supreme Court's approach to interpreting the Water Cess Act in the following excerpt from the *Andhra Pradesh Rayons Ltd. Case,* and compare it with the Kerala High Court's approach in the case of *Gwalior Rayon,* also excerpted below.

ANDHRA PRADESH STATE BOARD FOR PREVENTION AND CONTROL OF WATER POLLUTION v ANDHRA PRADESH RAYONS LTD.
AIR 1989 SC 611

SABYASACHI MUKHARJI, J.:   * * *

[T]he question which is sought to be raised in this petition is whether the respondent— Andhra Pradesh Rayons Ltd. which is manufacturing Rayon Grade Pulp, a base material for manufacturing of synthetics or man-made fabrics is an industry as mentioned in Schedule I of the Water (Prevention and Control of Pollution) Cess Act, 1977 for the purposes of levy on Water Cess under the Act.

* * *

Specified industry is one which is mentioned in Schedule I which is as follows:

'...

7. Chemical industry.

...

10. Textile industry.
11. Paper industry.

...

15. Processing of animal or vegetable products. ... '

* * *

Before us it was sought to be canvassed that Rayon Grade Pulp is covered either by Item No. 7 which is chemical industry or Item No. 10 which is textile industry or Item No. 11 which is paper industry. We are unable to accept the contention.

It has to be borne that this Act with which we are concerned is an Act imposing liability for cess. The Act is fiscal in nature. The Act must, therefore, be strictly construed in order to find out whether a liability is fastened on a particular industry. The subject is not to be taxed without clear words for that purpose; and also that every Act of Parliament be read according to its natural construction of words.

* * *

The purpose of the Act is to realize money from those whose activities lead to pollution and who must bear the expenses of the maintenance and running of the State Board. It is a fiscal provision and must, therefore, not only be literally construed but also be strictly construed. ... [W]e find nothing to warrant the conclusion that Rayon Grade Pulp is included in either of the industries as canvassed on behalf of the petitioner here. ...

In this case, we must also note that neither the Water Pollution Board nor any authorities under the Act nor the High Court proceeded on any evidence how these expressions are used in the particular industry or understood in the trade generally. In other words, no principle of understanding in 'common parlance' is involved in the instant case.

* * *

KERALA STATE BOARD FOR PREVENTION AND CONTROL OF WATER POLLUTION v GWALIOR RAYON SILK MANUFACTURING (WEAVING) COMPANY LTD.

AIR 1986 KER 256

ORDER: * * *

The Cess Act is not to be read in vacuum or in a manner dissociated with the Water Pollution Act.

The learned single Judge [in the lower court] felt that the Cess Act could be viewed in isolation. That is evident from the following observation contained in the judgment:

> The purpose of the Pollution Act is to control water pollution; but the purpose of the Cess Act is to levy and collect a cess, i.e., a tax for a special administrative purpose. You cannot make rules under the Cess Act to achieve *the purposes of another Act*. [Emphasis supplied by the court.]

The above observations overlook the background of the legislation on environmental protection in general and water pollution in particular. The Cess Act was enacted three years after the Pollution Act had been brought into force. By that time, the Parliament had before it the experience in the working of the Pollution Act. The financial constraints under which the State Boards had been functioning had received the attention of the Central Government. In light of that experience, ways and means were devised to overcome the situation of the financial constraints of the State Boards. That is specifically referred to in the Statement of Objects and Reasons of the Cess Act. ... Strong indications are available in the enactment itself about the intertwining and interlacing of the two enactments. The Cess Act is dovetailed into the Pollution Act. The charging section itself explicitly states that the levy of the cess is *for the purposes* of the Water (Prevention and Control of Pollution) Act 1974 and utilisation *thereunder*. [Emphasis supplied by the court]. In the face of such specific and express words, it is impossible to understand or construe the Cess Act, dehors the provisions of the Pollution Act. There are other indications also. Under S. 2(d) the words and expressions of the Cess Act not specifically defined are to have meanings as assigned under the Pollution Act.

* * *

NOTES AND QUESTIONS

1. The Supreme Court has impliedly overruled the Kerala High Court's determination that the Cess Act should be construed liberally. The Supreme Court emphasizes the need for clarity as to which enterprises will be subject to the cess. The court's rationale for its decision appears to be that individual companies should not be surprised by imposition of a cess. Given that the purpose of the cess is to fund the state boards, should a company which generates polluted water be surprised by imposition of the cess? The Kerala High Court read the entire Water Cess Act and focused on the preamble to the statute in its decision to construe it literally in light of the Water Act. Could one say that the Kerala High Court has actually construed the Water Cess Act more literally than the Supreme Court? Would the Water Cess Act be more effective if it provided that any person subject to the Water Act is also subject to the Water Cess Act, unless specifically exempted? Why should the government impose the cess on some polluters but not others?

2. In *Saraswati Sugar Mills v Haryana, State Board*,[48] the Supreme Court strictly construed the entry covering 'processing of animal or vegetable products industry' to *exclude* the manufacture of sugar from sugar cane. Following the *Andhra Pradesh Rayons Case*, the court preferred the common parlance meaning of 'vegetable' covering edible plants over the botanical definition which was applied by the High Court. The High Court held that the expression 'vegetable' was used in distinction to the word 'animal' and extended beyond common kitchen vegetables to include sugar cane. Adopting a line of reasoning similar to the *Saraswati Case*, in *Harrisons Malayalam Ltd. v Kerala State Pollution Control Board*,[49] the Kerala High Court ruled that the processing of latex was not covered under the entry 'processing of ... vegetable products' in Schedule I of the Cess Act.

---

[48] AIR 1992 SC 224. In view of this judgment, *Kisan Sahakari Mills v State of Uttar Pradesh* AIR 1987 ALL 298 and *Travancore Sugars & Chemicals Ltd. v Pollution Control Board* 1990 (2) KER.L.T. 924 are no longer good law. The strict construction test was reiterated by the Supreme Court in a 1995 decision reported at *Bihar State Pollution Control Board v Tata Engineering & Locomotive Co. Ltd.* 1998 (8) SCC 720.

[49] AIR 1992 KER 168.

3. The Allahabad High Court in *Sri Durga Glass Works v Union of India*,[50] adopted a very different approach. The petitioners pressed two issues before the High Court: (i) glass units were not liable to pay the cess since this industry was not specified in Schedule I to the Cess Act; and (ii) there was no 'consumption' of water in the factory and consequently no question of any pollution. The manufacture was carried out in dry conditions because moisture or water was harmful to the process. The Revenue Department argued that the glass industry fell within the ambit of 'ceramic industry', listed at item 8 of the Schedule. Despite the Supreme Court judgment in *Saraswati Sugar Mills* holding that the entries in the Schedule be construed strictly, the High Court found no force in this contention. The court preferred to apply a liberal interpretation based on the 'polluter pays principle' cited by the Supreme Court in *Vellore Citizens' Welfare Forum v Union of India*,[51] and *Indian Council for Enviro-Legal Action v Union of India*.[52]

Rejecting the arguments put forward by both the parties, the court found that glass units fell within 'Non-ferrous metallurgical industry' listed at item 2 of the Schedule. The second plea of the petitioners was dismissed thus: 'It cannot be imagined that this industry is not consuming water in the industry in any form. No industry can exist without water.' How persuasive is this reasoning? Does the polluter pays principle extend to taxing statutes?

4. The use of common raw materials in the manufacture of mill board and paper, persuaded the Allahabad High Court to hold that 'mill board' (card board or hard board) was covered by 'Paper industry' at item 11 of Schedule I.[53] The High Court did not notice the Supreme Court judgment in *Andhra Pradesh Rayons*.

5. The Central Government adopted the Water Cess Act without the approval of the state governments. Water is a subject in the State List under the Constitution. Many industries claimed that the Water Cess Act violates the constitutional separation of state and central powers. Most courts concluded that the water cess is a tax which Parliament is authorised to impose under Entry 97, List I of Schedule VII of the Constitution. The ruling in *Agra Engineering Industries v Union of India*[54] is typical of the reasoning applied by the courts in resolving this issue. In *Tata Iron & Steel Co. Ltd.(Tisco) v State of Bihar*,[55] a division bench of the Patna High Court also concluded that the cess imposed under the Act was within the legislative competence of Parliament.

6. In 1991 the Cess Act was amended. The charging section and the provisions relating to rebate are reproduced below.[56]

[50] AIR 1997 ALL 179.
[51] AIR 1996 SC 2715.
[52] AIR 1996 SC 1446.
[53] *Chandra Enterprises v Cess Appellate Committee* 1991 ALL. L.J. 729.
[54] 1987 ALL.L.J.41.
[55] AIR 1991 PAT 75.
[56] The italicised clauses were introduced by the 1991 amendment.

3. Levy and collection of cess

(1)   There shall be levied and collected a cess for the purposes of the Water (Prevention and Control of Pollution) Act, 1974 (6 of 1974) and utilisation thereunder.

(2)   The cess under sub-section (1) shall be payable by—
    (a) every person carrying on any specified industry; and
    (b) every local authority,

and shall be calculated on the basis of the water consumed by such person or local authority, as the case may be, for any of the purposes specified in column (1) of Schedule II, at such rate, not exceeding the rate specified in the corresponding entry in column (2) thereof, as the Central Government may by notification in the Official Gazette, from time to time, specify.

(2A) Where any person carrying on any specified industry or any local authority consuming water for domestic purpose liable to pay cess fails to comply with any of the provisions of Section 25 of the Water (Prevention and Control of Pollution) Act, 1974 (6 of 1974) or any of the standards laid down by the Central Government under the Environment (Protection) Act, 1986, cess shall be, notwithstanding anything contained in sub-section (2) of this section, calculated and payable at such rate, not exceeding the rate specified in column (3) of Schedule II, as the Central Government may, by notification in the Official Gazette, from time to time, specify.

(3) Where any local authority supplies water to any person carrying on any specified industry or to any other local authority is liable to pay cess [under sub-section (2) or sub-section (2A)][57] so supplied, then, notwithstanding anything contained [in those sub-sections],[58] the local authority first mentioned shall not be liable to pay such cess in respect of such water.

    Explanation: For the purposes of this section and Section 4, consumption of water includes supply of water.

* * *

7. Rebate

Where any person or local authority, liable to pay the cess under this Act, installs any plant for the treatment of sewage or trade effluent, such person or local authority shall, from such date as may be prescribed, be entitled to a

---

[57] Substituted for 'under sub-section (2)' and 'in that sub-section' respectively by Act No.53 of 1991.
[58] *Id.*

rebate of [*twenty five per cent*][59] of the cess payable by such person or as the case may be, local authority.

   Provided that a person or local authority shall not be entitled to a rebate, if he or it—

   (a) *consumes water in excess of the maximum quantity as may be prescribed in this behalf for any specified industry or local authority; or*

   (b) *fails to comply with any of the provisions of Section 25 of the Water (Prevention and Control of Pollution) Act, 1974 (6 of 1974) or any of the standards laid down by the Central Government under the Environment (Protection) Act, 1986 (29 of 1986).*

7. In *Tisco's Case*,[60] the High Court was concerned with the provisions of section 7 as they stood prior to the 1991 amendment. Tisco claimed rebate though its water treatment plant could treat only a part of the industrial effluent generated by the company. In its assessment order, the Bihar pollution control board refused to grant rebate due to the limited facilities. Accepting the company's claim, the court held that an assessee was entitled to rebate even where it was not in a position to treat the entire trade effluent or sewage in the water treatment plant. In reaching this conclusion, the High Court applied a liberal interpretation, holding that the rebate provisions were for the benefit of industry. Was this approach justified? Does it survive the 1991 amendment?

The Madras High Court followed *Tisco* in *Seshasayee Paper and Board Ltd. v The Appellate Committee*.[61] The High Court permitted rebate, finding that the company had installed a 'relatively successful' effluent treatment plant. The assessing authority had declined to grant the rebate since the treated effluent did not meet the norm for bio-chemical oxygen demand. Interpreting the provisions of section 7 (pre-1991 amendment), the court held: 'It will be most unreasonable in my view to say that a person can claim rebate only when the treatment by the plant installed by him is successful, in the sense that no further treatment of the effluent is required at all. ... ' The court held that once an assessee contributed towards the treatment of the effluent, the revenue ought to allow rebate.

8. The provisions introduced in 1991 create fresh interpretation difficulties. To enjoy the benefit of the *lower* cess rates (column (2), Schedule II rates as against the higher column (3) rates) and rebate, the assessee must: (i) comply with the provisions of section 25 of the Water Act; (ii) meet the standards laid down under the Environment (Protection) Act of 1986 (EPA); and (iii) consume water within the limits prescribed.[62]

---

[59] Substituted for the words 'seventy per cent' by Act No.53 of 1991.
[60] *Supra* note 55.
[61] 1994 (2) MAD L.J.REP. 394.
[62] The first two conditions are common to the levy and rebate provisions; the third condition applies only to rebate.

Section 25 of the Water Act requires the polluter to apply for consent of the state board. Is condition (i) above, met by merely obtaining consent or does it further require that the assessee *comply* with all the conditions in the consent? Is the expression 'standards laid down under the EPA' restricted to the norms for water pollution or does it embrace *all* standards in respects of air, solid waste, etc.?

The differential tariff structure under Schedule II and the rebate clause are apt to lead to needless disputes between the assessee and the state pollution control board. In view of the stringent 1991 amendments, the detailed norms prescribed under the EPA and the strict conditions mentioned in the consent issued by the boards, it is next to impossible for an assessee to benefit from the lower tariff or rebate. Should Parliament delete the rebate clause and introduce a uniform tariff structure?

9. Besides the specified industries, section 3 of the Cess Act requires every local authority to pay cess on water consumed or supplied. Regrettably, municipal bodies neither obtain consent under section 25 of the Water Act nor pay cess under the Cess Act. In this regard, almost every municipality and local authority in India is a tax dodger, liable to the penalties imposed under section 14 of the Cess Act. The result is that huge amounts of cess remain unpaid and the state boards are deprived of funds.

10. The Delhi Electric Supply Undertaking (DESU) has a thermal power plant on the banks of the river Yamuna. The plant draws water from the river to cool its turbines and discharges the water used back into the river. DESU challenged the assessment orders passed under the Cess Act on the ground that there was no 'consumption' of water and consequently the taxable event for the levy of cess had not occurred. In a brief order the Supreme Court declined to interfere with the reasoning and conclusions of the cess appellate authority. The authority held that the water drawn by the utility was 'consumed'.[63]

11. The Bombay High Court quashed and set aside a demand for differential cess where the assessing authority had failed to comply with the principles of natural justice. The court remanded the case to the authority with a direction to disclose to the assessee the basis on which it proposed to deny rebate and charge cess at the higher rate.[64]

12. In *Arvind Textiles Case*,[65] the Rajasthan High Court upheld the levy of an additional octroi on grey cloth brought into Balotara town. The octroi was imposed to finance the municipal board's scheme to put up a common effluent

---

[63] *Delhi Electric Supply Undertaking v Central Board* 1995 Supp (3) SCC 385. Whether recycled water returned to a stream is a 'trade effluent' is a mixed question of law and fact. *Rajasthan State Electricity Board v Cess Appellate Committee* 1991 (1) SCC 93.

[64] *Tata Hydroelectric Power Supply Co. Ltd. v Member Secretary* Writ Petition No. 2347 of 1998, 15 January 1999.

[65] *Arvind Textiles v State of Rajasthan* AIR 1994 RAJ 195.

treatment plant to treat discharges from 200 textile processing units in the area.

13. For further discussion of the use of the Water Cess Act, as amended, to reduce pollution, see A. Rosencranz, A. Pandian and R. Campbell, *Economic Approaches for a Green India* (1999). The authors argue that Water Cess is still too low to induce polluters to change behavior and install pollution measures.

C. THE ENVIRONMENT (PROTECTION) ACT

The Environment (Protection) Act of 1986 clearly extends to water quality and the control of water pollution. Section 2(a) of the Act defines the environment to include water and the interrelationship which exists among and between water and human beings, other living creatures, plants, micro-organisms, and property. The Act authorises the Central Government to establish standards for the quality of the environment[66] and for emission or discharge of environmental pollutants from any source.[67] The Ministry of Environment and Forests has published Environment (Protection) Rules establishing general standards and industry-based standards for certain types of effluent discharge.[68] The ministry has not yet promulgated rules establishing ambient inland water quality standards, though state boards must have regard to the assimilative capacity of receiving bodies.[69] In 1997, the Maharashtra pollution control board pioneered the development of ambient norms for fresh water bodies.[70] However, these norms do not have statutory sanction and serve only to guide industry in selecting a suitable location.

The Environment Act includes a citizens' initiative provision[71] and a provision authorising the Central Government to issue direct orders to protect the environment.[72] The Central Government may delegate specified duties and powers under the Environment Act to any officer, state government, or other authority.[73] For example, the power to issue directions under section 5 has been delegated to the state governments and the power of entry and the right to take samples under sections 10 and 11 have been delegated to various officers.

[66] Section 3(2)(iii).

[67] Section 3(2)(iv).

[68] Schedule I and Schedule VI, Environment (Protection) Rules. Industry-based standards override general standards.

[69] Annexure I, Schedule VI, Environment (Protection) Rules. In December 1998, the minister issued water quality standards for coastal waters. Entry 86, Schedule I, Environment (Protection) Rules.

[70] Maharashtra Pollution Control Board, *Classification of River Water & Guidelines for Location of Industrial Activity* (1997).

[71] Section 19(b).

[72] Section 5.

[73] Section 23.

D. NUISANCE LAW AND WATER POLLUTION

I. PUBLIC NUISANCE ACTIONS UNDER THE CODE OF CRIMINAL PROCEDURE

In the landmark *Ratlam Municipality Case*,[74] discussed in the previous chapter, the Supreme Court did not consider the effect of the Water Act on the availability of injunctive relief under section 133. There is a divergence of judicial opinion on this issue. Initially, the Kerala High Court in *Tata Tea* ruled that a court could not entertain a section 133 action to abate water pollution, even where the state board was remiss. According to this view, the Water Act was a complete code to prevent water pollution and impliedly repealed the provisions of section 133 of the Criminal Procedure Code in so far as they relate to the prevention and control of water pollution.[75]

In *Nagarjuna Paper Mills Ltd. v Sub-Divisional Magistrate*,[76] the Andhra Pradesh High Court established a less stringent rule, taking the position that section 133 injunctive relief was available as long as it did not interfere with an order of a state pollution control board issued under the Water Act. The court noted that the magistrate's decision to issue an order for injunctive relief was based on a report submitted by the superintendent engineer of the pollution control board itself, which stated that water pollution from the paper mills was harming people and cattle. This view was also adopted by a division bench of the Kerala High Court in *Krishna Panicker v Appukuttan Nair*,[77] overruling the contrary opinion expressed earlier in *Tata Tea*.[78] However, without considering *Panicker's Case*, the Karnataka High Court in 1997 followed *Tata Tea*,[79] then quickly retreated,[80] preferring the approach of the Andhra Pradesh High Court.

II. INJUNCTIVE RELIEF UNDER COMMON LAW

A private party who suffers an unreasonable interference with the enjoyment of his or her property, may bring a common law action to restrain the polluter. The following case, considers whether section 58 of the Water Act bars the jurisdiction of the civil courts to entertain private nuisance suits.

SREENIVASA DISTILLERIES v THYAGARAJAN
AIR 1986 AP 328

ORDER: * * *

Section 58 enacts two prohibitions. Firstly, not to entertain any suit or proceedings in respect of any matter which the appellate authority constituted under the Act is

---

[74] AIR 1980 SC 1622.
[75] *Tata Tea Ltd. v State of Kerala* 1984 KER. L.T.645.
[76] 1987 CRI.L.J.2071.
[77] 1993 (1) KER. L.T.771.
[78] *Supra* note 75.
[79] *Executive Apparel Processors v The Taluka Executive Magistrate* 1997 (4) KAR.L.J.181.
[80] *Harihar Polyfibres v Sub-Divisional Magistrate* ILR 1997 KAR 1139.

empowered to determine. Secondly, no injunction shall be granted in respect of any action taken by any authority under the Act in pursuance of the provisions of the Act. This is the only provision barring the jurisdiction of a Civil Court. The section is intended to preserve the statutory protection given to the Boards untouched by civil actions. Now, the present action is only preventing the defendant from polluting water. But this section is not directed to annul any orders passed by the authority constituted under this Act. Now it is admitted that no orders are passed under the Act, and, therefore, any order passed by the Civil Court will not take away the jurisdiction of authorities constituted under the Act. Hence, I am of the view that S. 58 does not prohibit the jurisdiction of the Civil Court to entertain any suit or proceeding restraining the defendant to cause pollution.

NOTES AND QUESTIONS

1. Do you find an intent of Parliament in the Water Act to bar private remedies for water pollution or is the Act intended to supplement other remedies for the control of water pollution?

2. The citizens' suit provisions of the Water Act and the Environment (Protection) Act do not provide for private damages. A private litigant, however, can seek damages rather than injunctive relief in a civil lawsuit. In view of section 58 of the Water Act can a court hearing a private lawsuit order the polluter to pay damages?

3. Does a statutory provision, such as section 58, bar the jurisdiction of a High Court to entertain a petition under Article 226 of the Constitution or the jurisdiction of the Supreme Court to entertain petitions under Article 32? Citizens have a fundamental duty to protect and improve the natural environment under Article 51A(g) of the Constitution: Should a statutory provision curtail availability of legal remedies which enable a citizen to discharge this fundamental duty?

E. RIPARIAN RIGHTS AND WATER POLLUTION

A riparian owner is one who has title to land adjacent to a natural stream. The Indian legal system has recognised the right of riparian owners to unpolluted waters at least since the adoption of the Indian Easements Act of 1882. Under section 7 of that Act every riparian owner has the right to the continued flow of the waters of a natural stream in its natural condition without obstruction or unreasonable pollution.

The legal system also recognises a common law riparian right to unpolluted water. This common law right is rarely invoked in contemporary litigation concerning water pollution. The Supreme Court, however, revived this doctrine in *M.C. Mehta v Union of India (Municipalities)* by stating:

In common law the Municipal Corporation can be restrained by an injunction in an action brought by a riparian owner who has suffered on account of the pollution of the water in a river caused by the Corporation by discharging into the river insufficiently treated sewage from discharging such sewage into the river.[81]

NOTES AND QUESTIONS

1. The Supreme Court in the *Mehta (Municipalities)* opinion noted that the Central and state water boards and the municipality that was releasing sewage effluent had failed to implement or enforce the laws, for controlling water pollution. Suppose an industrial manufacturer or municipality is releasing effluent in compliance with the consent orders of a state board. The effluent causes harm to a riparian landowner who uses the water for domestic purposes or irrigation. How should a court rule on the riparian landowner's request for an injunction restraining the polluter from releasing effluent?

2. Assume a court decides to issue a restraining order to protect a plaintiff's riparian rights. What should the order require of the polluter—primary treatment of the effluent, no discharge whatever of effluent, or removal only of those substances which interfere with the actual riparian uses of the water? Assume the riparian landowner requires water of very high quality for aquaculture. Assume also that the water in the stream in its natural condition—that is, not subject to any other use— is suitable for aquaculture. Must all users of water on the stream return the water in its natural condition? Should small farmers be exempt from this requirement? Should large industrial concerns be exempt if they apply the best available technology for treating the water?

F. THE GANGA ACTION PLAN

Amidst great fanfare in 1985, the Government of India announced an ambitious new plan for cleaning up the Ganges river. A newly created Ganga Authority, headed by the Prime Minister, is ultimately responsible for the river's restoration. The eight-member authority includes the Central Government's planning and environmental ministers and the chief ministers of the states through which the Ganges flows.

The Central pollution control board has produced an '*Action Plan for the Prevention of Pollution of the Ganga*' as a guide for steps in the cleanup. The government has established an inter-departmental steering committee to formulate detailed components of this Plan and to administer and monitor implementation of the Plan. A Ganga Project Directorate is included within the Department of Envi-

[81] AIR 1988 SC 1115.

ronment to appraise and clear projects prepared by field level agencies, release funds, and coordinate long-term activities under the Action Plan.

The Ganga Action Plan is based on a comprehensive survey of the Ganga Basin carried out by the Central board. About 80 per cent of the pollution in the river is caused by raw sewage discharged directly into the river. The first phase of the Ganga Action Plan focuses on construction of an extensive network of self-sustaining sewage treatment plants in the cities along the Ganga River as the first measure to reduce pollution. Most of the physical infrastructure for intercepting, diverting and treating municipal sewage has been created,[82] though the efficacy of these schemes remains uncertain.[83] In the second phase, the Plan envisages establishing similar facilities along the Ganga's major tributaries, including the Yamuna and Gomti. The Central Government has also initiated an ambitious scheme to replicate the Ganga model for cleaning up polluted stretches elsewhere in the country through a National River Conservation Plan (NRCP).

NOTES AND QUESTIONS

1. The governmental authorities charged with implementing the Ganga Action Plan are the same authorities that have the duty of implementing and enforcing the Water Act and Environment (Protection) Act. These authorities have drawn heavy criticism from commentators and the courts for proceeding at a snail's pace to implement environmental legislation. The Ganga Action Plan, however, calls for a different approach to preventing water pollution than the permit system of the Water Act. Instead of trying to force recalcitrant industries and public authorities into expending funds for water treatment, the Ganga Action Plan calls for coordinated expenditure of public funds from the Central Government. The agencies have direct control over implementation of the Ganga Action Plan and are not dependent on the willingness of polluters to comply with government orders and directions. Do polluters get a free ride at public expense, if such a scheme does not require polluters to pay fees for use of publicly funded treatment plants? Is it more economically efficient for polluters to pay for the reduction of pollution?

2. The organizational structure for the Ganga Action Plan designates a role for non–governmental organizations in preparation, execution, maintenance, and public participation in the cleanup of the Ganges but does not specify the means for incorporating the advice of these organizations. No citizen members are included in the Ganga Plan Authority or the Steering Committee. Should private organizations, whose leaders are not responsible to the electorate, have a say in the implementation

---

[82] Ministry of Environment and Forests, Government of India, *Annual Report: 1997–98* (1998).

[83] Shankar, *Purifying the Ganga* in *Down to Earth*, 30 September 1992, p. 25 and Banerji, *Change at Last* in *Down to Earth*, 28 February 1998, p. 20. The second article quotes a UK study suggesting some improvement in the water quality.

of the Ganga Action Plan? Should industry have a voice in implementation of the Plan? Could full public disclosure of proposed expenditure of funds and a forum for the public to comment on expenditures make the Plan more effective?

3. For a critical review of the Ganga Action Plan, see the Centre for Science and Environment's *State of India's Environment: The Citizens' Fifth Report* 91–108 (1999).

G. THE GANGA POLLUTION CASES

The *Ganga Pollution Cases* are the most significant water pollution cases to date. In 1985, M.C. Mehta, an activist Supreme Court advocate, filed a writ petition under Article 32 of the Constitution. Among other things, the petition was directed at the Kanpur Municipality's failure to prevent waste water from polluting the Ganga. Mehta asked the court to order governmental authorities and tanneries at Jajmau near Kanpur to stop polluting the Ganga with sewage and trade effluents.

The ensuing litigation involved hundreds of polluters and the Supreme Court noticed the action as a representative action under Order 1, Rule 8 of the Code of Civil Procedure. In the previous chapter, we carried an overview of the *Ganga Pollution Cases*. Here, we excerpt from three major opinions in the case, where the court ruled against the Kanpur tanneries, the municipalities on the Ganga and the Calcutta tanneries.[84]

While reading the following excerpts, consider particularly these issues: (a) the polluted condition of the river Ganga more than two decades after the enactment of the Water Act; (b) the basis for the court's jurisdiction under Article 32; and (c) the specific actions ordered by the court in each case.

M.C. MEHTA v UNION OF INDIA (KANPUR TANNERIES)
AIR 1988 SC 1037

VENKATARAMIAH, J.:

This is a public interest litigation. The petitioner who is an active social worker has filed this petition, inter alia, for the issue of a writ/order/direction in the nature of mandamus to the respondents other than Respondents 1 and 7 to 9 restraining them from letting out the trade effluents into the river Ganga till such time they put up necessary treatment plants for treating the trade effluents in order to arrest the pollution of water in the said river. Respondent 1 is the Union of India, Respondent 7 is the Chairman of the Central Board for Prevention and Control of Pollution, Respondent 8 is the Chairman, Uttar Pradesh Pollution Control Board and Respondent 9 is the Indian Standards Institute.

Water is the most important of the elements of nature. River valleys have been

---

[84] For convenience, these opinions are referred to as *Kanpur Tanneries*, *Municipalities* and *Calcutta Tanneries*.

the cradles of civilization from the beginning of the world. Aryan civilization grew around the towns and villages on the banks of the river Ganga. Varanasi which is one of the cities on the banks of the river Ganga is considered to be one of the oldest human settlements in the world. It is the popular belief that the river Ganga is the purifier of all but we are now led to the situation that action has to be taken to prevent the pollution of the water of the river Ganga since we have reached a stage that any further pollution of the river water is likely to lead to a catastrophe. There are today large towns inhabited by millions of people on the banks of the river Ganga. There are also large industries on its banks. Sewage of the towns and cities on the banks of the river and the trade effluents of the factories and other industries are continuously being discharged into the river. It is the complaint of the petitioner that neither the government nor the people are giving adequate attention to stop the pollution of the river Ganga. Steps have, therefore, to be taken for the purpose of protecting the cleanliness of the stream in the river Ganga, which is in fact the life sustainer of a large part of northern India.

When this petition came up for preliminary hearing, the court directed the issue of notice under Order 1 Rule 8 of the Code of Civil Procedure treating this case as a representative action by publishing the gist of the petition in the newspapers in circulation in northern India and calling upon all the industrialists and the municipal corporations and the town municipal councils having jurisdiction over the areas through which the river Ganga flows to appear before the Court and to show cause as to why directions should not be issued to them as prayed by the petitioner asking them not to allow the trade effluents and the sewage into the river Ganga without appropriately, treating them before discharging them into the river. Pursuant to the said notice a large number of industrialists and local bodies have entered appearance before the Court. Some of them have filed counter-affidavits explaining the steps taken by them for treating the trade effluents before discharging them into the river. When the above case came up for consideration before the Court on the last date of hearing we directed that the case against the tanneries at Jajmau area near Kanpur would be taken up for hearing first. [The court noted that only 47 of the 75 tanneries designated as parties to the lawsuit were represented before the court by counsel. The remaining tanneries did not appear before the court at the time of the hearing nor were they represented by any counsel. As authority for the importance and need to protect the environment, the court cited the directive principle in Article 48A of the Constitution which provides that the State shall endeavour to protect and improve the environment and to safeguard the forests and wildlife of the country, Article 51A which imposes a fundamental duty on the citizens to protect and improve the natural environment, and the proclamation adopted by the United Nations Conference on the Human Environment of 1972, including the common conviction of the participant nations that environmental pollution must be halted. The court also invoked the Water Act as an indication of the importance of the prevention and control of water pollution. The court emphasized that notwithstanding the comprehensive provisions contained in the Water Act the state boards had not taken effective steps to prevent the discharge of effluents into the river Ganga.

The court ruled that the fact that effluents are first discharged into municipal sewers did not absolve the tanneries from being proceeded against under the provisions of the law in force, since ultimately the effluents reach the river Ganga from municipal sewers.

The court also invoked the Environment (Protection) Act as further indication of the importance of prevention and control of water pollution and noted that not much had been done even under that Act by the Central Government to stop the grave public nuisance caused by the tanneries at Jajmau, Kanpur.]

There is not much dispute on the question that the discharge of the trade effluents from these tanneries into the river Ganga has been causing considerable damage to the life of the people who use the water of the river Ganga and also to the aquatic life in the river. The tanneries at Jajmau in Kanpur have themselves formed an association called Jajmau Tanners Pollution Control Association with the objects among others:

(1) To establish, equip and maintain laboratories, workshops, institutes, organisations and factories for conducting and carrying on experiments and to provide funds for the main objects of the Company.

(2) To procure and import wherever necessary the chemicals etc. for the purpose of pollution control in tanning industries.

(3) To set up and maintain common effluent treatment plant for member tanners in and around Jajmau.

(4) To make periodical charges on members for the effluent treatment based on the benefit it derives from time to time to meet the common expenses for maintenance, replacement incurred towards effluent treatment.

* * *

A study of the conditions prevailing at Jajmau, Kanpur was made by the Sub-Committee on Effluent Disposal constituted by the Development Council for Leather and Leather Goods Industries along with the various tanneries situated in some of the other parts of India and in its report submitted in April 1984, the Sub-Committee has observed in the case of the tanneries at Jajmau, Kanpur thus:

> In the case of Jajmau, Kanpur, the committee visited few tanneries where the effort has been made to have primary treatment of the effluent before it is discharged to the common drain/the river Ganges. There are 60 tanneries in Jajmau which will be covered under joint effluent disposal. The total production is to the tune of 12,000 hides with a total discharge of 5 million litres per day. The State Government has taken appropriate steps in preparation of the feasibility report under the guidance of the UP Pollution Control Board. This proposal was also supported by Central Pollution Control Board, Delhi by sharing the total fee of Rs. 80,000 to be paid to the Public Health Engineering Consultancy, Bombay. ...
>
> The report suggests that each tannery should make arrangement for the primary treatment of their effluent and then it will be discharged into common treatment plant.

There is a reference to the Jajmau tanneries in An Action Plan for Prevention of Pollution of the Ganga prepared by the Department of Environment, Government of India in the year 1985 which is as under:

* * *

'4.4.12 Effluent from industries: Under the laws of the land the responsibility for treatment of the industrial effluents is that of the industry. While the concept of "Strict Liability" should be adhered to in some cases, circumstances may require that plans for sewerage and treatment systems should consider industrial effluents as well. Clusters of small industries located in a contiguous area near the river bank and causing direct pollution to the river *such as the tanneries in Jajmau in Kanpur* is a case in point. In some cases, waste waters from some industrial units may have already been connected to the city sewer and, therefore, merit treatment alongwith the sewage in the sewage treatment plant. It may also be necessary in some crowded areas to accept waste waters of industries in a city sewer to be fed to the treatment plant, provided the industrial waste is free from heavy metals, toxic chemicals and is not abnormally acidic or alkaline.

In such circumstances, scheme proposals have to carefully examine the case of integrating or segregating industrial wastes for purposes of conveyance and treatment as also the possibilities for apportionment of capital and operating costs between the city authorities and the industries concerned.' (Emphasis added)

* * *

In the counter–affidavit filed on behalf of Hindustan Chambers of Commerce, of which 43 respondents are members, it is admitted that the tanneries discharge their trade effluents into the sewage nullah which leads to the municipal sewage plant before they are thrown into the river Ganga. It is not disputed by any of the respondents that the water in the river Ganga is being polluted grossly by the effluents discharged by the tanneries. We are informed that six of the tanneries have already set up the primary treatment plants for carrying out the pre-treatment of the effluent before it is discharged into the municipal sewers which ultimately leads to the river Ganga. About 14 of the tanneries are stated to be engaged in the construction of the primary treatment plants. It is pleaded on behalf of the rest of the tanneries who are the members of the Hindustan Chambers of Commerce and three other tanneries represented by [counsel] that if some time is given to them to establish the pre-treatment plants they would do so. It is, however, submitted by all of them that it would not be possible for them to have the secondary system for treating waste water as that would involve enormous expenditure, which the tanneries themselves would not be able to meet. It is true that it may not be possible for the tanneries to establish immediately the secondary system plant in view of the large expenditure involved but having regard to the adverse effects the effluents are having on the river water, the tanneries at Jajmau, Kanpur should at least set up the primary treatment plants and that is the minimum which tanneries should do in the circumstances of the case. In the counter-affidavit filed on behalf of the Hindustan Chambers of Commerce it is seen that the cost of pre-treatment plant for a 'A' class tannery is Rs. 3,68,000, the cost of the plant for a 'B' class tannery is Rs. 2,30,000 and the cost of the plant for 'C' class tannery is Rs. 50,000 This cost does not appear to be excessive. The financial capacity of the tanneries should be considered as irrelevant while requiring them to establish primary treatment plants. Just like an industry which cannot pay minimum wages to its workers cannot be allowed to exist, a tannery which cannot set up a primary treatment plant cannot be permitted to continue to be in existence for the adverse effect on the public at large which is likely to ensue by the discharging of the trade effluents from the tannery to the river Ganga would be immense and it will outweigh any inconvenience that may be caused to the management and the labour employed by it on account of its closure. Moreover, the tanneries involved in these cases are not taken by surprise. For several years they are being asked to take necessary steps to prevent the flow of untreated waste water from their factories into the river. Some of them have already complied with the demand. It should be remembered that the effluent discharged from a tannery is ten times as noxious when compared with the domestic sewage water which flows into the river from any urban area on its banks. We feel that the tanneries at Jajmau, Kanpur cannot be allowed to continue to carry on the industrial activity unless they take steps to establish primary treatment plants. In cases of this nature this Court may issue appropriate directions if it finds that the public nuisance or other wrongful act affecting or likely to affect the public is being committed and the statutory authorities who are charged with the duty to prevent it are not taking adequate steps to rectify the grievance. For every breach of a right there should be a remedy. It is unfortunate that a number of tanneries at Jajmau even though they are aware of these proceedings have not cared to even enter appearance in this court to express their willingness to take appropriate steps to establish the pre-treatment plants. So far as they are concerned an order directing them to stop working their tanneries should be passed.

[The court then ordered the tanneries which did not appear before the court to stop running their tanneries and releasing trade effluents into the river Ganga without subjecting the trade effluents to a pre-treatment process by setting up primary treatment plants as approved by the state board. The court made its order effective from 1 October 1987. The court also ordered that tanneries with primary treatment plants may continue production as long as the primary treatment plants are in sound working order.]

[Counsel] for the other tanneries who are members of the Hindustan Chambers of Commerce and the other tanneries who have entered appearance ... submits that they will establish primary treatment plants within six months and he further submits that in the event of their not completing the construction of the primary treatment plants as approved by the State Board (respondent 8) and bringing them into operation within the period of six months the said tanneries will stop carrying on their business. We record the statement made by the learned counsel and grant them time till 31 March 1988 to set up the primary treatment plants. If any of these tanneries does not set up a primary treatment plant within 31 March 1988 it is directed to stop its business from 1 April 1988.

We issue a direction to the Central Government, the Uttar Pradesh Board established under the provisions of the Water (Prevention and Control of Pollution) Act, 1974 and the District Magistrate, Kanpur to enforce our order faithfully. Copies of this order shall be sent to them for information.

* * *

NOTES AND QUESTIONS

1. Part III of the Constitution, which includes Article 32, contains the fundamental rights. The fundamental right to petition the Supreme Court is guaranteed in Article 32(1) which reads:

The right to move the Supreme Court by appropriate proceedings for the enforcement of the rights conferred by this Part is guaranteed.

In *Kanpur Tanneries*, the court does not explicitly invoke a fundamental right found in Part III of the Constitution as the basis for its jurisdiction to hear the writ petition. Is concern over this issue of constitutional authority mere quibbling? Is the Supreme Court's failure to expressly invoke a fundamental right under Part III bad jurisprudence?

2. Note that the *Ganga Pollution* litigation commenced before the introduction of the citizens' initiative provision into the Water Act. Could M.C. Mehta have proceeded against the tanneries under the Water Act? Is an Article 32 writ petition more effective than a citizens' prosecution under the Water Act?

3. Normally, an order issued in an Article 32 petition is directed at public officials or authorities who are instrumentalities of the 'State' under Article 12. In *Kanpur Tanneries*, the court issued direct orders to private tanneries, including orders to cease operations. Are private enterprises subject to the discipline of Part III of the Constitution? Should the court have moulded the relief differently?

M.C. MEHTA v UNION OF INDIA (MUNICIPALITIES)
AIR 1988 SC 1115

VENKATARAMIAH, J.:   * * *

Since it was found that Kanpur was one of the biggest cities on the banks of the river Ganga, we took up for consideration the case in respect of the Kanpur Nagar Mahapalika.

[The court reproduced excerpts from the Uttar Pradesh Nagar Mahapalika Adhiniyam which applies to the municipalities of Kanpur, Allahabad, Varanasi, Agra, and Lucknow. The excerpts list the following statutory duties of municipalities: Treat and dispose of sewage; provide a safe water supply; protect water used for human consumption; provide for public sanitation and disposal of human wastes; dispose of dead animals; limit agricultural operations; remove noxious weeds, abate public nuisances arising from tanks; and control disease. The court also cited the Uttar Pradesh Municipalities Act of 1916 and the Uttar Pradesh Water Supply and Sewerage Authority Act of 1975 which establish municipal statutory duties regarding the supply of water to cities and towns and the construction of sewerage systems.

The court enumerated the duties of the pollution control boards established by the Water Act and the Environment (Protection) Act. The court referred to the affidavits filed and the inspection reports placed before the judges.]

Shri M.C. Mehta, the petitioner herein, drew our attention to the Progress Report of the Ganga Action Plan (July 1986–January 1987) prepared by the Industrial Toxicology Research Centre, Council of Scientific and Industrial Research. At page twenty of the said report the details of the analysis of the Ganga water samples collected during August 1986 to January 1987 from Uttar Pradesh region are furnished. That report shows that the pollution of the water in the river Ganga is of the highest degree at Kanpur. [Data from the report on biological oxygen demand, chemical oxygen demand and bacterial contamination indicate that *water is not fit for drinking, bathing and fishing purpose.* The report recommended that all nullahs be trapped immediately and raw water be treated conventionally at water works and disinfected with chlorination.] In the concluding part of the said Progress Report it is stated thus:

The Ganga is grossly polluted at Kanpur. All nullahs are discharging the polluted waste water into river Ganga. But Jajmau by-pass channel, Sismau, Muir Mill, Golf Club and Gupta Ghat nullahs are discharging huge quantities of polluted waste water. To improve the quality of the Ganga all major nullahs should be diverted and treated. Combined treatment should be provided for Jajmau tanneries. Effluent treatment plants should be installed by all polluting industries.

It is needless to say that in the tropical developing countries a large amount of misery, sickness and death due to infectious diseases arises out of water supplies. [The court provided lengthy excerpts from Lall's *Commentaries on Water and Air Pollution Laws* (2nd Edition) describing water borne diseases, especially typhoid and cholera and quoted from *Water Pollution and Disposal of Waste Water on Land* (1983) by U.N. Mahida]

[The court discussed common law riparian rights to unpolluted water.] The petitioner in the case before us is no doubt not a riparian owner. He is a person interested in protecting the lives of the people who make use of the water flowing in the river Ganga and his right to maintain the petition cannot be disputed. The nuisance caused by the pollution of the river Ganga is a public nuisance, which is widespread in range and indiscriminate in its effect and it would not be reasonable to expect any particular person to take proceedings to stop it as distinct from the community at large. The petition has been entertained as a Public Interest Litigation. On the facts and in the circumstances of the case we are of the view that the petitioner is entitled to move this Court in order to enforce the statutory provisions which impose duties on the municipal authorities and the Board constituted under the Water Act. We have already set out the relevant provisions of the statute which imposes those duties on the authorities concerned. On account of their failure to obey the statutory duties for several years the water in the river Ganga at Kanpur has become so much polluted that it can no longer be used by the people either for drinking or for bathing. The Nagar Mahapalika of Kanpur has to bear the major responsibility for the pollution of the river near Kanpur.

It is no doubt true that the construction of certain works has been undertaken under the Ganga Action Plan at Kanpur in order to improve the sewerage system and to prevent pollution of the water in the river Ganga. But as we see from the affidavit filed on behalf of the authorities concerned in this case the works are going on at a snail's pace. We find from the affidavits filed on behalf of the Kanpur Nagar

Mahapalika that certain target dates have been fixed for completion of the works already undertaken. We expect the authorities concerned to complete those works within the target dates mentioned in the counter-affidavits and not to delay the completion of those works beyond those dates. It is, however, noticed that the Kanpur Nagar Mahapalika has not yet submitted its proposals for sewage treatment works to the State Board constituted under the Water Act. The Kanpur Nagar Mahapalika should submit its proposals to the state within six months from today.

It is seen that there [are] a large number of dairies in Kanpur in which there are about 80,000 cattle. The Kanpur Nagar Mahapalika should take action under the provisions of the Adhiniyam or the relevant bye-laws made thereunder to prevent the pollution of the water in the Ganga on account of the waste accumulated at the dairies. The Kanpur Nagar Mahapalika may either direct the dairies to be shifted to a place outside the city so that the waste accumulated does not ultimately reach the river Ganga or in the alternative it may arrange for the removal of such waste by employing motor vehicles to transport such waste from the existing dairies in which event the owners of the dairy cannot claim any compensation. The Kanpur Nagar Mahapalika should immediately take action to prevent the collection of manure at private manure pits inside the city.

The Kanpur Nagar Mahapalika should take immediate steps to increase the size of the sewers in the labour colonies so that the sewage may be carried smoothly through the sewerage system. Wherever sewerage line is not yet constructed steps should be taken to lay it.

Immediate action should also be taken by the Kanpur Nagar Mahapalika to construct sufficient number of public latrines and urinals for the use of the poor people in order to prevent defecation by them on open land. The proposal to levy any charge for the making use of such latrines and urinals shall be dropped as that would be a reason for the poor people not using the public latrines and urinals. The cost of maintenance of cleanliness of those latrines and urinals has to be borne by the Kanpur Nagar Mahapalika.

It is submitted before us that whenever the Board constituted under the Water Act initiates any proceeding to prosecute industrialists or other persons who pollute the water in the river Ganga, the persons accused of the offences immediately institute petitions under Section 482 of the Code of Criminal Procedure, 1973 in the High Court and obtain stay orders thus frustrating the attempt of the Board to enforce the provisions of the Water Act. They have not placed before us the facts of any particular case. We are, however, of the view that since the problem of the pollution of the water in the river Ganga has become very acute the High Courts should not ordinarily grant orders of stay of criminal proceedings in such cases and even if such an order of stay is made in an extraordinary case the High Courts should dispose of the case within a short period, say about two months, from the date of the institution of such case. We request the High Courts to take up for hearing all the cases where such orders have been issued under Section 482 of the Code of Criminal Procedure, 1973 staying prosecutions under the Water Act within two months. The counsel for the Board constituted under the Water Act shall furnish a list of such cases to the Registrar of the concerned High Court for appropriate action being taken thereon.

One other aspect to which our attention is drawn is the practice of throwing

corpses and semi-burnt corpses into the river Ganga. This practice should be immediately brought to an end. The co-operation of the people and police should be sought
in enforcing this restriction. Steps shall be taken by the Kanpur Nagar Mahapalika
and the Police authorities to ensure that dead bodies are not thrown into the river
Ganga.

Whenever applications for licences to establish new industries are made in
future, such applications shall be refused unless adequate provision has been made
for the treatment of trade effluents flowing out of the factories. Immediate action
should be taken against the existing industries if they are found responsible for the
pollution of water.

Having regard to the grave consequences of the pollution of water and air and
the need for protecting and improving the natural environment which is considered to
be one of the fundamental duties under the Constitution (vide clause (g) of Article 51-
A of the Constitution) we are of the view that it is the duty of the Central Government
to direct all the educational institutions throughout India to teach for one hour in a
week lessons relating to the protection and improvement of the natural environment
including forests, lakes, rivers and wild life in the first ten classes. The Central
Government shall get text books written for the said purpose and distribute them to the
educational institutions free of cost. ... This should be done throughout India.

In order to rouse amongst the people the consciousness of cleanliness of
environment the Government of India and the governments of the States and Union
Territories may consider the desirability of organizing 'Keep the city clean' week
(Nagar Nirmalikarana Saptaha), and 'Keep the town clean' week (Pura Nirmalikarana
Saptaha) and 'Keep the village clean' week (Grama Nirmalikarana Saptaha) in every
city, town and village throughout India at least once a year. During that week the
entire city, town or village should be kept as far as possible clean, tidy, and free from
the pollution of land, water and air. The organization of the week should be entrusted
to, the Nagar Mahapalikas, Municipal Corporations, Town Municipalities, Village
Panchayats or such other local authorities having jurisdiction over the area in question
... During that week all the citizens including the members of the executive, members
of Parliament and the State Legislatures, members of the judiciary may be requested
to co-operate with the local authorities and to take part in the celebrations by rendering
free personal service. This would surely create a national awareness of the problems
faced by the people of the appalling all-round deterioration of the environment which
we are witnessing today. We request the Ministry of Environment of the Government
of India to give a serious consideration to the above request.

What we have stated above applies *mutatis mutandis* to all other Mahapalikas
and Municipalities which have jurisdiction over the area through which the Ganga
flows. Copies of this judgment shall be sent to all such Nagar Mahapalikas and
Municipalities. The case against the Nagar Mahapalikas and Municipalities in the
State of Uttar Pradesh shall stand adjourned by six months. Within that time all the
Nagar Mahapalikas and Municipalities in the State of Uttar Pradesh through whose
areas the river Ganga flows shall file affidavits in this Court explaining the various
steps they have taken for the prevention of pollution of the water in the river Ganga
in the light of the above judgment.

NOTES AND QUESTIONS

1. The court relied on expert evidence to show the extent and consequences of the pollution of the Ganga. The evidence in *Municipalities* included affidavits from engineers employed by the Uttar Pradesh water pollution control board and the Progress Reports of the Ganga Action Plan. The court also gave judicial recognition to the book Lall's *Commentaries on Water and Air Pollution Laws* and *Water Pollution and Disposal of Waste Water on Land*. Compare this evidence with the requirements of the Water Act for taking and analysing samples admissible as evidence. Is it not more difficult to establish that pollutants are being released under the Water Act? Does the Water Act require that the government or citizen proceeding against a polluter show harm from the pollution?

2. Note that in this case there appears to be no dispute that the pollution of the Ganges has harmed the public health and welfare. Has the court acted in this case because of the overwhelming and admitted degradation of the Ganges? The Water Act empowers the state boards and the courts to issue orders if pollution appears likely. Can the Supreme Court, under Article 32, order measures to prevent pollution before harm has actually occurred, or is the court's power only remedial?

3. In *Municipalities*, the Supreme Court found that the nagar mahapalika of Kanpur had to bear the major responsibility for the pollution of the Ganga near Kanpur. The court ordered all municipalities and all nagar mahapalikas in Uttar Pradesh along the river to take steps to prevent the polluting of the Ganges. The court specifically addressed the problems in Kanpur by ordering the city to fulfil statutory duties including: Removal of dairies or the wastes from dairies at the city's expense; increase of the capacity of the sewers in labour colonies; provision of public latrines and urinals at the city's expense; stricter enforcement to prevent the placing of dead bodies in the Ganges; and submission of sewer proposals to the state within six months. Why has the city failed to take these steps in the past? Can the court order the city to raise the revenue if available funds will not cover the costs of taking these steps? Note that many of the statutory duties are imposed by state and central statutes. Can local governments be expected to fulfil these duties without sufficient funding?

4. The Supreme Court describes in great detail the laws, plans and administrative authorities at all levels of government—all directed towards restoring the water quality of the Ganges. Note, however, the court's observation that the sewers of Kanpur have not had adequate cleaning in almost twenty years. How can one explain this administrative failure to implement obvious and basic measures to prevent water pollution? Will the court's order to the Central Government to increase public education about pollution help change this situation?

5. The Supreme Court retained jurisdiction in *Municipalities* to review the steps taken by all the mahapalikas and municipalities along the Ganges in Uttar

Pradesh to control water pollution. Does the Supreme Court have the resources to undertake this review? Should the courts become involved in such massive administrative tasks?

M.C. MEHTA v UNION OF INDIA (CALCUTTA TANNERIES)
1997 (2) SCC 411

KULDIP SINGH, J.

This petition—public interest—under Article 32 of the Constitution of India was initially directed against the tanneries located in the city of Kanpur. This Court by the order dated 22–9–1987 (*M.C. Mehta v Union of India* AIR 1988 SC 1037) issued various directions in relation to Kanpur tanneries. While monitoring the said directions, the scope of the petition was enlarged and the industries located in various cities on the banks of River Ganga were called upon to stop discharging untreated effluent into the river. In this judgment we are concerned with the tanneries located at Tangra, Tiljala, Topsia and Pagla Danga the four adjoining areas in the eastern fringe of the city of Calcutta (the Calcutta tanneries). These areas accommodate about 550 tanneries. According to the examination report dated 30–9–1995 by the National Environmental Engineering Research Institute (NEERI), ninety per cent of the Calcutta tanneries use chrome-based tanning process, while the remaining utilise vegetable tanning process. The present status of the four tannery clusters in Calcutta, according to the NEERI Report, is as under:

> It was observed by the inspection team that no appropriate waste water drainage and collection systems are available in any of the tannery clusters. The untreated waste water flows through open drains causing serious environmental, health and hygiene problems. Also, no waste water treatment facilities exist in any of the four tannery clusters.

The observations by the NEERI team, regarding the Calcutta tanneries in the report are as under:

> Tannery units are located in highly congested habitations, offering little or no scope for future expansion, modernisation or installation of effluent treatment plants (ETPs). Tannery units are located in thickly populated residential areas.
>
> Surroundings of the tanneries are extremely unhygienic due to discharge of untreated effluents in open drains, stagnation of wastewater in low-lying areas around the tannery units, and accumulation of solid waste in tanneries.

It is thus obvious that the Calcutta tanneries have all along been operating in extremely unhygienic conditions and are discharging highly toxic effluents all over the areas.

This Court on the basis of the material on the record in Kanpur tanneries' order observed as under regarding the noxious nature of the tannery effluent:

It should be remembered that the effluent discharged from a tannery is ten times more noxious when compared with the domestic sewage water which flows into the river from any urban area on its banks.

Needless to say that the State of West Bengal and the West Bengal Pollution Control Board (the Board) are wholly remiss in the performance of their statutory obligations to control pollution and stop environmental degradation.

[The judgment refers to the principal interlocutory orders passed by the court; the response of the state government and the board to various solutions mooted during the hearings; and the steps taken for relocating the tanneries to a new site.]

This Court has been monitoring this petition for a long time primarily with a view to control pollution and save the environment. In the process the Calcutta tanneries have been extended all possible help to relocate themselves to the new complex. Despite repeated reports by the Board that the Calcutta tanneries were/are discharging highly noxious effluents and are polluting the land and the river, this Court did not order the closure of the tanneries because they agreed before this Court and had given clear undertaking that they would relocate to the new complex. In spite of all the efforts made by this Court to provide every possible facility to the Calcutta tanneries to shift to the new complex they remained wholly non-cooperative. With a view to control the pollution generated by the Calcutta tanneries this Court. ... agreed to examine the proposal regarding setting up of common effluent treatment plants at the existing areas where the tanneries are operating. This Court directed NEERI to examine the feasibility of the projects. NEERI submitted its report dated 30–9–1995. The report indicates that a four-member team inspected the existing sites of tanneries' clusters and examined the issues relating to the proposed common effluents treatment plants (CETPs) and their locations at Tangra, Tiljala, Topsia and Pagla Danga in Calcutta. The conclusions reached by the NEERI are as under:

5.0 Conclusions

On review of the proposed CETP schemes for tannery wastewater management at Tangra, Tiljala and Topsia by M/s KROFTA Engineering Ltd., Chandigarh and M/s BOC, Calcutta at Pagla Danga; and after detailed discussions with the consultants, the inspection team notes that:

The proposed schemes are neither scientifically sound, nor can be constructed on the existing locations without interfering with the normal life of the residents in above-mentioned areas.

The proposed CETP schemes are not capable of treating the wastewater laden with high total dissolved solids, chromium and nitrogenous constituents. Thus the proposed CETP designs cannot control pollution and odour in totality at the tannery clusters at Tangra, Tiljala, Topsia, and Pagla Danga.

The proposed designs have little scientific basis, and do not consider the industry-specific requirements of effective wastewater treatment in tannery clusters at Tangra, Tiljala, Topsia and Pagla Danga.

In view of categoric findings of the NEERI and also several reports by the Board there is no possibility of setting up of common effluent treatment plants at the existing locations of the Calcutta tanneries. In the facts and circumstances discussed in this judgment, we have no hesitation in holding that the Calcutta tanneries shall have to be relocated from their present locations.

[The court considered and rejected the tanneries' contention that the designated new site would damage an ecologically fragile wetland. The court summarised the steps taken under judicial supervision to facilitate relocation; set out the provisions of the Water Act that were being breached by the tanneries and after referring to the 'precautionary principle' and 'polluter pays principle' concluded:] It is thus settled by this Court that one who pollutes the environment must pay to reverse the damage caused by his acts.

We, therefore, order and direct as under:

1. The Calcutta tanneries ... shall relocate themselves from their present location and shift to the new leather complex set up by the West Bengal Government. The tanneries which decline to relocate shall not be permitted to function at the present sites.

2. The Calcutta tanneries shall deposit 25 per cent of the price of the land before 28-2-1997 with the authority concerned. The subsequent installments shall be paid in accordance with the terms of the allotment letters issued by the State Government.

3. The tanneries who fail to deposit 25 per cent of the price of the land as directed by us above shall be closed on 15-4-1997.

...

6. All the Calcutta tanneries who deposit 25 per cent of the land price shall be permitted to function at the present sites provided they keep on depositing the subsequent installments in accordance with the terms of the allotment letter.

...

8. The State Government shall render all assistance to the tanneries in the process of relocation. The construction of the tannery buildings, issuance of any licenses/permissions etc. shall be expedited and granted on priority basis.

9. In order to facilitate shifting of the tanneries the State Government shall set up unified single agency consisting of all the departments concerned to act as a nodal agency to sort out all the problems. The single window facility shall be set up by 31-1-1997. We make it clear that no further time shall be allowed to the State Government to set up the single window facility.

10. The use of the land which would become available on account of shifting/relocation/closure of the tanneries shall be permitted for green purposes. While framing the scheme the State Government may keep in view for its guidance the order of this Court in *M.C. Mehta v Union of India* 1996 (4) SCC 351, relating to the shifting of Delhi industries. The shifting tanneries on their relocation in the new leather complex shall be given incentives which are normally extended to new industries in new industrial estates.

11. The tanneries which are not closed on 15-4-1997 must relocate and shift to the new leather complex on or before 30-9-1997.

12. All the Calcutta tanneries shall stop functioning at the present sites on 30-9-1997. The closure order with effect from 30-9-1997 shall be unconditional.

Even if the relocation of tanneries is not complete they shall stop functioning at the present sites with effect from 30–9–1997.

13. We direct the Deputy Commissioner/Superintendent of Police of the area concerned to close all the tanneries operating in Tangra, Tiljala, Topsia and Pagla Danga areas of the city of Calcutta by 30–9–1997.

14. The State Government shall appoint an Authority/Commissioner who with the help of Board and other expert opinion and after giving opportunity to the polluting tanneries concerned assess the loss to the ecology/environment in the affected areas.

15. The said authority shall further determine the compensation to be recovered from the polluter-tanneries as cost of reversing the damaged environment. The authority shall lay down just and fair procedure for completing the exercise.

16. The amount of compensation shall be deposited with the Collector/District Magistrate of the area concerned. In the event of non-deposit the Collector/District Magistrate shall recover the amount from the polluter-tanneries, if necessary, as arrears of land revenue. A tannery may have set up the necessary pollution control device at present, but it shall be liable to pay for the past pollution generated by the said tannery which has resulted in the environmental degradation and suffering to the residents of the area.

17. We impose pollution fine of Rs. 10,000 each on all the tanneries in the four areas of Tangra, Tiljala, Topsia and Pagla Danga. The fine shall be paid before 28–2–1997 in the office of the Collector/District Magistrate concerned.

18. We direct the Collector/District Magistrate of the area concerned to recover the fines from the tanneries.

19. The compensation amount recovered from the polluting tanneries and the amount of fine recovered from the tanneries shall be deposited under a separate head called 'Environmental Protection Fund' and shall be utilised for restoring the damaged environment and ecology. The pollution fine is also liable to be recovered as arrears of land revenue. The tanneries which failed to deposit the amount of Rs. 10,000 by 15–3–1997 shall be closed forthwith and shall also be liable under the Contempt of Courts Act.

20. The State Government in consultation with the expert bodies like NEERI, Central Pollution Control Board and the Board shall frame scheme/schemes for reversing the damage caused to the ecology and environment by pollution. The scheme/schemes so framed shall be executed by the State Government. The expenditure shall be met from the 'Environment Protection Fund' and from other sources provided by the State Government.

21. The workmen employed in the Calcutta tanneries shall be entitled to the rights and benefits as indicated hereunder:

(a) The workmen shall have continuity of employment at the new place where the tannery is shifted. The terms and conditions of their employment shall not be altered to their detriment.

(b) The period between the closure of the tannery at the present site and its restart at the place of relocation shall be treated as active employment and the workmen shall be paid their full wages with continuity of service.

(c) All those workmen who agree to shift with the tanneries shall be given one year's wages as 'shifting bonus' to help them settle at the new location.

(d) The workmen employed in the tanneries which fail to relocate shall be deemed to have been retrenched with effect from 15–4–1997 and 30–9–1997 respectively keeping in view the closure dates of the respective tanneries provided they were in continuous service for a period of one year as defined in Section 25–B of the Industrial Disputes Act, 1947. These workmen shall also be paid in addition six years' wages as additional compensation.

(e) The workmen who are not willing to shift along with the relocated industries shall be deemed to have been retrenched under similar circumstances as the workmen in (d) above but they shall be paid only one year's wages as additional compensation.

(f) The shifting bonus and the compensation payable to the workmen in terms of this judgment shall be paid by 31–5–1997 by the tanneries which close on 15–4–1997 and by 15–11–1997 by the other tanneries closing on 30–9–1997.

(g) The gratuity amount payable to any workman shall be in addition.

We have issued comprehensive directions for achieving the end result in this case. It is not necessary for this Court to monitor these matters any further. We are of the view that the Calcutta High Court would be in a better position to monitor these matters hereinafter. The 'Green Bench' is already functioning in the Calcutta High Court. We direct the Registry of this Court to send the relevant records, orders, documents, etc., pertaining to the Calcutta tanneries to the Calcutta High Court before 10–1–1997. The High Court shall treat this matter as a petition under Article 226 of the Constitution of India and deal with it in accordance with law and also in terms of the directions issued by us. We make it clear that it will be open to the High Court to pass any appropriate order/orders keeping in view the directions issued by us. We give liberty to the parties to approach the High Court as and when necessary. The matter pertaining to Calcutta tanneries is disposed of with costs which we quantify as Rs. 25,000

NOTES AND QUESTIONS

1. A decade after the Supreme Court's rebuke to the Kanpur tanneries, the Calcutta tanneries were discharging untreated effluents into the Ganga. What does this say about the pollution control board; the polluters; the West Bengal government; the city of Calcutta; and more generally, public interest litigation as a vehicle for environment protection?

2. In many ways the acute and complicated problems of Calcutta are typical of the milieu in other cities. Environmental pollution continues unchecked because of negligent officials, a weak city administration, the absence of budgetary support and political will at the state level and persistent refusal on the part of polluters to clean up their act. Once the problem attains huge proportions, there is no single agency capable of tackling all the aspects: land acquisition, translocation, displacement, workers' compensation and the financial outlay. Does this mean that the Supreme Court and the High Courts must continue playing the role of a super-agency to tackle urban India's environmental woes? Is there an alternative?

3. Note the shifting stand of the tanneries. Initially, they bought time through a cooperative posture. When the alternative site was identified and re-location seemed imminent, resistance set in: Initially, on the ground that a CETP could be accommodated at the existing site and then an ironic plea that the new site would damage an ecologically fragile wetland.

4. The Supreme Court judgment attempts to sensitize many layers of the bureaucracy and the judiciary to the importance of environment protection. For example, apart from the officials directly involved in the case, the order casts implementation and oversight responsibilities on the collector/district magistrate, the deputy commissioner/ superintendent of police, and the 'Green bench' of the Calcutta High Court.

5. Review the directions issued by the court, especially the workers' entitlements crafted by the court. Were you a tannery operator, would you comply? Would you prefer to file for bankruptcy/dissolution? Is the fiscal burden imposed by the court disproportionately high?

6. Justice Kuldip Singh delivered the *Calcutta Tanneries* judgment on the eve of his retirement. What strategic considerations might have prompted the transfer of the case to the Calcutta High Court?

7. Is industrial relocation policy the province of the court? Should the court have shut down the violating units and issued time-bound directions to the state government to frame and implement a suitable relocation scheme? What are the pitfalls in this approach?

8. In *Vellore Citizens' Welfare Forum v Union of India*,[85] the Supreme Court issued a range of directions to bring to book the leather tanneries of Tamil Nadu. We carry a short excerpt of the case in a later chapter on international environmental law.

9. Where the chairman and secretary of the Uttar Pradesh pollution control board permitted Mohan Meakins' brewery to discharge its untreated effluent into the Gomti beyond the deadline imposed by the Supreme Court, contempt proceedings were initiated against the board officials. Finding the officials guilty of violation of the court's order, the judges administered a severe warning to both officers.[86]

H. JUDICIAL INITIATIVES IN GUJARAT

In early 1995, under the stewardship of Chief Justice B.N. Kirpal the Gujarat High Court embarked on a crusade against industrial pollution. Gujarat has large chemical and textile industries which have thrived at the cost of the environment. As the High Court discovered, untreated effluents from scores of units had blighted agricultural fields around Ahmedabad city. We carry a short excerpt from this landmark case,

[85] AIR 1996 SC 2715.
[86] *Vineet Kumar Mathur v Union of India* 1996(1) SCC 119.

focusing on the procedure adopted by the court and some of the contentious issues raised by the case.

PRAVINBHAI J. PATEL v STATE OF GUJARAT
1995 (2) GUJ.L.REP 1210

B.N. KIRPAL, C.J.:

Large scale pollution of the Kharicut Canal and the areas at least in the immediate vicinity thereof by some of the industrial units, which are now within the Ahmedabad Municipal limits, and the inaction of the Government Authorities in taking any effective steps to control it has led to the filing of the present writ petition. As we shall presently see, it is as if a Chemical War has been launched by some industrial units, against Man and Nature.

The two petitioners are agriculturists having agricultural land in Kheda District. In this petition, which has also been termed as 'a public interest litigation', it is alleged that the industries which have been set up in the industrial estates at Naroda, Vatva and Odhav in Ahmedabad are discharging their polluted effluents into Kharicut Canal which, in turn, leads to Khari river. It is further alleged that there are about 11 villages in Kheda District, whose only source of water for the purposes of agriculture is from Khari river. Due to the water pollution caused by the said industries, the water in the Khari river is no longer suitable for agriculture. In addition thereto, the agricultural lands in these villages have lost their fertility and the water drawn from the wells was having reddish colour even when it is from the depth of about 300 ft.

It is further alleged that in these 11 villages, which are commonly known as 'Kalambandi villages', there are about 8,000 acres of agricultural land wherein not only the agricultural operations are adversely affected by reason of the pollution of the Khari river, but even animals, like cattle, sheep, etc., are adversely affected due to consumption of the said polluted water. A specific allegation which has been made is that whereas before the industrial units had been set up in the said three industrial estates, the agriculturists were able to get yield of about 2 tons of agricultural produce per acre but after the pollution of the Khari river the present agricultural yield is hardly 0.50 ton per acre. Drinking water is also not readily available and even from the bore wells, the water which comes out is full of toxicants. Such polluted bore well water is common in villages like Bherai, Pinglaj, Navagam, Lali, etc.

It is further alleged that representations have been filed before the Gujarat Pollution Control Board (hereinafter referred to as 'G.P.C.B.') since about 1978 and other authorities, but no action has so far been taken. The contention of the petitioners is that the provisions of the three Acts, dealing with environment, have been infringed by the Industries, the three Acts being: [The Water Act, 1974; the Air Act, 1981; and the Environment Act, 1986]. The main prayer in the writ petition is that action should be taken against the respondents, viz., the State of Gujarat, the G.P.C.B., the Gujarat Industrial Development Corporation ('G.I.D.C.'), Ahmedabad Municipal Corporation ('A.M.C.') and the Gujarat Electricity Board for not taking steps to control and curb the water pollution of Khari river, which is resulting in the violation of the petitioners' fundamental rights under Art. 21 of the Constitution of India. Direction is also sought for taking steps to control the water and air pollution and there is also a claim made for payment of compensation due to the loss suffered due to air and water pollution. Another prayer is for directions to be issued for providing proper drainage/gutter facilities for letting out trade effluent/waste water after treating them in order to arrest the pollution of water.

Before dealing with the merits of the case, and the action taken by the Government, it is important to refer to and give background with regard to the legal provisions, including the parameters laid down by the G.P.C.B. [The court reviewed the legislative history of these laws and summarised the adverse impact of the pollutants on health and agriculture].

Looking at the averments in the petition and the state of the water in the Kharicut Canal, which was produced in bottles brought to Court by the petitioners' counsel and the obnoxious smell which it had, and treating this also as a public interest litigation, the approach of the Court was as follows:

Firstly, find out about the extent of pollution;
Secondly, determine as to who were responsible for causing pollution;
Thirdly, find out whether there is a remedy or treatment to the problem;
Fourthly, to see what has been the role of the Government to the problem so far;
Fifthly, to see what role industry has played till now in its obligation to meet the GPCB parameters;
Sixthly, to consider the submissions of the parties; and
Seventhly, what directions, if any, should be given on the basis of the facts emerging from above.

[The court set about the task of fact-finding through a committee of three advocates who surveyed the affected areas and submitted periodic reports. On the basis of the reports, the court issued interim directions requiring polluting units to forthwith achieve discharge standards or else, face closure. The court also appointed two other committees to examine the representations of affected industries and to recommend suitable solutions to the problem.

The court found that hundreds of industrial units were engaged in large scale pollution and had made little or no effort to comply with the law. 'Neither the industry, which causes pollution, nor the government nor the G.P.C.B. nor the G.I.D.C. have paid more than lip service to the Environmental laws. ... It will not be wrong to say that the continued violation of the law by the industrial units has become a habit and condoning it by the governmental authorities, a practice.'

The court was dismayed by the role of the enforcement agencies: 'Since 1980, till today not a single unit or person has been convicted of having violated any of the pollution laws. In fact, not in a single case [have] the prosecution proceedings ... been completed.' Later in the judgment the court observed that government 'has abetted or collaborated with the industry in breaking the law ...' and that the G.P.C.B. had neglected its duties despite citizen complaints.]

Closure of some of the units would, undoubtedly cause them a financial set back. From the report submitted by the counsel appearing for the state of Gujarat, it appears that in these 756 units, about 25,000 workers are employed. The main revenue, which is contributed by this group of industries is by way of sales tax, which comes to according to the state, approximately Rs. 6.50 crores per year. As against this, pollution which is being caused by these units is adversely affecting nearly 10 lacs of people. The sales tax which is paid represents less than 1% (one per cent) of the gross turnover of this industry which seems to imply that even sales tax may not have been fully paid by it. At the same time, large scale damage perhaps, some of it irreversible, is being done to the soil and the sub-soil and river water.

Such cases relating to environment cannot be merely regarded as being cases of *lis* between the petitioners and the respondents. The problem which are sought to be tackled are with regard to the effects which today's action or inaction will have on the posterity. But, even if it was to be regarded as a *lis* between the petitioners and the industry, we find that approximately five lacs of people are residing in the 11 villages, which are, admittedly, being directly affected by the pollution. It has been alleged in the writ petition that the agricultural yield has been reduced from 2.00 tons per acre to 0.50 tons per acre per year. There are approximately, 8,000 acres of land in these villages. This being so, the loss of agricultural yield has been estimated to be Rs. 6.40 crores per year. Therefore, whereas a closure of the industry till it is able to mend its ways and install the pollution control plants is only temporary, and the loss to be suffered by them will not be permanent, on the other hand; the loss to the agriculturists, relatively speaking, would be of much greater magnitude and the damage to environment more permanent. In fact, their grievance has been subsisting at least for last 15 years.

* * *

From the aforesaid discussion, the conclusions can be for the sake of convenience, summarized as follows:

1. There is admittedly, large scale pollution being used caused by about 756 industrial units situated in the G.I.D.C. Industrial Estates of Vatva, Naroda and Odhav and also by some textile units and processing houses situated in and around Narol.

2. The pollution has been caused since over 15 years with the continued discharge into Kharicut Canal by the Odhav, Naroda and Vatva industrial units, which has also resulted in increasing salinity and degradation of the quality of soil, which has the effect of drastically reducing the agricultural produce at least in the 11 villages around Kharicut Canal including the land of the petitioners.

3. Pollution can be controlled by giving primary and secondary treatment to the effluent.

4. The Government as well as G.P.C.B. and G.I.D.C. have been negligent in discharge of their statutory duties and they have, by their inaction connived or collaborated or abetted to the continued pollution by these 756 polluting units. The Government, in particular, has shown little or no concern to the environment's degradation in the state. It is guilty of total inaction in taking effective steps for protecting and/or improving the environment and thereby, the quality of life.

5. The individual units causing pollution have shown complete disregard to

the statutory provisions. For them, the rule of law did not exist as they seemed to have some protection or assurance that no effective action will be taken against them. Their industrial progress and affluence has been at the cost of environment.

* * *

The industrial units want time so as to enable them to meet the G.P.C.B. norms. Effort is made to set up common effluent treatment plant, after which effluent will be taken and mixed with the treated sewage which is discharged from the municipal works at Pirana.

* * *

We accordingly:
A.I. Issue a writ of mandamus to the state of Gujarat to direct the closure forthwith of the manufacturing operations of [highly polluting units enumerated in the order].
II. In order to ensure that production is suspended by those units, to whom the directions have been issued, the state will issue, where necessary, directions for the stoppage of supply of electricity and/or water in order to ensure compliance. These units, however, will be given the connection, if they require, for the purposes of satisfying the G.P.C.B. that the units are in a position to meet the G.P.C.B. norms. Electricity and water are required for sufficiently long time to enable the checking of the claim but till No Objection Certificate/Consent is obtained, no permission should be given for commercial production.
III. Furthermore, the units ordered to suspend or close their operations, as aforesaid, may start them only after obtaining the consent letter of the G.P.C.B.

* * *

B.(ii) The state of Gujarat, G.I.D.C. and A.M.C. are directed to lay separate/necessary pipes and/or drains to carry the treated industrial effluent to Pirana for mixing the same with the treated sewage before discharge into the river. The expense for this shall be borne entirely by the polluting units, who shall contribute *pro-rata* as and when demanded by the Government. The work on this should start immediately and be completed by 31st December, 1995, or within such extended time as the Court may allow on the proper application being made.

* * *

C. Orders are further issued to the following effect:
...

(xii) Since for the last number of years pollution has adversely affected the 11 Kalambandi villages of Kheda, as also villages of Lali, Navagam, Bidaj, Sarsa, Aslali, Jetalpur, Bareja, Vinzol and Vatva comprised in Dascroi and Mahemedabad Talukas, a lump sum payment should be made by the 756 industrial units, calculated at the rate of

1 per cent of their one year's gross turnover for the year 1993–94 or 1995–96, whichever is more and that amount should be kept apart by the Ministry of Environment and should be utilised for the works of socio-economic uplift of the aforesaid villages and for the betterment of educational, medical and veterinary facilities and the betterment of the agriculture and livestock in the said villages. Payment should be quantified by the G.I.D.C. within three months and the collections made within two months thereafter.

* * *

NOTES AND QUESTIONS

1. Four years after the judgment, a bench of the Gujarat High Court continues to monitor *Pravinbhai Patel's Case*. Applications for 'trial' production by defaulting units that were ordered shut (but have since installed treatment facilities), are routinely taken up in court. The High Court also periodically reviews progress on the construction of the effluent pipeline to Pirana and monitors compliance by industrial units. One effect of the continuing mandamus is that the GPCB displays little or no initiative, and leans on judicial directions to justify all its actions. Will the High Court's role inhibit the GPCB from growing into a strong, independent institution?

2. In a further order in *Pravinbhai Patel's Case* passed on 10 May 1996 the High Court extended by six months the compliance deadline of 31 December 1995. While doing so, the court required units availing the extension to abide by stringent compliance conditions. In view of the authorities' inability to maintain round-the-clock vigil, the court introduced a self-regulatory mechanism by which industry associations were directed to monitor the discharges by member units. Further, the May 1996 order established a coordinating committee under the chairmanship of M.D. Pandya, an advocate, to monitor compliance, coordinate action between industry and the authorities, and assist the court in matters relating to the implementation and enforcement of its orders.

3. One of the High Court's directions required polluting units to pay for the necessary pipes and drains to carry the effluent over 28 kms to Pirana. The estimated project cost in January, 1996 was Rs. 28 crores. The GIDC which laid out the industrial estates at Naroda, Vatva and Odhav invited entrepreneurs to establish units in these estates on the assurance that basic infrastructure including underground sewers and pipelines would be provided by the corporation. This assurance was a term of the contract between individual units and the corporation and each industry contributed a charge towards infrastructure development. When the Ahmedabad city limits were extended to cover the three industrial estates, the AMC assumed the obligations of GIDC in respect of the underground drains and sewers. AMC

was also under an independent statutory obligation to provide suitable sanitation and drainage facilities within city limits. Despite these obligations, both GIDC and AMC failed to lay the necessary pipelines causing untreated effluent from hundreds of units to seep into the Kharicut canal. In these circumstances was the court justified in requiring the polluting units to pick up the *entire* tab in respect of the pipeline? Does this approach dilute the citizen's right to require municipal bodies to discharge their fundamental public duty of providing drains and sewers?[87]

4. The pipeline to Pirana was required because the chemical units were incapable of achieving the Total Dissolved Solids (TDS) norm even *after* providing primary and secondary effluent treatment. The only way to attain these norms was to mix the treated industrial effluent with municipal sewage from the Pirana Treatment Plant, before its discharge into the river. Hence the pipeline to Pirana.

5. In requiring a unit to shut down or pay 1 per cent of its gross turnover towards 'socio-economic uplift' of the affected villages, which 'standards' should a court apply: (i) the unit-specific standards in the individual 'consent' issued to each industrial unit; (ii) the industry-specific standard prescribed under Schedule I to the Environment (Protection) Rules of 1986 (EPR); (iii) the national minimum standards prescribed in Schedule VI to the EPR; or (iv) the standards notified by the GPCB which though based on the EPR, depart from them in some respects? Remember, section 24 of the Environment (Protection) Act of 1986 (EPA) gives overriding effect to the provisions of the EPR.

Within the national minimum standards, should the norms in respect of inland surface water be applied or the irrigation norms? Kharicut Canal, which was the focus of judicial scrutiny, is a 'dry' canal for most of the year and carries effluent into the Khari river. Farmers along the canal draw the industrial discharges and use it for irrigating their fields. Is Kharicut canal an 'inland surface water'? If the court's principal concern was the harm suffered by agriculturists, shouldn't the national irrigation norms be the bench mark for testing whether a unit should be shut down or be required to pay 1 per cent of its gross turnover?

6. What is the nature of the 1 per cent levy? Is it a fee, a tax, a fine, a penalty, a charge or compensation by way of damages? What is the legal significance of the character of the levy?

7. The 1 per cent levy was imposed on all 756 polluting units, irrespective of the facts in each case. Some of the units were wilful defaulters, others deviated from the norms very slightly. Had the executive or legislature imposed such a levy without regard to the extent of compliance by individual units or the extent of pollution caused, what might have been the judicial response? Would an across the board levy on all polluting units be termed discriminatory, arbitrary or violative of the equal protection guarantee under Article 14? On the other hand, is such a levy

[87] See *Municipal Council, Ratlam v Vardhichand* AIR 1980 SC 1622 and *Virendra Gaur v State of Haryana* 1995(2) SCC 577.

akin to a case of 'mass-copying' where even some honest students suffer because of the misconduct of their peers?

8. Does the High Court's 1 per cent levy apply to those defaulting on the date of the judgment, the date when the petition was filed, or at any prior time?

9. The Gujarat High Court supplied a rationale for the 1 per cent payment in *Deepak Nitrate Limited v Ajit B. Padiwal*:[88]

> Looking to the large number of industries in large industrial estates and also at other places where industries are established, the affected people and those concerned for the environment would find it difficult, if not impossible, to point out the exact nature of damage being caused by an individual unit. Once an industrial unit is found to be violating the GPCB norms, it would follow that damage has been caused to the environment. Now, if an individual inquiry were to be made in respect of each industrial unit as to which particular area of soil was damaged or which particular sub-stratum of underground water level was affected on account of the discharge of untreated or improperly treated industrial effluent not meeting with the GPCB norms, either on account of percolation or on account of such effluent going on to the agricultural fields or into the water sources of the community, such inquiry would not lend itself to easy quantification in a civil suit for damages which would take years, if not decades, for final decision. On the other hand, in last two years, this Court has in a number of decisions applied the aforesaid formula of 1 per cent of the turnover as compensation for the betterment of the environment and allied purposes in various industrial areas of Ahmedabad, Nandesari (where the present unit is situated), Vapi and Ankleshwar and 1 per cent of the highest turnover has been found to be the lowest common denominator as the figure for compensation. If such inquiry is held, we are sure that the extent of damage would be more than 1 per cent as assessed. At this stage, we would also like to place on record that after the decision of this Court in the case of *Pravinbhai* covering industrial units of Ahmedabad, the formula of quantifying 1 per cent of the highest turnover as compensation for damage caused to the environment on account of violation of pollution control laws during the period prior to judicial cognizance has come to be widely accepted even by the industries in Baroda, Bharuch, Surat and other districts of Gujarat.

Do you agree with the justification? Is not establishing liability *after* applying rules of evidence and procedure, the quintessential judicial function? Would every deviation from a pollution norm necessarily imply 'damage to the environment', as the court suggests?

10. Impressed by the tough judicial approach in *Pravinbhai Patel's Case*, Taruben Gamit of Surat District moved the Gujarat High Court for relief against a

[88] 1997 (1) GUJ.L.HER.1062.

paper mill that discharged its effluent into a channel that led to Tapi river.[89] The long and rambling division bench judgment suggests that the debate in court centred about the respondent's liability to pay 1 per cent of its turnover on the same lines as *Patel's Case*. The mill argued that there were neither pleadings nor proof that any damage had occurred or was caused by the mill and there was no reason to impose the charge on the company.[90] The court steered clear from an inquiry into the harm suffered by the petitioner, *assuming* that damage had occurred. The judges preferred to focus on the company, finding that it had resumed operations in November, 1993 using an old rusted treatment plant which was inadequate to treat the discharges. Up to March 1997 (despite investment in new equipment), the water and air pollution standards were not attained.

Using a logic of its own, the court justified the 1 per cent charge on two grounds. The court found that the mill discharged 836,100 kilolitres of polluted water every month, rendering a huge quantity of water 'useless either for human consumption or cultivation'. Multiplying the water supply charge with the consumption figure, the court arrived at a value of Rs. 2,50,83,000 as being the approximate 'damage caused by the unit ... per year.'[91] The court also found that by delaying installation of the new effluent treatment plant by a couple of years, the unit had made an 'illegal saving' to the tune of about Rs. 4,32,00,000.[92] In these circumstances, the court characterised the 1% levy amounting to Rs. 1,11,00,000 as a 'very meagre amount'.

Taruben's Case is significant because the High Court held that in order to be branded a 'polluting unit' to attract the 1 per cent charge, it was sufficient if the unit failed to meet the norm for even a single pollutant.[93]

11. The Gujarat High Court judgments in *Pravinbhai Patel's Case* and *Taruben's Case* set out the harmful effects of some common pollutants.

12. Recalcitrant units that disobeyed closure orders passed in *Pravinbhai Patel's Case* faced stiff sanctions including heavy fines and prison terms for the officers.[94]

13. How does a writ court go about securing compensation in mass pollution cases? What procedure should be followed? There are several models to choose from.

(A) Where the damage is caused by the accidental handling of *hazardous* material, the Public Liability Insurance Act of 1991 and the National Environment Tribunal Act of 1995 provide a machinery to compensate victims on a 'no-fault' basis. The writ court may refer the victims to the alternate remedy or quantify an *ad hoc* entitlement where the damage is established.[95]

---

[89] *Taruben S. Gamit v Central Pulp Mills Ltd.* 1997 (2) GUJ.L.HER.1007.

[90] *Id.* at 1012.

[91] *Id.* at 1023.

[92] *Id.* at 1024.

[93] *Id.* at 1022–3.

[94] *Suo Motu v Bhavana Textile Pvt. Ltd.* 1997 (2) GUJ.L.HER.760.

[95] In *Consumer Education and Research Centre v Union of India* AIR 1995 SC 992 the Supreme Court directed payment of Rs. 100,000 to each factory worker found to be suffering from asbestosis.

(B) The polluter pays principle is illustrated by the *Bichhri Case*,[96] where remedial or clean-up costs to *restore the environment* may be recovered from the polluter under the writ jurisdiction. Here the Supreme Court directed the Secretary, Union Ministry of Environment and Forests to determine the amount required for remedial measures after granting the polluters an opportunity to be heard; and to recover the amount determined from the industries.[97] The polluter pays principle was also applied in the *Shrimp Culture Case*[98] and in *Vellore Citizens' Welfare Forum v Union of India*[99] where the Supreme Court directed the Central Government to constitute separate authorities under section 3(3) of the EPA and directed the authorities to assess the loss to the ecology/environment and recover the amount from the polluters. In the *Calcutta Tanneries Case*[100] the task of assessment and recovery of restoration costs was assigned to an authority appointed by the state government. Span Motel was directed to pay compensation for restitution of the environment and ecology in *M.C. Mehta v Kamal Nath*.[101] The Supreme Court in *In Re: Bhavani River: Sakthi Sugars Limited*,[102] directed an independent environmental agency, NEERI, to inspect the affected area and assess the damage caused by discharges from the sugar factory. NEERI was also asked to submit its report on the cost of restitution. On 30 July 1998 the court held: 'We are somewhat unhappy about the manner in which the Pollution Control Board gave its consent unmindful of the grave consequences, which have been amply demonstrated before us.'[103] The Supreme Court remanded the matter to the Madras High Court, with a direction to look into the NEERI reports and 'examine the question of the restitution of the areas damaged on account of the pollution already caused.'[104]

(C) On occasion, the Supreme Court has directed polluters to pay a '*pollution fine*' with the proceeds being credited to an environment protection fund for the restoration of the local environment.[105]

(D) When it comes to compensating the victims, widely disparate procedures have been adopted. In *Bichhri*[106] the Supreme Court declined to award damages despite seven years of litigation and directed the villagers to institute suits in the appropriate

---

[96] *Indian Council for Enviro-Legal Action v Union of India* AIR 1996 SC 1446. Subsequent orders are reported at 1997 (6) SCALE 17 (SP), 1999 (7) SCALE 610 and 2000 (1) SCALE 655.

[97] Two years after the judgment the ministry had made no progress beyond sending a notice to the industries. Katariya, *The Red Triangle* in *Down to Earth*, 15 January 1998 at 27, 31.

[98] *S. Jagannath v Union of India* AIR 1997 SC 811.

[99] AIR 1996 SC 2715.

[100] *M.C. Mehta v Union of India* 1997(2) SCC 411.

[101] 1997(1) SCC 388.

[102] 1998 (2) SCC 601. A previous order is reported at 1998 (1) SCALE 15 (SP).

[103] 1998 (4) SCALE 322, 323.

[104] *Id.* at 324.

[105] e.g. *The Calcutta Tanneries Case*, *supra* note 100; and *Vellore*, *supra* note 99.

[106] *Supra* note 96.

civil court. The *Vellore*[107] and *Shrimp Culture Case*[108] models appear more victim-friendly. In both these cases the authorities to be constituted by the Central Government under section 3(3) of the EPA were asked to indentify the victims of the pollution; assess the compensation to be paid; and determine the liability of individual polluters after following a just and fair procedure.

Perhaps the most effective approach was the one adopted by the Supreme Court in the *Patencheru Case*.[109] Here, the court was dealing with extensive loss suffered by farmers on account of damage to crops from contaminated surface water. The court accepted the loss estimated at Rs. 28,34,000 by a team of government officials, directed the state government to deposit the full amount (less contributions from industry) in court to enable distribution to the farmers; and ordered the state to recover the entire amount from industry.[110]

(E) Finally, there is the '1 per cent of the gross turnover' formula adopted by the Gujarat High Court in *Pravinbhai Patel's Case*.[111]

I. LAKES

Many of India's fresh water lakes are imperilled by civic and development pressures.[112] In the next case, the Supreme Court attempts to stem the rot by framing *ad hoc* regulations to preserve two lakes in Haryana. Is this a worthy regulatory model? Do we need *national* fresh water regulations (similar to the coastal regulations) to preserve the waterfront? Or in this field best left to *local* planning authorities? Consider these issues as you examine the excerpt.

M.C. MEHTA v UNION OF INDIA (BADKHAL & SURAJKUND LAKES)
(1997) 3 SCC 715

ORDER:

This Court by the order dated 10–5–1996 dealt with the question whether—to preserve environment and control pollution—mining operations should be stopped within the

---

[107] *Supra* note 99.

[108] *Supra* note 98.

[109] *Indian Council for Enviro-Legal Action v Union of India* 1995 (6) SCALE 578; 1996 (4) SCALE 36 (SP); 1996 (5) SCALE 412; 1997 (1) SCALE 21 (SP); 1997 (5) SCALE 405; 1998 (1) SCALE 5 (SP); 1998 (3) SCALE 664; 1998 (4) SCALE 1; 1998 (6) SCALE 5; 1999 (4) SCALE 331 and 2000 (2) SCALE 330.

[110] The estimate of Rs. 28,34,000 (1995(6) SCALE 578) was revised to Rs. 1,39,09,737 (1996(5) SCALE 412). The state government was directed to deposit the larger amount as well.

[111] The Association of Narol Textile Processors, Ahmedabad urged the Gujarat High Court to review its direction on the 1% payment in *Pravinbhai Patel's Case*. The review application was rejected by the High Court and eventually the Supreme Court dismissed the association's special leave petition (SLP[Civil] No. 18043/96) on 16 June 1996.

[112] See Narendra, *Kolleru Lake: The Broken Mirror* and Vania, *Pulicat Lake: The Salt of the Earth* in *Down to Earth*, 31 December 1993 at 26 and 32.

radius of 5 kms from the tourist resorts of Badkhal Lake and Surajkund in the State of Haryana. The Court gave five directions in the said order. Direction 4 is in the following terms:

We further direct that no construction of any type shall be permitted now onwards within 5 km radius of the Badkhal Lake and Surajkund. All open areas shall be converted into green belts.

The Haryana Pollution Control Board (the Board) has notified the ambient Air Quality Standards by the notification dated 11-4-1994. The notification fixes limiting standards of pollution in respect of sensitive areas, industrial areas and residential areas. The standards for sensitive areas are more stringent than the standards prescribed for industrial and residential areas. The Board has recommended that the area of 5 kms around the periphery of a centre of tourism be notified as 'sensitive area'. With a view to control pollution and save environment in the vicinity of Badhkal and Surajkund, the above-quoted direction was issued.

The Municipal Corporation, Faridabad, Haryana Urban Development Authority and builders having interest in the area have approached this Court for modification/clarification of the above-quoted direction. It is contended by learned counsel appearing for the parties that in the said area of 5 kms buildings are under construction, plots have been allotted/sold under various development schemes and the plot-holders have even been started construction. According to the learned counsel vested rights of several persons are likely to be adversely affected causing huge financial loss to them.

[The court observed that the direction was not intended to apply to plots under construction. It also took on record two plans showing the proposed green belts around Badkhal lake (Ex. 'A') and Surajkund (Ex. 'B')].

This court by the order dated 13-9-1996 in IA No. 18 [WP (C) No. 4677 of 1985] has directed the Central Government to constitute an authority (the Authority) under Section 3(3) of the Environment (Protection) Act, 1986. The said Authority shall have the jurisdiction over the National Capital Region as defined under the National Capital Region Planning Act, 1955. It is ... obvious that the area of Badkhal and Surajkund, with which we are concerned, comes within the jurisdiction of the said authority.

[Counsel] appearing for some of the builders had vehemently contended that banning construction within one km radius from Badkhal and Surajkund is arbitrary. According to him it is not based on technical reasons. He has referred to the directions issued by the Government of India under the Environment (Protection) Act, 1986 and has contended that the construction can at the most be banned within 200 to 500 metres as was done by the Government of India in the coastal areas. He has also contended that restriction on construction only in the areas surrounding Surajkund and Badhkal lakes is hit by Article 14 of the Constitution of India as it is not being extended to other lakes in the country. We do not agree with [Counsel]. The functioning of ecosystems and the status of environment cannot be the same in the country. Preventive measures have to be taken keeping in view the carrying capacity of the ecosystems operating in the environmental surrounding under consideration. Badkhal and Surajkund lakes are popular tourist resorts almost next door to the capital city of Delhi. We have on record the inspection Report in respect of these lakes by the National Environmental Engineering Research Institute (NEERI) dated 20–4–1996 indicating the surroundings, geological features, land use and soil types and archaeological significance of the areas surrounding the lakes. According to the report Surajkund Lake impounds water from rain and natural springs. Badhkal Lake is an impoundment formed due to the construction of an earthen dam. The catchment areas of these lakes are shown in a figure attached with the report. The land use and soil types as explained in the report show that the Badhkal Lake and Surajkund are monsoon-fed water bodies. The natural drainage pattern of the surrounding hill areas feed these water bodies during rainy season. Large-scale construction in the vicinity of these tourist resorts may disturb the rain water drains which in turn may badly affect the water level as well as the aquifers which are the source of ground water. It may also cause disturbance to the aquifers which are the source of ground water. The hydrology of the area may also be disturbed.

The two expert opinions on the record—by the Central Pollution Control Board and by the NEERI—leave no doubt on our mind that the large-scale construction activity in the close vicinity of the two lakes is bound to cause adverse impact on the local ecology. NEERI has recommended green belt at one km radius all around the two lakes. Annexures A and B, however, show that the area within the green belt is much lesser than one km radius as suggested by the NEERI.

[The judgment refers to the 'precautionary principle' which makes it mandatory for the government to anticipate, prevent and attack the causes of environmental degradation. The court concludes: 'We have no hesitation in holding that in order to protect the two lakes from environmental degradation it is necessary to limit the construction activity in the close vicinity of the lakes.']

In clarification of direction 4 quoted above, we order and direct as under:

1. No construction of any type shall be permitted, now onwards, within the green belt area as shown in Ex.A and Ex.B. The environment and ecology of this area shall be protected and preserved by all concerned. A very small area may be permitted, if it is of utmost necessity, for recreational and tourism purposes. The said permission shall be granted with the prior approval of 'the Authority', the Central Pollution Control Board and the Haryana Pollution Control Board.

2. No construction of any type shall be permitted, now onwards, in the areas outside the green belt (as shown in Ex.A and Ex.B) up to one km radius of the Badhkal lake and Surajkund (one km to be measured from the respective lakes). This direction shall, however, not apply to the plots already sold/allotted prior to 10–5–1996 in the developed areas. If any unalloted plots in the said areas are still available, those may be sold with the prior approval of 'the Authority'. Any person owning land in the area may construct a residential house for his personal use and benefit. The construction of the said plots, however, can only be permitted up to two and a half storeys (ground, first floor and second half floor) subject to the Building Bye-laws/Rules operating in the area. The residents of the villages, if any, within this area may extend/reconstruct their houses for personal use but the said construction shall not be permitted beyond two and a half storeys subject to Building Bye-laws/Rules. Any building/house/commercial premises already under construction on the basis of the sanctioned plan, prior to 10–5–1996 shall not be affected by this direction.

3. All constructions which are permitted under directions 1 and 2 above shall

have the clearance of 'the Authority', the Central Pollution Control Board and the Haryana Pollution Control Board before 'occupation certificates' are issued in respect of these buildings by the authorities concerned.

4. All development schemes, and the plans for all types of construction relating to all types of buildings in the area from one km to 5 km radius of the Badkhal Lake and Surajkund (excluding Delhi areas) shall have prior approval of the Central Pollution Control Board and the Haryana Pollution Control Board.

NOTES AND QUESTIONS

1. Most lakes in the sub-continent are fed by monsoon streams, springs and aquifers and extensive construction in the catchments could disturb the water systems. Should the precautionary principle be applied across the board to all riparian developments and lake-front properties or only to those like Badhkal and Surajkund which are tourist spots?

2. The judgment is significant because it recognizes a key environmental concept, namely, the 'carrying capacity' of an eco-system. This notion is central to the sustainable use of resources as well as the proper management of wildlife. Loading a river with excessive pollutants beyond its re-generative or carrying capacity may cause long term damage. To prevent such harm, source-specific effluent and emission norms are supplemented by general ambient water and air quality standards. The carrying capacity of a forest determines the size of its animal population. Reducing the size of a national park or permitting logging operations in a forest may reduce the carrying capacity of the ecosystem.

3. The builders' argument under Article 14 of the Constitution: 'Why pick on us—look at all the others'—is a refrain heard in many environmental cases. The court had little trouble rejecting the contention, holding that each ecosystem is unique and every case must be dealt with having regard to the specific facts and circumstances.

4. The Madras High Court in *Palani Hills Conservation Council v Union of India*,[113] considered a challenge to a holiday resort which threatened Kodaikanal lake and its environs. The court directed the state government to constitute an expert committee. Recognising the lake as a priceless and unique feature of the hill station, the committee recommended several measures specific to the hotelier, Sterling Resorts, and more general steps including setting up a common sewage treatment plant. The court directed the state government to take appropriate measures on the lines recommended by the committee.[114]

---

[113] Writ Petition No. 4257 of 1988, Madras High Court, 20 December 1991.
[114] The same citizens' group thwarted another hotelier in Kodaikanal in *Pleasant Stay Hotel v Palani Hills Conservation Council* 1995 (6) SCC 127.

5. Troubled by 'Nainital, a beautiful butterfly ... turning into an ugly caterpillar',[115] the Supreme Court stepped in to save the hill station's lake from degradation. Responding to a public interest litigation filed by a member of the Nainital Bachao Samiti, the court appointed a commissioner to inspect the town and report on the grievances. The September, 1994 report supported the petitioner's case:

> A perusal of that report shows that on local inspection it was found that the lake has turned dark green with an oily surface and is now full of dirt, human faeces, horse dung, paper-polythene bags and all sorts of other waste. Most of the sewer lines which leak, open into it. The Commissioner also found that wherever the drains open at the shores of the lake, big heaps of rubble used in construction of the buildings are collected and these materials ultimately settle down on the shores of the lake thereby reducing the length, depth and width of the lake, besides polluting the water to a great extent. It has been mentioned in the report that ecologists feel that if nothing was done to prevent this siltation then the lake will dry up.[116]

Accepting the recommendations made by the commissioner, the court urged the authorities to constitute a monitoring committee to implement remedial measures such as preventing sewage from entering the lake, maintaining the drains and restricting lakeshore construction.

J. GROUNDWATER

1. In many parts of India, industry, agriculturists and municipalities are increasing their dependence on groundwater resources. For the user this is an attractive option since the source is continuous (unlike monsoon-fed rivers and streams), the water is generally clean and the user need not depend on an external agency for the supply. The rights to the groundwater attach to the land and hence land owners may draw on the groundwater and use it as if it were their own private property.[117] According to Chhatrapati Singh this private ownership regime is inequitable because it leaves out all the landless and tribals who do not enjoy private ownership.[118]

Since the exploitation of groundwater has a bearing on the user's fundamental right to life under Article 21 of the Constitution, her right to dig bore wells cannot be restricted by an executive fiat. This right may be restricted or regulated only by an Act of the legislature.[119]

---

[115] *Ajay Singh Rawat v Union of India* 1995 (3) SCC 266, 267.
[116] *Id.* at 268.
[117] Singh, *Water Rights and Principles of Water Resources Management*, 39 (1991).
[118] *Id.*
[119] *Puttappa H. Talavar v Deputy Commissioner* AIR 1998 KAR 10.

There is no national statute regulating groundwater resources and apart from Gujarat none of the states have legislated in this field. The Gujarat amendments to the Bombay Irrigation Act introduced a licencing procedure for sinking tube wells and prohibited the sinking of tube wells beyond a depth of 45 metres.[120]

Until the Supreme Court judgment in *M.C.Mehta v Union of India*,[121] the Union Government was of the view that central legislation may not be permissible since 'Water' was a state subject under Schedule VII of the Constitution. Each state would need to introduce separate legislation to regulate and control groundwater resources and to assist the states, a model bill was circulated in 1970. The Supreme Court, however, expressed a *prima facie* view that Article 253 of the Constitution and the provisions of the Environment (Protection) Act of 1986 (EPA) empowered the Centre to regulate groundwater exploitation. The court's observations were made on an application filed by M.C. Mehta urging the Central Government to constitute a national authority under section 3(3) of the EPA to ensure that groundwater resources are managed sustainably. Noting the recommendations made by the National Environment Engineering Research Institute, Nagpur, the Supreme Court directed the Union Ministry of Environment and Forests to constitute the Central Ground Water Board as an authority under section 3(3) of the EPA to regulate the indiscriminate exploitation of underground water in the country.

2. The need for good management of groundwater resources was recognized earlier by the Kerala High Court in a public interest litigation filed by local islanders seeking to protect fresh water resources on the Lakshadweep Islands. The petitioners apprehended that the government scheme to pump out groundwater on the island would cause saline intrusions in the fresh water table which would, in turn, imperil the potable water supply on the islands. The Kerala High Court commissioned an expert report which opposed the government scheme. Recognizing the importance of fresh water to the islanders and holding that the right to fresh water was an aspect of the fundamental right to life, the High Court prohibited the government from implementing the scheme until it was reviewed and modified by the Union Ministry of Environment and the Ministry of Science and Technology.[122]

3. The citizens of Karaikudi town in Tamil Nadu challenged a government scheme which would carry away waters from an ancient spring named Sambai Uthu which was the principal source of water for the town from time immemorial. In 1987, the municipality of Karaikudi unanimously opposed the scheme which was intended to benefit Tirupattur. In the face of this opposition the state government suspended the scheme. Seven years later the government revived the project leading to a public outcry and allegations that the project was being hurried through to benefit a mineral water factory at Tirupattur, where a government minister had an interest. Though the

---

[120] *Supra* note 117.
[121] 1997 (11) SCC 312.
[122] *Attakoya Thangal v Union of India* 1990 (1) KER.L.T. 580.

High Court rejected the allegations against the minister in the absence of evidence, it directed the state government to review the scheme after taking into consideration the availablity of groundwater and also the views of the residents of Karaikudi.[123]

4. Responding to a public interest litigation alleging failure and neglect by the state in providing safe drinking water to villagers in Mandla district, a division bench of the Madhya Pradesh High Court directed the state to extend free medical treatment and compensation to the affected persons. Water drawn from hand pumps sunk by the state contained excessive fluoride which caused bone diseases, deformities and dental fluorosis.[124]

5. In January, 1996 an expert committee appointed by the Gujarat High Court submitted its report on pollution caused by Gujarat Fluorochemicals Ltd. (GFL) in the Panchmahals district. Several residents of the villages neighbouring GFL complained of crop failures, health problems and a loss of milk production. The report (a model of sound methodology and clear analysis) records that most water samples drawn from tubewells indicated fluoride and chloride concentrations exceeding potable water limits. *Prima facie*, GFL appeared to be responsible for the adverse environmental impact.[125]

6. Binani Zinc Ltd. was directed by the Kerala High Court to supply drinking water to the affected villagers after test samples drawn from neighbouring wells were found to contain 'acidic' water unfit for drinking. The water contained very high concentration of zinc, cadmium and total dissolved solids which may have been caused by seepages from the factory.[126]

7. A study conducted by a team of *Down to Earth* reporters in 1999 found that numerous factories deliberately inject untreated effluents into the ground, contaminating underground aquifers. Samples drawn from eight sites in Haryana, Gujarat and Andhra Pradesh, showed traces of heavy metals like iron and zinc in all the samples, cadmium in five samples and lead in three. All the samples contained dangerously high levels of mercury, known to cause Minamata disease, neurological disorders, retardation of growth in children and abortion. The reporters found that the Central Ground Water Authority and the state pollution control boards were completely ineffective in checking polluters.[127]

---

[123] *Pazha Karuppiah v State of Tamil Nadu* AIR 1997 MAD 144.

[124] *Hamid Khan v State of Madhya Pradesh* AIR 1997 MP 191. There is no indication in the judgment whether the excessive fluoride was a natural occurrence or caused by pollution.

[125] Gupta, Pandya, Rao & Shukla, *Report of the Expert Committee* (1996) submitted in *Andarsingh Parmar v State of Gujarat* Spl.Civ.Appln.No. 5280 of 1995.

[126] *Edayar Environment Protection Council v Government of India* Orig.Petition No. 4419/96, Kerala High Court, 10 April 1997.

[127] M. Tiwari and R. Mahapatra, *What Goes Down Must Come Up* in *Down to Earth*, 31 August 1999, p. 30.

6

AIR POLLUTION CONTROL

A. SCOPE OF THE PROBLEM

The environment magazine *Down to Earth* reports extensively on the air pollution problems afflicting Indian cities. The following report highlights the dangers posed by suspended particulate matter (SPM) to public health. The latter part of the excerpt links the high levels of SPM in Agra to the root causes of air pollution in that city and lays the ground for the *Taj Trapezium Case*,[1] discussed later in this chapter.

DEATH IS IN THE AIR; DOWN TO EARTH, 15 November 1997, p. 29

The number of people dying in urban India due to deteriorating air quality is rising every year and very little is being done to deal with pollution in Indian cities. A stupendous 51,779 people are estimated to have died prematurely in 36 Indian cities due to air pollution in 1995 as against 40,351 in 1991–92—a rise of 28 per cent over the three year period. Calcutta, Delhi, Mumbai, Kanpur and Ahmedabad account for 10,647, 9,859, 7023, 3,639, 3,006 premature deaths respectively. This accounts for 66 per cent of total premature deaths in India. The number of air pollution-related ailments requiring medical treatment and hospital admissions have sky-rocketed to 25 million cases, indicating an increasingly ruined state of health in Indian cities. The estimate was 19 million in 1991–92.

In Calcutta and Delhi, cases of hospital admissions and sickness requiring medical treatment due to air pollution have almost doubled in a span of three years, crossing the five million mark in 1995. Disturbing trends are also emerging in Kanpur, Chennai and Ahmedabad. The main culprit is suspended particulate matter (SPM), dust and ash particles sometimes laden with toxic chemicals. The primary sources of SPM are power plants, industrial units and auto emissions. SPM levels in the above-mentioned cities are three to five times higher than the acceptable limit set by the World Health Organization (WHO). Dust particles less than 10 microns in diameter—

[1] *M.C. Mehta v Union of India* AIR 1997 SC 734.

known as PM10 and PM2.5—can penetrate lungs easily and are detrimental to human health. PM10 has been associated with both premature mortality (death from respiratory illness and cardiovascular diseases) and increased morbidity (high incidents of chronic obstructive lung diseases, especially bronchitis and upper and lower respiratory tract infections).

Evaluation of these premature deaths suggests that economic and health costs due to growing levels of SPM range between Rs. 1,747 and 7,252 crores. Similarly, estimates of the monetary losses due to sickness caused by high levels of SPM is between Rs. 107 to 213 crore.

In a 1995 report titled *Valuing Environmental Costs in India: The Economy Wide Impact of Environmental Degradation*, World Bank (WB) staffers Carter Brandon and Kirsten Homman formulated a model to establish the relationship between air pollution and human mortality and morbidity. The model was subsequently used to assess environmental and health conditions in India. Using air quality data for 1991–92 provided by the Central Pollution Control Board (CPCB) from 290 monitoring stations in 92 Indian cities and towns, they found that air pollution results in 40,351 premature deaths in India. Calcutta, Mumbai and Delhi accounted for 5,726 (14 per cent) 4,477 (11 per cent) and 7,491 (19 per cent) respectively. Substituting the CPCB air quality data for 1991–92 by the corresponding 1995 data, the figure for number of premature deaths increased to 51,779, an alarming increase by all standards.

* * *

Agra: The Beauty and the Beast

The Taj Mahal is not the only thing monumental about Agra; so is the rising level of air pollution. Although data published by the Uttar Pradesh Pollution Control Board (UPPCB) shows a decline in SPM levels in the city between 1991 and 1994, it has steadily increased thereafter. Emissions from 70,000 generators used as a result of daily power shortages, increasing number of three-wheelers running on diesel and emissions from the Mathura Oil Refinery continue to be the major sources of high levels of SPM in Agra.

The closure of 212 coal-based industrial units in 1993 and shifting out of a thermal power plant are possible reasons for the decline in SPM levels between 1991 and 1994. But the reasons for the increase in pollution from 1994 to 1996 are not clear. Part of the blame goes to the frequent use of generators due to severe electricity shortages after the coal-based thermal power plant was shifted out.

Residents of Agra are of the opinion that the number of vehicles in the city have increased alarmingly over the past few years, although no data could be obtained on this. They blame diesel-run three-wheelers known as 'Vikrams' that are the main source of public transport. One of the largest manufacturers of these vehicles is the Lucknow-based government-owned Scooters India Ltd. (SIL). A surprise test conducted on new vehicles out of the SIL factory by the UPPCB revealed that emission from 15–20 percent of the 'Vikrams' were in violation of the minimal requirements of environmental safety. Government authorities also come in for flak for not dealing with vehicular air pollution effectively. The pollution under control (PUC) certificates for vehicles can be obtained for a paltry fee of Rs. 20 without taking the vehicles to the checking centre.

'On paper, the CPCB says that pollution has decreased. I don't know about scientific data, but judging by the health of my patients, I say that the level of pollution has definitely gone up,' says Deepak Goyal, a physician in Agra. 'The numbers and the severity of asthma cases has increased, as have cases of respiratory diseases, allergies and chronic bronchitis.' The views of residents indicate that hardly any steps have been taken to solve the problem of air pollution. And the steps taken have either been inadequate or have led to other problems. For example, the coal-based thermal power station has been shifted out of Agra. This has given rise to frequent power cuts, thereby increasing the use of generators.

The Mathura refinery, located about 40 km north-west of Agra, has been dogged by controversy ever since it started functioning. 'I feel the Mathura refinery surely contributes to air pollution in Agra. I have seen the Taj for the last 20 years and have noticed that the colour has definitely changed—its has turned yellow,' says Goyal. ' I may not be able to explain how this has happened but it definitely has to do with pollution. Even though the refinery is about 35–40 km from the Taj, they have a chimney that is constantly emitting pollutants. The smoke is bound to stay in the atmosphere and cause detrimental effects sooner or later.' Meanwhile, M K Dutta, senior technical services manager at the refinery, stressed that the pollution control equipment at the refinery has been upgraded and that the emissions are well within the acceptable standards. But he refused to provide data on the emission levels at present.

B. THE STATUTES

Unlike the Water Act, which was enacted by Parliament under Article 252(1) of the Constitution after securing enabling resolutions from 12 states, the Air (Prevention and Control of Pollution) Act of 1981 was enacted by invoking the Central Government's power under Article 253 to make laws implementing decisions taken at international conferences. The preamble to the Air Act states that the Act represents an implementation of the decisions made at the United Nations Conference on the Human Environment held at Stockholm in 1972. Although a central statute, executive functions under the Air Act are carried out in the states by state pollution control boards. This delegation of executive functions is permitted by Article 258(2) of the Constitution. Article 258(3) requires the Central Government to compensate the states for the cost of carrying out these delegated functions.

The Air Act of 1981, as amended in 1987, contains several interesting features. First, the Act grants discretion to each state government to designate particular areas as 'air pollution control areas'.[2] Within a declared air pollution control area,

---

[2] Section 19.

neither the board nor the state government may exempt a polluter from the purview of the Act.[3] Polluters located outside such air pollution control areas cannot be prosecuted by the state board, but every industrial operator within an air pollution control area must obtain a permit (consent order) from the state board.[4] Second, the Act enables a magistrate to restrain an air polluter from discharging emissions,[5] and empowers both the Central and state boards to give directions to industries which, if not followed, can be enforced by the board closing down the industry or withdrawing its supply of power and water.[6]

Third, citizens can not only sue to enforce the Act to gain compliance by the industries, but can also require the board to provide the emissions data needed to build a citizens' case.[7]

Procedurally, the Air Act follows the basic structure of the Water Act—with a Central board and state boards administering a system of consent orders, monitoring activities, and enforcement through fines and criminal prosecutions. The Air Act specifies that Central and state air pollution control authority is to be exercised by the Central and state water boards. (These boards have generally dropped the term 'Water' from their title and are usually known as 'State Pollution Control Board').

The state board is required to carefully examine all relevant facts including the measures taken to prevent pollution, when processing a consent application.[8] Although there is no express mandate in the Air or Water Acts requiring community consultation or transparency at this stage, the Supreme Court has intervened to review the board's decision, where the consent issued affected the community at large. The court termed 'incongruous' certain conditions in the consent requiring deferred compliance, despite the immediate impact of the pollution on the public.[9]

The Air Act as a matter of practice, operates in tandem with the Environment (Protection) Act of 1986 (EPA). Being a self-contained statute, the Air Act empowers the state boards to independently notify standards under section 17(g). There is an overlap, however. The EPA enables the Central Government to lay down emission standards[10] which are found in the schedules appended to the Environment (Protection) Rules of 1986 (EPR). By operation of section 24 of the EPA, the EPR norms take precedence and hence in practice the state boards generally re-notify the EPR standards under the Air Act.

---

[3] *K. Muniswamy Gowda v State of Karnataka* 1998 (3) KAR.L.J.594.
[4] Section 21.
[5] Section 22A.
[6] Section 31A.
[7] Section 43.
[8] *Mahabir Coke Industry v Pollution Control Board* AIR 1998 GAU 10.
[9] *Sugarcane, G. & S.S. Association v Tamil Nadu Pollution Control Board* AIR 1998 SC 2614. This case was a water pollution case.
[10] Sections 3 and 6.

The rules framed under the EPA prescribe emission norms for specific industries[11] and general emission standards which are 'concentration based', 'equipment based' and 'load/mass-based'.[12] The general standards apply in the absence of industry specific norms.[13] In addition to emission norms, National Ambient Air Quality Standards (NAAQS) are notified for industrial, residential and rural areas, and sensitive regions.[14] The NAAQS are levels of air quality intended to protect public health, vegetation and property with an adequate margin of safety. Two other major areas where standards have been issued under the EPR are ambient air quality standards in respect of noise[15] and emission standards for motor vehicles.[16] Both these topics are separately dealt with below.

C. AIR ACT CASES

In this section we digest air pollution cases including prosecutions, briefly dwelling on the role of the pollution control boards. As you read the opening excerpt of the Gujarat High Court judgment, critically review Justice Vaidya's opinion on the responsibilities of corporate management in pollution cases.

DWARKA CEMENT WORKS LIMITED v STATE OF GUJARAT
1992 (1) GUJ. LAW HERALD 9

K.J.VAIDYA, J:

The Dwarka Cement Works, a limited company and five others who are its Chairman, Directors and General Manager respectively, have by this Misc. Criminal Application, under Section 482 of the Code of Criminal Procedure, 1973, moved this court for quashing and setting aside the impugned order issuing process against them in Criminal Case No. 162/89, by the learned [Magistrate], Dwarka, for their alleged offences under Sections 21 (4), 21 (5), 31–A, 39 and 40 of the Air (Prevention and Control of Pollution) Act, 1981 (for short the Pollution Act).

[Counsel for the petitioners argued that the process deserved to be quashed since there were no specific averments in the complaint regarding the manner in which the petitioner Nos. 2 to 6 were directly in charge of and responsible to the company.] Now it true that in what manner each of the petitioner Nos. 2 to 6 were directly in charge and responsible to the conduct of the company, is not deftly and exhaustively stated in the complaint, but then at the same time, such minute details of evidence are

---

[11] Schedule I, Environment (Protection) Rules of 1986.
[12] Part D, Schedule VI.
[13] Rule 3.
[14] Schedule VII.
[15] Schedule III. Noise standards are also prescribed under the Noise Pollution (Regulation and Control) Rules of 2000 framed under the EPA.
[16] Schedule IV.

not necessary while filing the complaint for putting the criminal law in motion. The matter and material of details are always subject matter of the evidence to be led at the time of the trial while recording the evidence. At the initial stage of issuing the process, the court has to mainly find out whether the facts disclosed in the complaint contain a 'germ' of the alleged offence—the 'ingredient', to put the criminal law in motion or not. If that 'germ' or the 'ingredient' is found to be present in the complaint, there is no scope for any grievance that because the detailed description about the manner was absent in the complaint, the learned Magistrate was not justified in issuing the process. * * * The averment 'accused Nos. 2 to 6 are *responsible* for the management of the accused No. 1-company' is sufficient enough for any court to take cognizance of the offence and order issuance of process on the basis of the same. Thus taking into consideration the contents of the complaint, at this stage, it cannot be said that the averments made therein lack any vital ingredient showing no ground made out that the process could not be issued. In fact, to accept the first contention raised by the petitioners at this stage, would be simply prejudging the issue without affording a reasonable opportunity to the prosecution to substantiate allegations as held by the Supreme Court in the case of *State of Bihar v Narayan Sing*, reported in AIR 1991 SC 1308. Such an unwarranted interference at a preliminary stage, according to this Court would be nothing less than miscarriage of justice . * * *

[T]here is yet one more important angle or perspective from which the point is required to be looked at, viz., that of the social welfare jurisprudence. This perspective and angle none of us can ever afford to [lose sight of.] ... [E]xamining the point raised from that angle of social welfare jurisprudence, it is obviously clear—(i) That the offences alleged against the petitioner Nos. 2 to 6 are under an important social legislation, viz. the Pollution Act; (ii) That such proceedings under the Pollution Act, be it civil or criminal, the same needs to be attended to and disposed of as expeditiously as possible to make the provisions of the Act effective and meaningful enough to bring about the social justice; (iii) That the petitioner No. 1-company unlike an ordinary accused is a *limited company* (Emphasis supplied); (iv) That the petitioner Nos. 4 to 6 are sought to be prosecuted and tried for the alleged vicarious liability of the petitioner No. 1-company; (v) That the prosecution of the petitioner Nos. 2 to 6 by way of their vicarious liability under the Pollution Act stand distinctly apart and on different footings than that of the prosecution of the other accused under the ordinary criminal law; (vi) That unlike the accused in ordinary criminal cases, the petitioner No. 1 company and its Directors who are to be prosecuted and tried, maintain the record of their day-to-day business and names of persons concerned with the management in their ordinary course of the business. In this view of the matter, as to who in fact were the real persons at the relevant time of the alleged offences committed by the company concerned with the management of the company to be prosecuted for their vicarious liabilities is a *fact within the special knowledge of the company and so far as its Directors are concerned, they have at least access to that special knowledge.* (Emphasis supplied.) Under such circumstances, the vague assertions of the petitioner No. 2 to 4 by merely saying that there is nothing in the complaint to indicate as to how they were concerned with the management of the company and that they were prosecuted on mere assumptions, cannot be straightway accepted. In such type of criminal cases, both the offending company and its Directors owe a foremost duty to the court and to the cause of justice to place on record full and true disclosures of the facts and particulars (on the basis of the relevant notings, entries, etc. pertaining to the duty assignments and/or some other material) pointing out there from as to whether the particular Director or such other persons were or were not concerned with the management of the company at the relevant time when the alleged offence came to take place. This has got to be done and that neither the petitioner No. 1-company nor its Directors Nos.2 to 6 can ever be permitted to take shelter behind some technical pleas like the one taken in the instant case by either suppressing some material facts or stating half truth or by lying (for what ought we know the record of the company may expose themselves as total liers). There indeed can never be any scope for any legal battles to be fought by way of some strategies, trickeries of gaming to be played by the accused at the imminent cost and risk of society under the guise of some technicalities ultimately playing foul with noble object of the Act and overall beneficient interest of the society, (*at the cost of repetition) more particularly when the things are matter of record within the special knowledge of the petitioner No.1—company and its Directors.* Thus, in the opinion of this court, the bald assertion of the Petitioner Nos.2 to 6 that at the relevant time, they were not looking after day-to-day works and affairs of the company without placing on the record of the court any material from the record of the company is not *sufficient.* Instead of coming to this court praying for quashing the process, the petitioners Nos. 2 to 6 ought to have gone first before the concerned learned Magistrate who had issued the process and requested him for reasonable adjournment and exemption to appear before the court in order to point out as to if they were not concerned with the affairs of the management of the company, who else as per the record were the persons concerned with the same, so that they can be brought on the record for prosecuting them for their vicarious liabilities. The oft quoted dictum that the accused need not open his mouth in defence can be a good principle of criminal jurisprudence in the matter of ordinary prosecution and trials, but as stated earlier, in such types of cases under special statutes in the direction of social welfare, the petitioner No. 1-company which is a Public Limited Company and its Directors have got to open their mouth and point out who are the real persons concerned with the management and affairs of the company who can be held vicariously liable.

* * *

To lightly invoke the inherent powers of this Court under Section 482 of the Code, is itself abusing the discretion of the court and doing injustice to the society, which is allegedly the victim of the air pollution. The power under Section 482 of the Code is a discretionary power which has to be sparingly exercised 'to prevent the abuse of the process of law' or otherwise 'to secure the ends of justice'. The light exercise of such powers, in the opinion of this court, under such types of prosecutions, would frustrate the ends of justice. It is also true that such types of cases should be disposed of as expeditiously as possible. Now in this regard it is also the duty of the Pollution Board to be vigilant and insist upon the court to dispose of the matter as expeditiously as possible, if the court under the pressure of work, loses sight of that particular case.

In the result, this Misc. Criminal Application having no substance fails and is dismissed summarily. The learned Advocates for the respective parties are hereby directed to appear before the learned Magistrate on 25–10–1991 and take appropriate date for further proceeding. It is further directed that taking into consideration the gravity of the offence and hazards of the air pollution to the society, the learned Magistrate is directed to dispose of the case as expeditiously as possible.

NOTES AND QUESTIONS

1. Do you agree with the court's conclusion that under the scheme of the Air Act an accused company and its directors are obliged to disclose the identity of the managers who could be held liable? Are the six factors listed in the judgment sufficient to cast this burden on the accused?

2. In a part of the judgment which is not excerpted above, the High Court applied 'common sense' to repel the company's contention that there was no provision under the Act that cast a duty to disclose the responsible manager. According to the court, a common sense interpretation of the Act casts such a duty on the management. Is this strained reasoning or sage jurisprudence?

3. In *S.M. Dubash v V.M. Bhosale*,[17] the Bombay High Court quashed the prosecution of directors and officers of a company, since there was no specific sanction against them. In this case, the state board had approved the prosecution of the company alone. The court held: 'The authority and power of the Board cannot be delegated to an officer to pick and choose the accused against whom the prosecution can be launched.'[18]

4. The liability of corporate officials is also discussed in the previous chapter on water pollution where we carry excerpts from *N.A. Palkhivala v M.P. Pradushan Niwaran Mandal*[19] and *Haryana Pollution Control Board v Bharat Carpets Limited*.[20]

The Supreme Court followed the public interest litigation route pioneered in the *Ganga Pollution Cases*[21] to discipline kiln operators in Uttar Pradesh who were breaching emission norms. Responding to a petition filed by a citizens' group under the banner, World Saviors, the court directed the state board to check whether scores of industries operating kilns had installed abatement equipment and achieved the required standards. Show cause notices issued to units that met the norms were discharged by the court, though the board was directed to periodically inspect the

---

[17] 1996 (2) MAH.L.J.312.
[18] *Id.* at 315.
[19] 1990 CRI. L.J. 1856.
[20] 1993 FOR. L.T.97.
[21] *M.C. Mehta v Union of India* AIR 1988 SC 1037; AIR 1988 SC 1115; and 1997(2) SCC 411.

units and take action should a lapse occur. Industries operating kilns that had not installed air pollution control equipment or were not attaining the standards were ordered to shut down. Units that had invested in equipment but were unable to operate it due to the unavailability of energy, were permitted to resume operations only after the power was restored and the new equipment proven.[22]

Justice Sankaran Nair of the Kerala High Court expounds the dangers of air pollution in *Mathew Lukose v Kerala State Pollution Control Board*,[23] where the residents of Chingavanam organised themselves to confront Travancore Electro Chemicals Industries. The company manufactured calcium carbide and acetylene black in large quantities. In addition to the complaints about the slurry which was polluting streams in the neighbourhood, the petitioners claimed that the intense atmospheric pollution was causing pulmonary diseases and ailments. Though seven chimneys spewed carbon dioxide and sulphur dioxide into the air, the authorities did little to control the emissions. The state board conceded violations by the polluter but pleaded that it was doing its best in the circumstances. The company drew attention to its earnest efforts and claimed that raising the chimney heights and installing a Rs. 35 lakh 'multiple cyclone guided inlet dust collector' had reduced the problem. Holding that the sweep of Article 21 of the Constitution includes the right to a healthy environment, the court granted the company three months to attain the limits prescribed by the board. The board was directed to close down the plant if the company failed to achieve these norms. In prescribing the time frame, the court recognised that the company had over two years since the filing of the petition to eliminate the deficiencies.

Justice Nair's judgment is notable for introducing several features that came to be accepted by the Supreme Court in later judgments. Among these are the express articulation of the right to a wholesome environment as a facet of the right to life under Article 21; securing assistance from an *amicus curiae*; and reference to the emergent norm of inter-generational equity. The judge also urged the government to prescribe ambient air quality standards, ambient noise levels and environment impact assessment regulations, all of which now appear in the statute book.

For years, the residents of the Bombay suburb, Ghatkopar suffered very poor air quality due to the burning of garbage at the city's garbage dumping ground at Deonar, located a few kilometres upwind from the suburb. Thick clouds of smoke rose from Deonar and drifted over the residential localities in Ghatkopar, posing a nuisance and health hazard to the residents. The state board confirmed that the levels of ambient air quality exceeded the statutory limits. Considering the provisions of the Air Act, the ambient air quality norms and the statutory obligations of the municipal corporation, the High Court issued comprehensive directions to the respondents to

---

[22] *World Saviors v Union of India* 1996 (3) SCALE 32 (SP); and 1996 (4) SCALE 22 (SP). The same order is reported twice.
[23] 1990 (2) KER. L.T.686.

abate the nuisance. The directions included proper management of the solid waste disposal site.[24]

The issue whether the provisions of the Air Act operate to impliedly repeal the application of section 133 of the Criminal Procedure Code (dealing with public nuisance), arose before the Rajasthan High Court in *Lakshmi Cement v State*.[25] Having rejected the consent application, the board by its letter dated 19 September 1984 directed the company to stop operations[26] and endorsed a copy of the letter to the district collector with a request to take administrative action against the factory. The collector forwarded the letter to the magistrate, Mount Abu, who issued an order on 19 November 1984 under section 133 of the Code requiring Lakshmi Cement to abate the nuisance. By the time the High Court decided the company's petition challenging the magistrate's order, the petition was rendered infructuous by subsequent events. The board issued a provisional consent to the company shortly after the magistrate's order and the company installed air pollution control equipment which brought down the emissions to within the prescribed limits. Allowing the petition to 'secure the ends of justice' since the public nuisance had long abated, the High Court nevertheless rejected Lakshmi Cements' plea that section 133 stood impliedly repealed by passage of the Air Act.[27]

Throughout this book are cases where the statutory agency abdicates its responsibility, compelling judges to fill the regulatory vacuum. Several reasons contribute towards the ineffective functioning of the pollution control boards. A senior official in the Union Ministry of Environment and Forests counts corruption, a lack of independence and diffuse responsibilities among regulators as being some of the reasons for the administrative sloth.[28] The chairman of the Central pollution control board (CPCB) adds that the lack of funding and staff cripple effective administration.[29] Each inspector must cover 500 to 20,000 factories and the grants provided by the Central Government are paltry. On occasion, prosecutions are

---

[24] *Shanti Park 'Sorento' Co-op. Hsg. Soc. Ltd. v Municipal Corporation* Writ Petition No. 1138 of 1996, Bombay High Court, 6 August 1996.

[25] 1994 (2) RAJ.L.W.308.

[26] This direction was issued prior to the introduction of section 31A which was brought into effect from 1 April 1988.

[27] The Karnataka High Court has disapproved the execution of closure orders passed by the state board under the Water Act through the magistrate. *Executive Apparel Processors v Taluka Executive Magistrate* 1997 (4) KAR.L.J. 181. The judgments discussing section 133 of the Code of Criminal Procedure in relation to the Water Act are discussed in the water chapter.

[28] S.C. Maudgal, Senior Advisor to the Ministry quoted in Halarnkar, *Leaking Plugs* in *India Today*, 9 June 1997 p. 69.

[29] Dilip Biswas, Chairman, CPCB quoted in Halarnkar, *id.*

withdrawn without good reason.[30] All these factors add up to the bleak result of a 1997 survey: 'No one has ever gone to jail for pollution.'[31]

The laxity in implementing the Air Act is illustrated in the Division Bench judgment of the Gauhati High Court in *Mahabir Coke Industry v Pollution Control Board*.[32] Mahabir Coke operated its coke factory with a consent issued under the Water Act by the Assam board. On 12 May 1993, twelve years after the passage of the Air Act, the state government declared the whole of the state as an 'air pollution control area' under section 19 and thus extended application of the Act to Assam. Initially, the firm failed to apply for consent under the Air Act and submitted its application in August, 1995, after receiving a show cause notice from the board. In September 1995, the board refused consent on the ground that the factory was emitting 'black smoke' and no preventive measures were being taken to control the emissions. The board alleged that the firm had failed to control emissions for the past two years and directed the unit to shut down until anti-pollution measures were adopted. The firm informed the board that two out of three ovens had the necessary anti-pollution devices and in respect of the third unit, orders were placed and the equipment would be installed in six months. In the first week of November 1995, the board monitored the air quality in the locality and thereafter issued an order under section 31A of the Air Act, directing Mahabir Coke to close down its manufacturing units. The single judge of the Gauhati High Court rejected the writ petition which was carried in appeal to the division bench.

Reviewing the provisions of the Air Act, the division bench held that the appellant ought to have applied for consent and that its failure to do so clearly amounted to a breach of the provisions of the Act. Nevertheless, the division bench allowed the appeal, permitting Mahabir Coke to run its factory. The appellate court found that the state board had failed to prescribe emission standards under section 17(1)(g).[33] In the absence of standards and a chemical examination of the composition of the smoke emitted by the firm, it was not open to the board to issue a closure notice merely because a thick black smoke was spewing out from the factory chimney.

The judgment appears flawed. The division bench failed to notice the provisions of the Environment (Protection) Act of 1986 (EPA) and the national standards prescribed in the schedules to the Environment (Protection) Rules of 1986 (EPR).

---

[30] *Supra* note 23, at 694.

[31] Halarnkar, *supra* note 28.

[32] AIR 1998 GAU 10. The court found that emission standards had not been issued under the Air Act; the state board did not have a recognized laboratory to analyse emissions and lacked the equipment to measure emissions.

[33] When the board relied on a notification dated 11 July 1996 which declared that the Assam board would follow the CBCB standards issued from time to time, the High Court held that the notification could not be relied upon since it was issued *after* the closure notice dated 15 November 1995. Moreover, it appears that the notification was not published in accordance with law. The court also rejected the board's attempt to support its order on the basis of National Ambient Air Quality Standards.

Section 24 of the EPA gives overriding force to all rules framed under the Act. Rule 3 (3A) requires each and every industry, operation or process to comply with the minimum national standards set out in Schedule VI to the EPR from 1 January 1994. Schedule VI, Part D contains general emission standards which would apply to coke ovens. Once these standards are notified by the Central Government, they apply nation wide, without need for the state pollution control boards to re-issue these standards under the Air Act or the Water Act. Assuming that the EPR standards applied, could the Assam board have issued a closure direction under section 31A of the *Air Act* on the basis of *EPR norms*? While the court may have looked to the EPR to fill the gap in the Air Act standards, this may not have changed the outcome of the appeal: It is difficult to justify a section 31A closure direction in the absence of measuring equipment to analyse the composition of the emissions released by the firm.

The judgment is also marred by a misconstruction of section 31A. The division bench observes that a direction by the board under section 31A may be issued only where the Central Government has first issued a direction in that behalf. This appears incorrect. A Central Government direction is not a condition precedent for the issue of a direction by the state board; but where the board issues a direction, any such direction is 'subject to' overriding Central Government orders.

No less remarkable is the restrictive interpretation placed on section 31-A by Justice Jaspal Singh of the Delhi High Court in *Gopi Nath Pvt. Ltd. v Department of Environment.*[34] The petitioner ran an iron casting business in a residential premises without obtaining consent under the Air Act. Relying on its power to issue 'any directions in writing to any person, officer or authority' in the performance of its functions under the Air Act, the respondent directed the magistrate to seal the offending unit. Quashing the direction, the High Court held that though section 31A enabled the board to direct '*closure*' or discontinuance of the objectionable activity, *sealing* the unit and preventing access was unauthorized.

In *Suma Traders v Chairman, Karnataka State Pollution Control Board,*[35] the High Court came down heavily on the first respondent. The petitioner challenged a closure order passed by the chairman under section 31A of the Air Act. The impugned order was issued after local residents complained against the air pollution caused by the firm's food grain processing plant. The firm challenged the order on the sole ground that the chairman was incompetent to issue orders under section 31A in the absence of the proper delegation of authority by the board under section 15 of the Air Act. On the board conceding that there was no delegation in favour of the chairman, the court held that the impugned order was passed in flagrant violation of the provisions and amounted to a misuse of statutory power. The judge wondered whether the incumbent was suitable for

---

34 1998 (72) DEL.L.T.536.
35 AIR 1998 KAR 8.

the post of chairman and imposed personal costs on her, assessed at Rs. 2,500.[36]

In equally galling circumstances, the Gujarat High Court was more restrained in its approach. N.J. Industries was acquitted in an Air Act prosecution because the Gujarat pollution control board failed to produce before the magistrate the official gazette declaring Ahmedabad as an 'air pollution control area' and was also unable to produce any local newspaper where the declaration was notified.[37]

D. STONE QUARRYING

Limestone quarrying in the Dehradun Valley triggered the first major public interest environmental case in the Supreme Court.[38] The primary ecological concerns of the court were the devastation of forests, landslides and the impact of quarrying on the hydrological system in the Mussoorie Hill Range. In this section, we focus on air pollution problems caused by unregulated quarrying.

Over six months in 1993, a division bench of the Himachal Pradesh High Court guided a public interest litigation to prevent stone crushing in the hills around Shimla. Assisted by a team of lawyers appointed *amicus curiae*, the court framed a scheme that would protect Shimla's environs while cushioning the economic impact on the quarry owners.

COURT ON ITS OWN MOTION v STATE OF HIMACHAL PRADESH
1994 FOR.L.T. 103

KAMLESH SHARMA, J.:

By way of this writ petition, this Court took *suo motu* cognizance of the reports appearing in the daily edition of the Tribune on 31 December 1992 and Indian Express on 10 January 1993 that illegal mining and installation of stone crushers have caused havoc at twelve places in the suburbs of Shimla, including Kamla Nagar, Tara Devi, Dhalli Nal Dehra and Choora Chowki. Kamla Nagar is also known as Bhatha Kuffar.

[The court traced the stages through which the case developed. Interim injunctions prohibiting quarrying were issued against the mine lessees but were partially modified. The Himachal Pradesh pollution control board was repeatedly directed to file detailed affidavits, the first two efforts by the board being 'deficient'. The court recorded the opinion of the Controller of Mines that the air pollution was 'caused mainly due to mechanical operation of stone crushers and not from manual extraction of stones, in which case the emission of dust remains within the standards of Ambient Air Quality.' In a development parallel to the case, the state government

---

[36] Under the Water Act, the Gujarat High Court has upheld the chairman's right to accord sanction to prosecute a polluter where the state board delegates its function to her. *Gujarat Pollution Control Board v Indian Chemicals Manufacturer* 1990 (2) GUJ.L.R.1306.

[37] *Dahyabhai Solanki v N.J. Industries* 1996 (1) GUJ.L.HER. 466.

[38] *Rural Litigation and Entitlement Kendra, Dehradun v State of Uttar Pradesh* AIR 1985 SC 652.

constituted a high level committee headed by the Chief Secretary to look into environmental degradation caused by mining operations and polluting industries in the state. The committee recommended that Shimla and its suburbs be declared an Environment Protection Zone by the Central Government under rule 5 of the Environment (Protection) Rules of 1986. The High Court impleaded the committee and sought its recommendations in relation to the quarries around Shimla. In light of the deliberations of the committee, the state government urged the High Court to confirm the interim injunction in the interest of local residents, tourists and the environment. 'The lessees may apply for suitable sites outside the Zone for mining and establishment of crushers which will be considered on priority ... .' The respondent lessees (Nos. 9 to 27) resisted the injunction claiming that they had the requisite permits and were operating the mines manually.]

From the material on record, it is proved that the Government had practically closed its eyes to environment degradation and ecological imbalance being caused by mining and industrial activities in and around Shimla, which has been acknowledged as Queen of the Hills for the last one century. Though the Government has brought on record its declaration made in the Industrial Policy of 1991 (Annexure RA to the affidavit, dated 15th May, 1993 of the Secretary (Industries), that environment friendliness is viewed as basic criteria for selection of industrial projects in the State and industries causing air and water pollution, [toxic discharges], degradation of forests and soil erosion will be [discouraged] and industries detrimental to tourism will not be set up within the public view of National State Highways and main tourist traffic routes, yet no effective measures were taken to implement this policy, till interim injunction was issued by this Court in C.W.P. No. 865 of 1992, *Tejinder Singh v State of Himachal Pradesh* staying mining activities at Dhalli-Naldehra road and in the present writ petition stopping mining operations being carried out at 12 places in the suburbs of Shimla.

* * *

[T]he, next question [is] whether respondents No. 9 to 27 should be permitted to work their mines/quarries and to operate their stone crushers till the Shimla Environment Protection Zone is created. From the proceedings of the third meeting of the High Level Committee held on 11 May 1993, it appears that while it accepted the recommendations of the Sub-Committee headed by Sh. H.C. Sharma, Additional Chief Conservator of Forests, it did not keep in view that creation of Shimla Environment Protection Zone by the Central Government will take minimum six months' time and what will happen during the interregnum to the business of respondents No. 9 to 27 and how the needs of common man as well as the Government will be met who are consumers for their produce, that is, stones, grit and sand for the construction of buildings, roads, bridges and other development projects. The Sub-Committee headed by the Secretary, H.P. State Pollution Control Board had recommended that out of 18 mines and stone crushers seven mines and stone crushers may be permitted to function for a period of six months and five mines and stone crushers may be permitted for indefinite period, as these are located reasonably away from Shimla town and also for other reasons stated in its report but these recommendations have been rejected by the High Level Committee for the reason that these mines and stone crushers fall within the proposed Shimla Environment Protection Zone. The approach of the High Level Committee was not realistic and balanced. The responsibility of state government is not over by taking decision to make recommendations to Central Government to create Shimla Environment Zone. It must look into the problems which are fall out of its said decision. It has been brought on record by respondents No. 9 to 27 in their separate affidavits that since the operation of stay order and closure of their business, not only have they lost their source of livelihood and incurred heavy financial losses, the labourers engaged by them have been rendered unemployed and the consumers of their goods are also suffering heavily as they are paying four times the price for purchasing stones, grit and sand which are now required to be brought from far off places near Nalagarh and Kalka. Neither these allegations have been [rebutted] on behalf of the Government nor any inclination is shown to consider and find out solution to the difficulties of lessees or consumers.

It is correct that for the larger public interest of protection of environment and ecological balance, the interests of a group of individuals should be sacrified but eyes cannot be closed to the hard realities that mines and industries, even if hazardous to the environment and the health of the people, are required to be worked and set up since they are essential for economic development and advancement of the well being of the people. All efforts are required to be made, to minimise the element of hazards or risk to the environment and people by taking all necessary steps by locating such industries and mines at such places and adopting such safety measures which will pose least risk and hazard to environment and people. (*M.C. Mehta v Union of India* AIR 1987 SC 965).

[The High Court noted the stands of the state government and the state board as well as the latter's recommendations for controlling air pollution.]

Keeping in view the totality of facts and circumstances brought on record by the parties, in the opinion of this Court, it will be in the interest of justice and fair play to allow respondents No. 10 and 13 to 27 to work their mines and operate their stone crushers for a period of only six months from the date of this order or till Shimla Environment Protection Zone is created, whichever is earlier subject to their strictly complying will all the laws, rules, instructions and directions applicable and providing all measures under the Act of 1981 to prevent Air Pollution and also subject to their undertaking that they will implement the scheme of afforestation in the mined areas at their own cost. During the period of six months, alternative mining site for mining and installing their stone crushers will be selected and approved by the state government and they will be rehabilitated there. The contention of the Additional Director (Industries), Mr. S.K. Justa, in his affidavit dated 13th July, 1993 that rehabilitation of the lessees and owners of the stone crusher is not the responsibility of the Government does not seem to be reasonable in the facts and circumstances of the present case.

* * *

The result of the above discussion is that writ petition is disposed of with the following directions:

(1) The state government will approach the Central Government for creation of Shimla Environment Protection Zone by issuing notification under clause (v), subsection (2) of Section 3 of the Environment (Protection) Act, 1986 read with clause (a),

sub-rule (3) of Rule 5 of the Environment (Protection) Rules, 1986 within a period of fifteen days from the date of this order. The state government will depute a responsible officer not below the rank of Deputy Secretary to pursue the matter with the Central Government and supply all necessary documents and material required by it without any delay.

(2) The Government of India will finally decide and issue the notification, if it deems necessary, for creating Shimla Environment Protection Zone, within a period of six months from the date of receipt of the request of the state government. Since the Central Government is not a party to this writ petition, we direct that it be impleaded as party respondent No. 29 and a copy of this judgment be sent to it through the Secretary, Ministry of Environment, Government of India, New Delhi.

(3) Respondent No. 10 and 13 to 27 are permitted to work their mines and operate their stone crushers for a period of six months from the date of this judgment or till the notification creating Shimla Environment Protection Zone is issued by the Central Government, whichever is earlier. For working their mines and operating their stone crushers, they will strictly follow all laws, rules, instructions issued/to be issued by the state government for mining soil and forest conservation and other purposes and also the H.P. State Pollution Control Board for the prevention of environmental degradation. The period of six months will not be extended even if the notification creating Shimla Environment Protection Zone is not issued by the Central Government and mining, lessees and stone crusher owners are not rehabilitated on alternative site(s) within the period of six months. There will be no mines/quarries and stone crushers in the proposed Shimla Environment Protection Zone on the expiry of the period of six months from the date of the judgment and the mines/quarries and Stone Crushers of respondents No. 10 and 13 to 27 will be wound up.

(4) The state government is directed to rehabilitate respondents No. 10 and 13 to 27 on alternative site(s) by granting all necessary permissions within a period of six months.

* * *

NOTES AND QUESTIONS

1. In addition to the directions excerpted above, the High Court directed the lessees and stone crusher operators to contribute 20 per cent of their gross profit to a fund to be used for restoring the scarred hills and afforestation.

2. Six years after the High Court judgment, the Shimla Environment Protection Zone had not been notified. What factors might have stalled the move? Anumita Roychowdhury analyses the political and economic repercussions of the ban on quarrying in Himachal Pradesh in her thoughtful article, *Quarrying for Trouble* in *Down to Earth*, 15 May 1993 at page 25.

3. Several hill stations and mountain holiday destinations have been robbed of their charm by deforestation, poor town planning and sanitation, excessive tourist pressure and burgeoning hotels in response to the tourist influx. Among the earliest judicial efforts to stem the rot was the attempt to restore the Mussoorie Hills and Doon Valley in the *Dehradun Valley Case*.[39] Other cases to preserve hill station ecology are *M.C. Mehta v Kamal Nath*,[40] *Ajay Singh Rawat v Union of India*,[41] *Bombay Environmental Action Group v State of Maharashtra*[42] and *Bombay Environmental Action Group v State of Maharashtra*.[43]

4. Stone crushing operations around Delhi caught the attention of the Supreme Court on an application under Article 32 of the Constitution. M.C. Mehta objected to the quarrying because the dust particles polluted the air and the quarries violated town planning regulations.[44] The court directed the Central pollution control board to inspect the plants and verify the allegations.[45] On 15 May 1992, the court issued a detailed order 'for the reasons to be recorded and pronounced at a later stage'.[46] Quarries in Delhi and in the surrounding areas of Haryana were told to close down in three months. Quarry owners operating without licences from the town planning authorities or who were issued closure orders under section 31A of the Air Act or section 5 of the Environment (Protection) Act of 1986, were directed to forthwith cease operations. The Haryana authorities were asked to allot alternative sites in a new 'crushing zone' located at a suitable distance from the capital. (It is unclear whether the court considered what might happen to the persons residing in and around the new 'crushing zone'). The Supreme Court prefaced its directions with this observation:

> We are conscious that environmental changes are the inevitable consequences
> of industrial development in our country, but at the same time the quality of
> environment cannot be permitted to be damaged by polluting air, water and
> land to such an extent that it becomes a health hazard for the residents of the
> area. We are constrained to record that Delhi Development Authority,
> Municipal Corporation of Delhi, Central Pollution Control Board and Delhi
> Pollution Control Committee have been wholly remiss in the performance of

[39] *Rural Litigation and Entitlement Kendra, Dehradun v State of Uttar Pradesh* AIR 1985 SC 652.
[40] 1997 (1) SCC 388, 415. Directions to the Himachal Pradesh Pollution Control Board to inspect all hotels, institutions and factories in the Kullu-Manali areas and ensure that none of them discharged untreated effluents in the Beas river.
[41] 1995 (3) SCC 266. Directions to preserve Nainital.
[42] Writ Petition No.2754 of 1997, Bombay High Court, 18 November 1998. Directions to preserve Mahableshwar.
[43] Writ Petition No. 2773 of 1997, Bombay High Court, 4 December 1998. Quashing a letter of intent issued by the State to Sahara India Housing Ltd. in respect of the proposed Sahara Lake City in Pune district.
[44] *M.C. Mehta v Union of India (Stone Crushing)* 1992 Supp (2) SCC 85 and 86.
[45] *Id.* at 87.
[46] *M.C. Mehta v Union of India (Stone Crushing)* 1992 (3) SCC 256, 257. It is unclear whether any reasons followed. If so, the law reports appear to have missed them.

their statutory duties and have failed to protect the environment and control air pollution in the union territory of Delhi. Utter disregard to environment has placed Delhi in an unenviable position of being the world's third grubbiest, most polluted and unhealthy city as per the study conducted by the World Health Organisation. Needless to say that every citizen has a right to fresh air and live in pollution-free environment.[47]

Pushing the quarry operators away from Delhi and further into Haryana was fraught with danger. Haryana has an abysmal record for protecting bonded labourers working in stone quarries in the Faridabad district of the state. A few months earlier, the Supreme Court in *Bandhua Mukti Morcha v Union of India*[48] urged the state to ensure that 2000 quarry workers received better health care, education and other facilities. Anticipating the orders in the *Stone Crushing Case*, the court observed:

> The State of Haryana must come forward to play its role in a better way. As already pointed out these are quarries near about the industrial belt of Haryana and not far away from Delhi. Ecology is not only a local problem but must be taken to be a problem of Delhi also. Dust emanating from the working area in Haryana is bound to affect adversely the Delhi atmosphere. In fact, if adequate importance is given to the angle of pollution the industry itself has to be regulated or may have to be stopped.

The Haryana government permitted the quarry operators to re-locate their operations in the new 'crushing zones' around Pall and Mohabatabad. Predictably, the operators were quick to despoil the environment around the new sites, forcing M.C. Mehta to revive the case in the Supreme Court in late 1995. On 20 November 1995 the court directed a team of scientists and environmental engineers from the Central pollution control board to inspect the new locations. The report submitted to the court projected a dismal picture. The air pollution was intense, chiefly because the dust containment systems, although installed, were not being operated by any of the quarry owners and a water shortage prevented the sprinklers from being used. The report revealed that the mining operations were being conducted haphazardly and warned of an imminent ecological disaster. The Supreme Court directed the parties to arrange for the sprinkler water supply. The quarry owners were granted two months time to install necessary pollution control devices and the state government was asked to lay a road to the quarrying zone besides implementing the suggestions and directions given by the Central board.[49]

As a separate issue, one may wonder whether the Supreme Court of India can have the time and resources for the above sort of micro-management.

[47] *Id.*
[48] 1991 (4) SCC 177, 193, 195.
[49] *M.C. Mehta v Union of India (Delhi Stone Crushing)* 1996 (1) SCALE 29 (SP).

5. In *Navin Chemical's Case*,[50] the Allahabad High Court declined to interfere under Article 226 of the Constitution in a petition filed by a pharmaceutical manufacturer against Detchem Mineral Corporation, who were grinding and pulverising stone next to the drug unit. Navin Chemicals complained that the atmospheric pollution caused by Detchem was interfering in its manufacture of sensitive life saving drugs. Reviewing the material on record, the court declined to interfere since the Uttar Pradesh pollution board was alert to the matter. In declining relief, the court may have been influenced by the board's contention that Navin Chemicals too was guilty of breaching the Air Act. In the final paragraphs of the judgment, the court erroneously construed section 43 of the Air Act (prior to its amendment in 1987) as operating to bar a petition under Article 226 of the Constitution. The section 43 bar does not preclude a writ petition under Article 226 and operates in respect of criminal prosecutions under the Air Act. Generally, statutory provisions cannot curtail the constitutionally guaranteed writ jurisdiction of the Supreme Court and the High Courts.

6. In *Chaitanya Pulverising*, the Karnataka High Court quashed the decision of the respondent board to shut down the petitioner's unit which was pulverising dolomite stones on the ground that the board had no authority to do so. This judgment construed the provisions of the Air Act *before* the insertion of sections 22A and 31A by the 1987 amendment. The High Court held that the pre-amended statute entitled the board to prosecute the polluter for non-compliance of Air Act provisions but did not permit prohibitory orders.[51]

7. The failure of the Karnataka government and the state board to frame a suitable zoning policy for stone quarrying and crushing, compelled the High Court to issue general directions in *Obayya Pujari v Karnataka State Pollution Control Board*.[52] The petition challenged the board's consent permitting stone crushing. The petitioners feared that the new unit would damage their crops and adversely affect the health of residents in the locality. Extending the scope of the petition to cover stone crushing operations across the state, the High Court directed the government to immediately formulate a policy regulating the business and to identify 'safer zones' for such operations. The Karnataka High Court drew upon the Punjab and Haryana High Court decision in *Ishwar Singh v State of Haryana*,[53] to highlight the environmental damage caused by unregulated stone quarrying.

8. In *Kennedy Valley Welfare Association v Ceylon R.L.W. & S. Society*,[54] the Supreme Court restored a ban imposed by the single judge of the Madras High Court, prohibiting stone crushing operations within 500 metres of residential

---

[50] *Navin Chemicals Manufacturing and Trading Ltd. v New Okhla Industrial Development Authority* 1987 ALL.L.J.13.

[51] *Chaitanya Pulverising Industry v Karnataka State Pollution Control Board* AIR 1987 KAR 82.

[52] AIR 1999 KAR 157.

[53] AIR 1996 P&H 30.

[54] 2000 (2) SCALE 143.

colonies. Earlier, a division bench of the High Court in appeal had restricted the ban to 50 metres.

E. PRESERVING THE TAJ MAHAL

On the eve of his retirement, Justice Kuldip Singh delivered the Supreme Court judgment in the *Taj Trapezium Case*, culminating a long and arduous battle fought by M.C. Mehta for over a decade. In the winter of 1984, M.C. Mehta, a conscientious advocate practising at the Bar of the Supreme Court, placed before the court the material he had gathered and warned of damage to the Taj Mahal from air pollutants. The *Taj Case* was Mehta's first tentative step in the nascent field of environmental litigation.[55] In the following year, he filed Article 32 petitions to clean up the Ganga,[56] rid Delhi of hazardous and heavy industry,[57] close down and relocate Shriram's industrial complex in the heart of the capital[58] and regulate air pollution caused by automobiles, thermal power stations and industries.[59] Over time, each of these cases grew into full blown class actions involving scores of parties.

Mehta's cases rode on the passion of the presiding judge. The *Shriram Gas Leak Case* was the first to kick off under the stewardship of Chief Justice Bhagwati who was anxious to help the Bhopal victims by articulating the principles of mass tort liability.[60] The next of Mehta's cases to gain momentum was the *Ganga Pollution Case* where Justice Venkataramiah issued a series of opinions to discipline the Kanpur tanneries and riparian municipalities.[61] Troubled by the deteriorating air quality in Delhi and the soot on his shirt collar, Chief Justice Ranganath Misra pulled the *Motor Vehicles Case* off the back burner in 1991.[62] Although first among Mehta's cases, the *Taj Case* was the last to evoke interest. It was propelled to the fore in 1993 by a series of orders issued by Justice Kuldip Singh. We carry excerpts from the final judgment delivered almost four years after the periodic hearings commenced in January, 1993. Before perusing the judgment, review the opening reading in this chapter describing the air pollution problems of Agra. The 'Taj Trapezium Zone' referred to by the court is a 10,400 sq.km trapezium-shaped area covering the five districts of the Agra region.

---

[55] *M.C. Mehta v Union of India* Writ Petition (Civil) No. 13381 of 1984.

[56] *M.C. Mehta v Union of India* Writ Petition (Civil) No. 3727 of 1985.

[57] *M.C. Mehta v Union of India* Writ Petition (Civil) No. 4677 of 1985.

[58] *M.C. Mehta v Union of India* Writ Petition (Civil) No. 12739 of 1985.

[59] *M.C. Mehta v Union of India* Writ Petition (Civil) No. 13029 of 1985.

[60] See the judgments of Chief Justice Bhagwati in *M.C. Mehta v Union of India* AIR 1987 SC 965 and AIR 1987 SC 1086.

[61] See the judgments of Justice Venkataramiah in *M.C. Mehta v Union of India* AIR 1988 SC 1037 and AIR 1988 SC 1115.

[62] See the next section on vehicular pollution and Chief Justice Misra's judgment in *M.C. Mehta v Union of India* 1991 (2) SCC 353.

M.C. MEHTA v UNION OF INDIA (TAJ TRAPEZIUM CASE)
AIR 1997 SC 734

KULDIP SINGH, J.:

Taj Mahal—The Taj—is the 'King Emperor' amongst the World Wonders. The Taj is the final achievement and acme of the Mughal Art. It represents the most refined aesthetic values. It is a fantasy-like grandeur. It is the perfect culmination and artistic interplay of the architect's skill and the jewellers' inspiration. The marble in-lay walls of workmanship. The elegant symmetry of its exterior and the aerial grace of its domes and minarets impress the beholder in a manner never to be forgotten. It stands out as one of the most priceless national monuments, of surprising beauty and worth, a glorious tribute to man's achievement in architecture and engineering.

* * *

The Taj is threatened with deterioration and damage not only by the traditional causes of decay, but also by changing social and economic conditions which aggravate the situation with even more formidable phenomena of damage or destruction. A private sector preservation organisation called 'World Monuments Fund' (American Express Company) has published a list of 100 most endangered sites (1996) in the World. The Taj has been included in the list by stating as under:

> The Taj Mahal, marble tomb for Mumtaz Mahal, wife of Emperor Shah Jahan, is considered the epitome of Mughal monumental domed tombs set in a garden. The environment of Agra is today beset with problems relating to inadequacy of its urban infrastructure for transportation, water and electricity. The densest pollution near the Taj Mahal is caused by residential fuel combustion, diesel trains and buses, and back-up generators. Construction of the proposed Agra Ring Road and Bypass that would divert the estimated daily 6,50,000 tons of trans-India truck traffic awaits financing. Strict controls on industrial pollution established in 1982 are being intensively enforced following a 1993 Supreme Court order. The Asian Development Bank's proposed $300 million loan to the Indian Government to finance infrastructure improvements would provide the opportunity to solve the chronic problems. Agra contains three World Heritage Sites, including the Taj Mahal.

According to the petitioner, the foundries, chemical/hazardous industries and the refinery at Mathura are the major sources of damage to the Taj. The sulphur dioxide emitted by the Mathura Refinery and the industries when combined with oxygen— with the aid of moisture—in the atmosphere forms sulphuric acid called 'Acid rain' which has a corroding effect on the gleaming white marble. Industrial/Refinery emissions, brick kilns, vehicular traffic and generator-sets are primarily responsible for polluting the ambient air around Taj Trapezium Zone (TTZ). The petition states that the white marble has yellowed and blackened in places. It is inside the Taj that the decay is more apparent. Yellow pallor pervades the entire monument. In places the yellow hue is magnified by ugly brown and black spots. Fungal deterioration is worst in the inner chamber where the original graves of Shah Jahan and Mumtaz Mahal lie. According to the petitioner the Taj—a monument of international repute—is on its way to degradation due to atmosphere pollution and it is imperative that preventive steps are taken and soon. The petitioner has finally sought appropriate directions to the authorities concerned to take immediate steps to stop air pollution in the TTZ and save the Taj.

* * *

[The court considered the affidavit filed by the board and directed the board to issue a public notice.] Pursuant to the Court's order ... the Board filed affidavit dated 5–8–1993 wherein it stated that public notice was published in two local newspapers of Agra on 17–5–1993 and two national newspapers on 18–5–1993 calling upon the industries to file their replies during the extended time. The affidavit states that all the listed industries were polluting industries and 507 out of them had not even installed any air pollution control device. The 212 industries who did not respond to the notice and failed to take any steps towards installing the pollution control devices were closed by the order dated 27–8–1993 with immediate effect. The closure order was to operate till the time necessary pollution control devices were to be set up by the industries concerned.

[The judgment records subsequent developments in the case between 1993 and 1996. The court was assisted in its efforts to improve air quality in the TTZ by the reports prepared by the National Environment Engineering Research Institute (NEERI); inputs from the Gas Authority of India Ltd. (GAIL) on the supply of fuel gas to industries in the area; and the study conducted by the Vardharajan Committee which was constituted in May, 1994 by the Union Ministry of Environment and Forests at the prompting of the court. On 3 August 1995 the court formed a tentative view that polluting industries in the TTZ would have to be relocated and sought the assistance of the Union Government to devise an appropriate solution. However, in the words of the judgment: 'There being no helpful response from the Government of India, we finally heard the matter at length for several days and are disposing of the issues raised before us by this judgment.']

The Taj, apart from being a cultural heritage, is an industry by itself. More than two million tourists visit the Taj every year. It is a source of revenue for the country. This Court has monitored this petition for over three years with the sole object of preventing and protecting the Taj from deterioration and damage due to atmosphere and environmental pollution. It cannot be disputed that the use of coke/coal by the industries emits pollution in the ambient air. The objective behind this litigation is to stop the pollution while encouraging development of industry. The old concept that development and ecology cannot go together is no longer acceptable. Sustainable development is the answer. The development of industry is essential for the economy of the country, but at the same time the environment and the ecosystem have to be protected. The pollution created as a consequence of development must be commensurate with the carrying capacity of our ecosystems.

Various orders passed by this Court from time to time ... clearly indicate that the relocation of the industries from TTZ is to be resorted to only if the Natural Gas which has been brought at the doorstep of TTZ is not acceptable/available by/to the industries as a substitute for coke/coal. The GAIL has already invited the industries in TTZ to apply for gas connections. Before us ... learned counsel for the industries have clearly stated that all the industries would accept gas as an industrial fuel. The industries operating in TTZ which are given gas connections to run the industries need not relocate. The whole purpose is to stop air pollution by banishing coke/coal from TTZ.

* * *

Based on the reports of various technical authorities mentioned in this judgment, we have already reached the finding that the emissions generated by the coke/coal consuming industries are air pollutants and have damaging effect on the Taj and the people living in the TTZ. The atmospheric pollution in TTZ has to be eliminated at any cost. Not even one per cent chance can be taken when—human life apart—the preservation of a prestigious monument like the Taj is involved. In any case, in view of the precautionary principle as defined by this Court, the environmental measure must anticipate, prevent and attack the cause of environmental degradation. The 'onus of proof' is on an industry to show that its operation with the aid of coke/coal is environmentally benign. It is, rather, proved beyond doubt that the emissions generated by the use of coke/coal by the industries in TTZ are the main polluters of the ambient air.

We, therefore, hold that ... 292 industries [out of 511] shall as per the schedule indicated hereunder change over to the natural gas as an industrial fuel. The industries which are not in a position to obtain gas connections—for any reason—shall stop functioning with the aid of coke/coal in the TTZ and may relocate themselves as per the directions given by us hereunder.

We order and direct as under:

(1) The industries (292 listed [in the order]) shall approach/apply to the GAIL before 15–2–1997 for grant of industrial gas connection.

(2) The industries which are not in a position to obtain gas connections and also industries which do not wish to obtain gas connection may approach/apply to the UP State Industrial Development Corporation (UPSIDC)/Government before 28–2–1997 for allotment of alternative plots in the industrial estates outside TTZ.

(3) The GAIL shall take final decision in respect of all the applications for grant of gas connections by 31–3–1997 and communicate the allotment letters to the individual industries.

(4) Those industries which neither apply for gas connection nor for alternative industrial plot shall stop functioning with the aid of coke/coal in the TTZ with effect from 3–4–1997. Supply of coke/coal to these industries shall be stopped forthwith. The District Magistrate and the Superintendent of Police shall have this order complied with.

(5) The GAIL shall commence supply of gas to the industries by 30–6–1997. As soon as the gas supply to an industry commences, the supply coke/coal to the said industry shall be stopped with immediate effect.

(6) UPSIDC Government shall finally decide and allot alternative plots, before 31–3–1997, to the industries which are seeking relocation.

(7) The relocating industries shall set up their respective units in the new industrial

estates outside TTZ. The relocating industries shall not function and operate in TTZ beyond 31–12–1997. The closure by 31–12–1997 is unconditional and irrespective of the fact whether the new unit outside TTZ is completely set up or not.

(8) The Deputy Commissioner, Agra and the Superintendent (Police), Agra shall effect the closure of all the industries on 31–12–1997 which are to be relocated by that date as directed by us.

(9) The UP state government/Corporation, shall render all assistance to the industries in the process of relocation. The allotment of plots, construction of factory buildings, etc., and issuance of any licence/permission, etc., shall be expedited and granted on priority basis.

(10) In order to facilitate shifting of industries from TTZ, the State Government and all other authorities shall set up unified single agency consisting of all the departments concerned to act as a nodal agency to sort out all the problems of such industries. The single window facility shall be set up by the UP State Government within one month from today. * * * We make clear that no further time shall be allowed to set up the single window facility.

(11) The state government shall frame a scheme for the use of the land which would become available on account of shifting/relocation of the industries before 30–6–1997. The state government may seek guidance in this respect from the order of this Court in *M.C. Mehta v Union of India*. [1996 (4) SCC 351. In this case the court issued directions to shift industries from Delhi.]

(12) The shifting industries on the relocation in the new industrial estates shall be given incentives in terms of the provisions of the Agra Master Plan and also the incentives which are normally extended to new industries in new industrial estates.

(13) The workmen employed in the above-mentioned 292 industries shall be entitled to the rights and benefits as indicated hereunder:

(a) The workmen shall have continuity of employment at the new town and place where the industry is shifted. The terms and conditions of their employment shall not be altered to their detriment.

(b) The period between the closure of the industry in Agra and its restart at the place of relocation shall be treated as active employment and the workmen shall be paid their full wages with continuity of service.

(c) All those workmen who agree to shift with the industry shall be given one year's wages as 'shifting bonus' to help them settle at the new location. The said bonus shall be paid before 31–1–1998.

(d) The workmen employed in the industries who do not intend to relocate/ obtain Natural Gas and opt for closure, shall be deemed to have been retrenched by 31–5–1997, provided they have been in continuous service (as defined in Section 25–B of the Industrial Disputes Act, 1947) for not less than one year in the industries concerned before the said date. They shall be paid compensation in terms of Section 25–F(b) of the Industrial Disputes Act. These workmen shall also be paid, in addition, six years' wages as additional compensation.

(e) The compensation payable to the workmen in terms of this judgment shall be paid by the management within two months of the retrenchment.

(f) The gratuity amount payable to any workmen shall be paid in addition.

Before the parting with this judgment, we may indicate that the industries in the TTZ other than 292 industries shall be dealt with separately. We direct the Board to issue individual notices and also public notice to the remaining industries in the TTZ to apply for gas connection/relocation within one month of the notice by the Board. The Board shall issue notice within one month from today. The matter to come up for further monitoring in this respect before this Court on 4-4-1997.

We may also indicate that this Court by order dated 10-5-1996 has stopped the operation of all the brick kilns in the TTZ with effect from 15-8-1996. This Court by order dated 4-9-1996 has directed that the fly-ash produced in the process of the functioning of thermal plants may be supplied to the brick kilns for the construction of bricks. This would be a useful step to eliminate the pollution caused by fly-ash.

The Court is separately monitoring the following issues for controlling air pollution in TTZ:

(a) The setting up of hydro-cracker unit and various other devices by the Mathura Refinery.

(b) The setting up of a 50-bed hospital and two mobile dispensaries by the Mathura Refinery to provide medical aid to the people living in the surrounding areas (Court order dated 7-8-1996).

(c) Construction of Agra bypass to divert all the traffic which passed through the city. Under directions of this Court, 23 kms stretch of the bypass shall be completed by the end of December 1996 (Court order dated 10-4-1996).

(d) Additional amount of Rs. 99.54 crores sanctioned by the Planning Commission to be utilized by the State Government for the construction of electricity supply projects to ensure 100 percent uninterrupted electricity to the TTZ. This is necessary to stop the operation of generating sets which are major source of air pollution in the TTZ (Court orders dated 10-4-1996, 10-5-1996, 30-8-1996, 4-9-1996 and 10-9-1996).

(e) The construction of Gokul Barrage, water supply work of Gokul Barrage, roads around Gokul Barrage, Agra Barrage and water supply of Agra Barrage, have also been undertaken on a time-schedule basis to supply drinking water to the residents of Agra and to bring life into River Yamuna which is next to the Taj (Court order dated 10-5-1996 and 30-8-1996).

(f) Green belt as recommended by NEERI has been set up around Taj. Pursuant to continuous monitoring of this Court, the Green belt has become a reality.

(g) This Court suggested to the Planning Commission by order dated 4-9-1996 to consider sanctioning separate allocation for the city of Agra and the creation of separate cell under the control of Central Government to safeguard and preserve the Taj, the city of Agra and other national heritage monuments in the TTZ.

(h) All emporia and shops functioning within the Taj premises have been directed to be closed.

(i) Directions have been issued to the Government of India to decide the issue, pertaining to declaration of Agra as heritage city within two months.

We are mentioning these issues dealt with by this Court because it may be necessary to monitor some of these matter to take them to a logical extent. This Court may look into these matters on 4–4–1997.

The issue relating to 292 industries is thus disposed of.

NOTES AND QUESTIONS

1. Having survived the threat of Governor General William Bentinck to demolish the Mughal monuments at Agra and ship the marble to London, as well as outdoor balls, picnic parties, revellers and brigands,[63] the Taj may pull through its present ordeal. Environmentalists argue that the air pollution problem could have been avoided had the authorities heeded warnings not to build the Mathura Refinery in the 1970s. The debate over the suitability of the site is tracked by Darryl D'Monte in his study *Temples or Tombs?*[64] Within two years of commissioning the refinery in 1982, sulphur dioxide around the Taj increased three-fold.[65]

2. Would environment impact assessment (EIA) procedures have prevented the Mathura Refinery from coming up? Are the current EIA regulations strong enough to prevent recurrence of the folly? *Was* it a folly? In the wake of the controversy, several experts cleared the project in the 1970s.

3. The Supreme Court relied heavily on the NEERI report to support its re-location directives. But NEERI's methods, analysis and conclusions are questioned by experts and Agra's small industry owners. They refer to the Vardharajan Committee report of 1994 which found no evidence of pollution related damage to the monument and attributed deteriorating air quality mainly to non-industrial sources such as traffic and diesel generator sets. Some experts doubt the veracity of NEERI's air quality data; point to several archaeological errors; question why the Mathura Refinery was ignored by the report and criticise the over-estimates of emissions from Agra's foundries.[66]

4. Would you regard the court's approach too 'monument-oriented' and insensitive to economic realities? One study fears that shifting the small industrial units would render them financially unviable and might jeopardize the employment of over 50,000 people.[67]

5. The breadth of judicial activity in the *Taj Trapezium Case* is unmatched. The

---

[63] D'Monte, *Temples or Tombs? Industry versus Environment: Three Controversies* 91–92 (1985).
[64] *Id.*
[65] Raghuram, *The Trouble with the Trapezium* in *Down to Earth*, 15 April 1996, p.32, 35.
[66] *Id.* at 32–37.
[67] Report of the Tripathi Committee set up by the Uttar Pradesh government in 1994 to study the impact of pollution on the Taj. *Id.* at 37.

court supervised the installation of pollution abatement equipment; shut down violators; cajoled GAIL to pipe gas to the industries; urged development of a green belt around the monument; relocated industries; fashioned a labour compensation and entitlement scheme; expedited the construction of a highway to divert traffic away from Agra; prodded the government to speed up work on barrages that would revive the flow in the Yamuna; and generally monitored development activity in the Trapezium.

Was this a legitimate response to what Sriram Panchu calls 'the felt necessities of the times'[68] or a manifestation of the 'natural, self-aggrandizing instinct of altogether too many lawyers and judges ... to stand up and do something—anything at all—when any aspect of life seems less than perfect'?[69]

6. The judgment vigorously applies the 'precautionary principle'; casting the burden on industry to show that operating with the aid of coke/coal was environmentally benign.

7. The ringing tone of the judgment had little effect on the parochial approach of the UP State Electricity Board. Raising several technical quibbles, the board declined to supply power to the air quality monitoring station at the Taj Mahal. The objections were brushed aside by the court in January, 1998.[70]

8. In February, 1998 the Central Government informed the court that Agra did not qualify for declaration as a world heritage city because of its polluted atmosphere and haphazard growth.[71]

9. A key feature of the Supreme Court scheme to clean the air in the Taj Trapezium was the introduction of natural gas to replace dirtier fuels such as coke and coal. On 31 August 1999 the court reviewed the progress in respect of gas supply to the Trapezium and directed 53 iron foundries which had not agreed to accept the gas to close down. Seventy eight iron foundries that used cupola-based technology submitted that despite their best efforts no reliable technology was available to convert their units to gas. These foundries claimed that the new technology was in the last stages of development and that they would switch over to natural gas as soon as the technology became available. The Supreme Court declined to accept the plea for an indefinite extension. The court directed the district magistrate to ensure that no coal or coke was supplied to the cupola-based foundries after 15 September 1999. The foundries were permitted to operate after they converted to natural gas.[72]

10. In May 1999, the Centre constituted the Taj Trapezium Pollution (Prevention and Control) Authority under section 3 of the Environment (Protection) Act of 1986. The Authority, comprising eight government officials, is headed by

[68] Panchu, *Environmental Law in India: Key Environmental Issues; Legislation; Case Law; Enforcement; Lessons to be Learnt* 14 November 1997 (unpublished manuscript).

[69] Huber. *Safety and Second Best: The Hazard of Public Risk Management in the Court*, 85 Columbia L.Rev. 277. (1985).

[70] *M.C. Mehta v Union of India (Taj Trapezium Case)* 1998 (2) SCALE 7 (SP).

[71] *Down to Earth*, 28 February 1998 p. 29

[72] *M.C. Mehta v Union India* AIR 1999 SC 3192.

the Commissioner, Agra Division. It has wide powers to implement schemes for protecting the Taj Mahal and improving the environment including necessary measures to ensure compliance with emission standards by motor vehicles. The Authority is empowered to issue statutory directions under section 5 of the Act and initiate prosecutions under section 19.[73]

11. As a matter of practice, the Supreme Court is reluctant to entertain Article 32 petitions which relate to local air pollution problems. For example, a public interest petition received by post alleging air pollution by a cement factory at Ariyalur in Tamil Nadu was directed to be sent to the Madras High Court and to be disposed of under Article 226 of the Constitution.[74]

F. VEHICULAR POLLUTION

The Centre for Science and Environment, New Delhi periodically publishes well researched and authoritative reports on the state of the environment. The next excerpt focuses on emissions from mobile sources of pollution, an especially hard nut to crack for regulators. Note how the automobile industry in India has influenced standard setters in New Delhi to prescribe weak norms for new vehicles. While the tussle between industry and environmental regulators is a global feature, automakers in India appear especially persuasive.

CENTRE FOR SCIENCE AND ENVIRONMENT; SLOW MURDER: THE DEADLY STORY OF VEHICULAR POLLUTION IN INDIA, 16–19, 48–51, 109 (1996)

> Though industries, thermal power plants and domestic activity also contribute to air pollution in cities, the transport sector is the largest emitter of carbon monoxide (CO), nitrogen oxides (Nox) and hydrocarbons (HC) into the air. Gasoline-run vehicles contribute most of the CO, HC and lead (Pb), while diesel vehicles are the chief source of particulate and sulphur dioxide. Emission statistics indicate that vehicular pollution is responsible for a shocking 64 per cent of the total air pollution load from various sources in Delhi, 52 per cent in Mumbai and 30 per cent in Calcutta. As much as 97 per cent of HC emissions and 76 per cent of CO emissions in Delhi are from vehicles running on petrol. Presently, vehicles emit 1,300 metric tonnes of pollutants into Delhi's air everyday. This is almost 50 per cent more than 870 tonnes per day (tpd) emitted in 1987—more significantly, this is more than the sum of vehicular pollutants in Mumbai (659.57 tpd), Calcutta (310.62 tpd) and Bangalore (253.72 tpd).

* * *

[73] S.O. 350 (E) dated 17 May 1999.

[74] *V. Subramanian v Union of India* 1990 (Supp) SCC 775.

The measures publicized so far seem to indicate that to control vehicular pollution, it is the vehicle consumers who need to be brought to heel. Poor maintenance definitely increases emissions from old vehicles, and pollution checks are necessary to deal with this problem. But there are other culprits—vehicles manufactured in India have high levels of pollution, even when they are brand new; the fuel sold in petrol bunks across the country is of poor quality and often adulterated, resulting in increased emissions; and the increasing dependence on vehicular transport systems in general, and fuel-and-capacity-inefficient modes of road transport in particular, are taking their toll on atmosphere quality.

Standards for controlling emissions levels of new vehicles were incorporated into the Motor Vehicles Act (1989) only as late as 1991, enforcing some sort of quality control on the automobile industry. The existing Bureau of Indian Standards for fuel started incorporating emission parameters during the same period. But in both cases, the standards were set according to the terms and conditions dictated by the industry. Both the regulatory authorities and the manufacturers pleaded incapacity to make any drastic improvements, and so the standards they follow today are far too lax compared to those elsewhere in the world.

* * *

The petroleum sector picked up the gauntlet and provided unleaded fuel, although the benefits of using catalytic converters have been rendered questionable. [The catalytic converter is a device in the engine exhaust system which converts harmful gases like CO, HC and Nox into more benign constituents like carbon dioxide, water vapour, nitrogen, etc.] This is because unleaded fuel is being manufactured in India without investing in appropriate technology, resulting in an increase in carcinogenic benzene emissions. The petroleum sector is safe from reproach so far because, alarming as it sounds, nobody is measuring benzene levels in India as yet; even the WHO specifies that there are no safe levels for airborne benzene. The toxic effects of benzene inhalation by humans include damage to the circulatory, immune and central nervous systems. Benzene is a known human carcinogen classified as Group 1 (definite carcinogen) by the International Agency for Cancer Research, and known to cause lung cancer, skin cancer and leukaemia.

Meanwhile, even the catalytic converters do not seem to be working—tests carried out first by the Central Pollution Control Board (CPCB) in May and June 1995, and then by a local environmental group in January 1996, showed that some of the models fitted with converters, particularly the Maruti Zen, did not even meet CO emission standards set for cars without converters. The CPCB tested 23 Maruti vehicles with catalytic converters and eight exceeded emission limits. 'There is absolutely no regulatory mechanism to test the quality of catalytic converters that are being imported for Indian cars,' claims H B Mathur of the Indian Institute of Technology, Delhi. 'For all we know, the car companies have been importing boxes in place of converters.' So far, there are no norms for cars fitted with converters.

* * *

A long period of waiting ended in disappointment for the automobile industry in April 1996, after the government notified emission standards which the industry claimed would threaten the fate of its products. The industry registered its protest at a meeting convened by the Ministry of Environment and Forests (MEF) in August 1995, where the manufacturers dismissed many of the proposed standards as 'not achievable.' But, as the CPCB chairperson D K Biswas [assured], the government did not relent. 'Let them stop producing these vehicles now and start when they are ready with the technology,' Biswas said.

When the standards were being discussed, ministry sources said that several products will have to be phased out when the standards come into force. These included Yamaha RX 100, TVS Shogun, Bajaj Kawasaki RTZ (motor cycles), all petrol driven three-wheelers, Mahindra jeeps and Maruti Udyog Ltd's Gypsy. These models were withdrawn from the domestic market once the norms were issued in April 1996 and are now being sold in countries abroad where emission norms are less stringent. Only Bajaj has stopped manufacturing its Kawasaki RTZ model, which in any case constituted only 1 per cent of its total production, and replaced it with the KB 125 motorcycle.

The rest, with a higher stake in the market, claim they have 'modified' the product to meet standards. Escorts Ltd has withdrawn Yamaha RX 100, which constituted 50 percent of its production, but promptly replaced it with another two-stroke model, Yamaha RXG 135, which they claim meets the standards. They also claim they have modified TVS Shogun (20 percent of Escort's total production). Mahindra jeeps and Maruti Udyog also claim they have made modifications. Bajaj, the largest manufacturer of three-wheelers in India, modified the engine design of its three-wheelers.

* * *

Considering the ease with which the industry modified the polluting models once they were told to do or die, the fuss they kicked up when the standards were being discussed in August 1995 was entirely out of proportion. Their habit of throwing a tantrum and playing tug-of-war with a very indulgent ministry has often resulted in undermining the objective of improving air quality.

The exercise of fixing pollution norms meanwhile was knocked out of its scientific domain and assumed a political hue, with the contending parties—the automobile industry, the petroleum industry and the government—trying to pass on the onus of cleaning up the air to one another in order to reduce the load of each one's own obligations.

A committee was set up under H.B. Mathur of the Indian Institute of Technology (IIT), New Delhi, to recommend vehicular emission norms for 1995 and 2000. It based its recommendations on the deliberations of two sub-committees—one for petrol cars set up under S. Raju of the Automotive Research Association of India (ARAI), and another for diesel vehicles under B.P. Pundir of the Indian Institute of Petroleum. Ever since the Mathur Committee's report in 1991, conflicting arguments and counter-arguments have led to endless discussions, needless dilution and uncertainty of proposed standards despite the fact that the automobile manufacturers were represented in this committee and its sub-committees.

[T]he final notification issued by MEF in 1993 was a diluted version of the Mathur Committee recommendations and even more lenient than the initial proposal put up for consideration by the CPCB. This progressive dilution occurred even though the Mathur Committee rejected the recommendations of the Raju sub-committee [assuring it] of being sympathetic to the automobile industry and opting for softer norms. The Mathur Committee found that these norms were so lenient that more than 60 percent of the vehicles in India were already within the proposed limit. 'What is the point in setting norms which do not aspire to achieve higher targets,' exclaims Mathur, 'It is important to set higher targets than what is currently achievable to make technology more responsive.'

The MEF, under pressure from the automobile manufacturers, extended the deadline for meeting the standards from the original date of April 1995 to April 1996 and diluted the norms for CO, HC and NOx emissions. The Mathur Committee had recommended 5.0 to 9.0 gm/km for CO and 2.0 to 4.0 gm/km for HC and NOx emissions, according to the reference weight of petrol vehicles. Following this, MEF first agreed to 7.40 gm/km for CO and 1.97 gm/km for HC and NOx as a single standard for all vehicles irrespective of reference weight of the vehicles. But the Ministry subsequently, under continued political pressure, finalised the figures at around 8.68–12.4 gm/km for CO and 3.0–4.36 gm/km for HC and NOx according to the cubic capacity of the vehicles.

The Ministry further diluted the standards by replacing the cold start (engine condition when engine is started from cold) emission measurement recommended by the committee with warm start (warm condition of the engine when starting), since the industry was not prepared to adopt the required design changes by 1996. Emissions from vehicles is maximum at cold start or before the engine warms up. But Biswas defends the government's stand. 'The norms were set in accordance with the technical capacity of our industry. This is not adequate but we need to tighten them progressively to give industry some time to adjust.' The industry was allowed four years to adjust to the 1996 norms which came into force in April 1996.

TABLE 4.2 EFFECTS OF VEHICULAR POLLUTANTS ON HUMANS

Substance	Health effects
CO (from gasoline cars, 2–wheelers, 3–wheelers)	Fatal in large doses; aggravates heart disorders; affects central nervous system; impairs oxygen carrying capacity of blood.
NOx (from diesel vehicles)	Irritation of respiratory tract.
Ozone	Eye, nose and throat irritation, risk to asthmatics, children and those involved in heavy exercise.
Lead (from petrol vehicles)	Extremely toxic; affects nervous system and blood; can impair mental development of children, causes hypertension.
HC (mainly from 2–wheelers and 3–wheelers)	Drowsiness, eye irritation, coughing

Benzene	Carcinogenic
Aldehydes	Irritation of eyes, nose and throat, sneezing, coughing, nausea, breathing difficulties, carcinogenic in animals.
PAH (from diesel vehicles)	Carcinogenic

| CO: carbon monooxide | NOx: nitrogen oxides |
| HC: hydrocarbons | PAH: polycyclic aromatic hydrocarbons |

NOTES AND QUESTIONS

1. Why are mobile sources of pollution more difficult to regulate than stationary sources?

2. The principal statutes governing vehicular emissions are the Motor Vehicles Act of 1988 (MVA) and the Central Motor Vehicles Rules of 1989 (MVR) framed under the MVA. The Environment (Protection) Rules of 1986 (EPR) and the Air Act supplement the primary regulations.

The MVA was brought into force on 1 July 1989 repealing the predecessor Act of 1939. Section 110 of the MVA empowers the Central Government to prescribe emission standards for vehicles and to frame rules regulating the construction, equipment and maintenance of motor vehicles in relation to the emission of smoke, visible vapour, sparks, ashes, grit or oil. Any person committing a breach of the prescribed air pollution standards is liable to be punished with a Rs. 1,000 fine for a first offence and a Rs. 2,000 fine for subsequent offences.[75]

Rule 115 of the MVR prescribes nationwide emission levels for both diesel and petrol engine vehicles. Every motor vehicle is required to be maintained and driven so as to comply with the standards prescribed. No distinction is made between old and new vehicles. Rule 115(6) obliges the manufacturer to certify that every new vehicle conforms to the prescribed standards and that the vehicles are designed and constructed to meet these emission levels. Emission standards identical to those described under the MVR have also been issued under the EPR.[76]

Rule 115(7) specifies that year old vehicles must obtain a 'pollution under control' (PUC) certificate issued by the state government's authorised agency. The PUC certificate is required to be produced on demand to the officers referred to in rule 116(1). Each certificate is valid for a period of six months or a shorter period that may be prescribed by the state government.

Rule 115(9) of the MVR lays down 'mass emission standards' which were to

[75] Section 190 (2).
[76] Schedule IV, Environment (Protection) Rules of 1986.

be achieved by 1 April 1996. In the wake of the campaign conducted by citizens' organisations on release of the report *Slow Murder* (excerpted above), the Central Government introduced tougher emission norms for the year 2000.[77]

Rule 116 provides that any officer not below the rank of sub-inspector of police or inspector of motor vehicles may require the driver of a vehicle to get the automobile emissions tested. Where the vehicle does not meet the emission standards, the driver is required to rectify the defect within seven days. The failure to rectify the defects attracts penalties under section 190 (2) of the MVA.

3. The primary agency for enforcement of vehicular emission norms is the state/regional transport authority appointed under the MVA. The EPA adopts a consistent regulatory model. In exercise of its powers under section 10 of the EPA, the Central Government has empowered the state/regional transport authority to inspect motor vehicles and collect samples for the purposes of analysis under the EPA. As we shall see from the cases digested below, the rules to regulate vehicular emissions are mostly ignored or circumvented.

4. Section 17(1)(g) of the Air Act empowers the state boards to lay down standards of air pollutants released by automobiles in consultation with the Central board. Under section 20 of the Act, the state government is required to give necessary instructions to the vehicle registration authority under the MVA to ensure that automobile emission norms are complied with; and the authority is obliged to comply with such instructions.[78]

VEHICULAR POLLUTION CASES

At the time of writing, there is no final judgment delivered in the *Motor Vehicles Case* filed by M.C. Mehta in 1985.[79] In early 1998, the case took an abrupt turn with the Supreme Court welcoming the Central Government's proposal to constitute an authority under section 3 of the Environment (Protection) Act of 1986, to be called the Environment Pollution (Prevention and Control) Authority for the National Capital Region (EPPCA). Acknowledging this step as appropriate and timely, the Supreme Court clarified that the jurisdiction of the new authority would extend to the entire sphere of environmental pollution problems faced by the National Capital Region, not just vehicular emissions.[80]

The constitution of the EPPCA seemed to have come as a relief to the court. Despite numerous orders since early 1991 exerting pressure on the authorities to introduce ameliorative measures, the air pollution problem persisted. In many

---

[77] The Central Motor Vehicles (Amendment) Rules of 1997 introduced the new norms by inserting sub-rule (10) in rule 115. The amendment was notified *vide* GSR 493 (E) dated 28 August 1997.

[78] Dr. Mano Devi, *Air Pollution: Legal Control, Enactment and Enforcement Particularly in Reference to Vehicular Air Pollution in India* (1995) (unpublished manuscript).

[79] *M.C. Mehta v Union of India* Writ Petition (Civil) No. 13029 of 1985.

[80] *M.C. Mehta v Union of India* AIR 1998 SC 617 and 773.

ways, the *Motor Vehicles Case* is the least successful among the major litigations launched by Mehta. There are few tangible gains and a perusal of the orders reveals a colossal waste of judicial time and effort. In shifting responsibility to the EPPCA, the court tacitly recognized that Delhi's dirty air cannot be banished by judicial decree.

The petition when originally filed sought directions to close down hazardous industries located in the densely populated areas in Delhi, to regulate air pollution caused by automobiles operating in the capital and to reduce pollution from the thermal power stations generating energy for the Delhi Electricity Supply Undertaking.[81] However, most of the orders sought in the petition relate to vehicular pollution.

On 14 November 1990, the Union Ministry of Environment acknowledged on affidavit that air pollution in Delhi was chiefly caused by vehicular emissions. The court directed the city administration to place before it a complete list of prosecutions launched against defaulting vehicles and noted that heavy vehicles such as buses and trucks were the main contributing factor to pollution and ought to receive more attention from the authorities. The ministry was also asked to carry out appropriate experiments to test whether a pollution reduction device suggested by the petitioner could be adopted.[82] On 16 January 1991, the Supreme Court permitted the Association of Indian Automobile Manufacturers to intervene in the proceedings.[83] On 12 February 1991, the Additional Solicitor General assured the court that on the next date of hearing he would be able to 'demonstrate with reference to documentary evidence that the Delhi administration and the Union of India are taking effective steps to control pollution in Delhi.'[84] On 19 February 1991, a bench comprising of Chief Justice Ranganath Misra and Justice Kania adjourned the case after a protracted hearing to enable the Attorney General to file a scheme which would lead to setting up a committee for the purpose of controlling air pollution in Delhi.[85]

On 22 February 1991, the case came up before a bench of the Chief Justice and Justice K.N. Saikia. The record of proceedings states that an order adjourning the matter was passed by the court.[86] Justice Saikia retired in the following week, on 1 March 1991.[87]

On 14 March 1991, a bench presided over by the Chief Justice passed an interim order describing the problems of vehicular pollution in Delhi. Confronted by various technical issues that came up during the deliberations at the bar, the court directed the

[81] *M.C. Mehta v Union of India (Vehicular Pollution Case)* 1991 (2) SCC 353.

[82] Writ Petition (Civil) No.13029 of 1985, order dated 14 November 1990.

[83] *Id.*, order dated 16 January 1991.

[84] *Id.*, order dated 12 February 1991.

[85] *Id.*, order dated 19 February 1991.

[86] *Id.*, order dated 22 February 1991.

[87] Ministry of Law and Justice, Government of India, *Judges of the Supreme Court and the High Courts* 131 (1996).

Union Government to set up a high power committee.[88] The terms of reference required the committee:

(i) to make an assessment of the technologies available for vehicular pollution control in the world;

(ii) to make an assessment of the current status of technology available in India for controlling vehicular pollution;

(iii) to look at the low cost alternatives for operating vehicles at reduced pollution levels in the metropolitan cities of India;

(iv) to examine the feasibility of measures to reduce/eliminate pollution from motor vehicles both on short term and long term basis and make appropriate recommendations in this regard;

(v) to make specific recommendations on the administrative/legal resolution required for implementing the recommendations in (iii) above.

Recently retired Justice K.N. Saikia (who in the previous week sat on the bench which heard this case) was appointed as chairman of the committee and the court ordered: 'Shri Justice K.N. Saikia shall be entitled to all the benefits to which a retired judge of this court *while called back to duty is entitled.*'[89] The committee was directed to submit bi-monthly reports in the matter. On 27 March 1991, the Union Government constituted the high power committee.

Over the next several years, the Justice Saikia committee produced mounds of reports running into thousands of pages. The reports are prolix, lack analysis and are frequently little more than a string of quotations interspersed with platitudes. Some of the reports deal with subjects which appear unrelated to the task before the committee. For example, the Sixth Bi-monthly Report contains a tract on the absolute liability principle laid down in the *Shriram Gas Leak Case*,[90] a discussion on the Bhopal Gas Leak disaster[91] and a dissertation on water pollution.[92] It would appear that the committee found time to deliberate on limestone quarrying in the Doon Valley[93] and on why 'Personal Interest Petition cannot be masqueraded as Public Interest Petition by abusing the process of the Court'.[94] The reports also speak of cycling in German towns,[95] the traffic and transport structure in the Netherlands,[96] Mexico's efforts to control pollution,[97]

---

[88] *Supra* note 81. The judgment records that the Union Government agreed to the constitution of the committee for devising methods to solve the air pollution problems in Delhi.

[89] *Id.* at 359. (Emphasis supplied).

[90] Sixth Bi-monthly Report, paras 4.61–4.67; pages 487–530.

[91] *Id.*, para 4.65; page 498.

[92] *Id.*, paras 5.3–5.28; pages 508–551.

[93] *Id.*, para 5.22; pages 538–539.

[94] *Id.*, para 5.50; pages 571–576.

[95] Ninth Bi-monthly Report, para 8.12; pages 779–782.

[96] *Id.*, para 8.23; pages 790–791.

[97] Eighth Bi-monthly Report, para 7.33, pages 685–689.

the energy tax controversy in USA[98] and hi-tech parking garages in Japan.[99] The committee also suggested the best ways to prevent illegal parking in Indian cities.[100] The Supreme Court refers to the committee's junket to Canada,[101] doubtless 'to make an assessment of available world technologies ... by visiting selected countries.'[102]

The Supreme Court hardly ever relied on the Saikia committee reports and references to the reports in the court's orders are rare. Did the committee serve any purpose? Should it have been disbanded within a few months? Is this an instance of wasted public money?

During the course of the litigation, the Supreme Court shifted focus from one scheme to another. In 1990, the emphasis was on the prosecution of defaulters.[103] In 1991, the court was anxious to have buses of the Delhi Transport Corporation converted from diesel to gas operation.[104] In early 1992, the court's attention shifted to bringing down emissions from public buses.[105] Throughout 1994, the court exerted pressure on government to ensure that new vehicles are fitted with catalytic converters and that lead free petrol is introduced in the four metros by April, 1995.[106] Thereafter the court monitored the extension of the unleaded petrol distribution network and obtained assurances from the Centre in respect of reductions in the lead content of petrol and the notification of year 2000 emission norms.[107] In late 1996 and 1997, the Supreme Court pressed the Central Government to convert its vehicles to operate on a cleaner fuel—compressed natural gas (CNG)[108] and also sought technical solutions to reduce harmful emissions from two and three wheelers[109] and diesel trucks and buses.[110]

Shortly after the Supreme Court endorsed the Central Government's decision to set up the EPPCA,[111] the authority headed by Mr. Bhure Lal was constituted on 29 January 1998. There was little progress in the next few months, prompting the Supreme Court to censure the administration:

---

[98] Fifteenth Bi-monthly Report, para 15.45; pages 1048–1049.

[99] Sixteenth Bi-monthly Report, para 16.18; pages 1071–1072.

[100] *Id.* para 16.19; pages 1071–1072.

[101] 1997 (3) SCALE 24 (SP), 25.

[102] First Bi-Monthly Report, page 5.

[103] 1991 (2) SCC 137.

[104] Writ Petition (Civil) No. 13029 of 1985, orders dated 3 October 1991 and 25 October 1991.

[105] *Id.*, order dated 8 January 1992.

[106] Orders dated 12 August 1994; 21 October 1994 and 28 March 1995 reported at 1997 (4) SCALE 4 (SP), 1997 (4) SCALE 5 (SP) and 1997 (4) SCALE 6 (SP).

[107] Order dated 14 February 1996 reported at 1998 (8) SCC 648.

[108] Order dated 26 April 1996 reported at 1997 (4) SCALE 7 (SP).

[109] Orders dated 23 September 1996; 7 October 1996 and 9 December 1996 reported at 1997 (4) SCALE 9 (SP), 1997 (4) SCALE 10 (SP) and 1997 (4) SCALE 11 (SP).

[110] *Supra* note 101.

[111] *Supra* note 80.

We are not satisfied with the performance of the concerned authorities in tackling the acute problem of vehicular pollution and traffic regulations in Delhi. Environmental protection appears to have taken a back seat. In fact, we are distressed to find that the directions given by this Court, from time to time, have not evoked the response they were expected to evoke. ... The directions issued by this Court were aimed at making the state to effectively discharge their obligations. In their response the Delhi Administration and the Union of India have pleaded, among other factors, lack of manpower to deal with the growing menace of chaotic traffic and decline in the environmental quality.[112]

The tone of the order conveys the judges' despair. The bench even considered appointing *court officers* to assist the administration and had to remind the respondents of their obligation to 'act in aid of the Supreme Court', under Article 144 of the Constitution. The EPPCA was directed to submit in ten weeks a report and action plan to curb vehicular pollution.

On 28 July 1998 the court yet again expressed distress at the apathy of the state, but this time followed the litany with sweeping directions to axe New Delhi's obsolete commercial fleet. All commercial vehicles including taxis which were 15 years old were ordered off the road by 2 October 1998. The court also endorsed a time frame fixed by the EPPCA for eliminating leaded petrol; converting autorikshaws, taxis and buses to clean fuels; reducing the age of the commercial fleet; and strengthening the clean-fuel distribution network.[113] It is unclear from the court order whether the age-related embargo had a statutory basis, though section 59 of the Motor Vehicles Act of 1988 (MVA) does empower the Centre to notify age limits for different classes or different types of motor vehicles.[114]

On 16 April 1999, the Supreme Court targetted diesel vehicles, which the EPPCA blamed for more than 90 per cent of the Nitrogen Oxide and respirable particulate matter (RSPM) in Delhi's air. Noting that the California Air Resource Board had on 27 August 1998 formally designated diesel particulate as a toxic air contaminant, and the *amicus curiae's* request to suspend the registration of diesel vehicles in Delhi, the court adjourned the case to 29 April 1999 to consider submissions on the issue.[115]

On the adjourned date a bench headed by Chief Justice A.S. Anand imposed super norms for vehicles registered in the National Capital Region (NCR), which 'appeared appropriate' to the bench.[116] The court required all private vehicles

[112] Order dated 12 May 1998 reported at 1998 (6) SCC 60.

[113] 1998 (6) SCC 63. On 29 September 1998 the court modified the ban order by setting a time frame for a more gradual phase out of old commercial vehicles, AIR 1999 SC 291.

[114] Age limits for tourist vehicles (seven years) and national goods carriers (nine years) are prescribed under rules 82 and 88 of the Central Motor Vehicle Rules of 1989.

[115] 1999 (6) SCC 9.

[116] 1999 (6) SCC 12.

registered after 1 June 1999 to conform to Euro I norms and those registered after 1 April 2000 to meet the Euro II norms. Diesel taxi's were prohibited in the NCR unless they conformed to Euro II norms. The Euro norms are European Community standards that have been enforced across Europe. On 13 May 1999,[117] the court clarified that what it meant by the 'Euro I norms' were the India 2000 norms, notified by the Central Government on 28 August 1997.[118] In other words, the court advanced the statutory emission norms that were to come into effect on 1 April 2000 to 1 June 1999; and introduced more stringent emission standards (Euro II) with effect from 1 April 2000. The Euro II norms were re-christened 'Bharat Stage II' standards by the Central Government and were notified through the Central Motor Vehicles (Third Amendment) Rules of 2000.

What has been gained since the case was filed in 1985? Should the court have been more focused? Should the court have restricted the new emission regime to the NCR or extended it to all polluted metropolitan regions? Should other High Courts follow the lead and prescribe similar technology-forcing deadlines in respect of the polluted cities in their jurisdiction?[119]

Institutionally, each bench of the Supreme Court over a period of several years is likely to have different members with different degrees of interest in a particular environmental problem. The *Motor Vehicles Case* indicates the difficulty of the court's intermittent attempts to oversee a complex problem fraught with political, economic and technological considerations.

The Kerala High Court achieved a more modest agenda in requiring the Kerala government to strictly implement vehicular emission regulations framed under the MVA. The court directed the state to provide a smoke meter and gas analyser at every major town.[120] Similar directions were issued by the Gwalior bench of the Madhya Pradesh High Court.[121]

G. NOISE POLLUTION

Acute exposure to high noise levels and prolonged exposure at lower levels are known to adversely affect the health and social development of exposed persons.

---

[117] 1999 (6) SCC 14.

[118] *Supra* note 77.

[119] The Bombay High Court required compliance with the Euro I norms from 1 January 2000 and the Euro II norms from January 2001 in respect of private (non commercial) vehicles. *Smoke Affected Residents' Forum v Municipal Corporation* Writ Petition No. 1762 of 1999, 17 September 1999. In a later order the court issued comprehensive directions strengthening implementation of the emission norms; enhancing penalties against violators; allowing citizen participation in the PUC testing procedure; and constituting a committee to recommended measures to control vehicular pollution. Order dated 15 December 1999.

[120] *Murali Purshothaman v Union of India* AIR 1993 KER 297.

[121] *Santosh Kumar Gupta v Secy., Ministry of Environment* AIR 1998 MP 43.

The direct physiological effects include a loss of hearing, either temporary or permanent. The non-auditory effects include cardiac ailments, stress and fatigue, and sleep disturbances. Among the psychological effects documented by experts are a lack of concentration, loss of memory and an adverse impact on the education of children. Noise is also suspected of aggravating nausea, headache, insomnia and a loss of appetite.[122]

The Environment (Protection) Act of 1986 (EPA) recognizes noise as an environmental pollutant and empowers the Central Government to frame rules prescribing the maximum permissible limits for noise in different areas.[123] On 14 February 2000, the Centre framed the Noise Pollution (Regulation and Control) Rules. Two types of noise standards are prescribed: Ambient air quality standards in respect of noise[124] and emission limits for designated types of machinery, appliances[125] and fire crackers.[126]

Separate ambient levels are fixed for industrial, commercial and residential areas and silence zones. The prescribed day time levels (6.00 AM to 10.00 PM) are typically ten decibels higher than the corresponding levels for night time. The Noise Rules require the states to designate an authority or officer responsible for maintaining the ambient standards. The designated authority could be the district magistrate or police commissioner or any other official. Rule 3 requires the states to take measures to ensure that ambient air quality standards are met and imposes a duty on local bodies to have regard to noise pollution as a parameter of quality of life while planning development activity. Rule 5 prohibits the use of loudspeakers at night except in a closed premises. Day time use of loudspeakers is allowed after obtaining permission of the authority. The authority has jurisdiction to entertain complaints about excess noise and may issue directions under rule 8 to abate the nuisance. The cases discussed below relate to the period *prior* to the framing of the Noise Rules, 2000.

The emission equipment standards prescribed in Schedule VI of the Environment (Protection) Rules of 1986 relate to motor vehicles, air conditioners, refrigerators, diesel generators for domestic use and certain types of construction equipment.

The 1987 amendments to the Air Act specifically extended the provisions of the Air Act, including increased penalties and the issuance of injunctions by magistrates, to noise pollution. The definition of 'air pollutant' was expanded to include

---

[122] *Report of the Expert Committee on Noise Pollution*, paras 4.1–4.2.4. (1986). The committee was constituted by the Bombay High Court in Writ Petition No. 1879 of 1985 (*Dr. Y.T. Oke v State of Maharashtra*).

[123] Section 6 (2)(b).

[124] Rule 3 of the Noise Rules read with the Schedule to these Rules. Earlier ambient noise levels were prescribed in Schedule III, Environment (Protection) Rules of 1986. This schedule appears to have been impliedly repealed by the Noise Rules of 2000.

[125] Schedule VI, Part E.

[126] Entry 89, Schedule I, Environment (Protection) Rules of 1986.

noise. Besides these central statutes, local municipal legislation and the police Acts also regulate certain types of activity which generates noise. For example, in several states regulations governing the use of loudspeakers are framed under the local police Act.

The High Courts at Bombay and Calcutta have responded energetically to citizens' complaints about noise. On 30 September 1985, Justice Sujata Manohar of the Bombay High Court constituted an expert committee to report on the extent of noise pollution in the city and to recommend steps to improve regulation.[127] The petition was filed by doctors, including Dr. Oke, who were concerned about the adverse health impact on the citizens of Bombay from exposure to high noise levels. The report prepared by the expert committee provides an excellent survey of the problems faced by the citizens in the Greater Bombay area. Noting the recommendations of the expert committee, the High Court disposed of the petition by recording the decision of government to suitably amend existing legislation and to address the concerns expressed by the committee.

Despite these assurances, the Maharashtra government did little to regulate noise, prompting Dr. Oke to file another petition before the High Court in 1995. This time he challenged the loudspeaker rules framed under the Bombay Police Act which permitted the use of loudspeakers contrary to the national ambient air quality levels and the EPA. On 18 December 1995, the High Court ordered:

The potentiality of adverse effects on the human system resulting from prolonged exposure to noise and acute exposure to high noise levels has been established by studies of general population exposed to different levels of noise. Noise is especially troublesome in urban areas. People in or near cities are exposed to loud noise much of the time. Noise causes discomfort in people. It can cause several harmful effects which can be both physiological and psychological. Noise pollution can also cause some adverse sociological and psychological effects. Parliament has, therefore, while enacting the Environment Act, specifically dealt with the aspect of the noise pollution. ...

Considering the [Expert Committee Report of 1986] and the provisions of the Environment Act and Rules framed thereunder for restricting the noise pollutant as provided in Schedule III quoted above, it is the duty of the state government to frame the Rules under the various Acts including the Bombay Police Act in conformity with the said Rules. Section 15 provides for punishment to person or companies for contravention of the provisions of the Environment Act and the Rules. Section 17 provides for punishment of Government department for contravention of the provisions of the Environment Act and the Rules thereunder. It inter alia, provides that where an offence under the Environment Act has been committed by any department of Government, the

---

127 *Supra* note 122.

head of the department shall be deemed to be guilty of the offence and shall be liable to be proceeded against and punished accordingly. Therefore, prima facie it appears that permission for use of loud speakers which results in noise pollution in violation of Rule 3 cannot be granted. Hence, it would be just and proper to direct the respondents to find out and report to this court what actions can be taken under the provisions of the Environment Act and the Rules framed thereunder with regard to noise pollutant in conformity with the Environment Act and the Rules by taking into consideration the Report submitted by the committee appointed by Mrs. Justice Sujata Manohar on Noise Pollution as the said Report has taken into consideration various aspects in various areas on noise pollution of the Bombay city.[128]

The Bombay High Court declined to permit loudspeaker use beyond 11.30 PM during the Ganesh festival and Navratri celebrations. Quoting from an earlier judgment in *State of Bombay v Narasu Appa Mali*,[129] where the court drew a distinction between religious faith and belief and religious practices, as well as the Report on the National Commission on Urbanisation,[130] the court held:

While dealing with a similar application during the Ganesh festival, we have rejected it by our order dated 10th September, 1996 by observing that religious ceremony nowhere provides that on religious festival days loudspeaker is a must without which festivals cannot be observed. For us, it would be difficult to distinguish Ganesh festival from Navratri festival. We note that during Ganesh festival the respondents had taken proper steps for controlling the noise pollution. Therefore, we do not find any justifiable reason to grant permission to use loudspeakers as prayed for during Navratri festival which would result in increase in noise pollution. In any case, there is no question of granting any permission by us or putting an imprint or seal to do something which is in violation of the Environment Act and the Rules. It is for the State Government to implement the said Act and the Rules and prohibit certain activities which adversely affect the lives of persons who cannot oppose the noise pollution for various restraints. It is the duty of the State Government not to encourage the activities which will lead to violation of law. Nobody can object to Navratri festival or any festival for that matter. These festivals can be enjoyed even without loudspeakers. Garba or Dandiya during the Navratri festival without

[128]*Dr. Y.T. Oke v State of Maharashtra* Writ Petition No. 1732 of 1995, Bombay High Court, 18 December 1995.

[129]AIR 1952 BOM 82. 'A sharp distinction must between drawn between religious faith and belief and religious practices. What the state protects is religious faith and belief. If religious practices run counter to public order, morality or health or a policy of social welfare upon which the state has embarked, then the religious practice must give way before the good of the people of the state as a whole.'

[130] *Report of the National Commission on Urbanisation* , Vol. II, para 14.4.3. (1988).

noise pollution by the loudspeaker were played in the recent past and can be played without use of loudspeaker.

Hence, the State Government would take appropriate steps to control noise pollution created by loudspeakers during these festivals and protect the silent sufferers [who] may be students, old, infirm or others not interested. It is for the State to implement the law as it is.[131]

The Kerala High Court in *P.A. Jacob v Superintendent of Police*,[132] grappled with loudspeakers. The court held that the fundamental right to freedom of speech guaranteed under Article 19(1)(a) of the Constitution did not include the right to use a loudspeaker. The petitioner sought permission to use loudspeakers at a public meeting where he proposed to denounce the practice of an orthodox Christian sect which barred its members from marrying outside their denomination. When the sub-inspector of police withdrew loudspeaker permission, apprehending that the petitioner's view may cause public disorder, the petitioner moved the Kerala High Court. Justice Sankaran Nair's judgment reviewed in depth the authorities on freedom of speech and then discussed the right of the unwilling listener:

Apart from the right to be let alone,—freedom from aural aggression—Article 21 guarantees freedom from tormenting sounds. What is negatively the right to be left alone, is positively the right to be free from noise. Exposure to high noise, is a known risk and it is proved to cause bio-chemical changes in man, elevating levels of blood catecholamine, cholesterol, white cell counts and lymphocytes. Laboratory studies made by monitoring electroencephalographic (EEG) responses and changes in neurovegetative reactions during sleep, show that disturbance of sleep becomes increasingly apparent as ambient noise levels exceed about 35 db (A). ... Sound levels generally caused by loudspeakers transgress safe limits by a wide margin. Loudspeakers have become part of political, social, religious and cultural life of this country. To allow advocates of various persuasions to commit unlimited aural aggression on unwilling listeners, would be to allow them to subjugate the right of life of unwilling listeners, to their aggressions. Protests made by sufferers like the student community or sick, generally fall on heedless ears.

Finding that the authority had acted arbitrarily in refusing permission, the court held that the petitioner would be permitted to avail of loudspeakers in a reasonable manner so long as the output from the loudspeakers was modulated and reasonable. In an earlier case, Justice Nair declined to issue a mandamus to compel the respondents to grant loudspeaker permission, recognising that noise pollution was

---

[131] *Supra* note 128, order dated 11 October 1996.
[132] AIR 1993 KER 1.

an accepted danger and the indiscriminate use of loudspeakers could not be permitted.[133]

The approach of the Kerala High Court to loudspeakers has varied from case to case, with permission being granted to the Guruvayur temple management to use loudspeakers,[134] but a prohibition being imposed in respect of loudspeaker use at a congested junction.[135]

The Calcutta High Court was among the first to tackle public interest issues relating to noise. In *Rabin Mukherjee v State of West Bengal*,[136] the High Court recognized the nuisance created by noisy electric and air horns used in buses and trucks. The court directed the transport authorities to strictly enforce the provisions of the Motor Vehicles Act and the Bengal Motor Vehicle Rules which restricted the use of loud and shrill horns.

In 1996, the Calcutta High Court clamped down on the indiscriminate use of microphones and loudspeakers. In *Birangana Religious Society v The State*,[137] Justice Bhagabati Prosad Banerjee considered an application by a religious organization which was aggrieved by the respondents' refusal to permit microphones and loudspeakers during the daily poojas and other religious activities. The petitioners prayed for a mandamus directing the district magistrate to accord the necessary permission under the Police Act. Justice Banerjee used the case to frame detailed guidelines for the issue of loudspeaker permits and asked the authorities to accord permissions in accordance with the guidelines. The court directed the West Bengal pollution control board to maintain noise level registers; prohibited the use of loudspeakers between 9.00 PM and 7.00 AM; and required the authorities to calibrate and seal the apparatus amplifying the sound so that the noise did not exceed the prescribed limit. In the course of his judgment, Justice Banerjee recognized that every citizen has a right to leisure, a right to sleep, and a right *not* to hear. Noise generated from loudspeakers and microphones posed a serious threat to public health. Building on the principal order, the High Court proceeded to tone up the administration. In July 1996, Justice Banerjee urged the West Bengal government to sanction more posts so that the pollution control board had adequate personnel to effectively discharge their functions under the court order. The court also urged the police to be vigilant in the discharge of its duties and directed All India Radio and Doordarshan to disseminate information and create awareness on the harmful effects of noise pollution.[138]

Thereafter, taking judicial notice of complaints from the districts outside

---

[133] *Venu v Director General of Police* 1992 (2) KER L.T.86.

[134] *Chairman, Guruvayur D.M.C. v Superintendent of Police* AIR 1998 KER 122.

[135] *New Road Brothers v Commissioner of Police* AIR 1999 KER 262.

[136] AIR 1985 CAL 222.

[137] (1996) 100 CWN 617. C.O.No. 4303 (W) of 1995, 1 April 1996.

[138] *Id.*, order dated 23 July 1996. In a subsequent order passed in February 1997, the court urged all medias and newspapers to publish information regarding the method of lodging complaints with the pollution control board.

Calcutta, the court directed the district police authorities to strictly administer the judicial norms. The board was asked to devise suitable measures to regulate the noise from electric and air horns of public vehicles, fireworks and other sources of noise pollution.[139] When organizers of Durga Pooja festivities and hotels were found to have breached court orders, contempt proceedings were initiated against them. Generally, the contempt proceedings were dropped after securing an undertaking of good future behaviour and a goodwill contribution in favour of the West Bengal pollution control board.[140]

The Calcutta High Court quelled the clamour raised by the organizers of religious gatherings thus:

It is made clear that the effect of the judgment and order passed by this Court is to be followed by all sections of people including people of all communities irrespective of caste, creed and religion. In the parent order it was provided that the right to propagate one's religion means the right to communicate a person's belief to another or to expose the tenets of that faith. But, the right to propagate religion includes the right to use the loudspeakers and microphones for the purpose of granting religious tenet or religious texts also implies the duties not to indiscriminately use the microphone or loudspeakers during religious performance in the society by any religion. One can practice, profess and propagate religion as granted under Article 25 (1) of the Constitution, but that is not an absolute right, it cannot be said that a citizen should be coerced to hear anything which he does not like or which he does not require.

Accordingly, the Pollution Control Board is directed to issue notices to the District Magistrate, Superintendent of Police in the districts and the Commissioner of Police at Calcutta to take steps for controlling noise levels and/or restricting the noise level in the temples, mosques and churches, gurudwaras and/or other religious place at the time of religious functions which is a rising phenomenon and is creating sound pollution violating the permissible noise level. It is made clear that India being a secular State, the order passed by this Court should be complied with by all irrespective of caste, creed and religion and not by any particular community, otherwise it will be a discriminatory treatment which is not the intention of this Court. Steps should be taken in this regard so that the sound generated in the temples, mosques, churches or gurudwaras, etc. does not flow beyond the vicinity of such religious place.[141]

Referring to the national ambient noise levels prescribed under the Environment (Protection) Rules of 1986, the court directed the pollution control board to monitor

[139] *Id.*, order dated 30 September 1997.

[140] *Id.*, orders dated 9 January 1997 and 16 January 1997. The contributions ranged between Rs. 5000 and Rs. 25,000.

[141] *Id.*, order dated 29 November 1996.

noise levels at different parts of the city and directed the police to strictly enforce the provisions relating to silence zones.

On 3 March 1997, the High Court banned the use of microphones and loudspeakers around schools and colleges in Calcutta and any district of the state during the school board examinations. Moreover, during this period, the use of microphones in the entire state was prohibited between 6.00 PM and 7.00 AM.

Meanwhile, spurred by the directions issued on 30 September 1997,[142] the police prevented the sale of firecrackers which emanated noise exceeding 65 decibels. In a petition filed by the fire works dealers, the High Court declined relief since no person had a right to manufacture or sell fireworks that created sound beyond the ambient noise levels prescribed under the Environment (Protection) Act of 1986.[143] The Supreme Court approved the view taken by the High Court while dismissing a special leave filed by an aggrieved fire works dealer.[144] But the fire works dealers were quick to strike back. They successfully lobbied the Union Ministry of Environment and Forests to amend Schedule I to the Environment (Protection) Rules, 1986 by introducing statutory noise standards for fire crackers that allow noise levels up to 125 decibels.[145]

A division bench headed by Justice Banerjee in *Maulana Mufti Syed Barkati v State of West Bengal*,[146] repelled a challenge to the restrictions on loudspeakers imposed by the state between 9:00 PM and 7:00 AM. The petitioners assailed the restrictions on the ground that they violated their fundamental right to freedom of religion guaranteed under Article 25 of the Constitution. The petitioners claimed that Azan, which was integral to Islam was required to be called five times a day through loudspeakers. Without loudspeakers, it was not possible to reach the voice of Azan to the believers of Islam. The High Court dismissed the petition, holding that the use of loudspeakers was a technological development and was not a part of Islam.

Amidst the growing anti-noise jurisprudence, the Gujarat High Court struck a discordant note in *New GIDC Housing Association v State of Gujarat*.[147] The court dismissed a writ petition filed by a housing colony complaining about the noise pollution caused by an iron and steel factory. Since, the housing colony was located within the industrial estate, and was established after the factory, the court accepted the company's plea that the residents having 'come to the nuisance', could not be heard to complain. The High Court noted the ambient air quality standard prescribed

---

[142] *Supra* note 139.

[143] *Burrabazar Fire Works Dealers v Commissioner of Police* AIR 1998 CAL 121.

[144] Order dated 12 January 1998 in a petition filed by Mohan Fire Works. The order is reproduced in *Maulana Mufti Syed Barkati v State of West Bengal* AIR 1999 CAL 15, 26.

[145] Entry 89, Schedule I was inserted *vide* the Environment (Protection) (Second Amendment) Rules of 1999. The Kerala High Court considered these standards in *Anand Parthasarthy v State of Kerala* O.P. Nos. 11016 & 26161 of 1998, 1 December 1999. The division bench directed strict implementation of the norms and suggested that 'separate courts regarding noise pollution may be established'.

[146] AIR 1999 CAL 15.

[147] 1997 (2) GUJ.L.HER.221.

in Schedule III to the Environment (Protection) Rules of 1986 but erroneously declined to enforce these standards. Apparently, the purpose behind ambient air quality standards was not explained to the High Court, which could not appreciate where the ambient noise was to be measured. Unlike noise emission standards which mention the distance from which the noise level is to be measured, ambient levels should obtain throughout the area (irrespective of the distance from the source of the noise). The High Court ought to have directed the Gujarat pollution control board to measure whether the ambient noise levels around the housing colony were within the industrial zone levels under Schedule III. If the levels exceeded the norms, the company may have been required to abate noise from its factory. Quite possibly, the High Court was influenced by the importance of the iron and steel factory.

In *Fali Kumana v Municipal Corporation of Greater Bombay*,[148] the Bombay High Court directed the respondent telephone company to 'utilize the *best available technology* in the country for controlling the noise pollution' caused by the noisy airconditioning units installed at the telephone exchange.

[148] Writ Petition No. 2390 of 1996, 10 August 1998.

7

FORESTS

Despite recent efforts to increase forest cover through reforestation, India's forests are in a devastated condition, with less than 18 per cent of India under forest cover in 1997.[1] To ensure ecological stability, 30 per cent of the nation should be under adequate forest cover. Some of the domestic consequences of deforestation, particularly with regard to disrupted river flows, flooding, and drought, have been alluded to elsewhere in this book. Others, such as wildlife extinction, displacement of forest dwellers, and scarcity of forest products on which the survival of many depends, will be discussed in this and the next chapter. Still others of global proportion, such as climate change, desertification, and ozone depletion, are issues that have received international attention; however, comprehensive coverage of these latter consequences is beyond the scope of this book.

All sectors of the economy make demands on forest resources. Forest land is sacrificed for massive development projects, such as the Narmada Valley Project and the Tehri Project discussed in a later chapter. Large industrial interests use forests as the source of raw material for paper, pulp, and rayon mills. Export of timber products generate foreign revenue. Small businesses depend on forests as the source of wood for a myriad products. Almost half of the nation's city dwellers depend on firewood brought in from the forests for cooking fuel. Forests are crucial to many rural people, particularly tribal communities, as a source of fuel, fodder, building materials and minor forest products. In addition, these people traditionally use the forests as their homes, either permanently or seasonally. Forests and wildlife parks also generate tourist income. Finally, forests serve as a source of emotional and spiritual renewal for visitors from India and all over the world.

That some uses are incompatible with others is exemplified by both

[1] Reply by the Union Minister of Environment and Forests to Rajya Sabha. Unstarred Question No. 2673 answered on 24 March 1998. The question was on the status of forests in India. Dense forests cover only 12 per cent of the land. Centre for Science and Environment, *State of India's Environment: The Citizens' Fifth Report*, 111 (1999).

commercial logging and industrial strip mining on forested land. Such logging or mining destroys the integrity of the forest ecosystem, upon which both endangered wildlife and forest dwellers depend. Soil stability is lost. The resulting erosion and runoff lead to flooding and siltation of water courses, reservoirs and irrigation channels. Given the breadth of demands on India's forests, it is not surprising that the problem of deforestation has gained significant public attention, and that implementation of conservation and afforestation programmes has sparked intense controversy.

The most decisive and influential judicial intervention in the environmental field is the ongoing *Forest Conservation Case*.[2] The orders in this case form the core of this chapter. Before turning to this case, we outline the evolution of national forest policy, touching upon the gaps between the declared government objective and the field reality. We also examine the legal controversy of mining and other industrial uses on forest land, focusing on the *Dehradun Valley* litigation.[3] We then turn to the rights of forest dwellers in India—often tribals or indigenous people who have been offered scant legal protection. Notes and questions to more fully flesh out the issues and prompt further reflection are interspersed throughout the chapter.

A. FOREST LAWS AND POLICY

When India gained independence, forests were placed on the State List of the Constitution. Forest departments of individual states continued to regulate forests in accord with the Indian Forest Act of 1927, as implemented by state regulations. The Indian Forest Act gives the states jurisdiction over both public and private forests and facilitates the extraction of timber for profit. Public forests, those in which state governments have a proprietary interest, are divided into three categories: reserve forests, village forests and protected forests.

Forest land or wasteland may be notified as a reserve forest by a state government's declaration in the official gazette.[4] Previously recognized individual and community rights over the forest are extinguished upon such a notification[5] and access to the forest and forest products becomes a matter of privilege, subject to permission of forest officials acting under governing laws and regulations.[6] The Act includes procedures for making claims against the government for the loss of legal rights over the forest.

Village forests are established when a state assigns to a village-community the

---

[2] *T.N. Godavarman Thirumulkpad v Union of India* AIR 1997 SC 1228; AIR 1998 SC 769 and AIR 1999 SC 97.

[3] *Rural Litigation and Entitlement Kendra, Dehradun v State of Uttar Pradesh* AIR 1985 SC 652.

[4] Section 4.

[5] Section 9.

[6] Section 15.

rights over any land which has been constituted a reserve forest.[7] State governments make rules for managing the village forest and prescribe conditions under which the village community is provided with timber, other forest products or pasture. The rules may also assign duties to the village for the protection and improvement of the forest.[8]

State governments may designate as a protected forest any forest or wasteland in which the government has proprietary right or rights to any part of the forest's products.[9] Protected forests cannot be created from reserve forests.[10] The government must survey the rights and claims of private persons in forests being considered for protection but may declare the forest area a protected forest pending completion of the survey.[11] The Act authorizes state governments to close portions of the forests as long as the remainder of the forest is sufficient for individuals and communities to exercise their existing legal rights to use the forest.[12] State governments may prohibit certain activities such as grazing, cultivation, charcoal burning and stone quarrying.[13] The state government may also regulate all rights and privileges for use of the protected forest.[14]

In extending to forest lands which are not the property of the government,[15] the Indian Forest Act represents strong governmental intrusion into private rights. State governments may regulate timber cutting, cultivation, grazing and burning or clearing of vegetation on private forest land.[16] The Act also authorizes state governments to acquire private land for public purposes under the Land Acquisition Act of 1894.[17]

Countering governmental powers under the Act, the Indian Forest Act also provides protection and compensation for legally recognized individual or community rights to forest land or forest products. However, for most forest dwellers, particularly tribal people,[18] the crucial issue is not the *protection* of recognized legal rights but rather the threshold issue of *recognition* of legal rights over forests.

---

[7] Section 28.
[8] *Id.*
[9] Section 29.
[10] *Id.*
[11] *Id.*
[12] Section 30.
[13] *Id.*
[14] Section 31.
[15] Chapter V.
[16] Section 35.
[17] Section 37.
[18] Because of the diversity of racial origins, languages, and economic conditions, the exact description of 'tribal' people is impossible. Scholars have suggested numerous functional definitions of tribal people, most of which include cultural or racial distinctions and a lack of integration into the nation's predominant economic and political institutions. Legally, the Constitution incorporates the recognition of tribal people through the notion of 'Scheduled Tribes.' Under Article 342, the President of India, subject to review and modification by Parliament, may designate any tribe or tribal community or group within any tribe or tribal community as a Scheduled Tribe for purposes of the Constitution. About 40 million people in India are classified as tribal people. For more detailed descriptions of

The debate over how to balance the various demands of the nation on the forests intensified in the 1970s. The Forty-Second Amendment Act of 1976 transferred forests from the State List to the Concurrent List of the Constitution. This transfer empowered the Central Government to act directly in managing India's forests. The Ministry of Environment and Forests now has administrative jurisdiction over national forest policy, forestry development and the Indian Forest Service. Since 1976, the Central Government has taken three major actions with regard to forests: the Forest (Conservation) Act of 1980, an amendment in 1988 of this Act, and the adoption of a revised National Forest Policy in 1988.

The 1980 Act was Parliament's response to the rapid decline in forest cover. Until then, deforestation averaged 1 million hectares a year.[19] The Act prohibits the deletion of a reserved forest, or the diversion of forest land for any 'non-forest' purpose, and prevents the cutting of trees in a forest without the prior approval of the Central Government.[20] Contravention of the Act attracts up to 15 days in prison.[21]

The framework provided by the Indian Forest Act of 1927 continues to guide the forest bureaucracy to this day. This has meant that shifts in government policy since the colonial period have largely remained on paper. Moreover, the centralized policing regime under the 1980 Act undermines the 1988 policy to encourage local participation in forest management. This policy–law hiatus is explored in Kanchan Chopra's article below.

CHOPRA; FOREST AND OTHER SECTORS: CRITICAL ROLE OF GOVERNMENT POLICY, Economic and Political Weekly, 24 June 1995, p. 1480

The period up to the 1980s was marked by long sub-periods of comparative stability in policy. Two major policy statements appeared during this time, statements purporting to give direction to the role of the government in relation to the alternate functions performed by forests: the statements of 1894 and 1952. In practice, it was the Forest Act of 1927 that charted the course for much of the period.

Assertion of central control and emphasis on the role of forests as providers of timber and industrial raw material is the common thread running through these major statements of policy. A reading of the fine print suggests however, a shift in focus between different statements. The 1894 policy, when viewed as a policy enunciated by a colonial government, is surprisingly broad-based and capable of interpretation to suit local interests. The role of forests as essential on climatic and ecological grounds is

---

India's tribal people. For more detailed description, see N. Hasnain, *Tribal India Today* (1983); and C. von Furer-Haimendorf, *Tribes of India* (1982).

[19] World Bank, *India: Forest Sector Review* (1993). Between 1987 and 1989, a quarter million hectares of forests were lost. Society for the Promotion of Wasteland Development, *Need for Increased Funding for Forests* (1991).

[20] Section 2.

[21] Section 39.

realized, the significance of local user's rights is also pointed out. Note for instance the following, 'no restriction should be placed upon local demands merely in order to increase state revenue'. Also note, 'And, in the fourth place, cultivation must not be allowed to extend so as to encroach on the minimum area of forest which is required in order to supply the general forest needs of the country or the reasonable forest requirements of the neighbourhood in which it is situated.' With regard to pastures and grazing lands, it is stated 'it will generally be possible to lease or otherwise manage the unoccupied lands of a village through the agency of the village community ... at a moderate estimate of their value to them ...' Though the purpose of such concessions was stated to be the furtherance of cultivation, they nevertheless existed.

The most explicit shift in emphasis in the post-independence declared 1952 policy statement was with respect to the claims of communities living near forests. Referring to the claims of such communities, it is stated that 'local use should at no event be permitted at the cost of national interests' and that 'national interests should not be sacrificed because they are not greatly discernible'. While the protective and productive aspects of forests are referred to and the needs of future generations also receive a mention, the production of good timber in the national interest receives priority. 'Each type of land is to be allotted to that form of use under which it produces the most and deteriorates the least'. With a number of decades of scientific forestry behind it, the government's view of production was, fairly obviously, timber production.

A hiatus is bound to exist between the intent of a policy and its functioning. The nature and magnitude of such a hiatus depends on the awareness of the population and the countervailing power that it is able to exert. Evidence does exist of collective action and protest. It was intermingled with political protest and interpreted as such. In the absence of pronounced grass roots activity, the actual working of the policy at the practical level throughout much of the period up to the late 1970s and early 1980s continued to be governed by the Forest Act of 1927 and the corresponding state acts. The growing needs of industry and the centralized exercise of state power were the focal driving forces of this implementation of policy.

The declaration of a National Forest Policy in 1988 was the consequence of a number of factors. Local needs had grown with population and with no visible alternative to meet the fuel and fodder requirements emerging in large parts of the country. The post-independence environment, together with this pressure of local needs and support of some enlightened foresters result in the emergence of forest protection groups first in West Bengal and then in a number of other states. The apparent failure of policing of forests as a policy, the emergence of 'participation' as an almost unavoidable policy option and the increasingly significant countervailing power exercised by these local level groups resulted in the declaration of a new policy initiative in 1988.

The 1988 policy gave new direction in important areas. It emphasized the environmental protection and conservation role of forests, stated that organized industry must meet its needs from private lands and asked for an increase in participatory management of forests. In a sense, it constituted a small beginning in trying to create an enabling rather than a policing role for government. This general direction was pursued further in the form of the issue of a circular from the ministry of environment and forests to state forest secretaries in June 1990 providing guidelines for the involvement of village communities and voluntary agencies in the regeneration of degraded forests. Following this several state governments issued orders on joint forest management.

The National Forest Policy of 1988 also laid down that forest-based industry should meet its raw material needs by establishing a direct relationship with farmers rather than depending on forests, which would henceforth be maintained primarily for ecological functions and for meeting the subsistence needs of the people. It seemed that a two-pronged strategy with reliance on the market and on local institutions for alternative needs was to be followed.

* * *

The new thrust of forest policy was to be a stress on multiple products and ecological functions with local control replacing central control. The amended Forest Conservation Act belies any such hopes as a number of its provisions seem to contradict the provision of the Forest Policy. Note, for instance, the following:

(a) The prohibition on the plantation of horticultural crops which includes palms, oil-bearing and medicinal plants on forest lands, without prior permission of the government of India. While this may be good for banning some kinds of crops in forests, it could give rise to the suspicion that all usufruct trees, such as 'ber', 'mahua' and other medicinal herbs are to be limited.

(b) The ban on assignment or lease of forest land to people or institutions not wholly owned by government. The contradiction between this provision and the move towards participatory management is clear.

(c) The provision for distribution of minor forest products and other materials through depots at reasonable prices. This again brings in a centralized policing role for government.

(d) Introduction of regulations to govern the felling of trees on private holdings. This provision will come in the way of tree farming by farmers which was to provide for the needs of industry as per the Forest Policy of 1988.

NOTES AND QUESTIONS

1. The National Forest Policy was adopted by Parliament in 1988 shortly before the passage of the amendment to the Forest (Conservation) Act (FCA). Should judges use the policy statement to interpret the statute?

2. Activists working among tribal communities argue that the amended FCA prevents the restoration of degraded lands and watershed development. While the policy resolution encourages tree farming and plantations in degraded lands, the 1988 amendment prohibits the leasing of such lands to any non-government agency, except with the prior approval of the Central Government. Field workers complain that while the Centre routinely grants clearance to mega-projects involving the large scale destruction of natural forests, small projects directly benefiting forest dwellers are seldom permitted. Is the policy statement's concern for tribal welfare an eyewash?

B. THE FOREST CONSERVATION CASE

Beginning December, 1996 the Supreme Court issued sweeping directives to oversee the enforcement of forest laws across the nation. Assisted by an *amicus curiae* the court froze all wood-based industrial activity, reinforced the scope of the embargo on forest exploitation, issued detailed directions for the sustainable use of forests and created its own monitoring and implementation machinery through regional and state level committees. The case has no parallel, even by the expansive standards of India's pro-active judiciary. As we shall see, the court assumes the role of a super-administrator, regulating the felling, use and movement of timber across the country in the hope of preserving the nation's forests. There are a number of orders in the case and we excerpt from four principal orders dated 12 December 1996; 4 March 1997; 8 May 1997 and 15 January 1998.[22] The analysis that follows these excerpts focuses on the issues impacting the North-East region where the wood-based industry contributes substantially to the region's economy.

T.N. GODAVARMAN THIRUMULKPAD v UNION OF INDIA
AIR 1997 SC 1228

ORDER: * * *

After hearing all the learned counsel, who have rendered very able assistance to the Court, we have formed the opinion that the matters require a further indepth hearing to examine all the aspects relating to the National Forest Policy.

It has emerged at the hearing that there is a misconception in certain quarters about the true scope of the Forest Conservation Act, 1980 (for short the Act) and the meaning of the word 'forest' used therein. There is also a resulting misconception about the need of prior approval of the Central Government, as required by Section 2 of the Act, in respect of certain activities in the forest area which are more often of a commercial nature. It is necessary to clarify that position.

The Forest Conservation Act, 1980 was enacted with a view to check further deforestation which ultimately results in ecological imbalance; and therefore, the provisions made therein for the conservation of forests and for matters connected

---

[22] Some of the other orders in *T.N. Godavarman Thirumulkpad v Union of India* are 14 July 1997, 1997 (5) SCALE 2 (SP); 7 January 1998, AIR 1999 SC 97; 13 January 1998, 1998 (5) SCALE 8 (SP); 14 January 1998, 1998 (5) SCALE 10 (SP); 23 January 1998, 1998 (5) SCALE 11; 29 January 1998, 1998 (2) SCALE 5 (SP); 23 February 1998; AIR 1999 SC 43; 15 April 1998, 1998 (5) SCALE 13 (SP); 5 May 1998, 1999 (1) SCC 210; 16 July 1998, 1998 (5) SCALE 17 (SP); 21 July 1998, 1998 (4) SCALE 3 (SP); 28 July 1998, 1998 (5) SCALE 18 (SP); 29 July 1998, 1998 (4) SCALE 4 (SP); 17 August 1998, 1998 (4) SCALE 6 (SP); 10 September 1998, 1998 (5) SCALE 21 (SP); 17 September 1998, 1998 (6) SCALE 289; 10 December 1998, 1998 (6) SCALE 17 (SP); 20 January 1999, 1999 (1) SCALE 466 and 467; 16 April 1999, 1999 (5) SCC 736; 7 May 1999, 1999 (4) SCALE 12; 2 August 1999, 1999 (5) SCALE 187; 16 August 1999, 1999 (5) SCALE 189; 27 August 1999, 1999 (5) SCALE 422; and 6 September 1999, 1999 (5) SCALE 423; 17 December 1999, 2000 (1) SCALE 71; 13 January 2000, 2000 (1) SCALE 412; and 11 May 2000, 2000 (5) SCALE 125.

therewith, must apply to all forest irrespective of the nature of ownership or classification thereof. The word 'forest' must be understood according to its dictionary meaning. This description covers all statutorily recognised forests, whether designated as reserved, protected or otherwise for the purpose of Section 2(i) of the Forest Conservation Act. The term 'forest land', occurring in Section 2, will not only include 'forest' as understood in the dictionary sense, but also any area recorded as forest in the Government record irrespective of the ownership. This is how it has to be understood for the purpose of Section 2 of the Act. The provisions enacted in the Forest Conservation Act, 1980 for the conservation of forests and the matters concerned therewith must apply clearly to all forests so understood irrespective of the ownership or classification thereof. * * * This has become necessary also because of the stand taken on behalf of the State of Rajasthan, even at this late stage, relating to permissions granted for mining in such area which is clearly contrary to the decisions of this Court. It is reasonable to assume that any state government which had failed to appreciate the correct position in law so far, will forthwith correct its stance and take necessary remedial measures without any further delay.

We further direct as under:

I. General:

1. In view of the meaning of the word 'forest' in the Act, it is obvious that prior approval of the Central Government is required for any non-forest activity within the area of any 'forest'. In accordance with Section 2 of the Act, all on-going activity within any forest in any State throughout the country, without the prior approval of the Central Government, must cease forthwith. It is, therefore, clear that the running of saw mills of any kind including veneer or ply-wood mills, and mining of any mineral are non-forest purposes and are, therefore, not permissible without prior approval of the Central Government. Accordingly, any such activity is *prima facie* violation of the provisions of the Forest Conservation Act, 1980. Every state government must promptly ensure total cessation of all such activities forthwith.

2. In addition to the above, in the tropical wet ever-green forests of Tirap and Changlang in the State of Arunachal Pradesh, there would be a complete ban on felling of any kind of trees therein because of their particular significance to maintain ecological balance needed to preserve bio-diversity. All saw mills, veneer mills and ply wood mills in Tirap and Changlang in Arunachal Pradesh and within a distance of 100 kms from its border, in Assam, should also be closed immediately. The state governments of Arunachal Pradesh and Assam must ensure compliance of this direction.

3. The felling of trees in all forests is to remain suspended except in accordance with the Working Plans of the state governments, as approved by the Central Government. In the absence of any Working Plan in any particular state, such as Arunachal Pradesh, where the permit system exists, the felling under the permits can be done only by the Forest Department of the state government or the State Forest Corporation.

4. There shall be a complete ban on the movement of cut trees and timber from any of the seven north-eastern states to any other state of the country either by rail, road or water-ways. The Indian Railways and the state governments are

directed to take all measures necessary to ensure strict compliance of this direction. This ban will not apply to the movement of certified timber required for defence or other Government purposes. This ban will also not affect felling in any private plantation comprising of trees planted in any area which is not a forest.

[Directions specific to the States of Jammu and Kashmir, Himachal Pradesh, Uttar Pradesh, and West Bengal and Tamil Nadu are omitted.]

We also direct that notwithstanding the closure of any saw mills or other wood-based industry pursuant to this order, the workers employed in such units will continue to be paid their full emoluments due and shall not be retrenched or removed from service for this reason.

We are informed that the Railway authorities are still using wooden sleepers for laying tracks. The Ministry of Railways will file an affidavit giving full particulars in this regard including the extent of wood consumed by them, the source of supply of wood, and the steps taken by them to find alternatives to the use of wood.

* * *

T.N. GODAVARMAN THIRUMULKPAD v UNION OF INDIA
AIR 1997 SC 1233

ORDER: * * *

We are satisfied that there is need to constitute a High Power Committee to oversee the strict and faithful implementation of the orders of this Court in the North-Eastern region and for certain ancillary purposes. Accordingly we direct as under. [The court constituted the High Power Committee (HPC) and directed it to prepare an inventory of timber and timber products lying in the forests, transport depots and mills in the region. The HPC was empowered to permit the use or sale of timber products if it considered appropriate through the State Forest Corporation. Pending the final hearing, the expenses relating to the HPC were to be borne by the Central and State Governments.]

All unlicensed saw mills, veneer and plywood industries in the State of Maharashtra and the State of Uttar Pradesh are to be closed forthwith and the state governments would not remove or relax the condition for grant of permission/licence for the opening of any such saw mill, veneer and plywood industry and it shall also not grant any fresh permission/licence for this purpose. The Chief Secretary of the State will ensure strict compliance of this direction and file a compliance report within two weeks.

* * *

It is made clear that the orders passed by this Court in these matters, including the order dated 12–12–1996 [AIR 1997 SC 1228] and the present order shall be obeyed and carried out by the Union Government as well as the State Government notwithstanding any order of direction passed by a Court, including a High Court or Tribunal, to the contrary.

We further direct the Registrar General to communicate the order dated 12–12–1996 as well as the present order to the Registrars of all the High Courts to ensure strict compliance. It is also clarified that the orders passed by this Court including the order dated 12–12–1996 and this order will apply to all Autonomous Hill Councils in the north-eastern states as well as the union territories.

It is made clear that all the concerned authorities would, in the meantime, continue to examine the various aspects of the problems requiring solution and try to solve these problems in collaboration with the Central Government and the state governments. An efficacious exercise of this kind would enable reduction of the area which may require judicial scrutiny and adjudication in these matters.

[The court clarified/modified its previous order. The directions were not to apply to minor forest produce, including bamboo; plantations were permitted to fell fuel trees; and the golf courses at Kodaikanal and Udagamandalam were allowed to function until permission from the Union Government was received.]

T.N. GODAVARMAN THIRUMULKPAD v UNION OF INDIA
1997 (7) SCC 440

ORDER: * * *

In relation to the seven north-eastern states, it is further directed as under:

(a) The ban on felling and transportation of trees and timber as already imposed shall continue.

(b) As directed by the High-Powered Committee (HPC), the State Government shall take all measures necessary to bring the felled timber lying in the forest to the depots/storage points, and have it stacked.

(c) After the process of inventorisation is over, the HPC may permit saw mills and other wood-based industry to utilise their own legitimate stocks of timber for conversion into finished produce. Such finished produce may then be disposed of by these mills under supervision of the HPC and the State Forest Department. The permission granted by the HPC to these mills shall be on suitable terms to ensure that no malpractice occurs in the future, and the mills shall be required to file an undertaking to comply with such terms, any breach thereof having the same consequence as a breach of the order of this Court.

(d) After the inventory of the felled timber gathered at the depots/storage points is complete, the HPC may permit sale of such rounded timber for utilization within the state to the extent it is from a lawful source. The movement of rounded timber within the state as well as the movement of rounded timber within and outside the state shall be under transit passes—the issuance and disposal of which will be under the overall supervision of the HPC.

(e) No person other than a local inhabitant, a Forest Officer or Police Officer or any other personnel on official duty shall be permitted to enter the reserved forests except in accordance with permission in writing issued by the Principal Chief Conservator of Forests.

(f)   The ban on movement of cut trees, timber or veneer from any of the seven north-
      eastern states to any other state in the country in any manner applies also to the
      growth and/or felled timber from any private plantation.

* * *

T.N. GODAVARMAN THIRUMULKPAD v UNION OF INDIA

AIR 1998 SC 769

ORDER: * * *

Learned Attorney General submits that the perception of the Ministry of Environment
and Forests (MoEF) is as under:

1. It has been estimated by the HPC that about 1.20 lakhs cubic metres of
illicitly felled seized timber, belonging to the state governments is lying in the forests
and depots for varying periods of time between 1 to 2 years and is thereby getting
degraded on account of decay and rotting of the wood. It is necessary to dispose it off
at the earliest to minimise any further loss in its monetary value. There is, in addition,
considerable quantity of timber claimed by the private industry and local people. In
view of the approaching monsoon season (April 98) all such timber needs to be disposed
off with urgency to save further loss in quality, as also in value, albeit with proper
checks and balances.

2. Given the weak infrastructure in the north-eastern region, it does not seem
feasible to transport such huge quantities of timber for auction in markets outside the
region in a short time. Moreover, there would be uncertainty of the response in timber
markets far away from the source of timber which has been subject to elements of
degradation in varying degrees. There is also the likelihood of local resentment, in
an otherwise sensitive area, if all such material is removed from the region without
processing and value addition, which could be conceived as creating an adverse
effect on the region's economy.

3. Even though the proliferation of wood based industries has been the
main cause of degradation of forests in the north-eastern states, considering
the extent of forests (64 per cent of the geographical area) and the dependence of
the local people on the forest resources in the region it is neither feasible, nor
desirable, to ban completely either the timber trade or running of the wood based
industries. However, their numbers and capacities need to be regulated qua the
sustainable availability of forest produce and they are also required to be relocated
in specified industrial zones. Moreover, the industrial requirements have to be
subordinated to the maintenance of environment and ecology as well as *bona fide*
local needs.

4. There shall be no fresh fellings in the forests belonging to the Government,
District and Regional Councils till the disposal of their existing stocks of legal and
illegal timber.

5. In view of the multi-dimensional issues impinging upon forest protection, foolproof institutional arrangements need to be put in place, and made functional under the strict supervision of the North-East Council (NEC), Technical backstopping in the forestry matter will be provided by MoEF by opening a separate cell in the Ministry under an officer of the rank of Chief Conservator of Forests (CCF) and starting a satellite office of the Forest Survey of India at Shillong. * * *

We have heard the *amicus curiae*, the learned Attorney General and learned counsel for north-eastern states. In view of the report of the High Power Committee and taking into account the factors which require an order to be made by the Court for disposal of the felled timber and ancillary matters which are lying in the north-eastern states, we consider it appropriate to make the following order:

1. Disposal of timber shall commence only after the concerned Principal Chief Conservator of Forests irrevocably certifies that inventorisation of all felled timber in the state has been completed.

2. As a first measure all inventorised timber, including seized timber lying in the forests should be immediately transported to specified forest depots.

3. All illegal/illicit timber found in possession of an offender or abandoned in the forest shall be confiscated to the state government and shall be disposed off in accordance with the procedure to be adopted for disposal of Government timber.

4. Out of the seized timber, logs found suitable for manufacture of veneer and plywood shall be processed by the state governments within the own factories and by hiring such facilities. The finished product can be marketed freely.

5. The remaining timber belonging to Government and District Councils shall be offered for sale to Government Departments for their *bona fide* official use and the rest shall be sold in public auction or through sealed tender after fixing floor price by an Expert Committee with a representative from the MoEF. Private timber owners whose stocks have been cleared by HPC shall have the option of selling the timber either in the auctions organized by the State Forests Departments/Forests Development Corporation or directly.

6. The state government shall formally notify industrial estates for locating the wood based industrial units in consultation with the Ministry of Environment and Forests.

7. Timber as per inventory cleared by HPC may be allowed to

(a) be converted/utilized if the unit is located within the notified industrial estate. As the relocation in proposed industrial estates may take some time, existing units with only legal stocks may convert this timber, as one time exception, notwithstanding anything contained in para 12 hereunder, till such stocks last subject to the maximum period as per the norms prescribed by the High Power Committee (vide their III report) or six months whichever is less. Any stock remaining thereafter shall vest in the state government. However, fresh trees/timber will be allotted to these units only when they start functioning within the designated industrial estates. The territory Deputy Conservator of Forests/Divisional Forest Officer shall be responsible for ensuring that such units process the legal stocks only and will closely monitor the various transit permits (inward and outward) and maintenance of the prescribed records. All such record shall be countersigned (with date) by an officer not less than the rank of an Assistant Conservator of Forests.

(b) allowed to be sold to other units which are located in these industrial estates subject to the condition that such transactions are routed through an authority notified/constituted by the Principal Chief Conservator of Forests.

(c) The state governments shall ensure disposal of illegal timber before permitting the conversion/disposal of legal/authorized timber available with the wood based industries.

8. Transportation of auctioned timber (as well as legal timber) including sawn timber outside the North-Eastern Region shall only be done through railways under the strict supervision of the Forest Department. The Railway Board shall give priority for providing rakes/wagons for such transportation.

9. Modalities for transportation of timber/timber products and alternative modes in case of difficulties in transportation by Railways, will be worked out by the state government in concurrence of the Ministry of Environment and Forests.

10. Existing inventorized stock of timber originating from plantations in private and community holdings in the States of Meghalaya, Mizoram, Tripura, Manipur and Nagaland may be disposed of by their owners under the relevant state laws and rules. In states where such laws and rules do not exist, the necessary laws and rules may be framed within six months.

Pricing of Timber

11. The state governments shall ensure that timber/forest produce is supplied to industries, including Government Undertakings, at full market rate. The existing royalty shall be reviewed and revised upwardly by a Committee constituted under the Chairmanship of Principal Chief Conservator of Forests with representatives from the concerned Departments and shall also include a representative of the Ministry of Environment and Forests. The price of timber for which royalty has not been realized in full shall also be reviewed by this Committee and the concerned industry shall be required to pay the revised price or the royalty (including surcharge, fee etc.), whichever is higher after deducting the part of royalty already paid.

Licensing

12. Licenses given to all wood based industries shall stand suspended.

13. Wood based industries which have been cleared by the High Power Committee without any penalty shall have the option to shift to industrial estates which shall be identified by the states within 45 days and developed within six months thereafter.

14. Units which have been penalized because they were found to exceed normal recovery norms, but were within 15 per cent of the said norms, will have a right to approach the High Power Committee on or before 9 February 1998. The High Power Committee shall examine all relevant material, in particular the income-tax and excise records for the preceding three years. The High Power Committee shall dispose of all such applications within 45 days thereafter and such mills may

be granted licence if the High Power Committee finds that it is not against public interest so to do.

15. Units which have not furnished details /information to the High Power Committee so far or which have not been cleared by the High Power Committee, shall not be granted any licence and the stocks in their custody if any, shall be confiscated to the state government. In case of leased mills belonging to corporation/trusts/co-operative societies owned/controlled/managed by the state government and where the lessees have been penalized by the High Power Committee, the lease shall stand revoked. Such mills shall, however, be eligible for relicensing subject to the condition that these mills are not leased out in future except to a entity fully owned by the Government.

16. Units who do not want to shift to the designated industrial estates shall be allowed to wind up as per law.

17. Henceforth, licenses of units shall be renewed annually only in those cases where no irregularity is detected.

18. There shall be a complete moratorium on the issue of a new licenses by the state governments or any other authority for the establishment of any new wood based industry for the next five years after which the situation shall be reviewed with the concurrence of Ministry of Environment and Forests.

19. Number of wood based industries shall be determined strictly within the quantity of timber which can be felled annually on sustainable basis as determined by the approved working plans from time to time. If it is found that units after relocation in industrial estate have excess capacity then their capacities shall be reduced *pro rata* to remain within the sustainable levels.

Forest Protection

20. An action plan shall be prepared by the Principal Chief Conservator of Forests/Chief Forest Officer for intensive patrolling and other necessary protective measures to be undertaken in identified vulnerable areas and quarterly report shall be submitted to the Central Government for approval. The approved plan together with the modifications, if any, shall be acted upon.

21. To ensure protection of the forest wealth the forest officers in the north-eastern states may be empowered with authority to investigate, prosecute and confiscate on the lines of the powers conferred on the forest officers in many other states in the country.

22. The state government shall be responsible for providing all facilities including security and police force to strictly enforce forest protection measures to stop illicit felling, removal and utilization of such timber. The Chief Secretary shall review the various matters concerning from protection and development in his state at least once every six months with senior forest officers upto the rank of Conservator of Forests. Regional Chief Conservator of Forests of MoEF shall be invited to all such meetings.

Scientific Management of Forest

23. Working Plans for all forest divisions shall be prepared by the state governments and approved from the Government of India. Forest working shall be

carried out strictly in accordance with the approved prescriptions of the working plans. The working plans should be prepared within a period of two years. During the interregnum the forests shall be worked according to an annual felling programme approved by the MoEF which shall be incorporated in the concerned working plan. In case a working plan is not prepared within this time frame, further felling will remain suspended till the regular working plan is prepared and got approved.

24. The forests under the District, Regional and Village Councils shall be worked in accordance with working schemes which shall specify both the programme for regeneration and harvesting and whose period shall not be less than 5 years.

25. The maximum permissibly annual yield in the ad interim measures suggested above, shall not exceed the annual harvestable yield determined by Ministry of Environment and Forests. The plantation schemes raised on private and community holdings shall be excluded from these requirements but shall be regulated under respective state rules and regulations.

26. The states shall identify ecologically sensitive areas in consultation with leading institutions like the Indian Council of Forests Research and Education, Wildlife Institute of India, North Eastern Hill University, North Eastern Regional Institute of Science and Technology, leading NGOs. etc. and ensure that such areas are totally excluded from any kind of exploitation. The minimum extent of such areas shall be 10 per cent of the total forest area in the state.

Action against Officials

27. The state government shall identify within 45 days all those forest divisions where significant illegal fellings have taken place and initiate disciplinary/criminal proceedings against those found responsible. The first action taken report (ATR) in this regard shall be submitted to the Central Government within three months which shall be followed by quarterly reports (QRs) till culmination of the matter.

General

28. Timber extraction in forests irrespective of ownership, except in private plantations, shall be carried out by a state agency only. The states shall endeavour to adopt pattern obtaining in the State of Himachal Pradesh as described in para 25.3 of the Rajamani Committee Report.

If there be any local laws/customs relating to the forest in any state, the concerned state government may apply to this Court for the needed modifications, if any, with alternative proposal.

29. The penalties levied on the wood based industries as ordered by the High Power Committee shall constitute the revolving fund to meet the expenses involved in collection and transportation of seized illegal timber. These can be augmented by utilising the funds generated by the initial sales of illegal timber already available in the forest depots.

30. Each state shall constitute a State level Expert Committee for matters concerning the preparation of working plans, their implementation, development of industrial estates, shifting of industrial units to these estates, rules and regulations regarding the grant and renewal of licenses to wood based industry and other ancillary

matters, under the chairmanship of Principal Chief Conservator of Forests and with a nominee of Ministry of Environment and Forests as one of its members. Any decision of this Committee which is not acceptable to the state government shall be referred to the Central Government.

31. The existing permit system in Arunachal Pradesh shall stand abolished. The state government may provide financial assistance in cash or kind in the form of timber only for the *bona fide* use of the local tribals alone. Such concessional timber shall not be bartered or sold. Felling of trees for such purpose shall be carried out only by a Government agency.

32. The total sale proceeds from the sale of seized timber, as well as timber products manufactured and disposed by the state government (vide para 4) and penalties would be credited to the state revenues. Out of this, the state shall utilize one half of the amount for raising forest plantations by local tribal population and as assistance to the tribals. The remaining one half of the total sale proceeds, after deduction of the expenses there from, would go to the state coffers for other developmental activities in the state.

33. The state shall ensure that sufficient budgetary provisions are made for the preservation of biodiversity and protection of wildlife.

34. To ensure that timber/forest produce smuggled across the border may not be used as cover for trade in illegal timber, it is directed that all such timber seized by Customs/Border Security Force should not be redeemed in favour of individuals who are smuggling it but should be confiscated and handed over to the concerned State Forest Department along with offenders, vehicles, tools and implements for prosecution under the relevant Acts.

35. For the proper and effective implementation of these orders, Ministry of Environment and Forests will have the liberty to issue suitable directions consistent with this order.

36. Action taken report be filed by each state government and the Ministry of Environment and Forests every two months.

37. Liberty to apply for modification/clarification in case of need.

(NOTE: In this order the term 'state government' would include District Council also except where the context implies otherwise.)

On 17 September 1998, the MoEF constituted the Arunachal Pradesh Forest Protection Authority under section 3(3) of the Environment (Protection) Act of 1986 with powers to protect the environment and forests in the state. The Authority was asked to monitor and implement the directions of the Supreme Court in the *Forest Conservation Case*, in which the above orders were issued. The responsibilities of the Authority included issuing necessary directions for disposing felled timber; determining the sustainable number of wood based industries; approving industrial estates; managing the forests scientifically; pricing timber; and fixing the royalty payable to the state.

On the same day, the Supreme Court referred all pending applications in respect of Arunachal Pradesh to the Authority. The Authority was empowered to consider these applications and issue appropriate directions consistent with the orders of the Supreme Court.

NOTES AND QUESTIONS

1. In its order dated 23 February 1998 the Supreme Court noted the contents of the *State of Forests Report 1997* which was placed before the court by the *amicus curiae*. He submitted that between 1995 and 1997, 17,777 sq. kms. of dense forest were lost to the country. The court observed: 'This presents a rather dismal picture and is an alarming situation depicting deforestation on a large scale. We find from a perusal of the report that major defaulters appear to be the states of Andhra Pradesh, Madhya Pradesh, Assam, Manipur, Nagaland, Orissa and Meghalaya.'[23]

2. In a case of this complexity the role of the *amicus curiae* is extremely challenging. Whose interests should he protect? The forest dwellers? The forest? Persons whose livelihood depends on timber-related economic activity?

3. The court's interpretation of the expressions 'forest' and 'forest land' was timely. To overcome the Forest (Conservation) Act of 1980 (FCA), some state governments regarded section 2(i) of the Act as covering only those forests that were designated as 'reserved' forests and not forests classified as village forests or protected forests. This narrow interpretation enabled some states to de-reserve or re-classify forests. As a first step, these governments declared protected forest lands as 'non forest' and then allocated them to industries or other agencies. The court's clarification prevents such misuse. No forest, by whatever name designated, can now be re-classified and diverted to a non-forest purpose without prior Central Government permission.

4. Apart from the interpretation of the expressions 'forest' and 'forest land', the Supreme Court opinions take the form of detailed administrative directions. There is hardly a mention of the arguments advanced before the court by the *amicus curiae* or other parties appearing in the case. There is no weighing of rival contentions or analysis of the issues and the arguments made before the court. The court's directions are not supported by any reasons. Is this summary approach justified by the urgent need to prevent deforestation and degradation? Considering the finality of Supreme Court orders and their far reaching impact, should not the court have supplied reasons to support the directions issued?

In *Sabia Khan v State of UP*,[24] the petitioner claimed that the directions issued in the *Forest Conservation Case* were not 'judicial verdicts' but were '*ad hoc* orders.'

---

[23] AIR 1999 SC 43.
[24] AIR 1999 SC 2284.

The petitioner submitted that these orders breached the citizen's fundamental right under Article 19(1)(g) to operate saw mills. The Supreme Court rejected the petition with costs assessed at Rs. 10,000, holding that the petition was an abuse of process.

5. The orders issued by the Supreme Court cover a wide range of forest issues: felling trees; transport of timber; timber pricing; licensing of wood based industries; forest protection; scientific management of forests; action against errant officials and the spending of forest revenue. Is this a legitimate extension of the judge's role? Can the directions issued by the court be reasonably derived from the provisions of the FCA or any other statutory or constitutional provision?

6. In its order of 12 December 1996 (AIR 1997 SC 1228), the Supreme Court observed that the matter required an in depth hearing to examine all aspects relating to the National Forest Policy. Do the comprehensive directions issued more than a year later on 15 January 1998 (AIR 1998 SC 769) conform to the National Forest Policy resolution of 1988? Do they advance the policy objectives of promoting tribal welfare and encouraging joint forest management programmes between forest officers and local communities? Do the court's orders strengthen the policing and centralized decision-making features of the forest laws, to the exclusion of local people? Is such a regime of 'fencing' the forests equitable and sustainable?

7. On 12 December 1996 the court ordered the closure of all saw mills, veneer mills and plywood mills that were operating within any forest without prior Central Government approval. Several of these mills were operating openly for several years to the knowledge of government and revenue authorities. Likewise, mining within any forest was ordered to cease forthwith. On 15 January 1998 the court suspended all licenses given to wood based industries in the north-east region. Were the drastic directions fair to the mill operators? Keep in view that the closure and the suspension orders were passed without issuing show cause notices or granting a hearing to the affected mills. Contrast this approach with the *Ganga Pollution Case*,[25] where the Supreme Court directed closure only after granting an opportunity to the industries to explain whether they were functioning under a statutory 'consent' and whether they were complying with the norms. Which is a higher value—natural justice or ecological integrity? Can they be reconciled?

8. Were a zealous administrator to issue closure orders and suspend licenses in a like manner, would her action withstand judicial review? Should not the standards of fairness expected from an administrator apply with greater rigor to a 'super-administrator'?

9. The Supreme Court orders dated 8 May 1997, 14 July 1997 and 15 January 1998 refer to and rely upon reports submitted by the HPC. The content of the reports was not disclosed by the court. Moreover, copies of these reports were not released by the HPC and scores of affected mills and industries had no access to the material in the reports. Nevertheless, in its 15 January 1998 order the court issued numerous

---

[25] *M.C. Mehta v Union of India* 1992 Supp (2) SCC 633 and 1992 Supp (2) SCC 637.

important directions relating to the licensing of mills, the resumption of operations and the conversion of timber stock, on the basis of the HPC reports. Is it a fair procedure to pass orders on the basis of material that is not made available to the affected parties? Can you suggest a better procedure to overcome the problem?

10. The task before the HPC was to prepare an inventory of timber lying in the north-east region and to perform certain ancillary functions specified in the order dated 4 March 1997. After preparing an inventory, the HPC appears to have fixed 'norms' for plywood and veneer production from timber. Where the mill exceeded the norms, the HPC surmised that they used illegally felled timber and directed the state government to recover penalties running into several lakhs of rupees from individual units.

Was the imposition of penalty lawful? There does not appear to be any such power under the FCA or the Indian Forest Act. No power to impose penalties or fix norms was conferred on the HPC by the Supreme Court while constituting the committee on 12 December 1996. The norms were not disclosed to the mills. The method of arriving at these norms was not explained to the affected parties. The units were neither given notice nor granted an opportunity to explain their case before imposing the penalty. Is a penalty imposed without notice, without grant of an effective opportunity and hearing and without disclosing the norms, fair to the affected parties?

11. The procedure adopted by the Supreme Court and the HPC appears to fall far short of recognized rules of fair play. While forest conservation is a laudable end, has the court strayed from its primary function—to do justice *in accordance with law*?

12. Contempt of court proceedings were initiated against officials of the Jammu and Kashmir government who circumvented the court's orders. The officials permitted a private company to fell *khair* trees on the basis of the court's clarification that minor forest produce was not covered by the directions issued in the case. The court observed that *'katha'* which was extracted from *khair* wood was a minor forest produce but not *khair* which was timber. *Prima facie*, the permission to fell *khair* trees was a deliberate attempt to circumvent the order of the court.[26] Where under the garb of removing infected *saal* trees, healthy trees were being cut in the regions around Kanha National Park in Madhya Pradesh, the court restrained the state government from cutting any of the trees (whether considered diseased or not) until appropriate material was furnished to satisfy the court that its orders were not violated.[27]

13. In the course of this vast exercise, the Supreme Court responded to several administrative challenges. The court investigated complaints of illegal mining activity in the Doon Valley that were brought to its notice by an advocate.[28] It did so by constituting a fact-finding committee, summoning the Chief Secretary of Uttar Pradesh

---

[26] 1998 (2) SCALE 5 (SP) and 1999 (1) SCC 210.
[27] AIR 1999 SC 43.
[28] AIR 1999 SC 97; 1998 (5) SCALE 8, 10, 11, 13 (SP).

to court and censuring the Director of Geology and Mining, whose casual approach to the problem was 'evident from his demeanour in Court, before us.' In situations where local villagers and activists had been threatened with violence or were beaten up, the court directed the state to provide protection and security.[29] The Supreme Court asked the Karnataka government to prevent new encroachments and retrieve encroached forests in the Chickmagalur District.[30] A wide range of directions were issued to regulate saw mills in Jammu and Kashmir[31] and ban the felling of rare tree species in the state.[32] To reduce its administrative burden, the court required the Union Government to consider constituting authorities (similar to the Arunachal Pradesh Forest Protection Authority) under section 3(3) of the EPA for other states, and a national supervisory and appellate authority.[33] In the case of Madhya Pradesh, the court asked the Central Bureau of Investigation to investigate a case where files in the office of the District Forest Officer, Damoh were destroyed to cover up the illegal smuggling of teak wood.[34]

14. Applying the principles laid down by the court in the *Forest Conservation Case*, a division bench of the Bombay High Court, in *Goa Foundation v Conservator of Forest*,[35] quashed the permissions granted to the Tata Housing Development Company to construct a residential complex on a hill to the north of Mandovi river. The High Court directed Tata to remove all development work and restore the hill to its original vegetation. While so directing, the court rejected the developer's plea that 28 units in the residential complex had already been sold for Rs. 45 million and that more than Rs. 55 million was spent on the project.

15. In *Sriram Sah v State of West Bengal*,[36] a division bench of the Calcutta High Court held that the directions issued in the *Forest Conservation Case* did not apply to private plantations. Here, the petitioner confronted police and revenue officials who claimed that the Supreme Court order prevented him from cutting 14 old mango trees that had lost their fruit bearing ability and were infected by parasites!

16. To arrest the shrinking forest cover, most High Courts have leaned in favour of adjudging disputed acreage to be forest land. In a contest between a quarry operator and the forest department, the Bombay High Court held that the disputed area was indeed 'forest land' since the sale deed in favour of the operator described the tract as such.[37] In *Colorock Private Ltd. v Director of Mines and Geology*,[38] the

[29] 1998 (5) SCALE 8 (SP); 1999 (5) SCALE 189.
[30] 1998 (5) SCALE 4 (SP).
[31] 1998 (5) SCALE 21 (SP).
[32] 1998 (6) SCALE 21 (SP).
[33] 1998 (6) SCALE 17 (SP).
[34] 1999 (5) SCALE 187, 189, 422.
[35] AIR 1999 BOM 177.
[36] AIR 1999 CAL 10.
[37] *Kamaruddin N. Shaikh v State of Maharashtra* 1996 (4) BOM. C.REP. 209.
[38] 1990 FOR. L.T. 10.

Andhra Pradesh High Court rejected the petitioner's argument that the FCA would not apply to lands that were not designated in the revenue records as 'forest lands'. The court held that since the forest department was of the opinion that the land was forest land, it was not open for a revenue official to take a contrary view on the basis of revenue records.

17. Interpreting the expression 'forest produce' under the Kerala Forest Act of 1961, the Kerala High Court held it to include articles that are normally found in the forest and which are the spontaneous and wild growth in a forest. Coffee, cardamom, arecanut, pepper and rubber were products obtained by raising plantations, and could not be termed as the spontaneous or wild growth of a forest.[39] However, for the purposes of the Kerala Private Forests (Vesting and Assignment) Act of 1971, the Supreme Court held that the term 'agricultural crops' as commonly understood did not include a teak plantation, and hence lands that were covered by a teak plantation were not exempt from the purview of private forests under the Act.[40]

C. THE DEHRADUN VALLEY LITIGATION: FOREST CONSERVATION AND NATIONAL NEEDS

The *Dehradun Valley* litigation[41] is significant as the first case requiring the Supreme Court to balance environmental and ecological integrity against industrial demands on forest resources. The case arose from haphazard and dangerous limestone quarrying practices in the Mussoorie Hill Range of the Himalayas. Miners blasted out the hills with dynamite, extracting limestone from thousands of acres. The miners also dug deep into the hillsides, an illegal practice which resulted in cave-ins and slumping. As a result, the hillsides were stripped of vegetation. Landslides killed villagers and destroyed their homes, cattle and agricultural lands. Mining operations upset the hydrological system of the Dehradun Valley. Springs dried up and severe water shortages occurred in the Valley, an area formerly blessed with abundant water supplies. At the same time, mining debris clogged river channels and during the monsoon season severe flooding occurred.

The state of Uttar Pradesh failed to regulate the mining as required by existing mining laws. In 1961 the state minister of mines did sharply curtail mining in the

---

[39] *Aliyakutty Paul v State of Kerala* 1995 (2) KER. L.T. 93.

[40] *K.M. S Ubaida v State of Kerala* 1998 (2) SCALE 647. Likewise eucalyptus trees were also not exempt. *Gwalior Rayons Silk Mfg. (Wvg.) Co. Ltd. v Custodian* 1990 (Supp) SCC 785.

[41] *Rural Litigation and Entitlement Kendra, Dehradun v State of Uttar Pradesh.* The Supreme Court has issued numerous opinions and orders in this case, of which the principal orders are 12 March 1985, AIR 1985 SC 652; 13 May 1985, AIR 1985 SC 1259; 30 September 1985, 1985 (2) SCALE 906; 18 December, 1986, AIR 1987 SC 359, 19 October 1987, AIR 1987 SC 2426; 30 August 1988, AIR 1988 SC 2187; 16 December 1988, JT 1988 (4) SC 710; 4 May1990, JT 1990 (2) SC 391; 30 April 1991, AIR 1991 SC 2216; 1 August 1991, 1993 Supp (1) SCC 57 and 20 November 1991, 1993 Supp (1) SCC 426.

area. In less than a year, however, quarry operators successfully lobbied with the Chief Minister of the state to reopen mining operations. Mining leases were granted for 20 years. Illegal and destructive practices continued and existing mining safety rules were flouted with no enforcement by corrupt and ineffective state officials.

In 1982, eighteen leases came up for renewal. The state, finally recognizing the dimensions of the ecological devastation in the Valley, rejected all the renewal applications. The Allahabad High Court, however, issued an injunction allowing the applicants to continue mining, presumably in the belief that economic considerations outweighed ecological factors. At this point, in 1983, the Supreme Court treated a letter received from the Rural Litigation and Entitlement Kendra, complaining against the environmental degradation, as an Article 32 petition. The case developed into complex litigation as lessees of more than 100 mines joined the action, engaging an impressive array of the nation's top lawyers to argue for continued mining in the region.

The Supreme Court played an activist role in this litigation, essentially conducting a comprehensive environmental review and analysis of the national need for mining operations located in the Dehradun Valley. In addition, the court provided for funding and administrative oversight of reforestation of the region. The following synopsis highlights the major rulings in the case.

(1) In 1983, the court prohibited blasting operations pending a review to determine if the mines were being operated in compliance with the safety standards laid down in the Mines Act of 1952 and the relevant mining regulations. The court appointed an expert committee (the Bhargava Committee) to assess the mines.

(2) In March 1985, the court, upon the recommendations of the Bhargava committee, ordered that the most dangerous mines and those falling within the Mussoorie city board limits be denied leases and that their operations cease immediately. Operations of a second group of mines were restricted, pending review by another committee. This second committee (the Bandopadhyay Committee) was empowered to consider plans submitted by the miners to safeguard the environment and to hear the claims of people adversely affected by the mining. The Uttar Pradesh government was directed to provide the necessary funds for the Bandopadhyay committee as well as 'transport and other facilities for the purpose of enabling them to discharge their functions.'[42] The court determined that a third group of mines, including a major operation owned by the state of Uttar Pradesh, could remain open because the environmental damage was less clear.

(3) In 1987, the court concluded after review of the Bandopadhyay committee's report that based on ecological considerations alone, mining in the Valley should cease. The court, however, was concerned about the effect of closure on other national interests and made the following request for information from the Central Government:

[42] AIR 1985 SC 652, 656.

While we reiterate our conclusion that mining in this area has to be stopped as far as practicable, we also make it clear that mining activity has to be permitted to the extent necessary in the interests of the defence of the country as also for the safeguarding of the foreign exchange position. We call upon the Union of India in the relevant ministry or ministries to place before the Court on affidavit the minimum total requirement of this grade of limestone for manufacture of quality steel and defence armaments. The affidavit should also specify as to how much of high grade ore is being imported into the country and as to whether other indigenous sources are available to meet such requirements. This Court would also require an affidavit from responsible authorities of the Union of India as to whether keeping the principles of ecology, environmental protection and safeguards and anti-pollution measures, it is in the interests of the Society that the requirements should be met by import or by tapping other alternate indigenous sources or mining activity in this area should be permitted to the limited extent. The Court expects the Union of India to balance these two aspects and place on record its stand not as a party to the litigation but as a protector of the environment in discharge of its statutory and social obligation for the purpose of consideration of the Court by way of assisting the Court in disposing of the matters in issue. If the Court comes to the conclusion that the minimum requirement of limestone will be permitted to be lifted from some of the quarries, it shall be for the Court to indicate as to which of the quarries shall be operated for that limited purpose. We make it clear that whichever quarries may be permitted to be worked out the same shall be subject to strict control and regulations and would have to undertake acceptance of the obligation to maintain the green cover of the area by diverting a major portion of its profits.[43]

(4) The court rejected as unresponsive the first affidavit from the Central Government, submitted by the Director of Environment, Forests and Wildlife in the Ministry of Environment and Forests. The rejected affidavit detailed uses of limestone for industrial operations within Uttar Pradesh, but did not provide a satisfactory evaluation of other sources of the limestone within India and the extent to which national defence industries relied on the limestone. A second affidavit, submitted by the Secretary in the Ministry of Environment and Forests, contained the required evaluation and concluded that the requirements of the defence industries did not justify continuing operations of any mine in the Dehradun-Mussoorie region.[44]

(5) In 1988, the court concluded that all mines in the Dehradun Valley remain closed, except three operations. The court directed that the leases of the three remaining mines should not be renewed and that upon expiration of the existing leases the three remaining operations should close.

Although the Dehradun Valley mining operations occupied 800 hectares of

[43] AIR 1987 SC 2426, 2428.
[44] AIR 1988 SC 2187, 2204.

reserved forests and the Forest (Conservation) Act of 1980 was in effect in 1982, when the lessees applied to the state government for renewal of their leases, the state did not seek Central Government approval for the mining operations. This failure may have reflected confusion as to whether the requirement of the Act applied to renewal of leases which had originally been granted before the Act came into force. The Supreme Court resolved this question in *Ambica Quarry Works v State of Gujarat.*[45] The court held that state governments may renew pre-existing mining leases only with the review and approval of the Centre, as required under the Forest (Conservation) Act.

In the *Dehradun Valley* litigation, the court concluded in 1988 that continued mining in the Valley violated the Forest (Conservation) Act. Moreover, the court went beyond the requirements of the Act to merely conserve forest and issued orders to ensure that the Valley be reforested. The court noted that although the state of Uttar Pradesh had a reforestation programme, the record of reforestation was not encouraging. The court established a Monitoring committee comprised of Central, state, and local officials and two 'public-spirited' citizens to oversee reforestation, mining activities and 'all other aspects necessary to bring about normalcy in the Doon Valley'. The court also provided the Monitoring committee with funding by ordering that 25 per cent of the gross profit of the remaining mines be deposited in a fund controlled by the committee.

(6) Vijay Shree Mines, one of the lessees permitted by the court to operate until the expiry of its lease in 1990, misused the permission. The lessee continued to quarry limestone in an unscientific manner and in disregard of the directions issued by the Monitoring committee. In an application filed by the committee, the court held that the mining activity surreptitiously carried on by Vijay Shree Mines had caused immense damage to the area and directed the firm to pay Rs. 3 lakhs to the fund of the Monitoring committee.[46]

(7) An offshoot of the *Dehradun Valley* litigation was the *ARC Cement Case*. ARC Cement operated a cement factory in the Valley since November, 1982 until restrained by an order of the court. The company employed about 400 persons. In 1987 the Supreme Court declined permission to ARC to open its polluting cement factory and encouraged the company to shift it elsewhere. When the matter came up four years later, the Supreme Court was dismayed by the lack of progress, primarily because the company had failed to propose an alternative site. The court held:

> We cannot go back upon our earlier order that the cement factory shall not be permitted to run at the site. Shifting from this place has, therefore, got to be done. We permit the petitioner to indicate some alternative site so that there would be an option available to the State Government as also to the Pollution

[45] AIR 1987 SC 1037.
[46] 1991 (3) SCC 347.

Board to consider which of the sites offered may be acceptable to them for the purpose of shifting the cement factory from the present location.[47]

The court granted the petitioner two weeks time to come up with alternatives. On 20 November 1991 the Supreme Court recorded some of the terms of a general understanding between the company and the UP State Mineral Development Corporation for the supply of limestone and other related issues. However, no consensus was reached on a new site and while disposing the case the court acknowledged that certain aspects of the arrangement remained to be negotiated between the parties.[48] The efforts to relocate the cement factory apparently failed and the company was declared 'sick'. On 13 February 1995 ARC Cement was ordered to be wound up by the Board for Industrial and Financial Reconstruction.[49]

NOTES AND QUESTIONS

1. The Central Government became concerned about the destructive mining operations in the Valley at the same time that the Supreme Court took up the issue. In 1983, the Government of India appointed a Working Group to inspect the limestone quarries in the Dehradun-Mussoorie area. The same individual, D.N. Bhargava, headed both the government's Working Group and the court's first expert committee. Not surprisingly, the Working Group and the court's committee came to similar conclusions as to the harmful effect of the mines on the environment. The Working Group also prepared reports for the court on the few mining operations which were allowed to remain open.

2. During the course of the litigation, in 1986, Parliament enacted the Environment (Protection) Act. The mining operators contended that because the Act provides procedures to deal with the situation at issue, the court should dismiss the case and leave the issue to administrative authorities under the Environment (Protection) Act. Counsel for the miners relied on the following statement from a 1986 opinion issued in the case:

It is for the Government and the Nation—and not for the Court—to decide whether the deposits should be exploited at the cost of ecology and environmental consideration or the industrial requirement should be otherwise satisfied.[50]

In rejecting the miners' arguments for dismissal, the court relied on the fact that the litigation commenced and significant orders were issued before the adoption

---

[47] *ARC Cement Ltd. v State of UP* 1993 Supp (1) SCC 57.
[48] 1993 Supp (1) SCC 426.
[49] *ARC Cement Limited v Appellate Authority for Industrial and Financial Reconstruction*, 1998 (71) DEL. L.T. 213.
[50] AIR 1987 SC 359, 363.

of the Environment (Protection) Act. The court also addressed the potential effect of the Act in ousting the Court's jurisdiction over Article 32 public interest writ petitions as follows:

> The Act does not purport to—and perhaps could not—take away the jurisdiction of this Court to deal with a case of this type. In consideration of these facts, we do not think there is any justification to decline the exercise of jurisdiction at this stage. Ordinarily the Court would not entertain a dispute for the adjudication of which a special provision has been made by law but that rule is not attracted in the present situation in these cases. Besides it is a rule of practice and prudence and not one of jurisdiction. The contention against exercise of jurisdiction ... must stand overruled.[51]

3. In the *Dehradun Quarrying Case,* the opinions of the court and the Central Government did not conflict. Since the court's ruling, the Centre has designated the Valley as an ecologically fragile area under the Environment (Protection) Act. The Centre has also appointed a Doon Valley Board, under the chairmanship of the Minister for Environment and Forests, which is charged with conserving and restoring degraded areas of the Valley. Consider, however, a case in which the Central Government determines that a project that will cause significant environmental degradation is justified because the project fulfils other national interests. Do you think the court should permit the challenge of a project which has been reviewed under the Environment (Protection) Act? Why or why not? What experts will the court appoint in its evaluation of such a project? Note that in the *Dehradun Quarrying Case,* the government and the court relied on many of the same experts. What if the project is a government-owned operation and not a private operation—should the issue be analysed differently in such a case?

4. The Supreme Court concluded that mining in reserved forests in the Dehradun Valley violated the Forest (Conservation) Act. Note, however, that the Forest (Conservation) Act only prohibits non-forest activities on forest lands that do not have the approval of the Central Government.

5. In addition to ecological integrity and national interests, the Supreme Court was also concerned with the welfare of mine operators and labourers left unemployed by closure of the Dehradun Valley operations. The court issued the following directions to try to mitigate the effects of closing the mines:

(a) orders that mine lessees whose operations were terminated by the court be given priority for leases in new areas open to limestone mining; and

(b) orders that the Eco-Task Force of the Central Department of Environment reclaim and reforest the area damaged by mining and that workers displaced by mine closure be given priority for jobs with the Eco-Task Force operations in the region.

[51] AIR 1988 SC 2187, 2195.

6. In the *ARC Cement Case* the logic of the court seems to be: 'we cannot change our previous orders so the factory must move.' What kind of reasoning is that? Is it more important to preserve the integrity of court orders and consequent faith in the judicial system than to re-evaluate the merits of a case?

The court gave two weeks to ARC Cement to suggest alternative sites and four weeks to pick one: Is this adequate time for a comprehensive environmental impact assessment? Where did the court find those numbers? Are those even feasible deadlines? What expertise does the court have in assessing various environmental impacts of a cement factory?

Who is to blame for the commercial bankruptcy of ARC Cement: the entrepreneur for poor site selection; the management for failing to promptly suggest alternative sites; or the court for closing down operations without regard to the devastating impact on the company and its employees?

7. Building on the principles laid down in the *Dehradun Valley* litigation and the *Ambica Quarry Works Case*, the Supreme Court has clarified that the renewal of a lease should be in accordance with the law in operation on the date of renewal. Renewal was not a vested right and unless *prior* concurrence of the Central Government was obtained, mining in a forest area was completely prohibited.[52] The prior approval of the Central Government is a condition precedent and the grant of a lease or renewal without such approval renders the lease void.[53]

8. The Madras High Court reprimanded officials for granting a mining lease to Golden Granites in reserved forests in Tamil Nadu.[54] The court held that the impugned order permitting quarrying of black granite, though subject to a special condition that the commencement of operations should await Central Government concurrence, failed to give effect to the words 'prior approval' in section 2 of the Forest (Conservation) Act of 1980. 'The impugned order is a result of a blatant and patent transgression of law and smacks of sinister motives and ulterior objects and the same has not been passed in the public interest.'[55]

Likewise, the Andhra Pradesh[56] and Patna[57] High Courts have held that no mining operations may be carried out unless prior approval of the Central Government is granted in favour of renewing a mining lease in a protected or reserve forest.

---

[52] *Divisional Forest Officer v S. Nageswaramma* 1996 (6) SCC 442. Prior to this decision, a full bench of the Andhra Pradesh High Court held that a lease may be granted by a state government but no forest may be cleared until Central Government approval was obtained. This view may not be valid after the judgment in *S. Nageswaramma's Case. Hyderabad Abrasives and Minerals v Government of Andhra Pradesh* 1990 (1) ANDH. L.T. 180.

[53] *Samatha v State of Andhra Pradesh* AIR 1997 SC 3297, 3346, 3348.

[54] *Golden Granites v K.V. Shanmugam* AIR 1998 MAD 150, upholding the single judge order reported at *K.V. Shanmugam v State of Tamil Nadu* AIR 1997 MAD 338.

[55] *Id.* at 169.

[56] *Sakti v State of Andhra Pradesh* W.P No. 3734/1993, Andhra Pradesh High Court, 27 August 1993.

[57] *Nirmal Kumar Pradeep Kumar v State of Bihar* 1994 (1) BIH. L. J.REP. 524 and *Bihar State Mineral Development Corporation v State of Bihar* 1998(3) BIH. L.J.REP 1676.

In the *Nagarahole Hotel Case*,[58] a division bench of the Karnataka High Court struck a discordant note. Reversing the single judge,[59] the court held that the failure to obtain prior approval did not render a lease of forest land void at inception. In an approach similar to *Hyderabad Abrasives*,[60] the court held that the lessee may obtain Central Government approval *after* the lease but *prior* to carrying on any work in the forest. Having regard to the Supreme Court judgments in *S. Nageswaramma* and *Samatha* cases alluded to in note 7 above, is the Karnataka High Court opinion tenable? Will not the High Court's interpretation encourage clandestine quarrying and corruption?

Merely because forest land is quarried upon, it does not cease to be forest land for the purposes of forest laws.[61]

9. To protect the Saproon Valley from degradation, the Himachal Pradesh High Court followed the lead provided by the Supreme Court in the *Dehradun Valley* litigation. The mountains in Saproon Valley are rich in limestone deposits that have been quarried for over a century. The expansion of unscientific and unsystematic mining operations in the 1980s caused severe water pollution and erosion of the top soil. In a public interest litigation filed by the residents of Saproon Valley, the High Court abided by the recommendations of an expert committee and ordered the mines where scientific mining was not economically viable or technically possible to shut down. Other mines where further mining was possible subject to safeguards and precautions, were permitted to continue under the supervision of a monitoring committee.[62]

10. The guidelines for bureaucrats assessing an application to mine in a forest were set out by the Supreme Court in *Samatha v State of Andhra Pradesh*:

> Mining operations, though detrimental to forest growth, are part of layout of the industry, provision should be made for investment or infrastructural planning to reforest the area; and to protect environment and regenerate forest. The Ministry of Environment and Forests and all Secretaries of all the State Governments holding charge of Forest Departments have a duty to prevent mining operations affecting the forest. It is significant to note that, whether mining operations are carried on within the reserved forest or other forest area, it is their duty to ensure that the industry or enterprise does not denude the forest to become a menace to human [existence] nor a source to destroy flora and fauna and biodiversity. [In *State of Himachal Pradesh v Ganesh Wood Products*, 1995 (6) SCC 363, this Court] held that the application of sustainable development requires that the application of sustainable development requires

---

[58] *Gateway Hotels & Gateway Resorts Ltd. v Nagarahole Budakattu Hakku Sthapana Samithi* W.A. No. 1333/1997, Karnataka High Court, 11 April 1997. For a full discussion see the Wildlife chapter.
[59] AIR 1997 KAR 288.
[60] *Supra* note 52.
[61] *Kamaruddin N. Shaikh v State of Maharashtra* 1996(4) BOM. C. REP. 209.
[62] *General Public of Saproon Valley v State of Himachal Pradesh* AIR 1993 HP 52.

that appropriate assessment should be made of the forest wealth and the establishment of industries based on forest produce; other working should also be monitored closely to maintain the required ecological balance. No distinction can be made between the Government forest and private forests in the matter of forest wealth of the nation and in the matter of environment and ecology.[63]

11. In *Khanna Construction v State of Bihar*,[64] the petitioner challenged a demand for 'damages' claimed by the state government in respect of the unlawful mining of lands falling within a reserve forest. The petitioner argued that they had paid all legitimate taxes, royalty and statutory dues in respect of the mining. The government asserted that mining within the reserve forest was prohibited since no Central Government approval was obtained. The High Court rejected the state's plea since there was no statutory provision to back the claim for damages from a person who did not hold a valid mining lease in his favour. The High Court permitted the state to take appropriate action against the officers responsible for passing orders renewing the mining lease.

D. SUSTAINABLE DEVELOPMENT, FOREST DWELLERS AND COMMON PROPERTY

In a series of opinions delivered in the 1990s, the Supreme Court enjoined government officials to permit wood-based industries to operate only where forest resources were available on a sustainable basis.[65] 'The obligation of sustainable development requires that a proper assessment should be made of the forest wealth, and the entitlement of industries based on forest produce should not only be restricted accordingly but their working should also be monitored closely to ensure that the required balance is not disturbed.'[66] Forest-based industries do not have an absolute or unrestricted right to operate their units where forest resources are scarce.[67]

While this approach may in theory prevent the destruction of forests, it may be a while before the Supreme Court's aspiration that 'forest preservation and protection was no more to be separated from the life style of tribals,'[68] is realized.

Current law and policy governing forests allows wholesale destruction of forests for mega-projects but does not encourage or facilitate potentially less harmful

---

[63] AIR 1997 SC 3297, 3347.
[64] 1994 (1) BIH. L. J.REP. 586.
[65] *State of Himachal Pradesh v Ganesh Wood Products* AIR 1996 SC 149, 163; *UP Kathha Factories' Association v State of UP* 1996 (2) SCC 97; *T.N. Godavarman Thirumulkpad v Union of India* AIR 1998 SC 769, 772 and *Samatha v State of Andhra Pradesh* AIR 1997 SC 3297, 3347.
[66] *Ganesh Wood Products, id.*
[67] *Id.*
[68] *Samatha, supra* note 65.

uses of forest products by local peoples as seen in *Banwasi Seva Ashram v State of Uttar Pradesh.*[69] The case was initiated as a public interest writ petition under Article 32 of the Constitution, on behalf of local people protesting reservation of forest land by the state. People in 433 villages had lived in or near the forest for generations and relied on the forest products—fruits, vegetables, fodder, flowers, timber, animals and fuelwood—for their daily needs. The petitioners alleged that the state had ignored the claims of these people over the forest and that steps were being taken for the eviction of many of the forest dwellers. The petitioners further asserted that this curtailment of access to the forest violated the fundamental right to life of the local people guaranteed by Article 21 of the Constitution.

In 1983, the Supreme Court prohibited eviction of the forest dwellers pending investigation of their claims over the forest. It also ordered the formation of a high powered committee to investigate the claims of the people over the forest. The state responded that it had already formed such a committee. The state committee was chaired by the chairman of the State Board of Revenue and included the collector, Mirzapur and the local conservator of forests. These three state officials had a strong interest in reserving the forest to the state to ensure that the forest generate revenue for the state. The Supreme Court disapproved this biased committee and ordered that a new committee of retired High Court judges and two other officials be appointed to adjudicate the customary rights of the people to use of the forests. The court, however, failed to make the actual appointments and so a more objective committee was never formed.

In the meantime, the government informed the court that it wanted to site the proposed Rihand Super Thermal Plant of the National Thermal Power Corporation (NTPC) in the disputed forest lands. The NTPC intervened in the case, requesting that the court lift its order prohibiting evictions of local people and allow the NTPC to take possession of land for the project. The court responded by immediately lifting the prohibition of evictions on all 1800 acres of forest requested by the NTPC for the project. Although the court noted that forests are a 'much wanted national asset', it determined that a scheme to generate electricity is of equal national importance and cannot be deferred.

The court did not treat the claims of those dispossessed by the forest reservation with such dispatch and deference. First, the court dropped from the action entirely claims over land which the state had notified as reserved under section 20 of the Indian Forest Act. (Such notification is given when a state determines that it has disposed of all claims or that the time period for bringing claims has elapsed.) Although the court noted that claimants to this land could attempt to establish their rights 'in any other appropriate proceeding' the court gave no indication of what other proceedings are available to these claimants.

As to the remaining reserved forest land, the court appointed a Commission to

[69] AIR 1987 SC 374.

oversee administration of claims over that land and ordered that legal assistance be given to the claimants. The court, however, did not address the primary issue in the petitioners' claim—whether the local people could assert a claim to the forest arising from their dependence on the forest, based on the right to life guaranteed by Article 21 of the Constitution. The court established an elaborate administrative machinery for protecting rights already legally established, but begged the most important question for local people, viz., the question of the legal basis for establishing rights over the forest.

The Forest Settlement Officer decided the claims of the Adivasis and Banvasis on the basis of written as well as oral objections. Accepting some of these claims, he excluded parts of the area that were to be notified as a reserve forest; and vested in the village council certain other tracts that fell between agricultural lands. In appeals before the Additional District Judge, the claims were rejected on procedural grounds. The Judge held that oral objections could not be considered; that the claims were invalid since the written applications were not stamped; and that vesting the lands in the village council was unjustified.

In a writ petition challenging the District Judge's order, the Allahabad High Court restored the findings of the Forest Settlement Officer. The High Court held that the District Judge ought not to have extinguished the rights of Banvasis and Adivasis on procedural and technical grounds. Many claimants were illiterate or ignorant of their legal rights, and the object of the Supreme Court orders stood defeated by the lower court's restrictive approach.[70]

In February, 1992 the court disposed of the proceedings insofar as NTPC was concerned by issuing detailed directions for the rehabilitation of the tribals. The District Judge, Sonebhadra was asked to prepare a final list of the affected persons, who according to the petitioners numbered more than 1500 families. The rehabilitation package provided for housing plots, a shifting allowance, transportation, re-employment opportunities, infrastructure development and civic amenities such as schools, hospitals and sports centres.[71]

NOTES AND QUESTIONS

1. Chhatrapati Singh has pointed out that it is unlikely that tribal or forest dwellers will find the names of their ancestors on any written documents which may be used to establish rights to the land, even if the forest dwellers have occupied the forest for centuries.[72] How can legally cognizable rights of tribal and local peoples over forest land and forest products be established? Should any person currently using

---

[70] *UP Legal Aid and Advice Board v State of UP* AIR 1991 ALL 281.
[71] AIR 1992 SC 920.
[72] C. Singh, *Common Property and Common Poverty* 35 (1986).

forest land or forest products be given rights over the forest? Should the granting of rights be limited to communal rights of Scheduled Tribes recognized under the Fifth and Sixth Schedule of the Constitution as distinct communities? Should rights be based on reference to historical documents?

2. Even if a state government extends privileges over forests to local peoples, these privileges may be curtailed by oppressive actions of state forest department personnel. The opinion issued in *Fatesang Gimba Vasava v State of Gujarat*[73] documents such a situation. Petitioners were tribals granted privileges to obtain bamboo from a reserved forest. They fashioned the bamboo into articles which they sold to private traders. Petitioners charged that state forest department officials barred traders from transporting the bamboo articles by truck and had requested that the local railway administration cease transporting the goods. The alleged motive for these actions was a scheme between the forest officials and a local paper mill to force the tribals to sell raw bamboo to the paper mill.

3. Forest department personnel in many states have been prosecuted for conspiring with timber smugglers, referred to by the press as the 'forest mafia', in schemes to clearcut large expanses of forest. Meanwhile, local people have been prosecuted under the Indian Forest Act of 1927 for relatively minor offences. The corruption of some forest department officials makes many forest dwellers distrustful of any actions of these departments.

4. Article 46 of the Constitution, a directive principle of state policy, declares:

> The State shall promote with special care the educational and economic interests of the weaker sections of the people, and, in particular, of the Scheduled Castes and Scheduled Tribes, and shall protect them from social injustice and social exploitation.

Many forest dwelling people are members of Scheduled Tribes. Try to formulate a legal argument, based on Article 46, that a state government must pay special attention to the needs of tribal people when the government reserves or protects forest land under the Indian Forest Act.

5. In contrast to dereservation of forests, the Central Government has not adopted analogous legislation and rules governing a state's determination to reserve forest land and to limit the rights of indigenous peoples to the use of forest land. As an exercise, try to write legislation governing reservation of forest land that addresses the needs of people dependent on the forests. How would you balance the needs of the people with the need to protect the forest from over logging and over grazing? Who should make decisions about managing the forest? For example, should the state forest department or a representative body of forest dwellers make decisions as to which species of tree should replace harvested trees?

6. Although the Central Government has assumed a veto power over state actions

[73] AIR 1987 GUJ 9.

regarding forest use, it has not yet explicitly legislated priorities for forest use. In 1981, the Central Government did issue Forest (Conservation) Rules implementing the Forest (Conservation) Act of 1980. Rule 5 lists factors that the Central Advisory Committee should consider in approving a state action. These factors include:

(a) whether the forest land proposed to be used for non-forest purpose forms part of a nature reserve, national park, wildlife sanctuary, biosphere reserve or forms part of the habitat of any endangered or threatened species of flora and fauna or of an area lying in a severely eroded catchment;
(b) whether the use of forest land is for an agricultural purpose or for the rehabilitation of persons displaced from their residence by reasons of any river valley or hydro-electric project;
(c) whether the state government or other authority has certified that it has considered all other alternatives and no other alternatives in the circumstances are feasible and that the required area is the minimum needed for the purpose; and
(d) whether the state government or other authority undertakes to provide at its cost acquisition of land of an equivalent area and afforestation thereof.

How effective do you think a requirement 'to consider' these factors will be in protecting forests? Note that for the most part, these factors provide for a case-by-case analysis of each portion of forest proposed for dereservation or non-forest use. Should the total area of adequate forest cover in the nation be a major consideration? The rules do not require the states to consider alternatives for projects located on forest land. Whether an analysis of alternatives has been conducted is only one factor for consideration. Can the Advisory Committee make a principled determination under the Forest (Conservation) Act without an adequate analysis of alternatives to a proposed project?

7. The Central Government has not provided uniform national rules concerning forest issues such as a price structure for timber leases or protection for specific tree species or forest products. One commentator has noted that the lack of uniform rules makes it difficult for a state to effectively manage and protect its forests.[74] For example, Karnataka attempted to impose a price structure for forest produce supplied to industry that would give the state sufficient revenue to properly manage state forests and to provide for reforestation. The state's price was undercut by lower prices in other states. Should the Central Government adopt nationwide rules governing the sale of forest products to industry? Should the Centre require that all states set prices on forest products sufficient to cover the costs of reforestation and forest management? What is the overall effect on the forests of allowing each state to set its own prices for forest products? What interests benefit from the lack of uniform rules?

[74] C. Saldanha, *Forests in the New Forest Policy*, in FOREST ENVIRONMENT AND PEOPLE 46 (W. Fernandes ed. 1983).

8. Why are there 'protected forests' at all, since the state's powers in creating 'reserved forests' are so broad?

9. Tribal protests and marches have, over the years, led to many deaths and human rights violations. Occasionally, tribals have blown up train tracks, and resorted to other violent methods, countered by police violence, to win their rights. Is there another way to do this? Is the civil unrest worth the benefit to industry and development?

10. Why should the rights of indigenous people matter? And why should they deserve special protection? Consider the following argument.

> Perhaps the most compelling and widely cited argument for safeguarding indigenous environments (and hence their human inhabitants) is the environment's unequalled diversity of medicinal plants. The case has again been made by various researchers who say that many indigenous lands, especially rainforests, may hold the key to treating pernicious ailments like AIDS, cancer, and heart disease. Genetic scientists argue that preserving precious indigenous knowledge to unlock the secrets of plant species is an essential element in the equation.[75]

11. Anil Agarwal and Sunita Narain, pioneering eco-journalists, argue in favour of giving tangible and real control to local communities over forest resources. They fear that until forest dwellers are made stakeholders in the forest, corruption and exploitation will continue:

> The Gujjars, nomadic herdspeople, were faced with a peculiar problem in the autumn of 1992. The forest guards who normally 'granted' them entry into a state-owned forests (their winter abode in the foothills of the Himalaya) presented them with a new demand. The 'entry fee' had gone up. They were told that the prime minister had gone to a foreign land called Rio where it was agreed that human beings would not be allowed into the forest. Now the guards could allow the Gujjars in, but at a personal risk. Thus, instead of the usual rate of 1 kg of ghee per milking animal each month and 1 kg of milk per day for each animal, they need to double the bribe and for the *ghaas salami* (literally meaning salute for the grass) instead of Rs. 30 per animal, they now needed Rs. 80 per animal. The 'Rio payment', as this came to be known, is paid till date. Such payments are not unusual. Poor forest dwellers and villagers regularly pay them for their survival.[76]

12. In *V. Shankar Reddy v State of AP*,[77] the Andhra Pradesh High Court struck down a government order permitting the felling of trees and the transport of timber

---

[75] Stephen Mills, *Last Chance for First People: Efforts to Preserve Indigenous Peoples*, Omni, March, 1995.
[76] Agarwal & Narain, *Corruption and the Environment: The Method Behind the Madness,* in *Down to Earth,* 31 October 1998, p. 27, 34.
[77] 1992 (2) ANDH. L.T. 514.

from the forests in East Godavari District. Sakthi, a tribal welfare organisation, questioned the legality of the government order in favour of V. Shankar Reddy, a forest contractor, on the ground that it was contrary to Chapter III-A of the Andhra Pradesh Forest Act of 1967. The chapter prohibited the transfer of any forest or forest produce or the denudation of a forest, without prior approval of the district collector. The court held that Chapter III-A was introduced to safeguard the interests of Scheduled Tribes and to preserve forests. The impugned executive order being contrary to legislation was invalid.

In an emerging trend, judges are granting relief on the basis of common property rights. Take the case of *Nabipur Gram Panchayat v State of Gujarat*[78] where the residents of Nabipur in Gujarat objected to the construction of huts on their grazing lands. The villagers, among them Adivasis and Harijans, feared that the proposed diversion of the grazing land would aggravate the shortage of fodder already faced in the village. Allowing a writ petition based on this common property entitlement, the High Court quashed the orders of resumption, since 'the Collector [had] failed to apply his mind with regard to the actual requirement of grazing land for the people of village Nabipur and the actual availability of grazing land to them.'[79] The Allahabad High Court recognized the importance of Himalayan meadows in the case below.

OM PRAKASH BHATT v STATE OF UP
AIR 1997 ALL 259

RAVI S. DHAVAN, J.:

The petition by Shri Om Prakash Bhatt and others was basically brought to Court as the residents of the hills, particularly of Garhwal, and more particularly of the district of Chamoli, felt threatened by the invasion of state organisations and the erosion of the sanctity and the peace and tranquillity of the Bugiyal. Bugiyal in Garhwal basically means meadows and pasture land which exists above a certain altitude in the mountains no different than the Alpine meadows of Switzerland and Austria. Closer to home the meadows at Khilanmarg above Gulmarg in Kashmir are called 'marg'. The complaint to the Court was that these areas are pasture lands to the sheep and the shepherd. The submission was that the Bugiyal is basically an ecosystem in itself and this delicate balance between ecology and environment has to be understood and respected. It cannot be defiled and the intricate balance of nature does not suffer the presence of aliens on these pasture lands as it keeps away the sheep and shepherd, thus disturbing the ecology. This living phenomenon may be watched but cannot be tread upon.

[78] AIR 1995 GUJ 52.
[79] *Id.* at 54.

The complaint is that the Garhwal Mandal Vikas Nigam (hereinafter, in short, the Nigam) had put up pre-fabricated lodging houses as a hotel for tourists on the slopes of a bugiyal which is below the peak of the temple of Tungnath. This has happened at Chopta. Tungnath incidentally, is accepted and reported even by the State administration as one of the highest temples in India.

The next issue presented was that indiscriminate import of plastic and nonbio-degradable material is playing havoc with the environment of the hills as each seasons' plastic collects on the slopes of the hills to be covered by autumn leaves of one season and this exercise is repeated year by year with plastic being sandwiched between leaves, preventing rain water from seeping and percolating into the hill slopes and causing another ecological disbalance; the disappearance of little streams and water resources on which the hill people rely upon. The deposit of plastic material also kills the green life on the slopes of the mountains.

The third aspect is about the tourist and trekking pilgrimage routes, where the tourist, the pilgrim and the trekker devoid of all civic sense with no respect of the environment throw non-biodegradable material on the slopes of the hills and the moun-tain routes are being littered with indiscriminate evidence of deliberately created gar-bage. Besides on these mountain routes commercial activity, like kiosks and tea shops at places where they ought not to be, has been encouraged by the state administration. Court's attention was drawn on the garbage strewn on the slopes of the hills right up to the glacier of Gomukh and of man made deposits of synthetic and non-bio-degradable materials at the source of the river Ganga at above 14,000 feet.

* * *

The response from the Nigam was that this complex was established by the funds of the Government of India after due clearance from the Government of Uttar Pradesh and the Government of India. The Tourism Department has spent a lot of money on the construction of this complex. This complex takes the pilgrims and the tourists to the highest temple in the world 'Tungnath'. Tungnath temple is visited by pilgrims since centuries. Removal of these facilities from Chopta or Dugalbitta area will not benefit the area.

Merely because money has been spent is no ground to degrade ecology and environment. While conforming uses in urban planning were not permitted to be compromised by the Supreme Court, when it was held that such violations were illegalities which were not curable. (AIR 1974 SC 2177, *K. Ramdas Shenoy v The Chief Officers, Town Municipal Council, Udipi*). The violation of environment cannot continue and upsetting an ecological balance will be judged with even more strict standards. That money has been spent by the Nigam on putting prefabricated structures and tents on the bugiyal was a misplaced expenditure. The bugiyal be-longs to the people. It is an ecosystem in itself. Nature has tailored it. It is not for man to erode the sanctity of this area. It must be returned to nature to provide for whom it was meant; the sheep, the shepherd, the wild flowers, the micro-organ-isms and the plant and insect life below the turf and in the shrubs at the altitude. Clearly, putting a tourist lodging house on a bugiyal was a mistake. The Court had during the seasons 1994–95 and 1995–96 not interfered with the Nigam's occupation with this sensitive area, as the Court expected that by this time the Nigam would see the reality and unwind its occupation of running a camp tourist resort there. There is a danger looming on the horizon. If a state financed tourist camp has been planted on the bugiyal, there are other five star hotel groups waiting to encroach on this beautiful and tranquil area nestling in the mountains. The Court is afraid that the Nigam will have to unwind its occupation of the bugiyal next season before the end of March 1997. The Chief Conservator of Forests (Hills) will ensure that this will be done. Further, no allotment should be made in respect of occupation of the pasture lands and the meadows that are the bugiyals. The eco-system is to be preserved.

* * *

To discourage the entry of plastics and non-biodegradable materials into the hills, the state administration brought to the notice of the Court that it is adopting a legislation from the neighbouring state i.e. Himachal Pradesh. The process has begun and a legislation is contemplated to prevent, control and discourage plastic shopping bags, wrappers and other non-biodegradable materials from being brought to the hill areas. The Court is informed by a report that the name of the legislation which is on the anvil and is being drafted, will be Uttarkashi Environment Protection and Pollution Act, 1996. As the state of Uttar Pradesh is already considering a legislation for the purpose of discouraging plastic and like material to be kept away from the hills, the Court is of the opinion that another effort has been made in meeting the principle of protecting the ecology of this area. It will not be appropriate for the Court to make any comment on the proposed legislation except that it ought to be brought into effect for the entire area of the hills with due speed and as a matter of urgency.

* * *

The directions given to the Nigam, to withdraw occupation of its camp site on the slope of the bugiyal below the temple of Tungnath and above Chopta are to be carried by this public sector state organization running a hotel at this place. The Chairman and Managing Director of the Organization will ensure that the direction is followed and implemented by 31 March 1997. Hereinafter hotels and tourist lodges will ensure following the precautionary principle. There are several open patches made available by nature where barren terrain exists to take in tourist lodges provided they are spread out widely. The Chief Conservator of Forests (Hills) for Kumaun and Garhwal can indicate the specific sites in consultation with the village panchayats.

* * *

While High Courts have often followed the lead of the Supreme Court in taking an active role in balancing the interests of environmentalists and industrialists, there are exceptions. It is within the High Courts that one is likely to find more conservative, less activist opinions, more akin to British or American opinions. Consider, for example, the following opinion of the Kerala High Court, reversing the judgment of the lower court which had, in a detailed and scientifically analytical opinion, found in favour of environmental protection.

EXECUTIVE ENGINEER, ATTAPPADY VALLEY IRRIGATION PROJECT v ENVIRONMENTAL & ECOLOGICAL PROTECTION SAMITHY
AIR 1993 KER 320

JAGANNADHA RAO, C.J.:　　　* * *

These two writ appeals are connected and can be disposed of together. ... [One] is filed by the State of Kerala, the Chief Conservator of Forests and the Executive Engineer, Attappady Valley Irrigation Project, Agali P.O. Mannarkad. ... [The other] appellant is Sri O. Elamkovan, a contractor, who was the successful bidder for cutting the bamboo clusters. The contesting respondent in both the appeals is the writ petitioner, called the 'Environment and Ecological Protection Samithy', Agali, represented by its covener, one K. Rajan.

The relief claimed by the respondent-writ petitioner is for the issue of a writ of prohibition, prohibiting the appellants (in particular the appellant. ... who is the contractor) from cutting the spread bamboo reed forest in Attappady area, allegedly 4 kilometres long. The writ petition was filed on 17–11–1989.

* * *

[The] respondent-writ petitioner Samithy waited till the land occupied by the bamboo clusters was acquired by the Government for the purpose of the Project and huge compensation was paid to the land owners. ... [T]he present writ petition was filed ... after the contractor had paid Rs. 4,60,000 and cut the bamboo for more than two months and had spent about Rs. 1,86,000 for such cutting.

The learned single Judge directed appointment by the Government of an expert committee to go into the question of environmental degradation and the three-member Committee appointed by the Government submitted a report ... on 19–2–1990. Arguments were heard on various dates and judgment was delivered on 22–3–1991 allowing the writ petition, directing the appellants (respondents in the writ petition) in both appeals to 'forbear from cutting and removing bamboo clusters and other vegetation ...'

No direction was given in respect of the refund ... nor in respect of the expenditure ... said to have been incurred by the contractor during the period of two months and odd of his cutting. The expert committee had stated in its report:

The stacked bamboo poles may be roughly about 40 lorry loads, i.e. about 400 metric tonnes. The collected bamboos have dried and deterioration will set in shortly. Hence it is advisable to remove this produce at the earliest.

Even so, no directions were given in the judgment dated 22–3–1991 for removal of these 40 lorry loads of bamboo.

* * *

The question is whether interference is called for by this Court and if so, in what manner and how to now adjust the equities?

The learned single Judge has referred to various aspects of environment, ecology and forestry. That part of the judgment is highly academic and the learned Judge has taken great pains to refer to various scientific methods and principles. We have no quarrel with that part of the judgment.

But, while allowing the writ petition, the learned Judge ought to have considered whether all factors relevant to the case were considered by the Government. ... If the Court felt that relevant factors or considerations were not properly adjusted, the Court should have remitted the matter to the Government. The Court should have, at the same time, permitted the contractor ... to remove the cut bamboo which was decaying.

* * *

In view of our finding that [the Committee Report] is defective and a fresh look at the matter is necessary and the long lapse of time, we do not think it proper for us to take any final decision in the matter ... These are matters which, in our view, are to be left to the Government to decide, in light of any further expert opinion the government might take into consideration. It will also be for the government to consider the relevance of the Attappady Valley Irrigation Project and it is not for this Court nor to the expert committee to think that project will never materialize.

If Government is taking any opinion in favour of further cutting and removal of the bamboo clusters, it will be appropriate for the Government to issue a notice to the writ petitioner and to the contractor to make their submissions. It will be for the Government to consider whether a personal hearing is to be given or an opportunity to file a reply is to be given, to the said persons.

* * *

[I]t will be open to the contractor to seek such remedies by way of damages or otherwise against such persons, if any, who the contractor believes are responsible for any loss or losses incurred by him. We have ... permitted the contractor to remove the cut bamboo, whatever be its present condition. ...

As considerable delay has already occurred, the Government shall complete the entire exercise within four months from the date of this Judgment.

For all the aforesaid reasons, the writ appeals are allowed, the judgment of the learned single Judge is set aside and in place of the orders issued by the learned single Judge, the above orders shall issue. No costs.

NOTES AND QUESTIONS

1. In his opinion,[80] the single judge, Justice Sankaran Nair, considered the nature of deforestation, climate change, and the ecological impact of cutting bamboo. He relied not only on the findings of the expert committee, but also numerous texts and results of a forestry experts' meeting held in Kerala. The division bench found this exercise inadequate. Is it not the appropriate province of the trial judge to determine the facts and merits of the case?

2.The court finds it significant that the writ petition was filed only after the government acquired the land for the irrigation project. However, who would the writ petitioner have sued prior to the acquisition? The landowners for selling to the government? In addition, the court points out that the writ petition was filed two months after the contractor won the bid to cut the bamboo and had begun to do so. Is two months really an inordinately long time in which to prepare and file a writ petition? If the petitioner had filed before the auction, whom would he have sued? How was the petitioner expected to learn about the auction?

3. One constant complaint levelled against the Indian courts, is the backlog in cases and delays in litigation. Is the Kerala High Court's approach—punishing what it considers a belated action—the better response than that of the trial court? Should courts establish a more deferential attitude towards the administrative decisions, as the courts in the United States have done, thereby lessening the number of cases litigated? Is the Kerala High Court's approach an effective tool to clean up some of the problems plaguing India's court system? If so, at what cost to the environment?

---

[80] 1991 (3) ILR (KER) 125.

8

WILDLIFE PROTECTION*

For over a century, Indian wildlife has received sporadic protection through numerous, species-specific statutes. The primary intent of most early statutes was to preserve game animals for hunting. The Indian Forest Act of 1927 included provisions for hunting restrictions in reserved or protected forests and authorised the establishment of sanctuaries. In 1972, India adopted a comprehensive national law, the Wild Life (Protection) Act of 1972, intended solely to protect wildlife. The Forty-Second Constitutional Amendment in 1976 moved wildlife and forests from the State List of the Constitution to the Concurrent List. Subsequently, the Central Government has increased its role in developing national wildlife policy. The most recent statutory initiative is the 1991 amendment to the Wild Life Act.

Some of the current debates among conservationists are reflected in the cases discussed in this chapter. The people-park controversy, for example, raises core issues relating to the rights and livelihood of forest dwellers and villagers who live in and around protected areas. How should courts balance their immediate and acute community needs against the national agenda of minimizing human intervention in the national parks and sanctuaries? A second theme is the conflict between environmentalists and industrial interests in exploiting mineral resources and timber in the protected regions. Straddling the rival claimants are the state governments, many of which depend on mineral royalty or are keen to encourage industry in remote regions of the state. Finally, we examine cases where industrial lobbying and developmental pressures persuaded State Legislatures to 'de-reserve' protected areas. Writes Valmik Thapar,

> At the end of the twentieth century, and after nearly fifty years of independence, the Indian subcontinent can be justly proud of its enormously varied flora and fauna. In India alone, 13,000 species of flowering plants and 65,000 species of

---

* This chapter has benefited from the insights shared by Nandan Nelivigi.

fauna have been recorded, including 2000 fish, 1200 birds and 340 mammals. ... India now has 560 protected areas, including 80 national parks, but much remains to be done if the natural life of India is to survive human depredation.[1]

A. THE WILD LIFE ACT: SCOPE AND IMPLEMENTATION

The Wild Life (Protection) Act of 1972 provides the statutory framework for protecting wild animals, plants and their habitats. The Act adopts a two-pronged conservation strategy: *specified* endangered species are protected regardless of location, and *all* species are protected in designated areas, called sanctuaries and national parks.

The Wild Life Act was enacted by Parliament under Article 252, after eleven State Legislatures passed the required resolutions.[2] After the subject wildlife was moved to the Concurrent List by the Forty-Second Constitutional Amendment in 1976, Parliament was empowered to enact laws relating to wildlife without recourse to Article 252 (1). By the 1991 amendment to the Wild Life Act, Parliament extended the Act to the whole of India except Jammu and Kashmir, which has its own Wild Life Protection Act similar to the national law.[3]

The Wild Life Act provides for the establishment of wildlife advisory boards[4] and the appointment of wildlife wardens and other staff to implement the Act.[5] In several states, the office of the Chief Wild Life Warden and the Chief Conservator of Forests is united in a single post and the responsibilities under both statutes are discharged by the same person.

Except under specified conditions,[6] the Act prohibits hunting the animals listed in Schedule I, II, III and IV.[7] Under the Act, the state government may declare any area of adequate 'ecological, faunal, floral, geomorphological, natural or zoological significance' a sanctuary[8] or a national park.[9] In both sanctuaries and national parks, public entry is restricted[10] and the destruction of any wildlife or habitat is prohibited.[11]

---

[1] Thapar, *Land of the Tiger: A Natural History of the Indian Subcontinent* 11 (1997).

[2] *Pradeep Krishen v Union of India* AIR 1996 SC 2040. Article 253 (relied on to enact the Air Act in 1981 and the Environmental (Protection) Act in 1986) was not invoked by Parliament to introduce national wildlife legislation.

[3] Kothari, Panda, Singh and Variava, *Management of National Parks and Sanctuaries in India: A Status Report*, 107 (1989).

[4] Section 6.

[5] Sections 3 and 4.

[6] Sections 11 and 12

[7] Section 9

[8] Section 18.

[9] Section 35.

[10] Sections 27 and 35 (8). In *Bombay Burmah Trading Corporation v Field Director (Project Tiger)* AIR 2000 MAD 163, the High Court upheld restrictions on plying vehicles in the sanctuary.

[11] Sections 29 and 35 (6).

In theory, national parks enjoy a higher degree of protection than sanctuaries. For example, the grazing of live-stock is prohibited within a national park,[12] but permissible in a sanctuary.[13]

By the 1991 amendment, specified plants were brought under the protective umbrella of the Act.[14] The amendments also envisaged establishment of a Central Zoo Authority to regulate the management and functioning of zoos.[15] The boundaries of sanctuaries and national parks may not be altered except by a resolution of the State Legislature.[16] The Act regulates trade and commerce in wild animals, animal articles, trophies[17] and derivatives from certain animals.[18] Any violations of the provisions in the Act attract imprisonment and fines. Patterned on similar provisions in the Air and Water Acts, the 1991 amendments permit citizen prosecutions after giving sixty days notice of intent to the government.[19]

NOTES AND QUESTIONS

1. In *State of Bihar v Murad Ali Khan*,[20] the Supreme Court allowed the state government's appeals and restored the orders of the magistrate taking cognizance of offences under the Wild Life Act. The accusation against the respondents was that they had shot and killed an elephant in the Kundurugutu Range Forest and had removed its ivory tusks. In its judgment, the Supreme Court explained the object of the Wild Life Act:

> The policy and object of the Wild Life laws have a long history and are the result of an increasing awareness of the compelling need to restore the serious ecological imbalances introduced by the depredations inflicted on nature by man. The state to which the ecological imbalances and the consequent environmental damage have reached is so alarming that unless immediate, determined and effective steps were taken, the damage might become irreversible. The preservation of the fauna and flora, some species of which are getting extinct at an alarming rate, has been a great and urgent necessity for the survival of humanity and these laws reflect ... a grave situation emerging from a long history of callous insensitiveness to the enormity of the risks to mankind that go with the deterioration of environment. ... Environmentalists' conception of the ecological

---

[12] Section 35(7).
[13] Sections 29 and 33(d).
[14] Chapter IIIA.
[15] Chapter IVA.
[16] Sections 26A(3) and 35(5).
[17] Chapter V.
[18] Chapter VA.
[19] Section 35.
[20] AIR 1989 SC 1.

balance in nature is based on the fundamental concept that nature is 'a series of complex biotic communities of which a man is an inter-dependent part' and that it should not be given to a part to trespass and diminish the whole. The largest single factor in the depletion of the wealth of animal life in nature has been the 'civilized man' operating directly through excessive commercial hunting or more disastrously, indirectly through invading or destroying natural habitats.[21]

2. Nandan Nelivigi argues that the distinction between national parks and sanctuaries is artificial and is not linked to any real differences in their biotic features, the extent of human intervention or conservation functions. The absence of a clear and coherent policy unifying the Wild Life Act and the forest laws has enabled the state governments to completely ignore the differences in the objectives and roles of different habitats, to the detriment of wildlife.[22]

3. Section 2(16) of the Act defines 'hunting' to include (a) capturing, killing ... any wild animals, (b) driving any wild animals for any of the purposes specified in (a), and injuring or destroying any such animal. The Tehri Dam which is under construction is set to destroy twelve rare and endangered species.[23] Is constructing the dam covered under the definition of 'hunting'? If it is hunting, can construction of the dam be stopped?

4. Concerned by the lax enforcement of the Wild Life Act in several states, the Centre for Environmental Law, WWF, petitioned the Supreme Court under Article 32 seeking diverse directions to improve implementation. In an interim order dated 14 August 1997, the Supreme Court directed the states which had either not constituted wildlife advisory boards or where the term of the board had expired, to constitute boards within two months. State governments which had failed to appoint wildlife wardens were asked to appoint wardens for all the areas within the states. The court noticed several instances where despite notifications intending to establish sanctuaries and national parks, the concerned government had failed to take further steps to finally notify the protected areas. The states were directed to complete the process of determining the rights and acquisition of lands as contemplated by the Act, within a period of one year. To guard protected areas from 'de-notification' or 'de-reservation' the state governments were directed to refer the proposal to the Indian Board for Wild Life (IBWL) for its opinion and place the proposal and the opinion of the IBWL before the Legislative Assembly.[24]

---

[21] *Id.* at 3, 4.

[22] Nelivigi, *Bio-Diversity, Wildlife and Protected Area Management in India: A People Centred Approach* 37 J.I.L.I. (1995).

[23] Government of Uttar Pradesh, *Report of the Comptroller and Auditor General of India*, 238 (Vol.I, 1986–87).

[24] *Centre for Environmental Law, WWF v Union of India* 1997 (6) SCALE 8 (SP). 'WWF', the World Wide Fund for Nature, is a leading non-governmental organization working in the field of wildlife conservation. Subsequent orders in this case are reported at AIR 1999 SC 354, 1999 (3) SCALE 6 and 1999 (4) SCALE 333.

5. Earlier, the WWF approached the Delhi High Court seeking directions against the Union Government and the states to take effective steps to protect wild animals, tigers in particular, from being poached or illegally hunted. The petitioners also sought directions to curb the illegal trade in animal articles. The division bench judgment delivered by Justice Dalveer Bhandari refers to the Parliamentary debates that preceded enactment of the Wild Life Act, reviews India's international obligations under the Convention on International Trade in Endangered Species of Wild Fauna and Flora (CITES) and records the grim statistics and trends regarding seizures of animal skins by the Wild Life department.

The judgment looked closely at the problems confronting the tiger. Incidents of poaching were on the rise and census figures of the tiger population suggested that the gains made by the 'Project Tiger' initiative launched by the Union Government in 1972 might soon dissipate because of the tremendous demand of tiger skins and bones in Taiwan, China, Europe and United States. In an effort to improve implementation, the High Court directed the respondents to provide adequate staff and to equip the forest guards with modern weapons. The court urged the staff to enlist the aid of villagers living in the neighbourhood of sanctuaries. The postal and customs authorities as well as local police and revenue intelligence were told to strengthen the enforcement machinery to prevent the illegal traffic in animal articles. Finally, the High Court constituted a high power committee to implement the directions and to make recommendations for the preservation and protection of wild animals in national parks with particular reference to the tiger.[25]

So long as there remains an unbridled international demand for tiger products, will any of these well intentioned policing measures help? Is a well enforced international ban on tiger articles (similar to the ivory ban, which may have reduced the slaughter of African elephants for their tusks) the answer? If so, should WWF focus its energy to that end? Do lawyers and judges have a role in this effort?

6. In March 1997, a full bench of the Delhi High Court considered a spate of challenges to the constitutionality of the 1991 amendments to the Wild Life Act, in two batches of writ petitions: one set filed by ivory traders and a second set brought by dealers in animal skins.

In *Ivory Traders and Manufacturers Association v Union of India*,[26] the petitioners challenged provisions banning trade in imported ivory and articles made from this ivory on the ground that it violated their fundamental right to carry on their trade or business guaranteed under Article 19(1)(g) of the Constitution. Repelling the challenge, the High Court held that the prohibition was justified since the

---

[25] *World Wide Fund for Nature v Union of India* 1994 (54) DEL. L.T.286. The Supreme Court is considering tiger protection measures in a later case, *Navin M. Raheja v Union of India* 1999 (4) SCALE 333 and 2000 (5) SCALE 423.
[26] AIR 1997 DEL 267.

sale of ivory by the dealers would encourage poaching and killing of elephants to replenish the stocks held by the petitioners. 'Trade and business at the cost of disrupting life forms and linkages necessary for the prevention of biodiversity and ecology cannot be permitted. ...'[27] The High Court expressed concern at the serious threat to the Indian elephant, particularly in south India. The international ban on the trade in the ivory of the African elephant was likely to exert even greater pressure on the Indian elephant, necessitating a complete prohibition. The High Court concluded that under the Constitution, the trade in articles of ivory was similar to a pernicious activity like the business in intoxicants, and could be lawfully banned. The court also rejected a plea by traders in mammoth ivory,[28] who claimed that they posed no threat to elephants. The court found that it was difficult to distinguish between the two types of ivory and hence the ban applied to dealers in mammoth ivory articles as well.

The challenge by manufacturers, wholesalers and dealers in tanned, cured and finished animal skins was rejected by the Delhi High Court in *G.R. Simon v Union of India*.[29] The petitioners dealt in furs (coats, caps, gloves, blankets, stoles) and snake skin items (bags, shoes, brief cases). They argued that there was no nexus between the object of preservation of animals and banning the trade in animal skins; the 1991 amendment was colourable since the statement of the minister to Parliament conveyed the impression that the ban would apply to *specified* animals and not to *all* animals; that the provisions preventing the holding of stocks beyond the stipulated period was confiscatory; and that the impugned provisions would render unemployed the petitioners, who were engaged in a legitimate business. The court rejected each of these pleas. Wildlife formed a part of India's heritage and the amendments were inserted on the recommendations of the IBWF. The court held that the amending act was not a colourable exercise of power and that the provisions designed to eliminate stocking of animal skins was necessary to prevent accumulated stocks from serving as a cover for smuggling animal articles.[30]

The rigor of the ban introduced by the 1991 amendment was diluted by interim injunctions passed by the Delhi High Court in *Ivory Traders Case* as well as *G.R. Simon's Case*. The injunctions permitted the traders to continue their business for several years. Were the injunctions justified?

7. I.R. Coelho and other land owners living in the hilly tracts of Tamil Nadu had a different complaint: Animals listed in Schedules I to the Act were likely to damage their property, including standing crops.[31] Despite the threat to property,

[27] *Id.* at 286.

[28] Ivory drawn from mammoths, an extinct genus of elephants found as fossils.

[29] AIR 1997 DEL 301.

[30] On 9 July 1997 the Supreme Court dismissed a special leave petition (No. 11004/97) filed by the Mysore Super Reptile Corpn. assailing the Delhi High Court judgment.

[31] *I.R Coelho v State of Tamil Nadu* 1992 (1) MAD. L.REP.355.

the Act unreasonably prevented the hunting of these animals. The High Court rejected this plea, holding that the Act did not deprive the owner from holding, enjoying and protecting her property. The right claimed by the petitioners to hunt wild animals when they proved dangerous to property was without basis.

8. In 1997 the Bombay High Court was asked to prevent atrocious and cruel treatment to wild birds. The petitioners complained that Bombay served as a conduit for traffic of wild birds, as birds from reserve forests, sanctuaries and national parks were being transported to the city. The petition named the places where the illegal markets flourished. Responding to the petition, the court constituted a committee to suggest ways for ensuring compliance with the provisions of the Wild Life Act and directed the police to take immediate steps to prevent illicit trade in birds and animals. The committee was requested to submit monthly reports to the court regarding compliance by the authorities.[32]

9. Sukh Dev Singh Roy brought an unusual complaint to the Delhi High Court in 1992. Singh was a farmer in Ghaziabad, Uttar Pradesh. His crops were frequently damaged by wild boars and 'blue bulls' (Nilgai). Section 62 prior to its amendment in 1991 allowed the state government to declare any wild animals to be a 'vermin' for an area. (Vermin may be hunted without restriction). However, the 1991 amendment divested the state of this power and now the Centre alone was empowered to declare vermin. Singh considered the impugned provisions illegal since they divested the state government of lawful authority. The High Court dismissed the petition since the subject of wildlife was in the Concurrent List and Parliament had the power to legislate on this regard. Applying the doctrine of pith and substance, the court held that the impugned provision related principally to the protection of animals and birds and not agriculture (a state subject).[33]

10. In *Jaydev Kundu v State of West Bengal*,[34] The Calcutta High Court was asked to quash proceedings in the court of the Sub-Divisional Judicial Magistrate, Siliguri. In February 1992, the Range Officer at the Mahananda Wild Life Sanctuary seized a number of captive animals including a hyena and a leopard from the custody of the petitioner. The petitioner was arrested and charged with offences under the Wild Life Act and the custody of the animals was given to the forest department. The petitioner claimed that he was operating a zoo and was therefore entitled to possess the animals. The court was unimpressed. Merely because the petitioner was operating a zoo did not mean that he had acquired or purchased captive animals from an authorized person or another zoo. The petitioner had failed to establish a consistent case about the manner in which he acquired the animals and *prima facie*, the presumption under section 57 of the Act that he was in unlawful possession, applied to the case.

---

[32] *Viniyog Parivar Trust v Union of India* AIR 1998 BOM 71.
[33] *Sukh Dev Singh Roy v Union of India* 1993 (60) DEL.L.T. 319.
[34] 97 CWN 403.

B. PEOPLE VERSUS PARKS

The provisions to eliminate human intervention within national parks and sanctuaries operate harshly against forest communities, one of the poorest and politically weakest constituencies in India. It is estimated that there are nearly 5000 villages in protected areas with a population of about 250,000.[35] Tribal activists argue against protected areas because they deprive forest dwellers of access to common property resources, uproot communities, halt development activities and heighten tensions between local residents and the wildlife bureaucracy. Severing forest dwellers from their traditional access to forest produce 'criminalizes' honest citizens who have little choice but to tap the forests for fodder, fuel, food and minor forest produce. Conservationists sympathize with this view, but justify the extension of the national park and sanctuary network because of the degraded condition of our forests. They argue that the best preserved wildernesses in India are within the national parks and sanctuaries. Imperfect as the Wild Life Act is, it offers a proven legal framework to preserve our vanishing natural heritage. The task of balancing these competing interests fell on the Supreme Court in the cases below.

PRADEEP KRISHEN v UNION OF INDIA
AIR 1996 SC 2040

AHMADI, CJI:

The petitioner, an environmentalist actuated by public interest, has filed this petition under Article 32 of the Constitution of India challenging the legality and constitutional validity of an order issued by the state of Madhya Pradesh, Department of Forest, No. F.14/154/91/10/2 dated 28 March 1995, permitting collection of tendu leaves from Sanctuaries and National Parks by villagers living around the boundaries thereof with the avowed object of maintenance of their traditional rights. The petitioner contends that this act of the state government is *ultra vires* the provisions of the Wild Life (Protection) Act, 1972, as well as the petitioner's fundamental rights guaranteed by Article 14 and 21 of the Constitution and is even otherwise inconsistent with the Directive Principle contained in Article 48A and the Fundamental Duty cast on every citizen under clause (g) of Article 51A of the Constitution of India. The petitioner further contends that the said order is *mala fide* and against public interest. The order complained of [in pertinent part reads:]

> 1. Keeping in view the traditional rights of the villagers around the boundaries of those National Parks and Sanctuaries in respect of which the final notification U/s 26–A and 35 have not been issued, the blocks/areas earmarked for collection of tendu leaves would be reopened as done in the past.
>
> 2. In order to provide sufficient wages to the villagers living in these areas,

35 *Stressed Woods* in *Down to Earth*, 31 December 1995, p. 49.

labour intensive works should be provided to them to the maximum extent possible.

According to the petitioner, in the state of Madhya Pradesh, 11 areas have been declared as National Parks and 33 areas as Sanctuaries covering a total area of nearly 16,790 sq. kms. i.e. 12.4% of the total forest area of the state admeasuring 1,35,396 sq.kms. He refers to a news item published in 'The Sunday Times' dated 16 April 1995, headlined 'Forest cover shrinking in MP' and further refers to the report of the Comptroller and Auditor General of India stating that excessive grazing, reckless felling of trees and forest fires are responsible for the depletion of the forest area by 145 sq. kms. between 1991 and 1993. He further contends that indiscriminate felling of trees has resulted in a depletion of the forest area in the entire country including Madhya Pradesh, causing concern to not only environmentalists, but also referred to the criticism appearing in the media in regard to the issuance of the order dated 28 March 1995. * * *

The petitioner contends that while the impugned order dated 28 March 1995 permitting collection of tendu leaves has been issued ostensibly with a view to providing employment living in the vicinity of the National Parks and Sanctuaries, it has ignored the need to protect the flora and the fauna as well as wild life which are, so to say, nature's laboratory where evolutionary process of life in all forms takes place and which ought not to be interfered with. The presence of human beings, albeit in earmarked Parks, will not only adversely affect the flora and the fauna but will also scare away wild life. That is because, contends the petitioner, the collection of tendu leaves is a destructive process and can cause extensive damage to ecology and regeneration of trees etc. Besides, the destruction of organic matter is bound to affect the structure of the soil and there is the real apprehension of forest fires. The petitioner has, therefore, filed this petition with a view to preserving the National Parks and Sanctuaries which are likely to be adversely affected by the implementation of the impugned order. On the above pleadings and contentions, the petitioner has raised two contentions which have been formulated as under:

(i)   Whether an area declared as a Sanctuary and National Park under Section 18 and Section 35, respectively, of the Wild Life (Protection) Act, 1972 can be exploited for the collection of minor forest produce in violation of the restrictions contained in the said Act? and

(ii) Whether the state government has the right to exploit minor forest produce from the Sanctuaries and National Parks which have been so declared for the protection and preservation of ecology, flora, fauna, geomorphological, natural or zoological significance?

* * *

Dealing with the apprehension of the petition that setting fire to tendu bushes may set the forest on fire, the deponent states that the practice of setting fire to tendu bushes has been completely stopped and only pruning operations are permitted under strict supervision and no pruning is done by setting fire to bushes or trees in the forest. ... With a view to protecting the wild life and curbing poaching activities in the forest area, a special cell comprising police and forest officials under the control of the Inspector General of Police had been set up to supervise the forest area. There is, therefore, no real danger to the flora, fauna, trees and wild life in the National Parks and Sanctuaries. It is, therefore, contended that the entire petition is based on suspicion and misconceived apprehension

In his rejoinder ... the petitioner ... clarified that the petitioner does not challenge the right of the tribals living in and around the National Parks and the Sanctuaries to collect minor produce for their personal *bona fide* use, but only challenges the commercial exploitation thereof, in particular, the tendu leaves through contractors, since it is inconsistent with the object and spirit of the Act. * * * According to the petitioner, Sanctuaries which were declared as such under Section 18 of the Act prior to its amendment would continue as such even after the amendment and their status does not get affected by the amendment and therefore, in respect thereof, a second notification under Section 26A is unnecessary and non-issuance of a fresh notification cannot take way the protection extended by Sections 27 to 34 of the Act. This, in brief, is the stand taken in the rejoinder.

In the present proceedings, three persons (i) Bali Ram (ii) Shyam Lal and (iii) Munshi Lal, have filed I.A. No. 3 of 1995 seeking permission to intervene. These three persons, who claim to be tribals, contend that they are vitally interested in the present proceedings as they largely depend on minor forest produce for their survival. They contend that they collect tendu leaves during the forty-day season on a token payment to the state government and if the prayer sought in the writ petition is granted, their interest will be greatly prejudiced. They deny the allegation that during the process of collection of tendu leaves, they disturb the eco-system of the sanctuaries. They also deny that their presence is the prime cause for fires in the forest area. This, they say, is the handiwork of racketeers and contractors. According to them, what they earn from the tendu leaves is barely enough for their sustenance and is not a big commercial venture as is sought to be made out by the petitioner. They lastly contend that they have been enjoying this privilege for generations and the denial of this privilege to the small tribal population located around the sanctuaries would result in ruination of the entire tribal population since their survival is on minor forest produce only. ... They, therefore, contend that no fundamental right of the petitioner, for the matter of environmentalists, is violated and the Court should refuse to entertain the petition.

[The court set out the provisions of the Act and in the absence of reliable evidence, rejected the petitioner's apprehension in respect of forest fires.]

It is evident from the above pleadings that since neither the traditional rights of those living in the vicinity of these parks and sanctuaries have been acquired, nor have provisions been made to either compensate or rehabilitate them, the final declaration under Sections 26A and 35 has not been possible. That is the reason why the state government had to permit collection of tendu leaves by the impugned notification dated 28.3.1995.

[The court referred to the constitutional and statutory provisions relating to the declaration and the settlement of rights in national parks and sanctuaries.]

On a plain reading of these provisions, it is, therefore, obvious that the procedure in regard to acquisition of rights in and over the land to be included in a Sanctuary or

National Park has to be followed before a final notification under Section 26A or Section 35(1) is issued by the state government. In the instant case, it is not the contention of the petitioner that the procedure for the acquisition of rights in or over the land of those living in the vicinity of the areas proposed to be declared as Sanctuaries and National Parks under Section 26A and 35 of the Act has been undertaken. It was for this reason that the order of 28.3.1995 in terms stated that since no final notification was issued under the said provisions, the state government was not in a position to bar the entry of villagers living in and around the Sanctuaries and the National Parks so long as their rights were not acquired and final notifications under the aforesaid provisions were issued. It is, therefore, not possible to conclude that the state government had violated any provision of law in issuing the notification dated 28.3.1995 in question.

The matter, however, does not rest there. The petitioner contends that the forest cover in the state of Madhya Pradesh is gradually shrinking. As pointed out earlier, there is a shrinkage to the extent of 145 sq. kms. between 1991 and 1993. In our country, the total forest cover is far less than the ideal minimum of one-third of the total land. We cannot, therefore, afford any further shrinkage in the forest cover in our country. If one of the reasons for this shrinkage is the entry of villagers and tribals living in and around the Sanctuaries and the National Parks, there can be no doubt that urgent steps must be taken to prevent any destruction or damage to the environment, the flora and fauna and wildlife in those areas. If the only reason which compels the state government to permit entry and collection of tendu leaves is it not having acquired the rights of villagers/tribals and having failed to locate any area for their rehabilitation, we think that inertia in this behalf cannot be tolerated. We are, therefore, of the opinion that while we do not quash the order of 28.3.1995, we think that the state government must be directed to decide on the question of completing the process for issuing final notifications and then take urgent steps to complete the procedure for declaring/notifying the areas as Sanctuaries and National Parks under Sections 26A and 35 of the Act. We, therefore, direct that the state government shall take immediate action under Chapter IV of the Act and institute an inquiry, acquire the rights of those who claim any right in or over any land proposed to be included in the Sanctuary/National Park and thereafter proceed to issue a final notification under Sections 26A and 35 of the Act declaring such areas as Sanctuaries/National Parks. We direct the state government to initiate action in this behalf within a period of 6 months from today and expeditiously conclude the same showing that sense of urgency as is expected of a state government in such matters as enjoined by Article 48A of the Constitution and at the same time keeping in view the duty enshrined in Article 51A (g) of the Constitution. We are sure, and we have no reason to doubt, that the state government would show the required zeal to expeditiously declare and notify the areas as Sanctuaries/National Parks.

We dispose of the writ petition with these directions. We make the rule absolute as per the conditions given above with no order as to costs.

NOTES AND QUESTIONS

1. What is likely to happen to the tribals after their rights are acquired and the final notification is issued?

2. The directions requiring Madhya Pradesh to complete the procedure for finally declaring sanctuaries and national parks, was extended by the Supreme Court to cover all the states, in a petition filed by the WWF.[36] Why were so many states dragging their feet?

3. In recognition of the severe problems caused by the forced displacement of forest dwellers, section 24 of the amended Act enables the collector responsible for acquiring rights in the sanctuary to consult the chief wild life warden and permit forest dwellers to continue to live within the limits of a sanctuary. Is this wise? Will it perpetuate the conflict between tribals and foresters? Remember, though the village settlements may continue within a sanctuary post-1991, it is likely that these isolated villages will lose out on the benefits of development taking place outside the protected area. Forest dwellers residing in a national park must re-locate—there is no provision in the Act which enables continued residence within national parks.

4. *Niyamavedi v State of Kerala*,[37] is a rare case where a well known environmental group of Kochi petitioned the High Court to *prevent* a Biological Park from being established in 'Agasthayavanam', an extraordinarily rich ever-green forest, having 150 species of plants. Niyamavedi feared that the project would denude the forests and would oust the Adivasis from six ancient settlements. The court declined to interfere, accepting the respondents' case that the park would promote the conservation of flora and fauna of the Western Ghats.

5. Where the government of Mizoram was unable to produce the official gazette proving publication of the areas of Dampa Wildlife Sanctuary, the Guwahati High Court quashed government orders for shifting the villages which fell within the sanctuary. The court held that eviction proceedings must strictly accord to the requirements of the law.[38]

ANIMAL AND ENVIRONMENT LEGAL DEFENCE FUND v UNION OF INDIA
AIR 1997 SC 1071

SUJATA V. MANOHAR, J.:

The petitioner is an association of lawyers and other persons who are concerned with protection of the environment. They have filed the present petition in public interest challenging the order of the Chief Wildlife Warden, Forest Department, Government of Madhya Pradesh (second respondent) granting 305 fishing permits to the tribals formerly residing within the Pench National Park area for fishing in

---

[36] *Centre for Environmental Law, WWF v Union of India* 1997 (6) SCALE 8 (SP) and AIR 1999 SC 354. In *Kunapuraju Rangaraju v Government. of A.P.* 1998(3) ANDH. L.T.215, the Andhra Pradesh High Court directed the state to issue a final notification under section 26A within 6 months and permitted fishing operations in the meantime. The proposed sanctuary was in the Kolleru Lake area.

[37] AIR 1993 KER 262.

[38] AIR 1983 GAU 18.

the Totladoh reservoir situated in the heart of the Pench National Park Tiger Reserve.

* * *

Under S.26(1)(i) of the Indian Forest Act, 1927, any person who in contravention of any rules made in this behalf by the state government hunts, shoots, fishes, poisons water or sets traps or snares, shall be punishable in the manner provided in that section. According to the petitioner, in view of these provisions, the ancestors of the present tribals could not have acquired any fishing right in the Pench River. The present permits which are issued in lieu of this traditional right, therefore, are unwarranted and must be cancelled or set aside.

[The court reviewed the provisions of the Wild Life (Protection) Act, 1972 in respect of the declaration of sanctuaries and national parks. On 1 March 1983, the government of Madhya Pradesh notified its intention under section 35(1) to constitute the Pench National Park. Thereafter, claims were invited by the district collectors under sections 19 and 21 of the Act, but no claims were received. In the absence of any claim, final orders were issued under section 24. However, no final notification under section 35(4) was issued by the Madhya Pradesh government.]

As per the counter-affidavit filed on behalf of the second respondent it has been stated that although the necessary proclamations were issued earlier nobody came forward to claim their rights on account of illiteracy and unawareness. However, recently three applications regarding claims had been received pertaining to the traditional rights of villagers residing in 8 villages within the notified area which have now relocated outside the National Park area. These villagers are tribals. The villagers claim that they had a traditional right of fishing for their livelihood in the Pench river. They have claimed that their traditional right of fishing should be preserved as this is their only source of livelihood. Most of these tribals have been displaced from their original villages and have been resettled in villages outside the National Park area. Under an order dated 30–5–1996 these tribals have now been given permits to fish in the Totladoh reservoir which came into existence in 1986–87 on construction of a dam across the Pench river as a part of Pench Hydro Electric Project. The reservoir is in the center of the National Park area which partly falls in Maharashtra and partly in Madhya Pradesh. Apparently, fishing activity had been started in this reservoir by the Fisheries Development Corporation of the State of Madhya Pradesh despite protests from the forest department.

The petitioner as well as the state of Maharashtra have pointed out that if fishing is permitted in the heart of the National Park and as many as 305 fishing permits are issued, the bio-diversity and ecology of the area will be seriously affected. Fishing activity is a potential source of danger to the National Park because it may also lead to illegal felling of trees or poaching. It will be humanly impossible to monitor 305 licensees, their ingress and egress and to ensure that these licensees do not indulge in poaching and other ecologically harmful activities. ... The National Park is also a tiger reserve and all these other activities have a direct bearing on the protection of wildlife in the National Park area.

The petitioner is undoubtedly justified in expressing his apprehensions and in pointing out the dangers of permitting 305 licensees to fish in the Totladoh reservoir. The fishing permits, however, have been granted to the tribals in lieu of their traditional fishing rights. Although the petitioner relies upon the provisions of the Indian Forest Act in support of the contention that the tribals cannot have any rights in a Reserved Forest which has subsequently become a National Park, the Collector of Chhindwara, in his report has pointed out that in fact that there were four villages of tribals in Chhindwara District falling within the Reserved Forest-cum-National Park area where these tribals resided and fishing was their main source of livelihood. * * *

[W]hile every attempt must be made to preserve the fragile ecology of the forest area, and protect the Tiger Reserve, the right of the tribals formerly living in the area to keep body and soul together must also receive proper consideration. Undoubtedly, every effort should be made to ensure that the tribals, when resettled, are in a position to earn their livelihood. * * *

[The court issued detailed directions for the proper implementation of the license condition. The directions included the issue of photo identity cards for permit holders; restrictions on the route travelled while entering and leaving the Park; a prohibition on lighting fires for cooking or for any other purpose; and strict monitoring by the state government to ensure that there was no poaching.]

The intervenor organization which has intervened in this petition, namely, Jan Van Andolan Samiti, Totladoh shall explain to the concerned fishermen, the conditions, subject to which they are allowed to fish in the Totladoh reservoir and shall impress upon these fishermen their obligation to carry on the fishing activity in a manner which does not damage the ecology of the National Park or disturb its environment.

Since all the claims in respect of the National Park area in the state of Madhya Pradesh as notified under S.35(1) have been taken care of, it is necessary that a final notification under S.35(4) is issued by the state government as expeditiously as possible. In the case of *Pradeep Krishen v Union of India* AIR 1996 SC 2040, this Court had pointed out that the total forest cover in our country is far less than the ideal minimum of 1/3rd of the total land. We cannot, therefore, afford any further shrinkage in the forest cover in our country. If one of the reasons for this shrinkage is the entry of villagers and tribals living in and around the sanctuaries and the National Park there can be no doubt that urgent steps must be taken to prevent any destruction or damage to the environment, the flora and fauna and wildlife in those areas. The state government is, therefore, expected to act with a sense of urgency in matters enjoined by Art. 48A of the Constitution keeping in mind the duty enshrined in Art. 51A(g). We, therefore, direct that the state government of the state of Madhya Pradesh shall expeditiously issue the final notification under S.35(4) of the Wild Life (Protection) Act, 1972 in respect of the area of the Pench National Park falling within the state of Madhya Pradesh.

The petition is disposed of with these directions.

NOTES AND QUESTIONS

1. How persuasive is the reasoning of the court? Did the court have an answer to the petitioner's case that the tribals could not have acquired any

rights since the land was a reserved forest before conversion into a national park? Looked at differently, are not all statutory provisions subordinate to the right to life? If so, the court was justified in protecting the life and livelihood of the tribals.

2. The creation of the Rajaji National Park in the Shivalik ranges of the Himalayas, threatens the livelihood of thousands of villages who depend on 'bhabhar' grass, a minor forest produce, that is used to make rope ('baan'). Making baan is the major source of livelihood in this area. The park also serves as a winter base for the pastoral gujjars, who graze their flocks in the Tehri and Himachal Himalayas during the warmer months. The park authorities claim that all the rights have been settled and that the government has handed over the compensation to the village councils. The villagers refuse to move out, asserting that no proper rehabilitation scheme exists. The conflict and tensions at Rajaji are brought out in an article by Indira, *Conservation at Human Cost: Case of Rajaji National Park*.[39]

3. Apart from tribals residing in wilderness reserves, park administrators must confront encroachers who have settled on protected lands. The Guwahati High Court turned down the claims of villagers who sought protection against eviction when the state notified the Burachapari Reserve Forest to be a wildlife sanctuary. The petitioners claimed to represent two thousand graziers engaged in cattle rearing and the supply of milk. Justice Sharma found no infirmity in the procedure adopted by the government. Her judgement records: '[The] learned ... government advocate has submitted that these petitioners are not actual inhabitants of the area in question and they are recent encroachers through the unprotected border. I find sufficient merit in the submissions of the learned government advocate and prefer to take judicial notice of it as large scale influx of encroachers in such a forest land is a common phenomena, putting the forest authority in innumerable and unsolvable problems at the cost of the protection of precious endangered wildlife.'[40]

4. When judicial orders to relocate thousands of squatters from Borivali National Park in Bombay met with resistance, the Bombay High Court called in platoons of the state reserve police to assist in forcibly evicting the encroachers.[41]

---

[39] *Economic and Political Weekly*, 1 August 1992, p. 1647. Also see *supra* note 35 and the Supreme Court order in *UPSC & ST Welfare Assoc. v State of Uttar Pradesh* 1990 ALL.L.J.914.

[40] *Chandamari Tea Co. v State of Assam* AIR 2000 GAU 13, 21. The judgment disposed of a group of petitions some of which challenged the extension of the Kaziranga National Park. The state justified the extension on the ground that some poachers used the encroachments to sneak into Kaziranga.

[41] *Bombay Environmental Action Group v A.R. Bharati, Deputy Conservator of Forests* Writ Petition No. 305 of 1995. Orders dated 2 March 2000 and 13 March 2000. This case is discussed in greater detail in the public spaces and parks section of the Urban Problems chapter. For a softer approach to forest encroachers see *Nature Lovers Movement v State of Kerala* AIR 2000 KER 131.

C. INDUSTRY VERSUS PARKS

THE SARISKA CASE

The Tarun Bharat Singh is a non-governmental organization engaged in rural development in Rajasthan. One of the critical needs in Rajasthan's villages is water. The Aravalli range and its forests trap rain water during the brief monsoons and release the water over the dry months, like a soaked sponge being gently squeezed.

Widespread open-cast mining for limestone and marble in the Alwar District was disturbing the aquifers, springs and the water holding capacity of the Aravalli. The use of dynamite had scarred and devastated the hills. Rajinder Singh, the secretary of the Tarun Bharat Sangh was troubled by the impact of unregulated mining on the water resources in the region. These common property and development concerns prompted him to launch the *Sariska Case*, excerpted below.[42] The area, now popularly known as the 'Sariska Tiger Sanctuary' was an exclusive hunting reserve of the former Rulers of Alwar.

At the admission stage, the Supreme Court noted the apparent contradictions in the Rajasthan government's policy:

> The purpose of the notification declaring the area as a Game Reserve under the Rajasthan Wild Animals and Birds Protection Act, 1951; or the declaration of the area as a sanctuary under the Wild Life (Protection) Act, 1972 and the notification dated 1–1–1975 declaring the area as a protected forest under the Rajasthan Forest Act, 1953 is to protect the forest wealth and wild life of the area. It is, indeed, odd that the state government while professing to protect the environment by means of these notifications and declarations should, at the same time, permit degradation of the environment by authorising mining operations in the protected area.[43]

On 14 May 1992 the court framed the issues before it and set the tone for deliberations:

> This litigation concerns environment. ... The issues and concerns in this case far transcend the trivialities and inhibitions of an adversarial litigation. ... The issues of environment must and shall receive the highest attention from this Court.
>
> The primary issue in the case is the protection of the forest-wealth and wild life in Alwar district in the state of Rajasthan. The area in question has been declared a 'protected forest' by virtue of the notification dated 1st January, 1975 issued under Sections 29 and 30 of the Rajasthan Forest Act, 1953. Some areas are also declared as 'Reserved Areas, Sariska' under the Rajasthan Wild Animals & Birds Protection Act, 1951. Some parks have also been declared as 'National Park' under Section 35 of the Wild Life Protection Act, 1972. The

---

[42] Interview with Rajeev Dhawan, counsel for Tarun Bharat Sangh, 23 May 1994. Conducted by S. Divan.
[43] *Tarun Bharat Sangh, Alwar v Union of India* AIR 1992 SC 514, 516.

question that requires to be solved is whether in these areas which are covered by the various statutory notifications illegal mining activities are carried on and if so whether such activities require to be stopped by the intervention of the Court.[44]

TARUN BHARAT SANGH, ALWAR v UNION OF INDIA
1993 SUPP (3) SCC 115

B.P. JEEVAN REDDY, J.:

Tarun Bharat Sangh, a voluntary organization interested inter alia in protection of environment, approached this Court complaining that widespread illegal mining activity was going on in the area declared as tiger reserve in Alwar district of Rajasthan. In the interest of ecology, environment and rule of law, it said, the activity should stop.

The petitioner's case is that the area wherein the illegal mining is going on has been declared as a tiger reserve under Rajasthan Wild Animal and Birds Protection Act, 1951, as a Sanctuary and a National Park under Wild Life (Protection) Act, 1972, and as protected forest under the Rajasthan Forest Act, 1953. These various notifications, said the petitioner, prohibit all or any mining activity and yet the Government of Rajasthan had granted hundreds of licenses for mining marble, dolomite and other minerals in late 1980s, contrary to law.

* * *

Petitioner's case was that no mining lease/license can be granted within the protected forest except with the prior permission of the Government of India—Section 2 of the Forest (Conservation) Act, 1980 and Rule 4(6) of Rajasthan Minor Mineral Concession Rules—and that no such permission was obtained in fact.

By its order dated 26 November 1991, the court clarified that the order dated 11 October 1991 was not intended to permit the mine-owners to carry on their mining activity where such activity was prohibited by any Act, rule or notification having the force of law. In effect, the order said, it meant to prohibit—and not to permit—the mining activity.

In its order dated 14 May 1992, the court clarified the meaning of the expression 'protected area' used in the order dated 11 October 1991. The expression, it was clarified, was intended to and does refer to all the areas which have had legal protection against non-forest activities that devastated the environment including poaching, mining, felling of trees etc. It was further clarified that once an area is declared as protected forest, it becomes a protected forest notwithstanding the fact that a part of that area is waste. The idea behind declaring an area as protected forest, it was pointed out, is not merely the protection of the existing forest but also afforestation.

The committee submitted its report dated 28 September 1992. The report states that the committee verified and cross-checked the tracing maps furnished by the Revenue Department and found that both of them matched. After looking into the khasra numbers mentioned in the notification dated 1 January 1975 and all other material placed before it by the parties including the mine-owners, the report states,

[44] Writ Petition (Civil) No. 509/91; order dated 14 May 1992.

the committee identified the areas declared as protected forest. The report indicates that the area declared as protected forest under the said notification was not in one contiguous block but was comprised in several blocks or areas, as it may be called.

As per the said report, 215 mines mentioned in Appendix 'A' to the report fall completely within the areas declared as protected forest while 47 mines mentioned in Appendix 'B' to the report fall partly inside and partly outside the areas declared as protected forest. (These 262 mines are referred to hereinafter as 'listed mines'). To this extent, there is no difference of opinion among the members of the committee. Differing opinions have, however, been expressed when it came to making of recommendations for the consideration of this Court. The Chairman, Shri Justice M.L. Jain recommended that the mining operations in all the 215 mines listed in Appendix 'A' should be stopped forthwith to the extent they fell within the area declared as protected forest. Three other members of the committee (Collector, Alwar, the Chief Conservator of Forest and Chief Wildlife Warden, Rajasthan and the Additional Director of Mines) differed from the Chairman. They suggested that this Court be pleased to accept the representation of the State Government (appended as Appendix 'C' to the report) wherein it was prayed that the area covered by the mines should be allowed to be excluded from the protected forest, in lieu of which the Government of Rajasthan will provide an equal extent of area for being included in the protected forest. An application has also been filed by the State of Rajasthan to the same effect. It is stated therein that the protected forest area measures about 800 sq. kms, whereas the 262 mines mentioned in Appendices 'A' and 'B' cover only an area of 2.08 sq. kms including the area covered by the said mines to be allowed deleted from the protected forest. In lieu thereof, the Government of Rajasthan offered to place an equal extent for the purpose being declared as protected forest. It is submitted further that when the mining leases with respect to the said 262 mines were granted, the Government of Rajasthan was under the impression that the said mines did not fall within the protected forest area. Indeed, it was so clarified by the Forest Department. This happened because of want of clarity about the precise boundaries of the areas declared as protected forest.

[The court recorded the submissions made by the parties. The Central Government submitted that the Forest (Conservation) Act extended not only to reserve and protected forests but *all* areas recorded as forests in government records. No mining could be permitted in the absence of prior approval of the Central Government. On 7 May 1992, the Central Government had issued a notification under section 3 of the Environment (Protection) Act prohibiting mining in the Sariska National Park, Sariska Sanctuary and areas under Project Tiger. The petitioner argued that the government of Rajasthan was colluding with the mine-owners. The mining leases granted were illegal. Counsel for the state of Rajasthan urged the court to delete 5 sq. kms from the protected areas to enable mining to continue in the public interest. The mine owners disputed the demarcation by the committee and the maps put forward by the state. They disputed the claim that the mines fell in the tiger reserve and pointed to the unemployment, and economic loss that would result from closure.]

At the outset, we may be permitted to clarify an aspect. This is not a case where we are called upon to shut down an activity being carried on lawfully, in the name of higher considerations of ecology and environment. This is a simple case where we are called upon to ensure observance of enacted laws made by the state to protect the environment and ecology of the area. In such a case, we need not be oppressed by considerations of balancing the interests of economy and ecology. That has already been done by the Legislature and Parliament. The grievance of the petitioner is against the executive. Charged with the delegation of implementing the laws of the land, the executive is yet failing to do its duty by law and by people, when faced with the might of money; respect for law is dissolving into respect for Mammon, says the petitioner. Let us therefore first find out which laws are violated, if any, and then decide, what are the proper directions to make.

(A) Sections 2 of the Forest (Conservation) Act read with Section 29 of the Rajasthan Forest Act and Rule 4(6) of the Rajasthan Minor Mineral Concessions Rules:

* * *

Once an area is declared as a protected forest, it comes within the purview of the Forest (Conservation) Act, 1980. It becomes a forest land within the meaning of Section 2. The effect of this position is that no non-forest activity can be carried on in the said area except with the prior approval of the Central Government. Even the state government cannot carry on such non-forest activity in the said area without prior approval. That the mining activity amounts to non-forest purpose is beyond dispute. Thus, the grant of mining leases/licenses and their renewal by the state government, without obtaining the prior approval of the Central Government, in respect of the mines situated within the protected forest, after 1 January 1975 is contrary to law. All the mines listed in Appendix 'A' to the committee's report do fall within the areas declared as protected forest while the mines listed in Appendix 'B' fall partly within and partly outside such areas. According to Rule 4(6) of the Rajasthan Minor Mineral Concession Rules, 1986, too, no mining lease could have been granted or renewed within the forest 'without clearance from the Central Government in accordance with the Forest (Conservation) Act, 1980 and the rules made thereunder.' Admittedly no such prior approval or clearance of Central Government was obtained. The Chairman of the committee, Shri Justice M.L. Jain has recommended that 215 mines mentioned in Appendix 'A' to his report, which are situated wholly within the protected forest should be closed forthwith. There can hardly be any valid objection in law to the said recommendation. Similarly, with respect to 47 mines mentioned in Appendix 'B' to the report, the learned Chairman has recommended that they should be closed forthwith insofar as they fall within the protected forest. To this recommendation also, there can be no valid objection in law.

At this stage, it would be appropriate to consider the application filed by state of Rajasthan for permission to delete an extent of 5.02 sq. kms from out of the protected forest. The application is confined only to 208 mines out of 262 listed mines. Fifty four mines mentioned in para (9) of the application are proposed to be closed; indeed, according to the counsel for the state, they have already been closed. Reliance is placed upon the order dated 14 May 1992 in this behalf. It is pointed out that the said order does contemplate such modification, of course, with the permission of this Court and for valid reasons. It is pointed out that for such deletion or modification, the prior approval of the Central Government is not required. No such requirement is prescribed either in the Forest (Conservation) Act or Rajasthan Forest Act, it is submitted in this context, the submission of [counsel for the mine owners] may also be considered. He says that there are a number of mines around and outside the area declared as protected forests and that no purpose would be served by merely closing the mines within the protected forest and leaving those outside unhindered. He says that all these mines within and outside, are outside the sanctuary. Maybe so. But it cannot be forgotten that purpose of Forest Acts and purpose of Environmental Protection Acts may not always be the same. Such closure may not serve the environmental purpose—assuming that the factual situation asserted by the learned counsel is true, upon which aspect we need not and do not make any pronouncement— but it may serve the forest purpose. Be that as it may, both the purposes appear to be intertwined in this case. In this situation, we think it appropriate that the merits of the said proposal be examined by the Ministry of Environment and Forests, Government of India and a report submitted to this Court, within three months from today. Orders will be passed on the application for directions filed by the state of Rajasthan after considering the said report.

(B) Notification issued by the Central Government under Section 3 of the Environment (Protection) Act, 1986 on 7 May 1992

This notification expressly prohibits the carrying on of the mining operations, except with the Central Government's prior permission, in the 'areas covered under project tiger.' The prohibition extends to existing mining leases in sanctuaries/ National Park. All mining operations are prohibited therein. The table appended to the notification particularises the areas where carrying on of the processes and operations aforesaid is prohibited without the permission of the Central Government. They include all reserve forest, protected forest or any other area shown as forest in the land records maintained by the state government as on the date of the issuance of the said notification in relation to *inter alia* Alwar district of the state of Rajasthan. The table also includes 'all areas of Sariska National Park and Sariska Sanctuary notified under the Wild Life (Protection) Act, 1972 (53 of 1972).' We cannot agree with the learned counsel for mine-owners that the area declared as project tiger in the Alwar district has not been identified or that it is not properly identifiable. Both the state government and Central Government have demarcated them in exactly identical manner. The map produced before us by the state government is a detailed plan, prepared with great care. There is no reason to presume that it is not prepared by competent persons on the basis of the relevant material. The map delineates the area declared as sanctuary within the area declared as tiger reserve—though outside the sanctuary. A publication by the Forest Survey of India, Dehradun, Ministry of Environment and Forest, Government of India, entitled *'Status of Forest Covering in Project Tiger Reserve'* has been placed before us. At pages 92–94, we find the map of Sariska Tiger Reserve, Rajasthan. The boundaries, shape and dimensions of the said map tally fully and perfectly with the map prepared by the state of Rajasthan. Thus, there can be no legitimate dispute with respect to the correctness of map produced by Government of Rajasthan or with respect to the area declared as tiger reserve. Both the state government and Central

Government have delineated it. Maybe that the declaration as tiger reserve was without any statutory authority and is relatable to the executive power of the Union of India—but the notification issued under Section 3 of the Environment (Protection) Act puts the stamp of statutory authority over it. The Central Government has specifically stated in its affidavit that no 'prior permission' was obtained with respect to the mines located within the tiger reserve. On this ground, the mining operations being carried on in the tiger reserve, including the listed mines also appears to be contrary to law. Of course, this notification has come only in May 1992.

[The court directed the listed mines (those listed in Appendices 'A' and 'B') to stop forthwith. The Central Government was directed to submit a report within 3 months on the state government's proposal to delete 5.02 sq.kms from the protected area. Mines situated outside the protected forests within the tiger reserve were permitted to continue for 4 months, within which period they were permitted to approach the Central Government for permission to continue their operations. If no permission was obtained, they were directed to cease mining activity.]

NOTES AND QUESTIONS

1. In November, 1991 the mine owners turned violent. Rajinder Singh, secretary of the petitioners, was attacked and beaten by a crowd of mine owners when he accompanied the court-appointed committee on a site inspection. Ashok Agarwal, one of the mine owners, was convicted of criminal contempt and was sentenced by the court to imprisonment for seven days and a fine of Rs. 500. 'The atmosphere of show of force said to have been displayed by the mine-owners ... is really disturbing. We should make this case one which will unmistakably tell those like-minded with the contemner that this kind of crime against the course of justice and process of law does not pay. ...'[45]

2. Since its action in permitting mining was illegal, the state proposed to 'move the forest' by de-reserving about 5.02 sq. kms of protected forest and offering compensatory reservation of an equal area. Should the court have encouraged the forest swap proposed by Rajasthan? Does it set a dangerous precedent?

3. The Justice Jain committee submitted its report on 28 September 1992. The report was not signed by the environmentalist, Anil Agarwal, who submitted his dissent in November, 1992. Surprisingly, the principal judgment makes no reference to Agarwal's dissent. Agarwal was dissatisfied with the committee's obsession with the boundary disputes rather than the main environmental concerns.[46]

4. The Union Government's response to the court's directions was typical. It set up three committees: the first to recommend whether mining should continue in the areas *within* the Project Tiger Reserve, but *outside* the protected forest; the

---

[45] *Tarun Bharat Sangh, Alwar v Union of India* 1992 Supp (2) SCC 750, 754.
[46] *Supra* note 42.

second to advise on Rajasthan's forest swap proposal; and the third to look into the ecological aspects of Rajasthan's proposal.[47] Was this a practical approach? What would happen if the committees took divergent positions?

5. Why did the court not provide for the rehabilitation of the mine-owners elsewhere in the state, following the precedent of the *Dehradun Valley* litigation?[48]

6. Note that an administrative directive establishing the Project Tiger Reserve, by itself, affords no protection. To prevent mining activity, the prohibition must have statutory backing. In the *Sariska Case*, the backing was eventually provided by the 1992 notification under the Environment (Protection) Act of 1986 (EPA). Why should the Union Government single out Sariska for this additional protection? Why not issue similar EPA notifications for *all* Tiger Reserves?

7. On 12 April 1994 the Supreme Court rejected review applications filed by some of the aggrieved miners.[49]

JAMNAGAR MARINE PARK CASE

In 1998, Reliance Petroleum Limited (RPL) was well into setting up a giant refinery on the fringes of a marine national park and sanctuary close to Jamnagar on the coast of Gujarat. To transport crude oil from an offshore buoy to the refinery, the company requested the park authorities for permission to lay a pipeline which would run through a part of the sanctuary and park. When the chief wild life warden issued the permission, the Gujarat Navodaya Mandal challenged the permit, claiming that it was *ultra vires* the Wildlife Act.

GUJARAT NAVODAYA MANDAL v STATE OF GUJARAT
1998 (2) GUJ.L.HER.359

PANDIT, J.:

Gujarat Navodaya Mandal a registered society, registered under the Societies Registration Act as well as Bombay Public Trusts Act has filed the present petition to challenge the order passed by the respondent no. 2—Chief Wildlife Warden on 8 August 1997 in favour of respondent no. 4—Reliance Petroleum Ltd. (hereinafter referred to as RPL for short).

Respondent no. 4, RPL has undertaken 'Moti Khadi Refinery Project' for the production of petroleum products. RPL in order to function the said project has to import crude oil by sea fare and then to refine the same, and to produce the petroleum products in their refinery. For that purpose, they first applied on 2 September 1992 for getting clearance of their project from the state government. By its communication dated 1.10.92, the state government agreed to give clearance and supported the said project of the RPL. On November 19, 1992, the Gujarat Pollution Control Board

[47] *Id.*

[48] *Rural Litigation and Entitlement Kendra, Dehradun v State of Uttar Pradesh* AIR 1988 SC 2187.

[49] *Tarun Bharat Sangh Alwar v Union of India* 1994 (2) SCALE 68.

also issued necessary NOC for the purpose of setting up the project of RPL. Thereafter the respondent no. 4 RPL approached the Environment Department of the Government of India on 17 July 1996 in order to get clearance under the Environment (Protection) Act 1986. Government of India gave said clearance on certain conditions on 15 September 1995. Thereafter the respondent no. 4 applied for the permission under Section 2 of the Wildlife Protection Act 1972 (hereinafter referred to as the said Act) and Section 2 (ii) of Forest (Conservation) Act, 1980. After getting such clearance the respondent no. 4 approached the respondent no. 2 and respondent no. 2 has passed the order in this regard on 8 August 1997 by which he has permitted laying of pipeline in Marine National Park/Sanctuary, Jamnagar which is challenged by the present petitioner in this petition.

It is the claim of the petitioner that said order is purported to have been passed under Section 29 of the Wildlife Protection Act, 1972. It is the contention of the petitioner that in the permission granted and the work which the respondent no. 4 RPL is to undertake in pursuance of the said order, would not fall within the purview of Section 29. Consequently the respondent no. 2—the Chief Wildlife Warden has no jurisdiction to pass the said order. It is further contended by the petitioner that the said order is contrary to the provisions of the said Act. It is contended by the petitioner that the said order will cause damage to the forest as well as the marine life and would also cause damage to the environment. Thus, it is claimed that respondent no. 4's project will have disastrous effect on ecology and environment. Therefore, in the circumstances, the petitioner is seeking an order from this Court to strike down the order dated 8 August 1997 by holding that the respondent no. 2 has no power to pass such an order.

* * *

It is the claim of the respondent no. 4 that in order to see that the environment and ecology are not damaged and preserved, the RPL has engaged the Council of Scientific and Industrial Research (CSIR) as well as the National Institute of Oceanography (NIO) to survey the project and the area through which the pipeline was to be laid and the project to be implemented. It is the contention of the respondent no. 4 that these two organizations viz. CSIR and NIO are prime institutions for such survey and study and both of these institutions had carried out the survey and have cleared the project of RPL. It is further contended by respondent no. 4 that the NIO had also taken the approval of the Indian Resources Information & Management Technologies Pvt. Ltd., Hyderabad (IRIMT). Said IRIMT conducted a detailed study of the vegetation, morphology and ecological features of the intertidal area in question and only after their clearance NIO has recommended the special design as per the recommendations made by IRIMT. It is further contended against the claim of the petitioner that on account of the transfer of crude oil from Single Buoy Mooring (SBM) to the shore tank, because of the spillage control system adopted by respondent no. 4, they would not cause any damage to the marine life. They have taken necessary precautions and they are following the methods which are being followed for the first time in India to see that there is no damage to the marine life as well as to the ecology. It is further contended by the respondent no. 4 that by implementing the project in question, there will be the saving of 300 million dollars per year of foreign exchange. Thus it is in the national interest to have the project in question. Said project is also in the interest of state of Gujarat and therefore, in the circumstances also the claim of the petitioner that the respondent no. 4 should not be permitted to act on the said permission to start the work of the project should be rejected. Respondent no. 4 has further stated that the permission granted to the respondent no. 4 by the Government of India as well as the state government are conditional permissions. There are conditions which are put in the said permission are put with a view to see that there is proper protection of marine life as well as environment and ecology. Thus the respondent no. 4 contends that present petition should be rejected.

* * *

Section 29 runs as under:

> 29. *Destruction, etc. in a sanctuary prohibited without a permit.* No person shall destroy, exploit or remove any wildlife from a sanctuary or *destroy or damage the habitat of any wild animal or deprive any wild animal of its habitat within such sanctuary except under and in accordance with a permit granted by the Chief Wildlife Warden* and no such permit shall be granted unless the State Government being satisfied that such destruction, exploitation or removal of wildlife from the sanctuary is necessary for the improvement and better management of wildlife therein authorises the issue of such permit.
>
> (Emphasis supplied)

If the above provisions of Section 29 are considered, then it would be clear that under the said section everybody is prevented
(1) from destroying, exploiting or removing any wildlife from a sanctuary;
(2) from destroying or damaging the habitat of any wild animal;
(3) [from] depriving any wild animal of its habitat within such sanctuary except under and in accordance with a permit granted by the Chief Wildlife Warden.
Then it further lays down that in case of the destruction, exploitation or removal of wild life from sanctuary, the permission could not be granted unless state government is satisfied that it is for the improvement and better management. If this later part of Section 29 is considered, then it would be quite clear that this later part of Section 29 is only referring to the ... state government being satisfied only in case of destruction, exploitation or removal of wildlife. Therefore, if the Section 29 is considered as a whole, then it would be quite clear that the destruction or damage to the habitat or any wild animal being deprived of its habitat could be done only with the permission granted by the Chief Wildlife Warden. Section 29 does not say that for granting such permission, the Chief Wildlife Warden is required to obtain a permission from the state government which is to be satisfied that the same is necessary for better management and improvement of wildlife. That condition is applicable only in case if there is destruction or exploitation or removal of wildlife.
[The court referred to the conditions laid down by the authorities. RPL was

required to make financial contributions for cumulative impact assessment studies and for an environment management plan for the Gulf of Kutch region, the company was directed to transfer non-forest land to the state to compensate for the mangrove forest through which the pipeline would be laid; and the cost of compensatory afforesation was to be paid for by RPL.]

If the conditions which are put by the Central Government is giving clearance under the Memorandum dated 15 September 1996 as well as permitting of diversion of 1.9866 ha. of forest land by the letter dated 31 July 1997 are read together along with the conditions put by respondent no. 2 in his office order dated 8 August 1998, it would be quite clear that the Central Government as well as the state government have taken necessary precaution in order to see that there is proper protection for marine life, ecology as well as environment. If these conditions are taken into consideration, then it would be quite clear that when the respondent no. 2 has granted permission on 8 August 1997, he has passed the said order with a view to see that there is proper management of wildlife as well as their improvement.

[Counsel for the petitioner] very vehemently urged before us that the respondent no. 2 had not at all taken into consideration the fact that there was no improvement or better management of wildlife and consequently the order in question would be illegal and invalid. But in view of the material on record, we are unable to agree with his submission. In our opinion, when the conditions which the Central Government has put while granting clearance under the Environment Act on 15 September 1995 as well as the conditions in the letter of 21 July 1997 are read together, then it would be quite clear that the Central Government had taken necessary precaution to see that there is protection and betterment of wildlife and ecology and the respondent no. 2 has also granted permission in question to respondent no. 4 with conditions which show that the order in question is passed bearing in mind the provisions of the said Act. The Chief Wildlife Warden has filed his affidavit and the said affidavit is at page 162. In the said affidavit in paras 4 and 5 he has stated as under:

> I say that a pipeline which is being laid by Reliance Petroleum Ltd. through Marine National Park and Marine Sanctuary is most degraded area of the National park and the sanctuary which is presently devoid of any vegetation and is occupied by very little marine life.
>
> I say that Chief Wild Life Warden while permitting the Reliance Petroleum Ltd. for laying the pipeline had laid down certain conditions which ultimately would improve the habitat of the Sanctuary and National Park by planting mangroves and also providing protection to the Wild Life therein. So there is absolutely nothing wrong in permitting Reliance Petroleum Ltd. for laying pipeline through the Sanctuary and National Park within the conditions that it ultimately would improve the habitat of both sanctuary as well as National Park.

If the above statements made by the Chief Wildlife Warden in his affidavit dated 11 February 1998 are taken into consideration, then it would be quite clear that by permitting respondent no. 4 to make use of some portion of the land from the forest area and/or National Park, it could not be said that there is any likelihood of damage or destruction of the marine life, wildlife or ecology or environment.

Respondent no. 4 has stated in page no. 4 of additional affidavit that SBM is to be located at the water depth of 32 metres beyond the boundary of the sanctuary and Marine National Park and entire pipeline is to be certified and notified by Lloyds Register Shipping, London to ensure its safety. Then the underbody houses of the SBM have double carcass (double walled instead of single carcass). Then the pipeline in the intertidal area will be placed on a trestle (a bridge like construction) and the same will be above water level and will not interfere with the movements of water or any marine life. It is further stated that they have constantly consulted NIO and NEERI at every stage of implementing the project. It is further stated that the location of refinery and the pipeline connecting the SBM has been selected after giving paramount consideration that it would not affect adversely ecology and environment. There is no material to reject the above claims of the respondent no 4, RPL.

[The court quoted passages from Supreme Court judgments, including observations in *Indian Council for Enviro-Legal Action v Union of India* 1996(5) SCC 281 that 'development and environment must go hand in hand.']

In our humble opinion the above observation aptly apply to the proceedings before us. It has been mentioned by the respondent no. 4 in its affidavit, that by the project in question there will be savings of foreign exchange of 300 million US dollars per year. Said project will also generate employment opportunities and the project in question is for National interest and particularly in the interest of state of Gujarat. Therefore, taking into consideration this aspect and the fact that both the Central Government and state government have taken necessary precaution in seeing that neither the ecology nor environment is damaged while implementing the project in question, we are of the opinion that no interference is called for by this court by exercising the powers under Article 226 of the Constitution of India. We, therefore, hold that present petition deserves to be rejected. We accordingly reject the same with no order as to costs.

NOTES AND QUESTIONS

1. How convincing is the judgment? If pipelines are permitted, why not other types of industrial activity?

2. The court read the provisions of section 29 as enabling the chief wild life warden to grant permits that would damage the habitat. Is the power under section 29 meant to *promote* the objects of the Act or *defeat* them? What situations may require the destruction of wildlife or its habitat? Culling sick animals to prevent the spread of disease or protective measures in an emergency involving a natural disaster or forest fire are two such instances. Should section 29 be narrowly interpreted to cover only such situations?

3. Does the High Court's interpretation of section 29 square with the approach of the Supreme Court in the *Sariska Case*? Bear in mind the provision of sections 27 and 28 of the Act which prohibit entry into a sanctuary except for restricted purposes such as photography, scientific research and tourism.

4. Gujarat Navodaya Mandal (GNM) filed a special leave petition (SLP) in

the Supreme Court assailing the High Court judgment. During the pendency of SLP No. 10045/98 before the apex court, the government of Gujarat passed a fresh order dated 30 November 1998 ratifying the decision of the chief wild life warden dated 8 August 1997. On noticing the new order, the Supreme Court dismissed the SLP, without ruling on the correctness of the High Court decision. GNM were allowed to challenge the fresh order before the High Court in a new petition. In the second innings, the High Court ducked the section 29 issue raised by GNM, preferring to exercise restraint since the project was almost complete. However, the High Court issued a set of directions to minimize the environmental impact.[50]

THE NAGARAHOLE HOTEL CASE

The *Nagarahole Hotel Case* pitted a well reputed hotelier against environmentalists in Karnataka. In 1955, the royal hunting preserve along the Kabeni river was declared a sanctuary. The final declaration of the Nagarahole National Park in terms of section 35 of the Wildlife Act was issued in March, 1983. In November, 1994, the hotelier began renovating cottages and a reception centre within the National Park to set up a world class forest lodge. The state government considered the project necessary to encourage eco-tourism and cater to some of the 30,000 annual visitors to the Park. The hotelier claimed to having spent about Rs. 60 million on the project. In 1996, environmentalists and tribal welfare NGOs urged the state government to scrap the project and organized demonstrations and processions condemning the enterprise. As part of the campaign, a public interest writ petition was filed in the Karnataka High Court challenging the project. We excerpt two opinions in the case: Justice Bharuka's judgment dated 27 January 1997 allowing the petition; and the division bench judgment of 11 April 1997 partially allowing the hotelier's appeal. Contrast the rival approaches when you examine the excerpts below.

NAGARAHOLE BUDAKATTU HAKKU STHAPANA SAMITHI v STATE
AIR 1997 KAR 288

G.C. BHARUKA, J.:

This is a public interest litigation. The petitioner organizations claim to be working for the welfare of the tribals and are interested in ensuring the maintenance of ecological balance in Nagarahole National Park, which according to them, is essential to be maintained for the environmental reasons as also to protect the interests of the tribals residing in and nearby areas of the National Park.

In the present writ petition, the petitioners have challenged lease hold rights in certain properties situated in the midst of the Nagarahole National Park, under the lease deed dated 25–6–1994 (Annexure 'F') by the Government of Karnataka in favour of the 5th respondent, namely M/s. Gateway Hotels and Gateway Resorts Limited, a

---

[50] *Gujarat Navodaya Mandal v State of Gujarat* SCA No. 11251 of 1998; 12 May 1999.

private company for running its business of boarding, lodging and restaurant, for a period of 18 years.

The legality of the impugned grant of lease hold rights has been assailed by the petitioners on the ground that the same has been made in flagrant violation of the statutory restrictions contained in the Wild Life Protection Act, 1972, and the Forest (Conservation) Act, 1980. The propriety of the transaction has been questioned keeping in view the larger interest of the tribals residing in the forest and the apprehension that the promoting of such eco-tourism will spell doom for the precious undisturbed forest cover and will bring in modern day vices of the ultra urban culture.

FACTS NOT IN DISPUTE

The lease hold properties form part of the Nagarahole National Park which comprises of deep forestation having rich wild life like elephants, fourhorned antelopes, sloth bear, leopard, giant squirrel, adjutant stork, malabar pied hornbill, shahin falcon, etc. and also variety of birds of rare varieties.

Pursuant to a direction issued in the present proceedings the Asst. Conservator of Forests through an affidavit dated 9–1–1997 has stated that 'the land in question is forest one which form part of Hat Ghat reserve forest. The area in question falls in the buffer area of wild life sanctuary of Nagarahole.'

Admittedly, on 16–3–1983, the area was notified as National Park under Section 35 of the 1972 Act. A copy of the notification has been placed at Annexure 'A'.

It is a matter of record that even before the declaration of the area as wild life sanctuary, in the areas in question there existed a departmental saw mill which the Government has handed over to respondent No. 3—Karnataka State Forest Industries Corporation Order No. AFD 202 FDP 73 dated 27–3–1975 (Ann. 'R2').

It is further borne out from the records that pursuant to Government Order No. KHF:93:FPC:87 dated 10–4–1987, the aforesaid Saw Mill area at Murkal was transferred to M/s. Karnataka Forest Plantation Corporation, for establishment of a reception Centre with related facilities at a cost of Rs. 17,500,000. Accordingly, the said Plantation Corporation developed a project, namely, Murkal Complex and Wild Life India Cottages comprising of reception centre, super deluxe cottages, deluxe cottages, double bedroom dormitory, general toilets, staff quarters, manager's quarters, open air dinning hall, kitchens, bore wells, etc., the said complex with details of the structures spread over a large stretch of forest area measuring about 56.41 acres are ascertainable in greater details from the site plan of Murkal, which forms Schedules III to the impugned lease deed.

The said structures have now been leased out to the 5th respondent-Company, under the lease deed dated 25–6–1994 (Ann. 'F') for running its business of boarding, lodging and restaurant. Subsequent to execution of the impugned lease deed, the 5th respondent company has undertaken the work of reconstruction/renovation of the demised structures and construction of lease roads for providing required amenities and facilities to its customers intending to enjoy the flora and fauna of the National Park.

FACTS IN DISPUTE

The petitioners have alleged that under the guise of renovation of the structures, the 5th respondent-company is putting up new structures extending its operational activities to unworked forest lands by constructing metalled roads, cutting trees and is driving away the tribals residing around the area. They have also alleged that powerful generator sets have been installed which in due course will severely affect the unhindered natural movement of wild animals of the National Park, who had been coming to the nearby natural lake for drinking water. In support of the said facts, apart from making affidavit statements, they have also placed on record the photographs to substantiate their stand. The authenticity of the photographs has not been challenged by the respondents. But according to them the activities demonstrated in those photographs merely evidences renovation activities to make the resort habitable and comfortable for the visitors. According to them, they have not constructed any new structures. They have also seriously repudiated the allegations that they have cut any tree or are trying to make new metalled roads. According to them they have only placed boulders on pre-existing jungle path ways to make the roads motorable for an easy access to the resort.

ISSUES INVOLVED

In the aforestated factual background the legal issues which emerge for consideration are, whether the assignment of interest in favour of the 5th respondent company by way of lessee of otherwise was legally permissible under the provisions of (i) the Wild Life (Protection) Act, and/or (ii) the Forest Conservation Act.

Re: Wildlife (Protection) Act, 1972

Let me first refer to the relevant provisions of Wild Life (Protection) Act. ... Sec. 20 ... provides for bar of accrual of rights in any area declared as a sanctuary under Section 18. It reads thus:

'Sec. 20: *Bar of accrual of rights*: After issue of a notification under Sec. 18, no right shall be acquired *in, on or over* the land comprised within the limits of the area specified in such notification, except by succession, testamentary, or intestate.'

Section 35 of the 1972 Act empowers the state government to constitute an area as a national park for the purpose of propagating or developing wildlife therein or its environment for the reason of its ecological, fauna, flora, geomorphological or zoological association or importance. Sub-section (3) of the said section provides that: 'Where any area is intended to be declared as a national park, the provisions of Section 19 to 26 (both inclusive) shall, as far as may be, applied to the investigation and determination of claims, and extinguishment of rights, in relation to a land in such area as they apply to the said matters in relation to a land in a sanctuary.'

A conjoint reading of Secs. 20 and 35 (3) of the Act spells out a restriction on acquisition of any right in, on or over the land comprised within the limits of the area of a national park except by succession, testamentary or intestate. Therefore, it seems obvious to me that on and after the date of declaration by the state government of its intention to declare an area as a national park under Sec. 35(1), no one can acquire any right in on or over the land comprised therein either by way of a transfer within the meaning of Transfer of Property Act, 1882 or by easement or licence as understood under the Easement Act, 1882.

Re: The Forest (Conservation) Act, 1980

This Act was enacted to provide for conservation of forests by putting an effective check on further deforestation which ultimately results in ecological imbalance. Sec. 2 of the Act envisages restrictions on the dereservation of forests and use of forest land for non-forest purpose. The clause (iii) of Sec. 2 which is relevant for the present purpose is to following effect:

Sec. 2 Notwithstanding any thing contained in any other law for the time being in force in a state, no state government or other authority shall make, *except with the prior approval of the Central Government*, any order directing—
. . .

(iii) that any *forest land* or any portion thereof may be *assigned by way of lease or otherwise* to any private person or to any authority, corporation, agency or any other organization not owned managed or controlled by Government;

From the above mentioned restrictive provision, it is clear that no state government can assign by way of lease or otherwise any forest land or portion thereof to a person other than a governmental instrumentality except with the prior approval of the Central Government. In this context, the legal meaning of two expressions which has been made an issue at the bar namely, 'forest land' and 'assigned by way of lease or otherwise' needs to be appropriately ascertained.

[The court reviewed the case law on 'forest land']. Therefore, keeping in view the law declared by the Supreme Court as noticed above, if any land is identifiable as a 'forest land', then irrespective of the fact whether the same is virgin, broken or deforested, it will be incompetent on the part of the state government to permit the use of such land for the purposes referred to in Sec. 2 of the Act except with the prior approval of the Central Government.

* * *

From the above, it is clear that Sec. 2 (iii) of the 1980 Act restricts the right of the state government to transfer or create any right in or over a forest land or a portion thereof either by way of lease or otherwise. The expression 'otherwise' will, in my opinion, include assignment of rights even by way of easement or licence.

APPLICATION OF LAW TO THE PRESENT FACTS

Keeping in view of the facts as stated above, it cannot be seriously disputed that the state government has assigned a portion of the forest land by way of lease or otherwise thereby creating a right in the properties in question which forms part of the 'national park'-cum-'reserve forest' in favour of the fifth respondent, which is a private company, without seeking prior approval of the Central Government. There is an absolute prohibition on the grant of such rights under Sec. 20 read with Sec. 35(3) of the Wildlife (Protection) Act, 1972. As such the grant of lease in question is void and cannot be acted upon by the fifth respondent. Further, the transaction is also hit by Sec. 2 of the Forest Conservation Act, for want of prior approval of the Central Government.

The respondent have tried to resist the present public interest proceedings by raising the plea also of locus standi, mala fide and latches. So far as the objections based on the locus standi is concerned, apart from other considerations, in my opinion, if the Court finds that the question raised are of substantial public interest, then the issue of locus standi of the person placing relevant facts and materials before the Court becomes irrelevant. The legal position to the said effect is now more than settled. The allegations of mala fide have been raised on behalf of the fifth respondent company against the petitioner organisations on the plea that they are merely proxies on behalf of some interested parties. The allegations is too wild and sweeping requiring any serious consideration by this Court, inasmuch as no concrete foundations have been laid down to substantiate the said allegations. So far as the plea of latches is concerned that also cannot weigh in favour of the respondents, because, keeping in view the facts as emerging in the present case, through both the state government as well as the 5th respondent company, who are supposed to have well equipped legal assistance have been demonstrated to have tried to flout the mandatory environmental laws. The issues raised therein are quite fundamental in nature affecting the wider public interest requiring maintenance of ecological balance and environmental requirements. As such the Court cannot refuse to enter into the said issue on the plea of latches which has been evolved to subserve the equity and not to defeat the same. All the three pleas are therefore rejected without entering into any greater details.

For the said reasons, there cannot be any escape from directing the fifth respondent to immediately stop all its activities on the forest land in question and hand over its possession to the state government. The present public interest litigation thus succeeds and accordingly allowed with costs assessed at Rs. 10,000 to be paid equally by the state government and the 5th Respondent.

GATEWAY HOTELS & GATEWAY RESORTS LTD. v NAGARAHOLE BUDAKATTU HAKKU STHAPANA SAMITHI

Karnataka High Court
W.A.NO. 1333/1997
11 April 1997

R.P. SETHI, C.J.:

The admitted facts clearly indicate that after the declaration and notification of the National Park, the land in question was treated as an equity share of the KSFIC in 1984 and on 27–11–1985 the KFDC decided to construct boarding and lodging facilities with the object to encourage wild life tourism and to provide proper facilities for the public visiting the area.

[The court set out the clauses of the lease agreement, including the following: 'Now this indenture witnesses and it is hereby agreed by and between the parties that: 1. Effectively from the date of execution of this indenture the lessor do hereby demise to the lessee the premises more fully described in Schedule I (A) and (B) above and appended hereto forming a part of the agreement on an as is where is condition for a period of 18 (eighteen) years on terms and conditions as set out hereinafter and upon the lessee paying to the lessor the rent mentioned hereinafter.

* * *

6. The lessee shall run such business of boarding, lodging, restaurants, under the name and style in the demised premises as is deemed fit by the lessee.

* * *

11(f). The lessee shall not without previous consent in writing of the lessor make structural changes which are external to demised premises but this consent shall not be unreasonably withheld. However, the lessee will be entitled to carry on alterations within the existing structures without any previous consent of the lessor.']

A perusal of the aforesaid clauses of the lease agreement as noted herein above clearly show that no right in, on or over the land had been transferred. The appellants had been permitted to enjoy the existing structures after renovation and necessary modifications. No forest land or any part thereof has been acquired by the appellants. The lease deed is only for providing facilities to the nature lovers visiting the National Park area for the purposes specified in the Act for which specific permission has to be obtained. The lease is intended only to renovate and operate the forest lodges already existing with the declared object of meeting the demands of over 30,000 visitors claimed to be visiting the National Park every year. The purpose for which the visitors are to be allowed in the National Park is regulated by the provisions of Section 28 of the Act by which the appellants are bound. No person or group of persons can be permitted to enter or reside in the National park including the sites leased out to the appellants, without a permit, for the purposes specified under the Act.

What is prohibited by Section 20 is acquiring any right in, on or over the land regarding which declaration is issued under Section 18. The dictionary meaning of the word 'acquired' is 'to gain, to attain, that may be acquired'. In some cases it may be equated with the term 'transfer'. Transfer or acquisition with respect to a land may be something more than having the right of users of the property already in existence. Acquisition in relation to the land would mean getting the possession as an owner or purchaser or as a dominant user of the property according to his wishes and desires. Acquisition of a right by one would contemplate the deprivation of the right of others. Acquisition in relation to the property was held to mean and include the acquiring of entire title of the expropriated owner whatever the nature or extent of that title might be. The entire bundle of right which vested in the original holder are supposed to pass on acquisition to the person [acquiring], leaving nothing in the former. Acquire is something more than transfer. It would mean taking possession for its use to the exclusion of the real owner. The impugned lease deed, therefore, could not be termed to be amounting to acquisition of any right in, on or over the land forming part of the National Park.

* * *

Keeping in view the facts and circumstances of the case, we are of the opinion that the learned Single Judge was justified in holding that the state government had assigned a portion of the forest land by way of lease in favour of the appellant, which was a private company, admittedly without seeking prior approval of the Central Government. He, however, felt that in view of his finding that there existed an absolute prohibition on the grant of such rights under Section 20 read with Section 35(3) of the Wild Life Act, the lease itself was void which could not be acted upon by the appellant. We, are, however, of the opinion that in case the lease was contrary to the provisions of Section 2(iii) of the Forest (Conservation) Act, it could not be said that the lease agreement was void ab initio without conferring any right upon the appellant, particularly in view of our finding regarding interpretation of Sections 20 and 35(3) of the Wild Life Act. Even though the lease is not hit by the provisions of Section 20 of the Wild Life Act, yet it being contrary to the mandate of Section 2 of the Forest (Conservation) Act, cannot confer any right upon the appellant to carry on with their scheme, proposals and objects accorded to them on the basis of the lease deed executed in their favour, unless and until the approval of the Cental Government is obtained. In the absence of such approval no activity of renovation, repairs, etc. in terms of the impugned lease deed can be carried on till the approval of the Central Government in terms of Section 2 of the Act is granted.

* * *

Under the circumstances, the appeals are partly allowed by holding that—
(1) The judgment of the learned Single Judge in so far as it declares the impugned order and the lease deed to be contrary to Section 29 of the Wild Life (Protection) Act, is set aside.
(2) The respondents state and the appellants are at liberty to pray and seek the approval of the Central Government in terms of Section 2 of the Forest (Conservation) Act, 1980, which, if prayed or applied for, may be granted or refused strictly in accordance with the provisions of law.

The writ petitioners are held entitled to the payment of costs assessed at Rs. 5,000 to be paid by the appellant-hotel.

NOTES AND QUESTIONS

1. After the Appeal Court delivered judgment, Gateway Hotels moved the bench for permission to protect fifteen cottages from damage during the monsoon. The hotelier wanted to erect roofs on the cottages and lay roof tiles. When the High Court rejected the application, Gateway Hotels petitioned the Supreme Court under Article 136 of the Constitution. On 6 May 1997 the Supreme Court granted leave, recorded the statement of counsel for the hotelier that they were accepting the main judgment and permitted them to carry out the water proofing work.[51]

2. How convincing is the Appeal Court's interpretation of section 20 of the Wild Life Act? The Appeal Court asserts that if the petitioner's view is accepted, 'the purpose of the law would be defeated'. How so?

3. The Appeal Court concludes that an eighteen-year lease of several cottages, dormitories, a reception centre and other rooms and structures was *not* an acquisition of rights 'in, on or over the land'. Does the conclusion rest on sound first principles or frail logic? Was the Appeal Court swayed by the large amount—Rs. 60 million—spent by the hotelier?

4. What is so objectionable about putting up a hotel or renovating cottages and dormitories within a National Park? Across the world, wildlife parks have carefully designed hotels, hostels and other facilities for the convenience of tourists and visitors. Should India be an exception and permit hoteliers to set up their projects beyond the park boundries? Remember, sections 28 and 35 of the Wild Life Act recognise tourism and photography as legitimate activities within sanctuaries and national parks. Was this public interest litigation an instance of misplaced zeal on the part of environmentalists?

5. Do you agree with the Appeal Court's approach to the Forest (Conservation) Act (FCA)? There are at least three Supreme Court judgments which hold that a lease granted without the *prior* approval of the Central Government under the FCA is contrary to law and void.[52] Can the Appeal Court's judgment be reconciled with the Supreme Court rulings? If project proponents are permitted to execute leases first and then approach the Central Government for approval, will such permission be 'prior approval' as contemplated under section 2 of the FCA? Is the judicial construction wise or will it encourage clandestine and surreptitious exploitation of forest resources? In this case, the Central Government rejected Gateway Hotels' application under the FCA and the project stalled.

---

[51] 1997 (4) SCALE 18 (SP).
[52] *Tarun Bharat Sangh v Union of India* 1993 Supp (3) SCC 115, 125; *Divisional Forest Officer v S. Nageswaramma* 1996 (6) SCC 442 and *Samatha v State of Andhra Pradesh* AIR 1997 SC 3297, 3346, 3348.

D. DE-RESERVATION OF PROTECTED AREAS

Several sanctuaries are threatened by state government action to lift the protective shield provided by the Wild Life Act. Over 500 sq. km of tiger country in the Melghat Sanctuary in north Maharashtra were severed by a State Legislature resolution passed on 24 December, 1993. The ostensible purpose was tribal development in the region. In 1998, the state proposed to trim the Borivali National Park in Bombay so that slum dwellers who had encroached on park land would not be evicted. In 1994, the Orissa Government was under intense pressure to de-notify parts of the Bhitarkanika Wildlife Sanctuary, a unique mangrove ecosystem, to accommodate jetties for fishing trawlers.[53] A mix of environmental and political opposition has prevented the de-notification of Balukhand sanctuary, where the Orissa Government proposes to site a hotel complex.[54] In Gujarat, Sanghi Cement successfully lobbied the State Legislature to sever 320 sq. kms of the Narayan Sarovar Wildlife Sanctuary to enable the company to exploit limestone deposits in the region.

The provision which is used to de-reserve huge areas of protected land was introduced by the 1991 amendment and reads:

26–A (3) No alteration of the boundaries of a sanctuary shall be made except on a resolution passed by the Legislature of the State.

As you review the discussion below, consider whether the power to alter boundaries was intended by Parliament to be used to chop away huge tracts of land—over 500 sq. kms in the case of Melghat and over 300 sq. kms at Narayan Sarovar. The leading cases on the subject are the judgments arising from the Sanghi Cement plant.

SANGHI CEMENT CASE

In April, 1981, the Gujarat government declared 765 sq. kms of thorn forest in the Kutch Districts as the Narayan Sarovar Sanctuary. The sanctuary covers prime habitats for the Chinkara (a gazelle) and is the only protected area where the great Indian Bustard, the Houbara Bustard and the Lesser Florican occur together. A variety of migratory cranes pass through the area.[55]

In the 1990s, Sanghi Cement set up its plant on the southern fringes of the sanctuary. Among the locational advantages of the site was the proximity to rich limestone, lignite and bentonite deposits within the protected area. To run its fully

[53] A Kothari, *Environment and New Economic Policies*, in *Economic and Political Weekly* 29 April 1995, p. 924, 928. In *Centre for Environmental Law, World Wide Fund for Nature v State of Orissa* AIR 1999 ORI 15, the High Court issued a series of directions to protect the environment in and around the Bhitarkanika Wildlife Sanctuary.

[54] A. Kothari, *id.*

[55] Wildlife Institute of India, *Denotification of Narayan Sarovar Sanctuary: A Rapid Impact Assessment Study*, 6 (1996).

automated cement plants, the company needed access to the mineral deposits and the coast, along the western boundary of the sanctuary.

On 27 July 1993, the Gujarat government issued two notifications. The first claimed that the area of the sanctuary was 'substantially in excess of the requirements of the sanctuary' and proceeded to cancel the April 1981 declaration. Simultaneously, the second notification reconstituted a new Chinkara Wild Life Sanctuary of just 95 sq. kms The new 'sanctuary' comprised of islands of non-contiguous areas separated by broad bands of lands where mining activity could proceed.

Responding to a petition filed by the Consumer Education and Research Society, Ahmedabad, (CERS) the state traced its source of power to the rule in section 21 of the General Clauses Act which provides that the power to issue a notification includes the power to rescind it. The High Court rejected the defence and held that the 1993 notifications were *ultra vires*. Section 26A (3) applied to the case and in the absence of a resolution of the State Legislature, both the notifications were quashed.[56]

Unfazed by the reverse, Sanghi Cement lobbied the Vidhan Sabha to alter the boundary of the sanctuary. In July, 1995 the State Legislature resolved to reduce the sanctuary to 444 sq. kms by de-notifying over 320 sq. kms from the original limits. The de-notified area comprised lands holding rich deposits of limestone (7765 million tonnes), lignite (200 million tonnes) and bentonite (2.2 million tonnes).[57]

The Gujarat High Court upheld the resolution of the Legislature in a second round of litigation.[58]

CERS carried the matter to the Supreme Court.[59] On 14 May 1999 the Supreme Court constituted a ten member committee to survey the Narayan Sarovar Sanctuary as originally notified and in the light of its subsequent denotification to consider whether the area was adequate for the purpose of protecting the wildlife and its habitat. On 6 August 1999 P.K. Sen, Director, Project Tiger and Chairman of the committee submitted a dissonant report, with each member expressing his own view. Shortly before his retirement, Justice Nanavati delivered the judgment excerpted below.

CONSUMER EDUCATION & RESEARCH SOCIETY v UNION OF INDIA
2000 (1) SCALE 606

G.T. NANAVATI, J.: * * *

What we find from the debate that took place in the Assembly and the resolution is that the matter was discussed for two days, number of objections that were raised

---

[56] *Consumer Education and Research Society v Union of India* SCA. No. 13139 of 1993, Gujarat High Court, 22–24 March 1995.

[57] *Supra* note 55, at 8.

[58] *Ajit D. Padival v Union of India* 1996 (1) GUJ.L.R. 382.

[59] SLP (Civil) No. 13658/1996.

were considered and the decision was taken in overall public interest. ... We agree with [petitioner's counsel] that some aspect deserved better consideration and some other relevant aspects should also have been taken into account by the State Legislature. But it will not be proper to invalidate the resolution of the State Legislature on such a ground when we find that it took the decision after duly deliberating upon the material which was available with it and did not think it necessary to call for further information. The power to take a decision for reduction of the notified area is not given to state government but to the State Legislature. The State Legislature consists of representatives of the people and it can be presumed that those representatives know the local areas well and are also well aware of the requirements of that area. It will not be proper to question the decision of the State Legislature in a matter of this type unless there are substantial and compelling reasons to do so. Even when it is found by the Court that the decision was taken by the State Legislature hastily and without considering all the relevant aspects it will not be prudent to invalidate its decision unless there is material to show that it will have irreversible adverse effect on the wildlife and the environment.

The forest in the notified and de-notified areas is an edaphic thorn forest. It is a desert forest but with a large number of trees. It has been identified as a potential site for designation as a biosphere reserve by an Expert Committee constituted by the Ministry of Environment and Forests. It has been put in a 'Rich area category', from bio-diversity point of view, by the Gujarat Ecology Commission. Even the Union of India in its affidavit has stated that the de-notified area of the sanctuary includes many areas of high and very high floral and faunal value and these areas form integral part of the Narayan Sarovar Sanctuary. The Rapid Impact Assessment Report by the Wildlife Institute of India has also pointed out that any reduction in the area of that sanctuary will reduce the number of species of trees. It is also at the same time true, as pointed out by the Government, that this part of the Kutchh District is a backward area. There is no other possibility of industrial development in that area, though it contain rich mineral deposits. Therefore, if an attempt is made by the State Legislature and the state government to balance the need of the environment and the need of economic development it would not be proper to apply the principles of Prohibition in such a case. The reports of the three committees only point out the ecological importance of the area and express an apprehension, that any major mining operation within the notified area and large scale industrialization near about the sanctuary as originally notified, may adversely affect the ecological balance and bio-diversity of that area. It would, therefore, be proper and safer to apply the 'principle of protection' and the 'principle of polluter pays' keeping in mind the principle of 'sustainable development' and the 'principle of inter-generational equity'.

For the reasons stated above, we are not inclined to accept the contention raised by [petitioner's counsel] that the impugned resolutions and the notification deserve to be quashed. In our opinion the proper course to be adopted in this case is to permit restricted and controlled exploitation of the mineral wealth of that area, its effects for a period of about five years and direct a comprehensive study of the notified and denotified area from environmental point of view.

We accordingly direct that (1) the interim order passed by this Court shall continue for a period of one year. If a need arises to carry out mining operation in a larger area that may be permitted only after obtaining an order to that effect from this Court, (2) the state government shall constitute a Committee headed by a retired Judge of the Gujarat High Court and consisting of experts in the fields of hydrology, soil erosion and other related disciplines to make a comprehensive study of the relevant environmental aspects and also to study the effects of the present limited mining operation permitted by this Court. It shall also study the effect of running of the cement plant set up outside the old sanctuary area. The Committee shall, for this purpose, visit the area twice in a year, once before the monsoon and thereafter sometime after the monsoon, and submit its report to the state government and to this Court, (3) the state government is restrained from giving permission to others to carry on any mining operation or put up a cement plant within the area of 10 kms from the periphery of the old sanctuary area without obtaining an order from this Court. The state government shall also take steps to monitor air and water pollution in this area every three months through its officers and submit its report in that behalf. After considering the reports the state government shall take appropriate steps for controlling and improving the same. The state government shall also submit a yearly report to this Court as regards the action taken by it. This S.L.P. is ordered to be listed after a year for further orders. It will be open to the parties to approach this Court earlier if any clarification or modification of this order is required.

9

URBAN PROBLEMS

In many respects the citizens of 18th century Jaipur enjoyed civic facilities far superior to the contemporary urban Indian. The reasons for the slide in the quality of urban life are complex, involving an interplay of demographic factors, obsolete land-holding and rental laws, the failure of administrators to anticipate and plan for future needs and economic constraints. In addition, the model of urban development adopted by our planners ignores local, regional and cultural needs. Many of these factors are examined in the 1988 Report of the National Commission on Urbanization which recommends a set of measures to meet the needs of 350 million Indians who will live in urban settlements by 2001. Most of the National Commission's reform agenda, however, remain unimplemented.

As the edifice of many of our smaller towns crumbles[1] and the larger cities suffer from intolerable levels of air, water and noise pollution and a strain on the housing, energy and transport infrastructure, citizen groups have sprung up across the country to spur the civic administration into action. In this chapter, we analyse the judicial response to citizens' complaints. Many of these cases underscore the limitations of the judicial process and the need for even greater citizen pressure to secure better civic governance.

A. SANITATION

The leading case on sanitation and the duty of a municipality to dispose of human waste is the *Ratlam Case*,[2] discussed in the public nuisance section of the Judicial

---

[1] For an analysis of the problems plaguing Ludhiana, Tiruppur, Jetpur, Rourkela, Jaisalmer and Kottayam see Centre for Science and Environment, *State of India's Environment: The Citizens' Fifth Report*, 208 (1999).
[2] *Municipal Council, Ratlam v Vardhichand* AIR 1980 SC 1622.

Remedies chapter. In the *Koolwal Case*, a rather simple writ petition by citizens of Jaipur to compel municipal authorities to provide adequate sanitation, the court gets caught up in a somewhat adventurous constitutional interpretation. The court makes the questionable point that when every citizen owes a constitutional duty to protect the environment (Article 51A), the citizen must also be entitled to enlist the court's aid in enforcing that duty against recalcitrant state agencies.

L.K. KOOLWAL v STATE OF RAJASTHAN
AIR 1988 RAJ 2

ORDER: * * *

It is a happy sign that the citizens of Jaipur, through the present petitioner Mr. L.K. Koolwal has moved to this Court in the matter of sanitation of Jaipur City. Good number of affidavits have been filed by the citizens of Jaipur ... to show that the sanitation problem is acute in Jaipur which is hazardous to the life of the citizens of Jaipur. * * *

Article 51-A of the Constitution has been inserted in the Constitution of India vide 42nd Amendment in 1976. We can call Art. 51-A ordinarily as the duty of the citizens, but in fact it is the right of the citizens as it creates the right in favour of the citizens to move ... the Court to see that the State performs its duties faithfully and the obligatory and primary duties are performed in accordance with the law of [the] land. Omissions or commissions are brought to the notice of the Court by the citizen and thus, Art. 51-A gives a right to the citizen to move the Court for the enforcement of the duty cast on State, instrumentalities, agencies, departments, local bodies and statutory authorities created under the particular law of the State.

[Every citizen] has a right to know about the activities of the State, the instrumentalities, the departments and the agencies of the State. The privilege of secrecy which existed in the old times that the State is not bound to disclose the facts to the citizens or the state cannot be compelled by the citizens to disclose the facts, does not survive now to a great extent. Under Art. 19(1)(a) of the Constitution there exists the right of freedom of speech. Freedom of speech is based on the foundation of the freedom of right to know. The State can impose and should impose the reasonable restriction in the matter like other fundamental rights where it affects the national security and any other allied matter affecting the nation's integrity. But this right is limited and particularly in the matter of sanitation and other allied matter every citizen has a right to know how the State is functioning and why the State is withholding such information in such matters. ... Maintenance of health, preservation of the sanitation and environment falls within the purview of Art. 21 of the Constitution as it adversely affects the life of the citizen and it amounts to slow poisoning and reducing the life of the citizen because of the hazards created, if not checked.

Under Chap. VI of the Rajasthan Municipalities Act, 1959, S. 98 provides that it is the duty of every Board to make reasonable provisions referred therein within the Municipality under its authority. [Clauses] (c) and (d) of S. 98 read as under:

(c) cleaning public streets, places and sewers, and all spaces, not being private property, which are open to the enjoyment of the public, whether such spaces are vested in the Board or not, removing noxious vegetation and abating all public nuisances.

(d) removing filth, rubbish, night-soil, odour, or any other noxious or offensive matter from privies, latrines, urinals, cesspools or other common receptacles for such matter in or pertaining to a building or buildings.

It will not be out of place here to mention that Chapter VI deals with three of the duties of the Municipality namely, primary duty, secondary functions and special duty. Cleaning public streets, places and sewers, and all spaces, not being private property which are open to the enjoyment of the public, whether such spaces are vested in the Board or not, removing noxious vegetation and all public nuisances are the primary duties of the Municipality. Furthermore, it provides that it is the primary duty of the Municipal Council to remove filth, rubbish, night-soil, odour or any other noxious or offensive matter. The primary duties will have to be performed by the Municipal Board and there cannot be any plea whether the funds are available or not; whether the staff is available or not. It is for the Municipality to see how to perform the primary duties and how to raise resources for the performance of that duty. In the performance of primary duty no excuse can be taken and can be directed also as it is primary, mandatory and obligatory duty to perform the same.

*　*　*

Taking into consideration the serious allegations made in the affidavits and spontaneous submissions made by some of the eminent members of the Bar in the Court during the course of argument as well as taking into consideration the report of the Commissioner, which is the foundation for arriving at the conclusion, I am of the view that the problem of sanitation is very acute in Jaipur City and it is creating hazards to the life of the citizens. It is true that now after a lapse of time, the Municipality has awakened and is trying to do something and let us hope that they will do something within a short period.

In the result, I accept the writ petition and hereby direct the Municipality to remove the dirt, filth etc. within a period of six months and clean the entire Jaipur city and particularly in relation to the areas mentioned in the list submitted by the petitioner with this writ petition. Some applications have also been filed by some persons during the course of hearing about different areas and the Municipality will see that the sanitation is maintained in accordance with the provisions of Cls. (c) and (d) of S. 98, in those areas also. A team of five eminent Advocates of this Court is appointed as Commissioners in the case to inspect the city with the petitioner and Administrator, Municipality and to submit the report about the implementation of provisions of Cls. (c) and (d) of S. 98. ... [I]t was submitted by the Administrator, Municipal Council that it is very difficult to clean the entire city within the stipulated period of six months. It has been made very clear that it is not the duty of the Court to see whether the funds are available or not and it is the duty of the Administrator, Municipal Council to see that the primary duties of the Municipality are fulfilled.

Municipality cannot say that because of the paucity of funds or because of paucity of staff they are not in a position to perform the primary duties. If the Legislature or the state govt. feels that the law enacted by them cannot be implemented then the Legislature has liberty to scrap it, but the law which remains on the statutory books will have to be implemented, particularly when it relates to primary duty.

Order accordingly.

NOTES AND QUESTIONS

1. The court derives constitutional support from Articles 21 and 51A. Whereas Article 21 deals with a fundamental *right* clearly enforceable by the courts, Article 51A contains language implying that the citizen's *duty* to protect the environment is unenforceable. Can the court's exposition of Article 51A be justified in the light of the different constitutional significance of these two words?

2. One noteworthy contribution in the *Koolwal* judgment is the court's elaboration of Article 19(1)(a)—guaranteeing freedom of speech—to include the 'right to know'. In this case, the court extends the right to know to entitle the petitioner to full information about the municipality's sanitation programme, or the lack of it.

3. In its final paragraph, the court gives the administration six months to clean up the entire city, and dismisses any plea of lack of staff or funds. Is this a reasonable approach? Is this order enforceable? If six months pass and little progress is made, won't the result simply be a loss to the court's prestige?

4. *Janki Nathubhai Chhara v Sardarnagar Municipality*[3] was a public interest litigation which, like *Koolwal* and the *Ratlam Case,* involved unhygenic conditions within a municipality. The area, whose residents 'belonged to the lowest strata in the society', was filthy and unhygenic in normal times and become submerged during the monsoon. The Gujarat High Court, therefore, persuaded the municipality and the state government to install a permanent sewerage and drainage system.

The *Janki* Court's pursuit of mediation and accommodation contrasts with the classic adversarial approach in the *Koolwal* and *Ratlam* cases.

5. In *Koolwal* the court discusses the primary duties of a municipal authority, that may be enforced through the grant of mandamus. For a discussion by the Supreme Court on the same subject, see *Municipal Corporation for Greater Bombay v Advance Builders (India) Pvt. Ltd.*[4]

6. Following the lead given in *Ratlam*, the Madhya Pradesh High Court in *Dr. K.C. Malhotra v State of MP,*[5] directed the municipal authorities to cover an open drain, build public latrines and ensure that the drinking water supplied was not contaminated. The state public health department was told to adopt a range of

[3] AIR 1986 GUJ 49.
[4] AIR 1972 SC 793.
[5] AIR 1994 MP 48.

public health measures such as a vaccination programme against cholera and the distribution of chlorine tablets. The petition was moved by a physician who was concerned about the death of 12 children in 1991 due to insanitary conditions in Gwalior city.[6]

7. On a visit to Cuttack, the Supreme Court advocate M.C. Mehta discovered the rich cultural heritage marred by severe water pollution. Particularly offensive was the sight of the hundred year Taladanda irrigation canal which had been turned into a sewer carrying refuse. Likewise, the city's storm water drains were laden with sewage. A large section of the city's poor were forced to drink contaminated water. Responding to Mehta's public interest petition, a division bench of the Orissa High Court blamed the municipality, the state health department and the pollution control board for the 'horrendous state of affairs'. The court constituted a committee of senior government officials to devise measures to prevent water pollution and improve Cuttack's sanitation within a year.[7]

8. In 1973 the Haryana Urban Development Authority ('HUDA') sold plots in Ambala, assuring the purchasers 'all modern amenities'. Fifteen years later, the roads in the new layout were pot-holed and cess pools caused by the lack of sewerage and drainage were leading to the spread of malaria and jaundice in the locality. In reply to the plot holders' petition, HUDA disputed the facts, compelling the High Court to appoint a commission for local inspection. The Commissioner confirmed the lack of drainage and sewerage facilities.

The High Court was severe in its criticism of the Authority. Though the cost of providing amenities such as proper roads, sewerage, community buildings, parks etc. was collected from the plot purchasers, the amenities were not provided. '[HUDA's] inaction in spite of repeated requests from the residents of Sector 7 and failure to provide the promised amenities is not only arbitrary but even wholly illegal. ... In this situation, the Authority may well earn the dubious distinction of being dubbed as the "Haryana Urban Destruction Authority".' The court directed HUDA to provide within a year, and at its cost, basic amenities like drainage, sewerage, adequate potable water and parks.[8]

9. Despite several writs issued by the High Courts and the Supreme Court's judgment in the *Ratlam Case*, India's cities and towns continue to be swamped by sewage. Has the judicial system proved ineffective? Should aggrieved citizens turn to the consumer fora constituted under the Consumer Protection Act of 1986, for relief? Would a lack of proper sanitation constitute a 'deficiency in service' on the part of local bodies? What corrective measures can the consumer fora order? What advantages do these fora offer over the formal judicial system?

[6] For another sanitation case concerning Gwalior see *Citizens & Inhabitants of Municipal Ward, No. 15 v Municipal Corporation, Gwalior* AIR 1997 MP 33.

[7] *M.C. Mehta v State of Orissa* AIR 1992 ORI 225.

[8] *Ambala Urban Estate Welfare Society v Haryana Urban Development Authority* AIR 1994 P&H 288.

10. Consider this observation by a visitor to India: 'Indians are committed more to their family, caste and religion then to an abstract public. Their homes are immaculately clean inside—but litter begins on the doorsteps, even in prosperous areas, and the owners of new villas rent out their garden walls as billboards.'[9] Is the view justified? Or is the commentator being unnecessarily patronising?

11. Civic amenities, including road maintenance, lighting, sewerage and hospital maintenance were the subjects of a citizens' petition in the case of *Citizens Action Committee v Civil Surgeon, Mayo (General) Hospital*.[10] Of special interest in this case is the Bombay High Court's directions regarding specific remedial measures relating to de-congestion of crowded markets, road maintenance, sewage and sanitation infrastructure.

12. In *S.K. Garg v State of UP*,[11] the High Court noted the irony in the citizens of Allahabad not receiving any drinking water despite the city standing at the confluence of the Ganga and the Yamuna. Justice Katju was reminded of the Ancient Mariner's lament: 'Water, water everywhere but not a drop to drink.' The court set up the Allahabad Water Committee under a senior advocate to suggest measures to solve the potable water problem. The court directed the general manager of the Water Board to remain present in court on the next hearing date and respond to the recommendation of the committee.

Justice Katju had another occasion to deal with poor civic amenities in Allahabad in *Vinod Chandra Varma v State of UP*.[12] Directing the municipal corporation to take strong disciplinary action against safai karmacharis who neglected their work, the court observed:

> It is common knowledge that nowhere cleaning of the roads, garbage and sewer is done in Allahabad by the Nagar Nigam, although there are about 1800 permanent employees and 800 casual labourers working in the Nagar Nigam for this purpose, but they do not work and if they are told to work they threaten to go on strike. ... The citizens of Allahabad are paying [municipal taxes] without getting any corresponding benefits e.g. keeping the city of Allahabad clean and other basic amenities.

13. The facts in a petition filed by the residents of Kolhapur were equally stark. A United Nation's survey lists Kolhapur as among one of twelve cities in the

[9] Pope, *Billboards on the Garden Wall* in *Sierra* January/February 1999, p. 12.
[10] AIR 1986 BOM 136.
[11] AIR 1999 ALL 41. The Supreme Court constituted a monitoring committee to oversee measures for the supply of drinking water to Agra in *D.K. Joshi v Chief Secretary of H.P.* 1999 (7) SCALE 181. The efforts of the Patna High Court to ensure the supply of potable drinking water, after samples of contaminated water were drawn from 40 places in Patna including the Raj Bhavan, the High Court premises and the residences of High Court judges, are recorded in *Council for Protection of Public Rights and Welfare v State of Bihar* 1992 (1) BIH.L.J.REP. 822.
[12] AIR 1999 ALL 108.

world that supplies polluted water for drinking. Reprimanding the Kolhapur municipal corporation and the Maharashtra pollution control board for their neglect, the Bombay High Court issued directions to check the industrial pollution and monitor water quality in the Panchganga river which was the source of drinking water. The court also set up a committee of experts in water technology to augment the supply of potable water to Kolhapur.[13]

14. In an effort to upgrade the sewerage in Delhi, the Supreme Court in November, 1998 designated a senior official within each government department to take responsibility for implementing an improvement plan. A court-appointed committee had, over a 10 month period, surveyed the existing sewerage and drafted a time-bound action plan to improve sanitation.[14]

15. Sewage and drainage systems frequently get choked due to the indiscriminate disposal of plastic bags. Efforts to control this menace have been surveyed by the Centre for Science and Environment, New Delhi.[15] Several states, including Himachal Pradesh,[16] Sikkim,[17] Haryana[18] and Maharashtra[19] have made efforts to regulate or ban plastic bag usage, but with little success. On 2 September 1999, the Central Government issued the Re-cycled Plastics Manufacture and Usage Rules which prohibit the use of recycled plastic carrybags for dispensing or packing foodstuffs.

In *Wg. Com. Utpal Barbara v State of Assam*,[20] the Gauhati High Court quashed an order passed by the Additional District Magistrate, Kamrup, under section 144 of the Code of Criminal Procedure, banning the use of polythene bags throughout the district of Kamrup. The High Court held that while the district administration ought to take steps to regulate the use and disposal of polythene bags, it could not impose a total ban without resort to legislation. Moreover, the High Court found that there was no 'imminent danger' to public health or safety, justifying a prohibitory order under section 144.

---

[13] *Dhanjirao Jivarao Jadhav v State of Maharashtra* 1998 (2) MAH.L.J. 462. The Bombay High Court was more restrained when it came to drinking water supply to Nanded. The court declined to pass any directions in a public interest petition when it found that the authorities were 'alive to the situation'. *Nanded City Development Committee v State of Maharashtra* 1994 (2) BOM.C.REP. 7.

[14] *Sector 14 Residents Welfare Association v State of Delhi* AIR 1999 SC 308. A subsequent order dated 27 August 1999 (1999(5) SCALE 417) records that the Delhi Jal Board and Delhi Development Authority were at loggerheads and were unable to decide who was responsible for laying a 400 m sewer. In another public interest litigation, the apex court is monitoring the quality of water in the Yamuna at each of the 19 drains from which untreated sewage from Delhi flows into the river. *News Item Hindustan Times A.Q.F.M. Yamuna v CPCB* 1999 (5) SCALE 418; 2000 (1) SCALE 134; 2000 (1) SCALE 657; 2000 (3) SCALE 122 and 2000 (5) SCALE 127, 195, 196.

[15] *State of India's Environment: The Citizens' Fifth Report*, 258 (1999).

[16] Himachal Pradesh Non-biodegradable Garbage (Control) Act of 1995.

[17] Sikkim Non-biodegradable Garbage (Control) Act of 1997.

[18] Haryana Non-biodegradable Garbage (Control) Act of 1998.

[19] Order No. ENV.1098/899/C. R. 43/T.C-3 dated 8 March 1999 issued under section 5 of the Environment (Protection) Act of 1986 issued by the Environment Department, Maharashtra.

[20] AIR 1999 GAU 78.

B. SOLID WASTE MANAGEMENT

Municipal solid waste ('MSW') management or garbage disposal is another neglected area of urban development. In most cities nearly half of the MSW generated remains unattended.[21] The urban poor bear the immediate impact of the resulting unhygienic conditions but few city dwellers escape the periodic outbreaks of diseases that spread in unhealthy urban environments. A 1995 report prepared for the Planning Commission acknowledges the progressive decline in the standard of services with respect to the collection and disposal of household, hospital and industrial wastes.[22]

Chandigarh alone has a reasonably well managed MSW disposal programme.[23] Elsewhere, the collection, transport and disposal of MSW is haphazard or altogether absent. There is no system of segregation of organic, inorganic and recyclable wastes at the household level. Door-to-door collection is rarely practised; community collection bins are poorly designed and are usually no more than open dumps on the roadside. Municipal waste is generally carried to the city periphery where it is dumped in open land fills on neighbouring village lands.[24]

These dump sites are poorly managed and are swarmed by vermin and mosquitoes. Composting is seldom practised and the ground water in some areas is contaminated by leachate.[25]

The magnitude of the problem prompted Almitra Patel of Bangalore to file an Article 32 writ petition before the Supreme Court, seeking writs against the states and principal municipalities to implement 'cradle to grave' MSW management. In the wake of the Surat plague of 1994, Patel campaigned across the country urging municipalities to clean up their act. Though many of the municipal officers were receptive to her suggestions, few displayed the initiative to secure budgetary support and political backing to implement comprehensive MSW management measures.

On 3 March 1997, the Supreme Court directed the respondents to furnish details in respect of existing MSW practices adopted by them.[26] Since the affidavits filed by some municipalities and states were inadequate, in April, 1997 they were asked to report whether the recommendations made by the High Power Committee set up by the Planning Commission in 1995 and the 1994 report of the Central pollution control board on the management of municipal wastes, had been implemented.[27] On 28 July

---

[21] Government of India, Planning Commission, *Report of High Power Committee on Urban Solid Waste Management in India* 1 (1995).

[22] *Id.*

[23] Interview with Almitra Patel, Convenor, INTACH Waste Network; 2 March 1996. Conducted by S. Divan.

[24] *Id.* The villages are politically weak and are unable to resist the cities' search for fresh dumping grounds.

[25] *Supra* note 21 at 3.

[26] *Almitra H. Patel v Union of India* 1997 (6) SCALE 10 (SP).

[27] *Almitra H. Patel v Union of India* 1997 (6) SCALE 11 (SP).

1997 the respondents were told to frame time bound schemes for the disposal of MSW in a scientific and hygienic manner. In framing the schemes, the local bodies were directed to seek expert advice on vector control and were urged 'immediately to take steps to phase out the routine use of insecticides like DDT and BHC and similar dangerous insecticides on garbage heaps and dump sites.' Nearly a quarter century after the Water Act was passed, the Central and State pollution control boards were directed to ensure that local bodies complied with the provisions of the Act.[28]

In January, 1998, the Supreme Court constituted an expert committee to examine all aspects of MSW management in Class I cities (having a population over one lakh). The committee's charter extended to reviewing municipal laws, formulating standards and regulations for the management of MSW and suggesting suitable practices and proven technologies for the sorting, collection, transport, disposal, recycling and reuse of MSW in an eco-friendly manner.[29]

On 20 July 1998, the Supreme Court considered the interim report of the committee and approved its proposal to conduct regional workshops to sensitise and inform municipal officials about good MSW disposal practices.[30] On 12 April 1999, the court appreciated the work by the committee and directed the states to respond to the recommendations made in the final report.[31] On 13 August 1999,[32] the Supreme Court noted that the Central pollution control board had formulated draft MSW (Management and Handling) Rules, which were notified in the following month for inviting suggestions and objections. In subsequent proceedings, the court decided to take up the problems facing the four metropolises and Bangalore. Since a large proportion of the municipal revenue in the metros was being spent on wages for an inefficient staff, the court mooted the idea of privatizing garbage disposal services.[33] On 15 February 2000 the court issued directions specific to Delhi, ordering the authorities to identify land fill and composting sites, to recover fines for littering and to appoint magistrates to try offences in relation to littering, public nuisance and public health.[34]

Shortly before taking up the *Almitra Patel Case*, the Supreme Court had already directed its attention to garbage clearance in Delhi. Chastizing the authorities for permitting the Capital to become 'an open dust bin' with 'garbage strewn all over', the court issued a range of directions for the proper disposal of hospital wastes;

---

[28] *Almitra H. Patel v Union of India* 1997 (6) SCALE 12 (SP). The report misquotes the direction in respect of insecticides set out above.

[29] *Almitra H. Patel v Union of India* AIR 1998 SC 993.

[30] *Almitra H. Patel v Union of India* 1998 (4) SCALE 9 (SP).

[31] *Almitra H. Patel v Union of India* 1999 (2) SCALE 685.

[32] *Almitra H. Patel v Union of India* 1999 (5) SCALE 154.

[33] *Almitra H. Patel v Union of India* 1999 (7) SCALE 1 and 2000 (2) SCC 166.

[34] *Almitra H. Patel v Union of India* 2000 (1) SCALE 568. At the time of writing, the case was pending before the Supreme Court.

public education of residents; and the management of sanitary land fills. The court found that the municipal authorities had failed in their duties despite employing over 40,000 workers to keep the city clean. In an echo of the *Ratlam Case*, the court held:

> It is clear from various provisions of the [Delhi Municipal Corporation Act of 1957 and the New Delhi Municipal Council Act of 1994 that the Municipal Corporation of Delhi (MCD) and the New Delhi Municipal Council (NDMC)] are under a statutory obligation to scavenge and clean the city of Delhi. It is mandatory for these authorities to collect and dispose of the garbage/waste generated from various sources in the city. We have no hesitation in observing that the MCD and the NDMC have been wholly remiss in the performance of their statutory duties. Apart from the rights guaranteed under the Constitution the residents of Delhi have a statutory right to live in a clean city. The Courts are justified in directing the MCD and NDMC to perform their duties under the law. Non-availability of funds, inadequacy or inefficiency of the staff, cannot be pleaded as grounds for non-performance of their statutory obligations.[35]

The Bombay High Court addressed a more modest agenda in *Shanti Park 'Sorento' Co-op. Society Ltd. v Municipal Corporation of Greater Mumbai*.[36] The residents of Shanti Park complained against the daily burning of garbage at the municipal dumping site at Deonar. Thick plumes of smoke rose from Deonar and drifted over the suburbs of Chembur and Ghatkopar. The petitioners' investigations revealed that the garbage was being ignited by slum dwellers and rag pickers who recovered discarded metal from the waste. The High Court issued a series of orders requiring the municipal corporation to improve its MSW dumping practices and to prevent the burning of garbage at Deonar.

C. PUBLIC SPACES, PARKS AND PAVEMENTS

Among the strongest town planning judgments rendered by the Supreme Court is the *Bangalore Medical Trust Case*. It has two important pro-citizen dimensions. It lays down that power exercised under an environmental statute must further the legislative object of the Act. Further, it invalidates a favour by the Karnataka Chief Minister on the ground that it was in breach of public trust since it deprived Bangalore residents of a public park. We excerpt from Justice Sahai's opinion disapproving the intended change of user to enable a private nursing home to come up.

---

[35] *B.L. Wadehra v Union of India* AIR 1996 SC 2969. A further order in this case is reported at 1997 (5) SCALE 2 (SP).
[36] Writ Petition No. 1138 of 1996; 6 August 1996, 14 March 1997, 1 July 1997.

BANGALORE MEDICAL TRUST v B.S. MUDDAPPA
AIR 1991 SC 1902

R.M. SAHAI, J.:   * * *

Public park as a place reserved for beauty and recreation was developed in 19th and 20th century and is associated with growth of the concept of equality and recognition of importance of common man. Earlier it was a prerogative of the aristocracy and the affluent either as a result of royal grant or as a place reserved for private pleasure. Free and healthy air in beautiful surroundings was privilege of few. But now it is a 'gift from people to themselves'. Its importance has multiplied with emphasis on environment and pollution. In modern planning and development it occupies an important place in social ecology. A private nursing home on the other hand is essentially a commercial venture, a profit oriented industry. Service may be its motto but earning is the objective. Its utility may not be undermined but a park is a necessity, not a mere amenity. A private nursing home cannot be a substitute for a public park. No town planner would prepare a blueprint without reserving space for it. Emphasis on open air and greenery has multiplied and the city or town planning or development Acts of different states require even private house owners to leave open space in front and back for lawn and fresh air. In 1984 the [Bangalore Development Authority Act of 1976 as amended] itself provided for reservation of not less than 15 per cent of the total area of the layout in a development scheme for public parks and playgrounds the sale and disposition of which is prohibited under Section 38-A of the Act. Absence of open space and public park, in present day when urbanization is on increase, rural exodus is on large scale and congested areas are coming up rapidly, may give rise to health hazard. May be that it may be taken care of by a nursing home. But it is axiomatic that prevention is better than cure. What is lost by removal of a park cannot be gained by establishment of a nursing home. To say, therefore, that by conversion of a site reserved for low lying park into a private nursing home social welfare was being promoted was being oblivious of true character of the two and their utility.

* * *

Did the Division Bench commit any error of law? Was the conversion of site in accordance with law? Were any of the authorities aware or apprised of the provisions under which they could convert a site reserved for public park into a nursing home? Did the authorities care to ascertain the provisions of law or rules under which they could act? Was any precaution taken by the Chief Executive of the state to adhere to legislative requirement of altering any scheme? Not in the least. The direction of the Chief Minister, the apex public functionary of the state, was in breach of public trust, more like a person dealing with his private property than discharging his obligation as head of the state administration in accordance with law and rules. The government record depicted an even more distressing picture. The role of the administration was highly disappointing. This culture of public functionary, adorning highest office in the state of being law to himself and the administration acting on dictate, for whatever reason disturbs the balance of rule of law. What is more shocking is that this happened in 1976 and not even one out of various departments from which the papers were routed through raised any objection. And the statutory body like [The Bangalore Development Authority, (BDA)] with impressive members too succumbed under the pressure without, even, a murmur.

Financial gain by a local authority at the cost of public welfare has never been considered as legitimate purpose even if the objective is laudable. Sadly the law was thrown to winds for a private purpose. The extract of the Chief Minister's order quoted in the letter of Chairman of the BDA leaves no doubt that the end result having been decided by the highest executive in the state the lower in order of hierarchy only followed with 'ifs' and 'buts' ending finally with resolution of BDA which was more or less a formality. Between 21 April and 14 July 1976, that is less than ninety days, the machinery in BDA and government moved so swiftly that the initiation of the proposal by the appellant, a rich trust with 90,000 dollars in foreign deposits, query on it by the Chief Minister of the state, guidance of way out by the Chairman, direction on it by the Chief Minister, orders of Government resolution by the BDA and allotment were all completed and the site for public park stood converted into site for private nursing home without any intimation direct or indirect to those who were being deprived of it. Speedy or quick action in public institutions call for appreciation but our democratic system shuns exercise of individualized discretion in public matters requiring participatory decision by rules and regulations. No one howsoever high can arrogate to himself or assume without any authorization, express or implied in law, a discretion to ignore the rules and deviate from rationality by adopting a strained or distorted interpretation as it renders the action ultra vires and bad in law. Where the law requires an authority to act or decide, 'if it appears to it necessary' or if he is 'of opinion that a particular act should be done' then it is implicit that it should be done objectively, fairly and reasonably. Decisions affecting public interest or the necessity of doing it in the light of guidance provided by the Act and rules may not require intimation to person affected yet the exercise of discretion is vitiated if the action is bereft of rationality, lacks objective and purposive approach. The action and decision must not only be reached reasonably and intelligibly but it must be related to the purpose for which power is exercised. The purpose for which the Act was enacted is spelt out from the Preamble itself which provides for establishment of the Authority for development of the city of Bangalore and areas adjacent thereto. To carry out this purpose the development scheme framed by the Improvement Trust was adopted by the Development Authority. Any alteration in this scheme could have been made as provided in sub-section (4) of Section 19 only if it resulted in improvement in any part of the scheme. As stated earlier a private nursing home could neither be considered to be an amenity nor it could be considered improvement over necessity like a public park. The exercise of power, therefore, was contrary to the purpose for which it is conferred under the statute.

* * *

NOTES AND QUESTIONS

1. Justice Thommen in his concurring opinion emphazised the importance of public spaces. Referring to Indian and foreign statutes as well as English and American case law, he held that the reservation of open spaces for parks and playgrounds was a legislative attempt to eliminate the ill effects of urbanization. Open spaces for recreation and fresh air, playgrounds for children and promenades for residents were vital to any urban development scheme. These public spaces could not be privatized to the detriment of the citizenry.

2. Both Justice Thommen and Justice Sahai recognized the *locus standi* of residents to challenge government decisions destructive of the environment in their locality. The residents of a locality were the persons directly affected by an adverse town planning decision and could not be termed busybodies or interlopers.[37]

3. Section 65 of the BDA Act empowered the Karnataka government to give such directions to the BDA as were, in its opinion, necessary or expedient for carrying out the purposes of the Act. The BDA was bound by such directions. The state government argued that even if the BDA had not followed the statutory procedure for changing the user, the result was lawful since the Chief Minister's directions were protected by section 65. The Supreme Court rejected the plea. It was not open to the state government to give directions to the BDA that defied the very object of the Act. What was not permitted to be done by the BDA could not be legitimized by the state under section 65. For a direction issued under section 65 to be valid, it must advance the object of the Act.

4. Discretionary power under environmental statutes is sometimes exercised for ends that apparently conflict with the object of the law. For example, the power of government to alter the boundary of a sanctuary under the Wild Life Protection Act of 1972 has on occasion been exercised to de-notify large tracts and deprive wild life and its habitat of protection. This may not be permissible under the *Bangalore Medical Trust* judgment.[38] The court held that the exercise of discretionary power must be related to the purpose of the statute. In Justice Thommen's words, 'Any repository of power—be it the government or the BDA—must act reasonably and rationally and in accordance with law and with due regard to the legislative intent.'

5. What might have been the outcome of the case if a site reserved for a private hospital was converted on the diktat of the Chief Minister into a public park?

---

[37] A similar view was expressed in *K. Ramdas Shenoy v The Chief Officers, Town Municipal Council, Udipi* AIR 1974 SC 2177.

[38] In *Indian Council for Enviro-Legal Action v Union of India, (CRZ Notification Case)* 1996 (5) SCC 281, the Supreme Court went further and held that amendments to delegated legislation would be *ultra vires* where they were contrary to the object of the Environment (Protection) Act of 1986 or were likely to result in ecological degradation.

6. *Suresh Mehta v State of Rajasthan*[39] provides a startling contrast to *Bangalore Medical Trust*. Mehta petitioned the Rajasthan High Court to quash the allotment of open land to the Jodhpur Medical Research Centre Trust, which proposed to establish a hospital on the plot. The petitioner asked that the open land be used as a public park since in a previous litigation in respect of the same site, the government had assured the High Court that the land would be maintained as a park. On this assurance, the previous petition was dismissed. This time, in the absence of a land use map designating the site as a park, the High Court declined to hold the government to its assurance. 'The land was described as open land and could not be held to be meant for use of park.' The division bench made light of the *Bangalore Medical Trust* precedent: 'Each decision is an authority [for] what it decides'. One might expect greater deference to a Supreme Court judgment also dealing with the diversion of an open plot for a private hospital. Among the factors that may have persuaded the High Court to a different view were the doubt in respect of the petitioner's motive, the completion of the hospital during the pendency of the case and an 'unjustified outburst' by the counsel for the petitioner against the judges constituting the bench.

7. Justice N.L. Tibrewal of the Rajasthan High Court was more vigorous in applying the *Bangalore Medical Trust* ratio to save a park in Jaipur from being changed to a school.[40] Declaring the allotment in favour of the school illegal, the court held that the residents of a locality have a right to be heard before being deprived of a public space. The High Court also directed the respondent to list all open spaces in Jaipur and to prepare a scheme for preserving these spaces.

Contrast the outcomes of the *Suresh Mehta* and *Nizam* cases. Both are judgments of the Rajasthan High Court. Is the law relating to public parks and open spaces certain? Is it predictable?

8. The Bombay High Court[41] and the Allahabad High Court[42] have followed the Supreme Court's lead to preserve and create green belts within Nagpur and Ghaziabad. The Bombay High Court held that converting a public park into an area for housing was not permissible since it would disturb the basic feature of the Nagpur plan. The Ghaziabad Development Authority was reminded of its statutory duty to develop open places into parks with garden trees, flower beds, plants, lawns, promenades, etc.

9. The Supreme Court has done a fair bit to preserve Delhi's greenery. In *M.L. Sud v Union of India*,[43] the court secured an undertaking from the Delhi Development Authority (DDA) not to fell trees in a 435 acre forest belt known as the Jahapana Forest. The petitioner feared that the DDA was destroying the forest by cutting trees and constructing roads and buildings in the area. The court directed

---

[39] AIR 1993 RAJ 61.

[40] *Nizam v Jaipur Development Authority* AIR 1994 RAJ 87.

[41] *Hariyan Layout Sudhar Samiti v State of Maharashtra* 1997 (2) MAH.L.J.98.

[42] *D.D. Vyas v Ghaziabad Development Authority* AIR 1993 ALL 57.

[43] 1992 Supp (2) SCC 123.

the Conservator of Forests to visit the forest every quarter to ensure its preservation.

A green bonanza came the way of Delhi citizens in 1996. M.C. Mehta, a public-spirited advocate, asked the Supreme Court to enforce the Master Plan for Delhi which contemplated the shifting of heavy and hazardous industry away from the city. Having regard to the polluted atmosphere and the absence of 'lung spaces' in Delhi, the Supreme Court held that the land which belonged to the relocated industries ought to be used for the development of green belts and open spaces. Balancing the community need against the need of the factory owners who required resources to finance the shifting of industry, the court devised a land-use pattern which enabled the owner to develop a part of the land for her own benefit and to surrender the remainder for a green belt.[44]

In the same case, Mehta successfully obtained directions restricting the use of public parks for marriages or commercial purposes;[45] prohibiting the Delhi Chief Minister from running a camp office in a public park;[46] clearing the Delhi Ridge area from unauthorized encroachments,[47] including eleven places of worship;[48] and protecting Asola Wildlife Sanctuary within the National Capital Territory from degradation.[49]

10. In the case of *C.R. Dalvi v Municipal Corporation of Greater Bombay*,[50] a few Bombay residents brought an action to stop all commercial uses of a particular playground, claiming that those commercial uses illegally interfered with the enjoyment of the playground by the neighbourhood children. The court, on its own initiative, widened the scope of the case to include all playgrounds in Bombay. The court recognized both the importance and the scarcity of open recreational space within the city. It crafted a sensible and fair ruling, viz., that smaller playgrounds (less than 5000 square metres) are not to be hired out at all. Larger playgrounds (more than 5000 square metres) are to be divided into halves—one half to be reserved exclusively for recreation and the other half available for hire (but not for circuses, film shootings or fairs) for a period not exceeding one day. The *C.R. Dalvi Case* held the field for a decade until negated by an amendment to the Maharashtra Regional and Town Planning Act in 1997.[51] The amendment empowered the state government or the planning

---

[44] *M.C. Mehta v Union of India* 1996 (4) SCC 351.
[45] 1997 (6) SCALE 13 (SP).
[46] 1997 (6) SCALE 14 (SP).
[47] 1996 (1) SCALE 22 and 1996 (3) SCALE 51 (SP).
[48] 1996 (2) SCALE 55 (SP) and 1996 (3) SCALE 37 (SP).
[49] 1996 (2) SCALE 55 (SP); 1996 (2) SCALE 81 (SP); 1996 (3) SCALE 20 (SP) and 1996 (3) SCALE 37 (SP).
[50] 1987 MAH.L.J. 373.
[51] Section 37A was inserted by Mah. Ord. XIV of 1997 w.e.f. 6 August 1997. Prior to the Ordinance, the Bombay High Court rejected an application by the Municipal Corporation to relax the directions issued in *C.R. Dalvi's Case*. Notice of Motion No. 325 of 1996 in Writ Petition No. 2323 of 1985, 7 October 1996. The Ranchi Bench of the Patna High Court declined relief in *Citizens Council, Jamshedpur v State of Bihar* AIR 1999 PAT 1 since the petition challenging the permission to hold a handicraft exhibition on a playground lacked particulars and the exhibition had already started.

authority to permit playgrounds to be used for up to 30 days in a year for 'national events' and religious functions. To overcome the *C.R. Dalvi* judgment, the new provision declares, 'Notwithstanding anything contained in ... any judgment, order or direction of any Court ... such use shall not be deemed to be a change of user.' Is the new provision constitutional? On what grounds might you assail it?

11. The Borivali National Park is a unique preserve of wilderness within the densely populated Bombay metropolitan region. The park supports several species of birds, reptiles and large mammals including the leopard. The city exerts a constant pressure on the fringes of the reserve and according to the park authorities illegal quarrying and extensive encroachments by thousands of poor squatters are degrading the forest. Remote sensing imagery reveals that around 772 hectares of park land are encroached, mainly by hutments (512 ha.) and quarries (111 ha.). The continuous human intervention—vehicles, commercial shops and stores, slums, quarries—disturbs the wild life and damages the natural habitat.

In 1995, the Bombay Environmental Action Group filed a writ petition in the Bombay High Court seeking effective measures by government to protect the National Park.[52] Through a series of orders, the High Court attempted to strengthen the protective framework. On 12 February 1997, the court constituted a committee to recommend measures for preventing further encroachment of the forest and curbing illegal activities within the park. Based on the recommendations of the committee, on 7 May 1997, the High Court restricted public transport within the National Park area, ordered the disconnection of telephone lines, restrained the authorities from permitting any commercial or industrial activity within the park and directed the prosecution of persons refusing to vacate forest land. The state government was directed to increase the strength of the forest staff and to provide adequate infrastructure and equipment to enable effective policing of the region. The state government was also given 18 months to relocate thousands of slum dwellers outside the park boundary and to demolish the illegal structures.

Implementation of the court's directions were resisted by stall holders who catered food and beverages to visitors. Several of them claimed that they were running their business for more than three decades and that the High Court's directions would deprive them of their livelihood. The Bombay High Court declined to modify its 7 May 1997 order since unauthorized non-forest activities were not permissible within a National Park and the court's previous directions allowed sufficient time to the unauthorized occupants to vacate their premises.[53]

On 23 March 1998, the Bombay High Court issued further directions requiring a factory located within the park to shift out, directing the state to appoint two

[52] *Bombay Environmental Action Group v A.R. Bharati, Deputy Conservator of Forests* Writ Petition No. 305 of 1995.

[53] *Anil Kumar K. Parekh v Municipal Corporation for Greater Mumbai* Writ Petition No. 803 of 1997, Jun. 12, 1997. The Supreme Court dismissed SLP (Civil) No. 19050/97 on 20 October 1997.

public prosecutors to deal exclusively with forest cases and ordering the electricity utility to disconnect illegal power connections given in the National Park.

Reviewing implementation measures, in March 2000 the High Court found that several encroachers had refused to move away from the park and avail of alternative pitches under the court-approved relocation scheme. Finding that the time had come 'to send a clear message', the High Court gave a final opportunity to the squatters to shift out or else face forcible eviction.[54]

12. In *Almitra H. Patel v Union of India*,[55] the Supreme Court issued a warning against the encroachment of public lands. 'Establishment or creating of slums, it seems, appears to be good business and is well organised. ... Large areas of public, land, in this way, are usurped for private use free of cost. It is difficult to believe that this can happen in the capital without passive or active connivance of the land owning agencies and/or the municipal authorities. ... Rewarding an encroacher on public land with free alternate site is like giving a reward to a pickpocket. The department of slum clearance does not appear to have cleared any slum despite its being in existence for decades.' As a first step, the court directed the authorities to prevent fresh encroachments. How effective is this direction likely to be? Can slums be banished without addressing the underlying social and economic causes?

13. Responding to a public interest petition complaining about encroachments over a plot reserved for a park, the Andhra Pradesh High Court directed the respondent cantonment board to evict the encroachers and demolish the illegal constructions in accordance with law.[56]

In another case, the High Court declined to assist encroachers who lived in a slum on the bed of the river Moosi and were aggrieved by a project to clean and beautify the river. The court found that the government rehabilitation schemes was adequate and had been prepared in a thoughtful manner in consultation with environmentalists, social scientists, lawyers, journalists and urban planners.[57]

Across India the process of urbanization has been characterized by large migration from rural to urban areas. Migrants arriving in the city find that they do not possess the skills valued in the urban, industrial sector. Inevitably, most migrants are absorbed in low income occupations in the 'informal sector',[58] which is distinctive in the use of traditional technology, an unprotected labour market, ease of entry, low

---

[54] *Supra* note 52, orders dated 2 March 2000 and 13 March 2000.

[55] 2000 (1) SCALE 568, 570–1.

[56] *J.V. & S.A.C. Residents Welfare Association v Cantonment Board, Secunderabad* 1999 (3) ANDH.L.T. 657.

[57] *Kamal Nagar Welfare Association v Govt. of Andhra Pradesh* AIR 2000 AP 132.

[58] The segment of the labour force outside the organized labour market.

economic returns and a tendency for activity to operate on pavements and other public spaces. The informal sector makes a significant contribution to urban economies in the Third World. In Bombay, the informal sector accounts for two-thirds of the employment and provides citizens with a wide range of goods and services.

The conflict between hawkers and vendors who comprise the most visible segment of the informal sector and municipalities as well as citizens' groups anxious to protect public spaces from encroachment, is among the most vexing questions to reach the courts. In this section, we examine the case of Bombay, where hawkers and vendors choke principal thoroughfares, particularly streets and pavements around railway stations. For example, the main pedestrian corridor leading south from Churchgate station which handles approximately 15 lakh rail commuters daily (each way), is reduced from seven metres to just over one metre because of encroachments by hawkers all along the pavement. Who is entitled to use the pavement: the pedestrian or the hawker? Do the cases reviewed below resolve this issue?

BOMBAY HAWKERS' UNION v BOMBAY MUNICIPAL CORPORATION
AIR 1985 SC 1206

CHANDRACHUD, C.J.:   * * *

These writ petitions are filed by and on behalf of a large number of hawkers who carry on the trade of hawking their wares in Greater Bombay. They sell almost everything under the sun, from hairpins to hot food and vegetables to video cassettes. They hawk their wares standing or squatting on public streets, which constitutes a serious impediment to the free movement of pedestrian and vehicular traffic. Standing, of course, is safer than squatting because, it ensures easy mobility at the sight of Municipal or police officers. Mobile hawkers decorated with a hundred ball pens, like war-medals, is quite a common sight in Bombay. Constraints of modern times have created ingenious methods of trading. Some of the streets in Bombay are so incredibly flooded with mechandise sold by hawkers that it is impossible for the pedestrians to walk on those streets. The Bombay Municipal Corporation has been making herculean efforts to clear the streets of these and other obstructions but, those efforts have met with intense opposition from several quarters, not unexpectedly, even from those who wield considerable political influence. In the ultimate analysis, it is the ballot-box that matters. This tug-of-war or the game of hide-and-seek between Corporation and the hawkers led recently to a serious incident in which an officer of the Corporation engaged in the task of demolishing unauthorized constructions put up on public streets, was shot at. He survived but such is the magnitude of the problem.

Petitioner 1 is the Bombay Hawkers' Union, a Trade Union which has a large number of hawkers on its membership roll. It has been negotiating with the Municipal authorities for the creation of a hawkers' zone and for granting adequate number of licences to hawkers to enable them to carry on their trade and business. There are about 1,50,000 hawkers in the city of Bombay, 1/6th of them being women. Broadly, there are three types if hawkers—those who have four-wheeled carts, those who squat on the streets and those who have stalls. The largest amongst these are the squatting hawkers who number about 1,20,000. Petitioner 2 is the President of the Bombay Hawkers' Union and is also a Corporator. The other three petitioners carry on the business of hawking.

* * *

The contention of the petitioners is that they have a fundamental right to carry on their trade, business or calling and that the respondents are unlawfully interfering with that right. The petitioners complain that respondent 1 to 3 arbitrarily refuse to grant or renew licences for hawking, which renders the hawkers liable to be removed along with their goods, from places where they do their business. By these writ petitions, the petitioners ask for a declaration that the provisions of Ss. 313, 313-A, 314(3) and 497 of the Bombay Municipal Corporation Act, 1888 are void since, they confer upon the respondents an arbitrary and unguided power to refuse to grant or renew licences for hawking and to remove the goods without affording to the hawkers an opportunity to be heard.

* * *

In view of the fact that we are primarily concerned [with] the merits and feasibility of the scheme proposed by the Municipal Commissioner, it is unnecessary to consider the validity of the challenge made by the petitioners to certain provisions of the Bombay Municipal Corporation Act. We would, however, like to add that there is no substance in that challenge because, the right conferred by Article 19(1)(g) of the Constitution to carry on any trade or business is subject to the provisions of clause (6) of that Article, which provides that nothing in sub-clause (g) of Article 19(1) shall affect the operation of any existing law insofar as it imposes, or prevents the state from making any law imposing, in the interests of the general public, reasonable restrictions on the exercise of the right conferred by the said sub-clause. The affidavits filed on behalf of the respondents show in unmistakable terms that the impugned provisions of the Bombay Municipal Corporation Act are in the nature of reasonable restrictions, in the interests of the general public, on the exercise of the right of hawkers to carry on their trade or business. No one has any right to do his or her trade or business so as to cause nuisance, annoyance or inconvenience to the other members of the public. Public streets, by their very nomenclature and definition, are meant for the use of the general public. They are not laid to facilitate the carrying on of private trade or business. If hawkers were to be conceded the right claimed by them, they could hold the society to ransom by squatting on the centre of busy thoroughfares, thereby paralyzing all civic life. Indeed, this is what some of them have done in some parts of the city. They have made it impossible for the pedestrians to walk on footpaths or even on the streets properly so-called.

* * *

NOTES AND QUESTIONS

1. In *Bombay Hawkers' Union*, the Supreme Court asked the municipal commissioner to designate hawking and non-hawking zones within the city and to frame a scheme before 31 October 1985 in keeping with the guidelines indicated in the judgment. Despite the deadline, for over a decade the Bombay Municipal Corporation ('BMC') did nothing. In 1997, the BMC commissioned the Tata Institute of Social Sciences (TISS) and the Youth for Unity and Voluntary Action (YUVA) to carry out a socio-economic census survey of hawkers in all the 23 wards of Greater Bombay. The TISS survey covered 10 wards with 38,568 hawkers and showed that hawkers were concentrated in the central business district or near suburban railway stations and lanes leading from them.[59] The report noticed a huge racket in which police and civic officials received collective bribes ('hafta') from unauthorized hawkers to the tune of Rs. 500 crores annually. The YUVA survey which covered 13 wards and 68,383 hawkers found that the majority of hawkers conducted their activity on the footpath with the carriageway being the second most preferred location.[60]

2. In 1998, thirteen years after the Supreme Court deadline, the BMC designated hawking and non-hawking zones. The scheme stirred up a hornet's nest. Numerous residential colonies found that their streets and pavements were designated to accommodate 'surplus' hawkers who were to be shifted out from congested localities and main thoroughfares. Several citizens' groups protested at the lack of public consultation, before framing the scheme. In a batch of petitions filed before the Bombay High Court, the court directed the BMC to enforce its scheme only after considering fresh public comments on the draft scheme.[61] In July 1999, the BMC sanctioned its final scheme.

3. Supporting its scheme, the BMC claimed that out of approximately 100,000 hawkers in Bombay only 38,000 could be accommodated in all 23 wards of the city.[62] What is to become of the remaining 51,000 hawkers? Whose responsibility is it to find suitable accommodation: The state, the municipal corporation, the court, or the hawkers themselves?

4. Most initiatives by the BMC to remove unlicensed hawkers after the *Bombay Hawkers' Union* judgment, were stymied by court injunctions. The hawkers groups contended that they ought not to be evicted from their sites until the scheme directed by the Supreme Court was prepared and implemented. Many of these injunctions remained for years and encouraged fresh encroachments. The inability of the BMC to effectively resist these cases and quickly vacate the injunctions suggests a high

---

[59] Tata Institute of Social Sciences, *A Census Survey of Hawkers on BMC Lands*, para 3.1 (1998).
[60] Youth for Unit and Voluntary Action, *A Census Survey of Hawkers on BMC Lands*, para 4.1 (1998).
[61] *Avinash Tambe v Municipal Corporation of Greater Mumbai* Writ Petition No. 1722 of 1998 and *Citizen's Forum for Protection of Public Spaces v Brihanmumbai Municipal Corporation* Writ Petition No. 2324 of 1998, 30 November 1998.
[62] Affidavit dated 9 July 1999 filed in Writ Petition No. 1722 of 1998.

order of ineptitude on the part of the corporation to present its case or collusion between municipal officials and hawkers. To what extent are the courts to blame for the mess? What humane considerations might weigh with a judge in a hawker eviction case?

5. Within a week of the *Bombay Hawkers' Union* judgment, Chief Justice Y.V. Chandrachud rendered a judgment in *Olga Tellis v Bombay Municipal Corporation*,[63] concerning the poor who dwell on pavements. Upholding the right of the BMC to forcibly remove encroachments on footpaths over which the public has a right of passage or access, the Supreme Court held that footpaths and pavements are public property which are intended to serve the convenience of the general public. The main reason for laying out pavements is to ensure that pedestrians may go about their daily affairs with a reasonable measure of safety and security. Whatever may be the economic compulsion, public property may not be used for private purposes without requisite authorization. Olga Tellis recognized the right of a pavement dweller to a reasonable opportunity of putting forth her case before eviction.

6. In *Municipal Corporation of Delhi v Gurnam Kaur*,[64] the Supreme Court directed the Delhi administration to evolve an innovative plan along the lines suggested in the *Bombay Hawkers' Union Case* by creating hawking and non-hawking zones. In devising a scheme, the authorities were asked to preserve and maintain the aesthetic grandeur of Delhi by reducing congestion and at the same time rehabilitate persons forced to ply their trades on pavements and streets.

In a later Delhi case, a Constitution Bench of the Supreme Court recognized the right to carry on trade or business on streets and pavements (subject to proper regulation) as a part of the fundamental right guaranteed under Article 19(1)(g) of the Constitution. The Constitution Bench held that street trading cannot be denied on the ground that streets are meant exclusively for passing or repassing and for no other use.[65] Does the Constitution Bench judgment overrule the *Bombay Hawkers' Union* and *Olga Tellis* cases? Does the fundamental right to street trading extend to itinerant hawkers alone or persons squatting on pavements and streets? Who has a superior claim to the pavements: the 15 lakh commuters daily alighting from Bombay's Churchgate station or the 300–400 hawkers who eke out a living on the footpaths around Churchgate?

7. A division bench of the Calcutta High Court has held that the state is not under an obligation to provide alternative accommodation before the eviction of hawkers, although an appropriate scheme for rehabilitation ought to be framed.[66]

8. The plight of the pedestrian has been noticed by several High Courts. The Karnataka High Court prevented the Bangalore Municipal Corporation from permitting

[63] AIR 1986 SC 180. Regarding encroachments see *Ahmadabad Municipal Corporation v Nawab Khan* AIR 1997 SC 152.
[64] AIR 1989 SC 38.
[65] *Sodan Singh v New Delhi Municipal Committee* AIR 1989 SC 1988.
[66] *South Calcutta Hawkers' Association v Government of West Bengal* AIR 1997 CAL 234.

stalls on footpaths meant for pedestrians. The corporation proposed to use the pavement to rehabilitate shop owners temporarily displaced from their premises in an old market building, until the new market was constructed.[67] Earlier, a division bench of the Karnataka High Court held that the corporation could not lease land meant for a footpath in favour of a private business.[68]

In *Consumer Guidance Society of India v Bombay Municipal Corporation*,[69] a division bench of the Bombay High Court expressed concern at the failure on the part of the BMC to maintain footpaths. One of the grievances of the petitioners was that the electricity, telephone and water utilities habitually failed to restore the pavements after digging them up for servicing underground cables and pipes. The High Court directed the BMC to promptly restore pavements that were dug up and to construct pavements on streets where none existed so that road accidents were reduced. The Calcutta High Court in *Shankar Ladia v State of West Bengal*,[70] held that footpaths were essentially meant for pedestrians and could not be diverted for use as a car park. In a bizarre contest between a Town Area Committee and the Superintendent of Police, the Allahabad High Court chided the committee for seeking to construct shops on the side of a road in a manner that would obstruct highway traffic. The court held that the local body was obliged to keep roads absolutely free of obstruction.[71]

9. A division bench of the Allahabad High Court reviewed the case law on hawking and issued a mandamus to the administration to shift hawkers from sidewalks of Zahurul Hasan Road, Allahabad who were creating a public nuisance, causing congestion and choking the traffic. Since the administrative decision of 1986 to shift the 'Tehbazari market' (a street market) had not been implemented for 13 years, the court gave the city three weeks to remove the encroachments. 'To keep a public road or street and its sidewalks clear of encroachments is the statutory obligation of the administration in the performance of public duty. ... Tehbazari in modern times cannot be held on public roads.'[72]

10. In a public interest litigation filed by Nand Kishore Roy (C.W.J.C.No. 8175 of 1992), the Patna High Court directed the authorities to take necessary steps for the removal of illegal occupants, trespassers, encroachers and squatters from public land, particularly those who had erected hutments on the flanks of roads, streets and lanes in Patna. The order was issued to curb large scale encroachments which were constricting the movement of pedestrians and vehicular traffic in Patna. When the authorities moved to demolish illegal structures, a public interest litigation was filed by the occupants claiming that the demolition was illegal. The petitioners before the

---

[67] *G.R. Nagaraj v Bangalore Mahanagar Palike* 1997 (4) KAR. L.J. 348.

[68] *R. Neelakanta Rao v Bangalore City Corporation* 1994 (3) KAR.L.J. 209.

[69] Writ Petition No. 210 of 1996, 4 August 1998.

[70] 1991 (1) CAL.H.N.521.

[71] *Town Area Committee, Naraini, Banda v The Senior Superintendent of Police, Banda* 1988 ALL.L.J.1618.

[72] *Sanjay Agarwal v Nagar Mahapalika, Allahabad* AIR 1999 ALL 348, 355.

High Court were shopkeepers, traders and businessmen occupying the illegal structures as tenants. The High Court declined to exercise its discretionary power under the writ jurisdiction since none of the structures were legal. Moreover, the court found that the petition was not maintainable as a public interest litigation. The following extract from the judgment depicts the state of civic administration in Bihar's capital:

> Before parting with this case we are [compelled] to make a few observations. In the city of Patna, as also in other cities of this State, building laws and by laws have been observed in their breach. Their existence is completely ignored by those who raise structures within the Municipal area or the area covered by the provisions of the Regional Development Authority Act. The authorities, who are enjoined to enforce the provisions of the law have been equally indifferent to the violations of the laws, otherwise the problem presently faced by the citizens of Patna and other cities of this State would not have acquired such alarming proportion. One has to see to believe with what impunity the laws have been ignored, and illegal structures have been raised all over the city. The result is that the city of Patna is a veritable slum, and it will require a serious effort on the part of all concerned to make it a city worth living. Not only building laws, but even traffic laws and other such laws, which are intimately connected with the [enjoyment] of civic amenities and otherwise intended to make city life worthwhile, are also observed in their breach. This provides encouragement to the violators of the law. The impunity and obstinacy of the law breakers is only matched by the apathy and indolence of those responsible for enforcement of the laws. This has resulted in immense misery to the only sufferers, namely, the ordinary citizens of Patna, and other cities of the State, who have virtually raised their hands in despair. We can say from our judicial experience that even in ordinary routine matters, where actions must be taken in a normal way, without requiring any intervention by a court of law, large number of petitions in public interest are filed before this Court, and it is only under threat of court orders that the authorities are activated into action. This is a [sorry] state of affairs and has cast a heavy burden on the High Court with numerous writ petitions being filed in public interest for the purpose of enforcing the performance of normal statutory duties by the concerned authorities.[73]

11. In *Anthony Lawrence Quadros v Municipal Corporation of Greater Bombay*,[74] the secretary of a taxi drivers' union and a newspaper editor petitioned the High Court to direct the municipal authorities to improve badly potholed city roads. The court responded by constituting a committee of experts to recommend practical road improvement measures. Ultimately, after the municipal corporation

---

[73] *Shri Krishnapuri Boring Road Vyapari Sangh v State of Bihar* 1995 (1) BIH.L.J.REP.269, 280.
[74] Writ Petition No. 1129 of 1981, Bombay High Court, 11 April 1985.

agreed to implement the recommendations in the committee's report, the petitioners withdrew their case.

D. ZONING AND TOWN PLANNING

Zoning refers to the division of a city into districts within which building activity and land use are regulated by legislation. The responsibility for enforcing zoning laws usually vests in the city administration or a specialist planning authority. Most of the cases reviewed in this section are citizens' actions that arose when, in the petitioners' view, the concerned agency had failed to perform its enforcement duties.

I. DEVELOPMENT STOPPED

In July, 1999, the Supreme Court delivered a strong judgment against the illegal development of an underground market below a public park in Lucknow. The petitioners in the High Court were city corporators who challenged the agreement between the municipal corporation and the builder on the grounds that it was contrary to statute and was executed with doubtful motives.

M.I. BUILDERS PVT. LTD. v RADHEY SHYAM SAHU
AIR 1999 SC 2468

D.P. WADHWA, J.:

These appeals are directed against the judgment dated 23 August 1994 of a Division Bench of the High Court of Judicature at Allahabad, (Lucknow Bench). By a common judgment in three writ petitions, the High Court speaking through Shobha Dixit, J. held that the decision of the Lucknow Nagar Mahapalika ('Mahapalika' for short) (is now called Nagar Nigam or Corporation) permitting M.I. Builders Pvt. Ltd. (the appellant herein) to construct underground shopping complex in the Jhandewala Park ... situated at Aminabad Market, Lucknow, was illegal, arbitrary and unconstitutional. High Court set aside and quashed the relevant resolution of the Mahapalika permitting such construction and also the agreement dated 4 November 1993 entered into between the Mahapalika and the appellant for the purpose. Writ of mandamus was issued to the Mahapalika to restore back the park in its original position within a period of three months from the date of the judgment and till that was done, to take adequate safety measures and to provide necessary safeguard and protection to the public users of the park. High Court had noticed that the fact that the park was of historical importance was not denied by the Mahapalika and also the fact that [preservation] or maintenance of the park was necessary from the environmental angle and that only reason advanced by the Mahapalika for construction of the underground commercial complex was to ease the congestion in area. High Court, however, took judicial notice of the conditions prevailing at the Aminabad market. It said it was so crowded that it was bursting from all its seams. Construction of the underground shopping complex in question would only complicate the situation and that the present scheme would further congest the area. It said that the public purpose, which is alleged to be served by construction of the underground commercial complex, seemed totally illusory.

Aggrieved by the impugned judgment of the High Court, appellant has come to this Court.

* * *

Jhandewala Park, the park in question, has been in existence for a great number of years. It is situated in the heart of Aminabad a bustling commercial-cum-residential locality in the city of Lucknow. The park is of historical importance. Because of the construction of underground shopping complex and parking it may still have the appearance of a park with grass grown and path laid but it has lost the ingredients of a park inasmuch as no plantation now can be grown. Trees cannot be planted and rather while making underground construction many trees have been cut. Now it is more like a terrace park. Qualitatively it may still be a park but it is certainly a park of different nature. By construction of underground shopping complex irreversible changes have been made. It was submitted that the park was acquired by the state Government in the year 1913 and was given to the Mahapalika for its management. This has not been controverted. Under Section 114 of the [Municipal Corporation Act] it is the obligatory duty of the Mahapalika to maintain public places, parks and plant trees. By allowing underground construction Mahapalika has deprived itself of its obligatory duties to maintain the park which cannot be permitted. But then one of the obligatory functions of the Mahapalika under Section 114 is also to construct and maintain parking lots. To that extent some area of the park could be used for the purpose of constructing underground parking lot. But that can only be done after proper study has been made of the locality, including density of the population living in the area, the floating population and other certain relevant considerations. This study was never done. Mahapalika is the trustee for the proper management of the park. When true nature of the park, as it existed, is destroyed it would be violative of the doctrine of public trust as expounded by this Court in *Span Resort Case* (1997(1) SCC 388). Public Trust doctrine is part of Indian law.

* * *

It is not disputed that there is a Master Plan applicable to city of Lucknow. This Master Plan is prepared under the Development Act. It was submitted by the builder that the park could be exploited for commercial purposes as Aminabad has been shown to be a commercial area. No doubt Aminabad is a commercial area but that does not mean that the park can be utilized for commercial purposes. Rather using the park for commercial purposes would be against the Master Plan.

* * *

The facts and circumstances when examined point to only one conclusion that the purpose of constructing the underground shopping complex was a mere pretext and the dominant purpose was to favour the M.I. Builders to earn huge profits. In depriving the citizens of Lucknow of their amenity of an old historical park in the congested area on the specious plea of decongesting the area, Mahapalika and its officers forgot their duty towards the citizens and acted in a most brazen manner.

* * *

Now construction of shops will bring in more congestion and with that the area will get more polluted. Any commercial activity now in this unauthorized construction will put additional burden on the locality. Primary concern of the Court is to eliminate the negative impact the underground shopping complex will have on environment conditions in the area and the congestion that will aggravate on account of increased traffic and people visiting the complex. There is no alternative to this except to dismantle the whole structure and restore the park to its original condition leaving a portion constructed for parking. We are aware that it may not be possible to restore the park fully to its original condition as many trees have been chopped off and it will take years for the trees now to be planted to grow. But beginning has to be made.

* * *

NOTES AND QUESTIONS

1. The bench noticed that a number of cases were reaching the court pointing to unauthorized constructions at many places in the country. The Supreme Court held that in such cases, in addition to directing demolition, the court ought to direct an inquiry to bring the offenders to book.

2. Before the High Court, the municipal corporation resisted the petitions and in 1994 appealed to the Supreme Court against the High Court judgment. In August, 1996, the corporation resolved to withdraw the appeals and resist the developer. At the final hearing in the Supreme Court, M.I. Builders invoked the principle of estoppel by pleading, to tie down the corporation to its original stand. The Supreme Court rejected this plea, holding that the contract violated the statute and there could be no estoppel against a statute.

3. Though 80 per cent of the market was complete and 50 prospective allottees had paid the builder from their shops, the court directed demolition. The bench held: 'Unauthorized construction, if it is illegal and cannot be compounded, has to be demolished. There is no way out. Judicial discretion cannot be guided by expediency.'

The case of *T. Damodhar Rao v Hyderabad,* excerpted below, involved a municipal development plan earmarking 150 acres for a recreational park. Two public agencies bought 37 of these acres to build residential homes and the municipal corporation had already allowed several of these homes to be built.

The court held that neither the municipal corporation's permission nor the state government's relaxation of layout rules and building bye-laws could grant what the development plan prohibited, viz., residences on an area set aside for a park. Once approved, the development plan could only be altered by a complex procedure specified in the A.P. Urban Areas (Development) Act of 1975.

T. DAMODHAR RAO v SPECIAL OFFICER, MUNICIPAL CORPORATION OF HYDERABAD
AIR 1987 AP 171

ORDER:

The broad question that falls for consideration is whether the Life Insurance Corporation of India and the Income-tax Department, Hyderabad, can legally use the land owned by them in a recreational zone within the city limits of Hyderabad for residential purposes contrary to the developmental plan published in, G.O.Ms. No. 414 M.A. dt. 27–9–1975.

* * *

The present writ petition has been filed by some of the residents and rate-payers of the Hyderabad Municipal Corporation who live around the above mentioned area demarcated by the developmental plan as a recreational park. ... This writ petition is ... filed to direct the Municipal Corporation of Hyderabad and the Bhagyanagar Urban Development Authority, Hyderabad, to develop the entire area comprising of the land bounded in the West by Tank Bund, in the East by Ashoknagar Colony, in the North by D.B.R. Mills and in the South Domalguda locality as a public park in accordance with the approved developmental plan.

* * *

The matter may be examined from the view point of our legal and constitutional obligation to preserve and protect our ecology and environment.

Under the common law, the ownership denotes the right of the owner to possess the thing which he owns and his right to use and enjoy the thing he owns. That right extends even to consuming, destroying or alienating the thing. Under the doctrine of right to choose the uses to which a owner can put his land belongs exclusively to his choice. The right of use thus becomes inseparable from the right of ownership. The thrust of this concept of individual ownership is to deny communal enjoyment of individual property. This private law doctrine of ownership is comparable in its width and extent to the public law doctrine of sovereignty.

Into the domain of this doctrine of ownership, it is the collectivist jurisprudence of municipal administration that has made its first inroads. But in the recent past the law of ecology and environment has even more seriously shaken its roots. Under the powerful impact of the nascent but the vigorously growing law of environment, the unbridled right of the owner to enjoy his piece of land granted under the common law doctrine of ownership is substantially curtailed.

* * *

[I]t is clear that protection of the environment is not only the duty of the citizen but it is also the obligation of the state and all other state organs including the Courts. In that extent, environmental law has succeeded in unshackling man's right to life and personal liberty from the clutches of common law theory of individual ownership. Examining the matter from the above constitutional point of view, it would be reasonable to hold that the enjoyment of life and its attainment and fulfilment guaranteed by Article 21 of the Constitution embraces the protection and preservation of nature's gifts without [which] life cannot be enjoyed. There can be no reason why practice of violent extinguishment of life alone should be regarded as violative of Article 21 of the Constitution. The slow poisoning by the polluted atmosphere caused by environmental pollution and spoliation should also be regarded as amounting to violation of Art. 21 of the Constitution. In *R.L. & E. Kendra, Dehradun v State of UP,* AIR 1985 SC 652, the Supreme Court has entertained environmental complaints alleging that the operations of lime stone quarries in the Himalayan range of Mussoorie resulted in depredation of the environment affecting ecological balance. In [that case] the Supreme Court in an application under Art. 32 has ordered the closure of some of these quarries on the ground that their operations were upsetting ecological balance. Although Art. 21 is not referred to in these judgments of the Supreme Court, those judgments can only be understood on the basis that the Supreme Court entertained those environmental complaints under Art. 32 of the Constitution as involving violation of Art. 21's right to life.

It, therefore, becomes the legitimate duty of the Courts as the enforcing organs of Constitutional objectives to forbid all action of the state and the citizen from upsetting the environmental balance. In this case the very purpose of preparing and publishing the developmental plan is to maintain such an environmental balance. The object of reserving certain area as a recreational zone would be utterly defeated if private owners of the land in that area are permitted to build residential houses. It must, therefore, be held that the attempt of the Life Insurance Corporation of India and the Income-tax Department to build houses in this area is contrary to law and also contrary to Art. 21 of the Constitution.

Accordingly, I allow this writ petition and direct a mandamus to issue forbidding the Life Insurance Corporation of India and the Income-tax Department, Hyderabad, from raising any structures or making any constructions or otherwise using the land referred to above for residential purposes. I also direct the state government of Andhra Pradesh, the Hyderabad Municipal Corporation and the Bhagyanagar Urban Development Authority, Hyderabad, to enforce the law as contained in the developmental plan in G.O.Ms. No. 414 and to prevent and forbid the Life Insurance Corporation of

India and the Income-tax Department, Hyderabad, from using the above land for residential purposes. I also direct the state government of A.P., the Hyderabad Municipal Corporation and the Bhagyanagar Urban Development Authority, Hyderabad, to remove within sixty days any structures that might have been raised by the Life Insurance Corporation of India or the Income-tax Department, Hyderabad, during the pendency of this writ petition in this Court. I, however, make it clear that any residential houses or structures which have been built prior to the filing of this writ petition will not be covered by the judgment.

The writ petition is accordingly allowed with costs. Advocate's fee Rs. 500/-.

Petition allowed.

NOTES AND QUESTIONS

1. The court comes down hard on all the public agencies involved in this case, and is clearly intent on using the case as a vehicle to derive a constitutional basis for environmental protection. The court concludes that environmental protection and preservation is guaranteed by Article 21, and also ascribes an Article 21 rationale to the Supreme Court's decision in the *Dehradun Quarrying Case*[75] which 'can only be understood on the basis that the Supreme Court entertained those environmental complaints under Article 32 of the Constitution as involving violation of Article 21's right to life.' At the time, there was no Supreme Court decision expressly deriving the right to a healthful environment from Article 21.

2. Relief: The court's injunction and demolition order falls short of the affirmative relief sought, namely, a direction that the municipal authorities develop the area as a public park. What considerations might have dissuaded the court from granting this relief?

3. The leading case on public parks is the *Bangalore Medical Trust*[76] judgment discussed in the previous section.

4. In 1989, the residents of Besant Nagar challenged the decision of the Madras Metropolitan Development Authority re-classifying vacant lands from a residential area into an 'institutional zone'. The petitioners feared that their water source would dry up if office blocks came up in the area. The colony received no water from the public utility and was dependent on drawing ground water. The water table was falling rapidly—twelve feet in three years. Another fear related to a saline intrusion from the coast, should the office complex indiscriminately pump out the ground water. Justice Bhakthavatsalam found merit in the petitioners' case and held that the authority had failed to consider the issues relating to ecological balance. He quashed the impugned notification, stopped construction and permitted the authority to pass a fresh order of re-zoning after due regard to

[75] AIR 1985 SC 652.
[76] AIR 1991 SC 1902.

ecological factors.[77] The Appeal Court upheld the judgment and directed the authority to give an effective opportunity to the petitioners to present their objections.[78]

5. The residents of Banashankari Extension, Bangalore sued the state for permitting industry to operate in a residential zone. The administration took no action on the residents' complaints against the factories and workshops that were creating a din and fouling the air. Indeed, many of the industrial units were being aided by government permissions and licences, despite their non-conforming land-use. Allowing the petition, the High Court directed the closure of all industrial units in the layout and quashed the change of user permissions that did not conform to the development plan. It also made this suggestion to the affected industry: 'By allowing the writ petition, if calamitous consequences visit the concerned respondents as a result of non-feasance or malfeasance or misfeasance on the part of public authorities or public officials, the doors of justice are open to them to sue the public authorities for pecuniary relief by enforcing the principle of accountability.'[79] How practical is this advice?

6. Describing a cement godown in a residential area as a 'square peg in a round hole', the Kerala High Court quashed the permit issued to the cement dealer. The court found that the storage and handling of cement created a nuisance for residents in the locality.[80]

II. DEVELOPMENT ALLOWED

The developer does not always lose in Indian courts. In the *Calcutta Taj Hotel Case,* discussed later in this section the hotel project was eventually permitted to proceed, not only because the hotelier had taken environmental values into account in fashioning the project but also because there were obvious public benefits, viz., increased revenues from tourism, and general upgrading and beautification of the area.

Forward Construction Co. v Prabhat Mandal, excerpted below, involved a plot of land reserved, in the Bombay development plan, for a bus depot. The bus depot was to be operated by the Bombay Electricity Supply and Transport Undertaking (BEST), owned by the Bombay Municipal Corporation. BEST officials came up with a creative way to finance much needed employee housing: They would build not only a bus depot but also commercial buildings on the plot. The profit from the commercial buildings would finance the employee housing.

---

[77] *Besant Nagar Residents Forum v Madras Metropolitan Development Authority* 1990 MAD.L.J.REP.445.

[78] *Central Public Works Department v Besant Nagar Residents Forum* Writ Appeal No. 548 of 1990; 25 June 1991.

[79] *V. Lakshmipathy v State of Karnataka* AIR 1992 KAR 57, 90.

[80] *Antony v Commissioner, Corporation of Cochin* 1994 (1) KER.L.T.169.

FORWARD CONSTRUCTION CO. v PRABHAT MANDAL (REGD.)
AIR 1986 SC 391

R.B. MISRA, J.:   * * *

This leads us to the last but not the least in importance ... plea based on Building Regulation 3. In order to appreciate the contention it will be proper to read the regulation:

'The user of the following final plots will be as under, as per the sanctioned development plan:

Final Plot No.	User
10	Public Wall
12 Pert	Parking lot
14	BEST Bus Depot

Provided that the above users may be changed by the local Authority after modification of the Development Plan.'

It was this plea which prevailed with the High Court and the writ petition was allowed only on this score. The precise contention of the counsel for the respondents was that Building Regulation 3 will override the Development Control Rules for Greater Bombay. Rule 3 of the Development Control Rules for Greater Bombay reads:

'3(a)(i) All development work shall conform to the respective provisions made under these Rules. If there is a conflict between the requirement of these rules and the requirements of bye-laws in force the requirements of these rules shall prevail:

Provided however that in respect of areas included in a finally sanctioned Town Planning Scheme, the scheme regulations shall prevail if there is a conflict between the requirements of these rules and of the Scheme regulations.

(ii) The development work when completed shall not be used for any purpose except for the sanctioned use or such use as can be permitted under these rules.

(b) Change of use: No building or premises shall be changed or converted to a use not in conformity with the provisions of these rules.'

If the contention of the respondents that proviso to Building Regulation 3 overrides the Development Control Rules is accepted then the user of the plot as per sanctioned development plan can be changed by the local authority after modification of the development plan and as in the instant case there has been no modification of the development plan the change of user cannot be permitted. This is the crucial point on which the writ petition has been allowed. The other pleas taken by the respondents, as stated above, had been negatived by the High Court. What the proviso to Building Regulation 3 requires is that the change of user of the sanctioned plan can be made only after the modification of the development plan. The key word in this regulation is 'change'. What does the word 'change' mean? [The court set out the definitions of 'change' from the Collins and Oxford dictionaries.] So the general meaning of the word 'change' in the two dictionaries is 'to make or become different, to transform or convert'. If the user was to be completely or substantially changed only then the prior modification of the development plan was necessary. But in the instant case the user of the plot has not been changed. It has been used for a bus depot combined with a commercial use to augment the income of the Corporation for public purpose. In this view of the connotation of the word 'change' the proviso has no application to the present case and the High Court in our opinion was not quite justified in allowing the writ petition only on the basis of the proviso to Building Regulation 3. [The court proceeded to allow the appeals and set aside the judgment of the High Court].

NOTES

1. The Supreme Court might have insisted on a strict construction of the development plan. It might have faulted the project on the ground that the plot was designated for a public purpose—a bus depot—in the development plan, and was now improperly being put to a commercial purpose. Alternatively, the enlargement of the depot to include commercial space might have been regarded as a 'change' of building use, in violation of the applicable development control rules. But the court found an answer to these arguments. The use of part of the plot for commercial purpose was found unobjectionable because the proceeds would in turn fund a public purpose (employee housing). And the expansion of the plot's use to include commercial space was viewed as no substantial change at all, because there would still be a bus depot on the plot. The court even goes through an exegesis of two dictionary definitions of the word 'change'!

Evidently, the court in *Forward Construction* was impressed with the public benefit to be derived from the commercial space, and was determined not to let the project collapse under some minor technicality. The court actually went out of its way to say that commercial offices in a commercial zone would fulfil the Bombay Municipal Corporation's overall public purpose of improving Bombay.

2. *S.N. Rao v State of Maharashtra*[81] was another pro-development case in the Supreme Court. Here, the commissioner of the Bombay Municipal Corporation had refused permission to would-be developers of a five star hotel on a site designated as a green belt in a *proposal* to a draft development plan. The Maharashtra minister of state for urban development overruled the municipal commissioner and allowed the project to go forward, provided that 15 per cent of the land involved be dedicated to green and recreation space. The petitioners, members of various ecological action groups, argued that the entire area should be retained as a green belt. The court held that draft development plans may be binding on the authorities, but *proposals* to draft development plans have no such status.

In this case, the court evidently shared the minister's view of the public benefit that would derive from this project: 'It is ... apparent that in granting sanction to the

[81] AIR 1988 SC 712.

plan [the minister] was quite alive to public interest. ... The conditions show that considerable area out of the disputed land has been reserved for recreational ground or green belt.'

3. Overcoming the odds, a posh development comprising 270 villas survived a scathing decision by the Karnataka High Court.[82] The project was assailed in a public interest litigation on several grounds, among them the threat that the proposed garden colony posed to Bangalore's water supply. The developer, DLF Universal Ltd., obtained permission from the state to build country villas on the banks of Arkavati river which supplied fresh water to the city through Thippagondanahally reservoir. The High Court struck down the project on the ground that the conversion of agricultural lands for non-agricultural use was invalid and the state had failed to follow the statutory procedure for creating a new township. Allowing the appeal preferred by DLF, the Supreme Court found no infirmity in the land use change. The court held that the state government had taken into consideration all relevant factors and its approval was given after it was satisfied that the project did not imperil Bangalore's water supply.[83]

4. Obviously, each case is different. The judges involved have different inclinations and values; the quantum of public benefit varies from one development project to the next; and the court may sometimes be influenced —favourably or unfavourably—by the political status of the parties. While judges are seldom wholly 'pro-environment' or wholly 'pro-development', their preference for certain outcomes undoubtedly influences their response to particular arguments of the parties before them. It is hard to imagine how the judicial system can operate differently, and still enable judges to respond flexibly and creatively to grievances and disputes that reach the courts.

Sachidanand Pandey v State of West Bengal, excerpted below, is not merely another town planning case but a ringing statement of the courts' duty to protect the environment. Here, the duly authorized construction of a medium-rise five star hotel was alleged to interfere with the flight path of migratory birds, and the Supreme Court inquired extensively into this question. (If migratory birds are worthy of the court's attention, *a fortiori* the court's protection would extend to environmental issues of more direct impact on human beings.)

The land on which the hotel was to be constructed formerly belonged to the Alipore Zoological Garden and was put to important zoo-related uses. The zoo directors had withdrawn their objections to the hotel after the government promised them adjacent lands and relocation grants, and the hoteliers agreed to reconstruct all displaced facilities on the adjacent lands, at no expense to the zoo.

[82] *A. Lakshmisagar v State of Karnataka* AIR 1993 KAR 121.
[83] *DLF Universal Ltd. v Prof. A. Lakshmi Sagar* AIR 1998 SC 3369.

SACHIDANAND PANDEY v STATE OF WEST BENGAL
AIR 1987 SC 1109

CHINNAPPA REDDY, J.:   * * *

Today society's interaction with nature is so extensive that the environmental question has assumed proportions affecting all humanity. * * *

In India, as elsewhere in the world, uncontrolled growth and the consequent environmental deterioration are fast assuming menacing proportions and all Indian cities are afflicted with this problem. The once Imperial City of Calcutta is no exception. The question raised in the present case is whether the Government of West Bengal has shown such lack of awareness of the problem of environment in making an allotment of land for the construction of a Five Star Hotel at the expense of the zoological garden that it warrants interference by this Court. Obviously, if the Government is alive to the various considerations requiring thought and deliberation and has arrived at a conscious decision after taking them into account, it may not be for this Court to interfere in the absence of mala fides. On the other hand, if relevant considerations are not borne in mind and irrelevant considerations influence the decision, the Court may interfere in order to prevent a likelihood of prejudice to the public. Whenever a problem of ecology is brought before the Court, the Court is bound to bear in mind Art. 48-A of the Constitution, Directive Principle which enjoins that 'The State shall endeavour to protect and improve the environment and to safeguard the forests and wild life of the country,' and Art. 51-A(g) which proclaims it to be the fundamental duty of every citizen of India 'to protect and improve the natural environment including forests, lakes, rivers and wild life, and to have compassion for living creatures.' When the court is called upon to give effect to the Directive Principle and fundamental duty, the Court is not to shrug its shoulders and say that priorities are a matter of policy and so it is a matter for the policy-making authority. The least that the Court may do is to examine whether appropriate considerations are borne in mind and irrelevancies are excluded. In appropriate cases, the Court may go further, but how much further must depend on the circumstances of the case. The Court may always give necessary directions. However the Court will not attempt to nicely balance relevant considerations. When the question involves the nice balancing of relevant considerations, the Court may feel justified in resigning itself to acceptance of the decision of the concerned authority.

* * *

Bearing in mind the proper approach that we have to make when questions of ecology and environment are raised, an approach which we have mentioned at the outset, we are satisfied that the facts and circumstances brought out by the appellants do not justify an inference that the construction of the proposed hotel in the Begumbari land would interfere in any manner with the animals in the Zoo and the birds arriving at the Zoo or otherwise disturb the ecology: The proposed hotel is a garden-hotel and there is perhaps every chance of the ecology and environment improving as a result of planting numerous trees all around the proposed hotel and the removal of the burial ground and dumping ground for rubbish.

* * *

On a consideration of all the facts and circumstances of the case, we are satisfied that the Government of West Bengal acted perfectly bona fide in granting the lease of Begumbari land to the Taj Group of Hotels for the construction of a Five Star Hotel in Calcutta. The Government of West Bengal did not fail to take into account any relevant consideration. Its action was not against the interests of the Zoological Garden or not in the best interests of the animal inmates of the zoo or migrant birds visiting the zoo. The financial interests of the State were in no way sacrificed either by not inviting tenders or holding a public auction or by adopting the 'net sales' method. In the result, the judgments of the learned single Judge and the Division Bench of the Calcutta High Court are affirmed and the appeal is dismissed. In the circumstances of the case, we do not desire to award any costs.

NOTES AND QUESTIONS

1. *Sachidanand Pandey* is an exceptionally long and detailed case, a product of much painstaking effort by the court. Each major point is gone into several times. Was it worth all this effort? Most of the issues had already been resolved in negotiations among the zoo directors, the hoteliers and the state government. Was this a wise use of judicial time, especially when the courts have such a large backload of cases?

2. The proposed five star hotel in question was to be a medium-rise six story structure within an area containing several much taller structures. Should not the court have taken judicial notice of the areas' architectural configuration and dismissed the ornithological concerns on that count alone?

3. In a concurring opinion, Khalid, J. deplores the time, energy and expense involved in this public interest litigation, and suggests that a flood of rash or ill-conceived public interest litigations may abuse the judicial process and unduly impose on the hospitality and patience of the judiciary. He worries that instead of dispensing justice, the courts will be pushed by public interest litigants to assume administrative and executive functions.

4. The case of *Calcutta Youth Front v State of West Bengal*,[84] involved the development of an underground market below a neglected city park. The market would raise the park two metres above ground level. At their own costs the developers undertook to rejuvenate and replant the park with trees and grass. The Supreme Court upheld the High Court finding that the Calcutta Municipal Corporation

[84] AIR 1988 SC 436.

properly granted a licence to the developer. It agreed with the High Court that this development plan created an ecological benefit rather than a detriment. On its own initiative, the Supreme Court directed the developer and municipal authorities to renegotiate the rental terms which it found below market value. The developer subsequently agreed to a virtual doubling of the monthly rent and periodic upward revision of the amount.

Was it proper for the Supreme Court to look out for the municipality's financial interests when that matter had not been raised by any of the parties? Doesn't this intervention justify the fear of Khalid, J., that the courts may trespass into administrative and executive functions? Can you reconcile this decision with the judgment in *M.I. Builders*, excerpted earlier in this section.

5. In the *Calcutta Youth Front Case,* the petitioners were environmentally-minded citizens. In an earlier Supreme Court case, *B.K. Srinivasan v State of Karnataka,*[85] the petitioners were simply residents of a locality in Bangalore who protested against the city administration's plan to build high-rise structures in contravention of its published development plan. The developer argued that the municipal authorities had issued 57 building licences which contravened the development plan—evidencing their unawareness of the plan's requirements. The court gave short shrift to this plea, saying that it 'only exposes the deplorable laxity of the concerned authorities and emphasised the need for greater public vigilance. The present writ petitions, we hope, are forerunners of such vigilance.'

6. In *Parisar v State of Maharashtra,*[86] a division bench of the Bombay High Court refused to interdict the construction of a library hall and two small buildings to commemorate Dr. Ambedkar. The petitioners contended that the construction was illegal since the plot on Hanuman Hill, Pune was reserved for a garden. The court rejected the petition since only 50 sq.m. out of the 2 acre plot was intended for the new buildings. The rest of the plot would be developed into a garden. Moreover, the authorities had complied with the requirements for making a minor modification to the town plan.

III. Costs and Benefits

Should a court's desire to avoid economic waste persuade it to sanction a project which may be environmentally questionable?

A landmark Supreme Court zoning case, *K. Ramdas Shenoy v The Chief Officers, Town Municipal Council, Udipi,*[87] involved another violation of a town planning scheme by the responsible municipal authorities when they authorized a cinema building in a residential area. The court held:

[85] AIR 1987 SC 1059.
[86] 1990 (1) Bom.C.Rep. 79.
[87] AIR 1974 SC 2177.

An illegal construction of a cinema building materially affects the right to, or enjoyment of, the property by persons residing in the residential area. The Municipal Authorities owe a duty and obligation under the statute to see that the residential area is not spoilt by unauthorised construction. The Scheme is for the benefit of the residents of the locality. ... All the residents in the area have their personal interest in the performance of the duty. The special and substantial interest of the residents in the area is injured by the illegal construction.

Significantly, unlike the High Court below, the Supreme Court in *Shenoy* was not at all impressed by the argument that the illegal construction should be allowed because the respondent (cinema developer) had spent money: 'The Court declines to interfere for the assistance of persons who seek its aid to relieve them against express statutory provision.' Recently, in *M.I. Builders v Radhey Shyam Sahu*,[88] the Supreme Court revisited *Shenoy* and held: 'This court in numerous decisions has held that no consideration should be shown to the builder or any other person where construction is unauthorised. This dicta is now almost bordering rule of law.'

Noormohomed V. Siddiki v Municipal Corporation of Greater Bombay,[89] involved the impermissible operation of a bakery in a residential area in violation of development control rules adopted under the Maharashtra Regional and Town Planning Act of 1966. Citing *Shenoy*, the court restrained operation of the bakery and ordered that the alterations to the previous structure be demolished. In a further echo of *Shenoy*, the court observed that, 'Spending a large amount [of money] in pursuance of unauthorised activities cannot constitute a hardship, nor can it be a valid ground for denying relief to aggrieved persons.'

Are courts *ever* entitled to condone relatively minor statutory breaches when large economic costs are involved? Or is that only the province of the legislature? Consider the *Snail Darter Case*,[90] where the US Supreme Court stopped the construction of a large and nearly completed hydroelectric dam whose construction had cost over 100 million dollars. The court found that the subsequent flooding could harm the tiny snail darter, which was protected under the Endangered Species Act. Shortly afterward, the US Congress amended the Endangered Species Act to allow the dam to be completed.

E. BUILDING REGULATIONS

We now come to cases involving violations of building codes, specifically the FSI or floor space index. The Bombay Environmental Action Group has devoted considerable attention to this seemingly innocuous index, as will be seen from the following excerpt.

[88] AIR 1999 SC 2468.
[89] Writ Petition No. 2705 of 1983, Bombay High Court, 31 July 1984.
[90] *TVA v Hill* 437 U.S. 153; 57 L.Ed.2d 117.

CHAINANI; PEOPLE'S MOVEMENT: ROLE OF ENVIRONMENTAL
GROUPS IN ENVIRONMENTAL PROTECTION—THE EXPERIENCE OF
THE BOMBAY ENVIRONMENTAL ACTION GROUP, 28 October 1989
(Unpublished Manuscript)

Floor Space Index (FSI) otherwise known as 'Floor Area Ratio' (FAR) is defined as
'the quotient obtained by dividing the total covered area (plinth area) on all floors by
the area of the plot'.

$$\text{Thus FSI} = \frac{\text{Total covered area on all floors}}{\text{Plot area}}$$

FSI is a key planning tool since it determines the amount of built-up area on a given
plot of land and thereby governs the population density, which in turn affects the
pressure on civic amenities, etc.

* * *

In early 1981, Chief Minister Antulay [of Maharashtra] proposed that the floor
space index (FSI) should be raised. ... This move would at one stroke have nullified the
impact of all measures painfully agreed upon and undertaken in the recent past to
reduce further congestion of Bombay. It would have added greatly to the congestion of
Bombay taking civic amenities to the breaking point. 'The builders' lobby, as was
expected, was strongly in favour of the increase in FSI; the stakes for them were
enormous. The BMRDA, the Bombay Municipal Corporation (BMC), Department of
Urban Development etc., (and their officials) were all against the proposed increase
but could not press their opposition beyond a point. The state government was bent on
going ahead regardless of unanimous expert advice.

All the environmental groups separately and jointly conducted an extremely
vigorous and strong campaign against the proposal. As a result of this campaign, the
proposed increase in FSI, perhaps the single biggest threat to the environment of Bombay,
did not take place.

* * *

[In Bombay's FSI fraud scandal] several buildings have been built illegally in
excess of what the law permits. In one such case (that of Pratibha building), the Supreme
Court has permitted the Bombay Municipal Corporation to go ahead with demolishing
the top eight floors of the building. Two successive Municipal Commissioners have
been anxious to proceed with the work of demolition but the Standing Committee of
the Bombay Municipal Corporation (comprising of elected municipal councillors) has,
on one pretext or the other, stalled this demolition. The demolition work, though finally
started, is proceeding haltingly, if at all. Our group has a writ petition pending which
will be reactivated in case there is any going back on commitments already made to
demolish the illegal construction.

Honesty Builders, excerpted below, involves a fraud by the builders in mis-representing the actual FSI to the Bombay Municipal Corporation. On the basis of Honesty Builders' falsified documents, they were permitted to build a 17 storey building. The true FSI would have entitled them to build only 14 storeys. When the fraud was revealed, the municipal authorities denied Honesty Builders the right to occupy the building at least until the top three storeys were demolished. The peti-tioners purchased one of the flats in the top three storeys, occupied the flat illegally, and brought this action after the city turned off their water. The petitioners claimed that they were innocent third party purchasers and should not be denied possession of their flat.

PADAMCHAND J. KOTHARI v STATE OF MAHARASHTRA
Bombay High Court
O.S. Writ Petition No. 920 of 1985
13 June 1985

PENDSE, J.:   * * *

There is also another aspect of the matter which cannot be overlooked. The Corporation has framed Rules for the grant of occupancy certificate or part ... occupancy certificate for the benefit of the citizens who act in accordance with law. The provisions of grant of part occupancy certificate is obviously to remove the hardship to the holders of the building permit, in cases where entire building could not be constructed for reasons beyond the control of the owners. In case where the building could not be completed as per the permit for non-availability of cement or steel or for any other reasons which are genuine, the [Municipal] Corporation will certainly grant the part occupancy certificate. It is impossible to imagine that the builders, who produced the forged documents and secured the building permit should be granted part occupancy certificate in respect of area which according to the builders was constructed as per the available FSI. In case the courts start giving such reliefs to the builders, then it would promote the frauds on the part of the builders and would completely demolish the Municipal Administration. The submission that the petitioners are innocent and bona fide purchasers and should not be penalized for the wrong of builders is wholly inaccurate, because the petitioners, who are claiming through the builders cannot escape the consequences of fraud. It is well settled that fraud vitiates everything and the petitioners cannot harp upon the fact that they were the innocent purchasers. The flat purchasers have invested a large fortune and it is impossible to imagine that they had not taken precaution to ascertain whether the builder is constructing the building within the permissible limits. It has become a fashion to violate the law and construct high-rising buildings flouting all the rules and thereafter [to] approach the court and seek relief on sympathetic grounds. I am not inclined to grant any relief on such misplaced sympathy. In my judgment, the petitioners are not entitled to any relief whatsoever. It is open for the Society to demolish the top three floor's and then approach the Corporation for grant of occupancy certificate and completion certificate. It was entirely wrong on the part of the petitioners to forcibly occupy the premises in absence of completion and occupancy certificates. The petitioners must thank themselves for the mess in which they have put themselves and now they cannot make virtue out of their own doing. The writ jurisdiction is for advancing justice and not for defeating the law, and I am not inclined to assist the petitioners in any manner. It is required to be stated that the wrongful occupation of the petitioners of the flat in absence of an occupancy and completion certificate was in breach of Section 351 of the B.M.C. Act and such conduct is made punishable under Section 471 of the B.M.C. Act.

For these reasons, the petition is summarily rejected.

NOTES AND QUESTIONS

1. Was the court correct in tainting the purchasers of the flat with the builders' fraud? Suppose they really were innocent of any knowledge of the fraud? The court finds it 'impossible to imagine that they had not taken precaution to ascertain whether the builder is constructing the building within the permissible limits.' Do you find it impossible to imagine? Why would Honesty Builders be any more honest with their purchasers than with the municipal corporation?

2. The petitioners' innocence of fraud and misrepresentation should not affect the result in this case, but it could affect the court's reasoning. The court could have reasoned that it must choose between two policies, viz., its duty to protect the innocent third party purchasers and its greater duty to protect the community—for whose benefit the floor space index was developed (as a shield against congestion and excessive demand for water, sanitation and electricity).

3. Do the petitioners have any recourse to recover their investment?

PRATIBHA COOPERATIVE HOUSING SOCIETY LTD. v STATE OF MAHARASHTRA

AIR 1991 SC 1453

KASLIWAL, J.:

This petition under Article 136 of the Constitution of India is directed against the order of Bombay High Court dated 9 March 1990.

Facts necessary and shorn of details are given as under. Pratibha Co-operative Housing Society Ltd. (hereinafter referred to as 'the Housing Society') made some unauthorized constructions in a 36 storeyed building in a posh and important locality of the city of Bombay. The Bombay Municipal Corporation issued a show cause notice dated 7 August 1984 calling upon the Housing Society to show cause within 7 days as to why the upper eight floors of the building should not be demolished so as to limit the development to the permissible Floor Space Index (FSI). In the notice it was stated that additional FSI to the extent of 2773 sq. mts. was gained by the Housing Society and that the construction work had already reached 36 floors and that on the basis of the actual area of the building, the upper eight floors were beyond the permissible FSI limit and as such were required to be removed. The Housing Society submitted a reply to the show cause notice by their letter dated 13 August 1984. The Administrator of the Bombay Municipal Corporation made an order on 21 September 1984 requiring the Housing Society to demolish 24,000 sq. ft. on the eight upper floors of the building on the basis of 3000 sq. ft. on each floor.

* * *

We are also of the view that the tendency of raising unlawful constructions and unauthorized encroachments is increasing in the entire country and such activities are required to be dealt with by firm hands. Such unlawful constructions are against public interest and hazardous to the safety of occupiers and residents of multi-storeyed buildings. The violation of FSI in the present case was not a minor one but was to an extent of more than 24,000 sq. ft. Such unlawful construction was made by the Housing Society in clear and flagrant violation and disregard of FSI and the order for demolition of eight floors had attained finality right up to this Court. The order for demolition of eight floors has been substantially carried out and we find no justification to interfere in the order passed by the High Court as well as in the order passed by the Municipal Commissioner dated 13 November 1990.

In the result we find no force in the petition and the same is dismissed with no order as to costs. Before parting with the case we would like to observe that this case should be a pointer to all the builders that making of unauthorized constructions never pays and is against the interest of the society at large. The rules, regulations and by-laws are made by the Corporations or development authorities taking in view the larger public interest of the society and it is the bounden duty of the citizens to obey and follow such rules which are made for their own benefits.

* * *

NOTES AND QUESTIONS

1. The *Pratibha Case* demonstrates how pressure exerted by the media and environmental groups can force the authorities to take corrective action. In July, 1984 the press broke the story on the developer's fraud. The Bombay Environmental Action Group quickly moved a writ petition based on the news reports. Responding to the public outcry, the Bombay Municipal Corporation initiated action against the developer, culminating in an order for the demolition of the top eight storeys of the skyscraper.

2. One of the favourite decisions of lawyers defending illegal buildings is the

Supreme Court judgment in *Rajatha Enterprises v S.K. Sharma*.[91] Soon after Rajatha commenced building a shopping complex and school in Bangalore, the municipal commissioner initiated action against the builder, alleging deviations from the planning regulations. The upshot of these proceedings was an order by the commissioner directing Rajatha to reduce the height of the 6 storey building, failing which the upper three floors would be demolished. The High Court partly accepted Rajatha's contentions in a writ petition assailing the commissioner's order. The court set aside the demolition order in respect of the 4th and 5th floors. However, the demolition of the 6th floor was confirmed. In appeal, the Supreme Court set aside the 6th floor demolition as well. The Supreme Court found that the excess built up area was small and did not justify the harsh penalty of demolition since there was no evidence of any dishonesty or fraud or negligence on the part of the builder. The proposed government school in the building may have persuaded the court to take a lenient view.

3. A full bench of the Punjab and Haryana High Court in *Bakshish Kaur Saini v Union of India*,[92] construed the provisions of Chandigarh's planning laws to hold that unauthorized structures do not attain legal status by the passage of time. The full bench overruled an earlier decision of the court laying down that an unauthorized construction gained legitimacy over time.

4. As town planning laws and building regulations become more stringent, developers occasionally attempt to by-pass the prevailing regime by reaching back to building plans sanctioned a long while ago. This generally occurs where the project is delayed. In *Usman Khatri v Cantonment Board*,[93] the Supreme Court noticed the delay and required the owners of the plot to submit fresh building plans that conformed to the prevailing building laws. The Supreme Court held that the need for housing 'should always be subservient with the building restrictions and regulations made in the larger interest of the ... inhabitants of Pune and keeping in view the influx of population, environment hazard, sanitation, provision for supply of water, electricity and other amenities.'[94]

In another Pune Cantonment Board case, the Supreme Court reiterated its view that where the construction of a building was delayed and the original sanction to the building plan had lapsed, the proposed construction must conform to the prevailing scheme of building restrictions.[95] Builders do not acquire a vested right by mere submission of a plan for construction of a building. To acquire a right, the plans should be sanctioned.[96] Moreover, the time limit imposed on a planning authority for sanctioning

---

[91] AIR 1989 SC 860.
[92] AIR 1994 P&H 1.
[93] AIR 1994 SC 233.
[94] *Id.* at 243.
[95] *Pune Cantonment Board v MPJ Builders* AIR 1996 SC 2645. Also see *F.B. Taraporawala v Bayer India Ltd.* AIR 1997 SC 1846.
[96] *State of West Bengal v Terra Firma Investment and Trading Pvt. Ltd.* 1995(1) SCC 125.

plans, failing which the plans are 'deemed' to be sanctioned, would not apply where the plans are put before the authority on a remand by an appellate body.[97]

The case excerpted below, in the High Court's words, shows 'to what extent a powerful builder can ... throw to the winds all rules and regulations in respect of development of properties in the city of Bombay.' The case relates to Om Chambers, a multi-storeyed building at Kemp's Corner, an upper class district in South Bombay. The builder-appellant connived with officials in the city's land record department in forging documents and registers to reflect a larger plot area (and consequently greater FSI). The division bench judgment was severe on the builder. We carry an excerpt from the case relating to the developers' plea that the upper floors should not be demolished.

WEST COAST BUILDERS (P) LTD. v THE COLLECTOR
Bombay High Court
Appeal No. 92/1994 in Writ Petition No. 391/94
8 February 1994

PENDSE, J:　　　　　　　* * *

We are unable to find what is the demonstrable hardship to the appellants who has secured advantage by use of forged documents with the connivance of the Officers in the Collector's Office and possibly in the office of Bombay Municipal Corporation. A person who flouts the law and secures bogus entries in the Register can never seek equity from the Court and much less from the Writ Court. [Counsel for the appellants] referred to the decision of Supreme Court reported in A.I.R. 1989 Supreme Court 860 (*M/s Rajatha Enterprises v S.K. Sharma and others*) to urge that even if the construction is made in excess of permissible F.S.I., the Commissioner need not have directed demolition. The Supreme Court observed that if actual area is not large and neither public safety is endangered, nor section of public was inconvenienced by reason of construction, then the demolition need not be resorted to. We are not prepared to accede to the submission of the learned counsel that the Municipal Commissioner in the present case need not have directed demolition. There is a growing tendency amongst the builders to flout each and every regulation framed by the Bombay Municipal Corporation and State Government to regulate the construction in the City. The powerful lobby of the builders are under the impression that office of the Collector and the office of the Bombay Municipal Corporation can be taken for granted and the rules and regulations can be openly flouted by producing forged documents. The manner in which the appellants have constructed the building by flouting every rule and thereafter by

---

[97] *Bombay Metropolitan Region Development Authority v Gokak Patel Volkart Ltd.* 1995 (1) SCC 642.

manipulating the things to persist with violations makes it clear that the appellants have no respect for rules and regulations and purely out of monetary consideration are willing to bypass every restriction. It is fortunate that the Collector and the Municipal Commissioner in the present case have not fallen pray to the tactics of the appellant and have not hesitated to pass orders which are absolutely necessary. We hope and trust that the order passed by the Commissioner would be a lesson to all others who are still under the impression that everyone in this country can be purchased and any construction can be made with a view to earn huge profits. If such actions are permitted, then the day will not be long when the city and its surroundings will stand totally ruined. In our judgement, it does not lie in the mouth of the appellants that illegal construction should not be demolished. We refuse to accede to the desperate pleas made by the appellants that the demolition should be avoided on appellants seeking regularisation by payment of fine. In our judgement, the appellants cannot be permitted to regularize illegalities by offering payment of amounts.

* * *

NOTES AND QUESTIONS

1. On 29 April 1994 the Supreme Court rejected West Coast Builders' special leave petition against the Bombay High Court judgment.[98]

2. Generally, town planning laws vest discretion in matters relating to the demolition of an illegal building in a high official. The Calcutta High Court has held that such discretion ought to be exercised *bona fide* and not on extraneous considerations. Upholding a circular issued by the Calcutta Municipal Corporation that prevented illegal constructions from being regularized on the payment of a fee, the court found that such a general rule was desirable for the proper growth and development of the city. Justice Ajoy Nath Ray observed that it would be unjust for builders to buy their way out of trouble by paying penal charges where the structure was otherwise fit for demolition.[99]

3. In *Leena Fernandes v Planning Authority, Mangalore*,[100] a division bench of the Karnataka High Court distinguished the *Rajatha Enterprises* judgment for reasons similar to those adopted by the Bombay High Court in *West Coast Builders*. The Karnataka High Court found that the developer had ignored the sanctioned plans from the start and his conduct throughout lacked rectitude. Since there was a

---

[98] *West Coast Builders v Collector of Bombay* SLP (Civil) No. 5259/94.
[99] *Land & Bricks & Entertainment Ltd. v State of West Bengal* 1991 (2) CAL.H.N. 306.
[100] 1992 (3) KAR.L.J. 355.

deliberate attempt to benefit from the illegalities, the court responded to a public interest litigation and set aside orders passed by the state government relaxing the building norms for the benefit of the developer. The court directed the planning authority to consider the allegations of the concerned citizens and to take appropriate action in respect of the illegalities.

F. TRANSLOCATION OF INDUSTRIES

With few exceptions, Indian cities throb with industrial activity. Factories provide employment, pay taxes and more generally, vitalize the urban economy. Factories also pollute, despoiling the environment. Economic and political constraints prevent local bodies from vigorously pursuing an industrial location policy that would require factories to shift away from urban centres. As cities extend into the countryside and surround industrial plants that hitherto were located at a great distance from the urban population, the conflict between industry and neighbouring communities grows. In this section, we examine the controversial initiative by the Supreme Court, compelling hazardous industrial units to relocate beyond Delhi or shut down. Labour unions and a few non-governmental organizations have criticized the court for pursuing an elite agenda and depriving workers of their livelihood. Is the criticism justified? Should the court have refused to implement the Delhi Master Plan?

M.C. MEHTA v UNION OF INDIA
AIR 1996 SC 2231

ORDER:

The Master Plan for Delhi 1962 (MPD–62) was prepared and enforced under the Delhi Development Act, 1957 (the Act). At that point of time it was realized that the solution of the impending problems of the National Capital could only be found in regional context and as such the MPD–62 recommended that a statutory National Capital Region Planning Board should be set up for ensuring balanced and harmonised development of the region. The National Capital Region Planning Board Act, 1985 (Capital Region Act) came into force on 11 February 1985. The National Capital Region Plan—2001 (the Regional Plan) was published as a statutory document. In the words of the then chairperson, National Capital Region Planning Board, the purpose sought to be achieved by the Regional Plan was as under:

> The two important goals to be achieved by the Regional Plan are a balanced and harmoniously developed region, leading to dispersal of economic activities and immigrants to Delhi, thereby leading to a manageable Delhi. This is to be achieved by the progressive de-concentration of population and economic activities in the Region and their judicious dispersal to various priority towns as identified in the plan. The plan is a framework of policies relating to population distribution, settlement system, transport and communications,

physical and social infrastructure, regional land use, environment and eco-development, management structure for plan implementation and counter magnet areas for development. The focus of the plan is Delhi whose extraordinary growth has put great pressure on its essential services and civic facilities. It is expected that a vigorous implementation of the policies contained in the plan would help maintain the quality of life of our National Capital.

* * *

Delhi is recording heavy population growth since 1951. As the city grows, its problems of land, housing, transportation and management of essential infrastructure like water supply and sewage have become more acute. Delhi is one of the most polluted cities in the world. The quality of ambient air is so hazardous that lung and respiratory diseases are on the increase. The city has become a vast and unmanageable conglomeration of commercial, industrial, unauthorized colonies, resettlement colonies and unplanned housing. There is total lack of open spaces and green areas. Once beautiful city, Delhi now presents a chaotic picture. The only way to relieve the capital city from the huge additional burden and pressures, is to deconcentrate the population, industries and economic activities in the city and relocate the same in various priority towns in the National Capital Region (NCR).

The Master Plan for Delhi-perspective 2001 (the Master Plan) as approved by the Central Government under S. 11A(2) of the Act was published in the Gazette of India on 1 August 1990. The question for consideration, before us, is whether the hazardous/noxious/heavy/large industries operating in Delhi are liable to be shifted/relocated to other towns in the NCR?

The relevant part of the Master Plan is as under:

'Hazardous and Noxious Industries: Refer Annexure III, H (a).

(a) The hazardous and noxious industrial units are not permitted in Delhi.

(b) The existing industrial units of this type shall be shifted on priority within a maximum time period of three years. Project report to effectuate shifting shall be prepared by the concerned units and submitted to the authority within a maximum period of one year. * * *

(d) Action shall be taken by Delhi Administration to prepare a list of individual noxious and hazardous industrial units to be shifted and depending on the pollution/hazard, administration may force these industrial units to shift within a maximum prescribed period of three years.

Heavy and Large Industries: Refer Annexure III, H (b).

(a) No new heavy and large industrial units shall be permitted in Delhi.

(b) The existing heavy and large scale industrial units shall shift to Delhi Metropolitan Area and the National Capital Region keeping in view the National Capital Region plan and National Industrial Policy of the Government of India. * * *

(d) Modernization of heavy and large scale industrial units shall be permitted subject to the following conditions:

(i) It will reduce pollution and traffic congestion.

(ii) Whenever the unit is asked to shift according to the policies of the plan, no compensation shall be paid for assets attained because of modernization.'

It is thus obvious that under the mandatory provisions of the Master Plan the hazardous and noxious industrial units (H (a) industries) are not permitted to operate in Delhi. So far as the existing H(a) industries are concerned, they were required to be shifted within a maximum prescribed period of three years. The Master Plan came into force in August, 1990. H(a) industries should have been shifted by the end of 1993. It is unfortunate that no action in this respect was taken by the authorities concerned. The industries were required to prepare and submit the project reports to effectuate shifting. This was to be done within one year of the coming into force of the Master plan. None of the H(a) industries submitted the required project reports within the statutory period of one year. We have no hesitation in holding that the H(a) industries are operating in Delhi illegally and in utter violation of the mandatory provisions of the Master Plan. Delhi Administration was under a statutory obligation to prepare a list of H(a) industries. No such list was prepared within the statutory period of three years. It was only under the directions of this Court that the necessary lists were prepared.

There is no doubt that the H(a) industries have been operating in Delhi illegally during the last about three years. They must stop operating in Delhi and relocate themselves to some other industrial estate in the NCR. We are further of the view that the concerned officers of the Delhi Administration are equally responsible for continuous illegal operation of the H(a) industries in the city of Delhi. The Chief Secretary, Delhi Administration shall hold an inquiry and fix the responsibility of the officers/officials who have been wholly re-miss and negligent in the performance of the statutory duties entrusted to them under the Master Plan.

The Master Plan provides that 'no new heavy and large industrial units shall be permitted in Delhi'. Heavy and large industries have been categorized as H(b) under the Master Plan. It is further provided that the existing H(b) industries shall shift to Delhi Metropolitan Area (DMA) and the NCR keeping in view the Regional Plan and the National Industrial Policy of the Government of India. Although no period has been prescribed for the shifting of these industries ... in the absence of any such provision the shifting has to be done within a reasonable time period of six years from August 1990 when the Master Plan came into force. ... Some of these industries have, during the course of arguments, offered for modernization and also for conversion from polluting to non-polluting industries. The offers are simple ipse-dixit with no material. We are not impressed by the offers made by these industries at this late stage. They should have modernized or changed the process of manufacture during the six years they have been operating in violation of the Master Plan. We, therefore, reject these offers.

* * *

NOTES AND QUESTIONS

1. This order was passed on 8 July 1996. Earlier, under the supervision of the court, the polluting units were classified in the H(a) and H(b) categories. In the concluding portion of the order, the court directed 168 listed units in the 'H' categories to stop operating in Delhi from 30 November 1996. The authorities were directed to render all assistance in the process of relocating the units within permitted industrial zones.

Apart from the designated units, the court also directed the Delhi pollution control committee (DPCC) to identify additional units that would fall within the 'H' categories. In February, 1998, the DPCC confirmed the closure of 1,328 industries.[101]

2. The Supreme Court created entitlements for the workers employed in the 168 industries ordered for closure and relocation. They were guaranteed continuity of employment during the period of closure and shifting; assured equivalent terms of employment at the new site; assured full wages, during the transition; granted one years wages as 'shifting bonus'; and granted an option to claim retrenchment compensation if they chose not to move to the new site. In December, 1996 the court enhanced the compensation for workers opting for retrenchment. They were now entitled to six year's wages as additional compensation, over the statutory compensation under the Industrial Disputes Act of 1947. The court also made special provision for the residential accommodation of the workers.[102] Was this enough? What more might the court have done?

3. In February, 1996 the court directed the authorities and industry to construct common effluent treatment plants (CETPs) in all the industrial areas of Delhi. The CETPs were to be funded by government and industry with financial institutions assisting industry to meet the costs.[103]

4. The court's sweeping closure order appears to have improved the local ambient air quality in parts of Delhi and more significantly, reduced the risk to public health and safety.

The impact of the shut down on labour was harsh. According to one report published nearly two years after the November 1996 deadline, none of the workers, except those in a government textile mill had been paid their compensation.[104] Recourse to the courts to enforce the entitlements was a slow process, forcing most industrial workers to take up irregular, part-time, low-paying jobs.

Some managements used the court order as an excuse to shut down ailing

---

[101] N. Dasgupta, *Tall Blunders* in *Down to Earth* 30 September 1998, p. 22.

[102] *M.C. Mehta v Union of India* 1997 (11) SCC 327, 329. The Supreme Court's decisions in the *Calcutta Tanneries Case* 1997 (2) SCC 411 and the *Taj Trapezium Case* AIR 1997 SC 734 also contain directions to compensate and protect labour.

[103] *M.C. Mehta v Union of India* 1996 (2) SCALE 89 (SP).

[104] *Supra* note 101, at 24.

industry—a near impossible task under India's existing industrial law and policy.[105] Others avoided the compensation obligations, until the July and December, 1996 directions were clarified by the Supreme Court in December 1998, on the application of workmen.[106]

5. A letter petition from the residents of Chanditala, Calcutta, prompted the Supreme Court to appoint the National Environmental & Engineering Research Institute (NEERI) to inspect the locality and report on the state of pollution control facilities employed by industry. The report confirmed that emissions from factories were causing severe air pollution. In March 1996, when two years of efforts to persuade the offending units to relocate failed, the court directed the closure of five units, with an option to relocate by 30 June 1996. In recognition of the service rendered by the advocate Mr. M.C. Mehta, the State of West Bengal was asked to pay him Rs. 50,000 as costs.[107]

6. Responding to a public interest litigation, the Delhi High Court directed the relocation of a slaughter house away from the city in view of the severe environmental problems caused by the facility.[108] Since the authorities failed to expeditiously implement the court's orders, additional directions to abate pollution and improve hygiene were issued in 1994 in a fresh public interest petition. The court also appointed a committee under the chair of a retired High Court Justice to ensure compliance with its directions.[109] On 27 January 1995 the court ordered the closure of the slaughter house by the end of that year. In appeal, the Supreme Court balanced various factors including the consumer demand for meat against environmental considerations and then extended the closure deadline to 30 June 1997.[110]

7. The *Bayer Case* illustrates the unpredictability of the judicial process. In the aftermath of the Bhopal tragedy and the principle of absolute liability laid down by the Supreme Court in the *Shriram Gas Leak Case*,[111] a number of pharmaceutical and chemical factories urged the Thane Municipal Corporation (TMC) not to permit residential buildings to come up within a radius of one kilometre from the boundaries of these factories. The TMC was informed that the factories stored and used hazardous chemicals and that permitting multi-storeyed residential apartments in the industrial zone would increase the public risk posed by the units.

In January, 1990 the TMC issued an order rejecting building plans in the danger zone. In a writ petition filed by the developer assailing the TMC's refusal, the Bombay High Court quashed the TMC directive since according to the court, TMC had acted on a mere complaint and its action was not backed by the development plan. The

---

[105] *Id.*

[106] *M.C. Mehta v Union of India* 1999 (2) SCC 91.

[107] *D.P. Bhattacharya v West Bengal Pollution Control Board* 1996 (3) SCALE 41 (SP).

[108] *Mohd. Iqbal Qureshi v Manager, Delhi Slaughter House* 1992 (48) DEL.L.T.612.

[109] *Maneka Gandhi v Union Territory of Delhi* Civil Writ Petition No. 2961 of 1992, 10 March 1994.

[110] *Buffalo Traders' Welfare Association v Maneka Gandhi* 1996 (11) SCC 35.

[111] *M.C. Mehta v Union of India* AIR 1987 SC 1086.

success of the developer spawned 29 writ petitions by other builders, all of which were allowed with a direction to the TMC to re-examine the building plans without regard to irrelevant considerations such as the complaint by industry regarding the risk to local residents.

Bayer (India) Ltd. challenged the judgment before the Supreme Court, which permitted the company to approach the High Court in review. In a lengthy judgment rendered in Bayer's review petition, the High Court held that a safety zone with a radius of one kilometre was absolutely essential around the hazardous industrial units and that the TMC should not permit any new developments within the zone. The court found that the TMC was within its power to reject the building proposals in view of overriding public safety considerations. The High Court also rejected the contention of M.C. Mehta that the hazardous industries ought to move away. 'The units in question are not personal or proprietary businesses or small scale units, but are large industrial undertakings, shifting of which is hardly feasible. As of necessity, these chemical and pharmaceutical units have to be within the close proximity of area where the entire infrastructure is available and cannot be located at some isolated spot. ... The consequence of thousands of persons being rendered jobless, if the industries were to move, is a consideration of much seriousness, particularly in view of the present level of unemployment. We, therefore, feel ... that the best in the present situation would be to at least maintain a safety distance around the [hazardous industry].'[112]

In the Supreme Court, Bayer's initiative boomeranged. Back on his home turf, M.C. Mehta persuaded the court that the 1 kilometre prohibitory zone infringed on the right of the residents of Thane to reside in the locality, while leaving at the same time, a large number of persons already living in the area exposed to the risk of an industrial accident. The bench comprising Kuldip Singh and B.L. Hansaria, JJ. observed, 'it was thought by us that if the industrialists wanted to safeguard their interest in the event of some accident happening in their factories, it was for them either to obtain the ownership of the area in question or to shift their factories to such places where the residential areas could be kept wide apart from their factory premises.'[113] Encountering resistance from the industry to relocate, the Supreme Court directed the Central Government to constitute an authority under section 3(3) of the Environment (Protection) Act of 1986 to examine the issues arising in the case and to make a report to the Central Government. The TMC was asked to await the report of the authority before finally sanctioning the plans.

Which approach would you consider best from an environmental view point: The High Court's original decision, its judgment on Bayer's review petition, or the Supreme Court's judgment? Which decision is the most equitable? Does the environmental and public health interest diverge from the social welfare interest in each of these approaches?

---

[112] *Bayer (India) Ltd. v State of Maharashtra* 1994 (4) BOM. C.REP. 309, 353.
[113] *F.B. Taraporawala v Bayer India Ltd.* AIR 1997 SC 1846.

10

LARGE PROJECTS

A. INTRODUCTION

In this chapter we look at large development projects—dams, thermal power stations, ports and railway lines—and efforts to reduce their environmental impact.

India ranks among the most important dam building nations. It began building large dams shortly after independence. Large scale river development began in 1930 with the Mettur dam on the Cauvery and accelerated after independence with the Bhakra Nangal and Hirakud projects. By the mid-1980s, 1,553 large dams had been built, hydroelectricity generation had increased from 3.24 billion kilowatt hours (kWh) to 51 billion kWh and surface irrigation potential had increased from 9.7 million to 30.5 million hectares.[1] Currently however, India has tapped only 13 per cent of its total hydroelectric potential, estimated at 80,000 megawatts.

These dams are the cornerstones of large scale multi-purpose river valley projects intended to meet regional needs for irrigation, hydroelectric power and flood control. Since the 1950s, the governments, both state and national, have vigorously promoted dam building as a means to economic progress. Today, all major rivers in India are either dammed or in the process of being dammed.

In the past two decades, citizen protests and international human rights and environmental pressures have increasingly been brought to bear against these projects. The central issue in the citizen campaigns is the problem of displacement: the backwaters of a large dam generally displace many thousands of people—often tribals and forest dwellers who are the poorest and most powerless members of society. By the year 1990, an estimated 21 million people, primarily indigenous,

[1] Sharad Lele, *The Damming of India* in WORLD RIVERS REVIEW, Vol. 3, No.2, May / June 1988.

had been displaced over the years by large projects. Of these, only 25 per cent had been rehabilitated.[2] By the year 1999, according to Walter Fernandes of the Indian Social Institute who has studied displacement issues, the number of displaced people had risen to 30 million.[3] To compound this problem, the Indian Government's often extreme reactions to protests by potentially and actually displaced people has drawn unfavourable attention from the international human rights community. In addition, the structural design of dams built in seismically unstable areas has drawn even more attention to the potential loss of life and displacement that might result from a dam that fails.

To whom do the benefits of large dams accrue? Often the benefits go to large urban populations far downstream and not to the people who pay for the dam with their land and even their lives. In addition, funding for dams, often in the form of loans from other countries or multilateral development banks, raises international issues of responsibility and fault for unmitigated human and environmental damage.

Large dams are often ecologically unsound and economically unjustified if environmental and health costs are fully accounted for. These costs include the loss of forests and wildlife, waterlogging, siltation, loss of arable land and increases in water-borne diseases. Finally, the religious significance that many Indians attribute to the free flowing rivers and the communities endangered by faulty dam construction may not be adequately accounted for. Today, large dams are India's most controversial environmental issue, both domestically and internationally.

The environmental harm from a large project could be reduced if its probable environmental impacts were explored before the project's inception. In this chapter we examine the regulations that govern such environmental impact assessments in India and the land acquisition regime. We also review the legal dimensions of five important environmental campaigns—the successful campaign to conserve Silent Valley in Kerala, the ongoing battles to stop construction of the Tehri dam in Uttar Pradesh and the colossal Narmada Valley Project, the case to halt the Dahanu thermal power station and the Konkan Railway case. Notes and questions are interspersed throughout the chapter.

B. ENVIRONMENTAL IMPACT ASSESSMENT

Environmental Impact Assessment (EIA) is an effort to anticipate, measure and weigh the socio-economic and bio-physical changes that may result from a proposed project. It assists decision-makers in considering the proposed project's environmental costs and benefits. Where the benefits sufficiently exceed the costs, the project can be viewed as environmentally justified.

---

[2] Interview with W. Fernandes, Director (Tribal Studies) Indian Social Institute; *Down to Earth*, 15 February 1999.

[3] *Id.*

In view of the intricate web of relationships between the different parts of an ecosystem, a comprehensive EIA inevitably requires a multi-disciplinary approach. An environmental impact statement (EIS) for a dam, for example, might include inputs from geologists, forestry experts, wildlife experts, anthropologists, economists, agricultural scientists and social scientists.

Prior to January 1994, EIA in India was carried out under administrative guidelines which required the project proponents of major irrigation projects, river valley projects, power stations, ports and harbours, etc., to secure a clearance from the Union Ministry of Environment and Forests (MEF). The procedure required the project authority to submit environmental information to the MEF by filling out questionnaires or checklists. The environmental appraisal was carried out by the ministry's environmental appraisal committees. These committees held discussions with the project authority and on the basis of the deliberations, either approved or rejected the site. When approved, the project clearance was generally made conditional on specified safeguards.

On 27 January 1994, the MEF notified mandatory EIAs under rule 5 of the Environment (Protection) Rules of 1986 for 29 designated projects. The notification made it obligatory to prepare and submit an EIA, an Environment Management Plan (EMP), and a Project Report to an Impact Assessment Agency for clearance. The MEF was designated as the Impact Assessment Agency and was required to consult a multi-disciplinary committee of experts. Under the January 1994 notification any member of the public was to have access to a summary of the Project Report and the detailed EMPs. Public hearings were mandatory. This represented India's first attempt at a comprehensive EIA scheme.

On 4 May 1994 the MEF issued an amending notification substantially diluting the January 27 notification. The amendment was introduced furtively, without pre-publication of the draft. With these changes, the project proponent was no longer required to submit a 'detailed' Project Report (presumably, a summary report would do) and the previous requirement of preparing both an EIA and an EMP, was diluted to now require either of these documents to be submitted. The pre-requisite of securing environmental clearance from the Central Government before taking any measures at the site was weakened by the introduction of the expression 'construction', thereby restricting the prohibition to building activity. As amended, the clause permits the project proponent to initiate land acquisition proceedings and fell trees even before the clearance is given. Perhaps more invidious than the formal amendment to the parent notification, was an administrative guideline styled as an 'Explanatory Note' which was issued simultaneously by the MEF. The Explanatory Note restricted public access to an 'Executive Summary' of the environmental impact documents and further narrowed access to 'bonafide residents located at or around the project site or site of displacement or alleged adverse environmental impact'. Moreover, the Note diluted the comprehensive EIA report requirement (covering one year) to a single season report, termed as a rapid EIA report.

On 10 April 1997 some of the regressive changes introduced in May 1994 were undone by fresh amendments to the parent notification. The 1997 provisions restore public hearings, to be conducted in the manner prescribed. On the same day the MEF published a separate notification prescribing the EIA procedure for clearance of certain types of thermal power plants requiring environmental clearance from the concerned state government. The procedure to be followed under this notification mirrors the amended procedure prescribed for Central clearances.

In 1997, Parliament enacted the National Environment Appellate Authority Act which constitutes an authority headed by a retired Justice of the Supreme Court or Chief Justice of a High Court and comprising experts with technical knowledge on ecological matters. This Authority is empowered to hear appeals filed by persons aggrieved by the order granting environmental clearance in an area where industrial activity is restricted under sections 3(1) and 3(2)(v) of the Environment (Protection) Act. This includes project clearance granted by the Impact Assessment Agency. However, the Authority appears to have no jurisdiction to directly hear appeals by project authorities who are denied environmental clearance.

The state of Maharashtra has supplemented the central EIA regime with state EIA procedures notified on 7 August 1997. The state government resolution divides new development and industrial projects into three scheduled categories. The Maharashtra regime extends to all new scheduled projects including expansion, diversification and modernization of existing undertakings and prescribes a procedure similar to the 27 January 1994 MEF notification as amended on 4 May1994. However, the Maharashtra procedure does not provide for public hearings.

NOTES AND QUESTIONS

1. In *A.P. Pollution Control Board v Prof. M.V. Nayadu*,[4] the Supreme Court regarded the constitution of the National Environment Appellate Authority as approximating an ideal forum with judicial as well as technical expertise to adjudicate on complex environmental issues. The case concerned the siting of a vegetable oil factory close to the fresh water lakes supplying drinking water to Hyderabad and Secunderabad. In view of the complicated environmental issues, the court referred the matter to the Authority, holding that the High Courts and the Supreme Court may do so where the case required an investigation into scientific and technical aspects.

2. Why did Parliament restrict the jurisdiction of the Authority to appeals against the grant of a clearance? If the Authority has a special ability to correct erroneous decisions of the Impact Assessment Agency, on an application by an environmental group or project affected persons, would it not have the expertise to redress the grievance of the project proponent as well? What factors might have

[4] AIR 1999 SC 812.

prompted the legislature to limit the jurisdiction of the Authority? Does not the Supreme Court judgment in *APPCB v Prof. M.V. Nayadu* weaken the statutory limitation? In this case, the original authority, APPCB, refused site clearance to the industry. Nevertheless the matter landed before the Authority following a circuitous route through the High Court and the Supreme Court.

3. The Explanatory Note issued together with the 4 May 1994 notification is a curious document. It is certainly not subordinate legislation. What is the value of the Note? Is it a permissible aid to judicial interpretation? Is it open for a ministry to issue 'Explanatory Notes' that undermine the mandate of an environmental law which the ministry is supposed to vigorously enforce?

4. EIA procedure in India remains half hearted. Ashish Kothari, a leading environmentalist who served on the Environmental Appraisal Committee (EAC) for river valley and hydro-electric projects regards the procedure to be seriously flawed. He criticizes the practice of issuing 'conditional' clearances which result in most major projects receiving rubber-stamped approval, whether or not they pass muster on ecological considerations. The principal flaw in the method is that the MEF has an inadequate machinery to monitor whether or not the conditions are met. Kothari complains that there is not a single case of a violation of conditions where an environmental clearance was withdrawn or the concerned official prosecuted.[5]

5. In mid-1995 the MEF reviewed compliance by 300 project authorities that had been granted 'conditional' clearances for river valley and hydel projects over the past 15 years. The conditions frequently pertained to compensatory afforestation, rehabilitation of displaced persons and the treatment of the catchment and command areas to preserve bio-diversity. Reviewing the implementation record, the EAC found that the conditions were seldom honoured. The survey noted that over 88 per cent of river valley and hydel projects across India violated the EAC's terms and conditions. Frequently, the project authorities were ignorant about the conditions or had no idea how to implement the environmental measures.[6]

6. Whether a country is able or willing to enforce its own legislative and regulatory mandates depends on many factors: budgetary constraints, political popularity, and international pressure among them. What is the most likely reason behind India's failure to ensure that hydroelectric projects are properly assessed environmentally? Is the pressing need for the perceived benefits—irrigation, energy and drinking water—so great that it is unreasonable to expect the government to meet the stringent standards of a more developed country? Then should the legislation be more flexible? Is it better to have aspirational legislative goals in place and fail to meet them or to never put them in place to begin with? How would the international community react if the government were to 'throw up its hands' and admit that because it cannot meet the standards it will no longer seek to enforce them?

[5] Interview with A. Kothari, founder member, Kalpavriksh; 18 October 1999. Conducted by S. Divan.
[6] *Id.*

7. Once begun, is it a bigger waste of money to end a project that is out of compliance than to take the steps to ensure compliance? Consider the cost in terms of loss of jobs and the additional costs of monitoring progress. Does it make sense then to begin with a clean slate and only enforce regulations as applied to new projects, rather than go back and try to achieve compliance with respect to projects already in progress? Is there a way to assess the potential environmental damage of current projects and halt construction on only the worst ones?

8. The EAC found that one of the reasons for non-compliance was often ignorance on the part of project authorities of the conditions imposed for environmental clearance. What does this imply?

9. EIAs have been responsible for vast amounts of litigation in the United States with accompanying project delays and associated costs. Can India afford to litigate and delay each major project in this fashion? Can any government? Should there be a more efficient manner of settling disputes regarding environmental impacts, mitigating measures and the desirability of projects such as dams? Is the National Environment Appellate Authority the answer to these ills?

10. Since the 1970s, several international donor agencies that fund large development projects in the Third World insist upon an EIA. Indeed, international environmental consulting has grown into a big and profitable business with U.K. consultants earning $ 2.5 billion on overseas contracts in 1994.[7] Donor agencies, governments and the project authorities frequently treat the EIA process as just another regulatory hurdle to be jumped. Instead of the EIA process working towards improving the quality of locational decisions, the reports are used to legitimize projects that have already been decided to be built. EIAs rarely discuss whether the mitigation measures they recommend have been implemented or whether similar measures were successful for past projects.

11. On 2 March 2000, a division bench of the Gujarat High Court responded creatively to a petition filed by the Centre for Social Justice challenging the defective public hearing procedure adopted in the state. The High Court directed that (i) the venue of the public hearing be as near as possible to the site of the proposed project and no further than the sub-district (*taluka*) headquarters; (ii) the state pollution control board publish notice of the public hearing in at least two newspapers widely circulated in the region (one in the vernacular language); (iii) the first public hearing be held at least 30 days after the newspaper notice; (iv) a *summary* of the EIA report in the *local* language and the EIA report be made available to concerned citizens; (v) the quorum of the committee conducting the public hearing would be half its membership and the representatives of the pollution control board, state department of environment and one of the three senior citizens nominated by the Collector, would have to be present for a valid public hearing; (vi) the minutes of the public hearing be supplied to citizens on demand; and (vii) the gist of the environmental clearance

<hr />

[7] P. McCully, *Silenced Rivers: The Ecology and Politics of Large Dams*, 62 (1996).

be published in the newspapers in which notice of the public hearing was given.[8]

12. On 21 June 1999, the Union Ministry of Environment and Forests invited suggestions and objections from members of the public in respect of *draft* Environment (Siting for Industrial Projects) Rules. The proposed rules are intended to prohibit new industrial projects from being established within cities, around designated wetlands, around the periphery of national parks and sanctuaries, along national highways and rail lines, within the Taj Trapezium Zone and around designated archaeological monuments.

C. LAND ACQUISITION

Large projects require large tracts of land. To acquire the land, the State resorts to the Land Acquisition Act of 1894 which empowers the Union and state governments to take land for public purposes and for companies. The theory underlying this Act is the doctrine of eminent domain, which permits the state to reassert its right over a portion of the land for the public good. The exercise of eminent domain operates extremely harshly on the persons displaced, dishoused and uprooted.

The expression 'public purpose' has elastic import, including land for village development; town and country planning schemes; government corporations; educational, health, housing or slum clearance schemes or 'any other scheme of development sponsored by government.'[9] With the expansion of welfare activities by the state, land acquisition is resorted to in India for nearly all large industrial and development projects as well as for establishing institutions such as new universities. Sections 38A to 44B specifically relate to the acquisition of land for a company. For any such acquisition, the land must be needed for workers' housing, construction of buildings for industrial activity or a public purpose or for the construction of some work that is 'likely to prove useful to the public.'[10]

Under the scheme of the 1894 Act, government initiates acquisition proceedings by issuing a preliminary notification describing the land needed for the public purpose.[11] Objections to the acquisition must be made within 30 days. The jurisdictional collector hears the objections and makes a report to the government which then determines the land to be acquired.[12] Section 6 of the Act enjoins a secretary to the government to certify that the land is required for a public purpose and publication of this declaration is regarded as conclusive evidence of the need. Thereafter, the land is marked, measured and planned.[13] Next, the collector gives a notice to all interested

---

[8] *Centre for Social Justice v Union of India*, Special Civil Application No. 8529 of 1999.
[9] Section 3(f).
[10] Section 40.
[11] Section 4.
[12] Section 5A.
[13] Section 8.

persons of the government's intention to take possession of the land, inviting claims of compensation.[14] After conducting an enquiry, the collector awards compensation and apportions it among the interested persons.[15]

The criteria for determining compensation are set out in section 23 of the Act. The statutory factors include the market value of the land, the damage to standing crops or trees, damage for severance of other land and the damage to other movable or immovable property or any matter affecting the earning of the affected person. In addition to the market value, the state is required to pay interest at 12 per cent per annum on the market value from the date of publishing the notification under section 4 until the date of the award or the date of taking possession, whichever is earlier. The section also provides for solatium at the rate of 30 per cent of the market value. On payment of the compensation, the collector may enter and take possession of the land.

NOTES AND QUESTIONS

1. As we have noted in previous chapters, the poorest sections of our society depend heavily on common property resources for their basic needs of water, fuel, fodder and building material. The land acquisition regime in India completely ignores the real wealth of the poor: their access to common property resources, particularly biomass, in the locality where they live. As a result, the compensation measure under the statute operates to impoverish the poorest and weakest members of our society. Not only are these persons displaced from their traditional homes and their community life disrupted, but they are forced to migrate to urban centres where their access to common property resources is severely curtailed. Does a compensation regime that fails to adequately recompense persons for their real wealth—access to common property—meet the test of reasonableness under Article 14 or conform to the right to life guaranteed under Article 21 of the Constitution?

2. Traditional communities have preserved bio-diversity for centuries and have developed their livelihood around these resources. If common property resources are accepted as vital to the livelihood of traditional communities, should the Land Acquisition Act as framed, be repealed? If the loss of common property resources is to be compensated, how would you value the loss? Would monetary compensation suffice? Often, poor displaced persons who receive monetary compensation are unable to retain the monies since they are unaware of the working of the monetized economy and do not know how to invest funds. Is the taking regime in India with its 'market value of land' orientation, a just basis for recompensing tribals and forest dwellers, many of whom have little or no individual land holding in the strict property law sense?

---

[14] Section 9.
[15] Section 11.

3. Should government be entitled to acquire land for private companies under the Land Acquisition Act? Is it a legitimate extension of the theory of eminent domain?

D. THE SILENT VALLEY PROJECT

In the late 1970s, the Silent Valley project stirred up a hornet's nest in India's first major 'environment versus development' controversy. The proposed project, now abandoned, was to dam the Kuntipuzha river in Kerala's Palghat district. As it flows through the valley, the Kuntipuzha drops 857 metres, making the valley an attractive site for generating electricity. Those promoting the project claimed that it would produce 240 MW of power, irrigate 10,000 hectares of land and provide over 2000 jobs. Environmentalists, on the other hand, asserted that as home to one of the few remaining rain forests in the Western Ghats, the valley ought to remain pristine. They further contended that with over 900 species of flowering plants and ferns and several endangered species of animals and birds, Silent Valley was one of the world's richest biological and genetic heritages.

In the campaign to save Silent Valley, legal strategies played a peripheral role. The environmentalists' success was due to a combination of several other factors, including the grass-roots campaign led by the Kerala Sastra Sahitya Parishad (KSSP); intense lobbying by several non-governmental organizations and influential environmentalists within and outside government; and international pressure exerted on Prime Minister Indira Gandhi. Examine the judgment of the Kerala High Court in the *Silent Valley Case* (appended to the Prasad article, later in this section), in the backdrop of the larger campaign described in D'Monte's account.

D'MONTE; STORM OVER SILENT VALLEY, 9 India International Centre Quarterly 288 (1982)

> No other environmental issue has raised more heat and dust in the country than Silent Valley—a small and hitherto almost unheard of strip of dense forest in Kerala's western ghats. One reason is the very elemental nature of the controversy: whether or not to preserve this tropical forest belt, one of the few uninhabited areas in the entire country, for the future benefit of mankind.

> * * *

> It all started with a slim green report of the Task Force of the National Committee on Environmental Planning and Coordination, on the ecological planning of the western ghats. The group, appointed in 1976, was headed by the prominent environmentalist, Zafar Futehally. In the brief section on Silent Valley, it concluded: 'The task force feels very strongly that the project should be abandoned and the area declared a Biosphere

Reserve.' However, Futehally and his team were apparently under the impression that the Silent Valley multi-purpose project, then expected to cost Rupees twenty-five crores, was practically a *fait accompli* (though not as much as the Kudremukh iron mines in Karnataka, which it also studied). This is why it laid down several safeguards 'if the government feels the project cannot be abandoned for any reason'.

This triggered off an enormous row, the echoes of which have by no means died down, even five long years later. The two main opponents of the scheme in Kerala itself were the Kerala Sastra Sahitya Parishad (KSSP), a science-for-the-people organization which is to date the most effective grassroots environmental body in the country; and the Friends of the Trees, or more specifically, its indefatigable guiding spirit, Joseph John. They were given moral and material support from a 'Save Silent Valley' committee in Bombay, backed by individuals from the World Wildlife Fund, Bombay Natural History Society, and the Save Bombay Committee.

Pitted against these environmentalists were the Kerala government—irrespective of the particular party or the front in power at the time, the Kerala State Electricity Board (KSEB), which was to implement the project, and a group of scientists who banded together under the title, Parisara Asoothrana Samrakshana Samithy (PASS) which in Malayalam means Environmental Planning and Conservation Society.

Various international bodies jumped into the fray. Most were contacted to lend their considerable weight by environmentalists here. The most prominent of them was the International Union for Conservation of Nature and Natural Resources in Switzerland, which at its conference in Ashkabad in the USSR in September 1978, called upon the Kerala government to abandon the project. A few other foreign scientists also provided data in support of conservation; these were either experts in tropical rain forests, or zoologists who had studied the lion-tailed macaque. The IUCN, in fact, made its intentions quite clear from the very outset by offering the Futehally task force ten thousand dollars to help in its work, as part of its international campaign to save rain forests.

Before the NCEPC could even pronounce judgment on the task force recommendations, the Kerala government rushed to Delhi and convinced the Prime Minister, then Morarji Desai, that the scheme should be given the go-ahead. It did this armed with a unanimous resolution passed in the Kerala Assembly—in itself no mean feat, given the plethora of parties in that highly politicised state—accepting the task force report, together with all the safeguards. In fact, the only previous occasion when such unanimity was displayed was a resolution sanctioning pay rises for MLAs!

Belatedly, environmentalists realized that the seventeen safeguards listed by the task force wouldn't stop the forests from irretrievable damage. Futehally and the other members disowned their recommendations regarding safeguards and refused to serve on the Kerala government's Silent Valley Monitoring Committee. The debate grew really hot—on public platforms, where both KSSP and KSEB members spoke, and in the press. The furore at home, and its unexpected echoes at international forums, was sufficient to persuade the next Prime Minister, Charan Singh, to tell the Kerala government to stop further work on the project in late 1979.

In October that year, Central government, as much confused as anyone else by the charges and counter charges being traded in the dispute, decided to send the country's most reputed agricultural scientist to look at it. Dr. M.S. Swaminathan, who was then Secretary to the Union Agricultural Ministry, also endorsed the task force's opinion, recommending that the project be scrapped and that the entire area of Silent Valley and its environs—a total of 30,000 hectares—be converted into a rain forest Biosphere Reserve. The NCEPC was able to endorse these findings whole-heartedly on this occasion.

The Kerala authorities held a controversial seminar in April 1980 in Trivandrum, ostensibly with a view to clearing the air by allowing scientists and experts from either side to voice their opinion.

* * *

While genuflecting to the need for preserving the environment, the state-sponsored seminar concluded that 'a small disturbance in nature must be taken as a part of the game, when it comes to the question of prosperity of a region. Industries, projects and other developmental activities should not be stopped because of the fear of impending pollution'. It was believed that any threat to the environment could be contained, because of the great leaps made in pollution control technology.

Since the seminar in no way resolved the controversy, Mrs. Gandhi called a meeting in August 1980 with Chief Minister Nayanar. There it was decided to conclusively come to a decision on the fate of Silent Valley, by appointing yet another committee, this time headed by Prof. M.G.K. Menon, then Secretary of the Department of Science and Technology in Delhi. It was to consist of four members ... nominated by the Kerala government, and an equal number by the Centre.

The Menon committee report, originally due in three months, was finally submitted in the summer of 1983. Although the report's conclusions were ambiguous, a personal note appended by Menon made it clear that as chairperson he was in favour of preserving the Valley. Ultimately in November 1983, Kerala's electricity minister announced that his government had scrapped the Silent Valley project in deference to the wishes of Prime Minister Indira Gandhi.

In his book, *Temples or Tombs?* D'Monte offers a retrospective analysis of the decisive factors in the struggle to save Silent Valley. We carry a brief excerpt.

D'MONTE; TEMPLES OR TOMBS? INDUSTRY VERSUS ENVIRONMENT: THREE CONTROVERSIES, 57 (1985)

What finally tilted the scales in favour of the preservation of Silent Valley? One would like to think that it was primarily the groundswell of popular opinion stirred up by the ever-active KSSP, and secondly, the logic of those-environmentalists who cited alternatives and the scientists who put forward incontrovertible proof of the necessity of saving forests. The facts seem to tell a different story. It was as much the personality of the Prime Ministers which counted. Thus Morarji Desai, who has seldom displayed an aptitude for making unbiased decisions, was easily won over by specious arguments. * * * Mrs. Gandhi, on the other hand, did inherit some of her father's predilection for striving to appear 'modern' and 'scientific' in a huge, illiterate and superstitious country. More to the point, she—like Jawaharlal—was very concerned about her image abroad; so much so, that it proved her undoing when she decided to hold elections in the middle of the emergency in 1977 to stave off severe criticism in the West about her repressive measures and was unceremoniously bundled out of office.* * *

Mrs. Gandhi had replied to David Munro, the IUCN Director General, who had asked her to throw her weight behind the environmentalists, that she shared his concern but 'unless we can quickly identify some other way for them (the Kerala government), I am afraid that we may not be able to save the Valley.' Janet Barber, head of information of WWF-UK who visited Silent Valley in April 1981, wrote to a Kerala environmentalist that [when] she met Mrs. Gandhi in Delhi a little later, 'I congratulated her on what she had almost achieved in securing it for a Biosphere Reserve.' Prof. George Verghese, the PASS chemistry lecturer from Trivandrum's University College, commented sarcastically that the 'PM can't give Silent Valley the green signal because she is worried about her image abroad. It's as if the beginning of wisdom was in Morges!' (WWF's Swiss headquarters). Everyone—from officials in the Kerala government and the KSEB, environmentalists in Kerala and Bombay, officials in the DST and DoE in Delhi—is agreed on one thing: if it were not for Mrs. Gandhi, Silent Valley would be well on the way to being dammed forever.

It was a fascinating *pot pourri* of factors that went into the halting of the Silent Valley project, of which attitudes of the Prime Ministers concerned were perhaps the most important. At each stage, different scientific arguments were advanced: first, the loss of one of the last remaining tropical rain forests, then the lion-tailed macaque, then the question of it being a 'gene pool'. Correspondingly, the protagonists of the project tried to adduce their own facts to disprove each of these arguments. The weight of the national institutions which voted against the project was plainly far more impressive than that of local scientists whose command performance was orchestrated by the KSEB. When I asked Prof. M.G.K. Menon how the public was to choose between the two apparently contradictory sets of scientific data, he answered with a twinkle in his eye: 'Look at the credentials of the scientists.' Undeniably, the rallying force of the KSSP made Silent Valley a unique environmental campaign in the entire Third World because it took the issue out of lecture rooms and the columns of the press to the people. If many people in Kerala today are aware of the meaning of 'ecology', it is solely due to Silent Valley. This interplay of international pressure, lobbying in Delhi and counter-lobbying in the state, local agitation for the project, press campaigns and scientific deliberation, is witnessed, in varying proportions, in each of the three cases in this book. It bears testimony to the genuinely democratic process at work in this country, which will be hard to find anywhere else, in the Third World. In general, it can be concluded that the access of environmentalists to the highest echelons of power in Delhi turned the tables decisively in Silent Valley... while scientific opinion took a back seat.

PRASAD; SILENT VALLEY CASE: AN ECOLOGICAL ASSESSMENT, 8 COCHIN UNIVERSITY LAW REVIEW 128 (1984)

Lack of proper appreciation of environmental information may often lead to decisions going against the interest of the general public. Consequently, priority is given to developmental activities aimed at short term benefits over conservation oriented actions with a long term perspective of sustainable benefits. It is this unfortunate position that prompted the author to evaluate the judgment pronounced by the Kerala High Court on 2 January 1980 in *Society for Protection of Silent Valley v Union of India and others*.[16] The judgment was not reported. Hence I have given an extract in the appendix. Petitions were filed seeking a writ forbidding the state of Kerala from proceeding to construct a hydroelectric project at Silent Valley.[17] This venture was represented as fraught with adverse consequences deleterious to the environment. Experts including scientists attached to the Department of Science and Technology, Government of India had warned against the proposed construction. Environmentalists, scientists and conservation societies in India and abroad expressed great concern and joined the chorus of denunciation of the Silent Valley Hydro-Electric Project called SVHEP.

* * *

APPENDIX

EXTRACT FROM THE JUDGEMENT BY HON'BLE MR. JUSTICE V.P. GOPALAN NAMBIAR IN THE *SILENT VALLEY CASE*

There is, in the Palghat District of this state, 45 kilometres to the north of Mannarghadu, a stretch of forest, nearly 8952 hectares in extent, known as the 'Silent Valley'. The name is apparently derived from the peace, quiet and serenity of the place. But, paradoxically enough, as was once remarked in the far past in the Madras Legislature, the valley has been creaking and squeaking loudly on many occasions. The present noise and bustle are over the hydroelectric project sought to be built in this valley. These writ petitions, broadly stated, seek to forbid the state from proceeding with the project. As representatives of the arguments advanced, we may refer to O.P. No. 2949 of 1979. The government of Kerala is proposing to deforest the Silent Valley and to construct a dam for ... a hydroelectric project for power generation and supply of

---

[16] O.P. Nos. 2949 and 3025 of 1979.

[17] The petition pointed out that Silent Valley in the district of Palghat contained one of India's largest tropical evergreen forests and is the only vestige of virgin forest of the Western Ghats. It is estimated to have a continuous record of not less than 50 million years of evolutionary history, with diverse and complex flora and fauna. It is a unique vegetable food resource which contains mammals and birds in the valley. A number of endangered plants and animals live there. The forests perform very many important functions. They regulate water supply to the plains by retaining rain water in the soil and releasing it slowly down, maintaining the hydrological balance, averting floods and droughts in the plains. Soil erosion is prevented and the climatic condition of the whole area is regulated by the forests.

electricity. It is said that the dam is to generate 120 M. Watts of power by 1985. (The learned Advocate General rated the power generation much higher, viz., at 240 M. Watts). This venture has been represented as fraught with adverse consequences deleterious to the public. Experts have warned against the proposed construction of the dam and processing of the project. Scientists and technologists have joined the chorus of denunciation of the project.

The adverse effects from the conversion of the Silent Valley into a hydroelectric project were listed thus: first, the deforestation was bound to affect the climatic conditions in the state and even outside, by depriving the state of its legitimate share of rain during the Monsoon; second, that the preservation of the forests was needed for conducting research in medicine, pest control, breeding of economic plants and a variety of purposes, and third that deforestation was bound to interfere with the balance of nature, as between the forest land on the one side and arable and other types of lands on the other.

The argument stressed that a project like the hydroelectric project, if sanctioned and set up would have its impact on environment, and this has to be carefully considered. Copious citations were made from various treatises, reports, and publications, to show the importance of the environmental factor in industrial planning. [The court referred to some of these treatises and reports.]

It is pointed out that the Legislature of Kerala was of the unanimous view that the project was of crucial importance to the state. A resolution was unanimously adopted on 22-8-1978 expressing anxiety on the continuing delay. An all-party delegation from Kerala visited the Prime Minister on 7-4-1978. The various steps and developments of a similar nature are detailed in paragraph 20. They show clearly that the Government's mind was addressed to the question of the ecological aspects involved in the execution of the project and its impact upon the same. We were taken through copious extracts from various works, reports and other materials regarding the technical feasibility of the project and the importance of ecological considerations in assessing the worth and utility of a proposed project. But in this region we cannot substitute our judgment for that of the Government, on the question as to whether a national asset is to be more conveniently utilized as a hydroelectric project with prospects of greater power generation, or retained in its pristine glory for preservation of forests and wildlife, prevention of soil erosion, and avoidance of other deleterious effects on the community. The scope for interference with such policy decision of the Government, should, in the nature of things be limited. A wealth of material was cited and placed before us on the technical feasibility of the project and the impolitic decision to destroy the forest.

* * *

Counsel for the petitioner stressed the national importance of forests as having been responsible for certain amendments in the Constitution. Reference was made to Article 48A of the Constitution where by the preservation of forests and wildlife is one of the directive principles of state policy. Article 49 was also stressed giving obligation to protect every monument or place or object of artistic or historic interest, declared by Parliament to be of national importance from destruction, removal etc.

Rich and worthy material of a variegated nature was placed before us in regard to the national policy and environmental considerations. We are by no means satisfied that these aspects have not been borne in mind by the Government in planning and processing the project. We are also not satisfied that the assessment of these considerations made by the Government and the policy decisions taken thereafter are liable to be reviewed by this Court in these proceedings. Even if they be open to review no grounds for such review have been disclosed.

* * *

As for the danger of extinction of the lion-tailed monkey, the matter is dealt with in paragraph 8 of the counter-affidavit. We do not think it necessary to cover the entire gamut of the material—whether scientific, technical, technological or ecological—placed before us in great detail. It is not for us to evaluate these considerations again as against the evaluation already done by the Government. It is enough to state that we are satisfied that the relevant matters have received attention before the Government decided to launch the project. There has been no non-advertence of the mind to the salient aspects of the project. We are not to substitute our opinion and notions on these matters for those of the Government.

We find no reason to interfere. We dismiss these applications with no order as to costs.

NOTES AND QUESTIONS

1. Although the High Court eventually rejected the petitions, the legal action may have had a beneficial effect: A two week interim stay on the construction of the dam in August 1979 boosted the environmentalists' morale. The interim order might also have emboldened the NCEPC to record at its meeting in September 1979, that it did not favour the hydel project and that the valley should be preserved in its natural state.

2. Shouldn't the clear directive in Article 48A of the Constitution that 'the State shall endeavour to protect and improve the environment and to safeguard the forests and wild life of the country' have persuaded the Kerala High Court to subject the state government's decision to a more searching scrutiny?

3. In its 1987 judgment in the *Calcutta Taj Hotel Case*,[18] the Supreme Court inquired extensively into the government permission for the construction of a medium-rise hotel on the allegation that the building would interfere with the flight path of migratory birds. The Kerala High Court's deferential approach to the government in the *Silent Valley Case*—involving, as it did, the submergence of a pristine valley with its extraordinary wealth of flora and fauna—seems hard to reconcile with the Supreme Court's searching inquiry for what appears to have been a less momentous issue. What factors may account for this discrepancy?

[18] AIR 1987 SC 1109.

4. Has any government the authority to order the extinction of an endangered species—in this case the rare lion-tailed macaque? How could this issue be raised in a legal action? What constitutional provisions could be cited?

5. In 1979–80 when the case was argued and decided there was no statutory EIA in India. Now we have the statutory notification of 1994. Will this help preserve the environment? Or will the statutory mantle serve to shield weak scientific and technical opinions, like the ones used to advocate the Silent Valley project?

E. THE TEHRI DAM PROJECT

The rivers Bhagirathi and Bhilangana rise in the Garhwal Himalayas in northwestern Uttar Pradesh and flow south to the plains as the Ganga. As part of a larger plan to trap the waters of the Upper Ganga basin, a three billion dollar clay core, rock fill dam is being constructed at the confluence of the Bhagirathi and Bhilangana, close to the Garhwal town of Tehri. The lake created by the dam will extend upto 45 kms in the Bhagirathi Valley and 25 kms in the Bhilangana Valley with a water spread area of 42.5 sq. kms. It will submerge nearly 100 villages, including Tehri, a historical capital. As many as 85,600 families will be relocated as a result.[19] On the benefits side of the equation, the project is supposed to generate 2,400 MW of electricity, create irrigation facilities for 270,000 hectares of land, and create a supply of 500 cusecs of water to New Delhi.

The Tehri dam project has provoked controversy focused on three issues. The completed dam will displace many people and submerge several towns, among them the town of Tehri; the region is vulnerable to earthquakes and the dam may be structurally incapable of withstanding them or may perhaps even cause them;[20] and the possible failure of the dam could kill hundreds of thousands of people and destroy downstream towns of immense religious significance. Of particular concern are the 170,000 inhabitants of the downstreams Hindu holy towns of Hardwar and Rishikesh. Both the resettlement policies and the structural flaws of the dam have provoked civil protests, lawsuits and international attention that have repeatedly stalled the project which was begun in 1978.

The Tehri project was unsuccessfully challenged in the Supreme Court in a writ petition filed by the Tehri Bandh Virodhi Sangarash Samiti (TBVSS) in 1985. In April 1987 the Indian National Trust for Art and Cultural Heritage (INTACH), an 'intervenor' in this petition and a leading non-governmental organization in the field of conservation, sponsored an independent assessment of the economic feasibility of the dam. The principal finding of the multi-disciplinary team that conducted the appraisal was that the benefit to cost ratio of the Tehri dam, after calculating social and

---

[19] Paranjpye, *Evaluating the Tehri Dam: An Extended Cost Benefit Appraisal*, 23 (1988).

[20] Dams cause earthquakes if the weight of the water activates unnoticed faults in the earth as was the case in Koyna, Maharashtra in 1967 when 200 people were killed and 1500 were injured.

environmental costs and benefits, works out to 0.56:1, well short of the 1.5:1 ratio adopted by the Planning Commission to sanction such projects.

In addition, in 1986, the Soviet Union agreed to help fund the project with loans at extremely concessional terms. As a part of the agreement with the Indian Government, Soviet experts conducted a review of the proposed project and made several ominous findings, the most frightening of which was that the high seismicity of the Tehri area had not been adequately taken into consideration by Indian planners. The INTACH team, under the leadership of Vijay Paranjpye, also found that while the Indian Government projected a useful life of 100 years, the actual siltation rate would render the dam useless in 62 years or less. Finally, while the authorities put the number of displaced people, or oustees at 46,000, the INTACH team found that 85,600 people would be displaced by the project.[21]

The Supreme Court dismissed the petition in 1990 after a very limited enquiry. Although the Environmental Appraisal Committee had unanimously concluded that the Tehri project should not be approved, the Central Government relied instead on an opinion of the Department of Mines to convince itself and the court that the project was sound.

<h2 style="text-align:center">TEHRI BANDH VIRODHI SANGHARSH SAMITI v
STATE OF UTTAR PRADESH</h2>

1992 Supp (1) SCR 44

ORDER:

This petition under Article 32 of the Constitution of India has been filed in public interest by Tehri Bandh Virodhi Sangarsh Samiti and others. The petitioners have prayed that the Union of India, State of Uttar Pradesh and the Tehri Hydro Development Corporation be restrained from constructing and implementing the Tehri Hydro Power Project and the Tehri Dam.

The main grievance of the petitioners is that in preparing the plan for the Tehri Dam project the safety aspect has not been taken into consideration. It is asserted that the dam if allowed to be constructed poses a serious threat to the life, ecology and the environment of the entire northern India as the site of the dam is prone to earthquake. After this petition was filed a number of persons have intervened and the parties have filed affidavits and counter affidavits. The matter was heard by this Court at various stages. The controversy relating to the project has not only been debated in this Court but has also taken a good deal of Parliament's time.

[Counsel] appearing for the petitioners has argued that the seismic experts in India and abroad are of the view that past records of earthquake show that the likely length of fracture along the convergence boundary is of the order of 200–300 kilometers. According to him, it is thus possible that segment of such a length along the Himalayan belt covering the region from approximately Dehradun on the west and India-Nepal border in the east, could be the fracture area of a future large

---

[21] *Supra* note 19 at 31.

earthquake of magnitude 8 or so. According to him, the Government of India has not applied its mind to this very important aspect in preparing the project.

Shri V.K. Khanna, Joint Secretary, Ministry of Energy, Department of Power, New Delhi has filed an affidavit dated 5 November 1990 wherein relevant material has been placed before this Court showing that the Government of India, through its various departments and ministries has at every stage considered all relevant data and fully applied its mind to the safety and various other aspects of the project.

The project was initially considered by the Environmental Appraisal Committee of the Ministry of Environment and Forests and the said Committee, taking into consideration the geological and seismic setting, the consequent risks, and hazards, ecological and social impacts accompanying the project and the costs and benefits expected, came to the unanimous conclusion that the Tehri Dam Project did not merit environmental clearance and should be dropped.

The report submitted by the Environmental Appraisal Committee was considered and discussed in the meeting of the Committee of Secretaries held on 20 March 1990. The Committee of Secretaries came to the conclusion that the Environmental Appraisal Committee ought to have concerned itself with the environmental parameters within which the opinion of the said Committee was relevant. It was also opined by the Committee of Secretaries that the safety aspect of the design and earthquake engineering could be best looked into by the scientific and specialized organizations such as Geological Survey of India, National Geological Research Institute, Central Water Commission and Earthquake Engineering Department of the Roorkee University. In this context the Committee of Secretaries further observed that the safety aspect relating to the project ought to be resolved and in this regard directed the constitution of a High Level Committee of Experts to examine the issues relating to the safety aspects of Tehri Dam Project.

* * *

The High Level Committee of Experts under the Chairmanship of Shri D.P. Dhoundial, Director General, Geological Survey of India rendered its report on 6 April 1990. The affidavit filed by the Government of India stated as under regarding the said report:

The said Committee considered all safety aspects of the Tehri Dam and opined with reference to all the issues that were to be decided upon. The said Committee assumed the worst scenario of the possible occurrence of a large magnitude earthquake in the area and rendered an opinion to the effect that the design of the Tehri Dam incorporated adequate defensive measures in accordance with the recommendations of the International Congress of Large Dams on seismic design of dams made from time to time and that additional safety measures had been inbuilt to ensure an adequate and well evolved seismic design for this high dam.

The affidavit further gave details of the report of the High Level Committee in the following words:

The conclusions culled out from the said report of the High Level Committee are set out hereunder for the purpose of convenience:

'CONCLUSIONS OF HIGH LEVEL COMMITTEE:

I. Whether the earthquake potential of the zone in which the dam is being located has been fully taken into account in designing the dam:

a. Modern researches are being directed towards refining models of seismic potential in seismically active belts of the world. Different models suggesting probable source potentials in the Himalayan geotectonic setting around Tehri have been examined. In the absence of any definitive model the worst scenario of a Mag 8+ earthquake has been considered. The probable locale of such earthquake has been considered to be at a depth of 15 km below the dam site;

b. The seismic potential at a project site is characterized by the maximum intensity of ground motion due to earthquake occurrence on the likely seismic sources surrounding the site. The effective peak ground acceleration, considering earthquake events up to Mag 8 + has been evaluated at the dam site to be 0.22g.

c. The effective peak ground acceleration for which the design of the dam has been checked for stability is 0.25g. Thus, the seismic potential of the dam site has been fully taken into account in the design.

II. Whether the proposed dam would be safe as designed vis-a-vis earthquake potential of the area:

a. Cross section of the proposed dam would be safe vis-a-vis the maximum earthquake potential as indicated by the estimated effective peak ground acceleration (EPA) of 0.22g. on the following counts:

b. The design side slopes are stable with adequate factor of safety.

c. Settlement likely to occur in the height of dam, when subjected to an EPA of 0.25g will be within permissible limits and is taken care of by way of liberal free board provided in the design.

d. The shell material proposed to be used in the construction of the dam when subjected to an EPA of 0.25g does not show potential for liquefaction.

III. Whether there would be any threat posed by Reservoir Induced Seismicity (RIS) to the dam or civilian structures in the vicinity:

a. Seismicity induced by a large artificial reservoir can only act as a trigger to initiate a natural earthquake that would have occurred otherwise. Therefore, the presence of a reservoir does not increase the size of an earthquake event.

b. Since the design is considered safe for the worst case earthquake no additional consideration for RIS is necessary.

c. Earthquake vulnerability of the existing civil structures would depend upon the earthquake resistance built in the same. The construction of the dam would not in any way add to the vulnerability of the existing structures or affect the design requirements for the future constructions.

IV. Have all potential dangers arising out of seismicity been taken note of and adequate precautions taken in planning all aspects of the Project? If there are any lacunae in these respects, the same may be elaborated upon and action required in this regard spelt out.

All dangers arising out of seismicity have been taken note of and taken care of in the planning of the Tehri Dam Project.'

* * *

The report of the High level Committee was again considered by the Committee of Secretaries in its meeting dated 23 April 1990. The Committee of Secretaries found on a consideration of the report of the High Level Committee that the Tehri Dam as designed was safe and seismic potential of the site was taken into consideration by the experts. Meanwhile Dr. V.K. Gaur, a member of the High Level Committee of Experts, who had earlier agreed with the unanimous report, later on sent a note of dissent of 12 May 1990 wherein he questioned the conclusion of the High Level Committee of Experts in respect of the safety aspects of the project.

In the light of the letter of dissent sent by Dr. Gaur the Government of India decided to revive the High Level Committee of experts and referred the points raised by Dr. Gaur for further consideration of the Committee. The High Level Committee thereafter on 20 July 1990 rendered a supplementary report endorsing its earlier views rendered unanimously on 6 April 1990. This endorsement, however, was a majority view since Dr. V.K. Gaur this time issued a note of dissent stating that the opinion of the High Level Expert Committee was based on questionable grounds and formulations and that because of his dissent the entire matter ought to be referred to an independent seismological expert of international repute.

The Committee of Secretaries met again on 10 August 1990 and considered the recommendations of the High Level Committee along with the dissent of Dr. V.K. Gaur and in the circumstances requested the Department of Mines to refer the matter to an independent expert seismologist whose opinion should be taken as final. Pursuant to the said decision Prof. Jai Krishna a renowned expert of international repute examined the reports of the High Level Committee dated 6 April 1990, 20 July 1990 and also the dissenting note of Dr. V.K. Gaur. Prof. Jai Krishna submitted his report to the Department of Mines, Government of India on 8 September 1990 wherein he concurred with the conclusions arrived at by the High Level Committee of Experts. He did not agree with the view expressed by Dr. V.K. Gaur in his dissenting note. Prof. Jai Krishna confirmed that the recommendations of the High Level Committee of Experts were in accord with international experience and practice. He also opined that the design of the Tehri Dam as suggested by Indian and Russian experts was quite safe against the strongest expected earthquake in the region.

The aforesaid facts clearly show that the Union of India considered the question of safety of the project in various details more than once. It satisfied itself by obtaining the reports of experts and also took into consideration the dissenting view of Dr. V.K. Gaur. The project has been finalized after obtaining the expert report of Prof. Jai Krishna. In the circumstances, it is not possible to hold that the Union of India has not applied its mind or has not considered the relevant aspects of safety of the dam.

Learned counsel for the petitioners [has] urged that the report submitted by Prof. Jai Krishna should not have been relied upon, instead the matter should have been referred to a seismologist and that the safety of the dam is still in danger. In this connection he referred to the opinion given by Prof. James N. Brune to Dr. V.K. Gaur as well as to his dissenting opinion. The questions relating to the design of the dam, the seismic potential of the site where the dam is proposed to be constructed and the various steps which have been taken for ensuring the safety of the dam are a highly intricate question relating to science and engineering. This Court does not possess the requisite expertise to render any final opinion on the rival contentions of the experts. In our opinion the Court can only investigate and adjudicate the question as to whether the Government was conscious to the inherent danger as pointed out by the petitioners and applied its mind to the safety of the dam. We have already given facts in detail which show that the Government has considered the question on several occasions in the light of the opinions expressed by the experts. The Government was satisfied with the report of the experts and only thereafter clearance has been given to the project. The petitioners contend that the project has not as yet been cleared.

Mr. N.D. Jayal appearing for the intervenor—INTACH also referred to the various technical aspects of the matter and urged that the safety of the dam is still in danger having regard to the seismological aspects of the area where the dam is to be constructed. We need not discuss this matter any further, as in our opinion, the Government has already fully considered every aspect of the project including its safety.

We appreciate the petitioners' concern for the safety of the project which is of prime importance to the general public, however, in view of the material on the record we do not find any good reason to issue a direction restraining the respondents from proceeding ahead with the implementation of the project. The petition, therefore, fails and is accordingly dismissed with no order as to costs.

NOTES AND QUESTIONS

1. The campaign against the Tehri Dam began in the mid-1970s. The TBVSS initially enjoyed the support of all political parties. As the construction progressed the opposition weakened. With the freeze on government spending in old Tehri town due to its impending submergence, many local residents gave up active opposition. The struggle continues, inspired by Sunderlal Bahuguna, whose non-violent protests to save the Garhwal from environmental degradation have earned him recognition the world over.

2. The Tehri dam project was a hot potato for the Supreme Court. Expert opinion on the safety of the project was divided, more than 70,000 persons were going to be uprooted and the local people were opposed to the dam. At the same time, over Rs. 3 billion had already been spent on the project and powerful interests in the state and Centre were intent on seeing it through.

The court took an easy way out. It quite rightly disclaimed expertise to render any final opinion on the rival contentions of the experts, defining its narrow role thus: 'In our opinion the Court can only investigate and adjudicate the question as to whether the Government was conscious to the inherent danger as pointed out by the petitioners and applied its mind to the safety of the dam.' The court found that the government had indeed considered the question of safety, and hence rejected the petitioners' challenge.

3. While it is difficult to fault this broad approach, vigorous application by the court of its own standard would have made for more meaningful judicial review. For example, the court might have insisted on an affidavit by the Secretary, Ministry of Environment and Forests on the environmental aspects of the project. Under the present administrative framework, it is the Ministry of Environment that is charged with environmental impact appraisal. In particular, it is this ministry's job to assess and advise on environmental risks of the type created by the Tehri dam project. Nevertheless, the court did not seek the Environment Ministry's opinion, and instead relied on an affidavit filed by the Joint Secretary, Ministry of Energy, Department of Power! Considering that the Department of Power's primary task is to boost power generation (and the Tehri project would supply power to the Uttar Pradesh grid), wasn't it more than likely that the department would play down the risks involved? In this situation, was it wise for the court to rely exclusively on an affidavit from the Ministry of Energy?

Note that in the successful *Dehradun Quarrying Case*,[22] the Central Government filed an affidavit through the Secretary, Ministry of Environment and Forests.

4. The members of the Environmental Appraisal Committee (EAC)—an expert body within the Ministry of Environment and Forests—*unanimously* concluded that the Tehri project did not merit environmental clearance and should be dropped. Ordinarily, the government should adhere to the recommendations of its own expert agency or cogently explain any departure from the course of action suggested by its experts. Here, the committee of secretaries brushed aside the EAC's recommendations and the court, surprisingly, did not seek a detailed explanation from the government for departing from the EAC's report.

5. It appears that the Central Government took a political decision to proceed with the Tehri project and then structured an *ad hoc* administrative framework that would secure expert opinion to support that decision. Review of the safety aspect of the project was abruptly removed from the province of the Ministry of Environment and entrusted to the committee of secretaries, even though this committee had no expertise in environmental matters. Besides, by the nature of its composition— i.e., secretaries representing ministries that were committed to achieve developmental targets, not protect the environment—the committee was apt to discount environmental and safety factors. Note well that when it came to obtaining an additional opinion, in view of the note of dissent submitted by Dr. V.K Gaur, the committee of secretaries assigned this task to the Department of Mines. The Department of Mines

22 AIR 1988 SC 2187.

is an aggressive, 'pro-development' agency with a none too happy environmental record.

6. The Department of Mines' 'independent expert seismologist' Prof. Jai Krishna, was neither independent nor a seismologist. Prof. Jai Krishna was an earthquake engineer who had previously filed an affidavit in this case supporting the project.[23]

7. The only seismologist who gave an opinion on the project was Prof. James N. Brune. Based on the Brune opinion, Dr. V.K. Gaur's dissenting report disputed the High Level Committee's conclusions. Ordinary good judgment suggests that a seismologist's opinion ought to be verified or disputed by another seismologist—not an engineer. For reasons best known to it, however, the Supreme Court considered the opinion of an earthquake engineer, Prof. Jai Krishna, to be an adequate affirmation of the High Level Committee report.

8. In the language of the judgment, Prof. Jai Krishna 'opined that the design of the Tehri Dam as suggested by Indian and [Soviet] experts was quite safe against the strongest expected earthquake in the region.' The project being 'quite safe', the court declined to intervene.

Given the potentially catastrophic effect of a dam burst at Tehri, was it reasonable to accord approval on a 'quite safe' opinion? Shouldn't the standard for such project approvals be far more stringent? Would not an 'insignificant risk' standard be more appropriate? Is the project consistent with the precautionary principle?

9. Keeping in view that the expenditure incurred on the project exceeded Rs. 3 billion when the case was heard by the court, was the court ever likely to stop the project?

10. The fundamental right to freedom of religion is guaranteed under Articles 25 to 28 of the Constitution. Located downstream from the proposed Tehri reservoir are the towns of Rishikesh and Hardwar—considered by Hindus to be among the holiest of pilgrim centres. Both towns would probably be devastated in the event of a dam burst at Tehri. Is the project a threat to the right of Hindus to 'profess, practice and propagate religion'? Would the siting of a nuclear power project near Rishikesh and Hardwar threaten the community's fundamental right to freedom of religion?

11. Is there a temporal dimension to Article 21 and the right to equality guaranteed in Article 14, which recognizes 'intergenerational equity'? Consider this argument: All members of each generation of human beings, as a species, inherit a natural and cultural patrimony from past generations, both as beneficiaries and as custodians who are under a duty to pass on this heritage to future generations. Therefore, the right of each generation to benefit from and develop this natural and cultural heritage is inseparably coupled with the obligation to use this heritage in such a manner that it can be transmitted to future generations in no worse condition than it was received

---

[23] Interview with N.D. Dayal, Director (Natural Heritage), INTACH; 10 December 1990. Conducted by S. Divan.

from past generations. Do you agree with this argument? Is the Tehri dam project consistent with this argument?

In October 1991, about a year after the Supreme Court judgment, an earthquake measuring 6.1 on the Richter scale hit the Garhwal region, flattening villages in Uttarkashi and Chamoli, killing 2000 people, and causing some damage in the town of Tehri itself. Although the Power Ministry maintained that the dam works were not damaged in any way by the quake, its occurrence reignited the debate over the safety of the plans for a dam in such an earthquake-prone region, as well as the more specific controversy over exactly how great a quake the completed dam is designed to withstand.[24]

While project authorities have consistently maintained that the dam is designed to withstand quakes of up to 8 on the Richter scale, other experts disagree. In 1993, INTACH organized a workshop concerning the dam, which was attended by James Brune of the seismological laboratory at the University of Nevada, whose formula to determine quake resistance was relied upon by the Indian Government. Brune contended that the Indian Government misapplied his formula and consequently exaggerated the quake resistance potential of the dam and overestimated the dam's life. Moreover, he charged that the data concerning geological studies, silt load in the river and earthquake measurements were all incomplete.

In protest, on 14 December 1991, 5,000 people led by environmental activist Sunderlal Bahuguna brought work on the project to a complete halt through 'direct action' protests. They, in fact, placed their bodies on and around the site and the machinery, making any further work impossible. They maintained their 'sit in' for a full two months until finally Bahuguna and fourteen others were arrested on 29 February 1992. Following the arrests, Bahuguna went on a hunger strike that lasted for 45 days. Fearing more unrest in the event of the death of the popular activist, Prime Minister P.V. Narasimha Rao called a halt to all blasting and construction at the Tehri site, pending yet another review of the project. Despite these promises, dam construction work continued.

In April 1995, Bahuguna went on another hunger strike. He was arrested and forcibly hospitalized, only to be released following a court order. Two thousand protesters then marched on the dam site, only to be beaten back by police, who reportedly injured at least 150 of the protesters. After 49 days of fasting, the government again capitulated to Bahuguna's demands for review.

---

[24] The material in this part of the Tehri Dam section is drawn from wire service reports; M. Kishwar, *A Himalayan Catastrophe: The Controversial Tehri Dam in the Himalayas*, 95 Manushi 5 (1995) and P. McCully, *Silenced Rivers: The Ecology and Politics of Large Dams*, 336 (1996).

The government promised that this time, as opposed to the 1992 review, a panel of independent experts would be convened to consider the project. The government invited activists to select their own representative to work with officials on the review panel. In addition, the government promised that the panel would consider the ecological, economic, social and cultural impacts of the Tehri Project, all of which the 1992 panel had ignored. However, as the 1992 panel and the two prior reviews had considered the seismic safety of the project, that subject was, according to the Prime Minister, a dead issue.

In August, 1995 the government again broke its word. The Minister of State for Water Resources told the Rajya Sabha that there was no going back on the Tehri Dam on which huge amounts had already been spent. He claimed that the government was willing to look into new and substantial issues. As of early 2000, a review had yet to be commissioned.

NOTES AND QUESTIONS

1. Who pays for the Tehri Dam and who benefits?

2. One of the driving forces behind the continuation of the Tehri Project appears to be the vast amounts of money that have already been spent. The Indian Government's intractable stand based on money already spent raises economic questions. When, for example, is the cost of stopping construction greater than the cost of reassessing or abandoning the project? Does this take into account the cost of disaster relief if the dam does fail, as many predict that it will?

3. Another issue raised in any EIA cost benefit analysis is the cost assigned to human life, both in terms of resettlement and rehabilitation (R&R) and lives lost in the event of dam failure. Is it possible, as it appears from the disjointed nature of reviews of the Tehri project, that these costs have simply been ignored? If not, who assigns value to them? Should anyone?

4. Why, in a region as prone to earthquakes as the Tehri site, would the government reject the idea of several smaller hydroelectric projects, as opposed to the one gargantuan dam? Are lots of little projects perhaps not as conspicuous and therefore politically less appealing?

5. In the context of the Tehri project, how complete does an EIA or review need to be? How many things must the project planners take into account? The Supreme Court relied on a review from the Department of Mines, that the government submitted in lieu of the review by the EAC. Who decides which report is the most accurate? And should accuracy be measured in terms of irrigation and energy benefits or in terms of R&R and potential disaster? Where do environmental effects figure in the equation? Is it more important to preserve the environment or provide drinking water? How many 'experts' are needed and what if their opinions differ?

6. Finally, what is the role of popular protest in development and planning?

While protestors have successfully catalyzed further reviews, and probably account for delays in construction, they have not actually halted the project. Does this imply that their efforts have been futile? Has there been any sort of beneficial community empowerment as a result? If so, is that valuable in and of itself, despite the failure to halt the project?

F. THE NARMADA VALLEY PROJECT

The Narmada River springs from a holy pool amidst Hindu temples on the Amarkantak plateau in the forested Shahdol district of Madhya Pradesh, and then winds westward along a 1,300 kilometre course to drain into the Arabian sea. The Narmada is one of India's most sacred rivers. A verse in the ancient Matsya Purana commands those who wish to wash away their sins to bathe three times in the Saraswati river, seven times in the Yamuna or once in the Ganga, but if it is the Narmada that one visits—the mere sight of the river is cleansing enough.

The Narmada basin drains an area of 98,796 square kilometers and is home to 21 million people, nearly 80 per cent of whom live in villages. About a quarter of the basin is covered in moist and dry deciduous forests and about 60 per cent of it has black soils composed of silty clay with low permeability.

Although the Narmada Valley Project was conceived in 1946, final planning and work on it commenced only after the Narmada Water Disputes Tribunal passed its final orders in 1978. This tribunal was established in 1969 under India's Interstate Water Disputes Act of 1956 to resolve the dispute on river water sharing among the riparian states of Madhya Pradesh, Gujarat and Maharashtra. The tribunal also laid down conditions regarding resettlement and rehabilitation of the people to be displaced by the submergence—the 'oustees.'

The Narmada Valley Project, if and when completed, will rank as the largest irrigation project ever planned and implemented as a single unit anywhere in the world. By the year 2040, the project authorities hope to complete 31 major dams (11 on the Narmada and 20 on its tributaries), 135 medium dams and 3000 minor dams. Out of the 31 major dams, the ones most controversial are the Sardar Sarovar Project (SSP) in Gujarat and the Narmada (Indira) Sagar Project (NSP) in Madhya Pradesh. The NSP, which has the largest submergence zone and will create the biggest artificial reservoir in India, is years behind the SSP in construction. The SSP, however, is well under way and has become the rallying cry of international and Indian NGOs as a symbol of everything that is wrong with the way big dams are built, from international funding to environmental impacts to displacement and abuse of people.

The SSP is intended to bring drinking water to Kutch and other drought ridden regions of Gujarat. The dam will impound water in a 455 foot high reservoir that will submerge 37,000 hectares of land in the three states of Gujarat, Maharashtra and Madhya Pradesh. It will also divert 9.5 million acre feet (MAF) of water into a canal and irrigation system. The canal is the biggest in the world—450 kilometres long. The aggregate length of the distribution network will be 75,000 kilometres and will require 150,000 hectares of land, more than four times as the land submerged by the reservoir.

Because the Narmada Valley Project is such an enormous endeavour that has and will span such a significant length of time, it is impossible to cover every legal nuance of every step of the project, the protest and the plans. Narmada is plagued by many of the same problems discussed in the Tehri project section above, namely inadequate EIAs, funding setbacks and faulty construction. However, having examined these problems in the preceding section, we will not do so again in this one. This section is broken down into four subsections in which we highlight the major legal problems inherent in the Narmada Valley Project: International funding, resettlement and rehabilitation, human rights violations, and recent judicial developments.

I. INTERNATIONAL FUNDING

Although international aid for the Narmada Valley Project came from many sources, the most controversial was the World Bank assistance, which was to account for 15 per cent of the SSP.[25] In 1985 the Bank lent the three state governments of Gujarat, Maharashtra and Madhya Pradesh US $450 million to finance the SSP—both the dam and the canal. The three state governments then applied for an additional $350 million to complete the canal and $90 million for the related Narmada Basin Development Project. The financing initially represented two different things: international approval of the project itself and international satisfaction with the way in which the government of India went about planning for and executing the project. However, as events unfolded, Narmada came to symbolize instead the most embarrassing and citicized project in the World Bank's history. A centrepiece of the 'Fifty Years Is Enough' Campaign against the continued existence of the World Bank itself, the Narmada loan was the first in history to be terminated due to popular pressure, coupled with an independent Bank-ordered review of the project, known as the Morse Commission Report. It also provided the impetus for the traditionally secretive Bank to open its procedures to the public, reconsider and rewrite its guidelines on funding, improve upon its resettlement and rehabilitation policy and practice, and re-examine its currently funded projects.

We excerpt below a summary of the Narmada project, the World Bank's involvement and the effectiveness of NGO activism from *Silenced Rivers* by Patrick McCully of the US-based International Rivers Network.

[25] Omat Sattar, *Fair Deal Denied to People Displaced By Dam: Investigation of Maltreatment of People Displaced By the Sardar Sarovar Dam Projects*, New Scientist, 3 August 1991.

McCULLY; SILENCED RIVERS: THE ECOLOGY AND POLITICS OF LARGE DAMS, 301–306 (1996)

Medha Patkar was a 30-year-old social activist and researcher when she first came to the Narmada Valley in 1985 to work in the villages to be submerged by the Sardar Sarovar Dam. Over the next few years, Patkar travelled by foot, bus and boat throughout the nearly 200-kilometre-long submergence zone, which includes parts of three states and people speaking five different languages. Patkar lived with the villagers to be displaced, listened to their fears for the future, and urged them to organize to force the government to respect their rights.

Patkar spent most of her time among the adivasis in the remote and rugged Satpura hills of Maharashtra state. Her oratorical and organizing skills helped build the trust of many local people and also attracted a committed coterie of young outside activists to come to the valley. These activists, who included engineers, social workers and journalists, were to play a vital role in the Narmada movement. Early in 1986, Patkar and other activists and the Maharashtra villagers set up the Narmada Dharangrast Samiti (Committee for Narmada Dam-Affected People). The NDS villagers refused to be moved out or to cooperate with dam officials in any way until their demands for fair compensation and information about the impacts of the project were met.

The NDS also began to investigate the official claims of the benefits the project would provide. Among their findings were that crucial environmental studies had not been conducted, that the number of people to be displaced was not known, that estimates of the amount of land to get irrigation water were wildly optimistic, and that while the supply of drinking water to some 40 million people was supposed to be one of the project's main benefits, the massive sums needed to build the pipes and pumps to deliver this water had been left out of the estimated project costs. These findings led the NDS and two other oustees' groups they had helped to set up in Gujarat (the state where the dam is located) and Madhya Pradesh (the state where most of the reservoir would lie) to conclude that the claims of project benefits were fraudulent and just resettlement impossible. At six rallies held simultaneously in the three affected states on 18 August 1988 the NDS and their allies announced their total—but strictly non-violent—opposition to the dam.

National press coverage and awareness of the anti-Sardar Sarovar campaign burgeoned in the late 1980s and support for the Narmada activists mounted among environmental, human rights, religious, landless and *adivasi* organizations around the country. Within the valley, the activists built alliances across class and caste boundaries between *adivasi* and 'caste Hindu' areas, and between the reservoir oustees and people affected by the project in other ways—in particular, families losing land to the massive canal network. In 1989, this growing network of local and international groups was formally named the Save the Narmada Movement, or Narmada Bachao Andolan (NBA).

The International Front

Interest in the growing Narmada controversy within the international environmental community was boosted by two trips Medha Patkar made to Washington in 1987 and 1989. Lori Udall from the Environmental Defense Fund (EDF) in Washington was inspired by Patkar to take the lead role in raising the NBA's concerns with the World Bank. Udall also helped build a network of committed and informed activists in North America, Europe, Japan and Australia who become known as the Narmada Action Committee.

Medha Patkar met with some World Bank executive directors during her 1989 visit. 'When I hear what NGOs say about this project and then what the operations staff say,' one director remarked afterwards, 'it sounds like they are talking about two different projects.' Patkar also gave testimony at a congressional subcommittee hearing into the World Bank's performance on Sardar Sarovar. Congressional staff, journalists and environmentalists broke into spontaneous applause after her impassioned, hour-long presentation. A number of Congressmen later wrote to Bank President Barber Conable urging that the project be suspended.

The next foreign success for the NBA was a symposium in Tokyo in April, 1990. Influencing opinion in Japan was vital for the Narmada campaign as the Japanese government was lending some $200 million for the turbines for Sardar Sarovar. NBA and international activists joined Japanese NGOs, academics and politicians at the Tokyo symposium, which received considerable national press coverage. The activists later met with Japanese government officials. Within a month of the symposium, the Japanese withdrew all further funding for the dam. This was the first time that a Japanese aid loan had been withdrawn for environmental and human rights reasons.

The Long Road to the Indian Review

Back in India, the NBA had changed its straightforward 'no dam' position in March 1990, and, seeking a way of breaking the stalemate between pro-and anti-dam forces proposed the project be suspended pending a comprehensive and open review. In an attempt to pressure the government into holding the review, the NBA organized the most spectacular action of its long campaign. On Christmas Day 1990, 5,000 oustees and NBA supporters, including the widely respected veteran social activists Baba Amte, set off for the dam site from the town of Rajghat in Madhya Pradesh on a Struggle March Towards People's Development—to become known as the 'Long March'. Eight days later the marchers reached the village of Ferkuwa on the border with Gujarat and found their way blocked by the police and a counter-demonstration organised by the Gujarat government. An angry month-long stand-off ensued.

At first the NBA attempted to break through by sending forward groups of volunteers, their hands tied in front of them to symbolize their commitment to non-violence. The police repeatedly forced back the volunteers. Some were beaten and around 140 detained. Patkar and six others then began a fast by the side of the road. The days passed but the government remained unresponsive. Then, on 29 January, the twenty-first day of the fast, news came from Washington DC that the World Bank would commission a review of the project. The following day, the press coverage throughout India, greatly increased country-wide support for the NBA, and made Medha Patkar a national celebrity.

By 1991, full-scale construction on the dam had been under way for four years. Submergence was clearly possible during the upcoming monsoon, which hits the Narmada Valley between June and September every year. At a ceremony in Manibeli, the Maharashtra village closest to the dam, a group of oustees and activists vowed to be the first to face the waters rising behind the part-built dam. An NBA compound was set up at one of the lowest parts of Manibeli with a house where the *Samarpit Dal*, or 'Save or Drown Squad', would sit and wait to be engulfed by the new reservoir. In response, the government banned Patkar and other activists from the villages during the monsoon, and prohibited the villagers from holding anti-dam protests.

The NBA defied the bans, and hundreds of their supporters were arrested during the monsoon months. Members of the *Samarpit Dal* went into hiding to avoid detention and so be able to carry out their vow. A weak monsoon, however, meant that the water stayed several metres below Manibeli in 1991.

The following year the Narmada rose during one monsoon storm to within a metre of the lowest house behind the dam, Patkar was among 11 people in the house at the time. Also in 1992, police shot dead an *adivasi* woman while evicting her community from forest land which was to be given to resettled oustees.

The fiercely critical report of the World Bank-funded Independent Review team, headed by Bradford Morse, was released in June 1992, after nine months of research and writing. The NBA and its international supporters were delighted that the Review vindicated so many of their claims and they used it to step up pressure on the World Bank. Environmentalists wrote an open letter to World Bank President Lewis Preston which they published as a full-page advertisement in the London *Financial Times*. It warned that if the Bank refused to withdraw funding for Sardar Sarovar then NGOs would launch a campaign to cut government funding of the Bank. The letter was endorsed by 250 NGOs and coalitions from 37 countries. Full-page advertisements placed in the *Washington Post* and *New York Times* by US environmental groups made similar demands.

After the Bank

The Bank finally announced its withdrawal in March 1993. The Indian authorities initial reaction was to step up the use of violence and intimidation. In November, police shot dead an *adivasi* boy. Street demonstrations against the killing were met with *lathi* charges and yet more arrests.

Without World Bank funds, work on the canal system soon all but ground to a halt. Available financial resources were poured into raising the dam wall—most visible symbol of the project and the most intimidating to the people refusing resettlement. Large-scale submergence began during the 1993 monsoon with the dam wall 44 metres high. The lands of hundreds of villagers were inundated and the homes and possession of 40 families washed away. Police arrested the occupants of the lowest houses and dragged them to higher ground to prevent them carrying out their pledge to drown. Similar scenes were repeated during the 1994 and 1995 monsoons. In 1995 some villagers braved water which rose to chest height before receding.

With the World Bank out of the way, the NBA stepped up pressure on the Indian government to commission a comprehensive review, one which would look at all aspects of Sardar Sarovar—the terms of reference for the Morse Commission had covered only resettlement and the environment. In June 1993, Medha Patkar and Devram Kanera, a farmer from Madhya Pradesh, began a fast in downtown Bombay. After 14 days the government agreed to start the review process—but once the fast was called off it reneged on its promise.

Ever more frustrated with the government's duplicity, the continuing arrests and beatings of activists, and the submergence of homes in the valley, the NBA decided once again to use the strongest weapon at its disposal—the lives of its own members. In July 1993, the NBA announced that unless the review process began by 6 August, seven activists would throw themselves into the monsoon-swollen Narmada. Less than 24 hours before the deadline, the central government announced that it would establish a five-member group of experts nominated by both the NBA and dam supporters to 'look into all aspects of SSP'. The group met within hours of the announcement and called on the NBA to halt their action, while assuring them that they were committed to an unbiased and comprehensive review of SSP. The *jal samarpan*—'self-sacrifice by drowning'—was called off.

The review committee heard submissions from the NBA, affected people, central government ministries and the relevant state governments—except that of Gujarat, which boycotted the review. Scientists and engineers presented detailed suggestions for alternative methods of supplying water and power. The release of the report, however, was delayed indefinitely by legal action from the Gujarat government.

In May 1994, the NBA opened another front in its campaign by filing a comprehensive case against the project with the New Delhi Supreme Court. The case moved forward at a painfully slow pace with numerous postponements, delays and cancellations.

New hope for the campaign came in late 1994 when the Madhya Pradesh government announced that it had neither the land nor resources to resettle the state's huge numbers of oustees and that it wanted the planned dam height to be reduced. In an effort to pressure the upstream government to force Gujarat to halt the dam, the NBA decided the muster its resources for yet another round of fasts, this time to be held in Bhopal, the Madhya Pradesh capital. On 21 November 1994, Patkar and three men from the valley stopped eating. Twenty-six days later, the Madhya Pradesh government agreed to demand a halt to construction pending progress on resettlement. The NBA called off the fasts.

Three days before the end of the Bhopal fasts the Supreme Court ordered the government-commissioned review to be made public. The report questioned the basic data used to design the project and criticized the resettlement effort. The court asked the review team to investigate further the viability of the project.

The NBA received a significant boost in January 1995 when the central government in New Delhi forced Gujarat to suspend raising the dam wall with its lowest point 63 metres above the riverbed, just under half the planned final height. The suspension order came because the project was violating a court ruling that oustees must be resettled six months before their land is submerged.

As of August 1996, the result of the in-depth study of project feasibility ordered by the Supreme Court had still not been made public and no final decision had yet been reached by the Supreme Court on the future of the project. Construction on the dam wall remained stalled.

Whatever the final outcome, the long struggle of the people of the valley and their supporters within India and around the world has left deep scars on the World

Bank and the Indian and International dam industry. It is unlikely that the Bank will ever fund another river development project on such a scale in a democratic country. It is also unlikely for the forseeable future that the Indian dam lobby will succeed in pushing through any projects involving such large-scale displacement. 'We are not going in for large dams any more,' Indian power minister N.K.P. Salve told *International Water Power & Dam Construction* in late 1993. 'We want run of the river projects and to have smaller dams, if they are necessary at all, which will not cause any impediment whatsoever to the environmental needs.'

The NBA sees its role as much more than challenging a single dam or even dam building in general. Patkar and other NBA leaders have travelled throughout India supporting other struggles against destructive state and corporate development projects which strip the poor of their right to livelihood. Together with other leading environmental, women's lower-caste and Gandhian groups, the NBA has helped establish a National Alliance of People's Movements (NAPM). In March 1996, representatives from around 100 groups in 17 states drew up a 'People's Resolve', a common ideological platform for the NAPM around which it is hoped India's many thousands of diverse people's organizations can unite in a 'strong social, political force.'

II. RESETTLEMENT AND REHABILITATION

Of all the issues that have received attention during the development of the Narmada Valley Project and the international and domestic protests against it, none has generated as much controversy and litigation as the issue of resettlement and rehabilitation of Project Affected People (PAPs). The most widely known group of protesters, Save the Narmada Movement, known by its Indian acronym NBA, has built its widespread support and the primary focus of its protests around the displacement issue. This was also the issue most fully addressed and most roundly condemned by the World Bank independent review team and the international community.

Of particular significance is the fact that most oustees, particularly as a result of the SSP, are indigenous, or tribals. In other words, they are outside the Hindu caste system. And while many of them have been cultivating their land for generations, they lack formal title to it. In other areas, land that was traditionally theirs has been designated as state-owned forest reserves, cultivation of which is illegal. Consequently, many oustees will get no compensation for their land.[26] They will also lose access to common property resources, including agricultural and grazing land, water, forests and fish.

Beginning with the Narmada Valley Water Disputes Tribunal's order, through various private and public interest lawsuits by individuals and NGOs, up to and including the pending 1994 case filed before the Indian Supreme Court by NBA, the issue of resettlement and rehabilitation has generated vast amounts of litigation. An excerpt from the following 1994 *petition* under Article 32 of the Constitution,

[26] *Sacrifice at the Temple of India: Narmada*, International Dams Newsletter, Vol.1, No.1, Winter 1985–86.

highlights the intricacy of the issues and the desperate straits of the people of the Narmada Valley.

NARMADA BACHAO ANDOLAN V UNION OF INDIA

The humble Petition of the Petitioner abovenamed.
Most respectfully showeth:

1. That this writ petition is being filed in public interest for protecting the rights of life and livelihood of the persons directly affected by one of the biggest inter-state multi-purpose Project ever undertaken, with the largest irrigation network in any project in the world, known as the Sardar Sarovar Project (SSP) on the river Narmada. The impact of the project extends to an immense area and affects a very large number of people, especially tribals. At least 1,50,000 people, in 245 villages, live in the area affected by submergence. In Gujarat and Maharashtra almost all are tribals. In addition, the projects will displace lakhs of others from their lands and livelihood. ...

* * *

3. The grievance of the Petitioner in this Petition is that a large number of persons, mostly tribals and other marginalized sections of society are being forcibly displaced and uprooted from their homes and lands on account of this Project without giving them any opportunity to be heard and without properly compensating or resettling them and without even properly explaining to them the nature of the project for which they are being displaced. Moreover, Respondents are going ahead with the construction of the Project without even having completed the studies regarding the various effects and impacts of the project on the affected people or on the environment and are in the process of violating a large number of stipulations of the Narmada Waters Dispute Tribunal (NWDT) and conditions on the basis of which the Project had been conditionally cleared by the Ministry of Environment and Forests and the Planning Commission and the directives, principles, policies, accepted through the World Bank documents and even otherwise. ... The actions of the Respondents complained of in this Writ Petition are, therefore, violative of the Petitioner's fundamental rights under Articles 14 and 21 of the Constitution of India: [After reviewing the issue in 50 separate points, the petition states:]

54. The sum total of all this, therefore, is that

(a) There is [no] accurate estimate available of the number of oustees from the reservoir of the Sardar Sarovar Dam as proposed, as even basic surveys are not completed in Maharashtra & Madhya Pradesh and ... backwater effects are not computed in Madhya Pradesh.

(b) The land acquisition proceedings for acquiring land which would be submerged from the reservoir which will be filled up as per the present construction schedule within the next three years have not yet been completed in a number of villages. Even where this is said to be completed, the process has been wholly inadequate in as much as villagers have not received notices and have not been given any opportunity of objecting to the purposes of acquisition, or to the assumptions & viability of the project.

(c) No master plan exists about the places where the oustees would be resettled.

(d) Final estimates of costs of R&R not made and inter-state disputes exist about sharing the costs of rehabilitation.

(e) No land has been acquired for resettling the oustees of Madhya Pradesh as is evident from the 8th report submitted by the Union Ministry of Welfare to the Supreme Court even though several thousands of them would have to be resettled in Madhya Pradesh and some of the villages of Madhya Pradesh would come under submergence during monsoon this year itself. On 25 February 1994, the Chief Minister of Madhya Pradesh Shri Digvijay Singh confessed that two villages of the state will be totally submerged and 13 villages partially affected following the closure of the sluice gates in upper region of the dam constructed under the Sardar Sarovar Project. ... Comparing this with the 8th report submitted to the Supreme Court, one is surprised to find no mention or details about these fifteen villages or the status of rehabilitation of the people therein. Such confusion and contradictions abound all over the different documents. ...

(g) The only land made available for resettling the oustees in Maharshtra has been reserved forest land which has been de-reserved against the conditions of environmental and forest clearance for the Project.

(h) In Maharashtra, the govt. has refused to acquire any lands in Akrani Tehsil, claiming it to be govt. land, whereas the people have documents to prove & establish their rights over the lands. In village Surung (Akrani Tehsil, Dhule Dist, Maharashtra), the revenue lands which are not yet acquired are in the submergence zone of the coming monsoon.

(i) Even in Gujarat, till today only less than 14,000 hectares of land has been acquired which is enough for resettling maximum of 7000 oustees out of the more than 20,000 families that are to be rehabilitated in Gujarat as per the official estimates today. In fact, the then Director, Resettlement of Madhya Pradesh, Shri K.P. Singh had, after narrating the experiences of the govt. of Madhya Pradesh, written on 15 June 1993 to the Chief Secretary of Madhya Pradesh that even though Gujarat has been making tall claims about the availability of land for resettling the oustees, 'it is evidently clear from the above that Gujarat is not believable when it says that there is plenty of land available. ... at this stage, we can only ask Gujarat to stop further construction of the dam. ...'

(j) Now even the Chief Minister of Madhya Pradesh, the state having maximum number of reservoir oustees, has, seeing the impossibility of rehabilitation, asked for a reduction of height of the dam to reduce the number of people affected by the project [in a 4 March 1994 letter to the Prime Minister.]

(k) Out of about 7000 odd oustee families claimed to have been resettled by the authorities, till today many have not been satisfactorily resettled. They have been facing very serious problems at the resettlement sites which have forced many of them to return to their original homes and lands while many others too would like to do the same, but dare not. Some of the problems faced by these oustees in the resettlement sites are:

i) They could not get physical possession of the land which was allotted to them and the previous land owners still asserted their rights over the lands.

ii) The quality of the water was so poor that it was not drinkable.

iii) The land allotted to them was not cultivatable and was getting flooded during the monsoon.

iv) The land given to some of them was less than the two hectares that were promised.

v) Some of the other problems faced by the oustees at the resettlement sites include: lack of grazing lands, lack of source of firewood, lack of cremation facilities, problems of theft and robbery, and the problem caused by the host community.

vi) Even members of the joint families were given lands at different places and in different villages, thereby breaking up family units.

* * *

56. In conclusion we would like to say that in spite of all the good principles and policies on the paper, the experience till date of the implementation of the project and the policies clearly and unequivocally suggest that the policies are inadequate to put the principles in practice and that even the accepted policies are not followed. This has led to great suffering of the most deprived sections of the population in the name of development. In the process, the Tribunal stipulations, the World Bank agreements, the High Court and Supreme Court orders, and basic constitutional and human rights of the people are totally, abjectly and repeatedly violated. The tribals have lost their lands, their forests, their homes, their cultures and even their lives. All this is being tolerated in the name of pushing ahead with the dam and due to the political compulsions. No civil society can accept this. The work on the dam must be stopped if these violations are not to be tolerated.

* * *

NOTES AND QUESTIONS

1. The 'right to adequate housing' is one of the rights included in Article 11 of the U.N. Covenant on Economic, Social and Cultural Rights (CESCR), to which India is a State Party. In General Comment No.4 on the Right to Adequate Housing, adopted on 12 December 1991, the U.N. Committee on Economic, Social and Cultural Rights stated that, 'Instances of forced evictions are *prima facie* incompatible with the requirements of the Covenant and can only be justified in the most exceptional circumstances, and in accordance with the relevant principles of international law.' In further consideration of the right, the U.N. Commission on

Human Rights has declared the practice of forced evictions to be a 'gross violation of human rights, in particular, the right to adequate housing.'[27]

Is it possible that India's need to develop constitutes a 'most exceptional circumstance' that can justify the forced evictions of the villagers of the Narmada Valley? If not, should the U.N. intervene with a fact finding review of its own, to supplement the other international reviews, discussed above and below? Is India violating the CESCR? If India is found in violation, what difference would that make? Would it stop the project? Would it vindicate the villagers and the NBA? Should Covenants contain enforcement mechanisms to ensure that ratification is not just an empty promise? Would India have signed the CESCR if it did contain some sort of enforcement mechanism? What does it mean to be in violation of international human rights instruments? Would publicity against the project increase if the U.N. were to declare India a violator?

2. Another critical issue in terms of the Narmada Valley PAPs is their status as primarily indigenous people. While forced evictions of all people constitute a human rights violation, indigenous people, due to their traditionally exploited and marginalized status, have an especially protected status under international human rights laws. Perhaps the most respected and long-standing declaration of the rights of indigenous people is the 1957 International Labour Organization Convention Concerning the Protection and Integration of Indigenous and other Tribal and Semi-Tribal Populations in Independent Countries—ILO No. 107. India ratified ILO No. 107 in 1958. It provides in relevant part:

PART II, LAND
Article 11

The right of ownership, collective or individual, of the members of the populations concerned over the lands which these populations traditionally occupy shall be recognized.

Article 12

1. The populations concerned shall not be removed without their free consent from their habitual territories except in accordance with national laws and regulations for reasons relating to national security, or in the interest of national economic development or of the health of said populations.

2. When in such cases removal of these populations is necessary as an exceptional measure, they shall be provided with lands of quality at least equal to that of the lands previously occupied by them, suitable to provide

---

[27] *U.N. Commission on Human Rights Resolution on Forced Evictions,* U.N. Doc. No. 1993/77, adopted unanimously on 10 March 1993 during the 49th Session; *U.N. Sub-Commission on Human Rights Resolution on Forced Evictions,* U.N. Doc. No. 1991/12, adopted unanimously on 28 August 1991 during the 43rd Session.

for their present need and future development. In cases where chances of alternative employment exist and where the populations concerned prefer to have compensation in money or in kind, they shall be so compensated under appropriate guarantees.

3. Persons thus removed shall be fully compensated for any resulting loss or injury.

While the idea of compensating in equal terms sounds 'right', consider the practical realities involved. One of the largest problems facing the states concerned, especially Gujarat which bears the burden for the majority of the resettlement and rehabilitation (R&R) under the tribunal ruling, is that there simply is not enough land in the state of equal or greater value with which to compensate the PAPs. When forest reserves are taken out of reserve status to be given to the PAPs, as was done in Maharashtra, it may result in further displacement of tribals who have traditionally occupied these lands. In addition, 'de-reserving' forests is not an environmentally sound approach.

What then does this all imply? Who has a right to land? Displaced people or current inhabitants?

Should the PAPs take precedence over the forest dwellers? Is legal title determinative? According to ILO # 107 it is not, but *should* it be? If there is not enough land to properly compensate all PAPs under ILO # 107 in the event of any major development project, should countries such as India then be forced to cease developing?

An additional burden upon the state governments is the cost of monetary compensation for oustees. In March of 1992, the Supreme Court held that the loss of income from productive lands be included in compensation for oustees in a case against the Rihand thermal power station.[28] In a developing country, where resources are scarce, where is this money to come from? Is it fair to impose these standards on India now, when traditionally the already developed nations such as the United States not only displaced their native people, but often decimated them as well? If the United States had been held to these standards, would it have become as rich and industrialized and powerful as it is now? Is not this then a form of imperialistic standard setting that will prevent less developed nations from gaining a place in the world market equal to that of the industrialized countries? Or, if the global community is especially sensitive to the needs and value of indigenous people, should India and other developing countries be obligated to accept these special standards if they are to join the ranks of the developed nations?

3. In an article entitled *Displacement—Double Burden for Women*,[29] the author, Tanushree Gangopadhyay, pointed out that no land or home allotments are made to women under the R&R policies of the state governments. She also indicated that

[28] *Banwasi Seva Ashram v State of UP* AIR 1992 SC 920.
[29] INDIAN EXPRESS, Baroda, 4 April 1995.

among the human rights violations associated with the evictions and displacements, only women are subject to sexual abuse and abuses causing foetal endangerment. Finally, the article shows how domestic violence towards women increases under the stresses of dislocation through R&R. Why are men allowed compensation and not women? Is it continuation of a social structure designed to relegate women to a subservient role that should not be tolerated? Is it a violation of Article 14 of the Constitution of India guaranteeing equal protection?

III. HUMAN RIGHTS VIOLATIONS

Beyond the specific violations of human rights involved in mass displacements, evictions and the Narmada Valley Project's inadequate rehabilitation measures, there have been during the course of the project various and frequent human rights violations, primarily against protesters and NBA leaders. These violations have run the gauntlet from unexplained police detentions and abuse while in custody to beatings of non-compliant oustees and protesters by police and, in a few tragic cases, police shootings on crowds that resulted in injuries and death. It appears that the government of India has sometimes sought to deal with protesters through oppression and violence.

The repetitive nature of these violations had drawn the attention of the international human rights community, which has formed the Narmada International Human Rights Panel and now holds International Narmada Symposiums, to present the reports of fact finding missions by NGOs to chronicle abuses in India associated solely with the Narmada Valley Project. An excerpt from the third symposium follows:

UDALL & KLEINER; HUMAN RIGHTS VIOLATIONS ASSOCIATED WITH THE WORLD BANK FINANCED SAROVAR DAM PROJECT IN WESTERN INDIA, Third International Narmada Symposium, Tokyo, 29 April 1992

Since 1987, Narmada valley oustees and their NGO representatives have been non-violently protesting their forcible displacement caused by the construction of the Sardar Sarovar dam. As their protests have escalated so have state actions to stop the protests. Indian NGOs have sought national and international attention to expose the World Bank and Indian state governments for violating and abusing the basic human rights of the people protesting their displacement by Sardar Sarovar.

The human rights abuses in the Narmada valley include unprovoked, excessive physical police abuse towards non-violent protesters; discriminatory arrests based on fabricated, trumped up charges; arbitrary invocation of prohibitory orders to check the movement of activists; failure to provide charges upon arrest and witness before a magistrate within the constitutionally mandated period; failure to provide food and medical care to detainees; theft of personal property by police and other state officials; and the failure of law enforcement to be representative of, responsible and accountable to the community as a whole.

These are serious infringements of the International Declaration of Human Rights, the United Nations Code of Conduct for Law Enforcement Officials (1979), and the International Covenant on Civil and Political Rights (1966). Events over the last month in the village of Manibeli ... run counter to the 28 August 1991 resolution on Forced Evictions adopted by the United Nations Human Rights Sub-Commission on Prevention of Discrimination and Protection of Minorities.

When considered cumulatively as detailed below, these abuses must be seen as part of a systematic, official effort to intimidate rural poor and tribal people and to repress the views, demands and actions of a non-violent movement having clear social, environmental, and economic concerns about a large scale development project. ...

A majority of the oustees in the states of Madhya Pradesh and Maharashtra have been protesting their forcible displacement since 1987. Many have declared their total opposition to the project and are involved in a Gandhian, non co-operation movement, refusing to move from their villages. Numerous non-violent protests have been staged with the support of the grassroots organizations Narmada Bachao Andolan, including sit-ins, bridge blocking, rallies, and marches. Over the past few years, there have been an increasing number of human rights violations associated with these protests. The state has increasingly used repressive police force to stop these protests, silence the activists and intimidate the Narmada valley 'oustees'. This has generated an atrocious array of human rights violations.

As the oustees are outnumbered in their own villages by hordes of armed police, as the movements of dam opponents are blocked by police, and as inspirational activists are publicly beaten and carted off by police, some Narmada Valley oustees have been intimidated into accepting their own powerlessness and have accepted alternative land, resigning themselves to being displaced. However, a majority of oustees continue their opposition to Sardar Sarovar in the face of this repression. The tension has now reached new heights, as partial submergence of some villages due to the partially constructed dam is inevitable this monsoon. Currently there are daily collisions between resolute, but peaceful, villagers and armed police. The situation seems intractable and any acceptable resolution will depend on the government initiating an open and fair dialogue with the oustees and their supporters.

[The report goes on to list 72 specific instances of human rights violations over the period from 1988 through 16 April 1992 including invocation of the Official Secrets Act of 1923 in 1988, beating and intimidating protesters, including pregnant women, forcing villagers from their homes, abusing their family members and destroying their identification papers.]

NOTES AND QUESTIONS

1. The United States Department of State has twice listed the Narmada human rights abuses in its 1993 and 1994 annual *Human Rights Report*. Is simply monitoring human rights abuses going to change anything without more active intervention?

2. If India is to develop, some people will inevitably be displaced, others will

protest and conflicts will arise. In addition, it is virtually impossible to develop without environmental impact. However, without development, India will continue to suffer from the problems of all developing countries—including poverty, sickness, unemployment and a burgeoning population. Is it ever possible to reconcile the rights to development, a healthy environment, and the basic human rights of those displaced? Alternatively, one might argue that a decentralized, democratic, natural resource-based development involving self-reliant individuals and communities would be the right development path.

IV. RECENT SUPREME COURT ORDERS AND DEVELOPMENTS

The Narmada Water Disputes Tribunal (NWDT) established specific conditions regarding the resettlement and rehabilitation of the people that would be displaced by the creation of the Sardar Sarovar dam. The language of the tribunal award clearly states that all 'Project Affected Families' would be re-established as communities with access to water, education, and health (Clause IV(1)) on a 'land-for-land basis'. Clause IV(6) states that 'in no event shall any areas in Madhya Pradesh and Maharashtra be submerged under the Sardar Sarovar Project unless all payments of compensation and costs is made for acquisition of land and arrangements are made for rehabilitation.' This clause has served as the centerpiece for litigation by the Narmada Bachao Andolan (NBA).

The NBA focused its writ petition in the Supreme Court[30] on the rehabilitation of the affected people. It presented a comprehensive review of the project and requested that no further submergence or displacement take place. On 5 June 1995 the Supreme Court granted a stay, citing the questionable rehabilitation process. Construction was suspended at a height of 81.5 meters.

After four years of investigations and mounds of further litigation, the Supreme Court surprised many by issuing an interim order on 18 February 1999 which permitted the resumption of construction on the dam up to a height of 85 metres. One of the major reasons the court allowed work to resume was based on an affidavit provided by the states of Maharashtra and Gujarat that all oustees had been fully rehabilitated and indicating that arrangements had been made for those to be displaced by the increase of 3.5 metres in dam height. Overall, the court disregarded a great deal of the information prepared by the NBA. Instead, it used the government data as the basis for the deliberations. Although the court did allow work to continue, it also recognized a three member 'Grievance Redressal Authority', an independent committee appointed by Gujarat, which was to investigate two issues: (a) whether the rehabilitation of the resettled oustees had been completed in a satisfactory manner, in accordance with the NWDT award and other government policies; and (b) whether the preparations to resettle individuals who would be displaced if the height were to be raised to 90 meters were adequate. This committee was to report on the state of the displaced in

---

[30] *Narmada Bachao Andolan v Union of India* Writ Petition (Civil) No. 319 of 1994.

mid-April when the court would entertain the motion of raising the height of the dam to 90 metres.

The Sardar Sarovar Narmada Nigam Ltd. the corporation responsible for construction of the SSP, has stated that the dam will only be able to serve any purpose in terms of irrigation water or electricity once it reaches at least a height of 110 meters. Therefore even at a height of 90 meters the dam will not be functional.

Although the court did state in its decision that all those displaced by the increase to 85 meters needed to be adequately rehabilitated, what type of signal does the decision give to those displaced who now face the sudden and immediate threat of submergence? Do you believe individuals might end up accepting less advantageous rehabilitation packages than they might have otherwise? Why?

In this interim decision the court restricted itself to considering only issues of 'relief and rehabilitation.' Interestingly, the NBA argued strongly that the entire project ought to remain suspended until a full re-examination has been conducted. The NBA brought up environmental issues, cost-benefit issues, and constitutional and equity issues surrounding the displacement process itself. Is this narrowing of the issues problematic? Why? Do you believe the court erred in accepting the notion of displacement of individuals as long as they are rehabilitated? Can a community ever be 'rehabilitated'?

Not surprisingly, the court's 18 February 1999 decision to allow construction to resume touched off a flurry of activity within dam opposition groups. A series of marches, protests, and claims of government fraud ensued. Many opposition groups, with the NBA leading the cause, challenged the assertions that government officials made in court concerning land availability and the status of those currently displaced by the SSP. Citizen groups began their campaign against the pro-SSP ruling by testifying in front of the Grievance Redressal Committee. After conducting a detailed analysis of the resettlement process, people in the affected areas of the Narmada River Valley project concluded that the rehabilitation process that has occurred up to this point in regard to the SSP has been a violation of the most basic requirements laid out in the NWDT award. According to the NBA even the very first villagers displaced by the project 15–20 years ago have not been adequately resettled. Resettlement sites were plagued with problems including uncultivable lands limited drinking water, insufficient fuel supplies, limited grazing lands, and the total lack of other basic necessities. Furthermore, entire villages and family units had been completely disintegrated, constituting a direct violation of the NWDT award. Citizens also found that lands in at least 19 different sites claimed by government authorities to be set aside for those who would be displaced when the dam reached 90 meters were not available.

None of this is really surprising to groups such as the NBA, that have been conducting comprehensive research on displaced peoples for several years. Their January—February 1999 survey of the Madhya Pradesh oustees shows that out of 2,761 oustee families, 37 per cent are without land possession or title, 26 per cent have inadequate or bad land, and 26 per cent have fragmented of insufficient land.

Meanwhile Maharashata's own affidavit of September 1998 admitted that out of an allocated 4,200 hectares of land for rehabilitation, 836 were not suitable for cultivation and other sections of land were actually covered with forest.

In order to fully expose the incorrect government claims, the NBA and a host of other concerned groups representing oustees, women, dalits, tribals, farmers and other downtrodden people, organized marches and sit-ins throughout India, aimed particularly at dam sites and government buildings. Their purpose was to force the government to admit its untruths concerning the availability of land for the displaced. Several such protests were carried out between March and September, 1999. However, the most significant of these rallies, entitled the 'Manav Adhikar Yatra', or the Human Rights March, occurred in early April, 1999. This extensive march covered hundreds of kilometers and included thousands of participants. The march started in Badwani, Madhya Pradesh and wove through several dam-affected communities in the Narmada Valley, as well as numerous cities and towns before reaching New Delhi early April 8th.

It appears that campaigns conducted by citizen groups are having some positive outcomes. In March, 1999 the government of Maharashtra admitted that there was not land to sufficiently rehabilitate the families who would be submerged by the court sanctioned five meter rise in dam height. Remember that Maharashtra authorities had made earlier claims in the Supreme Court that there was land available for project affected families. Authorities have admitted that the number of displaced families they had cited in the affidavit submitted to the court was based on numbers of a survey conducted in 1983–1984. This figure represented only one tenth of the actual number of displacees. Earlier in March, authorities also admitted that land at four different sites which was claimed to be set aside for rehabilitation purposes had actually been claimed by local cultivators. Other tracts of land that the government of Maharashtra had requested for resettlement had not been approved. In other cases, government officials charged by the people to produce the actual lands where rehabilitation had occurred, simply claimed helplessness. If such admissions are being made by top level government officials, especially considering it was primarily the government affidavit figures that the court used to make its 18 February 1999 decision, how can the Supreme Court possibly permit the dam building process to continue? Can the Supreme Court as a legal institution retain any sense of legitimacy in the face of evidence of fraud if it does not order a re-examination of key issues cited by the NBA? If the court refuses to side with such challenges to the SSP project, what other channels are open to citizen groups? If fraud by the government is proved, can the Supreme Court undo what its order to increase the height has done to those affected?

Much of the recent controversy and litigation that has taken place is in response to the consideration of the court to allow building up to a height of 90 metres. However, recall the dam proponents admit that benefits will not accrue until the height of 110 metres (the final height planned is 138 metres). If completed as planned, opponents say that 320,000 people will be displaced by the SSP. Should the court be viewing the project in a more comprehensive manner considering the difficulties the government is having locating land for displacees at these lower dam levels? The issue of rehabilitation has been before the court for more than five years. Is there any likelihood that it will simply go away without a clear direction by the court to develop a comprehensive plan for the displaced, requiring hard proof of land availability? Interestingly, in April, 1999, the Supreme Court refused the Gujarat application to raise the dam height to 90 metres. It did, however, allow for the construction of three metre 'safety humps' which, in effect, raises the allowed dam height to 88 metres.

It is clear from all the facts given that this issue is incredibly complex, encompassing a variety of problematic issues. From an economic standpoint, India has invested a large sum of money in the Narmada Valley Project and is not prepared to see it fall apart completely. The Supreme Court has basically been charged with weighing the importance of economic gains versus issues of social equity. Large dams typically benefit urban populations located far from the actual projects themselves while poorer communities, often made up of tribal communities, bear the brunt of the costs. It appears that the Supreme Court has to decide between the rights of its citizens and the future path of India's major development projects.

Perhaps the only definitive thing that can be said about the SSP is that it will continue to stimulate debate. It is equally clear that the court has an opportunity to dictate how the planning, implementation, and administration of such massive projects are conducted in the future. It also has the chance to reaffirm India's commitment to social equity and environmental clearances for large projects. If one thing can be learned from the Narmada Valley Project as a whole, it is that such massive projects should not be started in haste. A comprehensive plan for all stages of the building process ought to be required before the first stone is laid. Committees ought to be established from the outset that are responsible for hearing grievances—social, political, and economic. Public input is a must. Furthermore, these committees ought to be delegated the ability to enforce their decisions. Most importantly, plans must be concise and schematic in nature. If these various requirements are impossible to fulfill, perhaps the government should reconsider the proposed undertakings.

The Narmada planning process seems to have been replete with false claims of benefits, even aside from the deeply flawed scheme for resettlement and rehabilitation. The governments involved continued to spend public money without environmental clearances, and presumably will do the same with future projects unless harsh penalties are imposed on them. Meanwhile, in the United States and France, large dams are being decommissioned as their high maintenance costs and damage to fisheries have become intolerable. Mega-dams may be a symbol of development in India, but they are beginning to seem an obsolete technology elsewhere in the world.[31]

---

[31] At the time of writing, the Supreme Court has not delivered judgement on NBA's petition. The court order discharging contempt of court proceedings against Medha Patkar, Shripad Dharmadhikari and Arundhati Roy in respect of their criticism of the order allowing the height of the dam to be raised to 85 m is reported at *Narmada Bachao Andolan v Union of India* AIR 1999 SC 3345.

G. THERMAL POWER PROJECTS

North of Bombay, on the west coast of India lies Dahanu, an ecologically sensitive region with a thriving agrarian economy. Dahanu is best known for its chikoo fruit. Its orchards also grow vast quantities of guava and coconut. It supplies fodder, rice, milk and poultry to the surrounding regions and the Bombay metropolitan area. Fishermen reap a rich harvest of fish, crabs and shrimp. According to the Dahanu Taluka Environment Welfare Association (DTEWA) nearly half of the sub-district is under forest cover. About 65 per cent of the Dahanu population is comprised of tribals who are engaged in cultivating their land and working on orchards.

The DTEWA and its energetic secretaries, Nergis Irani and Kitayun Rustom have vigorously campaigned against the despoliation of this area. Their campaign began in the late 1980s when the Bombay Suburban Electric Supply Company (BSES) decided to establish a 500 MW coal-fired thermal power station at Dahanu. BSES engaged a consulting firm to locate a suitable site for the power station to supply electricity to Bombay. Out of the nine sites investigated, only one—Bassein—was found to be technically viable. However, this site was discarded because it fell within the Bombay metropolitan region and would add to the existing high level of pollution in the area. Eventually, Dahanu was approved by the authorities.

The location of any thermal power station which draws on sea water to cool its turbines is bound to impact the marine environment. The warm water discharged by the plant alters the local ecology. Some species thrive in the warm water whilst others perish in the changed environment. Environmentalists feared that emissions from the proposed coal-fired plant, particularly sulphur dioxide, would adversely affect the chikoo crop. Another concern related to environmental harm from the disposal of ash in wetlands and reclaimed creek areas. The complex web of ecological issues and social impacts posed by the Dahanu siting were reduced to three easy-to-explain contentions before the Bombay High Court. The Bombay Environmental Action Group (BEAG) and DTEWA urged the court to stall the project since (i) the Central Government had issued environmental clearance contrary to the opinion of its Appraisal Committee of the Union Ministry of Environment and Forests (MEF); (ii) the project was being set up within 500 metres of the High Tide Line (HTL) mark, contrary to the guideline and condition imposed by the MEF; and (iii) the discharge of water would increase the sea temperature and adversely affect marine life.

A division bench of the Bombay High Court rejected the petitions finding that the site offered several advantages. The land was barren, no tree would be felled, there was no habitation at the site and consequently no relocation of villagers, and the use of marine water for cooling would help conserve scarce fresh water resources. Accepting the stand of the state government and BSES that the 500 metres distance from the HTL would be maintained, the court found that the concerned authorities had considered all the relevant factors, had imposed stringent safeguards and hence there was no justification for interfering with the project under Article 226 of the Constitution.[32]

The environmental groups petitioned the Supreme Court for special leave to appeal under Article 136 of the Constitution of India. We carry an excerpt from the Supreme Court judgment.

DAHANU TALUKA ENVIRONMENT PROTECTION GROUP v BSES
1991 (2) SCC 539

RANGANATHAN, J.:

The two petitioners, who are 'Environment Protection Groups' objected to the clearance, by the State of Maharashtra and the Union of India, of a proposal of the Bombay Suburban Electricity Supply Company Limited (hereinafter referred to as 'BSES') for the construction of a thermal power plant over an area of 800 hectares or thereabouts in Dahanu, Maharashtra. They filed writ petitions in the Bombay High Court challenging the decision of the Central Government to that effect dated 29 March 1989. After some hearing the Bombay High Court passed an order dated 30 March 1990 adjourning the hearing to enable the Government of India to consider the representations made by the two petitioners. Government of India did this and reaffirmed its decision to clear the project. A detailed affidavit was filed on behalf of the Union on 29 June 1990. To this was enclosed a memorandum dealing in seriatim with the various objections raised by the petitioners and setting out the government's findings thereon. After considering the same and hearing the counsel at length, the High Court, by a detailed order, dismissed the writ petitions by its order dated 12 December 1990. The objectors have thereupon filed these two petitions for leave to appeal before us.

* * *

We have come to the conclusion that there are no grounds to grant leave to appeal from the order passed by the High Court. We shall briefly deal with the contentions urged before us:

(1) The BSES undertook surveys some time in 1976 and selected about ten sites where its thermal power station could be located and Dahanu was not one of them. After consideration, a site at Bassein was cleared in 1985. But the state government objected to this site later on the ground that Bassein was located within a distance of one kilometer from the sea shore and 500 meters from the river banks. This region was reserved in a plan for extending Bombay metropolitan region and no construction activity could be permitted therein. When this happened, the company has manoeuvred to get approval for the plant location at Dahanu although even the company had not found it suitable earlier and although the objections raised about Bassein equally apply to Dahanu. This criticism is unfounded. The Bassein site fell within the extended

[32] *Bombay Environmental Action Group v State of Maharashtra* AIR 1991 BOM 301.

Bombay metropolitan region; Dahanu falls outside this region. That apart, there were also other reasons to discard the Bassein site which do not apply to the Dahanu site. If the Bassein site having been rejected, an alternate site in Western Maharashtra had to be chosen and Dahanu being close to Bombay after Bassein and beyond the metropolitan development region has been chosen, there is nothing wrong in this.

(2) The principal objection on behalf of the petitioners is that the clearance is in the teeth of the findings of an expert body appointed by the government itself to examine all the aspects of the proposed location at Dahanu. It is contended that this Appraisal Committee for Thermal Power Stations (EAC) held its meetings on 27 October 1988 and 29 December 1988. The meetings were attended by the members of the EAC, concerned officers of the state of Maharashtra, the representatives of the company and representatives of various public bodies and groups. The Committee, after examining the various aspects, considered the site at Dahanu unsuitable and listed nine reasons for this conclusion. It is pointed out that this conclusion of the EAC was arrived at on 29 December 1988. Surprisingly, counsel say, despite the opinion of the EAC, the Government of India cleared the proposal on 29 March 1989 without any reasons disclosed for rejecting the expert body's report. This, it is urged, shows absence of application of mind on the part of the government to the dimensions of the problem.

Prima facie, this appears to be very forceful objection. But it proceeds on the misapprehension that the views of the EAC represent a decision of the government and that the approval of the project is in the nature of a volte face. This is not correct. [Counsel for BSES] sought to brush aside the EAC papers relied upon as nothing but 'minutes' and as ex cathedra pronouncements. This may be going too far. But we are in agreement with counsel that the findings of the EAC cannot be treated as conclusive or binding on the Central Government. We find that the Central Government had before it not only this 'report' but also the findings of a State Expert Committee which had gone into the matter in detail and recommended the Dahanu site. The state government in turn had before it several reports of expert bodies. The details are fully explained in the affidavit ... on behalf of the Government of Maharashtra which has been referred to in the judgement by the High Court. It is also seen that a comparative study of the two sites on all aspects such as pollution, contamination of fresh water resources, effect on fisheries, effect on plantation, agriculture and forests and effect on the tribal population living in the affected areas was looked into.

After examining all the aspects, the state government approved the proposal subject to several stringent conditions. There were also a couple of reports received after 29 December 1988 but before 29 June 1990 when the final decision of the Central Government, after the reconsideration directed by this Court, was taken. The several expert reports expressed the view that the pollution of water on account of the hot water discharge from the cooling plant and the atmospheric pollution due to outlet of gases would be well within permissible limits. Though the EAC had pronounced against the location of the thermal station at Dahanu, the Government of India had before it the strong recommendations of the state of Maharashtra and the several reports referred to above. If, after considering all the material, the Central Government chose to accept the recommendations of the state government, its action cannot be said to be arbitrary.

* * *

(3) Another grievance of the petitioners is that the clearance in respect of the site in question had been issued contrary to the 'Environmental Guidelines for Thermal Power Plants' issued by the Government of India in 1987. The guidelines lay down various criteria, two of which, according to the petitioners, are very important. These are: (1) that thermal power plants should not be located within 25 km. of the outer peripheries of metropolitan cities, national parks, and wildlife sanctuaries and ecologically sensitive areas like tropical forests; and (2) that, in order to protect coastal areas, a distance of 500 meters from the high tide line (HTL) and a further buffer zone of 5 km. from the seashore should be kept free of any thermal power station.

It is pointed out that the EAC had decided against the Dahanu location as it is the only green belt left in the region having about 40 to 60 per cent of forest cover located in Thane district and also as Dahanu town has chikoo gardens and forest areas located at about 3 to 7 kms from the power station. It opined that the emissions of pollutants and the coal and fly ash contaminants are likely to have an adverse effect on the chikoo plant and forest. In the memorandum dated 29 June 1989, it is said, the Government of India has waved away this important objection with a very brief comment that there are no ecologically sensitive areas within 25 kms. of the project site.

* * *

The distances mentioned in the guidelines are only intended as a safeguard against possible pollution effects; it cannot be treated as rigid and inflexible irrespective of local conditions. It is, therefore, quite natural for the Government of India to decide that the site could be cleared subject to stringent conditions to prevent danger of pollution. They have insisted on the installation of a multi-fuel boiler making possible the utilisation of not merely coal but also oil, gas or LSHS to the maximum extent possible. They have insisted upon a tall stack of not less than 275 meters, electrostatic precipitators and a Flue Gas Desulphurisation Plant (FGD). Continuous monitoring of stock emissions and ambient air quality have been insisted upon. Taking into account the Expert Committees' reports, which have been referred to earlier, the Central Government was satisfied that if these conditions are adhered to there will be no significant impact on the environment either due to atmospheric or water pollution.

(4) The second objection based on the guidelines is that the present plant cannot be located in such a way as to ensure being away from HTL (high tide line) by more than 500 meters not to speak of its being beyond 5 kms. from the coastline. Here again attention is drawn to the EAC's report which says that 'the site falls within high tide line in Dahanu creek' and that 'the site is low-lying land virtually in the creek which gets submerged during high tide'. It is true that the plant is located within 5 kms. of the sea but, for the reasons already pointed out, it is impossible to rigidly apply this standard in the context of the present project. The second part of the objection regarding its being within 500 meters of the HTL is, however, based on a misconception. In the first place the restriction in the guidelines is only for the buildings of the thermal station and, for obvious reasons pointed out by [BSES], cannot be read so as to mean that no

part of the site of the thermal station of about 800 hectares should at all fall within the distance of 500 meters.

* * *

We would, however, like to place the matter beyond doubt by directing the Central and the state governments to monitor the construction of the buildings under the scheme to ensure that no building of the thermal power station comes up within a distance of 500 meters from the HTL.

* * *

For the reasons discussed above, we are satisfied that the clearance to the thermal power station was granted by the Central Government after fully considering all relevant aspects and in particular the aspects of the environmental pollution. Sufficient safeguards against pollution of air, water and environment have been insisted upon in the conditions of grant. However, in order to allay the apprehensions on the part of the petitioners that the company may seek and obtain relaxations or modifications of the conditions that may prove detrimental to environment, we direct that the condition requiring the installation of a FGD plant should not be relaxed without a full consideration of the consequences and that, if there is any proposal from the company to relax this or any other condition subject to which the plant has been cleared, neither the state government nor the Union Government should permit such relaxation without giving notice of the proposed changes to the petitioner groups and giving them an opportunity of being heard.

* * *

NOTES AND QUESTIONS

1. The Bombay High Court relied on the Supreme Court judgment in the *Calcutta Taj Hotel Case*.[33] There, the Supreme Court held that while it was the duty of the court to examine whether appropriate considerations had been borne in mind and irrelevancies excluded, the court should not attempt 'to nicely balance relevant considerations. When the question involves the nice balancing of relevant considerations, the Court may feel justified in resigning itself to acceptance of the decision of the concerned authority.'[34]

[33] *Sachidanand Pandey v State of West Bengal* AIR 1987 SC 1109.
[34] *Id.* at 1115.

2. Environmentalists complain that the conditions imposed by the MEF and state governments at the time of granting clearance are meaningless since there is no effective post-clearance machinery to monitor compliance. Once the project is cleared, the implementation of the conditions depends entirely on the good faith of the project proponent. The material in the following notes justifies the apprehensions of the DTEWA and BEAG in respect of the conditions that were imposed on BSES.

3. The High Court judgment was delivered on 12 December 1990. The Supreme Court's decision on the special leave petitions was rendered on 19 March 1991. On 21 May 1991, Dr. Maudgal, scientific advisor to the MEF filed a report in his ministry after conducting a site visit. His report notes diverse breaches by BSES and confirms that contrary to the assurances given by the company to the courts, the site was located within the high tide submergence zone and was within a distance of 500 meters from the HTL. BSES had pushed back the natural HTL by constructing artificial bunds. Dr. Maudgal notes:

> Considering the elaborate arrangements being made through creation of bunds and for the blocking of criss-crossing streams and inlets of the creeks and raising of the site level through dumping ... one has to come to the unmistakable conclusion that the proposed site is lying within the High Tide Line. This is further confirmed by aerial photographs as well as hydrographic maps of the area.

4. In view of the breaches noticed in this report, BEAG once again moved the Bombay High Court by filing Writ Petition No. 428 of 1992. The High Court summarily rejected the petition, observing that it was not open to a public interest group to re-agitate the same issue over and over again.

> The Petitioners cannot consider themselves to be the super monitors of the two Governments. The Supreme Court has expressed confidence by directing the two Governments to monitor the progress ... and we do not see any reason to doubt that the two Governments will ... discharge their duties.[35]

Was it strategically sound to move the Bombay High Court after the special leave petitions were rejected by the Supreme Court? Would it have been wiser for the environmental groups to directly approach the Supreme Court by an interim application in view of that court's direction that all the conditions including the 500 m distance from the HTL be strictly observed? Should the High Court have stalled the project in view of the misleading statements by BSES and the state government in respect of the distance from the HTL?

5. On 20 June 1991, the MEF declared Dahanu as 'an ecologically fragile area' and imposed restrictions on the establishment of industries under section 3 (2)(v) of the Environment (Protection) Act of 1986 (EPA). This notification lists the industries that are permitted and prohibited in Dahanu and also required the state government to

[35] Order dated 12 March 1992.

prepare within a year a regional plan based on the existing land use in the region. The state was asked to clearly demarcate on the plan the existing green areas, orchards, tribal areas and other environmentally sensitive areas. The Dahanu notification prohibited a change in land use and confined industrial activity in the Taluka to a maximum of 500 acres within designated industrial estates.

The notification was a triumph for the environmental groups which had long campaigned to preserve Dahanu's natural heritage. The notification remains the foundation of DTEWA's efforts to protect the Dahanu environment.

6. Predictably, local businessmen as well as the state have lobbied the MEF to dilute or repeal the notification. To thwart the challenge, in 1994, the environmental groups filed a writ petition under Article 32 of the Constitution before the Supreme Court complaining that despite the June 1991 notification, the state government and local authorities were permitting unchecked industrial growth which was irreversibly harming Dahanu.[36] The principal grievance was that the state government had failed to prepare a regional plan within a year under the terms of the notification.

In March 1996, the MEF approved the regional plan for Dahanu submitted belatedly by the state government. According to the environmentalists, this plan violated the Dahanu notification and at their request on 24 September 1996, the Supreme Court directed the National Environmental Engineering Research Institute, Nagpur (NEERI) to study the plan and report on whether it conformed to the Dahanu notification and the Coastal Regulatory Zone (CRZ) Notification of 1991. In its report of 19 October 1996, NEERI found that the plan breached the notifications and 'is also ecologically and environmentally unviable.' Turning specifically to the BSES Plant, the report observed that the thermal power station was located on wetlands in violation of the Coastal Zone Regulations. The report recommended that BSES should use natural gas as fuel in place of coal; that all obstructions to the free flow of sea water into the creeks should be removed by BSES; and that the company should improve the monitoring of hot water discharges as well as air quality and emissions. NEERI suggested that BSES should study the effect of gaseous emissions on horticulture, particularly chikoo and mango trees.

7. By an order dated 31 October 1996 the Supreme Court directed the state government to implement the regional plan subject to the conditions imposed by the MEF. The state was also asked to implement 'all the recommendations of NEERI' as reproduced in the Supreme Court order. The court directed the Central Government to constitute an authority under section 3(3) of the EPA to protect the ecologically fragile Dahanu Taluka and to control pollution in the area. The Supreme Court also transferred the petition to the High Court with a request to the Chief Justice of the Bombay High Court to constitute a 'Green Bench' for the purpose of adjudicating public interest environmental cases.

8. In its report to the Supreme Court, NEERI found that between October 1991

---

[36] *Bittu Seghal v Union of India* Writ Petition (Civil) No. 231 of 1994.

and October 1996, the ecology of Dahanu creek, where the BSES hot water discharges occurred, had dramatically altered. There was a steep decline in the bio-mass at all hierarchical levels contributing to the instability of the ecological pyramid. The number of fish and prawn varieties had decreased within five years of commissioning the thermal power plant. There was a drastic variation in the salinity within the creek due to the incomplete mixing of creek and sea waters. The drop in salinity was the principal reason for the sudden change in the aquatic fauna. NEERI observed that the power plant's operations had decreased the wetlands and caused disappearance of criss-crossing creeks and natural drains which functioned as the breeding ground for aquatic fauna and which aided nutrient recycling and erosion control.

9. On 19 December 1996, a day before the deadline, the MEF constituted the Dahanu Taluka Environment Protection Authority chaired by Justice C.S. Dharmadhikari, a retired judge of the Bombay High Court. The Authority was charged with protecting the ecologically fragile areas of Dahanu whilst having regard to the 'precautionary principle' and 'the polluter pays principle' as enunciated by the Supreme Court.

10. The next major challenge to the DTEWA came with the state government issuing a letter of intent on 17 February 1997 to the Indian subsidiary of P&O Ports, Australia for establishing a giant port at Vadhavan, Dahanu. The state was anxious to build a major port facility in North Maharashtra for the purpose of handling coal, hazardous chemicals and other international cargo. The special geological feature of Vadhavan that attracted P&O Ports was the natural rock strata in the harbour that could save the company substantial costs when building the port facilities.

DTEWA along with other local groups campaigned against the proposed port. Unlike the previous protest against BSES, this campaign enjoyed mass political support, with fishermen, agriculturists and tribals joining hands with the environ-mentalists. All of them feared that a major port would disrupt the community and deplete the natural resources on which they were dependent. On 13 April 1998, the Dahanu Authority restrained the government and P&O Ports from proceeding fur-ther in the matter until the Authority finally decided the question relating to the feasibility of the Vadhavan Port.

On 19 September 1998, the Dahanu Authority ruled that the proposed port would breach the CRZ Regulations of 1991, the Dahanu Notification dated 20 June 1991 and the regional plan for Dahanu. At the time of this writing, the order of the Authority had not been challenged by P&O Ports or the state government and the project appeared to have been shelved.

The next excerpt is drawn from an extremely lengthy division bench judgment of the Karnataka High Court. What factors did the High Court consider most important while exercising judicial review? The project power station was being established by the National Thermal Power Corporation (NTPC).

JANA JAGRUTHI SAMITHI v UNION OF INDIA
1991 (2) KARN. L.J. 524

MOHAN, C.J.:

In all these writ petitions which are filed as Public Interest Litigations, the petitioners are questioning the location of Mangalore Super Thermal Power Station as well as ash pond at Nandikur Village with the aid of USSR. ... Before acquiring the lands for the proposed project it is incumbent for the Pollution Control Board to obtain clearance from the Ministry of Environment. There is no such clearance, much less the location of ash pond at Yellur. It is a case of putting the cart before the horse inasmuch as even without obtaining approval or clearance from the Ministry of Environment and Forests the respondents have proceeded with the acquisition of lands. Acquisition proceedings are taking place in a hurried way even before the project is sanctioned.

* * *

In the detailed statement of objections filed by respondent 4 Corporation [NTPC], the averments are met in the following manner:

There is acute power shortage in the state of Karnataka. Big industries have been shying away from the state. The only solution to this problem is the establishment of big generating stations like the one envisaged by the project in question. As a matter of fact, the petitioners have nowhere stated that there is no need to generate electric power on such large scale as is contemplated by the impugned scheme; and they are unaware that the project has been conceived, examined and passed by the highest authorities, viz.

(a) Government of India—Planning Commission.
(b) Central Electricity Authority.
(c) Karnataka State Pollution Control Board.
(d) Dept. of Ecology & Environment.
(e) Administrative Ministry, Dept. of Power Govt. of India.
(f) Ministry of Environment, Govt. of India.
(g) Ministry of Finance, Govt. of India.
(h) Public Investment Board.
(i) Cabinet Committee on Economic Affairs.

The above authorities, except (f) and (i), have cleared the project. However, the Thermal Appraisal Committee of the Ministry of Environment and Forests has already recommended environmental clearance, and the Cabinet Committee on Economic Affairs is only a formal one and the actual starting of infrastructural work in respect of the project need not await the clearance from that authority as per memorandum of understanding between the NTPC and the Govt. of India. In fact in respect of several of the projects undertaken and completed, clearance from that authority came long after

NTPC starting the infrastructural work etc. and it is so understood by all the authorities including the Cabinet Committee based on the recommendation of the Public Investment Board. The said Board has already recommended the project for clearance of Cabinet Committee. The infrastructural work can start even before clearance of Cabinet Committee, and for such work an amount of rupees five crores is permitted to be spent.

The Central Electricity Authority conducted the Electric Power Survey of India in December 1987. It has been found that the southern region including Karnataka State is to face acute power shortage both in terms of peaking capacity as well as energy requirement. As per the survey, an addition of 38000 MW of electric power is contemplated during the 8th Plan.

* * *

As is rightly urged in the statement of objections, if there has been clearance from Government of India, Planning Commission, Central Electricity Authority, Karnataka State Pollution Control Board, Department of Ecology and Environment (Govt. of Karnataka), Administrative Ministry in the Department of Power (Govt. of India), Ministry of Finance and Public Investment Board, what remains is only the clearance by the Cabinet Committee on Economic Affairs which is stated to be formal. We are unable to see how the petitioners could complain of any environment pollution and non-application of mind. We have already extracted the observations of Ranganath Misra, J. as he then was, in AIR 1987 SC 359. We will only reiterate that a balance between preservation of ecology and utilisation of modern technology has been arrived at by an Expert Body on the basis of appropriate advices. Therefore, it is of no use for the petitioners to contend that unless there is clearance of the project, the lands could not be acquired. We have already seen how this is a time-bound programme. The matter cannot brook delay at all as it would cause to the public exchequer and the Nation serious financial implications. No doubt the petitioners may have a say in view of 1991 (2) SCC 539; but they cannot assume that they alone are interested in safeguarding the environment and that the authorities are oblivious to this.

* * *

In the result, these writ petitions fail and are dismissed. No costs.

NOTES AND QUESTIONS

1. In *Society for Clean Environment v Union of India*,[37] a division bench of the Bombay High Court considered a challenge to the permission to the Tata Electric Companies (TEC) for establishing a seventh unit in the Trombay-Chembur suburb of Bombay. One of the complaints of the petitioners was that the conditions imposed by the state government while granting clearance would not be adhered to by TEC. This

[37] 1992 (3) BOM.C.REP. 362.

had happened earlier. The earlier power plant, Unit No.6 was established in March, 1990 on the condition that Unit Nos.1,2 and 3 would be scrapped. However, TEC had continued using the old units to generate electricity. The petitioners feared that a similar condition in respect of Unit No.7 would again be breached. The High Court declined to intervene in exercise of its constitutional jurisdiction, holding that the issues raised by the petitioners ought to receive the serious attention of the Maharashtra pollution control board. While dismissing the petition, the court required strict implementation of the condition regarding the de-commissioning of Units 1 to 3 and held that the condition was 'inflexible and indilutable'.

2. The Dahanu, Mangalore and Bombay cases suggest that courts are reluctant to stall power projects, possibly due to widely experienced power shortages across the country. The judges examining thermal power plant clearances like to ensure that the project proceeds without delay on the conditions stipulated by the authorities. What type of judicial directions relating to transparency, publication of information and reporting by the project authorities might improve enforcement of the conditions imposed?

H. KONKAN RAILWAY CASE

THE GOA FOUNDATION v THE KONKAN RAILWAY CORPORATION
AIR 1992 BOM 471

JUDGMENT:

Very few people are fortunate to see their dreams fulfilled and people residing on the west coast saw fulfilment of their dream when the Central Government decided to provide a broad gauge railway line from Bombay to Mangalore and thereafter to extend to the state of Kerala. It was a long standing demand of the people in the region for a cheap and fast transport to improve the economic conditions and to make accessible the hinterlands in the state of Maharashtra, state of Goa and state of Karnataka. The Central Government was considering providing a railway line for a considerable length of time but the project was postponed from time to time due to lack of requisite funds. Ultimately the Central Government took a decision to provide the line and to achieve that purpose. The Konkan Railway Corporation Ltd., a public limited Company, was set up. The length of the line from Bombay to Mangalore along the west coast is to be 760 kilometres and out of that 106 kilometres line runs through the state of Goa, The cost of the project was envisaged at Rs. 1391 crores in the year 1991–92. The Central Government set up a Corporation as the total allocation of the Planning Commission was only to the order of Rs. 300 crores and, therefore, it was incumbent for the Corporation to raise the funds for seeking equity contribution from the Ministry of Railways and the beneficiary states of Maharashtra, Goa, Karnataka and Kerala, The Corporation was also conferred with powers to raise money with issuance of 9% tax-free bonds from financial institutions and public borrowings. The Konkan Railway alignment passes through different terrain in different states and the Corporation is required to construct large number of tunnels and projects over rivers. The Railway line will have 136 major bridges and 1670 minor bridges and there will be 71 tunnels with a total length of 75 kms. The Konkan Railway is the biggest railway project undertaken in the Indian sub-continent in the present century. The project was approved after detailed and long-drawn survey of various aspects of the matter and the Corporation was constituted in July, 1990 to undertake the exercise which is of an extensive magnitude. The project commenced on 15 October 1990 and the Government of Goa approved the alignment passing through the State of Goa on 17 December 1990.

The petitioner No. 1 is a society registered under the Societies Registration Act and claims to protect and improve the natural environment including forests, lakes, river and wild life and to have compassion for living creatures. The petitioners approached this Court by filing the present petition under Article 226 of the Constitution with the prayer that the Corporation should be compelled to procure environment clearance for the alignment passing through the state of Goa from the Ministry of Environment and Forests, Government of India, and until such clearance is secured all the work in respect of providing railway line should be withheld. The grievance of the petitioners is that the proposed alignment has been planned and undertaken without an adequate Environment Impact Assessment (EIA) and an Environment Management Plan (EMP). The petitioners claim that the proposed alignment is wholly destructive of the environment and the eco-system and violates the citizens' rights under Article 21 of the Constitution. The petitioners also claim that even though the ecological damage will not be felt immediately, such damage will be gradual and will lead to the deterioration of the land quality and will affect large number of people. The petitioners further claim that as the proposed alignment passes across the rivers, creeks, basins and backwaters, the Corporation cannot proceed to carry out the work without obtaining the statutory clearance required under the provisions of the Environment (Protection) Act, 1986. The petitioners claim that under the provisions of Section 3(2) (v) the Ministry of Environment has issued Notification dated 19 February 1991 and restrictions on the setting up or extension of industries, operations or processes in the coastal regulation zone (C.R.Z.) are prescribed. The petitioners claim that the Corporation cannot ignore the activities prohibited or regulated under the Notification and in the absence of clear sanction or approval from the Ministry of Environment it is not permissible to proceed with the project undertaken within the state of Goa. The petitioners further claim that certain correspondence which has transpired between Inter-Ministerial Departments reflects that the Environment Ministry is not inclined to permit the Corporation to undertake the project without examining the objections raised by various Organizations to the proposed alignment.

* * *

In our judgement, the claim of the petitioners that the alignment would have devastating and irreversible impact upon the Khazan lands is without any foundation, and even otherwise, the extent of damage is extremely negligible and a public project of such a magnitude which is undertaken for meeting the aspirations of the people on the west coast cannot be defeated on such considerations. It is not open to frustrate the project of public importance to safeguard the interest of few persons. It cannot be overlooked that while examining the grievance about adverse impact upon a small area of 30 hectares of Khazan lands, the benefit which will be derived by large number of people by construction of rail line cannot be brushed aside. The Courts are bound to take into consideration the comparative hardship which the people in the region will suffer by stalling the project of great public utility. The cost of the project escalates from day to day and, as pointed out by the Corporation, the extent of the interest and cost which will be suffered by the Corporation every day is to the tune of Rs. 45 lakhs. No development is possible without some adverse effect on the ecology and environment but the projects of public utility cannot be abandoned and it is necessary to adjust the interest of people as well as the necessity to maintain the environment. The balance has to be struck between the two interests and this exercise must be left to the persons who are familiar and specialized in the field. The Corporation has set up not only a specialized Committee but has also engaged the service of a renowned engineer from Goa and who is practical not only in experience of the surroundings in Goa and when both of them have given green signal to the project, we decline to exercise our writ jurisdiction to frustrate the project of such magnitude on the alleged damage to the ecology and environment of Khazan lands.

* * *

Relying on the CRZ Notification it was contended on behalf of the petitioners that the activity of bunding undertaken by the Corporation for the alignment is a prohibited activity. In the alternative, it was contended that even if the activity is permissible such permission has not been sought. In our judgement, both the submissions are misconceived and are required to be turned down for more than one reason. In the first instance, the assumption of the petitioners that the exercise undertaken by the Corporation for providing a rail line is an industry is entirely unjustified. The expression 'industries, operations or processes etc.' cannot bring within its sweep the activities of providing a rail line. The contention that the activities of bunding undertaken by the Corporation are prohibited activities is fallacious. The reference to the bunding in the Notification must be read in the context of setting up industries or any operations or processes in respect of such industries. Once it is found that providing rail line is not an industry, then it is not possible to jump to the conclusion that the work of bunding is a prohibited activity and, therefore, the Corporation should be prevented from proceeding with the work. The alternate submission that even if the activity is permitted within the stipulated limit beyond 100 meters from the High Tide Line but within the distance of 500 meters, the clearance is required from the Ministry, is without any substance. Apart from the fact that the Notification has no application to the work undertaken by the Corporation, the activities in respect of which clearance is required are those where permanent buildings or workshops or harbours or thermal power plants are erected and not for the purpose of providing a rail line. The rail line or a public road is provided for access to the public to the seas, bays, estuaries, creeks and backwaters and either a public road or a rail line is not a construction which demands clearance. It is beyond our comprehension to appreciate as to how a rail line can be or a road can be constructed without travelling over the bridges constructed over the rivers, creeks or seas. The Notification on which reliance is placed has no application whatsoever to the work undertaken by the Corporation.

The Corporation is also right in the contention that the provisions of the Environment Act have no application in respect of work undertaken in exercise of powers conferred under Section 11 of the Railways Act, 1989. Section 11, inter alia, provides that notwithstanding anything contained in any other law, the Railway Administration may, for the purposes of constructing or maintaining a railway, make or construct in or upon, across, under or over any lands, or any streets, hills, valleys, roads, streams, or other waters, rivers as it thinks proper. The wide ambit of the provisions of the Environment Act do not bind the construction or maintenance of a railway line. The Railways Act is a legislation enacted subsequent to the Environment Act and the Corporation is right in claiming that for the purpose of providing railway line, clearance is not required even though the line passes over the railways, rivers, creeks, etc. in view of the specific provisions of Section 11 of the Railways Act.

* * *

The state of Goa has abundant natural resources and the railway line would assist in ... the prosperity of the common man. The existing transport facilities by road are entirely inadequate to cater to the needs of the people in transporting their goods to the large towns. We hope and trust that unnecessary obstructions are not raised to the project of such huge public utility and which will herald the prosperity for the poor people on the western coast. It should be remembered that the project of such gigantic magnitude has become available after the people fought for over a century and the petty interest of a local area should not defeat the project in respect of which the Central Government has already spent a huge amount.

* * *

NOTES AND QUESTIONS

1. The court appears to have been overwhelmed by the magnitude of the project. Can you fault its extreme deference to the contentions advanced by the railways?

2. Are the railways exempt from all environmental laws? Does the High Court's interpretation permit the railways to pollute without regard to the Water Act and the Air Act?

3. The court sensibly disposed of the writ petition with a final judgment at the admission stage. This approach is commendable because it reduces the uncertainty in relation to large projects and prevents a waste of public funds which could get blocked, were an interim injunction issued.

4. Apparently troubled by the delays to infrastructure projects due to judicial intervention, the Supreme Court made these observations in a dispute relating to a government contract for the design, engineering and supply of large pipes to the Khaperkheda Thermal Power Station in Maharashtra:

> When a petition is filed as a public interest litigation challenging the award of a contract by the State or any public body to a particular tenderer, the Court must satisfy itself that the party which has brought the litigation is litigating *bona fide* for public good. ... Intervention by the Court may ultimately result in delay in the execution of the project. The obvious consequence of such delay is price escalation ... The party at whose instance interim orders are obtained has to be made accountable for the consequences of the interim order. The interim order could delay the project, jettison finely worked financial arrangements and escalate costs. Hence the petitioner asking for interim orders, in appropriate cases should be asked to provide security for any increase in cost as a result of such delay, or any damage suffered by the opposite party in consequence of an interim order. ... Stay order or injunction order, if issued, must be moulded to provide for restitution.[38]

Do these observations apply to environmental public interest litigations? What type of security can a citizens' group or non-governmental organization furnish? Should a court require security when the petitioners have no private stake in the dispute and are espousing a public cause? Does not the notion of security in an environmental public interest litigation cut at the root of this jurisprudence?

In *Goa Foundation v Diksha Holding Pvt. Ltd.,*[39] the Bombay High Court distinguished the Supreme Court judgment in *Raunaq International Ltd.*[40] while granting interim relief to a public interest petitioner. Finding *prima facie* violations of the Coastal Regulations, the division bench held that an injunction was warranted even though substantial expenditure had been incurred on the project. The High Court relied on its decision in *Goa Foundation v The Goa State Committee on Coastal Environment*[41] and issued a *status quo* order restraining further development by the hotelier.

---

[38] *Raunaq International Ltd. v I.V.R. Construction* AIR 1999 SC 393, 397–398.
[39] Writ Petition No. 427 of 1998, order dated 11 February 1999.
[40] *Supra* note 38.
[41] 1998 (1) GOA L.T. 364.

11

THE COAST, WETLANDS AND HERITAGE

In this omnibus chapter we examine three topics of recent concern to environmentalists, administrators and the judiciary. The campaigns to preserve the Indian coast have heightened tensions among the diverse interests that control or use coastal resources. The cases below illustrate the conflicts between the Union and the states; traditional fishermen and owners of mechanized trawlers; the shrimp industry and fisherfolk; hoteliers and non-governmental organizations; and town planners and environmentalists. The section on wetlands dwells on the ecological importance of inhospitable bogs and swamps and the growing realization of the range of 'nature services' that these regions provide. We finally look at initiatives to preserve the man-made heritage—chiefly architectural buildings and antiquities—that are now recognized as part of the seamless cultural and natural patrimony that each generation must preserve for the next.

A. PROTECTING THE COASTAL REGION

India's lengthy coast stretches over 6,000 kilometres, supporting numerous fishing communities and driving the economies of coastal villages, towns and cities. The importance of coastal ecology and the linkages between community life, economic development and the environment are explored in a lively report prepared by Claude Alvares of the Goa Foundation titled, *Fish Curry and Rice*.[1] The report argues that overfishing in the near shore waters, marine pollution, excessive sand extraction, shore line development and destruction of the *khazans*[2] are endangering Goa's 'fish-curry-and-rice' ethos, which had evolved over the centuries in harmony

---

[1] C. Alvares, *Fish Curry and Rice: A Citizens' Report on the Goan Environment*, 52–95 (1993). The chapter on the coastal region is authored by N. Dantas and V. Gadgil.

[2] Saline flood plains in Goa's tidal estuaries.

with the environment. Many of these problems confront other coastal communities as well.

Three broad classes of human intervention threaten India's marine environment: maritime trade, the exploitation of ocean resources and on-land coastal development. Although we briefly review developments relating to the former two categories, this section mainly focuses on efforts to regulate land use along the ecologically sensitive coast line.

I. MARINE POLLUTION

India's ocean resources are primarily threatened by terrestrial sources of pollution, seemingly regulated under the Water Act of 1974 and the Environment (Protection) Act of 1986. Several Indian coastal cities such as Bombay directly discharge untreated city sewage into the sea. Industrial wastes and pesticide runoff contaminate the ocean through rivers and creeks. Studies conducted since the 1970s confirm the presence of high levels of heavy metals such as mercury in the coastal waters around Bombay and Gujarat.[3] The legal issues relating to these sources of pollution have been discussed earlier in the book.

The legislative framework for controlling marine pollution is provided by the Territorial Waters, Continental Shelf, Exclusive Economic Zone and Other Maritime Zones Act of 1976. The Territorial Waters (TW) extend 12 nautical miles from the defined base line; the Continental Shelf (CS) is the natural prolongation of India's land territory to the outer edge of the continental margin or 200 nautical miles, where the continental margin does not extend up to that distance. The Exclusive Economic Zone (EEZ) extends beyond the TW, over a distance of 200 nautical miles. The Act asserts India's sovereignty over the natural resources in the CS[4] and EEZ.[5] Sections 6(3)(d) and 7(4)(d) confer exclusive jurisdiction on the Central Government to preserve and protect the marine environment and to prevent and control marine pollution within the CS and EEZ.

Apart from these general provisions, there are no specific regulations framed under the Territorial Waters Act to regulate the dumping of substances in the sea or other causes of marine pollution. The Indian Coast Guard patrols the maritime zones and is responsible for 'taking such measures as are necessary to preserve and protect that maritime environment and to prevent and control marine pollution.'[6]

Specific provisions under the Merchant Shipping Act of 1958 (MSA) govern the civil and criminal liability regimes in respect of oil spills. Part X-B of the MSA deals with the civil liability of the owner of an Indian or foreign vessel that

---

[3] Malviya, *Marine Pollution Control: An Appraisal* in LAW AND ENVIRONMENT 217–233 (P. Leelakrishnan ed. 1992); and Remedios, *Pomfret Nitrate and Surmai a la Zinc* in TIMES OF INDIA, Bombay, 11 April 1999.

[4] Section 6(3)(a).

[5] Section 7(3)(a).

[6] Section 14(2)(c). The Coast Guard Act of 1978.

damages the environment in the TW or the EEZ. Part XI-A of the Act contains provisions for preventing and controlling oil pollution. Both parts were inserted in the parent Act in 1983, to give effect to international conventions.[7] Taken together, they provide a comprehensive code for dealing with the civil liability arising from oil pollution damage, and being a special law would prevail over general pollution control statutes. The quantum of the owner's liability is limited under section 352J of the MSA where the damage occurs without fault of the owner. Conversely, limitation does not apply where the damage is caused by negligence. Section 436 of the MSA prescribes penalties for wrongful oil discharges into Indian coastal waters.

II. OCEAN RESOURCES

Until the 1950s, the coastal waters were fished by traditional fisherfolk, employing rowing and sailing boats. The catch was consumed mostly in neighbouring coastal communities. Fishery development in the post-independence era received a boost from governmental support to mechanized craft, development of refrigeration and canning facilities and the promotion of marine product exports. These changes threatened the lifestyles and livelihood of traditional fishing communities.

In the 1960s big business entered the fishery sector. The introduction of mechanized trawlers initially increased the fish catch by permitting trawling further off the coast, but gradually the fish landings plateaued and even declined. While some of the fisherfolk were able to adjust to the new capital and resource intensive fishery culture, the majority were threatened by depleting returns. The ensuing clashes between fisherfolk and mechanized trawlers were most intense in Kerala, where the agitation led to strikes, protest marches and violent clashes between the traditional fishermen and trawler owners. The campaign resulted in restrictions on trawling, including a ban during the monsoon months which is the breeding season for several important species of fish. The ban imposed in 1988 and 1989 resulted in a better harvest in the aftermath of the monsoons.[8]

The clash between the fishermen and mechanized trawler owners in Kerala has reached the courts. In 1980 the Kerala Government enacted the Kerala Marine Fishing Regulation Act. The operators of mechanized vessels challenged notifications issued under the Act that prohibited mechanized vessels from trawling within the territorial waters and banned the use of certain types of gear by the mechanized craft. In a detailed judgment reviewing the history of the conflict, the Supreme Court upheld the notifications. The court found that the ban was a reasonable restriction on the freedom to trade since it was necessary for protecting the source

---

[7] Part X-B gave effect to the provisions of the International Convention on Civil Liability for Oil Pollution Damage (1969); and Part XI-A gave effect to amendments to the International Convention for the Prevention of Pollution of Sea by Oil (1954).

[8] M. Gadgil & R. Guha, *Ecology and Equity*, 16, 81–83 (1995).

of livelihood of traditional fisherfolk and also to save the pelagic fish wealth within the territorial waters from depletion.[9]

III. COASTAL DEVELOPMENT

Development along coastal stretches is severely restricted under a regime comprising the Coastal Regulation Zone (CRZ) notification of 1991; the approved Coastal Zone Management Plans (CZMPs) for each state or region; ad hoc clarifications in respect of the 1991 notification and CZMPs issued by the Union Ministry of Environment and Forests (MEF); and local town and country planning laws to the extent that these do not conflict with the CRZ Regulations. In response to a series of Supreme Court orders berating the casual approach of the state to coastal protection, the MEF has constituted national and state level authorities to protect the coast.

Foreshore development was initially regulated by building rules under local town and country planning laws or the land revenue code. The first federal initiative came on 27 November 1981 when Prime Minister Indira Gandhi wrote to the state Chief Ministers:

> I have received a number of reports about the degradation and mis-utilisation of beaches in our coastal states by building and other activity. This is worrying as the beaches have aesthetic and environmental value as well as other uses. They have to be kept clear of all activities at least upto 500 metres from the water at the maximum high tide. If the area is vulnerable to erosion, suitable trees and plants have to be planted on the beach sands without marring their beauty.
>
> Beaches must be kept free from all kinds of artificial development. Pollution from industrial and town wastes must be also avoided totally.
>
> Please give thought to this matter and insure that our lively coastline and its beaches remain unsullied.[10]

Several coastal states urged the Centre to reduce the restriction to a distance of 200 m from the High Tide Line (HTL) since the prohibition discouraged tourism. In 1986, the Union Government set up an inter-ministerial committee to scrutinize proposals for setting up tourist resorts in Goa, Thiruvananthapuram, Mahabalipuram and Puri. In respect of these specific beaches, the limit of 500 m was relaxed to 200 m from the HTL. An early public interest litigation seeking to enforce the Prime Minister's directive against a hotel resort in Goa was rejected by the Bombay High Court in 1988. The court held that the directive was no more than an executive fiat, without the authority of law.[11] Nevertheless, the diktat was beneficial. Several large

---

[9] *State of Kerala v Joseph Antony* AIR 1994 SC 721.

[10] Archives, Bombay Environmental Action Group.

[11] *Sergio Carvalho v State of Goa* 1989 (1) GOA LAW TIMES 276, 289.

government projects re-located away from the coastal zone in view of the directive.[12]

In July 1983, the Union Department of Environment,[13] issued administrative guidelines to regulate the development of beaches.[14] Beaches were defined to cover the entire coast as well as the waterfront along rivers and lakes. These guidelines laid the foundation for the statutory regulations that followed in the next decade.

In February, 1991 the Union Ministry of Environment and Forests (MEF) framed regulations under the Environment (Protection) Act of 1986 (EPA), and the Environment (Protection) Rules of 1986, to preserve a coastal zone extending over a strip of land up to 500 m from the HTL along the entire Indian coast. These regulations, popularly known as the CRZ Regulations, severely restrict development on about 3000 sq. kms. of coastal India.

The CRZ Regulations are poorly drafted, leading to a great deal of uncertainty. The non-standard format of these regulations contributes to the confusion. The decisions of the Supreme Court and the High Courts have tried to clear the mess. The opening clause of the CRZ Regulations defines the regulatory zone:

> [T]he coastal stretches of seas, bays, estuaries, creeks, rivers and backwaters which are influenced by tidal action (in the landward side) upto 500 metres from the High Tide Line (HTL) and the land between the Low Tide Line (LTL) and the HTL.

When originally issued, the paragraph continued:

> For purposes of this Notification, the High Tide Line (HTL) will be defined as the line upto which the highest high tide reaches at spring tides.
>
> Note:— The distance from the High Tide Line (HTL) to which the proposed regulations will apply in the case of rivers, creeks and backwaters may be modified on a case by case basis for reasons to be recorded while preparing the Coastal Zone Management Plans (referred to below); however this distance shall not be less than 100 metres or the width of the creek, river or backwater whichever is less.

On 18 August 1994, an amending notification was issued substituting the clause quoted above, with the words:

> For the purposes of this notification, the High Tide Line means the line on the land upto which the highest water line reaches during the spring tide and shall be demarcated uniformly in all parts of the country by the demarcating

---

[12] Chainani, *Coastal Regulation Zone: CRZ Notification and Heritage Conservation*, 26 December 1998 (unpublished). Archives, Bombay Environmental Action Group.

[13] Predecessor to the Union Ministry of Environment and Forests.

[14] The Department of Environment, Government of India, *Environmental Guidelines for Development of Beaches* (1983).

authority so authorised by the Central Government in consultation with the Surveyor General of India.

Note:— The distance from the High Tide Line shall apply to both sides in the case of rivers, creeks and backwaters and may be modified on a case by case basis for reasons to be recorded while preparing the Coastal Zone Management Plans. However, this distance shall not be less than 50 metres or the width of the creek, river or backwater, whichever is less. The distance upto which development along rivers, creeks and backwaters is to be regulated shall be governed by the distance upto which the tidal effect of sea is experienced in rivers, creeks or backwaters, as the case may be, and should be clearly identified in the Coastal Zone Management Plans.

In *Indian Council for Enviro-Legal Action v Union of India*,[15] the Supreme Court held that the amendment reducing the width of the zone from 100 m to 50 m in respect of rivers, creeks and backwaters was contrary to the object of the EPA and was illegal. While the intention of the order is clear—restore the 100 m zone—the effect of the judicial declaration is uncertain. The judgment does not in clear words restore the original 100 m zone. It merely appears to strike down the words '50 metres' leaving a 'hole' in the regulations.[16]

Clause 2 of the CRZ Regulations prohibits 13 designated activities including establishing new industries and expanding existing units, except those that are directly related to the waterfront or which require foreshore facilities. The prohibition extends to land reclamation, bunding or disturbing the natural course of seawater; the mining of sand and rocks; and the harvesting of ground water.

Clause 3 provides for the regulation of permissible activities. Development clearance may be granted only where the activity requires water front and foreshore facilities. The clause designates certain activities such as construction for defence ports and harbours, and thermal power plants that require environmental clearance from the MEF. Clause 3(3) requires coastal states and union territory administrations to prepare within one year from the date of the principal notification, Coastal Zone Management Plans (CZMPs) identifying and classifying the CRZ areas within their respective territories. The CZMPs must be approved by the MEF. All development within the CRZ should conform to the CZMP. Pending approval of the CZMP, all development along the coast must comply with the restrictions in the notification. Clause 4 of the notification envisages monitoring and enforcement of the CRZ Regulations by the MEF, the state and union territory administrations or other authorities specifically designated for this purpose.[17]

---

[15] *The CRZ Notification Case*, 1996 (5) SCC 281.

[16] The Supreme Court order assumes that apart from having the power to strike down the invalid portion of the regulations, the court may also *modify* the wording to cure the provision of the *ultra vires* effect.

[17] There is no clause 5 in the main notification. Clause 5 of the draft notification dated 15 December

Clause 6(1) classifies the coast into four categories. The CRZ–I category comprises areas that are ecologically sensitive and important as well as areas between the LTL and HTL. Areas within municipal limits that are developed or substantially built up are classified as CRZ-II. Relatively undisturbed regions that do not belong to CRZ-I or CRZ-II fall under CRZ-III. This includes rural areas as well as areas within municipal limits which are not substantially built up. The coastal stretches of Andaman, Nicobar, Lakshadweep and other small islands fall under CRZ-IV.

Clause 6(2) prescribes the extent of permissible development activity within each of the four zones. Development of beach resorts and hotels within CRZ-III areas are regulated under clause 7. The project proponent must obtain the prior approval of the MEF before putting up the beach resort or hotel in conformity with the guidelines in clause 7.

Hoteliers were quick to criticize the new regime, claiming that the CRZ Regulations would stifle beach tourism. Responding to this lobby, the MEF constituted an expert committee headed by B.B. Vohra to examine whether the 1991 notification needed amendment. The Vohra Committee submitted its report on 31 December 1991 which was followed by the MEF diluting the parent CRZ notification on 18 August 1994.

The relaxation of norms was assailed by the Indian Council for Enviro-Legal Action (ICELA) led by M.C.Mehta, in an Article 32 petition before the Supreme Court. We carry an excerpt from the judgment later in this section.[18] As we shall see, the court struck down portions of the amendment that may have adversely affected coastal ecology and modified others to conform with the object of the CRZ Regulations.

Meanwhile, in interlocutory proceedings in ICELA's case, the Supreme Court took notice of widespread breaches of the law and issued a general moratorium on *all* development within 500 m of the HTL.[19] Several projects, big and small, were halted. Four months later, the Supreme Court lifted the ban, but required strict enforcement of the CRZ Regulations: 'The activities that have been declared as prohibited within the Coastal Regulation Zone shall not be undertaken by any of the respondent-States. The regulation of permissible activities shall also be meticulously followed.'[20] In a similar vein, in May 1995 the Supreme Court issued an interim injunction in the *Shrimp Culture Case*, prohibiting the setting up of new shrimp farms or the conversion of agricultural lands for aquaculture purposes in the coastal stretches of Andhra Pradesh, Tamil Nadu and Pondicherry.[21] This injunction was extended to all the coastal states in August, 1995.[22]

1990 invited objections from the public to the proposed CRZ Regulations. This clause was dropped from the final notification without renumbering the subsequent clauses.

[18] *Supra* note 15.

[19] *Indian Council for Enviro-Legal Action v Union of India* 1995 (2) SCALE 120. Order dated 12 December 1994.

[20] AIR 1995 SC 2252, 2253. Order dated 9 March 1995.

[21] *S. Jagannath v Union of India* 1995 (3) SCALE 126.

[22] 1995 (5) SCALE 66.

On 18 April 1996 the Supreme Court rendered judgment in the petition filed by ICELA.[23] Amongst the directions issued by the court was a deadline to all coastal states to file their CZMPs with the MEF by 30 June 1996. The MEF was directed to approve the plans by September, 1996. A flurry of activity ensued, culminating in the MEF issuing separate letters to each state on 27 September 1996 approving the CZMPs with modifications.[24] The conditions imposed by the MEF in each letter are part of the CZMP and are integral to the coastal regime in each state.[25]

On 31 January 1997 the CRZ Regulations were amended a second time to overcome the practical difficulties faced by the islanders of Andaman and Nicobar. A third set of amendments were introduced on 9 July 1997 to reduce 'the difficulties being faced by the local people and also for construction of essential facilities in the coastal zone.'

Apart from the statutory modifications, the MEF has issued letters explaining the scope of the regulations. On 27 March 1998 the MEF wrote to the Chief Secretary, Government of Maharashtra: 'In the areas categorized as CRZ-II, construction of buildings can be permitted on the landward side of the imaginary line drawn along the existing authorised structures.' On 8 September 1998 the MEF clarified that the imaginary line would run parallel to the HTL and connect authorized structures on adjoining plots. The ministry also explained the ambit of the expression 'existing authorized buildings' to cover buildings of a permanent nature that were constructed in accordance with building regulations prior to the coming in force of the 1991 notification.[26]

In terms of clause 4 of the CRZ Regulations, the MEF constituted a National Coastal Zone Management Committee (NCC) in August 1998. The NCC comprised eight officials and four representatives of fisherfolk and coastal communities. Its functions were chiefly to advise the MEF on matters relating to coastal policy, planning and enforcement of the regulations. The NCC was stillborn, yielding to a National Coastal Zone Management Authority (NCA) which was notified on 26 November 1998.[27]

The constitution of the NCA is identical to the NCC, with the same proportion of official and community representation. However, the NCA is conferred greater power to effectively protect the coast. The functions of the Authority include co-ordinating the actions by State Coastal Zone Management Authorities (SCAs);

[23] Supra note 15.

[24] The approval letters for all the states and union territories are published by the Goa Foundation in *The Coastal Regulation Zone Notification in India* (1997).

[25] The approval letters are in a standard format. Part 'A' enumerates general conditions applicable to all states. Part 'B' mentions specific conditions, modifications and clarifications particular to each state.

[26] Archives, Bombay Environmental Action Group.

[27] The NCA notification superseded the NCC notification and came to be issued after the Supreme Court expressed its dissatisfaction on 21 August 1998 regarding the designation and powers of the NCC. *Indian Council for Enviro-Legal Action v Union of India* 1998 (5) SCALE 5 (SP).

examining proposals for changes in the classification of coastal areas or in CZMPs; recommending suitable changes to the MEF; and ensuring strict compliance with the CRZ Regulations. For effective implementation, the NCA is empowered to review cases of CRZ violations and where necessary, to issue remedial directions under section 5 of the Environment (Protection) Act of 1986 (EPA). The Authority is also empowered to file complaints under section 19 of the EPA (to initiate prosecutions) and, in terms of section 10 of the EPA, may enter and inspect any place with a view to ascertain the facts. Moreover, the NCA is required to provide technical assistance to state governments, institutions and authorities that seek its guidance in matters relating to the coastal environment. It must also examine and accord approval to CZMPs submitted by the SCAs.

Simultaneous with the constitution of the NCA, the MEF issued a series of orders constituting separate State Coastal Zone Management Authorities for each coastal state and union territory. The SCAs comprise six or seven persons who are either officials in government departments or are experts on coastal issues. Unlike the NCA, the SCAs do not have any community or NGO representation. The functions and powers of the SCAs are similar to those of the NCA.

NOTES AND QUESTIONS

1. Are the CRZ Regulations consistent with India's federal system of government? Is it sound legislative policy to enable a ministry in Delhi to impose nationwide restrictions affecting 3,000 sq. kms. of coastal stretches through subordinate legislation? Remember, 'land', 'fisheries', and local authority administration are subjects in the State List (List II) of the Seventh Schedule to the Constitution of India. Do the CRZ Regulations encroach upon the powers of municipalities, local communities and the state governments to regulate and develop coastal stretches within their territory?

2. Are the CRZ Regulations 'democratic'? Do they allow local communities to participate in decisions relating to the nature of the development in their neighbourhood? Is it wise to impose a single set of regulations for the entire length of the Indian coast, without regard to regional factors such as population density, geography, social and community needs and aesthetic features?

3. Like forests, rivers and the air we breathe, the coast is a common property resource. Do the CRZ Regulations preserve the common property for the benefit of the community at large or do they operate as a 'fencing regime' similar to the Forest (Conservation) Act of 1980 and the Wild Life (Protection) Act of 1972? Are fencing regimes that alienate local communities from the immediate environment, a sustainable solution for the medium and long term management of natural resources?

4. The CRZ Regulations are framed under section 3(2) (v) of the EPA which enables the Central Government to impose restrictions on areas where any industry, operation or process or class of industries, operations or processes may be carried

out. Considering the power under which the CRZ Regulations are framed, it is hardly surprising that the framework of these regulations is exclusionary rather than participative. What changes might you introduce in the CRZ Regulations to allow community inputs in planning and development decisions?

5. The coastal regime is distributed over several documents, many of which are difficult to access. The principal notification of 1991 and its amendments apart, the CZMPs, the letters of approval issued by the MEF in respect of the CZMPs and the explanatory letters addressed by the MEF to the state governments are difficult to trace. Indeed, in Karnataka an environmental group found it difficult to inspect the CZMP since government officials could not locate the plan.[28] Is the coastal regulatory regime transparent? How is a person who seeks to develop a coastal plot expected to track down all this disparate paper?

6. The second and third amendments to the CRZ notification were introduced without inviting public comments, by recourse to rule 5(4) of the Environment (Protection) Rules of 1986 which permits dispensation with the pre-publication requirement if the 'public interest' demands. What considerations might have weighed with the MEF in bypassing the pre-publication procedure?

7. There is no provision in the notifications constituting the NCA and SCAs for budgetary support. One of the principal constraints that has impeded the proper functioning of the pollution control boards has been a lack of financial resources. How effective will these new authorities be, in the absence of an assured budget? Is it worthwhile setting up new environmental authorities without guaranteeing funds for the effective implementation of environmental laws?

The orders constituting the NCA and SCAs neither prescribe the procedure that these authorities should follow while hearing complaints about CRZ violations nor the frequency with which the authorities should meet. To effectively discharge their functions, it may be necessary for the authorities to frame rules of procedure for handling complaints and to meet at short intervals to redress grievances in a timely manner.

8. The constitution of the new authorities may reduce the public interest litigation burden of the High Courts. The High Courts may now direct the petitioners (in new as well as pending cases) to approach the authorities for relief. To assist the court in arriving at an informed decision, the High Courts may also seek the expert opinion of these authorities in cases relating to coastal ecology.

9. Some of the recurring difficulties in interpreting the CRZ Regulations arise from the non-standard format of these regulations. Most subordinate legislation in India opens with a definition clause where key expressions are defined. There is no definition clause in the 1991 regulations, leaving unclear critical expressions such as 'existing authorised structure', 'traditional rights and customary uses', and 'local architectural style'. The MEF has attempted to overcome some of the shortcomings

---

[28] Interview with Ranjan Rao Yerdoor, Trustee, Nagarika Seva Trust; 23 April 1999. Conducted by S. Divan.

through the 1997 amendment and explanatory letters written to the state governments.

Uncertainty in respect of the HTL has led to disputes between environmental groups and developers. The 1994 amendments require the Central Government to appoint an authority to demarcate the HTL uniformly in all parts of the country. This immense task has fallen on the Chief Hydrographer to the Government of India, who at the time of writing, had yet to complete the survey. (On 29 December 1998 an amendment to the CRZ Regulations required the Central Government to designate one or more authorities to demarcate the HTL uniformly 'in accordance with the general guidelines issued in this regard.')

Moreover, the HTL itself is a dynamic, shifting front which varies from region to region:

> In hydrographic surveying, the coastline is defined as the 'high water line'; on a cliffy coast, where the tide reaches the foot of the cliffs, or on a steep beach, the demarcation of the high-water line is clear; on a gently shelving beach, it is more difficult to judge but generally speaking the line of driftwood, flotsam and jetsam farthest up the beach gives the best idea of the position. In mangroves and salt water marshes where high tides flood the land, the seaward limit of the vegetation is taken as the coastline and is shown by a pecked line with the appropriate land symbol on the landward side.[29]

10. Dr. Prabhas Sinha of the Jawaharlal Nehru University has written extensively on ocean resources and the coastal environment. His writings survey the richness of India's marine biological wealth and make a persuasive case for not just strengthening the CRZ Regulations but also introducing Ocean Regulation Zones and Deep Sea Regulation Zones.[30] Elsewhere, Dr. Sinha argues that 'a critical evaluation of the health of the ocean around the coast of India, its islands, states and union territories, suggest that any grant of relaxation in delineating the CRZ categories in the backwaters, creeks, estuaries or other sensitive eco-systems need not be permitted. ... CRZ being a public-trust area, customary rights of coastal communities must be preserved in the coastal zone.'[31]

The *CRZ Notification Case* filed by the ICELA and excerpted below, was the first major judgment delivered by the Supreme Court on these regulations. It contains

[29] Hydrographer of the Navy; UK, *Admiralty Manual of Hydrographic Survey*, 1 (Vol. II, 1973).

[30] Sinha, *Marine Biological Diversity of India's Oceanic Space*, 5 JR. OF IND. OCEAN STUDIES 256, 265 (1998).

[31] Sinha, *Coastal Environment of India—Towards Their Integrated Management*, 4 JR. OF IND. OCEAN STUDIES 231, 239 (1997).

a strong indictment of administrators responsible for implementing our environmental laws. The main challenge in this case was directed against the dilution of the parent notification by the 1994 amendment:

INDIAN COUNCIL FOR ENVIRO–LEGAL ACTION v UNION OF INDIA
1996 (5) SCC 281

ORDER:

It is the case of the petitioner that with a view to protect the ecological balance in the coastal areas, the aforesaid Notification was issued by the Central Government which contained various provisions for regulating development in the coastal areas. It was contended that there had been a blatant violation of this Notification and industries were illegally being set-up, thereby causing serious damage to the environment and ecology of the area. It was also submitted that the Ministry of Environment and Forests except for issuing the main Notification, had taken no steps to follow up its own directions contained in the main Notification. The main prayer in the Writ Petition was that this Court should issue appropriate writ, order or direction to the respondent so as to enforce the main Notification.

* * *

According to clause [3(3)(i)] of the main Notification, the coastal States and Union Territory Administrations were required to prepare the Management Plans within one year from the date of the main Notification. This was essential for the implementation of the said Notification. The lack of commitment on the part of these States and Administrations, towards the protection and regulation of the coastal stretches, is evident from their inaction in complying with the aforesaid statutory directive requiring the preparation of Management Plans within the specified period. In view of the fact that there had been a non-compliance with this provision, this Court on 3.4.1995 directed all the coastal States and Union Territory Administrations to frame their plans within a further period of six weeks thereof.

A status report was filed in court by the Union of India which shows non-compliance of clause [3(3)(i)] by practically everyone concerned.

* * *

Explanations for the delay in preparation of the Management Plans and their approval have been offered, but they are far from satisfactory. If the mere enactment of the laws relating to the protection of environment was to ensure a clean and pollution free environment, then India would, perhaps, be the least polluted country in the world. But, this is not so. There are stated to be over 200 Central and state statutes which have at least some concern with environment protection, either directly or indirectly. The plethora of such enactments has, unfortunately, not resulted in preventing environmental degradation which, on the contrary, has increased over the years. Enactment of a law, relating to protection of environment, usually provides for what activity can or cannot be done by people. If the people were to voluntarily respect such a law, and abide by it, then it would result in law being able to achieve the object for which it was enacted. Where, however, there is a conflict between the provision of law and personal interest, then it often happens that self-discipline and respect for law disappear.

Enactment of a law, but tolerating its infringement is worse than not enacting law at all. The continued infringement of law, over a period of time, is made possible by adoption of such means which are best known to the violators of law. Continued tolerance of such violations of law not only renders legal provisions nugatory but such tolerance by the Enforcement Authorities encourages lawlessness and adoption of means which cannot, or ought not to be tolerated in any civilized society.* * * When a law is enacted containing some provisions which prohibit certain types of activities, then, it is of utmost importance that such legal provisions are effectively enforced. If a law is enacted but is not being voluntarily obeyed, then, it has to be enforced. Otherwise infringement of law, which is actively or passively condoned for personal gain, will be encouraged which will in turn lead to a lawless society. Violation of anti-pollution laws not only adversely affects the existing quality of life but the non-enforcement of the legal provisions often results in ecological imbalance and degradation of environment, the adverse effect of which will have to be borne by the future generations.

The present case also shows that having issued the main Notification, no follow-up action was taken either by the coastal states and union territories or by the Central Government. The provisions of the main Notification appear to have been ignored and, possibly, violated with impunity.

* * *

The Notification dated 18.8.1994 made six amendments in the main Notification. These amendments were made after the receipt of the report of a Committee, headed by Mr. B.B. Vohra, which had been set up by the Central Government. The validity of amended Notification was also challenged in I.A. 19/1995 which was filed by three environment protection groups, namely, the Goa Foundation, Nirmal Vishwa and Indian Heritage Society (Goa Chapter). In the said application, the applicants gave a table containing the main points of the main Notification, the recommendations made by the Vohra Committee and the amendments made by amended Notification of 1994. The said particulars are as follows:

Main CRZ Notification dated 19.21991 issues for relaxation	Vohra Committee recommendations	Amending Notification dated 18.8.94
1. 200 metres from HTL is no-development zone.	Relaxation allowed [for] rocky and hilly areas; No limit specified.	Blanket relaxation for all areas up to HTL if Central Government so desires.
2. No-development zone for rivers, creeks and backwaters: 100 metres.	Clarification demanded about limits; no relaxation suggested.	No-development zone relaxed to 50 metres.

Main CRZ Notification dated 19.21991 issues for relaxation	Vohra Committee recommendations	Amending Notification dated 18.8.94
3. No levelling or digging of sand dunes or sand.	Allows destruction of sand dunes.	No destruction of sand dunes allowed. However, goal posts, net posts, lamp posts allowed.
4. No-development zone area cannot be used for FSI calculations.	Recommends no-development zone area be permitted for FSI calculations.	Relevant section not amended but explanation added as an after thought in the Notification permitting no-development zone area to be included for FSI calculations.
5. No basements allowed; area not to be included in FSI.	Basement permitted.	Basement allowed.
6. No fencing permitted within 200 metre zone from HTL.	Only green fencing permitted, no barbed wire fencing allowed.	Allows green and barbed wire fencing.

* * *

According to the Union of India, while implementing the main Notification, certain practical difficulties were faced by the concerned authorities. There was a need for having sustainable development of tourism in coastal areas and that amendments were effected after giving due consideration to all relevant issues pertaining to environment protection and balancing of the same with the requirement of development. It has been specifically averred that a Committee headed by Mr. B.B. Vohra was set-up by the Government in response to the need for examining the issues relating to development of tourism and hotel industry in coastal areas and to regulate the same keeping in view the requirements of sustainable development and the fragile coastal ecology. According to the Union of India, the Committee also included three environmentalist members who had expressed their views and that the Government had accepted the recommendations of the Vohra Committee with slight modifications. According to it, there has been no blanket relaxation in any area as alleged and adequate environmental safeguards have been provided in the 1994 Notification.

* * *

The relaxation with regard to [No Development Zone (NDZ)] was sought by the Hotel and Tourism Industry and they desired concession only with regard to 20–30 kms of coastline. By the amended Notification, power had been given to the Central Government to make such relaxation with regard to any part of the 6,000 kms long coastline of India. The Central Government, has, thus, retained the absolute power of relaxation of the entire 6,000 kms long coastline and this, in effect, may lead to the causing of serious ecological damage as the said provision gives unbriddled power and does not contain any guidelines as to how or when the power is to be exercised. The said provision is capable of abuse. The Central Government also did not confine the relaxation to the extent as specified by the Vohra Committee. No satisfactory reason has been given by the Union of India as to why it departed from the opinion of the expert Committee and that too in such a manner that the concession which has now been given is far in excess of what was demanded by the Hotel and Tourism Industry.

We, accordingly, hold that the newly added proviso in Annexure III in paragraph 7 sub-paragraph (1) (item i) which gives the Central Government arbitrary, uncanalized and unguided power, the exercise of which may result in serious ecological degradation and may make the NDZ ineffective is ultra vires and is hereby quashed. No suitable reason has been given which can persuade us to hold that the enactment of such a proviso was necessary, in the larger public interest, and the exercise of power under the said proviso will not result in large scale ecological degradation and violation of Article 21 of the citizens living in those areas.* * *

Even the Vohra Committee which had been set-up to look into the demands of Hotel and Tourism Industry had not made such a proposal and, therefore, it appears to us that ... a reduction [to 50 metres] does not appear to been made for any valid reason and is arbitrary. This is more so when it has been alleged that in some areas like Goa, there are mangrove forests that need protection and which stretch to more than 100 metres from the river bank and this contention has not been denied. In the absence of any justification for this reduction being given the only conclusion which can be arrived at is that the relaxation to 50 metres has been done for some extraneous reason.* * * In the absence of a categorical statement being made in an affidavit that such reduction will not be harmful or result in serious ecological imbalance, we are unable to conclude that the said amendment has been made in the larger public interest and is valid. This amendment is, therefore, contrary to the object of the Environment Act and has not been made for any valid reason and is, therefore, held to be illegal.

* * *

We do not see any illegality having been committed by allowing the goal posts, net posts and lamp posts to be erected. In fact the erection of these would facilitate or lead to more enjoyment of the beaches. Therefore, the challenge to this amendment fails.

* * *

We, therefore, modify the amendment and direct that a private owner of land in NDZ shall be entitled to take into account half of such land for the purpose of permissible—FSI in respect of the construction undertaken by him outside the NDZ.

* * *

The primary effort of the Court, while dealing with the environmental related issues, is to see that the enforcement agencies, whether it be the state or any other authority, take effective steps for the enforcement of the laws. The Courts, in a way, act as the guardian of the people's fundamental rights but in regard to many technical matters, the Courts may not be fully equipped. Perforce, it has to rely on outside agencies for reports and recommendations whereupon orders have been passed from time to time. Even though, it is not the function of the Court to see the day to day enforcement of the law, that being the function of the Executive, but because of the non-functioning of the enforcement agencies, the Courts as of necessity have had to pass orders directing the enforcement agencies to implement the law.

* * *

With the increasing threat to the environmental degradation taking place in different parts of the country, it may not be possible for any single authority to effectively control the same. Environmental degradation is best protected by the people themselves. In this connection, some of the non-governmental organisations (NGOs) and other environmentalists are doing singular service. Time has perhaps come when the Government can usefully draw upon the resources of such NGOs to help and assist in the implementation of the laws relating to protection of environment. Under section 3 of the Act, the Central Government has the power to constitute one or more authorities for the purposes of exercising and performing such powers and functions, including the power to issue directions under section 5 of the Act of the Central Government as may be delegated to them.

* * *

NOTES AND QUESTIONS

1. In the two final paragraphs excerpted above, the court seems to sense that it is on the horns of a dilemma: It does not want to intrude on executive functions, and, indeed, recognizes that it lacks the resources to do so. At the same time, as 'the guardian of the people's fundamental rights', it needs 'to pass orders directing the enforcement agencies to implement the law.' But what can courts do when enforcement agencies flout court orders? Can NGOs be expected to step into this breach?

2. Conventionally, the role of the High Courts and the Supreme Court was limited to striking down invalid portions of delegated legislation. In this case, the Supreme Court went further, and where it considered appropriate, it modified the subordinate legislation by introducing beneficial provisions. Merely striking down the illegal amendments would have left a gap in the CRZ Regulations. What are the limits to this jurisdiction? What may happen if the High Courts went about 'modifying' regulations to cure the offending provision of the ultra vires effect?

3. In November 1998, more than two and a half years after the judgment, the MEF constituted National and State Coastal Zone Management Authorities, in response to the suggestion made by the Supreme Court. In one significant respect the suggestion of the court was ignored. In constituting the state authorities, the MEF did not draw on the expertise of NGOs and environmentalists.

4. The CRZ Regulations extend along rivers, creeks and backwaters that are affected by tidal action. In Goa, tidal action affects all the principal rivers, including the Zuari, the Mandovi and their tributaries. Tidal influence extends several kilometres up-stream from the mouth of these rivers. As a result, waterfront development is severely restricted on extensive stretches of riparian property. A similar situation arises along the backwaters of Kerala. Should these regions be exempted from the rigours of the CRZ notification?

The *Shrimp Culture Case* is the second important Supreme Court judgment on coastal ecology. The decision is controversial and an array of political and economic interests have joined hands to thwart effective implementation of the judicial orders. The case raised several complicated questions of fact and law, and involved intricate technical issues mixed with policy considerations. Shrimp farms along the coast were causing severe environmental degradation. The farms depleted drinking water supplies, caused salinisation, resulted in mangrove destruction, infringed the rights of traditional fisherfolk and damaged wetlands. Shrimp farming also earned foreign exchange for the country from the export of marine products and received strong government backing due to the economic benefits. Aquaculture projects appear to have benefited poor coastal communities that had invested in the shrimp farms by providing employment and income.

On 27 March 1995 the Supreme Court directed the National Environment Engineering Research Institute (NEERI) to visit coastal areas of Andhra Pradesh and Tamil Nadu and report on the prawn farms being set up. NEERI's assignment was later expanded to cover the other coastal states. Concerned at the severe degradation described in NEERI's reports, on 9 May 1995 the Supreme Court directed 'no part of agricultural lands and salt farms be converted into commercial aquaculture farms' and 'no groundwater withdrawal be allowed for aquaculture purposes.' The authorities were restrained from permitting new aquaculture farms from being set up and the local collectors and police superintendents were told to ensure strict enforcement of the interim directions. In August, 1995 the Supreme Court directed the coastal states and union territories as well as the Marine Products Export Development Authority (MPEDA) to issue individual notices of the case to the aqua-farms, to enable them to appear before the court.

In the judgment, the court relied on a paper prepared by Dr. Alagarswami,

Director of the Central Institute of Brackishwater Aquaculture, Madras (Alagarswami report), the NEERI reports and a report prepared by the Justice Suresh Committee which had visited several shrimp farms in Tamil Nadu and Pondicherry in July, 1995. We carry a short excerpt from this lengthy judgment.

S. JAGANNATH v UNION OF INDIA
AIR 1997 SC 811

KULDIP SINGH, J:

Shrimp (Prawn) Culture Industry is taking roots in India. Since long the fishermen in India have been following the traditional rice/shrimp rotating aquaculture system. Rice is grown during part of the year and shrimp and other fish species are cultured during the rest of the year. However, during the last decade the traditional system which, apart from producing rice, produced 140 kgs. of shrimp per hectare of land began to give way to more intensive methods of shrimp culture which could produce thousands of kilograms per hectare. A large number of private companies and multinational corporations have started investing in shrimp farms. In the last few years more than eighty thousand hectares of land have been converted to shrimp farming. India's marine export weighed in at 70,000 tonnes in 1993 and these exports are projected to reach 200 thousand tonnes by the year 2000. The shrimp farming advocates regard aquaculture as potential saviour of developing countries because it is a short duration crop that provides a high investment return and enjoys an expanding market. The said expectation is sought to be achieved by replacing the environmentally benign traditional mode of culture by semi-intensive and intensive methods. More and more areas are being brought under semi-intensive and intensive modes of shrimp farming. The environmental impact of shrimp culture essentially depends on the mode of culture adopted in the shrimp farming. Indeed, the new trend of more intensified shrimp farming in certain parts of the country—without much control of feeds, seeds and other inputs and water management practices—has brought to the fore a serious threat to the environment and ecology which has been highlighted before us.

This petition under Art. 32 of the Constitution of India—in public interest—has been filed by S. Jagannathan, Chairman, Gram Swaraj Movement, a voluntary organisation working for the upliftment of the weaker section of society. The petitioner has sought the enforcement of Coastal Zone Regulation Notification dated 19 February 1991 issued by the Government of India, stoppage of intensive and semi-intensive types of prawn farming in the ecologically fragile coastal areas, prohibition from using the waste lands/wet lands for prawn farming and the constitution of National Coastal Management Authority to safeguard the marine life and coastal areas.

* * *

Shri M.C. Mehta, learned counsel for the petitioner has taken us through the NEERI reports and other voluminous material on the record. He has vehemently contended that the modern—other than traditional—techniques of shrimp farming are highly polluting and are detrimental to the coastal environment and marine ecology.

According to him only the traditional and improved traditional systems of shrimp farming which are environmentally friendly should be permitted. Mr. Mehta has taken us through the Notification dated 19 February 1991 issued by the Government of India under S.3 of the Environment (Protection) Act, 1986 (the Act) (CRZ Notification) and has vehemently contended that setting up of shrimp farms on the coastal stretches of seas, bays, esturaries, creeks, rivers and backwaters up to 500 meters from the High Tide Line (HTL) and the HTL is totally prohibited under Para 2 of the said notification. The relevant part of the notification is as under:

'Prohibited Activities:

The following activities are declared as prohibited within the Coastal Regulations Zone, namely:

(i) Setting up of new industries and expansion of existing industries, except those directly related to water front or directly needing foreshore facilities;

(ii) Manufacture or handling or storage or disposal of hazardous substances as specified in the Notifications of the Government of India in the Ministry of Environment and Forests No. S.0.594 (E) dated 28 July 1989, S.O. 966(E) dated 27 November 1989 and GSR 1037 (E) dated 5 December 1989;

(iii) Setting up and expansion of fish processing units including warehousing (excluding hatchery and natural fish drying in permitted areas);* * *

(v) Discharge of untreated wastes and effluent from industries, cities or towns and other settlements. Schemes shall be implemented by the concerned authorities phasing out the existing practices, if any, within a reasonable time period not exceeding three years from the date of this notification;* * *

(viii) Land reclamation, bunding or disturbing natural course of sea water with similar obstructions, except those required for control of coastal erosion and maintenance or clearing of waterways, channels and ports and for prevention of sandbars and also except for tidal regulators, storm water drains and structures for prevention of salinity increase and for sweet water recharge;* * *

(x) Harvesting or drawal of ground water and construction of mechanisms therefore within 200 m of HTL; in the 200 m to 500 m zone it shall be permitted only when one manually through ordinary wells for draining, horticulture, agriculture and fisheries. ...'

According to Mr. Mehta the shrimp culture industry is neither 'directly related to water front' nor 'directly needing foreshore facility' and as such is a prohibited activity under Para 20(i) of the CRZ Notification. [Counsel for some of the respondents] on the other hand has argued that a shrimp farm is an industry which is directly related to water front and cannot exist without foreshore facilities. Relying upon Oxford English Dictionary, [he] contended that 'water front' means land abutting on the sea, that part of a town which fronts on a body of water. According to him 'foreshore' in terms of the said dictionary means the part of the shore that lies between the High Tide and the Low Tide. According to Webster Comprehensive Dictionary, International Edition the expression 'foreshore' means 'that part of a shore uncovered at low tide'.

It is, thus, clear that the part of the shore which remains covered with water at the High Tide and gets uncovered and become visible at the Low Tide is called 'foreshore'. It is not possible to set up a shrimp culture farm in the said area because it would completely submerge in water at the High Tide. It is, therefore, obvious that foreshore facilities are neither directly nor indirectly needed in the setting up of a shrimp farm. So far as 'water front' is concerned it is no doubt correct that a shrimp farm may have some relation to the water front in the sense that the farm is dependent on brackish water which can be drawn from the sea. But on a close scrutiny, we are of the view that shrimp culture farming has no relation or connection with the 'water front' though it has relation with brackish water which is available from various water-bodies including sea. What is required is the 'brackish water' and not the 'water front'. The material on record shows that the shrimp ponds constructed by the farm draw water from the sea by pipes, etc. It is not the 'water front' which is needed by the industry, what is required is the brackish water which can be drawn from any source including sea and carried to any distance by pipes etc. The purpose of CRZ Notification is to protect the ecologically fragile coastal areas and to safeguard the aesthetic qualities and uses of the sea coast. The setting up of modern shrimp aquaculture farms right on the sea coast and construction of ponds and other infrastructure thereon is per se hazardous and is bound to degrade the marine ecology, coastal environment and the aesthetic uses of the sea coast.

* * *

It is thus obvious that an industry dependent on sea water cannot by itself be an industry 'directly related to water front' or 'directly needing foreshore facilities'. The shrimp culture industry, therefore, cannot be permitted to be set up anywhere in the coastal regulation zone under the CRZ Notification.

We may examine the issue from another angle. Sea coast and beaches are a gift of nature to mankind. The aesthetic qualities and recreational utility of the said area has to be maintained. Any activity which has the effect of degrading the environment cannot be permitted. Apart from that the right of the fishermen and farmers living in the coastal areas to eke their living by way of fishing and farming cannot be denied to them. Alagarswami report states that 'the shrimp farms do not provide access to the beach for traditional fishermen who have to reach the sea from their villages. As farms are located and entry is restricted the fishermen have to take a longer route to the sea for their operation. This is being objected by traditional fishermen.'

The Alagarswami report further highlights the drinking water problem, salinization and destruction of mangrove by the shrimp culture industry. The relevant paragraphs have already been quoted above. The increase of stocking densities, heavy inputs of high energy feeds, use of drugs and chemicals result in the discharge of highly polluted effluent into the sea, creeks etc. and on the sea coast by the shrimp farms. It is, therefore, not possible to agree with [counsel for the respondents] that commercial shrimp farming has no adverse effect on environment and coastal ecology.

* * *

Under Para 2 of the CRZ notification, the activities listed thereunder are declared as prohibited activities. Various state governments have enacted coastal acquaculture legislations regulating the industries set up in the coastal areas. It was argued before us that certain provisions of the State legislations including that of the state of Tamil Nadu are not in consonance with the CRZ notification issued by the Government of India under Section 3(3) of the Act. Assuming that is so, we are of the view that the Act being a Central legislation has the overriding effect. The Act (the Environment Protection Act, 1986) has been enacted under Entry 13 of List I Schedule VII of the Constitution of India. The said entry is as under:-

Participation in international conferences, associations and other bodies and implementing of decisions made thereat.

The preamble to the Act clearly states that it was enacted to implement the decisions taken at the United Nations Conference on the Human Environment held at Stockholm in June 1972. The Parliament has enacted the Act under Entry 13 of List 1 Schedule VII read with Article 253 of the Constitution of India. The CRZ notification having been issued under the Act shall have overriding effect and shall prevail over the law made by the legislatures of the states.

* * *

We are of the view that before any shrimp industry or shrimp pond is permitted to be installed in the ... fragile coastal area it must pass through a strict environmental test. There had to be a high powered 'Authority' under the Act to scrutinize each and every case from the environmental point on view. There must be an environmental impact assessment before permission is granted to install commercial shrimp farms. The conceptual framework of the assessment must be broad-based primarily concerning environmental degradation linked with shrimp farming. The assessment must also include the social impact on different population strata in the area. The quality of the assessment must be analytically based on superior technology. It must take into consideration the inter-generational equity and the compensation for those who are affected and prejudiced.

Before parting with this judgment we may notice the 'Dollar' based argument advanced before us. It was contended before us by the learned counsel appearing for the shrimp acquaculture industry that the industry has achieved singular distinction by earning maximum foreign exchange in the country. Almost 100 per cent of the produce is exported to America, Europe and Japan and as such the industry has a large potential to earn 'Dollars'. That may be so but the farm-raised production of shrimp is much lesser than the wild caught production. * * *

It is obvious from the [United Nations] figures quoted above that farm raised production of shrimp is of very small quantity as compared to wild-caught. Even if some of the shrimp culture farms which are polluting the environment, are closed, the production of shrimp by environmentally friendly techniques would not be affected and there may not be any loss to the economy specially in view of the finding given by NEERI that the damage caused to ecology and economies by the acquaculture farming is higher than the earnings from the same of coastal acquaculture produce. That may be the reason for the European and American countries for not permitting their sea-coasts to be exploited for shrimp-culture farming. The UN report shows that 80 per cent of the farm cultured shrimp comes from the developing countries of Asia.

* * *

NOTES AND QUESTIONS

1. The Supreme Court Bench headed by Justice Kuldip Singh issued a range of mandatory injunctions and remedial directions. The Union Government was directed to establish a coastal authority under section 3(3) of the EPA, to be headed by a retired judge of a High Court. The authority was required to 'deal with the situation created by the shrimp culture industry', with power to issue remedial directions consistent with the precautionary principle and the polluter pays principle. The shrimp culture industry was prohibited in the coastal zone and existing farms were directed to be demolished. Special protective and remedial orders were issued in respect of Chilka Lake, Orissa and Pulicat Lake, Tamil Nadu. The workers rendered unemployed by the order of the court were awarded compensation, payable by the aqua-farm owners. Farmers operating traditional systems of shrimp cultivation were permitted to adopt improved technology to increase their yield.

2. The judgment met with stiff resistance from the Centre and the states. To overcome the decision, the Aquaculture Authority Bill of 1997 was introduced in Parliament 'to provide for the establishment of an Aquaculture Authority for regulating the activities connected with aquaculture in the *coastal* areas.' The Bill aimed at amending the CRZ Regulations with retrospective effect, by excluding shrimp farming from its purview.[32]

3. Shortly after Justice Kuldip Singh retired, review petitions were filed before the court. On 30 July 1997 a bench comprising Justices S.C. Sen and S. Saghir Ahmed referred the matter to a large bench, directed that the matter be heard 'with utmost expedition' and in the meanwhile stayed demolition of the aqua-farms.[33] In August, 1997, Justice A.S. Anand joined the other two judges and heard the matters in part. They directed the court registry to list the case on an appropriate day. The stay on the demolition was continued.[34] In December, 1997 Justice Sen retired, leaving the review cases unfinished.[35]

---

[32] A.K. Ganguli, *In Public Interest: A Review of PIL in the Supreme Court* in SUPREME COURT ON PUBLIC INTEREST LITIGATION A1, A15 (J. Kapur ed. Vol.I, 1998).

[33] 1997 (5) SCALE 406.

[34] 1997 (6) SCALE 7 (SP).

[35] At the time of writing, the review petitions are pending.

4. One of the review petitions filed before the Supreme Court alleged that the NEERI reports were unreliable. They questioned NEERI's competence, since the institute had earlier submitted a detailed report to a government undertaking where it encouraged the setting up of shrimp farms.[36]

Since the pollution control boards have proved unreliable, the Supreme Court has turned to NEERI on numerous occasions. What standards of disclosure apply to NEERI before accepting such assignments? So long as NEERI continues to act as a consultant to industry, should it accept these assignments? Is it time to look for other expert bodies in the field? Will they not suffer from a similar institutional bias?

5. In a part of the judgment which is not excerpted, the Supreme Court prohibited 'extensive, modified-extensive, semi-intensive and intensive' shrimp farm technologies. Were the respondents justified in resisting judicial intervention on the ground that the case involved difficult technical and economic policy issues apart from raising disputed questions of fact on the impact of aqua-farms?

6. There is a tradition in common law countries to construe laws strictly, and to base their violation on the narrowest possible grounds. In the above case, the court could have followed that tradition by holding that the CRZ notification was violated by the shrimp culture industry. Instead, the court went far afield, delving into inter-generational equity, the Stockholm Conference on the Human Environment (1972), the economies of shrimp farming and its impact on the country's foreign exchange. Is this good judicial reasoning? Is it sound jurisprudence?

7. In concluding that aquaculture was prohibited in the CRZ, the court interpreted the expression 'foreshore' to mean that part of a shore uncovered at low tide. Another popular meaning of foreshore is 'the part of the shore that lies just above the high-water mark.'[37] Would this interpretation have affected the outcome of the case?

8. The disputes between traditional fisherfolk, non-fishermen and the prawn culture industry around Chilka Lake were the subject of a division bench judgment of the Orissa High Court.[38] The court held that the state could not encourage intensive prawn culture to earn 'prawn-dollars' at the cost of the environment. The High Court modified the government policy on Chilka in an attempt to curb the 'mafia raj' that had gripped Chilka after the advent of the aquaculture industry. Though the Orissa High Court judgment deals with aquaculture issue in detail, the Supreme Court makes no reference to it in the *Shrimp Culture Case*.

9. Shortly after the principal judgment in the *Shrimp Culture Case*, three shrimp farm owners petitioned the Supreme Court under Article 32 of the Constitution, claiming that the decision rendered was not binding upon them. The petitioners submitted that since they were neither parties nor had the procedure under Order I, rule 8 of the Code of Civil Procedure (relating to class actions) been

---

[36] A.K. Ganguli, *supra* note 32.

[37] *Collins Dictionary of English Language* (1991).

[38] *Kholamuhana Primary Fisherman Co-op. Soc. v State of Orissa* AIR 1994 ORI 191.

followed, the directions issued by the court would not apply to their farms. The Supreme Court dismissed the petitions at the threshold, holding that the *Shrimp Culture Case* had received very wide publicity over a span of two years during which it was heard. The judges found it difficult to accept the petitioners' claim that they were unaware of the proceedings or the investigations and reports made by various authorities. The court held that the principles of Order I, rule 8 would not apply to public interest litigations since that would enable a few persons to rob the judgment of its efficacy by claiming that they were not parties and that the case should be heard again. The Supreme Court also refused to examine the merits of the petitioners' contention that the CRZ notification was ultra vires the Environment (Protection) Act of 1986 and the fundamental rights guaranteed under the Constitution.[39]

The next case arose on a remit by the Supreme Court. It pits citizens seeking strict enforcement of the CRZ Regulations against the Kerala government's project to connect the islands in the Cochin backwaters.

JACOB VADAKKANCHERRY v STATE OF KERALA
AIR 1998 KER 114

THULASIDAS, J.:

By Notification dt. 19–5–1991 issued in exercise of the powers conferred by sub-section (1) section 53-A of the Town Planning Act, the Government of Kerala constituted a Special Authority called 'Goshree Islands Development Authority' for the integrated development of the Vypeen, Bolgatty, Vallarpadam, Mulavukad, Thanthonnithuruthu and Kadamakudy islands within the Cochin Port limits. ... These islands are in Cochin backwaters, whose inhabitants will have to depend upon the main land for their basic needs and livelihood. The islanders have been agitating for a long time for constructing bridges to connect the islands with the main land. ... Though successive Governments felt the need to link the islands with the main land with bridges, nothing was done on account of financial constraints. The issue however became a matter of concern and the Government responded by constituting the Goshree Islands Development Authority as a self-financing project. As originally conceived it envisaged reclamation of 250 hectare of land during Phase I at two locations around Thanthonnithuruthu and Bolgatty Islands and construction of four bridges connecting the main land and the four islands, viz. Thanthonnithuruthu, Vallarpadam, Bolgatty and Vypeen and also envisaged reclamation of 110 hectare of land around Vallarpadam in Phase II. Infrastructural facilities over the reclamation of land were

---

[39] *Gopi Aqua Farms v Union of India* AIR 1997 SC 3519.

also proposed. The estimated cost of Rs. 520 crores was to be met by selling the reclaimed land in public auction for commercial purposes. The project was given environmental clearance by the Ministry for Environment and Forests, Government of India on 10–5–1995 subject to certain conditions. A No Objection Certificate was also given by the Kerala State Pollution Control Board on 5–4–1995. Sidco Ltd., Bombay was entrusted with the designing of the bridges. The project, however, ran into rough weather. Several scientific bodies and environmental scientists voiced their objections that received wide coverage in the media. Support to the project too came, but not in good measure. NEERI, which examined the project as directed by the Supreme Court, found it to suffer from several drawbacks. The report said that it was not environmentally viable, is bound to cause shrinkage of backwaters, affect its hydrological features, upset the acquatic ecology, and impair the life supporting systems of the most vulnerable population in the region violating the premises and pre-conditions for sustainable development.

* * *

[M]any of the findings and observations in the report, it was said, did not represent a correct appraisal of all that was relevant and material. There was also an allegation that it was either misinformed or was deeply committed to canvass its own views on the environmental and ecological matters, which are far off from ground realities. We do not wish to say upon the merits or otherwise of the objections, since the report is with respect to the project as originally envisaged that has now been given up for the one that would only require reclamation of 25 hectare of land abutting the sea wall in a continuous stretch from the existing Marine Drive. The number of bridges has been reduced to three and the estimated cost also brought down to Rs. 52 crores. In other words, the project profile is substantially different from the original one that therefore it seems to be not necessary to examine the report of the NEERI in detail. We are however unable to agree that the project as conceived and given shape to was without the necessary indepth study of the various aspects by competent scientists and scientific bodies.

* * *

As already stated, the new project would involve reclamation of 25 hectare near the Marine Drive and it was submitted that the entire water front abutting it, where reclamation is to be made, is retained by a rubble wall, as a result of which when the tides recede no land is exposed. It was said that high tide and low tide lines would both practically coincide as the water level against the rubble wall will merely go down to a lower level without touching the bed of the backwaters and therefore the land to be reclaimed would be outside the CRZ. Indeed it was not brought to our notice that there was a demarcation of HTL. ... Taking all aspects of the matter into account, we find it difficult to hold prima facie that the land proposed to be reclaimed will fall within the CRZ. ... Serious impairment to aquatic resources, ecology and environment are unlikely to result by reclamation of a small strip of land along the existing Marine Drive, that would not also involve violation of CRZ Regulations. The apprehensions, difficulties and dangers have been magnified out of proportion, that we do not wish to countenance, having regard to the public purpose the project will subserve. We are of the view that the objection to the reclamation of 25 hectare of land on the grounds stated do not deserve to be upheld.

* * *

We should however remind the Government that it is its duty to ensure that the islanders are provided basic infrastructural facilities and amenities and that their demand for bridges across the backwaters can ill-afford to be ignored, postponed or delayed. We do not doubt the bona fides of the Government, that has happily shed its lukewarm attitude and became more responsive. We agree that it was on account of sheer financial and other constraints and for no other external reasons that it decided that the project be implemented with resources of its own. The concept of self-financing is nothing new and has been widely accepted.

Though we do not prohibit reclamation of 25 hectare of land, we should put a caveat that it should be resorted to only after all attempts to implement the Project otherwise than by reclamation have failed to materialise. Indeed several agencies had come forward with their proposals, that should receive serious consideration by the Government.

* * *

NOTES AND QUESTIONS

1. At times, the overwhelming necessity for basic infrastructure may influence judges to discount ecological concerns. The full bench of the Kerala High Court that heard the case seemed anxious to permit the development project to proceed without further delay. It held that the proposed reclamation was not covered by the CRZ Regulations. In the operative part of the judgment, the court directed the state to commence work within two months. The Kerala High Court's approach was similar to the one adopted by the Bombay High Court while permitting the Konkan Railway Project. The Bombay High Court held that the CRZ notification did not apply to railways that travelled over bridges that spanned rivers, creeks or seas. 'The rail line or a public road is provided for access to the public to the seas, bays, estuaries, creeks and backwaters and either a public road or a rail line is not a construction which demands clearance.'[40]

2. The Kerala judgment exposes a lacuna in the CRZ regime. The High Court

[40] *Goa Foundation v Konkan Railway Corporation* AIR 1992 BOM 471, 476.

interpreted the notification strictly to cover the inter-tidal zone, but not stretches of the coast that are continuously submerged both during high tide and low tide. The High Court's interpretation enables unrestricted reclamation of the sea so long as the area reclaimed is not exposed during low tide. The upshot of this judgment is that reclamation may be undertaken where the sea is held back by a retaining wall or along a cliffy coast where no land is exposed during the low tide. Reclamation of the land just a few yards beyond the LTL towards the sea, is not covered by the CRZ Regulations.

3. Niyamavedi, a public spirited organization active in Kerala, petitioned the High Court in 1996 against the indiscriminate dumping of Ammonium Per Chlorate (APC), into the sea around Cochin. APC, a toxic substance, was generated by the Vikram Sarabhai Space Centre (VSSC), in the course of building rockets for space exploration. VSSC conceded that previous efforts to dispose APC into trenches in the plant premises had led to complaints from local residents, but claimed that disposal in the sea was 'the safest and most harmless [method of disposal] as it does not cause ... any damage to the mainland or inland water streams unlike ... other industries.' The respondents urged the High Court not to stall production since APC was required as an oxidiser for rocket propellants and any delay would upset the space programme. Moreover, APC was capable of being used to manufacture explosives and could be misused 'for anti-national purposes by unscrupulous persons'. Since the APC was being disposed in the sea, the respondents claimed that it was not necessary to secure the consent of the Kerala State Pollution Control Board (KSPCB).

Justice K. A. Abdul Gafoor had no trouble rejecting the respondents' defences. He held that VSSC was obliged to secure a valid consent from KSPCB and until an appropriate consent was issued, he restrained the Centre from disposing the effluent in the sea. The board was directed to pass final orders on VSSC's consent application within six weeks. In the event of the consent being granted, VSSC was ordered to alert the Coast Guard regarding the date and time of disposal on every occasion so that the coastal waters around Cochin were protected.[41]

4. The residents of Valmiki Nagar, Madras challenged a nearby housing project of the Tamil Nadu Housing Board on the ground that the development violated the CRZ Regulations. The impugned project comprised four buildings that were being constructed at a distance between 210 m to 370 m from the HTL. The petitioners argued that since the project investment exceeded Rs. 5 crores, clearance from the Union Ministry of Environment and Forests (MEF) under clause 3 (2)(iv) though mandatory, had not been obtained. Moreover, the petitioners sought a mandamus restraining construction on the ground that the applicable norm for urban areas— that no building shall be permitted on the seaward side of an existing road or on the seaward side of existing authorized structures—was breached.

Rejecting the writ petition, a division bench of the Madras High Court held that the requirement in clause 3(2)(iv) of the Regulations pertaining to clearance from

---

[41] *Niyamavedi v Chairman*, Pollution Control Board, O.P.No. 2553 of 1996, 21 May 1997.

the MEF should be read ejusdem generis (as being the same kind or class) with the preceding sub-paragraphs. Applying this principle of interpretation, the requirement for clearance from the MEF did not apply to the construction of residential buildings but was restricted to other projects in the nature of those enumerated in the earlier sub-clauses. The court also accepted the respondent's plea that since the housing project comprised four separate developments in respect of which four separate contracts had been awarded, it was wrong to club the value of all the works for the purpose of deciding whether the project cost exceeded Rs.5 crores. Individually, the contracts were within the monetary limit prescribed.

Surveying the extent of development in the neighbouring areas, the division bench found that there were well formed roads near the sea line both to the north-east and south-east of the plots under development. The disputed area was surrounded on three sides by built up areas where buildings had been constructed nearer to the seashore than the impugned structures. The High Court held:

> The fact that there are structures and roads on the north-east and south-east, is not in dispute. Nor is it disputed that Valmiki Nagar and Teachers' Colony are developed areas provided with all infrastructural facilities. Hence, the contention that because there is no existing structure or existing road directly in between the impugned construction and the sea, the norm prescribed in the government notification is violated, is without any substance. The norm cannot be tested with reference to each building situated on the seashore. That is why, the definition of Category—II uses the expressions 'area' and 'developed area'. Once it is seen that the area is a developed one and there are buildings and roads in the said area which are nearer to the sea than the impugned constructions, there can be no doubt whatever that the impugned constructions are situated on the landward side of the existing roads and structures and thus the norm prescribed in the notification is fully satisfied. We have no hesitation to reject the contention urged on behalf of the petitioners that the norm is violated.[42]

On 12 February 1998, the Supreme Court rejected a special leave petition seeking to assail the Madras High Court judgment. 'However, we make it clear that the questions of law argued and decided by the High Court are left open to be decided in an appropriate case by this Court. Findings of the High Court on facts are restricted to the special facts of these cases.'[43] Does the Supreme Court order denude the precedential value of the division bench judgment?

On 27 March 1998, in the context of Maharashtra's CZMP, the MEF wrote to the state explaining that in CRZ-II areas 'construction of buildings can be permitted on the landward side of the imaginary line drawn along the existing authorized

---

[42] K.V. Ramanathan v State of Tamil Nadu Writ Appeal No. 1287 of 1995 and Writ Petition No. 5971 of 1995, 14 December 1995.

[43] K.V. Ramanathan v State of Tamil Nadu SLP (Civil) Nos. 13463–64 / 96.

structures.'[44] On 8 September 1998, in another letter the MEF explained that the imaginary line would run parallel to the HTL; and that it would connect existing authorised structures on the adjoining plots.[45] Is this an attempt to defeat or revive the Madras High Court judgment?

5. The Bombay Municipal Corporation's effort to build a toilet block near the Gateway of India, irked Dr. P. Navin Kumar and the Indian Heritage Society. Rejecting the petitions, the High Court held that the CRZ notification did not prohibit the impugned activity.[46] In the course of its judgment, the High Court observed that the entire city of Bombay would fall within the ambit of CRZ-II and that once an area was covered under CRZ-II, it would not be covered by CRZ-I. In special leave petitions filed against the High Court judgment, the Supreme Court clarified: 'We do not think that it is anybody's case that whole of Mumbai would fall within the ambit of CRZ-II. Observations of the High Court that entire city of Mumbai would fall within the ambit of CRZ-II do not appear to be warranted.'[47] The judgment of the Supreme Court records that the petitioners gave up their challenge to the construction of the toilet block and were restricting their grievance to the High Court's observations that would adversely affect several other pending cases.

6. In *Sneha Mandal Co-op. Hsg. Soc. Ltd. v Union of India*,[48] a division bench of the Bombay High Court struck a balance between environmental concerns and development pressures. Here, the residents of Cuffe Parade, Bombay challenged the coastal location of a bulk receiving station and helipad owned by the Tata Electric Companies (TEC). The petitioners also assailed the change of land use on two plots in the locality that were reserved for a garden / playground but had been changed to government housing. All the plots abutted the coast.

In a lengthy judgment, the High Court referred to the mammoth reclamation programmes over two centuries that had transformed the local geography from seven islands into a single strip of land on which the metropolis stood. The court noticed the Madras High Court judgment in *Ramanathan's Case*[49] and the clarifications issued by the MEF on 27 March 1998 and 8 September 1998.[50] It relied on these letters to confer judicial recognition to the notion of an 'imaginary line', introduced by the MEF in correspondence with the state government. Referring to an authorized electricity sub-station that stood on an adjacent plot and a plan appended to the judgment, the court held: 'The imaginary line from the authorized structure [the sub-station] which is shown in red runs parallel to the High Tide Line. The impugned structure cannot cross the building line shown in red in the Plan. In the facts and

[44] Archives, Bombay Environmental Action Group.
[45] *Id.*
[46] *P. Navin Kumar v Bombay Municipal Corporation* AIR 1997 BOM 342.
[47] *P. Navin Kumar v Bombay Municipal Corporation* AIR 1999 SC 1816.
[48] AIR 2000 BOM 121.
[49] *Supra* notes 42, 43.
[50] Text accompanying *supra* notes 44, 45.

circumstances of the present case, therefore, we are of the view that the impugned proposed structure [bulk receiving station] does not violate the CRZ Notification.' Having regard to the huge costs incurred by TEC in laying electricity cables and the acknowledged need for a bulk receiving station in the locality, the High Court also observed that when two public interests compete, the greater public interest (the need for a bulk receiving station) should prevail. Despite rejecting the challenge to the electricity receiving station, the court accepted the petitioners' case that the helipad and change of user violated the CRZ notification.

7. Tourism is projected to grow rapidly in the coming decades. Though the surge in world tourism has so far bypassed India, the employment potential and economic benefits from this industry are likely to spur domestic growth in the near term. Equations is a non-governmental organization committed to growth through developing equitable tourism options. Hari Babu of Equations is concerned that vast tracts of the western coast are thoughtlessly being designated as 'special tourism areas' (STAs), where the states are encouraging the construction of hotels and resorts by extending concessions and financial benefits to promoters. One glaring instance is an unbroken 500 km. stretch of coastline extending from the Sindhudurg district in Maharashtra and running south through Goa and Karnataka upto Bekal in Kerala.[51] According to Hari Babu no impact studies preceded the designation of this STA.

The Goa Foundation on numerous occasions has petitioned the Bombay High Court against CRZ breaches by hoteliers. Their principal cases are digested in a citizens' report published in 1993.[52] The Goa Foundation has endeavoured to strictly enforce the 200 m 'no-development zone' in CRZ-III areas; extend CRZ compliance along Goa's rivers that are affected by tidal action; restrict building activity to 'dwelling units ... within the ambit of traditional rights and customary uses'; and freeze coastal development at the level of twice the number of dwelling units that existed in each coastal village in February 1991 when the regulations were enacted. At the time of writing, several petitions on these issues were pending in the High Court.

8. In *Raja Shiv Chhatrapati Cooperative Housing Society Ltd. v MHADA*,[53] the Bombay High Court held that in view of section 24 of the Environment (Protection) Act of 1986, the CRZ Regulations would override the local town planning regulations.

B. WETLANDS

Wetlands are bogs, swamps and marshes. They provide numerous ecosystem services including water purification, maintaining surface moisture, curbing soil erosion, reducing the impact of floods and droughts and re-charging wells. Wetlands support a host of wildlife such as birds, fish, reptiles, amphibians and insects. There is no specific

[51] Interview with Hari Babu, Equations; 23 April 1999. Conducted by S. Divan.
[52] C. Alvares, *supra* note 1 at 170–195.
[53] Writ Petition 442 of 1999, 17 August 1999.

statute regulating wetland use or conversion, leaving the field open to judicial control on a case to case basis. The pioneering judgment in this field was delivered by Justice Umesh Chandra Banerjee of the Calcutta High Court, who responded to a petition filed by PUBLIC, a citizens' group concerned about the rapid dredging and filling of the marshes near Calcutta.

PEOPLE UNITED FOR BETTER LIVING IN CALCUTTA v STATE OF WEST BENGAL
AIR 1993 CAL 215

ORDER: * * *

Turning attention on to the Calcutta wetlands we find that there are 40 species of algae and 2 species of fern, 7 species of monocods and 21 species of dicods. Latest datas suggest the presence of about 155 species of summer birds of which 64 species are resident birds and 91 are migratory. There are 90 species of winter birds of which 44 are residents and 46 are migratory. These migratory birds are mainly from Siberia and East Europe and they arrive at the city through Trans-Asia Migration Route. Admittedly, Calcutta has had around 20,000 acres approximately of wetland area, of which 10,000 acres have already been reclaimed and the sprawling metropolis under the name of Salt Lake City being a satellite township area of Calcutta exists, and the East Calcutta wetlands now therefore comprises of around 9,000 and odd hundred acres approximately on the eastern fringe of the city with a natural slope from the west to the east. The entire area comprises of low lands characterized by marshes and ponds etc. As regards the soil, there is no manner of doubt that it has very high moisture content of a mixed clay and alluvium type. On the issue of hydrology, the entire waste and drainage (sewer) water of Calcutta runs through a system of main and ancillary channels going through the wetlands; these flows are channelised into the sewage-fed fisheries for pisciculture and the wetlands purify the entire waste water through a natural process of oxidation, radiation, biological breakdown of organic wastes and pisciculture.

* * *

Calcutta wetlands presents a unique eco-system apart from the material benefit to the society at large. Within the Calcutta Metropolitan area the Calcutta wetlands can be easily identified as the most outstanding wetland cluster. As already mentioned, these wetlands bear the oldest tradition in the world of resource recovery from city's waste besides being the largest of such systems in the world. They have now become a subject of international interest. Since the beginning of this century, various forms of agriculture and pisciculture have been practised in the region. These wetlands are interdistributory marshes lying between the levee of the river Hugli to the west and of Bidyadhari to the east. The Bidyadhari can now be traced only by its aggraded bed presently under paddy cultivation. It was a tidal channel and the shallow marshes acted as spill basins. Gradually with diversion of city sewage, premature reclamation by building embankments for the then existing salt water fisheries and with silting up of the river, these marshes became stagnant and ceased to be saline. Since then they have become sewage receptacles for the city and with innovative enterprise of local people they have been used as waste water fisheries producing more than 10 quintals of fish per acre per year for the city. These wetlands also store run off from the adjacent areas during the rains, and are traversed by the sewage outfall channels of the city. These channels carry the wastewater eastwards to the Kulti river which eventually falls into the Raimangal which drains into the Bay of Bengal. These wetlands recycle waste water for efficient nutrient recovery, provide fresh fish to the market of Calcutta and employ thousands of rural people over an area of about 7,500 acres.

* * *

Before proceeding further, however, it is to be noted that India is a contracting party to the Ramsar Convention, an Inter Governmental Treaty on Wetlands under which she is obliged to promote the conservation of wetlands habitat in her territory. The Salt Lake Swamp is acknowledged as an important wetland by virtue of its socio-economic and ecological values. As a matter of fact, it is in the Directory of Asian Wetlands and a wetland of international importance—it meets all accepted criteria for identification of an internationally important wetland.

* * *

When considered as an ecosystem, the wetlands are useful for nutrient recovery and cycling, releasing excess nitrogen, inactivation of phosphates, removing toxins, chemicals, heavy metals through absorption by plants, and also in treating waste water. Removal of suspended solids from flowing water by reducing the flow also benefits the retention of water for sometime whereby biological, physical and chemical changes are made possible (Mitsch & Gosselink, 1986). Retention of sediments by wetlands also reduces siltation in the rivers. Wetlands also help in mitigating floods, recharging acquifers and in reducing surface run off and consequent erosion. Mangrove wetlands on India and Bangladesh act as buffers against devastating storms of the Bay of Bengal. Wetlands also influence microclimate of a locality. Besides these, they are also valued for their aesthetic qualities and recreational opportunities. A fresh water wetland checks underground salt water intrusion of an adjacent brackish water environment through interface pressure (US, EPA, 1985).

On a global scale the wetlands function significantly in maintaining air and water quality including nitrogen, sulphur, methane and carbon dioxide cycles.

* * *

There is no manner of doubt, therefore, that wetlands being a bounty of nature do have a significant rule to play in the proper development of the society—be it from environmental perspective or from economic perspective. Pollutionwise this metropolitan city of Calcutta tops the list in the country—can we in this city further endanger the environment by reclaiming the nature's gift to mankind when, in fact, such a reclamation is only for the purpose of expansion of the satellite township on the Eastern fringe of the city of Calcutta. The only developmental project spoken of is the World Trade Centre along with the Public Exhibition Centre which [has] already been dealt with in this order as above and apart therefrom no other developmental project has been spoken of during the course of submission in the matter. If, however, it is said that the reclamation is not for developmental projects, then and in that event, I am of the view that question of further consideration of the matter does not and cannot arise since wetland is precious, wetland ensures the benefit of the society at large and assists mankind to live in a cleaner and purer environment—which in my view, one cannot afford to lose neither the Court of Law can lend assistance to contra-belief or contra-action of a State Agency. Wetland acts as a benefactor to the society and there cannot be any manner of doubt in regard thereto and as such encroachment thereof would be detrimental to the society which the Law Courts cannot permit. This benefit to the society cannot be weighed on mathematical nicety so as to take note of the requirement of the society—what is required today may not be a relevant consideration in the immediate future. Therefore, it cannot really be assessed to what amount nature's bounty is required for the proper maintenance of environmental equilibrium. It cannot be measured in terms of requirement and as such, the Court of Law cannot, in fact, decry the opinion of the environmentalist in that direction. Law Courts exist for the benefit of the society—Law Courts exist for the purpose of giving redress to the society when called for and it must rise above all levels so that justice is meted out and the society thrives thereunder. I do not find any justiciable reason to disagree with the opinion expressed by the environmentalists that wetland should be preserved and no interference or reclamation should be permitted.

It is, however, placed on record that no issue as regards the maintainability of the writ petition or that of locus standi was raised before the Court during the entire course of hearing of the matter and as such I need not delve into the issue.

In that view of the matter, there shall be an order of injunction restraining the State Respondents from reclaiming any further wetland. There shall also be an order of injunction prohibiting the respondents from granting any permission to any person whatsoever for the purpose of changing the use of the land from agricultural to residential or commercial in the area as indicated in the map annexed to the petition and marked with letter 'C'. The State Respondents are further directed to take steps so as to stop private alienation and, if required, by extending the statutory provisions in regard thereto.

* * *

NOTES AND QUESTIONS

1. In this case, the court seems to take notice of the importance of wetlands and relies on that notion to restrain the state from reclaiming any further wetland. Is

there any statutory or common law basis for the judgment? Should a court simply nullify executive action based on its own notion of what is best for society?

2. Does the court's citing of the Ramsar Convention justify its nullification of executive action?

3. On 30 November 1994 Justice Banerjee modified his previous order on an application by the promoters of the World Trade Centre. Reiterating the importance of wetlands and the need to balance development with environment, the court modified the injunction to permit the project.

4. In *Consumer Action Group v Union of India*,[54] the Madras High Court prevented the destruction of wetlands in the Adyar estuary which were being reclaimed to erect a memorial to Dr. Ambedkar. The petitioners complained that while they had no objection to the construction of a memorial, they objected to the wetlands being converted into an auditorium and car park. Allowing the petition, the High Court directed the respondents to restrict construction to the eastern end of the 5 acre plot, restore the rest of the plot to its original condition and refrain from constructing an auditorium. The Madras Metropolitan Development Authority was told to preserve about 45 acres of low lying wetlands and not permit any construction in the area.

C. HERITAGE

India's rich and varied cultural heritage comprises a multitude of buildings and sites that link the present to the past. Due to their artistic or social significance these landmarks require special protection against the pressures of contemporary development and damage from the elements. Article 49 of the Constitution contains a directive principle obliging the state to protect every monument or place or object of artistic or historic interest declared by or under law made by Parliament to be of national importance from spoliation, destruction or removal. Parliament is conferred a corresponding legislative power under Entry 67 of List I, in the Seventh Schedule to the Constitution. The states have power to enact laws to preserve and protect lesser ancient and historical monuments.[55] The Union and the states have concurrent power to legislate on archaeological sites and remains other than those declared by Parliament to be of national importance.[56] The fundamental duty of every citizen under Article 51A (f) 'to value and preserve the rich heritage of our composite culture' may now be discharged by recourse to the writ courts, the Supreme Court having recognized that the right to life would extend to preserving 'the tradition and cultural heritage of the persons concerned.'[57]

These constitutional provisions have enabled Parliament to enact the Ancient

---

[54] 1994 (1) MAD. L.J. REP. 481.

[55] Entry 12, List II, Seventh Schedule.

[56] Entry 40, List III, Seventh Schedule.

[57] *Consumer Education and Research Centre v Union of India* AIR 1995 SC 922, 959.

Monuments and Archaeological Sites and Remains Act of 1958 covering monuments and sites of national importance and the Antiquities and Art Treasures Act of 1972 to prevent the export and smuggling of art treasures. State level laws such as the Maharashtra Ancient Monuments and Archaeological Sites and Remains Act of 1960 complement the national statutes. The Archaeological Survey of India (ASI) is the national agency responsible for preserving, protecting and restoring the nationally important sites. State departments of archaeology are supposed to protect the buildings, monuments and sites recognized under the state law.

Beyond this legislative framework but nevertheless worthy of conservation are a host of buildings, works, relics or places that are of historic, cultural, social, aesthetic or architectural significance. These comprise our environmental 'heritage'. In India, the notion of heritage would extend to natural features of cultural or social significance such as sacred groves, hills, hillocks, water bodies, open areas and wooded areas.

Over the past two decades several non-governmental organizations (NGOs) have worked to protect heritage sites and sensitize planning authorities on the importance of conservation. The role of NGOs in the heritage movement is vital, largely because neither the ASI nor the town planning authorities have displayed much initiative in the field. The Indian National Trust for Art and Cultural Heritage (INTACH) has developed models to preserve historic precincts, among them Chanderi, a weaving town in Madhya Pradesh and the Varanasi Ghats. A.G. Krishna Menon, who worked on these projects for INTACH, argues: 'While in the West, traditional settlements have been more or less destroyed, in India the past is truly a living presence. Indeed, the paradox is that authenticity in the Indian context need not be preserved, it can be continually created today. It is this precious quality that characterizes our living environment and establishes its identity.'[58] The Bombay Environmental Action Group (BEAG) has played a key role in introducing the first heritage regulations in India—The Heritage Regulations for Greater Bombay— framed in 1995 under the Maharashtra Regional and Town Planning Act of 1966. BEAG has also lobbied to extend heritage protection to other cities in Maharashtra, notably Pune, Nashik and Nagpur and the hill station of Mahabaleshwar. The Indian Heritage Society (IHS) is best known for the annual awards it presents for heritage conservation efforts in Bombay. The IHS has assisted the government in identifying heritage buildings and precincts and has petitioned the courts for redress against the despoliation of the urban heritage.

The Bombay Heritage Regulations grade heritage buildings and precincts into three categories based on their importance. Over 600 buildings and conservation areas are enumerated in a schedule appended to the Regulations. Heritage structures may be repaired or re-developed only after obtaining the prior written permission of the municipal commissioner, who in turn, is required to consult the statutory Heritage Conservation Committee (HCC). The constitution of the HCC includes an

---

[58] A.G. Krishna Menon, *Cultural Identity and Urban Development*, 4 (1989).

environmentalist, a city historian as well as structural engineers and architects. Several incentives compensate the owner of a heritage property for the loss of development rights. Under the regulations and the norms adopted by the HCC, heritage owners are entitled to 'transferable development rights',[59] change from residential to commercial use and special protection against government schemes for road widening or acquisition for public projects.[60] Adopting the Bombay model, in December 1995, heritage regulations were introduced to protect 152 buildings and 9 precincts in Hyderabad.[61]

The Union Ministry of Environment and Forests (MEF) has encouraged the states and union territories to adopt suitable local heritage regulations. In December, 1995, the MEF circulated model heritage regulations and asked the regional governments to frame suitable laws. The MEF followed this initiative with letters on 21 August 1998 and 8 April 1999 urging the states to quickly frame regulations to conserve the natural and built heritage.[62]

NIYAMAVEDI v GOVERNMENT OF INDIA

Kerala High Court
W.A.NO. 1427 / 1994–B
6 November 1995

SHANMUGAM, J.:

A public spirited organization 'Niyamavedi' interested in the preservation of precious archeological monument of the pre-historic ages viz. 'Sage Cages' in Marayur, Idukki District was the petitioner in the Original Petition ['O.P.'] and appellant before us. The O.P. was filed praying for the issue of a writ of prohibition prohibiting the respondents from [destroying], disfiguring and exporting the stone extracted from the Marayur ancient Sage Cage and for the issue of a writ of mandamus directing the respondents to set the law into motion as provided under the Antiquities and Art Treasures Act, 1972 to safeguard the ancient monuments of Sage Cages in Marayur from destruction, disfigurement and spoilage. The learned single Judge declined to grant the relief but only directed the authorities to take special care to see that quarrying operation by the 6th respondent [A.B.N. Granites Ltd.] is done strictly in accordance with the licence conditions. Aggrieved by the judgment the Association has filed the above appeal.

To understand the scope of the Original Petition a brief resume of the importance

---

[59] A right to build elsewhere in the city ward where the heritage building stands. TDR may be encashed by sale to a developer.

[60] S. Chainani, *Heritage Legislation & Heritage Movement in Bombay and Elsewhere: A Selective Personal Account*, 15 July 1998 (unpublished). Archives, Bombay Environmental Action Group.

[61] *Id.*

[62] Archives, Bombay Environmental Action Group.

and implications of the stone monuments found at Marayur Village, Devikulam Taluk, Idukki District is necessary. The 'Sage Caves' (Muniyara—Megalithic tombs) and the Eluthupara (pre-historic painting) are found distributed in the reserve forest area in huge natural rock of concave shape situated 3 kms from the ground level. The importance of Muniyaras is described by Komattil Achutha Menon in his book 'A Survey of Kerala History'. Under the heading 'Megalithic Culture' it is stated that the term 'Megalithic' (mega—great and lithoi—stone) means monuments erected out of large blocks of stones, as funerary edifices, either sepulchral or commemorative ... Under the heading 'Prehistory' it is stated that 'Mention may also be made in this connection of the alleged kinship of the South Indian megaliths in other parts of the world, e.g., the lands bordering on the Mediterranean and the Atlantic, in the Caucasus and in Iran'.

The 2nd respondent in the O.P. viz. the Director General, Archaeological Survey of India, New Delhi directed an inspection of the entire area on receipt of the notice in the above O.P. The Deputy Superintending Archaeologist, Trivandrum submitted a report Ext.R2(a) after visiting the site on 24.3.1994. ... According to him, the paintings of Eluthupara [were] protected by the Department of Archaeology, Government of Kerala in the year 1976. On the hill range there are few natural caverns also. Exploration revealed that there are quite a number of the 'Sage Caves' (Muniyara) widely disturbed in the hill area and also at the foot of the hill. Majority of them are in the reserve forest area and nearly 30 to 40 of such monuments are in groups forming a 'Cluster Zone'. The monuments are standing above the ground level. These types of monuments are widely distributed in may places of this area and the practical problem arises in protecting all the monuments. The structures lying in the village area may be considered for the protection with all infrastructure, otherwise the Kerala Archaeology Department may be asked to protect some of these monuments, since the pre-historic painting Eluthupara is already a protected monument of the State Department.

In the Writ Appeal the Division Bench by order dated 15.11.1994 called for a further report from the 2nd respondent in reference to specific questions viz. whether the blasting operations proposed to be conducted by the 6th respondent would endanger the safe existence of the 'Sage Cages' and what are the protective steps that are to be taken in the matter. The 2nd respondent was also directed to report whether the blasting operations would cause difficulties in maintaining the Sage Cages numbering 40 and forming a Cluster Zone as ancient monuments as recommended by the earlier report Ext.R2(a). In pursuance to this order there was a further inspection by the Deputy Superintending Archaeologist, Archaeological Survey of India, Madras Circle, which is marked as Annexure-R2A. The said officer inspected the site on 16.12.1994. In the report it is stated that on these hills, the megalithic tombs known as 'Dolmenoid-cist' are situated at different levels and the total number of ancient tombs are more than a hundred. Ancient people selected the hillrock to get the raw material on the spot and away from the residential areas (plains). The other portion of the report is worth quoting, which is as follows:

I have thoroughly examined the whole area of land which was earmarked for blasting operation and also the hillrock and its surroundings and come to conclusion that *the blasting operation cannot be allowed at all in the proposed site*. The reasons for arriving at this conclusion are:

1. The authors of 'Sage-Caves' (Dolmenoid cists) selected particular regions with specific topographical features for constructing such burials. Therefore, the whole topography is as important as the burials themselves in understanding them in proper perspective.

2. The disturbances caused by blasting will definitely have its repercussions in the safety of the dolmenoid-cists or burials as they are situated on different levels.

3. *No doubt 'Sage-Caves' can be protected by delimiting the area from quarrying but natural, ancient topography will be lost forever.* (Emphasis added)

A consideration of the study reports of the competent experts in the field of Archaeology would make one thing clear that the Muniyaras, Sage Caves or pre-historic ancient monuments are to be preserved and there can be no second opinion on that. The Government and the 6th respondent-Company who had been granted the quarrying lease admit the fact of importance and the preservation of this ancient monument. The only difference of view is whether the quarrying and blasting operations would in any way effect or interfere with the ancient monument. According to the 6th respondent it would not affect the ancient monument.

[The court set out the relevant provisions of the Ancient Monuments and Archaeological Sites and Remains Act of 1958, the Ancient Monuments Preservation Act of 1904, the Kerala Ancient Monuments and Archaeological Sites and Remains Act of 1968 and the Kerala Minor Mineral Concession Rules of 1967.]

It is no doubt true that so far these 'Sage Caves' have not been declared as ancient monuments by the Central or state governments excepting the Eluthupara paintings in that area which was declared as protected in the year 1976. It is very significant to note that the Director of Archaeology, Thiruvananthapuram had informed the Superintending Archaeologist, Archaeological Survey of India, Madras Circle by letter No.A2-2970/93/DA dated 29.6.1994 (Ext.R2(b)) that the Department proposes to protect and preserve the site in question, excluding the forest area. Therefore, based on these two inspections conducted by the Deputy Superintending Archaeologist, Trivandrum and Deputy Superintending Archaeologist, Madras Circle, 'Sage Caves' satisfy the definitions of 'ancient monument' and 'antiquity' in the Acts mentioned above. Therefore, there cannot be any semblance of doubt as to the importance and the necessity to preserve these ancient monuments. The fact of declaration under these Acts is only a question of time. The effect of declaration involves financial implications to the state as well as to the Centre. Further the Departments are rather slow in responding for immediate action. But the fact remains as per the reports of the experts that these 'Sage Caves' are ancient monuments and are to be preserved as such, in view of the admitted historic importance.

* * *

It is the duty of every citizen to protect and preserve the ancient and historic monuments for future generations. It is a basic source of study for the archaeologists and are of national and state importance which cannot be permitted in any way to be interfered with or affected. Even if there is possibility of remotest chance of being affected, we feel it the duty of this court to extend our jurisdiction to protect and preserve these ancient monuments. We are of the view that 'Niyamavedi', the appellant herein has made out a case for the issue of the writ prayed for.

Accordingly we issue a direction prohibiting the respondents from permitting any quarrying operation from Sy.No. 373 of Marayur Village, Devikulam Taluk, Idukki District. We further direct the 1st and 2nd respondents to take appropriate steps to declare these 'Sage Cages' (Muniyaras) of Marayur village as monuments and antiquity under the Act 24 of 1958, Act 7 of 1904 & Act 26 of 1969 respectively as expeditiously as possible. Writ Appeal is allowed in the above terms.

NOTES AND QUESTIONS

1. The archaeological site came within a reserved forest. What argument might the petitioners have used under the forest laws to prevent quarrying in the area?

2. Without specifically articulating the norms, the court appears to have been guided by the precautionary principle, as well as the principles of sustainable development and inter-generational equity. These international law norms have been assimilated into the domestic regime by the Supreme Court. The precautionary principle requires government authorities to anticipate the causes of environmental degradation and shifts the onus of showing that an action is environmentally benign on the developer. Sustainable development and intergenerational equity require the prudent use of natural resources so that economic growth is sustained and the cultural and natural heritage inherited from the previous generation is preserved intact for the next.

3. Responding to a petition filed by BEAG, the Bombay High Court directed the Maharashtra government to afford statutory heritage protection to designated buildings in the Mahableshwar region:

With regard to the Heritage Committee constituted by the State Government *vide* the Government Resolution dated 21 July 1998, we are informed that a meeting of this Committee was held on 9 November 1998. The Heritage Committee is directed to finalize the list of heritage structures and sites (both natural and man-made), including scenic points, walks, rides, etc. within four months from today. The Heritage Committee shall also, within the said period, formulate and finalize the draft Heritage Regulations for Mahabaleshwar-Panchgani Region in conformity with the Draft Model Regulations for Conservation of Natural and Man-made Heritage formulated by the Union Government's Ministry of Environment & Forests and which has been circulated to all State Governments in 1995. Within one month of the receipt of the said list and draft Regulations, the State Government shall publish and notify the same following the procedure stipulated in Sections 37 and 20 of the Maharashtra Regional & Town Planning Act, 1966. [63]

4. The Supreme Court has issued directions to the ASI to protect the monuments in the Fatehpur Sikri area,[64] as well as the tomb of Mirza Ghalib.[65] In *Surendra Kumar Singh v State of Bihar*,[66] the Supreme Court considered a special leave petition against orders passed by the Patna High Court preventing stone crushing operations within a distance of 500 m. of three hills that had been declared as protected monuments. Dismissing the petitions, the court directed the state electricity board to aid the petitioners in shifting their operations away from the prohibited zone. In *Rajiv Mankotia v The Secretary to the President of India*,[67] the Supreme Court delved into the history and origins of the Viceregal Lodge at Shimla and issued directions to preserve the building and prevent its conversion into a hotel. In *Ram Sarup v State of Haryana*,[68] the Punjab and Haryana High Court examined the provisions of the Ancient Monuments and Archaeological Sites and Remains Act, 1958 and upheld the government notification under section 4 of the Act declaring an area around Brahm Sarovar at Kurukshetra to be a controlled area for the purpose of the Act.

---

[63] *Bombay Environmental Action Group v State of Maharashtra,* Writ Petition No. 2754 of 1997, 18 November 1998.

[64] *Wasim Ahmed Saeed v Union of India,* 1997 (5) SCALE 451; 1999 (1) SCALE 683; and 1999 (1) SCALE 685.

[65] *M.C. Mehta v Archaeological Survey of India,* 1996 (8) SCALE 11 (SP); 1997 (2) SCALE 25 (SP); and 1997 (5) SCALE 1 (SP).

[66] 1991 SUPP (2) SCC 628.

[67] 1997 (4) SCALE 368.

[68] AIR 1993 P&H 204.

12

REGULATION OF HAZARDOUS SUBSTANCES

A. LEGISLATIVE FRAMEWORK

Hazardous substances pervade modern industrialized societies. Indian industry generates, uses, and discards toxic substances. Increasing numbers of farmers—encouraged by government agricultural policies—spray highly toxic chemical pesticides to protect their crops. Hazardous substances include flammables; explosives; heavy metals such as lead, arsenic and mercury; nuclear and petroleum fuel by-products; dangerous micro-organisms; and scores of synthetic chemical compounds like DDT and dioxins.

Section 2(e) of the Environment (Protection) Act of 1986 (EPA) defines a 'hazardous substance' to mean 'any substance or preparation which, by reason of its chemical or physico-chemical properties or handling, is liable to cause harm to human beings, other living creatures, plants, micro-organisms, property or the environment.'

Exposure to toxic substances may cause acute or chronic health effects. Acute effects occur soon after a high-level exposure and range in severity from temporary rashes to death. Chronic effects frequently result from long-term, low-level exposure and include cancers, birth defects, miscarriages and damage to the lungs, liver, kidneys and nervous system.

Toxic substances are extensively regulated in India. The first comprehensive rules to deal with one segment of the toxics problem, namely hazardous wastes, were issued by the Central Government in July, 1989. Framed under the enabling provisions of the EPA, the Hazardous Wastes (Management and Handling) Rules as amended in January 2000, apply to designated categories of waste that are enumerated in the Schedules to the Rules. Radioactive wastes, covered under the Atomic Energy Act of 1962, and wastes discharged from ships, covered under the Merchant Shipping Act of 1958, are explicitly excluded from the Hazardous Wastes Rules. The Rules also do not apply to waste water and exhaust gases regulated under the Water Act and Air Act.

Under rule 4, a person generating hazardous wastes and the operator of a hazardous wastes facility are 'responsible' for the proper handling, storage and disposal of wastes.

The Rules prescribe a permit system administered by state pollution control boards (or designated committees in respect of the union territories) for the handling and disposals of hazardous wastes: No person without board authorization may collect, receive, treat, transport, store or dispose of hazardous wastes. Moreover, the Rules provide for the packaging, labelling and transport of hazardous wastes and require state governments to compile and publish an inventory of hazardous waste disposal sites. Significantly, rule 11 prohibits the import of hazardous wastes into India for dumping and disposal. Until January 2000, the import into India of hazardous wastes for *recycling* was *not* prohibited under the Rules and a large quantity of hazardous wastes moved into India through this loophole until 1997. During this period, the international trade in hazardous wastes into India for *recycling* purposes fell under the Basel Convention of 1989,[1] where it was virtually exempt from controls.[2]

The judiciary tried to strengthen import barriers. On 5 May 1997, the Supreme Court banned the import of hazardous wastes as an interim measure in a writ petition filed by the Research Foundation for Science, Technology and Natural Resource Policy.[3] On 4 August 1997, the court noted that despite the lapse of several years, the authorities had not taken effective steps for implementing the Hazardous Wastes Rules: 'We are left with the impression that even now all the authorities do not appear to appreciate the gravity of the situation and the need for prompt measures being taken to prevent serious adverse consequences if the problem is not tackled immediately.'[4] In October, 1997, the court constituted a committee with a charter to examine in depth all matters relating to hazardous waste and to give their report and recommendations at an early date.[5] In December 1997, the committee was also requested to examine the quantities and the nature of the hazardous waste stock lying at docks and ports and recommend a mechanism for the safe disposal of these wastes or re-export to the places of origin.[6] The committee found containers holding hazardous wastes at Delhi and Bombay. Pending the committee's final report and recommendations, the customs authorities were restrained from releasing the goods until further orders by the court.[7]

---

[1] Convention on the Control of Transboundary Movements of Hazardous Wastes and their Disposal (Basel, 1989). *Reprinted in* 28 I.L.M. 657 (1989).
[2] Article 9 (b).
[3] Writ Petition (Civil) No. 657 / 1995.
[4] *Research Foundation for Science, Technology and Natural Resource Policy v Union of India* 1997 (5) SCALE 495.
[5] *Research Foundation for Science, Technology and Natural Resource Policy v Union of India* 1999 (1) SCC 223, 224.
[6] *Id.* at 225.
[7] *Supra* note 5. The directions issued by the court on 24 September 1999 are reported at 1999 (6) SCALE 345.

On 10 December 1999, the court permitted the disposal of hazardous wastes that were lying at the ports, in accordance with the recommendations of the committee. The Central pollution control board was directed to oversee the disposal of the imported wastes to industries that operated proper storage, processing and disposal facilities.[8]

Earlier, on 10 April 1996, a division bench of the Delhi High Court restrained the import of zinc and lead wastes into the country. The order was passed on the intervention of two non-governmental organizations, WWF India and Srishti, in a petition filed by a waste importer against the customs department. The customs had detained an incoming shipment of lead waste. Despite the High Court order, Greenpeace investigations revealed that the order was being flouted and 15,000 tonnes of hazardous waste entered India from 27 countries between April, 1996 and February, 1997.[9]

Spurred by the judicial initiative, in January 2000 the Centre introduced comprehensive amendments to the Hazardous Wastes Rules of 1989. The amendments extend the application of the Rules to hitherto unregulated processes and wastes, strengthen the existing permit system and introduce a new set of regulations to restrict the export and import of hazardous wastes for recycling and reuse. The Union Ministry of Environment and Forests is designated as the nodal agency to permit the transboundary movement of hazardous wastes.

In November, 1989 the central Department of Environment, Forests and Wildlife issued the Manufacture, Storage and Import of Hazardous Chemicals Rules. These Rules apply to industries that use or store specified hazardous chemicals. Rule 3 prescribes the duties of various governmental authorities. For example, the Central and state pollution control boards are required to enforce governmental directives and procedures pertaining to the isolated storage of hazardous chemicals, and the district collector (or other designated authority) is required to prepare off-site emergency plans to contain major chemical accidents. The responsibility of preparing and upgrading on-site emergency plans rests with the 'occupier' who controls the industrial activity. Rule 3 was amended in October, 1994 requiring each of the designated authorities to inspect the industrial activity at least once in a calendar year and annually report to the Union Ministry of Environment and Forests (MEF) on the occupier's compliance with the Rules. Under rule 4, an occupier must identify the major hazards posed by his industry, take steps to prevent and limit the consequences of an accident, and inform and train workers in occupational safety. The 1994 amendments strengthened the safeguards to prevent chemical accidents by requiring the authorities to inform the occupier about any lacunae in its systems needing rectification;[10] obliging the occupier to obtain site approval prior to commencing the indus-

[8] 1999 (7) SCALE 612.

[9] N. Jayaraman, *Poison Over Poverty* in FROM THE LAWYERS COLLECTIVE, October 1997, p. 4, 8–9. The article surveys the international regulatory regime and makes a persuasive case for better safeguards against the dumping of toxic waste in India by industrialized nations.

[10] Rule 5(5).

trial activity;[11] and mandating an independent annual safety audit of the industrial activity.[12]

Under rule 18, an importer of hazardous chemicals into India must disclose complete product safety information. Where the imported chemical is likely to cause a major accident, the designated governmental authorities are empowered to issue directions, including an order to stop the import. The importer must also ensure that the transport of the chemicals from the port of entry accords with the central Motor Vehicles Rules of 1989.

On 19 January 2000, the Central Government amended the Rules. The amendment redefined 'major accident', introduced fresh parameters to identify toxic chemicals, flammable chemicals and explosives and altered the Schedules, including the insertion of a revised list of hazardous chemicals in Schedule I.

Rules to regulate the manufacture, use, import, export and storage of hazardous micro-organisms and genetically engineered cells were issued under the EPA in December, 1989. These Rules cover industries, hospitals, research institutions and other establishments that handle micro-organisms or are engaged in genetic engineering. Committees of experts established under rule 4 play a pivotal role in administering the regulations. For instance, the Recombinant DNA Advisory Committee is required to review developments in biotechnology in India and abroad and to recommend suitable safety regulation in recombinant DNA research, use and applications. Procedures restricting or prohibiting production, sale, import and use of specified organisms are prescribed by the Review Committee on Genetic Manipulation. Rule 7 prohibits the handling, manufacture and use of hazardous micro-organisms except with the approval of the Genetic Engineering Approval Committee. Under rule 17, a District Level Committee, chaired by the district collector, is required to prepare off-site emergency plans to contain major accidents caused by the escape of harmful micro-organisms.

A fourth set of rules, the Chemical Accidents (Emergency Planning, Preparedness and Response) Rules were issued in August 1996, to strengthen the administrative response to hazardous substance accidents. These Rules supplement the Hazardous Chemicals Rules of 1989. The Rules require the Centre and the states to constitute 'crisis groups' at the national, state, district and local levels. The Central Crisis Group is responsible for dealing with major chemical accidents. Its tasks as set out in rule 5 include monitoring post accident situations, reviewing the adequacy of district off-site emergency plans, suggesting measures to reduce risks in industrial zones and rendering financial and infrastructural help to the states in the event of a chemical accident. Each state crisis group is required to assist the respective state government in managing chemical accidents and planning mitigation measures when accidents occur.[13] The district and local crisis groups are required

[11] Rule 7.
[12] Rule 10(4)–(7).
[13] Rule 7.

to conduct at least one mock drill of a chemical accident each year to strengthen the local response machinery.[14] The local crisis groups must also integrate the local emergency plans with district off-site emergency plans, prepared under rule 14 of the Hazardous Chemicals Rules of 1989.[15] The 1996 Rules emphasize the importance of disseminating information and oblige each crisis group to provide information regarding chemical accident prevention, preparedness and mitigation to members of the public on request.[16]

Hospitals, clinics, blood banks and other organizations generating bio-medical waste are regulated through a licensing and reporting system under the Bio-Medical Waste (Management and Handing) Rules of 1998. The Rules envisage the segregation, packing and disposal of ten categories of bio-medical waste which are listed in a Schedule to the Rules.

Although the statute book has several sets of rules to regulate hazardous substances, pollution control board officials and environment department representatives concede that there is no effective implementation. Most officers interviewed complained that a lack of personnel, funds and training prevented them from enforcing the stack of new rules.[17] In *Suo Motu v Vatva Industries Association*,[18] the Gujarat High Court reprimanded officers of the state pollution control board for neglecting their duties. Rather than proceed against the industries that were dumping hazardous wastes, the board officials chose to file a note before the judges and urged *them* to take action.

As we shall see later in this chapter, toxic substance regulation in India was largely a response to the Bhopal tragedy that occurred in December, 1984. Among the judicial responses to Bhopal was the Supreme Court judgment in the *Shriram Gas Leak Case*,[19] where the court articulated a new standard of absolute liability. The plight of the victims in the aftermath of Bhopal also underscored the need for a simple compensation regime that would assure a subsistence for chemical accident victims and their dependents. Parliament addressed these issues by enacting the Public Liability Insurance Act of 1991 (PLIA). The Statement of Objects and Reasons that accompanied the Bill recognizes that industry is seldom willing to compensate the victims of accidents, compelling the victims to engage in prolonged litigation. The PLIA gives statutory recognition to 'no-fault' liability and provides that where death or injury to any person or damage to property has resulted from a hazardous substance accident, the owner of the hazardous substance will be liable to give relief in the sum prescribed

[14] Rules 9(2)(g) and 10(2)(e).

[15] Rule 10(2)(b).

[16] Rule 13.

[17] Interviews with participating officials from several states at the Environmental Law Enforcement—Capacity Building Workshop organized by the National Law School, Bangalore, 22 September 1999. Conducted by S. Divan.

[18] AIR 2000 GUJ 33.

[19] *M.C. Mehta v Union of India* AIR 1987 SC 1086.

in the Schedule to the Act.[20] Section 3(2) provides that in any claim for relief under the Act, 'the claimant shall not be required to plead and establish that the death, injury or damage in respect of which the claim has been made was due to any wrongful act, neglect or default of any person.' The compensation figures mentioned in the Schedule are very low, with fatal accidents and cases of permanent disability entitling the maximum receipt of Rs.25,000. Section 8 of the Act clarifies that any relief under the PLIA would be in addition to the right to recover compensation under any other law.

To ensure that the victims receive compensation quickly, the Act requires every owner to obtain mandatory insurance cover[21] and provides an independent machinery administered by the district collector for the filing and adjudication of claims.[22] The collector is empowered to award relief under the Act after conducting an inquiry for which he may adopt a summary procedure.[23] The Act also contemplates the establishment of an Environment Relief Fund,[24] to which every owner must make a contribution.[25] The Rules framed under the PLIA, limit the liability of an insurer to Rs.5 crores for every accident.[26]

The 'no-fault' liability regime received further legislative endorsement in the National Environment Tribunal Act of 1995.[27] Section 3 of the Act provides that where death or injury to any person or damage to any property or the environment has resulted from a hazardous substance accident, the owner shall be liable to pay compensation under the heads specified in the Schedule to the Act on the principle of no-fault liability. The Schedule enumerates various heads including death; permanent, temporary, total or partial disability; loss of wages; medical expenses; damage to private property; expenses incurred by government in providing relief to victims or in coping with damage to the environment; damage to draught animals; claims arising from damage to flora and fauna; and loss of business or employment. To administer the no-fault liability regime, the Act empowers the Centre to establish the National Environment Tribunal,[28] to be headed by a sitting or retired judge of the Supreme Court or a High Court.[29] The tribunal is empowered to pass interim orders[30] and make final awards determining the compensation to be paid after granting the affected party an opportunity to be heard and complying with the principles of natural justice.[31] To prevent a

---

[20] Section 3(1).
[21] Section 4.
[22] Sections 5 and 6.
[23] Rule 5, Public Liability Insurance Rules, 1991.
[24] Section 7A.
[25] Section 4(2C).
[26] Rule 10.
[27] At the time of writing, the Act had not been brought into force.
[28] Section 8.
[29] Section 10.
[30] Section 6.
[31] Section 5(2).

double recovery, section 7 of the Act provides that any compensation awarded by the Tribunal must stand reduced by the relief or compensation paid under the PLIA or any other law.

In *UP State Electricity Board v District Magistrate, Dehradun*,[32] the Allahabad High Court held that the PLIA was a social welfare statute that applied the principle of strict liability shorn of the exceptions carved out to the rule in *Rylands v Fletcher*.[33] The High Court rejected the petition filed by the electricity board claiming exemption from the provisions of the PLIA. The court held that electricity was a hazardous substance for the purposes of the PLIA. 'In India, while rapid industrialization is absolutely essential for modernization of the country, we must try to avoid the evils caused by unplanned industrialization e.g. air and water pollution, discharge of harmful chemicals, explosion, etc., and where industrial accidents occur prompt compensation must be paid to the victims.'[34]

In addition to the EPA and the PLIA, provisions touching on certain other aspects of storage, transportation and regulation of hazardous substances are contained in the central Motor Vehicles Rules of 1989, the Insecticides Act of 1968, the Explosive Substances Act of 1908, the Inflammable Substances Act of 1952 and the Atomic Energy Act of 1962. In addition, the 1987 amendment to the Factories Act of 1948 introduced a section on hazardous industrial activities. This amendment aims at increasing plant safety by such measures as worker participation in the monitoring of safety measures and stiff penalties, including imprisonment, against employers for failing to comply with safety norms.

The next section of this chapter deals comprehensively with the *Shriram Gas Leak Case*. A few radiation and other hazardous substance cases are examined in the third section. In the next chapter we review recent developments in the Bhopal Gas Leak Case which was treated more fully in the previous edition of this book.

B. THE SHRIRAM GAS LEAK CASE

This case originated in a writ petition (No. 12739 of 1985) filed in the Supreme Court by the environmentalist and lawyer M.C. Mehta, as a public interest litigation. The petition sought to close and relocate Shriram's caustic chlorine and sulphuric acid plants located in a thickly populated section of Delhi. One month after the filing of this petition, oleum leaked from the sulphuric acid plant located in the same 76 acre industrial complex as the chlorine plant, affecting several people. The leak took place on 4 December 1985—a day after the first anniversary of the Bhopal gas leak—and caused widespread panic in the surrounding community.

The Inspector of Factories and the Assistant Commissioner (Factories) issued

---

[32] AIR 1998 ALL 1.
[33] 1868 LR 3 HL 330.
[34] *Supra* note 32, at 11.

separate orders on 7 and 24 December 1985 shutting down both plants. Aggrieved, Shriram filed a writ petition (No.26 of 1986) challenging the two prohibitory orders issued under the Factories Act of 1948 and sought interim permission to reopen the caustic *chlorine* plant.

On behalf of those affected by the *oleum* leak, the Delhi Legal Aid and Advice Board and the Delhi Bar Association filed applications for compensation in the original petition by M.C. Mehta. (Neither the claimants nor the legal aid bodies were parties in the original petition.)

The *Shriram Gas Leak Case* pitted the Supreme Court against one of India's largest corporations. But it was an unusual confrontation, because Shriram invariably bowed to the court's directions and willingly complied with its often unprecedented orders. Several of these orders required Shriram to deposit significant sums of money to finance the court's exercise of seemingly executive and legislative functions in the process of adducing evidence in the case.

Chief Justice Bhagwati, who presided over the Supreme Court bench, was deeply concerned for the safety of Delhi's citizens and was anxious to improve plant safety at the caustic chlorine unit—a task which the statutory agencies seemed incapable of performing. Moreover, the Chief Justice, who was a year away from the mandatory retirement age at the time of the oleum gas leak, saw in the Shriram oleum leak a way of influencing the pending and far more important *Bhopal Gas Leak Case*.

Reviewers of this case should focus on:

(a) instances of the judicial assumption of functions normally performed by executive and legislative bodies;

(b) the stringent standards that the court imposes before permitting Shriram to operate its caustic chlorine unit;

(c) the court's laudable contribution in introducing a new 'no-fault' liability standard ('absolute liability') for industries engaged in hazardous activities;

(d) the anomaly of making major reforms in the Indian law of liability and compensation without first deciding whether the court has jurisdiction over the company to which such liability attaches; and

(e) the court's creative approach to fact-finding and to securing scientific and technical advice regarding an industry whose government regulators were lax and ineffective.

There are six reported orders in the *Shriram Case*.[35] We excerpt from the three principal orders of 17 February, 10 March, and 20 December 1986.

---

[35] 31 January 1986, 1986 (1) SCALE 153; 17 February 1986, AIR 1987 SC 965; 24 February 1986, 1986 (1) SCALE 341; 10 March 1986, AIR 1987 SC 982; 20 December 1986, AIR 1987 SC 1086; and 24 March 1987, 1987 (1) SCALE 1271 (2).

M.C. MEHTA v UNION OF INDIA
AIR 1987 SC 965

BHAGWATI, C.J.:

Writ Petition No. 12739 of 1985 which has been brought by way of public interest litigation raises some seminal questions concerning the true scope and ambit of Articles 21 and 32 of the Constitution, the principles and norms of determining the liability of large enterprises engaged in manufacture and sale of hazardous products, the basis on which damages in case of such liability should be quantified and whether such large enterprises should be allowed to continue to function in thickly populated areas, and, if they are permitted so to function, what measures must be taken for the purpose of reducing to a minimum the hazard to the workmen and the community living in the neighbourhood. These questions which have been raised by the petitioner are questions of the greatest importance particularly since, following upon the leakage of MIC gas from the Union Carbide Plant in Bhopal, lawyers, judges and jurists are considerably exercised as to what controls, whether by way of relocation or by way of installation of adequate safety devices, need to be imposed on Corporations employing hazardous technology and producing toxic or dangerous substances and if any liquid or gas escapes which is injurious to the workmen and the people living in the surrounding areas, on account of negligence or otherwise, what is the extent of liability of such Corporations and what remedies can be devised for enforcing such liability with a view to securing payment of damages to the persons affected by such leakage of liquid or gas. These questions arise in the present case since on 4 and 6 December 1985, there was admittedly leakage of oleum gas from one of the units of Shriram Foods and Fertiliser Industries and as a result of such leakage, several persons were affected and according to the petitioner and the Delhi Bar Association, one advocate practising in the Tis Hazari Courts died. We propose to hear detailed arguments on these questions at a later date. But one pressing issue which has to be decided by us immediately is whether we should allow the caustic chlorine plant of Shriram Foods and Fertilisers Industries to be restarted and that is the question which we are proceeding to decide in this judgment.

* * *

Since there were conflicting opinions put forward before us in regard to the question whether the caustic chlorine plant should be allowed to be restarted without any real hazard or risk to the workmen and the public at large, we thought it desirable to appoint an independent team of experts to assist us in this task. We accordingly by an order dated 18 December 1985 constituted a Committee of Experts consisting of Dr Nilay Choudhary as Chairman and Dr Aghoramurty and Mr. R.K. Garg as members to inspect the caustic chlorine plant and submit a report to the court on the following three points:

1. Whether the plant can be allowed to recommence the operations in its present state and condition?
2. If not, what are the measures required to be adopted against the hazard or possibility of leaks, explosion, pollution of air and water etc., for this purpose?
3. How many of the safety devices against the above hazards and possibility

exist in the plant at present and which of them, though necessary, are not installed in the plant?

* * *

We have thus two major reports, one of Manmohan Singh Committee and the other of Nilay Choudhary Committee, setting out the recommendations which must be complied with by the management of Shriram in order to minimize the hazard or risk which the caustic chlorine plant poses to the workmen and the public. The question is whether these recommendations have been complied with by the management of Shriram, for it is only if these recommendations have been carried out that we can possibly consider whether the caustic chlorine plant should be allowed to be restarted.

* * *

There can ... be no doubt that there would be hazard to the life and health of the community, if there is escape of chlorine gas from the caustic chlorine plant, whether by reason of negligence of the management or due to accidental release. * * * We cannot therefore ignore the possible hazards to the health and well-being of the workmen and the people living in the vicinity on account of escape of chlorine gas. We also cannot overlook the old and worn out state of machinery and equipment, the negligence of the management in the maintenance and operation of the caustic chlorine plant and the indifference shown by the management in installing proper safety devices and safety instruments and taking proper and adequate measures for ensuring safety of the workmen and the people living in the vicinity. These are considerations which are very relevant in deciding whether the caustic chlorine plant should be allowed to be restarted. But as against these considerations, we must also take into account the proven fact that all the recommendations made in the reports of Manmohan Singh Committee and Nilay Choudhary Committee have been carried out by the management of Shriram and it is the opinion of not only Manmohan Singh Committee and Nilay Choudhary Committee but also of the last Committee appointed by us on January 31, 1986 that since all these recommendations have been complied with by the management in satisfactory manner, Shriram may be allowed to restart the caustic chlorine plant. There can be no doubt, particularly having regard to the opinion of Manmohan Singh Committee, Nilay Choudhary Committee and the last Committee appointed by us, that the possibility of hazard or risk to the community is considerably minimised and there is now no appreciable risk of danger to the community if the caustic chlorine plant is allowed to be restarted. We cannot also ignore the interests of the workmen while deciding this delicate and complex question. It could not be disputed either by the Government of India or by the Delhi Administration or even by the petitioner that the effect of permanently closing down the caustic chlorine plant would be to throw about 4000 workmen out of employment and that such closure would lead to their utter impoverishment. The Delhi Water Supply Undertaking which gets its supply of chlorine from Shriram would also have to find alternative sources of supply and it was common ground between the parties that such sources may be quite distant from Delhi.

* * *

We have ... decided to permit Shriram to restart its power plant as also plants for manufacture of caustic chlorine including by-products like sodium sulphate, hydrochloric acid, stable bleaching powder, superchlor, and sodium hypochlorite, vanaspati refined oil including its by-products and recovery plants like soap, glycerine and technical hard oil and container works. ... But we are laying down certain conditions which shall be strictly and scrupulously followed by Shriram and if at any time it is found that any one or more of these conditions are violated, the permission granted by us will be liable to be withdrawn. We formulate these conditions as follows:

[(1) The court constituted an expert committee to monitor Shriram's compliance with the recommendations of the Manmohan Singh and the Nilay Choudhary Committees. Shriram was asked to deposit Rs. 30,000 to meet the travelling, boarding and lodging expenses of the expert committee.

(2) The court stipulated that one operator be designated as personally responsible for each safety device in the caustic chlorine plant.

(3) The Chief Factory Inspector was directed to inspect the caustic chlorine plant at least once a week.

(4) The Central pollution control board was asked to depute an inspector to visit the Shriram plants at least once in a week to ascertain Shriram's compliance with the effluent discharge and emission standards prescribed in the consent orders under the Water Act and the Air Act.]

(5) The Management of Shriram will obtain an undertaking from the Chairman and Managing Director of the Delhi Cloth Mills Ltd. which is the owner of the various units of Shriram as also from the officer or officers who are in actual management of the caustic chlorine plant that in case there is any escape of chlorine gas resulting in death or injury to the workmen or to the people living in the vicinity, they will be personally responsible for payment of compensation for such death or injury and such undertakings shall be filed in court within one week from today.

[(6) The court constituted a workers's safety committee.

(7) Shriram was asked to publicize the effects of chlorine and the appropriate post-exposure treatment through charts placed at the gate of the premises and within the plant.

(8) Shriram was directed to instruct and train its workers in plant safety through special audio-visual programmes.

(9) Shriram was directed to install loudspeakers to alert neighbours in the event of a chlorine leak.

(10) Shriram was asked to ensure that the workers use safety devices like gas masks, safety belts, etc., and was directed to provide regular medical check-ups to the workers.]

(11) The management of Shriram will deposit in this court a sum of Rs. 20 lakhs as and by way of security for payment of compensation claims made by or on behalf of the victims of oleum gas, if and to the extent to which such compensation claims are held to be well founded. This amount deposited by the management of Shriram will be invested by the Registrar of this Court in fixed deposit with a nationalised Bank so that it earns interest and it will abide further directions of this Court. The management of Shriram will also furnish a bank guarantee to the satisfaction of the Registrar of this Court for a sum of Rs.15 lakhs which bank guarantee shall be encashed

by the Registrar, wholly or in part, in case there is any escape of chlorine gas within a period of three years from today resulting in death or injury to any workman or to any person or persons living in the vicinity. The amount of the bank guarantee when encashed shall be utilised in or towards payment of compensation to the victims of chlorine gas, the quantum of compensation being determinable by the District Judge, Delhi on applications for recompensations being made to him by the victims of chlorine gas. The amount of Rs. 20 lakhs shall be deposited and the bank guarantee for Rs. 15 lakhs shall be furnished within a period of two weeks from today and on failure of the management of Shriram to do so, the permission granted by us by this judgment to restart the caustic chlorine plant and other plants shall stand withdrawn.

* * *

It is ... necessary to point that when science and technology are increasingly employed in producing goods and services calculated to improve the quality of life, there is a certain element of hazard or risk inherent in the very use of science and technology and it is not possible to totally eliminate such hazard or risk altogether. We cannot possibly adopt a policy of not having any chemical or other hazardous industries merely because they pose hazard or risk to the community. If such a policy were adopted, it would mean the end of all progress and development. Such industries, even if hazardous, have to be set up since they are essential for economic development and advancement of well-being of the people. We can only hope to reduce the element of hazard or risk to the community by taking all necessary steps for locating such industries in a manner which would pose least risk of danger to the community and maximising safety requirements in such industries. We would therefore like to impress upon the Government of India to evolve a national policy for location of chemical and other hazardous industries in areas where population is scarce and there is little hazard or risk to the community, and when hazardous industries are located in such areas, every care must be taken to see that large human habitation does not grow around them. There should preferably be a green belt of 1 to 5 km. width around such hazardous industries.

There is also one other matter to which we should like to draw the attention of the Government of India. We have noticed that in the past few years there is an increasing trend in the number of cases based on environmental pollution and ecological destruction coming up before the courts. Many such cases concerning the material basis of livelihood of millions of poor people are reaching this Court by way of public interest litigation. In most of these cases there is need for neutral scientific expertise as an essential input to inform judicial decision making. These cases require expertise at a high level of scientific and technical sophistication. We felt the need for such expertise in this very case and we had to appoint several expert committees to inform the court as to what measures were required to be adopted by the management of Shriram to safeguard against the hazard or possibility of leaks, explosion, pollution of air and water etc. and how many of the safety devices against this hazard or possibility existed in the plant and which of them, though necessary, were not installed. We had great difficulty in finding out independent experts who would be able to advise the court on these issues. Since there is at present no independent and competent machinery to generate, gather and make available the necessary scientific and technical information, we had to make an effort on our own to identify experts who would provide reliable scientific and technical input necessary for the decision of the case and this was obviously a difficult and by its very nature, unsatisfactory exercise. It is therefore absolutely essential that there should be an independent Centre with professionally competent and public spirited experts to provide the needed scientific and technological input. We would in the circumstances urge upon the Government of India to set up an Ecological Sciences Research Group consisting of independent, professionally competent experts in different branches of science and technology, who would act as an information bank for the court and the government departments and generate new information according to the particular requirements of the court or the concerned government department. We would also suggest to the Government of India that since cases involving issues of environmental pollution, ecological destruction and conflicts over natural resources are increasingly coming up for adjudication and these cases involve assessment and evolution of scientific and technical data it might be desirable to set up Environment Courts on the regional basis with one professional Judge and two experts drawn from the Ecological Science Research Group keeping in view the nature of the case and the expertise required for its adjudication. There would of course be a right of appeal to this Court from the decision of the Environment Court.

* * *

Before we part with this judgment we would like to express our deep sense of appreciation for the bold initiative taken by the petitioner in bringing this public interest litigation before the court. The petitioner has rendered signal service to the community by bringing this public interest litigation and he has produced before the court considerable material bearing on the issues arising in the litigation. * * * Though lone and single, he has fought a valiant battle against a giant enterprise and achieved substantial success. We would therefore as a token of our appreciation of the work done by the petitioner direct that a sum of Rs. 10,000 be paid by Shriram to the petitioner by way of costs.

NOTES AND QUESTIONS

1. The court's order of 17 February 1986 makes clear in its first paragraph that the court is interested in a prospective application of its *Shriram* rulings to impose liability on Carbide in the pending *Bhopal Gas Leak Case*. Is the court's clear intention to affect the *Bhopal Case* objectionable?

2. Put yourself for a moment in Chief Justice Bhagwati's shoes: All government agencies with any responsibility over Shriram's operations have apparently been lax, and have made no move to change Shriram's operations, until the oleum leak. The Chief Justice wants to discover and remedy any problems that exist at the Shriram complex and the only person offering any assistance is M.C. Mehta—a single lawyer without substantial resources. In these circumstances, did he not act creatively and resourcefully in setting up an effective fact-finding and safeguard-implementing process?

3. Note that in its order of 17 February 1986, the court engages in an *ad hoc*

balancing of economic and health considerations (4000 jobs are at stake in the chlorine plant, and chlorine is needed to purify Delhi's water supply) with environmental and safety considerations (chlorine is hazardous and could harm Shriram's employees and the surrounding community). Ultimately, the court decides to reopen the chlorine plant 'temporarily'. Is not this balancing more properly the province of executive organs?

4. The court deserves praise for minimizing the danger to workers and the surrounding community by requiring Shriram to take stringent safety measures before restarting its hazardous caustic chlorine unit. Apart from compliance with the recommendations of the Manmohan Singh and Nilay Choudhary Committees, Shriram was required to 'strictly and scrupulously' follow eleven further conditions. Some of these conditions, viz., making senior level management responsible for hazardous industrial operations, introducing workers' participation in safety management, publicizing preventive measures in the case of an emergency and requiring trained and experienced personnel to handle hazardous substances—have been codified into the Factories Act by the 1987 amendment.

5. In its orders of 31 January 1986 (not excerpted) and 17 February 1986, the court periodically required Shriram to contribute substantial sums of money —15,000 and 30,000 rupees at a time—to support the expenses of the various committees and experts that the court designated to help it sort out the facts of the case. Is this sort of fund raising appropriate? Can you think of any alternative ways to accomplish (and finance) the court's purposes?

6. Should the sums of money contributed by Shriram in compliance with the orders have been returned to Shriram once the court declared that it would not decide whether it had jurisdiction over the case? (See the subsequent order dated 20 December 1986.) Does Shriram have a legal claim against the Indian treasury for reimbursement of these 'contributions'? What would be likely to happen if Shriram chose to pursue such a claim?

7. What would happen if, in the future, the respondent in a writ proceeding in a High Court refused to comply with the court's order to pay significant sums of money to support the court's fact-finding and advice-seeking? Would such refusal short circuit all proceedings and ultimately undermine the court's authority and prestige? Would the court be likely to take recourse to its contempt power? If so, the court would implicitly be asserting an *inherent power* to raise funds to do justice. But wouldn't a respondent on whom such a liability was imposed have any basis for resisting such a liability, or for shifting it to the public treasury?

8. Viewed from the court's perspective, the court's exercise of quasi-executive functions in creating agencies, appointing a safeguard committee, appointing a committee of inspectors, recruiting experts from all over India and paying for their air travel to and from Delhi and so on helps the court to ascertain the facts of the case and secure objective scientific advice. The court's creativity in marshalling these resources may deserve commendation rather than criticism. Similarly, the court manifests

creativity in attempting to ensure compliance with its orders—by appointing monitoring committees that must report back to the court regarding the measures taken to remedy Shriram's unsafe procedures and conditions.

9. Commendably in its 17 February 1986 order, the court requires Shriram to present a bank guarantee of Rs. 15 lakhs to ensure compensation for any future chlorine victims. The court also requires Shriram to deposit Rs. 20 lakhs as a condition to reopening the *chlorine* plant, with the money to be used to compensate the *oleum* leak claimants. Isn't this a bit of a Robin Hood-type remedy? If so, did the court exceed its authority?

10. In any case, when the court determined on 20 December 1986, that it would not assert jurisdiction over Shriram, should it not have returned to Shriram the Rs. 20 lakhs it had earlier ordered to be deposited? By normal standards of orderly judicial procedure, liability cannot be imposed on a company over which a court has no jurisdiction. Is there any justification for the court retaining Shriram's Rs. 20 lakhs?

11. The court suggested the creation of environmental courts consisting of one judicial member and two technical experts from the 'Ecological Sciences Research Group'. There would be a right of appeal to the Supreme Court. What do you think of this suggestion? To be responsive and effective, should there not be an environmental court in every state?

12. The court awarded Rs. 10,000 to be paid (by Shriram) to the petitioner M.C. Mehta. Considering the time, effort and resources expended by M.C. Mehta in this public interest litigation, what amount might you have awarded?

M.C. MEHTA v UNION OF INDIA
AIR 1987 SC 982

ORDER:

This application has been made by Shriram Foods and Fertiliser Industries (hereinafter referred to as 'Shriram') for clarification in respect of certain conditions set out in the Order passed by us on 17 February 1986 in Writ Petns. Nos. 12739 of 1985 and 26 of 1986 (AIR 1987 SC 965). Though the application has been styled as an application for clarification, it is really and in substance, an application for modification of some of the conditions contained in the Order. * * *

[The court modified condition No. 2 pertaining to safety devices.]

[Next, the court turned to condition No. 5 pertaining to the personal liability of the Chairman and Managing Director.] The contention of Shriram is that it is not clear as to who can be described as officer in actual management of the caustic chlorine plant and that this particular direction requires clarification so that the management can obtain the necessary undertaking from such officer. So far as this difficulty pointed out on behalf of Shriram is concerned, we would like to clarify that the officer whose undertaking is required to be taken under the directions given in our Order dt. 17 February 1986, is the officer who is the 'occupier' under the Factories Act, 1948 because he is the person who has actual control over the affairs of the factory and/or the officer who is in charge of the actual operation of the caustic chlorine plant and who is responsible to the management for the operation of the plant. But it was urged on behalf of Shriram that if we insist upon an undertaking to be given by any such officer or officers it would be impossible to secure the services of any competent officers because they would not be willing to accept employment in a situation where they are made responsible not only for their own acts or omissions but also for the acts or omissions of others over whom they have no control.

[W]e are not unmindful of the fact that if absolute unlimited liability were to be imposed on any officer or officers in the employ of Shriram for death or injury arising on account of possible escape of chlorine gas many competent persons would shy away from accepting employment in Shriram and that would make it difficult for Shriram to have really competent and professionally qualified persons to manage and operate the caustic chlorine plant. We would therefore modify the condition prescribed by us by providing that undertaking shall be obtained from the officer who is 'occupier' of the caustic chlorine plant under the Factories Act, 1948, and/or the officer who is responsible to the management for the actual operation of the caustic chlorine plant as its head and such undertaking shall stipulate that in case there is any escape of chlorine gas resulting in death or injury to the workmen or to the people living in the vicinity the officer concerned will be personally responsible, to the extent of his annual salary with allowances, for payment of compensation for such death or injury but if he shows that such escape of gas took place as a result of Act of God or vis major or sabotage or that he had exercised all due diligence to prevent such escape of gas, he shall be entitled to be indemnified by Shriram.

So far as the undertaking to be obtained from the Chairman and Managing Director of Shriram is concerned it was pointed out by Shriram that Delhi Cloth Mills Ltd. which is the owner of Shriram has several units manufacturing different products and each of these units is headed and managed by competent and professionally qualified persons who are responsible for the day to day management of its affairs and the Chairman and Managing Director is not concerned with day to day functioning of the units and it would not therefore be fair and just to require the Chairman and Managing Director to give an undertaking that in case of death or injury resulting on account of escape of chlorine gas, the Chairman and Managing Director would be personally liable to pay compensation. We find it difficult to accept this contention urged on behalf of Shriram. We do not see any reason why the Chairman and/or Managing Director should not be required to give an undertaking to be personally liable for payment of compensation in case of death or injury resulting on account of escape of chlorine gas, particularly when we find that according to the reports of various expert committees which examined the working of caustic chlorine plant, there was considerable negligence in looking after its safety requirements and in fact, considerable repair and renovation with and installation of safety devices had to be carried out at a fairly heavy cost in order to reduce the element of risk or hazard to the community.

* * *

NOTES AND QUESTIONS

1. Recognizing that many companies have named low-level officials as 'occupier' and 'manager'—posts liable for prosecution under the Factories Act of 1948—section 2(n) of that Act was amended in 1987 to specify that the 'occupier' of a factory 'means the person who has ultimate control over the affairs of the factory: Provided that ... in the case of a company, any one of the directors shall be deemed to be the occupier. ...' The last clause was somewhat ambiguous, leading to a divergence of opinion among the High Courts in respect of who might be an occupier. In *J.K. Industries Ltd. v Chief Inspector of Factories & Boilers*,[36] the Supreme Court resolved the issue, holding that after the 1987 amendment, a company could only nominate a director as an occupier and not any other employee or officer. The amended provision was constitutional and did not confer unguided power on the Inspector of Factories. It was for the board of directors of a company to notify the particular director who was to be treated as an occupier and only where the board failed, was it left to the Inspector of Factories to choose one among the directors as a deemed occupier.

2. Note that Shriram pursued an entirely different litigation strategy than Union Carbide did in the *Bhopal Gas Leak Case*. Shriram complied with all orders, including those requiring them to subsidize the court's fact-finding, without complaint or demur. Carbide seemed inclined to contest virtually every order of every court. What might account for the difference? The nationality of the company? The fact that Shriram is a going concern keen to continue its business in India, while the Union Carbide Corporation had no future stake in Indian business? The fact that feelings were running high against Carbide, and Shriram did not want to be tarred with the same brush? Other factors?

M.C. MEHTA v UNION OF INDIA
AIR 1987 SC 1086*

BHAGWATI, C.J.:

This writ petition under Article 32 of the Constitution has come before us on a reference made by a Bench of three Judges. The reference was made because certain questions of seminal importance and high constitutional significance were raised in the course of arguments when the writ petition was originally heard. * * * When applications for compensation came up for hearing it was felt that since the issues raised involved substantial questions of law relating to the interpretation of Articles 21 and 32 of the Constitution, the case should be referred to a larger Bench of five Judges and this is how the case has now come before us.

---

[36] 1996 (6) SCC 665.

* The report of the judgment in the All India Reporter is slightly different from the report carried in the Supreme Court Cases reporter. These differences are not material. At a few places we have departed from the AIR report since the SCC report appeared to be more accurate.

[The court then considered Shriram's preliminary objection. Shriram urged the court not to decide the issues arising from the compensation claims since no such claim was made in the original petition and the petitioner had not amended the pleadings to incorporate a compensation plea. The court, however, dismissed the objection, stating that a 'hyper-technical' approach would defeat the ends of justice.

Thereafter, the court examined the ambit of Article 32 of the Constitution and concluded that under that article the Supreme Court may award compensation in appropriate cases.]

The next question which arises for consideration on these applications for compensation is whether Article 21 is available against Shriram which is owned by Delhi Cloth Mills Limited, a public company limited by shares and which is engaged in an industry vital to public interest and with potential to affect the life and health of the people. * * * [W]e do not propose to decide finally at the present stage whether a private corporation like Shriram would fall within the scope and ambit of Article 12, because we have not had sufficient time to consider and reflect on this question in depth. The hearing of this case before us concluded only on 15 December 1986 and we are called upon to deliver our judgment within a period of four days, on 19 December 1986. We are therefore, of the view that this is not a question on which we must make any definite pronouncement at this stage. But we would leave it for a proper and detailed consideration at a later stage if it becomes necessary to do so.

We must also deal with one other question which was seriously debated before us and that question is as to what is the measure of liability of an enterprise which is engaged in an hazardous or inherently dangerous industry, if by reason of an accident occurring in such industry, persons die or are injured. Does the rule in *Rylands v Fletcher* (1868 LR 3 HL 330) apply or is there any other principle on which the liability can be determined. The rule in *Rylands v Fletcher* was evolved in the year 1868 and it provides that a person who for his own purposes brings on to his land and collects and keeps there anything likely to do mischief if it escapes must keep it at his peril and, if he fails to do so, is prima facie liable for the damage which is the natural consequence of its escape. The liability under this rule is strict and it is no defence that the thing escaped without that person's wilful act, default or neglect or even that he had no knowledge of its existence. This rule laid down a principle of liability that if a person who brings on to his land and collects and keeps there anything likely to do harm and such thing escapes and does damage to another, he is liable to compensate for the damage caused. Of course, this rule applies only to non-natural user of the land and it does not apply to things naturally on the land or where the escape is due to an act of God and an act of a stranger or the default of the person injured or where the thing which escapes is present by the consent of the person injured or in certain cases where there is statutory authority. * * * We are of the view that an enterprise which is engaged in a hazardous or inherently dangerous industry which poses a potential threat to the health and safety of the persons working in the factory and residing in the surrounding areas owes an absolute and non-delegable duty to the community to ensure that no harm results to anyone on account of hazardous or inherently dangerous nature of the activity which it has undertaken. The enterprise must be held to be under an obligation to provide that the hazardous or inherently dangerous activity in which it is engaged must be conducted with the highest standards of safety and if any harm results on account of such activity, the enterprise must be absolutely liable to compensate for such harm and it should be no answer to the enterprise to say that it had taken all reasonable care and that the harm occurred without any negligence on its part. Since the persons harmed on account of the hazardous or inherently dangerous activity carried on by the enterprise would not be in a position to isolate the process of operation from the hazardous preparation of substance or any other related element that caused the harm the enterprise must be held strictly liable for causing such harm as a part of the social cost of carrying on the hazardous or inherently dangerous activity. * * * This principle is also sustainable on the ground that the enterprise alone has the resource to discover and guard against hazards or dangers and to provide warnings against potential hazards. We would therefore hold that where an enterprise is engaged in a hazardous or inherently dangerous activity and harm results to anyone on account of an accident in the operation of such hazardous and inherently dangerous activity resulting, for example, the escape of toxic gas the enterprise is strictly and absolutely liable to compensate all those who are affected by the accident and such liability is not subject to any of the exceptions which operate vis-a-vis the tortious principle of strict liability under the rule in *Rylands v Fletcher*.

We would also like to point out that the measure of compensation in the kind of cases referred to in the preceding paragraph must be correlated to the magnitude and capacity of the enterprise because such compensation must have a deterrent effect. The larger and more prosperous the enterprise, the greater must be the amount of compensation payable by it for the harm caused on account of an accident in the carrying on of the hazardous or inherently dangerous activity by the enterprise.

* * *

NOTES AND QUESTIONS

1. Note that throughout the *Shriram Case*, the Supreme Court assumed legislative and executive functions to adduce evidence and to provide relief. Can this extraordinary assumption of power be justified in the face of legislative and executive agency inactivity regarding the control of hazardous industrial activity? Does this judicial activism set a healthy precedent? What can Parliament do to curb any judicial encroachment upon its own powers and prerogatives? What can the executive do to curb judicial encroachment on its powers and prerogatives? Bear in mind that neither the government nor Parliament has criticized the court's actions in the *Shriram Case*, indicating that a broad political consensus backed the court.

2. The Article 32 writ petition process is designed to alter the behaviour of government officials. *Shriram* is the first case in which an Article 32 petition was used to seek compensation from a private company, viz., Shriram. The court attempted to cope with this dilemma by drawing on American cases where private companies acting under the colour of State law (i.e., with the sanction and cooperation of state officials) are deemed to be engaging in *state action* (and hence

subject to the US Constitution's 14th Amendment, regulating the conduct of the states).

Does this imply that Shriram, and other private companies whose activities like Shriram's, have a 'public character'[37] should be treated as an instrumentality of the state for purposes of an Article 32 writ petition? If so, it could result in a deluge of writ petitions, and would expose countless private enterprises to writ proceedings asserting infringements of fundamental rights.

The court could undoubtedly counter this 'flood of litigation' argument by observing that it seeks only a very narrow expansion, namely those private corporations affected with a public purpose that allegedly deprive citizens of their right to life under Article 21. Is it likely that such a 'narrow' expansion would be maintained? This deluge was held back by the Chief Justice's failure to assemble a majority of his bench behind the 'state action' doctrine. Accordingly, if Shriram is not a state instrumentality under Article 12 of the Constitution then it must be a private party, and not capable of receiving a writ of mandamus. The court does not say that Shriram is not a state instrumentality, but clearly there is no majority for the view that it is, and so the court does not decide whether it has Article 32 jurisdiction over Shriram.

3. Suppose the chlorine plant *had* leaked and had resulted in numerous deaths and injuries. Would not the court have assumed jurisdiction over the case and have overcome the argument that Shriram is a private company and hence not subject to an Article 32 petition?

4. Do you believe that the court's massive response was a reaction to the *Bhopal Case*?

5. If the *Shriram* court was inclined to exercise judicial self-restraint, the case would have ended here: No affirmative holding on the threshold issue of jurisdiction means that the court will not decide the questions of liability and compensation. But the court, having come this far, and having a great desire to prospectively reach the *Bhopal Gas Leak Case*, doesn't let its lack of jurisdiction inhibit it from articulating a new absolute liability standard and a new standard also for determining the quantum of damages.

6. In its 20 December 1986 judgment, the court did not decide whether Shriram could be characterized as the 'State' within the meaning of Article 12. The court observed:

[W]e have not had sufficient time to consider and reflect on this question in depth. The hearing of this case before us concluded only on 15 December 1986, and we are called upon to deliver our judgment within a period of four days. ... We are, therefore, of the view that this is not a question on which we must make any definite pronouncement at this stage. ... (AIR 1987 SC 1086, 1098)

---

[37] We use the term 'public character' to summarize the court's description of Shriram as 'a private corporation under the functional control of the State, engaged in an activity which is hazardous to the health and safety of the community and is imbued with public interest and which the State ... proposes to exclusively run under its industrial policy. ...' (AIR 1987 SC 1086, 1097).

If four days were not sufficient time to reflect in depth on the Article 12 ('state action') question, how could it have been sufficient to radically change the liability and compensation laws of India, as the court then proceeded to do?

7. The final portion of Chief Justice Bhagwati's 20 December 1986 order makes two quantum leaps in the law, viz., the articulation of a new standard of a hazardous industry's *absolute liability* for the harm resulting from its activities—a standard which admits of no defences—and the declaration that damages are to be commensurate with the tortfeasor's ability to pay. Can one argue that these policies fall within the normal function of a common law judge to refine and extend reasoned principles articulated in earlier cases? Or are they simply judge-made laws?

8. Judge-made law can be far more potent than an act of Parliament: In the *Shriram Case*, for example, the court declares a new *absolute liability* standard and applies this standard to the instant case. If a legislature attempted to articulate a liability standard and to apply it to a gas leak that happened a year earlier, such action would very likely be challenged. It could be attacked as unreasonable and arbitrary, and violative of Article 14 of the Constitution. But a court encounters no such impediments: It merely announces that the newly revealed standard has *always* implicitly been the law of the land. The court has simply found the standard embedded in the common law and has interpreted it to apply to the instant case.

9. Note that the court justifies its formulation of a 'no exceptions' strict liability rule by observing, in part,

> as new situations arise the law has to be evolved in order to meet the challenge of such new situations. ... We have to evolve new principles and lay down new norms which would adequately deal with the new problems which arise in a highly industrialised economy. (AIR 1987 SC 1086, 1099)

Isn't the articulation of new principles and norms the quintessential legislative function?

10. There is nothing in the reported orders in the *Shriram Case* that justifies the expansion of the *Rylands v Fletcher* strict liability rule. It appears that Shriram offered none of the defences recognized as exceptions to *Rylands v Fletcher* (such as an act of God, the act of a third party, and statutory authority). Hence, there seems to have been no reason for the court to announce a new rule of absolute liability allowing no exceptions. This adds support to the supposition that the court's hidden agenda was to anticipate and nullify the third party 'saboteur' defence in the *Bhopal Case*.

11. Cost internalization and loss spreading arguments suggest that regardless of negligence, hazardous industries rather than innocent victims should bear the cost of injuries caused by hazardous substances. These two arguments support the court's articulation of a new 'absolute liability' standard.

Imposing absolute liability ensures that the cost of injuries from toxics are borne by the manufacturers who use, market and profit from these products. Cost internalization is intuitively just, in that victims obtain compensation from those who profit from their harmful activity. Moreover, cost internalization deters future tortious conduct.

Absolute liability guarantees that hazardous industries become insurers against risk of injury arising from their activity and through higher prices, the cost of injuries caused by the toxic substance is then distributed among the public as part of business costs rather than borne in entirety by the injured individual. Loss spreading is fair because everyone in society benefits from the products that the hazardous industries manufacture and, therefore, everyone should pay for a portion of the harm associated with these products.

12. But is an absolute liability standard that makes no allowances for war, a terrorist attack, or an act of God (storms, cyclones, lightning, tidal waves, etc.) consistent with notions of fundamental fairness and justice?

13. Each of the major new principles in the *Shriram Case*—absolute liability and the quantum of damages determined by the respondent's ability to pay— seems defensible, standing alone. They are much harder to defend together: Absolute liability admitting no defences, amounts to a 'no fault' system. In a no fault system, the person or company made liable needs to know in advance what the quantum of liability will be, so that he or she can obtain liability insurance. An *indeterminate sliding scale* seems unconstitutionally vague, as well as bad public policy.

14. Over the years, the Shriram principles have waxed and waned. In December, 1989 (three years after the *Shriram* judgment) a five judge bench of the Supreme Court upheld the validity of Bhopal Gas Leak Disaster (Processing of Claims) Act of 1985.[38] Certain observations in the opinions delivered in the *Bhopal Act Case* appear to weaken the *Shriram* court's standard that the quantum of damages should be on the basis of the monetary capacity of the delinquent. Referring to this standard, Chief Justice Mukharji (for himself and Saikia, J.) stated:

> This is an uncertain promise of law. On the basis of evidence available and on the basis of the principles so far established, it is difficult to see any reasonable possibility of acceptance of this yardstick. And even if it is accepted, there are numerous difficulties of getting that view accepted internationally as a just basis in accordance with law.[39]

Justice Ranganathan (for himself and Ahmadi, J.) concurred:

> Whether the [*Bhopal Case*] settlement should have taken into account [the Shriram standard of punitive liability] is, in the first place a moot question. Mukharji, C.J. has pointed out—and we are inclined to agree—that this is an 'uncertain province of the law' and it is premature to say whether this yardstick has been, or will be, accepted in this country, not to speak of its international

[38] *Charan Lal Sahu v Union of India*, AIR 1990 SC 1480.
[39] *Id.* at 1545.

acceptance which may be necessary should occasion arise for executing a decree based on such a yardstick in another country.[40]

Justice K.N. Singh (who was also a member of the *Shriram* court) did not express any opinion on the quantum of damages issue.

15. The absolute liability theory was examined by the Supreme Court when deciding the Bhopal Settlement review petitions,[41] as well as the *Bichhri Case*.[42] We carry a discussion on these judgments including an excerpt from the *Bichhri Case* in the Judicial Remedies chapter. Next to *Shriram*, the *Bichhri Case* is the most important judgment rendered by the Supreme Court on hazardous substances.

16. In its petition for review of the 20 December 1986 order, Shriram stated that it did not argue the question of exemplary damages since the court declared that it would not be considering the question. If this is correct, was it proper for the court to create a new standard for compensation without giving an opportunity to be heard to the party newly made liable?

17. The Supreme Court directed that the oleum gas leak claimants should file their claims in the Tis Hazari Courts (the lowest trial courts in Delhi, located quite close to the Shriram complex). After the Delhi High Court designated five judges to hear these claims, most other judges of the Tis Hazari Courts immediately filed claims against Shriram, claiming personal injury in the oleum gas leak!

18. In the 1990s, Shriram relocated some of its units at Patiala in Punjab.[43] Several other polluting industries in Delhi were also directed by the Supreme Court to move operations away from the National Capital Region.[44]

Eventually, Shriram settled with the claimants. Although Shriram considered many claims to be bogus, the company decided to pay reasonable amounts to every claimant, rather than risk a contest and an award in a few genuine cases that was linked to the company's 'ability to pay'. The settlement also involved a payout by Shriram's insurers.[45]

Rarely do courts stall a large project on environmental grounds. One successful case where economic interests were subordinated to safety concerns was filed by the Law Society of India which urged the Kerala High Court to restrain a giant public

---

[40] *Id.* at 1557.

[41] *Union Carbide Corporation v Union of India (Bhopal Review)* AIR 1992 SC 248.

[42] *Indian Council for Enviro-Legal Action v Union of India* AIR 1996 SC 1446.

[43] Interview with Ravinder Narain, Counsel for Shriram; 12 June 1999. Conducted by S. Divan.

[44] *M C Mehta v Union of India* AIR 1996 SC 2231. See the section on translocation of industries in the Urban Problems chapter.

[45] *Supra* note 43.

sector fertilizer company from operating its 10,000 ton ammonia storage tank in Cochin. The petitioners claimed that an accidental leakage of ammonia could devastate the entire city and its environs. A division bench of the High Court embarked on a detailed evaluation of the technical and legal aspects of the case and delivered a lengthy judgment, an excerpt from which follows.

LAW SOCIETY OF INDIA v FERTILIZERS & CHEMICALS TRAVANCORE LTD.

AIR 1994 KER 308

VARGHESE KALLIATH, J: * * *

In the petition the petitioner wants to spearhead and underscore the high potency danger involved in allowing to continue the operation by the first respondent a 10,000 tonne ammonia storage tank in Willingdon Island in Port Area.

The first respondent the Fertilizers and Chemicals Travancore Ltd. Udyoga-mandal is a public sector undertaking. It is engaged in the production of fertilizers. 0.27 per cent of the shares in the Company is held by the public, the balance being held by the Government of India, the Government of Kerala, the Government of Tamil Nadu and the Government of Andhra Pradesh. Its manufacturing units for production of chemical fertilisers are Cochin Division at Ambalamedu and Udyogamandal Division at Eloor.

From the counter affidavit of the first respondent it is seen that the Company is producing 4.24 per cent of the fertilizer production of the country. It is stated in the counter affidavit that it has a capital investment of Rs.520 crores and a staff strength of 8527.

Ammonia is a chemical and is used as the raw material for the production of fertilizers like Urea, NP 20:20:0, DAP 18:46:0, Ammonium Sulphate, Ammonium Chloride and petro-chemicals like caprolactum.

The ammonia stored in the storage tank is imported in special refrigerated ships and is pumped from the ships to the refrigerated storage tank at atmospheric pressure. Since the first respondent required ammonia for the purpose of production of fertilizers and caprolactum, it is importing ammonia after obtaining the required governmental sanction. The tank, which was designed in March, 1973 was commissioned in August, 1976 to receive liquid ammonia from ship. The ammonia stored in this tank is transferred into rail tank wagons and transported to first respondent's Cochin Division, where it is stored in a 5000 tonne capacity ammonia storage tank before being pumped to the consuming plants. Part of the ammonia that is stored in the tank is transported to Udyogmandal through barges specially made for the purpose of refrigeration.

* * *

The question posed before us is of stupendous consequence. We are fully informed of the fact if we order decommissioning of the plant, it will have multi-faceted repercussions and it may cause a seminal impact in the industrial and agricultural sectors of this state and perhaps to some extent the country as a whole, particularly in the agricultural sector. We are clearly informed of the fact that we will never be justified if we slur over the question or postpone the issue or refrain to take action only on the above said considerations since what is notched against these considerations is an avoidance of potential morbid genocide. We are certainly informed of the truth that when science and technology are put to the maximum use in producing goods and services calculated to advance the quality of life, there inheres a potent element of hazard or risk inherent in the very use of science and technology and it may not be possible to eliminate such hazard or risk in its entirety. It may be out of time, fatuous, asinine and thoughtless to adopt a policy of not having any chemical or other hazardous industries merely because they pose a hazard or risk to the community. Such industries in the modern set up may be necessary for the industrial, agricultural and economic growth of the country and the resultant well-being of the people. But we must strain every nerve to minimize the hazard or risk to the community, by taking all necessary steps for locating such industries in a manner which would pose least risk or danger to the community. If the court is convinced that it is possible to minimize the hazard or risk to the community in not allowing an industry to be run in a location inherent with potential additional danger and risk to the community certainly the court is bound to act and should give necessary directions.

* * *

We have to investigate two broad questions in this case. The first question is the possibility of the operational failure of 10,000 tonnes of ammonia storage tank and the consequent leak of ammonia and the degree of pollution of air and the resultant ecological imbalance they may cause thereby and as a result of this environmental pollution the hazards that have to be faced by the people of Willingdon Island and the city of Cochin. The second question that we have to answer is as to whether there is any reasonable possibility of catastrophic failure, of the tank resulting in a crack or break or a rupture which would result in an uncontrollable major leak of ammonia with its resultant devastation of the entire population in Willingdon Island and the city of Cochin and surrounding places on account of the seminal sensitive and strategical siting of the tank in the port area very close to the runway of the airport and very near to the Southern Naval Command.

* * *

Certain important facts and circumstances unfolded in the case and the findings.

(i)   In case of a catastrophic accident to the storage tank resulting in a major crack or rupture, it would lead to disastrous and devastating consequences of annihilating all living beings, inverting the city of Cochin, [into] a city of the dead and nearby places, a morbid grave-yard.

(ii)   The catastrophic failure of the tank is not an unreal or remote possibility, but a credible and contingent possibility to be reasonably anticipated on the facts unfolded in the case.

(iii)   Though the catastrophic event is only a possibility and when it would happen is unpredictable, it is unwise to forget or slur it. Once it happens, it is irreversible, so prudence dictates not complaisance, but positive action.

[The court concluded that the location of the tank endangered public safety.]

On the findings and conclusions we have decocted from the mass of materials placed before us, we have to make our own final decision in the matter. We are fully aware of the fact that directing the first respondent to decommission the ammonia tank would certainly involve very far reaching and serious economic issues as well as issues relating to loss of employment to large number of persons. Certainly these issues involve vital and serious consequences. But we have to balance these issues with the real and intelligible potential possibility of a catastrophic accident to the ammonia tank resulting in extermination of all living beings in Willingdon Island, City of Cochin and nearby places. We have found that the catastrophic failure of the tank not a remote possibility, but a credible and contingent possibility to be reasonably anticipated on the facts unfolded in the case. We feel that we have to discharge our obligation informed of the fact that the human population of the Cochin City and Willingdon Island should not be compelled to remain under the dark shadow of a genocide. Life on earth can never be peaceful if it is shrouded in perpetual anxiety and fear of extermination on account of an avoidable human activity. It is the plain and clear negation of the most basic human right and gross violation of the fundamental right guaranteed under Article 21 of the Constitution of India.

Deprivation of life under Article 21 of the Constitution of India comprehends certainly deprivations other than total deprivation. The guarantee to life is certainly more than immunity from annihilaton of life. Right to environment is part of the right to life. Apart from the rights under Article 21 of the Constitution of India and its refined articulation in Article 51(g), we have to remember that in 1984, United Nations adopted a resolution reading: 'All human beings have the fundamental right to an environment adequate for their health and well being.' A state of perpetual anxiety and fear of extermination of life is not an environment adequate for the health and well being of human race.

We hold that the continuation of the operation of the ammonia storage tank by the first respondent is a plain and clear violation of the fundamental right guaranteed under Article 21 of the Constitution of India and so we are obliged to stop it.

* * *

In the result, on an anxious consideration of the rival claims and competing concerns, we order the first respondent to de-commission and empty the ammonia storage tank at Willingdon Island within 3 months from today. Further we direct that the storage tank at Willingdon island should not be used for storing liquid ammonia after decommissioning the tank. The first respondent is directed to pay Rs. 5,000 ... to the petitioner as costs of this litigation.

* * *

NOTES AND QUESTIONS

1. Revealing a dimension of Article 21 of the Constitution, the court held that locating a dangerous industrial facility with potentially catastrophic effects in a city would violate the right to life of the citizens put at risk. In view of this judgment, is it permissible to continue, establish or expand an hazardous industry within or near a city?

2. FACT employed more than 8,500 persons, some of whom were directly concerned with the operation of the storage tank. The company staff perceived the petition as a threat to their livelihood and filed a strong affidavit opposing relief. The trade unions and workers' associations alleged that the petitioners were instigated by foreign multinationals interested in retarding India's development. The High Court, however, rejected the conspiracy theory out of hand.

A better point raised by the workmen was that several other ports in India and elsewhere in the world had similar storage installations and the petitioners' apprehensions were unjustified. This argument was turned down by the court after considering the special features at the Cochin facility, expert opinions on safety and after balancing the rival interests.

3. In a significant development the High Court implicitly laid down the standard which project proponents must adopt when introducing hazardous technologies capable of causing catastrophic damage. Three solutions were recommended by Dr. Kurt Mager to strengthen the defective foundation work. FACT selected the most economical and least time consuming method, although this was not the safest option. In paragraph 88 of the judgment (not excerpted above), the High Court disapproved the selection in view of the high risk involved and held that the safest solution, albeit more expensive and time consuming, ought to have been adopted. This is the first reported case in India where the court required the *best available technology* to be employed, irrespective of the financial costs.[46]

4. As in the *Tehri Dam*[47] and *Irish Butter*[48] cases, expert opinion was divided on the question of safety. The Central Building Research Institute (CBRI) gave a clean bill of safety to FACT with regard to repaired foundation work. The Indian Institute of Technology, Madras (IIT) was more ambivalent, reporting that the foundation was not in an 'alarming condition'. As against this, the Port Trust, the Southern Naval Command, the Kerala pollution control board and the Union Ministry of Environment emphasized the need to immediately shift the tank. Dr. Campbell,

---

[46] In *Fali Kumana v Municipal Corporation of Greater Bombay*, the Bombay High Court directed the respondents to adopt the best available technology to abate noise pollution from an air conditioning plant. Writ Petition No. 2390 of 1996, order dated 10 August 1998.
[47] *Tehri Bandh Virodhi Sangharsh Samiti v State of UP* 1992 Supp (1) SCC 44.
[48] *Dr. Shivarao Shantaram Wagle v Union of India* AIR 1988 SC 952.

the court-appointed Commissioner, pointed out that the proximity of the tank to the airport increased the risk of a catastrophe.

The court declined to defer to the expertise of CBRI and the IIT since important considerations were overlooked by both. After a detailed assessment of the expert reports, the High Court held: '[I]f the court is not satisfied with the manner of examination or investigation, the court is not bound to act on the experts' opinion. We do not think we are bound to follow blindly the opinion of experts.' The court's willingness to reject the CBRI and IIT reports probably stemmed from its anxiety to protect the entire city of Cochin from a disaster waiting to happen. In addition to the defective foundation work and the possibility of an air crash in the vicinity, the potential danger of an industrial disaster was recognized by several others. Indeed, the committee constituted by the district collector, Ernakulam to prepare a contingency plan threw up its hands since no contingency plan with a reasonable chance of success could be formulated.

5. In the *Tehri Dam Case*, despite the magnitude of the possible disaster in the event of a dam burst due to an earthquake, the Supreme Court accepted an expert opinion which considered the dam 'quite safe' and cleared the project. The Kerala High Court, however, required a much higher standard of safety when it rejected the IIT reports that concluded: 'Once [the suggested] repair works are successfully completed, it can be assumed that the structure is quite safe, say for another 10–15 years.' The High Court found the report to be casual and unreliable. Which standard would you consider appropriate for such projects: 'quite safe' or 'insignificant risk'?

6. Would the outcome of the case have been different had powerful government departments such as the Union Ministry of Environment and Forests, the Navy and the Port authorities not supported the petitioners?

7. The twists and turns in the *Bayer Case*[49] are discussed in the section on the translocation of industries in the Urban Problems chapter. Bayer was concerned that an accident at its chemical factory near Thane city in Maharashtra might endanger persons who came to live in the locality. The case rebounded on Bayer when the Supreme Court suggested that the industry, not the residents, shift away.

8. In *M.C.Mehta v Union of India (Re: Airport Authority of India Ltd.)*,[50] the Supreme Court permitted the Airport Authority of India to operate hot mix plants to enable the resurfacing of runways. M.C.Mehta opposed the application on the ground that the proposed units were a hazardous industry and ought not to operate within populated areas. Reiterating the necessity to balance environmental concerns and infrastructure needs, the court allowed the Airport Authority's application on conditions and safeguards mentioned in its order.

[49] *Bayer (India) Ltd. v State of Maharashtra* 1994 (4) BOM.C.REP. 309 and *F.B.Taraporawala v Bayer India Ltd.* 1996 (6) SCC 58.
[50] AIR 1999 SC 2367.

C. PESTICIDE AND RADIATION CASES

While the *Shriram Case, Bichhri*[51] and the *FACT Case* are undoubtedly the leading cases in the area of hazardous substances, they are not the only cases. Several cases have arisen involving the manufacture and use of pesticides, but most have involved issues of procedure rather than substance, and are not reproduced here. In *Dr. Ashok v Union of India*,[52] the Supreme Court treated a letter addressed to the Chief Justice of India as a public interest petition. Dr. Ashok complained that several widely used insecticides, colour additives and food additives ought to be banned since they were carcinogenic. Most of the 40 chemicals complained of were banned in the USA. The Union Government filed a detailed affidavit explaining the measures it had taken to prohibit these chemicals or restrict their use. In the judgment, the court acknowledged that broad spectrum pesticides upset the ecosystem and possibly caused cancer. The court was satisfied with the measures taken by the government in respect of the impugned items, but directed an inter-ministerial committee to review the cases of other chemicals and recommend additional measures in the future.[53]

Exposure to radioactive substances can occur in a variety of ways, most commonly through leaks from nuclear power plants, mining of radioactive compounds such as uranium and improper disposal or transportation of radioactive wastes. India is plagued by all these threats, but by far the most prevalent threat to human life and the environment is the decay of India's atomic energy programme. Not simply limited to one faulty plant, the entire national programme has been called into question by activists, journalists and international NGOs and their governments.

In 1996, a series of newspaper reports and editorials criticizing the safety record of the atomic energy programme appeared in the Indian press. The articles referred to a report prepared by the Atomic Energy Regulatory Board (AERB) listing about 130 safety violations and defects in various nuclear power plants in India and the statements of Dr. A. Gopalkrishnan, former chair of AERB, expressing his concern at safety features in the nuclear establishment. The People's Union for Civil Liberties petitioned the Bombay High Court demanding disclosure of the AERB report and also seeking appropriate directions against the respondents to rectify each of the defects. The petitioners asked for an expert body to investigate whether there were any incidents of negligence in respect of the nuclear installations. The respondents resisted disclosure, citing the secrecy provisions under the Atomic Energy Act of 1962. A division bench of the Bombay High Court held for the respondents. The court upheld the government's claim of privilege in respect of the report; upheld the constitutional validity of section 18 of the Atomic Energy Act which enabled the government to withhold information

---

[51] *Indian Council for Enviro-Legal Action v Union of India* AIR 1996 SC 1446. The case is discussed in the Judicial Remedies chapter.

[52] AIR 1997 SC 2298.

[53] The harmful effects of pesticides are surveyed in Centre for Science and Environment, *Homicide by Pesticides* (ed. A. Agarwal, 1997).

from the public; and found that the authorities were sufficiently alive to the safety concerns expressed by the petitioners, having themselves constituted a committee to review the regulatory framework.[54]

One widely publicized case decided by the Supreme Court involved imported Irish butter, which was alleged to have been contaminated by the radioactive fallout from the Chernobyl (USSR) nuclear disaster. Following the example of *Shriram*, the court in the *Irish Butter Case*[55] appointed a three person committee of experts to determine whether the butter was safe for human consumption. The expert committee concluded that the butter was indeed safe. On the basis of the committees' report, the Supreme Court rejected the petitioners' challenge and permitted distribution of the imported butter.

The expert committee seemed to rely heavily on the fact that India's AERB has stricter standards than most other countries for permissible radioactivity in dairy products. But no one really knows whether low levels of radioactivity are in fact harmless, and there will always be some reputable scientists advising against taking any risk. The court, its experts, the AERB, and the entire scientific community must simply do the best they can within the limits of scientific uncertainty.

One of the complicating factors in the *Shriram Gas Leak Case* was the proliferation of expert committees. In the *Irish Butter Case*, the Bombay High Court had already consulted the Bhabha Atomic Research Centre and the secretary of the AERB. Should the Supreme Court have deferred to the judgment of the Bombay High Court, based as it was on expert advice, and not have incurred additional expense and delay in appointing its own committee of experts?

Those advocating the view that all exposure to low level radioactivity should be avoided are undoubtedly frustrated by the difficulty in finding respected scientists in India with no ties to the government and, by implication, no axe to grind. Hence, the petitioner in the *Irish Butter Case* had to resort to the supposedly more objective views of Nobel Laureates from abroad. But was not the Supreme Court correct in associating these Nobel Laureates with 'a particular school of thought', and thus no more authoritative than the Indian scientists?

Sharma v Bharat Electronics, excerpted below, involved a petition brought by a union representing employees at Bharat Electronics Ltd., a public sector company, some of whom were exposed to X-ray radiation in the course of their work. They alleged that the company's failure to adequately protect their health and safety had

---

[54] *People's Union for Civil Liberties v Union of India* Writ Petition No. 1785 of 1996, order dated 30 January 1997.
[55] *Dr. Shivrao Shantaram Wagle v Union of India* AIR 1988 SC 952.

deprived the exposed workers of their fundamental rights and entitled them to compensation.

M.K.SHARMA v BHARAT ELECTRONICS LTD.
1987 (1) SCALE 1049

RANGANATH MISRA, J.:

This is an application under Article 32 of the Constitution and the petitioners are the Bharat Electronics Employees Union and the Secretary of that Union. Bharat Electronics Limited is a public sector undertaking. The company has its factory at Ghaziabad and manufactures electronic components and equipment including integrated circuits, TV picture tubes and sophisticated Radars used by the country's defence establishments. The respondent No. 1 has entered into technical collaboration with a French firm, TCSF. Respondent No. 2 is the competent authority appointed under the Radiation Protection Rules, 1971 framed under the Atomic Energy Act by the Central Government. This writ application is confined to employees working in the transmitter assembly room of the factory. The petitioners have alleged that in course of their employment those of the employees who are made to work in the transmitter assembly room are exposed to the baneful effects of X-ray radiation. The ill effects of such exposure has been detailed in the writ petition. They have alleged that respondent No. 1 has not been following the rules and no care and attention has been devoted to the safety and protection of the employees in such a sensitive place. They have further asked for a declaration that the failure of the respondents to provide adequate protection and adopt safety procedure has resulted in a violation of the transmitter assembly workers' fundamental rights and they have become entitled to compensation. Several other reliefs were prayed for. This Court on 5 May 1986 directed medical examination of 68 workers who complained of exposure to X-ray radiation by the Indian Council of Medical Research and when it was reported that there was no facility for appropriate examination at that place, on 21 July 1986, the Court directed those 68 workers to be examined in convenient batches by the Bhabha Atomic Research Centre (hereinafter referred to as 'BARC'). The said BARC also carried on a survey relating to radiological protection within respondent No. 1's installation and sent an interim report and later a detailed report has also been received. The BARC has also made certain suggestions for future protection of the worker from exposure to radiation.

* * *

The result of medical examination carried out shows that there is no clear proof of any injury or ill effect on the workers following the alleged exposure. It is, however, not disputed on either side that the evil effects take time to manifest and it is possible that even though no adverse effect is noticed now, on account of the exposure already suffered, the consequences may appear later. [Counsel] appearing for the employer-respondent No. 1—does not disown the responsibility to compensate the workmen in the event of proof of ill effects directly flowing out of employment at a future date. The only way in which this aspect of the demand can be dealt with is to say that as and when any related ill effect is manifested, the aggrieved workman or workmen would be entitled to lodge claim for compensation but as the matter stands no order for compensation at this stage is warranted. Safety rules have been framed and respondent No. 1 has undertaken before us that the same would be strictly complied with. Now that a competent officer has been appointed and is available at the spot, he will ensure that appropriate care and protective steps are taken.

The respondent-company has a system of film badges for measuring radiation absorbed during a month and the data which is collected on the basis of the aforesaid film badges would be regularly sent to the BARC for evaluation on monthly basis. The result of such analysis shall be duly publicized and would also be communicated to the petitioner-union at reasonable intervals.

The respondent-company has installed instantaneous measuring instrument near the transmitter to give immediate indication of radiation levels. In the event of fortuitous failure of the protective lead-shields, the transmitter has the primary lead-shield and also a secondary lead-shield. All care will be taken to keep these in use.

The electrical inter-locking device will ensure that the transmitter is not commissioned to service without primary lead-shield being in position.

Equally apprehensive of X-ray exposure are the officers who work in the sensitive areas of the factory. We direct the Union of India, respondent No. 3, to carry bi-annual checks by competent authority of strict compliance of safety devices.

In addition to all these, we are of the view that those of the officers and workers of the company who work within the sensitive portion of the factory should be covered by appropriate insurance cover and above general insurance, if any, to which as workmen at large they may have become entitled. Every workman should be insured for, a sum of Rs. one lakh and officers should be insured to the tune of Rs. two lakhs. It would be open to the respondent to get into group insurance arrangements with the insurer in case it is possible, otherwise individual insurance policies will have to be taken. The cost for these insurance policies would be borne by respondent No. 1 as a related and necessary expenditure of business. The benefit of insurance cover should be made available in terms of this direction by 30th of June, 1987. There will be no order for costs.

NOTES AND QUESTIONS

1. The court found no proof of injury and, therefore, no entitlement to compensation at this stage, but recorded the employers' assumption of responsibility to compensate workers in the event of future proof of injury resulting from present and continuing employment. This is a significant gain for the workers and their union. It has taken many years and much litigation for American workers to establish the right to recover compensation for the chronic effects of exposure to hazardous substances, i.e., effects which may take many years to manifest themselves.

2. It is unclear from this case as to who has the burden of proving a chronic injury, which may take years to show up in medical tests. The normal tort rule is

that the claimant has the burden of proof. In the United States, however, statutes have shifted the burden to the employer in certain cases involving exposure to hazardous substances. Should India follow this example and shift the burden of proof to the employer (or the state)?

3. If the burden of proof is kept on the worker, should it be enough to show that he or she has suffered health damage traditionally associated with exposure to the particular substance in question? What if the worker is a cigarette smoker, and it is shown, with toxicological or epidemiological data, that smoking significantly increases a worker's risk of contracting a particular long-term disease or condition, or significantly aggravates such condition? Should the compensation be negated or reduced by evidence of smoking?

4. The Bharat Electronics court evolves two important occupational health and safety policies, viz., that the workers' health status shall be periodically evaluated and *publicized*, and that this company—and presumably all others similarly involved in hazardous activities exposing workers to long-term health damage—must carry and pay for insurance for each exposed worker and officer.

5. The court requires that the company specially insure each exposed worker for Rs. 1 lakh and each exposed officer for Rs. 2 lakh. In light of the hue and cry that arose in the *Bhopal Gas Leak Case* over the supposed discrepancy in the value of an American life and an Indian life, isn't it strange that an officer should be entitled to twice as much life insurance as a worker?

6. Occupational health and safety were the primary concerns of the judges who heard CERC's petition filed against asbestos manufacturers. The Supreme Court used the case to direct safeguards for workers who were likely to be afflicted by asbestosis and other lung related diseases.[56] In another work environment case, the Supreme Court directed the payment of compensation to the victims of an accident at a fire cracker factory in Sivakasi, Tamil Nadu. Thirty nine workers perished in the accident.[57]

---

[56] *Consumer Education and Research Centre v Union of India* AIR 1995 SC 922. The Supreme Court is examining issues relating to pollution from asbestos factories in *Environment Society v Union of India* 1999 (1) SCALE 687 and 1999 (3) SCALE 9.

[57] *M.C. Mehta v State of Tamil Nadu* 1991 (2) SCALE 464 and 1991 (1) SCC 283.

13

THE BHOPAL GAS LEAK CASE

A. INTRODUCTION

The Bhopal disaster, which took place just after midnight on 3 December 1984, is undoubtedly the worst industrial accident in history. Forty tons of highly toxic methyl isocyanate (MIC), which had been manufactured and stored in Union Carbide's chemical plant in Bhopal, escaped into the atmosphere and was wind-borne directly towards the city centre. Initial estimates put the death toll at 3,500 people, while over 200,000 were estimated injured. Today, many years after the tragedy, the Indian government officially puts the death toll that evening at 2,500, while 2,800 have died since then from lingering effects of the toxic exposure. Activists however, place the number at closer to 8,000 that night with an equal number subsequently. The lack of documentation of deaths that fateful night, the subsequent chaos in administering aid to the victims since then, and the ongoing disputes over causes of illness, deaths, and the effects of the exposure all lead to the conclusion that the actual numbers of sick and dead will never be accurately fixed. What is true is that the estimates, official and otherwise, can never convey the enormity of the human tragedy—the families and communities disrupted, disabled, dislocated and impoverished then and those still suffering today. The numbers also fail to convey the anger, resignation, fear and suffering of many thousands of survivors who continue to evidence patterns of psychological and physical damage through exposure to the initial gas and the lingering fears of unknown illnesses and future genetic mutation.

To ensure that claims arising out of the disaster were dealt with speedily, and in alarm over the onslaught of American personal injury lawyers that flocked to Bhopal immediately after the gas leak, Parliament enacted the Bhopal Gas Leak Disaster (Processing of Claims) Act in March, 1985 (The Bhopal Act). The Act was held constitutional in a challenge by the survivor groups in December,

1989.[1] The Bhopal Act conferred the exclusive right on the Indian government, acting as *parens patriae*, to represent all claimants both within and outside India, and directed the government to organize a plan for the registration and processing of the victims' claims.

In April 1985, shortly after the Bhopal Act was passed, the Indian government sued Union Carbide in the United States. The government's preference for an American court stemmed from a lack of confidence in its own judicial system, the lure of large damages that an American jury might award, and its uncertainty about whether Carbide would submit to the jurisdiction of an Indian court. The American court, however, declined to try the Bhopal lawsuit, declaring that India was the more appropriate forum. Consequently, in September, 1986, nearly two years after the tragedy, the Indian government sued Carbide in the Court of the District Judge, Bhopal, for Rs. 3,900 crores (US\$ 3 billion) in damages.

The Bhopal case reached the Indian Supreme Court through the separate appeals of Carbide and the Indian government from the judgment of Justice Seth of the Madhya Pradesh High Court. In April, 1988, Justice Seth awarded interim damages of Rs. 250 crores (US\$ 192 million) on the basis of 'more than a *prima facie* case having been made out' against the defendants. Carbide's lawyers claimed that the judgment was unsustainable because it amounted to a verdict without trial. The Indian government appealed because Justice Seth had reduced by 30 per cent District Judge Deo's earlier interim payment award of Rs.350 crores (US\$ 270 million).

Surveying the Bhopal litigation in December 1988, the five judge Supreme Court bench must have been dismayed at the lack of progress in the principal lawsuit. The ineffectiveness of the Indian government's manoeuvers, combined with Carbide's apparent disregard for the victims, had dimmed the victims' hopes for early compensation. Proceedings in the original lawsuit before the Bhopal District Judge had stalled. Pretrial matters, such as discovery, had yet to be addressed. Four years after the tragedy, the government had yet to finalize its list of authentic claimants.

Rather than proceed rapidly with the trial of the original lawsuit and establish a legal claim on Carbide's American assets with a determinative final judgment, the government had preferred to pursue a risky short-cut. Encouraged by an early suggestion of Bhopal District Judge Deo, regarding an 'interim' award, the Attorney General of India's main litigation strategy was the pursuit of such a pretrial award. More than a year had been consumed in appeals from the award. In separate proceedings, additional efforts had been expended in a contempt of court action against Carbide, its Chairman and its lawyers. Indeed, there was little in the government's handling of the Bhopal case that might have impressed the Supreme Court judges with the government's capacity to devise legal strategies and introduce reformed trial procedures that could bring the Bhopal lawsuit to a swift conclusion.

---

[1] *Charan Lal Sahu v Union of India*, AIR 1990 SC 1480.

On 14 February 1989, the Supreme Court brokered an overall settlement of the claims arising from the Bhopal disaster. Under the settlement, Carbide agreed to pay US\$ 470 million to the Indian government on behalf of all the Bhopal victims in full and final settlement of all past, present and future claims, both civil and criminal, arising from the Bhopal disaster.[2] The entire amount had to be and was paid by 31 March 1989. In addition, the Supreme Court exercised its extraordinary jurisdiction and terminated all the civil, criminal and contempt proceedings that had arisen out of the Bhopal disaster and were pending in subordinate Indian courts.[3]

In December, 1989, the Supreme Court of India, in a long-winded judgment, upheld the constitutional validity of the Bhopal Act under which the Indian government gave itself the exclusive right to represent all Bhopal victims in civil litigation against Carbide. The court acknowledged that the Bhopal Act entitled the victims to notice and an opportunity to be heard on any proposed settlement, and the February 1989 settlement of US\$ 470 million failed to give such notice and hearing. Nevertheless, the court concluded that in the special facts and circumstances of the case, 'a post-decisional hearing would not be in the ultimate interest of justice.' The court noted that the hearings to be held during the *review* of the settlement (in review petitions filed by some of the victims in the Supreme Court), afforded a 'sufficient opportunity' to the victims. The court rationalized its view by declaring, '"To do a great right" after all, it is permissible sometimes "to do a little wrong".'

The Bhopal disaster raised complex legal, moral and ethical questions about liability—of parent companies for their subsidiaries, of transnational companies engaged in hazardous activities, and of governments caught between attracting industry to invest in business development while simultaneously protecting the environment and citizens. This chapter explores aspects of the legal strategies and decisions involved in the Bhopal lawsuit. Different decisions of the American and Indian courts are summarized and the resulting behaviour of the parties is presented from the time of the initial settlement through the fate of the victims today. We first approach the question of who was to blame and possible motivations for the behaviours that led to the disaster. Next, we examine the legal and political issues surrounding the choice of forum. We explore the role of the Indian government, both as a party to the lawsuit and as a sovereign nation responsible for the well-being of its citizens. Finally, we examine the settlement itself, what it represents to the victims, and how effective it is in terms of compensation for the victims. Questions and notes about the case are interspersed throughout the chapter.

---

[2] *Union Carbide Corporation v Union of India* AIR 1990 SC 273.

[3] The Supreme Court reinstated criminal charges against top executives at Union Carbide, including Warren Anderson, the CEO, while upholding the rest of the settlement, in October 1991. This judgment was rendered in petitions seeking review of the settlement and is reported at *Union Carbide Corporation v Union of India* AIR 1992 SC 248.

B. WHO WAS TO BLAME?

Many years after the Bhopal gas leak, the worst industrial catastrophe in history, it remains unclear who must bear legal responsibility.[4] Yet the question of moral responsibility is easily answered if one enters JP Nagar, a slum with 60,000 inhabitants. Not 200 metres away is the tower from which MIC used to be burned off.

BHOPAL: TEN YEARS LATER: Swiss Review of World Affairs, 1 February 1995

'A mass settlement, just a stone's throw from the production and storage center of highly poisonous substance—does it really need lawyers and judges?' asks R.L. Chouhan, a former chemical worker at the Carbide plant. Any visitor to the locale would find it hard to avoid the same conclusion: Neither the Union Carbide Corporation (UCC), an American firm well known for the strict management of its worldwide branches, nor the Indian government, could have been ignorant of the fact that a densely populated area was located immediately adjacent to a hazardous production site. And a review of the situation prior to the catastrophe shows that both of these main parties not only looked the other way, but knowingly accepted the risk.

Production of MIC first began at the Bhopal site in 1980, four years before the disaster. In the second year of operations there was an accident which prompted the workers' union to protest against inadequate safety measures. In 1982, M.N. Buch, the administrator of the city of Bhopal, requested that the government of the state of Madhya Pradesh shift the fertilizer factory to a remote region. The request was denied. Carbide was not eager for such a move, since Bhopal's central location in agrarian India was clearly advantageous for a fertilizer manufacturer. Then Arjun Singh, chief minister of Madhya Pradesh, did what most Indian politicians do with regard to the country's many illegal squatter settlements: In 1983, he legalized the slum known as JP Nagar. ...

Investigations following the Bhopal catastrophe showed that the responsibility of both the company and the government went far beyond the mere neglect of elementary safety measures. In an analysis in the British trade publication *Project Management*, a UN expert enumerated 16 factory shortcomings, 13 operational errors, 19 failures in communication and 26 system shortcomings. Many of these were the fault of company management, but many were also the government's fault.

Some of the 'mistakes' committed by a company of worldwide repute were astonishing: The cooling system which was supposed to keep the MIC at a temperature of zero degrees celsius to prevent a reaction, had been turned off six months before the accident; the same held for the burner in the tower for burning off the poison. Both steps had been taken with the approval of company headquarters. The scrubbers capable of neutralizing MIC exhaust fumes had been placed in 'passive mode' two months before the disaster. The spray system designed to pull escaping MIC fumes

---

[4] The case in chief was never adjudicated on the merits, nor have the criminal charges, still pending in India, been effectively pursued by the Indian government.

to the ground by surrounding them in a water mist was effective only to a height of 12 meters, but the MIC fumes were released at a height of 33 metres. The pipes attached to the MIC tanks were made of iron instead of the stainless steel called for by regulations; the iron ions in the rinse water were one of the major causes of the accident. The government authorities, responsible for monitoring adherence to safety regulations, had simply accepted management assurances that everything was in order. 'Bhopal', concluded the UN expert, 'was a catastrophe waiting to happen'.

NOTES AND QUESTIONS

1. Why would Carbide have allowed such flagrant safety violations as detailed in the UN expert's report?

2. Many volunteer organizations for the Bhopal victims have urged the Central Bureau of Investigation (CBI) to inspect Carbide's sister plant in Institute, West Virginia, to determine whether the safety standards are higher there. In fact, three such groups have petitioned an Indian court to order CBI to do so. Is it likely to be a useful investigation at this point, so many years later? In May, 1984, the Institute plant's safety system was completely revamped. Carbide had notified the United States Environmental Protection Agency of these changes, but not the Bhopal branch of operations. If indeed the Carbide plant in Bhopal was operated at unacceptably low standards, who is to blame? Will not all industries take cheaper, easier cost-cutting measures when allowed to do so? If industry in India were held to the same standards as industry in America, would Carbide have invested in the Bhopal operation? If industry will not regulate itself, and governments allow low standards to ensure foreign investment, who does regulate industry? Who should?

3. Perhaps the most devastating testimony against both Carbide and the Indian government is that of T R Chouhan, a chemical plant operator who used to work in the factory and has studied in detail the causes and implications of the accident. His book, *Inside the Killer Carbide Plant—A Bhopal Worker's Story* was published by Apex Press of New York in 1994. In his book, with the aid of charts, logs and chemical formulae, he alleges design faults, inadequate or non-existent safety measures, disregard of warnings and cost-cutting at the expense of safety. He also details the company's failure to divulge its research on the complex mixture of gases that escaped, their effects on the human organism and the best antidotes or treatment.

Chouhan also accuses the government of ignoring the problems at Carbide's Bhopal plant to a degree that smacks of a cover-up, or at least a wish to sweep the problem under the carpet. Even though the CBI used Chouhan's expertise to draw up charges against Carbide, Chouhan was transferred to a minor job as an industrial inspector in a small town 100 miles from his home in Bhopal.[5] The CBI has been ordered three times to provide evidence of the government's part in the disaster, yet

[5] John Rettie; *Out of Sight, Out of Mind*, THE GUARDIAN, 14 March 1994.

it has not complied. However, criminal prosecutions, for homicide not amounting to murder, have been brought against eight Union Carbide India Limited employees. Considering the government's role as exclusive plaintiff in all Bhopal disaster proceedings, is it conceivable that the government will ever be held accountable, or even forced to explain, its role in the disaster?

4. Finally, one of the major themes of many of the protests and demonstrations by the victims has been the culpability of Warren Anderson, the CEO of Carbide at the time of the disaster. In fact, he was often burned in effigy. Why is it so much more popular for victims to want the American CEO, rather than their own government leaders, brought to trial? How likely is it that prosecuting Anderson would prevent similar disasters in the future? Does it not make more sense to hold the Indian government accountable, thereby putting into place safeguards against future similar events?

C. THE FORUM

In a separate section of his 1988 order for interim compensation, High Court Justice Seth expressed the frustrations of an Indian whose government had preferred the American system to its own in a section entitled, 'A Word About Unbecoming Stand Taken By Plaintiff—Union of India Before U.S. District Court'.[6]

In 1993, the final wave of civil litigation in the United States courts was resolved against the plaintiff in *Bi v Union Carbide Chemicals and Plastics Co.*[7] The Second Circuit Court of Appeals dismissed the claims based on lack of standing. Excerpts from an American law journal article regarding both the *Bi Case* and the original dismissal on the basis of *forum non conveniens* in the original suit by the government in 1986,[8] follow.

HIGHET, KAHALE III, & VOLLMER; COMMENT, 88 American Journal of International Law 126 (1994)

> Faced with new attempts to assert claims in the United States arising from the gas leak disaster in Bhopal, India, after the termination of comprehensive proceedings in India, the court grappled for a theory to put an end to the litigation. It ultimately reached the right result, dismissing the claims, but for the wrong reasons, resting its decision on standing doctrine and using an unfortunate mix of politics and policy to

[6] *Union Carbide Corporation v Union of India* Civil Rev. No. 26 of 1988, 14 April 1988. The principal pleadings, judgments and orders in the *Bhopal Case* are reprinted in three volumes compiled by the Indian Law Institute: *Mass Disaster and Multi-National Liability: The Bhopal Case* (1986); *Inconvenient Forum and Convenient Catastrophe: The Bhopal Case* (1986) and U. Baxi & A. Dhanda, *Valiant Victims and Lethal Litigation: The Bhopal Case* (1990).

[7] 984 F. 2d 582 (2nd Cir.) (1993) *cert. denied*, 114 S. Ct. 179 (1993).

[8] *In re Union Carbide Corp. Gas Plant Disaster at Bhopal India in December, 1984*, 634 F. Supp. 842 (S.D. N.Y. 1986), *aff'd*, 809 F.2d 195 (2d Cir. 1986), *cert. denied*, 484 U.S. 871 (1987).

get there. The court ignored alternative rationales, such as recognition of foreign country judgments and the act of state doctrine, that would have permitted it to place the result on a sounder legal footing. ...

Affirming the dismissal of the complaints was wise and correct. Affirming on standing grounds with a soupcon of jingoistic civics and a splash of act of state was an approach that could have been improved. The Second Circuit's approach in Bi faltered in at least three significant ways.

First, the Second Circuit explicitly grounded its decision on standing although the case and the court's reasoning have nothing to do with traditional standing doctrine. Standing is a matter of US constitutional law that turns on several factors, including the requirement that the plaintiff suffer injury in fact. The doctrine does not depend on the type of government a foreign country has or the policies underlying the act of state doctrine. The appeals court understands this, of course, and therefore did not even venture a standard analysis of standing. ...

Second, the Court of Appeals engaged in the problematic exercise of appraising another country's government. It reviewed the political system in India, the independence of its judiciary and the guarantees of individual rights. Presumably it did so because the evaluation was relevant to its decision to defer to the Bhopal Act, and fortunately for India, the Indian system measured up. The court patronisingly decreed that 'India is a democracy.'

The Bi court should not have conducted this review. Few US actions are likely to cause greater foreign resentment and offense than the superficial examination by a federal court of the structure of a foreign country's government to determine whether it comports with our values. Such an examination is laden with value judgments and implies that systems of government differing from ours are not as worthy and do not produce laws that deserve our respect. It is also inconsistent with fundamental principles of international law and relations: the sovereign equality of nations and each state's sovereign authority to govern its territory. The United States is part of a plural world. Just as we expect tolerance and accommodations of our ways, so other nations generally deserve the same treatment from us.

NOTES AND QUESTIONS

1. In the article above, the authors describe the US Court of Appeals' tone as 'patronizing'. Justice Seth *felt* patronized. Yet, what the American courts seemed to have done with the government of India's efforts to litigate the Bhopal claims in the United States is to give full and fair respect to the Indian courts' abilities to remedy the situation. Why does this seem patronising to the authors and the Justice? Is it?

2. The party with the greatest lack of faith in the Indian courts throughout has always appeared to be the Indian government. After all, it was the government, as plaintiff, that initially tried to have the entire case heard in the United States. What does this say about the relationship between the executive and the judiciary in India? Or was the government of India merely shopping for a forum that could give it the largest tort damages?

3. Among the many reasons that various plaintiffs have continued to bring lawsuits in the United States are the large damages that American juries often give and that traditionally have not been available in India. However, in America, these often grossly disproportionate awards have been a topic of increased scrutiny, criticism and proposals for drastic reform. Might it therefore be wiser to maintain a system in which damages are kept to a proportionate level?

4. Another reason advanced for preferring the American court system is the experience of the American courts in coping with complex mass tort actions like Bhopal. Yet, how is another country's system supposed to develop if cases are tried elsewhere? The Indian courts took a long and circuitous path to the final settlement and the victims continued to suffer all the while. But such suffering may be endured in the initial stages of any case in any court system. Is there a better way to develop the judicial systems in developing countries, rather than at the expense of victims' lives, health and peace of mind? What about advisory judges from more developed countries?

D. THE GOVERNMENT

The role of the Indian government in the Bhopal disaster was that of an actor with multiple parts. The government was keen that transnational corporations such as Carbide set up shop in India, in the hope of creating jobs and drawing new technology and industry into this rapidly developing country. The government or its agents were also responsible for overseeing the construction and management of the Carbide plant, ensuring that applicable health and safety standards were met and maintained. Thus, its negligence in this role potentially could have made the government a defendant in the ensuing litigation, although this never transpired. Then with the passage of the Bhopal Act, the government named itself as sole plaintiff in all litigation arising from the gas disaster, a role that created enormous conflicts of interest. Finally, as a sovereign nation responsible for the welfare of its citizens, the Indian government had and continues to have the duty to care for its victims and act appropriately, through legislation, regulation and enforcement, to ensure that such a disaster never happens again. One newspaper reporter captured some of the conflicts inherent in the Indian government's many roles:

JOHN RETTIE; OUT OF SIGHT, OUT OF MIND, The Guardian,
14 March 1994

> In two articles written just after [the] settlement and never seriously challenged, the Supreme Court lawyer Prashant Bhushan said: 'The government has capitulated to Union Carbide for reasons that have nothing to do with justice or the plight of the victims, and the court has allowed itself to be used for that purpose.' In effect, he accused the government of doing the company's dirty work for it at the expense of

the victims, whose compensation was—and still is—long delayed so that, in despair, they would ultimately accept less.

Union Carbide was invited into India to bring new technology and provide jobs. ... ' The Madhya Pradesh government and Union Carbide: Partners in Progress' trumpeted the company's slogans as it set to work to build this dangerous factory—within the city limits. The government had no knowledge of MIC technology and designated the plant as a non-hazardous chemical plant because its final product, fertilizers, was just that. But the chemicals which went to make them were highly toxic.

Union Carbide all along maintained that the factory was not built in a built-up area and that people moved in around it later. This is true of Nanhe Khan's slum, Jai Prakash Nagar, but other densely populated areas nearby, in which thousands died, were there long before.

In this city of a million folk, the plant never provided more than 1,400 jobs, and on average fewer than 1,000. But it did give lucrative employment to the relatives of VIPs. It entertained politicians lavishly at its guest house, and invitations were always much sought after. It is widely believed to have contributed toward party funds, primarily those of the ruling Congress (I) party. It gave donations to such Congress-run, scandal-ridden charities as the Churhat Children's Relief Fund.

So the interests of Union Carbide were enmeshed with those of the Indian State and its elite. In such a corrupt society as India's the government, controlled by and in the last count representing that elite, could hardly be expected to confront the company by defending the opposing interests of the poor, the illiterate and the oppressed. It did not, of course. Instead it decreed that the victims, mostly illiterate, poor, ailing and bewildered, should run the gauntlet of the country's corrupt, bureaucratic and slothful apparatus. Almost as if they were guilty until proved innocent—or rather, healthy until proved ill. ...

Since the market reform programme launched in 1991, the government has become more keen than ever to attract foreign investment. It does not want Bhopal to spoil the prospects. So the bitter lesson of how a giant multinational behaves in a developing country is being ruthlessly brushed aside, at the expense of Indian victims. There are already many other dangerous factories in India, and many more will soon be coming in.

'Bhopal is like a window', says Sattinath Sarangi of the Bhopal Group for Information and Action. 'You can see the whole country through it.'

NOTES AND QUESTIONS

1. The CBI in December 1993, finally prepared the documents necessary to extradite Warren Anderson, the former CEO of Carbide.[9] Subsequently, an Indian court ordered the CBI to explain why extradition has not occurred. In September, 1994, the lawyer for CBI admitted there had been delays, but gave no reasons as to

---

[9] Press Trust of India News Agency, New Delhi; *Extradition Documents for Former Union Carbide Chairman Ready*, BBC Summary of World Broadcasts, 10 December 1993.

why. (As of April 2000, Anderson was still avoiding process service in the U.S.) Politically, does it make sense for the Indian government to demand Anderson's extradition? There are three different political perspectives involved, namely, the image the government has with its own constituents, many of whom are the most impoverished of its citizens; the political image of India in the international human rights community; and the political relationship India has with the United States. Which should take priority? Which has?

2. Were the Indian government to zealously pursue the prosecution of Anderson, what would be the likely reaction of other transnational corporations considering investment in India? Would this be good for India, in terms of protecting its people from exploitative and environmentally detrimental industry? Or would it be bad for India by inhibiting foreign investment in its economy and reducing its access to industry and technology that is so critical to gaining a foothold in the world market?

3. Consider the implications in the above article that the foreign investment only directly benefitted the elite in India, while the disaster affected the oppressed. Is this not true in every country, developed or developing? Is it true to a greater degree in India?

4. If, as the article maintains, there are indeed more Bhopal disasters lurking in India's future, and the government is actively recruiting such investments, who can prevent them? How should transnational corporate investment in developing countries be regulated? Should the United States bear the onus of overseeing the companies that are incorporated there, such as Carbide? How might that be possible? What would be the incentive to do so? Should an international oversight committee be created? Would this impinge on the sovereignty of nations, not to mention the fundamental principles of free trade?

5. Finally, which is more important, the right to a healthy environment or the right to development? Does it matter whether you ask an Indian citizen or an American citizen that question? Does it matter if either is rich or poor? Can the two rights co-exist?

E. THE SETTLEMENT

Whether a settlement was the preferable outcome of the disaster is a contentious point. In discussing the conflicts between groups formed to help the victims, the authors of one article have made the following observations:

ROSENCRANZ, DIVAN & SCOTT; LEGAL AND POLITICAL REPERCUSSIONS IN INDIA, in LEARNING FROM DISASTER: RISK MANAGEMENT AFTER BHOPAL, (S. Jasanoff, ed. 1994)

On one side were those—usually seriously affected victims—who wanted compensation from Carbide as quickly as possible. Many of the injured were unable to work and had severe and persistent medical problems. Without compensation they could not meet their medical bills, could not work, and often were unable to get enough to eat. Dependants of breadwinners who had been killed or disabled faced similar difficulties. The desire and need for speedy compensation caused all other issues to pale in comparison. The victims wanted relief and they wanted it as quickly as possible.

On the other side were those—often the leaders of the advocacy groups—for whom compensation was an issue but retribution against Union Carbide was at least as important. These advocates were opposed to any settlement not commensurate with what could be awarded in the United States for a disaster of comparable proportions. ...

Those who took the more strident stance were keenly sensitive to the historical inequalities of power between India and the United States. Conscious of India's long years as a colony, these groups did not want India to be under foreign influence of any kind. ...

NOTES AND QUESTIONS

1. As the excerpt illustrates, there are at least two sides to 'justice'—compensation and vindication. Which is more important? Does the status of the plaintiffs make a difference? Had the victims of Bhopal been primarily upper middle-class citizens, with enough savings to tide them over during litigation, would resolution on the merits have been more appropriate? Does this then imply that 'justice', in the retributive sense of the word, is a luxury, and not a right? If poorer people also have a 'right' to justice in the fullest sense of the word, what good does that right do them if they starve while attaining it?

2. The split in perspectives over a proper outcome often occurred between victims and leaders of advocacy groups who presumably were better off than most of the victims. Does this have any significance? Is it right to claim to represent a group when your goals are so divergent? When a lawyer represents any tort victim, is it more important to get the victim damages or have the tortfeasor found legally liable? Does it depend on the wishes of the client, or rather on what the lawyer perceives is in the client's best interest?

3. Most class action settlements require both the approval of the court and the notification, if not the approval, of the class. In the case of the Bhopal disaster, the victims were not even notified, and in a subsequent attack, the settlement was upheld. Thus, the victims were not allowed to sue on their own behalves, were denied resolution on the merits, and were not notified of the settlement of their claims. Can anyone truly say that the Bhopal disaster victims have received justice?

KIBEL & ROSENCRANZ; A BLANKET SPREAD TOO THIN: COMPENSATION FOR BHOPAL'S VICTIMS, Economic and Political Weekly, 2 July 1994, p. 1643

The existing Bhopal Settlement distribution scheme is based exclusively on compensating specific claimants for death or injury. This individual-based distribution scheme, by itself, fails to respond to the severe medical and social consequences of the Bhopal disaster unless it is integrated with 'community-based' distributions. These would fund institutions, programmes, and services that serve the larger, collective group of persons injured and adversely affected by the Bhopal accident, would provide effective long-term relief and assistance to survivors, and would serve as a landmark case of disaster relief. ...

Although the individual-based compensation scheme may appear as an appropriate, effective and fair response, the scheme possesses many flaws. These flaws render the scheme dysfunctional, and prevent the Indian government from achieving basic medical, social and justice-related goals. The three primary flaws concern (1) administrative burden and time delays; (2) the susceptibility of claimants to exploitation and manipulation; and (3) most importantly, the failure to provide for the future of the Bhopal community and affected unborn generations. ...

There is an alternative to the flaws and limitations of the individual-based distribution scheme—'community-based' compensation. Under this model, only a portion of settlement funds are distributed directly to individual claimants. A significant fraction of settlement funds are invested in institutions, programmes and services that will collectively benefit the entire class of claimants. The theory behind this alternative distribution scheme is simple. The claimants will derive the greatest benefit from pooling a portion of their individual claims, and developing an ongoing financial framework to deal with the Bhopal community's problems and needs.

NOTES AND QUESTIONS

1. Community based compensation, according to the authors, would be a more beneficial way of distributing some, if not most, of the settlement. One reason behind this contention is that the administrative burdens of an individual based compensation scheme are overwhelming. In fact, the Indian government has been neither prompt not efficient in distributing the individual awards, and many victims remain uncompensated today. However, the administrative burdens of long-term community investments, such as housing, hospitals and schools are also great. If the government is having such difficulty handing out money to individuals, what guarantees are there that it is any better equipped, or perhaps willing, to invest the energy and long-term planning in community benefits?

2. In fact, hospitals for the victims have been constructed, as has housing. However, the hospitals reportedly sell the medicine for the victims on the black market, thereby earning extra money and forcing victims to buy medicines from private pharmacies. In addition, housing developments lack the necessary public

transportation infrastructure and are at such great distances from the city's centre that many developments remain virtually uninhabited. With a track record like this, is it perhaps overly idealistic to suggest that the Indian government should construct its compensation awards on a community-based scheme?

The claims may be settled slowly, but despite delays, there has been an influx of money into Bhopal due to the policy of awarding compensation directly to victims. This, according to some, has had immediate mixed effects on the community. Ram Shankar Tiwari, Professor of Economics at the Academy of Administration in Bhopal, and his colleagues have conducted a survey of 21,000 survivors, before and after receiving compensation. According to Tiwari, the individual compensation awards seem to have done the community as a whole more harm than good. Among the beneficial impacts was an increase in the number of children going to school after the compensation was distributed and the remodelling and reconstruction of houses. On the whole, however, Tiwari and other authors of the study, cited primarily negative effects.

There was a paralytic effect on the community's work initiative; people who were self-employed before the disaster had sold off their assets and were living off the money. Intra-family disputes had increased due to quarrels over respective shares of cash awards. Along these same lines, instances of divorce and remarriage, in order to claim greater or multiple compensation awards, were reported. Finally, there was an alarming trend amongst compensation recipients to spend the money immediately, rather than invest the funds in long terms assets. Emphasizing the position that they were by no means opposed to the idea of compensation per se, Tiwari and his colleagues suggested that the money be distrubuted in cash only to the extent needed to pay medical bills, with the rest distributed in the form of insurance policies or government bonds for the victims.[10]

NOTES AND QUESTIONS

1. Judging from Tiwari's report, it appears that many of the fears of the advocates of the community based compensation scheme have in fact proved well grounded. Was the individual based scheme a mistake?

2. Doctors at a local government hospital maintain that some of the effects that Tiwari attributed to cash awards, such as lack of drive and initiative in the community, were actually 'a natural psychological sequel to such a traumatic event as the gas

---

[10] Sam Basir, *India-Bhopal: Relief Money May Spark Socioeconomic Crisis*, Inter Press Service, 9 December 1994.

disaster.' If this is the case, perhaps even a community based scheme would not have helped at least the first generation of disaster survivors. However, is it possible that after surviving such a disaster, the best compensation a victim could hope for is to be able to quit working and live off the award? Is that inherently a bad thing? Is there some benefit to making sick, traumatized, and possibly psychologically damaged victims invest their awards and get back to work?

3. What about future generations? Do they deserve compensation for potential genetic consequences?

F. THE COMPENSATION MACHINERY

The processing of claims filed by victims takes place in special courts established for the purpose of distributing the moneys received from Carbide under the settlement. To obtain compensation, a claimant has to obtain a medical certificate which puts her into various categories, graded on the seriousness of the injury. On the basis of the certificate, the victim files her claim before the special court.

Serious charges of graft have tarnished the integrity of the distribution machinery. Media reports recount numerous instances of kickbacks paid by victims to governmental officials, a racket involving counterfeiting of claim documents and even corruption by a compensation judge.

According to the Sambhavna Trust, Bhopal, Rs. 850 crores have been paid to 320,000 claimants as of November, 1998. A balance of Rs.100 crores remains to be distributed. More than 90 per cent of the claimants have been paid a sum less than Rs. 25,000 ($600) for personal injuries. From these modest awards 'nearly Rs. 10,000 have been routinely deducted against interim monetary relief paid by the government from 1990.'[11] The remaining sum does not begin to cover claimants' medical expenses, much less provide for future expenses.

Judges at the claims court seem 'completely ignorant of the medical consequences of toxic (chemical) exposure. ... [T]he administration of compensation is riddled with corruption, so that the claimants' inability to pay bribes [has often resulted] in the denial of compensation.'[12]

Over the years, the Supreme Court has overseen the distribution of settlement funds[13] and interim relief for the victims.[14] The court has also spent much time and resources over the construction of a hospital at Bhopal.[15] In 1992, it issued directions

[11] *The Bhopal Gas Tragedy: A Report from the Sambhavna Trust*, 15 (1998).
[12] *Id.*
[13] *Indian Red Cross v Union of India* 1992 (2) SCC 53.
[14] *Bhopal Gas Peerit Mahila Udyog Sanghatan v Union of India* 1992 (2) SCALE 498; 1992 (3) SCALE 251; 1993 Supp (4) SCC 481.
[15] *Union Carbide Corporation Ltd. v Union of India* 1994 (4) SCALE 973; 1996 (1) SCALE 14 (SP); 1996 (2) SCALE 46 (SP); 1996 (3) SCALE 64 (SP); 1998 (1) SCALE 32; 1998 (5) SCALE 2 (SP). Also see *Bhopal Gas Peedith Mahila v Sangat v Union of India* 2000 (1) SCALE 355.

for the transfer of settlement funds from the Supreme Court registry to the Welfare Commissioner,[16] and has since occasionally intervened to ensure that the victims receive compensation quickly.[17] In 1996, the Supreme Court upheld the award of Rs. 150,000 to the parents of a four month old girl who died in December, 1986. The child was born seriously disabled, nearly two years after the gas leak. The court relied upon the evidence of the doctor who had deposed on the adverse effects of the gas before the Deputy Commissioner. The doctor had treated patients after the MIC gas leak and found that newly born children suffered adverse effects even where the pregnancy was post gas leakage. The mother of the girl was one of the victims of the gas tragedy.[18]

One hopes that the Bhopal tragedy will never be repeated. But if a similar situation were ever to arise, would it not behoove the authorities not only to provide the victims with social and rehabilitative services, including health care, education, welfare, housing and job training, but also some financial planning services? Many victims have been reported to have lost their entire settlement awards to unscrupulous dealers, middlemen and other assorted predators.

During the 1990s, Indian courts were confronted primarily with two legal matters related to the Bhopal disaster. The first is the continual pressure from activist groups to bring criminal proceedings against Carbide Chairman Warren Anderson, mentioned earlier, and against officials of Union Carbide of India Ltd. (UCIL). On 13 September 1996, the Supreme Court concluded that the acts or omissions of Carbide officials on the night of the gas leak could not amount to culpable homicide, although other criminal charges might apply.[19]

The other main issue was the creation of the Bhopal Hospital Trust. To meet the needs of the gas victims, the Supreme Court, on 3 October 1991, ordered the Government of India to construct a 500-bed hospital. The costs of hospital construction and operation for eight years was to be borne by Carbide and UCIL. Carbide refused to put up the money but it was ultimately supplied by the Bhopal District Court's attachment and eventual liquidation of UCIL's shares when criminally charged Carbide officials failed to turn up in court to face trial.

Shortly after the Bhopal District Court attached Carbide's UCIL shares, Carbide registered a charitable trust in London to provide medical relief in Bhopal. Sir Ian Percival, a former UK solicitor-general, was named as sole trustee. Carbide pledged it's shares in UCIL to the Bhopal Hospital Trust, even though the Bhopal District Court had ordered that the money to construct the hospital must come from Carbide's own coffers. But in February, 1994, Sir Ian was able to persuade the

---

[16] Union Carbide India Ltd. v Union of India AIR 1994 SC 101.

[17] Krishna Mohan Shukla v Union of India 1995 (6) SCALE 410; Bhopal Gas Peerit Mahila Udyog Sanghatan v Union of India 1999 (3) SCALE 8.

[18] S. Said-ud-Din v Court of Welfare Commissioner 1996 (3) SCALE 28 (SP).

[19] Keshub Mahindra v State of Madhya Pradesh 1996 (6) SCC 129.

Supreme Court to allow him to sell the attached shares in UCIL to enable the trust to build the hospital.[20]

Sir Ian died in April, 1998. Financial accounts of the trust submitted to the Supreme Court show that between 1995 and 1998, Sir Ian spent Rs.10 crores (US $2.5 million) from Bhopal Hospital Trust funds to refurbish his London office, pay himself large trustee fees, and support his travel and office expenses.[21] In his four years as sole trustee, Sir Ian also persuaded the Supreme Court to use additional UCIL assets to expand the hospital to 500 beds and to add a cardio-thoracic unit— even though the international medical committee on Bhopal submitted an affidavit to the Supreme Court charging that Sir Ian's plans had no medical justification. Not only was there no need for more hospital beds, but the greatest need was for out patient services and community health care facilities. Also, there had been no cardiac disease reported amongst the gas-affected victims. The most commonly reported ailments are respiratory, neurological, neuro-psychological and eye disease.

Survivors' organizations have pointed out that Bhopal may already have more hospital beds per capita than anywhere else in the world, and that another hospital is not needed, except to shore up Carbide's image. Survivors want to take control of the Bhopal Hospital Trust funds to administer appropriate health care among gas-affected people.

Students of the Bhopal litigation may question whether a trust set up by a proclaimed absconder should be accorded recognition by any judicial or governmental body in India. Clearly, the Supreme Court seems to have been unduly impressed by Sir Ian Percival's status and reputation. It gave him what he asked for, and apparently looked the other way at his self-dealing.

---

[20] *Union Carbide Corpn. Ltd. v Union of India* 1994 (1) SCALE 811. A review of the 14 February 1994 order was rejected on 20 October 1994. 1994 (4) SCALE 189.
[21] *Supra* note 11, at 20.

14

TRANSNATIONAL ENVIRONMENTAL
POLICIES

Geographically, India is surrounded on the west, north and east, by Pakistan, China, Nepal, Bhutan, Burma, and Bangladesh, with Sri Lanka situated just off its southern tip. These countries share some of the world's great rivers, highest mountains, diverse wildlife, and air and ocean resources. India has been the dominant player in many of the bilateral and regional agreements to manage, share, and preserve these resources.

The most successful and simultaneously controversial efforts to manage transnational resources between India and its neighbours have focussed on fresh water resources, with the Indo-Pakistan Indus River Basin Treaty scheme representing the greatest success in terms of longevity. While other agreements have been reached concerning river waters with both Nepal and Bangladesh, these have proved less enduring. Bilateral or regional efforts in the areas of mountain ecosystem preservation and trade in wildlife are under way. Air pollution treaties among the South Asian countries, however, are conspicuous by their absence.

This chapter concentrates primarily on river management between India and its neighbours. Notes and questions are interspersed throughout the chapter and contain some information on the efforts to manage other resources.

Three interrelated issues should be kept in mind throughout this chapter. First, many, if not all, of these resources are life-sustaining. Thus, as opposed to some bilateral agreements concerning, for example, immigration or military security, these agreements need to be negotiated with increasing urgency. Second, all these resources are interrelated within regional ecosystems. One cannot consider any transboundary natural resource in a vacuum. Although we have separated them to a certain degree for the purposes of simplification, the separation is artificial. Finally, each negotiation takes place with political overtones. Many of these neighbouring countries have a long history of colonialism followed by political upheaval. Hence, agreements negotiated by any two governments are often not acceptable to newer regimes, or provide the foundation for political platforms by opposition parties.

Fresh water, in the form of rivers, is one of the most heated issues of our time, and controversy surrounding fresh water worldwide is predicted to escalate in the next few decades. In fact, experts predict that tomorrow's wars may be fought over fresh water, as the supply grows scarcer and the demand increases. Water is crucial for survival. Beyond the value of unpolluted and abundant drinking water, fresh water is needed for agriculture. Water is also necessary for livestock and industry, sustenance and commercial fishing, and transportation. Finally, especially in states that border mountain ranges, such as Nepal and India, water represents a huge, and largely untapped, source of energy. Hence, free flowing rivers are often a bone of contention between neighbouring countries, and South Asia is no exception.

A. THE INDUS RIVER BASIN

The Indus River Basin covers 930,000 square kilometres in India and Pakistan. It consists of the Indus River, which rises from the Tibetan Plateau to travel 2900 kilometres to the Arabian sea. Its major tributaries, ranging in length from 400–1450 kilometres long, are the Kabul, the Jhelum, the Chenab, the Beas, the Ravi and the Sutlej. Each year approximately 1700 million acre feet of water passes through the Indus system, 69 per cent from India, 19 per cent from Pakistan, and 12 per cent combined from Tibet and Afghanistan.[1]

One of the most successful bilateral agreements made by India is the agreement between India and Pakistan over the Indus River Basin. Negotiated by the World Bank, India and Pakistan signed the Treaty at Karachi on 19 September 1960.[2] Nearly four decades later, it is still in effect. Excerpts from this historic effort follow:

THE INDUS WATERS TREATY BETWEEN INDIA AND PAKISTAN;
19 September 1960

PREAMBLE. The Government of India and the Government of Pakistan, being equally desirous of attaining the most complete and satisfactory utilization of the waters of the Indus system of rivers and recognising the need, therefore, of fixing and delimiting, in a spirit of goodwill and friendship, the rights and obligations of each in relation to the other concerning the use of these waters and of making

---

[1] Data for this section was drawn from Concannon, *The Indus Waters Treaty: Three Decades of Success, Yet, Will it Endure?*, 2 GEORGETOWN INTL. L. REV. 55 (1989).

[2] The full text of the treaty, with annexures, is available in the United Nations Legislative Series, Legislative Texts and Treaty Provisions Concerning The Utilization of International Rivers For Other Purposes Than Navigation (1963), U.N. Doc. No. ST/LEG/SER.B/12.

provision for the settlement, in a cooperative spirit, of all such questions as may hereafter arise in regard to the interpretation or application of the provisions agreed upon herein, have resolved to conclude a Treaty in furtherance of these objectives * * *

ARTICLE I: *Definitions*

As used in this Treaty: * * *

(5) The term 'Eastern Rivers' means The Sutlej, The Beas and The Ravi taken together.

(6) The term 'Western Rivers' means The Indus, The Jhelum and The Chenab taken together ...

(8) The term 'Connecting Lake' means any lake which receives water from, or yields water to any of the Rivers; but any lake which occasionally or irregularly receives only the spill of any of the Rivers and returns only the whole or part of that spill is not a Connecting Lake.

(9) The term 'Agricultural Use' means the use of water for irrigation of household gardens and public recreational gardens.

(10) The term 'Domestic Use' means the use of water for:

    (a) Drinking, washing, bathing, recreation, sanitation (including the conveyance and dilution of sewage and of industrial and other wastes), stock and poultry, and other like purposes;

    (b) Household and municipal purposes (including use for household gardens and public recreational gardens); and

    (c) Industrial purposes (including mining, milling and other like purposes); but the term does not include Agricultural Use or use for the generation of hydro-electric power.

(11) The term 'Non-Consumptive Use' means any control or use of water for navigation, floating of timber or other property, flood protection or flood control, fishing or fish culture, wild life or other like beneficial purposes, provided that, exclusive of seepage and evaporation of water incidental to the control or use, the water (undiminished in volume within the practical range of measurement) remains in, or is returned to, the same river or its Tributaries; but the term does not include Agricultural Use or use for the generation of hydro-electric power. ...

(13) The term 'Bank' means the International Bank for Reconstruction and Development. ...

(15) The term 'interference with the waters' means:

    (a) Any act of withdrawal therefrom; or

    (b) Any man-made obstruction to their flow which causes a change in the volume (within the practical range of measurement) of the daily flow of the waters: Provided however that an obstruction which involves only an insignificant and incidental change in the volume of the daily flow, example, fluctuations due to afflux caused by bridge piers or a temporary by-pass, etc., shall not be deemed to be an interference with the waters. ...

ARTICLE II: *Provisions regarding Eastern Rivers*

(1) All the waters of the Eastern Rivers shall be available for the unrestricted use of India, except as otherwise expressly provided in this Article.

(2) Except for Domestic Use and Non-Consumptive Use, Pakistan shall be under an obligation to let flow, and shall not permit any interference with, the waters of the Sutlej Main and the Ravi Main in the reaches where these rivers flow in Pakistan and have not yet finally crossed into Pakistan. ...

(3) Except for Domestic Use, Non-Consumptive Use and Agricultural Use as specified in Annexure B, Pakistan shall be under an obligation to let flow, and shall not permit any interference with, the waters (while flowing in Pakistan) of any Tributary which in its natural course joins the Sutlej Main before these rivers have finally crossed into Pakistan.

(4) All the waters, while flowing in Pakistan, of any Tributary which, in its natural course, joins the Sutlej Main or the Ravi Main after these rivers have finally crossed into Pakistan shall be available for the unrestricted use of Pakistan: Provided however that this provision shall not be construed as giving Pakistan any claim or right to any releases by India in any such Tributary. If Pakistan should deliver any of the waters of any such Tributary, which on the Effective Date [1 April 1960] joins the Ravi Main after this river has finally crossed into Pakistan, into the reach of the Ravi Main upstream of this crossing, India shall not make use of these waters; each party agrees to establish such discharge observation stations and make such observations as may be necessary for the determination of the component of water available for the use of Pakistan on account of the aforesaid deliveries by Pakistan, and Pakistan agrees to meet the cost of establishing the aforesaid observations.

(5) There shall be a Transition Period [of 10–13 years] during which, to the extent specified in Annexure H, India shall

   (i) Limit its withdrawals for Agricultural Use,

   (ii) Limit abstractions for storages, and

   (iii) Make deliveries to Pakistan from the Eastern Rivers. ...

(9) During the Transition Period, Pakistan shall receive for unrestricted use the waters of the Eastern Rivers which are to be released by India in accordance with the Provisions of Annexure H. After the end of the Transition Period, Pakistan shall have no claim or right to releases by India of any of the waters of the Eastern Rivers. In case there are any releases, Pakistan shall enjoy the unrestricted use of the waters so released after they have finally crossed into Pakistan: Provided that in the event that Pakistan makes any use of these waters, Pakistan shall not acquire any right whatsoever, by prescription or otherwise, to a continuance of such releases or such use.

ARTICLE III: *Provisions regarding Western Rivers*

(1) Pakistan shall receive for unrestricted use all those waters of the Western Rivers which India is under obligation to let flow under the provisions of Paragraph (2).

(2) India is under an obligation to let flow all the waters of the Western Rivers, and shall not permit any interference with these waters, except for the following

uses, restricted ... in the case of each of the rivers, The Indus, The Jhelum and The Chenab, to the drainage basin thereof:

    (a)   Domestic Use;

    (b)   Non-Consumptive Use;

    (c)   Agricultural Use, as set out in Annexure C; and

    (d)   Generation of hydro-electric power, as set out in Annexure D. ...

(4)   Except as provided in Annexure D and E, India shall not store water of, or construct any storage works on, the Western Rivers.

ARTICLE IV: *Provisions regarding the Eastern Rivers and the Western Rivers*

(1)   Pakistan shall use its best endeavours to construct and bring into operation, with due regard to expedition and economy, that part of a system of works which will accomplish the replacement, from the Western Rivers and other sources, of water supplies for irrigation canals in Pakistan which, on 15 August 1947, were dependent on water supplies from the Eastern Rivers.

(2)   Each Party agrees that any Non-Consumptive Uses made by it shall be so made as not to materially change, on account of such use, the flow in any channel to the prejudice of the uses on that channel by the other Party under the provisions of this Treaty. In executing any scheme of flood protection or flood control each Party will avoid, as far as practicable, any material damage to the other Party, and any such scheme carried out by India on the Western Rivers shall not involve any use of water or storage in addition to that provided under Article III.

(3)   Nothing in this Treaty shall be construed as having the effect of preventing either Party from undertaking schemes of drainage, or from removal of stones, gravel or sand from the bed of the Rivers. ...

(6)   Each Party will use its best endeavours to maintain the natural channels of the Rivers, as on the Effective Date, in such condition as will avoid, as far as practicable, any obstruction to the flow in these channels likely to cause material damage to the other Party. ...

(8)   The use of the natural channels of the Rivers for the discharge of flood or other excess waters shall be free and not subject to limitation by either Party, and neither Party shall have any claim against the other in respect of any damage caused by such use. Each Party agrees to communicate to the other Party, as far in advance as practicable, any information it may have in regard to such extraordinary discharges of water from reservoirs and flood flows as may affect the other Party.

(9)   Each Party declares its intention to operate its storage dams, barrages and irrigation canals in such manner, consistent with the normal operations of its hydraulic systems, as to avoid, as far as feasible, material damage to the other Party.

(10)   Each Party declares its intention to prevent, as far as practicable, undue pollution of the waters of the Rivers which might affect adversely uses similar in nature to those to which the waters were put on the Effective Date, and agrees to take all reasonable measures to ensure that, before any sewage or industrial waste is allowed to flow into the rivers, it will be treated, where necessary, in such manner as not materially to affect those uses: Provided that the criterion of reasonableness shall be the customary practice in similar situations on the Rivers. ...

(12) The use of water for industrial purposes under Articles II (2), II (3), and III (2) shall not exceed:

    (a)   In the case of an industrial process known on the Effective Date, such quantum of use as was customary in that process on the Effective Date;

    (b)   In the case of an industrial process not known on the Effective Date:

        (i)   Such quantum of use as was customary on the Effective Date in similar or in any way comparable industrial processes; or

        (ii)   If there was no industrial process on the Effective Date similar or in any way comparable to the new process, such quantum of use as would not have a substantially adverse effect on the other Party. ...

ARTICLE V: *Financial provisions*

[Mandates India's payment to Pakistan of a contribution of Pounds Sterling 62,060,000 towards the cost of irrigation canals that will free Pakistan from its dependence on the supply of the Eastern Rivers. In the event that the transition period is extended from ten to thirteen years, the Bank will take over the payment of amounts deposited therein by India.]

ARTICLE VI: *Exchange of data*

[Mandates monthly exchange between the two countries of data on daily river discharges, daily extractions from and releases to reservoirs, daily withdrawals from the heads of canals, daily escapages from canals, and daily deliveries from link canals, plus any other information that might be available if requested.]

* * *

ARTICLE VII: *Future Co-operation*

[1.   The first section primarily reiterates the agreement to exchange data not specified by the Treaty at the request of a Party, and encourages agreement and cooperation in building new drainage and engineering works involving the Rivers.]

2.   If either Party plans to construct any engineering work which would cause interference with the waters of any of the Rivers and which, in its opinion, would affect the other Party materially, it shall notify the other Party of its plans and shall supply such data relating to the work as may be available and as would enable the other Party to inform itself of the nature, magnitude and effect of the work. If a work would cause interference with the waters of any of the Rivers but would not, in the opinion of the Party planning it affect the other Party materially, nevertheless the Party planning the work shall, on request, supply the other Party with such data regarding the nature, magnitude and effect, if any, of the work as may be available.

ARTICLE VIII: *Permanent Indus Commission*

(1)   India and Pakistan shall each create a permanent post of Commissioner for Indus Waters, and shall appoint to this post, as often as a vacancy occurs, a

person who should ordinarily be a high-ranking engineer competent in the field of hydrology and water-use. Unless either Government should decide to take up any particular question directly with the other Government, each Commissioner will be the representative of his Government for all matters arising out of this Treaty, and will serve as the regular channel of communication on all matters relating to the implementation of this Treaty. ...

(3) The two Commissioners shall together form the Permanent Indus Commission. [The Commission's responsibilities include inspection tours of the River at least once every five years and annual meetings alternating from Pakistan to India. Each Government shall grant the other's Commissioner the privileges and immunities that are granted to representatives of member States of the United Nations.]

ARTICLE IX: *Settlment of difference and disputes*

(1) Any question which arises between the Parties concerning the interpretation or application of this Treaty or the existence of any fact which, if established, might constitute a breach if this Treaty shall first be examined by the Commission, which will endeavour to resolve the question by agreement.

(2) If the Commission does not reach agreement on any of the question mentioned in Paragraph (1), then a difference will be deemed to have arisen, which shall be dealt with as follows: [In most cases, first a Neutral Expert is consulted. If the Neutral Expert cannot resolve the issue, then a dispute is deemed to have arisen. If the Commission cannot resolve the dispute, or one of the Governments feels that there has been undue delay, the two Governments may negotiate the dispute with mediators, finally resorting to a Court of Arbitration if necessary.]

* * *

ARTICLE XI: *General Provisions*

(1) It is expressly understood that
   (a) This Treaty governs the rights and obligations of each Party in relation to the other with respect only to the use of the waters of the Rivers and matters incidental thereto; and
   (b) Nothing contained in this Treaty, and nothing arising out of the execution thereof, shall be construed as constituting a recognition or waiver (whether tacit, by implication or otherwise) of any rights or claims whatsoever of either of the Parties other than those rights or claims which are expressly recognised or waived by this Treaty.

Each of the Parties agrees that it will not invoke this Treaty, anything contained therein, or anything arising out of the execution thereof, in support of any of its own rights or claims whatsoever or in disputing any of the rights or claims whatsoever of the other Party, other than those rights or claims which are expressly recognized or waived in this Treaty.

(2) Nothing in this Treaty shall be construed by the Parties as in any way establishing any general principle of law or any precedent.

(3) The right and obligations of each Party under this Treaty shall remain unaffected

by any provisions contained in, or anything arising out of the execution of, any agreement establishing the Indus Basin Development Fund. ...

NOTES AND QUESTIONS

1. Prior to the Treaty, Pakistan was heavily dependent on Eastern Rivers water to supply its irrigation and inundation canals, built by the British while both countries were united and under a single sovereign. The Treaty ends this dependence by mandating construction of independent storage works and link canals in each country that would enable the two countries to evenly partition the Basin Rivers, Eastern and Western. In order to do so, India agreed to compensate Pakistan for its loss of the Eastern Rivers water with a contribution to their construction of a new system. The rest of the financing however, took the form of a World Bank loan of $90 million and the establishment of another agreement, the Indus River Basin Development Fund Agreement. The agreement was signed on 19 September 1960, by the United States, Australia, West Germany, the United Kingdom, New Zealand and Canada.[3]

What does the role of the World Bank and foreign powers in negotiating and maintaining a successful treaty regime imply? Is it meaningful that the most successful of India's bilateral agreements is financially and politically multilateral? Is this an appropriate role for the World Bank to take?

2. Note that there is very little regarding water pollution in the Treaty. Article IV (10) addresses the issue of 'undue' pollution and prevention 'as far as practicable.' What do those words mean (they are not addressed in the definitions section)? If the standard is truly the 'customary practices in similar situations on the Rivers,' what incentive is there to clean up the pollution? Could evolving standards of pollution control over the last four decades be written into the Treaty? Is this a matter that the Commission or other dispute resolution procedures were meant to address?

3. Also missing from the Treaty is any mention of environmental degradation. Beyond water pollution, how are the issues of, for example, erosion, fisheries, or salination to be resolved?

4. Articles II(2), II(3) and III(2) all permit the use of water for industrial purposes, as limited by Article IV(12). With today's water intensive industries, is this perhaps the biggest flaw in the Treaty? Taken in conjunction with the 'customary practice' standard for water pollution discussed above, is this an invitation for both nations to dump as much industrial effluent into the waters as they please? Is Pakistan, as the downstream state, at a severe disadvantage here?

5. A major source of potential conflict between India and Pakistan, and one reason for the potential breakdown of the Treaty, is identified and addressed in the following excerpt:

[3] The Indus Basin Development Fund Agreement, signed at Karachi, Pakistan, 19 September 1960, 12 U.S.T. 19, 444 UNTS 259 (1960).

CONCANNON; THE INDUS WATERS TREATY: THREE
DECADES OF SUCCESS, YET, WILL IT ENDURE?
2 Georgetown Int'l. Envtl. L. Rev. 55 (1989)

The Indus Treaty and construction of works pursuant to it were based on the expectation that past climate patterns would continue into the future. Recent observations of the effect of greenhouse gasses in the atmosphere, however, indicate that the global climate [will] change to an extent not previously encountered in human experience. Consequently, the factual assumptions underlying the agreement may not be accurate in the future. ...

The Treaty itself contains no provisions to guide such a modification. ... The dispute resolution provisions of Article IX would not help either. They apply only to questions of interpretation, application, or breach of obligations, not to major adjustments to new conditions.

What the Treaty does allow, and even encourages, is unilateral action. ... Under the Treaty, India and Pakistan may each respond to the changing conditions brought about by global climate change. Although this arrangement will allow each state latitude and flexibility in its response and will minimize the opportunity for international friction, it may not allow the comprehensive and coordinated responses that the changes will require. The two countries have to work together, to modify the treaty or create a new agreement if they are to effectively respond to the challenges posed by global climate change.

Does this mean that the Treaty may eventually fail? Is not India's position the stronger one of the two, and if so, what incentive does India have to renegotiate? Will the World Bank have to step in to renegotiate the Treaty or help draft a new one? Should the Bank and other nations intervene sooner, rather than later?

6. Is the Treaty's endurance in the face of the painful history of Indo-Pakistan relations a testament to its strength, or at least to the two countries' continued mutual interest in water sharing arrangements?

B. THE GANGA-BRAHMAPUTRA RIVER BASIN SYSTEM

The South Himalayan watershed is hydrologically defined by the Ganga-Brahmaputra Basin, and makes up most of the northern half of the Indian subcontinent. The headwaters of the Ganga and the Brahmaputra rise in the Himalayas. The system covers 1.8 million square kilometers of northern and northeastern India, Nepal, Bhutan, Bangladesh and Tibet. The Basin has a monthly surface runoff of approximately 10 billion cubic metres for about eight months of the year. During the four months of the monsoon, average monthly runoff is 110 billion cubic metres.

Of the basin system, the most controversial dispute has centred on the sharing of the water of the Ganga. Some of the tributaries of the Ganga rise in Nepal and join the main river in India which flows into Bangladesh, before emptying into the Bay of Bengal. While the Arun III dam project in Nepal was scrapped in 1994, thereby saving India from the potentially disastrous diversion of Ganga water by Nepal, tensions between India, Nepal and Bangladesh over the Ganga have simmered over the past two decades. India blames Nepal for deforestation in the Himalayas, which India claims is disrupting the flow of the Ganga. In 1974, India completed the Farakka barrage, a short distance from the Bangladesh border, to divert Ganga water into the Hooghly River so as to improve navigation and increase water supplies for Calcutta. In 1977, Bangladesh and India made a short-term bilateral agreement to share the Ganga dry season flow and guarantee Bangladesh minimum amounts of water during periods of extremely low flows. This agreement expired in 1982, to be replaced by an informal accord between the two governments that did not contain a minimum amount guarantee clause for Bangladesh. A follow-up informal agreement expired in 1988.

For eight years thereafter an agreement eluded the neighbours until December, 1996 when two newly elected governments in Dhaka and Delhi pushed through a 30 year accord. On the Indian side, Prime Minister Deve Gowda's task of securing the consent of the riparian states of Bihar and West Bengal was made easier by regional political alliances. Both state administrations were political allies of Gowda's ruling coalition in Delhi. In Bangladesh, the treaty was a diplomatic triumph for Prime Minister Sheikh Hasina Wajed who was seen as having successfully negotiated a fair share of the Ganga waters for her country.

Under the December 1996 pact, both countries will receive 35,000 cusecs (cubic feet per second) of water in alternative 10 day periods during the dry months from March to May. If the flow is between 50,000–70,000 cusec at Farakka, both countries share equally. However, if the flow drops below 50,000 cusec in a 10 day period, the two sides must immediately meet to make adjustments on an emergency basis.[4]

Diversion of the Ganga in India has had severe environmental and economic effects on Bangladesh. In 1993, the dry season flow of the Ganga into Bangladesh was the lowest ever recorded. In the northwestern region of Bangladesh, one of the country's largest agricultural schemes, the Ganga-Kobadak Project, suffered an estimated US$ 25 million in losses. As the Ganga no longer reaches the Bay of Bengal during the dry season, a saline front has rapidly intruded from the sea and advanced across the western portion of the delta, damaging coastal mangrove forests, vegetation and fisheries. On the Indian side of the border, however, things are not much better. India's water shortage and pollution problems with the Ganga are notorious. To make matters worse, the port at Calcutta is being subsumed by layers of silt, even with the current levels of diversion of the Ganga via the Farakka barrage.

---

[4] *Finding the Course at Last*, in *Down to Earth*, 15 January 1997 and Ruben Banerjee, *Defying the Current*, INDIA TODAY, 15 January 1997

The Brahmaputra, while not as divisive an issue as the Ganges, also has its share of controversies. Its flow has also been disrupted by deforestation. In a geographically interesting twist, the rise in the silt levels in the Brahmaputra have begun to form a huge island in the Bay of Bengal, which both India and Bangladesh claim as their territory.

The disputes over water are often perceived as issues involving only two countries, primarily because India, a dominant player in South Asian policies, generally negotiates only bilaterally, as opposed to multilaterally. This, however, is an artificial scenario created by political preferences, rather than ecological realities—river basins are shared by many countries. The political, ecological and geographical aspects of water resource management are illustrated in the following excerpt:

SHARMA; THE FARAKKA FALLOUT, The Hindu, New Delhi, 29–30 April 1997

Although Bangladesh is blessed with 230 rivers flowing over 24,000 km., only one river counts, the Ganga. The issue of sharing its waters, following the construction of the Farakka barrage, has been the single most important reason for the deterioration in Indo-Bangla friendship.

* * *

The water sharing formula of the first treaty of 1977 worked reasonably well for some years. But since 1988, when the arrangement broke down altogether, the anti-India feeling centred around the Farakka issue has grown steadily in Bangladesh. As a result, the 1996 treaty, signed last December, has been met with considerable scepticism in the country. Within a few months of its existence, it has already been declared unworkable.

Officials in Dhaka doubt almost everything stated by the Indian side, including the validity of flow data, and accuse New Delhi of withholding vital information. Professor Aiunun Nishat, one of the negotiators from Bangladesh in the recent treaty, complains, 'What we read in newspapers is the level of knowledge at the Government level. It is important that we implement the 1996 treaty with full trust. But in the last four weeks (in March,1997) the treaty is not being implemented in toto.'

The problems clearly go deeper than what Prof. Nishat and others see as 'deception' by India on flow data. Take this lean season. It happens, as Dr Amjad Hossain Khan, former Chairman of the Bangladesh Water Resources Board, acknowledges, to be 'a bad hydrological year'. By mid-March it was already clear that water levels were dropping. By April, flow levels had fallen to below 50,000 cusecs.

Why was such an eventuality not envisaged by those who formulated, negotiated and subsequently signed the treaty? It is apparent that regardless of how the current problem is sorted out, there has been a certain measure of unreality on both sides. India seems determined not to acknowledge that developments upstream of Farakka, such as illegal lift irrigation schemes in Uttar Pradesh and Bihar, could be affecting low season flows substantially. And Bangladesh appears determined to deny a reality that has prevailed now for over two decades, that Farakka or not, there is less water in the Ganga and so its plans on using this water have to be modified.

* * *

Another adverse impact of the Farakka one is told about is the apparent 'desertification' of the Barind Tract in northern Bangladesh. This area—'an infertile tract' according to an environmental lawyer—with lower than average rainfall also had a lower density of population. In the 1970s, following the first treaty between India and Bangladesh, the latter decided to develop this area by encouraging ground water irrigation and by introducing high-yielding varieties of rice. The lower prices of land and the availability of water drew people to the region resulting in a dramatic increase in its population. And today, it is a [cultivated] area with paddy fields watered by an irrigation system comprising deep tube wells and an underground distribution network.

Although the system worked well initially, it began to crack under the strain of increasing demands on ground water and the lowered ability of the Ganga to replenish the underground aquifers during the lean season. As a result, there has been a substantial drop in ground water levels in the last decade. Irrigation engineers in the area will admit that there are two reasons for this—excessive drawing of water for irrigation and Farakka. However, officials in Dhaka prefer to mention only the impact of the low flows in the Ganga.

Of course, by Indian standards the fall in water levels does not appear drastic when you can strike water at 50–60 feet. But hardship is a matter of perception. For populations that could get water from shallow wells at 25 feet and who are used to an over-abundant supply of water, even worrying about water is akin to desertification.

While allegations of 'desertification' in northern Bangladesh might appear exaggerated, as you drive past lush paddy fields and over flowing natural ponds, where you do see a desert is in a major distributary of the Ganga. The Gorai starts 16 km downstream of the 1.1 km-long Hardinge Bridge across the Ganga in Bangladesh.

According to the Director of the Ganga-Kobadak Irrigation Project, Mr Mohammed Obaidur Rahman, the Gorai stopped flowing in 1988–89. This marks the period when the understanding between India and Bangladesh over sharing of the Ganga water had broken down. ...

For five months in the year, the Gorai is a veritable desert. Inadequate flows to carry the high silt load have raised the height of the river bed at its offtake point from the Ganga, three metres higher than the main river. As a result, the Gorai receives no water once water levels fall in the Ganga. The Bangladesh Government plans to dredge upstream for 31 km from the offtake point and divert 5000 cusecs from the Ganga into the Gorai. This, it is hoped, will help the river to start flowing again over time.

* * *

Why should any of this concern India?. ... Dr Swain, who hails from Orissa, has done extensive research in Bangladesh, particularly in the divisions bordering India. According to his studies, there has been a dramatic drop in the growth of the population in Khulna division in the last two decades which cannot be attributed to better population control measures. Between 1981 and 1991, Khulna division saw a population growth rate of only 1.62 per cent while the average in the country was over 2 per cent. In the past the population growth rate in this area has been higher than the national average. So what has happened?

Dr Swain found that many occupations, specially fisherfolk and agriculturists, had been marginalised by the environmental fallout of the low flow of the Ganga. While there has been a noticeable drop in the fish catch, rendering thousands of fisherfolk unemployed or forcing them into other professions, salt water ingress has affected the agricultural vitality of many farmers in the Khulna division. Dr Swain has backed his theory about 'environmental refugees' migrating to India by interviewing recent Bangladeshi migrants in India. Out of 52 that he spoke to, 43 said they were from this region. He has also quoted the Chief Minister of Assam, Mr P.K. Mahanta, as stating that a large number of people from Khulna were arriving in Assam.

While Dr Swain's sample seems very small to support such a far-reaching theory, it is evident that for people to move from these border regions of Bangladesh to India would prove to be no problem at all. At a small fishing village just outside Rajshahi town, where a large number of fishermen have stopped fishing and become rickshaw pullers, people spoke openly about the ease with which the border can be crossed. Also, while the decrease in Khulna's population is an undeniable fact, [it is uncertain whether] most of these migrants have joined the ranks of the urban poor in Dhaka or some other city within Bangladesh.

* * *

An inescapable fact about the Ganga, as well as the Brahmaputra and Meghna which run through Bangladesh, is that these rivers keep changing course. The Ganga has been gradually moving westwards in India. According to [a] study, in 1944 the distance between the Ganga and the Bhagirathi, its distributary just south of Farakka, was 5.9 km. Today it is a mere 1.4 km. If the two rivers join and become one in the next 10 years, there could be all kinds of environmental consequences.

NOTES AND QUESTIONS

1. The 1996 Treaty drew considerable flak in Bihar and West Bengal.[5] Bihar fears losing some of the Ganga water it draws for irrigation. In Calcutta, the primary concern is about the silting up of the city's port and the down river port of Haldia. India needs about 40,000 cusec of water in the Bhagirathi and the Hooghly to flush the ports of the silt brought in by the tides from the Bay of Bengal. The new lean season formula, it is feared, may reduce the flow in the Hooghly, jeopardizing navigation at both international ports.

2. One of the principal criticisms levelled against the Ganga pact is that it

[5] Id.

ignores the ground reality. During negotiations, Bangladesh refused to accept flow data after 1988, which was when the two countries stopped jointly monitoring the water level. The Indian figures since 1988 suggest that the lift irrigation schemes in thirsty Bihar and Uttar Pradesh have reduced the lean season flow to levels far below the Treaty claim.[6] Was this a sensible approach to treaty making? Will the pact endure? Or are we likely to see a return to prolonged squabbles over water sharing?

3. In 1995, the International Convention to Combat Desertification in those Countries Experiencing Serious Drought Particularly in Africa[7] came into force. India is a party to this Treaty. Although the Treaty mandates that affected country governments create national action programmes to combat desertification, it does not mandate the same for upstream countries. What then, will its effect be on India?

4. What steps are necessary to protect a shared river system such as Ganga-Brahmaputra? Consider the following:

POSTEL; WHERE HAVE ALL THE RIVERS GONE? World Watch, May/June, 1995

Saving water for nature will be far more difficult in developing countries, where demands for food and drinking water are arising apace with population growth. But in those countries as well, ensuring minimum water flows to satisfy ecological needs is critical to protecting fisheries, delta economies and—as the tragedy in the Aral Sea basin underscores—the health of local people.

In all water-scarce river basins, cooperation among countries is essential not only to optimising economic benefits from the river but to safeguarding its ecological functions. Unfortunately, while most water-sharing agreements have specified how much water each river basin country is allotted, they have allocated nothing for the river system itself. But if all countries in a basin agreed on a portion to be left in-stream to satisfy ecological needs, they could then divide up the remaining river water equitably among them.

If water is such a scarce resource, how is it possible for India and its neighbours to allocate some for the rivers themselves? How can long-term benefits be integrated into acceptable current strategies? Are these problems exacerbated by the survival problems inherent to a developing country?

5. In the summer of 1995, economists at the World Bank issued reports and news releases predicting that the wars in the next century will be over water. Among the data they used to reach their conclusions are the facts that 80 countries now face

---

[6] Banerjee, *supra* note 4.
[7] *Reprinted in* 33 I.L.M. 1332 (1994).

water shortages that threaten their health and economies; 40 per cent of the world—over 2 billion people—currently have no access to clean water or sanitation; and worldwide demand for water is doubling every 21 years. The primary culprit for water shortages is 'agricultural drought', the result of increased food needs of expanding populations and water-intensive high-yielding crop varieties that have been introduced to better meet those needs.[8]

India has achieved self-sufficiency in grain production. Does it make sense to save water and sacrifice this independence? And if India can get enough water to irrigate its crops and remain self-sufficient with its current use of the Ganga, what could induce India to change the arrangement in favour of Bangladesh?

6. Not surprisingly, transnational mountain resources have not garnered as much attention as water. However, in light of the new awareness stemming from the 1992 Earth Summit in Rio de Janeiro of the unique and fragile nature of the Himalayas, international efforts by India, its neighbours, and the global community have begun to focus on preserving the mountains. The Himalayas are the world's newest and highest mountains—stretching in an east-west arc for more than 1500 miles, from Arunachal Pradesh, Sikkim and Bhutan in the east to Pakistan in the west. West of Nepal lies the Garhwal region of India. This region contains 14 peaks over 7000 metres high. It is also home to the Nanda Devi Sanctuary.

In 1994, the first conference on protecting the environment of the mountains was held in Nepal by the International Center for Integrated Mountain Development. The threats to the mountain environment currently include soil erosion, deforestation and ill-planned development. If, however, the water problems have been this difficult to resolve, what chance do the mountains have? On the other hand, if the mountains are not as life-sustaining as water, is it possible that these agreements will be more easily reached?

7. Unavoidably, the same nations that share transboundary resources such as mountains and water also share wildlife. While protection of wildlife in India is examined in greater depth in an earlier chapter, this section focusses primarily on ending trade in wild animals and animal parts between the nations that actually share the wildlife.

In an attempt to preserve wildlife on a regional basis, India hosted talks in 1994 on protecting the Bengal tiger. Environmental ministers from Bhutan, Myanmar, India and Russia and experts from Bangladesh, Cambodia, China, Indonesia, Laos, Nepal, Thailand and Vietnam all met to try to formulate uniform domestic legislation to address the issue. The meeting was prompted by the 1993 census of Indian tigers which found that their numbers had dropped to 3,750, down from 4,334 in 1992—a drop of more than 13% in one year. It is very possible that this is an inflated figure, and that the actual number of wild Bengal tigers at the beginning on the 21st century is barely one-third of the 1993 census figure.

[8] John Vidal, *Water Wars*, THE VANCOUVER SUN, 12 August 1995.

Should India and its neighbours concentrate on saving tigers when Bangladesh may become drought-ridden and the Himalayan mountains may erode beyond repair? Or are tigers and other wildlife an intrinsic part of the ecosystem and therefore equally deserving of attention? Or is it just easier to talk about tigers than water?

8. What about the idea of 'eco-tourism' as a savior of mountain ecosystems and their wildlife? While the concept of 'eco-tourism' has been touted as a progressive influence in the mountains, most notably in the Annapurna Conservation Area Project in Nepal's Himalayas, it may augur the end of entire ecosystems. On occasion, under the guise of eco-tourism, large resorts develop within wilderness areas with swimming pools, shopping arcades, golf courses and other amenities designed to attract tourists.

Is eco-tourism always a bad idea? Is there any viable alternative that accomplishes what eco-tourism is designed to do, that is, make conservation worthwhile, economically speaking, on a local level, while increasing international awareness and appreciation of unique areas? What about the people who are displaced to create wildlife reserves? Does this imply that wildlife is more valuable than human life? Is it always necessary to displace people—cannot they remain on as caretakers or even residents of a protected reserve?

15

INTERNATIONAL ENVIRONMENTAL LAW AND GLOBAL ISSUES

A. INTRODUCTION

In international law, a distinction is often made between hard and soft law. Hard international law generally refers to agreements or principles that are directly enforceable by a national or international body. Soft international law refers to agreements or principles that are meant to influence individual nations to respect certain norms or incorporate them into national law. Although these agreements sometimes oblige countries to adopt implementing legislation, they are not usually enforceable on their own in a court.

If a treaty or convention does not specify an international forum that has subject matter jurisdiction, often the only place to bring a suit with respect to that treaty is in the member state's domestic court system. This presents at least two additional hurdles. If the member state being sued does not have domestic implementing legislation in place to hear the dispute, there will be no forum available. Even in the event that the domestic legislation provides for such suits, since the judges who decide the case are residents of the country against which it is brought, potential conflicts of interest arise.

Only nations are bound by treaties and conventions. In international forums, such as the International Court of Justice (ICJ), countries must consent to being sued. Thus, it is often impossible to sue a country. The final question in the jurisdictional arena is who may bring a suit. Often, only countries may sue countries. Individual citizens and non-governmental organizations (NGOs) cannot. This has huge repercussions. First, the environmental harm must be large and notorious for a country to notice. Second, for a country to have a stake in the outcome of the subject matter, some harm may have to cross the borders of the violating country into the country that is suing. Finally, even if transboundary harm does exist, the issue of causation, especially in the environmental field, is often impossible to prove with any certainty.

The enforcement issue is one where advocates for a safer environment often find themselves stymied. Even if a treaty or convention provides for specific substantive measures to be taken by a country (many treaties merely provide 'frameworks'), specifies a forum for dispute resolution and authorizes sanctions for non-compliance, international law remains largely unenforceable. A country cannot be forced to do what it is not willing to do. One can sanction the country, order damages, restrict trade, or, most frequently, publicize non-compliance. But beyond that, if a country will not comply, there is very little to be done.

International institutions are generally not responsible for directly implementing and enforcing international environmental law, but they often play important monitoring, informational and diplomatic roles. For example, the 1992 Convention on the Conservation of Biological Diversity (Biodiversity Convention)[1] created a new international body, the Committee on Sustainable Development (CSD). The CSD lacks the power to bring enforcement actions against either governments or private parties, but it plays a role in implementing the Biodiversity Convention. The CSD helps monitor national compliance efforts by requiring member nations to submit annual reports. Through its meetings and publications, the CSD also provides a forum to discuss and debate issues associated with global protection of biological diversity and forests.

NOTES AND QUESTIONS

1. Consider for a moment why any law is enacted—domestically or internationally. Some would maintain that it is a moral statement about behaviour that a society cannot tolerate. Some would argue that certain conduct is outlawed to deter that conduct, which is why we also attach a penalty. Some would argue, especially in light of the inefficiencies in enforcement, that laws socialize society's members to behave in a certain way by defining a code.

What is the purpose of international environmental law—is it a moral statement, a deterrence, or a socializing tool? If it is a moral statement, which many of the framework conventions seem to be, is it merely aspirational? Do we honestly believe that all nations will achieve all the ideals expressed in all the agreements? Or do we, as a global community, simply like to think of ourselves as the kind of people who believe in these things? If it is intended as deterrence, why are there not more international forums for dispute resolution, more international bodies empowered to enforce agreements, more substantive requirements, and more 'hard law' self-executing agreements? If there were, would any nation sign them? If it is intended as a socialization technique, is it working? Are nations more environmentally aware?

---

[1] *Reprinted in* 31 I.L.M. 818 (1992) and P. Birnie and A.Boyle, *Basic Documents on International Law and Environment*, 390 (1995).

2. If ultimately all international environmental law is unenforceable, what good is it? Does it accomplish anything to find a country out of compliance with a treaty? What about publicity? What if the economic benefits of a project such as the Narmada Valley Project, are believed by government officials to outweigh the negative effects of the publicity?

3. The practice of relying on domestic implementing legislation to enforce international environmental agreements leave state parties in the position of having different obligations under the same treaty, depending on how their legislative, executive and judicial bodies interpret and implement the treaty. Is this fair? What about the costs and administrative burdens that are associated with creating and enforcing legislation? Does this put richer countries in a better position to comply with treaties? Does not this mean that poorer countries, who may wish to comply, will often be unable to? Should they be held to the same standards? Is it patronizing to hold them to *lower* standards?

4. What is the purpose of the informational roles of international institutions? Will more knowledge about the global environment and our impacts on it lead to better compliance? Or will so many new issues lead to non-compliance due to uncertainty? If it appears to the average citizen that virtually everything she does has a negative environmental impact, will she not cease to try to change any behaviour?

5. What are the difficulties with the monitoring role of international institutions? If information gathered by monitoring bodies is generated by the governmental institutions, how accurate may it be? Is it better to have inaccurate information or no information? How much of a threat to a nation's sovereign status is an international monitoring institution? When does a nation's sovereignty have to be compromised for the greater global good? Who is to say?

B. INDIA'S INTERNATIONAL OBLIGATIONS

India has obligations under numerous international treaties and agreements that relate to environmental issues. As a contracting party, India must have ratified a treaty, that is, by adopting it as national law before it came into force, or by acceding to it after it has come into force. For a treaty to enter into force, the requisite number of countries must ratify the treaty, which then has the force of international law.

Specific obligations under any treaty vary, depending on the treaty itself. The nature and degree of compliance and implementation depend on a number of factors, among them: (1) the capabilities and staff of an international institution charged with coordinating national compliance efforts; (2) the willingness of other state parties to enforce or comply with the treaty; (3) the political agenda of the government and popular support; (4) trade and diplomatic pressures brought to bear by other countries; and (5) sometimes, judicial or NGO involvement through court cases and publicity.

INDIA'S TREATY OBLIGATIONS

1. The Antarctic Treaty (Washington, 1959) 402 UNTS 71. Entered into force 23 June 1961. India ratified with qualifications, 19 August 1983.

2. Convention on Wetlands of International Importance, Especially as Waterfowl Habitat (Ramsar, 1971). 11 I.L.M. 963 (1972). Entered into force 21 December 1975. India acceded, 1 October 1981.

3. Convention Concerning the Protection of the World Cultural and Natural Heritage (Paris, 1972). 11 I.L.M. 1358 (1972). Entered into force 17 December 1975. India signed, 16 November 1972.

4. Convention on International Trade in Endangered Species of Wild Fauna and Flora (Washington, 1973) 12 I.L.M. 1055 (1973). Entered into force 1 July 1975. India signed, 9 July 1974; ratified 20 July 1976.

5. Protocol of 1978 Relating to the International Convention for the Prevention of Pollution from Ships, 1973 (MARPOL) (London, 1978). Entered into force 2 October 1983. India ratified with qualifications, 24 September 1986.

6. Convention on the Conservation of Migratory Species of Wild Animals (Bonn, 1979) 19 I.L.M. 15 (1980). Entered into force 1 November 1983. India signed, 23 June 1979; ratified 4 May 1982.

7. Convention on the Conservation of Antarctic Marine Living Resources (Canberra, 1980). 19 I.L.M. 841 (1980). Entered into force 7 April 1982. India ratified, 17 June 1985.

8. United Nations Convention on the Law of the Sea (Montego Bay, 1982). 21 I.L.M. 1261 (1982). Entered into force 16 November 1994. India signed, 10 December 1982.

9. Convention for the Protection of the Ozone Layer (Vienna, 1985). 26 I.L.M. 1529 (1987). Entered into force 22 September 1988. India ratified, 18 March 1991.

10. Protocol on Substances That Deplete the Ozone Layer (Montreal, 1987). 26 I.L.M. 1550 (1987). Entered into force 1 January 1989. India acceded, 19 June 1992.

11. Amendments to the Montreal Protocol on Substances That Deplete the Ozone Layer (London, 1990). 30 I.L.M. 541 (1991). Entered into force 10 August 1992. India acceded, 19 June 1992.

12. Convention on the Control of Transboundary Movements of Hazardous Wastes and Their Disposal (Basel, 1989). 28 I.L.M. 657 (1989). Entered into force 5 May 1992. India signed, 5 March 1990; ratified 24 June 1992.

13. United Nations Framework Convention on Climate Change (Rio de Janeiro, 1992). 31 I.L.M. 849 (1992). Entered into force 21 March 1994. India signed, 10 June 1992; ratified 1 November 1993.

14. Convention on Biological Diversity (Rio de Janeiro, 1992). 31 I.L.M. 818 (1992). Entered into force 29 December 1993. India signed, 5 June 1992; ratified 18 February 1994.

15. Convention to Combat Desertification in Those Countries Experiencing Serious Drought and/or Desertification, Particularly in Africa (Paris,1994). 33 I.L.M 1332 (1994). Entered into force, 26 December 1995; India signed, 14 October 1994; ratified 17 December 1996.

16. International Tropical Timber Agreement (Geneva, 1994). 33 I.L.M. 1016 (1994). Entered into force 1 January 1997. India signed, 17 September 1996. India ratified 17 October 1996.

17. Protocol on Environmental Protection to the Antarctica Treaty (Madrid, 1991). Entered into force 15 January 1998.

C. ESTABLISHED NORMS OF INTERNATIONAL ENVIRONMENTAL LAW

Norms are general legal principles that are widely accepted. This acceptance is evidenced in a number of ways, such as international agreements, national legislation, domestic and international judicial decisions, and scholarly writings. The leading norms in the field of international environmental law are addressed below:

(1) Foremost among these norms is Principle 21 of the 1972 Stockholm Declaration on the Human Environment. Principle 21 maintains that 'States have, in accordance with the Charter of the United Nations and the principles of international law, the *sovereign right to exploit their own resources* pursuant to their own environmental policies, and *the responsibility to ensure that activities within their jurisdiction or control do not cause damage to the environment of other States or of areas beyond the limits of national jurisdiction'.*[2]

(2) Another widely shared norm is the *duty of a state to notify and consult* with other states when it undertakes an operation that is likely to harm neighbouring countries' environments, such as the construction of a power plant, which may impair air or water quality in downwind or downstream states.

(3) Over and above the duty to notify and consult, a relatively new norm has emerged whereby states are expected to *monitor and assess* specific environmental conditions domestically, and disclose these conditions in a *report* to an international agency or international executive body created by an international agreement, and authorised by the parties to the agreement to collect and publicize such information.

(4) Another emerging norm is the guarantee in the domestic constitutions, laws or executive pronouncements of several states, including India,[3] Malaysia, Thailand, Indonesia, Singapore and the Philippines, that all *citizens have a right to a decent and healthful environment.* In the United States, this fundamental

---

[2] Emphasis supplied. *Reprinted in* P.Birnie and A.Boyle, *id.* at 1.

[3] The fundamental right to life guaranteed under Article 21 of the Indian Constitution has been interpreted by the Supreme Court to include the right to a wholesome environment. *Subhash Kumar v State of Bihar* AIR 1991 SC 420, 424.

right has been guaranteed by a handful of states but not by the federal government.

(5) Most industrialized countries subscribe to the *polluter pays principle*. This means polluters should internalize the costs of their pollution, control it at its source, and pay for its effects, including remedial or cleanup costs, rather than forcing other states or future generations to bear such costs. This principle has been recognized by the Indian Supreme Court as a 'universal' rule to be applied to domestic polluters as well.[4] Moreover, it has been accepted as a fundamental objective of government policy to abate pollution.[5]

(6) Another new norm of international environment law is the *precautionary principle*. This is basically a duty to foresee and assess environmental risks, to warn potential victims of such risks and to behave in ways that prevent or mitigate such risks. In the context of municipal law, Justice Kuldip Singh of the Supreme Court has explained the meaning of this principle in the *Vellore Citizens' Welfare Forum Case*,[6] which is excerpted later in this section.

(7) *Environmental impact assessment* is another widely accepted norm of international environmental law. Typically, such an assessment balances economic benefits with environmental costs. The logic of such an assessment dictates that before a project is undertaken, its economic benefits must substantially exceed its environmental costs. India has adopted this norm for select projects which are covered under the Environmental Impact Assessment (EIA) regulations introduced in January, 1994.[7]

(8) Another recent norm is *to invite the input of non-governmental organizations (NGOs)*, especially those representing community-based grassroots environmental activists. This NGOs participation ensures that the people who are likely to be most directly affected by environmental accords will have a major role in monitoring and otherwise implementing the accord. This principle is mirrored in the Indian government's domestic pollution control policy[8] and the national conservation policy,[9] and is given statutory recognition in the EIA regulations of 1994. The Supreme Court has urged the government to draw upon the resources of NGOs to prevent environmental degradation.[10]

(9) In October 1982, the United Nations General Assembly adopted the World

---

[4] *The Bichhri Case (Indian Council for Enviro-Legal Action v Union of India)* AIR 1996 SC 1446; and *Vellore Citizens' Welfare Forum v Union of India* AIR 1996 SC 2715.

[5] Ministry of Environment and Forests, Government of India, *Policy Statement for Abatement of Pollution*, para 3.3 (26 February 1992).

[6] *Supra* note 4. In *A.P. Pollution Control Board v Prof. M.V. Nayudu* AIR 1999 SC 812 the Supreme Court traced the development of the precautionary principle.

[7] The EIA regulations are extensively dealt with in the Large Projects chapter.

[8] *Supra* note 5, at para 11.1.

[9] Ministry of Environment and Forests, Government of India, *National Conservation Strategy and Policy Statement on Environment and Development*, para 8.7 (June, 1992).

[10] *Indian Council for Enviro-Legal Action v Union of India (CRZ Notification Case)* 1996 (5) SCC 281.

Charter for Nature and Principles of *Sustainable Development*. The agreement expressly recognised the principle of sustainable development, defined as using living resources in a manner that 'does not exceed their natural capacity for regeneration' and using 'natural resources in a manner which ensures the preservation of the species and ecosystems for the benefit of future generations.' The principle of sustainable development was also acknowledged in the 1987 report Our Common Future, published by the United Nations World Commission on Environment and Development. This report defined sustainable development as 'humanity's ability ... to ensure that [development] meets the need of the present generation without compromising the ability of future generations to meet their needs.' The Supreme Court[11] as well as the Indian government have recognised the principle of sustainable development as a basis for balancing ecological imperatives with developmental goals.[12]

(10) *Intergenerational equity* is among the newest norms of international environmental law. It can best be understood not so much as a principle, but rather as an argument in favour of sustainable economic development and natural resource use. If present generations continue to consume and deplete resources at unsustainable rates, future generations will suffer the environmental (and economic) consequences. It is our children and grandchildren who will be left without forests (and their carbon retention capacities), without vital and productive agricultural land and without water suitable for drinking or for sustaining cultivation or aquatic life. Therefore, we must all undertake to pass on to future generations an environment as intact as the one we inherited from the previous generation.

Proponents of intergenerational equity maintain that the present generation has a moral obligation to manage the earth in a manner that will not jeopardize the aesthetic and economic welfare of the generations that follow. From this moral premise flow certain ecological commandments: 'Do not cut down trees faster than they grow back. Do not farm land at levels, or in a manner, that reduce the land's regenerative capacity. Do not pollute water at levels that exceed its natural purification capacity.'

In *State of Himachal Pradesh v Ganesh Wood Products*[13] the Supreme Court recognized the significance of inter-generational equity and held a government department's approval to establish forest-based industry to be invalid because 'it is contrary to public interest involved in preserving forest wealth, maintenance of environment and ecology and considerations of sustainable growth and inter-generational equity. After all, the present generation has no right to deplete all the existing forests and leave nothing for the next and future generations.'[14]

(11) At the 1982 United Nations Conference on the Law of the Sea

[11] *Vellore Citizens' Welfare Forum v Union of India* AIR 1996 SC 2715.
[12] *Supra* note 9, at paras 1.1, 1.3.
[13] AIR 1996 SC 149, 163. Also see *CRZ Notification Case, supra* note 10, where the court expressed its concern at the adverse ecological effects which will have to be borne by future generations.
[14] *Id.*

(UNCLOS),[15] developing countries, led by India, articulated the norm that certain resources, such as the deep seabed, are part of the *common heritage of mankind* and must be shared by all nations.

(12) The 1992 Rio de Janeiro Earth Summit articulated the norm of *common but different responsibilities*. With regard to global environmental concerns such as global climate change or stratospheric ozone layer depletion, all nations have a shared responsibility, but richer nations are better able than poorer nations to take the financial and technological measures necessary to shoulder the responsibility.

NOTES AND QUESTIONS

1. As mentioned, norms of customary international law evolve through custom and usage. Not all norms are of equal importance however, some being accorded the status of *fundamental norms*. The category of fundamental norms comes under the doctrine of *jus cogens*, or the doctrine of *peremptory norms*. The 1969 Vienna Convention on the Law of Treaties[16] serves to clarify the concept in Article 53 as follows:

A treaty is void if, at the time of its conclusion, it conflicts with a peremptory norm of general international law. For the purposes of the present Convention, a peremptory norm of general international law is a norm accepted and recognised by the international community of States as a whole as a norm from which no derogation is permitted and which can be modified only by a subsequent norm of general international law having the same character.

The doctrine of *jus cogens* is extremely limited and extends to only a handful of norms, the most long-standing of which are the prohibitions against the slave trade, piracy and genocide. Many scholars also believe that the norm expressed in Principle 21 of the Stockholm Convention has risen to *jus cogens* status. Principle 21 is based on the Roman maxim, *sic utero tuo et alienum non laedas*, which roughly means 'do not behave in a way that hurts your neighbour.' However, again the question arises, what good does an international peremptory norm, like an international agreement, achieve?

2. Consider some of the other norms addressed above, such as the right to a healthful environment. Is there to be one standard by which all environments are judged, or is it a relative concept? If cutting down trees for firewood destroys the environment, but provides life-sustaining fuel, which right will prevail? Which right *should* prevail? How much weight does each of the two rights carry when the concept of intergenerational equity is introduced?

[15] *Reprinted in* 21 I.L.M. 1261 (1982).
[16] *Reprinted in* 8 I.L.M. 679 (1969).

When considering moral ideals such as the principles of a common heritage and intergenerational equity, what incentives do countries have to try to mould their practices to achieve these ideals? How can countries be better motivated? Is saving the environment for its own sake going to appeal to the majority of people, or does there have to be a more direct benefit, like the idea that we may, by destroying an ecosystem, inadvertently destroy the cure for cancer?

3. What exactly is 'sustainable development'? What is 'sustainable'? Could not intelligent and informed people differ over whether producing more minerals or preserving a landscape is sustainable? If so, which is more important? And what is 'development'? Factories that employ thousands, may give a country more industry with which to compete in the world market, but discharge effluents into the water and produce piles of hazardous waste. Do some countries have more of a right to development and less of an obligation to ensure sustainability and vice versa? How much more do industrialised nations need to develop? Have they not gone far enough? Who is to judge?

At the end of a judicial career which earned him the sobriquet 'Green Judge', Justice Kuldip Singh of the Supreme Court issued comprehensive directions to clean up the mess created by the leather tanneries of Tamil Nadu. In the following excerpt from this leading case, Justice Singh borrows international law norms and applies them to the local milieu.

VELLORE CITIZENS' WELFARE FORUM v UNION OF INDIA
AIR 1996 SC 2715

KULDIP SINGH, J.:   * * *

The traditional concept that development and ecology are opposed to each other, is no longer acceptable. 'Sustainable Development' is the answer. In the International sphere 'Sustainable Development' as a concept came to be known for the first time in the Stockholm Declaration of 1972. Thereafter, in 1987 the concept was given a definite shape by the World Commission on Environment and Development in its report called 'Our Common Future'. The Commission was chaired by the then Prime Minister of Norway Ms.G.H.Brundtland and as such the report is popularly known as 'Brundtland Report'. In 1991 the World Conservation Union, United Nations Environment Programme and World Wide Fund for Nature, jointly came out with a document called 'Caring for the Earth' which is a strategy for sustainable living. Finally, came the Earth Summit held in June, 1992 at Rio which saw the largest gathering of world leaders ever in the history—deliberating and chalking out a blue print for the survival of the planet. Among the tangible achievements of the Rio

Conference was the signing of two conventions, one on biological diversity and another on climate change. These conventions were signed by 153 nations. The delegates also approved by consensus three non-binding documents namely, a Statement on Forestry Principles, a declaration of principles on environmental policy and development initiatives and Agenda 21, a programme of action into the next century in areas like poverty, population and pollution. During the two decades from Stockholm to Rio 'Sustainable Development' has come to be accepted as a viable concept to eradicate poverty and improve the quality of human life while living within the carrying capacity of the supporting eco-systems. 'Sustainable Development' as defined by the Brundtland Report means 'development that meets the needs of the present without compromising the ability of the future generations to meet their own needs'. We have no hesitation in holding that 'Sustainable Development' as a balancing concept between ecology and development has been accepted as a part of the Customary International Law though its salient features have yet to be finalized by the International Law Jurists.

Some of the salient principles of 'Sustainable Development', culled-out from Brundtland Report and other international documents, are inter-generational equity; use and conservation of natural resources; environmental protection; the precautionary principle; polluter pays principle; obligation to assist and cooperate; eradication of poverty and financial assistance to the developing countries. We are, however, of the view that 'the precautionary principle' and 'the polluter pays' principle are essential features of 'Sustainable Development'. The 'precautionary principle'— in the context of the municipal law—means:

(i)   Environmental measures—by the State Government and the statutory authorities—must anticipate, prevent and attack the causes of environmental degradation.

(ii)   Where there are threats of serious and irreversible damage, lack of scientific certainty should not be used as a reason for postponing measures to prevent environmental degradation.

(iii) The 'Onus of proof' is on the actor or the developer/industrialist to show that his action is environmentally benign.

'The polluter pays' principle has been held to be a sound principle by this Court in *Indian Council for Enviro-Legal Action vs. Union of India (The Bichhri Case)*, 1996 (3) SCC 212. The Court observed, 'We are of the opinion that any principle evolved in this behalf should be simple, practical and suited to the conditions obtaining in this country'. The Court ruled that 'Once the activity carried on is hazardous or inherently dangerous, the person carrying on such activity is liable to make good the loss caused to any other person by his activity irrespective of the fact whether he took reasonable care while carrying on his activity. The rule is premised upon the very nature of the activity carried on'. Consequently the polluting industries are 'Absolutely liable to compensate for the harm caused by them to villagers in the affected area, to the soil and to the underground water and hence, they are bound to take all necessary measures to remove sludge and other pollutants lying in the affected areas'. The 'polluter pays' principle as interpreted by this Court means that the absolute liability for harm to the environment extends not only to compensate the victims of pollution but also the cost of restoring the environmental degradation. [Remedying] the damaged environment is part of the process of 'Sustainable Development' and as such [the] polluter is liable to pay the cost to the individual [who] suffers as well as the cost of reversing the damaged ecology.

[The court then set out the provision of the Constitution as well as the Water Act, Air Act and Environment (Protection) Act]. In view of the above mentioned constitutional and statutory provisions we have no hesitation in holding that the precautionary principle and the polluter pays principle are part of the environmental law of the country.

Even otherwise once these principles are accepted as part of the Customary International Law there would be no difficulty in accepting them as part of the domestic law. It is almost accepted proposition of law that the rule of Customary International Law which are not contrary to the municipal law shall be deemed to have been incorporated in the domestic law and shall be followed by the Courts of Law. For support we may refer to Justice H.R.Khanna's opinion in *Addl. Distt. Magistrate Jabalpur vs. Shivakant Shukla* (AIR 1976 SC 1207), *Jolly George Verghese's case* (AIR 1980 SC 470) and *Gramophone Company's case* (AIR 1984 SC 667).

The Constitutional and statutory provisions protect a person's right to fresh air, clean water and pollution free environment, but the source of the right is the inalienable common law right of clean environment. [The court proceeded to quote a paragraph from Blackstone's commentaries on the Laws of England (1876) in respect of 'nuisance']. Our legal system having been founded on the British Common Law the right of a person to pollution free environment is a part of the basic jurisprudence of the land.

* * *

NOTES AND QUESTIONS

1. In the concluding part of the *Vellore* judgment (which has not been reproduced above), the Supreme Court issued a wide range of directions. The Central Government was required to establish an authority under section 3(3) of the Environment (Protection) Act of 1986 headed by a retired High Court judge, to deal with the situation created by the tanneries and other polluting industries in Tamil Nadu. The authority so constituted was asked to apply the precautionary principle and the polluter pays principle whilst identifying the individuals who had suffered due to the pollution, assessing the loss incurred and determining the compensation payable by the polluters. The authority was conferred wide powers by the court, including the power to direct the closure of industry and the relocation of units. The court also imposed a pollution fine of Rs.10,000 on each of the tanneries in five districts of the state.

2. The discussion in the judgment relating to the polluter pays principle is dissatisfactory. In *Indian Council for Enviro-Legal Action (The Bichhri Case)* the

Supreme Court recognized the distinction between the principle of 'absolute liability' applicable only to hazardous industries, and the wider 'polluter pays' principle which applies whenever an industry pollutes the air, water or land, irrespective whether it is a hazardous unit or not. The court in the *Vellore Case* appears to have mixed up these two distinct principles and rolled them into one. Would you interpret the Vellore judgment to mean that the 'no-fault' liability principle extends to all situations where the damage is caused by pollution, and is no longer restricted in India to damage caused by hazardous industries? Does this mean that in India a polluter is no longer entitled to the defences that are available to him under the law of torts?

D. CONFLICTS BETWEEN THE ENVIRONMENT AND FREE TRADE

To help promote responsible environmental practices at home and abroad, many countries have enacted legislation that contains certain trade restrictions that prevent the free flow of goods across borders. Such environmental restrictions often conflict with the terms of international free trade agreements, primarily with the General Agreement on Tariffs and Trade (GATT), which seeks to discourage or prohibit the use of import restrictions.

GATT was formed in 1947 in the aftermath of World War II, primarily to encourage global economic development by limiting the use of tariffs and import restrictions. The agreement is the initial 1947 document and its periodic 'rounds' of amendment. The World Trade Organization (WTO) is the administrative body that sits in Geneva, Switzerland whose purpose is to implement the terms and requirements of the GATT. One way that WTO achieves this end is through dispute resolution panels where member states can reconcile conflicting interpretations of GATT's provisions.

GATT allows nations to restrict the import of products from other member nations, so long as these restrictions do not discriminate between foreign and domestic products. For instance, under GATT the US may ban the importation of a dangerous pesticide so long as the use of the pesticide is also banned in the US. Article 20 lists the exceptions that justify a deviation from GATT's general free trade requirements. Among these exceptions are trade restrictions 'necessary to protect human, animal or plant life and health,'[17] and those 'relating to the conservation of exhaustible natural resources.'[18] Most of the controversy regarding the agreement's impact on environmental protection has centered on the WTO dispute panels' interpretations of the Article 20 exceptions. No trade restriction based on Article 20(b) or 20(g) has as yet been upheld by these dispute panels.

[17] Article 20 (b).
[18] Article 20 (g).

NOTES AND QUESTIONS

1. GATT is one of the most powerful international agreements in the world and often supersedes environmental treaties. Why is this? Is it because GATT, unlike most environmental treaties, has an institutional dispute resolution mechanism and enforcement procedures? Or is it because the global community puts greater emphasis on commodities and trade than on the environment and conservation?

2. Many treaties, recognizing the power of market-based incentives, have tried to turn environmental issues into commodity issues. Is the market the proper mechanism for saving the environment? Would not the unfettered operation of free trade, as pictured under GATT, lead to the eventual destruction of the environment? Has it not brought us perilously close to that point already? Why, then, are economic approaches and GATT so powerful? Is economic self-interest the only true motivator of people and nations? If so, is there a way to give greater economic value to the environment? Is there an economic theory or accounting mechanism that can take true environmental costs into account in the face of a project's touted economic benefits?

E. HUMAN RIGHTS, INDIGENOUS PEOPLE AND THE ENVIRONMENT

Although environmental protection and human rights are often treated as separate legal topics, there are many situations where the two fields overlap. First, many governments and international bodies have recognised the right of citizens to live in a clean and healthful environment. Second, environmental and natural resource policies may disproportionately affect poor and minority communities.

The rights of indigenous people are a 'cross-over' issue in that they may be protected under both international human rights law and international environmental law. (Any environmental right can theoretically be couched in terms of a human right, so this is not the only area where the two bodies of law dovetail.)

The rights of indigenous people may be seen in two basic lights: (1) the right to protect and manage natural resources located on traditional indigenous lands; (2) the right of citizens to live in a healthful environment. Many environmentally destructive development practices severely impact the traditional lands and lifestyles of indigenous communities. Therefore, their rights often provide another tool in the fight against such projects.

With respect to the protection of indigenous people as a means to conserve biodiversity, international environmental law can play an important role. Many native and indigenous people have opposed government policies that permit resource exploitation on traditional lands. Because this exploitation threatens to undermine the economic and spiritual fabric of their cultures, and often results in forced migration and resettlement, the struggle to protect the environment is often a part of the struggle to protect the cultures of indigenous people.

THE RIO DECLARATION ON ENVIRONMENT AND DEVELOPMENT

Out of the Earth Summit in 1992, three documents emerged, one of which was the Rio Declaration on Environment and Development.[19] In Principle 22, the Declaration states that '[i]ndigenous people and their communities and other local communities have a vital role in environmental management and development because of their knowledge and traditional practices. States should recognize and duly support their identity, culture and interests and enable their effective participation in the achievement of sustainable development.'

The same principle is echoed in the Biodiversity Convention[20] in Article 8(j). However, as discussed below in the section on Protecting Endangered Species, both the Declaration and the Convention lack substantive obligations and enforcement mechanisms. Thus, both are regarded as 'framework' conventions upon which truly binding rights and responsibilities can only be built through further agreements.

The combination of human rights and environmental obligations can provide a powerful tool to protect land and ecosystems where indigenous people reside. This protection is evidenced by the reservation of lands for indigenous peoples, such as the Yanomani lands in Brazil, that incidentally also contain some of the world's precious rainforests. As the conservation expertise of indigenous peoples becomes more widely acknowledged, indigenous rights are likely to play an increased role in national and international environmental protection efforts.

NOTES AND QUESTIONS

1. Why do indigenous people deserve special protection? Granted, they have traditionally been dispossessed and marginalized, but so have many other groups, such as women. What value do indigenous people add to the global community? Is 'saving' indigenous people akin to saving rainforests? Should we do it because they are 'there' and it is therefore morally wrong to destroy them? In preserving biodiversity, how much *human* diversity should we aim to preserve? Do we only protect indigenous people because there is 'something in it' (medicinal and agricultural knowledge) for the rest of us? Is it altruism, selfishness or guilt that motivates us?

2. What if a community that suffers from an environmental threat or hazard is *not* indigenous? Do they therefore deserve less protection? What if indigenous people are inhabiting fragile lands that ought to remain pristine? What if indigenous people are engaged in environmentally destructive practices? When does the protection of indigenous people, and their common property lands, conflict with their right to development and self-determination?

[19] *Reprinted in* P.Birnie and A. Boyle, *supra* note 1, at 9. The Supreme Court referred to Principle 13 of the Declaration requiring states to develop national laws to compensate the victims of pollution and other environmental damage in the *CRZ Notification Case, supra* note 10.
[20] *Supra* note 1.

F. ENVIRONMENTAL JUSTICE

I. ENVIRONMENTAL POVERTY LAW

There is a growing awareness of the close relationship between poverty and environmental pollution. It is broadly recognized that poorer citizens are more likely to suffer the consequences of environmental pollution than other citizens, on both the national and international levels. It has also given rise to environmental poverty law, or environmental justice, which seeks legal remedies to the disproportionate environmental abuse suffered by poorer citizens.

Internationally, less affluent nations tend to have more severe environmental problems than wealthier nations. Examples of these problems are easy to identify. Air pollution in Mexico and China is generally more severe than in France or Australia. Hazardous waste is treated less safely in Eastern Europe and Africa than in Western Europe and Canada. The reasons for this situation are frustrating but not difficult to understand. Less affluent nations lack the financial resources to purchase modern pollution control or energy efficient technologies, or to implement environmental protection policies.

At the 1992 Earth Summit in Rio, developing countries asked for increased technology transfers. These countries pointed out that if the developed world is truly concerned with stemming the environmental deterioration in developing countries, new technologies for environmental protection need to be made available at little or no cost to the developing world.

On the national level, there have also been important developments. In India, for example, judicial decisions have held that the urban poor must be treated fairly and that government policies must respect their human rights.[21] Similarly, the United States has also begun to address environmental poverty issues. In 1994, President Clinton issued an executive order calling on federal agencies to make certain that environmentally undesirable activities do not disproportionately burden certain economic or ethnic sectors of society.

II. NORTH-SOUTH TENSIONS

Tensions between the developed and developing world are found at the international level. Many transnational corporations headquartered in the developed world have chosen to move environmentally dangerous industrial activities to the developing world.

Why do transnational corporations relocate to these poorer nations? First, labour costs are much cheaper. Second, taxes are substantially lower. Finally, environmental standards in the developing world are generally lower (and therefore less expensive) than in the developed world. This means, of course, that workers are often exposed to hazardous materials or unsafe conditions.

---

[21] e.g., *Olga Tellis v Bombay Municipal Corporation* AIR 1986 SC 180.

The export of environmental harm to the world's poorer nations, and to non-European populations, has resulted in severe health and environmental problems. Two widely-publicized examples were the lethal 1984 Union Carbide gas leak in Bhopal, and the continuing logging of tropical rainforests by First World timber companies.

NOTES AND QUESTIONS

1. Environmental justice has become one of the 1990s most sensitive issues. It underlies almost all of the negotiating sessions and the disputes leading up to international environmental agreements. Poorer, less developed countries (LDCs) feel strongly that developed countries exercise 'eco-imperialism' in all arenas. Is this correct? Why? Does it help powerful nations stay powerful? By not transferring technology, do the rich get richer? At whose expense? Is it not in the best interest of the developed countries, who after all share the planet with the LDCs, to ensure that LDCs have the technologies and economic resources to invest in sustainable development projects and industries, in order to preserve the global commons (the deep sea, the atmosphere, Antarctica)? Keep in mind that global environmental degradation, like global climate change and stratospheric ozone depletion, recognizes no boundaries.

2. The United States' initial refusal under President Bush to sign the 1992 Convention on Biological Diversity (discussed below) was based on one of the most controversial environmental justice issues, namely intellectual property rights over plant genetic resources. The privatization of biotechnology and plant genetic resources, primarily derived from LDCs but patented in developed countries, has led to wide-scale protests and civil unrest, resulting in what has become known as 'seed wars'. Are not seeds, as well as all plant genetic resources, humankind's 'common heritage'? Should they be allowed to be patented? If so, should they be patented in their countries of origin? Would allowing countries of origin to patent, thereby obtaining royalties, provide an economic incentive to conserve them?

G. AIR POLLUTION AND PROTECTION OF THE ATMOSPHERE

During the 1980s, international environmental efforts shifted from transboundary or regional air pollution concerns, such as acid rain, to threats to the global atmosphere. This shift was prompted by scientific evidence that emerged in the mid 1970s. The evidence linked the release of chlorofluorocarbons (CFCs) and other chlorine-based substances with the destruction of the stratospheric ozone layer. The ozone layer shields human beings and plant life from the harmful effects of solar radiation. CFCs are used in refrigeration, air conditioning, and foam furniture among other applications. To reduce the use of these substances, and protect the global atmosphere, the 1985 Vienna Convention for the Protection of the Ozone Layer[22] and the 1987 Montreal Protocol on Substances that Deplete the Ozone Layer[23] were adopted. Because the 1987 protocol incorporated the 1985 convention's basic aims, the international regime to protect the ozone layer is usually referred to as the Montreal Protocol.

Another issue involving the world's atmosphere is global climate change. The issue of global climate change encompasses many underlying environmental concerns, including air pollution, energy consumption, deforestation and management of the global commons. For purposes of this chapter, the issue will be discussed in the present section on air pollution and protection of the atmosphere. The primary international agreements relating to global warming and climate changes are the United Nations Framework Convention of Climate Change (UNFCCC)[24] signed at the Rio de Janeiro Earth Summit in 1992, and the Kyoto Protocol to the UNFCCC, signed at Kyoto, Japan in 1997.

1987 MONTREAL PROTOCOL ON SUBSTANCES THAT DEPLETE THE OZONE LAYER

The 1987 Montreal Protocol on Substances that Deplete the Ozone Layer (Montreal Protocol) sets firm targets for reducing consumption and production of a range of ozone-depleting substances. The standards set forth in the 1987 Protocol were strengthened and expanded to cover additional ozone-depleting substances, through amendments adopted in 1990, 1992 and 1994. These amendments were prompted by the development of new technology and alternative 'ozone friendly' substances. The Protocol's ability to respond to and incorporate scientific/technological developments has been widely praised, and has provided a model of constructive flexibility for future international environmental agreements.

One of the major innovations of the Montreal Protocol is its recognition that all nations should not be treated equally. The agreement acknowledges that certain countries have contributed greatly to ozone depletion while other countries have made very small contributions. The agreement also recognizes that a nation's obligation to reduce current emissions should reflect its technological and financial ability to abate CFC pollution. Because of this situation, the agreement applies more stringent standards, and a more accelerated phase-out timetable, to the countries that have contributed the most to ozone depletion. Such countries must eliminate all CFCs by the year 2000. Developing countries have a 10 year 'grace period', and must phase out CFC use by 2010.

The Montreal Protocol also includes innovative funding provisions providing less affluent member countries financial and technical incentives (such as the transfer of technology and patents) to encourage a rapid switch to non-ozone depleting substances and production methods. Specifically, Article 10 of the Protocol established a fund to facilitate technical co-operation and technology transfer to assist developing states.

---

[22] *Reprinted in* 26 I.L.M. 1529 (1987) and P. Birnie and A. Boyle, *supra* note 1, at 211.

[23] *Reprinted in* 26 I.L.M. 1550 (1987) and P.Birnie and A. Boyle, *id*. at 224.

[24] *Reprinted in* 31 I.L.M. 849 (1992) and P.Birnie and A. Boyle, *id*. at 252.

This Multilateral Ozone Fund, now administered by the Global Environment Facility (GEF),[25] depends on the support of the developed countries. While this system seems fair, it also creates a loophole in the Protocol through which many less developed countries (LDCs) will be able to avoid meeting the standards set out in the Protocol if the developed countries do not meet their financial obligations.

Finally, the Protocol also contains provisions to deal with the problem of the few nations that have not signed the Protocol and continue to produce and consume ozone-depleting substances, by banning trade in these substances with non-member states. Thus, parties to the Protocol are prohibited from importing such substances, or exporting CFC production technology and equipment. This comprehensive trade ban places both economic and diplomatic pressure on all nations to join the Protocol.

1992 UNITED NATIONS FRAMEWORK CONVENTION ON CLIMATE CHANGE

The Climate Change Convention[26] was prompted by several scientific studies in the late 1980s which indicated that increased levels of carbon dioxide (CO_2) in the atmosphere were causing global temperatures to rise. This increase in temperatures was attributed to the 'greenhouse effect,' wherein the sun's heat is trapped between the earth's surface and the CO_2 in the earth's atmosphere (which prevents the heat from escaping). The Climate Change Convention was adopted to reduce the amount of CO_2 emitted into the atmosphere, and to preserve and increase the earth's carbon absorption capacities.

In addressing the global warming issue, the international community chose to follow the process successfully employed in the ozone/CFC context. Just as the general, aspirational 1985 Vienna Convention preceeded the highly specific 1987 Montreal Protocol, the 1992 Framework Convention represents the first step in the international community's attempt to stop global warming. Its purpose is to demonstrate and forge consensus, and to provide the diplomatic foundation for a more substantive agreement.

Article 2 of the Convention states that the 'ultimate objective' of the framework agreement is to stabilize the concentrations of greenhouse gases at a level which would prevent dangerous interference with the climate system. This broad and general phrasing provides participating countries with flexibility in implementation strategies.

The Climate Change Convention was only a broad blueprint, but some significant principles and provisions were negotiated. Most of these provisions reflect North-South (developed-developing world) tensions. First, it was agreed that financial commitments should be based on the principles of 'respective capabilities', and 'appropriate burden sharing' and 'equity', meaning that wealthier nations should be required to contribute more than poorer nations. Second, the Convention states that

---

[25] GEF was initially established in 1991 as a pilot programme of the World Bank, UNEP and the UN Development Programme. It was restructured in 1994 following the decisions taken at the Rio Conference. The 1994 instrument is *reprinted in* 33 I.L.M. 1273 (1994).

[26] *Reprinted in* 31 I.L.M. 849 (1992) and P.Birnie and A. Boyle, *supra* note 1, at 252.

developed countries 'shall take all practical steps to promote, facilitate and finance, as appropriate, the transfer of, or access to, environmentally sound technologies.' In addition, the Framework Convention specifies that the newly created Global Environmental Facility will act as the financial mechanism for allocating environmental resources to developing countries.

Although the Climate Change Convention is modelled on the Montreal Protocol/ CFC approach, the recent meetings at Kyoto (1997) and Buenos Aires (1998) show that it may be difficult to move from the aspirational 'framework' stage to the binding 'implementation' stage. This is because the global warming issue lacks many of the elements that formed the foundation for the Montreal Protocol/CFC regime. Most importantly, there is lack of available and affordable alternatives to thermal power, and all nations, North and South, contribute to the problem and must contribute to its solution.

In December, 1997, the Third Conference of Parties to the Framework Convention on Climate Change met in Kyoto, Japan. After much contentious dispute and negotiation, the parties agreed and signed the Kyoto Protocol. The major industrialized countries agreed to reduce their greenhouse gas emissions by an average of five per cent relative to their 1990 levels, in the period 2008 to 2012, Japan agreed to a reduction of six per cent, the US agreed to seven per cent, and the European Union agreed to eight per cent. (Most countries, including the US, have yet to ratify the Protocol.)

Developing nations rejected taking on any new commitments and only agreed at the last minute to allow emissions trading among all countries as part of a 'clean development mechanism'. India and China seem prepared to resist emissions trading schemes because they want developed nations to bear the major costs of global carbon reductions—even though such reductions may be achieved in energy-inefficient developing countries at much lower cost than in energy-efficient developed countries. The 'clean development mechanism' of Article 12 of the Protocol seemingly allows developed countries to implement (and pay for) carbon-reducing projects in developing countries. This provision is largely undefined.

NOTES AND QUESTIONS

1. Having gained the experience of moving from framework to substantive agreements in the case of the Montreal Protocol, why did the drafters of the Climate Change Convention seek to *repeat* the framework process? Now that we know it can be done, why not move directly to the implementing protocol and skip the framework step altogether? Are there formalities involved in international negotiations that must be observed? Is this an efficient way to solve environmental problems? What if the problems are extremely urgent?

2. Since virtually all climate scientists agree on the likelihood of global climate change, why has collective action been so slow in coming? What happened to the

precautionary principle discussed above? How accurate and reliable does data have to be before we act on it? What if the effects of waiting cause irreparable harm?

3. What about GEF involvement in these projects? GEF is sponsored, in part, by the World Bank; the two institutions share staff and are located in the same site. Is this a problem? If so, how can it be overcome?

H. PROTECTING ENDANGERED SPECIES

1973 CONVENTION ON INTERNATIONAL TRADE IN ENDANGERED SPECIES OF WILD FAUNA AND FLORA

As of 1995, over 113 nations had signed the 1973 Convention on International Trade in Endangered Species (CITES).[27] CITES does not seek to directly protect endangered species or the development practices that destroy their habitats. Rather, it seeks to reduce the economic incentive to kill endangered species and destroy their habitat by closing off the international market. CITES' sole aim is to control or prevent international commercial trade in endangered species or products derived from such species.

CITES regulates by means of an international permit system. For plant and animal species threatened with extinction, international import or export is strictly forbidden. For plant and animal species suffering decline but not yet facing extinction, international import/export permits must be secured. These CITES permits enable the trade to be controlled and monitored so that it does not lead to species extinction or decline.

Many environmentalists believe that CITES does not go far enough in protecting endangered species, and that it approaches protection from a philosophically questionable standpoint. The main animals that CITES protects are 'charismatic species'— so called megafauna or animals whose parts and pelts have a market value. This prioritising of species is objectionable to many. The only thing that CITES controls is trade; it does nothing to limit hunting or killing. Theoretically, if a nation wanted to kill all its species for domestic consumption, CITES could do nothing to prevent it. Many people believe that CITES' dependence on trade regulations to protect endangered species is inimical to a biocentric perspective.

1992 BIODIVERSITY CONVENTION

At the 1992 UNCED meeting in Rio de Janeiro, an agreement was reached on the conservation and sustainable use of the world's biodiversity. The Convention on Biological Diversity (Biodiversity Convention)[28] took effect on 29 December 1993, after it was ratified by the required minimum of 30 countries.

---

[27] *Reprinted in* 12 I.L.M. 1055 (1973) and P.Birnie and A.Boyle, *id.* at 415.
[28] *Supra* note 1.

Although the Biodiversity Convention sets forth numerous obligations, most of these are aspirational; there are no specific standards or methods to ensure compliance. Article 8(c) requires that signatory nations 'regulate or manage biological resources important for the conservation of biological diversity whether within or outside protected areas, with a view to ensuring their conservation and sustainable use.' Article 8(d) obliges countries to 'promote the protection of ecosystems, natural habitats and the maintenance of viable populations of species in natural surroundings.' Under Article 9(b), nations agree to 'adopt measures relating to the use of biological resources to avoid or minimise adverse impacts on biological diversity.'

The environmentally progressive provisions listed above, however, are balanced against provisions that reaffirm each nation's sovereign right to manage and exploit its natural resources. Countries may adopt nature protection standards that are appropriate to their own economic needs and priorities. Taken as a whole, the Biodiversity Convention is broad and vague enough to be consistent with almost all natural resource policies, whether these policies are environmentally protective or destructive. The loose and contradictory language of the agreement has been criticized by many environmentalists, who maintain that an important opportunity was missed to create more sustainable international nature protection standards.

The Convention has also been criticized for its lack of enforcement mechanisms. The Convention created an institution, the Committee on Sustainable Development (CSD), to monitor compliance and implement the agreement. The CSD, however, has so far been unable to establish precise definitions of the vague and contradictory language in the agreement. Without this basic clarification, it is difficult to implement the Convention or monitor compliance.

NOTES AND QUESTIONS

1. If Kenya decided to kill every elephant in its borders for purposes of internal domestic consumption, CITES would not prevent this policy from being carried out. What kind of environmental treaty is it, then? Is it not actually another commodities agreement in disguise? CITES is often mentioned as the environmental treaty most likely to be voidable under GATT. Why is this so?

2. Is it true, as many critics contend, that CITES is only good for the animals we humans find appealing? Do we not have a moral obligation to protect *all* animals? Or if we only conserve out of utilitarian motivations, all *useful* animals? Of course, we can't possibly know which animals will prove useful!

3. The Biodiversity Convention is regarded by many as an unsuccessful attempt to please all of the people all of the time. Can all its conservation principles truly coexist with its sovereignty principles? In fact, can inviolable sovereignty coexist with global environmental law in general?

4. While the Biodiversity Convention has been criticized for being only a framework, is it possible to create a treaty with more specific substantive obligations

covering a topic as large as the planet's entire biodiversity? Is it more manageable to attempt to conserve different ecosystems individually, rather than impose guidelines that try to apply to all types in one instrument?

I. PROTECTING THE GLOBAL COMMONS

There are some areas of sea, land, and air that do not fall within recognized national boundaries. These areas are referred to as the 'global commons.' A primary example of global commons is international waters at sea—waters located outside each country's 200 mile exclusive economic zone.

1982 UNITED NATIONS CONVENTION ON THE LAW OF THE SEA

The United Nations Law of the Sea Convention (UNCLOS)[29] established several duties regarding the marine environment. These obligations include the duty of nations to (1) 'protect and preserve the marine environment'; (2) 'take, individually or jointly as appropriate, all measures that are necessary to prevent, reduce and control pollution of the marine environment from any source, using for this purpose the best practical means at their disposal and in accordance with their capabilities'; (3) 'take all measures necessary to ensure that activities under their jurisdiction or control are so conducted as not to cause damage by pollution.'

UNCLOS also obliges nations to (1) cooperate on a global and regional basis with international organizations to formulate 'international rules, standards and recommended practices and procedures for the protection and preservation of the marine environment'; (2) 'cooperate in the promotion of scientific research and data exchange programme regarding marine pollution'; (3) cooperate 'in eliminating the effects of pollution and preventing or minimizing the damage'; and (4) establish appropriate scientific criteria for the formulation of international environmental 'rules, standards and recommended practices and procedures for the prevention, reduction and control of marine pollution.'

Implementation and enforcement of UNCLOS is left to individual member nations. One national strategy to ensure compliance is to prohibit dumping or destructive fishing techniques by all vessels registered in a particular country. Another strategy is to deny port privileges to vessels from nations that have failed to adopt national legislation implementing UNCLOS. Both of these strategies are means of controlling activity in international waters located outside national boundaries.

A major legacy of the Law of the Sea treaty process is the assertion by the so-called group of 77 developing nations that the deep seabed, and minerals contained there, are the 'common heritage of mankind.' It logically follows that the profits from any mining of the deep seabed must be shared with all countries. Thus far, it has not

---

[29] *Supra* note15.

proved cost effective to mine the deep seabed. Also, the United States has not accepted the 'common heritage of mankind' principle as applied to the deep seabed. Obviously, this is an area of international environmental law that is still evolving.

NOTES AND QUESTIONS

1. Why would the United States not accept the UNCLOS 'common heritage of mankind' principle? Is it because the US, as a richer, technically advanced nation, may be one of the first to mine the deep seabed?

2. One of the most difficult aspects of marine issues is the monitoring of behaviour on the open sea. How would any country know if another country observed the principles of international law in the middle of an ocean? Does this render all future international agreements with respect to oceans largely aspirational?

3. Given the difficult regulatory nature of the open sea, would it not make more sense to mandate design changes in ships, such as double hulling to insure against oil spills, that could be enforced in the port states or in the building process?

J. PROTECTING FOREST ECOSYSTEMS

1992 STATEMENT OF FOREST PRINCIPLES

At the 1992 Rio de Janeiro Conference, more than 178 states adopted a statement of principles for the sustainable management of forests. Although the principles adopted are non-binding and lack the force of international law, the statement does provide a good basis upon which a future legally-binding multilateral agreement may be built.

The agreement title, *Forest Principles: Non-Legally Binding Authoritative Statement of Principles for a Global Consensus on the Management, Conservation and Sustainable Development of all Types of Forests*,[30] reflects the difficult politics that surrounded its drafting and adoption. The Forest Principles statement calls for information and technological exchange among parties to the agreement. It encourages public participation, including that of indigenous peoples likely to be affected by a proposed forest project, acknowledges the extreme importance of sustainable forestry practices, and specifically states that 'special attention should also be given to the countries undergoing the process of transition to market economics.'

From the history of the development of the Forest Principles statement, it is evident that some international support does exist for a binding multilateral forest agreement. During the annual 'Group of Seven Industrial Nations' (G-7) economic summit in 1990, the G-7 heads of government endorsed negotiation of a forest protection treaty. Since the G-7 economic summit, the United States has favoured a

[30] *Reprinted in* 31 I.L.M. 881 (1992).

global forest management and protection treaty including both tropical and temperate forests. United States negotiators pursued their goal of a global forest treaty at the 1992 Earth Summit but several developing countries strongly resisted a binding treaty. Developing countries, in particular India and Malaysia, viewed industrialized nations' attempts at negotiating a binding agreement as a means of compromising their sovereign right to exploit their own resources.

What finally emerged from the Earth Summit was a non-binding 'soft' legal instrument containing fifteen principles. Thirteen of these merely recommend what states 'should do' to ensure sustainable forestry practices. While environmental organizations criticized the Statement of Forestry Principles in its final form, delegates to the Summit said that negotiations were so contentious that any agreement signified progress.

In May, 1995 the CSD established a Forestry Panel to develop more binding forestry principles, perhaps in the format of a separate forest protocol or amendment. At the time of this writing, the CSD Forestry Panel had not established specific standards for sustainable forestry or created any new institutions to ensure compliance with the 1992 Statement of Forest Principles. It had, however, set up an Intergovernmental Forum on Forests to continue the dialogue.

1983 AND 1994 INTERNATIONAL TROPICAL TIMBER AGREEMENT AND THE INTERNATIONAL TROPICAL TIMBER ORGANIZATION

Adopted in 1983 under the auspices of the United Nations Conference on Trade and Development, the International Tropical Timber Agreement (ITTA) was designed to regulate the $7.5 billion per year trade in tropical timber. The current ITTA is primarily a commodity agreement focused on tropical hardwood timber. Tropical timber is defined within the agreement as non-coniferous tropical wood for industrial uses produced in countries situated in the tropical zone.

The ITTA's objectives are to provide an effective framework for cooperation and consultation between producing and consuming countries. It aims to expand and diversify international trade in tropical timber and improve structural conditions in the market. Research and development projects are directed at improving forest management, including reforestation. Other projects cover wood use, improving market intelligence, encouraging the processing of tropical timber in producing countries, improving marketing and distribution of exports, and maintaining ecological balance.

To implement the agreement, the International Tropical Timber Organization (ITTO), which functions through the International Tropical Timber Council, was established. The ITTO, based in Yokohama, Japan, consists of 23 producing countries such as Brazil, Colombia, Peru, Malaysia, India, Indonesia and Peru and 26 consumer nations including Australia, China, France, Germany, Japan and the United States. The ITTO's functions are to promote international cooperation, coordinate statistical data and support research and development on use, reforestation and marketing of tropical forest products.

Although its major concern is with the tropical forest products trade, the ITTO has also focused on sustainable forest management. For example, the ITTO has required member nations to file detailed reports covering the legal and institutional framework for forest policies, areas and distribution of protected and producing forest, production levels, prices and stocks. The ITTO has also discussed the possibility of imposing conditions for 'labelling' timber from sustainably managed forests and reducing duties on those products. Such labelling might influence consumer choices especially in Europe and North America.

The 1994 ITTA[31] was agreed to on 26 January 1994 in Geneva. The new agreement's objectives are similar to those of the original ITTA. The 1994 agreement aims to (1) promote and support research and development, and to improve market intelligence to ensure greater transparency in the international timber market; (2) promote increased processing of tropical timber from sustainable sources in producing-member countries to promote industrialization and increase employment opportunities and export earnings; (3) improve marketing and distribution of sustainably produced tropical timber exports; and (4) encourage member states to develop national policies to sustainably manage and conserve forests.

The 1994 ITTA has a new provision calling for all tropical timber exports to come from sustaintably managed forests by the year 2000. This pledge, labeled 'Target 2000', calls upon ITTO member-nations to 'implement appropriate guidelines and criteria for sustainable management of their forests comparable to those developed by the International Tropical Timber Organization' and to work towards 'the national objective of achieving sustainable management of their forest by the year 2000.' The 'Bali Partnership Fund' was also established in which developed countries pledged to provide 'significant resources' to help developing countries pay for forest conservation efforts.

Forest protection NGOs have heavily criticized the 'Target 2000' and 'Bali Partnership Fund.' The criticism has focussed on the ITTO's refusal to establish objective standards for sustainable forestry, and the minimal amount of funding currently pledged to the forest conservation fund. These new provisions are viewed as environmental window-dressing for the ITTA/ITTO's primary purpose—namely to increase the supply of timber and the profitability of the timber industry.

NOTES AND QUESTIONS

1. There are many overlapping and inconsistent agreements dealing with global forest protection. Obviously, there are many different types of forests, and forests are implicated in many other issues, such as climate change, species habitat, and biodiversity. However, could the extremely valuable nature of timber account for

---

[31] *Reprinted in* 33 I.L.M. 1016 (1994) and P.Birnie and A.Boyle, *supra* note 1, at 556.

the great number of agreements about forests? If so, what can be done to effectively conserve a natural resource that supports such a huge industry world-wide?

2. If timber and other forest products are so valuable, how can environmental costs be added to the equation to increase their price on the world market, and slow their trade? What about wood substitutes? What about changes in consumption patterns? How does one coerce or convince participants in a global economy to change their consumption patterns? Education? Publicity?

3. Why is there an agreement on tropical timber but not on temperate timber? Is it because tropical timber producing countries are primarily LDCs and therefore more easily forced by more powerful countries to regulate their trade? Or is it because the tropical timber forests are richer in biodiversity and are therefore more important to the international community?

APPENDICES

APPENDICES

A

THE AIR ACT

AIR (PREVENTION AND CONTROL OF POLLUTION)
ACT, 1981[1]

[NO. 14 OF 1981]

An Act to provide for the prevention, control and abatement of air pollution, for the establishment, with a view to carrying out the aforesaid purposes, of Boards, for conferring on and assigning to such Boards powers and functions relating thereto and for matters connected therewith.

Whereas decisions were taken at the United Nations Conference on the Human Environment held in Stockholm in June 1972, in which India participated, to take appropriate steps for the preservation of the natural resources of the earth which, among other things, include the preservation of the quality of air and control of air pollution;

And whereas it is considered necessary to implement the decisions aforesaid insofar as they relate to the preservation of the quality of air and control of air pollution;

Be it enacted by Parliament in the Thirty-second Year of the Republic of India as follows:

CHAPTER I

PRELIMINARY

1. Short title, extent and commencement.—(1) This Act may be called the Air (Prevention and Control of Pollution) Act, 1981.

(2) It extends to the whole of India.

---

[1] Received the assent of the President on 29 March 1981, published in the *Gazette of India, Extraordinary*, Pt. II, Sec. 1, dated 30 March 1981, pp. 55–80.

(3) It shall come into force on such date as the Central Government may, by notification in the Official Gazette, appoint.

2. Definitions.—In this Act, unless the context otherwise requires,—

(a) 'air pollution' means any solid, liquid or gaseous substance [2][(including noise)] present in the atmosphere in such concentration as may be or tend to be injurious to human beings or other living creatures or plants or property or environment;

(b) 'air pollution' means the presence in the atmosphere of any air pollutant;

(c) 'approved appliance' means any equipment or gadget used for the burning of any combustible material or for generating or consuming any fume, gas or particulate matter and approved by the State Board for the purposes of this Act;

(d) 'approved fuel' means any fuel approved by the State Board for the purposes of this Act;

(e) 'automobile' means any vehicle powered either by internal combustion engine or by any method of generating power to drive such vehicle by burning fuel;

(f) 'Board' means the Central Board or a State Board;

(g) 'Central Board' means the [3][Central Pollution Control Board] constituted under Section 3 of the Water (Prevention and Control of Pollution) Act, 1974 (6 of 1974):

(h) 'chimney' includes any structure with an opening or outlet from or through which any air pollutant may be emitted;

(i) 'control equipment' means any apparatus, device, equipment or system to control the quality and manner of emission of any air pollutant and includes any device used for securing the efficient operation of any industrial plant;

(j) 'emission' means any solid or liquid or gaseous substance coming out of any chimney, duct or flue or any other outlet;

(k) 'industrial plant' means any plant used for any industrial or trade purposes and emitting any air pollutant into the atmosphere;

(l) 'member' means a member of the Central Board or a State Board, as the case may be, and includes the Chairman thereof;

[4][(m) 'occupier', in relation to any factory or premises, means the person who has control over the affairs of the factory or the premises, and includes, in relation to any substance, the person in possession of the substance;]

(n) 'prescribed' means prescribed by rules made under this Act by the Central Government or, as the case may be, the state government;

(o) 'State Board' means,—

---

[2] *Ins.* by Act 47 of 1987.
[3] *Subs.* by *ibid.*
[4] *Subs.* by Act 47 of 1987.

(i) in relation to a state in which the Water (Prevention and Control of Pollution) Act, 1974 (6 of 1974), is in force and the state government has constituted for that State a [5][State Pollution Control Board] under Section 4 of that Act, the said State Board; and

(ii) in relation to any other state, the State Board for the Prevention and Control of Air Pollution constituted by the state government under Section 5 of this Act.

CHAPTER II

CENTRAL AND STATE BOARDS FOR THE PREVENTION AND CONTROL OF AIR POLLUTION

[6][**3. Central Pollution Control Board.**—The Central Pollution Control Board constituted under Section 3 of the Water (Prevention and Control of Pollution) Act, 1974 (6 of 1974), shall, without prejudice to the exercise and performance of its powers and functions under that Act, exercise the powers and perform the functions of the Central Pollution Control Board for the prevention and control of air pollution under this Act.

4. State Pollution Control Boards constituted under Section 4 of Act 6 of 1974 to be State Boards under this Act.—In any state in which the Water (Prevention and Control of Pollution) Act, 1974, is in force and the state government has constituted for that State a State Pollution Control Board under Section 4 of that Act, such State Board shall be deemed to be the State Board for the Prevention and Control of Air Pollution constituted under Section 5 of this Act, and accordingly that State Pollution Control Board shall, without prejudice to the exercise and performance of its powers and functions under that Act, exercise the powers and perform the functions of the State Board for the prevention and control of air pollution under this Act.]

5. Constitution of State Boards.—(1) In any state in which the Water (Prevention and Control of Pollution) Act, 1974 (6 of 1974), is not in force, or that Act is in force but the state government has not constituted a [7][State Pollution Control Board] under that Act, the state government shall, with effect from such date as it may, by notification in the Official Gazette, appoint, constitute a State Board for the Prevention and Control of Air Pollution under such name as may be specified in the notification, to exercise the powers conferred on, and perform the functions assigned to, that Board under this Act.

(2) A State Board constituted under this Act shall consist of the following members, namely:

[5] *Subs.* by Act 47 of 1987.
[6] *Subs.* by Act 47 of 1987.
[7] *Subs.* by *ibid.*

(a) a Chairman, being a person having special knowledge or practical experience in respect of matters relating to environmental protection, to be nominated by the state government:

Provided that the Chairman may be either whole-time or part-time as the state government may think fit;

(b) such number of officials, not exceeding five, as the state government may think fit, to be nominated by the state government to represent that Government;

(c) such number of persons, not exceeding five, as the state government may think fit, to be nominated by the state government from amongst the members of the local authorities functioning within the state;

(d) such number of non-officials, not exceeding three, as the state government may think fit, to be nominated by the state government to represent the interests of agriculture, fishery or industry or trade or labour or any other interest which, in the opinion of that Government, ought to be represented;

(e) two persons to represent the companies or corporations owned, controlled or managed by the state government, to be nominated by that Government;

8[(f) a full-time member-secretary having such qualifications, knowledge and experience of scientific, engineering or management aspects of pollution control as may be prescribed, to be appointed by the state government:]

Provided that the state government shall ensure that not less than two of the members are persons having special knowledge or practical experience in respect of matters relating to the improvement of the quality of air or the prevention, control or abatement of air pollution.

(3) Every State Board constituted under this Act shall be a body corporate with the name specified by the state government in the notification issued under sub-section (1), having perpetual succession and a common seal with power, subject to the provisions of this Act, to acquire and dispose of property and to contract, and may by the said name sue or be sued.

6. Central Board to exercise the powers and perform the functions of a State Board in the Union Territories.—No State Board shall be constituted for a union territory and in relation to a union territory, the Central Board shall exercise the powers and perform the functions of a State Board under this Act for that union territory:

Provided that in relation to any union territory the Central Board may delegate all or any of its powers and functions under this section to such person or body of persons as the Central Government may specify.

7. Terms and conditions of service of members.—(1) Save as otherwise provided by or under this Act, a member of a State Board constituted under this Act, other than the member-secretary, shall hold office for a term of three years from the date on which his nomination is notified in the Official Gazette:

---

8 *Subs.* by Act 47 of 1987.

Provided that a member shall, notwithstanding the expiration of his term, continue to hold office until his successor enters upon his office.

(2) The term of office of a member of a State Board constituted under this Act and nominated under clause (b) or clause (e) of sub-section (2) of Section 5 shall come to an end as soon as he ceases to hold the office under the state government or, as the case may be, the company or corporation owned, controlled or managed by the state government, by virtue of which he was nominated.

(3) A member of a State Board constituted under this Act, other than the member-secretary, may at any time resign his office by writing under his hand addressed,—

   (a) in the case of the Chairman, to the state government; and
   (b) in any other case, to the Chairman, of the State Board, and the seat of the Chairman or such other member shall thereupon become vacant.

(4) A member of a State Board constituted under this Act, other than the member-secretary, shall be deemed to have vacated his seat, if he is absent without reason, sufficient in the opinion of the State Board, from three consecutive meetings of the State Board or where he is nominated under clause (c) of sub-section (2) of Section 5, he ceases to be a member of the local authority and such vacation of seat shall, in either case, take effect from such date as the state government may, by notification in the Official Gazette, specify.

(5) A casual vacancy in a State Board constituted under this Act shall be filled by a fresh nomination and the person nominated to fill the vacancy shall hold office only for the remainder of the term for which the member whose place he takes was nominated.

(6) A member of a State Board constituted under this Act shall be eligible for re-nomination [9][* * *]

(7) The other terms and conditions of service of the Chairman and other members (except the member-secretary) of a State Board constituted under this Act shall be such as may be prescribed.

8. Disqualifications.—(1) No person shall be a member of a State Board constituted under this Act, who—

   (a) is, or at any time has been, adjudged insolvent, or
   (b) is of unsound mind and has been so declared by a competent court, or
   (c) is, or has been, convicted of an offence which, in the opinion of the state government, involves moral turpitude, or
   (d) is, or at any time has been, convicted of an offence under this Act, or
   (e) has directly or indirectly by himself or by any partner, any share or interest in any firm or company carrying on the business of manufacture, sale or hire of machinery, industrial plant, control equipment or any other apparatus for the improvement of the quality of air or for the prevention, control or abatement of air pollution, or

[9] *Omitted* by Act 47 of 1987.

(f) is a director or a secretary, manager or other salaried officer or employee of any company or firm having any contract with the Board, or with the Government constituting the Board or with a local authority in the state, or with a company or corporation owned, controlled or managed by the Government, for the carrying out of programmes for the improvement of the quality of air or for the prevention, control or abatement of air pollution, or

(g) has so abused, in the opinion of the state government, his position as a member, as to render his continuance on the State Board detrimental to the interests of the general public.

(2) The state government shall, by order in writing, remove any member who is, or has become, subject to any disqualification mentioned in sub-section (1):

Provided that no order of removal shall be made by the state government under this section unless the member concerned has been given a reasonable opportunity of showing cause against the same.

(3) Notwithstanding anything contained in sub-section (1) or sub-section (6) of Section 7, a member who has been removed under this section shall not be eligible to continue to hold office until his successor enters upon his office, or, as the case may be, for re-nomination as a member.

9. Vacation of seats by members.—If a member of a State Board constituted under this Act becomes subject to any of the disqualifications specified in Section 8, his seat shall become vacant.

10. Meetings of Board.—(1) For the purposes of this Act, a Board shall meet at least once in every three months and shall observe such rules of procedure in regard to the transaction of business at its meetings as may be prescribed:

Provided that if, in the opinion of the Chairman, any business of an urgent nature is to be transacted, he may convene a meeting of the Board at such time as he thinks fit for the aforesaid purpose.

(2) Copies of the minutes of the meetings under sub-section (1) shall be forwarded to the Central Board and to the state government concerned.

11. Constitution of committees.—(1) A Board may constitute as many committees consisting wholly of members or partly of members and partly of other persons and for such purpose or purposes as it may think fit.

(2) A committee constituted under this section shall meet at such time and at such place, and shall observe such rules of procedure in regard to the transaction of business at its meetings, as may be prescribed.

(3) The members of a committee other than the members of the Board shall be paid such fees and allowances, for attending its meetings and for attending to any other work of the Board as may be prescribed.

12. Temporary association of persons with Board for particular purposes.—(1) A Board may associate with itself in such manner, and for such purposes, as may be prescribed, any person whose assistance or advice it may desire to obtain in performing any of its functions under this Act.

(2) A person associated with the Board under sub-section (1) for any purpose shall have a right to take part in the discussions of the Board relevant to that purpose, but shall not have a right to vote at a meeting of the Board and shall not be a member of the Board for any other purpose.

(3) A person associated with a Board under sub-section (1) shall be entitled to receive such fees and allowances as may be prescribed.

13. Vacancy in Board not to invalidate acts or proceedings.—No act or proceeding of a Board or any committee thereof shall be called in question on the ground merely of the existence of any vacancy in, or any defect in the constitution of, the Board or such committee, as the case may be.

14. Member-secretary and officers and other employees of State Boards.—(1) The terms and conditions of service of the member-secretary of a State Board constituted under this Act shall be such as may be prescribed.

[10][(2) The member-secretary of a State Board, whether constituted under this Act or not, shall exercise such powers and perform such duties as may be prescribed, or as may, from time to time, be delegated to him by the State Board or its Chairman.]

(3) Subject to such rules as may be made by the state government in this behalf, a State Board, whether constituted under this Act or not, may appoint such officers and other employees as it considers necessary for the efficient performance of its functions under the Act.

(4) The method of appointment, the conditions of service and the scales of pay of the officers (other than member-secretary) and other employees of a State Board appointed under sub-section (3) shall be such as may be determined by regulations made by the State Board under this Act.

(5) Subject to such conditions as may be prescribed, a State Board constituted under this Act may from time to time appoint any qualified person to be a consultant to the Board and pay him such salary and allowances or fees, as it thinks fit.

15. Delegation of powers.—A State Board may, by general or special order, delegate to the Chairman or the member-secretary or any other officer of the Board subject to such conditions and limitations, if any, as may be specified in the order, such of its powers and functions under this Act as it may deem necessary.

CHAPTER III

POWERS AND FUNCTIONS OF BOARD

16. Functions of Central Board.—(1) Subject to the provisions of this Act, and without prejudice to the performance of its functions under the Water (Prevention and Control of Pollution) Act, 1974 (6 of 1974), the main functions of the Central

[10] *Subs.* by Act 47 of 1987.

Board shall be to improve the quality of air and to prevent, control or abate air pollution in the country.

(2) In particular and without prejudice to the generality of the foregoing functions, the Central Board may—

(a) advise the Central Government on any matter concerning the improvement of the quality of air and the prevention, control or abatement of air pollution;

(b) plan and cause to be executed a nationwide programme for the prevention, control or abatement of air pollution;

(c) co-ordinate the activities of the State Boards and resolve disputes among them;

(d) provide technical assistance and guidance to the State Boards, carry out and sponsor investigations and research relating to problems of air-pollution and prevention, control or abatement of air pollution;

[11][(dd) perform such of the functions of any State Board as may be specified in an order made under sub-section (2) of Section 18;]

(e) plan and organise the training of persons engaged or to be engaged in programmes for the prevention, control or abatement of air pollution on such terms and conditions as the Central Board may specify;

(f) organise through mass media a comprehensive programme regarding the prevention, control or abatement of air pollution;

(g) collect, compile and publish technical and statistical data relating to air pollution and the measures devised for its effective prevention, control or abatement and prepare manuals, codes or guides relating to prevention, control or abatement of air pollution;

(h) lay down standards for the quality of air;

(i) collect and disseminate information in respect of matters relating to air pollution;

(j) perform such other functions as may be prescribed.

(3) The Central Board may establish or recognise a laboratory or laboratories to enable the Central Board to perform its functions under this section efficiently.

(4) The Central Board may—

(a) delegate any of its functions under this Act generally or specially to any of the committees appointed by it;

(b) do such other things and perform such other acts as it may think necessary for the proper discharge of its functions and generally for the purpose of carrying into effect the purposes of this Act.

17. Functions of State Boards.—(1) Subject to the provisions of this Act, and without prejudice to the performance of its functions, if any, under the Water (Prevention and Control of Pollution) Act, 1974 (6 of 1974), the functions of a State Board shall be—

[11] *Ins. by ibid.*

(a) to plan a comprehensive programme for the prevention, control or abatement of air pollution and to secure the execution thereof;

(b) to advise the state government on any matter concerning the prevention, control or abatement of air pollution;

(c) to collect and disseminate information relating to air pollution;

(d) to collaborate with the Central Board in organizing the training of persons engaged or to be engaged in programmes relating to prevention, control or abatement of air pollution and to organize mass-education programme relating thereto;

(e) to inspect, at all reasonable times, any control equipment, industrial plant or manufacturing process and to give, by order, such directions to such persons as it may consider necessary to take steps for the prevention, control or abatement of air pollution;

(f) to inspect air pollution control areas at such intervals as it may think necessary, assess the quality of air therein and take steps for the prevention, control or abatement of air pollution in such areas;

(g) to lay down, in consultation with the Central Board and having regard to the standards for the quality of air laid down by the Central Board, standards for emission of air pollutants into the atmosphere from industrial plants and automobiles or for the discharge of any air pollutant into the atmosphere from any other source whatsoever not being a ship or an aircraft:

Provided that different standards for emission may be laid down under this clause for different industrial plants having regard to the quantity and composition of emission of air pollutants into the atmosphere from such industrial plants;

(h) to advise the state government with respect to the suitability of any premises or location for carrying on any industry which is likely to cause air pollution;

(i) to perform such other functions as may be prescribed or as may, from time to time, be entrusted to it by the Central Board or the state government;

(j) to do such other things and to perform such other acts as it may think necessary for the proper discharge of its functions and generally for the purpose of carrying into effect the purposes of this Act.

(2) A State Board may establish or recognise a laboratory or laboratories to enable the State Board to perform its functions under this section efficiently.

18. Power to give directions.—[12][(1)] In the performance of its functions under this Act—

---

[12] *Renumbered* by Act 47 of 1987 and after sub-section (1) as so *renumbered* sub-sections (2), (3) and (4) *ins.* by *ibid.*

(a) the Central Board shall be bound by such directions in writing as the Central Government may give to it; and

(b) every State Board shall be bound by such directions in writing as the Central Board or the state government may give to it:

Provided that where a direction given by the state government is inconsistent with the direction given by the Central Board, the matter shall be referred to the Central Government for its decision.

[13][(2) Where the Central Government is of the opinion that any State Board has defaulted in complying with any directions given by the Central Board under sub-section (1) and as a result of such default a grave emergency has arisen and it is necessary or expedient so to do in the public interest, it may, by order, direct the Central Board to perform any of the functions of the State Board in relation to such area, for such period and for such purposes, as may be specified in the order.

(3) Where the Central Board performs any of the functions of the State Board in pursuance of a direction under sub-section (2), the expenses, if any, incurred by the Central Board with respect to the performance of such functions may, if the State Board is empowered to recover such expenses, be recovered by the Central Board with interest (at such reasonable rate as the Central Government may, by order, fix) from the date when a demand for such expenses is made until it is paid from the person or persons concerned as arrears of land revenue or of public demand.

(4) For the removal of doubts, it is hereby declared that any direction to perform the functions of any State Board given under sub-section (2) in respect of any area would not preclude the State Board from performing such functions in any other area in the State or any of its other functions in that area.]

CHAPTER IV

PREVENTION AND CONTROL OF AIR POLLUTION

19. Power to declare air pollution control areas.—(1) The state government may, after consultation with the State Board, by notification in the Official Gazette, declare in such manner as may be prescribed, any area or areas within the State as air pollution control area or areas for the purposes of this Act.

(2) The state government may, after consultation with the State Board, by notification in the Official Gazette,—

(a) alter any air pollution control area whether by may of extension or reduction;

(b) declare a new air pollution control area in which may be merged one or more existing air pollution control areas or any part or parts thereof.

(3) If the state government, after consultation with the State Board, is of opinion that the use of any fuel, other than an approved fuel, in any air pollution

[13] *Ibid.*

control area or part thereof, may cause or is likely to cause air pollution, it may by notification in the Official Gazette, prohibit the use of such fuel in such area or part thereof with effect from such date (being not less than three months from the date of publication of the notification) as may be specified in the notification.

(4) The state government may, after consultation with the State Board, by notification in the Official Gazette, direct that with effect from such date as may be specified therein, no appliance, other than an approved appliance, shall be used in the premises situated in an air pollution control area:

Provided that different dates may be specified for different parts of an air pollution control area or for the use of different appliances.

(5) If the state government, after consultation with the State Board, is of opinion that the burning of any material (not being fuel) in any air pollution control area or part thereof may cause or is likely to cause air pollution, it may, by notification in the Official Gazette, prohibit the burning of such material in such area or part thereof.

20. Power to give instructions for ensuring standards for emission from automobiles.—With a view to ensuring that the standards for emission of air pollutants from automobiles laid down by the State Board under clause (g) of sub-section (1) of Section 17 are complied with, the state government shall, in consultation with the State Board, give such instructions as may be deemed necessary to the concerned authority in charge of registration of motor vehicles under the Motor Vehicles Act, 1939 (4 of 1939), and such authority shall, notwithstanding anything contained in that Act or the rules made thereunder be bound to comply with such instructions.

21. Restrictions on use of certain industrial plants.—[14][(1) Subject to the provisions of this section, no person shall, without the previous consent of the State Board, establish or operate any industrial plant in an air pollution control area:

Provided that a person operating any industrial plant in any air pollution control area immediately before the commencement of Section 9 of the Air (Prevention and Control of Pollution) Amendment Act, 1987, for which no consent was necessary prior to such commencement, may continue to do so for a period of three months from such commencement or, if he has made an application for such consent within the said period of three months, till the disposal of such application.]

(2) An application for consent of the State Board under sub-section (1) shall be accompanied by such fees, as may be prescribed and shall be made in the prescribed form and shall contain the particulars of the industrial plant and such other particulars as may be prescribed:

Provided that where any person, immediately before the declaration of any area as an air pollution control area, operates in such area any industrial plant [15][* * *] such person shall make the application under this sub-section within such

[14] *Subs.* by Act 47 of 1987.
[15] *Omitted* by ibid.

period (being not less than three months from the date of such declaration) as may be prescribed and where such person makes such application, he shall be deemed to be operating such industrial plant with the consent of the State Board until the consent applied for has been refused.

(3) The State Board may make such inquiry as it may deem fit in respect of the application for consent referred to in sub-section (1) and in making any such inquiry, shall follow such procedure as may be prescribed.

(4) Within a period of four months after the receipt of the application for consent referred to in sub-section (1), the State Board shall, by order in writing, [16][and for reasons to be recorded in the order, grant the consent applied for subject to such conditions and for such period as may be specified in the order, or refuse such consent]:

[17][Provided that it shall be open to the State Board to cancel such consent before the expiry of the period for which it is granted or refuse further consent after such expiry if the conditions subject to which such consent has been granted are not fulfilled:

Provided further that before cancelling a consent or refusing a further consent under the first proviso, a reasonable opportunity of being heard shall be given to the person concerned.]

(5) Every person to whom consent has been granted by the State Board under sub-section (4), shall comply with the following conditions, namely:

(i) the control equipment of such specifications as the State Board may approve in this behalf shall be installed and operated in the premises where the industry is carried on or proposed to be carried on;

(ii) the existing control equipment, if any, shall be altered or replaced in accordance with the directions of the State Board;

(iii) the control equipment referred to in clause (i) or clause (ii) shall be kept at all times in good running condition;

(iv) chimney, wherever necessary, of such specifications as the State Board may approve in this behalf shall be erected or re-erected in such premises;

(v) such other conditions as the State Board may specify in this behalf; and

(vi) the conditions referred to in clauses (i), (ii) and (iv) shall be complied with within such period as the State Board may specify in this behalf;

Provided that in the case of a person operating any industrial plant [18][* * *] in an air pollution control area immediately before the date of declaration of such area as an air pollution control area, the period so specified shall not be less than six months:

16 *Subs.* by *ibid.*
17 *Ins.* by Act 47 of 1987.
18 *Omitted* by *ibid.*

Provided further that—

(a) after the installation of any control equipment in accordance with the specifications under clause (i), or

(b) after the alteration or replacement of any control equipment in accordance with the directions of the State Board under clause (ii), or

(c) after the erection or re-erection of any chimney under clause (iv), no control equipment or chimney shall be altered or replaced or, as the case may be, re-erected except with the previous approval of the State Board.

(6) If due to any technological improvement or otherwise the State Board is of opinion that all or any of the conditions referred to in sub-section (5) require or requires variation (including the change of any control equipment, either in whole or in part), the State Board shall, after giving the person to whom consent has been granted an opportunity of being heard, vary all or any of such conditions and thereupon such person shall be bound to comply with the conditions as so varied.

(7) Where a person to whom consent has been granted by the State Board under sub-section (4) transfers his interest in the industry to any other person, such consent shall be deemed to have been granted to such other person and he shall be bound to comply with all the conditions subject to which it was granted as if the consent was granted to him originally.

22. Persons carrying on industry, etc., not to allow emission of air pollutants in excess of the standards laid down by State Board.—No person [19][* * *] operating any industrial plant, in any air pollution control area shall discharge or cause or permit to be discharged the emission of any air pollutant in excess of the standards laid down by the State Board under clause (9) of sub-section (1) of Section 17.

[20][**22-A. Power of Board to make application to court for restraining persons from causing air pollution.**—(1) Where it is apprehended by a Board that emission of any air pollutant, in excess of the standards laid down by the State Board under clause (g) of sub-section (1) of Section 17, is likely to occur by reason of any person operating an industrial plant or otherwise in any air pollution control area, the Board may make an application to a court, not inferior to that of a Metropolitan Magistrate or a Judicial Magistrate of the first class for restraining such person from emitting such air pollutant.

(2) On receipt of the application under sub-section (1), the court may make such order as it deems fit.

(3) Where under sub-section (2), the court makes an order restraining any person from discharging or causing or permitting to be discharged the emission of any air pollutant, it may, in that order,—

[19] *Omitted* by Act 47 of 1987.
[20] *Ins.* by *ibid.*

(a) direct such person to desist from taking such action as is likely to cause emission;

(b) authorise the Board, if the direction under clause (a) is not complied with by the person to whom such direction is issued, to implement the direction in such manner as may be specified by the court.

(4) All expenses incurred by the Board in implementing the directions of the court under clause (b) of sub-section (3) shall be recoverable from the person concerned as arrears of land revenue or of public demand.]

23. Furnishing of information to State Board and other agencies in certain cases.—(1) Where in any [21][* * *] area the emission of any air pollutant into the atmosphere in excess of the standards laid down by the State Board occurs or is apprehended to occur due to accident or other unforeseen act or event, the person in charge of the premises from where such emission occurs or is apprehended to occur shall forthwith intimate the fact of such occurrence or the apprehension of such occurrence to the State Board and to such authorities or agencies as may be prescribed.

(2) On receipt of information with respect to the fact or the apprehension of any occurrence of the nature referred to in sub-section (1), whether through intimation under that sub-section or otherwise, the State Board and the authorities or agencies shall, as early as practicable, cause such remedial measures to be taken as are necessary to mitigate the emission of such air pollutants.

(3) Expenses, if any, incurred by the State Board, authority or agency with respect to the remedial measures referred to in sub-section (2) together with interest (at such reasonable rate, as the state government may, by order, fix) from the date when a demand for the expenses is made until it is paid, may be recovered by the Board, authority or agency from the person, concerned, as arrears of land revenue, or of public demand.

24. Power of entry and inspection.—(1) Subject to the provisions of this section, any person empowered by a State Board in this behalf shall have a right to enter, at all reasonable times with such assistance as he considers necessary, any place—

(a) for the purpose of performing any of the functions of the State Board entrusted to him;

(b) for the purpose of determining whether and if so in what manner, any such functions are to be performed or whether any provisions of this Act or the rules made thereunder or any notice, order, direction or authorisation served, made, given or granted under this Act is being or has been complied with;

(c) for the purpose of examining and testing any control equipment, industrial plant, record, register, document or any other material object or for conducting a search of any place in which he has reason to believe that

[21] *Omitted* by *ibid.*

an offence under this Act or the rules made thereunder has been or is about to be committed and for seizing any such control equipment, industrial plant, record, register, document or other material object if he has reasons to believe that it may furnish evidence of the commission of an offence punishable under this Act or the rules made thereunder.

(2) Every person [22][* * *] operating any control equipment or any industrial plant, in an air pollution control area shall be bound to render all assistance to the person empowered by the State Board under sub-section (1) for carrying out the functions under that sub-section and if he fails to do so without any reasonable cause or excuse, he shall be guilty of an offence under this Act.

(3) If any person willfully delays or obstructs any person empowered by the State Board under sub-section (1) in the discharge of his duties, he shall be guilty of an offence under this Act.

(4) The provisions of the Code of Criminal Procedure, 1973 (2 of 1974), or, in relation to the state of Jammu and Kashmir, or any area in which that Code is not in force, the provisions of any corresponding law in force in that state or area, shall, so far as may be, apply to any search or seizure under this section as they apply to any search or seizure made under the authority of a warrant issued under Section 94 of the said Code or, as the case may be, under the corresponding provisions of the said law.

25. Power to obtain information.—For the purposes of carrying out the functions entrusted to it, the State Board or any officer empowered by it in that behalf may call for any information (including information regarding the types of air pollutants emitted into the atmosphere and the level of the emission of such air pollutants) from the occupier or any other person carrying on any industry or operating any control equipment or industrial plant and for the purpose of verifying the correctness of such information, the State Board or such officer shall have the right to inspect the premises where such industry, control equipment or industrial plant is being carried on or operated.

26. Power to take samples of air or emission and procedure to be followed in connection therewith.—(1) A State Board or any officer empowered by it in this behalf shall have power to take, for the purpose of analysis, samples of air or emission from any chimney, flue or duct or any other outlet in such manner as may be prescribed.

(2) The result of any analysis of a sample of emission taken under sub-section (1) shall not be admissible in evidence in any legal proceeding unless the provisions of subsections (3) and (4) are complied with.

(3) Subject to the provisions of sub-section (4), when a sample of emission is taken for analysis under sub-section (1), the person taking the sample shall—

(a) serve on the occupier or his agent, a notice, then and there, in such form as may be prescribed, of his intention to have it so analysed;

(b) in the presence of the occupier or his agent, collect a sample of emission for analysis;

[22] *Ibid.*

    (c) cause the sample to be placed in a container or containers which shall be marked and sealed and shall also be signed both by the person taking the sample and the occupier or his agent;

    (d) send, without delay, the container or containers to the laboratory established or recognised by the State Board under Section 17 or, if a request in that behalf is made by the occupier or his agent when the notice is served on him under clause (a), to the laboratory established or specified under sub-section (1) of Section 28.

(4) When a sample of emission is taken for analysis under sub-section (1) and the person taking the sample serves on the occupier or his agent, a notice under clause (a) of sub-section (3), then—

    (a) in a case where the occupier or his agent willfully absents himself, the person taking the sample shall collect the sample of emission for analysis to be placed in a container or containers which shall be marked and sealed and shall also be signed by the person taking the sample, and

    (b) in a case where the occupier or his agent is present at the time of taking the sample but refuses to sign the marked and sealed container or containers of the sample of emission as required under clause (c) of sub-section (3), the marked and sealed container or containers shall be signed by the person taking the sample,

and the container or containers shall be sent without delay by the person taking the sample for analysis to the laboratory established or specified under sub-section (1) of Section 28 and such person shall inform the Government analyst appointed under sub-section (1) of Section 29, in writing, about the wilful absence of the occupier or his agent, or, as the case may be, his refusal to sign the container or containers.

    27. Reports of the result of analysis on samples taken under Section 26.— (1) Where a sample of emission has been sent for analysis to the laboratory established or recognized by the State Board, the board analyst appointed under sub-section (2) of Section 29 shall analyse the sample and submit a report in the prescribed form of such analysis in triplicate to the State Board.

    (2) On receipt of the report under sub-section (1), one copy of the report shall be sent by the State Board to the occupier or his agent referred to in Section 26, another copy shall be preserved for production before the court in case any legal proceedings are taken against him and the other copy shall be kept by the State Board.

    (3) Where a sample has been sent for analysis under clause (d) of sub-section (3) or sub-section (4) of Section 26 to any laboratory mentioned therein, the Government analyst referred to in the said sub-section (4) shall analyse the sample and submit a report in the prescribed form of the result of the analysis in triplicate to the State Board which shall comply with the provisions of sub-section (2).

    (4) Any cost incurred in getting any sample analysed at the request of the occupier or his agent as provided in clause (d) of sub-section (3) of Section 26 or when he willfully absents himself or refuses to sign the marked and sealed container

or containers of sample of emission under sub-section (4) of that section, shall be payable by such occupier or his agent and in case of default the same shall be recoverable from him as arrears of land revenue or of public demand.

28. State Air Laboratory.—(1) The state government may, by notification in the Official Gazette,—

(a) establish one or more State Air Laboratories; or

(b) specify one or more laboratories or institutes as State Air Laboratories to carry out the functions entrusted to the State Air Laboratory under this Act.

(2) The state government may, after consultation with the State Board, make rules prescribing—

(a) the functions of the State Air Laboratory;

(b) the procedure for the submission to the said Laboratory of samples of air or emission for analysis or tests, the form of the Laboratory's report thereon and the fees payable in respect of such report;

(c) such other matters as may be necessary or expedient to enable that Laboratory to carry out its functions.

29. Analysts.—(1) The state government may, by notification in the Official Gazette, appoint such persons as it thinks fit and having the prescribed qualifications to be Government analysts for the purpose of analysis of samples of air or emission sent for analysis to any laboratory established or specified under sub-section (1) of Section 28.

(2) Without prejudice to the provisions of Section 14, the State Board may, by notification in the Official Gazette, and with the approval of the state government, appoint such persons as it thinks fit and having the prescribed qualifications to be Board analysts for the purpose of analysis of samples of air or emission sent for analysis to any laboratory established or recognized under Section 17.

30. Report of analysts.—Any document purporting to be a report signed by a Government analyst or, as the case may be, a State Board analyst may be used as evidence of the facts stated therein in any proceeding under this Act.

31. Appeals.—(1) Any person aggrieved by an order made by the State Board under this Act may, within thirty days from the date on which the order is communicated to him, prefer an appeal to such authority (hereinafter referred to as the Appellate Authority) as the state government may think fit to constitute:

Provided that the Appellate Authority may entertain the appeal after the expiry of the said period of thirty days if such authority is satisfied that the appellant was prevented by sufficient cause from filing the appeal in time.

(2) The Appellate Authority shall consist of a single person or three persons as the State Government may think fit to be appointed by the state government.

(3) The form and the manner in which an appeal may be preferred under sub-section (1), the fees payable for such appeal and the procedure to be followed by the Appellate Authority shall be such as may be prescribed.

(4) On receipt of an appeal preferred under sub-section (1), the Appellate

Authority shall, after giving the appellant and the State Board an opportunity of being heard, dispose of the appeal as expeditiously as possible.

[23][**31-A. Power to give directions.**—Notwithstanding anything contained in any other law, but subject to the provisions of this Act and to any directions that the Central Government may give in this behalf a Board may, in the exercise of its powers and performance of its functions under this Act, issue any directions in writing to any person, officer or authority, and such person, officer or authority shall be bound to comply with such directions.

Explanation.—For the avoidance of doubts, it is hereby declared that the power to issue directions under this section includes the power to direct—

(a)   the closure, prohibition or regulation of any industry, operation or process; or

(b)   the stoppage or regulation of supply of electricity, water or any other service.]

CHAPTER V

FUND, ACCOUNTS AND AUDIT

32. Contributions by Central Government.—The Central Government may, after due appropriation made by Parliament by law in this behalf, make in each financial year such contributions to the State Boards as it may think necessary to enable the State Boards to perform their functions under this Act:

Provided that nothing in this section shall apply to any [24][State Pollution Control Board] constituted under Section 4 of the Water (Prevention and Control of Pollution) Act, 1974 (6 of 1974), which is empowered by that Act to expend money from its fund thereunder also for performing its functions, under any law for the time being in force relating to the prevention, control or abatement of air pollution.

33. Fund of Board.—(1) Every State Board shall have its own fund for the purposes of this Act and all sums which may, from time to time, be paid to it by the Central Government and all other receipts (by way of contributions, if any, from the state government, fees, gifts, grants, donations, benefactions or otherwise) of that Board shall be carried to the fund of the Board and all payments by the Board shall be made therefrom.

(2) Every State Board may expend such sums as it thinks fit for performing its functions under this Act and such sums shall be treated as expenditure payable out of the fund of that Board.

(3) Nothing in this section shall apply to any [25][State Pollution Control Board] constituted under Section 4 of the Water (Prevention and Control of Pollution) Act,

[23] *Ins.* by Act 47 of 1987.
[24] *Subs.* by *ibid.*
[25] *Subs.* by *ibid.*

1974 (6 of 1974), which is empowered by that Act to expend money from its fund thereunder also for performing its functions, under any law for the time being in force relating to the prevention, control or abatement of air pollution.

[26][33-A. Borrowing powers of Board.—A Board may, with the consent of, or in accordance with the terms of any general or special authority given to it by, the Central Government or, as the case may be, the state government, borrow money from any source by way of loans, or issue of bonds, debentures or such other instruments, as it may deem fit, for discharging all or any of its functions under this Act.]

34. Budget.—The Central Board or, as the case may be, the State Board shall, during each financial year, prepare, in such form and at such time as may be prescribed, budget in respect of the financial year next ensuing showing the estimated receipt and expenditure under this Act, and copies thereof shall be forwarded to the Central Government or, as the case may be, the state government.

[27][**35. Annual report.**—(1) The Central Board shall, during each financial year, prepare, in such form as may be prescribed, an annual report giving full account of its activities under this Act during the previous financial year and copies thereof shall be forwarded to the Central Government within four months from the last date of the previous financial year and that Government shall cause every such report to be laid before both Houses of Parliament within nine months of the last date of the previous financial year.

(2) Every State Board shall, during each financial year, prepare, in such form as may be prescribed, an annual report giving full account of its activities under this Act during the previous financial year and copies thereof shall be forwarded to the state government within four months from the last date of the previous financial year and that Government shall cause every such report to be laid before the State Legislature within a period of nine months from the last date of the previous financial year.]

36. Accounts and audit.—(1) Every Board shall, in relation to its functions under this Act, maintain proper accounts and other relevant records and prepare an annual statement of accounts in such form as may be prescribed by the Central Government or, as the case may be, the state government.

(2) The accounts of the Board shall be audited by an auditor duly qualified to act as an auditor of companies under Section 226 of the Companies Act, 1956 (1 of 1956).

(3) The said auditor shall be appointed by the Central Government or, as the case may be, the state government on the advice of the Comptroller and Auditor-General of India.

(4) Every auditor appointed to audit the accounts of the Board under this Act,

---

[26] *Ins.* by *ibid.*
[27] *Subs.* by *ibid.*

shall have the right to demand the production of books accounts, connected vouchers and other documents and papers and to inspect any of the offices of the Board.

(5) Every such auditor shall send a copy of his report together with an audited copy of the accounts to the Central Government or, as the case may be, the State Government.

(6) The Central Government shall, as soon as may be after the receipt of the audit report under sub-section (5), cause the same to be laid before both Houses of Parliament.

(7) The state government shall, as soon as may be after the receipt of the audit report under sub-section (5), cause the same to be laid before the State Legislature.

CHAPTER VI

PENALTIES AND PROCEDURE

[28][**37. Failure to comply with the provisions of Section 21 or Section 22 or with the directions issued under Section 31-A.**—(1) Whoever fails to comply with the provisions of Section 21 or Section 22 or directions issued under Section 31-A, shall, in respect of each such failure, be punishable with imprisonment for a term which shall not be less than one year and six months but which may extend to six years and with fine, and in case the failure continues, with an additional fine which may extend to five thousand rupees for every day during which such failure continues after the conviction for the first such failure.

(2) If the failure referred to in sub-section (1) continues beyond a period of one year after the date of conviction, the offender shall be punishable with imprisonment for a term which shall not be less than two years but which may extend to seven years and with fine.]

38. Penalties for certain acts.—Whoever—

(a) destroys, pulls down, removes, injures or defaces any pillar, post or stake fixed in the ground or any notice or other matter put up, inscribed or placed, by or under the authority of the Board, or

(b) obstructs any person acting under the orders or directions of the Board from exercising his powers and performing his functions under this Act, or

(c) damages any works or property belonging to the Board, or

(d) fails to furnish to the Board or any officer or other employee of the Board any information required by the Board or such officer or other employee for the purpose of this Act, or

---

[28] *Subs.* by Act 47 of 1987.

(e) fails to intimate the occurence of the emission of air pollutants into the atmosphere in excess of the standards laid down by the State Board or the apprehension of such occurence, to the State Board and other prescribed authorities or agencies as required under sub-section (1) of Section 23, or

(f) in giving any information which he is required to give under this Act, makes a statement which is false in any material particular, or

(g) for the purpose of obtaining any consent under Section 21, makes a statement which is false in any material particular,

shall be punishable with imprisonment for a term which may extend to three months or with fine which may extend to [29][ten thousand rupees] or with both.

[30][**39. Penalty for contravention of certain provisions of the Act.**—Whoever contravenes any of the provisions of this Act or any order or direction issued thereunder, for which no penalty has been elsewhere provided in this Act, shall be punishable with imprisonment for a term which may extend to three months or with fine which may extend to ten thousand rupees or with both, and in the case of continuing contravention, with an additional fine which may extend to five thousand rupees for every day during which such contravention continues after conviction for the first such contravention.]

40. Offences by companies.—(1) Where an offence under this Act has been committed by a company, every person who, at the time the offence was committed, was directly in charge of, and was responsible to, the company for the conduct of the business of the company, as well as the company, shall be deemed to be guilty of the offence and shall be liable to be proceeded against and punished accordingly:

Provided that nothing contained in this sub-section shall render any such person liable to any punishment provided in this Act, if he proves that the offence was committed without his knowledge or that he exercised all due diligence to prevent the commission of such offence.

(2) Notwithstanding anything contained in sub-section (1), where an offence under this Act has been committed by a company and it is proved that the offence has been committed with the consent or connivance of, or is attributable to any neglect on the part of any director, manager, secretary or other officer of the company, such director, manager, secretary or other officer shall also be deemed to be guilty of that offence and shall be liable to be proceeded against and punished accordingly.

Explanation.—For the purposes of this section,—

(a) 'company' means any body corporate, and includes a firm or other association of individuals; and

(b) 'director', in relation to a firm, means a partner in the firm.

41. Offences by Government Departments.—(1) Where an offence under

[29] *Ibid.*
[30] *Ibid.*

this Act has been committed by any Department of Government, the Head of the Department shall be deemed to be guilty of the offence and shall be liable to be proceeded against and punished accordingly:

Provided that nothing contained in this section shall render such Head of the Department liable to any punishment if he proves that the offence was committed without his knowledge or that he exercised all due diligence to prevent the commission of such offence.

(2) Notwithstanding anything contained in sub-section (1), where an offence under this Act has been committed by a Department of Government and it is proved that the offence has been committed with the consent or connivance of, or is attributable to any neglect on the part of, any officer, other than the Head of the Department, such officer shall also be deemed to be guilty of that offence and shall be liable to be proceeded against and punished accordingly.

42. Protection of action taken in good faith.—No suit, prosecution or other legal proceeding shall be against the Government or any officer of the Government or any member or any officer or other employee of the Board in respect of anything which is done or intended to be done in good faith in pursuance of this Act or the rules made thereunder.

[31][**43. Cognizance of offences.**—(1) No Court shall take cognizance of any offence under this Act except on a complaint made by—

    (a) a Board or any officer authorized in this behalf by it; or

    (b) any person who has given notice of not less than sixty days, in the manner prescribed, of the alleged offence and of his intention to make a complaint to the Board or officer authorized as aforesaid, and

no court inferior to that of a Metropolitan Magistrate or a Judicial Magistrate of the first class shall try any offence punishable under this Act.

(2) Where a complaint has been made under clause (b) of sub-section (1), the Board shall, on demand by such person, make available the relevant reports in its possession to that person:

Provided that the Board may refuse to make any such report available to such person if the same is, in its opinion, against the pubic interest.]

44. Members, officers and employees of Board to be public servants.— All the members and all officers and other employees of a Board when acting or purporting to act in pursuance of any of the provisions of this Act or the rules made thereunder shall be deemed to be public servants within the meaning of Section 21 of the Indian Penal Code (45 of 1860).

45. Reports and returns.—The Central Board shall, in relation to its functions under this Act, furnish to the Central Government, and a State Board shall, in relation to its functions under this Act, furnish to the state government and to the Central Board such reports, returns, statistics, accounts and other information as that

---

[31] *Subs.* by Act 47 of 1987.

Government, or, as the case may be, the Central Board may, from time to time, require.

46. Bar of jurisdiction.—No civil court shall have jurisdiction to entertain any suit or proceeding in respect of any matter which an Appellate Authority constituted under this Act is empowered by or under this Act to determine, and no injunction shall be granted by any court to other authority in respect of any action taken or to be taken in pursuance of any power conferred by or under this Act.

CHAPTER VII

MISCELLANEOUS

47. Power of state government to supersede State Board.—(1) If at any time the state government is of opinion—

    (a) that a State Board constituted under this Act has persistently made default in the performance of the functions imposed on it by or under this Act, or

    (b) that circumstances exist which render it necessary in the public interest so to do,

the state government may, by notification in the Official Gazette, supersede the State Board for such period, not exceeding six months, as may be specified in the notification:

Provided that before issuing a notification under this sub-section for the reasons mentioned in clause (a), the state government shall give a reasonable opportunity to the State Board to show cause why it should not be superseded and shall consider the explanations and objections, if any, of the State Board.

(2) Upon the publication of a notification under sub-section (1) superseding the State Board,—

    (a) all the members shall, as from the date of supersession, vacate their offices as such;

    (b) all the powers, functions and duties which may, by or under this Act, be exercised, performed or discharged by the State Board shall, until the State Board is reconstituted under sub-section (3), be exercised, performed or discharged by such person or persons as the state government may direct;

    (c) all property owned or controlled by the State Board shall, until the Board is reconstituted under sub-section (3), vest in the state government.

(3) On the expiration of the period of supersession specified in the notification issued under sub-section (1), the state government may—

    (a) extend the period of supersession for such further term, not exceeding six months, as it may consider necessary; or

    (b) reconstitute the State Board by a fresh nomination or appointment, as the case may be, and in such case any person who vacated his office under clause (a) of sub-section (2) shall also be eligible for nomination or appointment:

Provided that the State Government may at any time before the expiration of the period of supersession, whether originally specified under sub-section (1) or as extended under this sub-section, take action under clause (b) of this sub-section.

48. Special provision in the case of supersession of the Central Board or the State Boards constituted under the Water (Prevention and Control of Pollution) Act, 1974.—Where the Central Board or any State Board constituted under the Water (Prevention and Control of Pollution) Act, 1974, is superseded by the Central Government or the State Government, as the case may be, under that Act, all the powers, functions and duties of the Central Board or such State Board under this Act shall be exercised, performed or discharged during the period of such supersession by the person or persons, exercising, performing or discharging the powers, functions and duties of the Central Board or such State Board under the Water (Prevention and Control of Pollution) Act, 1974 (6 of 1974), during such period.

49. Dissolution of State Boards constituted under the Act.—(1) As and when the Water (Prevention and Control of Pollution) Act, 1974 (6 of 1974), comes into force in any state and the state government constitutes a [32][State Pollution Control Board] under that Act, the State Board constituted by the State Government under this Act shall stand dissolved and the Board first-mentioned shall exercise the powers and perform the functions of the Board second-mentioned in that State.

(2) On the dissolution of the State Board constituted under this Act,—

(a) all the members shall vacate their offices as such;

(b) all moneys and other property of whatever kind (including the fund of the State Board) owned by, or vested in, the State Board, immediately before such dissolution, shall stand transferred to and vest in the [33][State Pollution Control Board];

(c) every officer and other employee serving under the State Board immediately before such dissolution shall be transferred to and become an officer or other employee of the [34][State Pollution Control Board] and hold office by the same tenure and at the same remuneration and on the same terms and conditions of service as he would have held the same if the State Board constituted under this Act had not been dissolved and shall continue to do so unless and until such tenure, remuneration and term and conditions of service are duly altered by the [35][State Pollution Control Board];

Provided that the tenure, remuneration and terms and conditions

---

[32] *Subs.* by Act 47 of 1987.
[33] *Ibid.*
[34] *Ibid.*
[35] *Ibid.*

of service of any such officer or other employee shall not be altered to his disadvantage without the previous sanction of the state government;

(d) all liabilities and obligations of the State Board of whatever kind, immediately before such dissolution, shall be deemed to be the liabilities or obligations, as the case may be, of the [36][State Pollution Control Board] and any proceeding or cause of action, pending or existing immediately before such dissolution by or against the State Board constituted under this Act in relation to such liability or obligation may be continued and enforced by or against the [37][State Pollution Control Board].

50. [38][* * *]

51. Maintenance of register.—(1) Every State Board shall maintain a register containing particulars of the persons to whom consent has been granted under Section 21, the standards for emission laid down by it in relation to each such consent and such other particulars as may be prescribed.

(2) The register maintained under sub-section (1) shall be open to inspection at all reasonable hours by any person interested in or affected by such standards for emission or by any other person authorised by such person in this behalf.

52. Effect of other laws.—Save as otherwise provided by or under the Atomic Energy Act, 1962 (33 of 1962), in relation to radioactive air pollution the provisions of this Act shall have effect notwithstanding anything inconsistent therewith contained in any enactment other than this Act.

53. Power of Central Government to make rules.—(1) The Central Government may, in consultation with the Central Board, by notification in the Official Gazette, make rules in respect of the following matters, namely:

(a) the intervals and the time and place at which meetings of the Central Board or any committee thereof shall be held and the procedure to be followed at such meetings, including the quorum necessary for the transaction of business thereat, under sub-section (1) of Section 10 and under sub-section (2) of Section 11;

(b) the fees and allowances to be paid to the members of a committee of the Central Board, not being members of the Board, under sub-section (3) of Section 11;

(c) the manner in which and the purposes for which persons may be associated with the Central Board under sub-section (1) of Section 12;

(d) the fees and allowances to be paid under sub-section (3) of Section 12 to persons associated with the Central Board under sub-section (1) of Section 12;

(e) the functions to be performed by the Central Board under clause (j) of sub-section (2) of Section 16;

---

[36] *Ibid.*
[37] *Subs.* by Act 47 of 1987.
[38] *Omitted* by Act 47 of 1987.

[39][(f)]   the form in which and the time within which the budget of the Central
          Board may be prepared and forwarded to the Central Government under
          Section 34;

   (ff)   the form in which the annual report of the Central Board may be prepared
          under Section 35;]

   (g)   the form in which the accounts of the Central Board may be maintained
          under sub-section (1) of Section 36.

(2) Every rule made by the Central Government under this Act shall be laid,
as soon as may be after it is made, before each House of Parliament, while it is in
session, for a total period of thirty days which may be comprised in one session or
in two or more successive sessions, and if, before the expiry of the session
immediately following the session or the successive sessions aforesaid, both Houses
agree in making any modification in the rule or both House agree that the rule
should not be made, the rule shall thereafter have effect only in such modified form
or be of no effect, as the case may be; so, however, that any such modification or
annulment shall be without prejudice to the validity of anything previously done
under that rule.

54. Power of state government to make rules.—(1) Subject to the provisions
of sub-section (3), the state government may, by notification in the Official Gazette,
make rules to carry out the purposes of this Act in respect of matters not falling
within the purview of Section 53.

(2) In particular, and without prejudice to the generality of the foregoing
power, such rules may provide for all or any of the following matters, namely:

[40][(a)]   the qualifications, knowledge and experience of scientific, engineering
          or management aspects of pollution control required for appointment as
          member-secretary of a State Board constituted under the Act;]

[41][(aa)]   the terms and conditions of service of the Chairman and other members
          (other than the member-secretary) of the State Board constituted under
          this Act under sub-section (7) of Section 7;

   (b)   the intervals and the time and place at which meetings of the State Board
          or any committee thereof shall be held and the procedure to be followed
          at such meetings, including the quorum necessary for the transaction of
          business thereat, under sub-section (1) of Section 10 and under sub-section
          (2) of Section 11;

   (c)   the fees and allowances to be paid to the members of a committee of the
          State Board, not being members of the Board under sub-section (3) of
          Section 11;

   (d)   the manner in which and the purposes for which persons may be
          associated with the State Board under sub-section (1) of Section 12;

---

[39] *Subs.* by Act 47 of 1987.
[40] *Renumbered* by Act 47 of 1987 and before clause (aa) as so *renumbered* clause (a) *inserted* by *ibid.*
[41] *Ibid.*

(e) the fees and allowances to be paid under sub-section (3) of Section 12 to persons associated with the State Board under sub-section (1) of Section 12;

(f) the terms and conditions of service of the member-secretary of a State Board constituted under this Act under sub-section (1) of Section 14;

(g) the powers and duties to be exercised and discharged by the member-secretary of a State Board under sub-section (2) of Section 14;

(h) the conditions subject to which a State Board may appoint such officers and other employees as it considers necessary for the efficient performance of its functions under sub-section (3) of Section 14;

(i) the conditions subject to which a State Board may appoint a consultant under sub-section (5) of Section 14;

(j) the functions to be performed by the State Board under clause (i) of subsection (1) of Section 17;

(k) the manner in which any area or areas may be declared as air pollution control area or areas under sub-section (1) of Section 19;

(l) the form of application for the consent of the State Board, the fees payable therefore, the period within which such application shall be made and the particulars it may contain, under sub-section (2) of Section 21;

(m) the procedure to be followed in respect of an inquiry under sub-section (3) of Section 21;

(n) the authorities or agencies to whom information under sub-section (1) of Section 28 shall be furnished;

(o) the manner in which samples of air or emission may be taken under sub-section (1) of Section 26;

(p) the form of the notice referred to in sub-section (3) of Section 26;

(q) the form of the report of the State Board analyst under sub-section (1) of Section 27;

(r) the form of the report of the Government analyst under sub-section (3) of Section 27;

(s) the functions of the State Air Laboratory, the procedure for the submission to the said Laboratory of samples of air emission for analysis or tests, the form of Laboratory's report thereon, the fees payable in respect of such report and other matters as may be necessary or expedient to enable that Laboratory to carry out its functions, under sub-section (2) of Section 28;

(t) the qualifications required for Government analysts under sub-section (1) of Section 29;

(u) the qualifications required for State Board analysts under sub-section (2) of Section 29;

(v) the form and the manner in which appeals may be preferred, the fees payable in respect of such appeals and the procedure to be followed by the Appellate Authority in disposing of the appeals under sub-section (3) of Section 31;

[42][(w) the form in which and the time within which the budget of the State Board may be prepared and forwarded to the State Government under Section 34;

  (ww) the form in which the annual report of the State Board may be prepared under Section 35;]

  (x) the form in which the accounts of the State Board may be maintained under sub-section (1) of Section 36;

[43][(xx) the manner in which notice of intention to make a complaint shall be given under Section 43];

  (y) the particulars which the register maintained under Section 51 may contain;

  (z) any other matter which has to be, or may be, prescribed.

(3) After the first constitution of the State Board, no rule with respect to any of the matters referred to in sub-section (2) other than those referred to [44][in clause (aa) thereof], shall be made, varied, amended or repealed without consulting that Board.

THE SCHEDULE

[45][* * *]

---

[42] *Subs.* by Act 47 of 1987.
[43] *Ins.* by *ibid.*
[44] *Subs.* by Act 47 of 1987.
[45] *Omitted* by *ibid.*

B

THE WATER ACT

WATER (PREVENTION AND CONTROL OF POLLUTION)
ACT, 1974
[NO. 6 OF 1974]

An Act to provide for the prevention and control of water pollution and the maintaining or restoring of wholesomeness of water, for the establishment, with a view to carrying out the purposes aforesaid, of Boards for the prevention and control of water pollution, for conferring on and assigning to such Boards powers and functions relating thereto and for matters connected therewith.

Whereas it is expedient to provide for the prevention and control of water pollution and the maintaining or restoring of wholesomeness of water, for the establishment, with a view to carrying out the purposes aforesaid, of Boards for the prevention and control of water pollution and for conferring on and assigning to such Boards powers and functions relating thereto;

And whereas Parliament has no power to make laws for the states with respect to any of the matters aforesaid except as provided in Articles 249 and 250 of the Constitution;

And whereas in pursuance of clause (1) of Article 252 of the Constitution resolutions have been passed by all the Houses of the Legislatures of the states of Assam, Bihar, Gujarat, Haryana, Himachal Pradesh, Jammu and Kashmir, Karnataka, Kerala, Madhya Pradesh, Rajasthan, Tripura and West Bengal to the effect that the matters aforesaid should be regulated in those states by Parliament by law;

Be it enacted by Parliament in the Twenty-fifth Year of the Republic of India as follows:

CHAPTER I

PRELIMINARY

1. Short title, application and commencement.—(1) This Act may be called the Water (Prevention and Control of Pollution) Act, 1974.

(2) It applies in the first instance to the whole of the states of Assam, Bihar, Gujarat, Haryana, Himachal Pradesh, Jammu and Kashmir, Karnataka, Kerala, Madhya Pradesh, Rajasthan, Tripura and West Bengal and the Union territories; and it shall apply to such other state which adopts this Act by resolution passed in that behalf under clause (1) of Article 252 of the Constitution.

(3) It shall come into force, at once in the states of Assam, Bihar, Gujarat, Haryana, Himachal Pradesh, Jammu and Kashmir, Karnataka, Kerala, Madhya Pradesh, Rajasthan, Tripura and West Bengal and in the Union territories, and in any other state which adopts this Act under clause (1) of Article 252 of the Constitution on the date of such adoption and any reference in this Act to the commencement of this Act shall, in relation to any state or union territory mean the date on which this Act comes into force in such state or union territory.

2. Definitions.—In this Act, unless the context otherwise requires,—

    (a) 'Board' means the Central Board or a State Board;

  [1][(b) 'Central Board' means the Central Pollution Control Board constituted under section 3;]

    (c) 'member' means a member of a Board and includes the chairman thereof;

  [2][(d) 'occupier', in relation to any factory or premises, means the person who has control over the affairs of the factory or the premises, and includes, in relation to any substance, the person in possession of the substance;]

  [3][(dd) 'outlet' includes any conduit pipe or channel, open or closed, carrying sewage or trade effluent or any other holding arrangement which causes, or is likely to cause, pollution;]

    (e) 'pollution' means such contamination of water or such alteration of the physical, chemical or biological properties of water or such discharge of any sewage or trade effluent or of any other liquid, gaseous or solid sub stance into water (whether directly or indirectly) as may or is likely to, create a nuisance or render such water harmful or injurious to public health or safety, or to domestic, commercial, industrial, agricultural or other legitimate uses, or to the life and health of animals or plants or of aquatic organism;

    (f) 'prescribed' means prescribed by rules made under this Act by the Central Government or, as the case may be, the state government;

---

[1] *Subs.* by Act 53 of 1988.
[2] *Subs.* by *ibid.*
[3] *Ins.* by Act 44 of 1978.

(g) 'sewage effluent' means effluent from any sewerage system or sewage disposal works and includes sullage from open drains;

[4][(gg) 'sewer' means any conduit pipe or channel, open or closed carrying sewage or trade effluent;]

[5][(h) 'State Board' means a State Pollution Control Board constituted under section 4;]

(i) 'state government' in relation to a union territory means the Administrator thereof appointed under Article 239 of the Constitution;

(j) 'stream' includes—
   (i) river;
   (ii) water course (whether flowing or for the time being dry);
   (iii) inland water (whether natural or artificial);
   (iv) sub-terranean waters;
   (v) sea or tidal waters to such extent or, as the case may be, to such point as the state government may, by notification in the Official Gazette, specify in this behalf;

(k) 'trade effluent' includes any liquid, gaseous or solid substance which is discharged from any premises used for carrying on any [6][industry, operation or process or treatment and disposal system] other than domestic sewage.

CHAPTER II

THE CENTRAL AND STATE BOARDS FOR PREVENTION AND CONTROL OF WATER POLLUTION

3. Constitution of Central Board.—(1) The Central Government shall, with effect from such date (being a date not later than six months of the commencement of this Act in the states of Assam, Bihar, Gujarat, Haryana, Himachal Pradesh, Jammu and Kashmir, Karnataka, Kerala, Madhya Pradesh, Rajasthan, Tripura and West Bengal and in the Union territories) as it may, by notification in the Official Gazette, appoint, constitute a Central Board to be called the [7][Central Pollution Control Board] to exercise the powers conferred on and perform the functions assigned to that Board under this Act.

(2) The Central Board shall consist of the following members, namely:

(a) a full-time chairman, being a person having special knowledge or practical experience in respect of [8][matters relating to environmental protection]

---

[4] Ins. by ibid.
[5] Subs. by Act 53 of 1988.
[6] Subs. by ibid.
[7] Subs. by ibid.
[8] Subs. by Act 44 of 1978.

or a person having knowledge and experience in administering institutions dealing with the matters aforesaid, to be nominated by the Central Government;

(b) [9][such number of officials, not exceeding five] to be nominated by the Central Government to represent that Government;

(c) such number of persons, not exceeding five, to be nominated by the Central Government, from amongst the members of the State Boards, of whom not exceeding two shall be from those referred to in clause (c) of sub-section (2) of section 4;

(d) [10][such number of non-officials, not exceeding three] to be nominated by the Central Government, to represent the interests of agriculture, fishery or industry or trade or any other interest which, in the opinion of the Central Government, ought to be represented;

(e) two persons to represent the companies or corporations owned, controlled or managed by the Central Government, to be nominated by that Government;

[11][(f) a full-time member-secretary, possessing qualifications, knowledge and experience of scientific, engineering or management aspects of pollution control, to be appointed by the Central Government.]

(3) The Central Board shall be a body corporate with the name aforesaid having perpetual succession and a common seal with power, subject to the provisions of this Act, to acquire, hold and dispose of property and to contract, and may, by the aforesaid name, sue or be sued.

4. Constitution of State Boards.—(1) The state government shall, with effect from such date [12][* * *] as it may, by notification in the Official Gazette, appoint, constitute a [13][State Pollution Control Board], under such name as may be specified in the notification, to exercise the powers conferred on and perform the functions assigned to that Board under this Act.

(2) A State Board shall consist of the following members namely:

(a) a [14][* * *] chairman, being a person having special knowledge or practical experience in respect of [15][matters relating to environmental protection] or a person having knowledge and experience in administering institutions dealing with the matters aforesaid, to be nominated by the State Government:

[16][Provided that the chairman may be either whole-time or part-time as the state government may think fit;]

[9] *Subs.* by *ibid.*
[10] *Subs.* by *ibid.*
[11] *Subs.* by Act 53 of 1988.
[12] *Omitted* by Act 44 of 1978.
[13] *Subs.* by Act 53 of 1988.
[14] *Omitted* by Act 44 of 1978.
[15] *Subs.* by *ibid.*
[16] *Ins.* by *ibid.*

(b) [17][such number of officials, not exceeding five,] to be nominated by the state government to represent that Government;

(c) [18][such number of persons, not exceeding five,] to be nominated by the state government from amongst the members of the local authorities functioning within the state;

(d) [19][such number of non-officials not exceeding three,] to be nominated by the state government to represent the interests of agriculture, fishery or industry or trade or any other interest which, in the opinion of the state government, ought to be represented;

(e) two persons to represent the companies or corporations owned, controlled or managed by the state government, to be nominated by that Government;

[20][(f) a full-time member-secretary, possessing qualifications, knowledge and experience of scientific, engineering or management aspects of pollution control, to be appointed by the state government.]

(3) Every State Board shall be a body corporate with the name specified by the state government in the notification under sub-section (1), having perpetual succession and a common seal with power, subject to the provisions of this Act, to acquire, hold and dispose of property and to contract, and may, by the said name, sue or be sued.

(4) Notwithstanding anything contained in this section, no State Board shall be constituted for a union territory and in relation to a union territory, the Central Board shall exercise the powers and perform the functions of a State Board for that union territory:

Provided that in relation to any union territory the Central Board may delegate all or any of its powers and functions under this sub-section to such person or body of persons as the Central Government may specify.

5. Terms and conditions of service of members.—(1) Save as otherwise provided by or under this Act, a member of a Board, other than a member-secretary, shall hold office for a term of three years from the date of his nomination:

Provided that a member shall, notwithstanding the expiration of his term, continue to hold office until his successor enters upon his office.

[21][(2) The term of office of a member of a Board nominated under clause (b) or clause (e) of sub-section (2) of section 3 or clause (b) or clause (e) of sub-section (2) of section 4 shall come to an end as soon as he ceases to hold the office under the Central Government or the state government or, as the case msay be, the company or corporation owned, controlled or managed by the Central Government or the state government by virtue of which he was nominated.]

[17] *Subs.* by *ibid.*
[18] *Subs.* by *ibid.*
[19] *Subs.* by *ibid.*
[20] *Subs.* by Act 53 of 1988.
[21] *Subs.* by Act 44 of 1978.

(3) The Central Government or, as the case may be, the state government may, if it thinks fit, remove any member of a Board before the expiry of his term of office, after giving him a reasonable opportunity of showing cause against the same.

(4) A member of a Board, other than the member-secretary, may at any time resign his office by writing under his hand addressed—

(a) in the case of the chairman, to the Central Government or as the case may be, the state government; and

(b) in any other case, to the chairman of the Board,

and the seat of the chairman or such other member shall thereupon become vacant.

(5) A member of a Board, other than the member-secretary, shall be deemed to have vacated his seat if he is absent without reason, sufficient in the opinion of the Board, from three consecutive meetings of the Board, [22][or where he is nominated under clause (c) or clause (e) of sub-section (2) of section 3 or under clause (c) or clause (e) of sub-section (2) of section 4, if he ceases to be a member of the State Board or of the local authority or, as the case may be, of the company or corporation owned, controlled or managed by the Central Government or the state government and such vacation of seat shall, in either case, take effect from such date as the Central Government or, as the case may be, the state government may, by notification in the Official Gazette, specify].

(6) A casual vacancy in a Board shall be filled by a fresh nomination and the person nominated to fill the vacancy shall hold office only for the remainder of the term for which the member in whose place he was nominated.

(7) A member of a Board shall [23][be eligible for renomination].

(8) The other terms and conditions of service of a member of a Board, other than the chairman and member-secretary, shall be such as may be prescribed.

(9) The other terms and conditions of service of the chairman shall be such as may be prescribed.

6. Disqualifications.—(1) No person shall be a member of a Board, who—

(a) is, or at any time has been adjudged insolvent or has suspended payment of his debts or has compounded with his creditors, or

(b) is of unsound mind and stands so declared by a competent court, or

(c) is, or has been, convicted of an offence which, in the opinion of the Central Government or, as the case may be, of the state government, involves moral turpitude, or

(d) is, or at any time has been, convicted of an offence under this Act, or

(e) has directly or indirectly by himself or by any partner, any share or interest in any firm or company carrying on the business of manufacture, sale or hire of machinery, plant, equipment, apparatus or fittings for the treatment of sewage or trade effluents, or

---

[22] *Subs.* by *ibid.*
[23] *Subs.* by Act 53 of 1988.

(f) is a director or a secretary, manager or other salaried officer or employee of any company or firm having any contract with the Board, or with the Government constituting the Board, or with a local authority in the state, or with a company or corporation owned, controlled or managed by the Government, for the carrying out of sewerage schemes or for the installation of plants for the treatment of sewage or trade effluents, or

(g) has so abused, in the opinion of the Central Government or as the case may be, of the state government, his position as a member, as to render his continuance on the Board detrimental to the interest of the general public.

(2) No order of removal shall be made by the Central Government or the state government, as the case may be, under this section unless the member concerned has been given a reasonable opportunity of showing cause against the same.

(3) Notwithstanding anything contained in sub-sections (1) and (7) of section 5, a member who has been removed under this section shall not be eligible for renomination as a member.

7. Vacation of seats by members.—If a member of a Board becomes subject to any of the disqualifications specified in section 6, his seat shall become vacant.

8. Meetings of Board.—A board shall meet at least once in every three months and shall observe such rules of procedure in regard to the transaction of business at its meetings as may be prescribed:

Provided that if, in the opinion of the chairman, any business of an urgent nature is to be transacted, he may convene a meeting of the Board at such time as he thinks fit for the aforesaid purpose .

9. Constitution of committees.—(1) A Board may constitute as many committees consisting wholly of members or wholly of other persons or partly of members and partly of other persons, and for such purpose or purposes as it may think fit.

(2) A committee constituted under this section shall meet at such time and at such place, and shall observe such rules of procedure in regard to the transaction of business at its meetings, as may be prescribed.

(3) The members of a committee (other than the members of the Board) shall be paid such fees and allowances, for attending its meetings and for attending to any other work of the Board as may be prescribed.

10. Temporary association of persons with Board for particular purposes.—(1) A Board may associate with itself in such manner, and for such purposes, as may be prescribed any person whose assistance or advice it may desire to obtain in performing any of its functions under this Act.

(2) A person associated with the Board under sub-section (1) for any purpose shall have a right to take part in the discussions of the Board relevant to that purpose, but shall not have a right to vote at a meeting of the Board, and shall not be a member for any other purpose.

[24][(3) A person associated with the Board under sub-section (1) for any purpose shall be paid such fees and allowances, for attending its meetings and for attending to any other work of the Board, as may be prescribed.]

11. Vacancy in Board not to invalidate acts or proceedings.—No act or proceeding of a Board or any committee thereof shall be called in question on the ground merely of the existence of any vacancy in or any defect in the constitution of, the Board or such committee, as the case may be.

[25][**11A. Delegation of powers to Chairman.**—The chairman of Board shall exercise such powers and perform such duties as may be prescribed or as may, from time to time, be delegated to him by the Board.]

12. Member-secretary and officers and other employees of Board.—(1) The terms and conditions of service of the member-secretary shall be such as may be prescribed.

(2) The member-secretary shall exercise such powers and perform such duties as may be prescribed or as may, from time to time, be delegated to him by the Board or its chairman.

(3) Subject to such rules as may be made by the Central Government or, as the case may be, the state government in this behalf, a Board may appoint such officers and employees as it considers necessary for the efficient performance of its functions [26][* * *].

[27][(3A) The method of recruitment and the terms and conditions of service (including the scales of pay) of the officers (other than the member-secretary) and other employees of the Central Board or a State Board shall be such as may be determined by regulations made by the Central Board or, as the case may be, by the State Board:

Provided that no regulation made under this sub-section shall take effect unless,—

   (a) in the case of a regulation made by the Central Board, it is approved by the Central Government; and

   (b) in the case of a regulation made by a State Board, it is approved by the state government.]

[28][(3B) The Board may, by general or special order, and subject to such conditions and limitations, if any, as may be specified in the order, delegate to any officer of the Board such of its powers and functions under this Act as it may deem necessary.]

(4) Subject to such conditions as may be prescribed, a Board may from time to time appoint any qualified person to be a consulting engineer to the Board and

[24] *Ins.* by Act 44 of 1978.
[25] *Subs.* by *ibid.*
[26] *Omitted* by *ibid.*
[27] *Ins.* by *ibid.*
[28] *Ins.* by Act 53 of 1988.

pay him such salaries and allowances and subject him to such other terms and conditions of service as it thinks fit.

CHAPTER III

JOINT BOARDS

13. Constitution of Joint Boards.—Notwithstanding anything contained in this Act, an agreement may be entered into—

(a) by two or more Governments of contiguous states, or

(b) by the Central Government (in respect of one or more Union territories) and one or more Governments of states contiguous to such union territory or Union territories,

to be in force for such period and to be subject to renewal for such further period, if any, as may be specified in the agreement to provide for the constitution of a Joint Board,—

(i) in a case referred to in clause (a), for all the participating states, and

(ii) in a case referred to in clause (b), for the participating union territory or Union territories and the state or states.

(2) An agreement under this section may—

(a) provide, in a case referred to in clause (a) of sub-section (1), for the apportionment between the participating states and in a case referred to in clause (b) of that sub-section, for the apportionments between the Central Government and the participating state government or state governments, of the expenditure in connection with the Joint Board;

(b) determine, in a case referred to in clause (a) of sub-section (1), which of the participating state governments and in a case referred to in clause (b) of that sub-section, whether the Central Government or the participating state government (if there are more than one participating state, also which of the participating state governments) shall exercise and perform the several powers and functions of the state government under this Act and the references in this Act to the state government shall be construed accordingly;

(c) provide for consultation, in a case referred to in clause (a) of sub-section (1), between the participating state governments and in a case referred to in clause (b) of that sub-section, between the Central Government and the participating state government or state governments either generally or with reference to particular matters arising under this Act;

(d) make such incidental and ancillary provisions, not inconsistent with this Act, as may be deemed necessary or expedient for giving effect to the agreement.

(3) An agreement under this section shall be published, in a case referred to in clause (a) of sub-section (1), in the Official Gazette of the participating states and in a case referred to in clause (b) of that sub-section in the Official Gazette of the participating union territory or Union territories and the participating state or states.

14. Composition of Joint Boards.—(1) A Joint Board constituted in pursuance of an agreement entered into under clause (a) of sub-section (1) of section 13 shall consist of the following members, namely:—

   (a)   a full-time chairman, being a person having special knowledge or practical experience in respect of [29][matters relating to environmental protection] or a person having knowledge and experience in administering institutions dealing with the matters aforesaid, to be nominated by the Central Government;

   (b)   two officials from each of the participating states to be nominated by the concerned participating state government to represent that Government;

   (c)   one person to be nominated by each of the participating state governments from amongst the members of the local authorities functioning within the state concerned;

   (d)   one non-official to be nominated by each of the participating state governments to represent the interests of agriculture, fishery or industry or trade in the state concerned or any other interest which, in the opinion of the participating state government, is to be represented;

   (e)   two persons to be nominated by the Central Government to represent the companies or corporations owned, controlled or managed by the participating state governments;

   [30][(f)   a full time member-secretary, possessing qualifications, knowledge and experience of scientific, engineering or management aspects of pollution control, to be appointed by the Central Government.]

(2) A Joint Board constituted in pursuance of an agreement entered into under clause (b) of sub-section (1) of section 13 shall consist of the following members, namely—

   (a)   a full-time chairman, being a person having special knowledge or practical experience in respect of [31][matters relating to environmental protection] or a person having knowledge and experience in administering institutions dealing with the matters aforesaid, to be nominated by the Central Government;

   (b)   two officials to be nominated by the Central Government from the participating union territory or each of the participating Union territories,

---

[29] *Subs.* By Act 44 of 1978.
[30] *Subs.* by Act 53 of 1988.
[31] *Subs.* by Act 44 of 1978.

as the case may be, and two officials to be nominated, from the participating state or each of the participating states, as the case may be, by the concerned participating state government;

(c) one person to be nominated by the Central Government from amongst the members of the local authorities functioning within the participating union territory or each of the participating Union territories, as the case may be, and one person to be nominated, from amongst the members of the local authorities functioning within the participating State or each of the participating states, as the case may be, by the concerned participating state government;

(d) one non-official to be nominated by the Central Government and one person to be nominated by the participating state government or state governments to represent the interests of agriculture, fishery or industry or trade in the union territory or in each of the Union territories or the state or in each of the states, as the case may be, or any other interest which in the opinion of the Central Government or, as the case may be, of the state government is to be represented;

(e) two persons to be nominated by the Central Government to represent the companies or corporations owned, controlled or managed by the Central Government and situate in the participating union territory or territories and two persons to be nominated by the Central Government to represent the companies or corporations owned, controlled or managed by the participating state governments;

32[(f) a full-time member-secretary, possessing qualifications, knowledge and experience of scientific, engineering or management aspects of pollution control, to be appointed by the Central Government.]

(3) When a Joint Board is constituted in pursuance of an agreement under clause (b) of sub-section (1) of section 13, the provisions of sub-section (4) of section 4 shall cease to apply in relation to the union territory for which the Joint Board is constituted.

(4) Subject to the provisions of sub-section (3), the provisions of sub-section (3) of section 4 and sections 5 to 12 (inclusive) shall apply in relation to the Joint Board and its member-secretary as they apply in relation to a State Board and its member-secretary.

(5) Any reference in this Act to the State Board shall, unless the context otherwise requires, be construed as including a Joint Board.

15. Special provision relating to giving of directions.—Notwithstanding anything contained in this Act where any Joint Board is constituted under section 13,—

(a) the Government of the state for which the Joint Board is constituted shall

---

32 *Subs.* by Act 53 of 1988.

be competent to give any direction under this Act only in cases where such direction relates to a matter within the exclusive territorial jurisdiction of the state;

(b) the Central Government alone shall be competent to give any direction under this Act where such direction relates to a matter within the territorial jurisdiction of two or more states or pertaining to a union territory.

CHAPTER IV

POWERS AND FUNCTIONS OF BOARDS

16. Functions of Central Board.—(1) Subject to the provisions of this Act, the main function of the Central Board shall be to promote cleanliness of streams and wells in different areas of the states.

(2) In particular and without prejudice to the generality of the foregoing function, the Central Board may perform all or any of the following functions, namely:

(a) advice the Central Government on any matter concerning the prevention and control of water pollution;

(b) co-ordinate the activities of the State Boards and resolve disputes among them;

(c) provide technical assistance and guidance to the State Boards, carry out and sponsor investigations and research relating to problems of water pollution and prevention, control or abatement of water pollution;

(d) plan and organize the training of persons engaged or to be engaged in programmes for the prevention, control or abatement of water pollution on such terms and conditions as the Central Board may specify;

(e) organise through mass media a comprehensive programme regarding the prevention and control of water pollution;

[33][(ee) perform such of the functions of any State Board as may be specified in an order made under sub-section (2) of section 18];

(f) collect, compile and publish technical and statistical data relating to water pollution and the measures devised for its effective prevention and control and prepare manuals, codes or guides relating to treatment and disposal of sewage and trade effluents and disseminate information connected therewith;

(g) lay down, modify or annul, in consultation with the state government concerned, the standards for a stream or well:

Provided that different standards may be laid down for the same stream or well or for different streams or wells, having regard to the quality of

[33] *Ins. by ibid.*

water, flow characteristics of the stream or well and the nature of the use of the water in such stream or well or stream or wells;

(h) plan and cause to be executed a nation-wide programme for the prevention, control or abatement of water pollution;

(i) perform such other functions as may be prescribed.

(3) The Board may establish or recognize a laboratory or laboratories to enable the Board to perform its functions under this section efficiently, including the analysis of samples of water from any stream or well or of samples of any sewage or trade effluents.

17. Functions of State Board.—(1) Subject to the provisions of this Act, the functions of a State Board shall be—

(a) to plan a comprehensive programme for the prevention, control or abatement of pollution of streams and wells in the state and to secure the execution thereof;

(b) to advise the state government on any matter concerning the prevention, control or abatement of water pollution;

(c) to collect and disseminate information relating to water pollution and the prevention, control or abatement thereof;

(d) to encourage, conduct and participate in investigations and research relating to problems of water pollution and prevention, control or abatement of water pollution;

(e) to collaborate with the Central Board in organising the training of persons engaged or to be engaged in programmes relating to prevention, control or abatement of water pollution and to organise mass education programmes relating thereto;

(f) to inspect sewage or trade effluents, works and plants for the treatment of sewage and trade effluents and to review plans, specifications or other data relating to plants set up for the treatment of water, works for the purification thereof and the system for the disposal of sewage or trade effluents or in connection with the grant of any consent as required by this Act;

(g) to lay down, modify or annul effluent standards for the sewage and trade effluents and for the quality of receiving waters (not being water in an inter-state stream) resulting from the discharge of effluents and to classify waters of the state;

(h) to evolve economical and reliable methods of treatment of sewage and trade effluents, having regard to the peculiar conditions of soils, climate and water resources of different regions and more especially the prevailing flow characteristics of water in streams and wells which render it impossible to attain even the medium degree of dilution;

(i) to evolve methods of utilization of sewage and suitable trade effluents in agriculture;

(j) to evolve efficient methods of disposal of sewage and trade effluents on land, as are necessary on account of the predominant conditions of scant stream flows that do not provide for major part of the year the minimum degree of dilution;

(k) to lay down standards of treatment of sewage and trade effluents to be discharged into any particular stream taking into account the minimum fair weather dilution available in that stream and the tolerance limits of pollution permissible in the water of the stream, after the discharge of such effluents;

(l) to make, vary or revoke any order—

    (i) for the prevention, control or abatement of discharges of waste into streams or wells;

    (ii) requiring any person concerned to construct new systems for the disposal of sewage and trade effluents or to modify, alter or extend any such existing system or to adopt such remedial measures as are necessary to prevent, control or abate water pollution;

(m) to lay down effluent standards to be complied with by persons while causing discharge of sewage or sullage or both and to lay down, modify or annul effluent standards for the sewage and trade effluents;

(n) to advise the state government with respect to the location of any industry the carrying on of which is likely to pollute a stream or well;

(o) to perform such other functions as may be prescribed or as may, from time to time, be entrusted to it by the Central Board or the state government.

(2) The Board may establish or recognise a laboratory or laboratories to enable the Board to perform its functions under this section efficiently, including the analysis of samples of water from any stream or well or of samples of any sewage or trade effluents.

18. Power to give directions.—[34][(1)] In the performance of its functions under this Act—

(a) the Central Board shall be bound by such directions in writing as the Central Government may give to it; and

(b) every State Board shall be bound by such directions in writing as the Central Board or the state government may give to it:

Provided that where a direction given by the state government is inconsistent with the direction given by the Central Board, the matter shall be referred to the Central Government for its decision.

[35][(2) Where the Central Government is of the opinion that any State Board has defaulted in complying with any directions given by the Central Board under sub-section (1) and as a result of such default a grave emergency has arisen and it is

---

[34] *Renumbered* by Act 53 of 1988 and after sub-section (1) as so *renumbered* sub-sections (2) and (3) *Ins.* by *ibid.*

[35] *Ibid.*

necessary or expedient so to do in the public interest, it may, by order, direct the Central Board to perform any of the functions of the State Board in relation to such area, for such period and for such purposes, as may be specified in the order.

(3) Where the Central Board performs any of the functions of the State Board in pursuance of a direction under sub-section (2), the expenses, if any, incurred by the Central Board with respect to the performance of such functions may, if the State Board is empowered to recover such expenses, be recovered by the Central Board with interest (at such reasonable rate as the Central Government may, by order, fix) from the date when a demand for such expenses is made until it is paid from the person or persons concerned as arrears of land revenue or of public demand.

(4) For the removal of doubts, it is hereby declared that any directions to perform the functions of any State Board given under sub-section (2) in respect of any area would not preclude the State Board from performing such functions in any other area in the state or any of its other functions in that area.]

CHAPTER V

PREVENTION AND CONTROL OF WATER POLLUTION

19. Power of State Government to restrict the application of the Act to certain areas.—(1) Notwithstanding anything contained in this Act, if the state government, after consultation with, or on the recommendation of, the State Board, is of opinion that the provisions of this Act need not apply to the entire state, it may, by notification in the Official Gazette, restrict the application of this Act to such area or areas as may be declared therein as water pollution, prevention and control area or areas and thereupon the provisions of Act shall apply only to such area or areas.

(2) Each water pollution, prevention and control area may be declared either by reference to a map or by reference to the line of any watershed or the boundary of any district or partly by one method and partly by another.

(3) The state government may, by notification in the Official Gazette,—

(a) alter any water pollution, prevention and control area whether by way of extension or reduction; or

(b) define a new water pollution, prevention and control area in which may be merged one or more water pollution, prevention and control areas, or any part or parts thereof.

20. Power to obtain information.—(1) For the purpose of enabling a State Board to perform the functions conferred on it by or under this Act, the State Board or any officer empowered by it in that behalf, may make surveys of any area and gauge and keep records of the flow or volume and other characteristics of any stream or well in such area, and may take steps for the measurement and recording of the rainfall in such area or any part thereof and for the installation and maintenance for those purposes of gauges or other apparatus and works connected therewith, and carry out stream surveys and may take such other steps as may be necessary in order to obtain any information required for the purposes aforesaid.

(2) A State Board may give directions requiring any person who in its opinion is abstracting water from any such stream or well in the area in quantities which are substantial in relation to the flow or volume of that stream or well or is discharging sewage or trade effluent into any such steam or well, to give such information as to the abstraction or the discharge at such times and in such form as may be specified in the directions.

(3) Without prejudice to the provisions of sub-section (2), a State Board may, with a view to preventing or controlling pollution of water, give directions requiring any person in charge of any establishment where any [36][industry, operation or process or treatment and disposal system] is carried on, to furnish to it information regarding the construction, installation or operation of such establishment or of any disposal system or of any extension or addition thereto in such establishment and such other particulars as may be prescribed.

21. Power to take samples of effluents and procedure to be followed in connection therewith.—(1) A State Board or any officer empowered by it in this behalf shall have power to take for the purpose of analysis samples of water from any stream or well or samples of any sewage or trade effluent which is passing from any plant or vessel or from or over any place into any such stream or well.

(2) The result of any analysis of a sample of any sewage or trade effluent taken under sub-section (1) shall not be admissible in evidence in any legal proceeding unless the provisions of sub-sections (3), (4) and (5) are complied with.

(3) Subject to the provisions of sub-sections (4) and (5), when a sample (composite or otherwise as may be warranted by the process used) of any sewage or trade effluent is taken for analysis under sub-section (1), the person taking the sample shall—

(a) serve on the person in charge of, or having control over, the plant or vessel or in occupation of the place (which person is hereinafter referred to as the occupier) or any agent of such occupier, a notice, then and there in such form as may be prescribed of his intention to have it so analysed;

(b) in the presence of the occupier or his agent, divide the sample into two parts;

(c) cause each part to be placed in a container which shall be marked and sealed and shall also be signed both by the person taking the sample and the occupier or his agent;

(d) send one container forthwith,—

(i) in a case where such sample is taken from any area situated in a

[36] *Subs.* by Act 53 of 1988.

union territory, to the laboratory established or recognized by the Central Board under section 16; and

    (ii) in any other case, to the laboratory established or recognized by the State Board under section 17;

(e) on the request of the occupier or his agent; send the second container,—

    (i) in a case where such sample is taken from any area situated in a union territory, to the laboratory established or specified under subsection (1) of section 51; and

    (ii) in any other case, to the laboratory established or specified under sub-section (1) of section 52.

[37][(4) When a sample of any sewage or trade effluent is taken for analysis under sub-section (1) and the person taking the sample serves on the occupier or his agent, a notice under clause (a) of sub-section (3) and the occupier or his agent wilfully absents himself, then,—

(a) the sample so taken shall be placed in a container which shall be marked and sealed and shall also be signed by the person taking the sample and the same shall be sent forthwith by such person for analysis to the laboratory referred to in sub-clause (i) or sub-clause (ii), as the case may be, of clause (e) of sub-section (3) and such person shall inform the Government analyst appointed under sub-section (1) or sub-section (2), as the case may be, of section 53, in writing about the wilful absence of the occupier or his agent;

(b) the cost incurred in getting such sample analysed shall be payable by the occupier or his agent and in case of default of such payment, the same shall be recoverable from the occupier or his agent, as the case may be, as an arrear of land revenue or of public demand;

Provided that no such recovery shall be made unless the occupier or, as the case may be, his agent has been given a reasonable opportunity of being heard in the matter.]

(5) When a sample of any sewage or trade effluent is taken for analysis under sub-section (1) and the person taking the sample serves on the occupier or his agent a notice under clause (a) of sub-section (3) and the occupier or his agent who is present at the time of taking the sample does not make a request for dividing the sample into two parts as provided in clause (b) of sub-section (3), then, the sample so taken shall be placed in a container which shall be marked and sealed and shall also be signed by the person taking the sample and the same shall be sent forthwith by such person for analysis to the laboratory referred to in sub-clause (i), or sub-clause (ii), as the case may be, of clause (d) of sub-section (3).

22. Reports of the result of analysis on samples taken under section 21.— (1) Where a sample of any sewage or trade effluent has been sent for analysis to the

[37] *Subs.* by Act 44 of 1978.

laboratory established or recognized by the Central Board or, as the case may be, the State Board, the concerned Board analyst appointed under sub-section (3) of section 53 shall analyse the sample and submit a report in the prescribed form of the result of such analysis in triplicate to the Central Board or the State Board, as the case may be.

(2) On receipt of the report under sub-section (1), one copy of the report shall be sent by the Central Board or the State Board, as the case may be, to the occupier or his agent referred to in section 21, another copy shall be preserved for production before the court in case any legal proceedings are taken against him and the other copy shall be kept by the concerned Board.

(3) Where a sample has been sent for analysis under clause (e) of sub-section (3) or sub-section (4) of section 21 to any laboratory mentioned therein, the Government analyst referred to in that sub-section shall analyse the sample and submit a report in the prescribed form of the result of the analysis in triplicate to the Central Board or, as the case may be, the State Board which shall comply with the provisions of sub-section (2).

(4) If there is any inconsistency or discrepancy between, or variation in the results of, the analysis carried out by the laboratory established or recognized by the Central Board or the State Board, as the case may be, and that of the laboratory established or specified under Section 51 or Section 52, as the case may be, the report of the latter shall prevail.

(5) Any cost incurred in getting any sample analysed at the request of the occupier or his agent shall be payable by such occupier or his agent and in case of default the same shall be recoverable from him as arrears of land revenue or of public demand.

23. Power of entry and inspection.—(1) Subject to the provisions of this section, any person empowered by a State Board in this behalf shall have a right at any time to enter, with such assistance as he considers necessary, any place—

(a) for the purpose of performing any of the functions of the Board entrusted to him;

(b) for the purpose of determining whether and if so in what manner, any such functions are to be performed or whether any provisions of this Act or the rules made thereunder or any notice, order, direction or authorisation served, made, given, or granted under this Act is being or has been complied with;

(c) For the purpose of examining any plant, record, register, document or any other material object or for conducting a search of any place in which he has reason to believe that an offence under this Act or the rules made thereunder has been or is being or is about to be committed and for seizing any such plant, record, register, document or other material object, if he has reason to believe that it may furnish evidence of the commission of an offence punishable under this Act or the rules made thereunder:

Provided that the right to enter under this sub-section for the inspection of a well shall be exercised only at reasonable hours in a case where such well is situated in any premises used for residential purposes and the water thereof is used exclusively for domestic purposes.

(2) The provisions of [38][the Code of Criminal Procedure, 1973 (2 of 1974),] or, in relation to the state of Jammu and Kashmir, the provisions of any corresponding law in force in that state, shall, so far as may be, apply to any search or seizure under [39][Section 94] of the said Code, or, as the case may be, under the corresponding provisions of the said law.

Explanation.—For the purposes of this section, 'place' includes vessel.

24. Prohibition on use of stream or well for disposal of polluting matter etc.—(1) Subject to the provisions of this section,—

(a) no person shall knowingly cause or permit any poisonous, noxious or polluting matter determined in accordance with such standards as may be laid down by the State Board to enter (whether directly or indirectly) into any [40][stream or well or sewer or on land]; or

(b) no person shall knowingly cause or permit to enter into any stream any other matter which may tend, either directly or in combination with similar matters, to impede the proper flow of the water of the stream in a manner leading or likely to lead to a substantial aggravation of pollution due to other causes or of its consequences.

(2) A person shall not be guilty of an offence under sub-section (1), by reason only of having done or caused to be done any of the following acts, namely:

(a) constructing, improving or maintaining in or across or on the bank or bed of any stream any building, bridge, weir, dam, sluice, dock, pier, drain or sewer or other permanent works which he has a right to construct, improve or maintain;

(b) depositing any materials on the bank or in the bed of any stream for the purpose of reclaiming land or for supporting, repairing or protecting the bank or bed of such stream provided such materials are not capable of polluting such stream;

(c) putting into any stream any sand or gravel or other natural deposit accumulated which has flown from or been deposited by the current of such stream;

(d) causing or permitting, with the consent of the State Board, the deposit accumulated in a well, pond or reservoir to enter into any stream.

(3) The state government may, after consultation with, or on the recommendation of, the State Board, exempt, by notification in the Official Gazette, any person from the operation of sub-section (1) subject to such conditions, if any, as may

---

[38] *Subs.* by *ibid.*
[39] *Subs.* by *ibid.*
[40] *Subs.* by Act 53 of 1988.

be specified in the notification and any condition so specified may by a like notification be altered, varied or amended.

25. Restrictions on new outlets and new discharges.—[41][(1) Subject to the provisions of this section, no person shall, without the previous consent of the State Board,—

(a) establish or take any steps to establish any industry, operation or process, or any treatment and disposal system or any extension or addition thereto, which is likely to discharge sewage or trade effluent into a stream or well or sewer or on land (such discharge being hereafter in this section referred to as discharge of sewage); or

(b) bring into use any new or altered outlet for the discharge of sewage; or

(c) begin to make any new discharge of sewage:

Provided that a person in the process of taking any steps to establish any industry, operation or process immediately before the commencement of the Water (Prevention and Control of Pollution) Amendment Act, 1988, for which no consent was necessary prior to such commencement, may continue to do so for a period of three months from such commencement or, if he has made an application for such consent, within the said period of three months, till the disposal of such application.

(2) An application for consent of the State Board under sub-section (1) shall be made in such form, contain such particulars and shall be accompanied by such fees as may be prescribed.]

(3) The State Board may make such inquiry as it may deem fit in respect of the application for consent referred to in sub-section (1) and in making any such inquiry shall follow such procedure as may be prescribed.

[42][(4) The State Board may—

(a) grant its consent referred to in sub-section (1), subject to such conditions as it may impose, being—

(i) in cases referred to in clauses (a) and (b) of sub-section (1) of Section 25, conditions as to the point of discharge of sewage or as to the use of that outlet or any other outlet for discharge of sewage;

(ii) in the case of a new discharge, conditions as to the nature and composition, temperature, volume or rate of discharge of the effluent from the land or premises from which the discharge or new discharge is to be made; and

(iii) that the consent will be valid only for such period as may be specified in the order,

and any such conditions imposed shall be binding on any person, establishing or taking any steps to establish any industry, operation or process, or treatment and disposal system or extension or addition thereto,

---

[41] *Subs.* by *ibid.*
[42] *Subs.* by *ibid.*

or using the new or altered outlet, or discharging the effluent from the land or premises aforesaid; or

(b) refuse such consent for reasons to be recorded in writing.

(5) Where, without the consent of the State Board, any industry, operation or process, or any treatment and disposal system or any extension or addition thereto, is established, or any steps for such establishment have been taken or a new or altered outlet is brought into use for the discharge of sewage or a new discharge of sewage is made, the State Board may serve on the person who has established or taken steps to establish any industry, operation or process, or any treatment and disposal system or any extension or addition thereto, or using the outlet, or making the discharge, as the case may be, notice imposing any such conditions as it might have imposed on an application for its consent in respect of such establishment, such outlet or discharge.

(6) Every State Board shall maintain a register containing particulars of the conditions imposed under this section and so much of the register as relates to any outlet, or to any effluent, from any land or premises shall be open to inspection at all reasonable hours by any person interested in, or affected by such outlet, land or premises, as the case may be, or by any person authorised by him in this behalf and the conditions so contained in such register shall be conclusive proof that the consent was granted subject to such conditions.]

(7) The consent referred to in sub-section (1) shall, unless given or refused earlier be deemed to have been given unconditionally on the expiry of period of four months of the making of an application in this behalf complete in all respects to the State Board.

(8) For the purposes of this section and sections 27 and 30,—

(a) the expression 'new or altered outlet' means any outlet which is wholly or partly constructed on or after the commencement of this Act or which (whether so constructed or not) is substantially altered after such commencement;

(b) the expression 'new discharge' means a discharge which is not, as respects the nature and composition, temperature, volume, and rate of discharge of the effluent substantially a continuation of a discharge made within the preceding twelve months (whether by the same or a different outlet), so however that a discharge which is in other respects a continuation of previous discharge made as aforesaid shall not be deemed to be a new discharge by reason of any reduction of the temperature or volume or rate of discharge of the effluent as compared with the previous discharge.

26. Provision regarding existing discharge of sewage or trade effluent.— Where immediately before the commencement of this Act any person was discharging any sewage or trade effluent into a [43][stream or well or sewer or on land] the provisions

---

[43] *Subs.* by Act 44 of 1978.

of Section 25 shall, so far as may apply in relation to such person as they apply in relation to the person referred to in that section subject to the modification that the application for consent to be made under sub-section (2) of that section [44][shall be made on or before such date as may be specified by the state government by notification in this behalf in the Official Gazette].

27. Refusal or withdrawal of consent by State Board.—[45][(1) A State Board shall not grant its consent under sub-section (4) of Section 25 for the establishment of any industry, operation or process, or treatment and disposal system or extension or addition thereto, or to the bringing into use of a new or altered outlet unless the industry, operation or process, or treatment and disposal system or extension or addition thereto, or the outlet is so established as to comply with any conditions imposed by the Board to enable it to exercise its right to take samples of the effluent.]

[46][(2) A State Board may from time to time review—

[47][(a) any condition imposed under Section 25 or Section 26 and may serve on the person to whom a consent under Section 25 or Section 26 is granted a notice making any reasonable variation of or revoking any such condition.]

(b) the refusal of any consent referred to in sub-section (1) of Section 25 or Section 26 or the grant of such consent without any condition, and may make such orders as it deems fit.]

(3) Any condition imposed under Section 25 or Section 26 shall be subject to any variation made under sub-section (2) and shall continue in force until revoked under that sub-section.

28. Appeals.—(1) Any person aggrieved by an order made by the State Board under Section 25, Section 26 or Section 27 may, within thirty days from the date on which the order is communicated to him, prefer an appeal to such authority (hereinafter referred to as the appellate authority) as the state government may think fit to constitute:

Provided that the appellate authority may entertain the appeal after the expiry of the said period of thirty days if such authority is satisfied that the appellant was prevented by sufficient cause from filing the appeal in time.

[48][(2) An appellate authority shall consist of a single person or three persons, as the state government may think fit, to be appointed by that Government.]

(3) The form and manner in which an appeal may be preferred under sub-section (1), the fees payable for such appeal and the procedure to be followed by the appellate authority shall be such as may be prescribed.

(4) On receipt of an appeal preferred under sub-section (1), the appellate

[44] Subs. by ibid.
[45] Subs. by Act 53 of 1988.
[46] Subs. by Act 44 of 1978.
[47] Subs. by Act 53 of 1988.
[48] Subs. by Act 44 of 1978.

authority shall, after giving the appellant and the State Board an opportunity of being heard, dispose of the appeal as expeditiously as possible.

(5) If the appellate authority determines that any condition imposed, or the variation of any condition, as the case may be, was unreasonable then,—

(a) where the appeal is in respect of the unreasonableness of any condition imposed, such authority may direct either that the condition shall be treated as annulled or that there shall be substituted for it such condition as appears to it to be reasonable.

(b) where the appeal is in respect of the unreasonableness of any variation of a condition, such authority may direct either that the condition shall be treated as continuing in force unvaried or that it shall be varied in such manner as appears to it to be reasonable.

29. Revision.—(1) The state government may at any time either of its own motion or on an application made to it in this behalf, call for the records of any case where an order has been made by the State Board under Section 25, Section 26 or section 27 for the purpose of satisfying itself as to the legality or propriety of any such order and may pass such order in relation thereto as it may think fit:

Provided that the state government shall not pass any order under this sub-section without affording the State Board and the person who may be affected by such order a reasonable opportunity of being heard in the matter.

(2) The state government shall not revise any order made under Section 25, Section 26 or Section 27 where an appeal against that order lies to the appellate authority, but has not been preferred or where an appeal has been preferred such appeal is pending before the appellate authority.

30. Power of State Board to carry out certain works.—[49][(1) Where under this Act, any conditions have been imposed on any person while granting consent under Section 25 or Section 26 and such conditions require such person to execute any work in connection therewith and such work has not been executed within such time as may be specified in this behalf, the State Board may serve on the person concerned a notice requiring him within such time (not being less than thirty days) as may be specified in the notice to execute the work specified therein.]

(2) If the person concerned fails to execute the work as required in the notice referred to in sub-section (1), then, after the expiration of the time specified in the said notice, the State Board may itself execute or cause to be executed such work.

(3) All expenses incurred by the State Board for the execution of the aforesaid work, together with interest, at such rate as the state government may, by order, fix, from the date when a demand for the expenses is made until it is paid, may be recovered by that Board from the person concerned, as arrears of land revenue, or of public demand.

---

[49] *Subs.* by Act 53 of 1988.

31. Furnishing of information to State Board and other agencies in certain cases.—[50][(1) If at any place where any industry, operation or process, or any treatment and disposal system or any extension or addition thereto is being carried on, due to accident or other unforeseen act or event, any poisonous, noxious or pollution matter is being discharged, or is likely to be discharged into a stream or well or sewer or on land and, as a result of such discharge, the water in any stream or well is being polluted, or is likely to be polluted, then the person in charge of such place shall forthwith intimate the occurrence of such accident, act or event to the State Board and such other authorities or agencies as may be prescribed.]

(2) Where any local authority operates any sewerage system or sewage works, the provisions of sub-section (1) shall apply to such local authority as they apply in relation to the person in charge of the place where any industry or trade is being carried on.

32. Emergency measures in case of pollution of stream or well.—(1) Where it appears to the State Board that any poisonous, noxious or polluting matter is present in [51][any stream or well or on land by reason of the discharge of such matter in such stream or well or on such land] or has entered into that stream or well due to any accident or other unforeseen act or event, and if the Board is of opinion that it is necessary or expedient to take immediate action, it may for reasons to be recorded in writing, carry out such operations as it may consider necessary for all or any of the, following purposes, that is to say,—

(a) removing that matter from the [52][stream or well or land] and disposing it of in such manner as the Board considers appropriate;

(b) remedying or mitigating any pollution caused by its presence in the stream or well;

(c) issuing orders immediately restraining or prohibiting the person concerned from discharging any poisonous, noxious or polluting matter [53][into the stream or well or on land] or from making insanitary use of the stream or well.

(2) The power conferred by sub-section (1) does not include the power to construct any works other than works of a temporary character which are removed on or before the completion of the operations.

33. Power of Board to make application to courts for restraining apprehended pollution of water in streams or wells.—[54][(1) Where it is apprehended by a Board that the water in any stream or well is likely to be polluted by reason of the disposal or likely disposal of any matter in such stream or well or in any sewer or on any land, or otherwise, the Board may make an application to a court, not inferior to

---

[50] *Subs. by ibid.*
[51] *Subs. by ibid.*
[52] *Subs. by ibid.*
[53] *Subs. by ibid.*
[54] *Subs. by ibid.*

that of a Metropolitan Magistrate or a Judicial Magistrate of the first class, for restraining the person who is likely to cause such pollution from so causing.]

(2) On receipt of an application under sub-section (1) the court may make such order as it deems fit.

(3) Where under sub-section (2) the court makes an order restraining any person from polluting the water in any stream or well, it may in that order—

(i) direct the person who is likely to cause or has caused the pollution of the water in the stream or well, to desist from taking such action as is likely to cause pollution or, as the case may be to remove from such stream or well, such matter, and

(ii) authorize the Board, if the direction under clause (i) (being a direction for the removal of any matter from such stream or well) is not complied with by the person to whom such direction is issued, to undertake the removal and disposal of the matter in such manner as may be specified by the court.

(4) All expenses incurred by the Board in removing any matter in pursuance of the authorization under clause (ii) of sub-section (3) or in the disposal of any such matter may be defrayed out of any money obtained by the Board from such disposal and any balance outstanding shall be recoverable from the person concerned as arrears of land revenue or of public demand.

[55][**33A. Power to give directions.**—Notwithstanding anything contained in any other law, but subject to the provisions of this Act, and to any directions that the Central Government may give in this behalf, a Board may, in the exercise of its powers and performance of its functions under this Act, issue any directions in writing to any person, officer or authority, and such person, officer or authority shall be bound to comply with such directions.

Explanation.—For the avoidance of doubts, it is hereby declared that the power to issue directions under this section includes the power to direct—

(a) the closure, prohibition or regulation of any industry, operation or process; or

(b) the stoppage or regulation of supply of electricity, water or any other service.

CHAPTER VI

FUNDS, ACCOUNTS AND AUDIT

34. Contribution by Central Government.—The Central Government may, after due appropriation made by Parliament by law in this behalf, make in each financial year such contributions to the Central Board as it may think necessary to enable the Board to perform its functions under this Act.

---

[55] *Ins.* by Act 53 of 1988.

35. Contribution by state government.—The state government may, after the appropriation made by the Legislature of the state by law in this behalf, make in each financial year such contributions to the State Board as it may think necessary to enable that Board to perform its functions under this Act.

36. Fund of Central Board.—(1) The Central Board shall have its own fund, and all sums which may, from time to time, be paid to it by the Central Government and all other receipts (by way of gifts, grants, donations, benefactions [56][, fees] or otherwise) of that Board shall be carried to the fund of the Board and all payments by the Board shall be made therefrom.

(2) The Central Board may expend such sums as it thinks fit for performing its functions under this Act, [57][and, where any law for the time being in force relating to the prevention, control or abatement of air pollution provides for the performance of any function under such law by the Central Board, also for performing its functions under such law] and such sums shall be treated as expenditure payable out of the fund of that Board.

37. Fund of State Board.—(1) The State Board shall have its own fund, and the sums which may, from time to time, be paid to it by the state government and all other receipts (by way of gifts, grants, donations, benefactions [58][, fees] or otherwise) of that Board shall be carried to the fund of the Board and all payments by the Board shall be made therefrom.

(2) The State Board may expend such sums as it thinks fit for performing its functions under this Act, [59][and, where any law for the time being in force relating to the prevention, control or abatement of air pollution provides for the performance of any function under such law by the State Board, also for performing its functions under such law] and such sums shall be treated as expenditure payable out of the fund of that Board.

[60][**37A. Borrowing powers of Board.**—A Board may, with the consent of, or in accordance with, the terms of any general or special authority given to it by the Central Government or, as the case may be, the state government, borrow money from any source by way of loans or issue of bonds, debentures or such other instruments, as it may deem fit, for the performance of all or any of its functions under this Act.]

38. Budget.—The Central Board or, as the case may be, the State Board shall, during each financial year, prepare, in such form and at such time as may be prescribed, a budget in respect of the financial year next ensuing showing the estimated receipt and expenditure, and copies thereof shall be forwarded to the Central Government or, as the case may be, the state government.

39. Annual Report.—[61][(1) The Central Board shall, during each financial

---

[56] *Ins.* by Act 44 of 1978.
[57] *Ins.* By *ibid.*
[58] *Ins.* by *ibid.*
[59] *Ins.* by *ibid.*
[60] *Ins.* by Act 53 of 1988.
[61] *Subs.* by *ibid.*

year, prepare, in such form as may be prescribed, an annual report giving full account of its activities under this Act during the previous financial year and copies thereof shall be forwarded to the Central Government within four months from the last date of the previous financial year and that Government shall cause every such report to be laid before both Houses of Parliament within nine months from the last date of the previous financial year.

(2) Every State Board shall, during each financial year, prepare, in such form as may be prescribed, an annual report giving full account of its activities under this Act during the previous financial year and copies thereof shall be forwarded to the state government within four months from the last date of the previous financial year and that Government shall cause every such report to be laid before that State Legislature within a period of nine months from the last date of the previous financial year.]

40. Accounts and audit.—(1) Every Board shall maintain proper accounts and other relevant records and prepare an annual statement of accounts in such form as may be prescribed by the Central Government or, as the case may be, the state government.

(2) The accounts of the Board shall be audited by an auditor duly qualified to act as an auditor of companies under section 226 of the Companies Act, 1956 (1 of 1956).

(3) The said auditor shall be appointed by the Central Government or, as the case may be, the state government on the advice of the Comptroller and Auditor General of India.

(4) Every auditor appointed to audit the accounts of the Board under this Act shall have the right to demand the production of books, accounts, connected vouchers and other documents and papers and to inspect any of the offices of the Board.

(5) Every such auditor shall send a copy of his report together with an audited copy of the accounts to the Central Government or, as the case may be, the state government.

(6) The Central Government shall, as soon as may be after the receipt of the audit report under sub-section (5), cause the same to be laid before both Houses of Parliament.

(7) The state government shall, as soon as may be after the receipt of the audit report under sub-section (5), cause the same to be laid before the State Legislature.

CHAPTER VII

PENALTIES AND PROCEDURE

[62][**41. Failure to comply with directions under sub-section (2) or sub-section (3) of Section 20, or orders issued under sub-section (2) of Section 33 or Section 33A.**—(1) Whoever fails to comply with any direction given under sub-section (2) or

[62] *Subs.* by Act 53 of 1988.

sub-section (3) of Section 20 within such time as may be specified in the direction shall, on conviction, be punishable with imprisonment for a term which may extend to three months or with fine which may extend to ten thousand rupees or with both and in case the failure continues, with an additional fine which may extend to five thousand rupees for every day during which such failure continues after the conviction for the first such failure.

(2) Whoever fails to comply with any order issued under clause (e) of sub-section (1) of Section 32 or any direction issued by a court under sub-section (2) of Section 33 or any direction issued under Section 33A shall, in respect of each such failure and on conviction, be punishable with imprisonment for a term which shall not be less than one year and six months but which may extend to six years and with fine, and in case the failure continues, with an additional fine which may extend to five thousand rupees for every day during which such failure continues after the conviction for the first such failure.

(3) If the failure referred to in sub-section (2) continues beyond a period of one year after the date of conviction, the offender shall, on conviction, be punishable with imprisonment for a term which shall not be less than two years but which may extend to seven years and with fine.]

42. Penalty for certain acts.—(1) Whoever—

(a) destroys, pulls down, removes, injures or defaces any pillar, post or stake fixed in the ground or any notice or other matter put up, inscribed or placed, by or under the authority of the Board, or

(b) obstructs any person acting under the orders or directions of the Board from exercising his powers and performing his functions under this Act, or

(c) damages any works or property, belonging to the Board, or

(d) fails to furnish to any officer or other employee of the Board any information required by him for the purpose of this Act, or

(e) fails to intimate the occurrence of any accident or other unforeseen act or event under Section 31 to the Board and other authorities or agencies as required by that section, or

(f) in giving any information which he is required to give under this Act, knowingly or wilfully makes a statement which is false in any material particular, or

(g) for the purpose of obtaining any consent under Section 25 or Section 26, knowingly or wilfully makes a statement which is false in any material particular,

shall be punishable with imprisonment for a term which may extend to three months or with fine which may extend to [63][ten] thousand rupees or with both.

(2) Where for the grant of a consent in pursuance of the provisions of Section

---

[63] *Subs. by ibid.*

25 or Section 26 the use of a meter or gauge or other measure or monitoring device is required and such device is used for the purposes of those provisions, any person who knowingly or wilfully alters or interferes with that device so as to prevent it from monitoring or measuring correctly shall be punishable with imprisonment for a term which may extend to three months or with fine which may extend to one thousand rupees or with both.

43. Penalty for contravention of provisions of Section 24.—Whoever contravenes the provisions of Section 24 shall be punishable with imprisonment for a term which shall not be less than [64][one year and six months] but which may extend to six years and with fine.

44. Penalty for contravention of Section 25 or Section 26.—Whoever contravenes the provisions of Section 25 or Section 26 shall be punishable with imprisonment for a term which shall not be less than [65][one year and six months] but which may extend to six years and with fine.

45. Enhanced penalty after previous conviction.—If any person who has been convicted of any offence under Section 24 or Section 25 or Section 26 is again found guilty of an offence involving a contravention of the same proviso, he shall, on the second and on every subsequent conviction be punishable with imprisonment for a term which shall not be less than [66][two years] but which may extend to seven years and with fine:

Provided that for the purpose of this section no cognizance shall be taken of any conviction made more than two years before the commission of the offence which is being punished.

[67][**45A. Penalty for contravention of certain provisions of the Act.**—Whoever contravenes any of the provisions of this Act or fails to comply with any order or direction given under this Act, for which no penalty has been elsewhere provided in this Act, shall be punishable with imprisonment which may extend to three months or with fine which may extend to ten thousand rupees or with both, and in the case of a continuing contravention or failure, with an additional fine which may extend to five thousand rupees for every day during which such contravention or failure continues after conviction for the first such contravention or failure.]

46. Publication of names of offenders.—If any person convicted of an offence under this Act commits a like offence afterwards it shall be lawful for the court before which the second or subsequent conviction takes place to cause the offender's name and place of residence, the offence and the penalty imposed to be published at the offender's expense in such newspapers or in such other manner as the court may direct and the expenses of such publication shall be deemed to be part of the cost attending the conviction and shall be recoverable in the same manner as a fine.

[64] *Subs.* by *ibid.*
[65] *Subs.* by *ibid.*
[66] *Subs.* by *ibid.*
[67] *Ins.* by *ibid.*

47. Offences by companies.—(1) Where an offence under this Act has been committed by a company, every person who at the time the offence was committed was in charge of, and was responsible to the company for the conduct of, the business of the company, as well as the company, shall be deemed to be guilty of the offence and shall be liable to be proceeded against and punished accordingly:

Provided that nothing contained in this sub-section shall render any such person liable to any punishment provided in this Act if he proves that the offence was committed without his knowledge or that he exercised all due diligence to prevent the commission of such offence.

(2) Notwithstanding anything contained in sub-section (1), where an offence under this Act has been committed by a company and it is proved that the offence has been committed with the consent or connivance of, or is attributable to any neglect on the part of, any director, manager, secretary or other officer of the company, such director, manager, secretary or other officer shall also be deemed to be guilty of that offence and shall be liable to be proceeded against and punished accordingly.

Explanation.—For the purposes of this section—

(a) 'company' means any body corporate and includes a firm or other association of individuals; and

(b) 'director' in relation to a firm means a partner in the firm.

48. Offences by Government Departments.—Where an offence under this Act has been committed by any Department of Government, the Head of the Department shall be deemed to be guilty of the offence and shall be liable to be proceeded against and punished accordingly:

Provided that nothing contained in this section shall render such Head of the Department liable to any punishment if he proves that the offence was committed without his knowledge or that he exercised all due diligence to prevent the commission of such offence.

49. Cognizance of offences.—[68][(1) No court shall take cognizance of any offence under this Act except on a complaint made by-

(a) a Board or any officer authorized in this behalf by it; or

(b) any person who has given notice of not less than sixty days, in the manner prescribed, of the alleged offence and of his intention to make a complaint, to the Board or officer authorized as aforesaid,

and no court inferior to that of a Metropolitan Magistrate or a Judicial Magistrate of the first class shall try any offence punishable under this Act.]

[69][(2) Where a complaint has been made under clause (b) of sub-section (1), the Board shall, on demand by such person, make available the relevant reports in its possession to that person:

Provided that the Board may refuse to make any such report available to such person if the same is, in its opinion, against the public interest.]

[68] *Subs.* by Act 53 of 1988.
[69] *Ins.* by *ibid.*

[70][(3)] Notwithstanding anything contained in [71][Section 29 of the Code of Criminal Procedure, 1973 (2 of 1974),] it shall be lawful for any [72][Judicial Magistrate of the first class or for any Metropolitan Magistrate] to pass a sentence of imprisonment of a term exceeding two years or of fine exceeding two thousand rupees on any person convicted of an offence punishable under this Act.

50. Members, officers and servants of Boards to be public servants.— All members, officers and servants of a Board when acting or purporting to act in pursuance of any of the provisions of this Act and the rules made thereunder shall be deemed to be public servants within the meaning of Section 21 of the Indian Penal Code (45 of 1860).

CHAPTER VIII

MISCELLANEOUS

51. Central Water Laboratory.—(1) The Central Government may, by notification in the Official Gazette,—

(a) establish a Central Water Laboratory; or

(b) specify any laboratory or institute as a Central Water Laboratory, to carry out the functions entrusted to the Central Water Laboratory under this Act.

(2) The Central Government may, after consultation with the Central Board, make rules prescribing—

(a) the functions of the Central Water Laboratory;

(b) the procedure for the submission to the said laboratory of samples of water or of sewage or trade effluent for analysis or tests, the form of the laboratory's report thereon and the fees payable in respect of such report;

(c) such other matters as may be necessary or expedient to enable that laboratory to carry out its functioning.

52. State Water Laboratory.—(1) The state government may, by notification in the Official Gazette,—

(a) establish a State Water Laboratory; or

(b) specify any laboratory or institute as a State Water Laboratory, to carry out the functions entrusted to the State Water Laboratory under this Act.

(2) The state government may, after consultation with the State Board, make rules prescribing—

(a) the functions of the State Water Laboratory;

(b) the procedure for the submission to the said laboratory of samples of

[70] *Renumbered* by *ibid.*
[71] *Subs.* by Act 44 of 1978.
[72] *Subs.* by *ibid.*

water or of sewage or trade effluent for analysis or test, the form of the laboratory's report thereon and the fees payable in respect of such report;

(c) such other matters as may be necessary or expedient to enable that laboratory to carry out its functions.

53. Analysts.—(1) The Central Government may, by notification in the Official Gazette, appoint such persons as it thinks fit and having the prescribed qualifications to be Government analysts for the purpose of analysis of samples of water or of sewage or trade effluent sent for analysis to any laboratory established or specified under sub-section (1) of Section 51.

(2) The state government may, by notification in the Official Gazette, appoint such persons as it thinks fit and having the prescribed qualifications to be Government analysts for the purpose of analysis of samples of water or of sewage or trade effluent sent for analysis to any laboratory established or specified under sub-section (1) of section 52.

(3) Without prejudice to the provisions of sub-section (3) of section 12, the Central Board or, as the case may be, the State Board may, by notification in the Official Gazette, and with the approval of the Central Government or the state government, as the case may be, appoint such persons as it thinks fit and having the prescribed qualifications to be Board analysts for the purpose of analysis of samples of water or of sewage or trade effluent sent for analysis to any laboratory established or recognised under Section 16, or as the case may be, under Section 17.

54. Reports of analysts.—Any document purporting to be a report signed by a Government analyst or, as the case may be, a Board analyst may be used as evidence of the facts stated therein in any proceeding under this Act.

55. Local authorities to assist.—All local authorities shall render such help and assistance and furnish such information to the Board as it may require for the discharge of its functions, and shall make available to the Board for inspection and examination such records, maps, plans and other documents as may be necessary for the discharge of its functions.

56. Compulsory acquisition of land for the State Board.—Any land required by a State Board for the efficient performance of its functions under this Act shall be deemed to be needed for a public purpose and such land shall be acquired for the State Board under the provisions of the Land Acquisition Act, 1894 (1 of 1894), or under any other corresponding law for the time being in force.

57. Returns and reports.—The Central Board shall furnish to the Central Government, and a State Board shall furnish to the state government and to the Central Board such reports, returns, statistics, accounts and other information with respect to its fund or activities as that Government, or, as the case may be, the Central Board may, from time to time, require.

58. Bar of jurisdiction.—No civil court shall have jurisdiction to entertain any suit or proceeding in respect of any matter which an appellate authority constituted under this Act is empowered by or under this Act to determine, and no injunction shall be granted by any court or other authority in respect of any action taken or to be taken in pursuance of any power conferred by or under this Act.

59. Protection of action taken in good faith.—No suit or other legal proceedings shall lie against the Government or any officer of Government or any member or officer of a Board in respect of anything which is in good faith done or intended to be done in pursuance of this Act or the rules made thereunder.

60. Overriding effect.—The provisions of this Act shall have effect notwithstanding anything inconsistent therewith contained in any enactment other than this Act.

61. Power of Central Government to supersede the Central Board and Joint Boards.—(1) If at any time the Central Government is of opinion—

(a) that the Central Board or any Joint Board has persistently made default in the performance of the functions imposed on it by or under this Act; or

(b) that circumstances exist which render it necessary in the public interest so to do,

the Central Government may, by notification in the Official Gazette, supersede the Central Board or such Joint Board, as the case may be, for such period, not exceeding one year, as may be specified in the notification:

Provided that before issuing a notification under this sub-section for the reasons mentioned in clause (a), the Central Government shall give a reasonable opportunity to the Central Board or such Joint Board, as the case may be, to show cause why it should not be superseded and shall consider the explanations and objections, if any, of the Central Board or such Joint Board, as the case may be.

(2) Upon the publication of a notification under sub-section (1) superseding the Central Board or any Joint Board,—

(a) all the members shall, as from the date of supersession vacate their offices as such;

(b) all the powers, functions and duties which may, by or under this Act, be exercised, performed or discharged by the Central Board or such Joint Board shall, until the Central Board or the Joint Board, as the case may be, is reconstituted under subsection (3) be exercised, performed or discharged by such person or persons as the Central Government may direct;

(c) all property owned or controlled by the Central Board or such Joint Board shall, until the Central Board or the Joint Board, as the case may be, is reconstituted under sub-section (3) vest in the Central Government.

(3) On the expiration of the period of supersession specified in the notification issued under sub-section (1), the Central Government may—

(a) extend the period of supersession for such further term, not exceeding six months, as it may consider necessary; or

(b) reconstitute the Central Board or the Joint Board, as the case may be, by fresh nomination or appointment, as the case may be, and in such case any person who vacated his office under clause (a) of sub-section (2) shall not be deemed disqualified for nomination or appointment:

Provided that the Central Government may at any time before the expiration of the period of supersession, whether originally specified under sub-section (1) or as extended under this sub-section, take action under clause (b) of this sub-section.

62. Power of state government to supersede State Board.—(1) If at any time the state government is of opinion—

(a) that the State Board has persistently made default in the performance of the functions imposed on it by or under this Act; or

(b) that circumstances exist which render it necessary in the public interest so to do,

the state government may, by notification in the Official Gazette, supersede the State Board for such period, not exceeding one year, as may be specified in the notification:

Provided that before issuing a notification under this sub-section for the reasons mentioned in clause (a), the state government shall give a reasonable opportunity to the State Board to show cause why it should not be superseded and shall consider the explanations and objections, if any, of the State Board.

(2) Upon the publication of a notification under sub-section (1) superseding the State Board, the provisions of sub-sections (2) and (3) of Section 61 shall apply in relation to the supersession of the State Board as they apply in relation to the supersession of the Central Board or a Joint Board by the Central Government.

63. Power of Central Government to make rules.—(1) The Central Government may, simultaneously with the constitution of the Central Board, make rules in respect of the matter specified in sub-section (2):

Provided that when the Central Board has been constituted, no such rule shall be made, varied, amended or repealed without consulting the Board.

(2) In particular, and without prejudice to the generality of the foregoing power, such rules may provide for all or any of the following matters, namely:

(a) the terms and conditions of service of the members (other than the chairman and member-secretary) of the Central Board under sub-section (8) of Section 5;

(b) the intervals and the time and place at which meetings of the Central Board or of any committee thereof constituted under this Act, shall be held and the procedure to be followed at such meetings, including the quorum necessary for the transaction of business under Section 8, and under sub-section (2) of Section 9;

(c) the fees and allowances to be paid to such members of a committee of the Central Board as are not members of the Board under sub-section (3) of Section 9;

73[(d) the manner in which and the purposes for which persons may be

---

73 *Subs.* by Act 44 of 1978.

associated with the Central Board under sub-section (1) of Section 10 and the fees and allowances payable to such persons;]

(e) the terms and conditions of service of the chairman and the member-secretary of the Central Board under sub-section (9) of Section 5 and under sub-section (1) of Section 12;

(f) conditions subject to which a person may be appointed as a consulting engineer to the Central Board under sub-section (4) of Section 12;

(g) the powers and duties to be exercised and performed by the chairman and the member-secretary of the Central Board;

74[* * *]

(j) the form of the report of the Central Board analyst under sub-section (1) of Section 22;

(k) the form of the report of the Government analyst under sub-section (3) of Section 22;

75[(l) the form in which and the time within which the budget of the Central Board may be prepared and forwarded to the Central Government under Section 38;

(ll) the form in which the annual report of the Central Board may be prepared under Section 39;]

(m) the form in which the accounts of the Central Board may be maintained under Section 40;

76[(mm) the manner in which notice of intention to make a complaint shall be given to the Central Board or officer authorised by it under Section 49;]

(n) any other matter relating to the Central Board, including the powers, and functions of that Board in relation to Union territories;

(o) any other matter which has to be, or may be, prescribed.

(3) Every rule made by the Central Government under this Act shall be laid, as soon as may be after it is made, before each House of Parliament while it is in session for a total period of thirty days which may be comprised in one session or in two or more successive sessions, and if, 77[before the expiry of the session immediately following the session or the successive sessions aforesaid], both Houses agree in making any modification in the rule or both Houses agree that the rule should not be made, the rule shall thereafter have effect only in such modified form or be of no effect, as the case may be; so, however, that any such modification or annulment shall be without prejudice to the validity of anything previously done under that rule.

64. Power of state government to make rules.—(1) The state government may, simultaneously with the constitution of the State Board, make rules to carry

74 *Omitted* by *ibid.*
75 *Subs.* by Act 53 of 1988.
76 *Ins.* by *ibid.*
77 *Subs.* by Act 44 of 1978.

out the purposes of this Act in respect of matters not falling within the purview of Section 63:

Provided that when the State Board has been constituted, no such rule shall be made, amended or repealed without consulting that Board.

(2) In particular, and without prejudice to the generality of the foregoing power, such rules may provide for all or any of the following matters, namely:

(a) the terms and conditions of service of the members (other than the chairman and the member-secretary) of the State Board under sub-section (8) of Section 5;

(b) the time and place of meetings of the State Board or of any committee of that Board constituted under this Act and the procedure to be followed at such meeting, including the quorum necessary for the transaction of business under section 8 and under sub-section (2) of Section 9;

(c) the fees and allowances to be paid to such members of a committee of the State Board as are not members of the Board under sub-section (3) of Section 9;

(d) the manner in which and the purposes for which persons may be associated with the State Board under sub-section (1) of Section 10 [78][and the fees and allowances payable to such persons;]

(e) the terms and conditions of service of the chairman and the member-secretary of the State Board under sub-section (9) of Section 5 and under sub-section (1) of Section 12;

(f) the conditions subject to which a person may be appointed as a consulting engineer to the State Board under sub-section (4) of Section 12;

(g) the powers and duties to be exercised and discharged by the chairman and the member-secretary of the State Board;

(h) the form of the notice referred to in Section 21;

(i) the form of the report of the State Board analyst under sub-section (1) of Section 22;

(j) the form of the report of the Government analyst under sub-section (3) of Section 22;

(k) the form of application for the consent of the State Board under sub-section (2) of Section 25, and the particulars it may contain;

(l) the manner in which inquiry under sub-section (3) of Section 25 may be made in respect of an application for obtaining consent of the State Board and the matters to be taken into account in granting or refusing such consent;

(m) the form and manner in which appeals may be filed, the fees payable in respect of such appeals and the procedure to be followed by the appellate authority in disposing of the appeals under sub-section (3) of Section 28;

[78] *Ins.* by *ibid.*

[79][(n) the form in which and the time within which the budget of the State Board may be prepared and forwarded to the State Government under section 38;

(nn) the form in which the annual report of the State Board may be prepared under section 39;]

(o) the form in which the accounts of the State Board may be maintained under sub-section (1) of section 40;

[80][(oo) the manner in which notice of intention to make a complaint shall be given to the State Board or officer authorised by it under section 49;]

(p) any other matter which has to be, or may be prescribed.

---

[79] *Subs.* by Act 53 of 1988.
[80] *Ins.* by *ibid.*

C

THE ENVIRONMENT ACT

ENVIRONMENT (PROTECTION) ACT, 1986[1]

[NO. 29 OF 1986]

An Act to provide for the protection and improvement of environment and for matters connected therewith.

Whereas decisions were taken at the United Nations Conference on the Human Environment held at Stockholm in June, 1972, in which India participated, to take appropriate steps for the protection and improvement of human environment;

And whereas it is considered necessary further to implement the decisions aforesaid in so far as they relate to the protection and improvement of environment and the prevention of hazards to human beings, other living creatures, plants and property;

Be it enacted by Parliament in the Thirty-seventh Year of the Republic of India as follows:

CHAPTER I

PRELIMINARY

1. Short title, extent and commencement.—(1) This Act may be called the Environment (Protection) Act, 1986.

(2) It extends to the whole of India.

(3) It shall come into force on such date as the Central Government may, by

---

[1] Received the assent of the President on 23 May 1986, published in the *Gazette of India, Extraordinary*, Pt.II, Sec. 1, dated 26 May 1986, pp. 1–11.

notification in the Official Gazette, appoint and different dates may be appointed for different provisions of this Act and for different areas.

2. Definitions.—In this Act, unless the context otherwise requires,—

(a) 'environment' includes water, air and land and the inter-relationship which exists among and between water, air and land, and human beings, other living creatures, plants, micro-organism and property;

(b) 'environmental pollutant' means any solid, liquid or gaseous substance present in such concentration as may be, or tend to be, injurious to environment;

(c) 'environmental pollution' means the presence in the environment of any environmental pollutant;

(d) 'handling', in relation to any substance, means the manufacture, processing, treatment, package, storage, transportation, use, collection, destruction, conversion, offering for sale, transfer or the like of such substance;

(e) 'hazardous substance' means any substance or preparation which, by reason of its chemical or physico-chemical properties or handling, is liable to cause harm to human beings, other living creatures, plants, micro-organism, property or the environment;

(i) 'occupier', in relation to any factory or premises, means a person who has control over the affairs of the factory or the premises and includes in relation to any substance, the person in possession of the substances;

(g) 'prescribed' means prescribed by rules made under this Act.

CHAPTER II

General Powers Of The Central Government

3. Power of Central Government to take measures to protect and improve environment.—(1) Subject to the provisions of this Act, the Central Government shall have the power to take all such measures as it deems necessary or expedient for the purpose of protecting and improving the quality of the environment and preventing, controlling and abating environmental pollution.

(2) In particular and without prejudice to the generality of the provisions of sub-section (1), such measures may include measures with respect to all or any of the following matters, namely:

(i) co-ordination of actions by the state governments, officers and other authorities—

(a) under this Act, or the rules made thereunder; or

(b) under any other law for the time being in force which is relatable to the objects of this Act;

(ii) planning and execution of a nation-wide programme for the prevention, control and abatement of environmental pollution;

(iii) laying down standards for the quality of environment in its various aspects;

(iv) laying down standards for emission or discharge of environmental pollutants from various sources whatsoever:

Provided that different standards for emission or discharge may be laid down under this clause from different sources having regard to the quality or composition of the emission or discharge of environmental pollutants from such sources;

(v) restriction of areas in which any industries, operations or processes or class of industries, operations or processes shall not be carried out or shall be carried out subject to certain safeguards;

(vi) laying down procedures and safeguards for the prevention of accidents which may cause environmental pollution and remedial measures for such accidents;

(vii) laying down procedures and safeguards for the handling of hazardous substances;

(viii) examination of such manufacturing processes, materials and substances as are likely to cause environmental pollution;

(ix) carrying out and sponsoring investigations and research relating to problems of environmental pollution;

(x) inspection of any premises, plant, equipment, machinery, manufacturing or other processes, materials or substances and giving, by order, of such directions to such authorities, officers or persons as it may consider necessary to take steps for the prevention, control and abatement of environmental pollution;

(xi) establishment or recognition of environmental laboratories and institutes to carry out the functions entrusted to such environmental laboratories and institutes under this Act;

(xii) collection and dissemination of information in respect of matters relating to environmental pollution;

(xiii) preparation of manuals, codes or guides relating to the prevention, control and abatement of environmental pollution;

(xiv) such other matters as the Central Government deems necessary or expedient for the purpose of securing the effective implementation of the provisions of this Act.

(3) The Central Government may, if it considers it necessary or expedient so to do for the purposes of this Act, by order, published in the Official Gazette, constitute an authority or authorities by such name or names as may be specified in the order for the purpose of exercising and performing such of the powers and functions (including the power to issue directions under section 5) of the Central Government under this Act and for taking measures with respect to such of the matters referred to in sub-section (2) as may be mentioned in the order and subject

to the supervision and control of the Central Government and the provisions of such order, such authority or authorities may exercise the powers or perform the functions or take the measures so mentioned in the order as if such authority or authorities had been empowered by this Act to exercise those powers or perform those functions or take such measures.

4. Appointment of officers and their powers and functions.—(1) Without prejudice to the provisions of sub-section (3) of section 3, the Central Government may appoint officers with such designations as it thinks fit for the purposes of this Act and may entrust to them such of the powers and functions under this Act as it may deem fit.

(2) The officers appointed under sub-section (1) shall be subject to the general control and direction of the Central Government or, if so directed by that Government, also of the authority or authorities, if any, constituted under sub-section (3) of section 3 or of any other authority or officer.

5. Power to give directions.—Notwithstanding anything contained in any other law but subject to the provisions of this Act, the Central Government may, in the exercise of its powers and performance of its functions under this Act, issue directions in writing to any person, officer or any authority and such person, officer or authority shall be bound to comply with such directions.

Explanations.—For the avoidance of doubts, it is hereby declared that the power to issue directions under this section includes the power to direct—

(a) the closure, prohibition or regulation of any industry, operation or process; or

(b) stoppage or regulation of the supply of electricity or water or any other service.

6. Rules to regulate environmental pollution.—(1) The Central Government may, by notification in the Official Gazette, make rules in respect of all or any of the matters referred to in section 3.

(2) In particular, and without prejudice to the generality of the foregoing power, such rules may provide for all or any of the following matters, namely:

(a) the standards of quality of air, water or soil for various areas and purposes;

(b) the maximum allowable limits of concentration of various environmental pollutants (including noise) for different areas;

(c) the procedures and safeguards for the handling of hazardous substances;

(d) the prohibition and restrictions on the handling of hazardous substances in different areas;

(e) the prohibition and restrictions on the location of industries and the carrying on of processes and operations in different areas;

(f) the procedures and safeguards for the prevention of accidents which may cause environmental pollution and for providing for remedial measures for such accidents.

CHAPTER III

PREVENTION, CONTROL AND ABATEMENT OF ENVIRONMENTAL POLLUTION

7. Persons carrying on industry, operation, etc., not to allow emission or discharge of environmental pollutants in excess of the standards.—No person carrying on any industry, operation or process shall discharge or emit or permit to be discharged or emitted any environmental pollutant in excess of such standards as may be prescribed.

8. Persons handling hazardous substances to comply with procedural safeguards.—No person shall handle or cause to be handled any hazardous substance except in accordance with such procedure and after complying with such safeguards as may be prescribed.

9. Furnishing of information to authorities and agencies in certain cases.—(1) Where the discharge of any environmental pollutant in excess of the prescribed standards occurs or is apprehended to occur due to any accident or other unforeseen act or event, the person responsible for such discharge and the person in charge of the place at which such discharge occurs or is apprehended to occur shall be bound to prevent or mitigate the environmental pollution caused as a result of such discharge and shall also forthwith—

(a) intimate the fact of such occurrence or apprehension of such occurrence; and

(b) be bound, if called upon, to render all assistance to such authorities or agencies as may be prescribed.

(2) On receipt of information with respect to the fact or apprehension of any occurrence of the nature referred to in sub-section (1), whether through intimation under that sub-section or otherwise, the authorities or agencies referred to in sub-section (1) shall, as early as practicable, cause such remedial measures to be taken as are necessary to prevent or mitigate the environmental pollution.

(3) The expenses, if any, incurred by any authority or agency with respect to the remedial measures referred to in sub-section (2), together with interest (at such reasonable rate as the Government may, by order, fix) from the date when a demand for the expenses is made until it is paid, may be recovered by such authority or agency from the person concerned as arrears of land revenue or of public demand.

10. Powers of entry and inspection.—(1) Subject to the provisions of this section, any person empowered by the Central Government in this behalf shall have a right to enter, at all reasonable times with such assistance as he considers necessary, any place—

(a) for the purpose of performing any of the functions of the Central Government entrusted to him;

(b) for the purpose of determining whether and if so in what manner, any such functions are to be performed or whether any provisions of this Act or the rules made thereunder or any notice, order, direction or authorisation served, made, given or granted under this Act is being or has been complied with;

(c) for the purpose of examining and testing any equipment, industrial plant, record, register, document or any other material object or for conducting a search of any building in which he has reason to believe that an offence under this Act or the rules made thereunder has been or is being or is about to be committed and for seizing any such equipment, industrial plant, record, register, document or other material object if he has reasons to believe that it may furnish evidence of the commission of an offence punishable under this Act or the rules made thereunder or that such seizure is necessary to prevent or mitigate environmental pollution.

(2) Every person carrying on any industry, operation or process or handling any hazardous substance shall be bound to render all assistance to the person empowered by the Central Government under sub-section (1) for carrying out the functions under that sub-section and if he fails to do so without any reasonable cause or excuse, he shall be guilty of an offence under this Act.

(3) If any person wilfully delays or obstructs any person empowered by the Central Government under sub-section (1) in the performance of his functions, he shall be guilty of an offence under this Act.

(4) The provisions of the Code of Criminal Procedure, 1973, or, in relation to the State of Jammu and Kashmir, or any area in which that Code is not in force, the provisions of any corresponding law in force in that State or area shall, so far as may be, apply to any search or seizure under this section as they apply to any search or seizure made under the authority of a warrant issued under section 94 of the said Code or, as the case may be, under the corresponding provisions of the said law.

11. Power to take sample and procedure to be followed in connection therewith.—(1) The Central Government or any officer empowered by it in this behalf, shall have power to take, for the purpose of analysis, samples of air, water, soil or other substance from any factory, premises or other place in such manner as may be prescribed.

(2) The result of any analysis of a sample taken under sub-section (1) shall not be admissible in evidence in any legal proceeding unless the provisions of sub-sections (3) and (4) are complied with.

(3) Subject to the provisions of sub-section (4), the person taking the sample under sub-section (1) shall—

(a) serve on the occupier or his agent or person in charge of the place, a notice, then and there, in such form as may be prescribed of his intention to have it so analysed;

(b) in the presence of the occupier or his agent or person, collect a sample for analysis;

(c) cause the sample to be placed in a container or containers which shall be marked and sealed and shall also be signed both by the person taking the sample and the occupier or his agent or person;

(d) send without delay, the container or the containers to the laboratory established or recognised by the Central Government under section 12.

(4) When a sample is taken for analysis under sub-section (1) and the person taking the sample serves on the occupier or his agent or person, a notice under clause (a) of sub-section (3), then—

(a) in a case where the occupier, his agent or person wilfully absents himself, the person taking the sample shall collect the sample for analysis to be placed in a container or containers which shall be marked and sealed and shall also be signed by the person taking the sample, and

(b) in a case where the occupier or his agent or person present at the time of taking the sample refuses to sign the marked and sealed container or containers of the sample as required under clause (c) of sub-section (3), the marked and sealed container or containers shall be signed by the person taking the samples,

and the container or containers shall be sent without delay by the person taking the sample for analysis to the laboratory established or recognised under section 12 and such person shall inform the Government Analyst appointed or recognized under section 13 in writing, about the wilful absence of the occupier or his agent or person, or, as the case may be, his refusal to sign, the container or containers.

12. Environmental laboratories.—(1) The Central Government may, by notification in the Official Gazette,—

(a) establish one or more environmental laboratories;

(b) recognize one or more laboratories or institutes as environmental laboratories to carry out the functions entrusted to an environmental laboratory under this Act.

(2) The Central Government may, by notification in the Official Gazette, make rules specifying—

(a) the functions of the environmental laboratory;

(b) the procedure for the submission to the said laboratory of samples of air, water, soil or other substance for analysis or tests the form of the laboratory report thereon and the fees payable for such report;

(c) such other matters as may be necessary or expedient to enable that laboratory to carry out its functions.

13. Government Analysts.—The Central Government may by notification in the Official Gazette, appoint or recognize such persons as it thinks fit and having the prescribed qualifications to be Government Analysts for the purpose of analysis of samples of air, water, soil or other substance sent for analysis to any environmental laboratory established or recognized under sub-section (1) of section 12.

14. Reports of Government Analysts.—Any document purporting to be a report signed by a Government analyst may be used as evidence of the facts stated therein in any proceeding under this Act.

15. Penalty for contravention of the provisions of the Act and the rules, orders and directions.—(1) Whoever fails to comply with or contravenes any of the provisions of this Act, or the rules made or orders or directions issued thereunder, shall, in respect of each such failure or contravention, be punishable with imprisonment for a term which may extend to five years or with fine which may extend to one lakh rupees, or with both, and in case the failure or contravention continues, with additional fine which may extend to five thousand rupees for every day during which such failure or contravention continues after the conviction for the first such failure or contravention.

(2) If the failure or contravention referred to in sub-section (1) continues beyond a period of one year after the date of conviction, the offender shall be punishable with imprisonment for a term which may extend to seven years.

16. Offences by companies.—(1) Where any offence under this Act has been committed by a company, every person who, at the time the offence was committed, was directly in charge of, and was responsible to, the company for the conduct of the business of the company, as well as the company, shall be deemed to be guilty of the offence and shall be liable to be proceeded against and punished accordingly:

Provided that nothing contained in this sub-section shall render any such person liable to any punishment provided in this Act, if he proves that the offence was committed without his knowledge or that he exercised all due diligence to prevent the commission of such offence.

(2) Notwithstanding anything contained in sub-section (1), where an offence under this Act has been committed by a company and it is proved that the offence has been committed with the consent or connivance of, or is attributable to any neglect on the part of, any director, manager, secretary or other officer of the company, such director, manager, secretary or other officer shall also be deemed to be guilty of that offence and shall be liable to be proceeded against and punished accordingly.

Explanation.—For the purposes of this section—
   (a) 'company' means any body corporate and includes a firm or other association of individuals;
   (b) 'director', in relation to a firm, means a partner in the firm.

17. Offences by Government Departments.—(1) Where an offence under this Act has been committed by any Department of Government, the Head of the Department shall be deemed to be guilty of the offence and shall be liable to be proceeded against and punished accordingly:

Provided that nothing contained in this section shall render such Head of the Department liable to any punishment if he proves that the offence was committed without his knowledge or that he exercised all due diligence to prevent the commission of such offence.

(2) Notwithstanding anything contained in sub-section (1), where an offence

under this Act has been committed by a Department of Government and it is proved that the offence has been committed with the consent or connivance of, or is attributable to any neglect on the part of, any officer, other than the Head of the Department, such officer shall also be deemed to be guilty of that offence and shall be liable to be proceeded against and punished accordingly.

CHAPTER IV

MISCELLANEOUS

18. Protection of action taken in good faith.—No suit, prosecution or other legal proceeding shall lie against the Government or any officer or other employee of the Government or any authority constituted under this Act or any member, officer or other employee of such authority in respect of anything which is done or intended to be done in good faith in pursuance of this Act or the rules made or orders or directions issued thereunder.

19. Cognizance of offences.—No court shall take cognizance of any offence under this Act except on a complaint made by—

(a) the Central Government or any authority or officer authorized in this behalf by that Government; or

(b) any person who has given notice of not less than sixty days, in the manner prescribed, of the alleged offence and of his intention to make a complaint, to the Central Government or the authority or officer authorised as aforesaid.

20. Information, reports or returns.—The Central Government may, in relation to its functions under this Act, from time to time, require any person, officer, State Government or other authority to furnish to it or any prescribed authority or officer any reports, returns, statistics, accounts and other information and such person, officer, State Government or other authority shall be bound to do so.

21. Members, officers and employees of the authority constituted under section 3 to be public servants.—All the members of the authority, constituted, if any, under section 3 and all officers and other employees of such authority when acting or purporting to act in pursuance of any provisions of this Act or the rules made or orders or directions issued thereunder shall be deemed to be public servants within than meaning of section 21 of the Indian Penal Code.

22. Bar of jurisdiction.—No civil court shall have jurisdiction to entertain any suit or proceeding in respect of anything done, action taken or order or direction issued by the Central Government or any authority or officer in pursuance of any power conferred by or in relation to its or his functions under this Act.

23. Power to delegate.—Without prejudice to the provisions of sub-section (3) of section 3, the Central Government may, by notification in the Official Gazette, delegate, subject to such conditions and limitations as may be specified in the notification, such of its powers and functions under this Act (except the power to constitute an authority under sub-section (3) of section 3 and to make rules under section 25) as it may deem necessary or expedient, to any officer, State Government or other authority.

24. Effect of other laws.—(1) Subject to the provisions of sub-section (2), the provisions of this Act and the rules or orders made therein shall have effect notwithstanding anything inconsistent therewith contained in any enactment other than this Act.

(2) Where any act or omission constitutes an offence punishable under this Act and also under any other Act then the offender found guilty of such offence shall be liable to be punished under the other Act and not under this Act.

25. Power to make rules.—(1) The Central Government may, by notification in the Official Gazette, make rules for carrying out the purposes of this Act.

(2) In particular, and without prejudice to the generality of the foregoing power, such rules may provide for all or any of the following matters, namely:

(a) the standards in excess of which environmental pollutants shall not be discharged or emitted under section 7;

(b) the procedure in accordance with and the safeguards in compliance with which hazardous substances shall be handled or cause to be handled under section 8;

(c) the authorities or agencies to which intimation of the fact of occurrence or apprehension of occurrence of the discharge of any environmental pollutant in excess of the prescribed standards shall be given and to whom all assistance shall be bound to be rendered under sub-section (1) of section 9;

(d) the manner in which samples of air, water, soil or other substance for the purpose of analysis shall be taken under sub-section (1) of section 11;

(e) the form in which notice of intention to have a sample analysed shall be served under clause (a) of sub-section (3) of section 11;

(f) the functions of the environmental laboratories, the procedure for the submission to such laboratories of samples of air, water, soil and other substances for analysis or test; the form of laboratory report; the fees payable for such report and other matters to enable such laboratories to carry out their functions under sub-section (2) of section 12;

(g) the qualifications of Government Analyst appointed or recognized for the purpose of analysis of samples of air, water, soil or other substances under section 13;

(h) the manner in which notice of the offence and of the intention to make a complaint to the Central Government shall be given under clause (b) of section 19;

(i) the authority or officer to whom any reports, returns, statistics, accounts and other information shall be furnished under section 20;

(j) any other matter which is required to be, or may be, prescribed.

26. Rules made under this Act to be laid before Parliament.—Every rule made under this Act shall be laid, as soon as may be after it is made, before each House of Parliament, while it is in session, for a total period of thirty days which may be comprised in one session or in two or more successive sessions, and if, before the expiry of the session immediately following the session or the sucessive sessions aforesaid, both Houses agree in making any modification in the rule or both Houses agree that the rule should not be made, the rule shall thereafter have effect only in such modified form or be of no effect, as the case may be; so, however, that any such modification or annulment shall be without prejudice to the validity of anything previously done under that rule.

D

THE ENVIRONMENT RULES

ENVIRONMENT (PROTECTION) RULES, 1986

Notification No. S.O. 844 (E), dated 19 November 1986[1]

In exercise of powers conferred by sections 6 and 25 of the Environment (Protection) Act, 1986 (29 of 1986), the Central Government hereby makes the following rules, namely:

1. Short title and commencement.—(i) These rules may be called the Environment (Protection) Rules, 1986.

(ii)　　　They shall come into force on the date of their publication in the Official Gazette.

2. Definitions.—In these rules, unless the context otherwise requires,—

(a) 'Act' means the Environment (Protection) Act, 1986 (29 of 1986);

[2][(aa) 'areas' means all areas where the hazardous substances are handled;]

(b) 'Central Board' means the Central Board for the Prevention and Control of Water Pollution constituted under section 3 of the Water (Prevention and Control of Pollution) Act, 1974 (6 of 1974);

(c) 'form' means a form set forth in Appendix A to these rules;

(d) 'Government Analyst' means a person appointed or recognized as such under section 13;

(e) 'person' in relation to any factory or premises means a person or occupier or his agent who has control over the affairs of the factory or premises and includes in relation to any substance, the person in possession of the substance;

[3][(ee) 'prohibited substance' means the substance prohibited for handling;]

---

[1] Published in *Gazette of India, Extraordinary*, Pt. II, Sec. 3(i), dated 19 November 1986.

[2] *Ins.* by G.S.R. 931 (E), dated 27 October 1989.

[3] *Ins.* by *ibid.*

(f) 'recipient system' means the part of the environment, such as, soil, water, air or other which receives the pollutants;

[4][(ff) 'restricted substance' means the substance restricted for handling;]

(g) 'section' means a section of the Act;

(h) 'schedule' means a schedule appended to these rules;

(i) 'standards' means standards prescribed under these rules;

(j) 'State Board' means a State Board for the Prevention and Control of Water Pollution constituted under section 4 of the Water (Prevention and Control of Pollution) Act, 1974 (6 of 1974), or a State Board for the Prevention and Control of Air Pollution constituted under section 5 of the Air (Prevention and Control of Pollution) Act, 1981 (14 of 1981).

3. Standards for emission or discharge of environmental pollutants.— (1) For the purposes of protecting and improving the quality of the environment and preventing and abating environmental pollution, the standards for emission or discharge of environmental pollutants from the industries, operations or processes shall be as specified in [5][Schedule I to IV].

[6][* * *]

(2) Notwithstanding anything contained in sub-rule (1), the Central Board or a State Board may specify more stringent standards from those provided in [7][Schedule I to IV] in respect of any specific industry, operation or process depending upon the quality of the recipient system and after recording reasons, therefor, in writing.

[8][(3) The standards for emission or discharge of environmental pollutants specified under sub-rule (1) or sub-rule (2) shall be complied with by an industry, operation or process within a period of one year of being specified.]

[9][(3A)(i) Notwithstanding anything contained in sub-rules (1) and (2), on and from the 1st day of January, 1994, emission or discharge of environmental pollutants from the [10][industries, operations or processes other than those industries, operations or processes for which standards have been specified in Schedule I shall] not exceed the relevant parameters and standards specified in Schedule VI:

Provided that the State Boards may specify more stringent standards for the relevant parameters with respect to specific industry or locations after recording reasons thereof in writing;

(ii) The State Board shall while enforcing the standards specified in Schedule VI follow the guidelines specified in Annexures I and II in that Schedule.]

---

4 *Ins.* by *ibid.*

5 *Subs.* by G.S.R. 422 (E), dated 19 May 1993.

6 *Omitted* by S.O. 23 (5), dated 16 January 1991.

7 *Subs.* by G.S.R. 422 (E), dated 19 May 1993.

8 *Ins.* by S.O. 23(E), dated 16 January 1991.

9 *Ins.* by G.S.R. 422 (E), dated 19 May 1993.

10 *Ins.* by G.S.R. 801 (E), dated 31 December 1993.

[11][(3B) The combined effect of emission or discharge of environmental pollutants in an area from the industries, operations, processes, automobiles and domestic sources, shall not be permitted to exceed the relevant concentration in ambient air as indicated and set out against each pollutant in columns (3) to (5) of Schedule VII.]

(4) Notwithstanding anything contained in sub-rule (3),—

(a) the Central Board or a State Board, depending on the local conditions or nature of discharge of environmental pollutants, may, by order, specify a lesser period than a period specified under sub-rule (3) within which the compliance of standards shall be made by an industry, operation or process;

(b) the Central Government in respect of any specified industry, operation or process, by order, may specify any period other than a period specified under sub-rule (3) within which the compliance of standards shall be made by such industry, operation or process.

(5) Notwithstanding anything contained in sub-rule (3), the standards for emission or discharge of environmental pollutants specified under sub-rule (1) or sub-rule (2) in respect of an industry, operation or process before the commencement of the Environment (Protection) Amendment Rules, 1991, shall be complied with by such industry, operation or process by the 31st day of December, 1991.]

[12][(6) Notwithstanding anything contained in sub-rule (3), an industry, operation or process which has commenced production on or before 16 May 1981, and has shown adequate proof of at least commencement of physical work for establishment of facilities to meet the specified standards within a time-bound programme, to the satisfaction of the concerned State Pollution Control Board, shall comply with such standards latest by the 31st day of December, 1993.

(7) Notwithstanding anything contained in sub-rule (3) or sub-rule (6), an industry, operation or process which has commenced production after the 16th day of May, 1981, but before the 31st day of December 1991, and has shown adequate proof of at least commencement of physical work for establishment of facilities to meet the specified standards within a time-bound programme, to the satisfaction of the concerned State Pollution Control Board, shall comply with such standards latest by the 31st day of December, 1992.]

[13][(8) On and from the 1st day of June 2001, the following coal based thermal power plants shall use [14][raw or blended or beneficiated coal with an ash content not exceeding thirty-four per cent on an annual average basis], namely:

(a) any thermal power plant located beyond one thousand kilometers from the pit-head; and

(b) any thermal power plant located in urban area or sensitive area or critically

---

[11] *Subs.* by G.S.R. 7, dated 22 December 1998.

[12] *Ins.* by G.S.R. 95 (E), dated 12 February 1992.

[13] *Ins.* by G.S.R. 560 (E) dated 19 September 1997.

[14] *Subs.* by G.S.R. 378 (E), dated 30 June 1998.

polluted area irrespective of their distance from pit-head except any pit-head power plant.

[15][Provided that any thermal power plant using Fluidised Bed Combustion or Circulating Fluidised Bed Comubustion or Pressurised Fluidised Bed Combustion or Integrated Gasification Cycle technologies or any other clean technologies as may be notified by the Central Government in the Official Gazette shall be exempted from clause (a) and (b).]

Explanation: For the purpose of this rule—

(a) 'beneficiated coal' means coal containing higher calorific value but lower ash than the original ash content in the raw coal obtained through physical separation or washing process;

(b) 'pit-head power plant' means power stations having captive transportation system for its exclusive use for transportation of coal from the loading point at the mining end up to the unloading point at the power station without using the normal public transportation system;

(c) 'sensitive area' means an area whose ecological balance is prone to be easily disturbed;

(d) 'critically polluted area' means the area where pollution level has reached or likely to reach the critical level and which has been identified as such by the Central Government or Central Pollution Control Board or State Pollution Control Board.]

[16][(e) 'Urban area' means an area limit of a city having a population of more than 1 million according to 1991 census.]

4. Directions.—(1) Any direction issued under section 5 shall be in writing.

(2) The direction shall specify the nature of action to be taken and the time within which it shall be complied with by the person, officer or the authority to whom such direction is given.

[17][(3-a)] The person, officer or authority to whom any direction is sought to be issued shall be served with a copy of the proposed direction and shall be given an opportunity of not less than fifteen days from the date of service of a notice to file with an officer designated in this behalf the objections, if any, to the issue of the proposed direction.

[18][(3-b) Where the proposed direction is for the stoppage or regulation of electricity or water or any other service affecting the carrying on of any industry, operation or process and is sought to be issued to an officer or an authority, a copy of the proposed direction shall also be endorsed to the occupier of the industry, operation or process, as the case may be, and objections, if any, filed by the occupier with an officer

---

[15] *Ins.* by G.S.R. 378 (E), dated 30 June 1998.
[16] *Ibid.*
[17] *Renumbered* by S.O. 64 (E), dated 18 January 1988.
[18] *Ins.* by *ibid.*

designated in this behalf shall be dealt with in accordance with the procedures under sub-rules (3-a) and (4) of this rule:

Provided that no opportunity of being heard shall be given to the occupier if he had already been heard earlier and the proposed direction referred to in sub-rule (3-b) above for the stoppage or regulation of electricity or water or any other service was the resultant decision of the Central Government after such earlier hearing.]

(4) The Central Government shall within a period of 45 days from the date of receipt of the objections, if any, or from the date up to which an opportunity is given to the person, officer or authority to file objections whichever is earlier, after considering the objections, if any, received from the person, officer or authority sought to be directed and for reasons to be recorded in writing, confirm, modify or decide not to issue the proposed direction.

(5) In a case where the Central Government is of the opinion that in view of the likelihood of a grave injury to the environment it is not expedient to provide an opportunity to file objections against the proposed direction, it may, for reasons to be recorded in writing, issue directions without providing such an opportunity.

(6) Every notice or direction required to be issued under this rule shall be deemed to be duly served—

(a) where the person to be served is a company, if the document is addressed in the name of the company at its registered office or at its principal office or place of business and is either,—

(i) sent by registered post; or

(ii) delivered at its registered office or at the principal office or place of business;

(b) where the person to be served is an officer serving Government, if the document is addressed to the person and a copy thereof is endorsed to the Head of the Department and also to the Secretary to the Government, as the case may be, incharge of the Department in which for the time being the business relating to the Department in which the officer is employed is transacted and is either,—

(i) sent by registered post; or

(ii) is given or tendered to him;

(c) in any other case, if the document is addressed to the person to be served and—

(i) is given or tendered to him; or

(ii) if such person cannot be found, is affixed on some conspicuous part of his last known place of residence or business or is given or tendered to some adult member of his family or is affixed on some conspicuous part of the land or building, if any, to which it relates; or

(iii) is sent by registered post to that person.

Explanation.—For the purposes of this sub-rule,—

(a) 'company' means any body corporate and includes a firm or other association of individuals;

(b) 'a servant' is not a member of the family.

5. Prohibition and restriction on the location of industries and the carrying on processes and operations in different areas.—(1) The Central Government may take into consideration the following factors while prohibiting or restricting the location of industries and carrying on of processes and operations in different areas—

(i) Standards for quality of environment in its various aspects laid down for an area.

(ii) The maximum allowable limits of concentration of various environment pollutants (including noise) for an area.

(iii) The likely emission or discharge of environmental pollutants from an industry, process or operation proposed to be prohibited or restricted.

(iv) The topographic and climatic features of an area.

(v) The biological diversity of the area which, in the opinion of the Central Government, needs to be preserved.

(vi) Environmentally compatible land use.

(vii) Net adverse environmental impact likely to be caused by an industry, process or operation proposed to be prohibited or restricted.

(viii) Proximity to a protected area under the Ancient Monuments and Archaeological Sites and Remains Act, 1958 or a sanctuary, National Park, game reserve or closed area notified, as such under the Wild Life (Protection) Act, 1972, or places protected under any treaty, agreement or convention with any other country or countries or in pursuance of any decision made in any international conference, association or other body.

(ix) Proximity to human settlements.

(x) Any other factors as may be considered by the Central Government to be relevant to the protection of the environment in an area.

(2) While prohibiting or restricting the location of industries and carrying on of processes and operations in an area, the Central Government shall follow the procedure hereinafter laid down.

(3)(a) Whenever it appears to the Central Government that it is expedient to impose prohibition or restrictions on the location of an industry or the carrying on of processes and operations in an area, it may, by notification in the Official Gazette and in such other manner as the Central Government may deem necessary from time to time, give notice of its intention to do so.

(b) Every notification under clause (a) shall give a brief description of the area, the industries, operations, processes in that area about which such notification pertains and also specify the reasons for the imposition of prohibition or restrictions on the location of the industries and carrying on of processes or operations in that area.

(c) Any person interested in filing an objection against the imposition of prohibition or restriction on carrying on of processes or operations as notified under clause (a) may do so in writing to the Central Government within sixty days from the date of publication of the notification in the Official Gazette.

(d) The Central Government shall, within a period of one hundred and twenty days from the date of publication of the notification in the Official Gazette, consider all the objections received against such notification and may [19][within [20][three hundred sixty five days] from such date of publication] impose prohibition or restrictions on location of such industries and the carrying on of any process or operation in an area.

[21][(4) Notwithstanding anything contained in sub-rule (3), whenever it appears to the Central Government that it is in public interest to do so, it may dispense with the requirement of notice under Clause (a) of sub-rule (3).]

[22][**6. Procedure for taking samples.**—The Central Government or the officer empowered to take samples under section 11 shall collect the sample in sufficient quantity to be divided into two uniform parts and effectively seal and suitably mark the same and permit the person from whom the sample is taken to add his own seal or mark to all or any of the portions so sealed and marked. In case where the sample is made up in containers or small volumes and is likely to deteriorate or be otherwise damaged if exposed, the Central Government or the officer empowered shall take two of the said samples without opening the containers and suitably seal and mark the same. The Central Government or the officer empowered shall dispose of the samples so collected as follows:

(i)   one portion shall be handed over to the person from whom the sample is taken under acknowledgement; and

(ii) the other portion shall be sent forthwith to the environmental laboratory for analysis.]

7. Service of notice.—The Central Government or the officer empowered shall serve on the occupier or his agent or person in charge of the place a notice then and there in Form I of his intention to have the sample analysed.

8. Procedure for submission of samples for analysis, and the form of laboratory report thereon.—(1) Sample taken for analysis shall be sent by the Central Government or the officer empowered to the environmental laboratory by registered post or through special messenger along with Form II.

(2) Another copy of Form II together with specimen impression of seals of the officer empowered to take samples along with the seals/marks, if any, of the person from whom the sample is taken shall be sent separately in a sealed cover by registered post or through a sealed messenger to the environmental laboratory.

(3) The findings shall be recorded in Form III in triplicate and signed by the

---

[19] *Ins.* by G.S.R. 562 (E), dated 27 May 1992.
[20] *Subs.* by G.S.R, 884 (E), dated 20 November 1992.
[21] *Ins.* by G.S.R. 320 (E), dated 16 March 1994.
[22] *Subs.* by S.O.64 (E), dated 18 January 1988.

Government Analyst and sent to the officer from whom the sample is received for analysis.

(4) On receipt of the report of the findings of the Government Analyst, the officer shall send one copy of the report to the person from whom the sample was taken for analysis, the second copy shall be retained by him for his records and the third copy shall be kept by him to be produced in the Court before which proceedings, if any, are instituted.

9. Functions of environmental laboratories.—The following shall be the functions of environmental laboratories:

(i)   to evolve standardized methods for sampling and analysis of various types of environmental pollutants;

(ii) to analyse samples sent by the Central Government or the officers empowered under sub-section (1) of section 11;

(iii) to carry out such investigations as may be directed by the Central Government to lay down standards for the quality of environment and discharge of environmental pollutants, to monitor and to enforce the standards laid down;

(iv) to send periodical reports regarding its activities to the Central Government;

(v)   to carry out such other functions as may be entrusted to it by the Central Government from time to time.

10. Qualification of Government Analyst.—A person shall not be qualified for appointment or recognized as a Government Analyst unless he is a—

(a)   graduate in science from a recognised university with five years experience in a laboratory engaged in environmental investigations, testing or analysis; or

(b)   post-graduate in science or a graduate in engineering or a graduate in medicine or equivalent with two years' experience in a laboratory engaged in environmental investigations, testing or analysis; or

(c)   post-graduate in environmental science from a recognized university with two years experience in a laboratory engaged in environmental investigations, testing or analysis.

11. Manner of giving notice.—The manner of giving notice under clause (b) of section 19 shall be as follows, namely:

(1) The notice shall be in writing in Form IV.

(2) The person giving notice may send notice to,—

(a)   if the alleged offence has taken place in a union territory:

(A) the Central Board; and

(B) the Ministry of Environment and Forests (represented by the Secretary of the Government of India);

(b)   if the alleged offence has taken place in a State:

(A) the State Board; and

(B) the Government of the State (represented by the Secretary to the State Government incharge of environment); and

(C) the Ministry of Environment and Forests (represented by the Secretary to the Government of India).

(3) The notice shall be sent by registered post-acknowledgement due; and

(4) The period of sixty days mentioned in clause (b) of section 19 of the Environment (Protection) Act, 1986 shall be reckoned from the date it is first received by one of the authorities mentioned above.

[23][**12. Furnishing of information to authorities and agencies in certain cases.**—Where the discharge of environmental pollutant in excess of the prescribed standards occurs or is apprehended to occur due to any accident or other unforeseen act or event, the person in charge of the place at which such discharge occurs or is apprehended to occur shall forthwith intimate the fact of such occurrence or apprehension of such occurrence to all the following authorities or agencies, namely:

(i)   The officer-in-charge of emergency or disaster relief operations in a district or other region of a State or Union Territory specified by whatever designation, by the Government of the said State or Union Territory, and in whose jurisdiction the industry, process or operation is located.

(ii) The Central Board or a State Board, as the case may be, and its regional officer having local jurisdiction who have been delegated powers under sections 20, 21, 23 of the Water (Prevention and Control of Pollution) Act, 1974 (6 of 1974), and section 24 of the Air (Prevention and Control of Pollution) Act, 1981 (14 of 1981);

(iii) The statutory authorities or agencies specified in column 3 in relation to places mentioned in column 2 against thereof of] [24][Schedule V.]

[25][**13. Prohibition and restriction on the handling of hazardous substances in different areas:**—(1) The Central Government may take into consideration the following factors while prohibiting or restricting the handling of hazardous substances in different areas:

(i)   the hazardous nature of the substance (either in qualitative or quantitative terms) as far as may be in terms of its damage causing potential to the environment, human beings, other living creatures, plants and property;

(ii) the substances that may be or likely to be or readily available as substitutes for the substances proposed to be prohibited or restricted;

(iii) the indigenous availability of the substitute, or the state of technology available in the country for developing a safe substitute;

(iv) the gestation period that may be necessary for gradual introduction of a

[23] *Ins.* by S.O. 82 (E), dated 16 February 1987.
[24] *Ins.* by G.S.R. 422 (E), dated 19 May 1993.
[25] *Ins.* by G.S.R. 431 (E), dated 27 October 1989.

new substitute with a view to bringing about a total prohibition of the hazardous substance in question; and

(v) any other factor as may be considered by the Central Government to be relevant to the protection of environment.

(2) While prohibiting or restricting the handling of hazardous substances in an area including their imports and exports the Central Government shall follow the procedure hereinafter laid down:

(i) Whenever it appears to the Central Government that it is expedient to impose prohibition or restriction on the handling of hazardous substances in an area, it may, by notification in the Official Gazette and in such other manner as the Central Government may deem necessary from time to time, give notice of its intention to do so.

(ii) Every notification under clause (i) shall give a brief description of the hazardous substances and the geographical region or the area to which such notification pertains and also specify the reasons for the imposition of prohibition or restriction on the handling of such hazardous substances in that region or area.

(iii) Any person interested in filing an objection against the imposition of prohibition or restrictions on the handling of hazardous substances as notified under clause (i) may do so in writing to the Central Government within thirty days from the date of publication of the notification in the Official Gazette.

(iv) The Central Government shall within a period of sixty days from the date of publication of the notification in the Official Gazette consider all the objections received against such notification and may impose prohibition or restrictions on the handling of hazardous substances in a region or an area.]

[26][**14. Submission of environmental [27][statement]:**—Every person carrying on an industry, operation or process requiring consent under section 25 of the Water (Prevention and Control of Pollution) Act, 1974 (6 of 1974), or under section 21 of the Air (Prevention and Control of Pollution) Act, 1981 (14 of 1981), or both or authorisation under the Hazardous Wastes (Management and Handling) Rules, 1989, issued under the Environment (Protection) Act, 1986 (29 of 1986), shall submit an environmental [28][statement] for the financial year ending the 31st March, in Form V to the concerned State Pollution Control Board on or before the [29][30th day of September] every year, beginning 1993.]

---

[26] *Ins.* by G.S.R. 329 (E), dated 13 March 1992.
[27] *Subs.* by G.S.R 386 (E), dated 22 April 1993.
[28] *Ibid.*
[29] *Ibid.*

SCHEDULE [30][I]
(*See* Rule 3)

Sl. No.	Industry	Parameter	Standards
1	2	3	4
1.	Caustic Soda Industry		Concentration not to exceed, milligramme per litre (except for pH and flow)
		Total concentration of mercury in the final effluent*	0.01
		Mercury bearing waste-water generation (flow)	10 kilolitres/tonne of caustic soda produced.
		pH	5.5 to 9.0

*Final effluent is the combined effluent from (a) cell house, (b) brine plant, (c) chlorine handling, (d) hydrogen handling, (e) hydrochloric acid plant.

Sl. No.	Industry	Parameter	Standards	
2.	Man-made fibres (synthetic)		Concentration not to exceed, milligramme per litre (except for pH)	
		Suspended solids	100	
		[31][Bio-chemical oxygen demand, (3-days at 27°C)	30	
		pH	5.5 to 9.0	
3.	Oil-refinery		Concentration, not to exceed, milligramme per litre (except for pH)	Quantum, kg/1000 tonnes crude processed
		Oil and Grease	10	7
		Phenol	1	0.7
		Sulphide	0.5	0.35
		[31][Bio-chemical oxygen demand, (3-days at 27°C)]	15	10.5
		Suspended solids	20	14
		pH	6 to 8.5	

[30] *Renumbered* as Sch. 1 by S.O. 82 (E), dated 16 February, 1987.
[31] *Subs.* by G.S.R. 176 (E), dated 2 April, 1996.

Sl. No.	Industry	Parameter	Standards
1	2	3	4
4.	Sugar industry		Concentration not to exceed, milligramme per litre
		[31][Bio-chemical oxygen demand, (3-days at 27°C)]	100 for disposal on land
			30 for disposal in surface waters
		Suspended solids	100 for disposal on land
			30 for disposal in surface waters
5.	Thermal power plants		Maximum, limiting concentration, milligramme per litre (except for pH and temperature)
	Condenser cooling waters (once through cooling system)	pH	6.5–8.5
		Temperature	Not more than 5°C higher than the intake water temperature
		Free available chlorine	0.5
	Boiler blowdowns	Suspended solids	100
		Oil and grease	20
		Copper (total)	1.0
		Iron (total)	1.0
	Cooling-tower blowdown	Free available chlorine	0.5
		Zinc	1.0
		Chromium (total)	0.2
		Phosphate	5.0
		Other corrosion inhibiting material	Limit to be established on case by case basis by Central Board in case of Union territories and State Boards in case of states
	Ash-pond effluent	pH	6.5–8.5
		Suspended solids	100
		Oil and grease	20
6.	Cotton textile industries (composite and processing)		Concentration not to exceed, milligramme per litre (except for pH and bio-assay)

Sl. No.	Industry	Parameter	Standards
1	2	3	4

		Common:	
		pH	5.5 to 9
		Suspended solid	100
		[32][Bio-chemical oxygen demand, (3-days at 27°C)]	150
		Oil and grease	10
		Bio-assay test	90% survival of fish after 96 hours
	Special:		
		Total chromium (as Cr)	2
		Sulphide (as S)	2
		Phenolic compounds (as C_6H_5OH)	5

The special parameters are to be stipulated by the Central Board in case of Union Territories and State Boards in case of states depending upon the dye used in the industry. Where the industry uses chrome dyes, sulphur dyes and/or phenolic compounds in the dyeing/printing process, the limits on chromium of 2 mg/litre, sulphides of 2 mg/litre, and phenolic compounds of 5 mg/litre, respectively shall be imposed.

Where the quality requirement of the recipient system so warrants, the limit of BOD should be lowered up to 30 according to the requirement by the State Boards for the States and the Central Board for the Union Territories.

A limit on sodium absorption ratio of 26 should be imposed by the State Boards for the States and the Central Board for the Union Territories if the disposal of effluent is to be made on land.

7.	Composite woollen mills		Concentration not to exceed, milligramme per litre (except for pH and bio-assay)
	Common:		
		Suspended solids	100
		pH	5.5 to 9.0
		[33][Bio-chemical oxygen demand, (3-days at 27°C)]	10

[32] *Ibid.*
[33] *Ibid.*

Sl. No.	Industry	Parameter	Standards
1	2	3	4
		Oil and grease	10
		Bio-assay test	90% survival of fish after 96 hours
	Special:		
		Total chromium (as Cr)	2
		Sulphide (as S)	2
		Phenolic compounds (as C_6H_5OH)	5

The special parameters to be stipulated by the Central Board in case of Union territories and State Boards in case of States depending upon the dye used in the industry. Where the industry uses chromes dyes, sulphur dyes and/or phenolic compounds in the dyeing/printing process, the limits on chromium of 2 mg/litre, sulphide of 2 mg/litre and phenolic compounds of 5 mg/litre, respectively shall be imposed.

Where the quality requirement of the recipient system so warrants, the limit of BOD should be lowered up to 30 according to the requirement by the State Boards for the state and the Central Board for the Union territories.

A limit on sodium absorption ratio of 26 should be imposed by the State Boards for the States and the Central Board for the Union territories if the disposal of effluent is to be made on land.

[34][8.	Dye and Dye Intermediate Industries		Concentration not to exceed, milligrammes per litre (except for pH, temperature and bio-assay)
		Suspended Solids	100
		pH	6 to 8.5
		Temperature	Shall not exceed 5°C above the ambient temperature of the receiving body
		Mercury (as Hg)	0.01
		Hexavalent Chromium (as Cr)	0.1
		Total Chromium (as Cr)	2.0
		Copper (as Cu)	3.0
		Zinc (as Zn)	5.0

[34] *Ins.* by S.O. 393 (E), dated 16 April 1987. Entries 8 to 10 were inserted by this notification.

Sl. No.	Industry	Parameter	Standards
1	2	3	4
		Nickel (as Ni)	3.0
		Cadmium (as Cd)	2.0
		Chloride (as Cl)	1000
		Sulphate (as SO_4)	1000
		Phenolic Compounds (as C_6H_5OH)	1.0
		Oil and Grease	10
		Bio-assay Test (with 1:8 dilution of effluents)	90% survival of test animals after 96 hours

The standards of chlorides and sulphates are applicable for discharge into inland and surface watercourses. However, when discharged on land for irrigation, the limit for chloride shall not be more than 600 milligrammes per litre and the sodium absorption ratio shall not exceed 26.

9.	Electroplating		Concentration not to exceed, milligrammes per litre (except for pH and temperature)
		pH	6.0 to 9.0
		Temperature	Shall not exceed 5°C above ambient temperature of the receiving body
		Oil and Grease	10
		Suspended Solids	100
		Cyanides (as CN)	0.2
		Ammonical Nitrogen (as N)	50
		Total Residual Chloride (as Cl)	1.0
		Cadmium (as Cd)	2.0
		Nickel (as Ni)	3.0
		Zinc (as Zn)	5.0
		Hexavalent Chromium (as Cr)	0.1
		Total Chromium (as Cr)	2.0
		Copper (as Cu)	3.0
		Lead (as Pb)	0.1
		Iron (as Fe)	3.0
		Total metal	10.0

Sl. No.	Industry	Parameter	Standards
1	2	3	4
10.	Cement Plants		Not to exceed-milligrammes per normal cubic metre
	Plant Capacity:		
	200 tonnes per day	Total dust (All sections)	400
	Greater than 200 tonnes per day	Total dust (All sections)	250

The Central and State Pollution Control Boards may fix stringent standards, not exceeding 250 milligrammes per normal cubic metre for smaller plants and 150 milligrammes per normal cubic metre for larger plants if the industry is located in an area which, in their opinion, requires more stringent standards.

Where continuous monitoring integrators are provided on dust emission lines, the integrated average values over a period, to be fixed by the Central and State Boards but not exceeding 72 hours shall be considered instead of momentary dust emission values for conformity to standards.]

[35][11.	Stone-crushing unit	Suspended particulate matter	The suspended particulate matter measured between 3 metres and 10 metres from any process equipment of a stone-crushing unit shall not exceed 600 microgrammes per cubic metre.]
[36][12.	Coke ovens		Concentration in the effluents when discharged into inland surface waters not to exceed milligrammes per litre (except for pH)
		pH	5.5–9.0
		[37][Biochemical Oxygen Demand (3 days at 27°C)]	30
		Suspended Solids	100
		Phenolic Compounds (as C_6H_5OH)	5

[35] *Ins.* by S.O. 443 (E), dated 28 April 1987. Entry 11 was inserted by this notification.
[36] *Ins.* by S.O. 64 (E), dated 18 January 1988. Entries 12 to 24 were inserted by this notification.
[37] *Subs.* by G.S.R. 176 (E), dated 2 April 1996.

Sl. No.	Industry	Parameter	Standards
1	2	3	4
		Cyanides (as CN)	0.2
		Oil & Grease	10
		Ammonical Nitrogen (as N)	50
13.	Synthetic Rubber		Concentration in the effluent when discharged into inland surface waters not to exceed milligramme per litre (except for colour, and pH)
		Colour	Absent
		pH	5.5–9.0
		[37][Biochemical Oxygen Demand (3 days at 27°C)]	50
		Chemical Oxygen Demand	250
		Oil & Grease	10.0
14.	Small Pulp and Paper Industry		Concentration not to exceed milligramme per litre (except for pH and sodium absorption ratio)
	*Discharge into inland surface water	pH	5.5–9.0
		Suspended Solids	100
		BOD	30
	Disposal on land	pH	5.5–9.0
		Suspended Solids	100
		BOD	100
		Sodium Absorption Ratio	26

*[38][Note (1):] Waste water generation shall not exceed 250 cubic metre per tonne of paper produced.

15.	Fermentation Industry (Distilleries, Maltries and Breweries)		Concentration in the effluent not to exceed milligramme per litre (except for pH and colour & odour)

[38] *Renumbered* by S.O. 12 (E), dated 8 January 1990.

Sl. No.	Industry	Parameter	Standards
1	2	3	4

		Parameter	Standards
		pH	5.5–9.0
		Colour & odour	[39][All efforts should be made to remove colour and unpleasant odour as far as practicable]
		Suspended Solids	100
		[40][BOD (3 days at 27°C)]	
		—disposal into inland surface water/river/ stream	30 mg/l
		—** Disposal on land for irrigation	100 mg/l.]

[41][* * *]

16. Leather Tanneries — Concentration in the effluents not to exceed milligramme per litre (except for pH and per cent sodium)

	Inland Surface Waters	Public Sewers	Land for Irri- gation	Marine Coastal areas
	(a)	(b)	(c)	(d)
Suspended Solids	100	600	200	100
[42][BOD (3 days at 27°C)]	30	350	100	100
pH	6.0–9.0	6.0–9.0	6.0–9.0	6.0–9.0
Chlorides (as Cl)	1000	1000	600	—
Hexavalent Chromium (Cr + 6)	0.1	0.2	0.1	1.0
Total Chromium (as Cr)	2.0	2.0	2.0	2.0
Sulphides (as S)	2.0	5.0	—	5.0
Sodium per cent	—	60	60	—
Boron (as B)	2.0	2.0	2.0	—
Oil & Grease	10	20	10	20

[39] *Subs.* by S.O. 12 (E), dated 8 January 1990.
[40] *Subs.* by G.S.R. 176 (E), dated 2 April 1996.
[41] Notes *omitted* by G.S.R. 176 (E), dated 2 April 1996.
[42]*Subs.* by G.S.R. 176 (E), dated 2 April 1996.

Sl. No.	Industry	Parameter	Standards	
1	2	3	4	

17. Fertilizer Industry

Concentration in the effluents not to exceed milligramme per litre (except for pH)

Effluents—
Straight Nitrogenous Fertilizers, excluding the Calcium Ammonium Nitrate and Ammonium Nitrate Fertilizer

Parameter	Plants Commissioned 1 January 1982 onwards	Plants Commissioned prior to 1 January 1982
	(a)	(b)
pH	6.5–8.0	6.5–8.0
Ammonical Nitrogen	50	75
Total Kjeldahl Nitrogen	100	150
Free Ammonical Nitrogen	4	4
Nitrate Nitrogen	10	10
Cyanide as CN	0.2	0.2
Vanadium as V	0.2	0.2
Arsenic as As	0.2	0.2
Suspended Solids	100	100
Oil and Grease	10	10
*Hexavalent Chromium as Cr	0.1	0.1
* Total Chromium as Cr	2.0	2.0

* To be complied with at the outlet of Chromate removal unit.

Straight Nitrogenous Fertilizers, including Calcium Ammonium Nitrate and Ammonium nitrate Fertilizers

	Plants Commissioned 1 January 1982 onwards	Plants Commissioned prior to 1 January 1982

Sl. No.	Industry	Parameter	Standards	
1	2	3	4	
			(a)	(b)
		pH	6.5–8.0	6.5–8.0
		Ammonical Nitrogen	50	75
		Total Kjeldahl Nitrogen	100	150
		Free Ammonical Nitrogen	4	4
		Nitrate Nitrogen	20	20
		Cyanide as CN	0.2	0.2
		Vanadium as V	0.2	0.2
		Arsenic as As	0.2	0.2
		Suspended Solids	100	100
		Oil and Grease	10	10
		* Hexavalent Chromium as Cr	0.1	0.1
		* Total Chromium as Cr	2.0	2.0

* To be complied with at the outlet of Chromate removal unit.

	Complex Fertilizers, excluding Calcium Ammonium Nitrate, Ammonium Nitrate & Ammonium Nitrophosphate Fertilizers		Plants Commissioned 1 January 1982 onwards	Plants Commissioned prior to 1 January 1982
			(a)	(b)
		pH	6.5–8.0	6.5–8.0
		Ammonical Nitrogen	50	75
		Free Ammonical Nitrogen	4	4
		Total Kjeldahl Nitrogen	100	150
		Nitrate Nitrogen	10	10
		Cyanide as CN	0.2	0.2
		Vanadium as V	0.2	0.2

Sl. No.	Industry	Parameter	Standards	
1	2	3	4	

		Parameter		
		Arsenic as As	0.2	0.2
		Phosphate as P	5	5
		Oil and Grease	10	10
		Suspended Solids	100	100
		*Fluoride as F	10	10
		**Hexavalent Chromium as Cr	0.1	0.1
		**Total Chromium as Cr	2.0	2.0

Complex Fertilizers, including Calcium Ammonium Nitrate, Ammonium Nitrate & Ammonium Nitrophosphate Fertilizers

	Plants Commissioned 1 January 1982 onwards	Plants Commissioned prior to 1 January 1982
	(a)	(b)
pH	6.5–8.0	6.5–8.0
Ammonical Nitrogen	50	75
Free Ammonical Nitrogen	100	100
Nitrate Nitrogen	20	20
Cyanide as CN	0.2	0.2
Vanadium as V	0.2	0.2
Arsenic as As	0.2	0.2
Phosphate as P	5	5
Oil and Grease	10	10
Suspended Solids	100	100
*Fluoride as F	10	10
**Hexavalent Chromium as Cr	0.1	0.1
**Total Chromium as Cr	2.0	2.0

* To be complied with at the outlet of Fluoride removal unit. If the recipient system so demands, Fluoride as F shall be limited to 1.5 mg/l.

** To be complied with at the outlet of Chromate removal unit.

Sl. No.	Industry	Parameter	Standards
1	2	3	4
	Straight Phosphatic Fertilizers		
		pH	7.0–9.0
		Phosphate as P	5
		Oil and Grease	10
		Suspended Solids	100
		*Fluoride as F	10
		**Hexavalent Chromium as Cr	0.1
		**Total Chromium as Cr	2.0
	Emissions		
	—Phosphatic Fertilizers (Fluoride and	Phosphoric acid manufacturing unit	25 milligrammes per normal cubic metre as total Fluoride
	Particulate matter emission)	Granulation, mixing and grinding of rock Phosphate	150 milligramme per normal cubic metre of particulate matter
	—Urea (particulate matter emission)	Prilling Tower Commissioned prior to 1-1-1982	150 milligramme per normal cubic metre or 2 kilogramme per tonne of product
		Commissioned after 1-1-1982	50 milligramme per normal cubic metre or 0.5 kilogramme per tonne of product

* To be complied with at the outlet of Fluoride removal unit. If the recipient system so demands, Fluoride as F shall be limited to 1.5 mg/l.
** To be complied with at the outlet of Chromate removal unit.

18.	Aluminium	Particulate Matter Emissions:	
		—Calcination	250 milligramme per normal cubic metre of particulate matter
		—Smelting	150 milligramme per normal cubic metre of particulate matter
19.	Calcium Carbide	Particulate Matter Emission:	
		—Kiln	250 milligramme per normal cubic metre

Sl. No.	Industry	Parameter	Standards
1	2	3	4
		—Arc Furnace	150 milligramme per normal cubic metre
20.	Carbon Black	Particulate Matter Emission:	150 milligramme per normal cubic metre
21.	Copper, Lead and Zinc	Particulate Matter Emission in concentrator	150 milligramme per normal cubic metre
	Smelting	Emission of Oxides of sulphur in Smelter & Converter	Off-gases must be utilised for sulphuric acid manufacture. The limits of sulphur dioxide emission from stock shall not exceed 4 kilogramme per tonne of concentrated (one hundred per cent) acid produced
22.	Nitric acid (emission of oxides of nitrogen)	Emission of Oxides of Nitrogen	3 kilogramme of oxides of nitrogen per tonne of weak acid (before concentration) produced
23.	Sulphuric Acid (emission of Sulphur dioxide and acid mist)	Sulphur dioxide Emissions	4 kilogramme per tonne of concentrated (One hundred per cent) acid produced
		Acid Mist	50 milligramme per normal cubic metre
24.	Iron & Steel (Integrated)	Particulate Matter Emission	
		—Sintering Plant	150 milligramme per normal cubic metre
		—Steel making	
		—during normal operations	150 milligrammes per normal cubic metre
		—during oxygen lancing	400 milligramme per normal cubic metre
		—Rolling Mill	150 milligramme per normal cubic metre
		Carbon monoxide from coke oven	3 kilogramme per tonne of coke produced.]

Sl. No.	Industry	Parameter	Standards
1	2	3	4

43[25.	Thermal Power Plants	*Particulate Matter Emissions:	
		—generation capacity 210 MW or more	150 milligramme per normal cubic metre
		—generation capacity less than 210 MW	350 milligramme per normal cubic metre

* Depending upon the requirement of local situation, such as protected area, the State Pollution Control Boards and other implementing agencies under the Environment (Protection) Act, 1986, may prescribe a limit of 150 milligramme per normal cubic metre, irrespective of generation capacity of the plant.

26.	Natural Rubber industry		Concentrations in the effluents not to exceed milligramme per litre (except for pH)
	—Discharge into inland surface waters	Colour & Odour	Absent
		pH	6.0–9.0
		BOD	50
		COD	250
		Oil & Grease	10
		Sulphides	2
		Total Kjeldhal Nitrogen	100
		Dissolved phosphate (as P)	5
		Suspended solids	100
		Dissolved solids (inorganic)	2100
		Ammonical nitrogen (as N)	50
		Free ammonia (as NH$_3$)	5
	—Disposal on land for irrigation	Colour & Odour	Absent
		pH	6.0–8.0
		BOD	100
		COD	250

43 *Ins.* by S.O. 8 (E), dated 3 January 1989. Entries 25 and 26 were inserted by this notification.

Sl. No.	Industry	Parameter	Standards
1	2	3	4
		Oil & Grease	10
		Suspended solids	200
		Dissolved solids	2100]
44[27.	All types of Asbestos manufacturing units: (including all processes involving the use of Asbestos)	Emissions —Pure asbestos material —Total dust	4 Fibre*/cc 2mg/m^3 (normal)

* Fibre of length more than 5 micrometre and diametre less than 3 micrometre with an aspect ratio of 3 or more.

28.	Chlor Alkali (Caustic soda)	Emissions	Concentrations in mg/m^2 (normal)
	(a) Mercury Cell	Mercury (from hydro-gen gasholder stack)	0.2
	(b) All processes	Chlorine (from hypo tower)	15.0
	(c) All processes	Hydrochloric acid vapour and mist (from (hydrochloric acid plant)	35.0
29.	Large pulp and paper	Emissions	Concentration in mg/m^3 (normal)
		Particulate matter	250**
		H$_2$S	10

** This standard of 250 mg/m^3 (normal) shall apply only for a period of 3 years with effect from the date on which the Environment (Protection) Second Amendment Rules, 1989, came into force. After three years the standard to be applicable in 15 mg/m^3 (normal).

30.	Integrated Iron and Steel Plants:		
		I. Emissions	
	(a) Coke oven	Particulate matter	50
	(b) Refractory material plant	Particulate matter	150

44 *Ins.* by G.S.R. 913 (E), dated 24 October 1989. Entries 27 to 31 were inserted by this notification.

Sl. No.	Industry	Parameter	Standards
1	2	3	4

		II. Effluents	Concentration in mg/litre (except for pH)
	(a) Coke oven By product plant:	pH	6.0–8.5
		Suspended solids	100
		Phenol	1.0
		Cyanide	0.2
		[45][BOD (3 days at 27°C)]	30
		COD	250
		Ammonical nitrogen	50
		Oil and Grease	10
	(b) Other plants such as sintering plant, blast furnace, steel melting and rolling mill:	pH	6.0–9.0
		Suspended solids	100
		Oil and Grease	10

Sl. No.	Industry	Parameter	Standards (mg/Nm^3)
1	2	3	4

31.	Reheating (Reverberatory) Furnaces: Capacity: All sizes	Emissions	Concentration in mg/m^3 (normal)
	Sensitive area	Particulate matter	150
	Other area	Particulate matter	450]
[46][32.	Foundries: (a) Cupola Capacity (melting rate):	Emissions	
	Less than 3	Particulate Matter	450

[45] *Subs.* by G.S.R. 176 (E), dated 2 April 1996.
[46] *Ins.* by G.S.R. 742 (E), dated 30 August 1990. Entries 32 to 47 were inserted by this notification.

Sl. No.	Industry	Parameter	Standards (mg/Nm^3)
1	2	3	4

	MT/hr.		
	3 MT/hr. and above	Particulate matter	150

Note: In respect of arc furnaces and induction furnaces, provision has to be made for collecting the fumes before discharging the emissions through the stack.

	(b) Arc furnaces Capacity: All sizes	Particulate Matter	150
	(c) Induction furnaces Capacity: All sizes	Particulate Matter	150

Note: In respect of Arc furnaces and induction furnaces, provision has to be made for collecting the fumes before discharging the emissions through the stack.

33.	Thermal Power Plants	Stack height/limits *Power generation capacity:*	
		—500 MW and above	275
		—200 MW/210 MW and above to less than 500 MW	220
		—Less than 200 MW/ 210 MW	$H=14(Q)^{0.3}$ where Q is emission rate of SO_2 in kg/hr. and H is stack height in metres
		Steam generating capacity:	
		—Less than 2 ton/hr.	$2^1/_2$ times the neighbouring building height or 9 metres (whichever is more)
		—More than 2 ton/hr. to 5 ton/hr.	12
		—More than 5 ton/hr. to 10 ton/hr.	15
		—More than 10 ton/hr.	18
		—More than 15 ton/hr. to 20 ton/hr.	15
		—More than 20 ton/hr. to 25 ton/hr.	24

Sl. No.	Industry	Parameter	Standards (mg/Nm^3)
1	2	3	4

		—More than 25 ton/hr. to 30 ton/hr.	27
		—More than 30 ton/hr.	30 or using formula H=14(Q)$^{0.3}$ (whichever is more) where Q is emission rate of SO$_2$, in kg/hr. and H is stack height in meters.
34.	Small boilers	Emissions* Particulate Matter	
	Capacity of boiler		
		—Less than 2 ton/hr.	1600
		—2 to 15 ton/hr.	1200
		—More than 15 ton/hr.	150

* All emissions normalized to 12 per cent carbon dixode

35.	Oil Refineries (Sulphur dioxide)	Emissions	
		—Distillation (Atmospheric plus vacuum)	0.25 kg/MT of feed**
		—Catalytic cracker	2.5 kg/MT of feed
		—Sulphur recovery unit	120 kg/MT of sulphur in the feed

**Feed indicates the feed for that part of the process under consideration only.

36.	Aluminium Plants (a) Alumina plant:	Emissions	
	(i) Raw material handling	Primary and secondary crusher Particulate Matter	150
	(ii) Precipitation area	Particulate Matter	250
		Carbon monoxide	1% max.
	–Calcination	Stack height	H = 14(Q)$^{0.3}$ where Q is emission rate of SO$_2$ in kg/hr and H is stack height in metres

Sl. No.	Industry	Parameter	Standards (mg/Nm^3)
1	2	3	4

	(b) Smelter point		
	(i) Green anode shop	Particulate Matter	150
	(ii) Anode bake oven	Particulate Matter	150
		Total flouride (F)	0.3 kg/MT of Aluminium
	(iii) Potroom	Particulate Matter	150
		Total flouride (F)	
		VSS	4.7 kg/MT of Aluminium produced
		HSS	6.0 kg/MT of Aluminium produced
		PBSW	2.5 kg/MT of Aluminium produced
		PBCW	1.0 kg/MT of Aluminium produced
		Stack height	$H = 14(Q)^{0.3}$ where Q is emission rate of SO$_2$ in kg/hr. and H is stack height in metres

Note: VSS = Vertical stud soderberg
HSS = Horizontal stud soderberg
PBSW = Prebacked side worked
PBCW = Prebacked centre worked

37.	Stone crushing unit	Suspended Particulate Matter (SPM)	The standards consist of two parts: (i) *Implementation of the following pollution control measures:* (a) Dust containment cum suppression system for the equipment. (b) Construction of wind breaking walls. (c) Construction of the metalled roads within the premises. (d) Regular cleaning and wetting of the ground within the premises.

Sl. No.	Industry	Parameter	Standards (mg/Nm^3)
1	2	3	4
			(e) Growing of a green belt along the periphery.
			(ii) *Quantitative standard for the SPM:* The Suspended Particulate Matter contribution value at a distance of 40 metres from a controlled isolated as well as from a unit located in a cluster should be less than 600 mg/Nm^3. The measurements are to be conducted at least twice a month for all the 12 months in a year.

Sl. No.	Industry	Parameter	Standards (concentrations in mg/l except for pH, temperature, specific pesticides and Bio-assay test)
1	2	3	4
38.	Petrochemicals (Basic and inter-mediates)	Effluents	
		pH	6.5–8.5
		*[47][(BOD (3 days at 27°C)]	50
		**Phenol	5
		Sulphide (as S)	2
		COD	250
		Cyanide (as CN)	0.2
		***Fluoride (as F)	15
		Total suspended solids	1000
		Hexavalent Chromium (as CR)	0.1
		****Total Chromium (as CR)	2.0

[47] *Subs.* by G.S.R. 176 (E), dated 2 April 1996.

Sl. No.	Industry	Parameter	Standards (concentrations in mg/l except for pH, temperature, specific pesticides and Bio-assay test)
1	2	3	4

* State Boards may prescribe the BOD value of 30 mg/l if the recipient system so demands.

** The limit for phenol shall be conformed to at the outlet of effluent treatment of phenol plant. However, at the final disposal point, the limit shall be less than 1mg/l.

*** The limit for fluoride shall be conformed to at the outlet of fluoride removal unit. However, at the disposal point, fluoride concentration shall be lower than 5 mg/l.

****The limits for total and hexavalent chromium shall be conformed to at the outlet of the chromate removal unit. This implies that in the final treated effluent, total and hexavalent chromium shall be lower than prescribed herein.

Sl. No.	Industry	Parameter	Standards
39.	Pharmaceutical manufacturing and formation industry	Effluents	
		1. pH	5.5–9.0
		2. Oil and Grease	10
		3. Total suspended solids solids	100
		4. [48][BOD (3 days at 27°C)]	30
		5. Bio-assay test	90% survival of fish after 96 hrs. in 100% effluent
		6. Mercury	0.01
		7. Arsenic	0.20
		8. Chromium (Hexavalent)	0.10
		9. Lead	0.10
		10. Cyanide	0.10
		11. Phenolics (as C_6H_5OH)	1.00
		12. Sulphides (as S)	2.00
		13. Phosphates (as P)	5.00

[48] *Ibid.*

Sl. No.	Industry	Parameter	Standards (concentrations in mg/l except for pH, temperature, specific pesticides and Bio-assay test)
1	2	3	4

Notes:

1. Parameters listed as 1 to 13 are compulsory for formulators. However, the remaining parameters (6 to 13) will be optional for others.
2. State Board may prescribe limit for chemical oxygen demand (COD) correlated with BOD limit.
3. State Board may prescribe limit for total dissolved solids depending upon uses of recipient water body.
4. Limits should be complied with at the terminal of the treatment until before letting out of the factory boundary limits.
5. For the compliance of limits, analysis should be done in the composite sample collected every hour for a period of 8 hours.

40.	Pesticide Manu-facturing and For-mulation industry	Effluents	
		1. Temperature	Shall not exceed 5°C above the receiving water temperature
		2. pH	6.5–8.5
		3. Oil and Grease	10
		4. [49][(BOD (3 days at 27°C)]	30
		5. Total suspended solids	100
		6. Bio-assay test	90% survival of fish after 96 hours in 100 per cent effluent
		7. (a) Specific pesticides:	
		Benzene Hexachloride	10
		Carboryl	10
		DDT	10
		Endosulfan	10
		Diamethoate	450
		Fenitrothion	10

[49] *Ibid.*

Sl. No.	Industry	Parameter	Standards (concentrations in mg/l except for pH, temperature, specific pesticides and Bio-assay test)
1	2	3	4
		Malathion	10
		Phorate	10
		Methyl parathion	10
		Phenthoate	10
		Pyrethrums	10
		Copper oxychloride	9600
		Copper sulphate	50
		Ziram	1000
		Sulphur	30
		Paraquat	2300
		Proponil	7300
		Nitrogen	780
		(b) Heavy metals:	
		Copper	1.00
		Manganese	1.00
		Zinc	1.00
		Mercury	0.01
		Tin	0.10
		Any other metal like Nickel, etc.	Shall not exceed 5 times the drinking water standards of BIS
		(c) Organics:	
		Phenol and phenolic compounds as C_6H_5OH	1.0

Notes:

1. Limits should be complied with at the end of the treatment plant before any dilution.
2. Bio-assay test should be carried out with available species of fish in receiving water.
3. State Board may prescribe limits of total dissolved solids (TDS) sulphates and chlorides depending on the uses of recipient water body.
4. State Board may prescribe COD limit correlated with BOD limit.
5. Pesticides are known to have metabolites and isomers. If they are found in significant concentration, standards may be prescribed for those in the list by Central or State Board.
6. Industries are required to analyse pesticides in waste by advanced analytical method such a GLC/HPLC.

Sl. No.	Industry	Parameter	Standards (concentrations in mg/l except for pH, temperature, specific pesticides and Bio-assay test)
1	2	3	4

7. All the the parameters will be compulsory for formulators, for others, the 7th will be optional.

41.	Tannery (after primary treatment Disposal: Channel/Conduit Carrying waste waters to secondary treatment plants Type of tanneries	Effluents	
	—Chrome tanneries/ combined chrome and vegetable tanneries	pH SS Chromium concentration after treatment in the chrome waste water stream	6.5–9.0 Not to exceed 600 45
	—Vegetable tanneries	pH SS	6.5–9.0 Not to exceed 600

Note:
The above standards will apply to those tannery units which have made full contribution to a Common Effluent Treatment Plant (CETP) comprising secondary treatment. Those who have not contributed will be governed by earlier Notification No. S.O. 64(E), dated January 18, 1988.

42.	Paint industry (Waste-water discharge)	Effluents pH Suspended Solids [50][BOD (3 days at 27°C)] Phenolics as C_6H_5OH Oil and Grease Bio-assay test Lead as Pb	6.0–8.5 100 50 1.0 10.0 90 per cent survival in 96 hours 0.1

[50] Subs. by G.S.R. 176 (E), dated 2 April 1996.

Sl. No.	Industry	Parameter	Standards (concentrations in mg/l except for pH, temperature, specific pesticides and Bio-assay test)
1	2	3	4
		Chromium as Cr Hexavalent	0.1
		Total	2.0
		Copper as Cu	2.0
		Nickel as Ni	2.0
		Zinc as Zn	5.0
		Total heavy metals	7.0
43.	Inorganic chemical industry (Waste-water discharge) Part 1 (metal compounds of Chromium, Manganese, Nickel, Copper, Zinc, Cadmium, Lead and Mercury)	Effluents pH	6.0–8.5
		Chromium as Cr Hexavalent	0.1
		Total	2.0
		Manganese as Mn	2.0
		Nickel as Ni	2.0
		Copper as Cu	2.0
		Zinc as Zn	5.0
		Cadmium as Cd	0.2
		Lead as Pb	0.1
		Mercury as Hg	0.01
		Cyanide as CN	0.2
		Oil and Grease	10.0
		Suspended solids	30.0

In addition to the above, total heavy metals are to be limited to 7 mg/l.

44.	Bullion Refining (Waste-water discharge)	Effluents pH	6.5–8.5
		Cyanide as CN	0.2
		Sulphide as S	0.2
		Nitrate as N	10.0
		Free Cl$_2$ and Cl	1.0
		Zinc as Zn	5.0
		Copper as Cu	2.0
		Nickel as Ni	2.0
		Arsenic as As	0.1
		Cadmium as Cd	0.2
		Oil and Grease	10.0
		Suspended solids	100

Sl. No.	Industry	Parameter	Standards (concentrations in mg/l except for pH, temperature, specific pesticides and Bio-assay test)
1	2	3	4
45.	Dye and Dye Intermediate Industry (Waste-water discharge)	Effluents	
		pH	6.0–8.5
		Colour, Hazen Unit	400.0
		Suspended solids	100.0
		[51][BOD (3 days at 27°C)]	100.0
		Oil and Grease	10.0
		Phenolic as C_6H_5OH	1.0
		Cadmium as Cd	0.2
		Copper as Cu	2.0
		Manganese as Mn	2.0
		Lead as Pb	0.1
		Mercury as Hg	0.01
		Nickel as Ni	2.0
		Zinc as Zn	5.0
		Chromium as Cr Hexavalent	0.1
		Total	2.0
		Bio-assay test	90% survival in 96 hours

Sl. No.	Company	Standards, dB (A)
1	2	3
46.	Noise limits for automobiles (free field at one metre in dB(A) at the manufacturing stage) to be achieved by the year 1992	
	(a) Motorcycles, scooters and three wheelers	80
	(b) Passenger cars	82
	(c) Passenger or commercial vehicles up to 4 MT	85
	(d) Passenger or commercial vehicles above 4 MT and up to 12 MT	89

[51] *Ibid.*

Sl. No.	Company	Standards, dB (A)
1	2	3
	(e) Passenger or commercial vehicles exceeding 12 MT	91
47.	Domestic appliances and construction equipments at the manufacturing state to be achieved by the year 1993	
	(a) Window air-conditioners of 1 ton to 1.5 ton	68
	(b) Air-coolers	60
	(c) Refrigerators	46
	(d) Diesel generators for domestic purposes	85–90
	(e) Compactors (rollers) front loaders, concrete mixers, cranes (movable) vibrators and saws	75]

Sl. No.	Industry	Parameter	Standards
1	2	3	4
[52][48.	Glass Industry A. Sodalime and Borosilicate and other special glass (other than Lead) (a) Furnace: Capacity	Emissions	
(i)	Up to a product draw capacity of 60 Mt/Day	Particulate matter	20 kg/hr.
(ii)	Product draw capacity more than 60 Mt/Day	Particulate matter	0.8 kg/Mt. of product drawn
(iii)	For all capacities	Stack height	$H=14\,(Q)^{0.3}$ where Q is the emission rate of SO_2 in Kg./hr. and H is stack height in metres
	(b) Implemen-	Total fluorides	5.0 mg/NM^3

[52] *Ins.* by G.S.R. 93 (E) dated 21 Feburary 1991. Entries 48 to 55 were inserted by this notification.

Sl. No.	Industry	Parameter	Standards
1	2	3	4
	tation of the following measures for fugitive emission control from other sections:	NOx	Use of low NOx burners in new plants

(i) Raw material should be transported in leak proof containers.
(ii) Cullet preparation should be dust-free using water spraying.
(iii) Batch preparation section should be covered.

B. Lead glass
(a) Furnace:

	All capacities	Particulate matter	50 mg/NM^3
		Lead	20 mg/NM^3

(b) Implementaiton of the following measures for fugitive emission control from other sections.

(i) Batch mixing, proportioning sections and transfer points should be covered and it should be connected to control equipments to meet following standards:

		Particulate matter	50 mg/NM^3
		Lead	20 mg/NM^3

(ii) Minimum stack height should be 30 metre in lead glass units.
(c) Pot Furnace
at Firozabad

	Furnace:	Particulate matter	1200 mg/NM^3

Note:

Depending upon local environmental conditions, State/Central Pollution Control Board can prescribe more stringent standards than those prescribed above.

	Glass Industry (For all categories)	Effluents: pH	6.5–8.5
		Total suspended solids	100 mg/l
		Oil and Grease	10 mg/l
49.	Lime Kiln Capacity:–	Stack Height	
	Up to 5T/Day	Stack Height	A hood should be provided with a stack of 30 metre height from ground level (including kiln height).

Sl. No.	Industry	Parameter	Standards
1	2	3	4
	Above 5T/Day	Stack Height	$H = 14\ (Q)^{0.3}$ where Q is emission rate of SO_2 in Kg/hr and H = Stack height in metres.
	More than 5T/ Day and up to 40T/Day	Particulate Matter	500 mg/NM^3
	Above 40T/Day	Particulate matter	150 mg/NM^3
50.	*Slaughter House, Meat and Sea Food Industry:	Effluents	
A.	Slaughter house		
	(a) Above 70 TLWK	[53][BOD (3 days at 27°C)]	100
		Suspended solids	100
		Oil and Grease	10
	(b) 70 TLWK and below	[53][BOD (3 days at 27°C)]	500
B.	Meat processing		
	(a) Frozen Meat	[53][BOD (3 days at 27°C)]	30
		Suspended solids	30
		Oil and Grease	10
	(b) Raw Meat from own slaughter house	[53][BOD (3 days at 27°C)]	50
		Suspended solids	50
		Oil and Grease	10
	(c) Raw meat from other sources		Disposal *via* screen and septic tank
C.	Sea Food Industry	[53][BOD (3 days at 27°C)]	30
		Suspended solids	50
		Oil and Grease	10

Note:

(i) TLWK—Total Live Weight Killed. (ii) In case of disposal into municipal sewer where sewage is treated the industries shall install screen and oil and grease separation units. (iii) The industries having slaughter house along with meat processing units will be considered in meat processing category as far as standards are concerned.

[53] *Subs.* by G.S.R. 176 (E), dated 2 April 1996.

Sl. No.	Industry	Parameter	Standards
1	2	3	4

*The emission standards from Boiler House shall confrom to the standards already prescribed under E(P) Act, 1986, *vide* notificaton No. GSR 742 (E), dated 30–08–1990.

51.	Food and Fruit Processing Industry	Effluents	Concentration not to exceed mg/l except pH	Quantum gm/MT of product

Category:

A. Soft Drinks

   (a) Fruit based syn-
      thetic (More than

	0.4 MT/Day)	pH	6.5–8.5	—
	Bottles and	Suspended solids	100	
	tetrapack	Oil and Grease	10	
		[54][BOD (3 days at 27°C)]	30	

   (b) Synthetic   Disposal *via*
      (Less than   septic tank   —
      0.4 MT/Day)

B. Fruit and

	vegetables	pH	6.5–8.5	
	(a) Above 0.4	Suspended solids	50	
	MT/Day	Oil and Grease	10	
		[54][BOD (3 days at 27°C)]	30	

   (b) 0.1–0.4 MT/   Disposal *via*
      Day (10 MT/Yr)   Septic tank   —

C. Bakery

   (a) Bread & bread
      and biscuit

   (i) Continuous

	process (more	pH	6.5–8.5	
	than 20T/Day)	[54][BOD (3 days at 27°C)]	200	25

   (ii) Non-continu-   Disposal *via*
      ous process   Septic tank
      (less than 20
      MT/Day)

[54] *Ibid.*

Sl. No.	Industry	Parameter	Standards
1	2	3	4

	(b) Biscuit Production		
	(i) 10 T/Day and above	pH	6.5–8.5
		[54][BOD (3 days at 27°C)]	300 35
	(ii) Below 10 T/ Day		Disposal *via* septic tank
D.	Confectioneries	Effluents	
	(a) 4 T/Day and above	pH	6.5–8.5
		Suspended solids	50
		Oil and Grease	10
		[54][BOD (3 days at 27°C)]	30
	(b) Below 4 T/Day		Disposal *via* — septic tank

Note:

To ascertain the category of 'unit fails' the average of daily production and waste water discharge for the preceding 30 operating days from the date of sampling shall be considered.

The emission from the boiler house shall conform to the standards already prescribed under the Environment (Protection) Act, 1986, *vide* Notification No. GSR 742 (E), dated 30–08–1990.

52.	* Jute Processing Industry:	Effluents	Concentration in mg/l except pH and water consumption
		pH	5.5–9.0
		[55][BOD (3 days at 27°C)]	30
		Suspended solids	100
		Oil and Grease	10
		Water consumption	1.60 Cum/Ton of product produced.

Note:

1. Water consumption for the jute processing industry will be 1.5 Cum/ton of product from January, 1992.

2. At present no limit for colour is given for liquid effluent. However, as far as possible, colour should be removed.

[55] *Ibid.*

Sl. No.	Industry	Parameter	Standards
1	2	3	4

* Stack emissions from boiler house shall conform to the standards already prescribed under Environment (Protection) Act, 1986, *vide* Notification No. GSR 742 (E), dated 30–8–90.

53.	Large Pulp and Paper/News Print/ Rayon Grade Plants of Capacity Above 24,000 mt/annum		
		pH	7.0–8.5
		[56][BOD (3 days at 27°C)]	30
		COD	350
		Suspended solids	50
		TOCL	2.0 kg/Ton of product
		Flow (Total waste water discharge	
		**(i) Large pulp and paper	200 Cum/ton of paper produced
		(ii) Large rayon grade/ News print	150 Cum/Ton of paper produced

Note:

*The Standards for Total Organic Chloride (TOCL) will be applicable from January 1992.

** The Standards with respect to total waste water discharge for the large pulp and paper mills to be established from 1992, will meet standards of 100 Cum/ Ton of paper produced.

54.	Small Pulp and Paper, Plant of Capacity Upto 24,000 MT/Annum: Category:		
		Effluent	
A.	*Agro-based	Total waste-water Discharge	2000 Cum/Ton of paper produced
B.	**Waste-paper based	– do –	75 Cum/Ton of paper produced

[56] *Subs.* by G.S.R. 176 (E), dated 2 April 1996.

Sl. No.	Industry	Parameter	Standards
1	2	3	4

Note:

* The agro-based mills to be established from January, 1992 will meet the standards of 150 Cum/Ton of paper produced.

** The waste-paper mills to be established from January, 1992 will meet the standards of 50 Cum/Ton of paper produced.

55.	Common Effluent Treatment Plants: A. Primary Treatment	Effluents (inlet effluent quality for CETP)	(Concentration in mg/l)
		pH	5.5–9.0
		Temperature °C	45
		Oil and Grease	20
		Phenolic compounds (as C_6H_5OH)	5.0
		Ammonical Nitrogen (as N)	50
		Cyanide (as CN)	2.0
		Chromium (hexavalent) (as Cr+6)	2.0
		Chromium (total) (as Cr)	2.0
		Copper (as Cu)	3.0
		Lead (as Pb)	1.0
		Nickel (as Ni)	3.0
		Zinc (as Zn)	15
		Arsenic (as As)	0.2
		Mercury (as Hg)	0.01
		Cadmium (as Cd)	0.1
		Selenium (Se)	0.05
		Fluoride (as F)	15
		Boron (as B)	2.0
		Radioactive Materials	
		Alpha emitters, Hc/mL	10.7
		Beta emitters, Hc/mL	10.8

Note:

1. These standards apply to the small scale industries, *i.e.*, total discharge up to 25 KL/Day.

2. For each CETP and its constituent units, the State Board will prescribe standards as per the local needs and conditions, these can be more stringent than those prescribed above. However, in case of clusters of units, the State Board with the concurrence of CPCB in writing, may prescribe suitable limits.

Sl. No.	Industry	Parameter	Standards		
1	2	3	4		
			Into inland surface waters	On land for Irrigation	Into Marine Coastal areas
			(a)	(b)	(c)
B.	Treated Effluent	Quality of common effluent treatment plant	Concentration in mg/l except pH and Temperature		
		pH	5.5–9.0	5.5–9.0	5.5–9.0
		[57][BOD (3 days at 27°C)]	30	100	100
		Oil and Grease	10	10	20
		Temperature	Shall not exceed 40°C in any section of the stream within 15 metres downstream from the effluent outlet	—	45°C at the point of discharge
		Suspended solids	100	200	(a) For process waste waters 100 (b) For cooling water effluents 10 per cent above total suspended matter of influent cooling water
		Dissolved solids (Inorganic)	2100	2100	—
		Total residual chlorine	1.0	—	1.0
		Ammonical Nitrogen (as N)	50	—	50
		Total Kjeldahl Nitrogen (as N)	100	—	100
		Chemical Oxygen Demand	250	—	250

[57] *Ibid.*

Sl. No.	Industry	Parameter	Standards		
1	2	3	4		
		Arsenic (as As)	0.2	0.2	0.2
		Mercury (as Hg)	0.01	—	0.01
		Lead (as Pb)	0.1	—	0.1
		Cadmium (as Cd)	1.0	—	2.0
		Total Chromium (as Cr)	2.0	—	2.0
		Copper (as Cu)	3.0	—	3.0
		Zinc (as Zn)	5.0	—	15
		Selenium (as Se)	0.05	—	0.05
		Nickel (as Ni)	3.0	—	5.0
		Boron (as B)	2.0	2.0	—
		Percent Sodium	—	60	—
		Cyanide (as CN)	0.2	0.2	0.2
		Chloride (as Cl)	1000	600	—
		Fluoride (as F)	2.0	—	15
		Sulphate (as SO_4)	1000	1000	—
		Sulphide (as S)	2.8	—	5.0
		Pesticides	Absent	Absent	Absent
		Phenolic Compounds (as C_6H_5OH)	1.0	—	5.0

Note:

All efforts should be made to remove colour and unpleasant odour as far as possible.]

58[56.	Diary	Effluents	Concentration in mg/l, except pH	Quantum per product processed
		pH	6.5–8.5	—
		* 59[BOD (3 days at 27°C)]	100	—
		**Suspended solids	150	—
		Oil and Grease	10	—
		Waste water generation	—	3m³/Kl of milk

Note:

* BOD may be made stringent up to 30 mg/l if the recipient fresh water body is a source for drinking water supply. BOD shall be up to 350 mg/l for the chilling plant

58 *Ins.* by G.S.R. 475 (E), dated 5 May 1992. Entries 56 to 61 were inserted by this notification.
59 *Subs.* by G.S.R. 176 (E), dated 2 April 1996.

Sl. No.	Industry	Parameter	Standards
1	2	3	4

effluent for applying on land provided the land is designed and operated as a secondary treatment system with suitable monitoring facilities. The drainage water from the land after secondary treatment has to satisfy a limit of 30 mg/l of BOD and 10 mg/l of nitrate expressed as 'N'. The net addition to the groundwater quality should not be more than 3 mg/l of BOD and 3 mg/l of nitrate expressed as 'N'. This limit for applying on land is allowed subject to the availability of adequate land for discharge under the control of the industry, BOD value is relaxable up to 350 mg/l, provided the waste water is discharged into a town sewer leading to secondary treatment of the sewage.

** Suspended solids limit is relaxable upto 450 mg/l, provided waste water is discharged into a town sewer leading to secondary treatment of the sewage.

57.	Tanneries	Effluents	Concentration in mg/l, except pH	Quantum per raw hide processed
		pH	6.5–9.0	
		*[60][BOD (3 days at 27°C)]	100	
		Suspended solids	100	—
		Sulphides (as S)	1	—
		Total Chromium (as Cr)	2	—
		Oil and Grease	10	—
		Waste water generation	—	28m³/T

Note:

* For effluent discharge into inland surface waters BOD limit shall be made stricter to 30 mg/l by the concerned State Pollution Control Board

****58.	Natural Rubber Rubber Processing industry	Centrifuging and creaming units		Crape and crumb units	
		For disposal into inland surface water	For disposal on land for irrigation	For disposal into inland surface water	For disposal on and for irrigation
		(a)	(b)	(a)	(b)
		(Concentration in mg/l, except pH and quantum of waste generation)		(Concentration mg/l, except pH and quantum of waste water generation)	

[60] *Ibid.*

Sl. No.	Industry	Parameter		Standards		
1	2	3		4		
	pH	6–8	6–8	6–8	6–8	
	Total Kjeldahl Nitrogen (as N)	200 (100*)	***	50	***	
	Amonical Nitrogen (as N)	100 (50*)	***	25	***	
	[61][BOD (3 days at 27°C)]	50	100	30	100	
	COD	250	***	250	***	
	Oil and Grease	10	20	10	20	
	Sulphide (as S)	2	***	2	***	
	TDS	2100	NP**	2100	NP**	
	SS	100	200	100	200	
	Quantum of waste water generation	5 lit/kg of product processed	8 lit/kg of product processed	40 lit/kg product processed	40 lit/kg of product processed	

* To be achieved in three years.

** Not prescribed in case effluent is used for rubber plantation of their own, in other cases suitable limit, as necessary may be prescribed by the State Board.

*** Not specified.

**** These standards supersede the standards notified at serial No. 26 vide Notification No. S.O. 8(E), dated 3 January 1989.

59.	Bagasse-fired fired boilers	Emissions	(Concentration in mg/l)
	(a) Step grate	Particulate matter	250
	(b) Horse shoe/ pulsating grate	Particulate matter	500 (12% CO_2)
	(c)Spreader stroker	Particulate matter	800 (12% CO_2)

Note: In the case of horse shoe and spreader stroker boilers, if more than one boiler is attached to a single stack, the standard shall be fixed based on added capacity of all the boilers connected with the stack.

60.	Man-made fibre industry (semi-synthetic)	Effluents	(Concentrate in mg/l except for pH)
		pH	5.5–9.0
		Suspended solids	100
		[62][BOD (3 days at 27°C)]	30
		Zinc (as Zn)	1

[61] *Ibid.*
[62] *Ibid.*

Sl. No.	Industry	Parameter	Standards
1	2	3	4
61. A.	Ceramic industry Kilns	Emissions	(Concentration in mg/NM^3)
	(a) Tunnel, Top Hat, Chamber	Particulate matter	150
		Fluoride	10
		Chloride	100
		Sulphur dioxide	**
	(b) Down-draft	Particulate matter	1200
		Fluoride	10
		Chloride	100
		Sulphur dioxide	**
	(c) Shuttle	Particulate matter	150
		Fluoride	10
		Chloride	100
		Sulphur dioxide	**
	(d) Vertical shaft kiln	Particulate matter	250
		Fluoride	10
		Sulphur dioxide	**
	(e) Tank furnace	Particulate matter	150
		Fluoride	10
		Sulphur dioxide	**
B.	Raw material handling, processing and operations		
	(a) Dry raw materials handling and processing operations	Particulate matter	150
	(b) Basic raw materials and processing operations	Particulate matter	*
	(c) Other sources of air pollution generation	Particulate matter	*
C.	Automatic spray unit		
	(a) Dryers		
	(i) Fuel fired dryers	Particulate matter	150

Sl. No.	Industry	Parameter	Standards
1	2	3	4
	(ii) For heat re-covery dryers	Particulate matter	*
	(b) Mechanical finishing operation	Particulate matter	*
	(c) Lime/plaster of paris manufacture Capacity		
	Up to 5T/day	Stack height – do –	A Hood should be provided with a stack of 30 metre height from ground level (including kiln height)
	Above 5T/day	– do –	$H = 14(Q)^{0.3}$ Where Q is emission rate of SO_2 in kg/hr and H is Stack height in metres
	More than 5T/day and upto 40T/day	Particulate matter – do –	500 mg/NM^3 150 mg/NM^3

Note: Oxygen reference level for particulate matter concentration for kilns mentioned at A(c) is 18% and for those at A(b), A(d) and A(e) is 8%.

* All possible preventive measures should be taken to control pollution as far as practicable.

** The standard for sulphur dioxide in terms of stack height limits for kilns with various capacities of coal consumption shall be as indicated below:

Coal consumed per day	Stack height
Less than 8.5 MT	9 m
More than 8.5 to 21 MT	12 m
More than 21 to 42 MT	15 m
More than 42 to 64 MT	18 m
More than 64 to 104 MT	21 m
More than 104 to 105 MT	24 m
More than 105 to 126 MT	27 m
More than 126 MT	30 m or using formula $H=14 (Qg)^{0.3}$ (whichever is more)

Sl. No.	Industry	Parameter	Standards
1	2	3	4

Note: In this notification, H-Physical height of the stack, Qg-Emission of sulphur dioxide in kg/hr., MT-Metric tonnes and m-metres.]

[63][62. Viscose-Filament Yarn (sub-sector of man-made fibre semi-synthetic industry)

Effluents — (Concentration in mg/l except for pH)

pH — 5.5–9.0
Suspended Solids — 100
[64][BOD (3 days at 27°C)] — 30
Zinc (as Zn) — 5]

[65][63. Starch Industry (Maize products)

Effluents — Concentration not to exceed mg/l (except pH and waste water discharge)

pH — 6.5–8.5
BOD (3 days at 27°C) — 100
Suspended solids — 150
Waste water discharge — 8m³/tonne of maize processed

Notes: The prescribed limits for BOD and suspended solids shall be made more stringent or less stringent depending upon the conditions and local requirements as mentioned below:

(i) BOD shall be made stringent upto 30mg/l if the recipient fresh water body is a source for drinking water supply.

(ii) BOD shall be allowed upto 350 mg/l for applying on land, provided the land is designed and operated as a secondary treatment system with the requisite monitoring facilities. The drainage water from the land after secondary treatment has to satisfy a limit of 30 mg/l of BOD and 10 mg/l of nitrate expressed as 'N'. The net addition to ground water quality should not be more than

[63] Ins. by G.S.R. 80 (E), dated 31 December 1993. Entry 62 was inserted by this notification.
[64] Subs. by G.S.R. 176 (E), dated 2 April 1996.
[65] Ins. by G.S.R. 176 (E), dated 2 April 1996. Entries 63 to 78 were inserted by this notification.

Sl. No.	Industry	Parameter	Standards
1	2	3	4

3 mg/l of BOD and 10 mg/l of nitrate expressed as 'N'.

(iii) BOD shall be allowed upto 350 mg/l for discharge into a town sewer, if such sewer leads to a secondary biological treatment system.

(iv) Suspended solids shall be allowed upto 450 mg/l for discharge into a town sewer, if such sewer leads to a secondary biological system.

(v) In the event of bulking of sludge, the industry shall immediately apprise the respective State Pollution Control Board.

64.	Beehive hard coke oven	Emissions:	
	(i) New unit	Particulate matter (corrected to 6% CO_2)	150 mg/Nm^3
	(ii) Existing units	Hydrocarbons	25 ppm
		Particulate matter (corrected to 6% CO_2)	350 mg/Nm^3

Note: For control of emissions and proper dispensation of pollutants the following guidelines shall be followed:

(i) Units set up after the publication of this notification shall be treated as new units.

(ii) A minimum stack height of 20 metres shall be provided by each unit.

(iii) Emissions from coke ovens shall be channelised through a tunnel and finally emitted through a stack. Damper adjustment techniques shall be used to have optimum heat utilisation and also to control the emisson of unburnt carbon particles and combustible flue gases.

(iv) Wet scrubbing system or waste heat utilisation for power generation or byproduct recovery systems should be installed preferably to achieve the prescribed standards.

(v) After four years from the date of this notification, all the existing units shall comply with the standards prescribed for the new units.

65.	Briquette Industry (Coal)	Emissions:	
	(a) Units having capacity less than 10 tonnes	Particulate matter (corrected to 6% CO_2)	350 mg/Nm^3

Sl. No.	Industry	Parameter	Standards
1	2	3	4

| | (b) Units having capacity 10 tonnes or more | Particulate matter (corrected to 6% CO_2) | 150 mg/Nm³ |

Note: For control of emissions/proper disposal of pollutants, the following guidelines shall be followed by the industry:

(i) A minimum stack height of 20 metres shall be provided.

(ii) All ovens shall be modified to single chimney multi-oven systems.

(iii) Emissions from ovens shall be channelised through inbuilt draft stack. Optimum heat utilisation technique shall be used.

(iv) In case of units having capacity 10 tonnes and above, wet scrubbing system shall be provided to control air pollution.

| 66. | Soft Coke Industry | Particulate matter (corrected to 6% CO_2) | 350 mg/Nm³ |

Note: Wet scrubbing systems alongwith by product recovery system shall be provided.

Guidelines for Emission Control to Improve Work Zone Environment (applicable for industries at serial numbers 64, 65 and 66):

(a) Water used for quenching and wet scrubbing shall be recirculated and reused through catch-pits.

(b) Leakages in the oven shall be sealed by bentonite or by any suitable paste and by proper maintenance to avoid fugitive emission.

Guidelines for Coal Handling and Crushing Plant (applicable to indusries at serial numbers 64, 65 and 66):

(a) Unloading of coal trucks shall be carried out with proper care avoiding dropping of the materials from height. It is advisable to moist the material by sprinkling water while unloading.

(b) Pulversiation of coal shall be carried out in an enclosed place and water sprinkling arrangement shall be provided at coal heaps, crushing area and on land around the crushing unit.

(c) Work area surrounding the plant shall be asphalted or concreted.

Sl. No.	Industry	Parameter	Standards
1	2	3	4

		(d) Green belt shall be developed along the boundary of the industry.	
		(e) Open burning of coal to manufacture soft coke shall be stopped.	
67.	Edible oil & Vanaspati	Effluents:	
		Temperature	Not more than 5°C above ambient temperature of the recipient waterbody.
		pH	6.5–8.5
		Suspended solids	150 mg/l
		Oil & Grease	20 mg/l
		BOD (3 days at 27°C)	100 mg/l
		COD	200 mg/l
		Waste water discharge	
		(i) Solvent extraction	2.0 cum/tonne of product (oil)
		(ii) Refinery/Vanaspati	2.0 cum/tonne of product (refined oil/Vanaspati)
		(iii) Integrated unit of solvent extraction & refinery/vanaspati	4.0 cum/tonne of refined oil/Vanaspati produced.
		(iv) Barometric cooling water/Deodoriser water	15.0 cum/tonne of refined oil/Vanaspati

Note:

(i) The above standards shall be applicable to wastewater from processes and cooling.

(ii) BOD shall be made stringent upto 30 mg/l if the recipient fresh water body is source of drinking water supply.

(iii) The standards for boiler emissions shall be applicable as prescribed under Schedule I of these rules.

68.	Organic Chemicals manufacturing industry (a) Compulsory parameters	Effluents:	
		pH	6.5–8.5
		BOD (3 days at 27°C)	100 mg/l

Sl. No.	Industry	Parameter	Standards
1	2	3	4
		Oil & Grease	10 mg/l
		Bioassay test	Minimum 90% survival after 96 hours with fish at 100% effluent
	(b) Additional		(mg/l)
	parameters	Nitrate (as N)	10
		Arsenic	0.2
		Hexavalent Chromium	0.1
		Total Chromium	1.0
		Lead	0.1
		Cyanide as CN	0.2
		Zinc	0.5
		Mercury	0.01
		Copper	2.0
		Nickel	2.0
		Phenolics as C_6H_5OH	5.0
		Sulphide	2.0

Note:

(i) No limit for COD is prescribed but it shall be monitored. If the COD in a treated effluent is persistently greater than 250 mg/l, such industrial units are required to identify chemicals causing the same. In case these are found to be toxic as defined in Hazardous Chemicals Rules, 1989 in Part I of Schedule–I, the State Boards in such cases may direct the industries to install tertiary treatment system stipulating time limit. This may be done on case-to-case basis.

(ii) These standards are not applicable to small-scale detergent (formulating units).

(iii) The standards for boiler emissions shall be applicable as per the existing emission regulations.

(iv) Industry covered under this group are haloaliphatics, plasticizers, aromatics (calcohols, phenols, esters, acids and salts, aldehydes and ketone), substituted aromatics, aliphatic (alcohols, esters, acids, aldehydes, ketones, amines and amides) and detergents.

| 69. | Flour Mills | Effluents | |
| | | pH | 6.5–8.5 |

Sl. No.	Industry	Parameter	Standards
1	2	3	4

		BOD (3 days at 27°C)	100 mg/l
		Total Suspended solids	100 mg/l
		Oil & Grease	10 mg/l
		Waste water discharge	2 cubic metre per tonne of wheat processed.

Note:

(i) BOD shall be made stringent upto 30 mg/l if the recipient fresh water body is a source for drinking water supply.

(ii) BOD shall be allowed upto 350 mg/l for applying on land, provided the land is designed and operated as a secondary treatment system with the requisite monitoring facilities. The drainage water from the land after secondary treatment has to satisfy a limit of 30 mg/l of BOD and 10 mg/l of nitrate expressed as 'N'. The net addition to ground water quality should not be more than 3 mg/l of BOD and 10 mg/l of nitrate expressed as 'N'.

(iii) BOD shall be allowed upto 350 mg/l for discharge into a town sewer, if such sewer leads to a secondary biological treatment system.

(iv) Suspended solids shall be allowed upto 450 mg/l for discharge into a town sewer, if such sewer leads to a secondary biological treatment system.

70.	Boilers (Small)	Steam generation Capacity (ton/hour)	Particulate emission matter (mg/Nm^3)
		less than 2	1200*
		2 to less than 10	800*
		10 to less than 15	600*
		15 and above	150**

* to meet the respective standards, cyclone/multicyclone is recommended as control equipment with the boiler.

** to meet the standard, bag filter/ESP is recommended as control equipment with the boiler.

Note:

(i) 12% of CO_2, correction shall be the reference value for particulate matter emission standards for all categories of boilers.

(ii) These limits shall supersede the earlier limits notified

Sl. No.	Industry	Parameter	Standards
1	2	3	4

		under Schedule I at serial number 34 of Environment (Protection) Act, 1986 *vide* notification GSR 742 (E), datd 30 August, 1990	
		(iii) Stack Height for small boilers.	
		For the small boilers using coal or liquid fuels, the required stack height with the boiler shall be calculated by using the formula	
		$H = 14\, Q^{0.3}$	
		Where H—Total stack height in metres from the ground level.	
		$Q = SO_2$ emission rate in kg/hr.	
		In no case the stack height shall be less than 11 metres. Where providing all stacks are not feasible using above formula the limit of 400 mg/NM^3 for SO_2 emission shall be met by providing necessary control equipment with a minimum stack height of 11 metres.	
71.	Pesticide Industry	(i) Compulsory Parameters	mg/1 except pH
		pH	6.5–8.5
		BOD (3 days at 27°C)	100
		Oil & Grease	10
		Suspended solids	100
		Bioassay test:	Minimum 90% survival of fish after 96 hours with 90% eff-luent and 10% dilution water. Test shall be carried out as per IS:6502–1971.
		(ii) Additional Parameters	mg/l
		(a) Heavy metal	
		Copper	1.0
		Manganese	1.0
		Zinc	1.0
		Mercury	0.01
		Tin	0.1
		Any other like Nickel	shall not exceed 5 times the drinking water standards (BIS) individually.

Sl. No.	Industry	Parameter	Standards
1	2	3	4

		(b) Organics Phenol & Phenolic Compounds as C_6H_2OH	1.0
		(c) Inorganics	
		Arsenic as AS	0.2
		Cyanide as CN	0.2
		Nitrate as NO_3	50
		Phosphate as P	5.0
		(d) Specific pesticide	(microgram/litre)
		Benzene Hexachloride	10
		DDT	10
		Dimethoate	450
		Copper oxychloride	9600
		Ziram	1000
		2, 4D	400
		Paraquat	23000
		Propanil	7300
		Nitrogen	780
		Other/below mentioned pesticides Individually)	100

Other Pesticides:

(i) Insecticides:

Aluminium Phosphide	Lindane	Pyrethrum extract
Dichlorovos	Malathion	Quinalphos
EDTC Mixer	Methyl Bromide	Monocrotophos
Ethylene Dibromide	Nicotine Sulphate	Carbaryl
Ethion	Oxydemeton Methyl	Endosulfan
Fenitrothion	Methyl Parathion	Fenvalerate
Lime-sulphur	Phosphamidon	Phorate
Temephos		

(ii) Fungicides:

| Aurefungin | Organomercurials (MEMC & PMA) |
| Barium | Sulphur (Colloidal, |

Sl. No.	Industry	Parameter	Standards
1	2	3	4

	Polysulphide	Wettable & Dust)	
	Cuprous Oxide	Streptocycline	
	Ferbam	Thiram	
	Mancozeb	Zineb	
	Manab	Carbendazim	
	Nickel	Tridemorph	
	Chloride		
	(iii) Rodenticides:	(iv) Nematicides:	(v) Weedicides:
	Comafuryl	Metham N-Sodium	Fluchloralin
	Warfarin		Isoproturon
	Zinc		Butachlor
	Phosphide		Anilphos
	(vi) Plant Growth	(vii) Any other pesticide	
	Regulants:	not specified above	
	Chloromequat		
	Chloride		
	Nemphalene		
	Acetic Acid		

Note:

(1) Limits shall be compiled with at the end of the treatment plant before any dilution.

(2) From the 'Additional Parameters' specified in 71 (ii), only the relevant parameters (based on the raw-materials used and products manufactured) may be prescribed by the concerned State Board on a case-to-case basis.

(3) No limit for COD is prescribed. If the COD in a treated effluent is presistently more than 250 mg/l, such industrial units are required to identify the chemicals causing the same. In case, these are found to be toxic as defined in Schedule I of the Hazardous Chemicals Rules, 1989, the State Boards in such cases may direct the industries to install tertiary treatment, stipulating time limit. This may be done on a case-to-case basis.

(4) Solar evaporation followed by incineration is a recognized practice, provided the guidelines of solar evaporation as given below are followed.

Guidelines on solar evaporation system or waste water from pesticide industry.

Sl. No.	Industry	Parameter	Standards
1	2	3	4

(i) Solar evaporation pans shall be constructed in such a way that the bottom is atleast one metre above the ground level.

(ii) Solar evaporation pans shall be leak proof and of impervious construction and designed as per IS:7290.

(iii) The solar evaporation pans shall be designed on the basis of evaporation rate matching to the out put of wastewater.

(iv) Wastewater must be pre-treated as below before subjecting to solar evaporation:

(a) Oil and grease and floating organics shall be removed so that the rate of evaporation is not effected.

(b) Acidic/Alkaline waste must be neutralised before solar evaporation to maintain pH in the range of 6.5 to 8.5

(c) Toxic volatile matter shall be removed so as not to cause air pollution.

(v) During the rainy season, storm water shall not be allowed to mix with process waste and enter the pans. The wastewater shall in no case outflow from the evaporation pans. Alternative arrangements shall be made to hold the waste water in proper impervious tanks and if necessary, force evaporated.

(vi) In no circumstances, the liquid effluent shall be discharged without conforming to the minimum national standards or stored in a holding arrangement which is likely to cause pollution.

(vii) The sludge from the solar evaporation pans shall be incinerated or disposed as per the guidelines for management and handling of hazardous waste, published by the Ministry of Environment and Forests, Government of India, after obtaining authorization from the State Pollution Control Board under the Hazardous Wastes (Handling and Management) Rules, 1989.

(viii) The facility shall be protected from flood and storm to prevent embankments from erosion or any other damage which may render any portion inoperable.

Sl. No.	Industry	Parameter	Standards
1	2	3	4

		(ix) Facilities shall have protective enclosures to keep wildlife, domestic animals, unauthorised persons, *etc.* away.	
72.	Oil Drilling and Gas Extraction Industry		
A.	Standards for Liquid Effluent 1.0 On-Shore facilities (For Marine Disposal)		

pH	5.5–9.0
Oil & Grease	10 mg/l
Suspended solids	100 mg/l
BOD (3 days at 27°C)	30 mg/l

Note:

(i) For on-shore discharge of effluents. In addition to the standards prescribed above, proper marine outfall has to be provided to achieve the individual pollutant concentration level in sea water below their toxicity limits as given below, within a distance of 50 metre from the discharge point, in order to protect the marine aquatic life:

Parameter	Toxicity limit, mg/l
Chromium as Cr	0.1
Copper, as Cu	0.05
Cyanide, as CN	0.005
Fluoride, as F	1.5
Lead, as Pb	0.05
Mercury, as Hg	0.01
Nickel, as Ni	0.1
Zinc, as Zn	0.1

(ii) Oil and gas drilling and processing facilities, situated on land and away from saline water sink, may opt either for disposal of treated water by on-shore disposal or by re-injection in abandoned well, which is allowed only below a depth of 1000 metres from the ground level. In case of re-injection in abandoned well the effluent have to comply

Sl. No.	Industry	Parameter	Standards
1	2	3	4

only with respect to suspended solids and oil and grease at 100 mg/l and 10 mg/l, respectively. For on-shore disposal, the permissible limits are given below:

S.No.	Parameter	On-shore discharge standards (Not to exceed)
1	2	3
1.	pH	5.5–9.0
2.	Temperature	40°C
3.	Suspended Solids	100 mg/l
4.	Zinc	2 mg/l
5.	BOD	30 mg/l
6.	COD	100 mg/l
7.	Chlorides	600 mg/l
8.	Sulphates	1000 mg/l
9.	TDS	2100 mg/l
10.	% Sodium	60 mg/l
11.	Oil and Grease	10 mg/l
12.	Phenolics	1.2 mg/l
13.	Cyanides	0.2 mg/l
14.	Fluorides	1.5 mg/l
15.	Sulphides	2.0 mg/l
16.	Chromium (Cr + 6)	0.1 mg/l
17.	Chromium (Total)	1.0 mg/l
18.	Copper	0.2 mg/l
19.	Lead	0.1 mg/l
20.	Mercury	0.01 mg/l
21.	Nickel	3.0 mg/l

2.0 Off-shore facilities:

For off-shore discharge of effluents, the oil content of the treated effluent without dilution shall not exceed 40 mg/l for 95% of the observation and shall never exceed 10 mg/l. Three 8-hourly grab samples are required to be collected daily and the average value of oil and grease content of the three samples shall comply with these standards.

B. Guidelines for Discharge of Gaseous Emission:
1.0 DG Sets

Sl. No.	Industry	Parameter	Standards
1	2	3	4

1.1 DG sets at drill site as well as production station shall conform with the norm notified under the Environment (Protection) Act, 1986.

2.0 Elevated/ground flares

2.1 Cold Venting of gases shall never be resorted to and all the gaseous emissions are to be flared.

2.2 All flaring shall be done by elevated flares except where there is any effect on crop production in adjoining areas due to the flaring. In such cases, one may adopt ground flaring.

2.3 In case of ground flare, to minimise the effects of flaring the flare pit at Group Gathering Station (GGS) Oil Collecting Station (OCS) and Group Collection Station (GCS) shall be made of RCC surrounded by a permanent wall (made of refractory brick) of minimum 5m height to reduce the radiation and glaring effect in the adjoining areas.

2.4 A green belt of 100m width may be developed around the flare after the refractory wall in case of ground glaring.

2.5 If the ground flaring with provision of green belt is not feasible, enclosed ground flare system shall be adopted, and be designed with proper enclosures height, to meet the ground level concentration (GLC) requirement.

2.6 In case of elevated flaring, the minimum stack height shall be 30 m. Height of the stack shall be such that the maximum GLC never exceeds the prescribed ambient air quality limit.

3.0 Burning of effluent in the pits shall not be carried out at any stage.

C.   Guidelines for Disposal of Solid Waste:

1.0 Disposal of drill cuttings.

1.1 The drill cuttings shall be conveyed through a conveyor system to the disposal pit after proper washing.

1.2 No drill cuttings (of any composition) shall be disposed off-shore. For off-shore installation, drill cuttings separated from mud, shall be transported on-shore through supply vessels secured land-fill disposal as per Ministry of Environment and Forests' guidelines. The site shall be approved by the concerned authority (State Government/State Pollution Control Board).

1.3 The disposal of drill cuttings (on-shore/off-shore) shall conform to the guidelines provided by the Ministry of Environment and Forests.

1.4 The secured land-fill pit shall be covered with a thick layer of local top soil provided with proper top slope, after drilling operation is over.

2.0 Disposal of drilling mud.

2.1 The unusuable portion of the drilling mud (of any composition), after reclamation shall be disposed of only at a secured land-fill site approved by the

Sl. No.	Industry	Parameter	Standards
1	2	3	4

concerned authority (State Government/State Pollution Control Boards). The disposal of mud shall conform to the guidelines provided by the Ministry of Environment and Forests under the Hazardous Wastes (Management and Handling) Rules, 1989.

2.2 No mud (of any composition) shall be disposed off-shore. For off-shore installation, the unusable portion of the mud shall be brought back to the shore for disposal in a secured land-fill.

2.3 Only water-based mud system shall be used. Where oil-based muds are used, the muds, after they become unusual, shall be properly treated/incinerated, in a centralised treatment facility. In case of off-shore installation, these may be brought to the shore and treated.

3.0 Production stage solid waste disposal.

3.1 The dried sludge from waste-water treatment plant and other solid wastes at production stage shall be disposed in a secured land-fill.

3.2 In case all content in the sludge is high, it shall be properly treated/incinerated and ash shall be disposed of in a secured land-fill.

73.	Pharmaceuticals industry (Bulk Drugs)		
		(i) Compulsory Parameters	(mg/l except pH)
		pH	6.5–8.5
		Oil & Grease	10
		BOD (3 days at 27°C)	100
		Total Suspended solids	100
		Bioassay test	90% survival after 96 hours in 100% effluent test shall be carried out as per IS:6582–1971
		(ii) Additional parameters	mg/l
		Mercury	0.01
		Arsenic	0.2
		Chromium (Hexavalent)	0.1
		Lead	0.1
		Cyanide	0.1

Sl. No.	Industry	Parameter	Standards
1	2	3	4

		Phenolics (C_6H_5OH) 1.0	
		Sulphides (as S) 2.0	
		Phosphate (as P) 5.0	

Note:

(i) The limit of BOD (3 days at 27°C) shall be 30 mg/l if effluent is discharged directly to fresh water body.

(ii) The additional parameters are applicable to bulk drug manufacturing units depending upon the process and product.

(iii) No limit for COD is prescribed, but it shall be monitored. If the COD of the treated effluent is greater than 250 mg/l, such industrial units are required to identify chemicals causing the same. In case there are found to be toxic, as defined in the Hazardous Chemicals Rules, 1989 (Schedule I), the State Boards in such cases shall direct the industries to install tertiary treatment system within the stipulated time limit. This may be done on a case-to-case basis.

74.   Emission standards for brick kilns:

I.   Minimal National Emission Standards for Brick Kilns:

Size	Kiln Capacity	Maximum limit for the concentration of particulate matter (mg/N cu.m)
1	2	3
Small	Less than 15,000 bricks per day (less than 15 ft trench width)	1000
Medium	15,000–30,000 bricks per day (15–22 ft trench width)	750
Large	More than 30,000 bricks per day (more than 22 ft trench width)	750

Note: The above particulate matter emission limits are achievable installing fixed chimney high draught kilns and/or settling chamber.

II. Stack Height Regulation:

The following stack heights are recommended for optional dispersion of particulate matter:

Kiln Capacity	Stack Height
1	2
Less than 15,000 bricks per day (less than 15 ft trench width)	Minimum stack height of 22 m or, Induced draught fan operating with minimum draught of 50 mm. Water Gauge with 12m stack height.
15,000–30,000 bricks per day (15–22 ft trench width)	Minimum stack height of 27m with gravitational settling chamber or, Induced draught fan operating with minimum draught of 50mm. Water Gauge with 15m stack height.
More than 30,000 bricks per day (more than 22 ft. trench width)	Minimum stack height of 30m with gravitational settling chamber or, Induced draught fan operating with minimum draught of 50mm. Water Gauge with 17m stack height.

[66][III. Existing moving chimney Bull's trench kilns shall be dispensed with by 30 June 2000 and no new moving chimney kilns shall be allowed to come up.]

IV. Considering the immediate need to protect the top soil and to find ways for safe disposal/utilisation of flyash, it is provided that from 1 January 1997, all brick manufacturing units within a radius of 50 kms from any thermal power plant, shall utilise flyash in optimal proportion for making bricks.

75.   Soda Ash Industry (Solvay Process)

PARAMETER	MINAS (Recipient body specified)		
	Marine	Brackish	Inland surface water
pH	6.5–9	6.5–9	6.5–9
Temperature	45°C or less	45°C or less	45°C or less
Oil & Grease	2 mg/l	20 mg/l	10 mg/l
Suspended solids (SS)	500 mg/l	200 mg/l	100 mg/l
Ammonical nitrogen	5 mg/l	50 mg/l	50 mg/l
Bio-assay	96 hours 90% survival	96 hours 90% survival	96 hours 90% survival

[66] *Subs.* by G.S.R. 682 (E), dated 5 October 1999.

Note: MINAS for disposal in brackish and inland surface water are without any dilution.
Standards for Dual Process Soda Ash Plants:

Parameter	Minas
	(Inland Surface Water)
pH	6.5–8.0
Ammonical nitrogen as N (mg/l)	50
Nitrate nitrogen, as N (mg/l)	10
Cyanide, as CN (mg/l)	0.2
Hexavalent chromium (mg/l)	0.1
Total chromium (mg/l)	2.0
Suspended solids (mg/l)	100
Oil and Grease (mg/l)	10

Note: [67][The standards shall to be implemented by the industry in a time target
schedule by December, 1999.] The progress on the time targetted implementation
schedule shall be periodically submitted by the industry to the State Pollution Control
Board and Central Pollution Control Board.

76.   Emission Stand-
      ard for SO_2 from
      Cupola furnace:
      Standard for Sulphur Dioxide emission from Cupola Furnace:

Characteristics	Emission limit
Sulphur dioxide (SO_2) emission	300 mg/Nm^3 at 12% CO_2 correction

To achieve the standard, foundries may install scrubber, followed by a stack of
height six times the diameter of the Cupola beyond the charging door.
   Note: In case due to some technical reasons, installation of scrubber is not possible,
then value of SO_2 to the ambient air has to be effected through the stack height.

77.   Specification of Motor Gasoline for Emission Related Parameters:

Sl.No.	Characteristics	Requirement	Method of Test ref. to P:of IS:1448
(i)	Reid Vapour Pressure at 38°C, KPa	35 to 70	P:39
(ii)	Benzene, Percent by volume, Max	5.0 ([1])	P:104
(iii)	Lead Content as (Pb) g/l, Max	0.15 (low leaded)([2]) 0.013 (unleaded)	P:38

[67] *Subs.* by *ibid.*

Sl.No.	Characteristics	Requirement	Method of Test ref. to P:of IS:1448
(iv)	Sulphur, per cent by mass, Max	0.10 (unleaded) 0.20 (leaded)	P:34
(v)	Potential Gum, g/m³, Max	50	ASTM 873:8
(vi)	Gum (Solvent Washed) g/m³ Max	40	P:29
(vii)	Oxygenates Content Ether (MTBE, ETBE) Alcohol, per cent by volume, Max	15	
(viii)	Phosphorus	See Foot Note[3]	ASTMD 3231

(1) 3.0 per cent by volume maximum in metro cities by 2000 AD.

(2) 0.15 g/l by 31 December 1996 (for entire country);
0.13 g/l by 1 April 1995 (in four metro cities);
by 1 December 1998 (for all State capitals/UTs and major metro cities)
and by 1 April 2000 for the entire country.

(3) Phosphorous containing additives shall be absent.

Note:

(a) Above specifications applies to leaded as well as unleaded petrol except lead content.

(b) For new refineries coming up during or after 1997 the specification applicable by 2000 for existing refineries shall be applicable by 1997.

78. Specifications of Diesel Fuel for Emission Related Parameters:

Sl.No.	Characteristics	Requirement	Method of Test ref. to P:of IS:1448
(i)	Density at 15°C, kg/m³	820 to 880[1]	P:32
(ii)	Cetane Number, Min	45.0[2]	P:9
(iii)	Distillation 85 per cent by volume recovery at °C Max	350	
	95 per cent by volume recovery at C Max	370	P:18
(iv)	Sulphur, per cent by mass	0.50[3]	P:33

(1) 820 to 860 by 2000 AD.

(2) 48 by 31 December 1998 (except in the refineries—Digboi, Gauhati and Bongaigaon Refineries & Petrochemicals Ltd.)

(3) (i) 0.50 per cent by mass by 1 April, 1996 in four metros and Taj Trapezium.

(ii) 0.25 per cent by mass by 1 October 1996 in Taj Trapezium.

(iii) 0.25 per cent by mass by 1 April 1999 throughout the country.

Note:

(a)   Above specifications apply to HSD only.

(b)   For new refineries coming during or after 1997 specification applicable by 2000 for existing refineries shall be applicable by 1997.

(c)   'P' refers to parts of IS:1448.]

Sl. No.	Industry	Parameter	Standards	
			New Batteries	Existing Batteries
68[79.	Coke oven plants (by product recovery type)	Fugitive Visible Emissions		
		(a) Leakage from door	5 (PLD)*	10 (PLD)*
		(b) Leakage from charging lids	1 (PLL)*	1 (PLL)*
		(c) Leakage from AP Covers	4 (PLO)*	4 (PLO)*
		(d) Charging emission (Second/charge)	16 (with HPLA)*	50 (with HPLA)*
	Stack Emission of Coke Oven			
		(a) SO$_2$ (mg/Nm^3)	800	800
		(b) NOx (mg/Nm^3)	500	500
		(c) SPM, (mg/Nm^3)	50	50
		(a) SPM emission during charging (stack emission) mg/Nm^3	25	25
		(b) SPM emission during coke pushing (stack emission) gm/ton of coke	5	5
	Sulphur in Coke Oven gas used for heating (mg/Nm^3)		800	800

68 *Ins.* by G.S.R. 631 (E), dated 31 October 1997. Entry 79 was inserted by this notification.

Emission for quenching operation
Particulate matter gm/MT of coke produced   50   50

Benzo-Pyerine (BOP) concentration in work zone air (ug/m^3)		
–Battery area (top of the battery)	5	5
–Other units in coke oven plant	2	2
–Ambient standards (ng/m^3)	10	10

For control of emissions and to maintain environmental quality in work zone area, the following guidelines shall be followed, namely:

(i) New coke oven units shall follow any of the low-emission procedures, such as, coke dry cooling, non-recovery coke-ovens, Indirect Quenching Process, Jumbo coke oven reactor, Modified Wet Quenching System with appropriate environmental controls (e.g. baffles, filtering media, collection and treatment of residual water from quench tower and recycling; Use of process water as quenching water shall not be permissible.)

(ii) Effective pollution control measures (for e.g. Extensive maintenance and cleaning of oven doors and frame seals, ascension pipes, charging holes and lids and other equipment; On-main charging system (HPLA); Luting charging holes with clay-suspension; Modified guide/transfer car with emission control system, etc.) shall be taken to reduce coal charging and coke pushing emissions. The bleeder of the coke oven shall be flared.

(iii) In the case of existing coke ovens with wet quenching, the new procedure as in (i) and (ii) shall be adopted and emission standards achieved within four years (by 2001).

Note: Units set up after the publication of this notificatin shall be treated as new units.

* HPLA—Aspiration through high pressure liquor injection in goose neck.
* PLD—Percent leaking doors.
* PLL—Percent leaking lids.
* PLO—Percent leaking offtakes.]

[69][80. Specification of two-stroke engine oil:

Specifications	Standard	Test procedure
Two-stroke engine oil grade JASO-FC as per JASO M-345-93 specification and API TC is per specification No. ASTM D 4859.	Minimum smoke Index of 85.	JASO-M342-92 for for JASO-FC and ASTM D-4857 for API TC

The above specification shall be effective from the 1 day of April 1999].

[69] *Ins.* by G.S.R. 504 (E), dated 20 August 1998. Entry 80 was inserted by this notification

[70][81. Battery manufacturing industry—(i) Lead Acid Battery Manufacturing Industries.

Emission Standards

Source	Pollutant	Standards Conc. based (mg/Nm³)
Grid casting	Lead	10
	Particulate matter	25
Oxide manufacturing	Lead	10
	Particulate matter	25
Paste mixing	Lead	10
	Particulate matter	25
Assembling	Lead	10
	Particulate matter	25
PVC Section	Particulate matter	150

—To comply with the respective standards, all the emissions from above mentioned sources shall be routed through stack connected with hood and fan. In addition to above, installation of control equipment, viz., bag filter/ventury scrubber, is also recommended.
—the minimum stack height shall be 30 m.

Liquid Effluent Discharge Standards

Pollutant	Concentration based standards
pH	6.5–8.5
Suspended solids	50 mg/l
Lead	0.1 mg/l

(ii) Dry Cell Manufacturing Industry

Emission Standards

Pollutant	Concentration based standards (mg/Nm³)
Particulate matter	50
Manganese as Mn	5

—To comply with the respective standards, all the emissoins from above mentioned sources shall be routed through stack connected with hood and fan. In addition to above, installation of control equipment, viz., bag filter/ventury scrubber, is also recommended.
—The minimum stack height shall be 30 m.

[70] *Ins.* by G.S.R.,dated 22 December 1998. Entries 81 to 87 were inserted by this notification.

Effluent Standards

Pollutant	Concentration based standards
pH	6.5–8.5
Total suspended solids	100 mg/l
Manganese as Mn	2 mg/l
Mercury as Hg	0.02 mg/l
Zinc as Zn	5 mg/l
Lead as Pb	10 mg/Nm^3
Particulate matter	50 mg/Nm^3
Minimum stack height	30 m

82. Environmental Standards for Gas/Naphtha-based Thermal Power Plants
    (i) Limit for emission of NOx
    (a) For existing units—150 ppm (v/v) at 15% excess oxygen.
    (b) For new units effect from 1-6-1999.

Total generation of gas turbine	Limit for Stack NOx emission [(v/v, at 15% excess oxygen]
(a) 400 MW and above	(i) 50 ppm for the units burning natural gas
	(ii) 100 ppm for the units burning naphtha
(b) Less than 400 MW but up to 100 MW	(i) 75 ppm for the units burning natural gas
	(ii) 100 ppm for the units burning naphtha
(c) Less than 100 MW	100 ppm for units burning natural gas or naphtha as fuel
(d) For the plants burning gas in a conventional boiler	100 ppm

(ii) Stack height H in m should be calculated using the formula $H = 14Q^{0.3}$, where Q is the emission rate of SO_2 in kg/hr, subject to a minimum of 30 mts.
(iii) Liquid waste discharge limit

Parameter	Maximum limit of concentration (mg/l except for pH and temperature)
pH	6.5–8.5
Temperature	As applicable for other thremal power plants
Free available chlorine	0.5
Suspended solids	100.0
Oil and Grease	20.0
Copper (total)	1.0

Parameter	Maximum limit of concentration (mg/l except for pH and temperature)
Iron (total)	1.0
Zinc	1.0
Chromium (total)	0.2
Phosphate	5.0

83. Standards/Guidelines for Control of Noise Pollution from Stationary Diesel Generator (DG) Sets—(A) Noise Standards of DG sets (15–500 KVA).

The total sound power level, Lw, of a DG set should be less than, $94 + 10 \log_{10}$ (KVA), dB(A), at the manufacturing stage, where, KVA is the nominal power rating of a DG set.

This level should fall by 5 dB(A) every five years, till 2007, i.e., in 2002 and then in 2007.

(B) Mandatory acoustic enclosure/acoustic treatment of room for stationary DG sets (5 KVA and above)

Noise from the DG set should be controlled by providing at acoustic enclosure or by treating the room acoustically.

The acoustic enclosures/acoustic treatment of the room should be designed for minimum 25 dB(A). Insertion Loss or for meeting the ambient noise standards, whichever is on the higher side (if the actual ambient noise is on the higher side, it may not be possible to check the performance of the acoustic enclosure/acoustic treatment. Under such circumstances the performance may be checked for noise reduction up to actual ambient noise level, preferably, in the night time). The measurement for Insertion Loss may be done at different points at 0.5 m from the acoustic enclosure/room, and then averaged.

The DG set should also be provided with proper exhaust muffler with Insertion Loss of minimum 25 dB(A).

(C) Guidelines for the manufacturers/users of DG sets (5 KVA and above)—

01 The manufacturer should offer to the user a standard acoustic enclosure of 25 dB(A) Insertion Loss and also a suitable exhaust muffler with Insertion Loss of 25 dB(A)

02 The user should make efforts to bring down the noise levels due to the DG set,outside his premises, within the ambient noise requirements by proper setting and control measures.

03 The manufacturer should furnish noise power levels of the unsilenced DG sets as per standards prescribed under (A).

04 The total sound power level of a DG set, at the user's end,shall be within 2 dB(A) of the total sound power level of the DG set, at the manufacturing stage, as prescribed under (A).

05 Installation of a DG set must be strictly in compliance with the recommendations of the DG set manufacturer.

06 A proper routine and preventive maintenance procedure for the DG set should be set and followed in consultation with the DG set manufacturer which would help prevent noise levels of the DG set from deteriorating with use.

84. Temperature Limit for Discharge of Condenser Cooling Water from Thermal Power Plant—

A: New Thermal power plants commissioned after 1 June 1999—
New Thermal power plants, which will be using water from rivers/lakes/reservoirs, shall install cooling towers irrespective of location and capacity. For thermal power plants which will use sea water for cooling purposes, the condition below will apply.

B: New projects in coastal areas using sea water—
The thermal power plants using sea water should adopt suitable system to reduce water temperature at the final discharge point so that the resultant rise in the temperature of receiving water does not exceed 7°C over and above the ambient temperature of the receiving water bodies.

C: Existing thermal power plants—
Rise in temperature of condenser cooling water from inlet to the outlet of condenser shall not be more than 10°C.

D: Guidelines for discharge point—
1. The discharge point shall preferably be located at the bottom of the water body at midstream for proper dispersion of thermal discharge.
2. In case of discharge of cooling water into sea, proper marine outfall shall be designed to achieve the prescribed standards. The point of discharge may be selected in consultation with concerned State Authorities/NIO.
3. No cooling water discharge shall be permitted in estuaries or near ecologically sensitive areas such as mangroves, coral reefs/spawning and breeding grounds of acquatic flora and fauna.

85. Environmental Standards for Coal Washeries—
1. Fugitive emission standards:
— The difference in the value of suspended pariculate matter, delta (Δ); measured between 25 and 30 metre from the enclosure of coal-crushing plant in the downward and leeward wind direction shall not exceed 150 microgram per cubic meter. Method of measurement shall be High Volume Sampling and Average Flow Rate, not less than $1.1 m^3$ per minute, using Upwind Downwind Method of measurement.

2. Effluent discharge standards:
— The coal washeries shall maintain the close-circuit operation with zero effluent discharge.
— If in case due to some genuine problems like periodic cleaning of the system, heavy rainfall etc. it becomes necessary to discharge the effluent into sewer/land/stream then the effluent shall conform to the following standards at the final outlet of the coal washery.

Sl.No.	Parameter	Limits
1.	pH	5.5–9.0
2.	Total suspended solids	100 mg/l
3.	Oil & Grease	10 mg/l
4.	BOD (3 days 27°C)	30 mg/l
5.	COD	250 mg/l
6.	Phenolics	1.0 mg/l

3. Noise level standards:
— Operational/Working zone—not to exceed 85 dB(A) Leq for 8 hours exposure.
— The ambient air quality standards, in respect of noise as notified under Environmental (Protection) Rules, 1986 shall be followed at the boundary line of the coal washery.
4. Code of practice for Coal Washery:
— Water or Water mixed chemical shall be sprayed at all strategic coal transfer points such as conveyors, loading/unloading points etc. As far as practically possible conveyors, transfer points etc. shall be provided with enclosures.
— The crushers/pulverisers of the coal washeries shall be provided with enclosures, fitted with suitable air pollution control measures and finally emitted through a stack of minimum height of 30 m, conforming to particulate matter emission standard of 150 mg/Nm^3 or provided with adequate water sprinkling arrangement.
— Water-sprinkling by using fine atomizer nozzle arrangement shall be provided on the coal heaps and on and around the crushers/pulverisers.
— Area, in and around the coal washery shall be pucca either asphalted or concreted.
— Water consumption in the coal washery shall not exceed 1.5 cubic metre per tonne of coal.
— The efficiency of the settling ponds of the waste water treatment system of the coal washery shall not be less than 90%.
— Green belt shall be developed along the roadside, coal-handling plants, residential complex, office building and all around the boundary line of the coal washery.
— Storage bunkers, hoppers, rubber decks in chutes and centrifugal chutes shall be provided with proper rubber linings.
— Vehicles movement in the coal washery area shall be regulated effectively to avoid traffic congestion. High-pressure horn shall be prohibited. Smoke emission from heavy duty vehicles operating in the coal washeries should conform to the standards prescribed under Motor Vehicle Rules, 1989.

86. **Water quality standards for coastal water marine outfall.**—In a coastal segment marine water is subjected to several types of uses. Depending on the types

of uses and activities, water quality criteria have been specified to determine its suitability for a particular purpose. Among the various types of uses there is one use that demands highest level of water quality/purity and that is termed as 'designated best use' in that stretch of the coastal segment. Based on this primary water quality criteria have been specified for following five designated best uses:—

Class	Designated best use
SW-I (See Table 1.1)	Salt pans, Shell fishing, Mariculture and Ecologically Sensitive Zone.
SW-II (See Table 1.2)	Bathing, Contact Water Sports and Commercial fishing.
SW-III (See Table 1.3)	Industrial cooling, Recreation (non-contact) and Aesthetics.
SW-IV (See Table 1.4)	Harbour.
SW-V (See Table 1.5)	Navigation and Controlled Waste Disposal.

The standards along with rationale/remarks for various parameters, for different designated best uses, are given in Table 1.1 to 1.5.

Table 1.1

PRIMARY WATER QUALITY CRITERIA FOR CLASS SW-I WATERS

(For Salt-pans, Shell fishing, Mariculture and Ecologically Sensitive Zone)

Sl.No.	Parameter	Standards	Rationale/Remarks
1	2	3	4
1.	pH range	6.5–8.5	General broad range, conducive for propagation of aquatic lives, is given. Value largely dependent upon soil-water interaction.
2.	Dissolved Oxygen	5.0 mg/l or 60 per cent saturation value, whichever is higher	Not less than 3.5 mg/l at any time of the year for protection of aquatic lives.
3.	Colour and Odour	No noticeable colour or offensive odour	Specially caused by chemical compound like creosols, phenols, naphtha, pyridine, benzene, toluene etc. causing visible colouration of salt crystal and tainting of fish flesh.
4.	Floating Matters	Nothing obnoxious or detrimental for use purpose	Surfactants should not exceed an upper limit of 1.0 mg/l and the concentration not to cause any visible foam.

Sl.No.	Parameter	Standards	Rationale/Remarks
1	2	3	4
5.	Suspended Solids	None from sewage or Industrial waste origin.	Settleable inert matters not in such concentration that would impair any usages specially assigned to this class.
6.	Oil and Grease (including Petroleum Products)	0.1 mg/l	Concentration should not exceed 0.1 mg/l because it has effect on fish eggs and larvae.
[71][7.	Heavy Metals: Mercury (as Hg) Lead (as Pb) Cadmium (as Cd)	0.001 mg/l 0.01 mg/l 0.01 mg/l]	(i) Concentration in salt, fish and shell fish. (ii) Average per capita consumption per day (iii) Minimum ingestion rate that induces symptoms of resulting diseases.

Note: SW-I is desirable to safe and relatively free from hazardous chemicals like pesticides, heavy metals and radionuclide concentrations. Their combined (synergestic or antagonistic) effects on health and aquatic lives are not yet clearly known. These chemicals undergo bio-accumulation, magnification and transfer to human and other animals. Thorough test should be performed following appropriate methods for the purpose of setting case specific limits.

Table 1.2

PRIMARY WATER QUALITY CRITERIA FOR CLASS SW-II WATERS

(For Bathing, Contact Water Sports and Commercial Fishing)

Sl.No.	Parameter	Standards	Rationale/Remarks
1	2	3	4
1.	pH range	6.5–8.5	Range does not cause skin or eye irritation and is also conducive for propagation of aquatic lives.
2.	Dissolved Oxygen	4.0 mg/l or 50 percent saturation value, whichever is higher	Not less than 3.5 mg/l at anytime for protection of aquatic lives.

[71] *Subs.* by G.S.R. 682 (E), dated 5 October 1999.

Sl.No.	Parameter	Standards	Rationale/Remarks
1	2	3	4
3.	Colour and Odour	No noticeable colour or offensive odour.	Specifically caused by chemical compound like creosols, phenols, naptha, benzene, pyridine, toluene etc., causing visible colouration of water and tainting of and odour in fish flesh.
4.	Floating Matters	Nothing obnoxious or detrimental for use purpose.	None in concentration that would impair usages specifically assigned to this class.
5.	Turbidity	30 NTU (Nephelo Turbidity Unit)	Measured at 0.9 depth.
6.	Fecal Coliform	100/100 ml (MPN)	The average value not exceeding 200/100 ml. In 20 per cent of samples in the year and in 3 consecutive samples in monsoon months.
7.	Biochemical Oxygen Demand (BOD)(3 days at 27°C)	3 mg/l	Restricted for bathing (aesthetic quality of water). Also prescribed by IS:2296–1974.

Table 1.3

PRIMARY WATER QUALITY CRITERIA FOR CLASS SW-II WATERS

[For Industrial Cooling, Recreation (non-contact) and Aesthetics]

Sl.No.	Parameter	Standards	Rationale/Remarks
1	2	3	4
1.	pH range	6.5–8.5	The range is conducive for propagation of aquatic species and restoring natural system.
2.	Dissolved Oxygen	3.0 mg/l or 40 percent saturation value, whichever is higher.	To protect aquatic lives.
3.	Colour and Odour	No noticeable colour or offensive odour.	None is such concentration that would impair usage specifically assigned to this class.

Sl.No.	Parameter	Standards	Rationale/Remarks
1	2	3	4
4.	Floating Matters	No visible, obnoxious floating debris, oil slick, scum.	As in (3)above.
5.	Fecal Coliform	500/100 ml (MPN)	Not exceeding 1000/100 ml in 20 percent of samples in the year and in 3 consecutive samples in monsoon months.
6.	Turbidity	30 NTU	Reasonable clear water for recreation, aesthetic appreciation and industrial cooling purposes.
*7.	Dissolved iron (as Fe)	0.5 mg/l or less	It is desirable to have the collective concentration of dissolved Fe and Mn less or equal to 0.5 mg/l to avoid scaling effect.
*8.	Dissolved manganese (as Mn)	0.5 mg/l or less	

* Standards included exclusively for Industrial Cooling purpose. Other parameters same.

Table 1.4

PRIMARY WATER QUALITY CRITERIA FOR CLASS SW-IV WATERS

(For Harbour Waters)

Sl.No.	Parameter	Standards	Rationale/Remarks
1	2	3	4
1.	pH range	6.5–9.0	To minimize corrosive and scaling effect.
2.	Dissolved oxygen	3.0 mg/l or 40 percent saturation value whichever is higher.	Considering bio-degradation of oil and inhibition to oxygen production through photosynthesis.
3.	Colour and odour	No visible colour or offensive odour.	None from reactive chemicals which may corrode paints/metallic surfaces.
4.	Floating materials, oil	10 mg/l	Floating matter should be free from excessive living organism which

Sl.No.	Parameter	Standards	Rationale/Remarks
1	2	3	4
	grease and scum (including Petroleum Products)	Not exceeding... per cent of...	may clog or coat operative parts of marine vessels/equipment.
5.	Fecal coliform	500/100 ml (MPN)	Not exceeding 1000/100 ml in 20 percent of samples in the year and in 3 consecutive samples in monsoon months.
6.	Biochemical oxygen demand (3 days at 27°C)	5 mg/l	To maintain water relatively free from pollution caused by sewage and other decomposable wastes.

Table 1.5

PRIMARY WATER QUALITY CRITERIA FOR CLASS SW-V WATERS

(For Navigation and Controlled Waste Disposal)

Sl.No.	Parameter	Standards	Rationale/Remarks
1	2	3	4
1.	pH range	6.5–9.0	As specified by the New England Interstate Water Pollution Control Commission.
2.	Dissolved oxygen	3.0 mg/l or 40 percent saturation value whichever is higher.	To protect aquatic lives.
3.	Colour and odour	None in such concentrations that would impair any usages specifically assigned to this class.	As in (1) above.
4.	Sludge deposits, solid refuse, floating solids, oil, grease and scum	None except for such small amount that may result from discharge of appropriately treated sewage; and/or industrial waste effluents.	

Sl.No.	Parameter	Standards	Rationale/Remarks
1	2	3	4
5.	Fecal coliform	500/100 ml (MPN)	Not exceeding 1000/100 ml in 20 per cent of samples in the year and in 3 consecutive samples in monsoon months.

87.   Emission regulations for Rayon Industry:

(a) Existing plants

Estimation of uncontrolled emission quantity (EQ) of CS_2

For VSF,

EQ = 125 kg of CS_2/t of fibre

For VFY,

EQ = 225 kg of CS_2/t of fibre.

Stack Height (H) requirement, m	Remarks
11 $Q^{0.41}$ -3 VsD/u	A minimum of 80 per cent of total emission shall pass through stack. If the calculated stack height is less than 30 m, a minimum height of 30 m shall be provided.

Where Q-CS_2 emission rate, kg/hr

Vs—stack exit velocity, m/sec.

D—diameter of stack, m

U—annual average wind speed at top of stack, m/sec.

Multiple stacks:

1. If there are more than one stack existing in the plant, the required height of all stacks shall be based on the maximum emission rate in any of the stacks. In other words, all the stacks carrying CS_2 emission shall be of same heights (based on the maximum emission rate).

2. Number of stacks shall not be increased from the existing number. However the number of stacks may be reduced. The existing stacks may be rebuilt and if stacks are to be relocated, condition 3 below applies.

3. Spacing among the stacks (x) at the minimum shall be 3.0 H (in m). If distance, x, between two stacks is less than 3.0 H (in m), emission shall be considered as single point source and height of both the stacks shall be calculated considering all emisson is going through one stack.

(b) Ambient air quality monitoring.

The industry shall install three air quality monitoring stations for CS_2 and H_2S measurements in consultation with State Pollution Control Board (SPCB) to ensure attainment of WHO recommended ambient air quality norms ($CS_2 = 100$ ug/m^3 and $H_2S = 150$ ug/m^3, 24 = hr, average).

(c) For new plants/expansion projects being commissioned on or after 1 June 1999.

Permissible emission limits are:

$CS_2 = 21$ kg/t of fibre

$H_2S = 6.3$ kg/t of fibre

(Note: a. and b. above also apply to new plants/expansion projects)]

[72][88. Emission Standards for new generator sets (upto 19 kilowatt) run on petrol and kerosene with implementation schedule.

The emission standards for portable generator sets run on petrol and kerosene shall be as follows:

A. From June 1, 2000

Class	Displacement (CC)	CO (g/kw-hr)		HC+NOx (g/kw-hr)	
		2-stroke engine	4-stroke engine	2-stroke engine	4-stroke engine
1.	≤ 65	603	623	166	65
2.	> 65 ≤ 99	—	623	—	36
3.	> 99 ≤ 225	—	623	—	19.3
4.	> 225	—	623	—	16.1

B. From June 1, 2001

Class	Displacement (CC)	CO (g/kw-hr)	HC+NOx (g/kw-hr)
1.	≤ 65	519	54
2.	> 65 ≤ 99	519	30
3.	> 99 ≤ 225	519	16.1
4.	> 225	519	13.4

C. Test method shall be as specified in SAEJ 1088. Measurement mode shall be DI cycle specified under ISO 8178 (Weighting Factor of 0.3 for 100% load, 0.5 for 75% load and 0.2 for 50% load).

D. Following organisations shall test and certify the generator sets:

[72] *Ins.* by G.S.R. 682 (E), dated 5 October 1999. Entries 88 and 89 were inserted by this notification.

    (v)   Automotive Research Association of India, Pune.

    (vi)   Indian Institute of Petroleum, Dehradun.

    (vii)   Indian Oil Corporation, R&D Centre, Faridabad.

    (viii)   Vehicle Research Development Establishment, Ahmednagar.

These organisations shall submit the testing and certification details to the Central Pollution Control Board, annually. The Central Pollution Control Board may send the experts in the field to oversee the testing.

    89.   Noise standards for fire-crackers—

A.   (i)   The manufacture, sale or use of fire-crackers generating noise level exceeding 125 dB(AI) or 145 dB(C)$_{pk}$ at 4 meters distance from the point of bursting shall be prohibited.

    (ii)   For individual fire-cracker constituting the series (joined fire-crackers), the above mentioned limit be reduced by 5 log$_{10}$ (N) dB, where N = number of crackers joined together.

B.   The broad requirements for measurement of noise from fire-crackers shall be—

    (i)   The measurements shall be made on a hard concrete surface of minimum 5 meter diameter or equivalent.

    (ii)   The measurements shall be made in free field conditions i.e., there shall not be any reflecting surface up to 15 meter distance from the point of bursting.

    (iii)   The measurement shall be made with an approved sound level meter.

C.   The Department of Explosives shall ensure implementation of these standards.

Note: dB (AI): A—weighted impulse Sound Pressure Level in decibel.

dB (C)$_{pk}$: C—weighted Peak Sound Pressure Level in decibel.

[73][SCHEDULE II]

(See Rule 3)

SCHEDULE [74][III]

Ambient Air Quality Standards in respect of Noise

Area Code	Category of Area	Limit in dB(A) Day Time	Leg. Night Time
(A)	Industrial area	75	70
(B)	Commercial area	65	55
(C)	Residential area	55	45
(D)	Silence Zone	50	40

[73] *Omitted* by G.S.R. 80 (E), dated 31 December 1993.

[74] *Ins.* by G.S.R. 1063 (E), dated 26 December 1989.

Note-1 Day time is reckoned in between 6 a.m. and 9 p.m.

Note-2 Night time is reckoned in between 9 p.m. and 6 a.m.

Note-3 Silence zone is defined as areas upto 100 metres around such premises as hospitals, educational institutions and courts. The Silence zones are to be declared by the Competent Authority.

Use of vehicular horns, loudspeakers and bursting of crackers shall be banned in these zones.

Note-4 Mixed categories of areas should be declared as one of the four above mentioned categories by the Competent Authority and the corresponding standards shall apply.]

75[SCHEDULE IV

(*See* Rule 3)

Standard for Emission of Smoke, Vapour, etc. from Motor Vehicles

(1) Every motor vehicle shall be manufactured and maintained in such condition and shall be so driven that smoke, visible vapour, grit, sparks, ashes, cinders or oily substance do not emit therefrom.

(2) On and from the 1st day of March 1990, every motor vehicle in use shall comply with the following standards—

(a) Idling CO (Carbon monoxide) emission limit for all four wheeled petrol driven vehicles shall not exceed 3 per cent by volume;

(b) Idling CO emission limit for all two and three wheeled petrol driven vehicles shall not exceed 4.5 per cent by volume;

(c) Smoke density for all diesel driven vehicles shall be as follows—

Method of Test	Maximum smoke density		
	Light absorption coefficient m-1	Bosch Units	Harridge Units
(a) Full load at a speed of 60% to 70% of maximum engine rated speeed declared	3.1	5.2	75
(b) Free acceleration	2.3	—	65

(3) On and from the 1st day of April 1991, all petrol driven vehicles shall be so manufactured that they comply with the mass emission standards as specified at

---

75 *Ins.* by G.S.R. 54 (E), dated 5 February 1990.

Annexure 'I'. The breakdown of the operating cycle used for the test shall be as specified at Annexure 'II' and the reference fuel for all such tests shall be as specified in Annexure 'III' to this Schedule.

(4) On and from the 1st day of April 1991, all diesel vehicles shall be so manufactured that they comply with the mass emission standards based on exhaust gas opacity as specified at Annexure 'IV' to this Schedule.

(5) On and from the 1st day of April 1992, all diesel driven vehicles shall be so manufactured that they comply with the following levels of emissions under the Indian driving cycle—

Mass of Carbon Monoxide (CO) Max. Grams per KWH	Mass of Hydro carbons (HC) Max. Grams per KWH	Mass of Nitrogen Oxides (NO) Maxm. Grams per KWH
14	3.5	18

(6) Each motor vehicle manufactured on and after the dates specified in paragraphs (2), (3), (4) and (5) shall be certified by the manufacturers to be conforming to the standards specified in the said paragraphs and the manufactures shall further certify that the component liable to effect the emission of gaseous pollutants are so designed, constructed and assembled as to enable the vehicle, in normal use, despite the vibration to which it may be subjected, to comply with the provisions of the said paragraphs.

(7) Tests for smoke emission level and carbon monoxide level for motor vehicles—(a) Any officer not below the rank of a sub-inspector of police or an inspector of motor vehicles, who has reason to believe that a motor vehicle is by virtue of smoke emitted from it or other pollutants like carbon monoxide emitted from it, is likely to cause environmental pollution, endangering the health or safety of any other user of the road or the public, may direct the driver or any person incharge of the vehicle to submit the vehicle for undergoing a test to measure the standard of black smoke or the standard of any other pollutants.

(b) The driver or any person incharge of the vehicle shall upon demand by any officer referred to in sub-paragraph (a), submit the vehicle for testing for the purpose of measuring the standard of smoke or the levels of other pollutants or both.

(c) The measurement of standard of smoke shall be done with a smoke meter of a type approved by the State Government and the measurement of other pollutants like carbon monoxide shall be done with instruments of a type approved by the State Government.

ANNEXURE-I
(*See* paragraph 3)
Mass Emission Standards for Petrol driven Vehicles

1. Type Approval Tests:
Two and Three Wheeler Vehicles

Reference Mass, R(Kg)	CO(g/km)	HC(g/km)
1	2	3
R ≤ 150	12	8
150 R ≤ 350	$12 + \dfrac{18(R - 150)}{200}$	$8 + \dfrac{4(R - 150)}{200}$
R > 350	30	12

Light Duty Vehicles:

References Mass, rw (kg)	CO(g/km)	HC(g/km)
1	2	3
rw ≤ 1020	14.3	2.0
1020 < rw ≤ 1250	16.5	2.1
1250 < rw ≤ 1470	18.8	2.1
1470 < rw ≤ 1700	20.7	2.3
1700 < rw ≤ 1930	22.9	2.5
1930 < rw ≤ 2150	24.9	2.7
rw ≤ 2150	27.1	2.9

2. Conformity of Production Tests:
Two and Three Wheelers Vehicles

References Mass, R(kg)	CO(g/km)	HC(g/km)
1	2	3
R < 150	15	10
150 R < 350	$15 + \dfrac{25(R - 150)}{200}$	$10 + \dfrac{5(R - 150)}{200}$
R > 350	200 40	200 15

Light Duty Vehicles:

References Mass, rw (kg)	CO(g/km)	HC(g/km)
1	2	3
rw ≤ 1020	17.3	2.7
1020 ≤ rw ≤ 1250	19.7	2.7
1250 ≤ rw ≤ 1470	22.5	2.8
1470 ≤ rw ≤ 1700	24.9	3.0
1700 ≤ rw ≤ 1930	27.6	3.3
1930 ≤ rw ≤ 2150	29.9	3.5
rw ≤ 2150	32.6	3.7

For any of the pollutants referred to above of the three results obtained may exceed the limit specified for the vehicle by not more than 10 per cent.

Explanation: Mass emission standards refers to the gm. of pollutants emitted per km. run of the vehicle, as determined by a chassis dynamometer test using the Indian Driving Cycle.

ANNEXURE-II
(*See* paragraph 3)

Breakdown of the Operating Cycle used for the Tests

No. of Operation	Acceleration (m/acc 2)	Speed (Km/h)	Duration of each operation(s)	Cumulative time(s)
1	2	3	4	5
01. Idling	—	—	16	16
02. Acceleration	0.65	0–14	6	22
03. Acceleration	0.56	14–22	4	26
04. Deceleration	−0.63	22–13	4	30
05. Steady speed	—	13	2	32
06. Acceleration	0.56	13–23	5	37
07. Acceleration	0.44	23–31	5	42
08. Deceleration	−0.56	31–25	3	45

No. of Operation	Acceleration (m/acc 2)	Speed (Km/h)	Duration of each operation(s)	Cumulative time(s)
1	2	3	4	5
09. Steady speed	—	25	4	49
10. Deceleration	−0.56	25–21	2	51
11. Acceleration	0.45	21–34	8	59
12. Acceleration	0.32	34–42	7	66
13. Deceleration	−0.46	42–37	3	69
14. Steady speed	—	37	7	76
15. Deceleraton	−0.42	34–34	2	78
16. Acceleration	0.32	34–42	7	85
17. Deceleration	−0.46	42–47	9	94
18. Deceleration	−0.52	27–14	7	101
19. Deceleration	−0.56	14–00	7	108

ANNEXURE-III

(*See* paragraph 3)

Reference Fuel for Type and Production Conformity Tests

Sl.No.	Characteristic	Requirements		Method of test
		87 Octane	93 Octane	(ref. of P: or IS: 1448*)
1	2	3	4	5
1.	Colour, visual	Orange	Red	—
2.	Copper-strip corrosion for 3 hours at 50°C	Not worse than No. 1		P:15 (1968)
3.	Density at 15°C	Not limited but to be reported		P:16 (1967)
4.	Distillation:	Not limited but to be reported		
	(a) Initial boiling point	10	10	P:18 (1967)
	(b) Recovery upto 20°C per-cent by volume min.	10	10	

* Methods of test for petroleum and its products.

| Sl.No. | Characteristic | Requirements | | Method of test |
		87 Octane	93 Octane	(ref. of P: or IS: 1448*)
1	2	3	4	5
	(c) Recovery upto 125°C percent by volume.	50	50	
	(d) Recovery upto 130°C percent by volume min.	90	90	
	(e) Final boiling point, Max.	215°C	215°C	
	(f) Residue percent by volume, Max.	2	2	
5.	Octane number (Research method) Max.	87	94	P:27 (1960)
6.	Oxidation stability in minutes, Min.	360	360	P:28 (2966)
7.	Residue on evaporation mg/ 100 ml, Max.	4.0	4.0	P:29 (1960) (Air-jet solvent washed)
8.	Sulphur, total, per cent by weight Max.	0.25	0.20	P:34 (1966)
9.	Lead content (as Pb), g/l Max.	0.56	0.80	P:37 (1967) or P:38 (1967)
10.	Reid vapour pressure at 38 degree C, kgf/ cm³, Max.	0.70	0.70	P:39 (1967)

* Methods of test for petroleum and its products.

ANNEXURE-IV
(*See* paragraph 4)
Limit Values of Exhaust Gas Opacity applicable for Diesel Driven Vehicles
The engine tests at steady speed

Nominal Flow G(l/s)	Absorption Coefficient K(m-l)	Nominal Flow G(l/s)	Absorption Coefficient (km-l)
42	2.00	120	1.20
45	1.91	125	1.17
50	1.82	130	1.15
55	1.75	135	1.31
60	1.68	140	1.11
65	1.61	145	1.09
70	1.56	150	1.07
75	1.50	155	1.05
80	1.46	160	1.04
85	1.41	165	1.02
90	1.38	170	1.01
95	1.34	175	1.00
100	1.31	180	0.99
105	1.27	185	0.97
110	1.25	190	0.96
115	1.22	195	0.95
		<200	0.93]

[76][SCHEDULE [77][V]
(*See* Rule12)

Sl.No.	Place at which the discharge of any environment pollutant in excess of prescribed standards occurs or is apprehended tooccur	Authorities or agencies to be intimated	Appointed under
1	2	3	4
1.	Factories as defined under the Factories Act, 1948— (a) Owned by the Central Governmet and engaged in carrying out the purpose of	(i) Atomic Energy Regulatory Board (AERB)	The Atomic Energy Act, 1962

[76] *Ins.* by S.O. 82 (E), dated 16 February 1989.
[77] *Renumbered* by G.S.R. 422 (E), dated 19 May 1993.

Sl.No.	Place at which the discharge of any environment pollutant in excess of prescribed standards occurs or is apprehended to occur	Authorities or agencies to be intimated	Appointed under
1	2	3	4
	the Atomic Energy Act,1962.	(ii) The Ministry of Environment and Forests.	
	(b) Factories other than those mentioned in para (a)	(i) The Chief Inspector of Factories.	The Factories Act, 1948
		(ii) The Inspector of Factories having local jurisdiction.	Do
		(iii) The Ministry of Environment and Forests.	—
2.	Mine as defined under the Mines and Minerals (Regulation and Development) Act, 1957	[78][(i) Controller-General of Mines.]	The Mines and Minerals (Regulaton and Development) Act, 1957
		[78][(ii) Regional Controller of Mines having local jurisdiction.]	Do
		(iii) The Ministry of Environment and Forests.	—
3.	Port as defined under the Indian Ports Act, 1908	(i) Conservator of Ports.	The Indian Ports Act, 1908
		(ii) The Ministry of Environment and Forests.	Do

[78] *Subs.* by S.O. 64(E), dated 18 January 1988.

Sl.No.	Place at which the discharge of any environment pollutant in excess of prescribed standard occurs or is apprehended to occur	Authorities or agencies to be intimated	Appointed under
1	2	3	4
4.	Plantation as defined under the Plantations Labour Act, 1951	(i) The Chief Inspector of Plantations.	The Plantations Labour Act, 1951
		(ii) The Inspector of Plantations having local jurisdiction.	Do
		(iii) The Ministry of Environment and Forests.	
5.	Motor Vehicle as defined under the Motor Vehicles Act, 1939	(i) State Transport Authority.	The Motor Vehicles Act, 1939
		(ii) Regional Transport Authority having regional jurisdictions.	Do
		(iii) The Ministry of Environment and Forests.	
6.	Ship as defined under the Merchant Shipping Act, 1958	(i) Director-General of Shipping.	The Merchant Shipping Act, 1958
		(ii) Surveyor having jurisdiction	Do
		(iii) The Ministry of Environment and Forests.]	Do

[79][SCHEDULE VI]

(*See* Rule 3–A)

General Standards for discharge of environmental pollutants

PART A

Effluents

Sl.No.	Parameter	Standards			
		Inland surface water	Public sewers	Land for irrigation	Marine coastal areas
1	2	3			
		(a)	(b)	(c)	(d)
1.	Colour and Odour	See 6 of Annexure-I	—	See 6 of Annexure-I	See 6 of Annexure-I
2.	Suspended solids mg/l,Max.	100	600	200	(a) For process waste water— 100 (b) For cooling water effluent 10 per cent above total suspended matter of influent.
3.	Particle size of suspended solids	Shall pass 850 micron IS Sieve	—		(a) Floatable solids, max. 3 mm. (b) Settleable solids, max 850 microns.
	[80][* * *]				
5.	pH value	5.5 to 9.0	5.5 to 9.0	5.5 to 9.0	5.5 to 9.0
6.	Temperature	Shall not exceed 5°C above the receiving water temperature	—	—	Shall not exceed 5°C above the receiving water temperature

[79] *Ins.* by G.S.R. 422 (E), dated 19 May 1993.
[80] *Omitted* by G.S.R. 80 (E), dated 31 December 1993.

Sl.No.	Parameter	Standards			
		Inland surface water	Public sewers	Land for irrigation	Marine coastal areas
1	2	3			
		(a)	(b)	(c)	(d)
7.	Oil & grease mg/l, Max.	10	20	10	20
8.	Total residual chlorine mg/l, Max.	1.0	—	—	1.0
9.	Ammonical nitrogen (as N), mg/l, Max.	50	50	—	50
10.	Total Kjeldahl nitrogen [81][N], mg/l, Max.	100	—	—	100
11.	Free ammonia [81][NH_3], mg/l, Max.	5.0	—	—	5.0
12.	Biochemical oxygen demand (5 days at 20°C) [81][mg/l, Max.]	30	350	100	100
13.	Chemical Oxygen demand, mg/l, Max.	250	—	—	250
14.	Arsenic (as As), [81][mg]/l, Max.	0.2	0.2	0.2	0.2
15.	Mercury (As Hg) mg/l,Max.	0.01	0.01	—	0.01
16.	Lead (as Pb), mg/l, Max.	0.1	1.0	—	2.0
17.	Cadmium (as Cd), mg/l, Max.	2.0	1.0	—	2.0
18.	Hexavalent chromium (as Cr+ 6), mg/l, Max.	0.1	2.0	—	1.0

[81] *Subs.* by G.S.R. 80 (E), dated 31 December 1993.

Sl.No.	Parameter	Standards			
		Inland surface water	Public sewers	Land for irrigation	Marine coastal areas
1	2	3			
		(a)	(b)	(c)	(d)
19.	Total chromium (as Cr), mg/l, Max.	2.0	2.0	—	2.0
20.	Copper (as Cu), mg/l, Max.	3.0	3.0	—	3.0
21.	Zinc (as Zn) mg/l, Max.	5.0	15	—	15
22.	Selenium (as Se) mg/l, Max.	0.05	0.05	—	0.05
23.	Nickel (as Ni) mg/l, Max. [82][* * *]	3.0	3.0	—	5.0
27.	Cyanide (as CN) mg/l, Max. [82][* * *]	0.2	2.0	0.2	0.2
29.	[83][Fluoride] (as F) mg/l, Max.	2.0	15	—	15
30.	Dissolved phosphates (as P), mg/l, Max. [82][* * *]	5.0	—	—	—
32.	Sulphide (as S) mg/l, Max.	2.0	—	—	5.0
33.	Phenolic compounds [83][as C_6H_5OH] mg/l, Max.	1.0	5.0	—	5.0
34.	Radioactive materials: (a) Alpha emitters [84][micro curie/ml] Max.	10^{-7}	10^{-7}	[77][10^{-8}]	10^{-7}

[82] *Omitted* by G.S.R. 80 (E), dated 31 December 1993.
[83] *Subs.* by G.S.R. 80 (E), dated 31 December 1993.
[84] *Subs.* by G.S.R. 80 (E), dated 31 December 1993.

Sl.No.	Parameter	Standards			
		Inland surface water	Public sewers	Land for irrigation	Marine coastal areas
1	2	3			
		(a)	(b)	(c)	(d)
	(b) Beta emitters [micro curie/ ml] Max.	10^{-6}	10^{-6}	10^{-7}	$^{84}[10^{-6}]$
35.	Bio-assay test	90% survival of fish after 96 hours in 100% effluent	90% survival of fish after 96 hours in 100% effluent	90% survival of fish after 96 hours in 100% effluent	90% survival of fish afer 96 hours in 100% effluent
36.	Manganese (as Mn)	2 mg/l	2 mg/l		3 mg/l
37.	Iron (as Fe)	3 mg/l	3 mg/l		3 mg/l
38.	Vanadium (as V)	0.2 mg/l	0.2 mg/l		0.2 mg/l
39.	Nitrate Nitrogen	10 mg/l	—	—	20 mg/l
40.	Pesticides: (microgm per lit. maximum)				
	(i) Benzene hexachloride	10	—	10	10
	(ii) Carboryl	10	—	10	10
	(iii) DDT	10	—	10	10
	(iv) Endosulfan	10	—	10	10
	(v) Diamethoate	450	—	450	450
	(vi) Penitrothion	10	—	10	10
	(vii) Malathion	10	—	10	10
	(viii) Phorate	10	—	10	10
	(ix) Methyl Parathion	10	—	10	10
	(x) Phenthoate	10	—	10	10
	(xi) Pyrethrums	10	—	10	10
	(xii) Copper Oxychloride	9600	—	9600	9600
	(xiii) Copper Sulphate	50	—	50	50

Sl.No.	Parameter	Standards			
		Inland surface water	Public sewers	Land for irrigation	Marine coastal areas
1	2	3			
		(a)	(b)	(c)	(d)
	(xiv) Ziram	1000	—	1000	1000
	(xv) Sulphur	30	—	30	30
	(xvi) Paraouat	2300	—	2300	2300
	(xvii) Proponil	7300	—	7300	7300
	(xviii) Nitrogen	780	—	780	780

PART B

Waste Water Generation Standards

Sl.No.	Industry	Quantum
1.	Integrated Iron & Steel	$16^{85}[m^3/tonne]$ of finished steel
2.	Sugar	$0.4\ ^{85}[m^3/tonne]$ of cane crushed
3.	Pulp & Paper Industries	
	(a) Larger pulp & paper	
	(i) Pulp & Paper	$175\ ^{85}[m^3/tonne]$ of paper produced
	$^{85}[$(ii) Viscose Staple Fibre	$150\ m^3$, tonne of product
	(ii) Viscose Filament Yarn	$500\ m^3/tonne$ of product]
	(b) Small pulp & paper:	
	(i) Agro-residue based	$150\ ^{85}[m^3/tonne]$ of paper produced.
	(ii) Waste paper based	$50\ ^{85}[m^3/tonne]$ of paper produced.
4.	Fermentation Industries	
	(a) Maltry	$3.5\ ^{85}[m^3/tonne]$ of grain produced
	(b) Brewery	$0.25\ ^{85}[m^3/KL]$ of alcohol produced
	(c) Distillery	$12\ ^{85}[m^3/KL]$ of alcohol produced
5.	Caustic Soda	
	(a) Membrane cell process	$^{85}[m^3/tonne]$ of caustic soda produced excluding cooling tower blow down
	(b) Mercury cell process	$^{85}[m^3/tonne]$ of caustic soda produced (mercury bearing), 10% blow down permitted for cooling tower

[85] *Subs.* by G.S.R. 80 (E), dated 31 December 1993.

Sl.No.	Industry	Quantum
6.	Textile Industries: Man-made fibre	
	(i) Nylon & Polyster	120 [85][m^3/tonne] of fibre produced
	(ii) Viscose rayon	150 [85][m^3/tonne] of product
7.	Tanneries	28 [85][m^3/tonne] of raw hide
8.	Starch, Glucose and related products	8 [85][m^3/tonne] of maize crushed
9.	Dairy	3 [85][m^3/KL] of Milk
10.	Natural rubber processing industry	4 [85][m^3/tonne] of rubber
11.	Fertiliser	
	(a) Straight nitrogenous fertiliser	5 [85][m^3/tonne] of urea or equivalent produced
	(b) Straight phosphatic fertiliser (SSP & TSP) excluding manufacture of any acid	0.5 [85][m^3/tonne] of SSP/TSP
	(c) Complex fertiliser	Standards of nitrogenous and phosphatic fertiliser are applicable depending on the primary product.

PART C
Load Based Standards

1. Oil Refinery Industry:

Parameter	Quantum in [86][kg]/1000 tonnes of crude processed
Oil & grease	10.00
Phenol	0.70
BOD	10.50
Suspended solids	14.00
Sulphide	0.35

2. Large, Pulp & Paper, New Print/Rayon grade plants of capacity above 24000 [86][tonne]/annum:

Parameter	Quantum
Total Organic Chloride (TOCl)	2 kg/[86][tonne] of product.

[86] *Subs.* by G.S.R. 80 (E), dated 31 December 1993.

PART D
General Emission Standards

I. Concentration Based Standards:

Sl.No.	Parameter	Standard Concentration not to exceed (in mg/Nm^3)
1.	[86][Particulate Matter (PM)]	150
2.	[86][Total Fluoride	25]
3.	Asbestos	[86][4 Fibres/cc and dust should not be more then 3 mg/Nm^3]
4.	Mercury	0.2
5.	Chlorine	15
6.	Hydrochloric acid vapour and mist [87][* * *]	35
8.	Sulphuric acid mist	50
9.	Carbon monoxide [87][* * *]	[88][1% max (v/v)]
11.	Lead [87][* * *]	[88][10 mg/Nm^3]

II. Equipment Based Standards:

[81][For dispersal of sulphur dioxide, a minimum stack height limit is accordingly prescribed as below:]

Sl.No.	Parameter	Standard
1.	Sulphur dioxide	Stack-height limit in [88][metre]
	(i) Power generation capacity:	
	— 500 MW and more	275
	— 200/210 MW and above to	220
	— less than 500 MW	$H = 14(Q)^{0.3}$
	— less than 200/210 MW	
	(ii) Steam generation capacity	Coal consumption per day [87][* * *]
	— Less than 2 [88][tonne/hr]	
	— 2 to 5 [88][tonne/hr]	
	— 5 to 10 [88][tonne/hr]	
	— 10 to 15 [88][tonne/hr]	

[87] *Omitted* by G.S.R. 80 (E), dated 31 December 1993.
[88] *Subs.* by G.S.R. 80 (E), dated 31 December 1993.

Sl.No.	Parameter	Standard
	— 15 to 20 [88][tonne/hr]	
	— 20 to 25 [88][tonne/hr]	
	— 25 to 30 [88][tonne/hr]	
	— More than 30 [88][tonne/hr]	

Note—H—Physical height of the stack in [88][metre]

Q—Emission rate of SO_2 in kg/hr. [87][* * *]

III. Load/Mass-based Standards:

Sl.No.	Industry	Parameter	Standard
1.	[88][Fertiliser] (Urea)		
	Commissioned prior to 1.1.1982	[88][Particulate Matter (PM)]	2 [88][kg/tonne] of product
	Commissioned after 1.1.1982	[88][Particulate Matter (PM)]	0.5 [88][kg/tonne] of product
2.	Copper, Lead and [88][Zinc Smelter Converter]	Sulphur dioxide	4 [88][kg/tonne] of concentrated [88][(100%) and acid produced]
3.	Nitric Acid	Oxides of Nitrogen	3 [88][kg/tonne] of weak acid (before concentration) produced
4.	Sulphuric Acid	Sulphur dioxide	4 [89][kg/tonne] of concentrated (100%) acid produced
5.	Coke Oven	Carbon monoxide	3 [89][kg/tonne] of coke produced
6.	Oil Refineries		

(a) [89][For the oil refineries the following standards shall be applicable:]

Process	Parameter	Standard
—Distillation [89][(Atmospheric plus vacuum)]	Sulphur dioxide	0.25 [89][kg/tonne] of feed in this process
—Catalytic cracker	Do	2.5 [89][kg/tonne] of feed in this process

[89] *Subs.* by G.S.R. 80 (E), dated 31 December 1993.

Process	Parameter	Standard
—Sulphur Recovery Unit	Do	120 [89][kg/tonne] of Sulphur in the feed
[90][* * *]		
7. Aluminium Plants:		
(i) Anode Bake Oven	Total Fluoride	0.3kg/MT of Aluminium
(ii) Pot room		
(a) VSS	Do	4.7 kg/MT of Aluminium
(b) HSS	Do	6 kg/MT of Aluminium
(c) PBSW	Do	2.5 kg/MT of Aluminium
(d) PBCW	Do	1.0 kg/MT of Aluminium

Note:

VSS = Vertical Stud Soderberg

HSS = Horizontal Stud Soderberg

[89][PBSW = Pre Backed Side Work]

[89][PBCW = Pre Backed Centre Work]

8. Glass Industry		
(a) Furnace Capacity		
(i) Up to the product draw capacity of 60 MT/Day	Particulate matter	2kg/hr
(ii) Product draw capacity more than 60 MT/ Day	Do	0.8 kg/MT of product drawn

PART E

Noise Standards

A. Noise Limits for Automobiles [91][Free Field Distance at 7.5 Metre] in dB(A) at the manufacturing stage

(a) Motorcycle, scooters & three wheelers 80

(b) Passenger cars 82

(c) Passenger or commercial vehicles up to 4 MT 85

(d) Passenger or commercial vehicles above 4 MT and up to 12 MT 89

(e) Passenger or commercial vehicle exceeding 12 MT 91

B. Domestic appliances and construction equipments at the manufacturing stage to be achieved by 31 December 1993.

[90] *Omitted* by G.S.R. 80 (E), dated 31 December 1993.

[91] *Subs.* by G.S.R. 80 (E), dated 31 December 1993.

(a) Window air conditioners of 1 ton to 1.5 ton	68
(b) Air [91][coolers]	60
(c) Refrigerators	46
(d) Diesel generator for domestic purposes	85–90
(e) Compactors (rollers), front loaders, concrete mixers, cranes (movable), vibrators and saws.	75

ANNEXURE I
(For the purposes of Parts A, B and C)

The State Board shall follow the following guidelines in enforcing the standards specified under Schedule VI:

1. The waste waters and gases are to be treated with the best available technology [91][BAT] in order to acheive the prescribed standards.

2. The industries need to be encouraged for recycling and reuse of waste material as far as practicable in order to minimise the discharge of wastes into the environment.

3. The industries are to be encouraged for recovery of biogas, energy and reusable materials.

4. While permitting the discharge of effluents and emissions into the environment, State Boards have to take into account the assimilative capacities of the receiving bodies, especially water bodies so that quality of the intended use of the receiving water is not affected. Where such quality is likely to be affected, discharges should not be allowed into water bodies.

5. The Central and State Boards shall put emphasis on the implementation of clean technologies by the industries in order to increase fuel efficiency and reduce the generation of environmental pollutants.

6. All efforts should be made to remove colour and unpleasant odour as far as practicable.

7. The standards mentioned in this Schedule [91][shall also apply to all other effluents discharged such as] mining, and mineral processing activities and sewage.

8. The limit given for the total concentration of mercury in the final effluent of caustic soda industry, is for the combined effluent from (a) Cell house, (b) Brine plant, (c) Chlorine handling, (d) Hydrogen handling, and (e) Hydrochloric acid plant.
   [92][* * *]

10. All effluents discharged including from the industries such as cotton textile, composite woolen mills, synthetic rubber, small pulp and paper, natural rubber, petro-chemicals, tanneries, paint, dyes, slaughter houses, food & fruit processing

[92] *Omitted* by G.S.R. 176 (E), dated 2 April 1996.

and dairy [91][industries] into surface waters shall conform to the BOD limits specified above, namely, 30 mg/l. For discharge of an effluent having a BOD more than 30mg/l, the standards shall conform to those given above for other receiving bodies, namely, sewers, coastal waters and land for irrigation. [92][* * *]

12. In case of fertilizer industry the limits in respect of chromium and [91][fluoride] shall be complied with at the outlet of chromium and [91][fluoride] removal units respectively.

13. In case of pesticides:

(a) The limits should be complied with at the end of treatment plant before dilution.

(b) Bio-assay test should be carried out with the available species of fish in the receiving water, the COD limits to be specified in the consent conditions should be correlated with the BOD limits.

(c) In case metabolities and isomers of the pesticides in the given list are found in significant concentrations, standards should be prescribed for these also in the same concentrations as the individual pesticides.

(d) Industries are required to analyse pesticides in waste water by advanced analytical methods such as GLC/HPLC.

[93][14. The chemical oxygen demand (COD) concentration in a treated effluent, if observed to be persistently greater than 250 mg/l before disposal to any receiving body (public sewer, land for irrigaton, inland surface water and marine coastal areas), such industrial units are required to identify chemicals causing the same. In case these are found to be toxic as defined in the Schedule I of the Hazardous Wastes (Management and Handling) Rules, 1989 the State Boards in such cases shall direct the industries to install tertiary treatment stipulating time limit.

15. Standards specified in Part A of Schedule VI for the discharge of effluents into the public sewer shall be applicable only if such sewer lead to a secondary treatment including biological treatment system, otherwise these discharge into sewers shall be treated as discharge into inland surface waters.]

ANNEXURE II
(For the purpose of Part D)

1. The State Board shall follow the following guidelines in enforcing the standards specified under Schedule VI:

(a) In case of cement plants, the total dust (from all sections) shall be within 400 mg/[94][Nm^3] and 250 mg/[94][Nm]^3 for the plants up to 200 t/d and more than 200 t/d capacities respectively.

---

[93] *Ins.* by G.S.R. 80 (E), dated 31 December 1993.
[94] *Subs.* by G.S.R. 80 (E), dated 31 December 1993.

(b) In respect of calcination process (e.g. Aluminium plants), kilns and Step Grate Bagasse-fired-Boilers. Particulate Matter (PM) emissions shall be within 250 mg/[94][Nm^3].

(c) In case of thermal power plants commissioned prior to 1.1.1982 and having generation capacity less than 62.5 MW, the PM emission shall be within 350 mg/[94][Nm^3].

(d) In case of Lime Kilns of capacity more than 5 t/day and up to 49 t/day, the PM emission shall be within 500 mg/[94][Nm^3].

(e) In case of horse shoe/Pulsating Grate and Spreader Stroker Bagasse-fired-Boilers, the PM emission shall be within 500 (12% CO_2) and 800 (12% CO_2) mg/[94][Nm^3] respectively. In respect of these boilers, if more than attached to a single stack, the emission standard shall be fixed, based on added capacity of all the boilers connected with the stack.

(f) In case of asbestos dust, the same shall not exceed 2 mg/[94][Nm^3].

(g) In case of the urea plants commissioned after 1.1.1982, coke ovens and lead glas units, the PM emission shall be within 50 mg/[94][Nm^3].

(h) In case of small boilers of capacity less than 2 tons/hr and between 2 to 5 tons/hr the PM emissions shall be within 1600 and 1200 mg/[94][Nm^3]

(i) In cae of integrated Iron and Steel Plants, PM emission up to 400 mg/[94][Nm^3] shall be allowed during oxygen lancing.

(j) In case of stone crushing units, the suspended PM contribution value at a distance of 40 metres from a controlled isolated as well as from a unit located in the cluster should be less than 600 [94][micrograms/Nm^3] [95][* * *]

These units must also adopt the following pollution control measures:

   (i) Dust containment cum suppression system for the equipment;

   (ii) Construciton of wind breaking walls;

   (iii) Construction of the metalled roads within the premises;

   (iv) Regular cleaning and wetting of the ground within the premises;

   (v) Growing of a green belt along the periphery.

(k) In case of copper, lead and zinc smelting, the off-gases may, as far as possible, be utilized for manufacturing sulphuric acid.]

2. The total fluoride emissions in respect of glass and phosphatic fertilizers shall not exceed 5 mg/Nm^3 and 25 mg/Nm^3 respectively.

3. [94][In case of copper, lead and zinc smelting, the off-gases may, as far as possible, be utilised for manufacturing sulphuric acid.]

[96][4. In case of cupolas (Foundries) having capacity (melting rate) less than 3 tonne/hour, the particulate matter emission shall be within 450 mg/Nm^3. In these cases it is essential that stack is constructed over the cupola beyond the charging

[95] *Omitted* by G.S.R. 80 (E), dated 31 December 1993.

[96] *Ins.* by G.S.R. 80 (E), dated 31 December 1993.

door and the emissions are directed through the stack, which should be at least six times the diameter of cupola. In respect of Arc Furnaces and Induction Furnaces, provision has to be made for collecting the fumes before discharging the emissions through the stack.]

[97][SCHEDULE VII
(*See* Rule (3B))
National Ambient Air Quality Standards (NAAQS)

Pollutant	Time weighted Average	Concentration in Ambient Air			
		Industrial Area	Residential Rural and other area	Sensitive Area	Method of measurement
(1)	(2)	(3)	(4)	(5)	(6)
Sulphur Dioxide (SO_2)	Annual Average*	80 ug/m^3	60 ug/m^3	15 ug/m^3	—Improved West and Gaeke method
	24 hours**	120 ug/m^3	80 ug/m^3	30 ug/m^3	—Ultraviolet fluorescence
Oxides of nitrogen as NO_2	Annual Average*	80 ug/m^3	60 ug/m^3	15 ug/m^3	—Jacab & Hochheiser modified (Na-Arsenite) Method
	24 hours**	120 ug/m^3	80 ug/m^3	80 ug/m^3	—Gas Phase Chemiluminescence
Suspended Particulate Matter (SPM)	Annual Average*	360 ug/m^3	140 ug/m^3	70 ug/m^3	—High Volume Sampling
	24 hours**	500 ug/m^3	200 ug/m^3	100 ug/m^3	—[Average flow rate not less than m^3/minute]
Respirable Particulate Matter (size less than 10 um) RPM	Annual Average*	120 ug/m^3	60 ug/m^3	50 ug/m^3	—Respirable particulate matter sampler.
	24 hours**	150 ug/m^3	100 ug/m^3	75 ug/m^3	

Ins. by G.S.R. 176 (E), dated 2 April 1996.

Pollutant	Time weighted Average	Concentration in Ambient Air			
		Industrial Area	Residential Rural and other area	Sensitive Area	Method of measurement
(1)	(2)	(3)	(4)	(5)	(6)
Lead (Pb)	Annual Average*	1.0 ug/m^3	0.75 ug/m^3	0.50 ug/m^3	—AAS method after sampling using EMP 2000 or equivalent filter paper.
	24 hours**	1.5 ug/m^3	1.00 ug/m^3	0.75 ug/m^3	
Carbon Monoxide	8 hours**	5.0 mg/m^3	2.0 mg/m^3	1.0 mg/m^3	—Non disbursive, infrared spectroscopy.
	1 hour	10.0 mg/m^3	4.00 mg/m^3	2.0 mg/m^3	

* Annual Arithmetic mean of minimum 104 measurements in a year taken twice a week 24 hourly uniform interval.

** 24 hourly/8 hourly values shall be met 98% of the time in a year. 2% of the time, it may exceed but not on two consecutive days.

Note:

1. National Ambient Air Quality Standard: The levels of air quality necessary with an adequate margin of safety, to protect the public health, vegetation and property.

2. Whenever and wherever two consecutive values exceeds the limit specified above for the respective category, it shall be considered adequate reason to institute regular/continuous monitoring and further investigations.]

* * *

E

COASTAL REGULATIONS

THE COASTAL REGULATION ZONE NOTIFICATION

Notification No. S.O. 114(E), dated 19 February 1991[1]

Notification under section 3(1) and section 3(2)(v) of the Environment (Protection) Act, 1986 and Rule 5(3)(d) of the Environment (Protection) Rules, 1986 declaring Coastal Stretches as Coastal Regulation Zone (CRZ) and Regulating Activities in the CRZ.

S.O.114(E).—Whereas a Notification under section 3(1) and section 3(2)(v) of the Environment (Protection) Act, 1986, inviting objections against the declaration of Coastal Stretches as Coastal Regulation Zone (CRZ) and imposing restrictions on industries, operations and processes in the CRZ was published vide S.O. No. 944 (E) dated 15th December 1990.

And whereas all objections received have been duly considered by the Central Government;

Now, therefore, in exercise of the power conferred by Clause (d) of sub-rule (3) of Rule 5 of the Environment (Protection) Rules, 1986, and all other powers vesting in its behalf, the Central Government hereby declares the coastal stretches of seas, bays, estuaries, creeks, rivers and backwaters which are influenced by tidal action (in the landward side) upto 500 metres from the High Tide Line (HTL) and the land between the Low Tide Line (LTL) and the HTL as Coastal Regulation Zone; and imposes with effect from the date of this Notification, the following restrictions on the setting up and expansion of industries, operations or processes, etc., in the said Coastal Regulation Zone (CRZ).

[2][For the purposes of this notification, the High Tide Line means the line on

---

[1] Published in *Gazette of India, Extraordinary*, Pt. II, Sec.3(ii), dated 20 February 1991.
[2] *Subs.* by S.O.1122(E), dated 29 December 1998.

the land upto which the highest water line reaches during the spring tide. The High Tide Line shall be demarcated uniformly in all parts of the country by the demarcating authority or authorities so authorised by the Central Government, in accordance with the general guidelines issued in this regard.]

[3][NOTE:

The distance from the High Tide Line shall apply to both sides in the case of rivers, creeks and back waters and may be notified on a case by case basis for reasons to be recorded while preparing the Coastal Regulation Zone Management Plans. However, this distance shall not be less than [4][100] metres or the width of the creek, river or back-water whichever is less. The distance upto which development along rivers, creeks and back-waters is to be regulated shall be governed by the distance upto which the tidal effect of the sea is experienced in rivers, creeks or back-waters, as the case may be, and should be clearly identified in the Coastal Zone Management Plans.]

2. Prohibited Activities:

The following activities are declared as prohibited within the Coastal Regulation Zone, namely:

(i) setting up of new industries and expansion of existing industries, except those directly related to water front or directly needing foreshore facilities;

(ii) manufacture or handling or storage or disposal of hazardous substances as specified in the Notifications of the Government of India in the Ministry of Environment and Forests No. S.O. 594 (E) dated 28 July 1989, S.O. 966(E) dated 27 November 1989 and GSR 1037 (E) dated 5 December 1989 [5][except transfer of hazardous substances from ships to ports, terminals and refineries and vice cersa, in the port areas:

Provided that Government of India in the Ministry of Surface Transport, on a case to case basis, may permit storage of petroleum products as specified in Annexure-III appended to this notification within the existing port limits of existing ports and harbours and in those areas of ports that have not been classified as CRZ-I subject to implementation of safety regulations including guidelines issued by Oil Safety Directorate in the Government of India, Ministry of Petroleum and Natural Gas after ensuring proper location of site and availability of necessary equipment to meet the safety norms and the exigencies arising due to any accident or spillage.]

(iii) setting up and expansion of fish processing units including warehousing (excluding hatchery and natural fish drying in permitted areas);

---

[3] *Subs.* by S.O. 595(E), dated 18 August 1994.

[4] *Restored* by the Supreme Court by its order dated 18 April 1996 in *Indian Council for Enviro-Legal Action v Union of India* (*CRZ Notification Case*) 1996 (5) SCC 281. The distance of 100 metres provided by the original notification dated 19 February 1991 was reduced to 50 metres by the amending notification S.O. 595(E), dated 18 August 1994.

[5] *Ins.* by S.O. 494(E) dated 9 July 1997.

[5][Provided that existing fish processing units for modernization purposes may utilise twenty five per cent additional plinth area required for additional equipment and pollution control measures only subject to existing Floor Space Index/ Floor Area Ratio norms and subject to the condition that the additional plinth area shall not be towards seaward side of existing unit and also subject to the approval of State Pollution Control Board or Pollution Control Committee.]

(iv) setting up and expansion of units/mechanism for disposal of waste and effluents, except facilities required for discharging treated effluents into the water course with approval under the Water (Prevention and Control of Pollution) Act, 1974; and except for storm water drains;

(v) discharge of untreated wastes and effluents from industries, cities or towns and other human settlements. Schemes shall be implemented by the concerned authorities for phasing out the existing practices, if any, within a reasonable time period not exceeding three years from the date of this notification;

(vi) dumping of city or town waste for the purposes of landfilling or otherwise; the existing practice, if any, shall be phased out within a reasonable time not exceeding 3 years from the date of this Notification;

(vii) dumping of ash or any wastes from thermal power stations;

[6][(viii) land reclamation, bunding or disturbing the natural course of sea water except those required for construction of ports, harbours, jetties, wharves, quays, slipways, bridges and sea-links and for other facilities that are essential for activities permissible under the notification; or for control of coastal erosion and maintenance or clearing of water ways, channels and ports or for prevention of sandbars or for tidal regulators, storm water drains or for structures for prevention of salinity ingress and for sweet water recharge;]

(ix) mining of sands, rocks and other substrata materials, except those rare minerals not available outside the CRZ areas;

[7][Provided that in the union territory of the Andaman and Nicobar Islands, mining of sands may be permitted by the Committee which shall be constituted by the Lieutenant Governor of the Andaman and Nicobar Islands consisting of Chief Secretary, Department of Environment; Secretary, Department of Water Resources; and Secretary, Public Works Department. Committee may permit mining of sand from non-degraded areas for construction purposes from selected sites, in a regulated manner on a case to case basis, for a period upto the 31st day of March, 1998. The quantity of sand mined shall not exceed the essential requirements for completion

[6] *Subs.* by S.O. 494(E) dated 9 July 1997.

[7] *Ins.* by S.O.73(E) dated 31 January 1997. Clause 2(1)(b) of the notification purports to insert the proviso under sub-paragraph (x), which pertains to ground water harvesting. This appears to be an apparent error. We have reproduced the proviso under sub-paragraph (ix), since both the sub-paragraph and the proviso pertain to the mining of sands.

of construction works including dwelling units, shops in respect of current year and 1997-98 annual plans. The permission of mining of sand may be given on the basis of a mining plan from such sites and in such quantity which shall not have adverse impacts on the environment.]

    (x) harvesting or drawal of ground water and construction of mechanisms therefor within 200 m of HTL; in the 200 m to 500 m zone it shall be permitted only when done manually through ordinary wells for drinking, horticulture, agriculture and fisheries;

[8][Provided that drawal of ground water is permitted, where no other source of water is available and when done manually through ordinary wells or hand pumps, for drinking and domestic purposes, in the zone between 50 to 200 m from High Tide Line in case of seas, bays and estuaries and within 200 m or the CRZ, whichever is less, from High Tide Line in case of rivers, creeks and back-waters subject to such restrictions, as may be deemed necessary, in areas affected by sea water intrusion, that may be imposed by an authority designated by State Government/ Union Territory Administration.]

    (xi) construction activities in ecologically sensitive areas as specified in Annexure I of this Notification;

    (xii) any construction activity between the LTL and HTL except facilities for carrying treated effluents and waste water discharges into the sea, facilities for carrying sea water for cooling purposes, oil, gas and similar pipelines and facilities essential for activities permitted under this Notification; and

    (xiii) dressing or altering of sand dunes, hills, natural features including landscape charges for beautification, recreational and other such purpose, except as permissible under the Notification.

3. Regulation of Permissible Activities:

    All other activities, except those prohibited in para 2 above, will be regulated as under:

    (1) Clearance shall be given for any activity within the Coastal Regulation Zone only if it requires water front and foreshore facilities.

    (2) The following activities will require environmental clearance from the Ministry of Environment and Forests, Government of India, namely:

    (i) Construction activities related to Defence requirements for which foreshore facilities are essential (e.g. slipways, jetties, etc.); except for classified operational component of Defence projects for whieh a separate procedure shall be followed. (Residential buildings, office buildings, hospital complexes, workshops shall not come within the definition of operational requirements except in very special cases and hence shall not normally be permitted in the CRZ);

[8] *Subs.* by S.O. 494(E) dated 9 July 1997.

[9][(ii) Operational constructions for ports and harbours and light houses and constructions for activities such as jetties, wharves, quays and slipways.

Provided that for expansion or modernization of existing ports and harbours including fishing harbours operational constructions for ports and harbours and construction of jetties, wharves, quays, slipways, Single Point Mooring and Single Buoy Mooring and for reclamation for facilities essential for operational requirements of ports and harbours in areas within the existing port limits, except the areas classified as category CRZ-I(i), shall require environmental clearance from Government of India in the Ministry of Surface Transport, which shall take decision on these activities on the basis of Environmental Impact Assessment Report.

Provided further that reclamation for commercial purposes such as shopping and housing complexes, hotels and entertainment activities shall not be permissible.]

(iii) Thermal power plants (only foreshore facilities for transport of raw materials facilities for in-take of cooling water and outfall for discharge of treated waste water/cooling water); and

[9][(iv) All other activities with investment exceeding rupees five crores except those activities which are to be regulated by the concerned authorities at the state/union territory level in accordance with the provisions of paragraph 6, sub-paragraph (2) of Annexure I of the notification.]

(3) (i) The coastal states union territory Administration shall prepare, within a period of one year from the date of this Notification, Coastal Zone Management Plans identifying and classifying the CRZ areas within their respective territories in accordance with the guidelines given in Annexures I and II of the Notification and obtain approval (with or without modifications) of the Central Government in the Ministry of Environment & Forests;

(ii) Within the framework of such approved plans, all development and activities within the CRZ other than those covered in para 2 and para 3(2) above shall be regulated by the state government, union territory Administration or the local authority as the case may be in accordance with the guidelines given in Annexures I and II of the Notification; and

(iii) In the interim period till the Coastal Zone Management Plans mentioned in para 3(3)(i) above are prepared and approved, all developments and activities within the CRZ shall not violate the provisions of this Notification. state governments and union territory Administrations shall ensure adherence to these regulations and violations, if any, shall be subject to the provisions of the Environment (Protection) Act, 1986.

4. Procedure for monitoring and enforcement:

The Ministry of Environment & Forests and the Government of state or union territory and such other authorities at the state or union territory levels, as may be

[9] *Subs.* by S.O. 494(E) dated 9 July 1997.

designated for this purpose, shall be responsible for monitoring and enforcement of the provisions of this notification within their respective jurisdictions.

ANNEXURE—I

COASTAL AREA CLASSIFICATION AND
DEVELOPMENT REGULATIONS

6. Classification of Coastal Regulation Zone:

6(1) For regulating development activities, the coastal stretches within 500 metres of High Tide Line on the landward side are classified into four categories, namely:

Category I (CRZ—I):

(i) Areas that are ecologically sensitive and important, such as national parks/ marine parks, sanctuaries, reserve forests, wildlife habitats, mangroves, corals/coral reefs, areas close to breeding and spawning grounds of fish and other marine life, areas of outstanding natural beauty/historically/ heritage areas, areas rich in genetic diversity, areas likely to be inundated due to rise in sea level consequent upon global warming and such other areas as may be declared by the Central Government or the concerned authorities at the state/union territory level from time to time.

(ii) Area between the Low Tide Line and the High Tide Line.

Category—II (CRZ—II):

The areas that have already been developed upto or close to the shore-line. For this purpose, 'developed area' is referred to as that area within the municipal limits or in other legally designated urban areas which is already substantially built up and which has been provided with drainage and approach roads and other infrastructural facilities, such as water supply and sewerage mains.

Category—III (CRZ—III):

Areas that are relatively undisturbed and those which do not belong to either Category-I or II. These will include coastal zone in the rural areas (developed and undeveloped) and also areas within Municipal limits or in other legally designated urban areas which are not substantially built up.

Category—IV (CRZ—IV):

Coastal stretches in the Andaman & Nicobar, Lakshadweep and small islands, except those designated as CRZ-I, CRZ-II or CRZ-III.

Norms for Regulation of Activities.

6(2) The development or construction activities in different categories of CRZ area shall be regulated by the concerned authorities at the state/union territory level, in accordance with the following norms:

CRZ—I

No new construction shall be permitted within 500 metres of the High Tide Line. No construction activity, except as listed under 2 (xii), will be permitted between the Low Tide Line and the High Tide Line.

[10][Provided that construction of dispensaries, schools, public rain shelters, community toilets, bridges, roads, jetties, water supply, drainage, sewerage which are required for traditional inhabitants of the Sunderbans Bio-sphere reserve area, West Bengal, may be permitted, on a case to case basis, by an authority designated by the state government.]

CRZ—II

(i) [11][Buildings shall be permitted only on the landward side of the existing road (or roads proposed in the approved Coastal Zone Management Plan of the area) or on the landward side of existing authorised structures. Buildings permitted on the landward side of the existing and proposed roads/existing authorised structures shall be subject to the existing local Town and Country Planning Regulations including the existing norms of Floor Space Index/Floor Area Ratio.

Provided that no permission for construction of buildings shall be given on landward side of any new roads (except roads proposed in the approved Coastal Zone Management Plan) which are constructed on the seaward side of an existing road.]

(ii) Reconstruction of the authorised buildings to be permitted subject to the existing FSI/FAR norms and without change in the existing use.

(iii) The design and construction of buildings shall be consistent with the surrounding landscape and local architectural style.

CRZ—III

(i) The area upto 200 metres from the HTL is to be earmarked as 'No Development Zone'. [11][No construction shall be permitted within this zone except for repairs of existing authorised structures not exceeding existing FSI, existing plinth area and existing density, and for permissible activities under the notification including facilities essential for such activities.

[10] *Ins.* by S.O. 494(E) dated 9 July 1997.
[11] *Subs.* by *ibid.*

An authority designated by the state government/union territory Administration may permit construction of facilities for water supply, drainage and sewerage for requirements of local inhabitants.] However, the following uses may be permissible in this zone—agriculture, horticulture, gardens, pastures, parks, play fields, forestry and salt manufacture from sea water.

(ii) Development of vacant plots between 200 and 500 metres of High Tide Line in designated areas of CRZ—III with prior approval of Ministry of Environment and Forests (MEF) permitted for construction of hotels/breach resorts for temporary occupation of tourists/visitors subject to the conditions as stipulated in the guidelines at Annexure—II.

(iii) Construction/reconstruction of dwelling units between 200 and 500 metres of the HTL permitted so long it is within the ambit of traditional rights and customary uses such as existing fishing villages and gaothans. Building permission for such construction/reconstruction will be subject to the conditions that the total number of dwelling units shall not be more than twice the number of existing units; total covered area on all floors shall not exceed 33 per cent of the plot size; the overall height of construction shall not exceed 9 metres and construction shall not be more than 2 floors (ground floor plus one floor). [12][Construction is allowed for permissible activities under the notification including facilities essential for such activities. An authority designated by state government/union territory Administration may permit construction of public rain shelters, community toilets, water supply, drainage, sewer age, roads and bridges. The said authority may also permit construction of schools and dispensaries for local inhabitants of the area for those panchayats the major part of which falls within CRZ if no other area is available for construction of such facilities.]

(iv) Reconstruction/alterations of an existing authorized building permitted subject to (i) to (iii) above.

CRZ—IV

Andaman & Nicobar Islands:

(i) No new construction of buildings shall be permitted within 200 metres of the HTL;

(ii) The buildings between 200 and 500 metres from the High Tide Line shall not have more than 2 floors (ground floor and first floor), the total covered area on all floors shall not be more than 50 per cent of

[12] *Ins.* by S.O.494(E) dated 9 July 1997.

the plot size and the total height of construction shall not exceed 9 metres;

(iii) The design and construction of buildings shall be consistent with the surrounding landscape and local architectural style.

[13][(iv) (a) Corals from the beaches and coastal waters shall not be used for construction and other purposes;

(b) sand may be used from the beaches and coastal waters, only for construction purpose upto the 31st day of March, 1998 and thereafter it shall not be used for construction and other purposes.]

(v) Dredging and underwater blasting in and around coral formations shall not be permitted; and

(vi) However, in some of the islands, coastal stretches may also be classified into categories CRZ—I or II or III with the prior approval of Ministry of Environment and Forests and in such designated stretches, the appropriate regulations given for respective Categories shall apply.

Lakshadweep and small Islands:

(i) For permitting construction of buildings the distance from the High Tide Line shall be decided depending on the size of the islands. This shall be laid down for each island, in consultation with the experts and with approval of the Ministry of Environment & Forests, keeping in view the land use requirement for specific purposes vis-a-vis local conditions including hydrological aspects erosion and ecological sensitivity;

(ii) The buildings within 500 metres from the HTL shall not have more than 2 floors (ground floor and 1st floor), the total covered area on all floors shall not be more than 50 per cent of the plot size and the total height of construction shall not exceed 9 metres;

(iii) The design and construction of buildings shall be consistent with the surrounding landscape and local architectural style;

(iv) Coral and sand from the beaches and coastal waters shall not be used for construction and other purposes;

(v) Dredging and underwater blasting in and around coral formations shall not be permitted; and

(vi) However, is some of the islands, coastal stretches may also be classified into categories CRZ—I or II or III, with the prior approval of Ministry of Environment & Forests and in such designated stretches, the appropriate regulations given for respective Categories shall apply.

[13] *Subs.* by S.O. 73(E) dated 31 January 1997.

ANNEXURE—II

GUIDELINES FOR DEVELOPMENT OF BEACH RESORTS/HOTELS IN THE
DESIGNATED AREAS OF CRZ—III FOR TEMPORARY OCCUPATION OF
TOURIST/VISITORS, WITH PRIOR APPROVAL OF THE MINISTRY OF
ENVIRONMENT & FORESTS

7(1) Construction of beach resorts/hotels with prior approval of MEF in the designated areas of CRZ-III for temporary occupation of tourists/visitors shall be subject to the following conditions:

[14][(i) The project proponent shall not undertake any construction within 200 metres in the land ward side from the High Tide Line and within the area between the Low Tide and High Tide Lines;

Provided that the Central Government may, after taking into account geographical features and overall Coastal Zone Management Plan, and for reasons to be recorded in writing, permit any construction subject to such conditions and restrictions as it may deem fit;[15]

(ia) live fencing and barbed wire fencing with vegetative cover may be allowed around private properties subject to the condition that such fencing shall in no way hamper public access to the beach;

(ib) no flattening of sand dunes shall be carried out;

(ic) no permanent structures for sports facilities shall be permitted except construction of goal posts, net posts and lamp posts;

(id) construction of basements may be allowed subject to the condition that no objection certificate is obtained from the State Ground Water Authority to the effect that such construction will not adversely affect free flow of ground water in that area. The State Ground Water Authority shall take into consideration the guidelines issued by the Central Government before granting such no objection certificate.

Explanation:

Though no construction is allowed in the no development zone for the purposes of calculation of FSI, the area of entire plot including [16][half] the portion which falls within the no development zone shall be taken into account.]

(ii) The total plot size shall not be less than 0.4 hectares and the total covered area on all floors shall not exceed 33 per cent of the plot size i.e. the FSI shall not exceed 0.33. The open area shall be suitably landscaped with appropriate vegetal cover;

---

[14] *Subs.* by S.O. 595(E) dated 18 August 1994.

[15] Italicised portion declared *ultra vires* in the *CRZ Notification Case, supra* note 4, at 298.

[16] *Modified* by the Supreme Court in the *CRZ Notification Case, supra* note 4, at 299. Prior to the modification, the entire area of the no development zone could be regarded for calculating FSI.

(iii) The construction shall be consistent with the surrounding landscape and local architectural style;

(iv) The overall height of construction upto the highest ridge of the roof, shall not exceed 9 metres and the construction shall not be more than 2 floors (ground floor plus one upper floor);

(v) Ground water shall not be tapped within 200 m of the HTL; within the 200 metres—500 metres zone, it can be tapped only with the concurrence of the Central/State Ground Water Board;

(vi) Extraction of sand, leveling or digging of sandy stretches except for structural foundation of building, swimming pool shall not be permitted within 500 metres of the High Tide Line;

(vii) The quality of treated effluents, solid wastes, emissions and noise levels, etc. from the project area must conform to the standards laid down by the competent authorities including the Central/State Pollution Control Board and under the Environment (Protection) Act, 1986;

(viii) Necessary arrangements for the treatment of the effluents and solid wastes must be made. It must be ensured that the untreated effluents and solid wastes are not discharged into the water or on the beach; and no effluent/ solid waste shall be discharged on the beach;

(ix) To allow public access to the beach, at least a gap of 20 metres width shall be provided between any two hotels/beach resorts; and in no case shall gaps be less than 500 metres apart; and

(x) If the project involves diversion of forest land for non-forest purpose, clearance as required under the Forest (Conservation) Act, 1980 shall be obtained. The requirements of other Central and State laws as applicable to the project shall be met with.

(xi) Approval of the state/union territory Tourism Department shall be obtained.

7(2) In ecologically sensitive areas (such as marine parks, mangroves, coral reefs, breeding and spawning grounds of fish, wildlife habitats and such other areas as may notified by the Central/state government/union territories) construction of beach resorts/hotels shall not be permitted.

[17][ANNEXURE—III

[See paragraph 2, sub-paragraph (ii)]

LIST OF PETROLEUM PRODUCTS PERMITTED
FOR STORAGE IN PORT AREAS

(i) Crude Oil;
(ii) Liquified Petroleum Gas;

[17] *Ins.* by S.O.494(E) dated 9 July 1997.

    (iii) Motor Spirit;
    (iv) Kerosene;
    (v) Aviation Fuel;
    (vi) High Speed Diesel;
    (vii) Lubricating Oil;
    (viii) Butane;
    (ix) Propane;
    (x) Compressed Natural Gas;
    (xi) Naptha;
    (xii) Furnace Oil;
    (xiii) Low Sulphur Heavy Stock.]

F

ENVIRONMENTAL IMPACT ASSESSMENT
REGULATIONS

Notification No. S.O. 60 (E), dated 27 January, 1994

Whereas a notification under clause (a) of sub-rule (3) of rule 5 of the Environment (Protection) Rules, 1986 inviting objections from the public within sixty days from the date of publication of the said notification, against the intention of the Central Government to impose restrictions and prohibitions on the expansion and modernization of any activity or new projects being undertaken in any part of India unless environmental clearance has been accorded by the Central Government or the state government in accordance with the procedure specified in that notification was published as S.O.No. 80 (E), dated 28 January 1993;

And whereas all objections received have been duly considered;

Now, therefore, in exercise of the powers conferred by sub-section (1) and clause (v) of sub-section (2) of section 3 of the Environment (Protection) Act, 1986 (XXIX of 1986) read with clause (d) of sub-rule (3) of rule 5 of the Environment (Protection) Rules, 1986, the Central Government hereby directs that on and from the date of publication of this notification in the Official Gazette, expansion or modernization of any activity if pollution load is to exceed the existing one, or new project listed in Schedule I to this notification, shall not be undertaken in any part of India unless it has been accorded environmental clearance by the Central Government in accordance with the procedure hereinafter specified in this notification;

2. Requirements and procedure for seeking environmental clearance of projects:

I. (a) Any person who desires to undertake any new project in any part of India or the expansion or modernization of any existing industry or project listed in the Schedule I shall submit an application to the Secretary, Ministry of Environment and Forests, New Delhi.

The application shall be made in the proforma specified in Schedule II to this notification and shall be accompanied by [1][a project report which shall, inter alia, include an Environmental Impact Assessment Report] [2][Environment Management plan and details of public hearing as specified in Schedule IV] prepared in accordance with the guidelines issued by the Central Government in the Ministry of Environment and Forests from time to time.

(b) Case rejected due to submission of insufficient or inadequate data and [3][Plan] may be reviewed as and when submitted with complete data and [4][Plan]. Submission of [5][incomplete data or plans for] the second time would itself be a sufficient reason for the Impact Assessment Agency to reject the case summarily.

II. In case of the following site specified projects— -

(a) mining;

(b) pit-head thermal power stations;

(c) hydro-power, major irrigation projects and/or their combination including flood control;

(d) ports and harbours (excluding minor ports);

[6][(e) prospecting and exploration of major minerals in areas above 500 hectares.]

The project authorities will intimate the location of the project site to the Central Government in the Ministry of Environment and Forests while initiating any investigation and surveys. The Central Government in the Ministry of Environment and Forests will convey a decision regarding suitability or otherwise of the proposed site within a maximum period of thirty days. [7][The said site clearance shall be granted for a sanctioned capacity and shall be valid for a period of five years for commencing the construction, operation or mining.]

III. (a) [8][The reports] submitted with the application shall be evaluated and assessed by the Impact Assessment [9][Agency, and if deemed necessary it may consult] a Committee of Experts, having a composition as specified in Schedule-III of this Notification. The Impact Assessment Agency (IAA) would be the Union Ministry of Environment and Forests. The Committee of Experts mentioned above shall be constituted by the Impact Assessment Agency [10][* * *] or such other body under the Central Government authorised by the IAA in this regard.

(b) The said Committee of Experts shall have full right of entry and inspection of the site or, as the case may be, factory premises at any time prior to, during or after the commencement of the operations relating to the project.

---

[1] *Subs.* by S.O. 356 (E), dated 4 May 1994.
[2] *Subs.* by S.O. 318 (E), dated 10 April 1997.
[3] *Subs.* by S.O. 356 (E), dated 4 May 1994.
[4] *Id.*
[5] *Id.*
[6] *Id.*
[7] *Subs.* by S.O. 356 (E), dated 4 May 1994.
[8] *Id.*
[9] *Id.*
[10]*Omitted* by S.O. 356 (E), dated 4 May 1994.

[11][(c) The Impact Assessment Agency shall prepare a set of recommendations based on the technical assessment of documents and data furnished by the project authorities and supplemented by data collected during visits of sites of factories, if undertaken and details of public hearing.

The assessment shall be completed within a period of ninety days from receipt of the requisite documents and data from the project authorities and completion of public hearing and decision conveyed within thirty days thereafter.

The clearance granted shall be valid for a period of five years from commencement of the construction or operation of the project.]

[12][IIIA. No construction work, preliminary or otherwise, relating to the setting up of the project may be undertaken until the environmental and site clearance is obtained.]

[13][IV. In order to enable the Impact Assessment Agency concerned to monitor effectively the implementation of the recommendations and conditions subject to which the environmental clearance has been given, the project authorities concerned shall submit a half-yearly report to the Impact Assessment Agency. Subject to the public interest the Impact Assessment Agency shall make compliance reports publicly available.]

V. If no comments from the Impact Assessment Agency are received within the time limit, the project would be deemed to have been approved as proposed by project authorities.

3. Nothing contained in this Notification shall apply to:

    (a) any item falling under Entry Nos. 3, 18 and 20 of Schedule I to be located or proposed to be located in the areas covered by the Notifications S.O. No. 102(E), dated 1 February 1989; S.O. No. 114(E) dated 20 February 1991; [14][S.O. No. 416(E) dated 20 June 1991 and S.O. No. 319(E) dated 7 May 1992.]

    (b) any item falling under entry Nos. 1, 2, 3, 4, 5, 7, 9, 10, 12, 13, 14, 16, 17, [15][19, 21, 25] and 27 of Schedule I if the investment is less than Rs. 50 crores.

    (c) any item reserved for Small Scale Industrial sector with investments less than Rs. 1 crore.

4.   Concealing factual data or submission of false, misleading data / reports, decisions or recommendations would lead to the project being rejected. Approval, if granted earlier on the basis of false data, would also be revoked. Misleading and wrong information will cover the following:

— False information.

— False data.

— Engineered reports.

[11] *Subs.* by S.O. 318(E), dated 10 April 1997.
[12] *Ins.* by S.O. 356 (E), dated 4 May 1994.
[13] *Subs.* by S.O. 318(E), dated 10 April 1997.
[14] *Subs.* by S.O. 356(E), dated 4 May 1994.
[15] *Id.*

— Concealing of factual data.
— False recommendations or decisions.

SCHEDULE I

(See Paras 1 and 2)

LIST OF PROJECTS REQUIRING ENVIRONMENTAL CLEARANCE FROM THE CENTRAL GOVERNMENT

1. Nuclear Power and related projects such as Heavy Water Plants, nuclear fuel complex, rare earths.
2. River Valley Projects including hydel power, major irrigation and their combination including flood control.
3. Ports, Harbours, Airports (except minor ports and harbours).
4. Petroleum Refineries including crude and product pipelines.
5. Chemical Fertilizers (Nitrogenous and Phosphatic other than single super-phosphate).
6. Pesticides (Technical).
7. Petrochemical complexes (Both Olefinic and Aromatic) and Petrochemical intermediates such as DMT, Caprolactam, LAB, etc. and production of basic plastics such as LLPDE, HPDE, PP PVC.
8. Bulk drugs and pharmaceuticals.
9. Exploration for oil and gas and their production, transportation and storage.
10. Synthetic Rubber.
11. Asbestos and Asbestos products.
12. Hydrocyanic acid and its derivatives.
13. (a) Primary metallurgical industries (such as production of Iron and Steel, Aluminium, Copper, Zinc, Lead and Ferro Alloys).
    (b) Electric arc furnaces (Mini Steel Plants).
14. Chlor alkali industry.
15. Integrated paint complex including manufacture of resins and basic raw materials required in the manufacture of paints.
16. Viscose staple fibre and filament yarn.
17. Storage batteries integrated with manufacture of oxides of lead and lead antimony alloy.
18. All tourism projects between 200m–500 meters of High Water Line and at locations with an elevation of more than 1000 meters with investment of more than Rs. 5 crores.
19. Thermal power plants.
[16][20. Mining projects (major minerals with leases more than 5 hectares).]

[16] *Subs.* by S.O. 356(E), dated 4 May 1994.

21. [17][Highway Projects except projects relating to improvement work including widening and strengthening of roads with marginal land acquisition along the existing alignments provided it does not pass through ecologically sensitive areas such as National Parks, Sanctuaries, Tiger reserves, Reserve forests.]
22. Tarred Roads in Himalayas and or Forest areas.
23. Distilleries.
24. Raw Skins and Hides.
25. Pulp, paper and newsprint.
26. Dyes.
27. Cement.
28. Foundries (individual).
29. Electroplating.

SCHEDULE II

(See Sub-para I (a) of Para 2)

APPLICATION FORM

1.	(a) Name and Address of the project proposed	
	(b) Location of the project	
	Name of the Place	
	District, Tehsil	
	Latitude/Longitude	
	Nearest Airport/Railway Station	
	(c) Alternate sites examined and the reasons for selecting the proposed site	
	(d) Does the site conform to stipulated land use as per local land use plan	
2.	Objectives of the project	
3.	(a) Land Requirement	
	Agriculture Land	
	Forest Land and Density of vegetation.	
	Others (specify)	
	(b) (i) Land use in the Catchment/within 10 km. radius of the proposed site	
	(ii) Topography of the area indicating gradient, aspects and altitude	

[17] *Subs.* by S.O. 318(E), dated 10 April 1997.

	(iii)	Erodability classification of the proposed land	
	(c)	Pollution sources existing in 10 km, radius and their Impact on quality of air, water and land	
	(d)	Distance of the nearest National Park/Sanctuary/ Biosphere Reserve/Monuments/heritage site/ Reserved Forests	
	(e)	Rehabilitation on plan for quarries/borrow areas	
	(f)	Green belt plan	
	(g)	Compensatory afforestation plan	
4.		Climate and Air Quality	
	(a)	Windrose at site	
	(b)	Max./Min./Mean annual temperature	
	(c)	Frequency of inversion	
	(d)	Frequency of cyclones/tornadoes/cloud burst	
	(e)	Ambient air quality data	
	(f)	Nature & concentration of emission of SPM_2, Gas (CO, CO_2, SO_2, NOx, CHn, etc.) from the project	
5.		Water balance	
	(a)	Water balance at site	
	(b)	Lean season water availability Water requirement	
	(c)	Source to be tapped with competing users (river, lake, ground, public supply)	
	(d)	Water quality	
	(e)	Changes observed in quality and quantity of ground water in the last 15 years and present charging and extraction details	
	(f) (i)	Quantum of waste water to be released with treatment details	
	(ii)	Quantum of quality of water in the receiving body before and after disposal of solid wastes	
	(iii)	Quantum of waste water to be released on land and type of land	
	(g) (i)	Details of reservoir water quality with necessary Catchment Treatment Plan	
	(ii)	Command Area Development plan	

6.		Solid wastes	
	(a)	Nature and quantity of solid wastes generated	
	(b)	Solid waste disposal method	
7.		Noise and Vibrations	
	(a)	Sources of noise and Vibrations	
	(b)	Ambient noise level	
	(c)	Noise and Vibrations control measures proposed	
	(d)	Subsidence problem if any with control measures	
8.		Power requirement indicating source of supply: Complete environmental details to be furnished separately, if captive	
9.		Peak labour force to be deployed giving details of:	
		—Endemic health problems in the area due to waste water/air/soil borne diseases	
		—Health are system existing and proposed	
10.	(a)	Number of villages and population to be displaced	
	(b)	Rehabilitation Master Plan	
11.		Risk Assessment Report and Disaster Management Plan.	
12.	(a)	Environment Impact Assessment	Report prepared as per guidelines issued by the Central Government in MOEF from time to time
	(b)	Environment Management Plan	
	(c)	Detailed Feasibility Report	
	(d)	Duly filled in questionnaire	
13.		Details of Environmental Management Cell	

I hereby give an undertaking that the data and information given above are true to the best of my knowledge and belief and I am aware that if any part of the data/information submitted is found to be false or misleading at any stage, the project be rejected and the clearance given, if any, to the project is likely to be revoked at our risk and cost.

DATE:
PLACE: *Signature of the applicant with name and full address*

> Given under the seal of
> Organisation on behalf of whom
> the applicant is signing.

In respect to item for which data are not required or are not available as per the declaration of project proponent, the project would be considered on that basis.

SCHEDULE III

(See Sub-para III (a) of Para 2)

COMPOSITION OF THE EXPERT COMMITTEES FOR ENVIRONMENTAL IMPACT ASSESSMENT

[18][1. The Committees will consist of experts in the following disciplines:]
- (i) Eco-System Management
- (ii) Air/Water Pollution Control
- (iii) Water Resources Management
- (iv) Flora/Fauna conservation and management
- (v) Land Use Planning
- (vi) Social Sciences/Rehabilitation
- (vii) Project Appraisal
- (viii) Ecology
- (ix) Environmental Health
- (x) Subject Area Specialists
- (xi) Representatives of NGOs/persons concerned with environmental issues.

2. The Chairman will be an outstanding and experienced ecologist or environmentalist or technical professional with wide managerial experience in the relevant development sector.
3. The representative of Impact Assessment Agency will act as Member Secretary.
4. Chairman and Members will serve in their individual capacities except those specifically nominated as representatives.
5. The membership of a Committee shall not exceed 15.

[19]SCHEDULE IV

(See Sub-para I of Para 2)

PROCEDURE FOR PUBLIC HEARING

(1) Process of Public Hearing:—Whoever apply for environmental clearance of projects, shall submit to the concerned State Pollution Control Board twenty sets of the following documents namely:

[18] *Subs.* by S.O. 356 (E), dated 4 May 1994.
[19] *Ins.* by S.O. 318 (E), dated 10 April 1997.

   (i) An executive summary containing the salient features of the project both in English as well as local language.

   (ii) Form XIII prescribed under Water (Prevention and Control of Pollution) Rules, 1975 where discharge of sewage, trade effluents, treatment of water in any form, is required.

   (iii) Form I prescribed under Air (Prevention and Control of Pollution) Union Territory Rules , 1983 where discharge of emissions are involved in any process, operation or industry.

   (iv) Any other information or document which is necessary in the opinion of the Board for their final disposal of the application.

(2) Notice of Public Hearing:—

   (i) The State Pollution Control Board shall cause a notice for environmental public hearing which shall be published in at least two newspapers widely circulated in the region around the project, one of which shall be in the vernacular language of the locality concerned. State Pollution Control Board shall mention the date, time and place of public hearing. Suggestions, views, comments, and objections of the public shall be invited within thirty days from the date of publication of the notification.

   (ii) All persons including bona fide residents, environmental groups and others located at the projects site/sites of displacement/sites likely to be affected can participate in the public hearing. They can also make oral/written suggestions to the State Pollution Control Board.

Explanation: For the purpose of the paragraph person means,—

   (a) any person who is likely to be affected by the grant of environment clearance;

   (b) any person who owns or has control over the project with respect to which an application has been submitted for environmental clearance;

   (c) any association of persons whether incorporated or not likely to be affected by the project and/or functioning in the field of environment;

   (d) any local authority with any part of whose local limits is within the neighbourhood, wherein the project is proposed to be located.

(3) Composition of public hearing panel:— The composition of Public Hearing Panel may consist of the following, namely:

   (i) Representative of State Pollution Control Board;

   (ii) District Collector or his nominee;

   (iii) Representative of state government dealing with the subject;

   (iv) Representative of Department of the state government dealing with Environment;

   (v) Not more than three representatives of the local bodies such as Municipalities or panchayats;

   (vi) Not more than three senior citizens of the area nominated by the District Collector.

(4) Access to the Executive Summary:—The concerned persons shall be provided access to the Executive Summary of the Project at the following places namely:

    (i) District Collector Office;

    (ii) District Industry Centre;

    (iii) In the Office of the Chief Executive Officers of Zila Parishad or Commissioner of the Municipal Corporation/Local body as the case may be;

    (iv) In the head office of the concerned State Pollution Control Board and its concerned Regional Office;

    (v) In the concerned Department of the state government dealing with the subject of environment.]

EXPLANATORY NOTE REGARDING THE IMPACT ASSESSMENT NOTIFICATION

1. *Expansion and modernization of existing projects*

A project proponent is required to seek environmental clearance for a proposed expansion/modernization activity if the resultant Pollution Load is to exceed the existing levels. The words 'Pollution Load' will in this context cover emissions, liquid effluents and solid or semi-solid wastes generated. A project proponent may approach the concerned State Pollution Control Board (SPCB) for certifying whether the proposed modernisation/expansion activity as listed in Schedule I to the notification is likely to exceed the existing pollution load or not. If it is certified that no increase is likely to occur in the existing pollution load due to the proposed expansion or modernisation, the project proponent will not be required to seek environmental clearance, but a copy of such certificate issued by the SPCB will have to be submitted to the Impact Assessment Agency (IAA) for information. The IAA will however, reserve the right to review such cases in the public interest if material facts justifying the need for such review come to light.

2. *Availability of Summary Feasibility Report, EIA/EMP Report etc. to concerned parties or groups*

The project proponent will have to submit an executive summary incorporating in brief the essence of project details and findings of environmental impact assessment study which could be made available to concerned parties or environmental groups on request.

3. *Clarification about concerned parties or environmental groups*

The concerned parties or environmental groups will be the bona fide residents located at or around the project site or site of displacement or site of alleged adverse environmental impact.

4. *Public Hearing*

Public hearings could be called for in case of projects involving large displacement or having severe environment ramifications.

5. *Requisite information required for site clearance/project clearance*

(a)   Site Clearance:
       Site clearance will be given for site specific project as mentioned in para-2(ii) of the notification. Project proponents will be required to furnish information according to environmental appraisal questionnaires for site clearance, as may be prescribed by the IAA from time to time. Additional information whenever required

by the IAA will be communicated immediately to the project proponents who will then be required to furnish the same within the time frame specified.

(b)   Project Clearance:

In addition to the application form as mentioned in Schedule II to the notification, project proponents are required to furnish the following information for environmental appraisal:

    (i) EIA/EMP report (20 copies);

    (ii) Risk Analysis report (20 copies): however, such reports if normally not required for a particular category of project, project proponents can state so accordingly, but the IAA's decision in this regard will be final;

    (iii) NOC from the State Pollution Control Board;

    (iv) Commitment regarding availability of water and electricity from the competent authority;

    (v) Summary of project report/feasibility report (one copy);

    (vi) Filled in questionnaire (as prescribed by the IAA from time to time) for environmental appraisal of the project;

    (vii) Comprehensive rehabilitation plan, if more than 1000 people are likely to be displaced, otherwise a summary plan would be adequate.

As a comprehensive EIA report will normally take at least one year for its preparation, project proponents may furnish Rapid EIA report to the IAA based on one season data (other than monsoon), for examination of the project. Comprehensive EIA report may be submitted later, if so asked for by the IAA.

The requirement of EIA can be dispensed with by the IAA, in case of project which are unlikely to cause significant impacts on the environment. In such cases, project proponent will have to furnish full justification for such exemption for submission of EIA. Where such exemption is granted project proponents may be asked to furnish such additional information as may be required.

6. *Submission of insufficient or inadequate data*

Regarding cases liable to be rejected due to inadequacy of data, it is clarified that the IAA will make such rejection within 30 days from the date of submission of the proposal. While rejecting a proposal due to insufficient or inadequate data after the first evaluation, the IAA may also stipulate additional requirement of information/ clarification for impact assessment purposes. If deemed essential due to the specific nature of location of the proposed project whose data as prescribed is not available, the IAA can examine the project on the basis of available data.

7. *Application Form*

    (i) In order to remove any hardship to the project proponent in providing any information, the project proponent may, where some information is not available or would cause inordinate delay, mention this in their application form. The IAA may consider the project proposal based on the information available.

(ii) Quality and quantity of ground water.

If 15 years data on the quantity and quality variation of ground water is not available with the concerned Department or Authorities, the project proponent may mention this accordingly in the application form prescribed in Schedule–II to the notification. Further, in case of projects where ground water is not to be used and effluent are not to be discharged on the land, the requirement of ground water variation data for the previous 15 years will be dispensed with.

(iii) A project proponent may write the words 'Not Applicable' while filing the application form as mentioned in Schedule II to the notification in respect of items which are not relevant for the purposes of the proposed project.

8. *Exemption for projects already initiated*

For projects listed in Schedule I to the notification in respect of which the required land has been acquired and all relevant clearances of the State Government including NOC from the respective State Pollution Control Board have been obtained before 27 January 1994 a project proponent will not be required to seek environmental clearance from the IAA. However, those units who have not as yet commenced production will inform the IAA.

G

THE FOREST (CONSERVATION) ACT

FOREST (CONSERVATION) ACT, 1980

[NO. 69 OF 1980]

An Act to provide for the conservation of forests and for matters connected therewith or ancillary or incidental thereto.

Be it enacted by Parliament in the Thirty-first year of the Republic of India as follows:

1. Short title, extent and commencement.—(1) This Act may be called the Forest (Conservation) Act, 1980.

(2) It extends to the whole of India except the state of Jammu and Kashmir.

(3) It shall be deemed to have come into force on the 25th day of October 1980.

2. Restriction on the preservation of forests or use of forest land for non-forest purpose.—Notwithstanding anything contained in any other law for time being in force in a state, no state government or other authority shall make, except with the prior approval of the Central Government, any order directing:

(i) that any reserved forest (within the meaning of the expression 'reserved forest' in any law for the time being in force in that state) or any portion thereof, shall cease to be reserved;

(ii) that any forest land or any portion thereof may be used for any non-forest purpose;

[1][(iii) that any forest land or any portion thereof may be assigned by way of lease or otherwise to any private person or to any authority, corporation, agency or any other organization not owned, managed or controlled by Government;

(iv) that any forest land or any portion thereof may be cleared of trees which have grown naturally in that land or portion, for the purpose of using it for reafforestation.]

---

[1] *Ins.* by Act 69 of 1988.

[2][*Explanation.*: For the purpose of this section 'non-forest purpose' means the breaking up or clearing of any forest land or portion thereof for:

(a) the cultivation of tea, coffee, spices, rubber, palms, oil-bearing plants, horticultural crops or medicinal plants;

(b) any purpose other than reafforestation,

but does not include any work relating or ancillary to conservation, development and management of forests and wild life, namely, the establishment of check-posts, fire lines, wireless communications and construction of fencing, bridges and culverts, dams, waterholes, trench marks, boundary marks, pipelines or other like purposes.]

3. Constitution of Advisory Committee.—The Central Government may constitute a Committee consisting of such number of persons as it may deem fit to advise that Government with regard to:

(i) the grant of approval under Section 2; and

(ii) any other matter connected with the conservation of forests which may be referred to it by the Central Government.

[3][**3-A. Penalty for contravention of the provisions of the Act.**—Whoever contravenes or abets the contravention of any of the provisions of Section 2, shall be punishable with simple imprisonment for a period which may extend to fifteen days.

3-B. Offences by authorities and Government departments.—(1) Where any offence under this Act has been committed:

(a) by any department of Government, the head of the department; or

(b) by any authority, every person, who, at the time of offence was committed, was directly in charge of, and was responsible to, the authority for the conduct of the business of the authority as well as the authority;

shall be deemed to be guilty of the offence and shall be liable to be proceeded against and punished accordingly:

Provided that nothing contained in this sub-section shall render the head of the department or any person referred to in clause (b), liable to any punishment if he proves that the offence was committed without his knowledge or that he exercised all due diligence to prevent the commission of such offence.

(2) Notwithstanding anything contained in sub-section (1), where an offence punishable under the Act has been committed by a department of Government or any authority referred to in clause (b) of sub-section (1) and it is proved that the offence has been committed with the consent or connivance of, or is attributable to any neglect on the part of, any officer, other than the head of the department, or in the case of an authority, any person other than the persons referred to in clause (b) of sub-section (1), such officer or persons shall also be deemed to be guilty of that offence and shall be liable to be proceeded against and punished accordingly].

---

[2] *Subs.* by *ibid.*
[3] *Ins.* by *ibid.*

4. Power to make rules.—(1) The Central Government may, by notification in the Office Gazette, make rules for carrying out the provisions of this Act.

(2) Every rule made under this Act shall be laid, as soon as may be, after it is made, before each House of Parliament, while it is in session, for a total period of thirty days which may be comprised in one session or in two or more successive sessions and if, before the expiry of the session immediately following the session or the successive sessions aforesaid, both Houses agree in making any modification in the rule or both Houses agree that the rule should not be made, the rule shall thereafter have effect only in such modified form or be of no effect, as the case may be, so, however, that any such modification or annulment shall be without prejudice to the validity of anything previously done under that rule.

5. Repeal and saving.—(1) The Forest (Conservation) Ordinance, 1980 is hereby repealed.

(2) Notwithstanding such repeal, anything done or any action taken under the provisions of the said Ordinance shall be deemed to have been done or taken under the corresponding provisions of this Act.

H

THE NOISE RULES

NOISE POLLUTION (REGULATION AND CONTROL) RULES, 2000

Notification No. S.O. 123 (E), dated 28 February, 2000

Whereas the increasing ambient noise levels in public places from various sources, inter alia, industrial activity, construction activity, generator sets, loud speakers, public address systems, music systems, vehicular horns and other mechanical devices have deleterious effects on human health and the psychological well being of the people; it is considered necessary to regulate and control noise producing and generating sources with the objective of maintaining the ambient air quality standards in respect of noise;

Whereas a draft of Noise Pollution (Control and Regulation) Rules, 1999 was published under the notification of the Government of India in the Ministry of Environment and Forests vide number S.O. 528 (E) dated the 28th June, 1999 inviting objections and suggestions from all the persons likely to be affected thereby, before the expiry of the period of sixty days from the date on which the copies of the Gazette containing the said notification are made available to the public;

And whereas copies of the said Gazette were made available to the public on the 1st day of July, 1999;

And whereas the objections and suggestions received from the public in respect of the said draft rules have been duly considered by the Central Government;

Now, therefore, in exercise of the powers conferred by clause (ii) of sub-section (2) of section 3, sub-section (1) and clause (b) of sub-section (2) of section 6 and section 25 of the Environment (Protection) Act, 1986 (29 of 1986) read with rule 5 of the Environment (Protection) Rules, 1986, the Central Government hereby makes the following rules for the regulation and control of noise producing and generating sources, namely:-

1. Short–title and commencement.—(1) These rules may be called the Noise Pollution (Regulation and Control) Rules, 2000.

(2) They shall come into force on the date of their publication in Official Gazette.

2. Definitions.—In these rules, unless the context otherwise requires,—

(a) 'Act' means the Environment (Protection) Act, 1986 (29 of 1986);

(b) 'area / zone' means all areas which fall in either of the four categories given in the Schedule annexed to these rules;

(c) 'authority' means any authority or officer authorised by the Central Government, or as the case may be, the State Government in accordance with the laws in force and includes a District Magistrate, Police Commissioner, or any other officer designated for the maintenance of the ambient air quality standards in respect of noise under any law for the time being in force;

(d) 'person' in relation to any factory or premises means a person or occupier or his agent, who has control over the affairs of the factory or premises;

(e) 'State Government' in relation to a union territory means the Administrator thereof appointed under article 239 of the Constitution.

3. Ambient air quality standards in respect of noise for different areas / zones.—(1) The ambient air quality standards in respect of noise for different areas / zones shall be such as specified in the Schedule annexed to these rules.

(2) The State Government may categorize the areas into industrial, commercial, residential or silence areas / zones for the purpose of implementation of noise standards for different areas.

(3) The State Government shall take measures for abatement of noise including noise emanating from vehicular movements and ensure that the existing noise levels do not exceed the ambient air quality standards specified under these rules.

(4) All development authorities, local bodies and other concerned authorities while planning developmental activity or carrying out functions relating to town and country planning shall take into consideration all aspects of noise pollution as a parameter of quality of life to avoid noise menace and to achieve the objective of maintaining the ambient air quality standards in respect of noise.

(5) An area comprising not less than 100 metres around hospitals, educational institutions and courts may be declared as silence area / zone for the purpose of these rules.

4. Responsibility as to enforcement of noise pollution control measures.—(1) The noise levels in any area / zone shall not exceed the ambient air quality standards in respect of noise as specified in the Schedule.

(2) The authority shall be responsible for the enforcement of noise pollution control measures and due compliance of the ambient air quality standards in respect of noise.

5. Restrictions on the use of loud speakers / public address system.—(1) A loud speaker or the public address system shall not be used except after obtaining written permission from the authority.

(2) A loud speaker or a public address system shall not be used at night (between

10.00 p.m. to 6.00 a.m.) except in closed premises for communication within, e.g. auditoria, conference rooms, community halls and banquet halls.

6. Consequences of any violation in silence zone / area.—Whoever, in any place covered under the silence zone / area commits any of the following offence, he shall be liable for penalty under the provisions of the Act:

(i)   whoever, plays any music or uses any sound amplifiers,

(ii) whoever, beats a drum or tom-tom or blows a horn either musical or pressure, or trumpet or beats or sounds any instrument, or

(iii) whoever, exhibits any mimetic, musical or other performances of a nature to attract crowds.

7. Complaints to be made to the authority.—(1) A person may, if the noise level exceeds the ambient noise standards by 10 dB(A) or more given in the corresponding columns against any area / zone, make a complaint to the authority.

(2) The authority shall act on the complaint and take action against the violator in accordance with the provisions of these rules and any other law in force.

8. Power to prohibit etc. continuance of music sound or noise.—(1) If the authority is satisfied from the report of an officer in charge of a police station or other information received by him that it is necessary to do so in order to prevent annoyance, disturbance, discomfort or injury or risk of annoyance, disturbance, discomfort or injury to the public or to any person who dwell or occupy property on the vicinity, he may, by a written order issue such directions as he may consider necessary to any person for preventing, prohibiting, controlling or regulating:

(a) the incidents or continuance in or upon any premises of—

(i) any vocal or instrumental music,

(ii) sounds caused by playing, beating, clashing, blowing or use in any manner whatsoever of any instrument including loudspeakers, public address systems, appliance or apparatus or contrivance which is capable of producing or re-producing sound, or

(b) the carrying on in or upon, any premises of any trade, avocation or operation or process resulting in or attended with noise.

(2) The authority empowered under sub-rules (1) may, either on its own motion, or on the application of any person aggrieved by an order made under sub-rule (1), either rescind, modify or alter any such order:

Provided that before any such application is disposed of, the said authority shall afford to the applicant an opportunity of appearing before it either in person or by a person representing him and showing cause against the order and shall, if it rejects any such application either wholly or in part, record its reasons for such rejection.

SCHEDULE
(See Rule 3 (1) and 4 (1))

AMBIENT AIR QUALITY STANDARDS IN RESPECT OF NOISE

Area Code	Category of Area / Zone	Limit in dB(A) Leq *	
		Day Time	Night Time
(A)	Industrial area	75	70
(B)	Commercial area	65	55
(C)	Residential area	55	45
(D)	Silence Zone	50	40

Note: 1. Day time shall mean from 6.00 a.m. to 10.00 p.m.
2. Night time shall mean from 10.00 p.m. to 6.00 a.m.
3. Silence zone is defined as an area comprising not less than 100 metres around hospitals, educational institutions and courts. The silence zones are zones which are declared as such by the competent authority.
4. Mixed categories of areas may be declared as one of the four abovementioned categories by the competent authority.

*dB(A) Leq denotes the time weighted average of the level of sound in decibels on scale A which is relatable to human hearing.

A 'decibel' is a unit in which noise is measured.

'A', in dB(A) Leq, denotes the frequency weighting in the measurement of noise and corresponds to frequency response characteristics of the human ear.

Leq: It is an energy mean of the noise level over a specified period.

INDEX

References to Appendices are in italic type